Praise for *Carry Me Home*

"McWhorter contributes significantly to the historical record."
　　　　　　　　　—*The New York Times Book Review* (cover review)

"A tour de force, comparable in importance to J. Anthony Lukas's *Common Ground* and Taylor Branch's *Parting the Waters. Carry Me Home* is destined to become a classic in the history of the civil rights revolution."
　　　　　　　　　—David Herbert Donald, author of *Lincoln*

"Her narrative takes on the suspense of a detective novel. . . . *Carry Me Home* is an ambitious, panoramic history with enough personal memoir to make us see why Diane McWhorter cannot forget—and wants us to remember—the momentous events that took place during one historic year in one Alabama city."
　　　　　　　　　—Francine Prose, *O Magazine*

"*Carry Me Home* is a case study in how the privileged and powerful can operate behind the scenes to control and, when it is in their interests, undermine and corrupt the social fabric."
　　　　　　　　　—*The Washington Post Book World*

"McWhorter's own involvement in the story . . . reenergizes the struggle, serving as a reminder that history is always personal."
　　　　　　　　　—*The New Yorker*

"Fresh, sometimes startling details distinguish this doorstop page-turner told by a daughter of [Birmingham's] white elite. [McWhorter] brings a gripping pace and an unusual, twofold perspective to her account, incorporating her viewpoint as a child . . . as well as her adult viewpoint as an avid scholar and journalist."
　　　　　　　　　—*Publishers Weekly* (starred)

"No current book . . . delves more deeply into the nuances of the movement era than Diane McWhorter's *Carry Me Home.*"
　　　　　　　　　—Jack E. White, *Time*

"Diane McWhorter's powerful moral epic about the civil rights movement in Birmingham, Alabama, contains all the elements of first-rate history, including dauntingly thorough research, a sure grasp of the big picture as well as the tiny details that illuminate it, evocative writing that brings action and character springing off the page, and a novelist's sense of how to mold a compelling narrative arc out of the innumerable molecules of historical fact."
　　　　　　　　　—Harper Barnes, *St. Louis Post-Dispatch*

"Birmingham's story will strike a chord with every Southerner who lived through that crucible, but it is as much a tribute to McWhorter's gifts that readers will feel as if they walk Birmingham's streets during that period as if through their own hometown."

—Ellen Dahnke, *The Tennessean*

"The product of nineteen years of research, *Carry Me Home* is a brilliant work of history."

—Craig Flournoy, *The Dallas Morning News*

"A stunningly provocative and vividly written history."

—Bruce Clayton, *Pittsburgh Post-Gazette*

"A vivid, admirably nuanced, and wide-ranging history of the city that became ground zero in the civil rights struggle . . . dense, detailed, and insightful."

—*Kirkus Reviews* (starred)

"America gets a thoughtful dissection of one of the most turbulent periods in its history."

—Jim Lynch, *Milwaukee Journal Sentinel*

"*Carry Me Home* is a staggering book . . . a twentieth century Iliad."

—Kate Callen, *San Diego Union-Tribune*

"*Carry Me Home* reads like a detective story as McWhorter relentlessly pursues her prey. . . . A powerful memoir and an absorbing social history, *Carry Me Home* belongs with Taylor Branch's *Parting the Waters* and Howell Raines's *My Soul Is Rested*."

—James A. Miller, *The Boston Globe*

"The force of *Carry Me Home* comes from the scope of the author's reporting. . . . She sketches the players in bold strokes and summons her themes with light ones, shaping the story of Birmingham into a lucid, elucidating drama about democracy."

—Troy Patterson, *Entertainment Weekly*

"Powerfully written, vividly recounted, McWhorter's intimate yet magisterial narrative adds important insights to our understanding of the Ku Klux Klan and its connections with official power in the South."

—Ruth Rosen, *Los Angeles Times*

"Impeccable history . . . in the polished prose of a novelist . . . A terrifically brave book."

—Lauren F. Winner, *Newsday*

"Impressive . . . gutsy."

—*Elle*

CARRY ME

DIANE McWHORTER

HOME

Birmingham, Alabama

The Climactic Battle of the

Civil Rights Revolution

A TOUCHSTONE BOOK
PUBLISHED BY SIMON & SCHUSTER
New York   London   Toronto   Sydney   Singapore

TOUCHSTONE
Rockefeller Center
1230 Avenue of the Americas
New York, NY 10020

Copyright © 2001 by Diane McWhorter
All rights reserved,
including the right of reproduction
in whole or in part in any form.

First Touchstone Edition 2002
TOUCHSTONE and colophon are registered trademarks
of Simon & Schuster, Inc.

For information about special discounts for bulk purchases,
please contact Simon & Schuster Special Sales:
1-800-456-6798 or business@simonandschuster.com

Manufactured in the United States of America

3   5   7   9   10   8   6   4

The Library of Congress has cataloged
the Simon & Schuster edition as follows:
McWhorter, Diane.
Carry me home : Birmingham, Alabama : the climactic battle
of the civil rights revolution / Diane McWhorter.
p.   cm.
Includes bibliographical references (p.   ) and index.
1. Birmingham (Ala.)—Race relations.
2. Afro-Americans—Civil rights—Alabama—Birmingham—
History—20th century.   3. Civil rights movements—
Alabama—Birmingham—History—20th century.   I. Title.
F334.B69 N449   2001
976.1'781063—dc21   00-53827
ISBN 0-684-80747-5
0-7432-1772-1 (Pbk)

The author and publisher gratefully acknowledge permission
to reprint lyrics from "Bull Connor's Jail," by Ernie Marrs.
© 1963, 1990 Sing Out! Corporation. Used by Permission. All
rights reserved.

To the memory of my grandmother,

Marjorie Westgate McWhorter

CONTENTS

A landscape to be seen has to be composed,

and to be loved has to be moralized.

—George Santayana, *The Sense of Beauty*

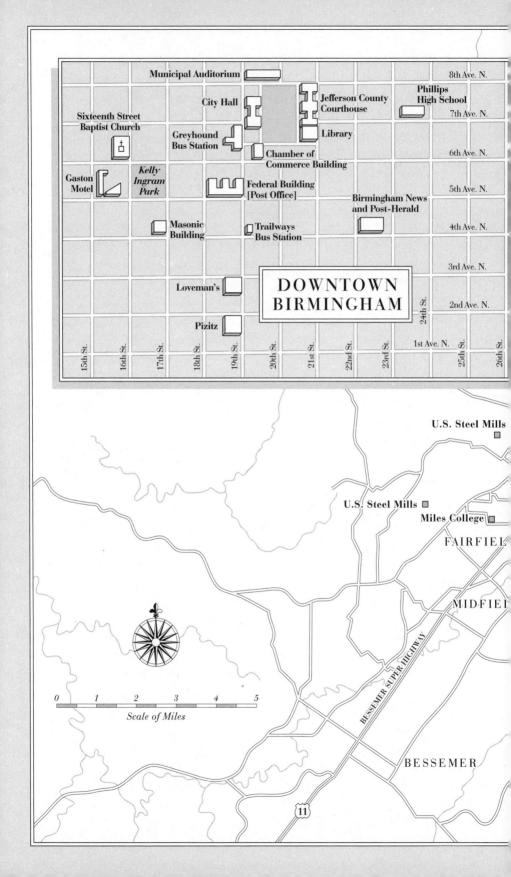

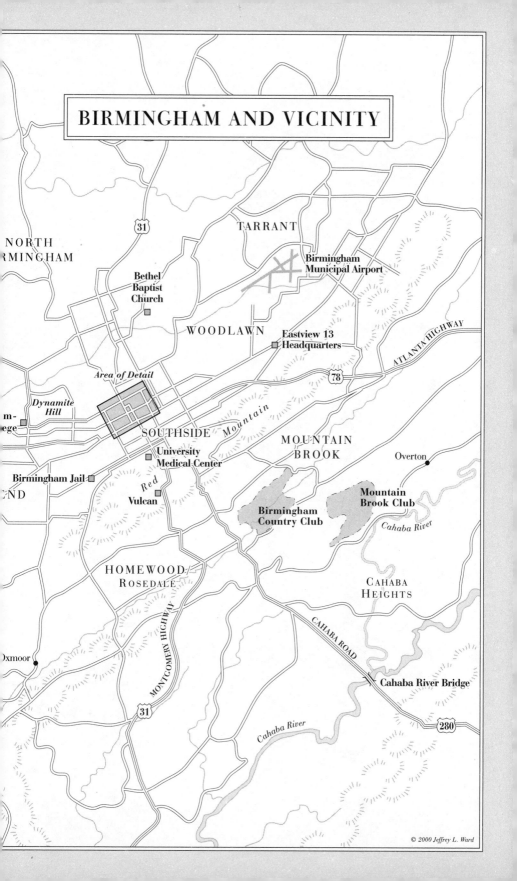

BIRMINGHAM AND VICINITY

31

TARRANT

NORTH
RMINGHAM

Birmingham
Municipal Airport

Bethel
Baptist
Church

WOODLAWN

Eastview 13
Headquarters

Area of Detail

ATLANTA HIGHWAY

Dynamite
Hill

78

m-
ege

SOUTHSIDE

Mountain

MOUNTAIN
BROOK

Overton

University
Medical Center

Red

Birmingham Jail

Mountain
Brook Club

ND

Birmingham
Country Club

Cahaba River

Vulcan

HOMEWOOD
ROSEDALE

CAHABA
HEIGHTS

MONTGOMERY HIGHWAY

)xmoor

CAHABA ROAD

Cahaba River Bridge

31

280

Cahaba River

© 2000 Jeffrey L. Ward

PREFACE

LIKE THE SPIRITUAL from which the title is taken, this book is about death, redemption, and race. It builds to the national turning point known in history as the Year of Birmingham, 1963, when two things happened there, in the country's most segregated city, that brought about the end of apartheid in America. The first milestone was the huge nonviolent demonstrations that Martin Luther King Jr. staged in the spring, as school-age witnesses for justice overcame the weapons of the state, including Commissioner Bull Connor's police dogs and fire hoses. The spectacle—something that seemed to belong in the Old Testament rather than the American midcentury—nationalized the faltering civil rights movement and galvanized public opinion behind federal legislation to abolish segregation.

But because this battle over black freedom was, in effect, a continuation of the Civil War, there were bound to be casualties. The second of the emblematic "events of Birmingham"—as President John F. Kennedy referred to the inspiration for his own Emancipation Proclamation, the bill eventually passed as the Civil Rights Act of 1964—was the Ku Klux Klan's bombing of the Sixteenth Street Baptist Church. In some ghoulish symmetry with the youth triumph of the spring, four black Sunday school girls were killed by the explosion.

I was a citizen of Birmingham in 1963, close to the age of the girls who died in the bombing. But I was growing up on the wrong side of the revolution. I knew nothing of what was happening downtown, even though my father, the renegade son of a prominent white Birmingham family, was taking an increasingly active role in opposing Martin Luther King's movement. In my quest to understand how a family of Ivy League–educated country clubbers could have produced a vigilante spirit like my father, I ended up discovering that the elite establishment of the city itself had nurtured the Ku Klux Klan and created the brutal conditions that incited a magnificent nonviolent revolution.

My education did not begin until after college, when I was living in Boston. The book review editor at an alternative weekly gave me (as a native of the tragicomic land of George Wallace) a copy of the Alabama volume in a 1976 Bicentennial series on the fifty states—not to review, God knows, but to get it off his shelf. Several years later, I finally opened the book, expecting the coverage of my city to be a salute to the Pittsburgh of the South. What I found instead would change my life, embarking me on a fifteen-year expedition back to Birmingham. The author of that Bicentennial tribute, a local historian named Virginia Van der Veer Hamilton, described the role of the power structure of Birmingham, the fathers and grandfathers of my schoolmates, who had materialized in the Chamber of Commerce building on a Tuesday in May 1963 to figure out how to make Martin Luther King stop the mass marches. They were so afraid of the social and economic consequences of dealing with King that only one man would agree to negotiate with him. He was a real estate executive named Sidney Smyer, and he was my cousin. It was only then that I realized that the events of Birmingham had anything to do with me.

The kinship between the Smyers and the McWhorters owed more to the place we had in common than to the distant ancestor we shared (one Lucy Haynie Harris, a South Carolinian of colonial Virginian stock). We were descendants of the tiny town of Gaylesville, Cherokee County, Alabama, of the Confederate States of America. There, in October 1864, Union troops bivouacked beside the Chattooga River within view of the McWhorter "plantation." My great-great-grandmother—whose husband, a regimental surgeon of the Forty-seventh Infantry, was at the Confederate Hospital in Richmond—led a delegation of local women over to the encampment and asked an unprepossessing man who identified himself as "General Sherman" if he would spare the gristmill downriver. "Madam," he replied gallantly, "if you ladies will recall your husbands and your brothers from the Army of the Confederacy, I shall be only too happy to leave it." Watching their main food source go up in Union flames, the community of women and children witnessed the beginning of the first modern war—against a civilian society—and the end of the great Confederate experiment. Sherman had earlier that month conceived his march "smashing things to the sea," to "make Georgia howl!"

Nearly a century later, in 1963, Sid Smyer found himself in the middle of a later war over emancipation, engineering the terms of the decisive battle. But it turns out that Smyer was a far more complicated character than the white savior of Birmingham that history would make him out to be. For nearly three decades, as businessman, politician, and even churchman, he had led the "polite" resistance to civil rights. He had also bankrolled a man who became one of the city's most rabid Klansmen. A hero as perverse as the city's history ("I'm a segregationist," he said to explain his change of heart, "but I'm not a damn fool"), Smyer embodied Birmingham's transformation from the Johannesburg of America to the proving ground of the civil rights movement.

BIRMINGHAM WAS DIFFERENT from other cities: It was southern and it had industry—steel, the business that built America. And because it had industry, it had a noteworthy concentration of workers. And because the workers were treated badly by the industrialists, the labor movement (as well as the Communist Party) paid Birmingham special attention, introducing it to a tradition of organized protest unheard of elsewhere in the South.

The forces of progress, however, had been no sweat for the forces of money until President Franklin D. Roosevelt sensationally wheeled the U.S. government around to the side of the have-nots in the 1930s, empowering the workers to unite against their bosses. And that is where the story of 1963 really begins, at the time Sid Smyer's own public career was launched, during the New Deal, when segregation itself was not only a racist ideology but also a means to an economic end. The civil rights movement was created from the rib of organized labor, and the industrialists answered it with a "grassroots" counteroffensive of hooded vigilantes and the queerest tory politician in history, a loudmouthed hick named Bull Connor.

The saga of African-American liberation is perhaps the most thrilling in our country's history, biblical in its subtexts and angles of moral instruction. But even though this book traces the Movement through its prime in Birmingham (and offers a somewhat unorthodox, pre-glory view of Martin Luther King), it is not merely about the civil rights struggle. I hope it also sheds insight on the segregationists and the respectable underpinnings of their violent resistance. Because of the city's industrially stratified demographics, the influence of class was more pronounced there than in other places in the South. The conflict that made Birmingham America's racial Armageddon in 1963 was the "class warfare" that had always threatened the confidence of a young nation founded on the preposterous principle of equality.

DIANE MCWHORTER
New York City, September 2000

INTRODUCTION

SEPTEMBER 15, 1963

B<small>Y NOON THAT SUNDAY</small>, people were arriving at the Mountain Brook Club's downstairs grill, soothingly dark, as if it had been designed with the hangover in mind. The after-church buffet table was spread with steamship roast beef (very rare), crabmeat au gratin, shrimp Creole, sweet potato and miniature marshmallow casserole, fresh turnip greens with homemade relish, and salads featuring canned white asparagus and Roquefort (never "bleu cheese") dressing. Amid this plenty, a sparse plate was the badge of one-upmanship.

The diners had a heavy-lidded, slow-glanced look, the air of having gotten there first and fashionably late at the same time. Theirs was a snobbery so exquisite that an evening over at the Birmingham Country Club—"that roadhouse," my uncle sneered charmingly, what with its ranch architecture and the acres of parking lot visible from the street—was considered slumming. The Mountain Brook was a whitewashed-brick plantation-style mansion (with tastefully unassertive columns) nestled in a piney glen. Sometimes a Mountain Brook man would deign to point out that the difference between the Birmingham and his club was the difference between Kiwanis, which ran the city, and Rotary, which owned it. The emotional distinction: Some of my best friends belong to the Birmingham, but I wouldn't want my caddie working for them.

For us children, the privilege of belonging meant that you knew which of your friends didn't, the same way you knew whose parents were divorced, whose father drank, who was a Catholic, and you instinctively redesigned your remarks, midsentence if necessary, not to call attention to the misfortune. My grandfather had been a charter member of the Mountain Brook, and his younger son, my uncle Hobart, felt entitled enough to indulge in unbecoming behavior, like flinging his racket down on the tennis court after a blown point, with a strangled cry of "God—bless America!" My father was another story. He had grown up at the club from infancy, swimming in its pool right through the polio scare, but he would not have been admitted there as an adult even if he had wanted to be. The shaky class structure on which Birmingham was built could disintegrate within a single family, in a single generation.

I was ten years old, and because my family was prominent enough to socially withstand any mortification my father could bring it, the Mountain Brook Club was the center of my universe. I would not understand for twenty-five years that it also contained the secrets of this fateful Sunday in 1963, when Birmingham earned a permanent place in history, not for the first time this year. Most of America knew of my city only as a sort of race circus—redneck freaks and Jim Crow wretches, clashing under the live fireworks of "Bombingham." But behind the scenes was a third set of principals, from whom I was learning the ordinary rituals of prosperity at the Mountain Brook Club. As the impresarios, they had provided the original economic motive for the gaudy performers, whom they themselves had lost sight of and finally disavowed.

The club's patriarchs—officially only men could belong—were known statewide as Big Mules, a perhaps unconscious tribute to the most prized members of the largely black work force that excavated their fortunes in coal and iron. "How many mules did we lose?" was their half-facetious response to a big mine explosion.

Founded after the Civil War, the heavy-manufacturing mecca of the South had been built by post-Emancipation slaves. Under a system popular all around the Old Confederacy known as the convict lease, the state of Alabama hired out half its prisoners to the tuberculosis-breeding coal mines of Birmingham's founding industrialists. The "crimes" of these mine slaves—the vast majority of them black—were often nothing more than gambling, indebtedness, or idleness. Young first offenders faced a double punishment, as "gal-boys" for the hardened criminals. The system had "all the evils of slavery without one of its ameliorating features," as one critic noted, like the slaveholders' vested interest in keeping their property alive. Slackers were hung on crosses, though with ropes rather than nails. Fugitives were mauled by bloodhounds and then whipped with wet leather straps until they begged for death. Those who got their wish were dumped in a common hole in the woods, saving the superintendent the nuisance of a funeral appearance. The lease raised money for the state at the same time that it provided the industrialists a cheap, strike-proof work force and a sense of moral purpose, for they insisted that a mine sentence was the best way to teach ignorant Negroes the lessons of citizenship.

The descendants of Birmingham's founding convict drivers were now the most venerated members of the Mountain Brook Club. One of them would soon lead the opposition to a campaign among the younger members to expand the club's parking facilities and, by extension, the circle of exclusivity that the iron makers shared with Ivy League–trained attorneys for the splendid corporations who, like my grandfather, had earned the accolade "Great Lawyer."

One Mountain Brook Club member was in a class all by himself. "A Great Man" was the way his peers described James Alexander Simpson, a distinguished corporation lawyer, founder of a bank, husband to a pedigree, and statesman. He was an imposing man with a handsome face composed dourly to convey toughness, the ultimate Birmingham virtue. His unapproachable bearing had prompted friend and foe to satirize him as "Sunny Jim" during the years he ruled the state legislature, where he was so attentive to the needs of business that he had fought for the unfettered entrepreneurship of loan sharks. It was the convert's zeal that had made him a larger-than-life member of his adopted aristocracy. For this confirmed elitist, the state's foremost capitalist ideologue, was the son of a communist.

Acquaintances still hailed Simpson as "Senator," to acknowledge not his beautifully crafted contributions to the state code as a state senator, but his one thwarted ambition, to be elected to the U.S. Senate. His 1944 campaign for the office, even though unsuccessful, had invented the future of politics in Alabama, one based on frank, unapologetic racism. And so it was that Simpson had created the enemies who had defined black America's struggle for freedom in this year of 1963, the Year of Birmingham, when segregation fell.

The most infamous of those enemies was Eugene "Bull" Connor, a former cornball radio personality whom Simpson had molded into the czar of Birmingham City Hall. The two men had written the laws, punished the dissenters, and generally made democracy safe for Simpson's mighty clients. Simpson's intimates were hard-pressed to understand what this Great Man could possibly have to do with a rube who signed official correspondence "Eugene 'Bull' Connor," in the rotund letters of someone proud of having mastered cursive writing. "At least ole Bull's *honest,*" the clubmen chanted, and when they mocked his gorgeous malapropisms—"White and Negro are not to segregate together!"—they did so with the same good-humored head-shake that punctuated their stories about the yardman's car breaking down again. The closest Simpson got to apologizing for Connor was to say, "He may be a son of a bitch, but he's my son of a bitch."

Their teamwork had produced the country's purest example of segregation, a civilization more peculiar than slavery, from which it had mutated. And that explained how Martin Luther King Jr. happened to have landed in town in the spring of 1963. Birmingham had become the do-or-die test for the civil rights movement, what King had pronounced "the most segregated city in America." It was the dreaded destination he had been hoping to avoid during the seven years since a bus boycott in Montgomery baptized him as the Negro* people's savior—America's Gandhi, according to *Time* magazine. But now the mantra of King's aides was, "As Birmingham goes, so goes the South."

From the relative safety of Atlanta, King had watched the trials of his Birmingham colleague Fred Lee Shuttlesworth, the proud creature of a city he said had "a heart as hard as the steel it manufactures and as black as the coal it mines." Shuttlesworth's ramrod carriage, arrogantly tilted head, and harsh intelligence contained in the package of an unpolished, rabble-rousing Baptist preacher contrasted with the Reverend Dr. King's intellectual Hamlet image, as the pampered product of the black bourgeoisie. Within the Southern Christian Leadership Conference, the organization he and King had founded, Shuttlesworth's ap-

---

* Like many historians of the era, I sometimes use "Negro," the contemporary designation of respect, to refer to African-Americans.

palling courage had earned him the nickname "the Wild Man from Birmingham."
He had been bombed, whipped with chains, and subjected to a Chinese-water-
torture dribble of legal harassments. His response had been: "We mean to kill segregation or be killed by it." By finally persuading—goading—the Movement to
take on Birmingham, Shuttlesworth had brought King to the crossroads of his career and of the long, rough passage of their people.

Frankly, Jim Simpson had not seen why there had been all that fuss about
Bull's using the police dogs and the fire hoses against King and the "outside agitators" who had rioted in Birmingham's streets in the spring. That was just standard
police procedure for crowd control. The national news media had overblown
King's "show"—all those marches, just for the right to eat a hot dog at a lunch
counter. And even so, it might have all gone away but for that news photograph of
a colored boy who had stepped into the jaws of one of the German police dogs. As
Eric Sevareid had said on the *CBS Evening News,* "A snarling police dog set upon a
human being is recorded in the permanent photoelectric file of every human
being's brain."

Where the photographer had made it look as if the dog were attacking the
youth, the Mountain Brook Club members knew that he was really being restrained on his leash by his officer. Those German shepherds had been treated as
VIPs ever since the city acquired them in 1961. Sergeant M. W. McBride had recently brought his "partner," Rebel, to our morning school assembly, where the
dog dutifully attacked a policewoman (in a protective suit) playing the role of
suspect. The awe-inspiring performance had caused me briefly to abandon my
ambition to make the U.S. equestrian team in favor of becoming a handler for the
K-9 Corps.

The local papers had had the good sense not to print the famous photo, but
we would have recognized the "victim," generically, as one of the colored boys we
saw pedaling undersized bikes with flat tires, as we drove through run-down
neighborhoods on our way to football games at Legion Field and, assuming that
the youths were budding juvenile delinquents, rolled up the car windows.

I had no idea that I was growing up under the reign of James A. Simpson,
even though I had attended first through fourth grade with his grandson, James A.
Simpson II, at a private school founded to spare our charmed circle of Mountain
Brook Club grandchildren from integration. Popsie, as everyone called the boy,
was the third generation of my family's friendship with the Simpsons. My grandfather had been a member of the "Senator's" kitchen cabinet in the 1930s, one of
the "best people" of Birmingham trying to redeem the state from the hookwormy
masses. Popsie's uncle Jimmy and my uncle Hobart had been in each other's weddings, and the senior Simpson's wife still marveled over the time my Ohio-bred
grandmother—what would those Yankees think of next?—brought a flaming
peach dessert to a formal dinner table right in the cast-iron skillet.

Popsie Simpson was our class clown. His Red Skelton routine at lunch period invariably concluded with the cracking of a hard-boiled egg on his head so

that he could feign a concussion. The day Popsie's maid accidentally put an un-cooked egg in his lunch box was the funniest moment of primary school, the kind of incident my mother would sorrowfully recall years later, when his name was being dragged through the papers in connection with Birmingham's society mur-der of the century. Even if Popsie's grandfather, the Great Man himself, had still been alive, it is unlikely he would have discerned in his namesake's sordid fate some rough justice from the gods who bind an individual life to public history.

For James A. Simpson, more than any of his esteemed collaborators, bore the political responsibility for what happened on this Sunday, September 15, 1963.

THE SIXTEENTH STREET BAPTIST CHURCH was the city's most elegant black church. It anchored the vital Negro cultural and commercial district a few blocks from the department store where I had bought my pale green Easter dress just before the "trouble" began that spring. The spacious balconied sanctuary had been the staging ground for Martin Luther King's demonstrations. Marchers gathered there to sing, clap, and pray until they caught the nonviolent spirit; then they filed out to face Bull Connor and the cameras. The picture of the black boy and the dog had been taken across the street from the church.

Sixteenth Street's stylish members had considered crusades for freedom the business of what they called "little niggers," and had only grudgingly consented to let King use their building. They were glad that by late summer the city's police dogs no longer fascinated the news media. King had moved on to Washington, where he had recently stood on the steps of the Lincoln Memorial and spoken to the multitudes about, among other dreams, the redemptive power of "unearned suffering." On this Sunday morning in September, eighteen days after the March on Washington, there was hardly an activist to be found at the Sixteenth Street Baptist Church, even if it had been stuck with the label "headquarters of the civil rights movement," subjecting it to bomb threats it did not "deserve."

Four girls around my age slipped out of their Sunday school class and went to a basement restroom to primp. Church clothes were, as white people knew, the acme of the Negro wardrobe, and Sixteenth Street was a continual fashion show. Today the girls were checking themselves in the mirror before going upstairs to take part in the regular church services for "Youth Day," inaugurated by the pas-tor in the hope of bringing new life to the stodgy congregation.

At 10:22, an exploding bundle of dynamite knocked a man-sized hole in the steel-reinforced stone-and-brick east wall of the church restroom. It blew the clothes off the Sunday school girls and stacked them like cordwood under a bliz-zard of debris. All four were killed. One had been decapitated.

At the Mountain Brook Club, the waiters—black by club policy—had been the first to know that the Sixteenth Street Baptist Church had been bombed. Some had heard the explosion as they set out for work, momentarily confused by the boom. However commonplace by night, the bombings against blacks had not yet occurred in broad daylight, let alone on a Sunday morning, in a place that called itself the City of Churches.

It had to have been the strangest day yet for the waiters—accustomed though they were to leading what one described as "two lives"—to go to their locker room and change into their tuxedos, uniforms identical to the formal leisure attire of the clubmen. The staff was a sort of magic mirror for the members, reflecting a wishful truth that contrasted with the example of previous black employees, the convict miners. "They have it better than we do," the clubmen said of the liveried servants, and pointed out that the late beloved doorman was commemorated at the club entrance with a bronze plaque ("In memory of Reginald B. Brown, major domo 1930–1947"). He had supposedly chosen the paternalistic perks of his club career—access to the biggest bankers, doctors, and lawyers in town—over a future in the Negro theater as the next Stepin Fetchit. It was as if the Big Mules had forgotten that oppressed, if not enslaved, Negroes were the cornerstone of their industrial success. Segregation—with its sentimental life force, racism—had kept their workers divided, wages depressed. The industrialists had not invented segregation, but they had honed it into the ultimate money-making instrument.

Brown's successor as the club's most favored employee in 1963, similarly dignified by being addressed by his last rather than his first name, was the headwaiter Lindsay Gaines, sleek as a fountain pen and openly proud of "working at the most prestigious club in the Southeast." Behind his back, his wait staff called him "Mr. Mountain Brook." For Gaines was no slouch in the art of ingratiation, spreading himself like balm over, for example, Jim Simpson's bickering grandchildren, Popsie and his three sisters. When Gaines's brick ranch house was bombed—presumably because it was in a formerly white neighborhood settled by upwardly mobile blacks—he had let his dismay show to the clubman who handled his insurance. Soon two white deputy sheriffs began standing guard at the house, serving notice on any predators that he was what blacks and whites alike called a "white folks' nigger."

The grandes dames who played bridge at the club had taken a special interest in him ("Gaines, you're a gentleman!"), arranging for him to visit the Sheraton Royal in Montreal and the fine dining rooms of New Orleans, where he learned to slice salmon, carve venison, and manipulate three sauce spoons in one hand. The ladies had been the first to introduce on club property the subject of the "trouble downtown." One said to Gaines: "What is it yall want? I do everything but go to bed with you." They would even drop the names of civil rights figures, to see if he would take the bait. But Gaines, whom they had taught "the value of discretion," never let on what became of some of the bills pressed into his palm after he flambéed the baked Alaska tableside, lowering the lights so that his white shirt and gloves stood out against the fire: The tips would be donated to the cause of Martin Luther King.

IF OUR HISTORY TEXTS listed *Uncle Tom's Cabin* among the Four Major Causes of the Civil War, so had the photograph of the police dog lunging at the black boy been a factor in the Emancipation Proclamation of the twentieth century. President John F. Kennedy went on national TV not long after the photograph was published (it had made him "sick," he said) and announced that he was sending to Congress a remedy for "the events of Birmingham": the first serious civil rights legislation since Reconstruction—ultimately the Civil Rights Act of 1964— which would end legalized racism in America.

Not so long ago, Our Way of Life, as the South preferred to describe segregation, had seemed immutable. "The world outlook was bad, yes," Walker Percy would write in *The Last Gentleman,* his novel set partly on the golf course of the Birmingham Country Club, across from where he grew up, "but not so bad that it was not a pleasant thing to say so of a gold-green afternoon, with a fair sweat up and sugared bourbon that tasted as good as it smelled."

"I'm going to tell yall the truth," one of the clubmen said, eyeing the distant black caddies waiting for the golfers to finish their whiskey refreshment. "If they want the country all that bad, I'm not all that much against letting them have it."

"Ain't nobody here but us niggers anyway," somebody finally answered. "Let's play golf."

Those old heavy-manufacturing warriors, who now channeled their killer instinct into the "dogfights" of golfers who teed off at half-hour intervals every Saturday morning, had once engaged in more direct forms of combat, using machine guns and, yes, dynamite, against the presumed enemies of free enterprise, notably the representatives of organized labor. The problem was, the vigilantes who had handled the industrialists' dirtiest work had not lost the habit of terrorism even after it ceased to serve the interests of business. The bombing of the Sixteenth Street Baptist Church was the endgame in the city fathers' long and profitable tradition of maintaining their industrial supremacy through vigilantism.

Not that anyone standing in the buffet line that Sunday had anything to do with the lethal package planted during those dark hours before the blast, when no sensible white person would be found in the colored section of downtown. The fuse had been lit years earlier, in the broad daylight of community approval, and even the cleanest hands at the Mountain Brook Club did their bit to keep it dry as it sizzled through bad neighborhoods and across many decades before it blew up four black Sunday school girls on September 15, 1963.

BIRMINGHAM WAS INITIALLY ENVISIONED, during Reconstruction, as a city upon a hill. It was to be the industrial summit of a New South sprung in full glory from the Alabama wilderness. And in its short life, it had indeed proved to be a spectacular American archetype, albeit as a city in a valley.

My father had been born in the last months of the roaring twenties, a time when the corporation-building efforts of men like *his* father had lent a glimmer of authenticity to Birmingham's wild self-promotion ("The Biggest City in America for its Age"). He had been weaned to an engraved silver cup, but now, at age thirty-four, he drank beer straight from the can at bars with tattooed men, the husky sort I mostly saw sitting in front of filling stations and leering behind their dark glasses as we asked for the key to the ladies' restroom.

Even before that Sunday-morning dynamite blast, the silhouettes had begun to haunt me, the intimations you have to stop your intelligence from trying to make sense of. One night in 1963, not long before Martin Luther King came to town, my grandmother, Papa's mother, was driving my mother and me to Birmingham-Southern College. Marjorie, as we called her, was a professor there, and we were going to see a play produced by the head of the theater department, whose flowing white hair and tendency toward Brecht were pretty much all Birmingham could call an avant-garde. Marjorie turned to Mama as we passed by the house of an acquaintance and in her tiniest voice said, "She was married to a sadist, you know."

"A what?" my mother said loudly.

Throughout Molière's *The Imaginary Invalid,* I mouthed "sadist, sadist, sadist"—Marjorie had pronounced it with a short *a*—so that I wouldn't lose it before I could get home to look it up. The dictionary described "one who derives pleasure from inflicting pain on others." Was the beautiful lady of the house, who seemed the picture of downy matronhood when I saw her dropping off her son at school, being tortured in a locked, shuttered room by a sadist—a breed evidently as homogeneous as werewolves?

One Saturday morning not long afterward, Mama came out of the kitchen drying her hands on a dish towel to tell my father that something awful had happened to one of the neighborhood dads. Jim LeBlanc* had been on his way back from Montgomery at dusk when a motorist motioned him off Highway 31, drove him into the woods, battered him, and left him stranded on a dirt road. His wife, Linda, a member of Mama's bridge club, had put him right to bed when he arrived home all black and blue.

Papa closed the *Post-Herald* and cocked his head. "Well, that dudn't sound right," he said in his grave morning voice. "Was he robbed?"

Mama didn't know. He shook his head slowly, as if a big idea were dawning, but simply said, "It dudn't add up."

After bridge club a few months later, my mother was getting in her car to come home when Linda LeBlanc, who lived across the street from where they'd all been playing, ran out of her house, screaming, "Jim's shot himself." Sometime later, Papa folded back a page of his morning paper and thumped at a news story. Funds had been embezzled from a local insurance company, Mama read out loud, by its vice president, the late Mr. LeBlanc.

Repeating the story later, Mama always marveled that Papa had realized right away that there was something fishy about Jim's beating. For me, his inkling of no-good, as well as the specter of sadists in my private-school world, had

* Not his real name.

opened up a new cognitive realm: One did not have to know what was wrong in order to know that *something* was wrong.

What were "civil rights"? I knew that they were bad and that my father was fighting against them, and this was why he rarely came home evenings: "at one of his civil rights meetings," my mother explained. At the mention of his "civil rights activities," Papa assumed the transcendent yet noncommittal look of Victor Laszlo in *Casablanca*. His own mother preferred not to know the nature of those meetings. I vaguely sensed a connection between his mission and the pistol stowed under his car seat and became worried that he would jeopardize the family's standing by doing something illegal. Soon those sensations of anxiety and shame would crystallize into a concrete fear: that my father was a member of the Ku Klux Klan.

I HAD HAD A TRAUMATIC EXPERIENCE in the summer of 1963 as a result of Birmingham's jail, though it had nothing to do with the recent notoriety of the place, as the address from which Martin Luther King had written what would become the most celebrated jailhouse epistle since St. Paul's. My family had taken out a membership at the Jewish Community Center, and my brothers and I had joined the swim team. One of our coaches had been picked up for drunk driving and while in jail had tried to hang himself with his shirt. He did not return to his summer job. My little brother, Stephen, quit the swim team; my big brother, Craig, had dropped out earlier, after pouring molten lead on his foot while making bullets. But I stuck with it.

I wore a shark's tooth necklace all summer for good luck. My father had brought it to me from one of his scuba-diving trips to Florida—I thought of him as Dixie's answer to Jacques Cousteau, with whom he had had his picture taken at a divers' convention in Chicago. I told everyone Papa had killed the shark that owned the tooth, although in the back of my mind I knew he would never have gotten around to having it mounted on a chain. I don't think he came to a single swim meet of mine, but he did ask me what my stroke was, and when I said fly, he cocked his head at me: He had held the state record for butterfly as a teenager, when he and his brother were the entire Mountain Brook Club swim team. "But I did it with a frog kick," he said.

I, too, alone on the team, used a frog kick instead of the standard dolphin. In the last meet of the season, I placed third in the state, sealing my bond with my father before he drifted beyond our rational grasp.

THE MORE MY FATHER BEHAVED like an outlaw, the more I clung to "ideals" like "responsibility" and "truth" and "citizenship." It was not unheard-of for my classmates and me to declare, "I'm very idealistic." In several years, I would achieve the platonic ideal of white Birmingham girlhood, as president of the ultra-elite high school sorority Theta Kappa Delta. With fond superciliousness, Uncle Hobart referred to me as "The Executive" and had his secretary, at the biggest law firm in Alabama, type my sorority bylaws. I controlled the expenditure of thousands of dollars and the social fate of hundreds of girls. Mothers telephoned me with clogged voices and asked whether their daughters were "TKD material." TKD material—"the three Bs," as our adult advisers defined it: "Beauty, Brains, and Breeding"—was the future that the policeman and his German shepherd were protecting from that black boy, who surely must have been breaking the law.

I believed that if you kept your nose clean you wouldn't get into trouble, and that if you got into trouble it was because you broke the rules and would have to "accept responsibility." There were rumors that the girls bombed at Sixteenth Street—even if they were the black version of TKD material—had been smoking in that basement restroom.

Keen moral certainty blesses both sides of a social revolution. "She believes that this world is a wonderful one in which to live," the headmistress of my school said of me, "and is the kind who helps make it so." Indeed, I was very much a part of my place. Sometimes, for a city as well as a person, growing up means becoming what one will unbecome. This is a story of Birmingham, of holocaust and redemption in the American citadel of segregation, but it is my story, too. It began as what I believed, became what I know, and now it is what I am.

PART I

Precedents
1938–1959

1.

THE CITY OF PERPETUAL
PROMISE

1938

A Local God

VULCAN WAS THE LARGEST cast-iron man in the universe. From his pedestal on the mountaintop, the fifty-six-foot-tall god of fire extended his nine-ton right arm in a salute to the valley of blast furnaces that made Birmingham, Alabama, what it was. Here was reputedly the only place on earth where the essential ingredients of iron-making existed in one spot—coal, iron ore, and lime. These mineral gifts had always been Birmingham's salvation and its damnation, and few natives could distinguish the two conditions. *Harper's* captured the local state of purgatory in a 1937 article about "this town, without parallel anywhere," called "The City of Perpetual Promise."

According to legend, the inspiration for Birmingham came to a Georgia-bred engineer named John Milner in 1858 as he stood near Vulcan's future site on the crest of Red Mountain, the Appalachian foothill named for the color of its iron-ore deposits. The valley below was dotted with the farms of the original squatters, Andrew Jackson's rowdy disciples from Tennessee. But Milner was struck by what it might one day become: a "great workshop town." He built a railroad to the mineral region, double-crossed some carpetbaggers who tried to horn in with their own railroad, and began selling the first plots of his city on December 19, 1871. Milner and his partners had thought they were naming Birmingham after "the best workshop town in all England," but at the time their urban model was world-famous as the manufacturing center of tawdry merchandise.

Birmingham remained a city of dubious superlatives, like its immortal but lame icon. Vulcan was the special patron of cuckolds as well as the god of the forge, unhappily married to the promiscuous Venus. His city, too, seemed to make the worst of enviable circumstances. The iron man had been Birmingham's grand prize–winning exhibit at the 1904 St. Louis world's fair, with an inscription at his base predicting that his city would "exceed all others in 'Time's March.'" Only three years later, the South's great industrial hope had become a backwater colony of Pittsburgh, the property of the United States Steel Corporation. Vulcan was staked at the state fairgrounds, a soot-blackened shill holding a sign honoring another great Pittsburgh industry, Heinz pickles, and later an outsize bottle of Coca-Cola, the business that made arch-rival Atlanta the fastest-growing city in the South.

There had been an earlier prophecy, dating back to the depression of 1894, that more accurately foretold the future: "Hard times come to Birmingham first and stay longest." Forty years later, the Great Depression of the 1930s had impoverished the one-industry town, darkening the steel mills clustered like a colony of dragons on the western periphery. Unemployed workers slept in the cold beehive coke ovens. The "pellagra ring" around the city had expanded into rickets, causing calcium-deprived children to go spastic. Adults coped with a V.D. epidemic. The writer James Agee had marveled at "the hard flat incurable sore of Birmingham" when he and the photographer Walker Evans passed through town on their way to find the Alabama sharecroppers who would be the subject of *Let Us Now Praise Famous Men.*

They were among the many journalists who made pilgrimages to Birmingham to gawk at the mess, generating more dubious superlatives. The homicide rate had earned the city the title of Murder Capital of the World. The illiteracy rate (also number one) had conspired with the poverty to produce a haven for loan sharks. Their profit margin humbled the industrialists quartered in the city's smattering of "tall buildings," the only skyscrapers in the state of Alabama, even if their architecture was perfunctory at best. Historically, the Big Mules had little patience for civic flourishes, including schools, so single-minded were they at converting minerals into cash. "Before God, I will be damned before I will put my hand in my pocket for anything," an early capitalist had pledged.

That was not quite true. For behind Vulcan, south of the bare buttocks that would be a perennial scandal to local Baptists, the coal and iron aristocracy had anted up for some of the most expensive houses in the South, including a replica of Mount Vernon. Pursuing a gracious life in the "improved estate section" of Mountain Brook, upwind from their mills and "over the mountain," the first families of Birmingham seemed immune from the Depression. They were far less upset about the plight of their workers, or even of the iron pipe they made, than about the "socialistic" remedies President Franklin Delano Roosevelt had proposed to mend the economy. The New Deal did more than threaten their businesses. It shook their sense of their identities, their caste. At the country club, the latest FDR joke—or a Poe-inspired poem about "the boresome Eleanor"—was a declaration of "I belong!"

Roosevelt had pronounced Birmingham the hardest-hit city in America, the superlative that most offended civic egos. Among the hundreds of millions of federal relief dollars the New Deal mobilized to the paralyzed district were $44,000, courtesy of the Works Progress Administration, to liberate Vulcan from his thirty-year confinement at the fairgrounds and move our symbol of perpetual promise, glittering with a new coat of aluminum paint, to a floodlit pedestal atop Red Mountain.

As it happened, Giuseppe Moretti, the Italian sculptor commissioned by the city fathers to make Vulcan for the St. Louis world's fair, had designed a companion deity to the god of industry—a soulful-looking marble head of Christ exhibited alongside him at the expo. Moretti had insisted that the two never be separated, as a reminder that a god dedicated to making money was the pagan—whose own creation, Pandora, had unleashed evil on earth. When Vulcan was rescued by Roosevelt, the city officials decided there was no room on the hilltop for Jesus.

Sometimes it seemed that all the profanity of industrial enterprise had collected in Birmingham. The worst fear of the heavy manufacturers was that their labor force might organize into a union and exercise self-determination in the workplace. In their exertions to prevent that from happening—forbidding the workers to grow corn in their gardens, lest the tall stalks serve as cover for union-organizing meetings—they had built a stunning example of what FDR had called the "latent fascism" of the American South. But by the very fact of its being capitalism's city in a valley, Birmingham had also produced the bravest, most electric practitioners of democracy. The profit motive had inspired, in the have-nots as well as the haves, a complex mesh of deformed ideals, and the struggle between those who owned the smokestacks and those who paid the human toll of industrialization had been by turns bloody and farcical.

Birmingham had carried into the modern industrial era the central dilemma of the South's agrarian past: the systematic subjugation of its black citizens. Founded during Reconstruction, the city seemed destined to become the postbellum host of the country's classic confrontations between Left and Right, between black and white, and ultimately between justice and power.

The first of these turning points took place in 1938. In late November, the New Deal arrived in Birmingham like some phantom made flesh—demon or angel, depending on which side you were on. At the Municipal Auditorium gathered the most remarkable group of world savers ever under one roof: academics and ironworkers, social scientists and poets, Communists and Klansmen, and a pageant of New Deal grandees led by Supreme Court Justice Hugo Black and First Lady Eleanor Roosevelt. This was the inauguration of the concerted struggle for freedom that would culminate in Birmingham a quarter century later. It was also Bull Connor's first challenge.

Great Men

JAMES ALEXANDER SIMPSON was within sight of the mountaintop. Perhaps the most powerful politician in Alabama at age forty-eight, he had styled himself the savior of free enterprise from the "socialism" of the New Deal. In Birmingham as

around the country, Big Business's crusade against Roosevelt had come to tran-
scend politics and even economics, taking on the intensity of a holy war against
infidels. It was not enough for Simpson and the elite interests he spoke for to complain that the federal government was telling its corporate betters how much
money to charge for their goods and how much to pay their employees. They also
made fun of the President's polio-crippled legs—the result, they contended, of
syphilis contracted from his wife's black lovers.

Fellow lawyers were sometimes startled at how emotional Simpson became
defending his corporate clients, and there did seem to be something Oedipal
about his pro-business passion. In 1899, nine-year-old Jim's father, a suffering
farmer, had given up all the family assets for them to join a utopian community in
Middle Tennessee run according to the principles of Karl Marx. The Simpsons
had been among the diehard crackpots who followed the dwindling Ruskin Commonwealth to the edge of the Okefenokee Swamp in South Georgia, settling in an
abandoned sawmill camp so squalid that Jim later said Roosevelt would have targeted it for slum clearance. The boy absorbed the social shame of his mother, a
country doctor's proud daughter, who cringed at the "comrades'" table manners,
and he later mocked the collective's notion of industry, such as "the roasting of
corn as a substitute for coffee." Though his Ruskin experience lasted only a year,
it left Simpson with a hatred of any government interference in the accumulation
of private wealth. The childhood taste of dysfunctional communism had marked
him as Alabama's patron saint of organized money.

"Organized money" was the epithet that the President and his lieutenant
Hugo Black employed to tweak the forces of reaction that men like Simpson had
mobilized against the New Deal. When he was Alabama's senior senator, Black
had been the congressional brains and brawn behind Roosevelt's programs, denouncing the "capitalist system," which favored the few "while others, equally
able and gifted, but less fortunately placed, are starved not only physically but
mentally." Black's legislative aggression against Big Business had bestowed national purpose on the equally ambitious Simpson. Inverted images of each other,
Simpson and Black, Alabama's Great Men, presided over the two dominant poles
in the state identity that also now defined American politics.

Back in the 1910s and 1920s, when they worked opposite sides of the Birmingham courts as "damage suit" lawyers, Simpson had always sucked hind teat
to "Old Ego," whose confidence drove adversaries to whine, "Look at that son of a
bitch, he thinks he's going to become President of the United States." Those cases
had been their first ideological standoff. Arguing for the voiceless drudges (including convicts leased to the mines), Black became the workshop town's Robin
Hood, wheedling outrageous jury awards for injured laborers. As the industrialists' shield against such "bolsheviks," Simpson refused to settle cases worth far less
than his legal fees, in order to deter dangerous precedents of "redistributing the
wealth." The two country boys on the make were respectful adversaries, performing essential functions of industrial hygiene, until the rise of the Ku Klux Klan set
them on their collision course in politics.

The Klan

OF THE MANY EXCUSES Hugo Black later gave for joining the Klan, the one that seemed most outlandish was probably the most accurate: The hooded brotherhood of white supremacists was also the liberal insurgent wing of the Democratic Party. The Klan was the flawed consummation of the have-nots' long flirtation with power, which had begun with the signal political phenomenon of the postbellum South: Populism. In a brief revolution during the early 1890s, oppressed farmers had seceded from the "Solid South's" Democratic monolith to form the People's Party and, most shockingly of all, entered into a coalition with former slaves.* The rebellion terrified the state's reigning "colonel and carpetbagger" oligarchy of big planters and Birmingham's fledgling but fierce industrialists. And so they quashed it, disfranchising the poor-white revolutionaries along with their Negro confederates with a stroke of the pen so indelibly clever that it passed into the language as shorthand for the South's peculiar brand of democracy, surviving segregation itself: the poll tax.† Populism's other legacy was the demagoguery of power against insurrection: The Pops were smeared as "nigger lovers and nigger huggers," a "communistic ring," and "simple-minded dupes to outside agitators."

The people's democratic impulse had not been squelched, however. They continued to rise up, next as Prohibitionists and then, after World War I, as Klansmen, seizing the racist propaganda for the common folks. In 1915, the Klan, fallow since Reconstruction, had been revived in Atlanta by an ex–Methodist preacher who had been inspired by a drunken hallucination of celestial night riders while staying with relatives in Birmingham. Initially just one of the many fraternal lodges of the day helping urban newcomers make the transition from country to city, the Klan was vaulted beyond its parochial horizon by a popular movie romanticizing the "true story" of the Reconstruction Klan, D. W. Griffith's *The Birth of a Nation*. Taking out after upwardly mobile ethnic Catholics more than the socially immobile Negro population, the Klan became the driving agency of postwar nativism, sweeping from Main Street to Zenith, through the Deep South to Middle America, claiming four million members at its height in the 1920s.

In 1921, *The Nation* declared Birmingham the "American hotbed of anti-Catholic fanaticism." That year, Hugo Black won an easy acquittal for a Klans-

---

*Populism was the formative political event in Simpson's and Black's lives. Jim was the son of a Populist extremist, one of Ruskin's communists, who had tipped the family's status from "marginal" to "lunatic fringe." Hugo's father was an enemy of the Populists, one of the prosperous storekeepers, or "furnishing merchants," they vilified for keeping the hurting farmers in perpetual hock through exorbitant interest rates. Like Simpson, Black (whose native Clay County was the birthplace of the Alabama People's Party) grew disillusioned with his father—bitterly certain that the only time he had been sober was when the whiskey that finally killed him ran out. So had the two men passed ideologically in the night.

†An annual "poll tax" of $1.50 was assessed each voter; it was cumulative until he (there were no she voters) reached forty-five. That is, a man who tried to register for the first time at forty had to pay $28.50. In Alabama's cash-scarce barter economy, the tax alone knocked out 98 percent of voting-age blacks and 17 to 23 percent of the whites. The property requirement and literacy test brought the percentage of disqualified white men to 35.

man—a gum-chewing Methodist parson—who had walked onto the rectory porch of the largest Catholic church in Alabama and fatally shot a priest who that day had married his daughter to a Puerto Rican. For once, Black and the industrialists seemed to be on the same side. The coal and iron men were humoring the Klan. As long as their "native-born" laborers were fighting the large Catholic-immigrant portion of the work force, there was no danger of union solidarity even among whites, let alone across color lines.*

On election day 1926, however, the bosses realized that the Kluxers they had thought they owned were nothing but damned populists. The surprise winner in the U.S. Senate race, Hugo Black, took the stage at a Klan Klorero held at the city auditorium to celebrate "Alabama's Super Government." The equally unanticipated governor-elect was the leader of the Montgomery klavern, Bibb Graves, a mix of Yale-educated intelligence, tobacco-chewing folk appeal, dictatorial temperament, and a history of Populist activism. As the Klaliff handed them gold plaques, Graves clasped Black's hand and asked, smiling, "We don't have to kiss, do we?" But the two friends embraced in an alliance that yoked the state's customary rulers, whom Graves had christened "Big Mules" because they munched hay from the heavy wagons drawn by little mules.

This was the pair that galvanized the right-wing political career of Jim Simpson. In the Klan's sweep of 1926, he was the sole anti-Klansman from the county elected to the state legislature, having courted the votes of "every man and woman in Jefferson County, white and black, Jew and Gentile, rich and poor—with no secret pledge to anyone." Thirty-six-year-old Simpson had become an aristocrat by marriage (his bride, a pig-iron heiress, had died from childbirth complications), the only candidate to list "Country Club" among his affiliations. Though he voted yes on Graves's first great act—the abolition of the convict lease in the last state where the New South's industrial slave system remained legal—Simpson began to understand that the governor's reforms (notably a $25 million bill to educate the poor) added up to a revolution, transforming government from an overseer of the status quo into an agent of social change.

A New Deal for Klansmen

EARLY IN 1933, Hugo Black waved from President-elect Franklin Roosevelt's motorcade at the farmers crowding the North Alabama crossroads. Their destination of Muscle Shoals was to be the hub of the Tennessee Valley Authority, the New Deal's radical electricity-making experiment intended to improve the lot of the struggling yeomen—and, by putting the federal government in competition with private industry, to shake up free enterprise in America. As Black's prominence in the presidential entourage implied, the old Klan leaders had reconstituted themselves as New Dealers. The following year, Bibb Graves made an

---

*Seventy-five years earlier, the southern slave oligarchy and northern slave traders had fomented another nativist anti-Catholic secret society, the Know-Nothing Party, to destabilize the northern anti-slavery consensus that had led to the slavery-restricting Missouri Compromise of 1820.

unprecedented comeback as governor after sitting out the term mandated by the state constitution (so that the executive branch, which the tory "Bourbon" Democrats couldn't control as easily as they did the legislature, would not amass too much power). Roosevelt acolytes had also captured two of the three spots on the Birmingham city commission. With point men in the governor's mansion and city hall as well as the White House, Hugo Black was positioned for maximum damage.

Jim Simpson's work was cut out for him. He returned to the state capital, this time as the senator from "Imperial Jefferson" County, to execute a smooth counterstroke against the New Deal. In the name of "ideals," he had figured out a way to divest Graves and the liberals on the Birmingham commission of their main political lever, patronage—the means by which the have-nots (like the Irish of Boston) had historically assimilated into the mainstream. Late in 1934, after a donnybrook over patronage slots in city hall had ripped apart even the janitorial staff of the women's restroom, Simpson began his maneuvers to replace the "spoils" system with a "merit" system based on the democratic principle that a public servant should be rewarded (or fired) on the basis of his performance, not his vote (or bribe). In reality, the civil service bill he proposed would have the effect of undermining the democratic process, for it effectively turned the people's elected executives into figureheads answerable to an oligarchy, the unelected personnel board.

Unfortunately for Simpson, Bibb Graves's top henchman—a Klan chieftain and radio demagogue who was a brilliant lawyer to boot—saw through the bill and mounted a torrid campaign to defeat it. Simpson, having adopted his new ruling class with a vengeance, no longer had the common touch to counter such a gifted rabble-rouser, who had already coined a new verb: "Simpsonize." He needed a folksy mouthpiece if he was going to turn the "grass roots" against the patronage protocols designed to uplift them. His new page, "George C." Wallace, seemed to have a promising instinct for stump politics, but he was only fifteen. Simpson's house delegation offered little relief. Virtually all Jefferson County's representatives were men who at least aspired to the country club. There was only one exception.

Bull

SOME SPORTS FANS had gotten together a petition nominating a popular baseball announcer to run for the state house of representatives in 1934. People used to say they would rather hear a game called by Eugene Connor than see it. Bull was his nickname, for his glibness and the hoarse bellow straining over the noisy Teletype. He flaunted the country inflection of his upbringing in the Black Belt village of Plantersville (hence "the Plantersville hog-caller"), where his schooling had been sporadic and largely unsuccessful. His parents, a railroad dispatcher and a farm girl, had given him the first name Theophilus, after a notorious bank robber of the day. After his mother died of pneumonia when he was eight, the widower, King Edward, passed his four boys among aunts and uncles, but he did find time to teach them all to read a ticker tape.

In 1921, twenty-four-year-old Eugene made his "sportscasting" debut at a baseball matinee in Dallas—the prototypic "media event," where fans gathered not to see the game but to hear an announcer "call it" on the strength of Morse code bulletins from the ballpark.* By the mid-twenties, Connor was a celebrity in Birmingham. Fans crowded into the billiard parlor below the radio station where he manned his telegraph machine, just to be near the voice. "Ouuuuuuuuuut!" he would roar. And "Now you pitchin', Candy Kid. Th'ow that onion, boy, th'ow it." And "Shine threw to Billy. Billy threw to Piccolo Pete Susko and now they're all OUUUUUUUUUUT. Now you goin', chilluns, now you goin'." His cornball idiom was lovingly mimicked all over town.

Baseball had been an opiate of the mine and mill masses at least since New York Giant pitcher Joe "Ironman" McGinnity dropped an ingot into Vulcan's mold before a paying crowd, to raise money for Birmingham's iron man. The mines and mills sponsored a highly competitive Industrial League of black teams and white teams, to encourage workers to exercise their collective impulses in company-sanctioned outlets rather than labor unions. The league begat the professional Black Barons, with their legendary trickster-pitcher from the 1920s, Satchel Paige. The (white) Barons were owned by the district's largest pig-iron manufacturer, A. H. "Rick" Woodward. It was at the state-of-the-art ballpark he built, Rickwood Field, that the cheeriest hour of the Depression took place—bigger, one sportswriter claimed, than Charles Lindbergh's Birmingham touchdown. In September 1931, in the World Series of southern white baseball, the Barons' aging second baseman batted in the winning run off Houston's bumptious Dizzy Dean. It was no wonder that Bull Connor, who had put the moment into words for thousands of hurting souls, became the voice of hope in Birmingham.† *The Sporting News* pronounced him the South's favorite announcer.

When Connor's fans begged him to run for the legislature the following year, he balked. He was shy about public appearances and self-conscious about his blind eye, the casualty of an air rifle during a boyhood game of war. But his gruff, friendly voice more than compensated for his physical flaws, which also included a high-waisted, chicken-chested body. "I'm going to tell the truth," he told the *Birmingham News*. "... I had no more idea of being elected than beating Lou Gehrig out for first base with the Yankees." Such "honesty" combined with his "efficiency" (he spent only $64 on his campaign) to elect an executive with mass as well as class appeal.

Bull had everything "Sunny Jim" Simpson lacked: bad grammar and the ear of the people. Simpson was only seven years older than thirty-seven-year-old

---

*Another gifted ad-libber, Ronald "Dutch" Reagan of Illinois, would also graduate from baseball chatter to politics.
†The Barons' batboy for the game was a resident of the nearby U.S. Steel neighborhood of Ensley, Charles O. Finley. One day he would own his own baseball team, the Athletics, whose farm system would include the Barons.

Connor, but he adopted him as his long-lost commoner son. Simpson called him Eugene, shunning like a punctilious father the nickname designed for mass intimacy that was listed in the phone book. Connor, in turn, felt gratefully entitled to chum up with the state's Great Man. "Me and Jim" was how Connor described the lasting partnership forged in the civil service legislation that he convinced his fans was a democratic reform rather than a Bourbon coup. The bill was signed into law in August 1935: the first step toward "Simpsonizing" Alabama.

In early 1937, Simpson and some Big Mules sat Connor down. Bull had been invaluable to the civil service fight and had otherwise been a regular "efficiency" beaver, blocking funding for a passenger elevator in the capitol. But he shouldn't be muffling his main asset—his popularity—behind closed doors in committees and subcommittees. An original like Bull needed his own show, down where he could mix with the folks. They wanted him to run for Birmingham's city commission, the public safety spot, and to purge city hall of the New Dealers. Governor Graves sent his operatives up from Montgomery to try to stop "Me and Jim" from colonizing Birmingham. But Bull struck back with his first recorded charge of "outside agitator" and won the spring election by a landslide.

Upon moving into his office in the fall of 1937, Bull promised *not* to improve his grammar and, as further proof of being a people person, removed the door from its hinges. Then he began systematically to undercut his police department's civil service policies, remaking the force as his personal militia. Simpson, whose commitment to "merit" was clearly situational, now would use his legislative skills to write laws that assigned more and more power to the police. By so extending the authority of the police Connor controlled, Simpson gained custody of the South's great workshop town.

Smyer

THE BIG MULES found an auspicious replacement for Connor as Simpson's steward in the statehouse. Sidney Smyer was a Cherokee County native—another country boy—who retained the blondish, raw-boned farmer look of the original Smeisser brothers who had emigrated from Bavaria to Pennsylvania in the mid-1700s. A bit earlier, the Ulster Scot Moses McWhorter had left Coleraine, Northern Ireland, for Pennsylvania after some Scottish Presbyterian kinfolk were strung up by the Catholics in a tree in front of their house. The two families had made their way down through the Piedmont, sweeping into Gaylesville with the great post–War of 1812 influx known as Alabama fever. Two years after Dr. Robert Lee McWhorter delivered Sid into the world, the Smyers set out for Birmingham, to run a dairy farm in gritty West End.

Sid grew up vowing never more to be "nursemaid to a cow." After graduating from the University of Alabama's law school, he joined the white-shoe practice of his wealthy uncle E.J. But he always felt a bit defensive around the country club set, having been called "dago" as a youth selling vegetables from a truck alongside first-generation vendors. When he took a night job at a drugstore to get a discount on his diabetic bride's insulin, Uncle E.J. chastised him, "Young man, make up your mind whether you want to be a lawyer or a soda jerk." And Smyer became a pretty fair real estate lawyer, earning his stripes by stopping the New Dealers in the county government from raising property taxes. The only clue to his civic destiny was that his main client was the Birmingham Realty Company, which was descended from the land company John Milner set up in 1871 after tricking the carpetbaggers out of their deeds to his great workshop town. The Big Mules believed that Smyer, with a little more hunger but less appetite than his rich clients, would make a perfect public servant of the status quo.

All the chips seemed to be falling into place for Jim Simpson's takeover of the state. He had his proxy in city hall and an able law writer lined up to take Connor's place in the statehouse. And then in August 1937, when Franklin Roosevelt rewarded Hugo Black with an appointment to the Supreme Court, Simpson's most important rival—the broker of practically every New Deal transaction in Alabama—was removed from the nitty-gritty of state politics.

But Simpson's real mission had only just begun. Black was about to return to Birmingham, leading the New Deal's charge against the South's feudal rulers.

The Communist

SOMETIMES IT SEEMED that the Big Mules were losing touch with reality. At the beginning of the Depression, when American society was on the verge of collapse, they had built their second country club to serve an ever smaller circle of elitedom. ("Persons who are fortunate enough to belong to the Mountain Brook Club," a visiting journalist observed, "... do not let the hour pass without somehow allowing the news to escape.") Isolated in their sylvan fortress, the industrialists had created such a caricatured portrait of the enemy—FDR, the "pig killer," cavorting with swarthy, wild-eyed bolsheviks—that they were not prepared to cope when the threat took the benign form of their own Joseph Gelders. Gelders was a Jew, true, but he was one of Birmingham's "pet Jews," from a prosperous and assimilated old German-Jewish family, which ran a fine restaurant downtown. Joe, the bookish son who had taken a while to find himself, was the last person the Gelderses' gentile friends would have suspected of being a real Bolshevik: a bona fide Communist.

Birmingham had become the Deep South headquarters of the American Communist Party not long after the Communist International decreed from Moscow in 1928 that the Negro peasants of America's plantation Black Belt (the dark band of humus-rich soil running from Virginia to Texas) were the potential advance guard of a Marxist revolution in the United States. "The right of self-determination of the Negroes of the Black Belt"—leading to secession if necessary—became a Communist objective. Agrarian though it was, the uprising was to be launched from the South's industrial hub.

The growing "Communist menace" earned Birmingham a visit in late 1930 from the right-wing New York congressman Hamilton Fish's committee investigating Communist propaganda, which seemed primarily interested in which of the revolutionaries' bland noms de guerre hid a Jew. In fact, few southerners had been moved by the Party's purely economic gospel, delivered by zealous young white intellectuals from the North who signed their letters "Comradely yours." It was as if Jesus had never gotten beyond fighting usury. The Party needed a crucifixion to translate dogma into passion, to tie capitalist evil to the South's central race drama, lynching.

The martyrs the Communists were looking for turned out to be nine illiterate black hoboes on the Chattanooga-to-Memphis freight train, which was chugging through the Tennessee River valley in northern Alabama an hour behind schedule on March 25, 1931. At the town of Stevenson, white hoboes debarked from a gondola car and told the stationmaster that some Negroes on board had beaten them up. All nine black males were seized by sheriff's deputies a couple of towns west. Two white hoboes taken off the train with them turned out to be overall-clad, snuff-dipping females—laid-off Huntsville cotton mill workers and occasional prostitutes—who told a deputy after twenty minutes of prompting that the black youths had raped them. A doctor's exam uncovered no evidence of rape, but the Negroes, whose ages ranged from thirteen to twenty, were taken to jail at the county seat, Scottsboro. Summarily sentenced to death, the "Scottsboro Boys" entered the realm of history, as the critic Edmund Wilson would write a few months later, where "the antagonism between hoboes in a freight-car bursts empires and lays commonwealths waste."

The "nigger rape case," as the locals called it, was soon seen around the world as a test of America's moral authority, thanks to the Communists' propaganda offensive—their first in the United States. In assuming charge of the death sentence appeals, the Communist Party embarrassed the National Association for the Advancement of Colored People, whose initial reaction to the case had been to wonder if the youths were guilty. By summer, the Party was showcasing Scottsboro moms—some of questionable authenticity—at fund-raising rallies around the country. As the headquarters of the defense, as well as the defendants' holding pen, Birmingham became the nerve center of the first southern working-class black movement. The ragtag Communist Party was challenging the NAACP's franchise, becoming an international symbol of what it called "Negro liberation."*

Birmingham's Communist Party was peaking in 1934, with a claimed membership of one thousand, before it touched the sheltered existence of Joe Gelders. In his thirties, Gelders had finally settled into a job that suited his sculpted fea-

---

*Besides the Scottsboro Boys, the Birmingham Communists stage-managed the decade's other black civil rights martyr: Angelo Herndon, who had joined the Party at nineteen after a couple of years mining coal for U.S. Steel. ("This is no life for a man and a Christian.") Too notorious to operate in Birmingham, Herndon was transferred to Atlanta, where, in July 1932, he was charged under an anti-insurrection statute left over from slavery. "You cannot kill the working class," he warned the court that sentenced him to eighteen to twenty years of hard labor, and he went on to become a Supreme Court test case for the Bill of Rights.

tures and wire-rim glasses, as a physics professor at the University of Alabama, in Tuscaloosa. In May 1934, a violent strike in Birmingham of mostly black U.S. Steel ore miners jolted his ivory tower world. Black strikers and strikebreakers had been murdered, and bombs, a choice instrument of labor strife, destroyed the homes of black scabs. Though anguished by the brutality, Gelders was fascinated by the *Birmingham News*'s view of the strike—"Reds Linked with Violence" and "Outbreak Believed Work of Agitators." Searching for his own explanation, he read Adam Smith, Charles and Mary Beard, and the English Fabian socialists. When he got to Marx and Engels, he believed he had found the answer. He sought out the Communist Party.

After receiving clearance to join, Gelders headed to New York, to be groomed outside Party officialdom as secretary of the National Committee for the Defense of Political Prisoners, a group of left-wing writers and artists including Aaron Copland, John Dos Passos, Theodore Dreiser, Lewis Mumford, Upton Sinclair, Jean Stafford, and Lionel and Diana Trilling, which had rallied to the Scottsboro Boys. In the summer of 1936, Gelders was sent back to Birmingham behind the front of the NCDPP as the Party's key stealth operator in the South. A quiet man, retaining much of the "bourgeois" propriety that had initially caused the Party to reject him, he was hardly a working-class hero spoiling to take on his hometown's Goliath—the United States Steel Corporation. Certainly he had no expectation of becoming a giant-slayer.

The Corporation

WHEN J. P. MORGAN created U.S. Steel in 1901, so intimidating was the resulting conglomerate—the biggest business in the world, combining Morgan's midwestern mills with Andrew Carnegie's Pittsburgh empire—that one British public figure said England's only hope was to become an American colony. "Big Steel," as the company was called, was the zenith of industry, the builder of an expanding America, and the hard foundation of the national defense. The "Morganization" of the country's economy would have been complete if it had not been for one of the principals strong-armed in the steel merger, the stock market rogue John "Bet a Million" Gates. A former wire salesman who had become the "King of Barbed Wire" (and transfigured the Texas landscape) on the strength of a stolen patent, Gates had vowed to get back at Morgan and seized control of Birmingham's largest steel producer, the Tennessee Coal, Iron, and Railroad Company. By 1907 he had turned it into a worrisome challenger to Morgan's young, overcapitalized corporation.

That fall, a panic in the financial markets presented Morgan with a solution to the problem of Birmingham, which Carnegie had long since pronounced "Pennsylvania's most formidable industrial enemy." The story of how he defused the Panic of 1907—gathering the country's major bankers to the red silk–walled library of his Manhattan townhouse for an all-night caucus on November 3—has become a cliché in the Morgan legend: the last hurrah of the world's supreme financier and the watershed in high finance that would lead to the establishment of the Federal Reserve System. Little notice was given to the fine print of the deal, which consigned Birmingham to limbo: The scheme Morgan proposed that night for averting a stock market crash was to buy the Birmingham-based Tennessee Company as a "favor" to the struggling Wall Street brokerage firm that happened to hold the majority stock of Gates's syndicate. President Theodore Roosevelt interrupted his breakfast the next morning to approve Morgan's instant monopoly—the banker's emissaries had convinced him, trustbuster though he was, that disaster would otherwise befall the country *within the week*. The announcement of the Tennessee Company sale was made that very day, November 4, 1907, and the stock market rallied.

Roosevelt remained plagued to his death by the feeling that he had been "either a fool or a knave" in permitting Morgan's takeover of Birmingham. For in what one analyst called "the most important occurrence in the iron trade" since the formation of U.S. Steel itself, the Corporation (as it liked to be known) acquired its strongest competitor for less than a fiftieth of its value. Morgan paid only $35.3 million for a company whose mineral properties alone were conservatively worth a *billion* dollars. Yet Congress's aggressive antitrust investigations into U.S. Steel's imperialism offended the Corporation's new southern subjects. Birmingham saw itself as a prince, however minor, in America's royal family, the "World's Largest Corporation." Even after the company imposed immediate layoffs and production cuts on its southern outpost, Birmingham did not understand what had been clear to a trade analyst of the day: that U.S. Steel had bought the district to prevent it from competing with the Pittsburgh flagship, where most of the Corporation's capital was invested, and that therefore the South's industrial potential would remain untapped. The once ascendant Tennessee Coal, Iron, and Railroad Company—TCI—was now the serf of an absentee baron.

The proletariat in a great workshop town that shut down at the drop of an economic indicator was bound to be frustrated and unstable. Which explained why Birmingham was so attractive to the Communist Party. The Party's inflammatory presence, in turn, justified any means the Corporation chose to prevent labor organizers from getting to its workers. U.S. Steel had virtually invented industry's union-beating game plan during the great, failed national steel strike of 1919, when its private detectives infiltrated the work force and supplied the propaganda that fueled that year's Red Scare—and established the authority for U.S. Attorney General Mitchell Palmer's famous raids on "radicals." The point of the propaganda was to equate organized labor with "bolshevism" and organized money with "Americanism." And this was the idea that still animated the civic-industrial complex that Joe Gelders would encounter nearly two decades later: a pageantry of repression that had landed his hometown on the American Civil Liberties Union's list of the three worst cities in the South.

Gelders's first project, in August 1936, was to rescue a young comrade from jail. Bart Logan (a.k.a. Jack Barton) had been put in charge of the Party's labor-organizing work in Bessemer, a satellite of Birmingham stripped of any civil pretense—what the reds called a wholly owned subsidiary of U.S. Steel. Logan had been sentenced to a shackled road crew for possessing "seditious" literature (including *The New Republic* and *The Nation*) in violation of a local ordinance designed to keep union organizers off the streets. Gelders made appeals on Logan's behalf to the Bessemer authorities, noting his tubercular condition, but a "committee" from TCI had visited a local bondsman and told him that if he sprung Logan, it would be the last business he ever saw.

Nearing midnight on September 23, Gelders was walking home from a meeting about the Logan case. On a deserted Southside street, four men clubbed him from behind, and bundled him into the back seat of a car. As they stomped his face and stomach, one read from the Scottsboro literature Gelders was carrying, making lewd noises about the rape details. Several hours later, the car stopped on a country road. The men dragged Gelders out of the car, stripped him down to his shorts and socks, then leather-strapped him on the back and blackjacked him in the face and stomach. When he came to in the woods, his body was covered with cuts and bruises, and he had chipped teeth, a broken nose, and a ruptured heart muscle.

Where the beatings of many "subversives"—commonplace enough for TCI to humorously designate them "fishing trips"—had been met with local indifference, the attack on Joe Gelders, a man from a fine Birmingham family, became a cause célèbre. The local newspapers joined the Communist Party and the American Civil Liberties Union in calling for the arrest of the floggers. Birmingham's chief of detectives vowed to catch them no matter "what organization they may belong to."

A week after the abduction, the police were summoned to a bedraggled eastern margin of downtown, where a witness had seen a man drive up to a corn patch in a green Chevrolet, loft some paper scraps into the breeze, and then pitch a bat into the field. A police search yielded a sawed-off baseball bat with human hair stuck to it and paper fragments that pieced together as Joe Gelders's American Legion card. But the authorities suddenly decided there was "nothing to it": The Chevy's owner was a man esteemed in high places.

Walter J. Hanna—known as Crack after his boyhood talent for pitching rocks at cans on the heads of Negro children—was at age thirty-four the hub of the city's anti-union machinery. He had proven himself by crushing the 1934 ore strike as a captain of the National Guard and had since moved on to the U.S. Steel payroll—with his own secret phone number—under the job description of "security." His duties included funneling the Corporation's money into anti-red "Americanization" efforts and coordinating "fishing trips" for radicals with the Birmingham police's Red Squad.

At a police lineup in mid-October (called under pressure from Governor Bibb Graves), the key witness in the case fearfully identified Crack Hanna as the short, stocky man he had watched throw the sawed-off bat in the corn patch. Gelders confirmed that it was Hanna who had struck the first blow against him on the street. Despite Gelders's positive identification of Hanna and two other assailants, the police made no arrests, and two grand juries refused to indict them, a diffidence that investigators understood to be related to the recent visit from the Corporation's officers ("like a royal family on progress," one writer noted) to announce a $31 million expansion for TCI.

Gelders realized that in the absence of justice, he might have to settle for truth. In Washington, Senator Robert M. La Follette Jr., Hugo Black's ally from Wisconsin, had begun hearings into the violence, industrial espionage, and repression of civil liberties that had greeted the New Deal's most serious affront to business: the government-protected right of workers, for the first time in history, to organize and bargain collectively with their employers. Perhaps because the Communists on La Follette's staff understood the impact Gelders's story might have on the World's Largest Corporation, his case was rushed to the front burner as the committee's second investigation.

Gelders's testimony, in January 1937, vindicated the Party's propaganda about life and liberty inside a U.S. Steel company town. But it was perhaps a state detective, unsympathetic to Communists, who explained the situation best: "You know, Senator, the T.C.I. owns or controls fifteen-sixteenths of that country around there, and any opposition against Captain Hanna, even by a court of misdemeanors or a $10 fine—anything that might bring a civil suit which would antagonize the T.C.I., and they are expecting an expenditure of $31,000,000 by the T.C.I.—" It was not necessary to say more, even though a parade of witnesses, including Communist victims of the Red Squad, unionist victims of the National Guard, Pinkerton agents, and even the chief prosecutor in Bessemer, did.

The city's institutions leaped to the defense of U.S. Steel, but it was astonishing how quickly the system collapsed under the force of the bad publicity. As the Birmingham police chief informed a colleague after a TCI executive paid a call on *him,* "Whippings, I believe, are over in this district." Indeed, within months, Birmingham had been taken off the ACLU's list of centers of oppression.

The era of payroll vigilantism came to a swift end. But the industrialists were hardly surrendering to organized labor. Now, instead of trying to crush the union with force, the Big Mules would wield a nonviolent club: the racism they had fomented whenever the have-nots threatened to organize across racial lines. Rather than give specific orders to the vigilantes, they would delegate political intermediaries to oversee strategic racial violence.

That was where Bull Connor, Birmingham's new commissioner of public safety, came into the picture. To prepare for his assignment, he would have to claim the issue of race as his personal badge. And Joe Gelders was plotting the perfect occasion.

Gelders Returns

HIS COMMUNIST PARTY membership still secret, Gelders had become a respected enough member of the New Deal's extended family by early 1938 to wangle an audience with Eleanor Roosevelt. She arranged for him to meet with the President, at Hyde Park, New York. In June, Gelders presented to Roosevelt his plan for a liberal takeover of the South.

By 1935, the Communist Party had shelved its hope of proletariat revolution in favor of a Popular Front (later Democratic Front) with the non-Communist Left, including former "mere" liberals. As the black masses were left in the lurch—the Birmingham party dwindled to thirty-four dues-paying members—Gelders was charged with organizing the enlightened white intelligentsia. He believed that if southern activists like those at the top of Roosevelt's alphabet agencies put their status and brains behind the goals of the labor movement, the South might be hauled out of the feudal system the President had decried recently as "the Fascist system" while campaigning against conservative southern senators. What Gelders proposed coincided with Roosevelt's ambitions for a midterm electoral sweep in Dixie: a convention of the great minds of the South, to form a counterestablishment to the reactionaries.

On his way back south from Hyde Park, Gelders stopped in Washington and asked Hugo Black if he would speak at his conference. The justice was pleased to, especially since it was going to take place in his hometown. With a figurehead like Black, Gelders's idea was now a live possibility. But he would need money and institutional resources to make it a reality. The benefactor he went to was the New Deal era's most muscular challenge to the vested interests, far more threatening than Gelders's own party. And accordingly it would bring down on Gelders's project one of the most vicious backlashes the anti–New Dealers could muster.

The CIO

IN THE Congress of Industrial Organizations, the labor movement had finally found its ultimate form. The CIO was the creation of John L. Lewis, the giant personality (he considered Roosevelt to be his only true peer) who headed the country's most powerful union, the United Mine Workers of America. By bolting the sagging American Federation of Labor in 1935 and forming the CIO, Lewis had ushered labor into the modern era of mass production, organizing workers according to the products they made rather than the jobs they performed (which management had cleverly subspecialized).

The CIO's make-or-break first quarry had been Big Steel. For the past twenty-eight years, the U.S. Steel Corporation had not bargained with a union it did not control, setting a reassuring example to industrialists nationwide that their employees were an extension of their property rights. And so the news of March 7, 1937, had been earth-shaking. U.S. Steel signed an agreement with the CIO conceding union recognition. As what Lewis called the "hyenas" of "Little Steel" saw it, the lion had given up its kingdom apparently over a thorn in its southpaw: "Unquestionably a large factor" in the Corporation's abdication, one journal stated, was the La Follette committee's revelations three months earlier about TCI's manhandling of Joe Gelders.

The CIO was the most dynamic force for progress in the South when

Gelders went to John L. Lewis's Birmingham-based southern deputy for help. Even after Gelders divulged his secret Communist Party membership, the CIO man did not flinch. The union agreed to take over the day-to-day planning of Gelders's conference and provided the chief subsidy for what was to become the CIO's southern conscience and think tank: this fusion of the South's liberal educated elite, left-wing ideological warriors, and grassroots working-man democrats, in an experiment called the Southern Conference for Human Welfare.

The President himself provided the agenda for the coming convention, a *Report on the Economic Conditions of the South* written by his southern kitchen cabinet and released over his name in August. He called the South "the Nation's No. 1 economic problem" and, like the report itself, made no mention of the black and white social one. But Gelders and the other southerners should have recognized the folly of thinking they could win their region's hearts and minds without confronting its soul of racism, especially in the place that was the country's laboratory of segregation, Birmingham.

Shuttlesworth

THE FIRST ELECTED MAYOR, James Powell, a former Pony Express rider turned prosperous mail coach operator, had given the great workshop town its two lasting names—Birmingham, of course, and the Magic City, both on the basis of a few surveyors' tents. In 1873, hoping to eventually make his still chimerical "El Dorado of the Iron Masters" the state capital, he had brought in trainloads of black Reconstruction Republicans to vote for Birmingham to become the seat of Jefferson County. A rumor was planted among these newly freed slaves that Powell, waving a saber astride a calico pony, was General Ulysses S. Grant. And so, believing they were on the side of the emancipators, local blacks used their one political opportunity for the next hundred years to anoint the toughest place their race would endure.

Many of these rural Negroes soon left their sharecropper plots to carry out the darkest underground labor or the hottest blast-furnace duty in the mines and mills of Birmingham. "If it were possible to employ horses and mules or oxen to perform this work," an iron expert said of one of the jobs reserved for blacks, "the Society for the Prevention of Cruelty to Dumb Beasts would have interfered long ago, and rightfully so." But the community recoiled from its black beasts of burden, who had given Birmingham the highest concentration of Negroes—more than 40 percent—of any large city. Law and industry conspired to restrain them, lest they "develop into human tigers," the *Birmingham News* warned, and "give vent to their hatred of some white men." First, the city's African-Americans were disfranchised through the all-white primary in 1888, and then they were legally erased from the landscape: streetcars (the front), public parks, white-zoned neighborhoods.

But it was the extralegal abuse, like the policeman's fatal bullet in the back of a thirteen-year-old Negro girl who had stolen a few lumps of coal in 1910, that had inspired the popular joke about a Negro in Chicago who informs his wife that Jesus came to him in his sleep and said He wanted him to go to Birmingham. She objects: "Did Jesus say He'd go with you?"

Her husband replied, "He said He'd go as far as Memphis."

Fred Shuttlesworth had gotten as far as Oxmoor, a disintegrating U.S. Steel scrapyard just southwest of Birmingham, where his stepfather, William Shuttlesworth, had mined ore for TCI until his lungs were ruined by ore dust. Now he was among the 75 percent of local Negroes on relief, nearly double the national average for working-age blacks. Fred's mother, Alberta Robinson, and his biological father (named Greene) had not married when their son was born on March 18, 1922, in a farming community outside of Montgomery, and Fred wore his mother's new, much older husband's name grudgingly: William cussed and beat the children and scrapped violently with their also fiery mother, whose eye was put out with a broomstick during one of their rows in 1937.

Fred reacted to the cruel authoritarianism of his household by finding acceptable expressions for his own combative spirit—meting out harsh discipline to his eight younger siblings and challenging schoolmates to boxing matches, after the black hero of the day, Joe Louis. The first glimpse Fred had of the complex world outside the tough life of subsistence in Oxmoor was when he was bused to high school in a nearby black community called Rosedale, which a prospectus on Mountain Brook had touted as "the home of many of the better type negro families" who would staff the new suburb's grand houses. These were the first Negroes he had encountered who had significant contact with white people.

If Shuttlesworth occasionally saw some white kids playing with his classmates after school, they were probably Martin, Gail, and Hobart McWhorter, who came to Rosedale to swim in the creek (where the churches held their baptisms) with the two children of the McWhorters' "shadow family" of retainers. The matriarch was the McWhorters' cook and house manager, Ruby Kenon Thornton. Her marriage to James Thornton, who worked across the street as butler to the McWane cast-iron family, forgers of Vulcan, placed the couple somewhere in the spacious median of a precarious black "middle class," on a tier below Pullman car porters, bellmen at white hotels, and barbers at white establishments. The proud maid who "worked over the mountain in Miss Ann's kitchen"—the generic term for domestic labor—might be called a "white folks' nigger" behind her back, but every Thursday, "maids' day off," she would be surrounded by less worldly acquaintances and questioned about "her white lady." Mama Ruby described the Gulf seafood recipe that her sophisticated Yankee lady was having her try out on the literary club, though such exotic rituals interested them less than the everyday things that Miss Ann had in common with black folks.

Shuttlesworth absorbed Rosedale's upwardly mobile ethic, distinguishing himself on the football field and, with what he called his "almost photostatic memory," in the classroom. But he did not adopt the strivers' assumption that "Negro liberation" was a function of making themselves acceptable to white people. Eventually Shuttlesworth would show the world that emancipation was a process that could not occur without the organized participation of his own humble kind. In the fall of 1938, however, as Joe Gelders's conference opened in Birmingham, liberals—white and black—still believed that democracy could be decreed from on high, that oppressors could be reasoned with, and that the oppressed could be "saved."

A City on a Hill

IN WHAT WOULD in retrospect seem a sort of skull-in-the-mirror image of the liberal millennium about to take place in Birmingham, the world had come to an end in late October when skyscraper-sized Martians bearing death rays invaded Grovers Mill, New Jersey, and then advanced on Times Square. It had turned out to be a Halloween prank by Orson Welles, the young actor, director, and producer, who had decided to dramatize H. G. Wells's *War of the Worlds* on his Sunday night radio program on CBS. But the nation was still naïve, unnerved by the Depression, and the next day's news—"Panic Grips Nation"—described riots of fleeing citizens. The world savers who gathered in Birmingham three weeks later (and for whom Welles became a fund-raiser) would cause a quieter maelstrom, but one that would turn into a cold civil war and finally a social revolution.

On the evening of November 20, 1938, more than 1,500 delegates—some 250 of them black—representing every state in the Old Confederacy, converged on Birmingham's tidy grid of a downtown, with the "so many vacant lots" that Jonathan Daniels, the New Deal liberal from an old North Carolina newspaper family, had described in his newly published *A Southerner Discovers the South* as "not so much areas of despair as shares in promise." At seven-thirty the men and women made their way inside the homely brick-and-concrete Municipal Auditorium. The biracial academic front included the University of North Carolina's president, Frank Porter Graham, and Fisk's eminent sociologist Charles S. Johnson, as well as an up-and-coming young historian, C. Vann Woodward. Barry Bingham and Mark Ethridge, of the *Louisville Courier-Journal,* led the press. The New Deal was liberally represented, foremost by Eleanor Roosevelt and Mary McLeod Bethune, the administration's most prominent Negro as the deputy chief of the National Youth Administration. Governor Bibb Graves arrived in the state limousine with his wife, a former suffragist. Five days earlier, he had made the decision of his career. By going against the advice of The Boss himself, Franklin Roosevelt, and refusing to release the Scottsboro Boys from prison, Graves would forfeit his chance of being remembered as Alabama's own FDR and he would instead go down in history as a Klansman who built schools and highways for the little people.

The VIPs, some dressed as if for the opera, mingled with sharecroppers and tenant farmers, able to attend because the CIO's support had held the registration fee to a dollar. The uncommon man among the overalls wearers was Hosea Hudson, a black iron molder who was the Communist Party's "authentic" working-class hero in Birmingham, the future subject of books as well as FBI memos trying to link Martin Luther King's own demonstrations to the great marches Hudson organized in the city during the 1930s. The handful of white leftists—mostly lapsed bourgeoisie like Gelders, including the Party's Deep South district organizer (a shabby-genteel product of Mobile)—took seats alongside such bastions of the economy as the president of the First National Bank, who were mollified by the conference's solid upper-middle-class roots. Observing it all, the Swedish social scientist Gunnar Myrdal, in the States researching what would become his groundbreaking book on race—*An American Dilemma*—was amazed at "this new and unique adventure."

Race, of course, was the dilemma the conference organizers were hoping to finesse, and keep progress uncontroversial. But it was broached unequivocally by the keynote speaker at the opening session Sunday night, UNC's Frank Graham. Three thousand people had now filled the auditorium, blacks having shunned the "Colored" entrance and walked through the front doors. Graham picked up on the (black) Industrial High choir's spiritual, "Deep River, My Home Is Over Jordan," and beckoned his colored brethren "into the promised land." Then he enunciated the issue to a standing ovation: "The black man is the primary test of American democracy and Christianity." For that one evening Joe Gelders had turned the hardest-hit city in a valley into a city upon a hill. Everyone "went away from there that night just full of love and gratitude," one participant recalled. "The whole South was coming together to make a new day."

But it was another memorable comment of Graham's that predicted the events of the following day. "Repression, whether it be of the Negro, Catholic, Jew, or laborer," he had said, "is the way of frightened power."

Connor's Baptism

AFTER A MORNING of integrated workshops—on the poll tax, education, wages, public health—delegates reported to the Municipal Auditorium to find it surrounded by black police wagons. A stout, jug-eared man with a mean squint maneuvered among them giving orders in a bullfrog voice. The rookie public safety commissioner of Birmingham uttered his first famous aphorism: "White and Negro are not to segregate together." And with that malapropism, Bull Connor nullified the agenda set by the President of the United States and made race the medium of the Southern Conference for Human Welfare.

Bull's men drove a peg into the lawn, tied a cord to it, and then teased it through the auditorium doors, down the central corridor, and onto the stage. History would record that Eleanor Roosevelt sat in the black section at a subsequent workshop until the police asked her to move, and then she defiantly dragged a folding chair into the center aisle. In the future context of Bull Connor's Birmingham, her action would be remembered as a gutsy moral stand rather than what it was: the wife of the President of the United States browbeaten by a crude radio personality. Connor had made his national debut.

The conference continued, heavily policed. Connor had pushed the SCHW to the left. Racial egalitarianism was hardly a condition of being a liberal at this time. Indeed, the only delegates militant enough to bring up civil rights—lynching, Negro enfranchisement—were the Communists. Forced by Connor to take a stand on segregation, the conference risked dissolving on its own in sectarian conflict. And though that was the Communists' specialty, they hung fire and stayed camouflaged, as Gelders tried unsuccessfully to persuade the conference's formal sponsors to disobey the ordinance. Twenty-five years later, the black Communist Hosea Hudson would maintain that if a few powerful white people had stood up to Connor then, "all that stuff that Reverend King and them went through trying to break down segregation, what they had to suffer, and some people's murder, could have been stopped that day."

The AP report on the day's events confirmed that Bull Connor had perfectly discharged his task. He had tarred the SCHW's mission with the no-win issue of segregation. The compromise resolution the conference passed—that it would hold no segregated meetings in the future—was played up in the lead as "a condemnation of the South's Jim Crow laws." The more conservative attendees turned heel over that, and the house was half empty on the last night, when Hugo Black received the "Thomas Jefferson Award"—Gelders's ploy to make liberalism seem as southern as the Ku Klux Klan. Black reverted to his old stump days, calling for the equal distribution of wealth, to the Communists' quiet delight. But the many Alabama politicians he had primed, including lame-duck Bibb Graves, who would gloomily conduct his last official business while swirling his "medicine" in a cracked cup, disowned their participation in this shining hour. And the New Deal went back north the next day.

The Southern Conference for Human Welfare had voted to become a permanent organization, but its key achievement would be its gift to posterity: It had initiated the key white players of the future civil rights movement—their names were Virginia and Clifford Durr, Aubrey Williams, Myles Horton, and James Dombrowski. At the current stage of American democracy, however, the SCHW proved to be no match for the anti–New Dealers' power, for which Connor had provided only the noise.

Uncle Charlie

JIM SIMPSON HAD MADE a political man out of his baseball announcer. With letters of congratulation pouring into city hall, Bull Connor followed up his segregation stand with a resolution condemning the SCHW as "a left-wing movement, financed in full or in part by Communists and extensively aided by W.P.A. and other federal employees"—thus deftly linking the New Deal with Communism. But the real powers of Birmingham had been sufficiently frightened that they weren't satisfied to let the functionaries handle the Southern Conference. The nation's entire right-wing bulwark would have to be engaged.

Charles DeBardeleben was the money and animus behind Jim Simpson, with a fixed smile that seemed at odds with his vehemence about everything including the football team of his alma mater, Auburn. The largest commercial producer of coal in the state, he was the son of Birmingham's founding father, Henry Fairchild DeBardeleben, who had built the city's great workshops out of the ashes of the Confederacy. The only local industrialist to have achieved robber baron status ("King of the Southern Iron World"), Henry had nearly made Birmingham an anomaly of home rule in a region dominated by Yankee capital. But in 1891, he had been toppled by stock market rascals ("and I clawed the rocks," he said of his devastation). Whereas Henry lost his kingdom to organized money, Charles DeBardeleben's own coal company was threatened from below, by organized labor.

To stop John L. Lewis from claiming his miners, "Uncle Charlie" (as he encouraged his employees to think of him) put machine-gun nests around his camps, dug trenches for his guards, buried battery-operated mines in the roads, and placed an "organizer trap"—an electrically wired dynamite bomb—next to the main entrance of one of the company villages. By 1934, DeBardeleben was a national figure of anti-unionism, the last major coal operator in America holding out against Lewis's United Mine Workers and a burr on Roosevelt's "infernal administration."* Legendary in union circles was the "mystery man" DeBardeleben sent into his mines (to intimidate the Negro workers), wearing a black robe, white gloves with black streaks on the fingers, and a mask with flickering flashbulbs as horns.

The DeBardeleben company had become labor's Alamo. In October 1935, 150 striking unionists drove out to "organize" the mines, to be greeted by an employee army personally headed by Charles and his son Prince. After fifteen minutes of machine-gun and rifle fire, a UMW member's corpse was recovered next to the public highway with thirty-two bullet holes in it. Nine DeBardeleben employees were charged with murdering him, but they beat the rap. And Charles, who was indicted for conspiracy to commit a felony, remained a hero to his class.

Because John L. Lewis's CIO was the infrastructure of the Southern Conference for Human Welfare, DeBardeleben was determined to destroy it. The weapon he would use spoke to the union policy that was both its strength and its vulnerability: The CIO organized black and white together, along the old "UMW formula" of biracial unionism that had made the Mine Workers a powerful vanguard of the otherwise lily-white trade union movement. DeBardeleben, identifying himself as "one of the greatest believers of White Supremacy," wrote to the SCHW's president, Frank Graham, and proclaimed his contempt for an or-

---

*DeBardeleben was sponsoring, through one of the companies he owned (and his son ran), the constitutional challenge to Roosevelt's Social Security Act.

ganization that let whites "mingle and associate with negroes." Then he carried the fight to the public through the slick *Time*-like weekly *Alabama: The News Magazine of the Deep South* that he and his peers had launched against the New Deal two years earlier. The magazine invented an estimate of six hundred "dyed-in-the-wool Communists" among the SCHW meeting's "long-haired men and short-haired women," but correctly identified Joe Gelders as its "prime mover," calling him the star of the La Follette committee's "Stalinized version of Jack the Giant Killer."

DeBardeleben and the Big Mules now had something bigger than the La Follette committee, a congressional attack dog of their own to sic on Gelders and his fellow travelers. The House Special Committee on Un-American Activities (it would become known as HUAC during the Cold War) had been created earlier that year as a sort of antidote to the left-leaning La Follette committee. Its chairman, Texas congressman Martin Dies, was the House's point man against the CIO. Dies defined un-Americanism as "to hate one's neighbor because he has more of this world's material goods."

Two weeks after the SCHW conference, the Dies committee set up a beachhead in Birmingham, announcing its arrival at an "America for Americans" rally staged by the Big Mules. Sharing the dais with Bull Connor* was Alabama's voice on the red-hunting committee, Congressman Joe Starnes. Starnes had earned a footnote in history during the Dies investigation of the Federal Theater Project; on learning that *Faustus* had been performed, he asked a witness if the playwright, Christopher Marlowe, was a Communist. But at the Birmingham rally, Starnes was more surefooted in his mission as he charged that the CIO was contaminated with reds, for indeed John L. Lewis did not discriminate ideologically when it came to hiring good organizers.

DeBardeleben had mobilized an awesome power bloc, spanning Birmingham's city hall and Capitol Hill. But he had one last gruesome trick in his bag. Birmingham's arch anti–New Dealer, it turned out, was more than just an angry capitalist championing the principles of free enterprise. His campaign against labor was rooted in the most extreme anti-democratic movement of the century. DeBardeleben had been high on the list of secret corporate benefactors of the Constitutional Educational League—one of the innocuous-sounding "patriotic" societies bankrolled by the big industrialists, including U.S. Steel, during the Red Scare of 1919. The current league, whose southern headquarters was in DeBardeleben's office building, was a clearinghouse of propaganda for the interlocking anti-Roosevelt action groups. But it was also part of a global network of pro-Nazi propagandists centered in Germany, where Adolf Hitler (who had been sponsored by the steel tycoon Fritz Thyssen) was red-baiting any progressive impulse, making liberals synonymous not simply with Communists but with

---

*One of Connor's fellow commissioners had asked the committee to investigate the SCHW, and Dies claimed to have sent a spy to the convention.

Jews.* The Constitutional Educational League had identified the demon-agent of Jewish-Communist internationalism in America. He was, of course, the CIO's John L. Lewis. The league's hero, the recipient of its 1938 "Americanism Award," was Martin Dies.

For hosting the SCHW meeting, *Alabama* magazine had pronounced Birmingham "the Munich of Southern capitulation." But this seemed to be a case of what Freud might call projection. Three weeks after the conference, on December 16, 1938, DeBardeleben's colleagues in the Constitutional Educational League held a banquet of the country's pro-fascist crusaders at New York's Hotel Biltmore, to honor the "man on horseback" chosen by Nazi agents in America to front a U.S. putsch. Major General George Van Horn Moseley, his name joined in a litany with Hitler, Mussolini, and Franco, was a natty, furtive career Army man based in Atlanta, who advocated sterilizing all Jewish immigrants to the United States.† Moseley's anti-Semitism was perhaps a bit obvious for his Park Avenue hosts, but he had a firm grasp of the main idea they had been trying to sell to the public: "Democracy, hell! It's nothing but Communism."

And democracy, after all, was the simple goal of DeBardeleben's enemies, the agenda of the labor movement as well as the Southern Conference for Human Welfare. If DeBardeleben had allowed the CIO to organize his employees and win them basic rights and privileges, the working-class revolutionaries he feared

---

*The head of the league was Joseph Kamp, the self-taught son of a German immigrant tailor from New York who was the most ambitious and prolific of the right-wing propagandists. *Join the C.I.O.*** *and Help Build a Soviet America* was Kamp's career-making pamphlet, published by the league in 1937, on the subversives in the labor movement—featured as a must-read in the Nazis' international propaganda organ, *World-Service*. Though the league published such discreetly anti-Semitic tracts as *Join the C.I.O.*, it also disseminated the notorious fake document of Jewish internationalism, *The Protocols of the Learned Elders of Zion*—a turn-of-the-century invention of the czar's secret police—and *Halt, Gentiles, and Salute the Jews!* He would write polemics against civil rights in the 1960s.

Fred Marvin, the Minnesota native who headed the league's Birmingham office, was the granddaddy of America's right-wing pamphleteers, a newspaperman who had been a professional union-baiter on the payrolls of the Rockefellers and their brethren since developing an antipathy for the union while covering the Western Federation of Miners' systematic bombing of Idaho's Coeur d'Alene mines in 1899. At sixty-eight, he was now a sort of chairman emeritus of the anti–New Deal hard core, spending his spare time accompanying "Uncle Charlie" to his anti-union coalfields and jotting down impressions of the beautifully landscaped mine entrances and the neat yards and homes of the employees ("no sign of slovenliness"). With almost a lover's tenderness, he described "Uncle Charley's ingratiating smile" and "indomitable energy" in the "history" DeBardeleben had commissioned him to write of the last great coal company in America: "A Story of a Visit to Happy Communities."

†Joining the Constitutional Educational League's Joe Kamp and Fred Marvin as the dinner's official sponsors was the A-list of pro-Nazi propagandists. John E. Snow was the avowed "gentleman fascist" of Park Avenue and pamphleteer for the National Association of Manufacturers. Another sponsor, John Eoghan Kelly, was a propagandist for fascist Spain. Allen Zoll was now pressing a Japanese propaganda campaign in the United States with help from the German-American Bund. Lawrence Dennis, a disillusioned Harvard-educated diplomat and Wall Street banker, claimed not immodestly to be "America's number one fascist theorist and intellectual"—and had the disciples to prove it, including the Museum of Modern Art's Harvard-educated tastemaker (and future architect) Philip Johnson. Dennis's swarthy complexion and kinky hair lent credence to later reports that the country's number one elitist was a former boy preacher from Atlanta, a Negro who passed as a "super-Aryan" at fetes in his honor in Germany and Italy.

might have turned into fine bourgeois citizens, with a respect for personal property very like his own. By blocking the union, DeBardeleben and his peers had deformed men who shared their own desire for comfort and security and indeed made them dangerous radicals.

Working Men

NOW NINETEEN, Troy Ingram had been born into Uncle Charlie's "family" of employees but was exiled after DeBardeleben discovered that Troy's father had joined the United Mine Workers. Troy himself would seek solidarity in a different sort of brotherhood and end up asserting his manhood through the thrilling tool of the trade DeBardeleben had taught him: dynamite.

Ingram's future best friend and fellow bomb maker, thirty-four-year-old Robert Chambliss, had also mined coal, in the particularly squalid camp of a local pig-iron company. His UMW union card was probably the best thing that had ever happened to him. But Chambliss's lifelong allegiance was to the Ku Klux Klan. And the Klan had redefined its mission during the 1930s as a union-fighting organization.* It had built up its largest membership in fifteen years during the CIO's organizing drives of 1937 by ranting against the Communism and "social equality" promoted by John L. Lewis, who DeBardeleben's enforcers insisted was "about three-quarters Negro himself."

These were the vigilantes to whom the industrialists would now assign the hands-on anti-union fight—under cloak and hood, and off the payroll. They would answer to city hall, specifically to the man the Big Mules had put there. Bull Connor had passed his first test. His next significant act as public safety commissioner would be to make Robert Chambliss his functionary within the Klan, bringing him purpose as well as material support, and a place in history.

---

*The Bourbon Democrats had expunged the Klan from politics (as they had neutralized the Populists) after Chambliss's klavern mate Hugo Black and Bibb Graves were elected in 1926.

2.

RING OUT THE OLD

1948

Prosperity

VULCAN WAS NOW KNOWN as the Symbol of Traffic Safety. In the hand that once held an iconographically correct spear, he raised an electric torch that shone green on days when there were no fatal car wrecks in Birmingham and turned red for twenty-four hours otherwise. Visitors might have been baffled at a god of fire clutching something that looked like a radioactive Popsicle, and a New York art critic had recently ruffled civic feathers by suggesting that this "artless monstrosity" be "bodily eliminated." But the natives were unamazed at the tricks Birmingham used to domesticate its erratic industrial idol. Traffic safety, after all, had been the topic of a ballyhooed series of radio talks that Bull Connor delivered right after taking office ten years earlier, when his city was sunk in the Depression and many of his constituents did not have food or shelter, let alone cars.

But what a difference a decade made! Steel had rebounded. World War II had turned Birmingham into a heavy-manufacturing boom town—the second-largest and fastest-growing city in the South, after New Orleans—making so much smoke that the white shirts of downtown pedestrians turned dark within hours. Birmingham had always embraced its air pollution as a welcome barricade against the rural wasteland around it, and one industrialist had to be arrested before he paid attention to a new smoke abatement ordinance. Enlarged by a war effort that their pro-fascist propaganda had helped undermine, the Big Mules seemed invincible. They had neutered the New Deal's southern do-gooders and had even divided and conquered organized labor, simply by calling the CIO "the nigger union."

Now, it was 1948: election year. With the unpopular Harry "To Err Is" Truman in an inherited presidency, the Big Mules were ready to make a run at the White House. They had been plotting a southern secession from the Democratic Party all spring. The man they had picked to front it was Bull Connor. He would have starring roles in two spectacles this time. At the first, he would kill off the vanguard of progress and civil rights, finishing the job he had begun when he faced down the Southern Conference for Human Welfare in 1938. At the second, he would fulfill the mission for which the Big Mules had originally tapped him and launch a "grassroots" political movement to serve the oligarchs, around the cause of white supremacy.

The year 1948 was the pivot into the modern era, when the future was still unrecognizable in the fastness of tradition. For even as the heavy-manufacturing elite appeared to be in their prime, they faced their decline. And the radicals who seemed most marginal and "extremist" were defining the nation's ultimate agenda. A short story by Shirley Jackson published to widespread offense in *The New Yorker* that year struck some deep readers as an obituary for the closing era of American capitalism. "The Lottery" was about an insular New England town that selected a citizen to be stoned to death every summer to appease the gods of prosperity: "Lottery in June, corn be heavy soon." In its new postwar role as a world power carrying the banner of global virtue, America, too, was beginning to wonder whether Vulcan's smokestack hegemony was extracting too harsh a sacrifice from the community.

A Bomb Threat

THE ABSOLUTISM of segregation in Birmingham had created a thriving Negro universe just northwest of the "white" retail center downtown. Fourth Avenue North was a grimy commercial strip of cafes, hotels, and shoeshine parlors whose proprietors worked the street like a convention of glad-handing mayors. A residential neighborhood tumbled into the business district—shotgun houses without plumbing right up against the white clapboard Victorian where Lionel Hampton spent his early childhood in the care of grandparents. On game days, the Black Barons caravaned down Fourth Avenue on the way to Rickwood Field, preening on the hoods of cars in their crisply laundered uniforms. This year's team was headed to the Black World Series, behind a teenage outfielder from TCI's black mill town, Willie Mays.

The Fourth Avenue district was a monument to the white man's fantasy that segregation was just and rational. But it also mirrored his most primitive anxieties, about sex, disease, and death. Racism was the province of Freud as well as Marx, of phobia as much as self-interest, and the fear that motivated segregationists most viscerally concerned the consummate act of integration—bodily contamination. That explained why the most successful businesses around Fourth Avenue were those that performed the compromising organic services. White entrepreneurs were so repelled by the idea of infusing Negro corpses with embalming fluids that black funeral homes operated free from Caucasian competition. Disgust for "burr heads" (on the part of both races) had exalted black hairdressers as alchemists who "conked" the kinks from Negro coiffures. "Dr." Ruth Jackson, who boasted a P.H.D., or Professional Hair Dressing degree, had lobbied the legislature to set standards for black beauticians and opened what was said to be the only beauty culture museum in America. Thus had Birmingham's Negroes finessed pride from shame.

Few white people would have suspected that a revolution was being hatched in a place that they saw as a joyful urban version of the cotton fields where happy slaves had sung their hearts out. But there were no secrets from Bull Connor in Birmingham. On April 26, 1948, three policemen went over to Fourth Avenue and walked into the district's architectural anchor, the "skyscraper" built by Alabama's black Masons, who boasted of having the largest fraternal lodge in the nation. The detectives' destination was the fourth-floor headquarters of the Southern Negro Youth Congress, a remarkably broad-based regionwide coalition of class and mass, professor and mill hand, conservative and radical. Over the past decade, they had been inventing the black struggle for freedom. And it was Bull Connor's good fortune that the spark plugs of the movement were Communists.

The youth congress was holding its annual convention that coming weekend. Connor saw it as an opportunity to establish himself as the toughest of patriots. For days he set the scene, promising a repeat of his showdown with the Southern Conference for Human Welfare. "All segregation laws of the City of Birmingham will be enforced and no community seating will be allowed," he warned. The once liberal *Birmingham Post* got the public behind Connor with a story headlined "Commies Sponsor Negro Youth Meet."

The object of the police's attentions at the SNYC offices was the organization's executive secretary, Louis Burnham, a thirtyish graduate of the City College of New York who seemed made for the expression "born leader." He was the last of the talented young black Communists who had come to Birmingham to command the congress's far-flung network of activists. And for that offense he was escorted a few blocks east to the stripped-down Art Deco tower that was city hall for an audience with Bull Connor.

The commissioner greeted him by waving a flyer Burnham had printed up to publicize the convention. " 'Young Southerners oppressed and beaten . . . , ' " he read from it, and then looked up at Burnham and demanded, "Who's oppressed and beaten?"

Connor continued, " 'Young Southerners burned and hung. . . .' Who's burned and hung?"

Then he read, " 'Young Southerners suffering daily the injustices of Klansmen's law.' " He fixed his eye on Burnham and said, "There's no Klan here, but there will be if you persist with this meeting." Not only did Connor know there was a Klan in Birmingham, he was its patron saint.

In the next few days, Connor rounded up the ministers who had volunteered their sanctuaries for the meeting and predicted "risk of damage to church property." He warned the most prominent of them, the pastor of Sixteenth Street Baptist, that if he opened his doors to the Southern Negro Youth Congress, God would "strike the church down." He told two more ministers which of God's agents would do the damage: the Ku Klux Klan. In one of many firsts, the SNYC had elicited the original threat of a church bombing in Birmingham.

A Dream of Freedom

THE SOUTHERN NEGRO YOUTH CONGRESS had become a big deal since announcing itself in 1937 with a resonating quotation from Frederick Douglass: "I had a dream of freedom." The young black college-educated Communists who had started the congress—to carry out indigenous centrist alternatives to the Comintern's hard-line directives on civil rights—moved their headquarters from Richmond to Birmingham after attending the 1938 founding of the Southern Conference for Human Welfare, with which they had continued to do business over the ensuing decade. According to the first black Rhodes scholar, philosopher Alain Locke, the SNYC was the most historic development among southern Negroes since Reconstruction. Notable among civil rights organizations for being black owned and operated, it seemed to have settled the class-mass dilemma that had plagued black activists since the NAACP was created in 1909 as a foil to the accommodationist leadership of Booker T. Washington. "Cast down your bucket where you are.... It is at the bottom of life we must begin, and not at the top," Washington had famously urged his fellow Negroes, ingratiating himself to the prominent white supporters of his black vocational school in Alabama, Tuskegee Institute. By contrast, the NAACP's chief theorist (and Harvard's first black Ph.D.), W.E.B. Du Bois, demanded unequivocal equality for the Negro. But his strategy for uplifting the race—training a college-educated "Talented Tenth" as "yeast" to "leaven the lump" of ignorant Negritude—further split the classes from the masses ("them asses"), who had figured in mainstream black protest only as a sort of forensic football passed among intellectuals: What should be "done" with them?

The Southern Negro Youth Congress, uniquely, decided to go for the full 100 percent of the community—the prestige of the classes and the manpower of the masses—not only to fight segregation but to promote trade unionism, full enfranchisement, and social equality. The young radicals captured the imagination of the race's celebrities. Despite its leadership of undeclared Communists, Booker T. Washington's own successor at Tuskegee called the SNYC "the flower of the Negro race" and joined the ultra-respectable elders on the SNYC's advisory board,* as did the black educator turned New Deal boss Mary McLeod Bethune (still active in the Southern Conference for Human Welfare). Other pa-

---

* The youth congress had a somewhat obscure relationship to the national Communist Party leadership. Although its Communist founders considered themselves advocates of a socialist revolution, they did not see the congress as an agent of that revolution. It was not a Party auxiliary as, say, the International Labor Defense had been. The FBI found no documentation that the CP donated money. However, Junius Scales, the SNYC's most active white Communist, a wellborn student at the University of North Carolina, had no doubt that the congress's leaders were getting their marching orders from the Party hierarchy. "If the Party coughed," he said, "they sneezed."

trons included the political scientist Ralph Bunche, the sociologist E. Franklin Frazier, and Howard University president Mordecai Johnson.* Joe Louis, heavyweight champion turned enlisted man, was named Southern Negro Youth of the Year at the 1942 convention in Tuskegee—not far from where he grew up on a sharecropper's plot as Joe Barrow. It was at that conference that Paul Robeson gave his first concert in the Deep South. President Roosevelt telegrammed patriotic good wishes.

From their offices in Birmingham, the SNYC leaders offered training and, when possible, money to affiliates all over the region, overseeing voter registration drives, anti–poll tax campaigns, and even a traveling puppet theater that proselytized Black Belt Negroes against the sharecropping system. They seemed like young gladiators poised to take Rome back—serious, profound, and convinced they were going to change the South, if only they didn't occasionally have to hock their typewriter to pay the rent. They dressed up in white "goin'-to-see-the-mayor" suits to call on Bull Connor at city hall, had served as research assistants for Gunnar Myrdal's exhaustive study of race in America, organized biracial fundraising dances (with Joe Gelders's daughter supplying the white kids), and generally made wild demands on behalf of their race. During the war, when Bechtel, the defense contractor, announced a mass hiring of 30,000 to rush the new B-29 bombers through production at its local plant, the SNYC cranked out handbills demanding 10,000 of those jobs for blacks. One of the new hirees was Fred Shuttlesworth, a Negro youth who would eventually fulfill the congress's dream of freedom.†

Shuttlesworth

FRED SHUTTLESWORTH HAD plummeted into shame only a few months after leading the graduation processional of the budding black bourgeoisie, as the valedictorian of Rosedale High School's class of 1940. A sheriff's deputy had appeared at the family homeplace and asked, "Where's the worm?" referring to the coil that distilled illegal whiskey out back. That moonshine still had been his wicked stepfather's chief source of income, but because William Shuttlesworth had died just before commencement, it was Fred who went to jail.

---

* A member of the SNYC's Fairfield, Alabama, council, Margaret Walker, would herself become famous, as the author of the novel *Jubilee,* considered "the black *Gone With the Wind.*"

† Bechtel's other noteworthy Birmingham employee was Arthur "Duke" Wolff, whose resplendent life as a con artist would be chronicled by his son Geoffrey in his book *The Duke of Deception.* At the plant, the Duke passed himself off as an aeronautics engineer and recruited dwarf workers from around the country; they not only offset the wartime manpower shortage, but also conveniently were able to get up into the wings of the aircraft they were outfitting. Wolff installed his family in a grand house opposite the Mountain Brook Club, where Geoffrey spent an afternoon swimming under circumstances too paradisiacal for him to recall when he described the scene in his book. Like most of the Wolffs' conned prizes, tenancy on Beechwood Road came to an unexplained end, and the family found itself in more modest quarters, a couple of doors down from my grandparents' house on Hastings Road. Wolff was fired on V-E Day. The dwarfs, who were laid off when the war ended, picketed outside the plant.

There had really been only one thing for a black valedictorian to do in Birmingham if he lacked the means for college and that was to become a preacher. Receiving no guidance, however, from the elders at his little Methodist church about how he might educate himself in God's direction, Shuttlesworth fell back on the Negro Depression gospel, "Let Jesus lead you and Roosevelt feed you." His first job was as a doctor's orderly with the National Youth Administration, Mary McLeod Bethune's controversial equal-pay-for-blacks New Deal agency. In the fall of 1941, six weeks before Pearl Harbor, Shuttlesworth married the relatively privileged Ruby Keeler, a fellow NYA employee, also nineteen, who was a few credits shy of her RN degree at Tuskegee. After his stint at Bechtel's B-29 plant, he followed the wartime boom to the Gulf port of Mobile. His job, ferrying cargo and passengers around the air base, involved a lot of waiting. He sat in his parked truck and read the Bible.

The local Methodist church hadn't touched his spirit. He fell in with a crowd from Corinthian Baptist. The thought of telling his devoutly Methodist, extremely definite mama that he was going to convert filled him with anguish, but after much prayer he took the baptismal plunge. Corinthian invited him to guest-preach regularly, and people "just solidified" around him. A white minister appointed as a "missionary" to Mobile Negroes urged him to enter an oratorical contest being sponsored by Selma University, an unaccredited but respected black Baptist college in the capital of the Black Belt. Shuttlesworth worked up a winning sermon around the obscure notion "It's a phrenological fact that. . . ."

The prize—admission to the school—put Shuttlesworth in a bind. He had a permanent government job that paid $200 a month. He had built a house with surplus government lumber and piped in his own gas. His wife had just had their third child—the much awaited son, Fred Jr. But Shuttlesworth sensed that God had "led" him to his painful breach with his mother's faith. Unlike regimented Methodism, the Baptist denomination was totally decentralized, with each church a fiefdom accountable to no constitution or theological authority. "The black preacher is the freest man on earth . . . ," Shuttlesworth realized, "especially the black Baptist preacher."

The Brown-educated president of Selma University (a member of the Southern Negro Youth Congress Advisory Committee) sweetened the offer with financial aid. In the middle of the hurricane of 1947, Shuttlesworth loaded a truck with his butane tank and 240 pounds of frozen beef from a cow he had slaughtered. The president bought him a milk cow and told him to give the school a daily quota and sell the rest. And so did Shuttlesworth arrive at his vocation, in the conspicuous style of the masses.

Red-Baited

THE SOUTHERN NEGRO YOUTH CONGRESS had peaked the year before, drawing a record thousand delegates to its ninth annual convention in October 1946 at Columbia, South Carolina. The celebrity lineup included Harlem con-

gressman Adam Clayton Powell; Howard Fast, the white Communist whose Reconstruction novel, *Freedom Road,* had become a youth congress bible; and, again,
Paul Robeson, who led the audience in a round of James Weldon Johnson's "Lift
Ev'ry Voice and Sing," known as the "Negro national anthem." The guest of
honor, W.E.B. Du Bois, gave his speech in a chapel so crowded that loudspeakers
were set up on the lawn. Its premise was memorable for its improbability. "The future of American Negroes is in the South," he said and declared over and over
that the revolution for black freedom worldwide would take root in that cradle of
segregation. He urged the audience to stay there and fight: " 'Behold the beautiful
land which the Lord thy God hath given thee.' "

There was only one delegate at the convention who would have a primary
role in vindicating Du Bois's "Behold the Land" speech. He was a fresh, confident
twenty-three-year-old Merchant Marine, who had made a big impression on the
SNYC's founders because of the boycott he had recently organized against a
racist grocery store owner in Miami, one of the youth congress's newer outposts.
His name was Hunter Pitts O'Dell, and to complete the jarring Irish impression,
the bantam-sized black man was known as Jack and was a Roman Catholic. This
was his first contact with the Communist Party. And because of it, he would be the
SNYC's most lasting legacy, as a top aide to Martin Luther King. The combination of O'Dell's Communist Party membership and his competence would bring
the entire investigative apparatus of the United States government down on the
civil rights movement.

The FBI had been spying on the youth congress's dry run of that movement
since Martin Dies's Committee on Un-American Activities fingered it as red in
1940. FBI director J. Edgar Hoover designated it "the most active communist
front organization among the Negro youth in the Southland." The SNYC's members had adopted a benign attitude toward the government's inept black informants (they usually ended up as converts), and it wasn't until America's wartime
friendship with the Soviet Union was displaced by the Cold War that the red-
baiting of the congress began to scare its wide lay membership. By the time the
SNYC landed on the U.S. attorney general's list of "subversive" organizations, in
December 1947 (the Central Intelligence Agency had already opened a file on it),
its moderate base was scattering. But the congress had one final scene to play.

Henry Wallace, FDR's one-term vice president and Harry Truman's former
commerce secretary (discharged for being soft on Stalin), was mounting a third-
party run for president that, despite the candidate's obvious deficiencies as a
politician, seemed to have delivered the Left to the mainstream of American life.
Wallace's Progressive Party platform, which he gamely conceded bore a marked
resemblance to the Communist Party's, called not only for peace with the Soviet
Union but also for a multi-pronged assault on the South's Way of Life. "I am here
to say: Jim Crow in America has simply got to go," Wallace had announced categorically. Besides supporting forty-five black candidates across the country, the
Progressive Party would hold more than two hundred well-publicized unsegregated meetings in the Old Confederacy. Because of the prominence of Commu-

nists in the campaign, liberals and conservatives alike considered Wallace the "Pied Piper of the Politburo." And indeed, the campaign's co-director in the South was Louis Burnham, the Communist Party member at the helm of the Southern Negro Youth Congress in Birmingham.

For the SNYC's 1948 annual conference that spring, Burnham decided to fuse his two roles and invite Wallace's running mate, Idaho senator Glen Taylor, to deliver the keynote address. A former cowboy bandleader with a grammar school education and an incredible hairpiece, Taylor had made his reputation as the champion of the returning GIs confronted by a postwar housing shortage. ("Oh, give me a home near the Capitol dome,/With a yard where little children can play.") Taylor arrived in Birmingham on May 1 with a harsh challenge to Bull Connor, calling him "a spokesman for a small and fast dying clique." Connor pledged to arrest any black person who even talked to a white while entering the convention, as well as the janitor and any speaker including the President of the United States.

At this point, it was a wonder that the meeting was taking place at all. In the wake of Connor's bomb threats, the pastor of Sixteenth Street Baptist had withdrawn the use of his church, as had at least one other minister. Hotels canceled the reservations of the white delegates. The conference opened at the tiny Alliance Gospel Tabernacle church on May 1, a day late because of the inflammatory front-page news stories. Someone called the SNYC offices to say that Ku Klux Klansmen would be patrolling the streets around the meeting place in a black car, carrying a tommy gun to use on Burnham.

Hosea Hudson, the Communists' prize prole who had ascended to the U.S. Party's all-important national committee, walked down Sixth Avenue toward the meeting. As one of the locals who had persuaded the SNYC to move to Birmingham, he wouldn't have missed it for the world. A black FBI informant, sitting on the sidewalk posing as a pencil salesman, hailed Hudson, asked him if he was interested in becoming a spy for the government too, and said helpfully, "They gonna arrest everybody."

Despite the vice presidential candidate and plenty of publicity, the intimidation and red-baiting worked. Fewer than two hundred people, mostly Negro college students, attended the meeting. The handful of whites, including a couple of newsmen and a stalwart from the Southern Conference for Human Welfare, were partitioned off by a board Connor had insisted be nailed horizontally across the sanctuary. Senator Taylor decided to cancel on account of the segregated seating. When he arrived by cab at 9 p.m. to make his regrets in person, the bulk of Birmingham's police force was guarding the small Negro church, giving professional thieves the opportunity to stage a major burglary downtown.

The waiting audience sang spirituals. Taylor ignored the side door designated "White Entrance," explaining later, "If they passed a law saying you had to spit in the face of any Negro you passed on the sidewalk, I would disobey it." When he tried to shoulder past a policeman at the front door, the cop seized the forty-three-year-old senator by the armpits and hoisted him off his feet. Other uniformed men backed him into a wire fence in the churchyard, ripping his suit, and then bustled him into the patrol car, saying, "Keep your mouth shut, buddy."

Next the policemen took Taylor on an ominous hospitality tour of Birmingham, driving him around to the city's steel mills and foundries, as if they were the great cathedrals of Europe. To point out how insignificant he was by comparison with the smokestacks silhouetted against the sky, the cops said over and over, "Here's Senator Taylor trying to be a hero." Then they took him to jail and locked him up in the drunk tank.

Louis Burnham and his wife had vacated their apartment that night after receiving the threats from the Klan. Crouched on the floor of a friend's car, they arrived with their baby daughter at the house of the youth congress's most active lay member, a schoolteacher named Sallye Bell Davis, whose four-year-old daughter was overjoyed by the unexpected company. Angela Davis herself would grow up to become a candidate for vice president of the United States, on the Communist Party ticket.

The following week, at Taylor's trial for disorderly conduct, assault and battery, and interfering with a police officer, the judge fined him $50, gave him a 180-day suspended sentence, and grumped, "This is a publicity stunt and had it been left to me, I never would have tried the case at all." Indeed, Taylor's attorney, Arthur Shores, had bigger plans for Taylor's misdemeanor.

The formal, dapper Shores was the NAACP's most prolific lawyer in the Deep South, the first Negro in Alabama to represent his clients in court rather than turn the case over to a white man for trial. Since World War II the NAACP had assumed charge of the civil rights struggle, seizing the advantage over the National Urban League as well as the Communist Party by making a cause of the bad faith of America's war against fascism abroad, when, as one Alabama sharecropper had put it, motioning toward the Big House, "Maybe the Hitler nearer me is the one to handle first." In the NAACP's venerable tradition of "legalism and gradualism," Shores had already gotten Alabama's white election primaries outlawed and had beat the notorious Boswell Amendment, cooked up by the Big Mules to deprive black people of the vote. Now he intended to use Taylor's guilty verdict to mount the first constitutional challenge to segregation in its most offensive manifestation, the physical barriers against Negroes in what would come to be known as public accommodations. But the Supreme Court was not ready to take on such a frontal assault on the South's Way of Life. Only two justices voted to review the lower court decision, one of them Hugo Black. And perhaps it was just as well: Shores's co-counsel on the case was the old La Follette committee lawyer, John Abt, who was a "semi-clandestine" Communist.

Back in Washington, Glen Taylor ruefully told his Senate colleagues that he had sung "Birmingham Jail" many a time in his bandleading days but now would be able to give it new feeling. He received only lukewarm sympathy—and went on to a career in wig manufacturing (Taylor Toppers) after being defeated for reelection two years later. On the other hand, the jailing of the senator had earned Birmingham two consecutive weeks' coverage in *Time*—which rather forgivingly quoted Bull Connor, "There's not enough room in town for Bull and the Commies." Thus was the world prepared for Connor's debut in a couple of months as the majordomo of what the pundits would pronounce the most momentous southern political occurrence since secession: the Dixiecrat revolt.

Simpson's Trial

PRESIDENT TRUMAN had enraged the southern Democrats by making a federal priority of a term previously cornered by the Left: "civil rights." He had appointed a blue-ribbon committee to look into what had been known as the "Negro question" and embraced its recommendations in a major address to Congress in February—nondiscriminatory employment practices, federal anti-lynching and anti–poll tax laws. As one Georgia congressman said, "Sounds like the program of the Communist Party." At the coming Democratic nominating convention in July, Truman was expected to adopt a strong civil rights plank. In response, the South would rise again.

There was some reason for the southerners to believe they had a chance at winning this war over slavery. In 1944, Alabama's crack crusader against Franklin Roosevelt, Jim Simpson, had run a path-breaking campaign for the U.S. Senate that had galvanized the nation's top-flight anti-Roosevelt talent. The race came to be seen as a referendum on the New Deal, partly because of the strategic importance of the office—southern senators were potentially the government's most entrenched oligarchs, elected and reelected into powerful seniority by a tiny poll tax–reduced fraction of those they governed. And the incumbent, Lister Hill, was an arch New Dealer whom Hugo Black, Governor Bibb Graves, and FDR himself had leveraged out of the House of Representatives and into Black's vacated Senate seat in 1938. Hill's influence in the administration had been telegraphed at the 1940 Democratic convention, where he had been given the honor of nominating Roosevelt.

Simpson was a reserved man, chilly even among intimates, but he had decided to go against type and gamble his future on the hot emotion of hate. Not since the Bourbons race-baited the Populists for consorting with freedmen had the ruling class claimed racism so crudely, and never again would the country's corporations so baldly foment racial strife. U.S. Steel set up a League to Maintain White Supremacy to spread "the white supremacy gospel of Simpson" among the grass roots (that is, its work force); Bull Connor supplied the organization's box-office appeal. The embattled Southern Conference for Human Welfare took out ads against the league, and the Southern Negro Youth Congress asked the U.S. attorney general to investigate its instigators ("Hitler's friends"). The league retaliated with flyers urging physical violence against the youth congress's female executive secretary, a "greasy haired coon."

The national cabal of anti–New Dealers mobilized its resources to Simpson's campaign through a colorful Texas-based and -sized promoter named Vance Muse, who had long been subsidized by an industrial who's who of Du Ponts,

Armours, General Motors' Alfred P. Sloan, the DeBardelebens of Birmingham, and, primarily, John Henry Kirby,* the Texas timber and oil baron behind Martin Dies's congressional career. The name of their current anti-labor "movement," the Christian Americans, alluded to the tried-and-true formula described by one of the industrialists' paid union-busters: "You ties in the niggers with the Jew, den you call the Jews Communists. That gets 'em." Birmingham's own anti-union prodigy, Charles DeBardeleben, had not lived to see his racist propaganda efforts become the substance of Simpson's political campaign—he died at age sixty-five of undisclosed causes in the summer of 1941, a few months after a Senate committee accused him of using armed deputies to coerce his employees to vote against Roosevelt the previous November. He insisted till the end that he was "preaching only what Jesus taught, the Golden Rule." It was his son who had acted as one of the go-betweens linking Simpson to the Christian Americans.

Among the specialized newspapers the group's seasoned propagandists published was a personal campaign tabloid for Simpson. Radical by every previous standard in the state, the *Alabama Sun* carried a weekly front-page "nigger" photo ("Eleanor Greets Nigger Again!") and issued knowing threats to "big shot coons" and other private black citizens, reflecting information that seemed to have come from Bull Connor's police files.

Lister Hill was astounded by the opposition's tactics—"the same pattern as the big industrialists of Germany used when they put Adolf Hitler in charge of the German government." President Roosevelt became so alarmed that his favorite financier, Bernard Baruch (of South Carolina), reputedly funneled some liberal outside funds into the Hill campaign. And in the end, the best-organized money and malice in the country could not prevail over Roosevelt's popular mandate. Simpson's defeat in the May primary was hailed by the moderate *Birmingham News* as a "sharp repudiation of the extreme and dangerous agitation of sheer racial prejudice." No one recognized quite yet that Simpson—"the most vindictive and vicious" politician the New Dealers had met—was the future of Alabama politics, any more than the country could imagine that FDR would be dead within a year. But Simpson had won 100,000 votes, nearly 45 percent, in his first statewide race, against a popular incumbent, with a manufactured cause so seemingly "spontaneous" that the candidate himself could turn to his more naive friends and deplore his advisers' overzealousness on the Negro Question.

Having counted on being the messiah, Simpson was too shattered to appreciate his John the Baptist warm-up role. "At least I have the satisfaction of knowing that the better people of the state voted for me," he told his wife, still trying to live

---

* Kirby's masterwork had been a Grass Roots Convention of Southern Democrats in Macon, Georgia, in 1936, with calico-clad extras shouting about the "dad-gummed foreigners" in Washington. In case the Jew-baiting went over anyone's head, tabloids had been placed on every seat picturing Eleanor Roosevelt touring Howard University with two black professors—or "Mrs. Roosevelt going to some nigger meeting." Senator Hugo Black had made a shameful public example of the backers of this convention through his Special Committee to Investigate Lobbying Activities, taking special relish in exposing the big donor from Alabama, Charles DeBardeleben.

down the social injury he had suffered in the Ruskin commune. Then in a fit of bad sportsmanship before leaving the state senate, he sponsored legislation forbidding Birmingham to accept federal money to build public housing for his district's poor, mostly black citizens. The law was precedent-setting obstruction, the first rebuff of the federal housing laws that the national real estate interests had sought unsuccessfully to scuttle in Congress. But the Big Mules were determined to put a stop to this "coddling" of the poor, convinced that all the Mountain Brook maids had joined "Eleanor Clubs" chartered to shove whites off the sidewalks.

Simpson's partner on the bill in the house was Sid Smyer, the big unpretentious guy with the stogie who had replaced Bull Connor in the Jefferson County delegation to the state legislature—and was the attorney for the big property owners who stood to lose their "investment" (verminous shotgun houses rented at a huge return) to the slum clearance that made room for the federal housing projects. Smyer had been Simpson's chief campaigner in Jefferson County, gamely warning rallies about the coming race Armageddon. And now as Simpson went into a sulky retreat from the action, the steady Smyer prepared to step into the Great Man's shoes. In conceding to Hill, Simpson had said, "The candidate acknowledges defeat, but the cause will be carried on to victory." And it was Smyer who would take Simpson's white supremacy gospel into national politics—to the White House, if all went as planned. Having beat Hitler, America would now have to confront its own, spiritual form of genocide, racism.

Bolt

SID SMYER WAS ASSIGNED the nuts and bolts of the South's secession from Truman's Democratic Party. Alabama's political mandarins considered him a mere apprentice—"our plump associate." The lofty stuff would be handled by Frank Dixon, the grandest of the Big Mule politicians besides Simpson himself. As governor from 1939 to 1943, Dixon had been so identified with the absentee corporate interests that New Deal wags called him the "Brooklyn overseer." Now the South's most rococo spokesman for white supremacy ("The Huns have wrecked the theories of the master race," he had lamented after Simpson lost to Hill), Dixon seemed to be following in the steps of his uncle Thomas Dixon, a versatile southern preacher (and Woodrow Wilson's roommate at Johns Hopkins), who had helped relaunch the Ku Klux Klan: He was the author of *The Clansman*, the best-selling novel about the Reconstruction Klan that David Wark Griffith of Kentucky made into a movie in 1915 named *The Birth of a Nation.**

Frank Dixon and Sid Smyer caucused all through the spring of 1948 with secession-minded politicians around the South. The southern bolt they were orchestrating was called the Birmingham Plan, in honor of its brain trust. The crowd-pleaser whom Dixon and Smyer had chosen as its mascot was Bull Connor.

---

* Thomas Dixon later denounced the 1920s Klan revival (probably because of its populist tendencies) and had gone on to become a spokesman for the anti–New Deal industrialists who had recently backed Simpson.

The second week in July, Connor arrived in Philadelphia as a delegate to the Democratic convention with the rest of the "States Rights Democrats" from Alabama. Amid weeping three-week-old bunting, left up in Constitution Hall by the cocky Republicans out of noblesse oblige, the bolters gloated through two and a half days of convention boilerplate, waiting to martyr themselves to Truman's "civil strife" plank. Connor whooped up and down the aisle in a feathered headdress, promoting "civil rights" for Indians. Then on July 13, the bolters got even more of a provocation than they had expected. The convention narrowly rejected Truman's civil rights program in favor of a more liberal minority plank eloquently promoted by the young mayor of Minneapolis, Hubert H. Humphrey. When the roll call on the vote ended in both cheers and jeers, Connor took his cue. With Alabama banners semaphoring around him, he bellowed for recognition from the floor. But the convention chairman, Sam Rayburn of Texas, ignored him and called a recess. Connor kept "hollering like the devil's own loudspeaker."

The Alabamians had to return to the convention after the adjournment in order to leave it. Recognized by alphabetical privilege, the chairman of the delegation announced, with a little bow, "We bid you goodbye."

"Good riddance," a Wisconsin delegate yelled.

The "walkers" stalked down the center aisle through a thunderclap of boos and out into a summer rainstorm. The Dixiecrats—christened by a derisive editor at the *Charlotte News*—had revolted!

Frank Dixon exulted, "The National Democratic Party has put a knife in the heart of the South." All was going according to plan. The bolters' own prearranged convention was to take place in Birmingham only three days later to nominate a presidential ticket. Their aim was to throw the election into the House of Representatives, where the southerners could broker its outcome. Dixon announced importantly that the Fox Movietone News Reel would film the proceedings. Bull Connor stepped off the *Silver Comet,* fresh from the spurned Democrats' convention, and pointed his thumbs down for the news photographers, beaming, "They crucified us."

The train station's signature welcome sign, MAGIC CITY, had never seemed more factual as on this third week in July, when the delegates arrived for the States Rights meeting and waded through the heat toward the Municipal Auditorium. It was not apparent that only three states (Alabama, Mississippi, and South Carolina) were seriously represented among them. And the free refreshments the Chamber of Commerce was handing out at the Tutwiler (the once luxurious hotel built to lodge the visiting members of U.S. Steel's all-powerful finance committee) were a flush gesture from the notably tightfisted Big Mules. The growing signs of economic decline, like the empty war plants, were out of sight, on the edge of town.

Inside the auditorium, *Time* and all three radio networks—100 to 150 journalists in all, the *Birmingham News* boasted—were setting up in the orchestra pit to record what one speaker called the rebirth of the Democratic Party. Standing on the sidewalk holding up an "End Lynching/ Win with Wallace" placard for the newsreel cameras was a creature of the last political renaissance, imperfectly midwifed under this roof by the Southern Conference for Human Welfare. She was one of the last diehard activists in the SCHW, a native Birminghamian whom Joe Gelders's daughter had recruited to the Communist Party as a high school student.

Dixie Wants Dixon

THE RAISED RING for Monday-night wrestling had been removed from the 6,000-seat auditorium. Even so, it was standing room only. Fifty-five Ole Miss frat boys were parked in front of the speaker's stand screaming, "To hell with Truman." A portrait-on-a-stick of Robert E. Lee was paraded around the floor. Ruby Mercer, star of the Metropolitan Opera and Broadway (in town for an unrelated performance), sang "Dixie" twice.

Bull Connor took the podium. The States Righters would find Birmingham's Municipal Auditorium "a lot more comfortable than the one they have up there in Philadelphia," he assured them. (At the climax of the Democratic convention, white pigeons had been released from a floral Liberty Bell and rained their regards on the delegates below.) Connor called the VIPs to their "seats of honor" onstage. Rebel yells broke out.

A hush of expectation settled on the hall as Frank Dixon made his deliberate way to the podium. He had lost a leg in the last days of World War I and was a rather stiff presence, with rimless spectacles and a prim expression. Normally his bigotry was the sly sort practiced at the country club. But today he found his uncle Thomas's voice and gored the Truman Democrats for trying "to reduce us to the status of a mongrel, inferior race, mixed in blood, our Anglo-Saxon heritage a mockery." To his refrain of "Do we belong in this kind of Democratic party?" the crowd screamed, "No!" Surreally aglow from the lights of the newsreel cameras, the conventioneers went wild for a full twenty minutes, cheering, stomping, and Confederate flag waving to the chorus of "Dixie Wants Dixon."

Dixon, however, declined his new party's presidential nomination. The honor went instead to South Carolina's forty-four-year-old governor, Strom Thurmond, who had recently been pictured in *Life* standing on his head for his twenty-one-year-old fiancée ("Virile Governor"). It was not Thurmond who immediately took the podium, however, but an altogether different (if also hormone-rich) governor, dwarfing the great men around him as he unfurled to his full height of six feet eight inches.

The Omen

IT WAS ALABAMA'S OWN forty-year-old chief executive, James Elisha Folsom: a spontaneously generated freak of liberalism, part genius, part buffoon, and 100 percent redneck. Known as the Little Man's Big Friend, this was the most flamboyant embodiment yet of the state's stubborn progressive streak, and Big Jim should have been a cautionary example to the militant conservatives hosting the States Rights convention. For well before they had been christened Dixiecrats, he had gone into politics to "cut those sons of bitches' nuts out."

Folsom's constituents were the "fokes" along the little-d democratic byways he called Buttermilk Road, and his message was as plain as the cornshuck mop and a cedar suds bucket he brought out at the high point of his rallies—to scrub and scrub the state capitol till a "green breeze out of the north" brought "the freshest, sweetest smell." Whereupon the crowd joined in the Folsom theme song, "Y'all Come," accompanied by his band of fiddlers, banjo pickers, and accordion players—the Strawberry Pickers—who occasionally included an alcoholic twenty-two-year-old named Hank Williams.

The pundits had declared Folsom's landslide victory in 1946 a "revolt of the 'outs' against the 'ins.' " The better classes braced themselves for national humiliation, as *Life* published pictures of the former small-time insurance man, naked in a bathtub, his bent legs looming in the foreground like oil derricks. But Folsom was not quite the rube the "gotrocks" (as he called the Big Mules) took him for. He caucused with the brass of the CIO—his chief source of support—and was an occasional dinner companion of Henry Wallace. His brand of democracy was the most potent the state had seen since Populism. In contrast to his predecessor Bibb Graves's special-interest New Deal liberalism—which had been an accretion of privileges for poor whites—Folsom's truly radical politics threatened the Bourbons with real class warfare: He pledged to give the vote to those with black faces as well as red necks and liked to comment on the number of so-called black people at his rallies who were as pale as he was: "There's a whole lot of integratin' goin' on at night."

And so it was that at the same time Birmingham's States Righters were beginning to contemplate their right-wing coup, Folsom's inauguration had led *The Nation* to declare Alabama "the most liberal state in the South." As it turned out, though, the innocent Folsom was no match for the Dixiecrats. They red-baited him for supporting Henry Wallace and called a press conference to introduce his illegitimate son, born to an attractive former hotel clerk during the gubernatorial race. His legislative program had been quashed, and he had even lost his recent bid to be a delegate to the Democratic convention.

On this hot day in July 1948, Folsom's equivocal greetings to the men he abhorred were greeted with boos. It did not seem possible that his time would come again so soon. Nor had the overconfident Dixiecrats taken any notice of the Big Jim acolyte who, three days earlier in Philadelphia, had stayed behind in Constitution Hall with Senator Lister Hill and the state's other delegates who remained loyal to the Democratic Party. He was a still obscure young state legislator from Barbour County who had sponsored some harsh anti–Big Mule bills, George Corley Wallace.

Carnival

WHEN STROM THURMOND strode onstage to accept the nomination, the audience again went into a frenzy. At the applause lines, the proud-poor Alabamian who was the last Deep South chief of the Communist Party U.S.A.—he was covering the convention for the *Daily Worker*—busily lit his pipe to deflect his seatmates' gestures of white supremacist fellowship. The candidate jabbed his index finger and promised, "There's not enough troops in the Army to break down segregation and admit Negroes into our homes, our theaters and our swimming pools." According to future biographers, however, Thurmond had not minded admitting them to his gene pool, when he fathered a daughter with a black house servant back in 1925. She was now a "high yaller" sorority girl at South Carolina State.

Most of the press, in Alabama and around the country, deplored the convention's "ugly carnival scene," and rebuked Frank Dixon for sounding as if he were "addressing the Ku Klux Klan convocation." A mob had set upon a booster whose placard carried a misspelling of Thurmond that too closely resembled Truman ("Thurman"). The American Broadcasting Company bailed out after a state legislator from Texas blamed the New England slave traders for importing "the howling, screaming savages."

Even Thurmond winced at the sight of Gerald L.K. Smith, the old Huey Long advance man who was the country's best-known professional anti-Semite, swaggering around the floor with two hundred followers from his current facade, the Christian Nationalist Crusade.* Smith still curried financial favor with the automobile manufacturers in his current home base of Detroit, with his assertions that the CIO was controlled by the Kremlin, but his Jew-baiting seemed quaintly opportunistic compared with that of the sincere young anti-Semite on the convention floor: the wave of the future.

J. B. Stoner, who believed that Hitler's program for dealing with the Jews had not been "modern" enough, was hoping to enlist Dixiecrat support behind his run for Congress in his native Tennessee on his very own Anti-Jewish Party ticket. He had already made his first of many print appearances, in the *Atlanta Constitution*, which had noted a resemblance between Stoner, crippled by polio, and his hero, Hitler's clubfooted propagandameister Joseph Goebbels. Eventually, Stoner would return to Birmingham as the most brazen church bomber of the civil rights era.

Harry S. Ashmore, the liberal young editor at the *Arkansas Gazette*, dismissed the Dixiecrat movement as "one of the most conspicuous failures in American political history." In the long run, he was right: Inflaming racial hatred was ultimately a counterproductive strategy for champions of economic growth. But if

---

* Charles DeBardeleben's old anti-Semitic axis from the 1930s was represented at the convention by the former Oklahoma governor Alfalfa Bill Murray, whom the Constitutional Educational League had sponsored on a speaking tour to attack the "Jew Deal."

the Dixiecrat convention was the last rites of a dying clique, those death throes would be creating tremors—the tremors of exploding dynamite—for the next fifteen years.

Chambliss

ROBERT EDWARD CHAMBLISS was in his own way as much a mascot of the Dixiecrats as Bull Connor. His exploits were performed under the shield of night. In earning his nickname Dynamite Bob, he also gave Birmingham one of its own: Bombingham.

At forty-four, Chambliss retained his bandy-legged figure. His face was perpetually ruddy, his eyes an intense, deep-in-the-head blue, and his mouth seemed on the verge of a pucker, as if he had been weaned on moonshine. A walking history of the Big Mules' labor practices, he was a vigilante charged with upholding the very system that controlled him. Chambliss was born in Pratt City, the largest of Birmingham's industrial suburbs and home to a huge prison stockade that had earned TCI the superlative of having the best facilities "ever erected by any convict contractor in the South." His family was Irish, the most chauvinistic of the immigrant groups in this unmelting pot, who were so renowned for their liquid appetites that Jack Daniel's temporarily relocated its distillery to Pratt City when its home state of Tennessee went dry. Birmingham's saloons—the most per capita in the country—had been safeguarded by the industrialists' anti-Prohibition crusades as an essential ingredient of the three Ds of "labor tranquility": Depress 'em, disperse 'em, and drug 'em. The first two were fulfilled simultaneously by the isolated company villages, with their communal outhouses hunched over open typhoid-hatching ditches. Epidemic disease was the leading cause of death in Birmingham, and Chambliss had lost four of his seven siblings, perhaps explaining why his mother suffered from depression on top of "female troubles."

Chambliss had reached adulthood with a taste for liquor and pride in being not only "100 percent Irish" but the bravest brawler in Birmingham. In 1924, unhappily married at age twenty to "some hellcat," he sought an outlet for his discontent by joining the Robert E. Lee klavern of the Ku Klux Klan—named after the same general that he was. Like his father (and Klan brother), Chambliss was embarked on a treadmill of subsistence. It was as a quarryman for Lone Star Cement that he first learned about dynamite: that it could blast away not only stone but tedium and futility. His education in explosives continued when the Depression drove him underground, into mines of the Sloss pig-iron company.

During the late 1930s and 1940s, the Klan's leadership directed its members to disrupt the CIO—the agent, ironically, of the only security these grunt laborers had ever had. Between the Klan's "boring from within" work and the employers' race-baiting, the rank and file had been so aroused against the liberal policies of the national union that the CIO's flagship union at TCI, the United Steelworkers of America, was becoming essentially an arm of management, with all its respect for the racial customs of the region.

In 1944, the Klan disbanded nationally after the federal government ordered it to pay $685,000 in back taxes, apparently to punish it for consorting with the German-American Bund. But the organization must have been crucial to Birmingham's ecosystem, for a year and a half later, in early 1946, one of the Big Mules' old Christian American tabloids called for the revival of the Klan to cope with the "problem" of the then flourishing Southern Negro Youth Congress. This was right after Louis Burnham, the SNYC's Communist leader, led fifty black veterans to the courthouse to assert their voting rights under a banner reading "Join Us to Register—Bring Your Discharge Papers." Within a week the SNYC had achieved another milestone: The Klan announced its postwar awakening with fiery crosses around Birmingham.

As the Federated Ku Klux Klan, Inc., the Klan now entered its Dixiecrat phase, under the guidance of Bull Connor. To take charge of the vigilantes, Connor needed a confidant inside the Klan. A charter member of the Federated, Robert Chambliss was now working in the city garage and flaunted his racist bona fides so aggressively that he had been arrested two years earlier for cussing out a group of Negroes. One of his duties at the garage was to clean police cars, which sometimes meant removing blood left on the back seat by "uncooperative" suspects. At police headquarters, he was known as the grease monkey who begged cops to let him go with them to investigate "Negro disturbances"—"You-all might need me along to kill a nigger."

Chambliss's semiannual efficiency ratings hovered at 93 or 94, even though his skills as a car mechanic—his official function—were summed up by Connor as, "He could about change a flat tire." And the bootlegging sideline that Chambliss pursued with impunity signaled that he was one of Connor's favorite informants. With the extra income, Chambliss and his second wife (his first wife had charged him with desertion and nonsupport of their two sons) could afford to move out of the foul mining town of Lewisburg and into a house they built in North Birmingham, using brick tiles as an economizing compromise between real bricks and concrete blocks. In the backyard, he kept a succession of dogs named Sport, all German shepherds.

That summer of 1947, Chambliss launched his new career, in the political applications of dynamite. On July 31, ruling on a lawsuit brought by the NAACP's Arthur Shores, a federal judge declared the city's 1926 Jim Crow zoning law unconstitutional. Nevertheless, the winning plaintiff, a black TCI ore miner and CIO man, was too scared to move into his new house in the formerly white neighborhood. On August 18, sports fans were arriving home from a night game at Rickwood Field at 10:45 when six sticks of dynamite exploded under the living room of the plaintiff's uninsured frame house, collapsing the dwelling that represented his entire life savings, $3,750 cash. Dynamite Bob had made his debut.

The Eyes of Fascism

CHAMBLISS WAS PROBABLY the divine agent Bull Connor had in mind in April 1948 when he warned the pastor of Sixteenth Street Baptist that God would strike down his church with the help of the Klan. But Connor had ended up handling the Southern Negro Youth Congress and vice presidential candidate Glen Taylor unilaterally.* It was Taylor's running mate on whom Chambliss would be sicced at the end of the summer. Former vice president Henry Wallace, the top of the Progressive Party presidential ticket, was coming to Birmingham on September 1 as part of his Jim Crow–bashing southern tour.

Flush from his fame at the Dixiecrat convention, Bull Connor noisily promised "Red Henry" a "nice clean cell." Sixty cops personally supervised by Connor patrolled the courthouse and the adjacent park, where an obstreperous crowd of 2,500 whites awaited Wallace's arrival, 400 black people separated from them by ropes and sawhorses. Wallace had already made the decision to cancel the speech, on the grounds that segregation was being enforced. Instead, his fifteen-car motorcade would ceremonially circle the courthouse.

As the sedans glided past the park, eggs ("fresh eggs," CBS's Edward R. Murrow noted) sailed by the candidate's entourage into some cops and spectators. A group of hecklers pressed their faces against the window of Wallace's tan Packard. "Look at that guy," one said about the candidate, his distinctive forelock hanging over one eye. "Send him out and we'll take him to Harlem to get a hair-cut." One of the men at the car window was recognized by a police detective on the scene. It was Robert Chambliss.

The police finally moved in on the mob, and the motorcade sped off to Bessemer, where another speech was to be canceled, at DeBardeleben Park. Chambliss followed in his own car.

Later that evening, Wallace delivered one of the strongest speeches of his long career over the local airwaves, while two hundred Klansmen paced around the radio station. He identified the forces behind Chambliss and the brethren who had menaced him: "northern steel corporations," he said, "those giants of great wealth who have sucked the South dry." He elaborated: "These rich and powerful men haven't been throwing eggs and tomatoes." No, he continued, "these men never do their own dirty work. They inflame the passions of others with deliberate falsehoods and lies." Privately, Wallace let aides see how shaken he was: "Now," he had told them, "I've seen the eyes of fascism." But arguably even he underestimated Chambliss and the nexus he was part of: Birmingham, as would soon become clear, was being run by a rump government of terrorists and their powerful handlers.

---

* The Klan had to settle for making a nocturnal raid a few weeks later—a hundred strong, in masks, pointed hats, and all—on a national Girl Scout training session outside Bessemer and asking one of the white instructors teaching black camp directors where her "hammer and sickle card" was. The instructor recognized the chief deputy from Bessemer, who later investigated the raid, as one of its leaders.

By the following spring, Chambliss was bombing houses with abandon. Once Jim Crow zoning was outlawed, the Klan became the last line of defense against the upwardly mobile Negroes moving into the pretty middle-class neighborhood of College Hills. By mid-1949, there were so many charred house carcasses that the area was informally renamed Dynamite Hill.

The bombers' exploits in Birmingham became an insult to the liberal governor, Big Jim Folsom, and with his attorney general he moved to "break up the Klan." The state threw a variety of charges (chiefly "flogging while masked") at Chambliss and thirteen Klan brothers, but nothing stuck in the courts of Birmingham. Indeed, the bombers blithely continued their demolition work on Dynamite Hill.

The attorney general had no doubt as to the source of the Klansmen's confidence (and of the high-priced lawyers who had been mobilized to their defense): U.S. Steel, the coal operators, and some notables in the Dixiecrat movement.* "That these Klan activities are handled from tall buildings," he wrote to his friend Senator Lister Hill, "THERE IS NO DOUBT,—I SAY, NONE AT ALL. . . . O, how careful one must be in the Birmingham District,—one will step in the wrong place if one does not watch one's step. I had never realized just how powerful the following group is: T.C.I. and the owners of the mines . . . BUT don't forget this: The Ala. Klan IS unquestionably and undoubtedly directed from tall buildings and, its [sic] most likely that its [sic] directed from one certain tall building." That would have been U.S. Steel's corporate offices on First Avenue, from which issued the paycheck of the Exalted Cyclops of the Robert E. Lee klavern, E.E. Campbell, a skilled worker in TCI's Fairfield plant. Campbell (who received free access to Bull Connor's police files) was also a member of the CIO and was thus the industrialists' insurance against solidarity across racial lines.

But Dynamite Hill was a phenomenon of the near future, and for now the Dixiecrats thought they could make their point through the ballot, as did their opposite numbers on the Left in the Progressive Party.

The Death of the Left

THE CLIMAX of the Henry Wallace campaign was a huge rally in New York a few weeks before election day. A young Merchant Marine and activist in Seamen

---

* The man the state investigators suspected of "financing and masterminding the show" was Bill Houseal, an insurance and real estate magnate long active in anti–New Deal politics. (Ten years earlier, he had arranged the America for Americans rally opposing the Southern Conference for Human Welfare and showcasing the Dies committee's Joe Starnes.) Houseal's suspected co-executive was Hugh Locke, an eminence of the Dixiecrat establishment (Hugo Black's oldest friend and once his fellow "liberal" klavern brother). Their liaison with the Graymont–College Hills Civic Association, the Klan's respectable front that was publicly protesting the sale of homes on Dynamite Hill to Negroes, was Olin Horton, an old Simpson political functionary who had been in charge of decorations at the Dixiecrat convention; he now held a sinecure as secretary-treasurer of the Alabama Mining Institute, the coal operators' lobby fingered by the attorney general as the other main institutional girder of the Klan.

for Wallace happened to ship in to New York just in time to go. Jack O'Dell, who
had been moving left since his introduction to the Communists at the 1946
Southern Negro Youth Congress convention, joined the 18,000 people, black and
white, who packed Madison Square Garden to hear Wallace. For O'Dell it was
like the millennium, listening to a mainstream politician speak of the dilemma of
race.* Out in the middle of the ocean, he had become convinced that Wallace's vision of "progressive capitalism"—and a Wallace presidency—was a practical possibility. "Because we read the *Daily Worker*," O'Dell later explained with a laugh.
Long after the Progressive Party disbanded, long after O'Dell helped organize
spectacular events of the next civil rights movement, he would still say that
Wallace's rally at Madison Square Garden had been the "most memorable" of his
career.

It was no wonder, then, that O'Dell and a million others were shattered by
Wallace's showing on November 2. The number of votes the Progressive Party
won—1,157,172—was considerably fewer than the 3.5 million that independent
analysts had predicted in the spring. Strom Thurmond's Dixiecrat take was only
12,000 more. In the end, poachers from both the Right and the Left had done
nothing to prevent Truman from beating Dewey.

The effects of the Progressive Party's collapse were severe. Henry Wallace's
civil rights movement turned out to be the last hurrah of the American Left, as the
Cold War dispatched popular-front liberalism. The Communist Party, having
thought it was going to anoint a president, now ran for cover. Louis Burnham dissolved the Southern Negro Youth Congress, but before returning to New York he
had given one last gift to the future civil rights movement: He had defined the ultimate agenda for the Southern Conference for Human Welfare, the one that
would make the difference.

SCEF

WHAT HAD BECOME of that great hope of the South since it inaugurated the
war against southern fascism ten years earlier? Though it continued to pursue a
relatively uncontroversial course of progress—its tireless campaign to abolish the
poll tax, for example—the Southern Conference for Human Welfare had lost all
potential for any real influence as a result of the anti-Communist investigations by the Dies committee as well as the propaganda churned out by the
industry-subsidized Constitutional Educational League (Charles DeBardeleben's old baby, which itself had been asked by Congress to answer to charges of
Nazi collaboration). In denying the red accusations, the liberals within the
SCHW began to doubt their own sincerity, especially since the conference's small
minority of Communists also constituted its most committed and vocal members,

* His comrade Louis Burnham had sensed the elusiveness of a racial promised land earlier, when a
sometime member of Wallace's brain trust, Lillian Hellman, the playwright with Stalinist leanings,
lost her composure during a policy argument and, perhaps reverting to her New Orleans roots,
called him "boy."

hewing to the diktats out of Moscow. Sectarian controversy sucked so much intramural oxygen out of the organization that the red-baiting achieved its goal: the alienation of the moderates.* The Southern Conference's most eminent champion, Eleanor Roosevelt, exited in 1946. So did the increasingly conservative CIO, cutting the SCHW's financial lifeline.

What remained of the conference in 1948 was the core of southern New Dealers who had been present at the creation, and their primary achievement was the vindication, still to come, of history. Louis Burnham, longtime SCHW board member (once he arrived for a meeting at a white hotel in Nashville wearing a turban, to get around the segregation ordinances as a "foreigner"), had been gracefully lobbying his white comrades, and as a result they had undergone a crucial transformation in their thinking about the future of southern democracy. Sensing that national politics was not the route to a southern utopia, they had begun to concentrate their energy on the issue they had recoiled from ten years earlier when Bull Connor ordered them not to "segregate together": They were out to destroy segregation. And the medium through which they were promoting this was the tax-exempt propaganda arm that the SCHW had created in 1946, the Southern Conference Educational Fund, or SCEF.

Though the SCHW disbanded along with the rest of the Progressive front after the Wallace candidacy flopped, SCEF endured. At a post-election interracial conference, the last of the South's New Deal liberals described their new abolitionist franchise in a Declaration of Civil Rights that began, "We still believe that all men are created equal." One of SCEF's officers had confidently told the *New York Times*'s southern correspondent, John Popham, "The next great liberal movement in this country will come from the South."† Although it took fifteen years, Fred Shuttlesworth would become president of SCEF, and the lonely movement these visionaries had barely dreamed of would capture the attention of the world and fulfill W.E.B. Du Bois's crazy prophecy: Behold the beautiful land.

---

* Regardless of the internal debate over the Communist influence within the SCHW, Communists supplied so much of the energy at the chapter level that they certainly believed they had the power to swing the organization. In June 1947, the House Un-American Activities Committee pronounced the SCHW a "deviously camouflaged Communist-front organization." Although it accurately identified many Party activists, the committee was in most respects far off the mark in terms of the Party's influence on the lay membership.

†The man most responsible for instigating that movement, Joe Gelders, never got to see the prediction come true. He had been eased out of the Southern Conference in mid-1941; the anti–poll tax campaign he had begun, which would prove to be the most vigorous project of the SCHW's nine-year life, was transferred to a coalition of organizations called the National Committee to Abolish the Poll Tax. Gelders confined his energies to Birmingham, issuing handbills picturing Bull Connor cracking a long red whip ("This is the kind of power that Hitler's secret police has in Germany"). Though Gelders never broke with the Communists ideologically, he refused after his war service to return to Alabama, where the Party felt his work was. He went back to graduate school at the University of California at Berkeley to get a Ph.D. in biophysics, and would suffer a fatal heart attack in the spring of 1950. Although his early death, at fifty-two, was often laid to the 1936 flogging that did damage to his heart muscle, contributing factors were a heavy diet of cream (to treat his ulcers) and a smoking habit.

By the end of the 1940s, the Communist Party had lost the battle. But its strange career in Alabama had been a dress rehearsal for a modern civil rights movement that would make Birmingham, as the Southern Negro Youth Congress had predicted, "the cradle of a reviving faith in the Negro people's destiny in the South." The SNYC had been conceived as a mass movement of churchgoing "basic folks"; before taking on the white world, it had set out to convert the race's own obstructionists—like the big preachers "frightened by Mr. Connor's bluff." With its capacity for accepting "integration" and black "nationalism" as simultaneous goals, the SNYC had attempted to prepare Negroes for becoming free black men and women, true to their own selves and not imitation whites. It had conducted "mass meetings" and "demonstrations," staples of the future movement. It had cast its lot with the young. Louis Burnham, whose heroes included not only Lenin but Gandhi, had even considered organizing a black political party under the slogan "Non-Violence and Non-Cooperation."

The SNYC had also made an anti-hero of Bull Connor, intuiting that a movement needed an enemy to bring it momentum—and the "pitiless, blatant publicity" that Du Bois had pinpointed as the catalyst of southern change in his 1946 speech. "We should be grateful to Mr. Connor," a delegate said at the final convention. "Mr. Connor's actions have made us more determined than ever to go back to our communities and fight all the harder for our rights as American citizens."

Indeed, looking back, Connor's last move against the SNYC leaders—running them out of town as red—may have been his first great favor to the civil rights movement. Though it was a "dialectic" that the Communists might not have appreciated, had they been allowed to maintain their influence within the civil rights struggle, the movement might well have been destroyed by red-baiting—and Jack O'Dell's apprenticeship in the Party would provide the segregationists ammunition enough. As the Old Left precedents of black protest were frozen and distorted by the Cold War, "Negro liberation" would find its ultimate mass vehicle in an institution that had been the Communists' steadfast enemy: the black church.

McWhorter 1948

BESIDES DELIVERING SID SMYER into existence, my general practitioner great-grandfather, Dr. Robert Lee McWhorter, had the distinction of owning the first automobile in the moonshine-soaked hills of Cherokee County, Alabama, and subsequently filled his barn and an old church on the property with his outdated Model Ts and a Red Devil Buick. When his son, Hobart Amory, my future grandfather, went off to the University of Alabama, the family had assumed he would get his medical degree and come home to be the third generation of McWhorter doctors. But instead, after teaching artillery to Army recruits during the Great War, he headed for Harvard Law School, where Professor Felix Frankfurter baited him about being from "the great South." The family lost him not only to an alien profession but also to a Yankee bride—a recent Wellesley graduate from Cleveland named Marjorie Westgate. And then Hobart moved to Birmingham, where the insecure new aristocrats feared having the junked cars in the yards of their past exposed.

On September 11, 1923, the couple were standing on a Southside sidewalk waiting for the streetcar to take them downtown to the movies when traffic was stopped by a parade of Klansmen on their way to the largest "naturalization" ever held in the South. Watching the 1,750 inductees file by, Marjorie said to her husband, "Oh, look, there's Hugo." Acquainted with Black mainly through his in-laws, who had taught the Yankee bride everything she needed to know about dealing with servants, the McWhorters didn't have much use for Black himself. "Of course Hugo was an ambulance chaser," my grandmother would explain to me, "and that would always be his mentality."

My grandfather would be one of Black's upstanding antagonists, a member of the anti–New Deal resistance led by his friend Jim Simpson. Hobart had become a lawyer for one of Black's favorite Big Business targets, the Alabama Power Company, though at a time when power meant light and progress. During the early 1920s, he went around the state condemning land for the great dams that would spread not only electricity but "education, enlightenment, culture," the company promised, throughout the benighted countryside. In 1926, as the firm's Harvard-trained lawyer, twenty-nine-year-old Hobart was sent to New York City to counsel with the House of Morgan. This time, the southern industrialists were suitors rather than prey, seeking Morgan capital to back a mammoth holding company of 165 utilities from around the country.* Like Morgan's other monopoly, U.S. Steel, Commonwealth & Southern would become an American icon— thanks largely to its president, a deceptively folksy young Indianan named Wendell Willkie, who had been Hobart's frequent bridge partner during the three years they worked together in New York.

Willkie and Commonwealth & Southern unexpectedly found themselves presiding over not the transformation of electricity from a luxury into a utility but an ideological conflict pitting business against government, which wound up squandering talent on both sides. At the center of the controversy was my grandfather's employer. In 1933, Birmingham's new great industrial hope was threatened when President Franklin Delano Roosevelt sold the Alabama Power Company down the river—the Tennessee River, even though the relevant properties were in Alabama. Roosevelt's experiment in electricity-making, the Tennessee Valley Authority, was to be inaugurated on Alabama

---

* Ironically, the electricity giant posed the only critical threat to Morgan's other megabase in Birmingham, the World's Largest Corporation, for one of the power company's major goals was to entice new industries to Alabama, to consume megacurrents of electricity—and compete for steel's laborers. The coal and iron companies relied on the harsh unelectrified countryside to provide them a steady supply of millbillies.

Power turf in the northwestern part of the state, on the Tennessee's rapids at Muscle Shoals.

This incursion upon private power became exhibit A in corporate America's brief against the "socialistic" New Deal. For the next six years, instead of using his legal skills to illuminate the backwoods, Hobart McWhorter helped obstruct the TVA in court.* Wendell Willkie, meanwhile, carried private electricity's PR banner nationally, with enough down-home charm ("a simple barefoot Wall Street lawyer," one opponent called him) to gain the 1940 Republican presidential nomination.

My grandfather was the heir apparent to the presidency of Alabama Power, and though he had named his first son Martin after the company's current president, he declined the job. The New Deal's attacks on business had made corporate lawyering a fulfilling challenge in itself. And in fact, though Hobart loathed Roosevelt and served in the brain trust that advised state senator Jim Simpson on how to wrest the state from "liberal" Klansmen like Governor Bibb Graves, his heart was not in politics either.

Hobart belonged to Birmingham's new ruling class of Great Lawyers. Their ethos was an obsession with personal "honesty" at the expense of public morality. Hobart was famed as the only social drinker in his crowd who had observed Prohibition. "He was the kind of person," my father would tell me bitterly, "who would arrest you for going thirty-eight in a thirty-five-mile-per-hour speed zone."

MY GRANDMOTHER once dressed the very young Martin in Little Lord Fauntleroy clothes for a mother-son portrait published in the *Birmingham Age-Herald,* illustrating the Joys of Reading. But he seemed to have never really fit in in Mountain Brook—"over the mountain," its residents called the suburb, as though it were a spiritual passage out of the workshops on the other side. The developer, a brilliant designer of residential neighborhoods named Robert Jemison Jr., had created this suburban masterpiece after being burned by the U.S. Steel Corporation. The first town he had built, in the 1910s, was a model TCI workers village— named Fairfield, after the rich bedroom community in Connecticut where U.S. Steel's president lived—but when it was nearly completed the Corporation had halted construction on the wire mill that was its whole reason for being, to punish Birmingham's congressman for voting against tariffs on wire imports. Carl Carmer, in his classic 1934 travelogue, *Stars Fell on Alabama,* saw a bit of anti-industrial aggression in Jemison's subsequent development of Mountain Brook Estates: "With an arrogant gesture," he wrote of Birmingham, "she builds her most luxurious homes on a mountain of ore yet unmined." But it was a more passive defeatism, described in an early Jemison prospectus, that perhaps best cap-

---

* There were three major constitutional challenges to the TVA, all brilliantly perverse. The most serious one, which my grandfather helped argue before the Supreme Court, was filed by nineteen power companies, led by Alabama Power but known, typically, as the Tennessee Electric Power Company, or TEPCO, case.

tured the values of the new suburban aristocracy, although Jemison was only referring to his care in not cutting down any trees unnecessarily when he declared,
"Nothing has been done brutally."

My grandparents were among the charter residents of Mountain Brook,
moving into a stucco-and-timber English "cottage" built by Hugh Martin, the architect who also designed the public library and a grander mansion beside the
Birmingham Country Club golf course, where Henry DeBardeleben's young
great-grandson Walker Percy was absorbing the material for his future novels.*
Amid these first families of Birmingham, Martin chose as his favorite playmate
the son of a neighbor's black live-in servant. One Saturday, after his lesson at
Jemison's Mountain Brook Riding Academy, he had shown up with his bamboo
fishing pole at the back door, but the boy's mother, the family maid, was standing
there. "Martin, yo' daddy called here," she said: Her son couldn't play with him
anymore. Martin's curious relationship with Negroes had begun, and as with
many of his eccentricities, this one would mock his community's instinct for social acceptability.

GROWING UP, I would learn that my Great Lawyer grandfather was Birmingham's most ethical man and his own son's nemesis. His children considered him
the toughest man alive. "We thought he was so tough that if you just touched him
it could kill you," said his younger son, Hobart Jr. "If he'd said, 'Boys, you have to
go to Washington and kill Franklin Delano Roosevelt,' we would have picked up
our guns." Martin, however, was coming up short on "toughness," a magnet for the
school bullies. What he would call his "salvation" came from his mother, the president of the Junior League. She recommended weightlifting classes at the Y.

Martin became obsessed with physical strength. The amount of food he consumed to bulk up and out of danger was unseemly, though it was not simply the
quantity that annoyed his father but his taste for bizarre food pairings like pimien-
tos and peanut butter, and for the most expensive thing on the menu. Relations at
home were further strained by his blighted school record and habits like shooting
squirrels out his bedroom window and then sticking their corpses in the freezer.
In 1943, he was shipped off to a disciplinary boarding school in Tennessee.

Another student at Battle Ground Academy, Sidney William "Billy" Smyer
Jr., the son of the rising Dixiecrat, was amazed at how his distant cousin defied the
hazing of the upperclassmen, not sure whether he was the bravest boy he had
known or the craziest. At home, Martin became Mountain Brook's stealth weapon
against the toughs of the great workshop town. When the sons of "millbillies"
picked on the rich Mountain Brook lads at the Pickwick dance hall, Martin
calmly beat them up. By the time he graduated from high school, he had earned
metropolitan fame as a country club warrior, the macho pride of the suburbs.
Home on vacation from Exeter and then Yale, Hobart Jr. won technical knockouts
simply by announcing to his aggressors, "I am Martin McWhorter's brother!"

---

* The architect's son, Hugh Martin Jr., would write the music for *Meet Me in St. Louis*.

THE FRIENDS Martin grew up with would mythologize him as the southern soul mate of the writer Jack Kerouac, who set off on the road across country at around the same time as my father, in 1948. Carrying only a change of clothes and an H.D. .22 high-standard target pistol, nineteen-year-old Martin camped out on the banks of Mississippi's Pearl River, where piney rooter hogs were running wild. "I caught me a shoat and dismembered it—killed it before dismembering it," he would say later, regaling his children with his feats, mostly of appetite. He swam with baby alligators (also in Mississippi), worked as a carny (in Nevada), laid fence for a wheat farmer (Texas), slept on a country club golf course (Flagstaff, Arizona). And finally he made it to Bakersfield, California, to the plaque commemorating the spot where his great-uncle Milton, the family's other eccentric, had struck oil, after inventing a death ray that could zap a cow at two miles.

At Christmastime 1948, Martin roared up on his Harley-Davidson to his house on a hill and came in through the back door. There was a dinner party in progress, which he ignored. Mama Ruby Thornton, the family housekeeper, informed Mrs. McWhorter that someone who resembled her son had gone upstairs. Martin had been away for several months, incommunicado except for the occasional postcard. But perhaps it was out of consideration for his parents' social pride that he neglected to let them know he was home or speak to the guests: A motorcycle accident had knocked out his front teeth.

The next day, Martin's older sister, Gail, was having her debut party, given jointly with a granddaughter of Robert Jemison, creator of Mountain Brook. It was an afternoon tea dance at the Mountain Brook Club, which had also been founded by Jemison. Gail and her friends had recently passed out campaign literature for Strom Thurmond at her father's suggestion, but not because he approved of his cousin Sid Smyer Sr.'s Dixiecrat shenanigans on the merits. (As my grandmother described the relationship between the two Gaylesville compatriots, "Your grandfather had lunch with Sid, not dinner.") As a Wendell Willkie Republican, Hobart simply thought the States Rights ticket might break up the Democratic monolith and bring a two-party system to the Solid South.

Although Gail had been rather cross with Martin ever since she returned from Wellesley one vacation to discover her phonograph welded to his workbench, blaring "The Ride of the Valkyrie," her brother was invited to her party provided he wore some teeth. His sally into Mountain Brook society proved to be as temporary as the bridge Dr. McClung put in his mouth that morning.

Martin was barely recognizable as the child of Hobart and Marjorie McWhorter by the time I was growing up as his daughter. But the fight he was fighting against "niggers" was a crude continuation of the resistance his father had helped mount against the New Deal. In light of his preference for his mother, Martin might easily have gone the other way, as a black sheep radical in the progressive tradition. For my grandmother had flirted with the left wing of the New Deal. A writer of produced children's plays, she had also taught young people under the auspices of the red-baited Federal Theater Project. In the fall of 1938, she was a delegate, in her capacity as a maternal welfare activist, to the Southern Conference for Human Welfare. A year later, she had written an eloquent but measured letter to the SCHW president, Frank Porter Graham, complaining that she had received suspiciously synchronized mailings from the SCHW's Communist-dominated Civil Rights Committee (headed by Joe Gelders) and from what she rather knowingly referred to as "the Party." Graham wrote her a gracious reply, commending her as one of the hundreds of brave southerners "willing to be smeared as Red or Black, or both in behalf of the people and the civilization of the South." But what Marjorie would eventually remember of her participation in the SCHW was that Eleanor Roosevelt had at one of her appointments snubbed a society matron in order to converse with a miner's wife.

When I quizzed my grandmother much later about why she didn't ask her son what he was up to on those nights while he was abroad in the workshop town foiling "civil rights," she replied, "Because I was afraid he would tell me." My great fear would be that my father had consummated another perverse pairing, between country clubber and Klansman, and that he had joined forces with the city's other "brave brawler," Robert Chambliss.

3.

MASS MOVEMENTS

1954–1956

Baseball

V ULCAN WAS ABOUT to be adopted statewide as the Alabama Symbol of Traffic Safety thanks to the efforts of Birmingham's Junior Chamber of Commerce. But glory seemed forever beyond the grasp of Sid Smyer. He was finally a bona fide Big Mule, the new president of the land company that had created Birmingham in 1871. But now that he had graduated from "plump associate" to the inner sanctum, the oligarchy he represented was sickly, and the cause he was defending was an apparently lost one: the Caucasian purity of baseball.

In one of their first acts of 1954, the city commissioners had done something unprecedented in Birmingham history. They had reversed segregation, gutting the signature ordinance that barred blacks and whites from sharing any recreational activity, up to and including checkers. The law had been causing problems for the sports-crazed city ever since Jackie Robinson desegregated big-league baseball in 1947, for it eliminated Birmingham from the pro exhibition circuit. And so, in consideration of the fans, the commission unanimously amended the statute so that blacks and whites could play certain spectator sports together— football and track, in addition to baseball.

The explanation for the commission's sudden softness on segregation was Bull Connor's departure from city hall, as a result of a police corruption scandal. "Honest Ole Bull" had for years run the police department as what one member of the media called a "small-time gestapo," controlling the force by rewarding loyalists ("my nigguhs") with plum assignments: the liquor detail, with payoffs from bootleggers, or the house-of-ill-repute beat, with flesh perks. And one of the nonloyalists had decided to expose just how deep Connor's hypocrisy ran.

Early on the evening of December 21, 1951, the disenchanted detective, Henry Darnell, arrived at the Tutwiler Hotel with a reporter in tow and began banging and kicking on the door of Room 760, hollering for Commissioner

Connor to come out. After a good twenty minutes, Connor finally opened the door. With him, also in coat and hat, was his secretary, Christina Brown. Connor was doubly compromised. Not only had he been married for thirty-one years, to the nice, overweight woman he had begun courting in sixth grade in Plantersville. But he had become quite the public moralist, denouncing girlie movies and even comic books. The ordinance under which he would be charged (by his own police department)—forbidding unmarried, unrelated men and women to occupy the same hotel room—had been written by his Great Man patron, Jim Simpson.

Bull was at the office Christmas party on Monday, drinking punch and yelling "Hey, Miss America!" to every female between sixteen and sixty, but his popularity could not offset this blow to his honesty. Impeachment charges against him were dropped only after he agreed not to run for reelection in 1953,* though Simpson did pull off one last feat of "Me and Jim" and successfully challenged the constitutionality of his own joint-occupancy ordinance.

When the new city commission, minus Connor, amended the notorious "checkers" ordinance on January 26, 1954—just in time for Jackie Robinson's Brooklyn Dodgers to announce an exhibition game with the Milwaukee Braves— it was only making legal the "integration" that the fans had long been practicing. Whites had flocked to see the superior Black Barons, with their star outfielder, Willie Mays. Now Mays was the darling of the New York Giants, and his Birmingham salutation, "Say, hey!" was the watchword of Gotham. Across town in the Bronx, another "ethnic" Birminghamian, Melvin "Mutt" Israel—a.k.a. Mel Allen, the Yankees' celebrity sports announcer—was patenting widely mimicked calls of his own: "How about that!" and "Going, going . . . gone!" †

Sid Smyer understood that more than just Jim Crow baseball was at stake; the commission had, incredibly, proclaimed, "Doing away with segregation is slowly, but surely coming to pass." His fifteen-plus years of political service were in danger of being canceled by a stroke of a pen. To safeguard Our Way of Life, Smyer figured he was going to have to revive the Dixiecrat movement. But it looked to be a tough course ahead.

The Dixiecrat monolith had crumbled in the six years since Smyer filled the Municipal Auditorium with governors, U.S. senators, and newsreel photographers to nominate Strom Thurmond for president. That revolt had turned out to be more than a failure. Truman's 1948 victory despite the South's opposition had

---

* Two impeachment trials had ended in hung juries. When Detective Henry Darnell got into his car to go to the courthouse to testify at one, he discovered five sticks of dynamite under the seat, with the fuse connected to the exhaust pipe. On the stand, Darnell pointed his finger at Connor and said, "You know who bombed all the Negro homes. You know. Admit it."

† Meanwhile, Birmingham was becoming a baseball purgatory. Jimmy Piersall had been shipped down to the Barons by the all-white Boston Red Sox midway into the 1952 season, to collect material, it turned out, for the memoir of his mental crack-up, *Fear Strikes Out*. After a few months of weird antics on and off the field, he woke up in the violence ward of a Massachusetts state mental hospital. "You acted more and more peculiar," his wife explained, "so they finally sent you to Birmingham."

proved that the national party didn't have to pander to its southern wing, any more than the Brooklyn Dodgers had humored Birmingham's Dixie Walker when he balked that year at playing in the same uniform as Robinson. (Celebrated as Brooklyn's "peepul's cherce," Walker was nonetheless traded.) By 1950, the Dixiecrats had even lost control of the state Democratic Party to the FDR liberals—Senator Lister Hill's faction. Smyer found himself lecturing dozing luncheon groups about the county sewer system.

Now, in the spring of 1954, Smyer resuscitated the Dixiecrat high command into the American States Rights Association, telegraphing his desperation by advertising the new group in practically every newspaper in the state. His canvassers went door-to-door collecting signatures for a petition demanding a voter referendum to resegregate baseball. After Smyer's colleague Hugh Locke (the Dixiecrat lawyer suspected of masterminding the Dynamite Hill bombings) accused the city commission of promoting "mongrelization" and warned that his supporters were going to get "red hot on this thing," a referendum vote was scheduled to coincide with the Democratic primary runoff on June 1, 1954.

The old Dixiecrat titans looked like spoilsports, sure losers. But then the highest-placed Birminghamian of all gave segregation's extremists new life.

May 17, 1954

As THE SENIOR ASSOCIATE JUSTICE of the U.S. Supreme Court, Hugo Black took his place to the right of the chief justice, Earl Warren. Though Black was about to execute a long-plotted coup, he wore the benignly distracted jury face he had perfected as a "damage suit" lawyer in Birmingham. The death of his wife in December 1951—a probable, though unacknowledged suicide—and his thankless Cold War role as the Court's minority defender of unpopular political beliefs had taken some of the starch out of him. There was no clue in his demeanor that the Court had swung to his side of the revolution.

For a decade, Justice Black had spearheaded the Court liberals' search for a case that would overturn the legal rationale for segregation, the Supreme Court's 1896 *Plessy* v. *Ferguson* decision. That case had ruled that Homer Plessy, a New Orleans Negro (one-eighth of his lineage, a great-grandmother, was black), had no standing under the Fourteenth Amendment to sit in the "white" car of a train that provided separate but equal facilities for his race. Over the past eight years the Court had outlawed segregation in political primaries, housing, interstate transportation, and even graduate schools without raising the Old Confederacy from the dead. But integrated primary and secondary schools meant mixing the races at the age that mating habits were being formed, raising the specter of miscegenation and, possibly, mass revolt. A collection of lawsuits challenging public school segregation had been stuck in the court since December 1952. Though the flagship case originated in South Carolina, the justices had selected Oliver Brown of Topeka, Kansas, to be the name plaintiff for all the suits, in order to deflect the spotlight from the South.

The late chief justice Fred Vinson had assumed that Black would write and take the fall for all the decisions on segregation, which Black had declared "Hitler's creed—he preached what the South believed." But the newly arrived chief, Earl Warren, had accepted the school cases with gusto, and had adroitly corralled his flock into unanimity. At 12:52 on May 17, Warren—seemingly President Dwight Eisenhower's least controversial appointee (Thomas Dewey's running mate, no less, and the former governor of California)—began without fanfare to read the decision of *Brown v. the Board of Education of Topeka, Kansas.* "We conclude, unanimously, that in the field of public education the doctrine of 'separate but equal' has no place" went the Court's verdict on segregation. "Separate educational facilities are inherently unequal."

The South's corrupt racial peace was over. And so was Sid Smyer's hiatus from the center stage of southern politics. Two weeks later, Birmingham's sports fans went to the polls and, encountering the American States Rights Association's referendum, voted separate and unequal baseball back in by a margin of 3 to 1.

In the same election, however, Big Jim Folsom, the bane of the Dixiecrats during the 1940s, reclaimed the governor's office, his popularity having survived the paternity suit, his "left-wing" politics, a prison corruption scandal, and the bibulous debaucheries he had hosted on the state yacht. His campaign manager for south Alabama was the young politician who had been his water carrier in the statehouse during his first term. George Wallace had rejoiced in Folsom's company, exulting to colleagues that when they visited the courthouse ring in his native Barbour County, the governor shook hands with the janitor first. Some believed that Wallace had written 90 percent of Big Jim's stump speeches, although George would insist that virtually the only scripted line in them was "Thanks for attending the rally."

The Folsom comeback moved the *New York Times* to praise Alabama for "underscoring the changing patterns of race relations in the South." With the Dixiecrats rising again, which face would the state now wear?

The Disciple

READING THE *Birmingham News*'s afternoon headline for May 17, Fred Shuttlesworth experienced a spiritual release the likes of which he hadn't felt since his conversion from Methodism to Baptism: "In Unanimous Decision—Court rules out Segregation in Schools." He was convinced that he was about to get his freedom. Remarkable! There it was, and he personally hadn't even gotten around to fighting for it.

Shuttlesworth had spent most of his thirty-two years dealing with the intraracial afflictions of racism, without even giving any serious thought to white people. The genius of segregation was the extent to which it had divided Negroes from their own, with a color prejudice said to be the vestige of pre-Emancipation distinctions between field hands and mulatto house slaves. "If you white, you all right," went the Negro saying. "If you brown, stick around. If you black, stay back."* Shuttlesworth had what was delicately known as a "dark complexion," or "stove-pan brown," and was a literal example of law enforcement's favorite epithet for shaming Negro men, "black bastard."

Shuttlesworth had never particularly worried about his station until he happened to be thrust out of it. After two years at Selma University (with the highest marks in the school's history), he had crossed a social chasm that seemed unnavigable. He was offered the pulpit at First Baptist of Selma, the oldest black church in the jewel of the Black Belt, one of whose deacons had once paid him fifty cents an hour to do chores. It was then that he learned how the black church only magnified the zero-sum mentality of a people seeking self-worth in a dominant culture that abominated them.

Shuttlesworth's youth, inexperience, abrasive ego, and preaching style—building toward the rhythmically gasping "whoop"—were probably factors along with his dark skin in his difficult relationship with the bourgeoisie of First Baptist. The suave deacons were annoyed when he consulted the congregation before selling church property to the state. "Don't fool with these other little niggers anymore," they advised him. Shuttlesworth replied, "God must have loved little niggers, he made so many of them."

Once Shuttlesworth understood that they expected him to step aside and let them run the church, he had to "face the cross." He confronted the head deacon: "You have as many faces as a city clock. You and I can't be friends. Go to hell." The deacons' resignation was Shuttlesworth's first achievement on behalf of the Negro masses, and the beginning of his leadership. It would be typical of his career that this group soon grabbed back its power and shoved him aside. At the end of 1952, he gave up his pulpit and moved to Birmingham.

It would have stunned Shuttlesworth to know that his unprepossessing two-hundred-member new church, Bethel Baptist, had been the first test of the Negro "mass movement" twenty years before. Bethel had then been the pulpit of a Big Preacher named Milton Sears, who received generous contributions from prominent whites, and the activists who brought him down were the Communists. Hosea Hudson, the Birmingham Party's top black rank and filer, had led an uprising against Sears after he betrayed a neighborhood man to the police. Seeing the unauthorized visitors march into his church, Sears had reached under his pulpit, pulled out a double-barreled shotgun, and waved it until the sanctuary emptied in a near stampede. The legend would come down that the intruders had been carrying picks, if not hammers and sickles.

Soon, Sears's church membership of two thousand plunged, and with it his influence in the neighborhood. Once he lost his value as an informant, the police withdrew his round-the-clock bodyguards, explaining, "Reverend, the reds are

---

* To call a Negro "black" was considered fighting words. It did not become the preferred description until 1966 and has lately ceded vogue to "African-American."

not threatening your life, they are just telling you to move out of that community." The Communists rejoiced in their one concrete victory in Birmingham, hooting at the bitter-end deacons guarding the parsonage with their Winchesters. Within a few years of Shuttlesworth's ministry, armed sentries would be protecting Bethel's pastor against a white rather than a red enemy.

Emory O.

FOR EMORY O. JACKSON, the initial euphoria over the *Brown* decision was an excuse for a morning-after hangover. Jackson was the editor of the *Birmingham World,* a twice-weekly black newspaper, and was the city's lone functioning "race man"—or the Negro Bull Connor said "ought to be run out of town." A cynical idealist in a perpetual state of heartbreak, Jackson had seen it all, several times. In 1938, he had attended the founding ceremonies of the Southern Conference for Human Welfare, and been escorted to his workshop in the Tutwiler by Eleanor Roosevelt after the hotel's white employees refused to reveal where it was taking place. Ten years later, in the same auditorium where the SCHW had been born, Connor had him escorted out of the Dixiecrat convention at the wrong end of a police revolver, even though he had considerately taken a seat in the balcony.

Emory O., as he was known to all, was out of place even in his own neighborhood. Though a member of the bourgeoisie (he had been student body president at Atlanta's revered Morehouse College), he spurned the strivers' conspicuous refinement. A badly dressed, unmarried loner, he held court in the disarray of his office, pounding on his desk, tossing newspapers in the air, and screaming in wheezy exasperation at the thankless civil rights labors that had been left to him since Bull kicked out his fond young Communist comrades from the Southern Negro Youth Congress.

Friends began to think that Emory O. had gone a little "Jim Crow crazy," so disillusioned with his race that he had begun to "feel like murdering somebody—myself, even." He was not surprised that the first objections to *Brown* were mounted by its presumed beneficiaries, like the Southern Negro Improvement Association that sprung up in Birmingham for the purpose of decrying the decision. Jackson understood something about black people that Fred Shuttlesworth did not. By pushing at last for real integration rather than equality within the framework of separateness, the NAACP had alienated its own constituency, the "Negro leadership class" that had learned to thrive within segregation. The axle of the black bourgeoisie—the schoolteachers—would be out of work if the schools merged. Jackson called segregation's black collaborators "the fat boys—fat because their bellies are full of crow: you know, Jim Crow."

Only a couple of things pierced Jackson's despair in the spring of 1954. Fred Shuttlesworth had managed to close down a well-known black bootlegger in North Birmingham and was praised in the *World* as a "solid thinking young citizen."* The other encouraging development was the installation of a new pastor at the Dexter Avenue Baptist Church in Montgomery. He was a bright doctoral candidate from Atlanta named Martin Luther King Jr. Jackson huzzahed his arrival, too, and made sure Shuttlesworth met him when he came through Birmingham.

Shuttlesworth did not immediately buy Emory O.'s enthusiasm for the young Atlantan, assuming that King was just another "high-type nigger preacher," as their ilk was called by the whites who gave them standing. But Jackson seemed to recognize in the two men a powerful complementarity—King with his instinct for conciliation, Shuttlesworth for confrontation.

The Seamstress

IT WAS SHUTTLESWORTH'S keen appreciation of the Negro church's obstructionist potential that explained his amazement at the circumstances under which he next encountered Martin Luther King, at the end of 1955. The young minister from Dexter had been thrust into the limelight of history, through no doing of his own. On the cold, overcast afternoon of December 1, a black woman had been riding the bus home from her $23-a-week job in alterations at the Montgomery Fair department store when the driver—J. Fred Blake, of Equality, Alabama—ordered her to surrender her seat to a white man who had gotten on after her, at the Empire Theater stop. Instead, the forty-two-year-old seamstress slid over from her aisle seat to the window and looked out on the colorful lights of seasonal good will and commerce.

Segregated public transportation was the most unavoidable daily insult of Negro life. Black people stepped into the front of the bus to pay their fare, then debarked, boarded through the rear door, and took their seats in the back. Some drivers glorified themselves as enforcers of the order and freely cursed black riders, shortchanged them, passed their stops, pulled guns on them. Fred Blake simply called the cops.

When two policemen arrived, the seamstress asked, "Why do you push us around?"

One of them replied, "I don't know," and then took her to jail.

The Zeitgeist, as King later put it, had tracked Rosa Parks down. Her action, spontaneous though it seemed, was actually the world-changing vindication of Alabama's long tradition of civil rights activism, mounted in obscurity and futility by the Southern Conference for Human Welfare and the Southern Negro Youth Congress. In the hindsight of Parks's stand, it would appear that the youth congress's signal protest had been its premeditated "direct action" against segregation on public transportation in 1942. Mildred McAdory, a young cook who moon-

---

* Shuttlesworth accomplished this under the auspices of the Civic Leagues, the loose-knit organization of neighborhood self-help groups that were a vestige of U.S. Steel's multi-pronged program from the 1930s to "control the thinking of the Negro workers." It was nominally headed by TCI's longtime top janitor, Will McAlpin, but controlled by the executive who had approved the abduction of Joe Gelders.

lighted as an organizer of steelworkers, had boarded a Birmingham streetcar with two SNYC colleagues and moved the "segregator," a wooden bar posted with a warning against touching it. After the police beat up McAdory and took her to jail, the SNYC had mounted a campaign to desegregate the streetcars. The local NAACP lawyer, Arthur Shores, took McAdory's case, but it never amounted to the intended legal challenge to segregation, what with the judge referring to him as "Arthur, boy." McAdory ended up moving to New York, where she became active in the Communist Party. But her protest had made an impression on Montgomery's premier black activist, E. D. Nixon.

Nixon, an energetic member of the youth congress's advisory board, was the founder of the local chapter of the Brotherhood of Sleeping Car Porters, the first significant black trade union. He was also a force in the NAACP, despite having the blue-black skin and creative grammar of a sharecropper's son. Nixon had shared an SNYC podium with Mildred McAdory, and perhaps he still remembered the exemplary pamphlet the congress had printed up to publicize her arrest ("For Common Courtesy on Common Carriers") when, not long after the *Brown* decision, he began looking for a solid citizen to front a constitutional challenge to bus segregation. Nevertheless, Nixon was taken by surprise when his very own secretary at the NAACP, Rosa Parks, called from the city jail on December 1 to say that she had refused to give up her seat.

Durrs

E. D. NIXON telephoned his lawyer, a courtly white southern gentleman named Clifford Durr. His wife, Virginia Foster Durr, was one of Rosa Parks's private sewing clients. She grabbed her coat too, and the couple went with Nixon to bail Parks out. The Durrs were back at the center of the biggest social revolution since the last one they had helped shape, as prominent New Dealers (Cliff was a member of the Federal Communications Commission), who were mainstays of the Southern Conference for Human Welfare. The *Report on the Economic Conditions of the South* that set the SCHW agenda had been written in their suburban Washington living room in the summer of 1938.

Virginia Durr was one of those larger-than-life figures who seemed marked for destiny, like her late sister's husband, Hugo Black. At the beginning of the New Deal, Black had brokered the Durrs' move to Washington from Birmingham, where Cliff had been a law partner of Hobart McWhorter (a member of the Durrs' wedding) and Virginia was in the Junior League with her fellow Wellesley alumna, Marjorie McWhorter. Aptly nicknamed Jinksie, Virginia had always been like a belle on phenobarbital. There had been times when Hobart gave his wife the hairy eyeball after Jinksie publicly betrayed some confidence Marjorie had shared about the law firm, Martin, Turner, and McWhorter. The truths Jinksie blurted out became morally as well as socially embarrassing once she was radicalized by Senator Robert La Follette's famous civil liberties hearings. Shocked by the revelations about how labor organizers were "taken care of" in her hometown of Birmingham, she had telegrammed her father's industrialist friends asking them to "refute this unwarranted lie." The rebuttals, of course, never came.

Virginia had looked up the star witness of the hearings, Joe Gelders, the next time she was in Birmingham. She became one of his co-conspirators in putting together the Southern Conference for Human Welfare, and her prominence at the 1938 Birmingham meeting had prompted the Big Mules' *Alabama* magazine to single her out as one of the "available pink Alabamians to give local color to the conference." Indeed, Virginia had not flinched from the Communists in either the Southern Conference or Henry Wallace's Progressive Party, on whose ticket she was the candidate for Senate in Virginia.

After Cliff refused reappointment to the FCC rather than submit to Truman's anti-Communist loyalty oath, the Durrs returned to his hometown of Montgomery, in 1951, the patrician Cliff having been forced into a professional diaspora as a defender of dissidents and pinkos—and E. D. Nixon's NAACP. Virginia, meanwhile, coped with her moral isolation by becoming a prolific letter writer. In early 1955, she received a request from one of her correspondents, a fellow architect of Rosa Parks's rebellion. Myles Horton, a poor white son of Appalachia, enlightened under the radical theologian Reinhold Niebuhr at Union Theological Seminary in New York, ran the Highlander Folk School in his native Tennessee, based on a concept originating in Denmark that an oppressed people collectively hold strategies for liberation that are lost to its individuals.* Highlander had been a haven for the South's handful of functional radicals during the thirties and the essential alma mater for the leaders of the CIO's fledgling southern organizing drives.

Though Horton's own revolutionary hero was Jesus, "who simply did what he believed in and paid the price," he had had no compunction about embracing the Communists—Don West, the young preacher-poet from Georgia who had founded Highlander with him, had moved on to the Party—and had declared in the 1930s that "the best radical work in the South was the exceptional work being done by the CP in the Birmingham area." Highlander had attracted both the financial blessings of prominent New Dealers like Eleanor Roosevelt and the ire of the South's great union beater, the coal magnate Charles DeBardeleben, whose propaganda organization, the Constitutional Educational League, had made the school a particular target.† As the Cold War thrust many of the league's ideas into the mainstream, the CIO broke with its left-wing think tank in Tennessee and the labor movement concentrated on protecting its hard-won power rather than advancing democracy. Like his close friends from the Southern Conference, Horton sensed that the next progressive frontier was race.

---

* As Karl Marx might have had it, Highlander's home county was also U.S. Steel country, site of the last tubercular vestige of the Tennessee Coal and Iron Company in its namesake state and the scene of the bloody 1892 uprising of coal miners that had led to Tennessee's abolition of the convict lease.

† The league named Highlander exhibit A in its 1940 "indictment" of the labor movement, a pamphlet called *The Fifth Column in the South.* DeBardeleben was rumored to have put up $5,000 to print the pamphlet.

The purpose of Horton's letter to Virginia Durr in early 1955 was to ask her to recommend a Montgomery Negro for a scholarship he had available for one of the workshops Highlander was holding to develop grassroots leaders for an offensive against segregation. Virginia had nominated her seamstress, Rosa Parks, who went to Highlander that summer to discuss the possibility of mobilizing blacks in her hometown. But Parks and everyone at the workshop came to the same conclusion: Montgomery was hopeless—the black people there would never stick together.

A Bus Boycott

NOW, SOME FOUR MONTHS LATER, the Durrs and E. D. Nixon bailed Rosa Parks out of jail. "Mrs. Parks, this is the case we've been looking for," Nixon said over coffee back at her house. Cliff Durr was already mentally preparing the constitutional brief against bus segregation. But after leaving the Parkses, Nixon had an even more ambitious idea. "Our people should just stop riding the buses," he told his wife when he got home. The plan was proselytized over the weekend in a frenzy of caucusing, mimeographing, organizing, and preaching. Leaflets were even passed around at the black dives, where patrons were sharpening switchblades to avenge their womenfolk from the insults of public transportation, complaining that "these bus drivers either dog 'em or date 'em." On Monday morning, the city buses rolled through black Montgomery, empty.

Standing with the crowd of some five hundred on the street outside Parks's trial later that morning, E. D. Nixon watched the drama of his race shift. In twenty years of going in and out of court, he had never seen a Negro male there except as a defendant or a relative of a defendant. It was time, he thought, for the black man to step into the spotlight. At a strategy meeting later that afternoon, he harangued the city's balky black preachers, "If we're gonna be mens, now's the time to be mens."

Fred Shuttlesworth recognized instantly that the bulletin out of Montgomery that day was "a big deal": the first mass protest in modern Alabama history. He drove ninety miles south to the state capital to attend the evening mass meeting at Holt Street Baptist. He was among the lucky thousand who got in; Virginia Durr was stuck out on the sidewalk with the estimated five thousand who didn't. To Shuttlesworth's mild surprise, the man welcomed to the pulpit as the leader of the boycott was the young minister to whom Emory O. Jackson had introduced him a year earlier.

No one could have been more surprised about his new position than Martin Luther King Jr. himself. Still in his twenties, languid and pampered-looking, he seemed a good fit for snooty Dexter Avenue Baptist, in the shadow of the state capitol—"a *big* nigger's church," said King's father, who had worked his way up from sharecropper's son to pastor of Atlanta's aspiring Ebenezer Baptist. The Dexter congregation "would prefer that you talk about Plato or Socrates or somebody like that," the Reverend Ralph Abernathy of First Baptist wryly warned his new best friend in Montgomery. Which was fine by King. Closing in on a doctorate in theology from Boston University, he loved to discuss his dissertation subject, Paul Tillich's idea of God, and salted his sermons with Greek words like *agape*.

That afternoon, King had been goaded by the city's established black leadership into assuming the presidency of the boycott organization, the unaffiliated Montgomery Improvement Association, which Abernathy had proposed as a cautiously moderate, demonstrably "native" alternative to the NAACP. "I figured on pushing him out so far that he couldn't run away," Nixon said later of King's ascension, which he and many of his MIA colleagues came to rue as they were relegated to extras in his life story. "And, with that bad guess, we got Moses."

A few hours later, in the packed sanctuary of the Holt Street Baptist Church, King opened with studied gravity his first speech as a civil rights leader. After dampening the eager audience with a bland recitation of the facts, he paused. "And you know, my friends," he continued, voice welling, "there comes a time when people get tired of being trampled over by the iron feet of oppression," Yeses and amens tested the stillness, and then there erupted a rolling roar over an undertow of pounding feet. King moved beyond preacher boilerplate to eloquence. "For many years, we have shown amazing patience . . . ," he said. "But we come here tonight to be saved from that patience that makes us patient with anything less than freedom and justice. . . . If you will protest courageously and yet with dignity and Christian love, when the history books are written in future generations the historians will pause and say, 'There lived a great people—a black people—who injected new meaning and dignity into the veins of civilization.' That is our challenge and our overwhelming responsibility."

The modern civil rights movement had been born. Eventually, it would seem to have a single father, Martin Luther King. Its multiple midwives would be eclipsed, and Rosa Parks would be seen as a simple woman with tired feet. As the news filtered out of Montgomery, one of the founders of the Southern Negro Youth Congress living in New York immediately thought back to the Columbia conference of 1946 and W.E.B. Du Bois's "Behold the Land" speech. The old Communist Party pipe dream of "self-determination in the Black Belt" was indeed coming true in the Cradle of the Confederacy.

Infatuation

THE EVENTS OF MONTGOMERY catapulted Emory O. Jackson out of his chronic gloom. The "refuse-to-ride movement," or "sacrifice for self-respect program," as his newspaper was calling the continuing bus boycott, made the new year worth living. During the early strategy sessions over tumblers of bourbon, Martin Luther King and Ralph Abernathy had assumed the protest would be the briefest interruption of their "real work," but Jackson recognized it as "a great questioning, an awakening," with "cosmic backing."

Jackson had become virtually a board member of the Montgomery Improvement Association, but he was having a problem with its goals. Despite its radical traces (Rosa Parks had met her husband when he was raising money for the Scottsboro Boys), the MIA was merely asking for a more polite form of back-of-the-bus: courtesy from the drivers and a plan of seating in which blacks still filled the buses from the rear, whites from the front, with the Jim Crow color line moving forward and backward according to the ride's demographics. King had quoted the champion of separate and unequal, Booker T. Washington, in his debut speech.

Emory O. Jackson denounced the MIA seating plan as having "all of the objectionable and despicable features of racial segregation." But as a former fellow traveler and survivor of Bull Connor's war on Communism, he realized that the boycott's vital significance was not in the ends as much as the means. Its indigenous leadership of clergymen promised to make it red-bait proof. Less than three weeks into the boycott, hoping to preempt those who might link this revolution to Lenin's, Jackson assigned King his historic role as America's answer instead to Mohandas K. Gandhi. "He often tells the story of how Mahatma Gandhi, the emaciated emancipator, liberated India with his nonviolence campaign," Jackson wrote in the *Birmingham World*. (At the time King himself professed "to know very little about" Gandhi.)

Fred Shuttlesworth watched the boycott with cautious awe. It seemed nothing less than a miracle that the capital city's contrarian black classes and masses had united behind a goal that demanded great physical and financial sacrifice and an esoteric strategy of nonviolence. Taxis and carpools were covering some bus routes, but most of the protesters were simply walking, making a witness as visible as a great black tide, as Virginia Durr saw it. Shuttlesworth began traveling regularly to Montgomery to caucus with King and Abernathy, whom he had met while getting a bachelor's degree at Alabama State College during the years he was preaching at First Baptist of Selma. The Montgomery phenomenon convinced him that God had chosen King for this hour. His might be next.

On January 22, Shuttlesworth delivered what Emory O. Jackson billed as his "first major speech before an NAACP-sponsored mass meeting." Shuttlesworth began by attacking the NAACP's own elite franchise. He urged the organization to get out of the "tree tops" and "launch a grass roots campaign to reach the masses." The finale paid homage to the "We are tired" refrain of King's speech. But he caustically expanded King's grievances: "Negroes are tired and fed up with their own leaders who rise to prominence and then do the Uncle Tom." Within a month, Shuttlesworth would declare an end to the NAACP's cherished legalism and gradualism.

Lucy

AT THE EMANCIPATION DAY festivities at Sixteenth Street Baptist Church on January 1, Emory O. Jackson had deferred to two young guests as the program's "real centers of attention." The more formidable was the tall, stylish but scrappy Pollie Anne Myers, who had gone to work for the *Birmingham World* as a student at

Miles College, a struggling local black Methodist school, and under Jackson's influence conceived an ambition to study journalism at the University of Alabama.
Her sidekick was another recent Miles graduate, an insecure farm girl from the
Black Belt named Juanita Lucy, who had thought about changing her detested
first name, Autherine, to Hilda until someone told her *that* name would make her
sound like a cow.

Three years earlier, the two young women had applied for admission to the
university as undergraduates—Lucy to the school of library science, because her
advisers assured her that the discipline was not taught at any black college in the
state and, what the heck, she loved to read. There was an ensuing interval of legalism and gradualism, during which Lucy and Myers heard occasional remarks
from their NAACP sponsors that they "were not the right type"—meaning, Lucy
understood, not that they weren't the race's best scholarly examples (which they
weren't), but that they were dark-skinned and humbly born. And then in the summer of 1955, the case landed in the court of Birmingham's newest federal judge,
a moderate Republican named Hobart Grooms. To the amazement of the
NAACP's lawyers, he amplified it to a class action and on July 1 enjoined the university's dean of admissions from excluding students on the basis of race.

The university appealed Grooms's decision, and the school year had already
begun when, in October, Justice Hugo Black unilaterally upheld Grooms's injunction. Since the students would have to wait until the winter term to enter the
university, the NAACP's much-delayed victory would now coincide with the
sensational developments in Montgomery.

Emory O. Jackson took Lucy and Myers to meet Martin Luther King. "Thank
God," King praised Lucy, his exact contemporary, "there are some people who can
rise above the old and broken down thoughts of their parents, who can rise above
their background and their heredity." Indeed, Milton Lucy, a Marengo County
sharecropper,* had explained to the white neighbors who threatened to kill him if
he didn't talk sense into his daughter, "That girl's grown. I raised her to know better. I always treated white people with respect. I always go to the back door."

A Peach Dress

EARLY ON THE GRAY, rainy morning of Wednesday, February 1, 1956, Lucy and
Myers met at the Masonic building to begin the two-hour trip to the University of
Alabama campus in Tuscaloosa. Myers's acceptance had been rescinded, on
grounds not of race but of "conduct and marital record": The university's hired
detectives had discovered that she had been pregnant and unwed at the time of
her application, though she had married before the baby was born. Lucy assumed
that the white folks figured that once they got rid of Myers, "Autherine would go
and sit down." But both women were determined.

---

* Autherine Lucy had never heard the word "sharecropper" until the news media began to roman-
ticize her rude beginnings.

For moral support, Lucy had asked a special friend to join the committee of concerned citizens who were accompanying her to Tuscaloosa. He had been the "smartest one" of her classmates at Selma University, from which she had graduated with the equivalent of a junior college degree before attending Miles, and in Latin class she had made sure she sat next to him so that she could cast her eyes over toward his paper "to get some ideas." Fred Shuttlesworth was delighted to go.

Once on campus, Lucy, in an aqua suit and high heels, was escorted into the dean's office. Pollie Anne Myers was dismissed. Students ambling down the hall where the black folks were waiting on a bench stopped to joke with Shuttlesworth, asking him why the NAACP didn't also "send down some basketball players about seven-two." Shuttlesworth replied that the university could use "some good football players, too." (Despite a decent quarterback named Bart Starr, the Tide had not won a single game in the 1955 season.) The friendly reception continued as Lucy and her large retinue made their way toward Bibb Graves Hall. A student came up to Emory O. Jackson and handed him a note: "Congratulations, many of us are with you all the way."

On Friday, Lucy, now wearing a pastel frock, took a center seat in her first class (geography), emptying the surrounding chairs. She was so grateful when a female student asked her name that she didn't even notice how gratuitous the question was. Shuttlesworth telegrammed Jackson in Birmingham, "Miss Autherine J. Lucy in class. Everything fine." But Lucy's entrance had acquired an iconography: Her arrival by Cadillac, the crisp hundred-dollar bill she had proffered for her registration fee, had become symbols of uppity Negritude.

"Ethel, do you know she wore a peach dress?" a white woman asked her maid, unaware that she was Autherine Lucy's sister.

Keep Bama White

ON FRIDAY NIGHT, February 3, 1956, after Lucy's first day of classes, a University of Alabama sophomore from Selma named Leonard Wilson found himself standing amid a group of male students who were plotting a panty raid. While other intense college loners pored over their stamp collections, Wilson spent an hour every day pasting clippings in segregation scrapbooks. Wilson diverted the young men away from the women's dormitories and led the growing crowd of students to the university president's house, sending up a chant of "Keep Bama white!" and "Hey, hey, ho, ho, Autherine's got to go." The president had left town for the weekend, and Wilson eased his schoolmates back to the Confederate war memorial, where he promised them bigger and better things for the following night. News photographs would confirm that Wilson presided over a full-scale riot on Saturday. A student following his instructions to stop cars with blacks and "make them believe" in segregation was pictured stomping the roof of an automobile filled with cringing Negroes. A Greyhound bus was ambushed. By Sunday, the campus mob included a large townie contingent, heaving rocks and firecrackers.

Among those drawn to this hot spot was Robert Chambliss. The birth of the civil rights movement had given his life meaning again. Since the late 1940s, the main source of his identity, the Ku Klux Klan, had been fragmented into "Bolshevik Klans," isolated terrorists in search of a revolution. During Governor Big Jim Folsom's anti-Klan campaign of 1949, Birmingham Klansmen had left the brotherhood in droves after their Grand Dragon was locked up in jail under state orders to surrender his membership rolls. Chambliss was finally fired from the city garage that year after assaulting a news photographer at a Labor Day Klan rally. Though Bull Connor had not been able to save Chambliss's job, he continued to protect him from being prosecuted for the Dynamite Hill bombings—including even the demolition of the new home office of Sid Smyer's own client, a prosperous black dentist he had known since he was a boy delivering milk. (It was not uncommon for segregationists to have conscience-saving "pet Negroes.") That apparently unauthorized mission, in the spring of 1950, had alienated the bombers' Dixiecrat sponsors and effectively brought an end to the fireworks on Dynamite Hill.

Since Connor's involuntary leave from office, Chambliss had been complaining about the Birmingham Klan "going soft." But now he had a new outlet— one that put him back under Smyer's wing. His current affiliation was a new phenomenon called the White Citizens Council, a resistance group started in the summer of 1954 in Mississippi by a Mississippi State football star turned plantation manager as a discreet alternative to the Ku Klux Klan. Its purpose was to mobilize the middle class behind the fight against the *Brown* decision. Its basic strategy was summed up by the Selma lawyer who had organized the first Alabama chapter: "We intend to make it impossible for any Negro who advocates desegregation to find and hold a job, get credit, or renew a mortgage."

For Sid Smyer, the White Citizens Councils offered a remedy to the identity crisis that had been plaguing his Dixiecrat spinoff, the American States Rights Association, since the successful baseball referendum turned it from a letterhead into a force. He had envisioned his group as sort of a war council to give orders to the troops, but didn't want to actually have to deal with the troops (the ASRA's $25 fee for voting privileges precluded mass membership). If he could graft the councils onto his organization, the top-heavy oligarchy would have an instant infrastructure. And so Smyer transposed the spreading Black Belt council movement to an urban setting—and a working-class constituency. "Dynamite Bob" Chambliss bragged of being the "first one in Jefferson County to join the White Citizens' Council." In that capacity, he was back at the University of Alabama the Monday morning after the riots, among the three thousand assembled at sophomore Leonard Wilson's urging to greet Autherine Lucy.

After her first class, as Lucy was whisked out a back door, the eggs came at her. They splattered the car she ducked into. A brick shattered the rear window. Ten or fifteen men charged the car. As Lucy ran inside Graves Hall for her next class, an egg hit her back. "Let's kill her, let's kill her," the crowd yelled. Gun barrels flashed. A mob of around a thousand shouted, "Hey, hey, ho, ho, where in the hell did that nigger go?" For three hours she remained locked in Graves Hall, praying for the courage to face death. Finally she was bundled by the state highway patrol onto the floor of a car and taken to the armed sanctuary of a black barbershop.

Only four arrests were made that day: Three were of the men who kneed the university chaplain in the groin as he came to the aid of Lucy's regular driver. The fourth was Robert Chambliss.

If the civil rights movement had been born in Alabama, the white resistance to it was also coming to maturity there. Beleaguered Dixiecrats and frustrated Klansmen were rallying to turn back this latest advance of the crusade for equal rights that had been launched by the New Deal. And their victories gave every impression of a successful counterrevolution in the making.

Autherine Lucy was the first black student in the history of desegregation to be greeted with organized violence. More than a thousand Negroes had already entered southern colleges and universities uneventfully. But the University of Alabama decided to settle the crisis on the mob's terms: That very Monday night, the trustees suspended Lucy until further notice, "for her protection and for the protection of other students and staff members."

Robert Chambliss, whose arrest was a formality, resulting in no trial, returned to the Union Building to celebrate his handiwork, blasting firecrackers, waving Confederate flags, and burning NAACP literature. The Lucy riot had worked. Or as the *New York Times* put it, "Because of the Lucy case and the Montgomery bus boycott, Alabama stands today as a symbol of Southern resistance to desegregation."

Alabama, it seemed, was leading a second secession. The state's recent "nullification" resolution, declaring *Brown* "null, void, and of no effect," inspired the Confederates in the U.S. Congress to rise again behind an integration-defying Southern Manifesto, its standard-bearer the Dixiecrats' old presidential candidate, South Carolina senator Strom Thurmond. This time, the old New Deal anti-Dixiecrat loyalist Lister Hill found he could not finesse "liberalism" from racism any longer, and capitulated.

The Dixiecrat rump caucus had finally enlarged into a mass phenomenon. Bankrolled by the same clique that had been behind the 1948 revolt, the White Citizens Councils were reaping a membership bonanza thanks to the double whammy of the bus boycott and Autherine Lucy. The biggest rally in Citizens Council history—ten thousand believers—took place on February 10 at Montgomery's giant "coliseum" auditorium, where Mississippi senator James Eastland, the VIP Dixiecrat who was a founding father of the councils, passed the torch of resistance from his state: "Thank God the state of Alabama has started the offense; from this day, the direction is forward."

Ace

UP IN BIRMINGHAM, Sid Smyer realized that he had a tiger by the tail. The Big Mules always seemed to be relearning the same lesson, as when the Klan they encouraged in the 1920s ended up electing Hugo Black: Given a little power, the people inevitably reverted to being "damn populists." And the man whom Smyer and the States Rights gang had put in charge of the North Alabama Citizens Councils was turning out to be an insubordinate with unauthorized ambitions and the talent to execute them.

As in many great dramas, a stranger had come to town, toting a vague résumé. Asa Earl Carter was a conservatively dressed, heavyset man in his late twenties, whose initial effect of sophistication was undercut by the ruddy country face and grammatical gaps of his rural Alabama youth. He admitted to having worked for Gerald L. K. Smith, the anti-Semitic rabble-rouser. But there was a competing rumor that he had been a member of the Communist Party. At any rate, his IQ—on file at the University of Colorado, which he had attended in the mid-forties following his discharge from the Navy—was high. His intelligence, combined with his on-air radio experience, had persuaded Smyer to hire him, toward the end of 1954, as the American States Rights Association's spokesman.

As the dashing Ace Carter, he had delivered the industrialists' message in a daily radio slot, managing to bring erudition to the single-note alarm of racial intermarriage. His sign-off, in the portentous cadences of Murrow and Paul Harvey, became as familiar as the Bullisms of the Big Mules' previous liaison with the folks. ("This is Ace Carter, and that is the history we are making. I thank you for your company.") The vehemence of his "Christianity"—let alone his white chauvinism—initially provoked little reaction, except from the Anti-Defamation League, the arm of B'nai B'rith that tracked dangerous anti-Semites.* But he had offended the wrong constituency in February 1955, and was forced off the air for denouncing the National Conference of Christians and Jews, whose local chapter was a hotbed not of the Communists Carter alleged but of the Chamber of Commerce's moderate members.

Smyer and the old Dixiecrat guard did not yet see Carter's anti-Semitism—or his binger's relationship with alcohol—as a liability. In the fall of 1955, they tapped him to head their newly formed North Alabama Citizens Council. By the time he appeared on the university campus to take advantage of the Autherine Lucy crisis, he was the Alabama Citizens Councils' most valuable asset, a brilliant demagogue, with two substantial Birmingham chapters to his credit. The vast majority of his members—by one estimate 75 percent—carried union cards. Like the other "white supremacist" offensives of the anti–New Dealers and their descendants, the Citizens Councils movement in Birmingham had a fairly simple goal: to devastate organized labor. Which explained why, in the wake of the Lucy riots, the newly merged American Federation of Labor and Congress of Indus-

---

* The ADL had tailed him as he headed to Michael's restaurant after recording his commentaries, got on an outdoor pay phone, called a local Jewish doctor, and spewed anti-Semitic obscenities into the receiver. The ADL sent a couple over from Atlanta, put them in turbans, and posed them as Arabs interested in buying the radio station he worked for. They stocked their hotel room with Carter's favorite whiskey, hid a tape recorder in the closet, and invited him over for a meeting. Once the "Arabs" let their feelings about Jews be known, Carter was up on his soapbox foaming at the mouth. But Carter saved the ADL the trouble of using its recording.

trial Organizations publicly condemned the White Citizens Councils, comparing their popularity to the rise of Nazism in the 1930s.*

As it turned out, there was a faction of the Citizens Council itself that had begun to characterize Ace Carter as a "Führer." His fiery underdog demeanor had always troubled the rich southern gentlemen-legislators who headed the councils' dominant Black Belt chapters. Carter did not share their hero worship of Robert E. Lee, considering his spiritual forebear to be Nathan Bedford Forrest, "the only red-neck in the army" and the founder of the Reconstruction Ku Klux Klan. The south Alabamians had worried that Carter might be leading a genuine folk movement rather than a grassroots version of the Dixiecrats, but they needed his recruiting skills too badly to act on their misgivings. Now that the Lucy case had brought a windfall of troops, the Black Belt gentry felt free to get rid of him.

At the end of February 1956, a sort of ghoulish Last Supper of the White Citizens Councils took place in Birmingham, as the apostles plotted to sell out their charismatic leader. Carter along with the Black Belt Judases held a banquet to honor a messiah from a bygone epoch, when the anti–New Deal elite, including Birmingham's first son, Charles DeBardeleben, had rented New York's Biltmore hotel to salute the figurehead of a putsch being plotted by Nazi agents in America. Now eighteen years later, their legacies nostalgically raised glasses to the Nazis' old "man on horseback," retired Major General George Van Horn Moseley. And then, two days after that, Carter's co-host of the George "Sterilize the Jews" Moseley banquet read Carter out of the movement, the trumped-up charge against him: anti-Semitism.

Carter's response was to lead his loyalists into a competing Citizens Council, causing the movement to cannibalize itself. Still, Sid Smyer and the Big Mules remained ambivalent about him, their urban agenda being somewhat different from that of the Black Belt whites surrounded by their Negro majorities. Carter was an embarrassment, yes, but he had done such wonders for Birmingham's labor problem, not only inciting a mutiny within AFL-CIO locals against the national union, but also corrupting labor's favorite politicians. Chief among them was the up-and-coming "damn populist" George C. Wallace, whose performance in the late forties as what one reporter called "the Number-One Do-Gooder in the legislature" had been sufficient for the Big Mules to circulate a grading of him as "radical."†

* To capitalize on the council's appeal with labor, the Big Mules recommissioned an old Klansman lackey from the Dixiecrat days—one of the accused floggers who beat the state's charges in 1949—to incite a southern secession from the AFL-CIO. In a wonderful coda to his epic anti-labor career, the Big Mules' proto-vigilante, Walter "Crack" Hanna, announced that he was joining the Citizens Council.

† Wallace had left the house of representatives after being flicked aside by Folsom's successor, a progressive but anti-populist governor who had a card in his secret office file noting: "George Wallace. Supported most of Folsom's legislation '47 & '49. Energetic, ambitious, liberal, smart, probably will be hostile . . ." Now an elected judge in his native Barbour County, he often slipped the bailiff a few dollars to buy hamburgers for black prisoners awaiting trial—and, more unprecedented, would switch their jury sentences to probation.

Solidarity

WALLACE REALLY HAD LESS an ideology than a gut passion for the hard-bitten country people he had grown up among in Barbour County, as the son of a layabout whose own father was a beloved country doctor. A sympathy for the "fokes" had sustained the bond between him and Big Jim Folsom. But now Wallace watched that star to which he was hitched sink erratically, and with it his own dream of becoming governor. Folsom had been coping with the stress of being the only white integrationist official in the state by disappearing into the bottle. "How drunk is the governor today?" had become the automatic opener on the capital's Goat Hill, as Folsom holed up in the Governor's Mansion making toasts to the spirit of Andrew Jackson. He had been on a "fishing trip"—a euphemism for his frequent lost weekends—when the University of Alabama campus erupted. But some believed that Folsom had deliberately abandoned Lucy to the mob in order to recover from the career-wounding racial gaffe he had committed the previous winter.

The governor had sent his limousine to the airport in December to meet Harlem congressman Adam Clayton Powell when he flew into town to help E. D. Nixon out with a voter registration drive (his last project before Rosa Parks got arrested). "How far can I go in talking about this?" the black New Yorker tactfully asked after he and Folsom enjoyed a Scotch and soda together.

"As far as you want," Folsom said.

"I just had a drink with the Governor," Powell announced to the press. "I doubt if I could have done that with the governor of my own state."* Folsom had finally crossed beyond the limits Alabama could be expected to bear. And a collateral consequence of those integrated cocktails was the unmaking of another progressive politician, his most promising protégé. Henceforth, George Wallace would fall back not on his populist sentiment, but on the fighting instinct he had honed as a young Golden Gloves bantamweight champion, with "as hard a lick as a little man could hit."

Wallace went into the pol-infested lobby of Montgomery's Jeff Davis Hotel and began cussing Folsom. A baffled old political hand asked for an explanation. Wallace shot back, as if he had been rehearsing, "Well, Big Jim's always been weak on the nigguh issue." This was from someone who had been as "soft" on race as they came, begging Folsom to appoint him to the board of trustees of Tuskegee Institute. Wallace had confided to a friend that his wartime service with Negroes convinced him that they were entitled to all the rights and privileges of whites.

On February 17, standing in an almost-empty high school lunchroom in

---

* And then there were rumors that Folsom had met secretly with E. D. Nixon and the bus boycott leaders and told them that their demands didn't go far enough. Back in 1944, on the train home from the Democratic National Convention in Chicago, the future governor had assured his Pullman porter, E. D. Nixon, "Let me tell you, the day is going to come when we will recognize the Negro."

Tuscaloosa, Wallace confronted the basic dilemma of every liberal southern politician before him, including his first hero, Governor Bibb Graves, as well as his former one, Big Jim. And that was how to advance a progressive political agenda—notably the interests of organized labor—without running afoul of the racist status quo. On this night, Wallace was the featured speaker at the first state meeting of the AFL-CIO's Committee on Political Education, the union's liberal political arm. But hardly any rank and filers had turned out to hear his ambiguous declaration that the "new South is going to be built on the shoulders of labor." Labor was building its house on the other side of town.

At the Tuscaloosa County Courthouse, hundreds of AFL-CIO men were attending the organizational meeting of the West Alabama Citizens Council, many of them the local B. F. Goodrich rubber workers who had been members of the Lucy mob. The chairman of the new council was the leader of the riots, the sophomore from Selma, Leonard Wilson, who had since been toughened under the tutelage of Ace Carter.

Wallace left Tuscaloosa a different man. Not long after, when the White Citizens Council filled the high school football stadium for its first meeting in his native Barbour County, George C. was there to receive the cheers of the crowd. He had made his choice: expediency over principle.

Co-Conspirators

AFTER AUTHERINE LUCY'S SUSPENSION, her lawyer, Arthur Shores, and his boss at the NAACP Legal Defense Fund, Thurgood Marshall, filed a complaint accusing the university officials of committing "conspiracy" with the mob to keep her out of school, naming four rioters specifically. At the top of the list was Robert Chambliss. Opening a hearing on the case on February 29, federal judge Hobart Grooms looked down upon a motley defense table, the University of Alabama's buttoned-down representatives alongside the most prolific bomber in the state.

As Marshall realized, the conspiracy charge had been a serious error: enough of a stretch to give the university some latitude. Thus, when Judge Grooms ordered the trustees to reinstate Autherine Lucy, their lawyers—the same firm that represented U.S. Steel and the DeBardelebens—countered by expelling Lucy permanently on the ground of her "outrageous, false and baseless accusations" of conspiracy. Meanwhile, another group of prominent lawyers compounded the bad faith by filing suit against the NAACP and Lucy on behalf of Robert Chambliss and the other three named rioters, seeking damages of $4 million.

And just like that, after less than three days on campus, the University of Alabama's first black student was gone. Though she felt stranded by the NAACP, Lucy was able to put the fear she had experienced on campus in perspective: "My whole life has been filled with fear—fear of growing up to be a nobody," she said. "Decidedly, America will never finish astonishing us." was how a French weekly put it, speaking for much of the world.

Eisenhower

IF AUTHERINE LUCY'S EXPULSION was a blow to the NAACP's policy of legalism and gradualism, President Eisenhower's refusal to reinstate her was a devastation. It had never occurred to the NAACP lawyers that the federal government would not back up its highest court, with troops if necessary. Nor that the man the President would now turn to for advice on his Negro problem was FBI director J. Edgar Hoover.

To address the injustices that sparked the Montgomery bus boycott, Attorney General Herbert Brownell had proposed a modest civil rights act, featuring voter protection and the establishment of a U.S. Civil Rights Commission and a civil rights division of the Justice Department.* Eisenhower invited Hoover to a March 9 meeting to discuss the legislation. The FBI director strode into the Cabinet Room with charts, easels, and soft-treading aides to present his top-secret twenty-four-page report, "Racial Tension and Civil Rights." Activist Negroes, it said, were the dupes of Communists. Hoover's position on the white resistance held that the "States Rights" offensive against *Brown* was a "resurgence of Jeffersonian principles"; the White Citizens Councils had attracted "the leading citizens of the South"—"bankers, lawyers, doctors, state legislators and industrialists." Whereas certain Negro leaders were fostering "racial hatred," segregationists were white parents frightened at the prospect of school integration because "colored parents are not as careful in looking after the health and cleanliness of their children."

At the Cabinet discussion, Eisenhower, too, rose to the segregationists' defense: "These people in the South were not breaking the law for the past sixty years," he said, "but, ever since the 'separate but equal decision,' they have been *obeying* the Constitution of the United States. Now, we cannot erase the emotions of three generations just overnight."

Fred Shuttlesworth was furious with the President—"Eisenhower is a president who sees nothing, hears nothing, thinks nothing, feels nothing, and winds up doing nothing." But he was also disillusioned with the NAACP—Lucy's lawyers had even made her read the inflammatory conspiracy charge before TV cameras. Shuttlesworth called the NAACP's game. "We've won legal victories," he told editor Emory O. Jackson. "Now is the time to massively overcome."

Bait

JACKSON HAD BECOME CONVINCED that the future of civil rights was in Montgomery. But now his euphoria over the bus boycott was deflating as well, for there had arrived at the capital, like some folkloric sage, a black man who had helped shape almost every form of Negro protest in the twentieth century, but who paradoxically risked bringing about the ruin of the boycott.

---

*The Civil Rights Act of 1957 would be the first civil rights legislation of the twentieth century.

Bayard Rustin, now forty-five, not only dressed like a dandy and (though raised outside Philadelphia) talked in a British-accented treble; he had also begun his civil rights career in the Communist Party, first fighting for the Scottsboro Boys, then organizing for the Young Communist League at the City College of New York. After leaving the Party in 1941, he joined up with A. Philip Randolph, the Harlem-based self-taught socialist intellectual who had turned the Brotherhood of Sleeping Car Porters into a force that exceeded its distinction as the first Negro trade union in the A. F. L. (though Randolph had never worked the trains himself).* Rustin then moved on to A. J. Muste's Fellowship of Reconciliation, an influential international pacifist organization that yoked Gandhi's system of spiritual ethics to Marx's economic ends. Rustin was forced to separate from the FOR in 1953, after being arrested for "copulating [the] private parts" of two men in a parked car. But now it was three years later, and in Montgomery the leader of an until now theoretical Negro mass movement was in over his head. In February 1956, Muste and his frequent ally Philip Randolph asked Rustin, who had recently been in India and West Africa experiencing "decolonization" firsthand, to head to Alabama.

As soon as he arrived in Montgomery, Rustin took charge of the boycott, advising the ninety prominent Negroes who had just been indicted under a 1921 anti-boycott statute that they should cheerfully turn themselves in—embrace the opposition in the manner of Gandhi, to dramatize that the real enemy was the system. Emory O. Jackson, who had watched Bull Connor denounce the Southern Negro Youth Congress's mass movement as "Communistic rattlesnakes" and "fleas," looked on with dread. Alabama's white people, including the reporter covering the protest for the *Montgomery Advertiser,* were already convinced that the reds were directing the bus boycotters as well as Autherine Lucy, who held a teary press conference in New York denying that she was a Communist.† And now here was Rustin, tailor-made for the opposition. On top of his homosexuality and his old Communist Party membership, there was his World War II prison sentence as a pacifist draft resister. He was, from the white South's point of view, a Commie pervert draft-dodging carpetbagger, and a "black bastard" to boot, having been raised under the impression that his mother was his older sister.

Jackson felt that he had to run Rustin off before the boycott was toppled by white propaganda. He dropped sour hints in his newspaper that outsiders were "offering services which if accepted by the protest group could obviously damage and setback their program." A week after his arrival, under penalty of exposure in the *World,* Rustin exiled himself to Birmingham and influenced the boycott at arm's length, like a football coach sending in plays from the sidelines. Rustin

---

* E. D. Nixon, the founder of the chapter in Montgomery, credited Randolph for his own dramatic transformation from "George" (the generic name passengers called Pullman porters) into "a different type of man" after hearing him speak at a black Y in St. Louis in the late 1920s.

† Meanwhile, the woman who had led Lucy to the University of Alabama, Pollie Anne Myers, had finally given up, after being snubbed by the NAACP. On a cold February night not long after her last futile trip to the university, she had gotten in her car, with instructions from her mother to get directions from policemen if she got lost, and had driven to Detroit; within three years she would have her first of two master's degrees from Wayne State University.

would remain a key (and controversial) figure in the developing movement, but for now Emory O. believed he had saved the day.

Daddy-O

A CYNIC LIKE JACKSON should have realized that appeasing the red-baiters was a slippery slope. There was no such thing as a civil rights movement that would pass ideological muster with segregationists. And indeed, Jackson had barely scared off Rustin when an even more lethal radical arrived: Hunter Pitts "Jack" O'Dell, the black ex–Merchant Marine introduced to the Communists' "dream of freedom" by the Southern Negro Youth Congress a decade earlier, was moving to Birmingham.

O'Dell was now one of the Party's top southern policy makers (under the pseudonym Daddy-O) and had begun to stake out his reputation as the most notorious black Communist in the country. In February, he had left his home base of New Orleans a step ahead of the local red squad and a subpoena from Senator James Eastland's Communist-hunting internal security subcommittee (which had interrogated Virginia Durr and Highlander's Myles Horton there two years earlier). Agreeing to face the committee in Washington, O'Dell had turned in a performance of considerable effrontery. His years in the South (chiefly Miami and New Orleans) had failed to blunt the no-nonsense style of his upbringing by his Catholic grandmother in a labor-conscious neighborhood of Detroit auto workers, and he informed Eastland how it felt to be fighting for the basic human rights of his people and have the standard-bearer of the White Citizens Councils accuse *him* of un-Americanism. The senator seemed stricken, and the committee's lawyer interjected, "Now, wait a minute. Will you stop talking?"

O'Dell: "What do you mean, stop talking? I have as much right to talk here as you. What are you? Some kind of dictator or something? I am making a statement here, and I intend to finish it."

By now, the government's aggression against the Communists was being rendered redundant by the American party's natural death. The new Soviet premier Nikita Khrushchev's revelations that February about the mass exterminations committed under Stalin's dictatorship had caused many thousands of the faithful to leave the American party, depleting the membership rolls. O'Dell stayed in; the black apparatchiks still considered the Party their best hope to gain equality and dismissed Martin Luther King as "the Baptist preacher." O'Dell explained, "I didn't get in because of Stalin, so I didn't get out because of him. The reason I was in was that the Communist Party analyzed the black problem as systemic to capitalism." And ironically he was about to take a job in the most fruitful vineyard of black capitalism, burial insurance.

One of his old Southern Negro Youth Congress comrades in New York had introduced O'Dell to a Birmingham man named H. D. Coke, the editor of the *Birmingham World* in the 1930s, who had been one of the SNYC's big lay supporters and would brag ruefully that he "didn't have the sense" to fear the

Communists.* Now an insurance executive, Coke was so impressed with O'Dell that he asked him to come work for him. Coke's old protégé Emory O. Jackson, who succeeded him as editor of the *World,* began listening for the other shoe to drop. Soon it would be clear how absurd was his ambition of saving the movement from the red taint: The first "Communist" enemy that the state of Alabama decided to go after was the stodgy NAACP.

Patterson

THE MAIN QUALIFICATION that thirty-five-year-old John Patterson possessed for his job as Alabama's attorney general was his father's assassination. Two years earlier, Albert Patterson had been shot in the face with a .38 revolver outside his law office in Phenix City, less than three weeks after he won the primary for state attorney general. He had campaigned on a pledge to clean up his hometown, "the Viceland of the South," which commercially indulged sins that included drugs, gambling, prostitution, and baby trafficking. The pillars of that hundred-million-dollar-a-year economy, which made crime one of Alabama's biggest industries, had responded harshly. The assassination not only won the attorney general's job for John Patterson, sentimentally given the nomination by the Democratic executive committee. It also made a folk hero of Walter "Crack" Hanna, U.S. Steel's old "security" hand, who had unintentionally brought about the end of the industrialists' payroll vigilantism by beating up Joe Gelders. Now commander of the Alabama National Guard, he led his battle-equipped troops into Phenix City and smashed the slot machines, closed the loaded-dice factory, and destroyed stills holding nearly 4,000 gallons of moonshine.

Because of his inexperience, Attorney General John Patterson relied gratefully on his kitchen cabinet—the lawyers for the Big Mules. And they were telling him that the agency through which the Communists were preying on the colored people of Montgomery, as well as Autherine Lucy, was the northern-based, integrated, Jewish-tinged EnDoubleAyeCeePee.† In May 1956, after discussing the

---

* O'Dell's old comrade James Jackson, a founder of the Southern Negro Youth Congress, had surfaced from five years underground to face trial in the second wave of Smith Act indictments of the Communist Party's national leadership. The Smith Act was a rider to the Alien Registration Act of 1940, which made it a crime to advocate the forcible overthrow of the government or organize or join a group that conspired to do so. Eleven top Party officials had been convicted under the act in 1949, in what was considered the government's official declaration of Cold War on the Communists. Jackson sent O'Dell down to Birmingham, where he had run the youth congress for eight years, to see if Coke would be willing to testify at his Smith Act trial. Coke did, as did W.E.B. Du Bois. Jackson would be saved from serving his two-year sentence when the Supreme Court, in the *Yates* decision of 1957, rendered the law unenforceable.

† Before the war the NAACP had indeed tolerated the Communists at their conventions. "They had no control," Thurgood Marshall explained, "and they were nice guys." But after the war, when a Communist faction tried to get the convention to protest the Marshall Plan, Thurgood Marshall had tricked them into making fools of themselves, earning a "verbal recommendation" from no less than J. Edgar Hoover, who gave the NAACP a "clean bill of health." Marshall himself wore his 33rd degree Mason ring as a badge of his 100 percent Americanism.

problem with the segregationist establishment around the South, Patterson filed suit to put the NAACP out of business in Alabama. Though it cited the Lucy case and the bus boycott, the suit's legal hook was that the NAACP was a "foreign corporation" that had failed to register with the secretary of state.

The suit landed in the court of the state's senior judge, Walter B. Jones, who had presided over the indictments of Albert Patterson's alleged assassins.* On June 1, without a hearing, Jones issued a temporary restraining order against the NAACP, halting its operations. The following month, he ordered the NAACP to turn over all membership and contribution records, as well as correspondence concerning the bus case and Lucy, or pay a daily fine of $10,000, raised to $100,000 after five days. The NAACP saw its legal-and-gradual life flash before its eyes.

Patterson's suit shut down not only the local NAACP chapter but the Birmingham-based regional headquarters for seven southern states as well. The entire South followed his ingenious blueprint. By 1957, Texas, Virginia, Florida, South Carolina, Georgia, Tennessee, and Arkansas had hogtied their NAACP chapters with litigation, although only Alabama had managed to obliterate it completely, becoming the South's research-and-development center of obstruction. For the next eight years, the NAACP would seek relief in the U.S. Supreme Court, whose orders to the Alabama courts to try the case on the merits were ignored.

In the new Gandhian age, however, where the oppressors saw their ploys turned against them, closing down the NAACP might have been the best thing the segregationists could have done for the civil rights movement.

"Doctors"

FRED SHUTTLESWORTH happened to be at the local NAACP office when a deputy arrived to serve Judge Jones's injunction. Shuttlesworth had not seen law enforcement in action since his arrest as a teenage bootlegger, and the document the officer brandished was so long that it looked as if "it reached from his shoulders to the floor," only slightly less intimidating than the gun on his hip. On the news that evening, Shuttlesworth watched a state legislator brag about having silenced the NAACP, killing "the goose that laid the golden egg at last."

"Yeah, you got the goose," Shuttlesworth said to his television set. But his people had the eggs, and they just might hatch.

After receiving numerous phone calls asking him what they should do, Shuttlesworth and a few NAACP board members met to discuss their options at a loan office—they didn't dare hold it on NAACP property. The organization's lawyer,

---

* These included Phenix City's district attorney and its chief deputy (or "underworld dictator"), as well as the state's outgoing attorney general, Si Garrett, who had committed the second unforgivable crime of giving Arthur Shores his tacit cooperation in the Autherine Lucy case. Garrett's indictment had been served on him at a psychiatric facility in Galveston; he would be declared mentally incompetent to stand trial.

Arthur Shores, was still cautious. "You can't violate a court order without going to jail," he warned.

"They can't enjoin us from being free," Shuttlesworth replied, and proposed a mass meeting.

At three o'clock the next morning, Shuttlesworth sat bolt upright in bed and said, " 'You shall know the truth and the truth shall make you free.' " He was having what he later considered a divine revelation. God was telling him to take his case straight to the masses.

At a strategy meeting on Monday, June 4, Shuttlesworth announced that he would call a mass meeting for the following night to form a new organization to replace the NAACP. That night, Luke Beard, the longtime pastor of the venerated Sixteenth Street Baptist, called Shuttlesworth and said, "Doctor, the Lord told me to tell you to call the meeting off."

"Doctor," Shuttlesworth said, "when did the Lord start sending my messages through you?"

"I'm not afraid, Doctor," the Reverend Beard insisted. "I just don't think it's the right thing to have this meeting."

"Pray for me," Shuttlesworth said and hung up.

At eleven-thirty, Beard called back and said the Lord still wanted him to call it off. Perhaps he was remembering the threat Bull Connor had made to destroy his church eight years earlier, intimidating him to withdraw Sixteenth Street Baptist as the final meeting place of the Southern Negro Youth Congress.

Shuttlesworth replied, "Tell the Lord that if He wants me to call it off, He better come down here in person, and He better have identifying marks on His hands and spear marks on His side. Then I'll call the meeting off."

Movement

ON TUESDAY, June 5, hourly radio bulletins announced the mass meeting for that evening. White stations specified that it had been called by "Fred Shuttlesworth, Negro minister, of 3191 North 29th Avenue," so that, to Shuttlesworth's mind, "the Klan would know where to put the bomb." All five hundred seats were filled at Ensley's Sardis Baptist—Emory O. Jackson's church—with half again as many people outside trying to get in. Ministers led the crowd in singing and prayer, a sort of spiritual wading-in after the model established in Montgomery. The speakers tipped their hats to those protesters as well as to the Negroes of Tallahassee, Florida, who had begun a bus boycott in May. But it was clear that this was going to be a dramatic departure from Martin Luther King's organization.

The Montgomery boycott, now concluding its fifth month without forcing a single concession, was a magnificent show protest, uniting virtually all the city's 50,000 Negroes. But it was a case of radical means serving conservative ends: the "polite segregation" of the buses. The one certain lesson that the boycott had yielded so far was the impossibility of reasoning with segregationists, who had become only more recalcitrant as the bus company verged on bankruptcy.

One of the old-guard ministers whom Bull Connor had cowed out of offering his church to the Southern Negro Youth Congress in 1948 beseeched the crowd at Sardis, "Y'all aren't going to get people killed now." He was roundly booed. Yet that was precisely the sort of sacrifice Shuttlesworth was willing to make. "We gonna wipe it out, or it's gonna wipe us out," he said about segregation. "Somebody may have to die." Three separate times, Shuttlesworth made the people vote on whether they were up to the risk of organizing.

Unlike the Montgomery Improvement Association, which had been the top-down creation of old-style lay activists, Shuttlesworth's organization was born in the church, of the masses. It would not stoop to appeasement, as the Montgomery group had. "We seek nothing which we would deny others," he shouted. (And then with his ability to turn piety on its head, he became conversational and asked the audience if they would be willing to sit next to a white man—"Then you believe in integration.") The declaration of principles pledged flatly to "press forward persistently for freedom and democracy, and the removal from our society of any forms of second-class citizenship." But neither did Shuttlesworth intend to "carry on the NAACP's work." Its Pyrrhic victories "do not lead us to embrace 'Gradualism.' We want a beginning NOW! WE HAVE ALREADY WAITED 100 YEARS!"

The declaration—written in Ruby Shuttlesworth's neat longhand and read aloud by a spellbinding young minister named Nelson H. Smith—brought a noisy ovation. Shuttlesworth was elected president by acclamation. Smith was made secretary. All the officers were ministers, with the exception of the treasurer, a successful undertaker named William E. Shortridge, famed among the CIO families who were his main clients for the "petrified man" on view in a back room. In destroying the NAACP, the state of Alabama had pushed Negro protest into its revolutionary form: a mass struggle, based in the church and on the notion not of an organization but of a movement. "Because you can outlaw an organization," Shuttlesworth said, "but not a movement."

There was a slight risk in the term. "Movement" had been a self-conscious left-wing word—the Communist martyr Angelo Herndon had used it to christen the Southern Negro Youth Congress in 1937. But Shuttlesworth knew instinctively how to foil the red-baiters. His would be "first, foremost, and always" a Christian movement, he said, naming his organization the Alabama Christian Movement for Human Rights. Its members called it simply "The Movement," pronounced "mooove-mint," with both syllables stressed equally. Shuttlesworth had found the word that would define the era.

4.

REHEARSAL

1956–1959

Your Basic Churchpeople

THE BUS BOYCOTT grinding on in the late-summer heat of Montgomery seemed at odds with America's current obsession, the automobile. *Time's* 1956 Man of the Year was the president of General Motors, while Ford was hoping to regain the edge with its still top-secret vehicular be-all, end-all, the Edsel. President Dwight Eisenhower inaugurated his multimillion-dollar interstate highway program. The blacks of Montgomery who took buses because they could not afford cars seemed remote from the American state of mind.

Indeed, it was mainly the bus boycott's young leader, Martin Luther King, who held the attention of the white world—a Negro who could awe reporters (from as far away as Japan and Australia) with lectures on Kant and Hegel and *agape*. King's sophisticated appeal underscored the shortcomings of Fred Shuttlesworth's lowly "mass movement" in Birmingham. Shuttlesworth himself was what was known as a "cussing preacher." (As he put it, "When I say Yea, I mean yea. When I say Nay, I mean nay. And after that it's Hell, Nay!")

And then there were his followers: "shouters" disdained by King's congregation. Two-thirds of the members of his Alabama Christian Movement for Human Rights were early-middle-aged women of low income, many of whom came straight to meetings from working as maids in "Miss Ann's kitchen." The Movement's men were janitors, cooks, dishwashers, and helpers on Coca-Cola delivery trucks (blacks were not allowed to actually drive), the sort who said defensively, "My daddy didn't go to Morehouse or no house." Whereas the bus boycott had involved the whole spectrum of Montgomery's Negroes, Birmingham's striving elements dismissed Shuttlesworth's followers as "your basic churchpeople," even though two-thirds of them had overcome their limitations (as well as the schemes of segregationists) to get registered to vote. As Shuttlesworth said, "Many of the upper-class persons who worked in the N.A.A.C.P.

are professional people who seem to feel that it is almost taboo to align actively with us."

A tiny one-half of one percent of the ACMHR's membership—basically three people, including Shuttlesworth and Emory O. Jackson—had belonged to the NAACP. The Negro bourgeoisie believed that the way to get freedom was to become more "white," by forming clubs, holding socials, and "talking white" with Latinate fastidiousness. Its members would have squirmed at the ACMHR's regular Monday-night sessions, called Mass Night or Movement Night, when the preacher of the evening "found his tune" midway through his sermon and began to "whoop" as though the Holy Spirit were kneading his tongue. A woman or two in the audience might go into a trance, arms stuck out and head thrown back, and then moan and shout and toss in an orgiastic frenzy until an usher carried her out.

But despite the Movement's common touch, the plain black folks had stayed away from the ACMHR too. Out of Birmingham's 209,000 plus Negroes, Shuttlesworth's organization had attracted a mere 600 active members—400 fewer than the Birmingham Communist Party claimed at its peak in 1934. The main problem: preacher politics. Once it became clear that the ACMHR was Shuttlesworth's store, J. L. Ware, the rival "activist" minister in town, had forbidden the hundred preachers in his Jefferson County Betterment Association to patronize it. His comment on one of Shuttlesworth's earlier initiatives to petition the city to hire Negro police: "My position is, don't say nothing good about it, don't say nothing bad. Let it alone and it'll die in two or three weeks, just like everything else little niggers get up causes around."

One evening, Shuttlesworth went to a meeting of the "Ware group" to enlist its cooperation. Another minister was speaking when he arrived, so Shuttlesworth slipped unnoticed into a back pew to wait for him to finish. It turned out that Ware's man was already denigrating Shuttlesworth's movement, saying, "Shuttlesworth got these little niggers around, and I'm not going to *bow.*" After he pledged several more times not to *bow,* Shuttlesworth decided that he ought to stand up and make his presence known. As he moved to the front of the church, another Ware man grimaced to catch the speaker's attention, and finally tried to quiet him, "You talking pretty loud."

"Yeah, I'm talking loud, and I'm not going to *bow,*" he said.

Finally his frustrated colleague said, "The man is here. Why don't we let him talk."

Shuttlesworth watched his detractor's feathers fall as he walked to the pulpit. "I think preachers should always be brothers," he told his colleagues. "That's what the Bible says. I will never be an enemy to other ministers." He asked them, in return, simply to refrain from criticizing him publicly. But Ware remained hostile. He was supporting a sure winner, donating the money his group raised to Martin Luther King, while encouraging the "little niggers" of Birmingham to remain on the back of the bus.

And so Shuttlesworth prepared to take a ride into the future of the civil rights movement, alone if necessary, but right up next to the driver's seat.

"Whatever Action Is Necessary"

ON TUESDAY, November 13, 1956, a week after President Eisenhower was re-elected by a landslide (still convinced that *Brown* had set back race relations), the U.S. Supreme Court held that segregation on the buses of Montgomery, Alabama, was unconstitutional. "God Almighty has spoken from Washington, D.C.!" a boycotter proclaimed.

The desegregation of Montgomery's buses had not come about as a result of the heroic protest by the city's masses. It was the fruit of the NAACP's lawsuit stemming from Rosa Parks's arrest. "All that walking for nothing!" the NAACP's chief legal strategist, Thurgood Marshall, said disparagingly. He had missed the larger truth, however. The legal victory highlighted the flaws of the NAACP's strategy of patience since the decision affected only the buses of Montgomery; theoretically, every other community in the South would have to take to the courts for similar relief. The NAACP's legal triumphs would henceforth be a preamble to the civil rights movement—the book of an Old Testament prophet. The bus boycott had introduced a new gospel. The struggle had moved out of the hands of the talented tenth and into the streets.

On Thursday, December 20, when federal marshals served the Supreme Court's order on Montgomery officials, Shuttlesworth was ready up in Birmingham to force the next frontier. He and the ACMHR secretary, Nelson Smith, went up to one of the TV studios alongside Vulcan on Red Mountain to audition a future Movement axiom: Sometimes an oppressed people had to provoke their oppressors. Through a prepared statement, the ministers delivered an ultimatum. In light of the Montgomery ruling, if Birmingham did not repeal its own bus segregation laws by December 26—the next meeting of the city commission—the Negroes of Birmingham were going to desegregate the buses themselves. "If there is any interference with the Negroes riding the buses unsegregated, we will take whatever action is necessary," Shuttlesworth threatened.

The news cameras, however, were still trained on Martin Luther King in Montgomery. At 5:45 a.m. he claimed a front seat, now within his full legal rights, on the first bus of December 21. "I believe you are Dr. King," the bus driver beamed, in a sort of Stanley-to-Livingstone statement of the obvious.

Shuttlesworth began rounding up volunteers to desegregate the buses of Birmingham. Where the Montgomery boycotters had merely refused to participate in a system they felt was immoral, he intended to flout it actively, escalating passive resistance to direct action. And that would necessitate a sacrifice that Shuttlesworth had broached back at the founding meeting of the ACMHR: going to jail.

Godsent

BULL CONNOR had recently asked his mentor, Jim Simpson, to lay out the game plan for his return to politics. Connor had been a man without purpose since leaving office in 1953. He was bored with the gas station his backers had set him up with and had made a failed bid to revive his sportscasting career. He still went down to the precinct stations and played dominoes with his former "nigguhs." Aching for a comeback, he had run, poorly, for sheriff in 1954 and, again unsuccessfully, for the public improvements spot on the city commission in the spring of 1956, making so many appearances before Ace Carter's White Citizens Councils that the FBI started to keep track. His old spot on the commission was coming up for grabs in the spring of 1957.

Jim Simpson had never quite gotten over his loss to Lister Hill in the Senate race of 1944. He had withdrawn into the life of a Big Mule lawyer, nursing his ulcers with milk cocktails at the Mountain Brook Club. Leaving the Dixiecrat movement in the hands of Frank Dixon and Sid Smyer, he had looked inward and backward, writing letters to the State of Tennessee seeking information about the communistic colony of Ruskin, where he had spent a year as a young boy. But now he seemed ready to vindicate his thirteen-year-old failure and revive that old Senate strategy in the service of "Me and Jim": Connor's campaign for the commission would be based purely on race. Blessed with the timely appearance of dangerous radicals throughout his career, Connor had lucked out again, with a bête noire worthy of single-name invocation: Shuttlesworth. If Connor could tie the rise of Shuttlesworth to his absence from office, he might have a winning cause.

An old friend of Connor's was also looking for meaningful work. Like Connor, "Dynamite Bob" Chambliss had broken with his old Citizens Council master, Ace Carter, and was ready to reclaim his nickname. This time his aim would be to destroy not merely property but life.

On Christmas morning 1956, Shuttlesworth said from his pulpit, "If it takes being killed to get integration, I'll do just that thing, for God is with me all the way." Over the weekend he had been organizing Birmingham's first mass protest since the Southern Negro Youth Congress's voting-rights march of black veterans in 1946. Around 250 men and women had signed nonviolence oaths to integrate the city buses the next day if the commission failed to repeal bus segregation at its morning meeting.

Shuttlesworth lay on his bed in shorts and a T-shirt on Christmas night, going over plans for the freedom ride with one of his deacons. In the dining room, ten-year-old Fred Jr. strutted around in his Tide-crimson football uniform from the University of Alabama, by way of Santa.

Sometime after nine-thirty, according to an FBI "confidential source," Robert Chambliss alighted from a dark sedan and scurried toward the parsonage of Bethel Baptist Church, carrying six sticks of dynamite. He threw them at the wall where the church met the parsonage. They exploded directly behind Shuttlesworth's bed. The wall and the floor were blown out, and the mattress heaved into the air, supporting Shuttlesworth like a magic carpet. The roof caved in on a tangle of blackened bedsprings. In the back of the house, appliances were ripped from the kitchen wall.

Chambliss's driver panicked and hit the gas. A block down the street, he composed himself enough to turn around, but still wouldn't stop. Chambliss had to run after the car and, grabbing onto a door handle, was dragged for a distance before he could hoist himself in.

Residents of the surrounding black neighborhood rushed to the scene with their pistols and sawed-off shotguns. Fire trucks arrived, shining their spotlight on the scene. "Is he dead?" a Movement vice president asked a policeman, surveying the collapsed front porch. A giant hole had also been ripped out of the adjacent church basement.

"No, he's in there," the cop said.

A voice rose from the wreckage: "I'm not coming out naked." And, after a few moments, Shuttlesworth emerged in the raincoat someone threw into the parsonage's rubble. He was not crippled, not bloodied or blind; he was not even deaf, though the blast had blown windows out of houses a mile away. His family and the deacon had also gotten off with minor injuries. Shuttlesworth raised a biblical hand to the concerned neighbors, and said, "The Lord has protected me. I am not injured."

Somebody called out that Fred Shuttlesworth was "Godsent." As if to illuminate the claim, Christmas tree lights still burned inside the wreckage.

A big cop was crying. "Reverend, I know these people," he said of the bombers. "I didn't think they would go this far. If I were you, I'd get out of town. These people are vicious."

"Well, Officer, you're not me," Shuttlesworth said. "Go back and tell your Klan brothers that if the Lord saved me from this, I'm here for the duration. The fight is just beginning." Then he surveyed his well-wishers—some five hundred now—and told them to lay down their arms. "This is not gonna turn us around."

As Shuttlesworth would later put it, with his gift for making the holy earthy, "And this is where I was blown into history."

Freedom Riding

THE NEXT MORNING, the mayor gaveled the Birmingham City Commission meeting to a close without mentioning the bombing or the bus controversy—his reticence perhaps owing to the glowering presence of 150 White Citizens. Arriving late, Shuttlesworth (in a borrowed suit) and his lieutenants spoke privately to Public Safety Commissioner Robert Lindbergh—a moderate former deputy sheriff with a night-school law degree—describing their intentions to violate the bus segregation ordinance. Bull Connor was now entering Lindbergh's peripheral vision for the commission race, and he must have been having second thoughts about his repeal of segregated baseball three years earlier. "If you ride the buses," Lindbergh replied, "we're going to put you in jail."

Some two hundred potential bus riders repaired to a nearby black funeral home. "I'm alive to ride, gentlemen," Shuttlesworth announced to the waiting reporters, but begged their patience on the exact timing of the protest. Lindbergh had the impression that the ride would take place the following day, Thursday.

Inside the funeral home, some ACMHR board members begged Shuttlesworth to call the protest off. A man in the audience, weeping, beseeched him, "We came here to hear you, Reverend. We didn't come to hear these scared folk."

"Hell, yeah, we're going to ride," the cussing preacher said and addressed his board. "Find you any kind of crack you can to hide in if you're scared, but I'm walking downtown after this meeting and getting on the bus. I'm not going to look back to see who's following me." His voice deepened into the preacher register. "Boys step back," he ordered, "and men step forward." Most of the disciples who trailed him out the door were women.

Shuttlesworth instructed the protesters—there had been quite a bit of bomb-related attrition—not to sit together, explaining, "You have to leave space for the white folks." Then he turned to the daughter of Bethel's head usher. "Come ride with me," he told her. "I'm going to make you famous."

Shuttlesworth and she boarded the bus for University Hospital, where his thirteen-year-old daughter, Pat, was being treated for burns (suffered a few days earlier when her nightgown caught fire from an open heater). Shuttlesworth was calm, supremely civil. At one point he said to a white woman standing over him, "Would you like to have my seat?" for which she thanked him. Complaints were occasionally lofted from blacks in the back of the bus, suggesting that he join them in their proper place. The preacher had long since reached his daughter's bedside when the police boarded the buses, and some protesters were on their third or fourth freedom ride by the time twenty-one of them were finally arrested.[*]

"The fight is on," Shuttlesworth told the press. He had pushed the Movement into its next phase of nonviolent strategy, civil disobedience.

The New Guard

UP UNTIL NOW the campaign for civil rights had been organized by integrated, northern-based groups, either bureaucratically inhospitable to mass action (the NAACP), too ideologically rarefied for mainstream temperaments (Muste's pacifist Fellowship of Reconciliation), or compromised by ulterior agendas (the Communist Party). The country's leading connoisseur of black protest, Bayard Rustin,

---

[*] Arthur Shores represented the freedom riders at their summary conviction. To prevent the defendants from mounting a constitutional challenge, the city craftily changed the charges from violation of segregation ordinances to disorderly conduct and breach of peace. Regardless, Shores filed suit on January 11 to have the bus segregation laws overturned for violating the Fourteenth Amendment. The commission would simply rewrite them along the peace-over-justice premise that segregation was essential to "the tranquility among people." City court judge Ralph Parker took it upon himself to declare the Fourteenth Amendment "null and void" and fined the riders $50 each. Although twenty-one southern cities voluntarily desegregated their buses within a month of the Supreme Court's Montgomery decision, bus segregation in Birmingham would remain under litigation, but legally enforced, until 1962.

had come to share Emory O. Jackson's view that a southern civil rights movement could succeed only if it was completely indigenous. Throughout the bus boycott, Fred Shuttlesworth and Joseph Lowery, Mobile's activist black minister, had traveled to Montgomery for monthly brainstorming sessions, to which Martin Luther King and Ralph Abernathy invariably showed up late with a peace offering of fried chicken. Rustin decided to formalize the budding southern coalition of black preachers.

With his usual disdain for fine points, he turned for help to a Jewish-Communist atheist from New York and a black woman with a confirmed distaste for Baptist ministers (because of a failed marriage to one). The former was Stanley Levison, who had amassed a small fortune through mundane exercises in capitalism—real estate, a car dealership, a wholesale laundry firm in Ecuador—that were, according to an informant for the FBI, "front" businesses to launder Moscow's secret annual subsidy to the American Communist Party. The latter was Ella Baker, a fifty-one-year-old black North Carolinian who was the NAACP's top-ranking female. She had concluded from her Depression contacts with Communists that the Party's method of organizing by small units—cells—could not be improved upon. Out of their confab of left-wing jargon around Levison's kitchen table in New York City that December came the "congress of organizations" that would epitomize the South's homegrown, preacher-led mass movement for civil rights: the Southern Christian Leadership Conference.

Although Fred Shuttlesworth had already created an authentic test model in the Alabama Christian Movement for Human Rights, the man Rustin had in mind to preside over his southern movement was the young minister-scholar who throughout the year-long boycott had shown leadership and courage, finesse with preacher politics, and excellent rapport with the white press. Martin Luther King also seemed passive enough to be guided—or controlled, as some saw it—by Bayard Rustin. To prod King into action, however, he needed someone confrontational, and it was Shuttlesworth whom Rustin tapped to get King to call the first meeting, three weeks after the Bethel bombing, of the new organization.

Shuttlesworth had been profoundly affected by what he saw as his divine deliverance from the dynamite. Before, he had conviction but phobias as well. He had been afraid, for example, to fly on airplanes. Now he began to court death. (His son, by contrast, had developed a stutter.) "I literally tried to get myself killed," he said: " 'He who loses his life for the sake of Mine shall find it.' " He refused to repair or raze the wreckage of his parsonage, and when a policeman complained about the debris, Shuttlesworth retorted, "Let the people see what America is."

On March 6, Shuttlesworth performed his second direct action. He and his wife, Ruby, had announced they would desegregate the white waiting room of the Birmingham train station. Wearing a top hat and a starched handkerchief in his suit pocket, and carrying an empty suitcase to use as a shield, Shuttlesworth barreled through the waiting-room door past a greeting committee of Klansmen in mufti, including Robert Chambliss. The Shuttlesworths made it to their destination of Atlanta unmolested by either mob or police,* and Fred exulted that "the city had abandoned segregation," calling Public Safety Commissioner Lindbergh a "man of high morals." But Shuttlesworth's bow to Lindbergh had an unintended effect. Much of the city's white population was beginning to think that Birmingham needed a man tough enough to keep the "niggers" in their place.

Ingram

THROUGHOUT THE CAMPAIGN for the city commission, Bull Connor had been chiseling away at the only fault in Lindbergh's record—the vote to repeal segregated sports (with his incredible prediction that segregation was coming to an end). And perhaps it was Connor who had revived the racial cause about which the white population was less ambivalent than it was about all-white baseball: residential zoning. After six years of quiet, the house bombings had resumed. The new Dynamite Hill was a transitional neighborhood called Fountain Heights, east of the original one, and affording a clear view of the classic dome of the Sixteenth Street Baptist Church. Negroes had just begun buying houses there when the first bomb exploded on New Year's Eve, 1956. It was similar to the one Robert Chambliss had used to dynamite Shuttlesworth's parsonage a week earlier. As the city commission race warmed up in April, two more houses recently bought by Negroes were wrecked by dynamite, and Chambliss was boasting that he would bomb any other "nigger" who dared to move in.

As Connor's good fortune would have it, the Ku Klux Klan was a force in the South again. In 1955, Eldon Lee Edwards, a spray painter at the Fisher body shop in Atlanta, had parlayed the Georgia Klan he headed into a regionwide organization, as the U.S. Klans, Knights of the Ku Klux Klan, Inc. Chambliss's klavern, the Klan's main lodge in the Birmingham area (descended from the original Robert E. Lee), was one of Edwards's chief assets, but like all great colonies had begun to feel twitches of independence, resenting especially that dues collected in Alabama ended up in Atlanta. The klavern voted to withdraw from the U.S. Klans and form the independent Alabama Knights. Elected Exalted Cyclops of the klavern was Troy Ingram, a dark horse of untested white supremacist conviction despite his being Robert Chambliss's official best friend. Yet Ingram had a certain compelling aura, perhaps because he could trace his roots to the mightiest of the white supremacists, Charles DeBardeleben.

If Chambliss was an uninflected caricature of nastiness, Troy Ingram was tragedy, the rejected bastard grandson of Birmingham's first family. Now in his thirties, he still mined coal from a stingy bed not far from where he had grown up,

---

* It was a white comrade of theirs, a twenty-nine-year-old TCI filing clerk and protest political candidate named Lamar Weaver, who was chased from the scene by the screaming mob, among which he recognized some fellow U.S. Steel employees. Weaver had taken Shuttlesworth to the Terminal Station only recently, when he heard that Harry Truman was passing through; the three men had posed in front of the train for a *Birmingham News* photographer while the former president congratulated Shuttlesworth for "doing one of the damnedest things in the damnedest town."

at DeBardeleben's Overton camp, the union-free challenge to organized labor. The dynamite he used to blast out his meager living was perhaps the most vigorous symbol of his manhood, still conferring a sense of power and self-respect as well as a certain macabre control over his destiny. Ingram had been in a company elementary school at the outset of the Depression when Charles DeBardeleben moved out to the camp to personally guard his employees against the influences of John L. Lewis's United Mine Workers. In anticipation of class war, he had surrounded his own house with a barbed-wire fence that carried 220 volts of electricity, to the final regret of three dogs that encountered it.

In the summer of 1934, "Uncle Charlie" had given fifteen-year-old Troy his first lesson in the ideological uses of dynamite. In response to a rumor that the Mine Workers were marching on the camp, DeBardeleben summoned his employees to the Overton company store. He had already expelled eighty "traitors" who had gone over to Lewis. Though Troy's father, Sam Ingram, had signed a union card, too, he had not yet been found out. "This switch leads to the dynamite placed on the road," DeBardeleben told his men. "That road leads to my house, and when they start toward my house, I am going to blow them up." DeBardeleben's lawyer reassured them that he would beat any rap that might result from their defense of their homes. The union canceled the march. But the impressionable Troy Ingram had learned that laws against murder, for example, were insignificant as long as one's crimes were committed in the service of "God-given principles," such as the "right to work," invoked by men like DeBardeleben.

After Sam Ingram and ninety other employees voted to join the United Mine Workers that summer, DeBardeleben shut down the Overton mine and evicted their families. Sam was not bitter. But Troy's sense of justice had been aroused. Under the influence of the UMW's lawyers, he and another son of an ousted unionist sued DeBardeleben and even returned to Overton to "visit friends," or perhaps incite more insurrection. Company agents intercepted them, inflicted a bit of pain, drove them eight miles into the country, and put them out in the rain. Troy's bravery earned him a nice write-up in the *Southern Worker,* the newspaper the Communist Party published out of Birmingham.* Having gained his first notoriety as a working-class hero of the reds, however, Ingram would go on to use his proletariat skills to commit one of the most heinous "class" crimes in history.

Troy Ingram's transformation may be comprehensible only under the terms of the Greek playwrights. Probably it was his friend Chambliss's persistence rather than ideology that lured him into the Klan, for he still subscribed to the old mining cliché that there was no difference between black and white when they were covered with coal dust underground. But joining the Klan turned out to be a homecoming for Ingram. It seemed that many of DeBardeleben's legatees were attracted to this form of solidarity, and one of the klavern's most gung-ho activists

---

* He was the second ex-DeBardeleben ward to be adopted by the Communists: Angelo Herndon's first mining job, at age thirteen, had been in a DeBardeleben-owned camp in Kentucky, and he had a permanent scar on his hand from an accident there.

was a fellow son of an Overton miner who had also lost his job after joining the biracial brotherhood of mine workers.

Walter Earl "Shorty" Thompson Jr. was a redhead with a fireplug build (he claimed to be "five foot five and three quarters") and squinty eyes that could turn suddenly mean. An FBI source identified Thompson as the driver of the automobile that carried Chambliss and his bundle of dynamite to Fred Shuttlesworth's parsonage on Christmas night, though if Chambliss's driver was in fact Thompson, his panicky flight from the scene suggested that he was not a seasoned bomber.* And neither was Troy Ingram, despite his ease with dynamite. Even the klavern brothers who elected him Exalted Cyclops agreed that he was an unlikely Kluxer—a "higher-type individual than the average Klansman." He even did his banking business in Mountain Brook. But the Klan, too, was reacquiring its shadow-establishment standing, reflected in its headquarters in the downtown meeting hall of the Fraternal Order of Police. The golden era of Klan-police relations was about to be reinstated by popular election.

In what would turn out to be one of Birmingham's poignant "if onlys," the incumbent Robert Lindbergh had narrowly failed to gain a majority in the first primary for the city commission, thus forcing a runoff with Bull Connor. The race-baiting tactics that Jim Simpson had designed for his candidate were so ugly that the *Birmingham News,* supporting Lindbergh, ignored the election. The turnout for the rematch was heavy. The final vote was 15,891 to 15,788. Birmingham's history had been dictated by 103 votes, Connor's way.

It was hardly a mandate for "Me and Jim," and even though they were back, they were no longer under the control of the city elite. They were now fusing with Birmingham's ascendant Ku Klux Klan into the last vital remnant of the South's great anti–New Deal empire. And as fate would have it, those old agents of anti-democracy were about to clash again with the underdog forces of democracy. Connor's career-making enemy from the 1930s, the Southern Conference for Human Welfare, was also undergoing a transformation. What remained of the organization—the Southern Conference Educational Fund, or SCEF—was rematerializing in Birmingham, in the person of Fred Shuttlesworth.

Fearing to Begin

MARTIN LUTHER KING sometimes seemed like a tourist in his own life, overwhelmed by the itinerary history had handed him. Fred Shuttlesworth admired King's gifts—particularly his touch with the masses, and from a man of his station—but wished that he would use them more aggressively. It was as if King had been domesticated by *Time* magazine, whose February cover story on him had hammered home the nonviolent nature of the Montgomery boycott and certified its twenty-eight-year-old leader as innocent of "the excesses of radicalism." Bayard Rustin had had to rely on Shuttlesworth to "put the persuasion" on the over-

---

* "I wasn't guilty of it," Thompson now says. "That's all in the past. I've given up all that stuff I used to do back then with the Klan. I give all my time to the church."

scheduled King to get him to show up at his own coronation—a "Prayer Pilgrimage" in Washington that Rustin had cooked up to introduce him as a "national Negro leader." The pilgrimage took place at the Lincoln Memorial on the third anniversary of *Brown,* May 17, 1957, and Shuttlesworth's self-effacing speech reflected his deference to Rustin's King-enhancing agenda—"I'm glad to be alive today, a follower of M.L. King, Jr."—though he did manage to frame the conflict succinctly: "This is the real battle for America." King, the last speaker, paused to say a few words about *agape* before returning to his theme—*Give us the ballot!*—and won *Ebony's* top rating as "the No. 1 Negro leader of men."

A few months later, Shuttlesworth had put King on notice before the third meeting of Rustin's group of southern preacher-activists, taking place in Montgomery in August. "It appears that the Southern counter-offensive has all but stymied our progressive attacks upon Fortress Segregation," Shuttlesworth wrote King. "I would certainly hope that we would never be found fighting as our enemies expect; that is, as they plan for us to fight. And I fervently pray that most of all, we shall never be found fearing to begin."

But the only thing substantive to come out of the meeting was a permanent name for the group: the Southern Christian Leadership Conference, following Shuttlesworth's use of the word "Christian" in his Alabama Christian Movement for Human Rights. As Rustin's co-conspirator Ella Baker, shaping the organization behind the scenes, put it, "You would, perhaps, avoid being tagged as 'Red' by being called Christian." Yet red was a label Shuttlesworth was willing to risk. He had become the first member of the new civil rights guard to return to the left-wing prototypes of the 1930s and 1940s.

Braden

ANNE McCARTY BRADEN was a link between the past and the future. She had taken a train from Louisville to Birmingham that summer to pay her first professional call on Shuttlesworth—and finish some old business. A graduate of a genteel Virginia women's college, she had been a green young reporter for the *Birmingham News* in 1946 when she covered the story that changed her life: the black veterans' march that the Southern Negro Youth Congress's Louis Burnham had led to the courthouse to demand the right to vote. McCarty recognized the SNYC march as a seminal bolt of democracy. And when the main outcome of the protest was the revival of the Klan, she decided she couldn't bear Birmingham any longer. She moved on to the *Louisville Times* and married the paper's socialist labor editor, Carl Braden. In the spring of 1954, the Bradens performed their own first "direct action" by buying a house for a black couple in an all-white Louisville neighborhood. After the house was twice dynamited, it was Carl rather than the bombers who was charged—with sedition. He began serving a fifteen-year sentence in December 1954.

The case had sparked the institutional memory of two men who (along with their great friends Cliff and Virginia Durr) had been among the towering southern liberals of the New Deal era: James Dombrowski and Aubrey Williams. They had kept the flame alive through the Southern Conference Educational Fund (SCEF). Williams, the impoverished son of an alcoholic blacksmith from Birmingham ("We were poor, but we were dirty," he liked to quip), had been one of the stars of the New Deal, the deputy to the relief architect Harry Hopkins and the founding chief of the most racially progressive of the alphabet agencies, the National Youth Administration. (Fred Shuttlesworth's first employer, the NYA had also found work for young George C. Wallace.) Along with Dombrowski, a Christian socialist from Tampa who at the time had been Myles Horton's right-hand man at the Highlander Folk School, Williams had helped Joe Gelders put together the Southern Conference for Human Welfare in 1938. Dombrowski had gone on to become the executive director of the Southern Conference, in which capacity he had been arrested along with Henry Wallace's running mate, Senator Glen Taylor, at the final, 1948 meeting of the Southern Negro Youth Congress in Birmingham.

In Carl and Anne Braden, Dombrowski and Williams believed they had found their heirs. They used SCEF funds to post an appeal bond for Carl and were trying to figure out how best to use the Bradens when, at the end of 1955, Williams's comrade, the sleeping-car porter E. D. Nixon, provided the answer by helping launch a bus boycott. Williams, who was now living in Montgomery and publishing a progressive newspaper for Alabama farmers, considered the boycott "the most important thing to happen in the nation's history." To be SCEF's liaison with the newborn movement, he and Dombrowski put the Bradens on the payroll.

Since Williams shared E. D. Nixon's growing dislike of Martin Luther King, SCEF decided to use Fred Shuttlesworth as its artery into the Movement. Thus, in June 1957, the Bradens caught the train to Birmingham to meet him. Dombrowski came up from the fund's headquarters in New Orleans, Williams from Montgomery. Shuttlesworth received them warmly at the motel where he was bunking while his parsonage was being rebuilt. The visitors were relieved by his welcome: SCEF was Senator Jim Eastland's favorite red-bait, its principals having been subpoenaed by his internal security subcommittee in 1954 along with Horton and Virginia Durr. Indeed, Shuttlesworth would be virtually alone among his clerical colleagues in embracing his Movement's radical antecedents. His retort to the professional anti-Communists was simple: "I don't need a Communist to tell me what democracy is."

Birmingham seemed to produce absolutists—on the Supreme Court Hugo Black had adamantly (and unsuccessfully) promoted First Amendment protections for Communists. But however admirable their certitude, sometimes men like Black and Shuttlesworth did not take reality into account, and the reality was that the civil rights movement faced a genuine dilemma in dealing with its radical past. Martin Luther King was about to be initiated into the rites of Cold War America.

A few months after sealing SCEF's pact with Shuttlesworth, Anne Braden met King for the first time, at the twenty-fifth anniversary celebration of the Highlander Folk School over Labor Day weekend. Myles Horton had also invited the folksinger Pete Seeger and another longtime Communist, Abner Berry, a

Daily Worker columnist from a family of black tap dancers, who had covered the Southern Negro Youth Congress's terminal 1948 conference. But the most "extremist" guest proved to be a sanitation expert from Georgia just "passing through," who took pictures of King and Ralph Abernathy in the company of Berry (as well as Aubrey Williams). The photographs would be distributed—by the tens of thousands—by a Georgia state commission chartered to uphold segregation. They accompanied an exposé pamphlet, *Highlander Folk School: Communist Training School, Monteagle, Tenn.* Eventually, as King's fame grew, billboards of the photograph would compete for highway shoulder space with the John Birch Society's "Impeach Earl Warren" signs.

Regardless of the perils of the red stigma, to purge the Movement of its radical influences would have been not only self-defeating but inconceivable. When Anne Braden gave King a ride from the Highlander anniversary festivities to his next appointment, in Louisville, he spoke approvingly of the "haunting" refrain of an old labor song that Pete Seeger had performed: "We Shall Overcome."

Mayhem

FRED SHUTTLESWORTH was going to make Martin Luther King justify his claim on the leadership of the civil rights movement. The Montgomery Improvement Association had all but collapsed since the bus boycott—"the old class split," Virginia Durr lamented. The MIA's treasurer, E. D. Nixon, had written King a bitter "Dear Sir" letter of resignation in June, explaining, "I do not expect to be treated as a child." Rosa Parks had taken a job at Tuskegee's equivalent in Virginia, the Hampton Institute. King's other project, the Southern Christian Leadership Conference, was going nowhere slowly. Its first project, a Billy Graham–inspired Crusade for Citizenship to register blacks to vote, was a resounding flop. Shuttlesworth began to wonder whether SCEF might be a more effective institutional sponsor for the Movement. Meanwhile, instead of waiting for King to find his way, he decided to move unilaterally on "Fortress Segregation."

The gentlemen segregationists thought they had solved the problem of the *Brown* decision with a cunning state law, imitated regionwide. It was called the Pupil Placement (or Freedom of Choice) Act, and theoretically it allowed parents to choose whether to send their children to black, white, or mixed schools; practically, the school superintendent would permit no integration to take place.* In

---

* The superintendent could reject any "free choices" that represented a threat to "the peace." But even though there would be no "mixed" schools, the state would appear to be in compliance with *Brown*, because the language of mandatory school segregation would be deleted from the Alabama constitution. Unexpected encouragement for the southerners had come from the Supreme Court, whose 1955 decree for implementing *Brown* ordered that school desegregation proceed with "all deliberate speed." The Court was basically leaving desegregation to the discretion of the individual states, the same states that the justices ruled had violated the fundamental rights of millions of black schoolchildren in the first place. "One of the worst things I've done was to go along with Felix on that," Hugo Black said of Justice Frankfurter's masterpiece of doublespeak. Which may have explained Black's peremptory ruling making Autherine Lucy the first college admission under *Brown Two.*

late August 1957, Fred Shuttlesworth became the first petitioner under the law, seeking with nine other black parents to admit their children to the (white) schools closest to them. The superintendent said he would take the matter up at the board of education's September 6 meeting—the day before school opened. By then, segregation's nonviolent defenders would be forced to rethink their relationship with their old hands-on practitioners.

Ace Carter, Sid Smyer's front man in the White Citizens Councils, had moved off the fringe into some mythical realm of southern gothic—*Look* magazine had run a big picture of him, hirsute and boar-necked, inciting a riot in Clinton, Tennessee, over school desegregation there the previous fall. And later in 1956, after effectively killing the Citizens Council movement in Alabama, Carter had convened thirty-five men around a bonfire of concrete "skulls" to inaugurate his rogue alternative to Troy Ingram's "establishment" Klan, a paramilitary offshoot called the Ku Klux Klan of the Confederacy. Arguments over the treasury led to a much publicized shoot-out at the abandoned movie theater, with its greasy popcorn popper still in the lobby, that was the Klan's headquarters. Charged with assault with intent to murder (but never tried), Carter went into one of his temporary remissions, replete with drinking jags that made him not merely mean but "weird." And the Confederate Klan collapsed.

In the summer of 1957, however, Carter's lieutenant, Jesse Mabry—who had carried out an assault on Nat King Cole during a performance at the Municipal Auditorium the previous spring—decided to revive the Confederate Klan. He was treasurer of the new klavern and, at forty-five, its elder statesman—a mattress company foreman and homeowner. On Labor Day evening, the officers met on a special order of business. The group had elected an Exalted Cyclops, a thirty-one-year-old construction worker named Joe Pritchett, but the time had come to promote someone to the number two job, Captain of the Lair. To earn it, the candidate would have to do more than just put on his hood and "scare a nigger."

At eight-thirty, six of the Klansmen drove to a drugstore and bought razor blades and a bottle of turpentine. They had a Negro in mind as their victim, but he turned out not to be home, so they drove around trying to figure out what to do next. They spied a black couple walking along the side of the Tarrant-Huffman road. The Confederates jumped out of the car, grabbed the man, who was slight of build, and threw him into the back seat, where the top captain contender, Bart Floyd, sat on him and pistol-whipped him. They took him back to the lair, a cinder-block cube with a dirt floor and windows fitted with blackout curtains. On this night, the lair was being referred to as "the slaughter pen." Floyd told the victim to "make like a dog" and held him by the nape of the neck as he crawled into the hut. The Klansmen lit kerosene lamps and looked him over. They didn't know his name and never asked.

Kneeling in the dirt, he watched the Klansmen suit up in hoods of white pillowcases with slits for the eyes. Exalted Cyclops Pritchett solemnly lifted his hood—his was red—and said, "Look up at me, nigger! Do you know me, nigger?"

"Naw suh," he replied. "I ain't never seen you." Pritchett kicked him in the eye and, replacing his own hood, ordered him to look around at all the other Klansmen, who barraged him with questions.

"Look at me, nigger! You think you're as good as I am?"

"You think any nigger is as good as a white man?"

"You got any children? You think nigger kids should go to school with my kids?"

"You think you got a right to vote?"

"Or eat where I eat?"

"Or use the same toilet I use?"

Finally, the rat court got to the point. "Do you know Shuttlesworth?" someone asked.

"Naw suh," the Negro replied.

"Well, I want you to carry a message to Shuttlesworth," Exalted Cyclops Pritchett said. "I want you to tell him to stop sending nigger children and white children to school together or we're gonna do him like we're fixing to do you."

Bart Floyd struck the victim with a wrench and dazed him. Pritchett ordered Floyd to do his "duty." The only time the negro was allowed to stand was when he was ordered to drop his pants. The Klansmen pinned him spread-eagled to the ground. Floyd dropped to his knees over the half-naked man and, with the newly purchased razor blade, sliced off his scrotum. The Klansmen passed around their new captain's credentials for inspection. One of the Klansmen, a thirty-two-year-old grocery clerk named William Miller, whom Ace Canter had personally anointed "captain of intelligence," vomited. But Pritchett plopped the scrotum in a paper cup to take home for a souvenir.

The men of the lair bundled their victim into the trunk of the car and drove him out to the Tarrant-Huffman highway, where they tossed him out on the shoulder. A passing motorist telephoned the police that a wounded Negro was staggering along the road. The police who took him to the hospital said that he "looked like he had been dipped in blood from the belt down." He survived, partly because the turpentine the Klansmen had poured on his penis to drive the pain deep into his gut had sterilized it against infection.

Finally, the community beheld, in terms starker than death, the ideology that Sid Smyer and the Dixiecrats had spun into laws and political campaigns. If the house bombings had come to seem technical, and even lynching could be rationalized as a misguided application of justice, these "castrationists"—as Governor Folsom was calling them, evoking the "segregationists" they spoke for—had gone beyond the pale. But before the public felt free to exercise its full outrage, the innocence of the victim had to be confirmed. A state investigator checking his background discovered that Edward "Judge" Aaron, a thirty-four-year-old painter's helper and veteran who lived with his mother, was considered a "white folks' nigger." Once it was determined that Aaron had not whistled at a daughter or sister or wife of his emasculators, the arrests were swift. Two of the suspects, both grocery store clerks, confessed and turned state's evidence in exchange for suspended sentences. But Jesse Mabry, Bart Floyd, Joe Pritchett, and Grover

McCullough did not understand that the polite institutions of the community could no longer absorb deeds like theirs. They pleaded not guilty to the charge of "mayhem," not believing for a minute that a white male jury would convict them. And besides, they had twice asked Aaron if he preferred death or emasculation.

The four men would be tried separately. None denied the crime, or claimed to have been drinking when he committed it. In each trial, the women were escorted out of the courtroom when the state brought Judge Aaron to display his mutilated groin to the white men of the jury. All the juries returned prompt guilty verdicts, and the maximum sentence of twenty years—not "nearly commensurate with the crime," the horrified judge said.

But nothing was simple in Birmingham. In a sense, the castrationists had illustrated their point too well. Precisely because the crime was so abominable, the polite segregationists were able to let the law do its job and dismiss these Klansmen as aberrations. Sid Smyer, as Ace Carter's original sponsor, felt a lingering dismay that he might be in the same club as castrationists, but his doubts were not confined to humanitarian concerns.

As his fellow civic leaders had begun to warn, "hoodlumism in racial difficulties" was hurting the local economy: Companies did not want to invest in—and employees did not want to relocate to—locales of civil unrest. The "timidity of northern capital" had been a source of worry for the city's promoters since the post-Reconstruction beginnings of the New South. But this time around, the Yankee-offending conditions were not Populism or railroad regulation but the very racism that had always accounted for the South's low wages, and thus its appeal as a colony.

And no one had felt the pinch like Smyer, the city's main real estate developer. Smyer's Birmingham Realty Company essentially controlled downtown, but business had gotten so slow that the second floor of his once elegant offices on First Avenue—with teller cages and a balcony like a frontier hotel—was converted to cobwebby storage rooms.

The Dixiecrats' era of bare-knuckled capitalism was over, especially now that the business of Birmingham, steel, was in crisis, as new competition from abroad exposed the American steelmakers' inferior, overpriced product and antiquated systems. U.S. Steel's local president cut a sad figure before the Rotary Club, badmouthing federal depreciation laws and striking workers. Atlanta, meanwhile, had wagered that a world-class airport would be its route to New South supremacy, and was not only the headquarters of Delta Air Lines, but also the regional hub of Eastern. Birmingham's city fathers had begun to fixate on the inevitable layover in the rival city: If you die in Birmingham, went the catechism of all air travelers, you have to go through Atlanta to get to hell.

Smyer had been certain that it was Fred Shuttlesworth and Martin Luther King and the New Negro who were disturbing the peace essential to profits, but now he realized that the problem was the enforcers of segregation he had bankrolled. And so, the custodian of his city's prosperity began his slow, strange reformation, from enemy of democracy to friend of the civil rights movement.

The Price of Freedom

ALABAMA'S RESISTANCE TO INTEGRATION had infected the rest of the South. In Little Rock, Arkansas, nine black children arrived to desegregate all-white Central High on the morning after Judge Aaron's castration and were halted by a barricade of National Guardsmen. For the first time since the Civil War, a state was militarily blocking the will of the federal government, whose courts had ordered the integration of the school. Lawyers from the NAACP immediately understood that the federal government's inaction during the Autherine Lucy riot the year before had given a green light to the armed segregationists at Little Rock—a model of racial temperateness until now, as was the man who called out the Guard, Governor Orval Faubus, the son of an unreconstructed Eugene V. Debs man from the hills, a socialist and "nigger lover."

Meanwhile, the ante had been upped in Birmingham. On September 6, when the board of education met to consider Shuttlesworth's petition to integrate all-white Phillips High School, the superintendent temporized. He "would be foolish to decide before an investigation is completed." Shuttlesworth had had about all the proper channels he could stand. On September 9, despite the warning the castrators had issued via Judge Aaron, he, Ruby Shuttlesworth, their daughters, Pat and Frederika ("Ricky"), and two young men also named on the petition drove up to the redbrick citadel of white secondary education.

That day, Eisenhower signed the toothless Civil Rights Act of 1957, which had survived a record filibuster of twenty-four hours and eighteen minutes by the ever virile Dixiecrat Strom Thurmond (who had gone to the Senate steamroom beforehand to dehydrate himself, so that he wouldn't have to relinquish the floor to go to the bathroom).* Despite what was happening in Little Rock, Ricky Shuttlesworth had every expectation of matriculating at Phillips. Then she spied the greeting committee that had responded to the $19 worth of telegrams her father had sent to the various white institutions, following the Gandhian mandate to keep the authorities informed. Besides the TV crews and a negligible police presence were twenty or so civilian white men.

To the child's disbelief, her father stepped out of the car. The men lunged at Shuttlesworth, baring brass knuckles, wooden clubs, and chains. Scampering west across the sidewalk, he was repeatedly knocked down. Someone had pulled his coat up over his head so that he couldn't lower his arms. Standing with the mob in what appeared to be a supervisory capacity was a man who looked like Ace Carter. "We've got this son of a bitch now," a man yelled. "Let's kill him," the crowd screamed. From a white female cheering section came advice to "kill the mother-fucking nigger and it will be all over." Men began smashing the windows of the car. One opened the door and took a chain to the Reverend J. S. Phifer, the Move-

---

* On September 24, after a marathon weekend of golf and bridge, President Eisenhower made good on his debt to Autherine Lucy and sent in the riot-equipped 101st Airborne Division to enforce the desegregation of Little Rock's Central High.

ment vice president who had driven Shuttlesworth to the school (against his better judgment). Phifer swung what he called "a nonviolent right hook."

The attack had been going on for several minutes, as reporters noted, before "half a dozen motor scouts and four patrol cars moved as if by prearranged plan" to the scene. A cop grabbed Phifer's attacker. Ruby Shuttlesworth tried to get out of the back seat and, fending off an assailant with her pocketbook, was stabbed in the hip. Phifer stepped on the gas and began to nose through the mob. Shuttlesworth had been struck by a chain and was beginning to see through a pre-blackout haze. He scrambled to the car and stumbled into the front seat as Phifer sped away. His daughters were so traumatized that they never spoke of that day to each other. Shuttlesworth, however, remained preternaturally composed. He instructed Phifer as they headed for the hospital, "Don't run the stop sign."

At University Hospital, police had to disperse what the *News* described as "curious groups" of a hundred white people who had gathered outside his hospital room to get a glimpse of *the* Fred Shuttlesworth. "I guess this is the price you pay for freedom," he said from his stretcher, smiling widely. ("I always smile when white folk are around," he explained sardonically, "because I don't want them to think I'm mad.") He suspected that part of what made him such a freak show was that his badly scraped face looked almost as white as theirs.

Shuttlesworth was X-rayed stem to stern and was found to have only some minor kidney damage. The doctor came into the room to order more pictures of his head, wondering that there were no fractures.

"You must have a hard skull," he said.

"Doctor," Shuttlesworth replied, "the Lord knew I was in a hard town so He gave me a hard head."

Then, according to Shuttlesworth, he heard the Lord saying to him, "You down there; get up. I've got a job for you to do." Ignoring the doctor's orders to remain in the hospital, he checked out that afternoon and announced to the reporters, "I believe I have been sent to lead God's army in our fight for freedom, as today is the second time within a year that a miracle has spared my life." His private doctor stopped by the house. To his amazement, Shuttlesworth was completely relaxed, his pulse and blood pressure normal. He smiled sweetly and said, "We're making progress, Doc."

For the mass meeting that night, supporters lined up half a block around the church as Shuttlesworth limped slowly by them, as if on his way to Calvary. From the pulpit, he again forgave his attackers, for they knew not what they did. As the story of the beating was retold many times, focusing more and more on the chains, Shuttlesworth would say as he lay on the sidewalk, "I shall be dead before I will ever be a slave again."

To his growing but still relatively small following, Shuttlesworth seemed ready to take his people "into the promised land" that had beckoned the Southern Conference for Human Welfare nearly twenty years earlier. Not only had he become part of that tradition with his new ties to SCEF; he had also found the ultimate form of the modern civil rights movement—the church-based "Christian" model. He had even pioneered the still avant-garde tactics of direct action. Though for now the mainstream—black as well as white—considered him crazy rather than prophetic, Shuttlesworth had understood early that the oppressors were essential "witnesses" for freedom, their wickedness often more eloquent than the victims' virtue. Now he would assume the lead in the greatest theater of the civil rights era, Shuttlesworth versus Bull Connor, who was sworn back in at city hall in November.

Endgame

CONNOR'S RETURN TO POWER—and with it the spirit of cooperation between Klan members and law enforcement—had been previewed by the police handling of Shuttlesworth's Phillips High School misadventure. By way of explaining their delay in arriving at the scene, officers prankishly noted that a bogus stolen car report was being dispatched over the police radio at the same moment that a lieutenant at the high school was calling headquarters for help. The decoy "stolen car," it turned out, belonged to Bull Connor.*

The old vigilante system the Big Mules had created was still in place, but no longer with the authority of the business elite. Connor, former mascot, had become autocrat. And the complex machinery of law, politics, and ideals that he had once operated had been reduced to the bitter ambition of his loyal handler, Jim Simpson. Meanwhile, the local Klan flagship that Connor still indulged had become too unruly for even its new Exalted Cyclops, Troy Ingram. His moderate leadership was under siege by a trouble-loving faction, and the treasury was being raided by one of his fellow officers. Citing the bad publicity over the castrationists, Ingram resigned. He still seemed to be something of a Boy Scout.

The Klansmen who remained were extremists like Ingram's best friend, Robert Chambliss. Since Bull Connor's November swearing-in, Chambliss had been rejoicing over his restored paraprofessional status. He monitored his police-band radio. If he beat officers to the crime scene, he pistol-whipped the suspect or made a "citizen's arrest." Shortly after midnight on December 7, a black couple's new house in Fountain Heights was nearly demolished by two separate bombs— the seventh explosion since the house bombings resumed. Connor announced his attitude toward the nocturnal vigilantes with clarity: He blamed the black home-owners for the terrorism and ordered them to fix their dynamited structure within thirty days or see it razed.

* Only three of Shuttlesworth's estimated twenty attackers were arrested, even though the assault was clearly photographed. No one was indicted, despite Shuttlesworth's positive identification of them. One of the three, a cafe owner named Jack Cash, had an active future in the Klan. It had been not a Klansman but a steelworker named Ivey Ford Gauldin who had brought along a bicycle chain when he drove his son to Phillips that morning—a CIO man had provided the enduring symbol of slavery.

Opening Act

THE FIRST CONFRONTATION, in the city commission's wood-paneled chamber, was deceptively farcical. Back in his perch at the dais, Bull Connor glared at a
delegation of forty-three black people, fixed his good eye on one of them, and
said, "You're Shuttlesworth, aren't you."

It was June 3, 1958, the end of a spring characterized by what Emory O. Jackson saw as a "suspicious quiet." Shuttlesworth had stuck to the courts since his
licking at Phillips High School,* and he was at city hall this Tuesday to petition
for the hiring of Negro policemen.

"I'm not gonna promise you nothin'," Connor said. "And I want you to know,
I believe you the worst thing that ever happened to the Negro in this city."

"History will judge both of us and decide who's good for my people," Shuttlesworth said. "All I'm asking you to do is vote for Negro police. If you do that—"

"I'm not promising you nothing!" Connor said.

"I'm not asking you to promise me nothing," Shuttlesworth said. "I'm just
asking you to tell the people of Birmingham that you're a city father rather than a
city tyrant."

At home forty-five minutes later, Shuttlesworth turned on the noon news.
Connor was on TV saying that some of the boys on the police force believed
Shuttlesworth knew more than he was saying about the Christmas bombing of his
parsonage. The *Birmingham News* that afternoon quoted from Connor's letter to
his police chief: "Since Shuttlesworth seems to be seeking more publicity for the
Northern newspapers and agitators," he suggested that his detectives give him a
lie detector test "to clear up some of the rumors that have been circulating." The
minister responded in a story headlined "Shuttlesworth Challenges Connor";
he'd be glad to take a lie detector test, provided Connor also took one and answered some questions: "One, does he hate Negroes? Two, is he a member of the
Klan?" The list went on, making for a worthy opening scene.

By proving himself a "crazy nigger," the only kind white southerners feared,
Shuttlesworth seemed to have gotten the slight edge, what with Connor reduced
to protesting that he was not a member of the Klan. But he was new to the show,
and still innocent about the enormity of the segregationists' big lie. Two police
officers were suspected of having personally bombed two houses in their neighborhood; their colleagues kidded them about it. And as Connor was implying that
Shuttlesworth had bombed his own church, two of the commissioner's undercover policemen were plotting a second bombing of Bethel Baptist Church with a
man who made Connor's usual collaborator, Robert Chambliss, look bush league.
J. B. Stoner, the Anti-Jewish Party founder who had first encountered Connor at
the Dixiecrat convention, was back doing business in Birmingham. And the right-
ward drift of Connor beyond the pale mirrored politics in the rest of the state.

---

* In May, a panel of three judges hearing Shuttlesworth's school desegregation suit, filed three
months after the visit to Phillips, upheld the state's masterly Pupil Placement Law.

Outniggered

THE TUESDAY that Shuttlesworth had his first showdown with Bull Connor was also election day, the day of the runoff between George Wallace and Attorney General John Patterson for governor. Shuttlesworth cast his vote for "the lesser evil," Wallace, in a fitting finale to the progressive career that might have been.

This was the day Wallace had been politicking for since leaving the legislature in 1952, touring the state, garish in chartreuse pants and burgundy corduroy shirt, his ducktail swiped back with a pocket comb. He had confidently begun with a classic populist campaign, complete with deliberate mispronunciations, Big Jim style (as in "I-dee-ho" for Idaho), and sheepish apologies for the big-finned Cadillac lent to him by a supporter. But early on he breezed into a town right after John Patterson had ended a rally, only to find the folks still damp-eyed over the orphan attorney general, whose baby face was barely matured by "the bald spot creeping abashed back on his skull," as the journalist Murray Kempton put it. Patterson had no shame about exploiting his father's assassination by the vice merchants. He larded his TV commercials with excerpts from a liberally fictionalized B movie called *The Phenix City Story*.

But Patterson's martyred father was the least of Wallace's handicaps. Not only was Patterson running on his record of killing off the NAACP, he also had actively courted the support of the dominant statewide Ku Klux Klan, referring to Alabama Grand Dragon Bobby Shelton in letters to voters as "our mutual friend." A Black Belt newspaper charged that Patterson was holding conferences with Klan leaders. The implications were astounding: The sitting attorney general, the chief law enforcement officer in the state, had struck an overt alliance with a group dedicated to terrorism.

Going into the June 3 runoff, having trailed Patterson in the May primary by 34,000 votes, Wallace had lost twenty pounds and was haggard with the knowledge that his dream had been snatched from him. Patterson took the race by nearly 65,000 votes, or 56 percent of the ballots, and would use his mandate to chart new frontiers of racial viciousness—banning black school marching bands from his inaugural parade, to begin with. One of the incurable romanticizers of Alabama's lost liberal tradition would later say, "I still think Wallace and the state both would have been entirely different if he had won that first time." Driving the stake into Wallace's progressive former self, two-thirds of the working-class voters of Birmingham had rebuffed their steadfast champion as well as the recommendation of the union leadership and gone with Patterson.

Looking to one of his cronies "like a hermit who had just come out of the woods," Wallace walked into a smoke-filled room in Montgomery's Jeff Davis Hotel and announced with a flat resolve that contradicted his porcupine stump style, "John Patterson out-nigguhed me. And boys, I'm not goin' to be out-nigguhed again."

"That's a Bomb"

BULL CONNOR SEEMED to be on the verge of solving an embarrassing law enforcement problem, and in the bargain getting rid of his biggest political headache, Fred Shuttlesworth. Unauthorized bombers had moved onto his turf that spring. On Monday morning, April 28, a blue canvas bag holding fifty-four sticks of dynamite had been discovered by a janitor on a basement window well of Birmingham's Temple Beth El; two twenty-foot fuses had burned to within five feet of the blasting caps. That weekend in Jacksonville, Florida, a Negro junior high school had been dynamited forty-five minutes after a bomb exploded across town at Temple Beth-El. A "General Ponce de León" from the Confederate Underground telephoned local officials and said, "We have just blown up a Jewish center of integration. Every segregationist in the South must go free. All integration must stop."

Because there had been recent synagogue and school bombings in Miami and Nashville (and a dynamite attempt against another Temple Beth El, in Charlotte), southern police departments decided to pool their resources to counter what was apparently an orchestrated regional bombing campaign. Connor and three detectives went to Jacksonville on May 3 to the founding meeting of the intelligence-gathering Southern Conference on Bombing. On a list of the South's active Jew-bashers passed around by the former FBI agent who handled investigations for the Anti-Defamation League were the key members of Ace Carter's defunct Klan (including the castrator Bart Floyd), Robert Chambliss, Troy Ingram, and "Connor, Eugene (Bull)." The ADL's national director quickly wired Connor apologies for the "clerical error."

A few days later, on May 8, there appeared in Connor's office—in the form of an old Birmingham legend—an opportunity to redeem himself in the eyes of his colleagues around the region. Hugh Morris was the Federated Klan chieftain who had spent sixty-seven days in jail during Governor Folsom's Klan hunt in 1949, before finally divulging the brotherhood's membership (and effectively bringing down the curtain on the Dixiecrat phase of the Klan). Connor almost didn't recognize him, not only because he had gotten even fatter but also because he was sober. Morris had come up to city hall from Montgomery, where he was working as a roofer, because he had become alarmed about an acquaintance of his named J. B. Stoner. Morris was a garden-variety anti-Negro racist who had been considered a stickler for Klan protocol ("Klancraft") and had no use for Stoner's rantings about the Jews and their "pigpens," or synagogues.

Morris told Connor that he thought Stoner was responsible for the recent rash of bombings around the South. "If he didn't do it, then he is the kingpin who had it done." Morris also said that he thought Stoner and his "boys," as he called the guys who actually planted the bombs, might be homosexuals. The evidence? Stoner was a bachelor, with a "silly laugh" (plus he drank 7UP instead of Coke). And then there was the question of why someone from landed gentry in Tennessee, educated at Chattanooga's exclusive McCallie School, would choose to hang out with Kluxers.

Connor suggested to Morris that he tell Stoner that there was a group of men in Birmingham wanting to do business with him. Two of Connor's trusted detectives would pose as steelworkers who were the moneymen's intermediaries. If the sting Connor had in mind worked, he would kill two birds with one stone: nail J. B. Stoner and, at the very least, run Fred Shuttlesworth out of town.

On Saturday, June 14, in anticipation of meeting with the "steelworkers," Stoner and Morris took a spin out to Shuttlesworth's small brick church amid the foundries of North Birmingham in Morris's Studebaker. Stoner was scrupulous about not abusing his company car, a cream and yellow 1957 Chevy, for his day job as a claims adjuster for State Farm Insurance out of Dublin, Georgia. (His six-year-old law degree from a night school in Atlanta had gone unused.) When forced to use the State Farm car for extracurricular work, he made sure he disconnected the odometer wires.

Stoner stopped at Bethel Baptist, walked up to one of the guards out front, and said, "I want to see Reverend Shuttlesworth." The guard asked him what for. "I want him to pray for me," Stoner said. "I'm in trouble."

Stoner's original price for the Shuttlesworth job was $5,000, but he had come down to $2,000 before he and Morris were out of North Birmingham. If there were at least two more bombing sites, he could offer a discount bulk rate of $1,000 apiece.

The following Saturday, June 21, Stoner met with Connor's two detectives ("steelworkers") in Morris's Studebaker in a Birmingham hotel parking lot. One of the detectives said he had always been opposed to violence but that the "niggers" had been causing a lot of trouble. Shuttlesworth was the biggest pain in the butt. The detectives explained that the group they represented wanted a "responsible person" who could arrange to have Bethel Baptist "blown completely off the map and not leave one brick standing." Their aim was to force Shuttlesworth to "leave Birmingham and go up North where he belonged." The money for the bombing was not yet available. They were waiting for "some big businesspeople" who had promised "substantial donations." They would get in touch with Morris as soon as Stoner's $2,000 fee came through—"within the next ten days or two weeks." Then, as a show of good faith, one of the detectives gave Stoner $100 to cover his expenses so far. The conversation in the Studebaker ended.

Sitting in a car observing the conference from across the street were Bull Connor and his buddy Clarence Kelley, the future head of the FBI, who was the special agent in charge of the Birmingham bureau. Two more FBI agents were in another big plain car. In a pickup truck nearby were a police detective and a radio technician, who was supposedly recording Stoner's remarks, transmitted by the wire one of the detectives wore. Despite "technical" coverage that seemed like overkill, the recording equipment was said to have failed; probably the tape was destroyed because of the damaging material it contained. The evidence suggests that the detectives proposed to Stoner that he assassinate Fred Shuttlesworth.

A week later, after midnight on Sunday morning, June 29, the usual guards from the Alabama Christian Movement for Human Rights were on duty at Shuttlesworth's church. Since the Christmas 1956 bombing, they had been protecting Bethel with their "nonviolent Winchesters," the first such contingent since deacons had protected Shuttlesworth's predecessor against the reds twenty-five years before. Occasionally, Jack O'Dell volunteered his services, though his insurance job had kept him too busy to get very much involved in the ACMHR other than to urge his clients to attend Movement meetings. The guards took staggered breaks in a little shack near Shuttlesworth's new house, rebuilt across the street from the church.

At around one-thirty, at least two of Stoner's "boys" from Atlanta pulled up alongside the church. Richard Bowling, an unemployable twenty-five-year-old product of Atlanta's housing projects whose long rap sheet included wife beating, would soon insist to one of Connor's detectives that the assignment was his. One of them deposited a sizzling five-gallon paint can next to the church's east wall, and then they cruised off. A waitress walking home from her shift at the Lomax Sandwich Shop spied smoke near the church and yelled for the guards. Two church elders who also acted as Shuttlesworth's bodyguards trotted toward the smoke and called to the guards inside the building to get out. "That's a bomb," one said. "That's a bomb," the other agreed.

One of the guards, Will Hall, a sixty-three-year-old retired miner known as John L. after his old union president, was something of a civil rights pioneer himself. He had been the plaintiff in attorney Arthur Shores's career-making 1939 victory—a police brutality prosecution against a whiskey-loving, rubber hose–happy police officer, which made it into the *Daily Worker.* Priding himself on being able to handle dynamite, he picked up the hissing can, walked briskly to the side of a road, and set it down in the street twenty-five feet from the church. He turned and ran, falling on his face as the blast tore through the night. The windows on the east side of the church blew out. Shrapnel sliced through the facade of a house across the street. Shuttlesworth got out of bed and greeted the two arriving policemen, Captain G. L. Pattie and Sergeant Tom Cook. They were the "steelworkers" who had proposed the bombing.

Stoner never got paid, and Pattie and Cook berated him for proceeding without a go-ahead. Connor tried to have Stoner prosecuted, but the district attorney felt that the case was too fishy, entrapment being one of the problems.* The commissioner continued to dangle job possibilities in front of Stoner, still

---

* Connor then took the case to Washington and made an impassioned pitch to the Justice Department, noting particularly the jeopardy that his brave detectives were in. But Justice rebuffed him. "Bull's record had preceded him to Washington," the assistant D.A. who accompanied him observed. "I think they just didn't buy Bull." In 1980, the Alabama attorney general prosecuted Stoner for the Shuttlesworth bombing. When Hugh Morris was asked to testify against Stoner, he said that he was not sure the police didn't do the bombing, adding that he "would make a better witness for the defense if the defense only knew it."

through Hugh Morris. Morris typed up a hit list of ten Negroes and gave it to Stoner. Topping it was Fred Shuttlesworth. Martin Luther King was also high up. Stoner began promoting his murder line at greatly reduced rates. He would consider killing King for, say, $1,500.

Meanwhile, Bull Connor's policemen "investigated" the bombing by pulling up in front of Bethel at four one dark morning and lighting matches, miming dynamiters at work. Shuttlesworth wrote to the FBI asking it to investigate the harassment. Despite what it knew, the bureau maintained no official interest in the church bombing. But it must have had some qualms about the conversations its agents overheard between the Birmingham police detectives and J. B. Stoner. The month after the bombing, the FBI, which prided itself on having close relations with local law enforcement, instructed its Birmingham office to "hold contacts with Connor to a minimum because of his unsavory background."

A Shining New Alloy

THE FBI WOULD SOON BEGIN a collaboration of its own with racist terrorists in Birmingham, as segregation's institutions rose in one great finale to hold the system together. If the magnitude of the opposition was only just becoming clear to Fred Shuttlesworth, his frustration over the Southern Christian Leadership Conference's failure to meet it was widely shared. Desperate to get something off the ground, Bayard Rustin and King's white guru, Stanley Levison, had persuaded their capable co-conspirator, Ella Baker, to become SCLC's acting director, but she was meeting resistance from the Baptist preachers—"glory seekers." That epithet included, especially, Martin Luther King, who "wasn't the kind of person you could engage in a dialogue with," Baker believed, "certainly if the dialogue questioned the almost exclusive rightness of his position."

Fred Shuttlesworth was the only minister in SCLC with whom Baker had established a bond, a distinction probably related to the fact that he was the only minister in SCLC who "let" his wife participate in the Movement, heavy-handed patriarch though he was. It was with some hope mixed with relief that Baker watched him assume the civil rights initiative that fall, when a medical emergency took King out of the action. In September 1958, while in a Harlem department store signing copies of his new book about the bus boycott, *Stride Toward Freedom,* King had been stabbed in the chest by a schizophrenic black woman and withdrew into a long recovery. But as Shuttlesworth stepped into the spotlight, it was apparent that the time for his ideas had not yet come. He was heading for a devastating personal setback, which in turn would drive the Movement deeper into entropy.

The Alabama Christian Movement for Human Rights's bus desegregation suit, filed by Arthur Shores in January 1957, had reached Judge Hobart Grooms's court in mid-October 1958. To moot that case, Bull Connor's adviser, Jim Simpson, made an unusual personal appearance at city hall and minted an ordinance to replace the one under contention; the new one had dropped the offending racial language and simply turned the seating arrangement over to the authority of the bus driver.

Shuttlesworth had an axiom to describe segregationist justice: "If the Klan don't get you, the police will; and if the police don't get you, the courts will." As the lawyers dutifully prepared to contest the new ordinance, it was obvious to Shuttlesworth that direct action was the Movement's only true option. He circulated the nonviolence oaths for the first organized protest in over a year, not counting the personal direct action he had staged against the bus driver who always refused to let his children off at the stop by his church (he had wheeled his car in front of the bus, halting it in the middle of the street). On Monday, October 20, around thirty Negroes boarded the front of the buses. For thirteen of them the last stop was jail. Shuttlesworth had decided not to ride ("to show 'Bull' that it was not just I, but many Negroes in Birmingham desirous of obtaining their civil rights"). But he was arrested anyway. As he was being loaded into a police wagon after cheerfully turning himself in, he told reporters, "I don't suppose I could do anything to make Mr. Connor happy except to commit suicide." Fred Shuttlesworth had finally become a political prisoner.

Thousands of Negroes knelt in silent prayer on the city hall lawn till after midnight as the "Birmingham fourteen" inside were being convicted in recorder's court. It was the first mass demonstration of the local Movement. Emory O. Jackson, still nursing his disillusionment over the bus boycott's outside influences, perked up with an editorial in the *World* comparing oppression in Birmingham to South African apartheid. On Monday afternoon, October 27, three ministers from the still fractious Montgomery Improvement Association followed the scent of bus protest to Birmingham and joined an emergency ACMHR board meeting at the jailed president's house. Tipped off by a wiretap on Shuttlesworth's phone, four plainclothes detectives (including, again, G. L. Pattie, the "steelworker" who had set up the sting on J. B. Stoner) walked in without a warrant, took the Montgomery men to headquarters on suspicion of "vagrancy," and grilled them for five hours about whether they were there to plan a bus boycott.

That evening, an overflow crowd of thousands attended the mass meeting, and in a miracle that some saw as equaling Shuttlesworth's survival of bombings and chain beatings, his obstructionist rival, the Reverend J. L. Ware, rallied more than a hundred ministers behind the Movement that many of them hadn't allowed to meet in their big churches. By the end of the night, a Birmingham bus boycott had indeed been called, with perilously little planning, for shortly after Halloween.

The jailing of the Montgomery ministers prompted the first national outcry against Bull Connor since his comeback, proving the benefits for the ordinary Negro of proximity to Martin Luther King's fame. The recuperating King, however, was able only to send telegrams to concerned northerners and statesmen, deploring Birmingham's "virtual reign of terror." He wrote Shuttlesworth an impassioned apology for his absence: "Your wise restraint, calm dignity and unflinching courage will be an inspiration to generations yet unborn." But he never mailed the letter, perhaps because it had been written on stationery from Detroit's Sheraton-Cadillac Hotel, the souvenir of King's jet-setting other life, far off the bus routes of his followers, that apparently had not been crimped by his convalescence.

King asked Glenn Smiley to go to Birmingham in early November to guide the bus protest. Smiley, a white Methodist minister from Texas, was the foremost tactical nonviolence specialist working in the South, a full-time field secretary for the Fellowship of Reconciliation who had gone to Montgomery early in the bus boycott to replace his "guru," the controversial Bayard Rustin. On December 21, 1956, Smiley had sat next to Martin Luther King at the front of the first integrated bus of Montgomery. By the time he flew into Birmingham two years later, on the evening of November 3, the nation's black press was focused hopefully on a new bus boycott, with its promising leader—"a shiny, new impelling civil rights alloy," the influential *Baltimore Afro-American* pronounced Shuttlesworth, "adept at blending homespun humor, ridicule and biting sarcasm into fire-and-brimstone emotionalism."

Smiley was less enamored of Shuttlesworth's spunk and would have felt more comfortable with J. L. Ware in charge. When Shuttlesworth told him, "I'm afraid of neither man nor devil," Smiley replied, "Fred, don't ever ask me to go with you on a project because if you're not afraid on occasions, and there's plenty to be afraid of here, I don't want to be around you."

Smiley left town a week later, in some doubt as to whether Birmingham could pull a Montgomery. The local media were imposing a blackout on the protest. And Bull Connor was exercising all the privileges of his office. He vowed to jail anyone "assisting in the bus boycott." His detectives had started to attend all the Movement's mass meetings, sitting in the back pew of the church and taking notes while a microphone transmitted the proceedings to a shortwave radio in a patrol car parked outside. Occasionally, firemen stampeded the church dragging hoses. Shuttlesworth informed them, "The kind of fire we got here you can't put out with axes and firehoses."

In mid-November, with the boycott only a week old, Connor's detective— again it was Captain G. L. Pattie, J. B. Stoner's contact—arrested a black minister who had been encouraging his congregation to walk in dignity rather than ride in humility. Later that month, another Movement mainstay, the Reverend Charles Billups, was arrested for "interfering with an officer" after touching the lapel of one of the surveillance detectives at the mass meeting. Perhaps worrying that his number might be up next, J. L. Ware went back to carping about Shuttlesworth's dangerous methods. Meanwhile, Shuttlesworth taunted the detectives, daring them to arrest him. "Only God can tell me what to preach in my own pulpit, and I am going to tell my people to stay off these buses, even if I have to go to Kilby Prison!"

Though Shuttlesworth was Bull Connor's theatrical match, he was still powerless against the resources of the commissioner's police state, as was even the attorney general of the United States. When William Rogers ordered a federal grand jury investigation into the illegal jailing of the Montgomery ministers, Connor retorted, "If Mr. Rogers thinks he can scare me or the Birmingham Police Department into permitting this city to become a scene of rioting which would follow just to please Negro voters, he is mistaken." He told *Time* that the attorney general was a "jackass ... yapping his brains out." To a black reporter from the *Baltimore Afro-American,* he boasted about arresting Senator Glen Taylor back in 1948. "Damn the law, we don't give a damn about the law," he explained. "Down here we make our own law."

The prematurely born bus boycott died without so much as an obituary at the end of November. At around that time Shuttlesworth also received his biggest blow yet on the constitutional front. In *Shuttlesworth* v. *the Board of Education of Birmingham,* the Supreme Court upheld Alabama's *Brown*-circumventing Pupil Placement Act, definitively turning over the job of implementing the five-year-old school decision to the very men who had necessitated it in the first place. Calling the case a depressing turning point, *New York Times* columnist Arthur Krock predicted "generations, not years" before school desegregation would take place. And soon Shuttlesworth, the vanguard alternative to legalism and gradualism, would be neutralized.

Neurotic

IN DECEMBER, when Glenn Smiley returned to Birmingham for a brief visit, Captain G. L. Pattie entered his room at the Tutwiler Hotel and helped himself to the contents of his briefcase, notably a personal letter, a chatty "word from the wars," that Smiley had written to an FOR colleague. As Smiley later recalled his own reaction, "I could have jumped off a cliff." On December 21, Bull Connor released the letter to the *Birmingham News,* which printed Smiley's personal observations about Fred Shuttlesworth: "Shuttlesworth is a courageous leader, but devoid of organizational knowledge, headstrong and wild for publicity, almost to the point of neurosis, undemocratic and willing to do almost anything to keep the spotlight on himself." He continued, "Nevertheless his group is the only one that is moving, and he cannot be boxed in. Must be helped, as he has power to cast us all into hell."

"Shuttlesworth marched to a different drummer from the rest of us," Smiley would say in retrospect, unconsciously comparing him to the civil disobedience master Henry David Thoreau. Smiley also complained that Shuttlesworth "craved publicity for the Movement, feeling that if you could get beat up badly it was good for the Movement." Later, Smiley conceded, "Now we all know it's true."

Shuttlesworth's two previous spiritual crises—leaving the Methodist church and facing down the deacons at First Baptist of Selma—faded before this Gethsemane. Bayard Rustin called him from New York. "They're trying to split the Movement up," he said. "The only way you can defend yourself is to defend Glenn."

"But 'neurotic'?" Shuttlesworth said

"We are all neurotic at certain points," Rustin said knowingly.

Shuttlesworth was personally crushed. He began developing physical symptoms, like leg aches. But the effect on the Movement was more damaging than all the dynamite blasts in the valley. As Shuttlesworth had feared, the Smiley debacle gave the NAACP's temperamentally conservative attorney Arthur Shores a pretext to refuse to take on the ACMHR's legal cases.* Shuttlesworth accused Shores of seeing the Movement only as "a chance to make big money" and, alternately, of being afraid he would be "attacked for stirring up litigation"—perhaps a veiled reference to Shores's friendly relationship with Bull Connor. In unguarded moments, Shores called Connor "a good close friend of mine" who "made officers do whatever I wanted done in a case." The quid for the quo was that he swung the black vote for Connor.

Now approaching age thirty-seven, Shuttlesworth found himself isolated with his dwindling band of "nobodies." Compounding the Movement's troubles, Martin Luther King, who had turned thirty in January, was blossoming as what one historian would call "a glorified after-dinner speaker." Ella Baker, who had now grown close to Shuttlesworth's entire family, began referring darkly to a "cult of personality," a term that, from the mouth of this sophisticate, had a malicious Stalinist subtext. Nevertheless, Baker's comrade Bayard Rustin continued to plump King, showcasing him in April at A. Philip Randolph's second Youth March for Integrated Schools on Washington. The event was barely reported, but it had an unintended effect that would prove pivotal.

Making his thank-yous, Randolph had singled out Stanley Levison for his organizing help. The mention of this onetime protagonist of the FBI's Communist Party files renewed J. Edgar Hoover's flagging sense of mission. The utter failure of the American party after Khrushchev's "secret speech" in 1956 had thrown his bureau into the mirror-image spy-versus-spy identity crisis of an enemy bereft of its enemy. But now, even if Levison had been off the FBI's active CP list for two years, Hoover had a patriotic pretext to take on the civil rights movement. And Hoover hadn't known the worst—or best—of it.

The man who had gathered scores of the signatures on the youth march's petitions, who had rustled up many of the demonstrators, was Jack O'Dell. The House Un-American Activities Committee had tracked O'Dell down in Alabama the previous summer† and after a typically brassy performance, he had moved back to New York to help an old Southern Negro Youth Congress colleague turned Party apparatchik, James Jackson, plot a youth movement for

---

* Shores had named a prohibitive "runoff" fee to sue to desegregate the city parks, and the ACMHR turned to a ringer from Jacksonville, Florida, Ernest Jackson, who filed suit on March 2. Jackson was headed off at the pass by a federal court order requiring that out-of-town counsel associate with a local lawyer in order to try cases in Alabama. It was believed in Movement circles that Shores and his black bar brethren had sought the order.

† HUAC had politically outlived its founder Martin Dies, who decided not to run for reelection in 1944 after being targeted by the CIO's political action committee.

the South.* But O'Dell had begun to sense that the Party was not going to be the Second Coming of civil rights. He had connected with Rustin and Randolph through his contacts in the left wing of the Democratic Party, and in August he wrote a letter offering his good wishes, if not yet his services, to Martin Luther King.

As O'Dell moved right toward SCLC, Fred Shuttlesworth was moving left away from what he felt was an empty organization.† The week after Randolph's march, Shuttlesworth wrote to King: "When the flowery speeches have been made, we still have the hard job of getting down and helping people to reach the idealistic state of human affairs which we desire." He concluded, "We must move now or else [be] hard put in the not too distant future, to justify our existence." Shuttlesworth was being pulled increasingly toward the Southern Conference Educational Fund, whose board he had joined in 1958. He had come to rely on Carl and Anne Braden as his lifeline to the outside world; they publicized the atrocities of Birmingham (ignored by the local newspapers) in SCEF's *Southern Patriot* or through friendly northern reporters. Shuttlesworth began to promote his own Movement separately from SCLC through a pamphlet Anne Braden wrote about the history of the ACMHR, *They Challenge Segregation at Its Core!* Sent out in a large mailing, it was more polished and ambitious than anything SCLC had yet produced. Shuttlesworth encouraged SCEF to take over the freedom struggle. Urging executive director Jim Dombrowski to redefine SCEF as a grassroots organization, he offered his own congregation as a seedbed.

The Movement's right wing took a nervous accounting of Shuttlesworth's drift. The NAACP had excluded him—along with its also leftward-traveling founder, W.E.B. Du Bois—from its fiftieth anniversary convention that summer. The Communist press covered the double rebuff, providing grist for the Birmingham police's "subversive" dossier on Shuttlesworth.

Methodists

AS THE CIVIL RIGHTS MOVEMENT struggled to come to terms with its radical past, so did the right-wing resistance. Both had turned to the church for solutions. For white Birmingham, Methodism was the quintessential, and most popular, denomination, its governing bishops and doctrinal manifestos (the stringent "method" that had inspired its originally pejorative name) perfect for a city whose class boundaries were little more than the wall of air pollution that separated the

---

* The Southern Negro Youth Congress had finally come back to haunt the Alabama movement when, the previous year, segregationists made much of the SNYC membership of Dr. Charles Gomillion, a Tuskegee educator who was leading a store boycott there to protest the gerrymandered districts that diluted black voting strength. His lawsuit would ultimately end up as one of the cases in the one-man-one-vote Supreme Court landmark decision.

† Despite King's star power, SCLC had raised only around $25,000 since its founding, less than half what Shuttlesworth's "little niggers" had come up with.

workers from their bosses. Sid Smyer was a staunch Methodist, not having followed the more socially ambitious Big Mules into the Presbyterian church, which sanctified their corporate status (as well as the damnation of their workers) as divinely "predestined." Four years earlier, Smyer had organized a militantly segregationist lay Methodist group as a sort of spiritual auxiliary to his main show, the American States Rights Association, its purpose to fight back against the national church officers' endorsement of *Brown*. Now, his discombobulated Dixiecrat oligarchy had moved further from the center ring of politics and was situated almost exclusively in the church.

That spring of 1959, Smyer's old ad hoc Methodist organization was revived, in more rabid form, as the Methodist Layman's Union. Some 1,800 lay Methodists from around Alabama and Florida met in March at Birmingham's Highlands Methodist Church to resolve that integration was "a betrayal of unborn generations and a monstrous crime against civilization." The MLU would prompt the *New York Times* to pronounce Birmingham the epicenter of "Christian" racism. But if Smyer still even believed that such groups were the answer to racial tension, he no longer had the fire to lead them, and the best-known Methodist layman at the meeting was Bull Connor. The balance of power had changed. Once the vested interests' "son of a bitch," Connor alone now ruled and ruined—the "big voice in Birmingham," *Time* magazine had called him in a December 1958 article titled "Integration's Hottest Crucible."

A strange scene occurred the day after the MLU meeting, suggesting that Connor no longer had control of *his* son of a bitch. Robert Chambliss, who had gotten a job driving a delivery truck for a rebuilt-auto-parts distributor since losing his city job, crashed a meeting of the state Democratic Party executive committee at the ballroom of the Tutwiler Hotel and began haranguing committeeman Bull Connor. First he called Connor a liar, and when the commissioner retreated to the back of the room, he followed, shouting, "You drug me out of bed at three a.m. and threw me in old sol [the lingo for solitary confinement]. You treated me worse than a goddamn nigger."* Clearly, he felt that Connor had reneged on some longstanding commitment—one that obviously gave him the authority to curse the city's ruling politician in public. Connor spoke placatingly as a policeman escorted Chambliss out of the room, the latter persisting, "You're a nigger lover and a liar."

Perhaps Connor felt that Chambliss's breed of vigilante was obsolete in a climate where the governor took phone calls from the Grand Dragon and the Klan posted "Welcome" signs on public highways, as if it were a civic club like the Lions or the Civitans. For now, Connor had managed to disguise the toxins of racism as Methodist holy water. But decommissioning vigilantes like Chambliss

---

* Apparently, Chambliss had been taken in for questioning about the impending trial of three Klanmen for a house bombing in July 1958—the first indictments for a dynamiting, and only because the targeted homeowner's friends ran the Klansmen down and beat them up. Chambliss, rumored to have been the driver of the getaway car, had reputedly thrown a second bomb in the vicinity that same night (and boasted that his "wasn't a dud," like that of his very inebriated brothers).

was not going to be easy, and it would ultimately be he who brought meaning to Birmingham's nickname, "The City of Churches."

McWhorter 1959

I BELIEVE THAT MY FATHER'S DRIFT from the establishment to the periph- ery was accelerated by the last, sarcastic words his father spoke in his presence: "He's free, white, twenty-one, and *married*." They were addressed to a nurse in the hospital where my grandfather, in his prime at age fifty-four, had been taken by ambulance after his Lincoln stalled in front of a Roadway truck on the Atlanta highway. Within a day of his comment to the nurse, he hemorrhaged to death from undetected internal injuries. The eulogy on the front page of the December 15, 1950, *Birmingham News*—in a column signed, ironically enough, by "Vulcan," patron saint of traffic safety—called Hobart McWhorter "a real gentleman, toler- ant and even tempered, who quietly held to principle. . . . It is good for the town that he left a deep imprint among us." The legacy's effects on his elder son were proving to be both alarming and heartbreaking.

Just six weeks earlier, Martin had gotten married at Parris Island, South Car- olina, where he was taking his basic training in the Marine Corps after a botched semester at Birmingham-Southern. He had gone to college under his father's or- ders following his cross-country motorcycle trip, and had even joined the socially desirable fraternity, Sigma Alpha Epsilon. His Brando-esque reserve inspired a certain fascination over at the Kappa Delta house, and one of the KDs, Betty Gore, a college beauty queen, had caught his eye. Visiting her in her small home- town, Martin found her family's temporary rental house everything that a Moun- tain Brook home was not—messy, dark, and smoky. When they married, his father did not attend the wedding.

After his discharge from the Marines, Martin moved his wife and baby son to Cherokee County near the McWhorter "plantation" in Gaylesville. Perhaps Martin expected his eccentricities to receive a bit more latitude in the place his own father had abandoned. His grandfather, Dr. McWhorter, had reputedly owned every acre in the county at one time or other, and Martin once said that he would have carried on the family medical tradition if he hadn't had a "lazy streak." But instead of returning to the fatherland as a doctor, he set up shop as a TV and radio repairman in an old Gulf gas station.

The men and women who grew up with Martin in Mountain Brook would use the term "mechanical genius" to rationalize how such a manual labor type could have sprung from the same family as his siblings, Hobart Jr., a well-known lawyer and country club wit, and Gail, an intellectual with the cocked brow and cigarette holder of Bette Davis. "He could take two rubber bands and a paper clip and turn it into a television set," one of the debutantes he once dated told me. But televisions either did not exist or did not break down in Cherokee County, and the radio repair jobs were few and far between. His business floundered.

To pass the time, Martin took up skin diving in nearby Little River Canyon—the "Grand Canyon of the South"—where his great-grandfather, the Civil War surgeon, had eluded Yankee scouts on his way back to the Confederate hospital in Richmond. Since there were no air compressors around to fill his diving tanks, Martin decided to build his own. After becoming somewhat proficient at rebuilding compressors salvaged from the Army, he went into business under the grand-sounding name McWhorter Engineering Company. That was in November 1952, around the time that my pregnant mother returned to her Mississippi hometown so that a trusted family doctor could deliver me. Which explained how I was stuck with the birthplace of Tupelo, the natal village of Elvis Presley.

We moved to Centre, the county seat and former site of the Cherokee Indian capital of Turkey Town. Its most impressive feature was a bewilderingly wide main street, as if heavy traffic were expected. We rented a shotgun house from the county patriarch Hugh Jordan,* and experienced the ordinary novelties of country life: the plump redheaded babysitter who showed us her freckled bottom, the wild boy who shot my brother in the face with BBs, the waterheaded baby at the county fair. One winter evening, while warming myself in front of a blue-gas space heater, I caught on fire but lived to brag that five nurses had to hold me down at the hospital when they peeled the charred skin off my bottom.

We could not have been further from our gracious, servant-filled world in Birmingham. Once puritanical, my father started crossing the state line out of our dry county into Georgia on Saturday nights to drink beer. The locals were not proving to be the best of influences. Uncle Hobart drove over one weekend for a visit and, creeping down our semi-paved road, spied an adult neighbor on his porch holding a knife to my brother's throat. As Hobart bolted from the car with his Army .38, the man explained, "We're just having fun."

Our Cherokee County experiment did not seem to be working, but in the end it was not social dysfunction but economics that drove my father away. The McWhorter Engineering Company was growing, and Papa tried to find land to build a shop on. He discovered that Old South property—the pine-covered red dirt where Nathan Bedford Forrest had tricked the Yankee Colonel Abel Streight into retreating by simulating cannons with logs and sawhorses—cost about three times the going rate for New South land. So in 1957 he bought a lot in Birming-

---

* Jimmy, the scion of Centre's first family, who had been in a Boy Scout troop my father started, would spend his adulthood in and out of prison, dating from the discovery of stacks of counterfeit $20 bills in caskets stored on a high shelf in Jordan's Department Store, an archeological formation of discontinued goods, hardware, clothes, feed, mule shoes, and auto parts that was Centre's social hub. Jimmy had moved from counterfeiting to drug dealing, eventually doing extra time in Georgia for paying a state senator a $10,000 bribe to spring him from a ten-year drug sentence. When he got out, the Jordans filed a breach of contract suit against the futilely bribed legislator. In 1990, Jimmy and his wife were shot at their lakeside Cherokee County cabin.

ham and moved us back to the Magic City. We children immediately joined in the local obsession known as "What color's Vulcan's light tonight?" Assuming that every motorist was magically wired to the iron man, I aspired to witness the moment the beacon switched from green to red.

Papa built his "plant," as we called it, using as collateral for his bank loan the small settlement Roadway had paid the family for killing Hobart McWhorter. (On the basis of the skid marks, it was calculated that the truck was doing 70 in a 50 m.p.h. zone.) My father roared through the fatal intersection on his way to work every day.

CENTRE WOULD GRADUALLY BECOME just a blur on my urban pedigree. We seemed to be back where we belonged. My older brother and I were enrolled in the charter first grade of Highlands Day School, founded in order to spare the elite children of Mountain Brook from a situation like the Business at Little Rock. My new friends included Popsie Simpson, with his inevitable hard-boiled egg at lunch, and my know-it-all soul mate, Sam Upchurch, whose family was renowned for the Statue of Liberty replica—with a flame—on top of its insurance company headquarters. Sam controlled the agenda of playground disputation: Do you belong to the Mountain Brook Club or the Birmingham? Are you for Alabama or Auburn? Do you believe in Predestination? Are you double-jointed? And, after Christmas vacation, Do you believe in Santa Claus? Sam had seduced me into temporarily renouncing my Bama allegiance to root for Auburn, which his family had largely endowed.

My most meaningful new classmate at Highlands Day, however, was the link to Cherokee County, Sidney William Smyer III. He was a plump blond boy with a quietly goofy sense of humor and wide blue eyes that seemed to know more than he let on. Young Sid and I addressed each other incessantly as "cousin," in those days when it was comforting to know that everyone was related through Adam and Eve. We were allowed to call his mother by her first name, Ingrid. Papa was still friendly with his old Battle Ground boarding schoolmate, Billy Smyer, young Sid's father. Occasionally we were invited out to the family retreat on Smyer Lake, which was my only inkling that Sid belonged to the real estate dynasty that would ultimately connect my own history with Birmingham's.

WE LIVED WITH MY GRANDMOTHER for our first months in Birmingham. The family had sold the Hastings Road house a decade earlier to one of "King Henry" DeBardeleben's grandsons and bought a grander mansion, a stone and dirty-redbrick Tudor in one of Robert Jemison's early developments on top of Red Mountain. Marjorie (as we called our grandmother) moved purposefully through her house with a swaying gait, professorially elegant in tweedy suits, earrings, good hosiery, and—always—high heels. After her husband died, she had gone to Harvard to get a master's in education and in 1953, at fifty-four, became a professor of education at Birmingham-Southern College, although my brothers and I thought she was a child psychologist because she took us out to the campus and let her students "observe" us. Once when I was in the back seat of her Chevrolet singing at the top of my lungs, she turned to my mother and asked ingenuously, "Does Diane always sing so loud?" My singsong fell to a quaver. Following Marjorie's example, my brothers and I "used psychology" on one another.

Instead of Holsum white bread and Campbell's chicken noodle, Marjorie fed us lasagna, fondue, herbed French bread, stick pretzels, homemade quince jelly, raspberries and sour cream, fresh ground pepper on our fried eggs—served on her everyday Wedgwood. There were no plastic toys or even television at 3516 Redmont Road. We improvised fun by scooting across the oriental rugs on a camel saddle Marjorie had brought back from Egypt. One day I called time-out from a game of hide-and-go-seek and ran to Marjorie, who was in her bedroom reading and listening to the Metropolitan Opera's afternoon broadcast. "I have to write a poem," I announced. She transcribed my verse, called "Holly Fairy," and put it away for safekeeping.

Her Doulton figurines and Mexican candlesticks were left unchildproofed in the living room. I used to sit on the camel saddle and fix my mind on all her worldly artifacts—souvenirs of her trips abroad every summer since my grandfather's death—and arouse myself to a tingling state of "art appreciation." On a piecrust end table were a brass bowl of unshelled nuts and a framed picture of my father at around age twenty-one. He wore his Marine uniform, the khaki cloth cap resting low on his forehead, and he was handsome. There was hardly any resemblance to the Papa I knew, with the beer beginning to show on his belly and the grease under his fingernails. For this slender, idealistic-looking young man seemed to belong in this sedate living room, still under the vigilance of a large portrait of his father done in undertaker hues by a popular Mountain Brook artist, who my father would say had painted some kindness into the eyes.

Martin never did acknowledge any breach of continuity between his past and his present. But his rebellion had not yet intersected with the racial warp of the place and time.

PART II

Movement
1960–1962

5.

BREAKING OUT

The New Dimension

"WOULD YOU LIKE TO STOP and see where the sit-ins are going on?" B. Elton Cox greeted Fred Shuttlesworth at the Greensboro, North Carolina, airport on February 11, 1960. Shuttlesworth had flown in for a midweek speaking engagement at the activist young Congregational minister's church in nearby High Point, and would leave with new hope for his Movement. Eleven days earlier, a student at North Carolina Agriculture and Technical, a local black college, had said to his mother, "Mom, we are going to do something tomorrow that may change history, that might change the world." And on Monday afternoon, February 1, Ezell Blair Jr. and three A&T classmates went down to the classiest intersection of downtown Greensboro, walked into Woolworth's, bought some school supplies, sat down at the lunch counter, and ordered a doughnut and coffee.

"I'm sorry, we don't serve colored here," the waitress said. Blair pointed out that she was mistaken and held up his receipt from a nearby cash register. The young men stayed on their stools until the manager turned off the lights thirty minutes before closing time.

Before the week was out, hundreds of students from the college-dense area were sitting in at Kress as well as Woolworth's. By Monday, when Woolworth's closed in conditional surrender, the protests had caught on in nearby Winston-Salem and Durham.

Shuttlesworth was knocked out by what Elton Cox showed him: Here was the sort of mass action he had futilely been urging on Martin Luther King for nearly three years. He sat at the counter with the students awhile, helped them maintain their nonviolence as a white man poked his belly in their way, and was disappointed not to be arrested. The kids seemed as disciplined as mature adults, yet as direct-action troops they had distinct advantages over their elders: no job to lose, no family to support. And they had not forgotten that twirling upon a stool at a soda fountain—something they had seen only white children do—had once seemed the joyous essence of freedom.

As soon as he got to Cox's house, Shuttlesworth called the person he was sure would get it: Ella Baker, in Atlanta. Her headaches as the acting director of the Southern Christian Leadership Conference had just been aggravated by Martin Luther King's recent move back home to Atlanta, to serve as Daddy King's absentee co-pastor and basically devote his full time to SCLC. "You must tell Martin that we must get with this," Shuttlesworth said, "and really this can shake up the world." This, he said, was "the new dimension of the Movement."

The sit-ins were actually an old dimension, not some spontaneous plague on the lone white preserves of a fully integrated consumer economy. More than anything else, the protesters were descendants of the Southern Negro Youth Congress. One sit-in, a student at Greensboro's Bennett College, was the daughter of one of the SNYC's three co-founders, Ed Strong. Another early SNYC activist, Francis Grandison, who headed Bennett's psychology department, was acting as a sort of big-daddy adviser to the students. James Jackson, the SNYC co-founder still high in the Party hierarchy, returned to his native Richmond later in February to report ecstatically for *The Worker* (formerly the *Daily Worker*) on the sit-ins spreading through the Upper South. He considered them sort of a memorial to the dear SNYC comrade he had just buried. On February 14, Frederick Douglass's birthday, Louis Burnham—the SNYC's final executive in Birmingham—was giving one of his gorgeous speeches to a Harlem writers' club. "Pardon me, I feel somewhat indisposed," he said. And then one of the last charismatic leaders of the previous Negro liberation movement died of a heart attack.

Moving

ON FEBRUARY 25, the sit-ins came to the Deep South. Thirty-five students from Alabama State College in Montgomery went to the state capitol, headed downstairs to the cafeteria, asked for food, and were marched out single file by a club-wielding sheriff. They walked two abreast back to the college, chanting, "If we can't go to Alabama, we go to Auburn."

Fred Shuttlesworth caught the student leader of the demonstration, Bernard Lee, on the news that night and was charmed by him. Lee, an Air Force veteran and father of three, known as Jelly after his favorite food, said something to the effect that "tomorrow we are going to meet at the capitol and *move*." Shuttlesworth and his security entourage (including Will "John L." Hall, the dynamite handler who once offered to do a bit of strategic bombing for the movement) drove to Montgomery the next day. Martin Luther King arrived from Atlanta that Friday, too, on a different errand: The previous week, two deputies had appeared at Daddy King's Ebenezer Baptist Church with extradition orders from Alabama. Upholding his reputation as the Movement slayer, Governor John Patterson had accused King of perjuring himself when he signed his 1956, 1957, and 1958 tax returns; ordinarily this would have been a misdemeanor, but the state's charge was felony tax evasion.*

Shuttlesworth shared the stage at the packed mass meeting with King, Ralph Abernathy, and Bernard Lee, who in a few years would be an insider himself, as King's personal minder. Shuttlesworth's praise of the "*moving* students" contained a joyous edge of vindication. But in fact the sudden sit-in movement had left him in a quandary about how to proceed on his own turf. His matron-heavy Alabama Christian Movement seemed unequal to sit-ins on a scale proportionate to Birmingham's size.

On Friday, February 26, Bull Connor threw down the gauntlet—a press release proclaiming that he would "*not* permit organized, planned and deliberate efforts to foment violence and interfere with the rights of others," such as the unspecified incidents "throughout the Southeast." Shuttlesworth retorted that the commissioner had insulted the intelligence of Birmingham's Negroes. But he was hoping that the local college students would spare him from having personally to prove Connor wrong.

A student movement had been struggling for definition at Miles, the city's only four-year black college, situated on the thirty most barren acres of U.S. Steel's model mill town of Fairfield. While the cachet of Morehouse, Fisk, Tuskegee, Talladega, and Howard attracted the children of Birmingham's black bourgeoisie, Miles—named after a bishop of the Colored (or Christian, as of 1956) Methodist Episcopal denomination that established the school in 1905— drew from the enterprising offspring of Birmingham's working class, such as Pollie Anne Myers, as well as promising rural youth, such as Autherine Juanita Lucy. The iron-handed college president, W. A. Bell, scraped and cajoled to sustain Miles's second-class accreditation (specifically for black schools), and it would have surprised the students that the dull old man had nurtured the Southern Negro Youth Congress radicals who had made Miles their base in the 1940s. He had even served on its advisory board until Bull Connor red-baited the final SNYC conference in 1948, and Bell testily told SNYC's Communist leaders that they had brought it on themselves. Bell kept his distance from "extremists" like Shuttlesworth, having come to believe that "Negro betterment" was a function of ambassadorship into white America rather than organized struggle.

The student body president, Jesse Walker, was the son of hard-working menial laborers. He had a good part-time job, a car, a little disposable income, and, recently, a rebellious impulse. Walker belonged to a longstanding Y-sponsored interracial group of college students motivated mainly by religious faith. Its current leader was Tommy Reeves, an asthmatic, bespectacled (white) Birmingham-

---

* In downtown Montgomery the next day, the *Montgomery Advertiser*'s young photographer Charles Moore got a clear shot of a white man cracking a black female shopper over the head with a baseball bat. The attacker was identified in the caption of the page-one picture, but it was Moore who got the death threats. His brilliant career making segregation graphic for a mass audience was under way.

Southern ministerial student with a Phi Beta Kappa key, who a year earlier had stood up at the organizational meeting of the Methodist Layman's Union and told the judges, lawyers, real estate suzerains, and Bull Connor that what they were doing was not Christian, that there were no slaves in Christianity. He was shouted down from the rostrum and followed back to campus by Kluxers—or perhaps policemen in unmarked cars. And then within two days, the MLU had had him fired from the small Methodist church he pastored.

Reeves had been captivated by the student sit-ins spreading across the South, and he went over to Miles College on Sunday night, February 28, to work up a plan with Walker and a couple of other students. Rather than just pile down to the lunch counters with everyone else, the students were hoping to do something with more spiritual verve. They settled on a round-the-clock prayer demonstration—a Vigil for Freedom—to coincide with the southern senators' "round-the-clock filibuster" against the feeble Civil Rights Act of 1960; Alabama's once liberal hope, Senator Lister Hill, was fueling up with oatmeal and wheat germ.

At around 6:45 Monday evening, Jesse Walker led twelve students into Kelly Ingram Park downtown, carrying placards of high moral aim—"The Law of God Will Be Fulfilled." Fred Shuttlesworth was there to greet them. He had decided not to butt in on the students' protest, but told them not to be alarmed or ashamed if the police hauled them off, that he would get them legal representation. Walker and another student leader followed Shuttlesworth into the adjacent Gaston Motel to talk more strategy.

Before they emerged, Bull Connor's police had wheeled up to Ingram Park, in the maiden run of a "strictly confidential" new police maneuver for racial emergencies: "Signal 31-Green." The cops must have felt somewhat deflated at the sight of the well-dressed young men armed with nothing but piety, but they took them to headquarters. The authorities just wanted to "get acquainted with them," the police chief explained upon releasing them without booking them, adding, "Should the students demonstrate again, we will get acquainted with more of them." The students called off their vigil, wanting no further acquaintance with Bull Connor, who had met this new law enforcement challenge by calling up 433 firemen for riot training. A police officer had just gone to Baltimore, the pioneer K-9 city, to train Birmingham's first dog cop, King.

In Montgomery the next day, March 1, after another strategy session with Ralph Abernathy, who had succeeded Martin Luther King as president of the Montgomery Improvement Association, Bernard Lee led half the Alabama State student body—more than a thousand—two by two to the capitol, which was closed for Mardi Gras. King and Abernathy had dissuaded them from sitting in, out of concern for the college president, whom Governor John Patterson had ordered to expel his student troublemakers. Instead, the protesters assembled in the portico and sang "The Lord's Prayer" and "The Star-Spangled Banner." The following week, embattled Alabama State administrators shooed student pickets off the campus into a waiting barricade of policemen bearing tear gas, carbines, and submachine guns. Thirty-five were arrested, the first jailings of the new youth movement in Alabama.

Shuttlesworth, who had been in and out of Montgomery fanning the protest, was appalled at what happened next. Despite Abernathy's urging, the Montgomery Improvement Association abandoned the students. Normally, Shuttlesworth ribbed his Montgomery colleagues that the MIA tended toward "a million dollars' worth of discussion and thirty-five cents' worth of action." Now, he told Abernathy how disappointed he was in his stewardship. "Fred, *I'm* not a dictator," Abernathy said, pulling out the standard charge against Shuttlesworth (whose standard response was, "God is a dictator, a benevolent dictator"). Then Abernathy pointed out that Birmingham's student movement wasn't exactly a ball of fire either.

Nor was it likely to become one after March 12, when the knock on the door came for the Miles College football star Robert "Jug" Jones, one of the praying Vigil for Freedom students whose names and addresses the *Birmingham News* had printed. Jones's mother let in five white men who identified themselves as police officers. Three more came in through the back door carrying guns, pipes, and leather blackjacks studded with razor blades. Mattie Jones reputedly said they would get to her son "over my dead body," and was nearly obliged. Multiple head wounds and a broken leg landed her in the hospital, where she recognized the two deputies who visited her the next day as her assailants. Jug Jones had been beaten, too, but he had been spared serious injury, perhaps in deference to his gridiron talent.

On March 15 in Atlanta, when students staged their first lunch-counter sit-ins, Martin Luther King—who had been praising student activists elsewhere—did not object when the black city fathers nixed future protests. Shuttlesworth, by contrast, found himself in the odd role of avant-garde elder statesman, spurring on rather than reining in his apprentices. Student body president Jesse Walker was making little militant headway at Miles. In a private meeting with W. A. Bell, he found the college president surprisingly sympathetic, but the old man's first priority was shielding his school from controversy. Walker told him he couldn't stop history. Bell would die trying, his anguish heightened by how well he had enforced a peace he did not quite approve of.

On March 30, Shuttlesworth issued a press release calling sit-ins a "necessary tonic for a sickened democracy"—and couldn't resist a sly dig at the recent arrivals on the law enforcement scene, "horseback riders, firemen and fire hoses, and even dogs." If the police are so shorthanded, he said, "many Negroes are qualified, available, and willing." Then, despairing of recruiting sit-in volunteers at Miles, he sent one of his toughest lieutenants to the city's other black (two-year) college, Daniel Payne, affiliated with the African Methodist Episcopal church.

Thirty-five-year-old Charles Billups, an assistant pastor and Boy Scout leader, was slender and wore glasses, and did not look like someone who had survived a Navy shipwreck during World War II; as a gunner's mate in Korea he had

earned a Medal of Honor as well as a metal plate in his head. Next to Shuttlesworth he was the Movement's luckiest survivor. The previous April, leaving his
shift at Hayes Aircraft at 1 a.m., Billups and two black co-workers had been blind-
folded and hustled into the back of separate cars by rifle-waving white men.
Billups had been in the news a few months earlier when he was sentenced to ninety
days and $95 for touching a detective's lapel at a Movement meeting. The white
men drove him into the woods and grilled him about the ACMHR's plans. Then
they beat him numb with chains, tied him to a tree, and branded his stomach with
"KKK" while ordering, "Nigger, stop that praying." Billups told Shuttlesworth afterward, "I know you want to know what I felt. I felt sorry for them." And indeed
when one of his remorseful attackers came to his house later and offered to turn
himself in to the police, Billups had suggested that they pray together instead.

Billups had no trouble coaxing a handful of Daniel Payne students into his
car for a ride to Shuttlesworth's house. Jesse Walker came over from Miles in a
borrowed car, to throw the cops off the scent. In his living room, Shuttlesworth
told the students, "Bull's not God, and we can't let him act like it."

The next morning, ten volunteers, wearing coats and ties, met with Shuttlesworth, pledged nonviolence, synchronized their watches, and at around ten
departed in pairs for the five largest food-serving stores downtown, written down
on a list at Shuttlesworth's the night before. They were to go to a department
some distance from the lunch counter and make a purchase. At Woolworth's, Jesse
Walker bought handkerchiefs and a birthday card for a friend. The students were
to be on the lunch counter floor at 10:27, and by 10:29 within sight of it. At exactly
10:30, each of five counters around the city had two black customers.

Within ten minutes, Bull Connor's men had blocked off traffic around the
stores and arrested all ten students for trespassing after warning. In front of Newberry's, Shuttlesworth argued with an officer about his right to stand on the sidewalk and was loaded into a squad car, along with the Reverend J. S. Phifer
(Shuttlesworth's driver at Phillips High School). They were taken to jail on
charges of vagrancy.

Right after posting bond, Shuttlesworth and Phifer were rejailed for "aiding
and abetting" the sit-ins: Before the youths bailed out, they had told detectives
about the list of target stores they had drawn up at Shuttlesworth's house the
night before. As another Shuttlesworth precedent set out for the Supreme Court,*
a telegram arrived from Martin Luther King. "You have transformed the jail from
a dungeon of shame into a haven of freedom and a badge of honor," he wrote to
the first of the Movement elders to be jailed for sitting in (and he hadn't even sat
in). "I know you will face this situation with the same courage that has always
guided your epic-making career. Continue the great work with the conviction
that unearned suffering is redemptive."

---

* Justice Hugo Black would recognize the name of Shuttlesworth's bail bondsman as the now dis-
barred lawyer Jim Esdale, who had been his kingmaker as the state boss of the Ku Klux Klan in its
"liberal" political heyday of the 1920s.

Oliver's Return

THE DANIEL PAYNE NINE went from jail to a meeting of cheering students at the college chapel. But by the next day, Saturday, April 2, the temperature on campus had dropped. Bull Connor had been massaging Payne's president, Howard Gregg. The commissioner was offering to drop the trespassing charges against the students in exchange for their testimony supporting the conspiracy case against Shuttlesworth. Gregg ordered them to accept Connor's generosity. Most were ready to capitulate until Robert King, the student body president, and James Kidd, a favorite social studies teacher, bustled them off to the professor's campus residence for a little pep talk.

Jesse Walker and Tommy Reeves drove up to Kidd's house at around seven. Reeves was in a bit of hot water himself for sending Governor Patterson a statement—signed by ninety-seven fellow Birmingham-Southern students, mostly women—protesting the expulsion of the Alabama State "ringleaders." (Patterson had immediately forwarded photocopies to the Birmingham police and the local media.) A third mediator was at Kidd's house when Reeves and Walker arrived. He was one of Birmingham's early, accidental civil rights gladiators, an uncommon preacher named C. Herbert Oliver, now returning to the arena.

Oliver had once hoped, like many an ambitious black youth, to find freedom through one of the white-approved areas of Negro achievement, sports or entertainment. And like many graduates of Birmingham's Industrial High School for Negroes, he had wanted to become a musician, after the example of the school's famous bandmaster, John T. "Fess" Whatley. He was practically a one-man underground railroad for talented blacks out to New York, supplying the orchestras of Louis Armstrong, Cab Calloway, Duke Ellington, and Billie Holiday. But a profession of faith had propelled young Oliver instead to an unaccredited Bible school in Nyack, New York, and then to Wheaton College in Illinois for a B.A. degree. He was a "nice-looking Negro," as white people called his light-skinned, pebble-faced type, with a demeanor somewhere between serious and lugubrious. He had had no plans to preach the controversial social gospel when he returned home in 1947, until the police shot an old black minister, a father of thirteen, who had, allegedly, been peeping into the homes of white people.

In late April 1948, Oliver read in the paper that Bull Connor had intimidated Sixteenth Street Baptist's pastor into withdrawing his church as the host of the Southern Negro Youth Congress's annual convention. Oliver, whose hero Fess Whatley had put on "Musical Extravaganza" fund-raisers for the SNYC, called the executive secretary, Louis Burnham, and asked if the congress was either a Communist or Communist front organization. Burnham said no. Oliver offered his Christian Missionary Alliance church, a tiny house on the same block as Sixteenth Street Baptist.

Oliver had been one of those arrested at his church during the convention, along with SCEF's Jim Dombrowski and Senator Glen Taylor. When Oliver was defrocked by the white officials of his segregated denomination (a splinter of

Presbyterianism), Burnham had tried to persuade him to start his own church, one that he felt could capture the spirit of rank-and-file defiance that was a by-product of the SNYC debacle. But Oliver did not share Burnham's view of the revolutionary potential of the black church. "Jesus had established the church, and I couldn't see starting a movement around my arrest," he said.

Oliver left Birmingham, worked in New York as a clothes presser (his father's trade), earned a master's from Philadelphia's Westminster Theological Seminary, pastored a small white congregation in Holton, Maine, and returned home at age thirty-four following the death of his father, in 1959. He was a pastor with impressive credentials—he had published a book, *No Flesh Shall Glory*—but no inclination to sit around with Big Preachers and laugh at "little niggers." Still, Shuttlesworth's ACMHR could offer him no suitable leadership role. "My heart was with Fred, but I couldn't lay down my mind and go along with everything he wanted," Oliver said. So he put his energies behind an idea that he hoped would reengage the Reverend J. L. Ware, who had been sulking since the failed bus boycott of 1958.

Oliver formed the Inter-Citizens Committee*—including Ware and six other clergymen, plus two white members—to target the heart of the segregationist beast: the police department. Since the force-wide blue wall of silence made federal statutes covering police brutality virtually impossible to enforce, Oliver decided to appeal to the court of public opinion. Clergymen, U.S. senators, and Justice Department officials, as well as friendly local politicians and Big Mules, made up the mailing list for his affidavits professionally documenting police abuse of blacks. His first was the Miles football player Jug Jones's mother's account of her beating. The second would be his own current predicament.

His friend on the Payne faculty, James Kidd, had called Oliver to the emergency session at his house. Oliver reasoned quietly with the kids that they simply ought to consult a lawyer, while Jesse Walker played the bad cop and scolded them. With Payne's Robert King holding on to his courage, the students telephoned President Gregg to inform him of their decision not to sell Shuttlesworth out. Gregg called the Birmingham police on the "outside agitators." Three squad cars pulled up in front of Kidd's house.

Gregg had begged the police not to embarrass him further by making the arrests on college property, so Oliver, Reeves, and Walker were safe as long as they stayed inside. At six in the morning of Sunday, April 3, during the police's shift change, they slipped off the campus. Seven hours later, a plainclothes policeman found Tommy Reeves at the little Methodist church where he served as music director, charged him—at his place of employment—with vagrancy, and took him to jail. (The Methodist Layman's Union had put out the word that the NAACP and the Communist Party were paying Reeves's new church a thousand dollars a

---

* Fess Whatley, a strong Shuttlesworth supporter, chewed Oliver out for teaming up with Shuttlesworth's rival. But Oliver believed that Ware liked Shuttlesworth and admired what he was doing, yet felt that the mission was an exercise in frustration he had already gone through.

month to keep him there for his integration work.) That evening, the police came for "Hubert" Oliver, yanking the hook off his screen door and dragging him onto the sidewalk by his bathrobe. Only upon checking his rap sheet would Bull Connor realize that Oliver was the same man he had run out of town with the Communists a dozen years before, even though the officer who arrested him should have known: He was the department's new "subversives" specialist, Detective Tom Cook, one of the "steelworkers" who set J. B. Stoner up to bomb Shuttlesworth's church in 1958.

At two the next morning, the police finally arrived at the Miles campus and hauled Jesse Walker to jail, accusing him of "intimidating a witness." Walker said later, recalling his harsh words for the Payne students at Kidd's house, "Well, I guess I was guilty of that." For a night, with Fred Shuttlesworth also in jail again, Birmingham's streets were free of civil rights agitators. Arthur Shores bonded them out the next day, returning provisionally to a Movement that was no longer Shuttlesworth's lonely battle. The battery of defense lawyers that Shores led into lowly recorder's court on Monday night—virtually the entire local black bar (with Ella Baker on hand as an observer for SCLC)—announced his intention to take this claim to the Supreme Court:* And this time, in the due course of legalism and gradualism, he was finally going to end segregation in the field of "public accommodations," which he had pioneered unsuccessfully twelve years before when Senator Glen Taylor tried to walk through the "Colored" entrance of Herb Oliver's church.

"Saulsbury"

HARRISON SALISBURY, a celebrated reporter for the *New York Times*, arrived in Birmingham on April 6. A few years back from his Pulitzer-winning tour in the Soviet Union, he had been assigned to do a series on southern cities as "a thorough situationer on the sit-downs." Standing next to Vulcan on top of Red Mountain, where John Milner had dreamed up his great workshop town, Salisbury had conceived what would prove to be another history-making view of Birmingham. His apocalyptic two-part story began on the front page of the *New York Times* on April 12, under the headline "Fear and Hatred Grip Birmingham":

> From Red Mountain, where a cast-iron Vulcan looks down 500 feet to the sprawling city, Birmingham seems veiled in the poisonous fumes of distant battles.
>
> On a fine April day, however, it is only the haze of acid fog belched

---

* Bull Connor answered the challenge the day after the routine convictions by beefing up the city's trespassing ordinance such that they subjected "almost any Negro customer to arrest," Emory O. Jackson noted in the *World*. Oliver, who was charged with vagrancy and intimidating a witness, was found not guilty at his trial that Monday night. Payne president Howard Gregg was a witness for the prosecution. Jesse Walker was acquitted of the intimidation charge but convicted of trespassing (in the sit-ins).

from the stacks of the Tennessee Coal and Iron Company's Fairfield and Ensley works that lies over the city.

But more than a few citizens, both white and Negro, harbor growing fear that the hour will strike when the smoke of civil strife will mingle with that of the hearths and forges. . . .

Every channel of communication, every medium of mutual interest, every reasoned approach, every inch of middle ground has been fragmented by the emotional dynamite of racism, reinforced by the whip, the razor, the gun, the bomb, the torch, the club, the knife, the mob, the police and many branches of the state's apparatus.

Salisbury's paint-stripping prose described white men—a pastor, a lawyer, a college president, a newspaperman—fearful as children about telling civic tales out of school to a Yankee reporter. "Be careful of what you say and who you mention," said a rabbi whom Salisbury disguised in his piece as a businessman. "Lives are at stake." Herb Oliver had given Salisbury his affidavit on the beating of Jug Jones's mother, providing the article's most sensational anecdote. But only Shuttlesworth had spoken of fear fearlessly and for the record. "He seemed to get a kick out of his role," Salisbury noticed. His expression in the *Times* photograph was a goofy sort of smirk.

The local white reaction to the article bypassed shame and went straight to outrage. The two newspapers led a hysterical counteroffensive—"Radio Moscow please copy," one columnist wrote. Both dailies reprinted the story in full. "Can this be Birmingham?" read the *News*'s page-one headline. "N.Y. Times slanders our city." What perhaps wounded white Birmingham's dignity more than the inventory of police brutality, false arrest, vigilante skull-crushing, and dynamiting (twenty-two bombings, all unsolved, of black homes and churches) was the catalogue of stupidity: libraries banning a book about white and black rabbits, whites rallying to keep "Negro music" off the airwaves (a project of Ace Carter, a pure country fan). The story's comic relief was provided by Bull Connor. His malapropisms—Salisbury had quoted his 1938 debut line to the Southern Conference for Human Welfare, "White and Negro are not to segregate together"—had a certain cracker charm when repeated over a Scotch at the country club. But in the black-and-white columns of the *Times,* Bull's eccentricities tainted the city fathers' hard-earned gentility.

Though Birmingham was growing accustomed to the outside media hits known in Chamber of Commerce jargon as "black eyes," the Salisbury article was finally the "pitiless, blatant publicity" that W.E.B. Du Bois had advocated as a catalyst of change in his "Behold the Land" speech fourteen years earlier. The dean of local columnists resentfully compared the piece to *Uncle Tom's Cabin,* which had helped start the Civil War. A visiting *Washington Post* reporter likened its impact on the city to "a bucket of cold water in the face." A psychologist might have characterized the shock as cognitive dissonance, this trauma of confronting a truth that contradicted the country club consensus once described by Sinclair Lewis as the "ecstasy of honest self-appreciation."

Sid Smyer found himself denouncing "Saaaalzbury's damn lies," but he was one of those in a position to be grateful for what the reporter had not mentioned—Judge Aaron's castration, for example. The old pragmatist had begun to take the city's problems seriously enough to have gone on the offensive against the bad press. Two years earlier, he and a few other Chamber of Commerce muck-a-mucks had hired a Louisville-based consulting firm, the Southern Institute of Management, to conduct an objective study of Birmingham, a "Metropolitan Audit" to gird them with "good points" against a "growing body of outside criticism." The results had not come back yet, in time to block Salisbury's mortal blow.

Smyer's old mentor, Jim Simpson, was not so encumbered by self-doubt. He took the *Times* affront personally: After all, he had helped create the "state's apparatus" Salisbury had so witheringly invoked. And the self-important Salisbury was the sort of journalist who could stir up Simpson's testosterone. When Simpson received copies of the article in the mail from Bull Connor, he proposed that the city commission sue the *Times* and "this man Saulsbury" for their "ruthless attacks on this region and its people." To pave the way for the lawsuit, he sent the *Times* a demand for a retraction over the commissioners' names, covering virtually every unattributed statement in Salisbury's story (plus the headline and photo captions), particularly the observation that Bull's 1957 comeback campaign—the one Simpson had micromanaged—was based on "race hate." Simpson's temper tantrums had a way of creating public melodramas, and this one marked his return to a national stage he had vacated after his precedent-setting "Cry Nigger" Senate campaign in 1944. This racial vendetta would be diverted into a First Amendment crisis, a constitutional landmark battle over libel law ultimately known as *The New York Times* v. *Sullivan*—and another Supreme Court precedent for Fred Shuttlesworth.

SNCC

SHUTTLESWORTH NEVER LET HIMSELF get too hung up on what the white folks were up to, and on April 15, the day Simpson was plotting with the commissioners, he was on his way to Raleigh to help Ella Baker formalize the student movement that had coalesced around lunch counters across the South. This was her gift to the civil rights struggle before handing the reins of SCLC over to a new executive director, Wyatt Tee Walker, a bracing combination of intellect and irreverence from Petersburg, Virginia, who had attended his first SCLC board meeting that December, in Birmingham. Though a Baptist preacher, Walker spoke the same "progressive" idiom as Baker. In the 1940s, while spending summers in Harlem (he went to high school in New Jersey), he had joined the Young Communist League after hearing Paul Robeson speak, and though he still kept up his subscription to the *Daily Worker,* he had never seriously bought into the discipline. The main attraction of the YCL was that he was "fascinated with the prospect of having a social relationship with white girls." Walker, needless to say, was something of a scandalist, and this radical edge, combined with his being on "Mike" terms with Martin Luther King (that had been his boyhood name, still used by his intimates), made Baker believe that he might have better luck waking up SCLC than she had.

In her farewell maneuver, Baker persuaded King to raid SCLC's treasury for $800 to fund the conference of young sit-in veterans to be held over Easter weekend at Raleigh's Shaw University, where she had been class valedictorian a few decades earlier. King received no mention in Baker's press release announcing it, except obliquely, in her endorsement of the students' group-centered rather than leader-centered approach as "refreshing indeed to those of the older group who bear the scars of battle, the frustrations and disillusionment that come when the prophetic leader turns out to have heavy feet of clay."

Baker had turned to her closest ally among that "older group," Shuttlesworth, who understood that the students' revolt was against not only the white South but also the "Negro leadership" of the past fifty years. She asked him to be on hand to help her resist the pressure she feared that King would exert to make the student movement an arm of SCLC. At the meeting, Baker's program went off without a hitch. King made a nice speech, but the three hundred young people resolved to form a decentralized, democratically run independent organization: the Student Nonviolent Coordinating Committee, whose acronym— SNCC (or Snick)—echoed its SNYC predecessor.

Bernard Lee and Jesse Walker, who had driven up to Raleigh with Shuttlesworth's lieutenant Charles Billups, were named to the coordinating committee from Alabama. Attending from Daniel Payne, Robert King, whose own activist days would end at commencement, was most impressed by Guy Carawan, the Highlander Folk School's resident folklorist, a Californian with southern parents hired at the recommendation of Pete Seeger. He encouraged the crowd to come up with new verses for one of the most stirring melodies King had ever heard, a "powerful, welling thing," one reporter wrote, called "We Shall Overcome." A white student at the meeting said of the song, "It was inspiring because it was the beginning, and because, in a sense, it was the purest moment."

And in a way this was the beginning, Shuttlesworth's "new dimension." With the creation of SNCC, "direct action" had now become a given, and not simply the "neurotic" compulsion of the SCLC renegade known to his colleagues as the Wild Man from Birmingham.

G-Man

AS THE MOVEMENT GAINED its new dimension, so did the resistance. The outcasts had gathered in the wings, as if for some long-awaited opening night. The arch-villain was Robert Chambliss, a deceptively banal bit of business; he was no more mysterious than city hall itself, though the relationship between the two now seemed a bit rocky. His sidekick, Troy Ingram, had more tragic glamour, as the bastard prince of the King of the Southern Iron World, Henry Fairchild De-Bardeleben, but he was still evolving. The other notorious rogue, J. B. Stoner, was Atlanta's gift to Birmingham, the "outside agitator." Ace Carter, the country folks' revenge, was quiescent for now, but his lawyer had convinced George Wallace's aides as he was being outniggered by John Patterson that what their campaign needed was someone who could "get those rednecks all stirred up." He gave them Ace's name.

Together, these characters told a familiar civic story: that Birmingham brought the worst on itself and then blamed Atlanta. But the man who would complete the cast for Birmingham's coming tragedy really did justify the orgy of civic self-pity currently being directed at the *New York Times.* He was the deus ex machina, no fault of the city's, and the fate that sent him here had taken the guise of the United States Justice Department.

Gary Thomas Rowe Jr. was a lost mercenary soul, an overweight, florid-faced guy with a law enforcement complex. With more education and grooming, this eighth-grade dropout from Savannah, Georgia, might have indulged his fantasies on the police beat of a newspaper. Instead, at age twenty-seven, he worked in the pasteurizing room of the White Dairy Company. By night, however, hunched over his Formica booth, brew and cigarette in hand, at the VFW club near city hall, he was Captain Law Enforcement. He claimed to be a real policeman, but that got him into a spot, since cops and his ilk tended to hang around the same watering holes. Though many policemen chummily indulged Rowe's fantasies, a few had gotten to resent him as "a Disney character," and he had been fined $30 for impersonating an officer in September 1956. Recently, however, he had gone for a bigger lie. He was saying he worked for the U.S. government—an FBI man.

FBI nuts like Rowe were an unfortunate consequence of J. Edgar Hoover's PR masterpiece, the romance of the G-man, and Birmingham's special agent in charge, Clarence Kelley, assigned this routine wrist slap to a twenty-eight-year-old rookie agent, a recent law school graduate named Barrett Kemp. In early April, Kemp went out to Rowe's house, and after several minutes of small talk the suspect said, "Well, why are you here? What have I did?" Kemp explained, but did not seem upset.

Kemp asked Rowe if he had any contacts in the Ku Klux Klan. Rowe replied that as a matter of fact the bartender at the VFW had just invited him to apply. His name was Loyal McWhorter. Perhaps what explained the FBI's sudden interest in the klavern was the law of action and reaction, the fear that the flowering of civil rights protest around the South was bound to be answered. Instead of penalizing Tommy Rowe for impersonating an FBI man, Special Agent Barry Kemp made his wildest dreams come true: He offered him a job spying on the Klan for the FBI. "If it is in the best interests of my country" was how Rowe would later say he accepted, a romantic from the start.

On April 18, the FBI officially opened its informant file on Gary Thomas

Rowe Jr. The timing was priceless. The power center of the Klan in America was about to move from Georgia to Alabama.

Grand Dragon Bobby Shelton, the highest Alabama official in Eldon Edwards's Atlanta-based U.S. Klans, had been feeling his oats ever since becoming a player on Governor John Patterson's team. A blank-eyed, malapropism-prone member of the Tuscaloosa klavern, Shelton had been one of the local rubber workers in the mob that kept the University of Alabama Autherine Lucy–free. In light of Patterson's well-publicized political indebtedness to him, B. F. Goodrich had promoted Shelton off the factory floor and named him the company's representative to sell tires to the state. But despite his access to the governor and the $1.6 million government contract he had secured for the company, Goodrich must have had second thoughts about all the Klan publicity and had recently let Shelton go.

Shelton had no use for the Imperial office in Atlanta, which had been accusing him of misappropriating funds (that is, refusing to give the home office its share of the province's dues). On April 11, a week before Tommy Rowe became an FBI informant, Imperial Wizard Edwards advised the Alabama secretary of state that Shelton was no longer the "authorized agent" of the U.S. Klans, Knights of the Ku Klux Klan, Inc. Shelton countered that he was organizing an independent Klan and taking Edwards's Alabama franchisees with him. On May 17, Shelton incorporated the Alabama Knights, Knights of the Ku Klux Klan, Inc. One of the Big Mules' old retainers inside the Klan claimed that John Patterson was behind Shelton's power grab, seeing in him a built-in political base.

The flagship klavern of what would indeed become the mightiest Klan organization in the world was Eastview 13, the newest incarnation of Birmingham's hard-core Klansmen: Robert Chambliss, Earl "Shorty" Thompson, and Loyal McWhorter, who had recruited Rowe. The FBI seemed unperturbed by the red flags in Rowe's background—Klan informants were bound not to be Jaycee material. That Rowe had added three years to his age to qualify for the Georgia National Guard when he dropped out of school in eighth grade might have struck the agents as the sort of noble white lie told by underage World War II enlistees. Rowe had also been arrested at eighteen in Savannah for carrying a pistol without a permit and had shot himself, perhaps accidentally. Special Agent Barry Kemp and his superiors seemed so kindly disposed to Rowe that they apparently accepted his explanation that the bar owner who had accused him of impersonating a Birmingham police officer in 1956 was lying, even though the bureau's acquaintance with Rowe was a result of his having impersonated an FBI agent.

The bureau's embrace of Rowe seemed odd in light of a memo Washington had sent to the FBI field offices five months earlier, warning that a "potential informant on Klan matters" who didn't make the cut later misrepresented himself as "a former FBI agent." Headquarters had urged a "thorough, intensive background investigation and careful personal scrutiny," to check for "some weakness as to stability and reliability." Instead of proceeding cautiously with Rowe, the

Birmingham bureau congratulated itself on its great fortune in finding him in the nick of time: Almost as soon as he infiltrated the organization, Klan violence in Birmingham flared, and would burn for as long as he remained in town.

Sullivan

THE BEST LAWYERS in Alabama had now joined forces with the public officials against the *New York Times* to create another state "apparatus" to muzzle unpopular opinion, in this case from the national press. While plotting his offensive against Harrison Salisbury, Jim Simpson had been talking strategy with his opposite numbers at Montgomery's leading corporate law firm, and on April 19 his colleagues there filed libel suits against the *Times* for $1.5 million on behalf of Montgomery's three city commissioners. Whereas Simpson was at least contesting the paper's news coverage, the Montgomery team had abandoned all pretense of fair play and was claiming that its officials had been defamed by a *Times* advertisement.

The ad in question was the handiwork of Bayard Rustin, who was now working for SCLC out of its small New York office. Ever since the state of Alabama indicted Martin Luther King on tax violations the previous month, Rustin had been beating the bushes of public outrage, while lawyers from New York, Chicago, and Alabama (notably Arthur Shores) bickered over how best to handle King's defense—the "Yankees" were fobbing the technical work off on the southerners and paying them half their own $300 day rate for court appearances. To raise the legal fees, Rustin had persuaded Philip Randolph to chair a Committee to Defend Martin Luther King, with a letterhead ornamented by Harry Belafonte, Marlon Brando, Nat King Cole, Van Heflin, Eartha Kitt, Sidney Poitier, John Raitt, Jackie Robinson, and Shelley Winters. Within a week it had $10,000 toward its $200,000 goal.

The committee's full-page ad had run in the *New York Times* on March 29, taking its title, "Heed Their Rising Voices," from the headline of a March 19 *Times* editorial praising the South's "growing movement of peaceful demonstrations by Negroes." The ad copy concerned not King's tax case but the sit-ins in the South. Rustin described King as the movement's "spiritual leader"—with a narrowly technical accuracy, bordering on bad faith, that would have choked Ella Baker and Fred Shuttlesworth, who was plotting actual sit-ins in Birmingham on the day the ad was published. The state of Alabama's harassment of the Montgomery students was the meat of the ad, though it mentioned no official by name or title.

One of segregation's many clever lawyers, however, decided that the ad—and by extension the *Times*—had defamed Montgomery's public safety commissioner, L. B. Sullivan, a quiet, moonfaced former state director of public safety elected after the bus boycott on a pledge to attract business to Montgomery. That is, defamed a public servant who, three weeks before the ad ran, had praised the spirit of "cooperation" between a mob of five thousand whites and the police, fire-men, and a mounted "race riot" posse who had turned back Negroes marching to the capitol to protest the Alabama State expulsions.

Despite Sullivan's well-publicized professional attitude toward blacks, the *Times* was not taking the commissioners' suits lightly. The plaintiffs had found four excuses to file in state court rather than federal court (which was likely to be less hostile to the Yankee press). To the lineup of luminaries—now including Eleanor Roosevelt, Diahann Carroll, the playwright Lorraine Hansberry, Langston Hughes, Mahalia Jackson, Howard University's Mordecai Johnson, the actors Hope Lange and Maureen Stapleton, A. J. Muste—Rustin had at the last minute added the Southern Christian Leadership Conference's board members: Ralph Abernathy and Fred Shuttlesworth, followed by Wyatt Tee Walker, Joe Lowery, and Solomon Seay, the MIA board member who was "the most argumen-tative person" Shuttlesworth had ever met, even when he agreed with you.* Their names—under the line "We in the south who are struggling daily for dignity and freedom warmly endorse this appeal"—conferred indigenous authenticity on what Rustin feared might have otherwise seemed like a giant celebrity backrub.

Shuttlesworth, Abernathy, Lowery, and Seay were named as co-defendants in L. B. Sullivan's lawsuit against the *New York Times.* It was their Alabama resi-dency that gave the Montgomery plaintiffs the entree needed to get the case be-fore a state judge. But then again, another school of thought was that Sullivan and his handlers were merely using the *Times* as a pretext to go after the four ministers and shut down civil rights activities in Alabama.

Any "truth is the best defense" strategy the *Times* might have mounted against the libel charges went out the window when the paper's Montgomery stringer, assigned to fact-check the ad, discovered that Rustin had been a bit cre-ative. The Alabama State students had sung "The Star-Spangled Banner" on the capitol steps, not, as the ad claimed, "My Country 'Tis of Thee," and "police armed with shotguns and teargas" had not exactly "ringed" the campus, but merely repulsed the students who were leaving it. The most serious error was the colorful line about the Alabama State dining hall being padlocked to starve the students into submission. "Absolutely no truth," the beleaguered college presi-dent told the stringer.

The *Times* retracted the errors—an unprecedented action in response to an ad, as the *Chicago Daily News* fretted. The *Times* had earlier taken the also unusual measure of publishing, on its front page, the Birmingham Chamber of Com-merce's "rebuttal" to the two-part Harrison Salisbury article. But Birmingham's pride had not been salvaged. The *Post-Herald* complained that the chamber's "timid, almost apologetic" statement should have been "thrown into the waste basket." On May 6, seventeen days after Sullivan et al. sued the *Times,* Jim Simp-son brought the Birmingham city commissioners' $1.5 million libel suit against

---

* Seay had been one of the three Montgomery ministers whose incognito jailing by the Birming-ham police during the brief 1958 bus boycott had caused national outrage.

the paper and Harrison E. Salisbury, for subjecting them to "public contempt, ridicule, shame and disgrace."

O'Dell Redux

FRED SHUTTLESWORTH did not see the "Heed Their Rising Voices" ad until he was in New York around the first of May and dropped by Bayard Rustin's office. His first reaction was amazement that so many celebrities had signed it—"people about whom I had read in the newspaper." The ad was turning him into a celebrity, too: a protagonist in a First Amendment crisis over the freedom of the press to criticize the government, leading to landmark constitutional law. But *New York Times* v. *Sullivan* was not the sort of notoriety Shuttlesworth's co-defendants had been bucking for. Ralph Abernathy, Joe Lowery, and Solomon Seay were pained that Rustin had not gotten their permission to use their names and complained to Martin Luther King. Shuttlesworth felt that Rustin's detractors inside SCLC were worrying too much about what the white folks might think. "I was not an apologetist for segregation," he said. "If the ad was wrong in some respects, it was practically right in all respects." But *Sullivan* was not the least of the troubles Rustin's Committee to Defend Martin Luther King would bring upon the civil rights movement.

Early that year while planning an SCLC benefit for the May 17 anniversary of *Brown*, Rustin had remembered the crack organizer who had surprised everyone a year earlier by recruiting southern college students for the Youth March for Integrated Schools on Washington. Jack O'Dell had begun to sense that the civil rights movement was about to take off—"When black people suddenly figured out that one hundred years after the Emancipation Proclamation they still couldn't get a cup of coffee at a lunch counter, I knew all hell was going to break loose." Though he had no beef with the Communist Party—FBI sources had him elected to its national committee as Cornelius James in December 1959*—he figured that "we were likely to get civil rights before we got socialism." He had let his Party membership lapse (after 1958, he claimed) by the time Rustin recruited him to the Committee to Defend Martin Luther King.

In February, hard at work in Rustin's office, O'Dell had received another subpoena from the House Un-American Activities Committee. In his previous appearance before HUAC, in the summer of 1958, he had frostily asked the committee's staff director, Richard Arens, if he knew "about the subversive activities in this country that began with the slavery of the Negro people, and have been going on for 300 years." Arens drew himself up indignantly and said, "Do you honestly feel, and are you trying to make this committee and the people of this country believe, that you, a member of the Communist conspiracy, responsive to the will of the Kremlin, are in truth and in fact, concerned with the welfare of the

---

* "When I heard that, I was as surprised as anyone," O'Dell said. "How could I be on the national committee and not stand for election?"

Negro people of this country?" O'Dell had replied, "I wouldn't try to make you believe anything." (A sage position, given that Arens was a paid consultant on a project bankrolled by a New York millionaire to prove that black people were genetically inferior.)

This time, O'Dell took the First and Fifth Amendments so impassively that he was dismissed forthwith. He went straight to Rustin to tell him about the hearing. The tone-deaf Rustin said fine, no problem. O'Dell's first official signature as an associate of Martin Luther King had been dated March 28, the day before the "Heed Their Rising Voices" ad ran, when he took the minutes as "acting recorder" of the Committee to Defend. And now the federal government, in the form of the FBI, would have a pretext to join the state of Alabama in harassing Martin Luther King.

As it happened, Rustin needn't have opened up so many cans of worms at all. King's attorneys had discovered that their client kept such immaculate financial records, including a diary of his daily expenses, that on May 28 twelve white men in Montgomery found him not guilty of tax evasion. "Something happened to the jury," a stunned King told his congregation back in Atlanta. The sore loser, Governor John Patterson, who had joined the queue of plaintiffs who were filing suit against the *New York Times* and the four Alabama ministers, added King to his list of defendants.

Brotherhood

ON JUNE 23, 1960, Gary Thomas Rowe Jr. was "naturalized" as a member of the Eastview 13 klavern of Bobby Shelton's new Alabama Knights, Knights of the Ku Klux Klan, Inc. FBI agents warned him that if he ever got mixed up in any Klan violence, the bureau would disown him and treat him like a common criminal. But that is not how things turned out in a bureaucracy whose ultimate mission was to avoid getting on the bad side of J. Edgar Hoover. When Rowe did participate in violence, when he perhaps instigated violence, the agents not only did not discipline him, they also covered it up.

Shelton's new Klan had imposed an impressive spirit of reciprocity among the district's klaverns, particularly between the reigning Eastview 13 and the club across the "Cut-Off" in Bessemer. Klokann chiefs from each klavern would have "Klonversations" over coffee by day to discuss problem individuals, white or black, who needed to have some sense knocked into them. A Klokann squad would then make a nocturnal hit on a neighboring klavern's territory, where they were less recognizable to civilian witnesses. Not that there was actually much chance of their getting caught. In Bessemer particularly, the Klan had indebted itself to the community by performing, as the Klokann chief put it, "certain acts which the Sheriff's Office could not legally do"—which was how one Birmingham policeman had characterized the beating of Shuttlesworth in front of Phillips High School (that is, something that the police would like to have done).

There had been a recent influx of younger men into the Klan, answering the civil rights movement's own youthful trend. Veterans of the 1940s and 1950s considered some of the youngsters riffraff, "ignorant idiots" whom Shelton was letting in to fatten his own pocketbook. But the newcomers undeniably provided a fresh audience for what seemed to be the Klan's major activity: spouting off at the regular Thursday-night meeting about the damnable condition of the country. "Senator John Kennedy *is* a member of the *N.A.A.C.P.* and has been a card carrying member since sometime in *1953*," Hubert Page announced at one meeting. As the Grand Titan of the North Alabama region, Page was Eastview's Mr. Big, one of the Klan's higher-ranking tradesmen as an electrician. He was imposing and bitter. Twice captured by the Germans in World War II, he had taken advantage of his veteran's right to sugar back home and opened a doughnut concession in Smithfield. The black residents who boycotted it launched an influential racist career. Page's intimidating smugness was perhaps related to his access to Bull Connor and his friendship with detective Tom Cook.

The Klan meetings were held on the second floor of Morgan's Department Store, a stately orange brick building in the very white eastern neighborhood of Woodlawn, which had been the city hall until the community was annexed into Birmingham in 1910. The Klansmen gathered in what had been the city court, reflecting their role as alternative administrators of justice, though they called the klavern hall "church," as when they told their wives, "I'm going to church." Indeed their regular Thursday nights were sort of an "oppressed whites" version of the Movement mass meetings taking place at black churches every Monday, with the unschooled rank and file responding to the speakers' claims with grunts and cries. As with the Movement, much of the business had to do with getting the members to part with their dues.

After the Klan meetings ended, Tommy Rowe would ride around for fifteen to thirty minutes to make sure he wasn't being followed, as the bureau instructed; then he would call his FBI handler from a public telephone, no matter what the hour. The next day, he would write a report, in which he referred to himself in the third person, and mail it to a blind post office box under the intriguing name of Karl Cross. Once or twice a month, he would get his cash payment.

On August 18, there was great cause for celebration at the Birmingham FBI office, high atop the 2121 Building downtown. His Klanhood less than two months old, Rowe was invited into the klavern's inner sanctum, elected Night-Hawk-in-Chief of Eastview 13. In addition to carrying the fiery cross at all public exhibitions, Rowe would be responsible for investigating new Eastview applicants and shepherding them through initiation. The reason a rookie like Rowe had been elected—by acclamation—was that no one else wanted the time-consuming job.

Rowe's reports began to reflect a quickening of violent purpose in Eastview 13 immediately after he became an officer. In late August, Grand Titan Hubert Page told the members that the law wasn't doing enough about Negroes riding the buses and sitting at the lunch counters (there had been a brief reprise of sit-ins) and that it was up to the Klan to "strike down at the niggers." He and other leaders were planning a "Wholesale Day," during which hundreds of Klansmen would ride the buses and attack any front-of-the-bus Negro with bicycle chains, blackjacks, and custom-"modified" baseball bats loaded with four or five ounces of lead and plugged and varnished at the end. Around a hundred of them were stacked like dynamite in a box in the klavern hall.

The regular meeting of September 1 concluded with a little light reading—a news clipping revealing that the Russians had referred to Negroes as monkeys. "That's the first time the Klan could go along with the Communists," the speaker quipped. Afterward, in a private room off the main hall, the inner circle discussed the opening of school. Eastview men were planning to rent a room overlooking Phillips High School and get a high-powered rifle with telescopic sights to stop any Negro. At the end of that meeting, twelve teams of three men blanketed the city to carry out the annual cross-burnings at the public schools, which were reputedly carried out under the direction of Detective Tom Cook.

Medicine

Rowe's reports—all big talk so far—made it hard to imagine a time when the Klan was close to the center of economic power, with a line from the klavern hall to the tall buildings and high-priced lawyers to fight off the aggressions of Governor Big Jim Folsom. The diminution of the Klan reflected the parallel decline of the heavy-manufacturing industry that had given it courage, and those attuned to the nuances of the great workshop town could hear the dying gasps of that old oligarchy in the drama that was being played out at the end of the summer in Bessemer, the wholly owned subsidiary of U.S. Steel that had been the setting of so much of the district's industrial vigilantism.

The town of Bessemer was preparing extraordinary "criminal libel" charges against Harrison Salisbury, since the most shocking atrocities in his story had taken place there (launching a thousand civic Hail Marys in Birmingham proper). The last time the statute had been invoked was in 1934, and the offending reporter was from the *Daily Worker.** Salisbury was charged with forty-two counts of criminal libel, and the *Times* ordered its reporters to steer clear of Alabama lest they be served with his indictment. With the nation's paper of record thus silenced, the *Chicago Tribune* called the Alabama lawsuits "the most important challenges to freedom of information to have arisen in many years."

But that national First Amendment predicament was really only a secondary effect of the Bessemer grand jury's primary aim: to get at a local young white man

---

* That first criminal libel defendant was the playwright John Howard Lawson, one of the prominent artist-radicals who made pilgrimages to Birmingham as a sort of domestic alternative to fighting in the Spanish Civil War. He was thrown in jail after criticizing the city in the *Daily Worker*. The Communist Party's cultural commissar in Hollywood and the founding president of the Screen Writers Guild in 1933, he would become the most militant of the "Hollywood Ten" blacklisted during the McCarthy era. His most enduring accomplishment as a scriptwriter was *Algiers,* in which Charles Boyer says to Hedy Lamarr, "Come with me to the Casbah."

who had provided the documentation for a good half of the material in Salisbury's story. Robert Hughes was a slight, pious ordained Methodist minister, but his was no ordinary flock. The reason he had become the main target of the Dixiecrats' newest desperate incarnation, the Methodist Layman's Union (the Bessemer prosecutor was a member), was that the constituency he represented was the rising industrial counterestablishment that would ultimately supplant the coal and iron titans now stumbling into obsolescence.

A new kind of carpetbagger—with moral rather than financial motives—had descended on Birmingham, recruited to a legitimate growth industry, a true rival to steel. The great workshop town was becoming a center of medicine and scientific research. The University of Alabama's medical college had grown to occupy sixty downtown blocks, thanks to a million-dollar federal appropriation in 1950. And so had a window of enlightened opinion opened in the fortress of heavy manufacturing.

This showdown among Methodists had its origins in the Unitarian Church. Dr. Joseph F. Volker, the dean of the Tufts University Dental School, who had been recruited to set up the medical center's dental school and head its research department, was like many a good Bostonian, a committed Unitarian. He had founded a church to accommodate his religion after coming to the city in 1948, fresh from working in Europe on the dental rehabilitation of Germany and Austria. The charming Volker had convinced the growing nonindustrial power base of medium-sized mules that his empire would be the salvation of Birmingham, and pretty soon Magic Citians were saying "medical center" in the same breath as "We're just as good as Atlanta." Yet, the independent-minded young scientists he lured to Birmingham with promises of federal money, research space, and benign neglect were not likely to sympathize with the Chamber of Commerce's controversy phobia.

When his young liberal recruits began to arrive, from California and Massachusetts, Volker had asked them just to observe the local scene for the first year, without committing to any moral action. Obligingly, the medical center's freethinkers kept their unsavory thoughts confined to the Unitarian church, whose minister, Alfred Hobart, had been the only local white clergyman to speak out frankly in support of *Brown*. At the close of Volker's year-long embargo on conscience, they joined the Alabama Council on Human Relations.

The organization was the local affiliate of the Southern Regional Council, the Atlanta-based research and education watchdog on race relations. The Alabama leadership was a collection of high-placed white and black moderates—an insurgent Presbyterian minister, a do-gooder Community Chest executive, and union officials (all white), plus a college president, ministers, a lawyer, a newspaper editor, and an NAACP official (black). They had made no inroads against segregation until a new full-time director was hired shortly after the *Brown* decision.

That was Salisbury's future source Bob Hughes. The twenty-six-year-old son of a Gadsden doctor and recent graduate of Emory University's Methodist seminary, he had trouble finding a church after informing potential employers of his doubts about southern Christianity's double standard on race. ("All I can say is that I am now seriously searching for the truth.") He set up the Alabama Council's office in Montgomery, where the local membership included Virginia Durr and Martin Luther King. Hughes's baptism had come during the first week of the Montgomery bus boycott, when he arranged for King to meet with the city commissioners and transit company representatives. "To say the least, it was premature" was how Hughes characterized that hostile encounter.

In 1956, after his boycott connections cost him his office lease, Hughes moved the council to Birmingham. His role was reduced to being a sort of professional witness to tactics—Shuttlesworth's—he did not entirely approve of. Hughes had been standing quietly in the mobs at both the Terminal Station when Shuttlesworth desegregated its waiting room and at Phillips High School, appalled at Shuttlesworth's folly despite his sympathy for the cause.

Public Safety Commissioner Robert Lindbergh had left the Alabama Council alone—Hughes conferred with him on the Q.T., and found him deeply concerned but vulnerable. And in truth, the council wasn't rocking many boats. For most of its white members, the meetings at black churches under cloak of night were occasions of spiritual growth rather than political action. "I think I was slightly in love with every black person I came into contact with," one medical center doctor said of the euphoria of encountering blacks as equals in Birmingham, Alabama. But the returning Bull Connor did not intend to brook even these mild forms of dissent. Shortly before he took office, in October 1957, police detectives—with reinforcements that Hughes believed were from the Ku Klux Klan—stormed a council meeting. Members' employers and neighbors received anonymous letters informing them of the Communists in their midst. Half the membership of one hundred dropped out, and average attendance fell to five. One of the most dedicated participants had been an informant, Asa Carter's disciple William Miller, whose collegiality with the council's black members perhaps explained why he had thrown up while joining in the castration of Judge Aaron.

And then in the spring of 1959, the Methodist Layman's Union had taken over the harassment of the council from Bull Connor and the Klan. The MLU issued a four-page letter to every Methodist congregation in the state exposing Hughes's "small group of whites and Negroes who, for several years, have been preaching full racial integration on all levels in all areas of the church." Hughes wrote to his Southern Regional Council bosses in Atlanta, "This is doubtless the beginning of a series of developments, the anticipation of which for four and a half years is almost as bad [as] what lies ahead." He began getting death threats, against his children as well as himself. On July 26, he watched through his living room window as a traffic jam formed out front and seventy-five men in white robes got out of cars, drove a stake into his yard, poured gasoline over it, and lit it. After the Karavan drove off, Hughes got out his garden hose and put out the burning cross. The next day, a neighborhood boy playing with his daughter spied the charred remnant and informed Hughes, "You had a visitor last night. Jesus Christ was here."*

Harrison Salisbury had noticed that Hughes seemed a little distressed when he arrived at his house by cab in early April 1960—the driver might be too talkative. The Methodist Layman Union's network of spies was so proficient that it had found out when Birmingham-Southern's Tommy Reeves, Hughes's protégé, had come out for dinner the previous fall. Hughes, who had just advised Reeves and Miles student body president Jesse Walker on the Vigil for Freedom, closed his curtains and opened his files to the visiting reporter. By the time he drove Salisbury back to the Tutwiler Hotel, at midnight, Hughes had brought Birmingham to a turning point. His only criticism of the resulting article, which some of Salisbury's colleagues feared exaggerated, was that it "didn't go far enough."

"Governor"

IN LATE AUGUST, a deputy sheriff served Hughes with the Bessemer grand jury's subpoena ordering him to surrender the Alabama Council's membership and financial records, including canceled checks, dating back to January 1958. It was a replay of Attorney General Patterson's attack on the NAACP. In the middle of the night, the medical center renegades who were Hughes's main council constituents sat in the office of Frederick Kraus, a dentistry professor who also ran the dentistry department of the Veterans Administration Hospital. Kraus was an Austrian who had become Joe Volker's student at Tufts after the Nazis ended his medical studies in Prague, and his ninth-floor office at the V.A.—exempt from local statutes because it was federal property—had become a sort of safe house for gatherings of controversial intent. Earlier that summer, Kraus had invited Fred Shuttlesworth there to meet his starstruck daughter, Ingrid. Tonight their guest was a brilliant young white lawyer named Charles Morgan Jr. In asking him to represent Bob Hughes, they fully understood the effect such a case would have on his well-known ambition to be governor of Alabama.

Chuck Morgan was shaping up as the best chance that Birmingham's growing coalition of liberals had at executing a progressive coup against the wobbling segregationists. He had the charisma of a great politician, and the drive and intelligence to manipulate large numbers of people. When his father, a Kentucky insurance man, had moved the family to Birmingham, fifteen-year-old Chuck immediately ingratiated himself with the sleek Mountain Brook crowd, joining one of the top high school fraternities. He was one of those people who, in adopting an attitude or a city, glamorized it far more than anyone born to it could. And so it was with the City of Lawyers. He could be seen middays politicking over fried Gulf shrimp and cole slaw at the "in" businessmen's restaurant, John's, whose

---

* No arrests were made, even though two deputy sheriffs had greeted the Klansmen at their meeting site, taken car tag numbers, and been assured there would be no "trouble."

proprietor already called Chuck "Governor." Strolling back to the office, Morgan greeted everybody along the way, exuding the radiance that haloes public figures. "Try your case on the streets . . . ," he explained. "That's your jury, fellows."

Chuck Morgan had only recently come to accept how unfeasible was his hope of pursuing a liberal program without tackling "the Negro question"—and thus committing political suicide. The previous spring, a young lawyer who was an old University of Alabama acquaintance had asked Morgan to represent Tommy Reeves when he was arrested after conspiring in the sit-ins; the friend's own bosses, at the city's top establishment law firm, had forbidden him to take the case. When Harrison Salisbury came to town a few weeks later to report on Reeves's arrest, the normally publicity-happy Morgan spoke to him only under guarantee of anonymity, in "the veiled double-talk" Salisbury had once heard from "Soviet dissidents fearful of the KGB." But it turned out that Bull Connor's real target had been Birmingham-Southern's president (who had refused to expel Reeves), not the small-fry student. Reeves's case had been continued pending "further investigation" until he graduated that spring, sparing Morgan from having to go public on his behalf.

Now, in Kraus's office, for the second time in six months Chuck saw his political ambitions turn to ghosts. He agonized with the doctors until three in the morning over whether to reap Salisbury's grief. The next night, Morgan, his partner, and a secretary were holed up in their office writing a motion to quash the subpoena of Bob Hughes.

Faithful

ON FRIDAY SEPTEMBER 2, Hughes and Morgan drove out to Bessemer to face the grand jury. Morgan's motion had been denied by the state supreme court. Hughes asked Morgan what he thought would happen next. "That's for the court and the Lord to decide, Bob," Morgan said. "I'll do my best in court. The Lord is your jurisdiction."

The courthouse lobby was clogged with Klansmen handing out leaflets that called Hughes a "nigger lover." Morgan was momentarily taken aback to confront the crude, shirt-sleeved version of the bigotry he had seen only in its genteel form at the country club. But his faith in his own political magic remained such that he spoke to the Klansmen, reminding them that the shoe had once been on the other foot and the Klan's Hugh Morris had been jailed in 1949 on exactly the same grounds—refusing to produce records. The Klansmen—perhaps swayed as much by Morgan's burly physique as by his clever argument—provided what would prove to be the high point of his day, by heeding his suggestion that they leave.

Before the grand jury, Hughes declined to turn over his records. He was sent to jail for contempt. Morgan, who now turned to the Supreme Court for relief, supplied milk for his client's ulcers and for his spirit a copy of *Profiles in Courage,* by the Democratic candidate for president. To Morgan's surprise, he began getting tacit pledges of support from white clergymen. First the Klan turning hide and now this. He was revved up and happy when Will Campbell, the poor-white Mississippian who was the National Council of Churches' race man, arrived from Nashville to help. "You another one of them nigger-loving preachers?" Morgan jested, and reassured him about Hughes. "Those bastards can't do this. Not even in Alabama. Now let's go eat."

Morgan was right. The Supreme Court was still reviewing his brief—it had apparently been expedited by Hugo Black—when Hughes was summarily released on the Tuesday after Labor Day, September 6. With the law no longer doing its duty, the Methodist Layman's Union pressured the Methodist conference, then meeting in Birmingham, to take away Hughes's ministerial standing. Some sympathetic churchmen, aware that Hughes had once applied for missionary work in Africa but had been disqualified by his health, persuaded the Methodist bishop in Southern Rhodesia to wire the conference that he needed Hughes there. His credentials restored, Hughes was thrown, ulcers and all, into the briar patch.

Driving home on the afternoon he had been temporarily stripped of his ministry, Hughes had passed a black boy kicking a can in the gutter and wondered if in some way he had made the child's future brighter. Suddenly it struck him that the opposition didn't matter. "The acceptance or rejection of others was not nearly as important as whether or not I had done my best," he realized. "Certainly, we are called on to be faithful before we are called on to be effective."

Even if he did not yet realize it, Hughes had won a moral victory over the Methodist Layman's Union. The "industrial" complex of medical scientists he presided over would now team up with ambitious politicians like Chuck Morgan to make a run at the Dixiecrats' embattled rampart. And they would have the unlikeliest ally in the man who had been synonymous with that old guard: Sid Smyer.

"Metropolitan Audit"

THE HARRISON SALISBURY ARTICLE ended Hughes's mission in Birmingham but it fulfilled it as well: "Blatant, pitiless publicity" had finally gotten the attention of the local power structure. The rest of the Chamber of Commerce might still be trying to kill the messenger, but Smyer knew that the city had no more defenses against black eyes.

In September, Smyer received the preliminary findings of the "Metropolitan Audit" he and some concerned city fathers had ordered two years earlier to redeem the city. The supposedly empirical study read like Greek tragedy. There was a citywide "conviction that somehow their community is lacking, that it is not as 'good' as other cities, that something is out of kilter." Powerful men—"able persons with excellent qualities," including a surprising number of scholars—mistrusted one another, as did bosses and subordinates. "Together they fearfully watch outsiders and the public." The essence of Birmingham was fear. Not of "anything real," but "of responsibility, of what others may think; of innovation.

All this boils down to a chilling and inhibiting fear of failure which, in terms of the individual, is a doubt of self."

The four most important goals the leaders of Birmingham named were: succeeding in their careers, enhancing the growth of their companies, personal prestige, and wealth. In other words, getting into the country club and being able to afford the dues. What explained the Babbittry of the city fathers? More than half of them, like George Babbitt himself, had come to the big city from the country.* That is, the core of Birmingham's "aristocracy" was actually made up of those "white country people teeming in from the piney woods," as *Time* had rudely put it two years earlier, to make up a "melting pot of raw men as well as raw material." We had done such a good job of covering our traces—we knew to say "nice to have met you" instead of "nice meeting you"—that the auditors were surprised that we were not "backward people who have become industrialized with consequent lack of taste." But the elite, preoccupied with buffing their "good breeding" at the country club, were not inclined to take on the socially compromising civic problems that were making Birmingham, as *Time's* headline had put it, "Integration's Hottest Crucible."

The community seemed arrested in adolescence, preoccupied with appearances, conformity, and pre-moral conditions of status. What of the central dilemma? Race was "much on Birmingham's mind"; yet any criticism on that score only incited "defensive measures." Coming in dead last on the city fathers' list of goals was "bringing about general social progress."

Smyer fired the auditors. That would be his last act of civic denial.

Impressing the Jury

THE WEEK BEFORE the presidential election in November, Fred Shuttlesworth was inside a Montgomery courtroom, at the defense table with his three fellow black ministers and a few pallid *Times* executives, looking up at the "big, foreboding bald head" of Judge Walter B. Jones. *Sullivan et al.* v. *New York Times* and Shuttlesworth, Ralph Abernathy, Joe Lowery, and Solomon Seay had landed in the court of the judge who had outlawed the state NAACP and then gone on to write a weekly column for the *Montgomery Advertiser* titled "I Speak for the White Race." Such good fortune for the plaintiffs could hardly have been an accident. There were rumors that Jones had dreamed up Sullivan's suit in the first place, and in rebuffing the *Times's* challenge to the state court's jurisdiction, he had had to overrule the textbook he literally wrote on Alabama courtroom procedure.

Waiting for the session to open, Shuttlesworth said something mirthful to his colleagues. "Fred, Fred," Lowery chided him in a stage whisper, "impress the jury." Shuttlesworth made a wide-eyed appraisal of Lowery and said, "Negro, you trying to impress the jury wearing a hundred-and-fifty-dollar green iridescent

---

* Only a quarter of the business elite were Birmingham natives, with an equal number from out of state, accounting for the agents of absentee capital.

suit and a shoe with a hole in it and that hole focused toward the jury?" Lowery uncrossed his legs. "You not fooling the white folk," Shuttlesworth said. "You're the victim and the bait."

The jaded Shuttlesworth considered the *Sullivan* case just another rogue farce coming out of the home state and had airily assured the reporters that he would be vindicated "upstairs" in the Supreme Court. The trial did bear all the parochial absurdities of Alabama justice, with some basic southern gothic thrown in: The *Times* attorneys had noticed that the gavel Judge Jones wielded, notwithstanding the SAE fraternity pin on the front of his robe, was plastered with pictures of pretty young boys. ("What Tennessee Williams could do with this!" one lawyer said.) After being turned down by all the white-shoe firms, the *Times* had finally managed to sign on the required local attorney for this and the concurrent Salisbury suits—Eric Embry, whose father had been part of Charles DeBardeleben's stable of lawyers, was a member of the prominent Birmingham criminal firm that briefly represented the Scottsboro Boys. The prejudices of that case echoed across thirty years as Embry registered the *Times*'s chief attorney in a motel far outside Birmingham, under a fictitious name that did not betray the New Yorker's Jewishness. Though Embry would gain history's approval as the attorney of record on the right side of this landmark constitutional case, he had also been one of the lawyers representing Dynamite Bob Chambliss in his post–Autherine Lucy lawsuit against the NAACP.

As for the plaintiffs' lawyers, one substituted the word "nigger" for "Negro" upon reading aloud the "Heed Their Rising Voices" ad, and another wheeled around to the defense table, pointed at the *Times* attorneys, and said, "When you write about a citizen of this town, you tell the truth, Mr. New York Times—the whole truth."

The national press did not in this instance share Shuttlesworth's sense of the absurd. *Sullivan* was a novel First Amendment nightmare: That a paper could be held accountable for inaccuracies in its *advertising* was a revolutionary notion. The paper's lawyers were not bothering to point out that the ad, far from damaging Commissioner Sullivan, had turned him into a local hero. Their mild claim that the ad had intended no "malice" hardly seemed fodder for a Supreme Court precedent.

Defending the ministers was Fred Gray, the lawyer who had been the attorney of record for the constitutional challenge (ghosted by Clifford Durr) of bus segregation in Montgomery. The plaintiffs' attorneys called him "Lawyer Gray" to circumvent the honorific "Mr.," but he had gotten a friendly laugh out of the courtroom when he demanded to know how his clients could be expected to "retract something, if you'll pardon the expression, that they didn't 'tract.' "* Still, the ministers were not exempted from the damages when after two hours of delibera-

---

* Gray had threatened to withdraw from the case because the Committee to Defend Martin Luther King refused to divert any of the considerable funds it had raised to the defense of the *Sullivan* defendants it had created.

tion the jury awarded Commissioner Sullivan half a million dollars—the largest sum in Alabama history. "State Finds Formidable Legal Club to Swing at Out-of-State Press," a *Montgomery Advertiser* headline crowed. Libel law, which was intended to protect individuals against institutional abuses, had been transformed into an instrument of state-sponsored censorship and intellectual terrorism.

Hall of Mirrors

FRED SHUTTLESWORTH had now entered the hall-of-mirrors stage of the revolution, when the inevitability of the cause equals the hostility of the status quo. On one wall was a reflection of Shuttlesworth the walking Supreme Court precedent, in a defendant class with the country's paper of record (which was appealing the October verdict). In November, he had filed a $9 million lawsuit against Greyhound, seeking damages over the treatment of his teenage children, Pat, Ricky, and Fred Jr. the previous August.

On their way home from summer camp at the Highlander Folk School (on a scholarship courtesy of the singer-activist Harry Belafonte), the Shuttlesworth kids had been pulled off the front of the bus and jailed in Gadsden, the piney woods metropolis northeast of Birmingham. (Shuttlesworth and his rescue convoy were stopped outside Gadsden by a roadblock of what must have been fifty policemen, providing him his first glimpse of a riot gun.) The Greyhound suit had occasioned high-level caucuses between SCLC and the NAACP to consider launching a national boycott against the bus company.

Within SCLC, Shuttlesworth was still the voice differentiated most loudly from that of Martin Luther King. For example, while King himself remained officially neutral about the presidential race,* Shuttlesworth was an outspoken supporter of John F. Kennedy. He had little use, however, for his candidate's Cold War rhetoric, and continued to taunt the red-baiters—chummily referring, in his regular ("A Southerner Speaks") column for the *Pittsburgh Courier,* to Kennedy's bête rouge, Khrushchev, as "Mr. K."

While SCLC tussled with SCEF over which organization would get to send out the press releases on his exploits, Shuttlesworth remained the "little nigger" in his own town, ineligible for respect from the lawyers of his own race. Arthur Shores, though he was representing Shuttlesworth et al. in the sit-in appeals en route to the Supreme Court, was still refusing to initiate any ACMHR suits.

---

* It would be King who got credit for delivering the black vote to Kennedy. On October 19, King, whom Bayard Rustin had seven months earlier designated the "spiritual leader" of the sit-ins, committed his first act of civil disobedience and was arrested after joining eighty Atlanta college students for synchronized sit-ins at the close of SNCC's third convention. When a judge had him transferred to the state penitentiary for hard-core criminals, Kennedy's civil rights advisers maneuvered the candidate into making a noncommittal sympathy call to Coretta King. Kennedy's campaign manager, brother Robert, called the judge and got King released on bail the next day. Topping off the empty gestures of self-interest, Daddy King told an overflowing rally at Ebenezer that he had been planning to vote against Kennedy because of his Catholicism, but "I've got all my votes and I've got a suitcase, and I'm going to take them up there and dump them in his lap."

Shuttlesworth had ventured even further left to an outside lawyer he had met through Anne Braden, a freewheeling black militant from Norfolk, Virginia, via Tuscumbia, Alabama, named Len Holt. ("You got no rights. Don't look for logic. You got no rights. You're black and you ain't got no rights.") He had been active in the formation of SNCC and was affiliated primarily with the left-wing, much red-baited National Lawyers Guild. Holt was so brilliant, Shuttlesworth said, that he could "write up a lawsuit on the plane from Atlanta to Birmingham." He had sued to desegregate the Birmingham airport's restaurant and limousine service while he was in Alabama in September to represent the Shuttlesworth children in Gadsden—the kids were found guilty of delinquency in juvenile court, which was deluged by outraged telegrams from around the country solicited by SCLC and SCEF.

Three weeks after the *Sullivan* trial, Shuttlesworth was in the segregationist federal judge Seybourn Lynne's court acting as his own lawyer. Following Holt's advice to "type the suit up yourself and file *in pauperis!*" he and his trusty lieutenant, Charles Billups, had sued Bull Connor and his chief of police, seeking $97,000 in damages and an injunction to bar police detectives from Movement meetings. In questioning Connor on the stand, "Attorney" Shuttlesworth lived up to the blowhard histrionics of Kingfish, the *Amos 'n' Andy* character with whom he wryly claimed an affinity. But his star witness turned out to be the black *Baltimore Afro-American* reporter who had been the audience for Connor's signature aphorism, "Damn the law, we don't give a damn about the law. Down here we make our own law."

Shuttlesworth's boilerplate "That is all"s and "Do you recall"s proved no match for the Great Lawyer representing Connor, Jim Simpson. Besides, his aim was not so much to win the case as to "harass the harasser." Judge Lynne (who once dismissed a suit filed by Thurgood Marshall on grounds of being "prolix and redundant") denied the injunction, fortunately for future historians: No more intimate and moving a record of the civil rights movement would survive than Connor's police surveillance reports.

BH 248

In November, Clarence Kelley, the special agent in charge of the FBI's Birmingham office, wrote Washington recommending that Gary Thomas Rowe Jr. be elevated from potential informant to full informant: BH 248-PCI (RAC), as he would go down in the files, for "Birmingham, ID number, Potential Confidential Informant (Racial)." The memo read like the report of a high school teacher who has finally had the honor of teaching a student gifted enough for Harvard. The information of "unusual value" furnished by Rowe—besides the descriptions of Klansmen and their cars—concerned the relationship between the Klan and local law enforcement. Irondale's police chief, Robert Olin Bragg, called on Klansmen for "assistance or advice." Rowe had gotten a pistol permit from the Jefferson county sheriff's office by showing his Klan membership card.

Kelley's glowing account curiously overlooked the magnificent coup of Rowe's election in August as Night-Hawk-in-Chief of Eastview. Perhaps at this stage the bureau was not admitting even to itself what it would later be embarrassed to explain: that it was a necessary evil for Rowe to penetrate the hard core of the klavern. The Klan's "missionary work" was executed by exclusive "action squads"—Klansmen of proven courage and loyalty. In order to be truly useful, the FBI would realize in retrospect, Rowe had to infiltrate the action squad and, to protect his cover, participate in violence. What was perhaps too unsettling for the bureau to acknowledge was that the action squads weren't carrying out any real violence until the arrival of Rowe, who had given a judo demonstration at a recent Eastview meeting, showing how to break a man's back.

In December, seven black college students, mostly from Atlanta, sat in at the lunch counter of the Greyhound Bus Terminal. Tom Cook and another detective had to handle the situation themselves, and they were somewhat constrained by the Constitution. The following day, Bull Connor called Eastview's Hubert Page—so Page claimed—and said that the Klan "better wake up." Page relayed the wake-up call to the hard-core Klansmen who met after Eastview's December 15 open session.

Rowe's December 15 report to the FBI, mentioned that the Klan was planning a statewide mobilization of squads to "crush" the black pickets expected at the department stores during the Christmas season. There was no indication in the FBI's files of any coordinated Klan attacks that year. Rowe, however, would claim that beatings did take place and that he administered some of them. Investigators combing the records later wondered if Rowe reported violence orally but that his handlers omitted it from the file. Some of them admitted that they did.

6.

ACTION

The Gridiron

ALL THE CULTURAL IDOLS seemed to be smiling on Bull Connor as he looked ahead to reelection in 1961. He had a new sports allegiance, and its inspiration was Paul "Bear" Bryant. In 1958, Bryant became head football coach at the University of Alabama, declaring "I ain't nothin' but a winner"—even though the team had won only four games in the three previous years. True to his word, the Bear had a winning rookie season, rekindling visions of the Crimson Tide's Rose Bowl squad of the 1930s, on which Bryant himself had been a so-so player. Birmingham proclaimed itself "The Football Capital of the South" on the strength of the annual "Iron Bowl" grudge match at Legion Field between Alabama and Auburn, which the fans pointed out was always broadcast on *national* TV.

By 1961, the year Bryant would win his first national championship, Birmingham barely noticed that Rickwood Field was about to go dark, the Barons having lost their spot in the Detroit Tigers system because of Sid Smyer's ordinance forbidding them to play integrated teams. Baseball, the old opiate of the masses, had been supplanted by football, a religion better suited to the fierce mood of white Birmingham. Connor was about to ride Crimson Tide football fever to political omnipotence.

The coming city elections held a potential bonus for Connor. The commission president, Jimmy Morgan, had decided not to seek reelection. Morgan had been a baseball man once, a minor-league third baseman turned Philco radio distributor, who had been elected to the commission along with Connor in the 1937 anti–New Deal sweep. Somehow he had avoided the faults of race politics, consistently casting lone votes in favor of hiring Negro police and lavishing honorifics on attorney Arthur Shores. A "friend-made" politician from the old "joiner" school, Morgan tried to "tote fair" with everyone. But a year after Connor's return to the commission, Morgan was quoted in *Time*'s scalding 1958 article: "I used to enjoy going to the City Hall. I don't anymore." Few were surprised when he announced he was turning in his gavel.

Few were more elated than Connor. Over the years, his constituents wondered why he never ran for the presidency of the commission (with its honorary title of mayor), not understanding that in Birmingham he who commanded the police commanded the power. Throughout his tenure in city hall, Connor had had to contend with moderate mayors. But now he had the chance to put his own president on the commission, a football man toughened against the forgiving racial rites of baseball. In the course of creating a mayor, Connor would reach the peak of his imperialism—and at the same time doom the future of segregation.

Football, Methodism, and the FBI

IN JANUARY 1961, Lewis Jeffers was sitting in a Washington, D.C., hotel room wondering if the snowstorm was going to let up in time for the inauguration of the thirty-fifth president of the United States. The phone rang. It was another Birmingham supporter of the Kennedy-Johnson ticket, Bull Connor, who was also staying at the Sheraton Park. "Come on up, Lew," Connor said to Jeffers. "I want to talk to you."

That Connor was summoning Jeffers to *his* room was proof that the city's old industrial potentates had lost control of their former mascot, and that Connor was willing to flaunt their impotence. Lew Jeffers—a right-leaning loyalist Democrat in Senator Lister Hill's large circle—was one of the city's biggest mules. As president of the Hayes Aircraft Corporation, he ruled over the city's largest employer after TCI, the epitome of the second generation of absentee-owned industries that had favored the South since World War II: the federal contractor—military bases, space laboratories, and defense industries like Hayes. Founded after the war by Chiang Kai-shek's American aviation adviser, Hayes modified aircraft for specific climates out of Bechtel's abandoned B-29 war plant, which had employed young Fred Shuttlesworth. The Korean War boom vaulted Hayes into the upper ranks of the district's industrial bullies. But a decade later, Lew Jeffers found himself doing the bidding of his onetime lackey. When Bull Connor called him, he jumped.

"Lew, we got to do something about the president of the city commission," Connor said when Jeffers arrived at his room. "We got to elect someone president."

Jeffers knew Mayor Jimmy Morgan was stepping down, but why was Connor consulting him?

"We want Art Hanes," Bull said. He was referring to Hayes Aircraft's chief of security. In a plant that handled top military secrets, Hanes's sensitive position demanded discretion combined with an intimidating toughness. But it was not a springboard for a political career.

"Why Art?" Jeffers asked Connor.

"He's the son of a Methodist minister, a football player, and an FBI man. We can elect him. We got to have him."

Hanes's father had been a beloved and flamboyant circuit rider, and Art had had the good political fortune to play football at (Methodist) Birmingham-

Southern. (He had also played semi-pro baseball, but that would not be stressed in his campaign biography.) Best of all, after law school he became an FBI agent, serving tours of duty in Washington and Chicago before Jeffers lured him to Hayes. With its stoic rites of brotherhood and clandestine derring-do, the bureau held a particular appeal to the southern male.

What Connor neglected to mention was his candidate's main asset: Hanes had been a speaker in demand by the Ace Carter Citizens Council faction that had kept Connor before the voting public during his exile. But unlike Connor, Hanes could pass. He approximated the grammar of gentlemen segregationists when speaking in book-lined dens to small over-the-mountain gatherings of the Big Mules' "conservative" in-group, the John Birch Society.

"Get him on the phone," Connor said to Jeffers. He wanted Hanes to be clear on who was handpicking him, and he wanted to have Jeffers as a witness.

Fatigue

AT THE ALABAMA CHRISTIAN MOVEMENT for Human Rights' inaugural day mass meeting, Fred Shuttlesworth attempted handshakes with Bull Connor's detectives and informed them that "the Movement put Kennedy in." ACMHR regulars believed that Officer Marcus Jones, who took an artist's pride in his surveillance reports, identifying each hymn sung by the Movement choir, "has become one of us." It was not unheard of for detectives to cry during meetings and put a dollar in the collection box.

At the January 23 meeting, a young jackleg preacher sent more than a dozen women into writhing trances by comparing the sorry affairs of the black community to the misconnected "dry bones" of Ezekiel. Shuttlesworth's second vice president, J. S. Phifer, began hollering "Praise the Lord" and "Oh, Jesus." Another minister screamed, "This is a nice place tonight" and "Khrushchev of Russia and Macmillan of England should be here." And then, almost as if the whole spectacle had been a "nigger frenzy" put on for the white visitors, Phifer told everyone to "look at the detectives how happy they look. No white church in Birmingham has religion like we have."

Shuttlesworth persevered in his strange career, commuting between the ridiculous and the sublime, though it was sometimes difficult to tell them apart. On February 1, he had on his insouciant "what white people?" face back in the Montgomery courtroom of Judge Walter B. Jones (who, the *Times* lawyers had learned, had pictures of boys—some nude—on the walls of his home study as well as on his gavel). Back at the defendants' table with the *New York Times,* Shuttlesworth, Ralph Abernathy, Joe Lowery, and Solomon Seay faced the second plaintiff in the *Sullivan* suits, Montgomery's Mayor Earl James. Five jurors as well as James were cultivating beards for the coming Civil War centennial, during which Judge Jones (whose father carried the Confederate truce flag at Appomattox, and went on to be a Bourbon governor of Alabama) was to administer the oath to "Jefferson Davis." Before the day's end, the modern-day Yankee invaders, and their southern black collaborators, had been socked with another half-million-dollar judgment. If the trend continued, the *Times* estimated that its exposure for the five Montgomery suits that had been filed over the "Heed Their Rising Voices" ad would reach $3 million, enough to threaten the paper's survival. The Salisbury suits—from the Bessemer city commission as well as Connor and his colleagues and a city detective—increased the exposure to $6,150,000.

The state pounced on the relatively poor Alabama defendants to collect the libel awards, even as the verdict was being appealed to the state supreme court. Abernathy's five-year-old sedan was seized first. By the time two sheriff's deputies came to confiscate Shuttlesworth's 1957 Plymouth on February 7, he had replaced the good tires with rejects. Watching a deputy pump a flat tire up so the car could be towed, Shuttlesworth stood outside his parsonage and laughed: "I never let the camera catch me frowning." And then he was off to New York, where he was the featured speaker at a Carnegie Hall concert to benefit the embattled Highlander Folk School. A state prosecutor had raided the school in 1959 and built an illegal-liquor-sale case around a confiscated bottle containing half an inch of gin. (The school's founder, Myles Horton, did serve guests martinis in Vienna sausage cans, complete with olive.) Highlander continued to operate by the grace of an appeal bond after the state of Tennessee technically shut it down.

Shuttlesworth's taste of renown had subtly begun to alienate him from his humble Bethel Baptist Church. He had been blessed with a congregation that never complained about his motto: "The world is my pulpit. Be glad when you see me, and pray for me when I'm gone." But lately he had found himself irked by his flock. Sewage problems plagued Bethel as a result of the 1956 bombing, and the building committee still hadn't managed to fix the damaged plumbing. Shuttlesworth hadn't been able to resist mentioning at a recent mass meeting that he had turned down a job in Cincinnati. The ACMHR took the hint and immediately started a fund to get him a new car—"in the name of Jesus," the Movement's first vice president, Edward Gardner, said, because "Mr. Sullivan can't take the car from the Lord."

Martin Luther King privately pleaded with Shuttlesworth to stay in Birmingham, while lobbying to get an Atlanta pulpit for Ralph Abernathy, who was also suffering from Alabama fatigue. Even though King had left the state, the Southern Christian Leadership Conference remained largely an Alabama phenomenon, with Abernathy as treasurer, Mobile's Joe Lowery as second vice president, and Shuttlesworth as secretary and SCLC's only functioning mass leader. But the state's equally adamant segregationists seemed to be wearing down SCLC's warriors.

Who Speaks?

COULD IT REALLY BE that bad down there? CBS News wanted to know. The network had sent a producer to Birmingham to check out the furor over Salisbury's article for a special *CBS Reports*. The *New York Times* had kept its reporters out of the state since the previous fall, but CBS was not intimidated. Despite the popular surge of two droll young newscasters over at NBC, Chet Huntley and David Brinkley, CBS remained the oracle of television journalism. The correspondent for its Birmingham documentary was television's sternest soothsayer, Edward R. Murrow, who had risen to the rung of statesman since his televised 1954 lashing of the Communist-bashing Senator Joseph McCarthy.

Murrow's producer, David Lowe, had begun the preliminary research on Birmingham in the fall of 1960, while finishing up their most recent collaboration, a sort of factual *Grapes of Wrath* that would become a standard of documentary filmmaking, "Harvest of Shame." Over pictures of a squalid camp of migrant fruit pickers, Murrow had narrated, "This . . . has nothing to do with Johannesburg or Capetown." Their Birmingham report was tentatively being titled, after a phrase in Salisbury's story, "The Johannesburg of America."

For background, David Lowe talked to Salisbury himself, who told of totalitarianism and police states, of how he had checked into the Tutwiler Hotel only to be switched from one room to another, presumably tapped. Editors had cut one of the overheated passages he had composed on the night plane back to New York from Birmingham: "To one long accustomed to the sickening atmosphere of Moscow in the Stalin days the aura of the community which once prided itself as the 'Magic City' of the South is only too familiar. To one who knew Hitler's storm troop Germany it would seem even more familiar." Lowe, too, thought the old Kremlinologist must be exaggerating.

Still, Lowe avoided the Tutwiler and registered at Birmingham's Travelodge Motel. His journalistic strategy was a sort of studied openness, an assumption that the white people would be delighted to rebut what they were calling "Salisbury's damn lies." A law school dropout, Lowe was a teddy bear, balding and harmless-looking, capable of eliciting trust and unforgettable footage from dead-eyed migrant workers. But Birmingham's white people remained inscrutable. Why, they didn't see what they could offer because there was really nothing *wrong* with Birmingham, they told him with sweet smiles. Not even a ham like Bull Connor would open up. Lowe had lunch with Salisbury back in New York and challenged his assessment: The fear in Birmingham was worse than he had said. The documentary's title was updated to "Who Speaks for Birmingham?"

The explanation for the silence was a phenomenon named Vincent Townsend, the editorial boss of the *Birmingham News* and the city's power broker, in the sense that power was wielded actively rather than as resistance to change. He had unchallenged rule not only of the most widely circulated newspaper in Alabama, but also of *News*-owned WAPI, Channel 13, the local television affiliate for both NBC and CBS, as well as WAPI Radio, the most powerful airwaves in the state. "I know how to pick the wheelers and dealers," he boasted to friends, "and I know how to make 'em do what I think is best." His leverage was predicated on the vast fund of information that never made it into the paper: Townsend had his own personal reporter-spy, whose resources rivaled the surveillance capacities of the Birmingham police.

Townsend loved Birmingham—a strange attraction shared by almost everyone who lived there, black and white. Now sixty-one, he had worked for the *News*, with one brief defection, since he was a sports stringer at Birmingham-Southern College. His management style as executive editor, according to one employee, was "to grab people by the throat and ears and kick 'em in the butt." The adversarial impulse did not extend toward the subjects of *News* articles. In the late fifties, a cub reporter had turned in a story about a housing scam in Ensley, and after overruling his city editor to kill it, Townsend invited the reporter out for one of his famous heart-to-heart lunches. "We don't do exposés. We make a lot of money as things are," he said. Warming to the role of "Big Daddy," as he encouraged favored staffers to call him, he moved from newsroom maxims ("Not failure, but low aim, is the crime") to broader philosophical wisdom. "There's only one thing the nigras want," he said. The reporter retained a polite, filial silence. Townsend glared at him through his glasses and said, "The subjugation of the white race."

The *News* avoided racial matters and concentrated on "constructive" things. In sponsoring two great annual causes, the Soap Box Derby and the Miss Alabama Pageant, the *News* promoted traffic awareness in young boys and, in girls all over the city, a collective dream of becoming an opera singer (the preferred talent of our emissaries to Atlantic City). Once, the *News* had been the intelligent, independent voice of the establishment, part of the conservative wing of the New Deal and no enemy of labor; the longtime publisher, Victor Hanson, had forcefully opposed his own lawyer Jim Simpson's challenge of Lister Hill in 1944. But upon Hanson's death the following year, the paper fell into the soft lap of his nephew, Clarence B. Hanson Jr., who appeared only occasionally in the city room, in his bespoke suit, to confer with the outdoors columnist on where the doves were flying.

When Clarence Hanson sold the *News* to the New York publishing baron Samuel I. Newhouse in 1955, Vincent Townsend stepped into the power vacuum, claiming he got his much-cited mandate directly from old man Newhouse: The *News* will do well only if the city of Birmingham does well. To keep the advertisers happy he banned "trouble" from the paper, and to satisfy the readers he decked his front page with controversy-free disasters—car wrecks and drownings the most popular. The real dirt had been so minimized that Townsend took Harrison Salisbury's article as a professional rebuke. And then his hysterical counteroffensive only bared his inadequacies as a wheeler-dealer. Townsend had armed a team of reporters with fine-tooth combs to refute what its columnist had called the *Times*'s "big lie." But Salisbury's minor errors were hardly fodder for civic indignation; one of the two dynamite attempts he had mentioned against local synagogues, for example, was merely a bomb threat.

The CBS documentary promised Townsend redemption from the Salisbury debacle. Big Daddy had instructed his reporters not to help Lowe (an order some would not obey). Then Townsend tapped a stable of presentable Birminghamians and sent them to New York to confront CBS president Frank Stanton.

In his long career at the network, Stanton had received many such delega-
tions of hyperventilating city fathers. Once, he had entered the CBS conference
room as some gentlemen from Tennessee were on their knees praying. The Birmingham businessmen who filed into Stanton's Madison Avenue office did not
appear so unsophisticated. Their spokesman, Clarence Hanson, quickly let Stanton know that he controlled not only the city's biggest newspaper but also the
television station that might or might not broadcast "Who Speaks for Birmingham?"—or any future CBS programming.

"Dr. Stanton," Hanson complained, "Edward R. Murrow is coming down and
is only interested in representing half the population of Birmingham."

Stanton was not inconsiderate of the racial mores of his southern audiences;
the network had recently blacked out all Negro speakers at the Democratic and
Republican presidential conventions. And as it turned out, there came an expedi-
ent solution to the Birminghamians' problem. Murrow and Stanton had been on a
philosophical collision course since both men arrived at CBS Radio in 1935, Stanton with a Ph.D. in industrial psychology from Ohio State, as a "research specialist" charged with maximizing the commercial potential of its audience. The
brasher Murrow believed in giving audiences what they needed rather than what
they wanted, and he had become publicly disaffected with the network even before the quiz show scandals of 1959. Stanton, the implied target of this criticism,
heartily recommended his colleague to the newly elected John F. Kennedy for the
job of director of the U.S. Information Agency.

Fresh from covering Kennedy's inauguration, Murrow went to Birmingham
to get down to work on the documentary. The atmosphere there reminded him of
a place he had previously reported on, Nazi Germany. He was chain-smoking and
caucusing in the Travelodge with his producer, David Lowe, the Reverend C.
Herbert Oliver (one of Salisbury's main sources as well), and a couple of medical
center imports who belonged to the Alabama Council on Human Relations. The
phone rang. It was President Kennedy, wanting to know if Murrow would head
the U.S. Information Agency. Murrow's decision to take the job was eased by his
dismay over CBS's newest people-pleasing product—westerns and a state-of-
the-art sitcom, *The Beverly Hillbillies.*

The Birmingham assignment fell to his good friend and fellow war correspondent, now the CBS Washington bureau chief, Howard K. Smith. Since Smith
was a southerner, the Birmingham men who had importuned Frank Stanton
believed that his stepping into Murrow's shoes represented a great concession
from the network. The son of a fallen-aristocrat ne'er-do-well from Ferriday,
Louisiana,* Smith had won an academic scholarship to Tulane, where he was also
a track star, and had gone on to Oxford as a Rhodes scholar. But Smith happened
to be CBS's resident radical, "a socialist at heart," he would say. He had been the
first American president of the campus Labour Party at Oxford and had been fin-

---

* A billboard there would one day boast of being the Birthplace of Jimmy Swaggart and Howard K.
Smith, omitting Jerry Lee Lewis.

gered by McCarthyites as red. Still, he put on his best southern accent and courtly air when he arrived in Birmingham, to be swept up in Plan B of Vincent Townsend's image-protection program.

Every day on a front-page corner, Townsend's newspaper carried a peppy fact about Birmingham under the headline "Fly the Banners of Confidence." The content of the feature was supplied by the Women's Committee of 100, a sort of ladies' auxiliary to the Chamber of Commerce that had formed after the menfolk botched the Salisbury rebuttal. Like Townsend, the women believed Birmingham's problems came from bad press, and so the ladies had sponsored "happy things," such as showcases for Art Linkletter, the bandleader Fred Waring, and Olivia de Havilland. If anyone could awaken CBS to Birmingham's virtues, it was these women, their charm summed up in the most coveted of all feminine compliments, "She just *loves* flowers."

Most of these women had more style and money than political sophistication. And so, to be the Women's Committee ambassador to CBS, Townsend had appealed to a rather special flower-lover, Eleanor Bridges. Her garden was reputed to have all the plants that had been in Eden, including acanthus. Though a vegetarian who had a daughter named London and for a time constituted the local following of Krishnamurti, Bridges had more recently followed her husband (a recovering alcoholic sculptor who had Frenchified his name to Georges) into the John Birch Society. It was her motto—"Keep your words soft and sweet, because you'll never know when you might have to eat them"—that gave Vincent Townsend confidence in her ability to cope with CBS.

Eleanor Bridges's interview with Lowe took place at The (pronounced "Thee") Club. This semi-private, amply plate-glassed dining room, attached like a tick to the top of Red Mountain right next to Vulcan, was the place where high school seniors supped before the prom on reservations made by their fathers, and it was the last stop on any Women's Committee tour of Birmingham; Harrison Salisbury had been taken to lunch there by the editor of the Chamber of Commerce's magazine, who was a local stringer for the *Times*. Bridges briskly described the city's booming arts scene, "a saturate solution of culture." Then Lowe got down to business: "Mrs. Bridges, were you personally aware of prejudice in Birmingham?" She was not. She admired the Negro race, but was worried. "I think that's one of the contributing factors to our creativeness in the South, is sort of a joyousness of the Negro," she explained. But it had been four or five years since she had "heard Negroes just spontaneously break into song"—"and that's bad, because they're not happy and we're not happy about it."

As the state chairman of UNICEF, she had sponsored a children's art exhibition and solicited submissions from Negro schools as well as white. Not long after the winner was announced, Bridges told the camera, a distress call came from the main library downtown, where the art show was mounted. The parents of the grand prize winner couldn't get in to see his entry because, as Bridges put it, "it's against the city ordinance for the Negro people to come into the white library." Bridges had absolutely no problem getting the black family in to see their son's winning picture. One phone call, and a special escort came to guide them through the exhibit. "I think art and culture belongs to everyone, and on that level I think we have very little prejudice," she said.*

Thus did the ladies "fly the banners of confidence." To the extent that the men spoke at all, they faithfully mouthed Townsend's script. "I think the racial unrest in Birmingham is existing largely in the minds of people outside of Birmingham," said the aging Dixiecrat (and Klan) lawyer Hugh Locke, suspected of underwriting the Dynamite Hill bombings. Townsend seemed so pleased with his image-repair work that he made a rare appearance in the foreground, telling Lowe with truculent directness: "There's been really no real disturbances in Birmingham."

It seemed that even Birmingham's Negroes were cooperating with Townsend's blackout. Lowe could barely find any to go before the camera. Finally, at Herb Oliver's suggestion, he showed up with his crew at the Alabama Christian Movement's March 14 mass meeting. After a number of his questions went unanswered, a young woman rose and began talking about how she had been abused by the police. This elicited testimonials from twenty others. The Reverend Calvin Woods told of being sentenced to six months of hard labor during the 1958 bus boycott—"Yeah!" said the crowd—and fined $500 "for preaching the truth ... that God created all men equal." The Reverend Charles Billups described his war wounds ("My face is plaster surgeon. I got a plate in my head"), told of being abducted by "evil mens" and "beaten with chains until the blood run down."

Fred Shuttlesworth's account of surviving two bombings and the Phillips High mob lacked passion by comparison: "If you can't take it, you can't make it." Throughout his interview, he wore a strange half-smile, as if he were pinching himself to confirm that he might be on national TV. "We mean to kill segregation or be killed by it," he concluded for the camera with a bright grin.

The Race

FOR NOW, thanks to Bull Connor's limitless reach, segregation seemed more vital than ever. The proof of how well Connor had finessed the rich men who had once thought he worked for them was that funds for his mayoral candidate, Art Hanes, were reputedly being raised at the Mountain Brook Club. The clubmen had no idea Hanes was Bull's boy; they thought he was, almost, one of them. He wore his suits well. He was tall and lean; his slightly protruding eyes and an underbite made him a handsome version of J. Edgar Hoover. That his sister, the beloved Margaret Hanes, was the principal of Mountain Brook Elementary School almost offset Hanes's graduation from déclassé Woodlawn High School. And Art Jr. was in his freshman year at Princeton.

* Bridges had been one of the funders of the Southern Negro Youth Congress's Negro art exhibition, billed as a first, at its 1939 convention in Birmingham. It had been added to the program after a black high school boy had won a prize in a citywide art show and then was denied admission to the exhibit.

Despite a campaign base that bridged Bull Connor's office, the country clubs, and U.S. Steel (TCI's president was a supporter), Hanes was not a sure thing for the May primary. The city's rogue liberal tradition that had bedeviled the Big Mules since the Populists first joined forces with Birmingham's fledgling labor movement seemed finally ready for prime time.

Hanes's main opponent was a thirty-seven-year-old lawyer named J. Thomas King. Though short, uncharismatic, and Baptist, King represented the biggest threat to Connor's authority since Detective Henry Darnell banged on the door at the Tutwiler Hotel and caught his boss in near flagrante. The progressive coalition King fronted had tentacles in Mountain Brook, Birmingham-Southern College, the backrooms of the state Democratic Party, and the University of Alabama medical complex, which had grown into a community of 2,500 employees, with an operating budget of $10 million—the third-largest industry in town after TCI and Hayes Aircraft. And at the center of it all was the irrepressible young lawyer Chuck Morgan, who was seemingly about to fulfill his promise, if through the proxy of Tom King for now.

King, too, seemed primed for political destiny, as the son of an old Bibb Graves man appointed to the bench by Big Jim Folsom. (Judge Alta King had presided over the Judge Aaron castration trial, pronouncing the crime the "most cowardly, atrocious and diabolical" in his experience.) As a first-year law student at the University of Alabama in 1948, Tom had attended a creek-side powwow of the Machine, a consortium of fraternities that was a microcosm of the state's genteel conservative establishment.* In that momentous political year, the Machine was proving to be a sort of bellwether of the drift of state politics beyond the control of the Dixiecrat oligarchy, and the relatively nonelitist King was tapped as the Greeks' candidate for the presidency of the Student Government Association, the state's most reliable political catapult.

One of the main gears in the Machine had been a Delta Tao Delta (Delt) freshman, Chuck Morgan, who was already showing signs of political genius, with his ability to cozy up to an array of cliques without exactly betraying his own essence. After helping elect King SGA president, Morgan moved confidently into the role of Big Man on Campus. Although his major "political" accomplishment was to organize week-long "spontaneous demonstrations" protesting the exclusion of Alabama from the 1950 Orange Bowl, he graduated to working on the 1954 reelection campaign of Big Jim Folsom, to the consternation of his upwardly mobile Mountain Brook parents. "Boy," Folsom told Morgan, dispensing an important lesson about the white man's shame, "them goddamned Dixiecrats'll sleep

---

* The Machine's official name was Theta Nu Epsilon, whose Greek letters spelled ONE, and it had been founded in 1870 at Wesleyan University in Middletown, Connecticut, as a national suprafraternity to secure ruling-class prerogatives amid an industrial revolution. It was said to have been brought to the Alabama campus by an ambitious member of Delta Kappa Epsilon from Montgomery, Lister Hill, who was elected Student Government Association president in 1914.

with 'em at night and eat the breakfast they give 'em the next morning. But they'll never let 'em sit down to eat with 'em. That's the difference. Letting 'em sit down."

Morgan and his Birmingham pals formed a band of Angry Young Men who had gone to the University of Alabama, not because they weren't smart enough to go elsewhere, but because they were planning careers that would be enhanced by the nostalgia of shared football games as well as the secret bonds of the Machine whose tory values they had come to question. They had coalesced loosely in the Young Men's Business Club, a luncheon group formed in 1946 by returning veterans who were leery of the fogies at the Chamber of Commerce. The Young Turks were hoping to carry out a progressive takeover of the city through economic diversification, moving the city's industrial base from heavy manufacturing to services such as those being supplied by their comrades at the University Medical Center. Like many white liberals before them, they were optimistically tiptoeing around the tar pit of race—notwithstanding the cautionary example of one of their cronies, Hugo Black Jr.

At his father's urging, young Hugo had gone to the University of Alabama as an undergraduate. He came back to Birmingham in 1949, after finishing Yale Law School, to mine Hugo Sr.'s old client base at the city's preeminent labor law firm, which was co-headed by the son of the old southern CIO chief who had put up the money for the Southern Conference for Human Welfare. Hugo Sr. and his dear friend Lister Hill had long been mapping Junior's path to the Senate, and by 1954 young Hugo was ready to declare for Birmingham's House seat. His father summoned him to Washington. Reminding his son of the school segregation cases pending before the Court, he warned, "I agree with old Justice Harlan's dissent in *Plessy* v. *Ferguson*. I don't believe segregation is constitutional." Hugo Jr. returned to Birmingham and told his powerhouse advisers he wasn't ready. *Brown* was handed down soon after the primary, and the name Hugo Black became an instant case of political leprosy. When the justice appeared at the Birmingham Country Club the following year, a table of lawyers walked out, and the club's board reputedly threatened to kick out any member who invited him again.

The coveted House seat went to another congressional legatee, George Huddleston Jr. His father had represented the district in the House of Representatives for twenty-two years until 1937, during which time he had transformed from "bolshevik" to frothing anti–New Dealer. Huddleston Jr. asked a young lawyer with the Birmingham U.S. attorney's office to become his administrative aide. Tom King, the old university SGA president, considered the job as Huddleston's liaison with the county voters to be an excellent foundation for a "great long career" in Alabama politics.

Chuck Morgan's reluctant initiation into racial politics, the Bob Hughes case of 1960, temporarily set back his own ambitions. Late-night phone calls had begun, heavy breathers phoning in death threats till dawn. But when Jimmy Morgan decided to give up the presidency of the city commission in 1961, Chuck Morgan thought of a comrade whose absence had made him free of controversy.

Tom King and he had renewed their college acquaintance because of Congress-man Huddleston's policy of acknowledging every piece of constituent mail. King had ghosted an earnest thank-you to Morgan's facetious letter about the con-gressman's proposed legislation to outlaw piranha fish. Their correspondence went on for around five generations of thank-you-for-your-thank-you-for-my-thank-you letters. King, whose feeling had become "let George's piranha fish take care of the constituent mail," appreciated the comic relief.

Morgan urged King to come home and run for Jimmy Morgan's job in the spring of 1961. King asked himself, "Why not start with being mayor? What's wrong with that?" Morgan took command of King's campaign headquarters at the Molton Hotel. Occasionally, he took an hour off to serve as David Lowe's favorite off-the-record source for his CBS documentary in progress. One day, Lowe an-nounced to Morgan that he had hit upon Birmingham's essence: depressed. He cast his eyes sardonically toward Red Mountain and said, "Hell, what you need up there is not a statue of Vulcan but a giant psychiatrist."

The House of Morgan

VIRTUALLY THE ONLY RECENT TIDBIT from Gary Thomas Rowe that the local FBI office had seen fit to pass along to J. Edgar Hoover in Washington was an any-way-I-can-be-of-service telegram from Congressman George Huddleston, read at an open Klan meeting in February. The congressman's former administra-tive aide, Tom King, who might otherwise have composed the telegram, was now back in Birmingham, mapping out his own political career with Chuck Morgan.

As Morgan saw things, the really important business of the city was run by the Consensus, an amorphous body of bankers, industrialists, real estate tycoons, and other major businessmen that exercised veto power over policies that threat-ened profits. Otherwise, the Consensus "really did not give a damn whether Tweedledee or Tweedledum occupied office space in City Hall." To the extent that there was a conventional political machine, it was the outgoing mayor Jimmy Morgan's network of faithful employees and interested city contractors. And it was this House of Morgan, as its members cheekily called it, that the King cam-paign first wooed.

At a meeting at a "secret" place that one member called "the Burgundy room," Morgan's gang had rejected the frumpy King in favor of a man's man, an FBI man, a football man, but also a Methodist Sunday school teacher. Apparently they were not aware that these qualities of Art Hanes's had already impressed Bull Connor. But for the first time, Morgan's council was not unanimous in its support of a candidate. The lone holdout also happened to be the gang's most for-midable member, Vincent Townsend, who personally commanded the most pow-erful "machine" of all, the two major news organs in the state. With some coaching from Chuck Morgan, Tom King had managed to flatter an endorsement out of Townsend.

For all the potential skulduggery of an election pitting Townsend's apparatus against the House of Morgan and Bull Connor, the seven-man mayor's race leading up to the primary was subdued. King's main regret was that he had let a stage manager talk him into standing on a Coca-Cola crate for a television appearance, leading some voters to remark when they saw him in person, "Gosh, Mr. King, I thought you were a lot taller than that."

Meanwhile, Art Hanes was distracted by an unexpected patriotic task. His most macho colleagues at Hayes Aircraft, the test pilots, had been among eighty local airmen trained by the Central Intelligence Agency to assist a ragtag band of Cuban expatriates in an amphibious attack on Fidel Castro's new Communist government in Cuba, descending on a small inlet on the island's southern coast called the Bay of Pigs. Beginning on April 17, the Brigade waged suicidal battle against 20,000 Cuban troops for two days, waiting in vain for the Alabama airmen to come to their defense. But President Kennedy had called off the air cover, apparently after the planned assassination of Castro was foiled. A handful of the frustrated Alabama boys got into their stripped-down B-26s anyway and left their base in Nicaragua for the Bay of Pigs. Four of Hanes's close friends were among them, the only American fatalities among the 200 men killed by Castro's troops. To ensure that the Americans' participation remained a secret, an FBI buddy in Washington representing the CIA called Hanes and asked him to inform the aviators' wives of their widowhood, distribute the government's cash regrets, and tell them "just to be quiet about it."

In the May 2 primary, Hanes placed second among the seven candidates for mayor. Tom King beat him by a mere 1,500 votes. The two would face each other in a runoff. Counting on a gentlemanly race, King had been shocked while watching the returns on TV when Hanes appeared on Channel 6—Bull's old station— and pointed out that King had carried the "Legion Field boxes," a racial code for the black neighborhood whose lawns turned into an impromptu parking lot when there was a Crimson Tide football game at the stadium.

In the race for the public safety spot on the commission, meanwhile, Bull Connor had bested his three opponents without a runoff by doing little more than parading his K-9 Corps. Now, he prepared to enlist the Ku Klux Klan to deflect Tom King's challenge.

One Hundred Percent

WALTER "CRACK" HANNA, the granddaddy of Birmingham vigilantes and now an "industrialist" in the steel-plate-seconds business, was building himself a country club. Not even his friendship with the president of his old employer, TCI (whom Hanna introduced at business meetings, "Now here comes Jesus"), had been able to get him into the Mountain Brook Club. There were rumors that repeated blackballs had driven Hanna to fire shots into the clubhouse's colonial white facade, biting the hand that had once fed him but did not want him at the table. His Green Valley Country Club was situated in a new over-the-mountain suburb being developed by a right-wing insurance mogul named William

Hoover, who had been a suspected architect of the Dynamite Hill bombings and one of Ace Carter's benefactors.

Vigilantism in Birmingham was about to undergo another transformation. Bull Connor was embarking on a new relationship with the Klan for a new civil rights age, calling for a kind of coordinated action beyond the meager capacities of his old guerrilla fighter, Robert Chambliss. Eastview 13's dealings with the police department had acquired a new hierarchical etiquette, involving the klavern's star rookie Gary Thomas Rowe. Rowe was now on buddy-buddy terms with his fellow Klansmen—"Baby Brother" (sounded like "Baby Bruh"), they called him, in an endearment akin to nicknaming the bald man "Curly." The Birmingham FBI special agent in charge, Thomas Jenkins, who had recently succeeded the Memphis-bound Clarence Kelley, sent headquarters a summary of Rowe's major contributions during his first three months as an official informant—during which he earned $155, plus $57.66 for expenses. Jenkins singled out his informant's intelligence on the Klan's membership and new state officers, Eastview expenditures for 1960 ($4,811), and the names of all Eastview recruits. One of the applicants Rowe reported must have given the G-men quite a shock. He was a former FBI colleague, and now a mayoral candidate, Art Hanes.

But Rowe was already vexed by the dilemma of his role. After pleading first-time jitters on his initial "missionary" action—the chain-beating of a man who was allegedly molesting his sixteen-year-old stepdaughter—Rowe told his FBI handlers, "Hey, you can't go out with carloads of fifteen men and say, Hey, I'm going to stand off on the side and look at you while you beat these damn people. You either got to get in there or leave it alone or you're gonna get killed." According to Rowe, one handler explained that by law they had to tell him he couldn't get involved, but the FBI's main concern was that he not get caught. "Be careful," Rowe said the agent said. Rowe began "whipping ass" at lunch counters and on buses, telling the FBI about the attacks sometimes before the fact, sometimes after. In its file on Rowe, the FBI would not mention any violent incidents until April 1961, when Rowe made his official debut as a government-protected lawbreaker.

After the regular Eastview 13 meeting of April 6, fourteen members, including Rowe and his recruiter, Loyal McWhorter, were told to stick around to help "move some heavy equipment"—one of the new Klan Kodes that had just gone into effect, along with "Have you ever studied English 7?" ("Come to Phillips High School at once") and "Have you got five dollars?" ("Get over to Woolworth's"). They piled out to Odenville, a town northeast of Birmingham, to confront an elderly couple who were caring for the "fudge ripple baby" of a white mother and a Negro military man. The mission had ended ignominiously with the old woman firing a German Luger at the fleeing Klansmen, one of whom was so unnerved that he retched by the side of the road. Rowe would take pride in the fact that he never associated with this unworthy Klansman again.

A few weeks later, perhaps trying to work off the mortification of that performance, Rowe began flashing what looked like CIA credentials, leather encased, and showing off back sores he claimed to have sustained at the Bay of Pigs. And indeed his status was about to soar, as his klavern graduated from Mickey Mouse missions to matters of state urgency. On April 20, the Klan's top executive, Bobby Shelton, and Eastview 13's Exalted Cyclops, Robert Thomas, instructed Rowe to get in touch with Sergeant Tom Cook of the Birmingham Police Department. This was big. Cook was Bull Connor's favorite detective, famed for his photographic memory.* He reported directly to Connor, from an office on the third floor near the commissioner rather than in the police department's headquarters in the basement of city hall. A veteran of the botched J. B. Stoner sting of 1958, he now had the "subversives" beat, with standing orders to investigate anyone suspected of being "mixed up in this Shuttlesworth crowd." His investigative partners were often Klansmen.

Assured by Bobby Shelton that Rowe was "one hundred percent," Cook met Rowe that day at Ivan's, a pit barbecue cafe north of downtown. Cook brought Rowe an agenda he had apparently worked out in advance with Eastview's Robert Thomas, who was interested in identifying the Jews behind Birmingham's integration movement. To that end, Cook handed Rowe his file on the Alabama Council on Human Relations, which had barely been limping along since Bob Hughes's departure for Africa. Cook wanted Rowe to get some reliable Klansmen to go to the council's integrated meetings, take license tag numbers, and inform the members' employers of their dangerous affiliation. Cook showed Rowe a list of known council members, telling him to ignore the asterisked names; they were working for him. Rowe recognized one of the starred informants as one of Eastview's more affluent members.

Cook gave Rowe a report he had done tracing the Communist and Jewish "connections" of the Alabama Council and its parent, the Southern Regional Council. He also produced a memo, "Re: Martin Luther King, Jr., and Communism," that he had submitted to Connor a year earlier, detailing the "power hungry" King's attendance at the Highlander Folk School's twenty-fifth anniversary and his association with Bayard "Ruskin" ("King's Manager," "a sex pervert," and "Communistic fronter") and A. J. Muste ("the infamous Pacifist Communist Collaborator"). Cook wanted Rowe to give the material to Robert Thomas to reproduce on the Klan printing press.

Four days later, on April 24, Rowe returned the documents to Cook's office, where the detective confided that someone was leaking information out of Eastview 13. He knew this because the FBI had tipped off the police about the klavern's planned violence at the Reverend Alfred Hobart's Unitarian Church, the spiritual headquarters of the medical center liberals. Rowe had indeed informed the bureau a month earlier that Hobart had invited John Ciardi, poetry editor of the *Saturday Review*, to speak at his church after the Alabama Education

---

* Cook had helped make the only bombing arrest of the Dynamite Hill era. The suspect, a TCI miner accused of the April 28, 1951, dynamiting of a house where his ex-common-law wife was staying, was a Negro.

Association canceled his address in response to the White Citizens Councils' protest of his article "Jim Crow Is Treason." Some of the Eastview boys had taken oaths to God that they would wipe out Hobart's church if that's what it took not to let Ciardi "ruin and degenerate the children of the white race."

Cook told Rowe that efforts were being made to find the snitch and prosecute him for something or other. "The jury could be fixed to have the individual sent to the penitentiary," he reassured Rowe. Then Cook opened several filing cabinet drawers and told Rowe that the Klan was welcome to his investigative records, cautioning that if Connor found out about his largesse, Cook would be looking for a job. Rowe thought Cook was exaggerating: When he had shared the earlier booty from Cook with Robert Thomas, the Exalted Cyclops had said, hell, he'd seen that tame stuff already, apparently courtesy of Connor. Rowe's FBI handlers had not been so blasé about the material; they sent photocopies to Washington. And in fact, Cook's documentation of King's subversive connections was more sophisticated than anything the bureau had yet produced on the civil rights movement.*

Bull Connor was going to have to step personally into police-Klan affairs, given the second-place showing of his candidate in the mayoral primary. Soon after the election, a Birmingham police detective named W. W. "Red" Self, who had gotten on a "Baby Bruh" basis with Rowe while working as a part-time bouncer at the VFW Hall, summoned Rowe to a meeting with him and Detective Tom Cook at Ivan's Restaurant. The police wanted Eastview 13 to know about "a group of niggers and whites coming into the State of Alabama on what was to be a so-called Freedom Ride." They were members of a civil rights organization called the Congress of Racial Equality, or CORE. Cook was asking the Klan to give them a welcome that would go down in the history books. "I don't give a damn if you beat them, bomb them, murder, or kill them," Cook said, according to Rowe. "I don't give a shit. We don't ever want to see another nigger ride on the bus into Birmingham again."

At Eastview's May 4 meeting, Robert Thomas and the klavern's other top contact with the Birmingham police, Hubert Page, announced grimly that CORE had started its tour of the southern states. Page said, "All Klansmen present should remain in close touch with their telephones."

Freedom Ride

THE CONGRESS OF RACIAL EQUALITY, historically white, northern, and elite, had found itself with a mass black constituency in 1960, when southern college students began duplicating the restaurant sit-ins it had pioneered in Chicago in the 1940s. CORE had become a combination brain trust and traffic control

---

* Twenty years later, after his relationship with Rowe was made public, Cook confidently declared that Rowe had made it all up. He said he knew Rowe was an FBI informant and wouldn't be stupid enough to turn documents over to him. Cook was unaware that the photocopied proof was in the files at the bureau.

center for the sit-in movement. The white men who ran the organization out of Manhattan decided it was about time to put a charismatic Negro at the helm.

Their man was forty-one-year-old James Farmer, another key pivot between the Left and the civil rights movement. The cloistered son of the first black Ph.D. in Texas, Farmer had gotten his first taste of organized activism as a college student in 1937, when he drove his dad's Dodge from Marshall, Texas, to Richmond for the founding meeting of the Southern Negro Youth Congress. While Farmer was getting his Ph.D. at Howard University's school of religion (where his father was on the faculty), the theologian-ethicist Howard Thurman introduced him to the teachings of Gandhi—and to an old friend who worked for the Fellowship of Reconciliation. Seeing meager potential in the black church, Farmer joined the FOR staff upon his graduation in 1941 as its race relations secretary in Chicago and soon presented A. J. Muste with a memorandum proposing an interracial organization that would use Gandhian direct action to attack segregation. The Congress of Racial Equality was spun off from the FOR shortly thereafter.

Farmer became frustrated by the doctrinaire pacifism of Muste and his sidekick, Bayard Rustin ("Rusty and Muste"), and left in 1945. It was Rustin who, two years later, organized the FOR's path-breaking protest, an integrated bus ride through the Upper South to test the Supreme Court's recent *Irene Morgan* decision, which outlawed segregated seating on interstate buses and trains. This "Journey of Reconciliation" by sixteen blacks and whites—mostly professional pacifists—had sparked little sound or fury, despite Rustin's arrest and sentence to a chain gang, but it introduced the prototype of civil rights protest that Farmer would undertake immediately upon assuming charge of CORE. He was calling his bus tour of the South a Freedom Ride.

This newest Birmingham turning point on the horizon was in part the work of Justice Hugo Black. The previous December, he had delivered the Supreme Court's opinion on a case filed by a fellow Alabamian, Bruce Boynton, the son of Selma's premier black activist, who had been arrested for defying Jim Crow in the Richmond Trailways bus terminal restaurant on his way home from law school. Black's *Boynton* decision expanded the Court's 1946 *Morgan* ruling to include the terminals—waiting rooms, restrooms, and restaurants.

CORE's Freedom Ride would thus be a departure from the student sit-ins' civil disobedience against state segregation ordinances. Though the Freedom Riders were not breaking the law, they were indeed, as white southerners liked to point out, looking for trouble. Farmer's avowed aim was to provoke "the racists of the South to create a crisis so that the federal government would be compelled to enforce the law."

Jim Farmer and his cadre of twelve black and white men and women were a cross-generational, polysectarian group. In addition to the usual veteran pacifists with trust funds, the fledgling Student Nonviolent Coordinating Committee had fielded a leader of its all-star Nashville chapter, a former boy preacher from Alabama named John Lewis, who had "saved" the chickens on the family farm ("The henhouse itself seemed a holy place to me") before moving to Tennessee for seminary there. At what one of the riders called a "last supper" at a Chinese restaurant in Washington, another rider, B. Elton Cox, the young North Carolina minister who had introduced Shuttlesworth to the sit-in movement, called for a prayer, which Farmer countered with the suggestion of a moment of silence, in deference to the atheists among them.

On May 4, they boarded two buses, a Trailways and a Greyhound, for a journey through the South to end in New Orleans. The buses had their usual complement of garden-variety segregation-observing passengers and only three reporters, all black. The mainstream press was preoccupied with astronaut Alan Shepard's first space shot, scheduled for the following day.

The Black-Hand Treatment

BULL CONNOR PREPARED for the Freedom Ride's arrival in Birmingham, in what promised to be a perfect campaign opportunity for his candidate for mayor, Art Hanes. As the runoff race took off, handbills from the "Committee to Keep Birmingham White" announced that Tom King's campaign had received $3,000 from the NAACP, that King had been sent down from Washington, D.C. ("cesspool of integration"), to desegregate the local schools. Even the centerpiece of the King campaign, the chestnut of getting Birmingham a decent airport, was being portrayed by the Hanes forces as a blueprint for integration. King was trying "to make Birmingham into another Atlanta," Hanes charged, tying the rival town's heavy air traffic with its self-aggrandizement as the "City Too Busy to Hate."

Chuck Morgan and the still wet-behind-the-ears Young Turks around Tom King panicked. Morgan arranged a summit meeting at the *Birmingham News* offices with Vincent Townsend. Townsend believed that King ought to pay a courtesy call on Bull Connor. King had reservations about courting the segregationist vote, but because of Townsend's beaming editorials he felt beholden.

On Monday, May 8, King arrived at city hall in a mood to get the errand over with. He was admitted to Connor's chambers without delay. After some small talk, Bull said, "You got quite a campaign," and referring to his own primary victory said, "I'm glad to be out of it." King said he didn't want to take up too much of the commissioner's time. "If elected, I see no reason why we can't work together," King said.

"These nigras," Bull said, changing the subject, "they gon' be here on a bus next week. They gon' be here. We have advance ways of knowing."

"I'm sure you will be ready for 'em, Commissioner," King said, then thanked Connor for his time.

King exited through the Art Deco front doors of city hall and made his way down the sidewalk. A voice behind him called out, "Mr. King, Mr. King." He turned and instinctively offered his hand to a tall man, about 280 pounds, in his thirties. His purposeful grip, as well as the color of his skin, made doom wash over King's body. The Negro man said nothing, just held the handshake for about thirty seconds and hurried away. Three days later, the Young Turks confirmed that the opposition had a photograph of Tom King committing the ultimate taboo.

The "black-hand treatment" against Tom King would become a Birmingham political legend. Most people assumed Bull Connor was its mastermind. But the proof of Connor's power was that he did not even have to do the dirty work for his handpicked candidate. The handshake had been set up by one of the "House of Morgan" operatives behind Art Hanes's campaign: Clint Bishop, Mayor Jimmy Morgan's executive secretary, had received a firm commitment from Hanes that he would keep his job in the new administration. The morning King came a-courting, Bishop asked Bull to do him a favor and buzz him down the hall when his visitor left. Bishop and a photographer then slipped into a room off the commission's public chambers and aimed out the window at the black man Bishop had paid to hail King.

Hanes blanched when he was shown the picture: "That's liable to kill us." Bishop suddenly realized that his candidate might not be the politician of everyone's dreams. "No," Bishop corrected him, "that got you elected."

At the Movement mass meeting that Monday night, Fred Shuttlesworth announced almost as an afterthought, "Next Sunday our bus riders will be here," a mixed group of whites and Negroes riding and eating under the auspices of "a real action organization."

The Point of No Return

ON THURSDAY, MAY 11, Bull Connor's personal detective, Tom Cook, went to Atlanta to get information on the buses' schedule for the coming Sunday, the date of the Freedom Riders' arrival in Birmingham. Cook passed the intelligence along to his best friend in the Eastview klavern, Hubert Page. That night, Page announced at the Eastview meeting that all Klansmen were to stay away from the Greyhound bus terminal on Sunday unless specifically instructed to participate in the "intervention" against the bus riders. On orders from the state's top Klansman, Bobby Shelton, sixty men would be selected to take care of the integrationists, thirty at the bus depot and thirty reinforcements stationed nearby at the Molton Hotel, which happened to be Tom King's campaign headquarters. After the meeting, Page conveyed a special message to the action squads from Bull Connor. "By God, if you are going to do this thing, do it right," the public safety commissioner of Birmingham reportedly said.

Connor would give them fifteen to twenty minutes to work over the Freedom Riders before any officers arrived. Police headquarters were virtually across the street from the Greyhound bus terminal. If Negroes went into the restrooms, Connor advised, the Klansmen were to beat them till they "looked like a bulldog got ahold of them." Then, Connor said, take the "nigger's" clothing off and carry it away so that he would have to walk out into the depot naked; he would be immediately arrested and sent to the penitentiary. If a Klansman overstayed the fifteen-minute grace period and was unavoidably arrested, he was to insist that the Negroes had started it. And if wires really got crossed and a Klansman was convicted, Connor would finagle a light sentence. The commissioner warned: Do not carry your Klan membership card or a pistol unless you have a permit.

Squad leaders from various klaverns around Alabama met at Eastview head-quarters above Morgan's Department Store in Woodlawn to put together the list of their best men. The lucky sixty would be called at nine the morning of the event. Hubert Page charged one of Eastview's toughest members with notifying the chosen Klansmen to bring leaded baseball bats and clubs. That was Earl "Shorty" Thompson, the feisty redheaded product of the DeBardeleben coal camp, who himself was said to favor Uncle Charlie's weapon of choice, a subma-chine gun. Gary Thomas Rowe was one of the squad leaders involved in planning the assault against law-abiding citizens.

The FBI had another problem. Normal bureau procedure required agents to pass their intelligence on to the local police and let them handle the enforcement. As J. Edgar Hoover vehemently maintained, FBI agents were only observers and information gatherers, not hands-on law enforcers per se. Otherwise, he insisted, the country would have a national police corps. But the problem with following standard operating procedure was that local law enforcement—reportedly Bull Connor himself—was at the heart of the plot. To compound the bureau's quandary, alerting the police would jeopardize their prize informant. But to say nothing would essentially make the FBI part of the Klan's plot. The local bureau had entertained the possibility that Rowe was a double agent, working them for information he could feed the Klan.

On Friday, May 12, Special Agent in Charge Thomas Jenkins teletyped Rowe's report on the Thursday-night Eastview meeting to the "seat of govern-ment," as Hoover referred to the FBI's headquarters on the Department of Justice building's fifth floor. Tom Cook had already telephoned a Birmingham FBI agent that day to feel out what he knew, asking point-blank if he had gotten any infor-mation that the Alabama Knights planned a reception for CORE. The Birming-ham bureau told headquarters that it didn't tell Cook anything, for fear of compromising its informant. The FBI was on the verge of making its own pact with the Ku Klux Klan.

Mother's Day Eve

WORD WAS OUT that hundreds of black-hand photographs of Tom King were ready for distribution. Art Hanes's henchmen had fanned the hysteria of King's aides by making them scheme and manipulate to get hold of a copy. On Saturday afternoon, May 13, King was at a barbecue in Ensley, given by a prominent Ford dealer, when he received an emergency summons to campaign headquarters.

Chuck Morgan was sensing his own political extinction once again. He had decided to set up another meeting with Vincent Townsend. Townsend issued an edict to King and his aides: Run a preemptive ad in the *News,* publishing the picture to expose Hanes's dirty tricks. King's heart thudded. Townsend pushed on. "We've got to get it in the paper tomorrow. That'll leave us two weeks before the election."

That same day, after nine days on the road, the Freedom Riders were welcomed to Atlanta by Martin Luther King and SCLC's executive director, Wyatt Tee Walker. The Upper South leg of the ride had been so uneventful that one of the protesters commented, "They heard we were coming and baked us a cake." Jim Farmer's cancer-racked father had been following his son's progress from his hospital bed in Washington. He had scoffed twenty years before when "Junior" told him of his plan to attack segregation through Gandhian means: "One question: are you Gandhi? The British threw him in jail. The Bamians and Mississippians would shoot him. Dead." Now he consulted his son's itinerary. "Oh, tomorrow he goes through Bama," he said to his wife. Then he died. Jim Farmer headed for the airport to get to the funeral. Mrs. Farmer was convinced that her husband had timed his passing to spare Junior from Birmingham.

At nine-thirty that night, Birmingham's police chief, Jamie Moore, informed Special Agent in Charge Thomas Jenkins that he would be out of town the next day, at a memorial service for his family in Albertville. Holding down the fort in his place, Moore told Jenkins, was Sergeant Tom Cook. Commissioner Connor would also be on hand.

Meanwhile, Howard K. Smith stood at the plate-glass window of The Club, taking in the sparkly city in the valley. The air date for "Who Speaks for Birmingham?" was less than a week away, and Smith was being treated to a bon voyage dinner by a delegation of impressive citizens, liberal-minded men and women including a businessman-lawyer who had been a Rhodes scholar with him at Oxford. The host was Cecil Roberts, an Englishwoman who had married into one of the first families of coal. Her keen satirical sense of her adopted city, a tartness sometimes bordering on the perverse, gave her enormous appeal to visiting journalists, and she had been acting virtually as an unpaid staff person on the CBS documentary.

The conversation at The Club was erudite, the cocktails were sublime. Enjoying the view from the top of Red Mountain, Smith asked his hosts, "Where does the other half live?"

"Oh, they live over in West End," a guest said. "You don't want to go there at night."

Before leaving Birmingham, Smith had one last lead to follow up. He and his producer, David Lowe, had been having a bite at their motel earlier that day when a tipster informed them, "Be sure to be at the bus station tomorrow, because you're going to see action."

7.

FREEDOM RIDE

Dr. Fields

THE TELEPHONED TIP to Howard K. Smith foretold a dramatic development in the vigilante vanguard of Birmingham: On the eve of their most
important assignment to date, the Klansmen who had always been the "authorized" enforcers of the segregationist status quo now faced serious competition
from a fringe element whose motives were suspect. J. B. Stoner had returned to the
action in Birmingham* and was hoping to move from the margins to the center of
the resistance.

Smith's caller was Edward Fields, a professional anti-Semite who was the titular head of Stoner's most recent anti-Jewish political organization, the National
States Rights Party. Because Fields was handsome and once had a legitimate career as a chiropractor, he seemed to stand a chance of "passing" as normal. "Dr.
Fields," as he preferred to be called, was an Atlanta native and, like Stoner, was
from a "good family"—a prep school product whose father was the local comp-
troller for Armour & Co. He had already been a seasoned anti-Semite when he
met Stoner in 1952 at the Atlanta Law School, having found his first mentor in
Atlanta's retired general, George Van Horn Moseley, the figurehead for the
Nazis' proposed American coup in 1938, whom the Ku Klux Klan periodically
tried to coax back into action. When Fields registered for the draft in 1952, listing

---

* Since being decommissioned after his collaboration with Bull Connor in the bombing of Fred
Shuttlesworth's church, Stoner had gone into hibernation. Georgia officials had arrested his followers for the October 1958 bombing of the Reform Jewish Temple of Atlanta. (Among them was
Richard Bowling, who had apparently handled the Shuttlesworth bombing.) Though the state authorities were not expecting to get convictions, they did correctly calculate that the arrests would
take the perpetrators out of circulation. As they hoped, two of the suspects named J. B. Stoner as the
supplier of dynamite. Amid the ensuing publicity, State Farm Insurance fired him, depriving him of
the company car that had ferried him around the southern bombing circuit. Desperate to raise the
money to buy a new car, Stoner told Hugh Morris, the old Klansman who had been his liaison to
Connor, that Martin Luther King could be disposed of for $2,500. His boys "would blow him up or
do whatever was necessary," Stoner said, "he or his family or anybody who was in the house." They
could also shoot him if that was preferable.

his job as "Anti-Jewish Crusader," a Navy psychiatrist classified him as an "S-4, paranoid, and a dangerous type," or "one step away from being totally insane." Instead of signing him up, the Navy brought Fields to the attention of the FBI. Fields abandoned law school and went to Davenport, Iowa, to study chiropractic.

Fields and Stoner had been running their National States Rights Party out of Louisville, Kentucky, for nearly two years when Harrison Salisbury's article on Birmingham appeared in the *New York Times* in April 1960. Soon after, Fields wrote a piece for the NSRP's organ, *The Thunderbolt* (its thunderbolt logo was also the emblem of Hitler's SS Elite Guards), which pretty much regurgitated Salisbury's assessment of the Magic City, though his viewpoint was one of approbation. Within a couple of months, the NSRP had moved to Birmingham.* Though Stoner returned to Atlanta, Fields and the party set up shop in a fieldstone house in the working-class neighborhood of Central Park, right down Bessemer Road from the abandoned theater that had headquartered Ace Carter's Klan of the Confederacy.

In January 1961, Fields sent Bull Connor an ingratiating letter advising him to refuse to cooperate with CBS ("owned and run by Jews") on its Birmingham documentary. But by May, when Fields called Howard K. Smith at his motel to say there was going to be "action" at the bus station, he had come to see CBS as a potential collaborator, a vehicle for publicizing the NSRP's first big splash in Birmingham. Fields and Stoner planned to be at the depot on Sunday to meet the Freedom Riders.

On to Bama

SMITH AND HIS PRODUCER, David Lowe, passed Fields's tip on to the Reverend Herb Oliver when he arrived at the motel to show the journalists bloodstained pants that had belonged to one of the subjects of his Inter-Citizens Committee affidavits, a young black boy who had been murdered and thrown into a pond, evidently for trying to fish in white boys' territory. Oliver, in turn, relayed the rumor of impending bus station violence to Fred Shuttlesworth. At 7:39 Sunday morning, under the Gandhian mandate to keep the authorities informed, Shuttlesworth and Oliver telegrammed Bull Connor and his police chief, seeking protection for the travelers, due in that afternoon.

Soon after, Tommy Rowe went down to the Greyhound station, a classic grimy squat box of a depot across the street from city hall, in whose basement the police department was housed. He called Detective Tom Cook at home from a pay phone. Cook asked Rowe how he was dressed so that he could have a patrolman stand at one of the phones to keep the line open all day for Rowe to call him. Rowe looked across the street to city hall and saw dozens of officers bunched on the sidewalk in front. He didn't mind telling Cook that this police

---

* Perhaps feeling some qualms over his past dealings with Stoner, Bull Connor wrote Fields in Kentucky and told him the NSRP was not welcome in Birmingham.

presence alarmed him. Cook reassured him. The Klan would have fifteen minutes, guaranteed.

Before noon, Shuttlesworth got a long-distance call from a Freedom Rider named James Peck. A forty-six-year-old Harvard-educated New Yorker and scion of the Peck & Peck retail family, Peck was a veteran of the original 1947 freedom ride through the South, the Fellowship of Reconciliation's Journey of Reconciliation, during which he had been impressed most by the Jim Crow Bibles used in southern courts to swear in black witnesses—COLORED printed on the page edges. He told Shuttlesworth that he and his fellow Freedom Riders—now around sixteen—were about to leave Atlanta for Birmingham.

At one minute before noon, the Atlanta FBI office wired Birmingham that the Greyhound freedom bus had left and would arrive in Birmingham at 3:30; a second group, with ten Freedom Riders, would arrive via Trailways at 4:05.

At city hall, Bull Connor waited. By now he had seen the morning's *Birmingham News*. What a pleasant surprise it contained: a full-page ad showcasing the notorious black-hand photograph—a rather innocuous distant aerial shot—under all-cap headlines: "TOM KING IS FIGHTING MACHINE POLITICS AT ITS WORST!" The picture was reaching more people than a truckload of handbills would have, and the *News* had made the King campaign pay for the ad.

Poison

BETWEEN PHONE CALLS to Tom Cook, Tommy Rowe was in and out of the Klan's room at the Molton Hotel. The Eastview elite—Rowe, Hubert Page, Robert Thomas, Earl Thompson—were supposed to refrain from landing blows at the bus station and save themselves for the real work: They would follow the CORE leaders back to their hotel or motel and beat them there, without a fifteen-minute restriction.

One unforeseen development had Bobby Shelton's nose out of joint: The National States Rights Party had decided to horn in on the Klan's show at the bus depot. In the year since the party had made Birmingham its home, the Klansmen had come to the conclusion, as had the old-fashioned Klansman Hugh Morris, that these anti-Semites were nutcases. There were the spoken doubts about their sexuality and the unspoken ones about why educated, highborn men like Fields and Stoner would be spending Sunday afternoon at a bus station. *The Thunderbolt*, written almost entirely by Fields except for the canned copy from Gerald L.K. Smith's *The Cross and the Flag* and such, was pitched to people who owned a hardcover dictionary and had heard of the Trilateral Commission. Whereas the Klan acted on orders from city hall, the anti-Semites' motives seemed private and psychological: Freud versus Marx. The official Klan line on Fields was that he should be treated as "poison." Shelton deeply resented his presence at the Greyhound station. And it was worse than that: J. B. Stoner himself had come over from Atlanta.

Page, Rowe, and Thompson approached Stoner. Page spoke for the group:

"Get your goddamn people out of here. When we get through whippin' ass here, we're going to whip yours too." Stoner explained that they had been invited to participate. When Fields came to his colleague's side, Page cussed him too. Rowe repaired to his bus station hot line, called Cook, and told him that Dr. Fields's group was not to be confused with his, and if anything went wrong, don't blame the Klan. Cook tried to placate him by saying, "You boys should work together." But Cook and his police cronies planned to deal with the States Righters themselves. After all, they might have to arrest *somebody* to justify their badges.

Roast 'Em

IN THE MIDDLE OF THE AFTERNOON, the Greyhound freedom bus rolled into Anniston, Alabama, a miniature Magic City of country club industrialists and their workers. It was the hometown of Kenneth Adams, an Ace Carter confederate who had led the attack on Nat King Cole at Birmingham's Municipal Auditorium in the spring of 1956, and though the klavern Adams headed was not affiliated with Bobby Shelton's Klan, he had cooperated by rustling up a gang to greet the Freedom Riders at the Anniston depot. His men began thrashing at the bus with iron bars. A uniformed policeman walked up and chatted with some of them before clearing a trail for the bus to leave.

A fifty-car convoy pursued the riders out of town, with a Ford truck in front of the bus to keep it from picking up too much speed. Five miles west of Anniston, a tire that had been slashed back at the station blew. As the driver scampered off the bus, two hundred men swooped in from their cars, waving chains, clubs, and pipes, some screaming "Sieg, heil!" A firebomb was tossed through a smashed rear window, landing with a hiss. The attackers held the door shut and shouted, "Let's roast 'em."

Eli Cowling, a gray-haired but still hardy plainclothes investigator for the state of Alabama who had boarded the bus at Governor Patterson's direction in Atlanta (probably for surveillance rather than protection), forced open the door of the burning bus, pulled his gun, and ordered the mob, "Now you get back and let these people off, or some of you are going to die." Passengers bailed out through the windows. The crowd began to disperse as Cowling fired into the air. Late-arriving state patrolmen sat in their cars and laughed. One officer later gave one of the confiscated weapons, a two-foot-long wooden club, to his son as a souvenir. The charred steel frame of the Greyhound bus was towed to an automobile graveyard in Birmingham.

Back in the Loop

TROY INGRAM HAD DRIVEN over the mountain to North Birmingham that morning, supposedly to visit a childhood friend from DeBardeleben's Overton camp. It had been nearly four years since he had resigned from the Klan amid the Judge Aaron castration scandal, and other than joining the White Citizens Council that met over at the Carnegie library in Ensley, he had largely confined his civic activities to the Cahaba Heights Volunteer Fire Department.

After hearing a report on his car radio that the freedom bus was heading toward Birmingham, Ingram would claim, he detoured to the Greyhound station and, seeing the crowds, decided to park in back of the depot and sit in his car. The FBI's later discovery that no local radio station reported the Freedom Riders' progress suggests that Ingram was moving back into the Klan loop. Perhaps he had met up with his best friend, Robert Chambliss, who was no longer the first brother the Klan turned to when it needed a job done. Dynamite Bob had not been among the Klan's chosen sixty on this assignment, having been supplanted by men like Tommy Rowe and Hubert Page as the klavern's contact with city hall. Though Ingram left the station after two hours, he would claim, before the bus arrived, Chambliss stayed on, not one to miss a Klan show like this.

Back of the Bus

JIM PECK AND HIS COMPANIONS on the Trailways freedom bus made it to Anniston an hour after the Greyhound, unaware of the reception their comrades had gotten. Most of the lay passengers got off there. Eight young white men boarded. "Niggers, get back," one announced. "You ain't up north. You're in Alabama, and niggers ain't nothing here." The whites broadsided Charles Person, a black Morehouse freshman whose parents had begged him not to go to Bama. Peck and Walter Bergman, a sixty-one-year-old retired white college professor from Michigan—an old Socialist—rose from their back-of-the-bus seats to reason with the attackers and were battered to the floor with Coke bottles. "Don't kill him," one of the white men cautioned the friend jumping up and down on Bergman, who incurred brain damage that would be permanent and life-threatening.

The white newcomers dragged their victims down the aisle to the back of the bus and stacked them "one-atop-the-other like pancakes." A policeman boarded the bus, smiled at the batterers, and said, "Don't worry about no lawsuits. I ain't seen a thing." The freedom bus then headed for Birmingham, escorted by four police cars, and in light of the eight-hundred-man mob said to have gathered on the regular route, detoured through Oxford, Alabama, where Ace Carter was reputedly in retirement on his farm.

Give 'Em Hell

TO THE SAVVY JOURNALISTS in the vicinity of Birmingham's Greyhound station, the presence of the Klan's Alabama chief, Bobby Shelton, cruising in his black Cadillac or pacing on foot, screamed "big news." Howard K. Smith noticed that two elderly men wearing black hats and suits with carnations in the pocket (Governor John Patterson's own fashion signature) seemed to be giving signals to the younger toughs—the two kept ostentatiously switching places.

During their next phone conversation, Detective Tom Cook told Tommy Rowe about the ambush of the Freedom Riders outside Anniston, saying it might have resulted in some deaths. "Hang in there," Cook said, "because there are still some buses coming into Birmingham." He reminded Rowe to get the hell away from the scene. The police were hoping just to arrest Dr. Fields's crowd, for unlawful assembly. Cook might get J. B. Stoner yet. Cook signed off, "Give 'em hell."

A motorcycle policeman received orders from his sergeant, which he assumed came down the chain of command from his lieutenant. Do not come within six blocks of the depots, he was told. "If a call goes out to go to the bus station," the sergeant continued, "you don't hear it."

Just Another Bus

TOM LANKFORD had spent most of the day with Connor and his detective, Tom Cook, monitoring the freedom buses. He was the subterranean player in the depot drama, a young man whom one admirer believed had "more potential than a nuclear bomb." Officially, he was a police reporter-photographer for the *Birmingham News,* a recent University of Alabama graduate who had edited the college newspaper, *The Crimson-White.* A boyish towhead who could have stepped out of a reading primer illustration, Lankford was also Townsend's personal reconnaissance man, with an expense account to buy the latest breakthroughs in modern information-gathering technology—reputedly wiretap and photographic surveillance equipment that outclassed that of the Birmingham Police Department.

Besides being Townsend's golden boy, Lankford was the police department's pet reporter, especially since his opposite number on the *Post-Herald,* the exprizefighter Bill Mobley, had accompanied Detective Henry Darnell to the Tutwiler Hotel on the evening of December 21, 1951, and snapped the compromising pictures of Connor and his secretary. Mobley now went into the commissioner's office and asked to borrow a police dog as protection against the mob gathered at the depot. Connor told him it was "just another bus coming in" and tipped him off that the real story was in Anniston, where Freedom Riders had been firebombed. As Mobley drove down the Atlanta highway toward Anniston, the freedom bus passed the city limits, coming from the opposite direction.

Meanwhile, Rowe took in the scene at the Greyhound station. Howard K. Smith was camped out with the local reporters (who were chilly, per Townsend's orders). Rowe's brothers were concealing their bats and clubs in an affectation of nonchalance. Suddenly Rowe was struck by the magnitude of it. He half expected to see the National Guard march in formation around the corner. His stomach did a flip: He had the feeling that if troops were called in, his handlers would desert him.

One of the Klansmen asked Smith what he was interested in "those niggers" for. At around 3:45, Smith observed a migration of squad cars into police headquarters, in the basement of city hall. At 4:10, a dispatcher at the Trailways station a couple of blocks away watched several Birmingham policemen leave the nearby parking lot where they had been hanging out. One of them was Red Self, the detective who had tipped Rowe off about the Freedom Ride. Back at Grey-hound, Rowe was approached by Conraid Creel, father of the Bessemer klavern's Exalted Cyclops, Robert Creel—two more refugees from Charles DeBardele-ben's coal mines to the Klan. Creel, who was probably one of the elderly men Smith had noticed, said that the action was going to happen at the Trailways sta-tion instead of the Greyhound. Bobby Shelton wanted Rowe, Earl Thompson, and the other squad leaders to get over there.

Three journalists from the *News* were drinking Cokes in a car parked in an alley behind the Trailways station, a block and a half away from where most of the reporters were still waiting at Greyhound; the press had not confirmed which bus line was carrying the second wave of Freedom Riders. A bus marked "Dallas" rolled into the alley at around 4:15. Because it was a late model, sleek and shiny, the *News* managing editor didn't figure it was the right one, evidently assuming that an integrated bus would be like those smoking jalopies known as "nigger cars" that ornamented downtown intersections.

Inside the bus, the eight white men who had boarded at Anniston advised Walter Bergman and his wife, Frances, that "you Communists ought to go back to Russia," then exited into a crowd of colleagues holding Coke bottles and lead pipes. Peck gave his black partner, Charles Person, a look intended to suggest cau-tion, but Person said, "Let's go."

Peck ignored his designated "escort" from the elite Eastview 13 squad (as Rowe described Gene Reeves, a bookbinder who he reported had a part in the Odenville "fudge ripple baby" visitation) and tried to shoulder through the white men surging around him and Person. Rowe was close enough to hear Peck address the mob, "Before you get my brother, you will have to kill me." Five men set upon Person, six on Peck, who blacked out within seconds.

The Klansmen had not worked out how they were going to distinguish the Freedom Riders from the ordinary, segregation-abiding passengers debarking along with them. Someone shouted, "Let's get them, let's get all of them." Inside the depot, Rowe caught sight of George Webb, a light-skinned twenty-nine-year-old black man who was at the baggage claim to pick up his fiancée, Mary Spicer. Rowe grabbed him and held him down while a man who was not part of the East-view team smashed Webb's ear and temple with a lead pipe wrapped in a paper bag. Spicer recognized the pipe wielder as one of the men who had gotten on the freedom bus (on which she was a regular, segregated passenger) in Anniston and beaten Jim Peck and Walter Bergman. One of Eastview's more gallant members encouraged Spicer to "get the hell out of here unless you want to get the same thing."

Tommy Langston, a photographer for the *Post-Herald,* was looking in the window of Acton's Camera Store in the alley behind the depot when Spicer came screaming out the station's back door. Langston entered through the swinging doors and, before his eyes had adjusted to the fluorescent light, aimed his camera at what sounded like a commotion. As his flash went off, a man yelled, "Get that camera."

Rowe and the mob released Webb, who had managed to kick one of the white men before escaping out the door with only a bloody face and a torn-off pants leg. They turned on Langston as he ran behind the parked freedom bus. By the time the three *News* men sipping their Cokes in their car realized they were missing their story, Langston was on the ground curled fetally around his camera, being kicked and pummeled by the mob. Hubert Page, natty in a suit befitting the Grand Titan of the Invisible Realm, was apparently supposed to supervise, but, no longer able to defer his missionary zeal, he jumped on the photographer (according to Rowe) and kicked him five or six times. Another reporter heard a man of Page's description ask Langston in a soft voice if he was hurt. Langston struggled to his feet and limped down the alley.

Bleeding black casualties were crawling and staggering from the station, amid screams of "Run, nigger, run." *Birmingham News* photographer Bud Gordon had gotten three good shots of the melee and was heading for his car when the man who was presumably Page yelled to the gang, "Get him." Rowe and Earl Thompson and a dark-skinned Eastview action squad leader named John "Nigger" Hall surrounded Gordon and tried to remove the film from his camera. "You are ruining my camera," Gordon complained and offered to remove the film pack himself. He then handed it to Rowe, who tore it apart and dropped it on the ground. The man with the lead pipe—none of the Eastview Klansmen recognized him—urged Rowe to "knock hell out of" Gordon, and Gordon later credited Rowe with restraining the rogue vigilante.

Vincent Townsend's eyes and ears, Tom Lankford, had gotten a few shots of his *Post-Herald* rival, Langston, on the ground and had then watched as the thugs exposed Gordon's film. Now he walked up to the muggers and volunteered his film. Someone brought yet a third camera to sanitize, turning the melee into a sort of Alphonse and Gaston chain of courtesies.

Rowe had begun to club a black woman when someone came up and grabbed his arm. He spun around right into the face of Detective Red Self. "Hey, get the fuck out of here, Tommy," Self said, according to Rowe. "Your fifteen minutes is up. All goddamn hell is going to break loose. Get these guys out of here. The police are coming." Rowe yelled out a warning, and all around him Klansmen began hollering, "Take off, take off, the police are coming."

The Freedom Rider Walter Bergman had propped up the bleeding Jim Peck and asked Howard K. Smith for help. Smith waved over a cabbie, who took one look at the fare and sped off. Smith set out to fetch CBS's rental station wagon at the Greyhound depot. But by the time his camera crew drove it over, the brouhaha had ended, as if on the cue of a maestro. Peck and Bergman were gone. Smith snagged three bloodied Negroes and drove them to his motel. Their interviews would provide CBS's only footage of the first public mass assault in modern civil rights history—Smith's roughest assignment since the opening of the Nazi concentration camps.

Leaving the Trailways station via the alley toward Nineteenth Street, Rowe and Earl Thompson's son-in-law, Ray Graves, ran into another Eastview man,

Billy Holt. A smallish man with a receding hairline and a ruddy, angry face, Holt was one of Eastview's elder statesmen, a forty-four-year-old second-generation brickmason at U.S. Pipe, whose wife was a sort of Klan moll, as dedicated to the cause as the men. According to an FBI source, Holt had been riding lookout in the car that the same source said Thompson had driven to deposit Robert Chambliss and his bomb at Bethel Baptist on Christmas night 1956. Now armed with pipe, Holt had been part of the backup unit outside the station. Detective Red Self just shook his head at them and smiled.

Halfway down the block on Nineteenth Street, Rowe, Graves, and Holt spotted Clancy Lake. An old Vincent Townsend protégé at the *Birmingham News,* Lake was the news director of the *News*-owned WAPI. He had run to his car, radioed the station, and begun broadcasting (from the driver's seat) an eyewitness account of George Webb's beating. The Klansmen trotted over to his car.

Rowe's later description of his attack on Lake to the FBI resembled a juvenile delinquent's account of a misdemeanor to a gullible mother who wants to believe the best of her son. Reportedly, Lake cursed the three men—"I saw you bastards"—and "upon hearing the language," Rowe said he, Holt, and Graves demanded the "camera." When Lake, sitting in the driver's seat, continued speaking, Holt took his baseball bat and smashed the window. Rowe went around to the passenger's side and broke the window with his shoe.

A police car stopped at a red light a few car lengths away and then rolled by, just as Holt was getting in his second lick. "Help, help, police," Lake screamed. "Send the soldiers, the people have gone crazy."

The passing police cruiser was Car 25, responding to a radio order to "check on 19th Street between 5 and 6 Avenues North on a 32"—code for a fight. After creeping by Lake's besieged car, one of the two uniformed officers, Floyd C. Garrett, radioed back, "Nothing to it." Garrett was a nephew of Robert Chambliss, who himself had apparently been a mere observer at the bus station.

Graves tore Lake's microphone loose from the radio. Rowe would tell the FBI that Lake continued to swear at them as they backed him up against the post office wall. Lake begged the gathering crowd for help, but nobody moved as Holt swung at him with a pipe. Lake broke south for the bus station. His assailants walked casually north, toward the police station. Out of Lake's sight, they got into the back seat of Bobby Shelton's waiting Cadillac. He dropped his Eastview guys at their own cars behind the Greyhound station. After beating up some Negro men (one of them sixty-five years old) who were taking down their license plate numbers, the Klansmen drove to Rowe's house for a victory celebration, marred by the wrath of Dot Rowe over her husband's involvement in such garbage.

Bloody as a Slaughtered Hog

AT BETHEL BAPTIST, Fred Shuttlesworth was leading an afternoon service. CORE had made no formal arrangements with him, other than wiring him $500 the day before for any local expenses. When a cab dropped off the Freedom Riders at his church, he dismissed the congregation in deference to Jim Peck, skull exposed and "as bloody as a slaughtered hog." Black people had never thought it possible that white folks would beat up their own kind like that. An ambulance was called. The Alabama Christian Movement for Human Rights chief of security followed Peck to the emergency room at University Hospital and wrapped his hand around a dime, with instructions to call Shuttlesworth when he was ready to leave. In a last flick of malice, Bull Connor phoned Shuttlesworth and threatened to arrest him for harboring the white casualties.

Double Agent

THE LAME-DUCK MAYOR, Jimmy Morgan, had fallen asleep at home listening to a baseball game over the radio. He was awakened by a long-distance phone call from an acquaintance, Douglas Edwards, the Troy, Alabama, native who anchored the CBS *Evening News.** What had their state come to? Edwards wanted to know. Meanwhile, Edward R. Murrow prepared to move his first big story—datelined Birmingham—over Voice of America from his new post as head of the U.S. Information Agency.

At the *News,* Vincent Townsend raged. All his efforts to manipulate the CBS documentary had been undone in fifteen minutes. To add journalistic shame to civic injury, his four men—the largest press contingent at the scene— had come back with no pictures, their cameras confiscated by the mob. But maybe that would turn out to be a blessing: Suppose the hoodlums had played into Townsend's general news blackout; suppose they had been so thorough that there were no pictures of the beatings. The atrocity might be contained inside the city limits. That would require a certain amount of intervention.

Howard K. Smith, the only national reporter on the scene, rushed the film of his interviews (two of his battered subjects were bystanders, and only one was a Freedom Rider) up Red Mountain to the WAPI studios. As he was about to begin his live report for the CBS *Evening News,* the floor director announced, "We aren't getting any signals." Smith assumed that an underling trying to please the boss had pulled the plug on his eyewitness account, unaware that no one at the TV station owned by the *Birmingham News* made a move without consulting Big Daddy Townsend.

The *Post-Herald* photo desk tracked down Tommy Langston, who had been checked out at the hospital for broken ribs. A reporter had found his smashed camera at the bus station. "Looks like the film hasn't been fogged," the desk man told him and asked if he wanted him to expose the film. The suggestion did not

---

* Frank Stanton persuaded Edwards, who had just distinguished himself as the commentator for the 1948 presidential conventions—the first to be televised—to give up his job as a second-tier CBS Radio journalist to host the network's first nightly television newscast (which was considered a step down at the time). "Doug, I guarantee you," Stanton said, "if you do this TV broadcast, you'll soon be as well known as Lowell Thomas."

surprise Langston, who, too, had soaked up the local gospel of no controversy, and he paused. He had no idea what he had photographed; it had been "like shooting in the dark." If he got something good, his photo credit would probably mean death threats to him and his seven-months-pregnant wife, and another black eye for Birmingham.* But Langston met the challenge and said, "Nah."

Rescue

THE FREEDOM RIDERS who had been firebombed en route to Birmingham were still in Anniston in the hospital, where doctors and nurses refused to treat them. In the emergency-room parking lot, state and local police, including the Anniston chief, mingled with the native warriors. Concerned newsmen phoned Governor John Patterson, but he maintained that the state could not "act as nursemaids to agitators."

"I am going to get my people," Shuttlesworth said in a radio interview. "I'm a nonviolent man, but I'm going to get my people." James Armstrong, the Movement's chief of security, talked Shuttlesworth out of leading the rescue mission, perhaps because Shuttlesworth had instructed him, "We can't take guns—we can't have any weapon." As the ACMHR's third vice president, Armstrong was one of the few non-preachers in the hierarchy, a barber whose neighbors had accused him of joining the Movement to help his business and then refused to patronize his barbershop for fear it would be bombed. The previous June, he had filed a class-action suit on behalf of his sons and the 33,715 black schoolchildren of Birmingham to desegregate the public school system. The NAACP's top lawyer in town, Arthur Shores, had declined this test of *Brown* (the NAACP's biggest triumph) because, Armstrong jested, "he was always at the bank."

Armstrong organized a convoy of fifteen cars to go to Anniston and outfitted his men with rifles and shotguns. At around ten, they picked up the stranded Freedom Riders without interference from either the state police or the mob outside the hospital.

Back at Birmingham's University Hospital, Jim Peck lay on the operating table. White doctors tended to him, while the afternoon's black casualties, one of them a back-of-the-bus Negro from the old DeBardeleben mining "family," were tended by Indian doctors. As the five gashes on Peck's head and face were sewn up—fifty-three stitches—he gave an interview to the *Birmingham News*'s Bud Gordon, who had recently cooperated with the Klansmen in destroying the photographic evidence of their handiwork.

---

* Langston had been on duty four years earlier when Fred and Ruby Shuttlesworth desegregated the Terminal Station, and had gotten a clear shot of a bunch of white thugs trying to overturn the car of Lamar Weaver, the white TCI filing clerk who had sat with the Shuttlesworths in the waiting room. He had been chased from the scene by the screaming mob, among whom he recognized some fellow U.S. Steel employees. Despite that and Langston's page-one shot of his assailants, the police made no arrests.

A Goddamn Shame

DETECTIVE RED SELF, Tommy Rowe would claim, had told him at the Trailways station, "Y'all did a good job. Now why don't you just go on home and get a good night's sleep." But Rowe was too excited to turn in. He and Eastview's toughest forty-four-year-old, Billy Holt, went back out late that night and picked a fight with some Negroes on a railroad track along Tenth Avenue. Holt fell back, but Rowe pursued them, figuring he could take on the whole group alone. One of the black men whipped out a knife and cut at Rowe's throat.

Rowe told his handler at the FBI that he had gotten the injury when he and some Klansmen intercepted a second wave of CORE riders at the Greyhound at around six that night, triggering a melee (in which the Negroes were the armed aggressors) that spread over the *entire* block. But Rowe hadn't called the bureau till after midnight, just after a Klan doctor in Pinson put eight stitches in his neck. And the agent's response was not to wonder why Rowe had waited six hours to get medical treatment for a life-threatening wound. Nor did he question Rowe about that second group of CORE riders, knowing there were no further buses. Instead, his agent said, according to Rowe, "It's a goddamn shame," and assured him that the bureau would reimburse him for the doctor's bill. It was not the first time Rowe had lied to his handlers, but it may have been the first time that they couldn't pretend not to know he was lying.

Ambush

AT 2:15 IN THE MORNING, Jim Peck phoned Shuttlesworth from the hospital to come get him. "If we're not back in thirty minutes, alert the FBI," Shuttlesworth told the black and white Freedom Riders and their supporters in his living room. He would call his decision to go fetch Peck "one of those divine urges that the Lord interposes."

Waiting outside the emergency room, Peck looked like a mummy. Though Shuttlesworth had instructed him to stay inside until he saw the car, hospital personnel had told him that discharged patients could not remain there. Once he was out on the sidewalk, a policeman threatened to arrest him for vagrancy. After getting Peck in the car, Shuttlesworth told his driver, "Don't go over twenty miles an hour." The police vehicles outside the hospital eased onto the street right behind. Halfway across the viaduct over the train tracks bisecting downtown, the police pulled them over.

"What's yo' name, boy, this yo' car?" a cop asked the driver and pretended to jump to the conclusion that it was stolen.

Shuttlesworth said, "No, officer, it's not stolen."

"Who the hell are you?" he asked.

"You know me, I'm Shuttlesworth. Oh, all of you know me," he repeated. "I'm Reverend Shuttlesworth. Tell me what you intend to do."

The cop relayed that information back to the patrol car. "Oh, hell, Shuttlesworth," his partner called. "Let 'em go."

Shuttlesworth believed that Peck had been selected for a fatal ambush. But whether or not his suspicions were exaggerated, by daylight it would become clear that the era of lynching—and of police business as usual—was drawing to an end in Birmingham.

The Picture

TOM COOK CALLED ROWE on Monday morning and congratulated him on "a goddamn good job down there. People always love you for it." But then he turned somber: "I thought you boys got all the film." Telling Rowe to go find his morning paper, he explained, "Some asshole got a picture of you or Holt, I'm not sure which, beating on a nigger. Don't worry, though. I'll take care of it."

Rowe unfurled his *Post-Herald*. Tommy Langston's photograph, plastered across five columns of the front page, pictured heavyset white men, wearing the sturdy shoes of laborers, wielding weapons in brown paper bags. Two gaping guys, one cocking a lead pipe, were beating George Webb (misidentified in the caption as Peck), while two crew-cut toughs in the foreground held him down. Tommy Rowe recognized himself as one of the crew-cut men, but at least his back had been to the camera. The clearest shot was of the man with the pipe. Who in the hell was he? Cook asked. Rowe didn't know either. Cook said it was probably one of Dr. Fields's men and asked Rowe whether he recognized anyone else in the picture. In the left foreground Rowe saw Eastview's Robert Conaway, who by day butchered the lamb chops for the patrons of the Western Supermarket in Mountain Brook. (It was he who had urged Webb's fiancée to flee.) Rowe could also make out Billy Holt. Cook hoped that the unauthorized assailants might enable the police to wangle some arrests from the incident. But the crime had fallen short of perfect.

"To the Day You Die"

THE FBI HAD PHOTOGRAPHIC PROOF that its best informant was not only a liar but a violent liar. "The Old Man's going to shit. He's going to climb the wall," Rowe would say his handler said as the two of them looked at the picture. The Old Man, as Rowe knew, was the director, J. Edgar Hoover.

Then the handler composed himself. "Who does that look like to you?" Rowe says he pointed at the large foreground figure.

"Me," Rowe said.

"Just think very carefully," the FBI man said. "Who else does that look like besides you?"

Rowe looked at it again and reconsidered. "I tell you the truth," he said, "kind of like Arnie Cagle." Charles Arnie Cagle, a preacher's son, was another husky Eastview regular. "That's it," the agent said. "Cagle. To the day you die, if you're ninety-nine damn years old, I don't care who asks you—if the director comes down and looks you in the eyes and says, 'Goddamnit, Gary Thomas Rowe, Jr., I know that's you'—you're going to look him in the eye and say, 'No, sir. That's not me. That's Arnie Cagle.' "

As fantastic as Rowe's story seems, it is one of the few plausible explanations for the FBI's even more fantastic behavior. The reports that flew from Birmingham to Washington were a frenzy of breast-beating and track-covering. On the one hand, the agents catalogued how many times the bureau had alerted the Birmingham police to the trouble. On the other hand, they couldn't resist flaunting their inside knowledge of the complicity between the Birmingham cops and the Klansmen. As for the man in the middle, Rowe, Special Agent in Charge Thomas Jenkins assured Hoover that he "advised he was not personally involved in the fighting at the Trailways bus depot" and had only "obtained film from photographers' cameras peacefully and without incident." Jenkins included Tommy Langston's incriminating photograph of Rowe in the material he sent to Washington, without accurate comment.

Not only did the Birmingham FBI office have a picture of its informant holding down a bystander while his buddies pummeled him, they also had numerous eyewitness accounts all consistent on one point: Only a handful of men— eight or so—administered the beatings at the bus station. Rowe estimated that there were eighty to a hundred Klansmen in the immediate area. Inescapably, that meant that Rowe, who later owned up to having worked over six to twelve people, could have refrained from violence without looking conspicuous, particularly since the original plan had called for his elite corps to beat up the CORE leaders in the privacy of their hotel rooms.

When Rowe's initial report about Bull Connor's fifteen-minute deal with the Klan had reached the local bureau the previous week, an agent's response had been, according to Rowe, "Jesus Christ, I can't believe this. This could never be allowed to happen. The American people would never stand for this." The agent had pledged to "get five thousand marshals or ten thousand troops in here, if necessary. We've got the 82nd Airborne, the 101st Airborne. We can pull more damn people in here than the Klan ever heard of. The Old Man will not allow this to go down." Yet the FBI did nothing, would claim not even to have sent any agents over to observe an event that they had gone through reams of paper anticipating. Rowe again offered a more believable account, swearing that several FBI agents had been at the Trailways, some taking movies.

"Where Were the Police?"

VINCENT TOWNSEND'S HOPES of suppressing the news out of Birmingham were dashed, but because his *News* was an afternoon paper, he had time to compose himself. The *Post-Herald* had given him an idea. Most of the rival paper's coverage was devoted to the outrages against its photographer, Langston. But an editorial mentioned, almost as a peevish afterthought, that no policemen had been on hand to prevent the violence; nor had any arrived expeditiously to end it. The depot was only a minute and a half by car away from the police station. "Where Were the Police?" the *Post-Herald's* headline asked.

Bull Connor's claim to competence was his "efficient" police force. Two weeks earlier, Townsend had given him the *News's* unqualified endorsement for reelection to his sixth term, using language that now had a certain inverted clairvoyance: "The newspaper has full confidence that not only will Mr. Connor serve well in preventing outsiders from using our city for agitating purposes, but that he will continue his determination to see that law and order prevail and that riot or other outbreak will be suppressed with dispatch regardless of who initiates it."

Connor, who had been returned to city hall by the largest landslide of his career, would have to be punished for spoiling Townsend's vengeance on the national news media.* Not to mention that Townsend would now personally look like a jackass for lecturing CBS on camera that Connor was certainly "not going to let any agents of turmoil, whether they are white or Negro, to cause any breaches of the peace in Birmingham."

Townsend and the polite businessmen for whom his paper spoke had for years attributed the city's problems to "agitators" who were "looking for trouble" or the lunatic-fringe Ku Kluxers who gave it to them. His umbrage at previous racial bombings and mutilations had been in the spirit of such *News* headlines as "An Ugly Act Sure to Hurt the South." But this time Townsend declined to point his finger at the usual suspects. The *News's* lead story on Monday afternoon, an editorial played above the logo and written by Townsend himself, also demanded in its headline, "Where were the police?" But he offered an answer that would become the civic equivalent of a tectonic shift.

Connor was claiming that the police were where all good boys should have been that afternoon: at home with their mamas. Sunday, May 14, was Mother's Day. And that was not the most egregious bad faith Townsend's reporters had been privy to. After the beatings had been going on for twelve minutes, Tom Cook, with whom the *News* men had been discussing the Freedom Rides all afternoon, breezed into the station and said he had received a report about a fight, as if for all he knew he was walking into a whiskey brawl.

"We fell, this city of Birmingham, into the trap, like a stupid beast falls into a pit in the jungle," Townsend wrote. For once, it seemed, the fault was not in our stars but in ourselves, as Edward Murrow had earlier chided a public still tolerant of McCarthyism. On Mother's Day 1961, it was plain to any good reporter at the bus station, to any careful reader of Townsend's editorial, that the man the voters had put in charge of city hall for twenty years was baldly collaborating with the armed "maniacs," if not actively directing them. The enormity of the conspiracy

---

* Howard K. Smith had made a radio report after Townsend cut off his TV access. It had been incorporated into the front-page story of the *New York Times,* which had been constrained by threat of subpoena from sending its own correspondents.

had been only hinted at in Townsend's strangely casual identification of them as members of the Ku Klux Klan.

Tom Lankford had a Machiavellian soul to match Townsend's own, and even though he was supposed to be the boss's eyes and ears, he had not been entirely straight with him about the events of that Sunday. Lankford's excuse for not having gotten any pictures of the fracas was that his film, which witnesses had seen him go out of his way to relinquish, had been wrested from him with a threat which "might very well have meant death if a wrong move were made," as Townsend wrote in his editorial. It is conceivable that Lankford believed by participating in the blackout he was enforcing his boss's "doctrine of wishful truth" (Chuck Morgan's term for the local civic creed) as well as cosseting his police sources and was perhaps trying to atone for another conspiracy that he had carried out against Townsend's interests.

A photograph of Lankford's had made it into the *News* on Mother's Day, albeit uncredited. It had been taken the previous Monday, through a third-floor window of city hall, in the company of one of his best sources, Mayor Morgan's executive secretary, Clint Bishop: Tom King shaking hands with a black man whom Lankford's *News* colleague Bud Gordon had paid $20 for the favor. Using the fancy surveillance equipment that Townsend had bought for him, Lankford had snapped the "black hand" photograph that was about to sink Townsend's candidate for mayor.

Old Pat

AS TOMMY LANGSTON'S PICTURE of the action inside the Trailways depot made its way to the far corners of the world, many Americans grasped before the Freedom Riders themselves did that the buses of Alabama had made history once again. Bayard Rustin was in London when he saw Langston's photograph, along with a picture of his old friend Jim Peck's bandaged head. His and Peck's 1947 Journey of Reconciliation now acquired John the Baptist status in the history of a Movement that had essentially rejected Rustin since the *Sullivan* setback.

Robert Kennedy would say that the first he knew of the Freedom Ride was when he saw the photograph of the smoke-spewing Greyhound bus at Anniston in his morning paper. The President's immediate worry was that the "adverse publicity," on top of the botched Bay of Pigs invasion, would embarrass him at his imminent Vienna summit meeting with Khrushchev: "Tell them to call it off," Kennedy told his brother. "Stop them."

The attorney general phoned Shuttlesworth and asked, "What do you think I should do?" Shuttlesworth asked for some protection for the riders. Kennedy called back in a few minutes: "Governor Patterson is ready."

Shuttlesworth led the Freedom Riders to the Greyhound station, which was surrounded by police cars and a growing press contingent, to catch the three o'clock bus to Montgomery. At the depot, Jim Peck recognized in the reconstituted mob some faces from the day before. But now the police were holding them back. A cop grabbed a drunken white man who approached Shuttlesworth, saying, "There's the one I want." The minister flashed him a beatific grin.

But there were two small problems. The bus drivers' union was refusing to let any of its members make the trip. And the governor was reneging on his promise of a state police escort to Montgomery.

Though Patterson had been courting just such a racial reckoning for his nearly seven unprecedentedly provocative years in public office, the Freedom Ride posed a dilemma for him. Patterson had fallen in love with the Kennedys in 1959 when Robert Kennedy, as counsel for the Senate Rackets Committee, gave a speech in Alabama about his "Get Hoffa" work investigating labor unions. At considerable political risk (and not to the complete delight of the candidate), Patterson had been the first major southern politician to support John Kennedy for president, prompting Shuttlesworth to predict that the endorsement from "Old Pat" would be the death of the Kennedy candidacy. Toward the end of the 1960 campaign, the governor had flown to New York to alert Kennedy that the CIA was training the Alabama Air National Guard for an invasion of Cuba and that if it occurred successfully before the election, Nixon would surely win.* Patterson sulked when President Kennedy failed to come through with a federal appointment for his "great pal in the South," as Robert Kennedy came to ruefully call him.

For all his segregationist moxie, Patterson was no cock of the walk. Around the capital, "Jittery John" was considered so inaccessible and skittish that even a rock-ribbed Black Belt legislator waxed nostalgic for former governor Folsom. Patterson blamed his wilting popularity on the deposed Phenix City syndicates that had his father assassinated; fences and armed guards were deployed around the Governor's Mansion. Hoping to counter his reputation as a crybaby, Patterson went on the offensive against the Freedom Riders, echoing a statement Bull Connor had just made: "When you go somewhere looking for trouble, you usually find it."

At the bus station, Shuttlesworth was on and off the phone with Robert Kennedy all afternoon. The attorney general pleaded with him to talk the bus driver into the assignment. Somewhat taken aback by Kennedy's insensitivity toward a labor versus management issue, Shuttlesworth said, "I don't work for the bus company. We'll just stay here."

At 3:15, an exasperated Kennedy called the local Greyhound superintendent, George Cruit. "Surely somebody in the damn bus company can drive a bus, can't they?" Kennedy asked. Finally he was pushed by Cruit's stonewalling to say, "Well, Mr. Cruit, I think you should—had better get in touch with Mr. Greyhound or whoever Greyhound is and somebody better give us an answer to this question." The conversation, tape-recorded by Cruit and released to the public by the Alabama attorney general, would turn up in future made-for-television movies as an example of the hands-on, can-do Kennedy style. But for the citizens of Alabama, it was proof that the federal government was masterminding the civil

---

* He also brought Kennedy $10,000 in cash, in a paper bag.

rights movement. The smoking gun: "I am—the Government—is going to be very much upset if this group does not get to continue their trip. . . . Somebody better get in the damn bus and get it going and get these people on their way."

In fact, Kennedy's ultimatum was an example of neither. The administration was so ignorant that its attorney general had tried to persuade Cruit to get "a driver of one of the colored buses" to take the Freedom Riders to Montgomery, apparently not having learned from the Montgomery bus boycott that there were no colored buses and certainly no colored drivers.

Shuttlesworth advised Kennedy: "Call Bull." But Connor was one southern politician the ultra-pragmatic Kennedy administration refused to deal with directly. After negotiations in which the local FBI office was the intermediary, Kennedy informed Shuttlesworth that Connor had agreed to usher the bus to the city line. "Are you kidding?" Shuttlesworth said. "Don't you know what happened outside the city limits of Anniston?" The riders would stay at the station until assured of a state police escort to the Mississippi line.

The resolve of the exhausted pacifists was wearing down. Facing an overnight stay in a bus station for the privilege of getting to Montgomery, they decided to catch the 6:15 Eastern Airlines flight to New Orleans. At least they would reach their destination in time for the scheduled *Brown* anniversary on Wednesday, May 17.

Bob

EASTVIEW'S HUBERT PAGE phoned a bomb threat in to Eastern. Police Chief Jamie Moore had assured the FBI's Thomas Jenkins that "there would be no trouble," and when Page and some friends showed up at the airport to see CORE's reaction (Eastern evacuated the plane), the heavy police contingent did not extend a welcome. Page told Tommy Rowe by phone that things had "gotten too hot" at the airport and they had left.

In Washington, the attorney general summoned his specialist on the South, thirty-two-year-old John Seigenthaler, a former reporter for the *Nashville Tennessean* who had met Kennedy while doing exposés on the Teamsters and had helped him write his Hoffa memoir, *The Enemy Within*. Seigenthaler was soon on a military jet to Birmingham, with orders "just to hold their hand and let them know that we care."

Shuttlesworth left the airport to get to the mass meeting. When he arrived, the warm-up act, his humorous first vice president, the Reverend Ed Gardner, was doing his version of "Where were the police?" saying, "Our commissioner sends them here each Monday night, but we can't find them when we need them." Shuttlesworth was darting in and out of a side door to check on the situation at the airport. Taking the pulpit, he said, "I talked to Bob Kennedy (I call him Bob) six times." He then excused himself—"I have a long-distance call from Bob"—and returned a minute later to assure the crowd, "Bob said he would keep in touch with the situation." He said that "Bob" had invited him to call him at the White

House if he couldn't reach him at the Justice Department. The crowd of 350 answered with whoops. At ten o'clock, an hour before the Freedom Riders' plane finally left under Seigenthaler's escort, Gardner's familiar sign-off to end the meeting had taken on the ring of destiny. "There is only one F. L. Shuttlesworth!"

Speaking for Birmingham

SID SMYER WAS HALFWAY AROUND THE WORLD, in Tokyo for a convention of the International Rotary Club. For the first time, he had been experiencing his city's "black eye" personally. "When you said you was from Birmingham," he said of the businessmen he ran into there, "boy, they didn't have anything to do with you." The fragile Frances Smyer, proud of her Mayflower pedigree, smarted. But her husband, who had just assumed the presidency of the Chamber of Commerce, took the cuts as a challenge. He had been assuring the men who had based their opinion on that article in the *New York Times* that Saaalzberry hadn't talked to a single responsible citizen.

And then, out of the blue, an advertisement for his city appeared on the front page of the Tokyo newspapers, and all over the world: Tommy Langston's photograph of white men in sports shirts bludgeoning interstate travelers inside a Birmingham bus station.

Back home, Smyer's fellow responsible citizens were already protesting that the people who beat them up "weren't even *from* Birmingham!" The talk at the country club would soon return to more pressing affairs—the passing of Gary Cooper, astronaut Alan Shepard's evanescent space shot, the *News*'s improved stock coverage. They did not yet understand that the story out of Birmingham had superseded them all. Furious letters from Minneapolis, Philadelphia, Denver, Palm Springs, swamped city hall. In one typical editorial cartoon, Khrushchev munched merrily on a watermelon labeled "U.S. Race Riots." And a man from Pittsburgh wrote, "Your city is sick! And I do mean SICK."

On the other side of the globe, out of the civic cocoon, Smyer suddenly saw the lie in his business ethos. Perhaps he even acknowledged in his soul the extent to which he had nurtured the Klansmen in the photograph. The doubting Dixiecrat now began working on a "Birmingham Plan" diametrically different from the one he had spearheaded thirteen years before: This one was to end segregation.

The Arrests

AS SID SMYER TURNED on the vigilantes who had once served his political ends, the Klan itself acquired its ultimate benefactor: the federal government. Until now, Gary Thomas Rowe might have believed that the FBI's cover-up of his violence at the bus station was in the interest of a greater law enforcement good, that his intelligence would be used to develop independent witnesses and move against the Klan. The suspects that the FBI began interviewing immediately after the attack were indeed Eastview 13's top performers—Billy Holt, Earl Thompson, Hubert Page, Robert Conaway, and Robert Thomas. Most said they had just happened to end up at the Trailways bus station that Mother's Day. Exalted Cyclops Robert Thomas just happened to be driving the head of the Gadsden Klan, Ace Williams, to the nearby Greyhound station. Robert Conaway just happened to walk in on the fight, and the only thing he could think about at the time was how to get away. The FBI agents pointed to him in the foreground of Tommy Langston's shot, his face in partial view, and commented that it did not look as if he were trying to get away. Why was his hand doubled into a fist? Conaway looked at the photograph and said his hand was not doubled into a fist. When agents interviewed Hubert Page, the man whom witnesses consistently said they would be able to identify again because of his prominent forehead, they did not take down the customary physical description.

On Tuesday, May 16, Detectives Melvin Bailey and Vernon Hart of the Birmingham police arrested three men for the bus station violence. They were identifiable subjects of the photograph who did not belong to the Eastview Klan or any of Bobby Shelton's clubs. They were troops from the remains of the late Eldon Edwards's U.S. Klans, who had been summoned to the bus station by the NSRP's Edward Fields. Tarrant City Klansman Jessie Oliver Faggard, a twenty-year-old doughnut-machine operator, was charged with assault with intent to murder; his father, Jessie Thomas Faggard, a carpenter, was accused of disorderly conduct. Melvin Dove, their Tarrant City compatriot who was also arrested, came up with the most imaginative excuse for his presence in Langston's picture—in the very foreground, the only man staring at the camera, like a tourist before a monument. A forty-year-old maintenance man at Anderson Electric, considered by a colleague to be a "slippery, agile liar and very unscrupulous," Dove claimed to have recently had a fistula operation and, needing frequent recourse to a bathroom, had felt the urge as he was walking by the Trailways station. Dove also had an answer for the FBI men when asked to account for his clenched fist. He had been smoking a cigarette, which fell out of his mouth when a Negro kicked him in the chest, but his right hand still clutched his lighter.

Dove's explanation for his fist certainly beat Robert Conaway's, but he had the poor luck of not knowing either Tommy Rowe or Tom Cook. He would be tried in recorder's court for disorderly conduct, fined, and sentenced to a short jail sentence, as were the two Faggard men. The most serious charges against the younger Faggard—assault and battery—were never prosecuted, although police suspected that he had done most of the damage, in a separate beating, to Jim Peck's head.

The stars of the photograph—the men in the center, one brandishing a lead pipe, the other baring his teeth in a hyena laugh—also turned out to be outside the magic Eastview circle. The pipe holder, Howard Thurston Edwards, was one of the men whom Mary Spicer saw board the bus in Anniston, with his weapon in a paper bag, and attack the riders along the way to Birmingham; he was an angry young man from the forlorn Birmingham suburb of Irondale, a print shop foreman, volunteer fireman, ham radio operator, and avid scuba diver. The other man, Herschel Acker, was a paper mill worker from Rome, Georgia, the inevitable outside agitator.

Chickens

"THE CHICKENS ARE BOXED," Diane Nash told Fred Shuttlesworth over the phone on Wednesday morning. Nash, a member of the Student Nonviolent Co-ordinating Committee's flagship squad, in Nashville, was a "comely coed" (*Jet*) at Fisk, a middle-class Catholic girl from Illinois whose beauty and charm had made her a runner-up in Chicago's Miss America trials even though she was black. Those qualities, and perhaps her blue eyes, disarmed opponents even as she was emerging as the most militant and stubborn voice in SNCC. Now she was achieving what Shuttlesworth had hoped the youths would do when he first saw the sit-ins in High Point: forcing the Movement elders' hands.

The previous Monday night, after the original Freedom Riders had bailed out and flown to New Orleans, Nash had telephoned Shuttlesworth from the church where she and the members of the Nashville movement had been meeting around the clock. "Violence can't stop the rides or we are lost," she told him. "I'm ready to send the students down."

Shuttlesworth was shocked to find another Negro willing to brave Birmingham. "Well, young lady, don't you know you could get killed in Birmingham?" he said. "It's a hell of a place." Nash replied that some of her volunteers had written wills.

Shuttlesworth told her to come before the weekend, "because if anyone gets killed, they can hide it then, and it'll never get out." They worked out a code to save a few surprises for the eavesdropping cops. "Dominecks" meant a racially mixed group, and "roosters" and "hens" would indicate the male-female ratio. If all the riders were students: "pullets." At noon on Wednesday, Shuttlesworth, ACMHR vice presidents James Armstrong and Ed Gardner, and the *World*'s Emory O. Jackson, in a reportorial capacity, were at the bus station, ready to meet seven roosters and three hens.

Even though he had been duly informed by Shuttlesworth's telegrams, Bull Connor had feared a trick and had his daughter, posing as a certain white liberal, call the minister to confirm the details. A Birmingham policeman stopped the bus at the city line and arrested a black student and a white student who had insisted on riding integrated on this preliminary leg of their "Truth Ride." At the depot, other cops got on the bus, released the lay passengers, and held all young people whose tickets read Nashville to New Orleans. Then they pasted over the windows with newspapers. One rider, Lucretia Collins, tried to engage the police guard in Gandhian solidarity against the "system."

"Are you a Christian?" she asked. He was. "Do you believe Christ died for all people?" she said.

"Yes," he said, "but look, this is my job. I'm sorry I have to do this."

Officially, the students were being held on the bus so that they could be transferred to the three o'clock bus to Montgomery. At 2:55, a student slipped a note out the bus window to Shuttlesworth, who immediately called Robert Kennedy's secretary. The freedom luggage had been loaded onto the three o'clock, but the bus remained in its bay. The driver told the students when they were finally allowed onto the loading platform, "If you get on, I will not drive the bus." A bomb threat was telephoned into the station. Governor Patterson announced that he couldn't "guarantee the safety of fools."

At 4:05, Chief Jamie Moore marched the riders to the waiting room. Shuttlesworth led them to the whites-only cafeteria but found the door locked. The students were then herded into a police wagon, to the cheers of the depot mob. When Shuttlesworth protested, he, too, was arrested, for refusing to obey an officer and interfering with an officer. As the crowd became aggressive, the police department's new German shepherds, the K-9 Corps, arrived for their first major assignment, if not against the race they had been intended for.

Shuttlesworth posted bond within five hours. Len Holt, the lawyer he had met through SCEF's Anne Braden, had flown in from Norfolk, Virginia. (Arthur Shores and his fellow NAACP lawyers did not approve of the Freedom Rides.) The police were telling the students (under "protective custody" in jail) that they could be out within half an hour if they promised to leave town. When Shuttlesworth learned that Holt was negotiating with Chief Moore to find the young people alternative ways out of Birmingham, he exploded: "I am the Kingfish of this organization. I am running it. We are not going anyplace. Just go back and tell them we are not going anyplace until we ride out on the bus."

While the rest of the riders sang through their first night in Birmingham Jail, a rally of one thousand in New Orleans honored CORE's original Freedom Riders. In his riproaring address, "Beltin' Elton" Cox confirmed the white South's darkest suspicions by encouraging "marry-ins," saying, "The whole world knows love is color-blind."

Marshals

IN WASHINGTON, the ranking Birminghamian in the Kennedy administration was holding a dinner party. Louis Falk Oberdorfer, the forty-two-year-old head of the Justice Department's tax division, came from one of Alabama's most prominent and conservative Jewish families. His father, Leo, had written the legal textbook of record for the state. After Dartmouth and the Army, Lou had attended Yale Law School with Byron White, now Robert Kennedy's deputy attorney general. Then he had clerked for his father's great friend Hugo Black in 1946 and 1947, while White clerked for Chief Justice Fred Vinson.

Since his appointment to the number two spot at Justice, Byron White had been staying with the Oberdorfers until he could move his family from Colorado. Joining them for dinner that night was Douglas Arant, one of the many Birmingham contacts Oberdorfer maintained and Hobart McWhorter Jr.'s boss at Alabama's leading white-shoe law firm. Arant was such a slick operator that he had managed to acquire a national reputation as a liberal and remain a member in high standing at the Mountain Brook Club (in whose bylaws he had stuck a never-enforced clause forbidding discrimination on the basis of race and creed, though not sex). Arant was working himself into a panic—should he return to Birmingham to protect his home? He, White, and Oberdorfer stood gloomily by the dining room table. White said of the Freedom Riders: "We're going to have to get those people out of there and keep them moving somehow." He believed they might have to use soldiers. Oberdorfer proposed instead a civilian force of federal marshals. By the time the dinner party broke up, they had worked out a standby plan to send twenty or thirty federal escorts to Birmingham.

The first thing the next morning, May 18, Byron White and Robert Kennedy went to the White House to see the President. John Kennedy put in a call to Governor John Patterson, who had told his secretary to say he had gone fishing. Lou Oberdorfer's marshal plan moved to the front burner. He racked his brain for ways to fill out a respectable contingent. In his office that day was another Alabama connection, his senior trial lawyer, Vincent Russo, who used to regale him with lore from his younger years as a Birmingham-based "Revenooer"—an officer with the Treasury Department's alcohol-tax unit—chasing rumrunners and busting up stills in the southern hills. Considering their experience with weapons and radio signals, these were the kind of "civilians" Oberdorfer needed, and he had the commissioner of Internal Revenue alert his southeastern agents. Then he called his Yale Law classmate Najeeb Halaby, the head of the Federal Aviation Administration,* to arrange air transportation for the marshals and agents.

For some reason, Oberdorfer's mind kept turning to a seminal event from his youth in Birmingham: the kidnapping and beating of his family friend Joe Gelders—Lou had gone out on a date with Gelders's daughter Marge—by Walter "Crack" Hanna, the respected captain of the National Guard. That had been Oberdorfer's first understanding of how men in uniform could moonlight as terrorists. He had described the episode to Byron White, trying to communicate that they were not up against an isolated bunch of "rednecks" and that military force might have to be used.

Smyer's Conversion

As soon as Sid Smyer returned from Tokyo, he named a "study group" to address the city's racial problems. It was backed not by well-meaning, statusless liberals or a charity organization but by the Chamber of Commerce. The committee of twelve was made up of the biggest of the Big Mules—U.S. Steel's local man—as well as utilities chiefs, a bank president, and the *News* publisher, Clarence Hanson. The radical thing about it, however, was Smyer's insistence that it "enlarge its membership to such number and persons as they deem necessary."

---

* He was the future father-in-law of King Hussein of Jordan.

The *Wall Street Journal* translated: The elite committee of powerful businessmen would include black people.

Certainly this, Smyer's first official progressive act, was motivated by the sudden decision of an Ohio concern he had wooed to Birmingham to take its $40 million plant investment instead to New England, the old seat of abolition. But for someone of his background, the study group meant a frank change of heart and mind. White men had mortgaged their conscience, as well as their livelihood, on the conviction that the Negro, though he might be a beloved servant or an amusing child (but more often a disease-ridden criminal), was less than a human being. As Big Jim Folsom had marveled to young Chuck Morgan, the culture's strict injunction against social equality had somehow centered on the symbolism of "sitting at a table" with a Negro, whether over a meal or a discussion. Physical intimacy was hardly the issue. The slaveholders had written the book on miscegenation, and one of the prominent New Dealers in the Southern Conference for Human Welfare used to tell the true story of a white country girl from his native Georgia who visited her mulatto love child at the colored orphanage and declined the administration's invitation to join the four-year-old boy for lunch. "Well, I couldn't do it. Eat with niggers?" No, it was the indirect consequences of "mixing" that terrified whites: that other white people might ostracize them.

Not only did Smyer break with a "sacred pattern" of his history, he went public. Vincent Townsend, the power broker behind the committee, noted pointedly that it had been formed the very day after the paper editorialized that "steps should be taken to define the city's policies, not the policies of the police or elected officials, but of the people, in the racial situation." That alluded to the second major realignment signaled by Smyer's move. The city fathers were going to take back some of the authority they had long ceded to Bull Connor and his police. They were going to speak for Birmingham.

Their inauspicious debut took place on national TV Thursday, May 18. The day that the *News* announced the formation of Smyer's committee was also the air date for CBS's documentary on Birmingham. And the irony of it was that "Who Speaks for Birmingham?" was as much the work of Vincent Townsend as of CBS. To be the "official" voice of the city, Townsend had selected a columnist from the rival *Post-Herald,* John Temple Graves, who had also led the charge against Salisbury. The gray eminence of local journalism, once widely syndicated, Graves had in the course of his long career transformed from New Deal liberal to arch-reactionary tribune of the White Citizens Councils. As the opening speaker on *CBS Reports,* he looked the epitome of the southern gentleman, white-haired and still handsome, sitting in front of a vase of flowers. "Reign of terror" indeed, he scoffed, and implored CBS to redress Salisbury's wrong: "I'm amazed to find that in your mind, and in the mind of so many, we're the villain of the Southern peace."

Testimonials to that peace followed. A grandfatherly lawyer pointed out that "even the dumbest farmer in the world" knows to put his white chickens and black chickens in separate yards. A sigh from a CBS crew member could be heard on the

air, and the camera jerked. And then there was an encrypted epitaph for Sid
Smyer's old era. Another white-haired lawyer, lips and wattle trembling, shook his
head balefully over his trusted yardman's remarks that some particularly beautiful flowers he was tending came from Russia. It was hard to believe that this was
Smyer's longtime colleague Hugh Locke, who had evolved from Hugo Black's
best friend, to the Ku Klux Klan's candidate for governor in 1928, to Dixiecrat, to
suspected architect of the Dynamite Hill bombings, to bankroller of the American States Rights Association and the White Citizens Councils, to, finally, this di-
nosaur.

The flower-loving high point, of course, was Eleanor Bridges's speech about
happy things, singing Negroes and budding Negro artists, filmed in The Club's
"pigeon room." Sometimes the club manager let his trained birds putter around
unrestrained, but on this day they nestled amid rubber plants in large cages. And
sometimes Bridges wore hats that resembled a tropical forest or a banana boat, but
on this day her selection was a relatively demure floral number. The Club's
trained pigeons were not roosting in it; it just looked that way on TV.

If that had been the worst of it, perhaps "Who Speaks for Birmingham?"
would have been an exercise in camp. But John Temple Graves had issued CBS a
challenge, demanding evidence of Salisbury's "instruments of violence and torture": "the rope, the knot, the whip, the razor." And history had obliged.

Howard K. Smith delivered his stand-up in front of a huge photograph of
Bull Connor. His measured reading betrayed no evidence of the expletives that
had flown during the final editing of the documentary that week. A CBS executive
had complained that the program presented Birmingham's Negroes in a better
light than the whites. (CBS's solicitude toward the feelings of the segregationists
came less than a week after Kennedy's Federal Communications Commission
chairman, Smith's friend Newton Minow, pronounced American television "a
vast wasteland.") It had been thanks to *CBS Reports*'s executive producer, Fred
Friendly, the revered ramrod personality who had gotten Murrow's McCarthy attack on the air, that the only thing Smith had ultimately given up was an ominous
quotation from Edmund Burke in his closing: "The only thing necessary for the
triumph of evil is for good men to do nothing."

Smith gamely described the bloody scene at the bus depot, where "men in
sports shirts" worked over their victims. The police—he pronounced it in the
southern manner, "poh-lease"—"did not arrive at this scene until ten minutes
later," he reported. "After ten minutes of undeterred savagery," he noted, the assailants "had, as if on signal, dispersed and had gone further down the street,
where I saw some of them discussing their achievement of the day right under the
windows of the police commissioner's office."

In little more than a year, what the *News* had called Salisbury's "big lie" had
come graphically true: "Fear and hatred did stalk Birmingham's streets yesterday," Townsend's editorial had conceded, putting him on the side of the national
news media. And that was hardly the oddest alliance struck that Thursday.

A Terrible Thing

GARY THOMAS ROWE fully understood the immunity his FBI status had given him when he saw the bureau's contrasting treatment of Mother's Day's other criminals. Agents had been all over the Anniston bus burning, swamping the FBI lab with debris samples. In less than two hours, the U. S. attorney in Birmingham had located a relevant federal statute: Section 33, Title 18, "Destruction of motor vehicle engaged in interstate commerce."

The prosecution of the Anniston case gained momentum on Thursday when the wife of a state investigator told the FBI that the man who threw the firebomb into the Greyhound bus was a Klan youth named Cecil Lamar Lewallyn. To the Eastview suspects it had identified even before the crime was committed, however, the FBI did nothing. It was almost as if the bureau shared the reasoning advanced by Eastview's Billy Holt in his FBI interview. The burning of the bus at Anniston—a property crime—was "a terrible thing," while the Freedom Riders beaten in Birmingham "got what they deserved."

Talking Loud

WHILE THE NASHVILLE STUDENTS remained in Birmingham Jail on a hunger strike, the Southern Christian Leadership Conference high command—executive director Wyatt Tee Walker, Joe Lowery of Mobile—met at Shuttlesworth's house to formulate a position on the Freedom Rides: Would they consider a compromise such as Martin Luther King had recently endorsed in Atlanta, where the "responsible Negro leaders" cut a deal with the Chamber of Commerce to call off the sit-ins, with the understanding that the lunch counters would be desegregated on the same indeterminate date as the schools? Shuttlesworth reported the consensus to the press: "These students came here to ride out on a regular scheduled bus and that's what they still hope to do. That is our irrevocable position. The challenge has to be made."

That night, Shuttlesworth went on trial in recorder's court. Encountering Bull Connor in the hall, he could have sworn that the commissioner wanted to shake his hand, but Connor recovered his dignity by going up to one of his policemen and asking him who that man was. "That's Reverend Shuttlesworth," came the incredulous reply. Shuttlesworth had gotten the last word that night on national television, as the only person who had an answer for the question "Who Speaks for Birmingham?" He shed some light on Connor's "rough voice," saying, "He wants the white people to believe that just by his being in office, he can prevent the inevitable, so he has to talk loud, he has to talk loud, because when the sound and fury is all gone, then there'll be nothing. There'll be emptiness."

The State Line

AT ELEVEN-THIRTY, a few hours after the airing of "Who Speaks for Birmingham?" Bull Connor arrived at the jail with a solution to the Freedom Rider problem that did not displease the frantic Kennedy administration. He rousted the students out of bed, introduced himself and two *Birmingham News* reporters— Tom Lankford and Bud Gordon—and said, "You people came in here from Tennessee on a bus. I'm taking you back to Tennessee in five minutes under police protection." Connor had explained jovially to the Justice Department through the FBI intermediaries that all their hymn singing was driving him crazy.

Two cars awaited them outside, one a hearselike rental. At the stroke of midnight, policemen picked up the students, who had gone limp in protest, and deposited them in the cars. The windows were rolled up tight. "Those windows may keep bullets out," Lucretia Collins observed, "but they can't keep God out." Connor bantered charmingly with the people he would publicly call "white women of immature age traveling around . . . with a bunch of Negro men . . . expenses paid by the NAACP, CORE, Communists, and other people who have never been in the South." One of the black women insisted that he join them for breakfast back at Fisk.

Four hours and ten minutes after leaving Birmingham, the cars stopped a few feet from the Tennessee state line, in the pre-dawn middle of nowhere. The luggage was dumped by the road. "You can take the bus back to Nashville" were Connor's parting words. One of the women called to the cars' receding taillights, "Tell Bull thanks, we'll see you at the Greyhound Bus Station today about noon."

The students, who were picked up by a car that Diane Nash sent from Nashville, reached Shuttlesworth's house at around three. Soon eleven more "packages," in Nash's code, arrived by train from Nashville and Atlanta. Shuttlesworth had decided to take the freedom bus to Montgomery with the kids. "I'm a battlefield general, not an armchair general," he explained to a horrified Robert Kennedy. A mob of thousands greeted Shuttlesworth and the SNCC students at the Greyhound station. The Movement locals were growing fond of the K-9 Corps on the scene. "Birmingham has good dogs," the ACMHR's Ed Gardner would say. "They don't know the Freedom Riders, the mob men, or nobody." The bus to Montgomery, idling in its bay, was canceled.

The afternoon news flashes came from Mobile. John Temple Graves, the local columnist who had been the first to speak for Birmingham on TV the night before, was defending the "eternal law" of segregation before a luncheon group when he keeled over dead. "Old Temp died like he lived—backwards," Shuttlesworth said. "He had to kick the bucket, not the mob." Clarence Hanson, the *News* publisher, charged that Graves had been killed by CBS's unfair editing, hinting at the First Amendment crisis that Birmingham would now spread to broadcast news.

The Whole World in His Hand

JOHN PATTERSON HAD FINALLY AGREED to meet with John Seigenthaler. Late Friday afternoon, the Kennedy aide headed down to the capital and entered the governor's office, his Tennessee accent "dripping sorghum and molasses."

Patterson, surrounded by his full cabinet, greeted him by boasting that "there's nobody in the whole country that's got the spine to stand up to the goddamned niggers except me."

Among Patterson's entourage was the Kennedys' only reliable contact in Alabama officialdom, the state's public safety director, Floyd Mann. The forty-year-old redhead had started in law enforcement as a company guard battling unionists at a Gadsden steel mill, and more recently, as chief of the Opelika Police Department, he had assisted Crack Hanna in the cleanup of nearby Phenix City after the assassination of Patterson's father. Mann had come to see Patterson's repeated statements to the effect that "You just can't guarantee the safety of fools" as an insult to his professionalism. Now he broke in to give his personal guarantee of protection for the riders. Seigenthaler picked up Patterson's phone to convey the state's new spirit of cooperation to Robert Kennedy.

That afternoon, Shuttlesworth was arrested at his home on separate counts of conspiracy and disturbing the peace*—Vincent Townsend had proposed in the *News* that the minister's telegrams notifying the press and government officials were the equivalent of crying "Fire!" in Justice Oliver Wendell Holmes Jr.'s hypothetical crowded theater. That is, Shuttlesworth was being held responsible for the mob that greeted the Freedom Riders. He bailed out in time to join what had become a high-spirited slumber party at the bus station. The Freedom Riders watched pay TV, depleted the vending machines, and made use of the white restrooms—"They washed their faces and combed their hair and fixed up much more than was necessary, because they had to look good in the waiting room," Shuttlesworth commented. When the police disconnected the TVs and the phones and locked the toilets, Shuttlesworth urged the students to lie down on the "nice benches." King, the German shepherd, and the rest of the K-9 Corps kept the mob at bay.

At six Saturday morning, a stocky driver walked over to the riders who had lined up to board his bus and told them, "I understand there is a big convoy down the road and I don't have but one life to give and I don't intend to give it to CORE or the NAACP, and that's all I have to say." Bull Connor arrived at around eight-thirty, preceded by a newsman who revealed that Robert Kennedy had finally made his point with "Mr. Greyhound." What was rumored to have done the trick was his threat to send down a Negro driver in an Air Force fighter plane. The driver reemerged from the employees' lounge and boarded the freedom bus.

"Man, what this state's coming to!" Shuttlesworth said, watching the phalanx of rifle-toting cops close ranks around the bus. "An armed escort to take a bunch of niggers to a bus station so they can break these silly old laws." He marched up

---

* He was accused of conspiring with unknown persons to cause a mob to gather at the Trailways station—the same sort of reckless "conspiracy" charge that had so outraged whites when Autherine Lucy's attorneys, Arthur Shores and Thurgood Marshall, leveled it against the white mob at the University of Alabama.

and down the police line and addressed them: "Now we're gonna assault Missis-sippi!" He turned to the lined-up Freedom Riders and led them in a few rounds of "He's Got the Whole World in His Hand," running through verses of "Pat" and "Bull." He was about to board the bus when Police Chief Jamie Moore came into the station and said, "Friend, why don't you go home. I don't want to arrest you." Shuttlesworth showed him his ticket to Montgomery. "Freddie Lee," Moore said wearily, "I'm ordering you to go home." When Shuttlesworth politely declined, Moore had him arrested for "refusing to move."

The officer who took Shuttlesworth to jail struck him, kicked him in the shin, called him a monkey, and then goaded him, "Why don't you hit me?" Shut-tlesworth replied, "Because I love you." He folded his arms and smiled the rest of the way to jail, where, forbidden to sing or pray, he took a nap.

Montgomery

THE SPLIT-LEVEL SCENICRUISER pulled out of the Greyhound station with a sirening motorcycle escort. At the Birmingham city limits, sixteen state police cars and a highway patrol airplane waited to usher the bus down Highway 31. Some riders slept; some laughed in giddy relief. At the Montgomery city line, an unmarked police car carrying two detectives fell in behind the bus. Twenty min-utes earlier, the state public safety director, Floyd Mann, had gone to Mont-gomery police commissioner L. B. Sullivan to confirm that he had men posted at the station. But just before the bus rolled in, at 10:23, a motorcade of policemen sped away from the depot area downtown. No police were in sight, only NBC cameraman Moe Levy and a few journalists. Among them was the *News* reporter Tom Lankford, who had "dressed like the mob."

John Lewis, the SNCC leader from Nashville via Troy, Alabama, who was the only current rider who had been in the original CORE crew, debarked with Birmingham's Katherine Burke onto the loading dock. As they talked into the NBC cameras, a hundred white men and women surged around the bus, swinging metal pipes, sticks, bats, and pocketbooks. First, they disposed of Moe Levy, smashing his camera on the street and hitting him on the head. Some of the twenty-one students still on board suggested exiting through the back door to placate the mob, but Jim Zwerg, a white dentist's son from Wisconsin in his junior year at Fisk, led the way out the front.

"Filthy Communists, nigger lovers, you're not going to integrate Mont-gomery," someone shouted as Zwerg took the first blows. Some riders broke for the post office, only to be nabbed in a roaring pursuit that would have done credit to the Bama secondary.

The only law enforcement presence was a stone-faced FBI agent, writing his description of the flying bodies on a bureau notepad.

Massacre

T H E *Birmingham News*'s Tom Lankford hustled toward his car, instructing a *New York Herald Tribune* reporter to take off his tie. "If anybody asks you, you're a Ku Kluxer, remember that." Over his police radio, Lankford heard that only two squad cars were being dispatched to the Greyhound station. The first cop arrived at least fifteen minutes after the outbreak. The state's Floyd Mann asked a city patrolman why he hadn't called Commissioner Sullivan. "The men he would send out probably would join the mob," the cop replied. Sullivan himself drove up and sat on his car. Three bleeding black victims limped over to him, spoke with him, and resumed their futile search for a taxi. "We have no intention of standing guard for a bunch of troublemakers coming into our city and making trouble," he told a reporter, apparently unconcerned that he was in the middle of a landmark libel case to defend his professional virtue. "I really don't know what happened. When I got here all I saw were three men lying in the street. There was two niggers and a white man." *

One of the "two niggers" was John Lewis, who had been brained by a wooden crate. A car driven by the *Sullivan* judge, Walter B. Jones, pulled up next to Lewis. The attorney general of Alabama, MacDonald Gallion, got out of it and dodged a flying Coke bottle in order to serve Lewis with Jones's injunction barring integrated bus riding in Alabama.

The mob howled despite the growing police presence. An unsuspecting black pedestrian was doused with flammable fluid, set afire, and left (alive) in the street after the flames flickered out. One cop turned his back on a black rider being savaged and began to direct traffic. The police finally made some arrests: A young white couple out shopping, Frederick and Anna Gach (a law school graduate, she had gone to high school in Phenix City with John Patterson), tried to protect some riders and were jailed on charges of disorderly conduct. As a man in the mob explained, "Anything we hate worse than niggers is nigger lovers."

Up the street from the main action, John Seigenthaler, wearing borrowed casual clothes, stopped his U-Drive-It rental car to rescue a white female Freedom Rider and was dragged out and smashed over the ear with a pipe. He lay unconscious in the gutter for twenty-five minutes until a police car took him to the hospital (all the "white" taxis had mysteriously "broken down").† The Justice Department's lone white friend in Alabama, Floyd Mann, drew his pistol on a gang of men beating a Birmingham TV cameraman and pulled one of John Lewis's Nashville classmates from the baseball bats and feet of another gang. "I'll

---

* A year earlier, Sullivan had told a White Citizens Council "rally" of fifty, "We want these outside meddlers to leave us alone," and then drawled meaningfully, "If they do otherwise, we'll do our best to 'accommodate' them here in Montgomery."

† Governor Patterson would later make much of the fact that Seigenthaler had left his ID back at the motel, as if that were the reason he had been left lying in the street. In subsequent correspondence with southerners, the Justice Department would stress that it was a young *white* girl Seigenthaler was trying to help.

shoot the next man who hits him," he shouted, the only officer who intervened in behalf of the riders.

A wide-eyed white Alabama boy named Bob Zellner fled the melee into the nearby law office of Clifford Durr, having unknowingly witnessed his future as one of the Movement's guerrillas. A student at Huntingdon College—a local white Methodist school—he and four others had interviewed Martin Luther King and Ralph Abernathy for a sociology paper the previous semester on racial problems and solutions, disobeying the professor's instructions to get their research from the Klan and the White Citizens Council. The college president pressured the "hoodlums" to withdraw from school, only to have to announce three days later that Zellner had won the college's highest scholastic award. Zellner successfully fought the expulsion with the help of his father, a Methodist minister and former Klansman who had become so liberal that he had accompanied his son to a SNCC meeting at Highlander Folk School that spring. They had met John Lewis and the other Nashville stalwarts now getting their heads bashed.

Zellner, who had become practically a son to the Durrs, found Virginia frantically watching the riot from the law office's second-story window. "Decca's down in the mob," she said, referring to Jessica Mitford, of the bizarre English Mitfords, who had lived with the Durrs in Washington as a young war bride and then widow. An open Communist turned journalist,* Mitford had recently been commissioned by *Esquire* to do a southern American version of her sister Nancy's famous essay on English class distinctions, coining the terms "U" and "non-U." Decca had come to Montgomery to avail herself of Virginia's attunement to the distinction between the "you-alls" and "non-you-alls."

Zellner had retrieved Mitford by the time police tear gas finally dispersed the mob at about one-thirty. Other than the "nigger-loving" white couple, no one was arrested. Visiting Seigenthaler in the hospital, Floyd Mann wept in frustration. Visiting John Lewis and some other battered Freedom Riders in the hospital, Zellner thought he might join the Freedom Riders, "if my mother would let me." He would catch up with them later, on the staff of SNCC.

When Fred Shuttlesworth got the news from Montgomery, he thought, "If they did that to Seigenthaler, think what they would have done to a black nigger like me." He became convinced that Robert Kennedy had personally intervened to have him arrested in Birmingham in order to save his life.

Pat

UP IN WASHINGTON, Birmingham's contribution to the Justice Department, Lou Oberdorfer, was having lunch at the Mayflower Hotel with the tax section of the American Bar Association. He had a feeling he ought to check in at the office.

---

* At home in Oakland, California, Mitford was a comrade of Joe Gelders's daughter, Marge Gelders Frantz, on whom she sometimes sloughed off tedious Party assignments.

"All hell broke loose," Justice's press officer, Edwin Guthman, told him. Oberdorfer returned to the office, where Robert Kennedy, who had been summoned from a baseball game with his children, told him to get five hundred U.S. marshals down to Alabama. Then Kennedy added, in his classic delegating style, "You take those marshals and go down there." Oberdorfer had qualms about being in charge of this mission. "I am from Alabama. I am Jewish," he told Byron White. "This thing will be very controversial." White, who was recovering from an ulcer operation, went into their boss's office and came back a couple of minutes later: "We will both go."

White, Oberdorfer, and a few other Justice men headed for Montgomery that evening in FAA chief Najeeb Halaby's Gulfstream turbojet. Oberdorfer had not considered it a good omen that Vincent Russo, the old Revenooer from Alabama, had refused to join their delegation. On board, they scoured the law books Russo had given them to find a legal rationale for invading Alabama. Oberdorfer was puzzled when White kept saying, "Do we have the right to protect a church?" He did not know what White knew: Martin Luther King was planning to hold a mass meeting at Ralph Abernathy's church the following night over the telephoned objections of Robert Kennedy.*

Oberdorfer was worried about White's career. Assuming that White would eventually be appointed attorney general when Robert Kennedy moved on to electoral politics, he said, "Byron, if this thing is a fiasco, which it may be, bringing in a disorganized group like this, and we get clobbered or somebody gets killed, if it goes wrong at all, you'll never be confirmed for anything by the Senate again." White grinned.

At eight o'clock central time, the Justice gang moved into a makeshift command post at Maxwell Air Force Base on Montgomery's outskirts. Still weak from surgery, White went to bed. Oberdorfer stayed up most of the night, directing the marshals and the tax agents filtering onto the base. Federal prison guards flew in from Atlanta and Chillicothe, Ohio. There were also Alcohol, Tobacco and Firearms agents (the "Revenooers") and Texas border patrolmen, the only crack shots among them. Capping Oberdorfer's growing sense of the surreal was that his wife's family lived only a few miles away and he dared not let them know he was in Montgomery.

The Press Freed

ON SUNDAY MORNING, caucuses took place at the highest executive level of the *New York Times.* Claude Sitton, a native of Conyers, Georgia, who had met Martin Luther King at the 1957 ceremonies officiating Ghana's independence when he was a press attaché there for the U.S. Information Agency, had sat on his porch in Atlanta the day before, listening to the news from Montgomery on his

---

* Eventually they found a Reconstruction statute that President Ulysses Grant had pushed through Congress in 1871, to enable him to send troops to put down Klan terrorism in South Carolina.

radio and "gnashing his teeth" over missing the biggest story of his three-year tour as the *Times* southern correspondent. Since his paper's prohibition on sending reporters to Alabama as a result of the Salisbury case, he had made one trip to the state, only to leave after being tipped off by the Montgomery AP bureau chief that he was wanted by some authorities with a subpoena.

The *Times*'s front-page stories on the Birmingham beatings were courtesy of the wire services. Sitton said over the phone to the national editor in New York, "How much longer are we going to let the goddamn lawyers tell us how to cover the story?" The executives finally relented. After nearly a year, the muzzle was lifted from the nation's paper of record.

We Asked for It

JOHN PATTERSON WAS MEETING with Byron White that Sunday, again surrounded by his full cabinet and joined by the national press corps. Patterson baited White, threatening to arrest the federal marshals if they tried to quell any race riots. (He asked White, "You know where some of these Freedom Riders are, don't you?" White replied, "Yes, in the hospital.")

Patterson's constituents no longer seemed amused by his snideness. Vincent Townsend's third front-page editorial of the week, in the Sunday *News,* referred overweeningly to Governor Patterson's term for the mob, "interested citizens." The headline read, "We asked for Federal intervention—we got it." Townsend even called Byron White by his nickname, Whizzer, a tribute to the football prowess that had earned him a brief career with the Detroit Lions.

"Out of the Way"

MARTIN LUTHER KING ARRIVED in Montgomery shortly after noon Sunday. Fifty federal marshals met him at the airport "like he was the president of the United States," the governor complained. Only twelve marshals were there to meet Fred Shuttlesworth later that day. Awaiting him at Abernathy's First Baptist was his brash new soul mate in SCLC, executive director Wyatt Walker. They watched the gathering crowd of chanting white people outside as bus boycott veterans began trickling into the sanctuary at around five. Len Holt, the fastest lawyer in the South, looked out a crack in the church door and saw "a living mass of formless hate." A skeleton crew of marshals, wearing yellow armbands over mufti, their jackets concealing sidearms, ringed the church, but there were no city policemen. King sat in Abernathy's office, working on his speech for the evening.

Jim Farmer, the mastermind of the Freedom Ride, was due in soon from Washington, having buried his father. Shuttlesworth departed with his bodyguards to go pick him up at the airport.

"Can you get me into that church, Fred?" Farmer asked.

"Wrong question, Jim. The only question to ask is: How will I get you in?"

A few blocks from First Baptist, Confederate flag wavers surrounded Shuttlesworth's car and began to rock it. Shuttlesworth smiled at the assailants as his driver shifted into reverse and made a screeching U-turn. At a black taxi stand, Shuttlesworth consulted a cabbie ("I have Jim Farmer"), who prescribed a circuitous path by way of Oakwood Cemetery. Stymied again by the mob, Shuttlesworth got out of the car. Coke bottles shattered car windows around him as he paused to register a strange smell, his first whiff of tear gas. Then he beckoned Farmer out of the car and strode into the mob. Farmer followed, "scared as hell," trying to shrink his bon vivant's ample body into Shuttlesworth's thin shadow. The goons parted, their clubs went slack, and Shuttlesworth walked up to the doors of First Baptist without a thread on his jacket disturbed. "Out of the way" was all he had said. "Go on. Out of the way."

"I'm only a little fellow," Shuttlesworth said, "but so was Jesus Christ."

The torching of a parked Buick signaled a quickening of mob momentum. Cliff and Virginia Durr owned the car. (Their houseguest, Jessica Mitford, in a "perfect Southern lady" costume of green chiffon and pearls, had driven it down to the church and gone inside.) "We'll get you, too," the crowd yelled at a local news photographer shooting the flaming car. *Newsweek*'s Joe Cumming was among a hefty national press contingent inside the church. He missed the Montgomery melee because he had overslept in Birmingham. He watched out the window as a potbellied man with a two-by-four went toe-to-toe with a marshal and announced, "We want to go to church with the niggers." The marshal tossed a canister in the mob's direction and pulled on his mask. Tear gas mingled with the vapors of the white folks' stink bomb and wafted into the church. Black teens repaired to the church's rec room to get some bats before being stopped by their elders.

Farmer and Shuttlesworth found King, Abernathy, and Diane Nash (who would soon be the subject of a *New York Times* profile by David Halberstam) dispiritedly awaiting the next bulletin from the Justice Department. The phone rang, and after a few minutes King came out of Abernathy's office to give Farmer a message from the attorney general: He wanted them to call off the Freedom Rides and have a "cooling-off period" to buy the administration time to work things out. Farmer replied, "We have been cooling off for three hundred and fifty years. If we cool off any more, we will be in the deep freeze."

A Sin and a Shame

"It's going to be very close, very touch and go," Byron White was telling Robert Kennedy at ten o'clock. The open phone line from Maxwell Air Force Base to Justice was being monitored by a switchboard operator who was keeping Patterson informed of all the conversations. Oberdorfer was working on one last tactical problem: how to transport the five hundred marshals to the church. Although Army troops were on standby across the Georgia state line at Fort Benning, the Alabama Army brass refused Justice the use of their cars. So the Montgomery postmaster had sent Oberdorfer scores of mail trucks, a good number of whose drivers were black.

Oberdorfer and White went down to the parking lot and began waving at them, hollering, "Get going. What are you waiting for?" The trucks were roaring out the gates before one of the Justice officials realized that they contained no federal marshals. White put his hand on his head and said, "Oh, my God, another Bay of Pigs."

Around 1,500 Negroes waited inside the church. Those looking anxiously out the windows felt little relief when they saw the advancing mail trucks. Nor would they have been reassured to know that many of the Revenooers they had been manned with were from Mississippi. When White was informed that they had arrived at the church, he quipped, "Whose side are they on?"

The mob had reached the church door. In the sanctuary, some men were retrieving weapons secreted in their jackets. From the pulpit, Solomon Seay shouted for everyone to be calm and sing—"and mean every word of it." Local lawmen finally began to arrive; a brick hurled by white teens hit L. B. Sullivan's car.

Sometime after ten, King took the pulpit. The crisis prompted him to drop his prepared remark that Alabama had "sunk to a level of barbarity comparable to the tragic days of Hitler's Germany." Instead, he urged equanimity on his audience, calling for "the right balance." At his elbow, Shuttlesworth seethed. When it was his turn to speak, he shouted in full preacher throat, "It's a sin and a shame before God that these people who govern us would let things come to such a sad state. But God is not dead. The most guilty man in this state tonight is Governor John Patterson."

At 10:10, a new uniformed presence began moving among the marshals and police outside First Baptist. Their white steel helmets shining in the night, National Guardsmen took sentry posts on the church stairs. After Robert Kennedy had informed him that federal troops would soon be flown in, Governor Patterson had declared martial law and chewed Kennedy out for causing the violence. "Now, John, you can say that on television," Kennedy replied. "You can tell that to the people of Alabama, John, but don't tell me that, John."

At five minutes before midnight, Robert Kennedy officially turned his marshals over to the command of the state of Alabama. Just after midnight, National Guard General Henry Graham, a Birmingham real estate executive in civilian life, strode into the church and ordered the occupants to stay put "for your own safety"—"I appreciate your cooperation," he said. "In fact, I insist upon it." It was not clear whether the fixed bayonets of the 150 or so Guardsmen, who had been warned against "taking sides," were repulsing the mob or checking the 1,500 black churchpeople.

King was appalled that the administration had acceded to a plan that put the federal marshals under the authority of the governor whom he and Shuttlesworth had both just damned from the pulpit as the wickedest man in the country. Shocked at the lack of gratitude, Kennedy pointed out over the phone that if he had not intervened, King would be "dead as Kelsey's nuts."

As King paused to ponder that Irish simile, Shuttlesworth grabbed the phone. "Oh, you made it," Kennedy said. Shuttlesworth told the attorney general that he had betrayed innocent church-bound hostages to their worst enemy. He wanted federal, not state troops. "You look after your end, reverend, and I'll look after mine," Kennedy said, and in a slight based on the distinction between a "doctor" and a mere "reverend," instructed him, "You go talk with somebody else. I was talking to Dr. King."

Sensing calm in Montgomery, Kennedy let a United Press reporter snap a fin-de-debacle photograph: the attorney general on the phone, wearing rumpled weekend wear and a cardigan, his dirty sneakers propped up on his desk. In Alabama, the photograph would be cited as more proof of the Kennedy administration's "bobby-sox" unprofessionalism—"Mickey Rooney just in from a touch football game," the *Montgomery Advertiser* jeered—subliminally echoing the famous caricatures of Reconstruction Negro solons putting their bare feet on the tables of the capitol.

By four-thirty in the morning, the mob had dispersed. National Guard jeeps rolled in to ferry home the Negroes whose transportational rights Alabama had gone to so much trouble to deny. "All right, nigger," they said, "where do you live?" Shuttlesworth sat high on his jeep, surveying the scene as if he were Patton—the general to whom he sometimes compared himself—overseeing a maneuver.

8.

PIVOT

Hoover

THE FREEDOM RIDES were proving to be one of history's rare alchemical phenomena, altering the structural makeup of everything they touched. They had engineered what was perhaps Birmingham's major civic turning point since Joe Gelders revealed to the La Follette committee that U.S. Steel had terrorists on its payroll. In the continuing evolution of vigilantism in Birmingham, the Freedom Riders' welcome to the city marked the end of Bull Connor's long life as the intermediary between the Big Mules and the Klan, alienating him with finality from his old sponsors. As Sid Smyer's study group proved, the business elite was finally distancing itself from the militantly segregationist ideology it had long shared with the Klan.

As Jim Farmer intended, the Freedom Rides had engaged the federal government in a symbiosis with the civil rights movement, but they had also made the government a shield for the Ku Klux Klan. The FBI's cover-up of Gary Thomas Rowe's actions would taint the Justice Department for decades, and that was only one of the bureau's insults to the civil rights movement. The most historic result of the Freedom Rides was perhaps the least well known: J. Edgar Hoover's enduring vendetta against Martin Luther King.

That Hoover's career path had wound its way to Birmingham had a certain logic: His profession as a hunter of subversives had been launched by U.S. Steel. To squelch the union movement among its workers in 1919, the Corporation had helped foment the Red Scare that led Congress to create an anti-radical general intelligence division of the Justice Department. Hoover was appointed its first chief, a green twenty-four-year-old who grafted his prejudices as a product of Jim Crow Washington on to his anti-red mission; Hoover's first black target had been America's pioneer "mass" leader, the Jamaican immigrant Marcus Garvey, whom he had bagged in 1923 on mail fraud charges.

Hoover's division was dissolved the following year, and he became director of the Bureau of Investigation, which acquired the prefix "Federal" during the New Deal. He never met a civil rights figure he didn't hold in suspicion—Philip

Randolph, W.E.B. Du Bois, Paul Robeson, even Mary McLeod Bethune. Truman's Committee on Civil Rights he considered pink at best. And his agents had cooperated with Bull Connor in closing down the Southern Negro Youth Congress. In 1953, the bureau opened a Communist-infiltration investigation of CORE, the cause of Hoover's current dilemma.

The Justice Department had been getting big doses of the FBI's aggressive passivity all week. Frustration over the Birmingham bureau's dodges had prompted the attorney general to buzz Hoover, technically his subordinate, and ask him how many agents "we" had in Birmingham. "We have enough, we have enough," the director said, and let loose a flood of words that neither answered the question nor didn't answer it. On Sunday night during the siege at Ralph Abernathy's church, the complaints about the FBI from Justice's "riot squad-ders"—as the lawyers on these ad hoc assignments were henceforth known—had grown so persistent that Robert Kennedy called his brother, who called Hoover at midnight. Hoover regarded any criticism of an FBI employee as "an attack on me personally," and he responded by scrounging around for a scapegoat. By morning he had found someone to take the blame for his staff's shortcomings in Alabama: It was the man responsible for the Sunday-night mess, Martin Luther King.

Making a target of King would solve another problem for Hoover. Three months earlier, his new attorney general had declared war on the Mafia, an organ-ization that Hoover insisted did not exist—possibly, as students of the FBI would later claim, because mobsters had evidence that the director had a taste for makeup and women's clothing. Hoping to divert Kennedy from the Mafia, Hoover declared that "the Communist Party U.S.A. presents a greater menace to the in-ternal security of our Nation than it ever has." Kennedy practically laughed, say-ing that the Party's membership consisted primarily of FBI agents. But Hoover could now get the upper hand over his boss if it was proved that the civil rights movement currently being protected by the attorney general's men was under the thumb of the Communist Party.

On Monday, May 22, Hoover ordered a report on King. Later in the day he received some spotty intelligence. The only potential red bait was that after King had been stabbed in the New York department store in 1958, Ben Davis, the black Harvard-educated Stalinist who was Angelo Herndon's lawyer before becoming Harlem's Communist councilman, had donated blood to his fellow Atlantan. Also, there was King's speech at the twenty-fifth anniversary commemoration of the Highlander Folk School, which the bureau, along with the rest of the segrega-tionist world, referred to as a "Communist Party training school." Indeed, the FBI document's details, as well as its spirit, echoed the report that Detective Tom Cook had done on King a year earlier for Bull Connor. On the new report's ad-mission that King had not been investigated by the FBI, Hoover annotated a pee-vish "Why not?" Hoover's minions needed no further directive to get to the bottom of the civil rights mess—this "latest form of the eternal rebellion against authority," as Hoover characterized Communism.

Alabama's Big Man

ON MONDAY NIGHT, King faced the first public challenge to his leadership from within the Movement. Fred Shuttlesworth had so far kept his beefs with him private, in the family, but now a showdown between the Southern Christian Leadership Conference and the Student Nonviolent Coordinating Committee was taking place at Montgomery's black YMCA. The students were asking King to put his "body" in the Movement and accompany them to Jackson, Mississippi, on the freedom bus. His excuse—that he was on probation for his arrest during the Atlanta sit-ins—stunned them. They, too, were on probation, for they had *sponsored* the sit-ins. "Well, now, I think I should choose the time and place of my Golgotha," King said, referring to the site of Jesus' Crucifixion. The students laughed at the man whom they had seen as a messiah and from then on mocked him as "de Lawd."

To the student vanguard, the black leader of choice was Shuttlesworth, whose star was rising that night in Birmingham as King's was in eclipse in Montgomery. Shuttlesworth arrived at the mass meeting in the middle of the Alabama Christian Movement for Human Rights treasurer Bill Shortridge's startling announcement that people had "run him down on the street" all week to give him money. Spying Shuttlesworth, the submissive first vice president, Ed Gardner, rushed to the pulpit and roused the assembled to their feet for a screaming ovation. Second vice president Abraham Lincoln Woods's introduction of Shuttlesworth hailed a Second Coming. "Nothing has happened in the South until God let this big man be born in Alabama," he said. Even Connor's surveillance men seemed to sense what Shuttlesworth had understood that Christmas night more than four years earlier when a bomb blew up his house: He had entered history. "They are trying to make Shuttlesworth very big and important," the detectives observed.

Shuttlesworth returned to Montgomery on Tuesday "to keep all the symbols all together in one place." Twelve hundred National Guardsmen in combat garb, along with more than six hundred federal marshals, patrolled the capital with fixed bayonets and stood guard at the homes of black activists, costing the Alabama taxpayers $30,000 a day. Rather than seeing "Pat's soldiers" as a nuisance, Shuttlesworth encouraged King, Abernathy, and Wyatt Walker to make nuisances of themselves, insisting that they report to the militia command before making the least move.

Meanwhile, the SNCC students prepared to die. Early on Wednesday morning, they took a bus out of Montgomery bound for Jackson. Escorted by forty-two vehicles containing Guardsmen, state police, and journalists, plus three L-19 reconnaissance planes and two helicopters, the twelve riders were outnumbered by the sixteen reporters—one of them the *Times*'s Claude Sitton, who had flown to Alabama on Monday. The Freedom Rides were turning out not to be the containable political crisis the Kennedys had assumed they would be when they gave state authorities the green light to arrest the riders on Monday ("I'm sure they would be represented by competent counsel," the starchy Byron White told reporters). A second freedom bus, carrying mostly CORE members, including a foot-dragging Jim Farmer, left a few hours after the first. Robert Kennedy dismissed these trips as unauthorized.

The Kennedys' irritation increased as their own peer group joined the bus protest. William Sloane Coffin Jr., the thirty-six-year-old son of New York's Sloane furniture family who was the chaplain of Yale University, had decided to become a Freedom Rider after seeing a picture in his Sunday paper of John Lewis lying on a Montgomery street, bleeding. Coffin and six other Ivy Leaguers, including an old Yale Divinity classmate originally from Montgomery and a black Yale Law student, rolled into the Montgomery Greyhound station late Wednesday afternoon, May 24. They debarked through a column of National Guard bayonets into the embrace of Fred Shuttlesworth and Wyatt Tee Walker, who took them to Ralph Abernathy's house for a fried chicken supper. Martin Luther King took a testy call from Robert Kennedy and after hanging up reported to Abernathy's guests that the Kennedys didn't have a clue that the Freedom Rides were part of "the social revolution going on in the world."

On the morning of Thursday, May 25, Shuttlesworth stalked up and down Abernathy's porch, lecturing the National Guardsmen about the evils of segregation. He had decided to accompany Coffin's group on the eleven-thirty bus to Jackson. Guardsmen escorted them through the barricade of troops around the Trailways station. Shuttlesworth, Abernathy, Walker, and the old Alabama State sit-in leader Bernard Lee bought tickets along with Coffin's people and went to get coffee at the white lunch counter. Shuttlesworth noticed that General Henry Graham, whose "very nice" bearing had so impressed him at Abernathy's church Sunday night—and whose voice had broken the day before in wishing the Montgomery-bound riders "a safe journey"—had "gotten tired of us." Graham gave the nod to the Montgomery County sheriff to arrest all eleven men. Walker, who was telephoning his wife in Atlanta to tell her he would be home that night, protested that he didn't see any "Colored" sign over the phone booth, but General Graham said wearily, "Now everyone is happy. This is what they wanted and we have accommodated them." Although Coffin received top billing, Shuttlesworth once again made it onto the front page of the *New York Times*.

The Klan's Day in Court

THE KU KLUX KLAN was experiencing its first tremors of vulnerability. Barely a week earlier, the FBI had observed that the Klan's chief, Bobby Shelton, was in Birmingham "expecting calls from the governor's office." But apparently, after four Klansmen were indicted on federal charges in the Anniston freedom bus firebombing on Monday, John Patterson began to rethink their collaboration. More recently, an FBI informant overheard him tell a Klansman, "You need not think that because you all supported me you can take the law into your own hands. I'm going to start arresting you every time you get out of line and start causing trouble."

The Justice Department had already moved against the Klan. John Doar, a Justice lawyer who happened to be in Alabama working on a voter registration case, had sought a novel injunction restraining the Klan from interfering with the safe travel of persons in the state. A Republican from Wisconsin, Doar was an Eisenhower holdover who had become the imperturbable Gary Cooper of the Kennedy civil rights team, and the Montgomery-based federal judge who gave him his injunction—in the dark hours of the morning following the Saturday riot in the capital—was a fellow tall Republican, from the "Free County of Winston," the anti-secessionist stronghold in North Alabama that had contributed a cavalry detail to the Union Army. Judge Frank Johnson had by now desegregated Montgomery's parks (which the commission promptly closed, in 1959) and, three years before, had delivered an unmerciful dressing-down to his old law school chum George Wallace, when the "fighting little judge" defied the "errand boys of the Civil Rights Commission" who had subpoenaed his district's voting records. Wallace had reputedly showed up at the judge's house one night with a paper bag over his head to cut a deal.

On Friday, May 26, Judge Johnson, whose house was being guarded by U.S. marshals, hosted the Ku Klux Klan in his courtroom for a hearing on his restraining order against it. The cocksure Klansmen who had hijacked the Greyhound bus in Anniston had become shaky boys. Cecil Lamar Lewallyn, the youth charged with throwing the firebomb, cowered behind the witness stand. When his voice could not carry beyond the bench, Johnson acidly informed his court, "He's trying to plead the Fifth Amendment." Then Johnson summoned a federal marshal to "commit this man to jail for contempt of court." Watching Lewallyn being led from the courtroom was his attorney J. B. Stoner, who was enjoying his emerging alliance with the Klan at the same time that he was rallying his National States Rights Party behind another defendant, Adolf Eichmann, who was about to go on trial in Jerusalem for the war crimes he had committed as Hitler's operations man.

The chief quarry of the Justice Department's Klan injunction, Bobby Shelton, further provoked Judge Johnson when he took the witness stand and proceeded to ignore John Doar's questions.* Fiddling with his glasses and furrowing his brow, Shelton finally answered Doar's query about whether he knew any members of the Alabama Klans: "To authenticate this information, I do not." Judge Johnson turned furiously on him and said, "That's not responsive." Ultimately, Shelton admitted that he knew Robert Thomas, Hubert Page, and the sus-

---

* Birmingham detective Tom Cook had just counseled Shelton to duck the marshal who tried to serve an injunction on him.

pected organizer of the Anniston attack, Ace Carter's old crony Kenneth Adams, who was also represented by Stoner.*

Johnson had put on an exhilarating performance. But as his earlier rout of George Wallace had proved, often in Alabama to lose was to win. Wallace had used his showdown with Johnson and the U.S. Civil Rights Commission to turn a simple "niggering" antic into a protest against the aggression of Big Government. And similarly, Wallace's future ally, Shelton, shed crocodile tears and condemned Johnson in a press release. The Freedom Rides, among their many turning points, were about to crown Shelton the undisputed king among Kluxers.

Anticlimax

THE MOVEMENT was facing the inevitable letdown that follows moral victory. The collegiate protesters had posted bond after only a day in jail and boarded a plane north under National Guard watch. (General Graham had recovered his country club manners to wish the departing visitors "a return to the South under more favorable conditions.") Still in the Montgomery jail, Fred Shuttlesworth, Wyatt Walker, and Ralph Abernathy kept their spirits up by baiting one another in the way that preachers socialize. When Walker goaded deputies with a chorus of "Come by here, milord, come by here," Shuttlesworth teased him for trying to "get in tune to upset the guard" even though he did not have the "tune" of a self-respecting "shouters'" pastor like him. Walker hoped to put the kibosh on the preachers' proposed hunger strike, arguing that it would be more of a hardship to actually drink the coffee. Shuttlesworth tweaked him, "I know you're skinnier than the rest of us, but you're gonna do without."

Even as more Freedom Riding reinforcements headed toward Montgomery on Saturday, Shuttlesworth surprised everyone by posting his $1,000 bond. He had to end this "glorious experience" in order to preach on Sunday at Revelation Baptist Church in Cincinnati. The urgency of the engagement would soon become woefully clear.

On Monday, May 29, Robert Kennedy petitioned the Interstate Commerce Commission to draw up federal regulations to convert into national policy the

---

* One of those named in the anti-Klan injunction was Claude V. Henley, a burly, cigar-smoking former reserve policeman and used-car salesman who had assaulted NBC cameraman Moe Levy and had locked his knees around Freedom Rider James Zwerg's head so that his comrades could beat him. Henley had gone to a young lawyer who had been his rural neighbor in Mount Meigs (Fred Shuttlesworth's birthplace): Morris Seligman Dees Jr., a Baptist whose father had been named after an admired Montgomery merchant. After assuring Doar that his client would abide by the injunction, Dees was accosted by a Freedom Rider who asked, "Don't you think black people have rights?" He would date his resolve to be on the right side of the civil rights struggle from that first, indirect encounter with Bobby Shelton. In the many face-offs with Shelton that would follow, Dees would be on the opposite side of the courtroom: As founder of the Klan-bashing Southern Poverty Law Center in 1971, he would become a man hunted by the country's white supremacist vigilantes and would effectively put Shelton's organization out of business in 1987.

Supreme Court's *Boynton* mandate barring discrimination against interstate travelers. Jim Farmer had gotten the coveted federal involvement, but ironically the government's petitions siphoned the melodrama from the protests themselves. The Kennedys had worked out an arrangement with Mississippi senator James Eastland (whom they really did consider their great pal in the South) whereby the continuing waves of Freedom Riders would be locked up as soon as they got off the buses in Jackson. Soon, the trickle of riders would be ignored by the news media and thus made invisible to the public.

Extremists on Both Sides

ON TUESDAY, MAY 30, it became plain that the Justice Department was attempting to force a truth that the public was not ready to hear. In proposing his anti-Klan injunction, John Doar had decided also to go after the Kluxers' high-level co-conspirators: the elected officials of Birmingham and Montgomery. Though the FBI agents Doar had interviewed for his brief neglected to divulge Bull Connor's fifteen-minute deal with the Klan, Judge Johnson agreed to name the commissioner and his police chief, Jamie Moore, in his restraining order, as well as Montgomery commissioner L. B. Sullivan and his police chief. The government's charge that Sullivan "deliberately failed to take measures to insure the safety of the students and to prevent unlawful acts and violence upon their persons" must have bemused the lawyers for the *New York Times.*

In Judge Johnson's court that Tuesday, defending himself against the injunction, Commissioner Bull Connor mugged for the gallery, principally for Shuttlesworth, who had made a special trip to the capital to see his nemesis squirm. Connor's advocate, Jim Simpson, assumed his famous courtroom indignation and hammered a single assertion: The only reason the Birmingham police were not at the Trailways station was that they thought the freedom bus was coming into the Greyhound station. If Gary Thomas Rowe still needed any proof that the FBI was willing to tolerate the complicity between local law enforcement and the Klan, it was provided by the appearance of Special Agent in Charge Thomas Jenkins as a witness in Connor's defense. In confirming on the stand Simpson's contention that nothing was said about a Trailways bus, Jenkins may have been technically correct. But in light of Rowe's reports, it appears that the FBI was content to ignore the larger truth of what Connor had done.

Judge Johnson removed Connor from his injunction against the Klan. And even he seemed uncomfortable with treating civil rights activists as citizens due the protections of the Constitution rather than provocateurs looking for trouble. In response to a motion from L. B. Sullivan's lawyer, he issued a last-minute second temporary restraining order, against Shuttlesworth, Martin Luther King, Wyatt Walker, and Ralph Abernathy, enjoining them from "sponsoring, financing, assisting or encouraging" any Freedom Rides. The most liberal judge in Alabama had fallen for that oft-invoked fallacy of "extremists on both sides."

In yet another front-page editorial, Vincent Townsend, the man who had first publicly linked Connor and the Klansmen at the bus station, praised Johnson for saving Birmingham from "intense embarrassment." Townsend's and Sid Smyer's civic epiphanies were beginning to look like fleeting aberrations. Connor had never seemed more in charge. Even Howard K. Smith had been humbled. In his regular Sunday radio commentary, on May 21, he had taunted the President of the United States to clear up the "confusion in the Southern mind" over where the responsibility lay for the Birmingham violence and—amazingly, given his "pink" vulnerability—demanded, "Do we really deserve to win the cold war?" The no-holds-barred radio piece gave the *New York Times* TV critic Jack Gould a pretext ("Smith at his best") to criticize the networks' increasingly namby-pamby policy of "fairness" and "objectivity," which seemed to accord segregationists equal time with integrationists. But CBS News's response was to suspend Smith from his job as Washington bureau chief.

Runoff

THAT TUESDAY of Connor's exoneration by Judge Johnson was the day of the mayoral runoff election between Tom King and Art Hanes. It was Connor's richest historical moment. He had gotten Mayor Jimmy Morgan's machine to do his mayoral candidate's gutter work, even using Townsend's surrogate son, Tom Lankford, to take the "black hand" photograph. On Mother's Day, Connor had handed Art Hanes a foolproof "racial incident." While Tom King deplored the bus station violence, Hanes insisted that a King victory would mean the fall of Birmingham as a "segregation stronghold." And he was right.

In the days after the Trailways beatings, King's campaign went straight to hell. When the *News* tried to refute the propaganda that King was a "captive of the Negro bloc," Hanes retorted that the editors were stooges of the paper's owner, Samuel Isaac (read: Jew) Newhouse. King extended his blackened hand to voters, only to have it rejected.

It was almost a relief when the May 30 election finally put King out of his misery. The surprisingly small margin of his loss—21,133 to 17,385—would be a poignant reminder of how close he and the Young Turks had come to pulling off their coup and rescuing Birmingham from its fate. The mastermind of King's campaign, Chuck Morgan, went incommunicado for a week, some said to take the bourbon cure.

Cincinnati

FRED SHUTTLESWORTH had found himself finally at the center of a real civil rights extravaganza. The Freedom Rides had pulled together all the various branches of the Movement (even the NAACP had begun to pitch in on the legal front). But ultimately what they had made Shuttlesworth realize was that in its four years of existence SCLC had failed to find an identity. The Freedom Rides were CORE's baby, reared to maturity by SNCC—which was now on a collision course with SCLC over money, strategy, philosophy, and credit.

Shuttlesworth was growing more frustrated at being stuck in Martin Luther King's orbit. He brandished yellowing press clippings. "Ole Bull says the riders only came here because of me and they been coming from New York and all over," he told a mass meeting in mid-June. "Well, all I know is I'm catching hell for being somebody." Yet he wasn't getting enough respect from Atlanta and sent King a letter pointing out that the ACMHR was doing all SCLC's work and getting none of the money.

"My native state would like to disown me," Shuttlesworth told the faithful at the fifth anniversary celebration of the ACMHR in June. But he had decided to save Alabama the trouble: He was accepting the pulpit at Revelation Baptist in Cincinnati. Although he would retain the presidency of the Alabama Christian Movement, the SCLC brass in Atlanta faced the departure of the Wild Man from Birmingham with the same dismay that Lincoln might have felt if William Tecumseh Sherman had resigned his commission in the middle of the first war for emancipation. "You have done a tremendous job in Birmingham," Wyatt Walker wrote Shuttlesworth, enclosing a check to the ACMHR from SCLC, in response to his earlier remonstration, "and I still don't believe the Lord called you to Cincinnati (smile)." Indeed, the only one who seemed to think the move was a good idea was Shuttlesworth's deposed rival, J. L. Ware, who had said to him, "Fred, we've had our differences, but we were never enemies. The Lord may be wanting you to go to Cincinnati. Don't feel like you have to stay here."

Shuttlesworth seemed glum about the decision. A heavy speaking schedule had left him fatigued and short-winded. The detectives at a late-July mass meeting noted with satisfaction that a collection for Shuttlesworth's going-away gift yielded "very little money." But, as Shuttlesworth was fond of saying, God worked in mysterious ways, and perhaps the ACMHR needed to shed its showy foliage if it was ever going to develop a root system that could sustain a mass movement.*

Mobilizing Some Strategies

THE ACMHR OFFICER most dry-eyed over Shuttlesworth's departure was its secretary, Nelson Smith, whose esteem for J. L. Ware had led some to question his loyalty to his president. Smith's distinction as the only big-church pastor in the inner circle had created tensions within and around him. As the son of a prominent minister from Monroeville, the idealistic young orator known as Fireball wanted to become what he called "a world-renowned preacher." Toward that end he rehearsed constantly, pantomiming at the steering wheel in contempt of traffic safety.

But Smith understood that the Movement needed to be liberated from its preacher mystique. Sometime around the beginning of the school year, not long

---

* As a bon voyage present, Bull Connor hatched a state law, passed unanimously in August, outlawing Freedom Rides in Alabama. Connor credited his "personal attorney," Jim Simpson, for drafting the bill, which prohibited any act calculated to offend Alabamians' "sense of decency." It was the Great Man's most tenuous constitutional standard to date.

after Shuttlesworth left, Smith paid a visit to Miles College, where he found some students under the trees, in their idiom, "mobilizing some strategies." The student-body presidency had passed from Jesse Walker, SNCC's first man in Birmingham, to Frank Dukes, one of the instigators of the aborted 1960 prayer vigil at Kelly Ingram Park. Dukes was at thirty-one only a year younger than Martin Luther King, a strapping Korean War veteran who had worked at a Chrysler plant in Detroit before coming home in 1959 and enrolling at Miles on the GI Bill. "This is the place for a man to start," he had decided, reborn in the Movement. "Right here. Right now."

Since Jesse Walker's graduation, the Miles militants had fallen out of the SNCC axis. Isolated in the valley of segregation, they were more philosophers than activists. If they had a spiritual father, it was the *World* editor, Emory O. Jackson. One of Frank Dukes's co-conspirators under the trees, a Navy veteran named Charles Davis, traced his enlightenment to his boyhood paper route and the NAACP slogan printed on the *World*'s front page: "A voteless people is a hopeless people." Jackson was one of the few members of the black power structure—many activist ministers included—who escaped the youths' encyclopedic classifications of Uncle Toms. (Tom #1 is opportunistic, may or may not be smart; Tom #2 fears reprisals; Tom #3 "loves white people.") But Jackson was still more gadfly than leader, his satirical style too cranky for mass appeal.

Although the Miles students supported Shuttlesworth's Movement and were willing to show up for protests and go to jail, they didn't attend mass meetings and they didn't pray. "A lot of us remained in the trenches because we didn't embrace all that continuous fellowship in Christ," Davis said. "We just knew that white people didn't have a monopoly on brains."

On the Miles campus, Nelson Smith surprised the young cynics who snickered at the canned flourishes of the clergy and quoted not the Scripture but Shakespeare.* His overtures on behalf of the ACMHR "caught our imagination," Charles Davis recalled. By the time he left them in the shade, the Alabama Movement had acquired a militant youth arm—and, thanks to a changing of the administrative guard at Miles, a reliable grown-up emissary to white Birmingham as well.

The previous January, the new college president, Lucius Pitts, had been rushed in from Atlanta to succeed W. A. Bell, who had died of a heart attack. A Christian Methodist Episcopal minister and educator, Pitts was such a dynamic combination of spiritual, intellectual, and managerial talent that Martin Luther King and Ella Baker had wooed him, unsuccessfully, in 1957 to become the first executive director of SCLC. He was the inverse of King himself: a man of the

---

* Perhaps Smith, too, had become disillusioned with the preacher culture. In early September, he had been part of a flying wedge of civil rights ministers who had literally tried to seize power from the czar of the National Baptist Convention, J. H. "Old Jack" Jackson, at the NBC's annual convention, in Kansas City. Amid the ensuing slugfest ultimately ended by riot police, a chair holding a Jackson yes-man was shoved off the stage, injuring him fatally. J. H. Jackson accused Martin Luther King of murdering a Baptist brother. Smith would soon become one of the powers in the civil rights–friendly Progressive National Convention that splintered off from the National Baptists; he served as its president from 1974 to 1976.

masses who could speak to the classes. Tall, well dressed, and handsome, he had a cultivated silvery voice, yet he retained the austere soul of the sharecropper's son who had washed dishes to pay his way through Georgia's Paine College and, despite temporary blindness caused by undiagnosed diabetes, earned a doctorate in theology.

"Miles College has a very fine president now," Ed Gardner, the ACMHR vice president who held down the fort for Shuttlesworth, said at a mass meeting in October. "He is not an intellectual Uncle Tom." Yet despite Pitts's militance, he claimed an asset that had been virtually unimagined among Birmingham's civil rights activists. As his Poitier-esque debut in CBS Reports's "Who Speaks for Birmingham?" proved, he could veil his threats in the language of accommodation. "It's a painful thing to be a reading Negro," he had told CBS's producers with a rueful smile, "well, say an educable Negro in the South, with a family, to try to decide how much to tell your child and how you interpret the situation to him, so that he doesn't develop the kind of hatred and fear and conditioning that I have had to strive to try to get rid of."

Birmingham blacks finally had the Good Colored Person to complete the equation of intimidation that until now had boasted only the "Bad Nigger," Fred Shuttlesworth. He would be featured in the coming SCLC newsletter as "the most courageous man on the civil rights scene in the South," though he no longer lived in the South. There was a faction in CORE trying to recruit him to replace Jim Farmer.

Southern Justice

SINCE ASSUMING the martyr's cross of a federal injunction, Bobby Shelton had gained control of the Ku Klux Klan in the South. Earlier in the summer, the honchos of what remained of Eldon Edwards's Atlanta-based United Klans—sundered since his death in 1960—had agreed to fold Shelton's Alabama Knights into their organization, perhaps not realizing that Shelton was a knight on a Trojan horse. At a powwow of the South's leading Klansmen at Indian Springs, Georgia, in July, Shelton was elected the Imperial Wizard of the new United Klans by acclamation. He began touring the South, proclaiming a "new, modern, jet-age Klan."

The headquarters of the United Klans were moved to Shelton's hometown of Tuscaloosa, and its flagship klavern, Eastview 13, now became the most important club in the entire Invisible Empire. Tommy Rowe's grandiosity grew accordingly. He considered himself not a mere informant ("a bad word to me") but—"absolutely"—an undercover agent for the FBI. And that made the FBI the guardian angel of a Klan that, having otherwise lost its establishment support, might have slipped into oblivion.

Unable to surmount the bad faith of both the FBI and southern justice, the Justice Department saw its seemingly open-and-shut cases against Cecil Lamar Lewallyn and Ken Adams for the Anniston bus burning wash out that fall. (Local

FBI agents wrote a memo depicting John Doar, the government's lawyer, as a pest.) The courtroom chapter of the Freedom Rides effectively closed in Alabama at the end of November with the trial of the last remaining defendant in the Birmingham beatings, Herschel Acker of Rome, Georgia, the tooth-baring assailant dead center in Tommy Langston's picture. Although Acker's victim, George Webb, identified him in court, the jury acquitted Acker of assault with intent to murder after thirty-one minutes. Howard Thurston Edwards, the pipe wielder next to Acker, was tried three times. All the trials ended in hung juries; the victim had failed to identify Edwards in a lineup after he restyled his pompadour.

No members of Eastview were tried for the beatings they had orchestrated. Despite the crimes he committed in the line of duty on Mother's Day, Gary Thomas Rowe received a $125 bonus. Within a month, his handler, Barry Kemp, left the bureau.

Head

THE DEMOCRATS on the federal bench like to slough the racial cases off on their junior Republican colleague, Hobart Grooms. October had been a busy month for the judge, his busiest since the winter of 1955–56, when he had presided regretfully over the ordeal of Autherine Lucy (and had futilely encouraged her to keep pressing her claim). He had set up shop in Anniston at the end of the month to oversee the hung jury mistrial of the accused bus bomber, Cecil Lamar Lewallyn, nearly jailing the NSRP's Dr. Edward Fields for contempt after he called up and harassed members of the jury panel. (In the trick-or-treat spirit of the season, a man wearing a mask showed up in the middle of the night at the door of a juror's motel room.) But before that trial, Grooms had heard the final arguments of a case that would traumatically force the white establishment to speak for Birmingham.

Fred Shuttlesworth's lawsuit to desegregate the city's sixty-seven public parks (as well as its eight swimming pools, the public golf courses, and the Kiddieland amusement park) had been going on for two years—another encounter with segregation that might have been scripted by the Marx Brothers. (The best legal argument the city had advanced was that the zoo was only "semisegregated," with racially separate concession stands and toilets.) Judge Grooms considered himself "a good conservative, but not so conservative that I can't see what the law is." As of January 15, 1962, he decreed, the city parks of Birmingham would be open to Negroes.

Whether the Negroes would be able to get past the police was a different matter. Bull Connor announced that he would simply close the parks.

When Sid Smyer formed his "study group" on race relations in the wake of the Freedom Rides, he surely did not guess that he would be supporting what amounted to a referendum on segregation only five months later. He must have assumed that Birmingham's crises of "image" would continue to be brought on by "outsiders"—the *New York Times,* Howard K. Smith, Freedom Riders—requiring the business leaders' rear-guard attention. But the closing of the public parks was the unilateral act of the man they had tolerated in city hall for twenty years, covering over their doubts by calling his counselor, Jim Simpson, a Great Man. This turn of events forced the Chamber of Commerce to take a positive, controversial stand: To fight to keep the parks open was also a fight to integrate them.

The open-parks campaign represented the coming of age of the lonely bourgeois southern white liberal, struggling for a voice since the New Orleans novelist George Washington Cable coined the term "silent South" in 1885 to describe the region's enlightened minority of "quality" if not "quantity." This was the group that the Southern Conference for Human Welfare had hoped to tap, underestimating the ability of the opposition to red-bait liberalism into the fringes. The dilemma of the decent progressive urbanite in Alabama was that "liberalism" had been cornered by the likes of Bibb Graves and the Ku Klux Klan or Big Jim Folsom. In the absence of any common ground with these morally flexible "rednecks," the intelligent, cultured, "honest" citizens of Birmingham had almost been forced into the camp of Jim Simpson. And so it was that James Head, the businessman who was going to lead this new challenge to segregation, was not only one of the establishment's most remarkable renegades, but was also the client and dear friend of Simpson.

Head was the co-sponsor of Smyer's study group, and as president of the Chamber of Commerce's activist arm, the Committee of 100 (chartered to bring new industry into Birmingham), he was a power in the power structure. It had been with a rueful amusement that Head had listened to Smyer's by-golly promises to take charge of race relations, for he understood the long history (of Smyer's making) that would have to be reversed. Head was an unreconstructed New Dealer, his rather prosaic business life as owner of the city's largest stationery and office supply company belying his identity as what he facetiously called "a radical disturber of the peace." He was currently in trouble with his peers for inviting Ralph McGill, the liberal *Atlanta Constitution*'s editor who was synonymous with the rival town's progressivism, to speak at the Rotary Club the Wednesday after Freedom Rider Sunday. Meanwhile, the Rotarians were saying they were happy to do something about the race problem—as long as it entailed no concession of any sort to the Negroes.

Head lived in a good Mountain Brook neighborhood, but perhaps because a hard-luck childhood following his father's early death had given him a sympathy for the underdog, the over-the-mountain air had not gone to his head. "Plowing a rock garden" was how he described his liberal efforts. His favorite cause, public education, had been a pet peeve among rich southerners since the slave states passed laws against Negro literacy after Nat Turner, taught to read by his parents, led Virginia slaves to massacre white people in 1831. (The feeling was also that "when you educate a Negro, you spoil a good field hand.") Head's friend Vincent Townsend repeatedly rejected his suggestions for worthy journalistic campaigns, saying, "Head, you're too idealistic. You've got to be *realistic.*" His biggest achievement so far had been to get Ace Carter fired from his radio station after broadcasting the attack on the National Conference of Christians and Jews, whose

Alabama chapter Head had helped found in 1928 to counter the anti-Catholic prejudice against the presidential candidacy of Al Smith. ("You're the known Communists I've been talking about," Carter had told Head and his delegation of prominent citizens when they confronted him.)

Until 1961, Head "passed" among the Big Mules. He was personally attractive—robust, congenial, confident—and he golfed with Republicans (the Dixiecrats' newest designation) at the Birmingham Country Club. He had humored Townsend by joining his mission to CBS's Frank Stanton; Head had barely contained himself from cheering when Stanton asked, in reference to the city's Negroes, "Why don't you take the other half of the population and educate them so they won't be such a *drag* on you all?" But the dovetailing fiascos of the Freedom Rides and "Who Speaks for Birmingham?" made Head realize that, even as an image-maker, Townsend was about as effective as the city fathers of Dayton, Tennessee, who had encouraged a schoolmaster named John Scopes to get himself arrested for teaching Darwin back in the twenties, thinking the publicity would be a magnet for new business.

At any rate, Townsend seemed to have made his point with CBS. Howard K. Smith, who had continued to do his Sunday radio "analyses" after being removed as Washington bureau chief, had in October broadcast another barbed comment about Kennedy's leadership. In November, Smith was gone from the network. "Birmingham reaped a small amount of revenge when C.B.S. relieved that Communist sympathizer, Howard K. Smith, from his lucrative job," an Alabamian wrote Bull Connor. Jim Simpson decided to take advantage of CBS's vote of no confidence in Smith and muzzle the country's network of record as well as its newspaper of record. In early December, he would file libel suits against CBS seeking $1.5 million on behalf of Connor and the two other commissioners.

At this stage in his radical's progress, Jim Head was still trying to finesse the race situation by explaining to his friends, "I'm a businessman. I'm only going to talk about the economic wrongs of segregation." And so he decided to mount an assault against segregation based purely on the New South doctrine of business progressivism, which held that what was good for business was automatically good for the community. Atlanta was a case in point. Its mayor, William "Never do anything wrong that they can take a picture of" Hartsfield, was basically a rubber stamp for Coca-Cola chairman Robert Woodruff, commander of the largest personal fortune in all the South, and Woodruff had decided that Atlanta would integrate its schools and its lunch counters that autumn, explaining, "Coca-Cola cannot operate from a city that is reviled." "The City Too Busy to Hate" was such a hit that the national news media did not notice that the restrooms in city hall still had "White" and "Colored" signs.

But Birmingham was a coke, not Coke, town, and as Chuck Morgan was fond of saying, no one was going to wake up one day and say, "Gee, Marge, I don't like what U.S. Steel did yesterday; I think I'll boycott steel." Moreover, segregation had been crucial to the industrialists' profits. It would not be easy to enlist the city's top businessmen to speak up in favor of open, integrated parks. Because Head was too controversial to front the effort, he turned to the only Big Mule he knew who might be able to pull it off: a lawyer, a scholar, and a gentleman on top of his privileged position in the heavy-manufacturing hierarchy.

Monaghan

As ONE of the most brilliant lawyers in the city, Bernard Monaghan had in 1956 transformed the Birmingham Slag Company—a homely business that ground out road construction materials from the hard ebony by-product of steelmaking—into one of the nation's biggest producers of crushed aggregate. Now running Vulcan Materials, Monaghan was an anomalous industrialist in a number of ways. Although he felt the regional pressure to define himself as a conservative, he was troubled that the label was usually a euphemism for bigot. At Harvard Law, his mentor, Felix Frankfurter, had reassured him that there was no shame in being a conservative, and afterward at Oxford, Monaghan had disapproved of the socialist high jinks of his fellow southern Rhodes scholar, Howard K. Smith. Despite three Irish Catholic grandparents, Monaghan had been propelled into Mountain Brook Club society thanks to his to-the-manner-born aplomb, and his refusal to accept a job as Justice Hugo Black's first clerk hadn't hurt; Monaghan was certain that Black had been one of the robed Klansmen who marched around his parochial school.

In early November, after Connor announced he would close the parks, Monaghan and Head drafted a statement, titled "Some Facts to Face," that laid out the "business progressivism" case for keeping the parks open. The trick would be in getting Birmingham's power structure to sign what was essentially a declaration of the end of segregation. The most important Big Mule signature belonged to Art Wiebel, U.S. Steel's man in Birmingham.

Wiebel exercised stern veto power over the business community's civic agenda, flexing his muscles through his purchasing department. One of his lieutenants might inform, say, a salesman for TCI's ball bearings supplier that the Corporation was displeased with a position taken by his boss on some issue that would threaten Steel's tax rate.* Dutifully, TCI's suppliers, as well as banks holding its deposits, toed the line. But Monaghan's Vulcan Materials was in an unusual position. TCI was not its biggest customer. On the contrary, Vulcan bought Wiebel's slag, rendering its sales force immune from TCI's blackmail.

Monaghan took time out from his executive schedule to drive out to TCI's corporate headquarters in Fairfield—"Fort Wiebel." After skimming "Some Facts to Face," Wiebel said, "Barney, you didn't need to come all the way out here. You

---

* One of the progressives' perennial causes was the merger of the suburbs into the city of Birmingham. U.S. Steel and the other major iron and steel companies had eluded municipal taxes by building their plants outside the city proper, where they enjoyed absurdly nominal assessments. Ever since the last major annexation of 1910, when not even the steel mills had escaped the city limits (with the exception, thanks to God knows what blackmail, of U.S. Steel's furnaces in the heart of annexed Ensley), the Corporation had made sure merger was a dirty word in the district.

could have just read me the statement over the phone and signed my name to it."
But knowing that Wiebel would hardly be receptive to pitches for keeping the
city attractive to outside industry, Monaghan knew he needed to put him on the
spot in person. And he continued to take time away from the office to pay personal calls on the power structure so that each man could see, without having to
ask, that Wiebel had signed.

On November 12, 1961, "Some Facts to Face" was published in a *News* ad
over the signatures of the 189 most powerful men in Birmingham. It was doubtful
that any of them had set foot in a city park since joining the country club, but
presently every civic organization in town sent emissaries to the commission
chambers to read pro-parks "whereases" and "be it resolved's." It was an amazing
referendum on Our Way of Life.

The city commission's response to it was to close the parks, effective January 1, 1962.

Jim Head recognized the flaw in the moderates' blueprint for change, which
had inspired this, the second uprising of reformers in six months. In both the
Young Turks' campaign to elect Tom King mayor and the open-parks movement,
the progressives had concentrated on business concerns without addressing the
"Negro question." The defect in the businessmen's familiar pledge of "We're taking care of this thing ourselves" was the same as in segregation itself: white men
"taking care" of race relations.

Now it was the Big Mules' turn to realize, as the Populists had briefly understood seventy years earlier, that if there was to be progress, Negroes would have
to be included in the process. But how? Even Head's front man, the sophisticated
Barney Monaghan, could not bring himself to sit down across a table from a black
man. It seemed as if the only way to avoid charges of being soft on race was to
turn race relations over to someone who was not soft on race. Head's thoughts settled on the "most typical" southerner, "one hundred and ten percent segregationist." He was his business neighbor on First Avenue, a Big Mule legislator,
Dixiecrat organizer, integrated-baseball battler, chief lay Methodist segregationist, and now president of the Chamber of Commerce. He was also Head's
co-sponsor of the "biracial" study group that had not yet invited any actual Negroes to study with it.

On December 1, 1961, prodded by Head, Sid Smyer called a biracial meeting
to discuss the parks closing. Reassured by Smyer's sterling segregationist credentials, white men who had never been within a $20 cab ride of controversy sat down
at a table with black men: Lew Jeffers, president of Hayes Aircraft and former boss
of Art Hanes; the president of Royal Crown Cola; the insurance magnate Frank
Samford, proprietor of Birmingham's Statue of Liberty; William Pritchard, the
lawyer who had promoted segregated chicken farming on "Who Speaks for Birmingham?" TCI's Art Wiebel came in person rather than by proxy. The lineup—
forty-five in all, black and white—bore a remarkable resemblance to an "Interracial Committee" of prominent whites and Negroes that had operated for several
years in the early 1950s under the auspices of "charity" (the Red Cross and the

Community Chest). The committee—its boldest action had been a campaign to hire Negro police—had been hounded out of existence in the spring of 1956 (along with the NAACP) by the man who was now reconstituting it, Sid Smyer.

Smyer had invited Mayor Art Hanes to attend, on the strength of his campaign promise "to sit down and talk to any group." By now, even the politically last-to-know Mountain Brook crowd was aware of the invisible hand behind Hanes's mayoralty. Soon after his election, he had told a group of prominent businessmen who urged him to prevent unfortunate incidents such as the Trailways trouble: "Well, before I can promise you anything, I've got to check with Bull." At the swearing-in ceremony in November, during the part where they vowed to uphold the United States Constitution, Hanes, forty-four years old, and Connor, sixty-two, had put their left hands behind their backs and crossed their fingers, like fourth-graders neutralizing a fib.

Upon being asked to Smyer's biracial meeting, Hanes told the press: "Don't worry about the Negroes. I'm not going to meet with 'em. I'm not a summertime soldier, I don't give up when the enemy shows up." The country clubbers' onetime darling had become the sort of embarrassment that got Birmingham, again, into *Time* magazine, whose reporter showed up one rainy December night at an open meeting on the parks closing. "I don't think any of you want a nigger mayor or a nigger police chief," Hanes addressed his constituents. "But I tell you, that's what'll happen if we play dead on this park integration."

The Colored Guests

THE CHASM between blacks and whites in Birmingham had never seemed wider, even as the city's ruling white men were breaking their first racial taboo to sit down with Negroes, almost man to man. The controversy that was making integrationists of segregation's former custodians had barely registered in the black community. The imminent closing of the parks was "a minor problem," a black spokesman told the *Wall Street Journal,* compared to the whites-only lunch counters and the police department. "We will not miss what we have never had," ACMHR vice president Ed Gardner pointed out. When Fred Shuttlesworth and the Movement's security chief, the barber James Armstrong, had showed up at the all-white public golf course in the fall of 1959 to set up the constitutional test to integrate the parks, they had had to borrow golf clubs and were happy to have been arrested before revealing their ignorance of how to swing them.

Shuttlesworth's attitude toward the white country clubbers trying to save parks they wouldn't deign to use was condescension: "They just don't all of a sudden love us, but let's pretend that they do and maybe it will come to be." The *World* editor, Emory O. Jackson, actively resented them. In a foul humor, he reported to Sid Smyer's integrated meeting on December 21, in the study of the Episcopal bishop at the Church of the Advent downtown (which had been the Interracial Committee's old haven). There were thirty-eight men at this one, including the Reverends J. L. Ware and Herb Oliver, and, on the white side, *News* publisher Clarence Hanson, Birmingham-Southern College's liberal president Henry King Stanford, and Jim Head, who felt that the only thing that could be said for Smyer's previous meetings on the parks issue was that they took place at all, and under Chamber of Commerce auspices.

Before this one, Head had gone to the chambers of Judge Hobart Grooms, a friend of his and a fellow Big Baptist in a town dominated by Methodists. Grooms had agreed to grant a sixty-day stay, similar to the plan approved by the federal court in Memphis, during which the parks could remain open on a segregated basis. Smyer's opening speech at the December 21 meeting solicited the black men's opinion of the plan.

The "colored guests," as Herb Oliver viewed them, spoke noncommittally of the need to "go forward," until the Reverend C. E. Thomas, bishop of the C.M.E. Church (and a former Interracial Committee member), offered some sharp words about the newspapers' coverage of racial matters. After feebly defending the *News,* Clarence Hanson left the meeting early with another white "host"—to play golf. Emory Jackson took the opportunity to huff out, in protest of the meeting's being declared off the record—which did not prevent him from announcing to his *World* readers that the Big Boys, as he called his black establishment peers, were "selling them down the river."

Miles College's talented new president, Lucius Pitts, recognized the territorial Jackson's rants for what they were: a gauntlet thrown down at him to justify his presumption to speak for Birmingham's blacks. The parks meetings had been Pitts's first venture as a "Negro leader" willing to do business with white folks. He responded to Jackson's challenge by nudging the Movement into its next stage.

"Demonstrations"

UNTIL RECENTLY, the word "demonstrations" had an anachronistic Old Left ring. Demonstrations had been the pride of the Communists in the thirties and the last refuge of the fifties' anti-nuke pacifists, but they had not been mustered by the modern civil rights movement until the spring of 1960, when the militant youths of Nashville led a mass march downtown that froze white onlookers into a glacier of fear and awe. Confronted softly at the end of the demonstration by Diane Nash, the moderate mayor, Ben West, admitted that it was not "morally right for someone to sell 'em merchandise and refuse 'em service," and he had desegregated his city's lunch counters.

In the past couple of months, demonstrations had joined the canon of modern liberation art. In Albany, a pecan and cotton center in southwest Georgia ("the tenth fastest booming city in the U.S.A.") that the locals called Al-BIN-ee, a scrappy SNCC field secretary named Charles Sherrod, veteran of sit-ins and Freedom Rides, had ignited the broadest-based community campaign since the Montgomery bus boycott five years earlier. A hotheaded twenty-two-year-old Baptist minister who had grown up on a squalid street in Petersburg, Virginia, Sherrod had staged the first Albany sit-in at the Trailways white waiting room on

November 1, the day that the new Interstate Commerce Commission ruling desegregating bus and train facilities in response to Robert Kennedy's petition went into effect. Soon after, in spectacular defiance of legendary black factionalism (as well as of the "massah" tradition bred by the nearby hunting retreats—"plantations"—of industrialists such as Coca-Cola's Robert Woodruff), the entire local black community, from the NAACP, to the Federation of Women's Clubs, to the ministerial alliances, banded together as the Albany Movement. Its goal was to stamp out segregation—not simply seating on buses or at lunch counters but, for the first time, the entire system.

The Albany Movement had gone demonstration crazy since spontaneously enacting, in late November, the first major demonstration after Nashville. There had been so many arrests that the Movement for the first time had a real shot at the Gandhian goal of filling the jails. Albany became a new civil rights mecca. SNCC was sending pilgrims there, and on the weekend of December 16 came "de Lawd" himself. Martin Luther King was arrested along with Ralph Abernathy, who had just moved to Atlanta to take over a church there at King's urging. Abernathy bailed out the night of his arrest in order to be back at his church in time to introduce his Men's Day speaker, Fred Shuttlesworth, but King vowed to spend Christmas in jail.

Albany now had a world-class martyr, and the news coverage to match. The campaign seemed to be soaring into history, as the Movement's long-awaited follow-up to the Montgomery bus boycott. But after less than two days in jail, King changed his mind and bailed out. The Albany Movement went into a tailspin of sectarian recrimination, with SNCC furious at SCLC's Wyatt Walker for trying to take command of their fight, in his crisp field marshal fashion. The news media, which hadn't really had the vocabulary to cover a sustained grassroots protest, now played the story not as one of black against white, but of black against black: "Rivalries Beset Integration Campaign," read the *New York Times* headline. Albany was "one of the most stunning defeats" of King's career, according to the *New York Herald Tribune,* "a devastating loss of face."

Somehow the story always came back to King, but strategic miscues had also hampered the Albany campaign. The protesters had aimed their demands at city hall, essentially asking elected officials to commit political suicide by abolishing segregation. In Birmingham, where Bull Connor was jailing the Greyhound station manager for desegregating his cafe in compliance with the ICC ruling, the Movement was realizing that it was time to stop fighting city hall. The activists had decided to take advantage of their new "friendship" with the city fathers since the parks misfortune and apply pressure to white men who were motivated not by politics per se but (as their embarrassment over the Freedom Rides had proved) by the economic consequences of "bad" politics.*

---

* Several months earlier, both Fred Shuttlesworth and Emory O. Jackson had begun urging a boycott of the local department stores—something Jackson had tried back in 1934 when a store fired a black truck driver.

By December, the new Miles College contingent of the Movement—President Lucius Pitts as well as Frank Dukes and his classmates—was ready to move beyond politics and take on the real power, as Bob Zellner had discovered the previous month. He had arrived in Birmingham hoping that his grandfather, an unregenerate local Klan racist who had disowned Bob's "nigger-loving" father, wouldn't find out he was there. Zellner had become SNCC's first white field secretary not long after the Freedom Rides capped off his education at Huntingdon College. The person who had recruited him was Anne Braden, of the Southern Conference Educational Fund, which had close ties to the student movement. It was SCEF that paid Zellner his modest salary, to carry on the old Southern Conference mandate as the SNCC staff member designated to proselytize white students. So far, however, Zellner had been busy bonding with his black comrades. On the steps of the courthouse in McComb, Mississippi, where SNCC was conducting a voter registration campaign, he had recently been choked by white men, gouged in the eyes, and kicked in the face, and then, still clutching his Bible, hauled off to jail. That baptism had made him a SNCC legend by the time he showed up in Birmingham and headed for Miles College to see if he could be of assistance.

Though they received him politely, Frank Dukes and his classmates were eager to avoid any appearance of being "agitated by outsiders." Zellner respected their concerns and unofficially helped Dukes and his lieutenants draft a statement, "This We Believe," whose dignified wording hardly disguised its radical intent: "We do not intend to wait complacently for those rights which are legally and morally ours to be meted out to us one at a time." Forming an Anti-Injustice Committee, the students began conducting a quiet investigation of local department stores. For a "school project," Dukes got figures from the unsuspecting Chamber of Commerce. The stores, he learned, operated on a 12 to 15 percent profit margin. "Negro dollars" made up 25 percent of the gross, or $4 million in an average week. This meant that cutting black business by half could tip the balance into the red. They began discussing a boycott that would paralyze the city's retail trade.

By chance, Sid Smyer's historic biracial meetings had suddenly put the Miles College president, Lucius Pitts, in a position to get his students' message across. Pitts was a crafty man. During the parks "talks," he had been reasonable without being subservient. He was the type of black man who made whites—liberals like Head, conservatives like Smyer—feel comfortable. And Pitts had plans for their budding "friendship." He knew that intimations of a department store boycott alone would fall under the "empty threat" category of what J. L. Ware called "little nigger causes." For a boycott to succeed, there would also have to be demonstrations—a presence of Negroes to offset their boycotting absence—to trigger a white person's worst nightmare of rampaging black people. This would incite a secondary boycott by white customers wanting to stay away from potential violence.

Fred Shuttlesworth had never proposed demonstrations for his town because he knew he had neither the troops nor the support of the middle class. And in truth, Pitts was hardly counting on actual demonstrations; the white folks merely had to *think* that they were going to happen. He began "tipping off" his new white acquaintances that he was trying to maintain order but didn't know how long he was going to be able to keep the Shuttlesworth crowd off the streets—massive demonstrations, you know.

"Niggers at the Krystal"

NOW THAT the Klan's old sponsors were joining forces with their former common enemy to phase out segregation, the vigilantes turned desperate to guard their diminishing domain. As if to restore the authority of the DeBardelebens to the enterprise, Troy Ingram had recently returned to the Klan fold; and when he did he was welcomed into the highest Imperial councils. He was the new old face in the usual lineup of bored husbands at the United Klans' November meeting of the North Alabama Province. The Eastview rank and file had grown fidgety, basically having done nothing since the Freedom Rides. Exalted Cyclops Robert Thomas seemed to be losing control of the klavern. Rather than giving or withholding approval for the "missionary work," he would say he didn't want to hear about it one way or the other.

When Klansman Al Peek had left a recent Thursday Eastview meeting to go get a sack of burgers down the street at the Krystal Kitchen, he had gotten so upset at the sight of "niggers at the Krystal" that he had barely been able to spit out the password for the Night Hawk to let him back in. On the first Saturday in December, Eastview's all-stars, including Gene Reeves and Tommy Rowe, teamed up with some rookies to defend the klavern's unofficial mess hall. The Krystal was crowded when they arrived. One of Troy Ingram's new recruits, from the old DeBardeleben precincts, was so hepped up by all the "nigger" talk—brainwashed, he later said—that when a black customer stood beside him, he cocked his fist and knocked "hell out of him." Another novice, Buddy Galyean, considered "mentally deficient" by one of his ex-employers, hit him with brass knuckles, according to Rowe's report to the FBI, and knocked out his eye. As the veteran Klansmen piled on, two football players from Woodlawn High School and another white man, Rodney Cooper, came to the victim's aid. The senior Klansman in the group, Gene Reeves, who had been one of the select Klansmen on the Freedom Rides detail, wrestled the white defenders out onto the sidewalk. Tommy Rowe swung at anyone handy.

Policemen appeared in the parking lot and arrested a bystander who had been "acting like a bantam rooster," according to Ingram's recruit, "doing a lot of crowing but no fighting." The police department's continuing sympathy with the Klan was perhaps a function of sentimental reflex, now that the stakes of the collaboration had degenerated from the industrial economy of a great workshop town to a ten-cent hamburger.

Cities Are What Men Make Them

ON NEW YEAR'S DAY, 1962, the undefeated Crimson Tide beat Arkansas 10–3, giving Bear Bryant his first national championship. Over the weekend, the Bear's number one fan, Bull Connor, had the parks—1,500 acres, valued at $9 million—posted with "No Trespassing" signs and announced that he would sell off the people's property to private investors. After golfers sneaked onto the public links, the holes were plugged with cement.

Smyer's biracial meetings had bogged down, breaking no ground at all. Jim Head took the last-ditch measure of making an appointment to see Connor face-to-face. Then he and Barney Monaghan drafted a "Plea for Courage and Common Sense," quoting from the commissioners' campaign promises to expand the city's playgrounds. Approved by thirty-seven power structure men in January, the statement had 1,260 signatures within the week, including Marjorie Mc-Whorter's, twice.

The moment of truth had come. On Tuesday morning, January 9, five men representing Birmingham's most impressively decent citizenry met at breakfast to caucus about their imminent meeting with Bull Connor. Joining Head and Monaghan were Birmingham-Southern's president, Henry King Stanford; David Cady Wright, the minister at a small, fancy Episcopal congregation; and Mayer Newfield, lawyer and son of the city's late, most beloved rabbi. The Reverend Mr. Wright surprised, if not alarmed, his lay colleagues. "The Chamber of Commerce is always stressing business and the city's 'reputation,' but I think we ought to put it on a spiritual basis," he said. "I'd like to open the meeting on the basis of brotherly love."

At ten o'clock, the five men took their petition into the commission chambers on the third floor of city hall. The three elected leaders of Birmingham sat on a walnut-colored platform, Mayor Hanes in the middle. To his right was Public Works Commissioner James "Jabo" Waggoner, a rubber stamp for Connor, though he kept so strictly to his street sanitation duties that he had been nicknamed the Garbageman. Connor was on the left, squinting down at the delegation.

The Reverend Mr. Wright began, "Some of my parishioners are concerned—"

Connor cut him off, knowing that most of Wright's congregation was from Mountain Brook. "If they live outside of Birmingham, I don't give a damn what they think. I want names and addresses."

Wright began again, "A number of members of my congregation *who live in Birmingham* are concerned—" Connor again demanded names and addresses. On his third try, Wright said, "I want to put this on the basis of brotherhood. I want to look to God."

"But remember God's commandment to Moses to keep the race lines clear," Connor replied.

Even the seasoned Henry King Stanford, who had discreetly rolled his eyes over breakfast when Wright invoked brotherly love, had not expected such a reception. He had been sparring with Connor since refusing to bow to pressure from both his board of trustees and city hall to expel Tommy Reeves, the ministerial student who had stood up to the Methodist Layman's Union and consorted with the black student sit-ins. (Harrison Salisbury had tipped his hat to Stanford in the *New York Times.*) "Mr. Connor," he said, "it looks as if you won't let him talk."

Grateful for the bait, Connor turned on him: "Doctor Stanford, you gonna integrate Birmingham-Southern? Because if you are, I want to let everyone in Alabama know so they won't send their kids there."

Jim Head spoke up for the first time. "Look, Bull," he said, "Doctor Stanford is not under a court order, but you are about to be."

"You wastin' yo' time if you think I'm about to let niggers in the parks," Connor replied. "Now, Doctor Stanford, you gon' integrate Birmingham-Southern?"

Barney Monaghan, who under normal circumstances charmingly quoted *The Iliad* and discussed the fine points of French succession law, sat mute. He had been convinced that Connor could be reasoned with, that his vulgarity was political calculation. He had thought Birmingham was a City of Lawyers.

Connor scowled at the petition of 1,260 good names and said, accurately, "I bet half the people on this list don't even live in Birmingham."

Judging from their shocked faces, Head knew that his distinguished friends were really seeing Connor for the first time. Birmingham had auditioned its most chivalrous leaders, in the most impressive mobilization of moderates ever undertaken in a southern city, yet they might as well have been a group from Cleveland proposing a law that the firstborn of every white family marry a Negro. How had Bull Connor been their political leader for a generation?

The answer, of course, was there for Head and his friends to read on their way out of the commission chambers. Lettered in gold above the doorway was Birmingham's motto: "Cities are what men make them." The long adolescence of the power structure, its belief in omnipotence without responsibility, had come to an end in a single hour on January 9, 1962.

9.

THE FULL CAST

Cherry Bomb

NINETEEN SIXTY-TWO opened in Birmingham with a bang. Three churches were dynamited between 9 and 10 p.m. on January 16. It seemed like amateur hour all the way. Damage was minimal at all three, and as the newspapers reported rather indignantly, none had a civil rights identity other than the similarity of New Bethel Baptist's name to that of Fred Shuttlesworth's old church. "We know that the Negroes did it," Bull Connor was saying. The proof was that two cops who happened to be in their car seventy-five yards from one explosion spied a black teenager running from the scene.

Perhaps Connor really didn't know anymore who was bombing churches, the vigilante system over which he had presided having had its grand finale at the Trailways bus station on Mother's Day of the previous year. The suspects that Gary Thomas Rowe offered his new handler, Special Agent Byron McFall, two hours after the blasts were journeyman members of the action squad commanded by Earl Thompson, a suspected bomber of Shuttlesworth's church on Christmas 1956. Only one of the names mentioned by Rowe would prove memorable.

Bobby Frank Cherry was a thirty-two-year-old in-city trucker with an eighth-grade education, no upper front teeth, a "Bobby" tattoo on his arm, seven kids, and a wife he beat and cheated on. Cherry (and reputedly his brass knuckles) had participated in the attack on Fred Shuttlesworth at Phillips High School and, as a former member of Ace Carter's anti-Semitic Klan, had turned up on the Birmingham police's checklist of suspects for the 1958 attempted bombing of Temple Beth El. Indeed, the training in explosives he received in the Marine Corps had given him informed opinions about the relative merits of hand-lit fuses, electrical blasting caps, and chemical detonators—and the nickname Cherry Bomb. Rowe had told the FBI that Cherry was in on Eastview's Keystone Kops raid on the mixed-race baby the year before. If the bureau had found a reason to investigate Bobby Cherry for the January 16 bombings, it might not have had to open a Birmingham church bombing file twenty months later.

Instead, the FBI was investigating Martin Luther King. After seven months of vetting, J. Edgar Hoover had confirmed that the civil rights movement was a Communist plot. The smoking gun was discovered on January 4, 1962, when a reliable informant told the bureau that an important speech King had made the previous month before the AFL-CIO's annual convention, in Miami, had been written by Stanley Levison, King's confidant of four years, who had attracted the FBI's attention in the early 1950s as the Communist Party's financial whiz.

For Hoover the scoop couldn't have come at a better time. Since the Kennedys had taken over the White House, the attorney general's standard reply to inquiries about the enduring problem of Hoover had been, "Just wait." The President was finally about to dump him after more than four decades of service. But now Hoover recovered his footing. He told his boss, Robert Kennedy, that King was in the thrall of a secret member of the Communist Party. By extension, since both Kennedys were on lunch terms with King, so was the United States government. Justice officials pressed the bureau for supporting details so that they could warn King about Levison's connections. Given that FBI intelligence strongly suggested that Levison had had nothing to do with the Party since 1956, Hoover refused, explaining, "King is no good anyway."

A Welcome Martyr

EVEN FROM ACROSS the Mason-Dixon line in Cincinnati, Fred Shuttlesworth still seemed to be the Southern Christian Leadership Conference's most effective activist. Though he had been prevented from making the expected weekly trips to Birmingham by a hectic out-of-town speaking schedule and the Alabama Christian Movement for Human Rights's strapped treasury, his leadership style—the kamikaze leaps into the spotlight—was actually well suited to absenteeism. His limited virtues as an organization man were often exceeded by his value as an icon, and now he offered SCLC some symbolic redemption from its embarrassment in Albany, Georgia. He was about to become the jailhouse martyr King had fallen short of being over Christmas.

On January 8, the day Hoover informed Robert Kennedy that King was under the influence of a Communist, the Supreme Court ended a three-year appeal and let stand Shuttlesworth's conviction in the bus protest of October 1958—the second integrated ride, in which he had not participated. The Court ruled on a technicality (his lawyers missed the deadline for the state court appeal), and Shuttlesworth went before the Birmingham mass meeting that night ridiculing Arthur Shores as a "Calhoun" for exposing him and his co-defendant, the Reverend J. S. Phifer, to ninety- and sixty-day jail terms, respectively. Legal recourse had become a joke in Alabama. A week later, Judge Hobart Grooms handed down sentences of probation to five men who had confessed to their part in firebombing the freedom bus in Anniston, in his own way reflecting the local feeling that as long as no one was badly hurt, bombs were to be regarded as big firecrackers—misdemeanors. Those who had destroyed a bus would not serve a day in jail, while Shuttlesworth stood to be locked up for three months even though he had not even sat on the buses that Judge Grooms himself had finally desegregated.

On January 25, Bull Connor threw Shuttlesworth and Phifer in jail. Shuttlesworth was so blasé that he liked to complain that he had yet to have the pleasure of staying in the new addition to the Southside jail. But his arrest galvanized the black masses, who overflowed the mass meetings. SCLC was overjoyed to have a bona fide political prisoner to offset King's premature bailout in Albany. The propaganda gears engaged. King wired Robert Kennedy that "hundreds of segregationists, in and out of jail would like nothing better than to do bodily harm to Reverend Shuttlesworth." Wyatt Walker hastened to Birmingham and fired off a letter to "friends of freedom" ("HE IS IN JAIL NOW!"), encouraging "public scrutiny so that no 'accident' befalls Fred in his jail." The extended palm came none too subtly after the appeals, presumably to raise money for SCLC's operating costs rather than Shuttlesworth's legal fees.

Shuttlesworth made the most of a jail stay sweetened by the black market sugar that regular inmates cadged for his coffee. On potato-peeling duty, he serenaded the staff with Movement songs. He sent out a steady stream of press releases, taped under the T-shirt of a jail janitor. Mayor Art Hanes went on TV to denounce Shuttlesworth's letter requesting the end of segregation at city hall. "Ordinarily I don't deal with jail birds," he said, sneering, but in this case he was sending Shuttlesworth a response—"to let you know that action is being taken immediately." And then he threw Shuttlesworth's correspondence into the wastebasket.

Though Fred Shuttlesworth did not cut quite the saintly figure that Rosa Parks had, there was at least one Movement veteran, the Reverend C. Herbert Oliver, who saw his jailing, like Parks's in 1955, as the kind of constructive affront that might spark the first full-community protest in Alabama since the Montgomery bus boycott. Lucius Pitts, the president of Miles College, was in a position to marshal that outrage behind the department store boycott his students were planning, and he intended to use the opportunity to further his own, personal ambitions as well.

Consciousness-Raising

PITTS HAD BEEN inviting Oliver, who was teaching philosophy and history at Miles, to his office in the evening. Sometimes till one in the morning, he picked Oliver's brain about who was who in the Movement, taking advantage of Oliver's unique access to the Shuttlesworth group, the Ware group, and the black and white liberals who sat with him on the Alabama Council on Human Relations. It was only after duly laying out the various rivalries that a chagrinned Oliver realized Pitts was "getting his bearing so that he could make his move" on Shuttlesworth's franchise. Pitts was putting together a brief on the disunity of the black leaders and drumming up a consensus that the absent Shuttlesworth was losing the confidence of Birmingham's Negroes.

What Pitts undeniably had that no one in the ACMHR did was the ear of the white power structure, and a week or so after Shuttlesworth's jailing he had begun to manipulate his white "friends." He phoned a business leader—the smart money would say it was Jim Head—and said he didn't know how much longer he was going to be able to hold the radicals off from taking to the streets. The businessman agreed to a meeting. Pitts promised to have a "demonstration" scheduled for the next Saturday postponed, provided that the whites could offer something in return.

The biracial meetings Head had maneuvered Sid Smyer into holding during the parks crisis made Head realize that the "powerlessness" of the power structure was really a cocoon of complacency. It wasn't that the Big Mules couldn't act; they simply didn't have to. Even if the white men at those meetings were the heart and soul of segregation, they weren't in an immediate position to remove its ugliest manifestation, the "White Only" and "Colored" signs. But there was a species of private businessmen who were: the owners of department stores and lunch counters, the men Pitts's students happened to be preparing to hit with a boycott. It was those segregationists that Head had to deliver to Lucius Pitts in order to forestall future "demonstrations."

For the first meeting of the New Year, Head rounded up a couple of store owners to appear at Episcopal bishop C.C.J. Carpenter's study at the Church of the Advent. Since this affair did not have the blessing of the Chamber of Commerce, the men came in secret, and Carpenter (who had blasted the 1960 sit-ins and deplored *Brown* in "Who Speaks for Birmingham?") "preferred not to know anything about it," as Head gathered. Pitts, his student body president Frank Dukes, and a few campus activists arrived in a low-key mood, hoping to raise consciousnesses more than alarms. Dukes spoke of watching a white buddy from the Korean War recoil from him on the street back home, even when no one else was around. "I said to myself, What in the world is going on?" The department store owners listened, gravely shook their heads, and wondered what any of this had to do with them.

The Big Boys

IN ORDER TO GET the white folks to take him seriously, Lucius Pitts would have to recruit one last man to his team. He was A. G. Gaston, the biggest of what Fred Shuttlesworth called the Big Boys and the most famous Negro in Birmingham. White folks pointed to this short, bespectacled roly-poly man who made no attempt to talk white, this punctual, dependable grandson of slaves, and said, Look what any Negro could do if only he worked hard enough. "That's the best nigger in town," Bull Connor said when the two passed on the street. While on business in New York, Gaston occasionally ran into U.S. Steel's Art Wiebel, who would slap him on the back and say, "Let's have lunch," and they did dine together a few times at the Waldorf. Though never extended back home, the invitation was heady recognition for a man whose first job had been as a common laborer for

Tennessee Coal and Iron in the 1920s. He had gotten his entrepreneurial start lending money to spendthrift black co-workers at twenty-five cents on the dollar every two weeks—an annual interest rate of 650 percent.

The Fourth Avenue Negro business district now virtually belonged to A. G. Gaston. In addition to the Booker T. Washington Insurance Company—"air conditioned," the stationery boasted—he had built a funeral home, a savings and loan bank ("to encourage thrift and confidence among our people"), a realty firm, and, in 1954, the boxy-modern brick Gaston Motel, at last giving Negro visitors a "nice place to stay" in Birmingham. Gaston's own utter faith in the Horatio Alger formula had brought him, at the age of sixty-six in 1962, to the not so unusual circumstance of trusting—he might allow, "loving"—the white man. As a destitute sharecropper's son in the Black Belt, he had seen a Negro being lynched on the sidewalk and assumed the killers must have had good cause simply because they were white.

Gaston had never put himself out for the cause of civil rights (though his bank had been happy to deposit the Montgomery Improvement Association's money during the flush days of the bus boycott). Which perhaps explained why Mayor Art Hanes had sought him out during the parks controversy to strike a compromise that would have spared the swimming pools from Judge Grooms's order, completing a circle that began when the Southern Negro Youth Congress persuaded the city to provide its first "Negro pool" in the 1940s. But Gaston had stood up to Hanes, saying, "We will never accept the status quo." And on February 12, he took an even more affirmative step and accompanied Pitts—as well as the other Big Boys the Miles president had been cultivating, J. L. Ware and Shuttlesworth's own treasurer, Bill Shortridge—to meet with the white store owners.

As a businessman, Gaston soon realized that, for all Pitts's skill at coalition-building, conferences like these accomplished nothing. His white friend Jim Head agreed. Most of the downtown retailers who showed up were Jewish and considered themselves as marginal to the power structure as Pitts himself. Head's thoughts turned once again to the most invulnerable man in the community, immune from the charge of "nigger lover." He said to Gaston, "Let's go see Sid Smyer."

The Continuing Education of Smyer

HEAD AND GASTON entered the offices of the Birmingham Realty Company through the back alley. Smyer, who had been getting middle-of-the-night phone calls since hosting the biracial sessions on the parks closing, received them more graciously than Head had feared—Head was running against Smyer's son for a spot on the state Democratic executive committee. Head began with platitudes about "our beloved city" but quickly moved to the "Colored" water fountains at the county courthouse. "We're not talking about hotels, now," Head said, pointing out that the courthouse was where Negroes carried out the ordinary functions of citizenship. But Smyer waved him to the next topic: the Frank Nelson Building downtown, owned by Smyer's realty company. The many blacks who came into the building for debtor's court had to climb as many as seven flights if the freight elevator happened to be hauling freight. "You mean those niggers can't even get an elevator?" Smyer asked, finally interested.

Head then repeated the story that a female Daniel Payne College student had recently told in Bishop Carpenter's study of her interrogation by the voting registrar as to the number of illegitimate children she had. Other young black female applicants were asked if they had V.D. Smyer said nothing, but Head noticed that his face had turned red. "We're happy you heard us out," Head said as he and Gaston picked up their hats. Smyer grabbed his own hat and walked out the alley door with them, saying, "By God, I'll do something about it."

First, Smyer went to the courthouse and began the negotiations that would get the "Colored" and "White Only" signs removed from the water fountains. Then he desegregated the elevators at the Frank Nelson Building. Most of the other office buildings in town followed suit. (The First National Bank had done so already, after Gaston threatened to close his account there.) Smyer worked the back channels to have a relatively tolerant former U.S. attorney appointed to succeed the rudest of the voting registrars, who had recently died. Finally, Smyer appeared at Bishop Carpenter's study for a secret session with Lucius Pitts and his crew.

Although Frank Dukes had been impressed at how quickly he and his fellow students had graduated from "niggers" to "boys," the "concessions" Smyer had arranged were not all they had in mind. They also wanted desegregated restrooms and lunch counters and the hiring of blacks in nonjanitorial positions—demands directed at the department stores. The liberal owner of Parisian, Emil Hess, had seemed unfailingly agreeable to the demands, but he had stopped coming to the meetings, and the Miles students suspected that he had been banned by his peers, who resented the fact that his store did not have a lunch counter to desegregate.

Junta

WITH SHUTTLESWORTH remaining in jail, Lucius Pitts's junta consolidated more power in the Movement. A. G. Gaston made his first appearance before the masses at the Movement meeting on Lincoln's Birthday, February 12. He did a fairly politic job, praising the "leaders" of the ACMHR, but he couldn't resist putting in a word for the "good white people in Birmingham." Privately, he had been criticizing Shuttlesworth for commanding the loyalty of no more than half the local blacks, unaware that such a large percentage would have been an inconceivable following for such a revolutionary.

The Reverend J. L. Ware, Pitts's point man in the ministerial bloc, took the podium to introduce the night's guest speaker, Martin Luther King. Even though Pitts considered him "naive" and "under the influence of his staff," King was sharp enough to have picked up on Pitts's power plays. He opened with a Christly allusion to Shuttlesworth, "who is presently in jail for all of us." After complimenting the "second-line leadership"—"Dr. Gaston" and "Dr. Pitts"—he turned cautionary: "Too many Negroes distrust other Negroes. The same with our Negro leaders." King then described "a wonderful meal" he had had recently with President and Mrs. Kennedy, making it clear that he had himself transcended the intramural jousting.

During his tour of the White House, King had spied the Emancipation Proclamation on the mantle in the Lincoln Room. He told the President that he would like to see him sign the Second Emancipation Proclamation in the same room. Birmingham would become the impetus for such a proclamation. But for now only Herb Oliver could see a destiny larger than SCLC's (or Lucius Pitts's) fortunes in the community spirit—up to three mass meetings' worth each week—aroused by Shuttlesworth's jailing.

Oliver urged the ACMHR first vice president, Ed Gardner, to seize the momentum and make real the boycott of downtown department stores. But the sweet-natured, unambitious Gardner balked. His role was to protect Shuttlesworth's authority, and he compared his position as vice president to the "vise" that you "put things in to hold it together until the real thing comes along." Rather than trying to take advantage of Shuttlesworth's martyrdom, he exulted that "Birmingham is a better 'ham" on February 26, when the Supreme Court ordered Judge Hobart Grooms to release Shuttlesworth on bail if the Alabama state courts had not done so within five days. And so did Gardner cede the Movement leadership to Shuttlesworth's detractors.

Lucius Pitts had scheduled a putsch for March 2. Shuttlesworth was released that day, after thirty-six days in jail, and flew to Cincinnati. Oblivious of the council of Big Boys taking place without him, he was bogged down in tomorrow's news: On February 19, the Supreme Court had turned away defense efforts to move the *Sullivan* suit to federal court, thus abandoning the four Alabama defendants' personal assets to the state. Shuttlesworth ignored Herb Oliver's warnings that Pitts was after his job.*

Boycott

PITTS WAS GOING TO launch the department store boycott himself. On March 6, his student body president, Frank Dukes, sent polite letters to the downtown retailers noting that the coming Easter season was not only "a period of goodwill" but one in which Negroes could be expected to spend more than the weekly average of $4 million. He asked the store owners to join the black students in "improving the human relations in our community" by hiring Negroes in noncustodial positions and desegregating the restrooms, water fountains, and lunch counters. Emil Hess replaced the dual drinking fountains at Parisian with a single

---

* Oliver would be dismissed from his teaching job at Miles at the end of the term, with no explanation from Pitts, who never spoke to him again.

fountain and a paper cup dispenser, and urged his fellow merchants to do the same. Hess asked Jim Head to bring some of his gentile Rotary friends into the negotiations, but Head knew that was hopeless.

Dukes's deadline of March 14 came and went. Pitts finally realized that a boycott could not succeed without an enthusiastic ACMHR. He arranged a hearing with Shuttlesworth. Shuttlesworth looked upon Pitts with respectful ambivalence, as one of the bourgeoisie who "would sandwich themselves between the white people and the poor blacks." Pitts mentioned his talks with the white men and said, "Fred, I told 'em if they didn't take down those signs, I was going to join the picket line myself." Shuttlesworth diplomatically told him he didn't see any reason he should jeopardize Miles's standing—just leave the theatrics to his students and professionals like himself.

On Saturday night, Frank Dukes and the core members of the Miles College Anti-Injustice Committee loaded church pulpits and nightclubs throughout the city with handbills announcing the department store boycott, or "selective buying" campaign, in deference to an anti-boycott statute that turned out to be no longer on the books. Within a few days, most black people were familiar with the committee's slogans—"Use a Dime's Worth of Common Sense" and "Wear Your Old Clothes for Freedom." Those who didn't heed them were intercepted on the sidewalks by "educating committees" and asked to return their purchases. One shopper, seeing her $15 Easter bonnet stomped on the pavement, retaliated with her umbrella.

Bull Connor overconfidently threatened to "sic the dogs" on any blacks who came downtown, assuming, like most white people, that "they" wouldn't be able to forgo their fancy Easter church clothes. But a few weeks into the boycott, the six-block shopping district was magnolia white, to the extent that the white shoppers hadn't also been scared off by the "trouble." Some departments, such as children's clothes, virtually shut down, although the rich folks were suspected of receiving their orders by mail. Herb Oliver threw himself into the campaign despite his disappointment that the ACMHR had let Pitts take credit.

Into the Spotlight

"It's on and it's hurting," a merchant admitted anonymously. When Fred Shuttlesworth returned to Birmingham toward the end of March, he found himself the beneficiary of the most unified effort of blacks in the city's history. "Our Big Boys are behind us," he said, amazed, and instead of acknowledging the intrigue among the disciples, he turned the other cheek. "I'm glad to see Dr. Pitts has come to town to our college," he said. Herb Oliver cringed, and ACMHR vice president J. S. Phifer reminded the mass meeting that "Shuttlesworth is God himself." The president, as he was billed more and more, was so primed for the rapture of leadership that he "went into a raging fit, hollering," according to the detectives' description, as the crowd "went wild, like a bunch of cannibals." But Shuttlesworth seemed equally at home with the higher-toned adulation bestowed on him three days later at a $10-a-plate testimonial dinner at the Cincinnati Hilton, where Martin Luther King paid tribute to what he hoped would be Shuttlesworth's fundraising appeal. "It makes the Tutwiler Hotel look like a hut in the cotton patch," said the ACMHR's Ed Gardner, who drank more coffee than he ever had in his life, just so the white waiters would keep filling his cup.

Bull Connor took Shuttlesworth's celebrity personally. When Gardner boasted at a mass meeting that the president lived in a fine three-story house in Cincinnati, a detective placated Connor with surveillance photographs of a two-story frame dwelling with siding. On March 28, shots were fired into the Movement treasurer Bill Shortridge's house. An anonymous white caller told him that Connor had induced a Greek barbecue victualer to put up $2,000 for a black police pimp to assassinate Shortridge, who (with a white grandfather and Howard business degree) the commissioner felt was the brains behind the ACMHR.

Finally the reprisals brought Birmingham pitiless, blatant publicity. At the April 3 meeting of the city commission, Connor announced, "I am reliably informed that the Shuttlesworth crowd met, and there was a lot of bragging about the boycott of our downtown stores. . . . A boycott can work both ways. I don't intend to sit here and take it with a smile." He proposed that the City of Birmingham cut off its $45,000 contribution to a $100,000 county-run program that distributed government-surplus food to 20,000 needy, predominantly black families. When Mayor Art Hanes proposed that they go slow, Connor slammed his fist on the desk. Hanes recovered, saying, "If the Negroes are going to heed the irresponsible and militant advice of the NAACP and CORE leaders, then I say let these leaders feed them."

The next day, Connor had Shuttlesworth arrested on a downtown street, along with Phifer, and jailed for "obstructing the sidewalk." Sentenced to 180 days for standing on a public street, the two bailed out immediately, their martyrdom no longer necessary to inspire the masses. The *News* lifted its traditional news blackout on Negro protest the following day, urging Birmingham to "face facts."

Deciding to take advantage of Art Hanes's halfheartedness, Lucius Pitts sent him a flattering letter requesting a permit for a "Mile of Dimes Parade" on Sunday to raise money for the school library, one of the liabilities that had cost the college its accreditation in 1958. In the mayor's office the next afternoon, the two reached a gentleman's agreement that the parade could go on. At eleven that night, Connor's executive secretary called Pitts to overrule his mayor.

The next afternoon, Pitts and Frank Dukes went on the premier black radio station, WENN, and delivered sly tearjerkers. Dukes trotted out his Korean War stories—"and I come back to Birmingham and the freedom for which I fought is denied because I am black." Pitts's voice quavered as he wondered aloud, "What meaning is there in the city's slogan: 'It's Nice to Have You in Birmingham'?" Any whites who happened to be listening could not have known that the "It's Nice to Have You in Birmingham" signs, which a new merchants' association had put up all over town, were a cynical inside joke among black people.

Publicity over the canceled Mile of Dimes Parade netted Miles enough donated books from around the country to rival the Library of Congress. The *Birmingham News* published a collage of news clips from *Time, Newsweek, Business Week,* and the major northern dailies describing Connor's cruelty to starving black families. Care packages of food deluged Birmingham, not only from the NAACP but from the American Zionist Council and the AFL-CIO. At a closed meeting of the merchants' trade organization in mid-April, the consensus was that the boycott "would have a drastic and far-reaching economic effect on the metropolitan area" if it went on much longer.

Oedipus in Alabama

BIRMINGHAM SEEMED POISED, as a Movement preacher might put it, between sweet progress and bleak retrogress. The Negro community was mounting its first united campaign at the same time the white power structure's racial consensus was coming apart. Sid Smyer's Tokyo epiphany had provided a glimpse into the future: Segregation could not last. Yet Connor seemed willing to go further than ever to enforce an unstable status quo. The state of Alabama was at a similar crossroads, as the spring's gubernatorial race to succeed John Patterson was turning into a battle for what remained of the soul of populism.*

Big Jim Folsom had entered the contest as the frontrunner, simply as a force of nature. Ironically, now that his racial tolerance no longer seemed scandalous to many Birmingham businessmen, he was unlikely to be tossing any bouquets to Negroes. That was because his main challenger was George Wallace, who was ready and willing not only to betray his liberal principles but also to slay his political godfather.

At rallies around the state, the gaunt farmers who had been Folsom's reclamation projects now came out to hear Wallace recycle the "pool-mixin' " horror that Strom Thurmond had warned about in his 1948 Dixiecrat acceptance speech and attack a Supreme Court that "did not have the brains to try a chicken thief." No matter what the pioneering race-baiters like Jim Simpson and Frank Dixon had said, they sounded like Louis XIV. But Wallace had transformed racial attack into the peasants' fight, as urgent as next season's corn crop. And when these saturnine men in denim occasionally removed their hands from their overall bibs to clap, Wallace aides flashed one another simian grins—Folsom was a goner. The phrase that seemed to be getting the most applause was Wallace's pledge to "Stand in the Schoolhouse Door," to personally block any court order to desegregate the schools.

To make good on his vow four years earlier never to be "outniggered" again, Wallace embraced his old nemesis's power base, the Ku Klux Klan. As John Pat-

---

* Bull Connor was making his quadrennial bid for governor, one of the few moneymaking scams in which "Honest Bull" indulged. (It was unclear what became of the campaign funds he raised.) He was setting the floor in the eight-man racial sweepstakes, slamming King and Shuttlesworth ("If they're preachers, then I'm a watchmaker") and pledging to meet the civil rights crisis with "100 German police dogs."

terson freely acknowledged, the boys couldn't be topped when it came to grunt-work. Not only would they nail their candidate's posters to telephone poles, but they would also use the other side of the hammer to remove opponents' signs. The Wallace campaign breathed oxygen into an old Klan hand. Robert Chambliss, who had not been among the protagonists of Gary Thomas Rowe's FBI reports, now reemerged in an uncharacteristic political role, organizing Klansmen to put up Wallace signs. Chambliss told his buddies that the candidate had promised them an all-expenses-paid fishing trip to the Gulf if he was elected. Chambliss furnished his own car, a jackhammer, and a saw. Eastview supplied the campaign an old bread truck rigged with radio equipment and a stolen license plate to conceal the vehicle's ownership. In it the Klansmen hauled Wallace literature, including a huge pile of *Thunderbolts* that the National States Rights Party's Edward Fields had delivered to an Eastview meeting. Klan gossip had it that Wallace had forwarded $7,500 to Imperial Wizard Bobby Shelton to cover the boys' expenses.

Sing Along with Big Jim

WHILE EASTVIEW SESSIONS were alive with plans for a Wallace administration, Movement mass meetings sometimes seemed like rallies for Folsom, who had sent a campaign letter to the ACMHR, signed "Jamelle and Big Jim." Ed Gardner told the audience, "You can all come if Big Jim is elected," quoting Folsom's old "Y'all Come" theme song. (On the other hand, an ad of one of his opponents read, "He said Y'all come, but who came? Adam Clayton Powell.") It was not a good sign, however, that Folsom had allowed Wallace to establish the racial debate. Though Folsom had telephoned Attorney General Robert Kennedy the previous year to praise him for using marshals to protect the Freedom Riders, he was now saying that if he had been governor he would have jailed them for their own protection. "I would have put fifty of the biggest, blackest country bucks I could find in the jail cells with them and the next morning those integrators would have come out saying 'Lord! Give us segregation!' " Folsom was even sanitizing his libertine image. Instead of succumbing to "wine, women, and song to which I plead guilty," he was preaching "Metrecal, one gal, and sing along with Big Jim." (Of the vice he and Wallace shared, Folsom explained, "George don't drink, but he always was bad to fuck.")

Confident of a runoff berth, Folsom bought TV time on the night before the May 1 primary for a statewide address that had been taped in advance. At the last minute, the film disappeared. Folsom decided to go on the air live with his family, against the vigorous objections of his aides: Big Jim had been into the juice. Introducing his eight children before the cameras, he faltered: "Now which one are you?" And true to his "Sing along with Big Jim" billing, he dismissed his opponents as "Me, too!" candidates by crooning a singsong "Me, too, me, too, meee, tooo!" The next day at the polls, Wallace workers hollered greetings: "Did you see Governor Folsom drunk last night?"

As the late returns flickered across his television set at home in Cullman, Folsom wept. It was a tribute to his legend that he failed to make the runoff by only 1,100 votes. He walked out into the fragrant spring night, peeled the campaign stickers off his car, and set out for Arkansas, in search of some private conclusion to his errand in the political wilderness.

He Listens!

THE MOUNTAIN BROOK CROWD did not understand the significance of the election returns. They had been jesting that they were supporting the Crimson Tide's national-championship football coach, Bear Bryant, but unfortunately the governor's job was "beneath him." The "nigger-baiting" of the first primary's leading vote getter, George Wallace, had struck them as no better or worse than Big Jim's tomfoolery. Both were damned populists, rednecks. Wallace, in turn, was so sensitive to the scorn of Mountain Brook that he sometimes rode around the suburb looking for just one of his campaign posters. The lone member of the power structure who had actively supported Wallace probably had too much class insecurity of his own to advertise his candidate on his lawn. But Jim Simpson had been working hard for his old senate page.

The old order was dying. Just as the post-bellum southern whites had clung to segregation as the phantom trace of slavery, so now did the polar relics of a moribund political/economic order, George Wallace and Jim Simpson, embrace around the emotional essence of segregation, racism. The consolation for Simpson's corporate constituents was that the balm Wallace was offering Alabama's poor was race hate rather than the old panacea of "redistribution of the wealth." If Simpson's relationship with Bull Connor had been excused at the Mountain Brook Club as a marriage of pure convenience, his alliance with Wallace was a love match, consummated in a passion that spurned even the economic indicators pointing to segregation's end.

Jim Head, the liberal businessman still licking his wounds over the open-parks campaign, was horrified by the rumor that his onetime political hero, Simpson, was the largest single contributor to Wallace's campaign. Head had encouraged Simpson to take on Lister Hill in 1944, raised a lot of money for him, and had been shocked at his white supremacist platform, for Head, like so many of Simpson's social associates, had not understood that the candidate was part of a coordinated anti-democratic movement. Simpson had reassured friends like Head that he had lost control of his campaign, but after the election, as the two men were driving to Montgomery together, Head had finally figured it out. Simpson had traveled to Italy presumably before the war, and was reminded of that trip as he looked out the car window, at the Negro field hands bent over rows of cotton. He said to Head, "Mussolini was on the right track."

"He was a dictator," Head pointed out.

"Ah, that's just a term," Simpson said. "He really got things done over there. You know, there are some people who want to educate *everybody*. But if you do that, who in the hell are going to be your bootblacks?" He looked out the car window. "Who in the hell is going to pick the cotton?"

Their once warm friendship was now on what Head called a "He put up with me and I felt sorry for him" basis. And now Simpson's association with George Wallace woke up the rest of the Great Man's moderate peers, liberating them to take a positive stand on state matters that they had previously left to the "rednecks." Head and his fellow moderate, Barney Monaghan, had been charmed out of their post–parks disaster funk by Wallace's surprise opponent for the gubernatorial runoff.

Ryan deGraffenried was a handsome thirty-six-year-old scion of Old Tuscaloosa who had been endorsed by the *Birmingham News* for the primary ("He *listens!*"). He had chalked up a progressive (pro-labor) record in the legislature, and on the race issue he was courageously ambiguous. "In the field of segregation, we have got to take the offensive," he said, leaving it to his listeners to figure out what that meant. Monaghan decided to see if he could rally some industrial money behind him and arranged for an array of Big Mules—including Frank Samford, the Statue of Liberty insurance magnate, and Art Wiebel, the Corporation's man—to hear deGraffenried's pitch. DeGraffenried answered their questions with candor, even the ones about school desegregation (inevitable) and taxes (yes, he would raise the minuscule corporate income tax of 3 percent to equal the personal rate of 5 percent).

All the industrialists opened their checkbooks, except U.S. Steel. Wiebel had gotten assurances from Wallace that the corporate tax rate would not increase. In the chaos of Alabama politics, Big Business's top citizen stuck with the candidate once labeled pink.

Toward the end of May, just before the runoff election, Wallace rode into Birmingham and gazed triumphantly at the tall buildings, basking in the knowledge that, thanks to his poll numbers, their occupants were ready to jump out of them. It could be taken as a sign of U.S. Steel's growing political irrelevance that Wallace did not carry Birmingham in an election that delivered to him the most votes ever cast for a gubernatorial winner. Wiebel, meanwhile, must have forgotten that damned populists did not abide by the Big Mules' standards of "honesty." One of Governor Wallace's first acts would be to propose raising the corporate tax rate.

The Demise of the Moderates

THE NEW WHITE FRIENDS of the civil rights movement were now learning the lesson that the Montgomery Negroes had been enduring since they boycotted the city buses. Uprisings often ended up reaping their participants a backlash worse than the conditions they started out with. Now, so soon after rallying to keep the parks open, Birmingham's white moderates toppled one by one. Birmingham-Southern's long-suffering guardian of academic freedom, Henry King Stanford, accepted the presidency of the University of Miami, his powerlessness having

been recently flaunted when a radio station on campus accused the Alabama
Council on Human Relations of being a Communist front. The remaining council activists saw their jobs once again in jeopardy, and the turnout was light for a
council panel that spring moderated by a young psychiatrist named Robert Coles,
who was in the South studying the effects of segregation on children. When sixty
citizens met at the medical center liberals' Unitarian church in April to discuss
the impending crisis over school desegregation, they were identified in a front-
page *News* "exposé."

Jim Head, too, was becoming vulnerable. For nearly a year, he had been secretly assembling a conclave of businessmen to function as a shadow city government, like the Coca-Cola chairman's cabal in Atlanta, although Head's project
was called the Dallas Plan in deference to the local Atlanta complex. For the annual May black-tie dinner of the Chamber of Commerce's industry-seeking
Committee of 100, of which he was president, Head had lined up Kennedy's secretary of commerce, Luther Hodges, to speak about the high priority he had
given to public education as governor of North Carolina. Head had assumed that
Hodges's anti-labor record as a textile magnate would make him acceptable to his
colleagues, but the first sign that the dinner might hit a snag came when Clarence
Hanson, publisher of the *Birmingham News*, picked Hodges up at the airport in the
company limousine and scolded him for buckling his seat belt: "Don't you trust
my driving? We're only going five miles down the road to the Tutwiler."

The audience that night for Hodges's understated reprimand against philis-
tinism was equally divided between men in their tuxedos and place settings with
unfolded napkins. Many committee members had paid for their dinners, but had
decided to boycott Head and a United States Cabinet member. Collaborating in
the destruction of a nearly century-old order of institutionalized racism was not
coming easily to the city fathers. Head's industrial accounts would soon drop him
"like an anchor of a ship." That same month, when Head unveiled the Dallas Plan
before the full Chamber of Commerce—it called for the hiring of Negro policemen and the desegregation of restaurants—Bull Connor walked out, fussing at no
one in particular.

Backsliding

THE DEPARTMENT STORE BOYCOTT, too, was eliciting the reaction of previous "successful" protests: white intransigence and retaliation. The merchants had
hung tough, refusing to negotiate. The manager of Newberry's fired his black employees. Woolworth's followed suit. In the face of shopper recidivism, Shuttlesworth warned the backsliders that the Movement, nonviolent though it was,
could not be responsible for what might happen to folks who didn't stay away
from downtown.

In June, Bull Connor began arresting the boycott picketers—Frank Dukes
was picked up three times in a single week—creating a brief revival of protest

spirit around the so-called Walking Seven. But with no results to show, the black classes went back to buying what Dukes bitterly described as "thirty-five-dollar segregated shoes." The masses again thronged the corner of Second Avenue North and Nineteenth Street in front of Newberry's turquoise siding, looking the way white Birmingham liked its Negroes to look, poignantly pathetic, wearing shower caps under sunny skies. One Saturday, after counting the black shoppers downtown, Herb Oliver went home and cried.

Martin Luther King pronounced Birmingham the "most difficult big city in the United States in race relations." But it was the failure of the promising campaign in Albany, Georgia, that currently preoccupied SCLC. SNCC was still there fighting a thankless fight six months after SCLC had skulked out. At its May executive board meeting in Chattanooga, SCLC's leaders had engaged in some stilted soul-searching over their responsibility to the student radicals who played picador to SCLC's sluggish matador. The discussion over whether SCLC should turn over a percentage of its annual budget to SNCC was shelved. And then Fred Shuttlesworth made a proposition so far out in left field that it didn't even make it into the minutes. He turned to King and suggested that they move on from Albany: Come into Birmingham, he said, and face Bull Connor.

But SCLC was confronting obstacles more daunting than Connor's crumbling police state. It would have to contend with a feistier than ever J. Edgar Hoover, whose tenure had been secured on March 22. During a four-hour lunch with the President that day, Hoover had divulged his awareness of the mistress in Los Angeles, Judith Campbell, whom Kennedy shared with Sam Giancana, the Mafia boss enlisted by the administration in its mission to assassinate Castro. And now, to advance his joint crusades against the Kennedys and Martin Luther King, Hoover was willing to enter reckless alliances of his own, beyond the slippery-slope collusion of his Birmingham office with the Ku Klux Klan.

Scoop

THE NATIONAL STATES RIGHTS PARTY'S newspaper, *The Thunderbolt*, printed out of Birmingham by one of the propagandists behind the anti-Semitic labor-bashing tabloids of the 1940s, was about to get its first big scoop.* A front-page article in the May issue alleged that John F. Kennedy had had a brief marriage in 1947 to a Florida socialite named Durie Malcolm. J. Edgar Hoover and Richard Nixon had reputedly discussed using this rumored union as a dirty trick in the 1960 election, and at the height of his job insecurity, in November 1961, Hoover dispatched an FBI agent to the New York Public Library to read a pri-

---

* The man who printed it, Fred Short, had been a charter member of the propaganda empire behind Jim Simpson's political career. Short had been a stockholder in the *Industrial Press*, the union-disrupting organ aimed specifically at TCI workers. In the 1950s, he had been a Citizens Council booster.

vately published Malcolm family history, which listed John F. Kennedy as Durie's third husband.*

Compared with the paranoid rants that Edward Fields generally published in *The Thunderbolt*, his Kennedy story had such a ring of authenticity that once it spread around the right-wing-fringe press, it seeped into the public domain. Under pressure to rebut it, the President tapped his pet scribe, *Newsweek*'s Washington bureau chief, Ben Bradlee, to receive (for one night only) "exculpatory" FBI documents. Hoover thus doubly toyed with Kennedy, helping refute a story he had apparently leaked. The problem for Kennedy was the depth of the well: Presently, *The Thunderbolt* would publish another exposé, on which Hoover's fingerprints were even more discernible. Headlined "JFK Accused of Adultery," it chronicled an item from Hoover's "Official and Confidential" file of dirt on public officials: Kennedy's affair as a senator with his twenty-year-old secretary, Pamela Turnure, who was now First Lady Jacqueline Kennedy's press secretary.

And yet the Kennedys persisted in incurring "favors" from Hoover. On June 27, while on a trip to California, the attorney general appeared at the home of Marilyn Monroe, his brother's recently discarded mistress. The Cadillac convertible Kennedy was driving had been lent to him by the FBI's special agent in charge in Los Angeles, William Simon, who duly informed the director.

Entangled Background

HOOVER MOVED seamlessly from the sexual blackmailing of the Kennedys to the ideological manhandling of the civil rights movement. Birmingham's snarky busybody, Emory O. Jackson, was typically the first in the Movement to sound the alarm. In July, Jackson used a speech Martin Luther King made before the NAACP's annual convention as a pretext to attack SCLC's voter registration campaign as amounting to "little more than the press releases from Dr. King's publicists." Though Jackson editorialized mercilessly in the *World* about SCLC's "gusty halls-of-talk rallies" ("let them be early in the morning when the weather is cooler") and abhorred the Movement's "let King do it attitude," the real burr in his flank was what he warned was "the entangled background" of one of the most effective and creative members of King's staff. Six years after running Bayard Rustin out of Montgomery, Jackson again found himself playing Cassandra about a new problem aide, Jack O'Dell.

Stanley Levison had set up O'Dell, now thirty-eight, in a tiny Harlem office of SCLC. (The two had not known each other in the Party, though Levison told O'Dell he had been a member.) On June 20, a conversation between Levison and O'Dell was picked up by the wiretap that FBI agents had installed on Levison's work phone in March, with the approval of Attorney General Kennedy. Levison

---

* Seymour Hersh concluded in his 1997 study of Kennedy, *The Dark Side of Camelot*, that the marriage had taken place, impulsively. He interviewed Charles Spalding, the Kennedy intimate who had removed the marriage certificate from the Palm Beach County Courthouse.

told O'Dell that Wyatt Walker needed executive assistance in Atlanta and that he had convinced King that O'Dell was the man for the job. Suddenly, everything made sense to J. Edgar Hoover: Levison was maneuvering the Communist Party into direct contact with King and the day-to-day operations of SCLC.

One of Emory O. Jackson's own sacred cows, Fred Shuttlesworth, had also become part of Hoover's conspiracy theory. Shuttlesworth's close relationship with the Southern Conference Educational Fund was providing steady fodder for the Birmingham police's "subversives" dossier on him, with supporting news clippings forwarded over by the FBI. All the anti-red antennae had been activated the previous February when SCEF's Carl Braden came to Birmingham to "get Shuttlesworth out of jail." Braden himself had just been let out of federal prison, having served nearly a year on a contempt-of-Congress charge stemming from his refusal to answer the House Un-American Activities Committee's questions about his political affiliations. ("Integration is what you are investigating," he had retorted to the committee counsel's assertions that it was investigating Communism.)

As Braden's case had become a cause célèbre in leftist circles, Shuttlesworth had forced SCLC to stand up to the red-baiters, pressuring a reluctant King to sign Anne Braden's petition protesting her husband's jailing. When the Bradens had held a civil rights conference in boycott-happy Birmingham in April, SCEF's proposed joint sponsors, SCLC and even SNCC, had gotten cold feet and those brave enough to attend, including Bob Zellner and the lawyer Len Holt, ran a gauntlet of police photographers and squad cars manned with police dogs. It was sort of a re-creation in miniature of the confrontation between Bull Connor and the Southern Conference for Human Welfare twenty-four years earlier, and it was still hard to fathom how progress was going to win against the reactionary forces once again arrayed against it.

A few weeks after the SCEF affair, though the FBI's Atlanta field office had concluded in a thirty-seven-page report that there was no significant Communist influence on either King or SCLC, Hoover placed King on the FBI's second-echelon enemies list, to be detained in the event of a national emergency. The leader of the civil rights movement had been classified as a security risk by the same organization that had deemed Gary Thomas Rowe essential to the nation's security.

Assassins

AS THE FAMILIAR POLAR FORCES reconverged on Birmingham, Eastview 13 rose to its mission. On the evening of July 19, 1962, when Tommy Rowe arrived upstairs at Morgan's Department Store for the klavern's regular Thursday meeting, a fellow officer diverted him into a side room for a discussion of Judge Hobart Grooms's recent ruling desegregating the Dobbs House restaurant at the airport. According to Rowe, Detective Tom Cook told big shot, Eastview's Hubert Page, that Bull Connor and Mayor Art Hanes were "tired of the way things are going in

the racial situation in Birmingham but that their hands are tied." Cook said that
Fred Shuttlesworth was planning to lead a delegation to the restaurant on July 21
or 22, and that city hall was relying on the Klan: Shuttlesworth would have to be
assassinated.

Page told his men that the police had pledged their cooperation in the plot.
The plan was for the older of the two policemen on duty at the airport to fake a
heart attack, and the other would be subdued by Klansmen. Another Klansman
would then stab Shuttlesworth. The Eastview veteran who volunteered to do the
cutting was John Wesley Hall, an alcoholic truck driver and larcenist specializing
in thefts from interstate truck shipments. Because of his dark complexion, he was
known as "Nigger."

Rowe's revelations put the FBI in a familiar bind. Rowe himself had been assigned the job of subduing one of Shuttlesworth's bodyguards. Unlike the attack
on the Freedom Riders, which implicated practically the entire Klan population
of North Alabama, this operation would involve only six men, causing serious
risk to the informant. Still, the next day, Henry Fitzgibbon, who had succeeded
Thomas Jenkins as Birmingham's special agent in charge, told Chief Jamie
Moore—and the old FBI man Art Hanes—about the assassination plan. Moore
promised to assign extra men to the Dobbs House.

Then an FBI agent warned Shuttlesworth in person. Shuttlesworth thanked
him, and for once, the battlefield general consented to be an armchair general.
The Klansmen who worked the airport in shifts over the appointed weekend were
unnerved by the police presence and left the Movement diners who arrived without Shuttlesworth to a peaceful meal at the Dobbs House.

Afterward, Hubert Page cornered Rowe, told him that the police had been
put wise, and vowed that once they caught the informant, his life "would not be
worth a plug nickel." Only one of the six conspirators, Billy Holt, the brickmason
who had reputedly tried to finish off Shuttlesworth back in 1956 by bombing his
church, suspected Rowe and campaigned to throw him out of the Klan. In the saga
of Gary Thomas Rowe, the rescue of Shuttlesworth would be his one legitimate
achievement, although before it was over the FBI agents who worked with him
would undoubtedly come to wonder whether he had been the one proposing the
assassination in the first place.

The collaboration between the Ku Klux Klan and the United States government, though it served no client other than a small group of men who felt the
need to dress up in sheets, was outlasting a relationship that had once cast the vigilantes as the defenders of free enterprise. But that era of heavy manufacturing
had finally drawn to a close, and so, too, was ending the political phenomenon it
had inspired: the reign of Bull Connor.

McWhorter 1962

CRESTLINE PARK came as a shock after we spent our first few months in Birmingham at my grandmother's mansion on the hill. We moved to the neighborhood in the spring of 1959, a grid of matchbox bungalows on streets as straight as bowling alleys. My grandmother Marjorie planted some wisteria to cover the chain-link fence. But her donated furniture could not defeat the scuffed Sheetrock and grimy Formica of the interior. Though a few of our neighbors planned to cross the magic border into adjacent Mountain Brook, most measured their social advancement in the accumulation of single-application kitchen gadgets (electric knives, electric popcorn poppers). I was not sure whether we were on our way up to Mountain Brook, or headed further out-of-bounds. We ate our meals off plastic dishes the color of teeth.

Papa remained very much the warrior. We had a standing invitation to sock him in the stomach as hard as we could, and as our wrists buckled on impact, he would wheeze, "Come on, I ain't got all day." On the nights he came home before our bedtime, he greeted me with an affectionate elbow lock under the chin—"How ya doin', Babe?"—flexing his biceps against my larynx and pulling me back on my heels until I coughed out, "Fine as frog's hair." He challenged us to crush his empty beer cans and then, after we failed to make a dent, scrunched them with one hand, to the sound effect of a belch.

After a few beers, he would have his one meal of the day—enough calories to keep him in sumo shape. His father, though slim and apparently fit, had had a heart attack at forty and popped nitroglycerin like jujubes. Papa liked to surprise the old ticker by jerk-lifting a file cabinet. "Do you believe I can do ten push-ups on three fingers of my left hand with my right hand tied behind my back?" he asked us every Sunday after dinner. "Not bad," he said as he got up off the floor, "for someone with one foot in the grave."

At the time, we thought the joke referred to his advancing age of thirty-three, but he was actually alluding to his paying hobby, out-toughing his father on his own turf, as the wildcat troubleshooter for Alabama Power. Whenever the company hit a snag building a dam that its union construction crew couldn't handle—or wouldn't because it was too dangerous—my father reported to the site ("my playpen") with his scuba gear and performed some life-threatening underwater repair. Once he gouged his leg on a steel reinforcing bar while plugging up a hole in a dam, and when the wound became grossly infected he operated on himself with his Marine knife. Doctors ceased to impress him after he had to grab the lance from the family physician, who had turned green ministering to a suppurating coral burn on his arm. "I didn't have the heart to send him a bill," Papa quipped.

Of course we knew he would never die. Even as his face grew scarred from car wrecks, he could drive as fast as he wanted and I felt safe, in spite of the smell of Scotch wafting to the back seat where the centrifugal force of his corner-turning had flattened me. He had gone to the highway to measure the skid marks

of the Roadway truck that hit his father and could still tell you what they measured—one hundred fifty-three feet.

THE SUMMER OF 1962 had opened like a hot oven door, but we over-the-
mountain children were cool in our valley. I negotiated my double life, commuting between the tiny house on Hoadley Drive and the pool of the Mountain
Brook Club. The only hint I got of the parallel public lives being lived came during a shopping excursion my mother and I took downtown to buy my annual
white leather sandals. She stopped our car shy of the business district, at Avondale
Park, and got out. "Isn't it a shame," she said. "They closed the parks." I looked at
the weedy swing sets, but had no idea what she was talking about. "They didn't
want colored people using them," she explained. It had never occurred to me that
people might "use" a public park. Why, when Birmingham had the most beautiful
country clubs in the world?

We, the grandchildren of Birmingham's suzerains, had "graduated" from
Highlands Day School. Most of us girls were moving on to fifth grade at the
Brooke Hill School—and we had also "flown up" from Bluebirds to Camp Fire
Girls, the only such troop in a city of public school Girl Scouts. Our troop's leader
was married to one of the bigwigs of the John Birch Society, and we would sometimes come across anti-Communist pamphlets in the living room. The fiercest of
the manufacturing families, once the money and passion behind the Dixiecrat
movement, had now congregated in the Birch Society, withdrawing further from
the political hub into a truculent sect educating its members about the Communist threat—the old union-busting ruse now abstracted into pure ideology. As it
turned out, the society was a good medium for my father to reconcile his vehement present with his elegant past.

The Birchers' guiding light, Robert Welch ("The Founder" to himself), had
come to Birmingham the previous fall and given a speech at the armory where I
was soon to begin ballroom dancing lessons. My grandmother attended the event
as a sentimental rather than an ideological gesture. Welch had introduced her to
my grandfather in 1920, when the men were roommates at Harvard Law School.
(Welch's fiancée, a former Wellesley classmate of Marjorie's, had arranged their
double date to the Harvard-Princeton game.) Welch, an academic prodigy from
North Carolina, left Harvard a semester shy of graduation, bought a recipe from
an old man who sold fudge in Harvard Square, and went on to make a fortune with
the Welch Candy Company. Gradually, he gave up control of the firm to his
brother and turned full-time to the exposure of the Communist threat to capitalism. That had been his preoccupation in the 1930s as the propaganda chief of the
National Association of Manufacturers.

Grandfather Hobart McWhorter, who had remained friendly with his old
roommate, had died by the time Welch founded his "conservative" society, in
1958, and named it after a Baptist fundamentalist OSS officer, John Birch, who
had gotten himself killed by Chinese Communists in 1945. Some of Hobart's
pallbearers had become members, meeting in small consciousness-raising clus-

ters—an imitation of the Communist cells that obsessed Welch—to hear lectures from "insiders" like the former FBI agent Art Hanes. My grandmother laughed out loud at the absurdity of the Birch Society and had not given a dinner party for Welch when he came to town. But her older son, my father, began speaking with affected furtiveness about a group he may or may not have been a member of called the Minute Men. I think this was the first time I realized that my peculiar father might be part of some organized resistance movement, though I did not know the Minute Men was one of the Birch Society's more militant "fronts," moving beyond armchair subversive-slaying.

My father was in the process of crossing over into the historical dimension. He was, as his parents' generation might say, "losing his caste." Until now his idiosyncratic relationship with the English language had been on the order of humorous eruptions such as "That's an ostentatious dis-play of your erudition!" He said "O'Hara Airport" and, of late, "Viet Nan" with the savoir faire of those who pronounce foreign capitals in the native accent. But he was also beginning to absorb the vernacular of the white T-shirted men with whom he drank beer after work. Orient was "orinate," and inundate, "oniondate." He said "he don't," "no" instead of "any," and pronounced only one of a double consonant, as when he referred to his younger son 'Tephen.

Worst of all, he said "nigger." The word was so taboo among over-the-mountain children that we facetiously referred to chiggers, those burrowing red mites, as "Chegroes." But Papa had become obsessed with "the nigger bit," as he called the race's growing insistence on itself. "You know why you won't ever see no nigger quarterbacks?" he would say on Sunday afternoons in front of the TV, as we watched Jim Brown run through the New York Giant defense. "The nigger will never be a quarterback because the nigger is orinated to rote memory only. That's right, rote memory." It was not that Papa disliked Negroes—"I grew up with 'em!" They were just part of The Plan, dupes of the Communists who were out to take over the world. John F. Kennedy was a Fabian Socialist! The Communist takeover was coming any day, and the regional headquarters for the coup, Papa said knowingly, was "that Communist training school in Monteagle, Tennessee." One morning, I was certain, we would wake up and find guard towers protruding from the kudzu that draped over our telephone poles and power lines. We called the vine "Communist weed," because it took over everything.

One of Papa's diving buddies, a bit younger than he, was a print-shop foreman named Howard Edwards, whose hobby was local Indian lore. Edwards had been the man with the distinctive pompadour who had been arrested for wielding a lead pipe in the melee at the Trailways bus station on May 14, 1961. The Freedom Rides had represented a turning point for my father, quite different from the change of heart they occasioned in his cousin Sid Smyer. His outrage—and perhaps that of the majority of Birminghamians—was directed not at Bull Connor and the violent mob but at the Freedom Riders. They were the aggressors, the first wave of latter-day Reconstructionists who would also have to be met by vigilante force. Was Papa one of the vigilantes?

MY FATHER AND his younger brother, my uncle Hobart, always greeted each other by clasping right hands and butting heads with the histrionic finesse of professional wrestlers. We children couldn't quite believe we were watching grown men—they looked like a two-man subspecies, foreshortened limbs and flat-backed heads that turned into neck without warning. But despite their similarities, the civilized values of the parents had taken in Hobart. Hobart did a patriotic stint in the Army after Exeter and Yale and then went to law school at the University of Virginia, where the classmate who impressed him most with his physical courage was Ted Kennedy. He joined the white-shoe law firm and in 1960 married Gordon Crawford Jackson, a six-foot-tall, husky-voiced bon vivant who was the daughter of a great lawyer.

With the exception of my father, Hobart's groomsmen were the golden boys of Birmingham, still more children of great lawyers—Jimmy Simpson, for example—settling into the profession themselves. (One groomsman, a lawyer's son named William Rogers, had come to Hobart's wedding from Hollywood, where he starred, as Wayne Rogers, in the TV series *Stagecoach* and eventually became Trapper John on *M*A*S*H.)* "Lotus-eating"—as the young men themselves called the cushy life in Birmingham—had been kind to Hobart. Only three years out of law school, he had recently become the youngest partner in the most powerful firm in the state.

I thought White, Bradley, Arant, Rose & All was the most beautiful sequence of words in the English language. Sometimes when my brothers and I were downtown with Mama, we stopped in at the Brown-Marx Building to see Uncle Hobart. He would swivel-walk into the foyer, and we would reciprocate his smirk even before he delivered himself of some obligatory joke about my brothers being "sissies." ("I didn't realize they were having a sissy parade downtown today!") Taking in the plush red carpet and leather chairs around me, I was reassured by how safe and orderly Birmingham seemed from inside a law firm.

Hobart was becoming a legend as a corporate litigator. "Look out, Hobart's got on his jury clothes," people said when he showed up in court, a button hanging on a thread from his back pants pocket like a wilting daisy. Coca-Cola was the client that had made him famous. Since the Depression, when enterprising down-and-outers put bugs in bottles of Coke and sued for damages, the company had had a strict policy against settling lawsuits. One of Hobart's fabled tactics as the defender of the Birmingham bottler was to take a lusty swig of months-old varmint- or glass-infested Coke, slam the bottle down on the exhibit table with a gratified sigh, and inform the jury in his terrible Oz voice, "I feel fine!" It never occurred to me that there could be better uses for my uncle's talents than drinking from a bottle with his clenched teeth forming a sieve for foreign objects. As far as I was concerned, he was the greatest lawyer in the city and—as guardian of perhaps the South's most positive modern myth, the international triumph of a soft drink—one of its most moral men.

In 1962, Uncle Hobart was the same age as the Young Turks bucking to reform Birmingham. He could have been one of them, as he knew most of them well. Hobart was in a position to merge with history on the right side. He was even mentioned (in a friendly context) in a book Chuck Morgan wrote about his exploits as a civil liberties lawyer years after he left Birmingham. But Hobart defined himself by the country club, and it was my father who had decided to engage with Morgan, from the opposite side. In the years to come, Papa chuckled in fond memory over his brother in Chi Sigma Chi, the elite high school fraternity, and said, "Good ole Chuck. We ran his ass out of town."

10.

PROGRESS

Vann

WHILE DRIVING TO WORK at White, Bradley, Arant on August 14, 1962, a young associate at the firm named David Vann had his brainstorm. It was the dog days of summer. The public swimming pools were open concrete pits, soon to be planted. Vann's car radio was tuned to Dave Campbell's call-in show, *People Speak,* and the intrepid host was delivering one of his "fish or cut bait" editorials: Either get behind the city commission or change the form of municipal government. The listeners were probably befuddled; almost everyone in Birmingham assumed that the commission was an immutable condition, synonymous with Bull Connor. For Vann, though, Campbell's proposition imposed a trajectory on the fuzzy realignment of power that had been taking place in the year since a picture shot inside a bus depot radicalized Sid Smyer. Suddenly the way to bring about change in Birmingham seemed simple: Get rid of Connor by abolishing his office.

Vann was Chuck Morgan's most active comrade among the bushy-tailed lawyers in the Young Men's Business Club who for the past two years had been trying to engineer a progressive takeover of their city. Though Vann had a basic awkwardness and Morgan was the personification of charm, the two men were doppelgängers, even down to the hefty physique that tended, as Morgan put it, "toward the weight of a chief deputy." They had met at the University of Alabama when Vann, the son of a circuit judge from Auburn, ran unsuccessfully for student government president against Morgan's Greek machine. There remained a certain tension between them. For Vann's ambition seemed to spring from spiritual yearning, transcending his cohort's zeal to make a mark. He did not care about popularity, financial success, all the things that dazzled Morgan, who felt a social pressure to maintain good standing with the old Chi Sigs (some of whom remembered the days when he had driven with them to "niggertown" to throw eggs at black pedestrians).

Now a colleague of Hobart McWhorter Jr.'s at the city's establishment firm, Vann was also a member of Alabama's most controversial fraternity. He had been a law clerk for Justice Hugo Black in 1954, when the Supreme Court handed down *Brown* v. *Board of Education*. Returning to Alabama two years later, Vann, like Black, had gravitated toward what the partners in his firm distastefully termed "politics." Nor did he share his fellow liberals' squeamishness about transgressing the racial norms. He was a member of his good college friend Bob Hughes's Alabama Council on Human Relations, though his mentor at White, Bradley, Arant—the very secret liberal Douglas Arant—had forbidden him to represent Hughes when he defied the subpoena in the Harrison Salisbury criminal libel case (which explained how it landed in Chuck Morgan's lap). Vann had confronted the Methodist bishop for North Alabama when the Methodist Layman's Union was formed at his church, and he had sat in a car with his Alabama Council colleague Herb Oliver and helped him draw up the mailing list of opinion shapers who would receive his Inter-Citizens Committee affidavits.

It was Vann who had presented the Young Men's Business Club's resolution in favor of open parks to the city commission in December 1961. Bull Connor had bellowed at him, trotting out his all-purpose retort, "David, you don't even live in Birmingham." Vann said, "Yessir, I do," and bit his tongue. The house next door to his was in Mountain Brook.

Vann lived on Monarch Avenue in the humble neighborhood of Crestline Park, in the same house that my father had used as a crash pad several years earlier when he would come to Birmingham from Cherokee County to see about bank loans for his new air-compressor business. Vann's roommate had been Martin's SAE fraternity brother at Birmingham-Southern, and on his way back to Centre my father would stop by George and Dave's house, end up tying one on, and get his sleeping bag out of the car trunk to take a snooze before heading back to his young family.

Now his Crestline Park neighbor, my father no longer had anything in common with Vann. But my uncle passed him every day in the corridors of White, Bradley, Arant—was one of the partners grousing about the impact of Vann's "political activities" on the firm. Earnest and dogged, Vann did not have Chuck Morgan's ability to disarm. He could not hobnob sardonically over cocktails or even practice great law. But he could change history.

End Run

THE COMMISSION FORM of government had been the result of a coup the ruling class executed on city hall in 1910. The "Great Annexation" that year had incorporated the surrounding municipalities into Birmingham and in the process expanded the board of aldermen, or city council, to include many former "suburbanites," Bible-thumping reformers from old Populist stock, who were not timid about raising taxes on the vested interests.

The gentleman delegated to restore the rule of his peers was Walker Percy, a son of one of the great Mississippi Delta plantations and the last person one would have expected to build the throne for a cracker like Bull Connor. Percy

had married a daughter of the old King of the Southern World, Henry F. De-
Bardeleben, and became the lawyer for Henry's son, his brother-in-law Charles,
as well as U.S. Steel, speaking out for the high-mindedness of J. P. Morgan when
he took over TCI in 1907. Preferring golf at the country club to the nitty-gritty of
politics, Percy ran reluctantly for the state house of representatives in 1910 to
push through a Progressive reform known as the city commission. A handful of
"professionals"—like the country's charter commissioners in Galveston, Texas,
who had recently proved their mettle in the tidal wave–torn town by building a
hardy seawall—would run city hall as a cost-conscious business. Replacing the
unwieldy mayor-aldermen system with three "honest men" (who, incidentally,
could be controlled by his industrial clients), Percy had turned efficiency into an
ideology that gave the gentlemen the moral upper hand against the "corrupt"
democrats. Which explained how "honesty" came to be Bull Connor's most vivid
asset.

But as Percy's nephew William Alexander Percy would write in his memoir,
Lanterns on the Levee: "Nothing is so sad as defeat, except victory." For the 1915
commission race, Walker was unable to persuade any businessman to make the financial sacrifice to run against a socialist druggist. Percy, who tended toward
melancholia, spared himself the coming anti-gentleman revolution, led by Hugo
Black and the Ku Klux Klan. On February 8, 1917, at age fifty-three, he took his
hunting gun up to a trunk room in his dark Southside mansion, disrobed, and shot
himself in the heart.

The city fathers of Birmingham had only belatedly begun to share Percy's
agony about the commission. Upon becoming Chamber of Commerce president
in 1961, Sid Smyer had asked the Birmingham Bar Association to study the three
forms of city government authorized by the state constitution (besides the commission, there were a mayor-council system and a compromise manager-council
model) and determine which would best serve Birmingham. The bar sat on
Smyer's request until the parks controversy reaffirmed that the city commission
had created a dictator. In February 1962, a committee of fifteen lawyers came
back with its verdict: Jettison the commission and replace it with a mayor and city
council—in the interest of "efficiency," the committee deadpanned, reprising
Walker Percy's half-century-old rationale for displacing the democratic clutter of
aldermen. The Big Mules had gotten the commission into city hall, and, by God,
they could get it out.

Since the heartbreaking defeat of Tom King for president of the commission
in the spring of 1961, David Vann had not given much thought to the government
reform proposal that the bar committee had been floating at luncheon groups.
Like most Birminghamians, he had learned to live with Bull Connor, maintaining
a utilitarian relationship with him through the local Democratic Party. (When
Vann had asked him to sit on the dais at a Kennedy rally in 1960, Connor replied
with a certain self-satire, "You know I'm for the ticket. But somebody's got to stay
at city hall and watch the niggers.") Lately, Vann, Chuck Morgan, and the other
lawyers of the Young Men's Business Club had been preoccupied with a more

feasible democratic exercise: emancipating the state legislature from the overrepresented reactionary Black Belt, whose nonvoting black majorities were counted in determining the size of a district's (all-white) house delegation.

Since malapportionment was its own best insurance, the Young Turks realized that the lawmakers would never vote to reapportion themselves out of power. So they had decided to end-run the legislature. In August 1961, following an increasingly popular path toward liberal reform, they had sued a roundup of state officials in federal court. Morgan made the plaintiffs' closing arguments the following April, claiming that "one boll weevil" in the Black Belt had more of a voice in the capitol than the "builders and bankers, the brokers and butchers," of urban Alabama. Thirty minutes later, a panel of three federal judges, including the busy Frank Johnson, returned their decision in favor of reapportionment. *Reynolds* v. *Sims* would be one of the landmark cases by which the Supreme Court would four years later make one man, one vote the law of the land. Morgan was riding high. The next time he got a middle-of-the-night crank call, he telephoned Mayor Art Hanes at home and informed him that he would ring him, at any hour, each time he was harassed in the future.

A special election was called for August 28 to choose the ten new legislators that the court order had added to Jefferson County's delegation of seven. David Vann was wrapped up in that event, two weeks away, when Dave Campbell's editorial riveted him back onto the problem of city hall. Upon arriving at his law office, he looked up the Mayor-Council Act to see how many signatures were required to force an election on the form of government.

Vann telephoned the lawyer Abe Berkowitz, the Young Turks' elder guru, who had served on the stacked bar committee that recommended the change in city government. Vann told Berkowitz he had figured out how to run Bull out of office: Set up petition booths at the polls on the imminent election day and get the necessary signatures for a referendum—10 percent of the electorate, or roughly 7,000. If they could collect them in a single day, Bull Connor's famed espionage team would not have a chance to counterattack.

Berkowitz telephoned a roster of distinguished businessmen. They were willing to meet that afternoon. His prime mark, Sid Smyer, guaranteed the attendance of his Chamber of Commerce colleagues, including the head of Pepsi-Cola. (Coke, less progressive, was not invited.) In Berkowitz's office, Vann made his pitch about abolishing Bull's office. But the businessmen who had come to figure out a way to oust Connor were paralyzed at the thought of antagonizing him. Smyer spoke up, volunteering to pull together a steering committee of twelve unimpeachable community leaders to sponsor the petition for an election to change the city government.

At a meeting two days later, on Thursday, August 16, Smyer was red-faced with exasperation. Having come to progress late, he had believed change in Birmingham would be dictated from the top down, Atlanta-style. But the twenty-five businessmen he approached had, to a man, said, "We cain't get involved." It was with a certain sense of liberation, from a class that had never made him feel fully welcome, that the old Dixiecrat told his comrades, "If we can't get twenty-five silk-stocking people, let's get five hundred anybodies."

Smyer would get much recognition for the anti-Bull movement that Abe Berkowitz had christened Citizens for Progress. But the irony of this, Smyer's first liberal achievement, was how much of the credit for it belonged to his old enemy, organized labor. At the group's founding meeting, it had been the union's local head—participating at Vann's insistence, and over the objections of the business-men—who finally goaded the balking gentlemen into action, saying that the question was not whether they should move against Bull but why they had waited so long. And ultimately, the only person who would put himself on the line to chair the campaign was a union man, a house painter on the AFL-CIO's political action committee. No Big Mules went public (most couldn't meet the Birming-ham residency requirement anyway), and Vann lay low, hoping to avoid being ex-posed as an accessory to Hugo Black.

On Tuesday, August 28, Citizens for Progress's booths had been assembled at strategic polls around the city, excluding the predominantly black "Legion Field boxes," to deprive the opposition of race bait. The only problem was, half of the booths were empty. Many of the volunteers who had come to a meeting on Sun-day to be trained to man them had been sent by Bull Connor, and they simply made off with the Citizens for Progress materials. Vann got on the phone and rus-tled up some emergency troops, but Connor also had a backup plan. He lined up twenty-five Negroes at the courthouse to sign the reformers' petition while his police movie cameras rolled.

Headway

THE MOVEMENT'S Miles College contingent had chosen this election Tuesday to confront Bull Connor in person for the first time. Frank Dukes, the student body president, led five other scholars into the city commission's weekly public meet-ing. They brought their own petition, signed by 833 blacks, urging the commis-sioners to repeal ordinances segregating lunch counters, restrooms, and drinking fountains. Connor interrupted the student body vice president, U. W. Clemon, with his standard "Where do you live?" Clemon told him Westfield, the black TCI mill village where Willie Mays had grown up. "You don't even live in Birmingham, and you have the nerve . . . ," Bull thundered. When Dukes came to Clemon's de-fense, Mayor Art Hanes broke in and asked if he had ever considered leaving Bir-mingham.

"I have a stake in Birmingham," Dukes said. "My family is here. I love Bir-mingham just as you do."

"You wastin' my time comin' down here and talkin' about integration," Con-nor said.

Jonathan McPherson, a Miles chemistry professor active in Shuttlesworth's movement, spoke up. He had, as one of the Alabama Christian Movement for Human Rights' early projects, become the first Negro to pass the civil service exam for joining the police force. But his name kept disappearing from the list of eligibles until finally he disqualified himself by moving outside the city limits. Connor now asked him if he would arrest a white man. "I would uphold the law," McPherson said.

"Before we let niggers be policemen," Connor said, "we'll have nigra deacons at First Baptist."

As the meeting wound down, Dukes asked the reporters present whether it would be possible to have a press conference. "Yes, have a press conference," Bull said mincingly. "You probably have already arranged it. I'm surprised NBC isn't here." Then he turned to Clemon and said, "You an outside agitator from West-field. If you ever come downtown, I'll have you arrested."*

The Miles delegation was the least of Connor's problems: He accused the students of being stooges of the integrationist Citizens for Progress, whose petitions to change Birmingham's form of government were currently being signed. By the time the polls closed, nearly 12,000 signatures had been collected, 5,000 more than required. Until they could be secured in a bank vault the next morning, one of the Young Turk lawyers guarded them overnight with his shotgun.

Bull Connor, a midwife of the civil service system, promised to fire any city employee who had signed, accounting for the seven names that had been razored out of the petition when it was filed at the courthouse the following week. Having exhausted themselves earning the simple right to hold a vote, Citizens for Progress now looked ahead to the even rougher task of winning the election.

On Monday evening, Labor Day, thousands of families cut short their holiday weekends and converged on a downtown corner to watch the ceremonial lighting of the Bank for Savings Building, the first skyscraper to spring from Birmingham's parking lots in thirty years. Chuck Morgan's family joined other neatly groomed Mountain Brook residents, ruddy steelworkers from Ensley, black people from Smithfield, all craning their necks to watch, greeting each illuminated story with sighs of wonder, until all seventeen were ablaze. Birmingham was so desperate for even a glimmer of progress that the *News* hailed the event as the beginning of "a new era." Morgan moved his law office into the building, as if rubbing a rabbit's foot.

Beyond Albany

SUMMER WAS OVER, and it was back to school for SCLC. The civil rights chapter that would go by the bittersweet name Albany had come to an end in July, when King returned to the Georgia town and (in contrast to SCLC's earlier efforts to keep Fred Shuttlesworth *out* of jail) gratefully accepted a forty-five-day sentence on his arrest for demonstrating the previous December. King was hoping to redeem his campaign-ruining bail-out at Christmas, but less than two days

---

* In 1980, Clemon would become Birmingham's first black federal judge, appointed by President Jimmy Carter.

after scrubbing their cell's commode into "the finest looking toilet in Albany," he and his loyal jailmate, Ralph Abernathy, were released. Their fine had been paid by an unidentified "well-dressed Negro man"—a fiction created by Albany's power structure, with the blessing of the Kennedy administration—prompting mirthful whodunit stories in the mainstream press. After ten months of discipline, courage, and self-sacrifice, the demoralized Albany Movement's rank and file hung up their marching shoes. To echo the common acronym for SNCC, "Snick," wags had begun to call SCLC "Slick."

SCLC was holding its annual convention in Birmingham on September 25–27, marking the beginning of a new season in the history of civil rights, the Year of Birmingham. Shuttlesworth knew it would be impossible to pull off a direct-action campaign in time for the convention. White folks, however, did not understand that demonstrations were not simply spontaneous acts, but had to be planned—recruits trained in nonviolence and bail bond money raised. Happily, some black folks didn't understand that, either. Toward the end of August, Shuttlesworth had begun to out-Pitts Miles's suave president Lucius Pitts, and let rumors of demonstrations "slip" to some of the Big Boys. They in turn clued their "white friends" in on the big secret: Martin Luther King was coming to Birmingham to march.

Dreading "another Albany," Sid Smyer formalized the historic move he had made eight months earlier in getting blacks and whites to "sit down" together over the parks controversy. On August 24, on top of raising money and bodies to oust Bull Connor, he had tapped the most influential members of the Chamber of Commerce. Also included were twelve black Big Boys. The *News's* wheeler-dealer Vincent Townsend did the white hand-picking, purposely excluding Jim Head, despite his having been the co-chair of the original "study group" from which this official "Senior Citizens Committee" had evolved.

Ever the good cop, Lucius Pitts let his white contacts know in mid-September that he had just "led" a delegation to Washington—a verb that might have been disputed by delegate Shuttlesworth. They were to have met with Robert Kennedy to discuss the dangers that might greet SCLC's convention in Birmingham, but found the attorney general preoccupied with another matter. Justice Hugo Black had recently ended a series of obstructionist lower-court maneuvers and categorically ordered the University of Mississippi to admit its first Negro student, a thirty-year-old Air Force veteran named James Meredith.

A black man entering an institution that in four years had produced two Miss Americas was unthinkable to most white southerners.* But the Kennedys had believed they could deal gentleman-to-gentleman with Mississippi's governor, Ross Barnett, a "humble plowboy," as editorialists romanticized him, turned $100,000-a-year damage-suit lawyer. He had declared that to integrate Ole Miss (the school

---

* That a pale-skinned Navy veteran had "passed" for the 1945–46 school year had not yet come to light. "What else?" he would reply when asked if he dated white girls.

nickname taken from the traditional honorific for plantation mistresses) would be to "drink from the cup of genocide."

As he met with the Birmingham delegation, the attorney general had run back to his telephone to take calls from Barnett or one of the "riot squadders" he had sent to Mississippi. Shuttlesworth and his treasurer, Bill Shortridge, urged him to use the full power of his office against Barnett, but Kennedy replied, "You don't just use power because you've got it."

When Shortridge persisted, Kennedy asked, "Mr. Shortridge, what would you do with Governor Barnett?"

"Jail him," Shortridge replied. Kennedy explained that that would make a martyr out of him. He said, "My purpose is to put Meredith in the institution"— even "if it takes all the troops in the United States."

On the office wall beside the charts mapping the Justice Department's voter registration battlefields was a shiny silver rifle. "That's a civil rights rifle," Kennedy told Shuttlesworth, who replied with equally droll ambiguity, "You know what, Mr. Kennedy? I'm sure you know that there are a lot of people you're dealing with who'd like to be using it right now."

Jimerson's Debut

IN THE MONTHS since Bull Connor closed the city parks, the soft-spoken, poker-faced Norman "Jim" Jimerson, the white nonpracticing Baptist minister who had succeeded Bob Hughes as head of the interracial Alabama Council on Human Relations, had expanded his white contacts well beyond the "Yankees" at the University Medical Center. As soon as he arrived the previous summer, he had several conferences with Sid Smyer, who had told him he was ready "to take the bull by the horns." Jimerson had since worked his way through the industrial elite. It was as if the natives had been waiting for years to unleash their pent-up moral confusion on a stranger—Jimerson was from New York State—who wouldn't tattle on them at the country club. His only negative meeting had been with U.S. Steel's Art Wiebel, who had an assistant screen him: "Are you a Communist?"

"No, I'm a Christian," Jimerson replied, "and you can't be a Christian if you don't believe in God."

In the black community, Jimerson's preferred contact was Lucius Pitts, who was known to throw an arm around him and say, "Jim, you've got a black heart." It was not Pitts, however, who had brought Jimerson into the current controversy, but David Vann, a member of the Alabama Council search committee that hired him. Vann was exercised over the coming "demonstrations." They would kill the referendum to oust Bull Connor that he had managed to get on the November ballot. Vann approached Jimerson: "We're asking you to go to Atlanta to convince them not to have demonstrations."

Though Jimerson viewed this assignment without relish, he did have a special entree with SCLC. In 1957, having attended the University of Michigan, seminary at Andover-Newton in Massachusetts, and graduate school in psychology and religion at Martin Luther King's alma mater, Boston University, he had taken a job as chaplain at the federal reformatory in Petersburg, Virginia. The pastor of the most elegant black church in town was Wyatt Walker, who, though he was given to provocative pronouncements such as "White folks is white folks, polite or heinous," had invited Jimerson to preach at his church, serve communion with him, and bring his family over for dinner.

Despite this connection with SCLC's executive director, Jimerson was not able to get a firm appointment with King, who was talking to *Time* when he showed up at SCLC's Atlanta office. Eventually, Jimerson headed back to the airport to wait for the next plane to Birmingham. Wyatt Walker rushed up to his gate and launched into a long tirade, demanding to know why SCLC should care about what the white people of Birmingham were up to. "Just out of curiosity, you might want to listen," Jimerson said, reminding him that being a white liberal in the South was such a trial that one's motive could not be anything other than a commitment to human dignity. Then he described how demonstrations would give Bull Connor the backlash he needed to defeat the referendum on his office. Walker made no promises, but the two men shook hands.

Upon his return, Jimerson and Vann urged Smyer to call Lucius Pitts. On Sunday, September 16, nine days before the SCLC convention was to begin, Smyer drove down from his house on Shades Mountain to talk to the three men. Pitts told Smyer that only some real and immediate concessions from the department stores could mollify Shuttlesworth and King. The "White Only" signs would have to be removed from restrooms and water fountains. Smyer deemed this "reasonable"; he'd try to have the signs down in forty-eight hours. To Pitts's request for a "status-backed" biracial committee, he said it was as good as done.

To white folks, "status" meant "Responsible Negroes," like the dozen blacks on Smyer's Senior Citizens Committee—Negroes who had the good manners not to actually attend the committee meetings, such as the one held with the three city commissioners at the Chamber of Commerce the following afternoon, Monday, September 17, to discuss SCLC's arrival. Though Jimerson admired Smyer's pluck, he realized that the power structure was "absolutely uninformed and incompetent in respect to the task they have before them," which was to defuse the coming "explosion" during the SCLC convention.

Jimerson's board of the Alabama Council appealed to the American Jewish Committee, the New York–based human-relations monitor that had been drawn into Birmingham's civil rights drama because of the vulnerability of the local Jews: Would the committee send down a specialist to "workshop" the businessmen on how to "stave off what could be quite catastrophic"? An Atlanta AJC member, a liberal lawyer named Morris Abram (future president of Brandeis University), asked King to postpone demonstrations.

Smyer was ready to negotiate with Pitts, but the great manipulator had manipulated himself into a corner. Having no authority to speak for SCLC, Pitts knew that only Fred Shuttlesworth could make any negotiations meaningful. Pitts passed the buck to the one Negro with the standing to persuade the white men to deal with Shuttlesworth: the millionaire A. G. Gaston. Pained though he must have been, Gaston went back to the white friends to whom he had recently denounced Shuttlesworth as a rogue elephant and said, "Fred's the man that's got the folks. I got some money, but that's all. Money don't run this thing now. He's the man with the marbles. You have to talk to the marbles."

Shuttlesworth, who had never even dealt with white clergymen or professional moderates, let alone the power structure, had to ask for directions to the Chamber of Commerce building—catty-corner from city hall—whose drab, unadorned facade was pictured on most Chamber literature, as if to advertise the community's no-frills business attitudes. In one of the private meeting rooms, the blacks and the whites took opposite sides of the table. Dapper as always, Shuttlesworth was flanked by Pitts and Arthur Shores. Gaston made a less than gracious introduction: "I told them, Fred, that they had to talk to you."

Smyer greeted Shuttlesworth, "Oh, Doctor, I'm so glad to meet you."

"I'm not a doctor," Shuttlesworth said, "and I'm not a good boy. I been here now suffering for five and six or seven years. I didn't hear from you when they bombed my church."

Smyer's hands trembled. All he was interested in, he said, businesslike, was how they could keep King out of Birmingham.

"Well, on your slogan at the airport and elsewhere, 'It's So Nice to Have You in Birmingham,' " Shuttlesworth began. "We think that means King too. We think he's nice enough to come in here. He's nice as anybody else, and there are some things wrong, the mere fact that we have to invite him in." Shuttlesworth's ego couldn't resist a dig about how funny it was that no one had wanted to see him when it was just Fred Shuttlesworth in town. He asked the men to get to the point: "If you've got some reason for calling me, what can you offer? That's what I'm here for, not to hold a conversation, because I don't think we're that brotherly."

"Well, ah, we, ah, we cain't, ah, make promises for the merchants," Smyer said.

"Well, I'm talking to the wrong crowd then," Shuttlesworth said pleasantly. "Let's go, gentlemen. Y'all wasting my time. I'm busy. I'm fighting segregation."

After the meeting, Pitts and Gaston fell all over Shuttlesworth with praise. Gaston admitted he had been afraid Fred would blow the white men out of the water. "You're a true spokesman," they told him. Although Shuttlesworth respected Pitts's "finesse to speak with people of all classes," he didn't necessarily envy it, and he certainly didn't warm to the backhanded compliment. Still, he was rather amazed at how fast the white folks could pull together a meeting when they wanted to. A second conference was called: nine or ten men of each race (compared with four or five at the first), including representatives from all the major department stores.

"All right, gentlemen," Shuttlesworth said, "what have you got to offer? You don't want King in here. We want him."

Isadore Pizitz led the merchants' chorus of negatives. His department store was the biggest in the state, the first to have escalators, but it still had the feel of an overgrown country store, catering to folks who looked as if they had put on their Sunday best to come into town. Black shoppers were said to prefer Pizitz, perhaps because it had Colored restroom facilities. Many stores didn't, and practically every black mother on a shopping expedition had endured a humiliating rite of passage: watching her child urinate in public, against a curb if no alley could be found in time.

Still, Shuttlesworth addressed "Mr. Pizitz"—he mispronounced the name, with the accent on the first syllable—when he complained, "Well, our women tell us they can't refresh themselves in your store. We want to desegregate the bathrooms."

Pizitz said he couldn't help him there.

"Mr. Pizitz," Shuttlesworth said, "it might interest you that I have decided exactly how it's going to be." He, Martin Luther King, and Ralph Abernathy would sit in Pizitz's store. "We won't walk out. We'll be dragged out by Bull Connor's efficient police. And while we're in jail, we won't shower or eat, and all the world will see how bad we look and how bad this city is."

A. G. Gaston had a soft spot for the merchants. He had spent his early childhood in the beautiful Southside home—tended by his mother, the live-in cook— of the Lovemans, the German-Jewish family that owned the store that was Pizitz's higher-toned competition. But Shuttlesworth's speech made Gaston realize that there had been no progress since the days when he built replicas of the four-story Loveman store with Adolph Loveman's young son, Berney. "Your father and I started in business at the same time," Gaston said to Pizitz. "You made your business off colored folks."

Isadore's Polish immigrant father, Louis Pizitz, had been an itinerant back peddler and had become one of Birmingham's outstanding progressive citizens—a dear friend of Hugo Black's. During the great coal strike of 1908, Pizitz had delivered food and supplies by the truckload to the evicted miners' tent villages. Louis's heir, Isadore, whose nickname, Bud, broadcast his assimilation, seemed trapped rather than enlarged by material success. He humored Bull Connor, whom he despised privately, accompanying the commissioner on his rounds checking for expired parking meters, and Pizitz would just as soon not know about one of Bull's favorite quips: that a Jew was nothing in the world but a "nigger turned inside out."

It was the only Protestant country clubber among the merchants who spoke affirmatively to Shuttlesworth. Roper Dial, the manager of the local Sears, said, "Well, I'll be glad to desegregate the water—"

"Not just water, gentlemen," Shuttlesworth cut him off. "Toilets!"

Dial recalled that his janitor had "accidentally" painted over the "White Only" sign on Sears's restroom door. "I'll just tell him to leave it."

"Well, that was accidental wisdom," said Shuttlesworth, who had no doubt as to what color the janitor was.

Which brought them to the last demand: jobs, noncustodial jobs, for Negroes in the stores. "Jobs," Smyer said. "That's chicken feed. We got plenty of jobs. I got quite a few niggers working in my rock quarries." One of them was the father of Miles College's old activist student president, Jesse Walker.

"Don't you know the English language?" Shuttlesworth's first vice president, Ed Gardner, asked.

"That's the way I was brought up," Smyer explained.

Nevertheless, Shuttlesworth had a feeling that the old Dixiecrat was no ordinary segregationist. As the meeting broke up with an agreement that the stores would be partly desegregated—not the lunch counters, but the elevators and water fountains and, the real breakthrough, the toilets—Smyer bounded around the table and, breaking another taboo, said, "Doctor, I give you my hand."

"No, no, I'm no doctor," the preacher said. "Fred Shuttlesworth."

"I'm so glad, so glad," Smyer kept repeating.

This was Shuttlesworth's first inkling that the segregationist power structure was not the solid monument he had assumed it to be. He agreed to make no public Bull-baiting statement and simply announced with a straight face at a press conference that demonstrations (which had never been planned in the first place) were being postponed for sixty days.

Unwitnessed Accidents

THE RUMORS OF DEMONSTRATIONS seemed to have worked too well. In mid-September, Imperial Wizard Bobby Shelton summoned to Tuscaloosa possibly as many as five hundred Klansmen from around the South to prepare to stop Martin Luther King's invasion of Birmingham. Anticipating collateral fallout, a Birmingham Jewish organization demanded—in a directive aimed specifically at the Right's old bête noire, the Anti-Defamation League—that outside Jewish agencies stay out of Birmingham.

The Alabama Advisory Committee of the U.S. Civil Rights Commission held a crisis meeting in mid-September, five days before the SCLC convention. Jim Head warned the commission's representatives of another Freedom Ride–type collaboration between the police and the Klan—an ambush that Connor "won't know anything about," a committee member agreed, but which will be "calculated to put these 'trouble-makers' in their places or in their graves." Connor had canceled press passes for all media, even local reporters. The worst of the rumors was that the Klan had been authorized to "finish off Martin Luther King once and for all in one of those unwitnessed accidents that can happen in the dark after the meeting."

In one of Birmingham's invisible turning points, the power structure implicitly acknowledged that it had control over the actions of the Ku Klux Klan. Sid Smyer's Senior Citizens Committee, in a rare public document, drafted an advisory for all the members of the Chamber of Commerce to post at their businesses, informing their employees that participating in demonstrations would not be tolerated. Cleverly worded to apply most obviously to would-be black demonstra-

tors, it was really aimed at the whites who might be involved in the Klan's welcome for SCLC. For good measure, Smyer and a couple of Senior Citizens met
with the city commissioners on September 24, the day before the convention
opened, and put them on notice. The city fathers had always claimed that they
were "taking care of things" themselves and actually doing so at long last carried
unpleasant truths: The Senior Citizens' scheme to discourage the white vigilantes
appeared to work, exposing the fraudulence of their insistence that the city's
"black eyes" had been the work of isolated hoodlums.

Upstaged

Wyatt Walker's bravado at a mass meeting on the eve of the convention—"I have come to Birmingham to ride the Bull"—was met coolly by the locals. As virtually the only functioning mass movement SCLC could claim, the
ACMHR had begun to chafe at high-handedness from Atlanta. King had raised
the hackles of his "connection man," as he called ACMHR treasurer Bill Shortridge, who was old enough to be his father, by informing him, via a special delivery
letter, of the board meeting during the convention. (Shortridge tersely responded
that "living in Birmingham should suggest that automatic cooperation on my part
is a 'must.' ") To mollify the locals, King agreed to give the ACMHR 40 percent of
the proceeds from the convention rather than the customary one-third.

On Tuesday, September 25, Martin Luther King and SCLC came to town, a
surprisingly innocuous-looking crew of three hundred or so. It was probably no
coincidence that Mayor Art Hanes was at the airport when they arrived. One of
his first official acts, a year earlier, had been the dedication of the remodeled ter-
minal-to-rival-Atlanta's, which had had to forswear segregation in order to qualify for federal money. Bull Connor and Jabo Waggoner had showily refused to
attend the ribbon-cutting ceremonies, as if they had not approved the desegregated facilities, and sent the mayor as the fall guy for a project built before he took
office. Which explained why Hanes was in no mood to offer any of the official
greetings expected of his position when he was joined at the only integrated uri-
nal in Birmingham by Martin Luther King.

The convention seemed to be skidding toward another SCLC anticlimax.
Not only had the Klan stayed away, but the reporters there taking notes were the
B-team press corps. The first-stringers were in Oxford, Mississippi, where Gover-
nor Ross Barnett had personally barred James Meredith from the University of
Mississippi "now and forevermore," handing him the gold-sealed document from
which he read as a souvenir.

From his new post as president of the University of Miami, Birmingham-
Southern's departed Henry King Stanford telegrammed Barnett a warning that,
in his capacity as college accreditation chairman of the Southern Association of
Colleges and Schools, he would recommend that all Mississippi schools be disac-
credited. In the aftermath of the ensuing disaster, Robert Kennedy would tell

Stanford that he had been "more effective than federal marshals," and the sad truth of the matter was that he was probably right.

In Birmingham, the press nearly got its page-one story on the convention's last day, Friday, September 28. At A. G. Gaston's auditorium, as King announced Sammy Davis Jr.'s coming benefit for SCLC, a 200-pound white youth got out of his seat right next to Gaston and walked toward the stage. Most people assumed he was a white supporter wanting to shake King's hand. Instead he began punching King in the mouth. King did not defend himself.

The conventioneers, after a stunned moment, rushed toward the stage. Joe Lowery was, with Abernathy, the first to get to King's side with fists ready and was astounded to watch King become his assailant's protector. He held him solicitously and, as the audience began singing Movement songs, told him that their cause was just, that violence was self-demeaning, that "we're going to win." Then King introduced him to the crowd, as though he were a surprise guest. Roy James, a twenty-four-year-old native New Yorker who lived in an American Nazi Party dormitory in Arlington, Virginia, began to weep in King's embrace. The police insisted on dragging him off to recorder's court for an immediate trial. James would explain that he had been driven to his deed by the mention of Sammy Davis—a black man converted to Judaism who was married to a white woman.

Was It Worth Two Lives?

ONE REASON that the only racist newsmaker for the SCLC convention was an "outside agitator" was that Birmingham had sent its homegrown agitators to Mississippi. Troy Ingram had been organizing groups to go help the other "patriots" keep Meredith out of Ole Miss. Responding to rumors that Dr. Edward Fields had taken "1,800 men" to Mississippi, FBI agents checked hotels and motels in the Jackson area but found no evidence of the National States Rights Party. They had not looked hard enough: Richard Bowling, the Atlantan who claimed to have been the hands-on bomber of Shuttlesworth's church in 1958 (and four months later had been charged in the bombing of a synagogue in Atlanta), was among the Stonerites at Ole Miss when it finally blew.

The Kennedy administration had had twenty phone conversations with Governor Ross Barnett and endured three rebuffs of James Meredith and his Justice Department escorts before the unflappable student was sneaked onto campus Sunday, September 30. The previous day, Governor Barnett whipped up the halftime crowd at the Ole Miss–Kentucky game in Jackson, in a spectacle that resembled "a big Nazi rally," according to one student, "just the way Nuremberg must have been!" Hung-over frat boys and sorority sisters had arrived back in Oxford on Sunday afternoon to find nonmatriculated patriots on the campus shouting "Barnett, yes; Castro, no" and wielding Molotov cocktails, rocks, iron spikes, shotguns, and rifles. Most prominent was General Edwin A. "Ted" Walker, who had been forced out of the Army for indoctrinating NATO troops in Germany with

John Birch literature and now seemed to be working off his regret over having commanded the paratroopers enforcing integration in 1957 at Little Rock's Central High School.

By eleven o'clock Sunday night, a French reporter had been shot in the back at close range and killed, and a jukebox repairman also fatally shot, in the head. By the time U.S. soldiers—along with the federalized Mississippi National Guard led by William Faulkner's nephew—arrived, 160 federal marshals had been injured, 28 by bullets. On Monday morning, Meredith, dressed in a conservative suit and carrying a briefcase, rode in a bullet-pocked Border Patrol car across a campus strewn with the green shards of Coke bottles. On his way to his nine o'clock class, Colonial American history, a student yelled at him, "Was it worth two lives, nigger?"

Thank God for Mississippi

DAVID VANN AND SID SMYER found fresh comfort in the old cliché "Thank God for Mississippi," the only place more benighted than Alabama. The specter of "another Oxford," a town now occupied by 23,000 federal troops, wafted east, haunting particularly the tall buildings where Vann and Smyer's ouster of Bull Connor was being plotted. The disaster at Oxford—and the "Stand in the Schoolhouse Door" that Governor-elect George Wallace was planning for Tuscaloosa—lent a sense of urgency to their campaign to get rid of the politician who had already stood in the bus depot door.

Suddenly, Citizens for Progress, until now something of a "grassroots" mirage, became as real as steel. The city fathers reached into their notoriously shallow pockets—$30,000 all told—for a palace coup being called the Birmingham Plan, this one a diametrical departure from the last Birmingham Plan they had bankrolled in 1948, the Dixiecrat secession. The men who sent in brown envelopes with $100 bills were not only the typical progressives such as Jim Head, who also donated office equipment. (Federal Judge Hobart Grooms gave $10 cash.) They were an industrial Who's Who, men whose response to change had historically ranged from "We cain't get involved" to obstruction: the major bankers, insurance executives, chairmen of utility companies, and the *News*'s Clarence Hanson, who gave $100. Flower-lovers on the Women's Committee of 100 gave. White, Bradley, Arant lawyers gave—$500 from Arant himself.

The most dramatic sign that Bull's old oligarchy had deserted him was the $200 contribution from the Stockham Valves family—Richard had been one of Hobart McWhorter Sr.'s pallbearers—which had not only cast the iron bull that ornamented Connor's lawn but also had financed the anti-Semitic, anti-union propaganda that had secured so many hearts and minds for "Me and Jim" in the 1940s. Absent from the benefactors was TCI's Art Wiebel, who had typically let the locals pay their own way.

The Referendum on Segregation

CITIZENS FOR PROGRESS faced a crucial obstacle: how to prevent the man on the street from figuring out that changing the form of city government was really a referendum on segregation. Before lunch groups all around town, the steering committee wielded elaborate flow charts to demonstrate that the reform was an academic imperative of political science. How could they be trying to get rid of Bull? If he was so wonderful, they pointed out, why force him to share power with two other commissioners? Elect him mayor.

There was indeed a possibility that the progressives would end up only consolidating Connor's power unless he somehow collaborated in his downfall. David Vann found the chink in his armor one day in court. Waiting for a case to be called, he caught the testimony of a young policeman named Jim Parsons, who told the truth on some point of police procedure about which cops customarily lied to get a conviction. Vann asked him to lunch.

Parsons, the son of an illiterate stalwart of the United Mine Workers, told Vann that a frustrated group of young patrolmen was in mutiny against Bull. Unlike the city fathers, Parsons's insurgents didn't give a damn about civic "black eyes." They were motivated by professional pride and ambition, and objected to the routine brutalization of Negro "suspects" as unpoliceman-like. More than anything they wanted to be detectives, the rank Connor had removed from the domain of civil service to use as carrot and stick. "I run it, and I'm gonna pick it," Connor had chided Parsons. "You're a bunch of soreheads."*

Parsons and some buddies sneaked into Connor's office after hours to get incriminating material to pass along to Tom Lankford, Vincent Townsend's police reporter and personal spook. Townsend was marshaling all his print and broadcast resources behind the change-of-government forces—new blood, new vitality—and now Parsons provided fodder for stories on police corruption. One described a Bull-sanctioned unlicensed Negro "shot house" that they hoped would put Connor on the "nigger-loving" defensive. Connor retaliated, charging that Citizens for Progress had been cooked up "at a Jewish Club."

Resegregation

IN LATE OCTOBER, the "White Only" signs that had been removed in honor of SCLC's arrival began going back up at the department stores. As the legend would develop, Bull Connor was harassing the merchants who had compromised with Fred Shuttlesworth by ordering impromptu fire inspections of the stores, uncovering all manner of violations of fire and building safety codes. One store, it was said, was ordered to buy $9,000 worth of elevator equipment and $100,000 worth of fireproofing. No one has produced any evidence to back the stories.

* The Young Turk policemen successfully took Connor to court to get the rank of detective put under civil service. "I don't have to take a damn one of them," Connor said to Art Hanes and Jabo Waggoner when the exam scores were posted, revealing that Parsons had scored number one.

Indeed, before Martin Luther King had come to town, Isadore Pizitz and some fellow retailers had gone to Connor's office and tried to humor him, recalling his ploy of providing separate entrances into the same restroom, or some such, at the new airport. "We aren't doing anything you didn't do at the airport," they said. "You put federal funds above your convictions." Perhaps some quid pro quo courtesy had been exchanged that day: The Jim Crow signs would go back up within a decent interval after SCLC departed. As Shuttlesworth had told King during the convention, "They took those signs down because you were coming to town, and they'll put 'em up again just as soon as you leave."

Within a couple of weeks before the November referendum on Connor's office, Birmingham had been resegregated. The discussions that had continued between black leaders and Smyer's Senior Citizens broke down too. Lucius Pitts, who had initially reported to the Alabama Council's Jim Jimerson that the white men were "getting with it," began telling his white friends, "I'm going to march my *self*." Smyer and his Senior Citizens would make the extraordinary claim that they offered to raise legal fees for the Movement to test the segregation ordinances, but that the blacks tartly suggested that the store owners get themselves arrested if they wanted to challenge them. In any case, the businessmen's proposed course of a discreet constitutional challenge was now a civil rights relic.

Thirteen months after his initial overtures to the store owners, Miles College's Frank Dukes said he had no choice but to revive the "Selective Buying Campaign." Or as the ACMHR vice president Abraham Woods put it at a mass meeting, "Keep your black feet and knock knees out of downtown." The Senior Citizens countered that they should have known all along that the Negroes couldn't be trusted.

In mid-October, at a caucus with Alabama's civil rights leaders in Montgomery, Martin Luther King announced, still not mentioning Birmingham, that SCLC's confrontation with segregation would begin in the state in six weeks. Kicking off a frenetic membership drive, the ACMHR ordered members to advertise their Movement support by wearing skullcaps emblazoned with "M."

COMINFIL

ON OCTOBER 23, J. Edgar Hoover launched the FBI's full-scale "Communist infiltration," or COMINFIL, investigation into SCLC. His professional impunity had been fully restored on the weekend of August 4, when his nominal boss Robert Kennedy's increasingly unstable ex-lover, Marilyn Monroe, was found at her home in Los Angeles dead of an overdose of barbiturates. In the ensuing decades of speculation surrounding her suicide, a variety of witnesses would say that Kennedy had been in Los Angeles that day, and others would claim to have heard surveillance tapes of a conversation the two had hours before her death. FBI agents immediately went to General Telephone's offices to remove the records of Monroe's final phone calls. The next morning, Kennedy attended mass in San Francisco, where he was staying with his family at the Saint Francis Hotel, and left for the Seattle World's Fair. There he doffed his hat to J. Edgar Hoover. "I hope he will serve the country for many, many years to come," he told reporters.

Immediately after opening the COMINFIL investigation into SCLC, Hoover had the FBI forward its Jack O'Dell file to a few friendly newspapers. In late October, virtually identical exposés appeared in five right-wing dailies in New Orleans; St. Louis; Augusta, Georgia; Birmingham, Alabama; and on Long Island. Apparently unmindful of the dampening effect this might have on his campaign against Bull Connor, Vincent Townsend put the story on the *News*'s October 26 front page, under the headline "Communist in High Post with King's Mixing Group." The story seemed especially urgent in light of the current U.S. naval quarantine around the island of Cuba, which was turning away missile-bearing Soviet ships. ("Can they hit Oxford, Mississippi?" Robert Kennedy had quipped two weeks earlier, when an American U-2 spy plane photographed some fifty sites for the Cuban missiles.)

O'Dell's red aura had been an object of nervous curiosity at SCLC. "If I was a Communist I would tell you," he assured anyone who broached the subject. But he would heartily volunteer, "Sure I know Communists. You want to meet some?" And he was serious. No enemy of the reds either, Wyatt Walker—a boss who told his workers, "Like Ray Charles said, 'I'm not hard to get along with, darlings. I just have to have perfection' "—counted O'Dell as SCLC's most effective staffer ever. King tried to finesse the issue. He declared that O'Dell had resigned "pending further inquiry," a phrase intended to indemnify the organization against the fact that he had not quit at all.

A City with a Great Future

IF THE O'DELL AFFAIR echoed those early days of the Cold War fifteen years before, when Bull Connor red-baited O'Dell's first Communist affiliation, the Southern Negro Youth Congress, out of existence, the latest contest between Connor and the moderates recalled the somewhat later moment when city fathers had teamed up with disgruntled police officers to force the commissioner from office. The element so far missing from this go-round was the equivalent of Connor's adultery at the Tutwiler Hotel.

It was at Carpenter Hall downtown where Connor had found himself in a compromising position on Wednesday, October 17. He and his fellow embattled commissioners had summoned the city's firefighters to a closed meeting to offer them 8 to 10 percent retroactive raises in exchange for their votes. A fireman asked, "Do we get the raise regardless of how the election comes out next Tuesday?"

"Absolutely not," Art Hanes said. "You don't get your raises unless *we* are here to give it to you."

Until now the *News*'s Tom Lankford had used his "technical capability" most dramatically to do the segregationists' dirty tricks, notably the "black-hand" photograph that destroyed Tom King's shot at city hall. A few months later, Lankford had reportedly burst in on a meeting of the Alabama Council on Human Relations and snapped pictures that were said to have ended up in Connor's files. But this time, Lankford had signed on with the other side and had bugged the commissioners trying to bribe the fire department.

A transcript of the skulduggery appeared in the next afternoon's *Birmingham News*. An unidentified messenger delivered a tape of the meeting to David Vann, who turned it into a radio ad, with a booming voice punctuating each of the commissioners' sleazy promises with "Stop corruption in city hall. Vote Mayor-Council."

The commissioners fought back. Hanes boasted of Bull's performance at the Southern Conference for Human Welfare convention—"Connor told Mrs. Roosevelt to break up the meeting or he would put her in jail." Connor pointed out that David Vann had clerked for Hugo Black "and probably had something to do with the lousy decision to integrate the schools." Meanwhile, Vann closed his crusade for progress where it had begun: on Dave Campbell's call-in radio show. "We took every nut in Birmingham for about two hours," Vann would recall. It was the fittingly absurd end to a contest for a city whose people, famously, would not speak.

On election day, November 6, Barney Monaghan, the progressive executive at Vulcan Materials, still smarting over his encounter with Bull Connor during the parks campaign, phoned Vann, worried about his young friend's mental health if the referendum was defeated. Vann assured him that he had prepared two statements, "one if I win, one if I lose." At six that evening, after 37,176 ballots had been cast, Vann took out a brief typescript and read before the newsmen: "This has been an historic day for Birmingham. We have seen one of the most dramatic demonstrations of democracy that any of us will ever witness. We have proved that Birmingham is a city of great vitality—a city with a great future."

The gods had finally cut Vulcan's great workshop town some slack. By barely a 700-vote majority, Birmingham's promise was perpetuated, by a new form of government.

PART III

The Year of Birmingham
1963

11.

NEW DAY DAWNS

An Unauthorized Bombing

AT 9:15 ON DECEMBER 14, 1962, television sets in the North Birmingham neighborhood of Collegeville went dead in the middle of *The Beverly Hillbillies*. A cast-iron-pipe shrapnel bomb had ripped out power lines and shattered the windows of Bethel Baptist, Fred Shuttlesworth's former pulpit. Children were still in the basement rehearsing for a Christmas pageant, and two were taken to the hospital to be treated for facial cuts.

Apparently, the bombing was unauthorized, for Bull Connor went to see the site for himself. "Dammit, they ought to be hung when they're caught," he said, explaining to the *News* that Shuttlesworth's replacement at Bethel permitted no civil rights activities. Though he would later recover his bluster and assert, "We know that Negroes did it," it was the first serious sign that the vigilantes who had begun to act outside Connor's loose supervision paid no attention to contingencies like the possibility of killing children in a church basement.

The day before, Thomas E. Blanton Jr. had missed work at Hayes Aircraft and alerted a friend that something big was going to happen. Tommy had become one of Eastview 13's more troublesome members, who reflected badly on the red-blooded all-Americans in the group, motivated by alcohol and a desire to get away from their underprovided-for wives and children at night. Blanton, his eighty-year-old father, Pop (who, unlike most Klansmen, did not drink), and their great friend Robert Chambliss had formed a sort of extremist Eastview subculture that had begun to worry Gary Thomas Rowe. He had singled out the Blantons as bellyaching weirdos in his reports to the FBI.

If Pop Blanton wore his racism on his ferocious face, Tommy was more of an enigma, with moods swinging from dazed indifference to explosive anger. By many accounts he had seemed a normal "quiet young man" until he emerged from the Navy with an "I don't give a damn attitude," reflected in his inability to please his string of brief employers, including Walter "Crack" Hanna's prospering steel company. Although he had earned a high school diploma while in the Navy, Tommy didn't have the attention span even for Klan meetings. He was always enlisting Klansmen in marginal schemes, such as surveilling Catholic churches to identify Catholics so that he could put acid on their cars, or painting Catholic statuary black. His West End neighbor, a Catholic widow, received constant "anonymous calls," easily recognizing Tommy's voice since she had known him for eighteen years: "Niggers and Catholics have to die," he said. She assumed that it was he who had thrown a mustard jar filled with red paint onto her new white Fairlane and slashed the tires on both her cars.

Tommy's anti-Catholicism might have been dismissed as some old-fashioned Klan mannerism except that he had been raised Catholic by his mother, who died of cancer when he was eight. Tommy was confirmed in the Catholic church in Washington, D.C., where Pop's peripatetic life in construction had taken the family. Tommy's Klan friends seemed amused by his dirty little secret. The loss of his mother may also have accounted for his intense attachments to other men. Tommy confided to a girlfriend that he had homosexual experiences.

Tommy had turned on his once-doting, much older half sister, who lived as the family pariah in Apartment 2 of Pop's rental property in West End, where father and son shared Apartment 4. Both Blanton men accused Nellie of having a "mental condition," because she had frequented restaurants that served black people. In the summer of 1962, Pop had committed Nellie to Bryce, the state mental hospital at Tuscaloosa. One of Blanton's tenants told him he was sending the wrong child to the loony bin.

For some time now, Tommy had been talking about the ultimate Klan act: church bombing, albeit of Catholic rather than Negro congregations. His associates pronounced him not intelligent enough to make a bomb but dumb enough to place it. His comrades who seemed capable of both were Chambliss and Bobby Frank Cherry, the Eastview man Rowe named as a suspect in the triple-church bombing of January 1962. And of course, there was Chambliss's dynamite-savvy best friend, Troy Ingram, the most apparently "normal" member of this emerging Klan cabal.

Though the December 14 bombing of Shuttlesworth's old church was just inches from murder, the FBI did not investigate it, and the detectives from the Birmingham police left Eastview alone, focusing instead on an "outside agitator," a Klan-connected private eye from Atlanta who was staying at the Redmont Hotel, bragging of owning camera equipment that could take nude pictures of women wearing nylon clothes. It turned out that his main agenda in Birmingham was to prove that the Klan had not been responsible for the castration of Judge Aaron, who, coincidentally, had gotten a bit of good news recently.

Dissension

THE REVEREND HERB OLIVER had taken pity on the beggar Aaron had become since his brief confinement in the psychiatric ward at Tuskegee's V.A. hospital, and had lobbied to get him veterans' benefits to cover his $20-a-month injections of the synthetic male hormone Delastryl. After Alabama's congressional delegation ignored Oliver's entreaties, New York senator Kenneth Keating intervened, and in December the benefits started coming. Aaron and his mother soon joined family members in a northern city, where he was able to escape the stigma of the event he referred to as "when I was hurt." Aaron completely recovered his speech and became a babysitter to the kids in his neighborhood. In his wallet he carried pictures, cut from newspapers, of Oliver and Keating.

For all his effectiveness, Herb Oliver had not yet found a niche in the Movement. From the outside, he had watched the balance of power in the ACMHR destabilize in October when Vice President J. S. Phifer, a staunch Shuttlesworth loyalist, accepted a pulpit in White Plains, New York. Lucius Pitts was about to move on Shuttlesworth again. On the night of the Bethel bombing, Pitts called Shuttlesworth's old rival, J. L. Ware, and asked him to pull together some ministers to register a protest. Thrilled to be recognized as the broker of pastoral power, Ware confided to Oliver (sorrowfully, since he knew he was talking to a Shuttlesworth man) that Pitts was about to execute a coup. Pitts called a meeting for December 17—putatively out of concern for Shuttlesworth's old church, but excluding Shuttlesworth himself, though he was in town—and held it rather brazenly at the altar of Shuttlesworth's disgruntled lieutenant, Nelson "Fireball" Smith, who had brought Miles College into the Movement axis.

The fact of Pitts's meeting turned out to be more ominous than the substance—the usual airing of complaints about the police. Oliver left to attend the Movement mass meeting, where his protectiveness toward Shuttlesworth converted to wounded pride. As Oliver was reciting a poem he had written to drum up support for a renewed retail boycott ("When I enter a store, I want to be more/Than a market exploited each day;/I want to be able to sit at a table/And order some food and be gay"), Shuttlesworth cut him off. Oliver's special status as a friend and confidant to all the black factions seemed to have turned.

Unaware that SCLC's flagship there was in a state of critical disruption, Martin Luther King guided the nation's attention toward Birmingham. After the Bethel bombing, he telegrammed President Kennedy, demanding federal protection in what was "by far the worst big city in race relations in the United States." When he and several other national black figures met with Kennedy three nights later to discuss African affairs, King again brought up the Bethel explosion, pressing the President to make a public commitment to civil rights. Kennedy, who was now playing down the Ole Miss debacle as an obstacle to his education bill, was noncommittal.

Hardening

ON NEW YEAR'S DAY, Alabama faced Oklahoma in the Orange Bowl—not, alas, for the national championship. Bama had lost 7–6 to Georgia Tech late in the season after missing a two-point conversion. (It was a point of honor that Bear Bryant never went for the tie.) Vincent Townsend's editorial page editor, E. L. "Red" Holland, had written to the Justice Department's civil rights chief, Burke

Marshall, in December, saying he understood that "Governor Bryant" had invited President Kennedy to attend the game in Miami. Usually, Bryant was linked with church rather than state—"The Bear walks on water." His televised post-game recap, *The Bear Bryant Show*, had become the City of Churches' strictest Sunday ritual, as the archdruid took to the airwaves to apologize for letting his "fine boys" down—failing to scout the other team's punt returner or some such—while sampling the show's sponsors' products, Coca-Cola and Golden Flake potato chips. (The sackcloth-and-ashes routine went down quite easily, given that the team had won the day before.) And so Holland suggested that Kennedy take advantage of the Bear's mystique and wrote in careful code, "The presence of the President very conceivably could do much, in subtle ways, to the thinking of many people."

The week after Christmas, President Kennedy was indeed at the Orange Bowl in Miami, but addressing a rally honoring the returning heroes of the Bay of Pigs. The Justice Department's ranking Birminghamian, Lou Oberdorfer, had been in charge of putting together a ransom package of pharmaceuticals and medicines that Fidel Castro had demanded in exchange for the 113 badly deteriorating Brigade members (including three CIA agents) captured during the invasion a year and a half earlier. (The four dead Alabama Air National Guardsmen would lie unclaimed for years in the Havana morgue.) At the Orange Bowl rally, the President made an unscripted remark that the Brigade's flag would one day fly over "a free Havana." Forty thousand Cuban exiles began weeping and, to the horror of some dovish Kennedy aides, chanting "Guerra! Guerra!"

When the President returned to the Orange Bowl four days later, more than half the capacity crowd was screaming "Roll, Tide!" Before the game, Kennedy stopped by the locker room to bestow go-get-'ems on the Oklahoma team and its coach, Bud Wilkinson, his recent appointee to head the President's Council on Physical Fitness. Bryant received no audience, and his team not even cursory benedictions. As Kennedy tossed the pre-kickoff coin, Alabama's captain, Lee Roy Jordan, eyed him as if he were the opposing center. The bourbon toasts that followed Bama's 17–0 win had the cold taste of secessionist revenge.

Celebration

ON THAT FIRST DAY of 1963, Tommy Blanton took his girlfriend on a joyride through Fountain Heights, the much-dynamited "transitional" neighborhood going black. Blanton liked to impress dates with jokes about the bombings in Birmingham, most recently the Bethel blast. New Year's Day seemed to demand a special feat of braggadocio. Spotting a Negro man step into the intersection, he veered right, toward the pedestrian, who made a dive for the curb. As his date screamed, Blanton complained that he had wanted to "kill the black bastard." He continued down Sixteenth Street in his white-on-blue 1957 Chevy, toward the famous black Baptist church.

On January 10, a few blocks from Blanton's swerve, Maurice and Ann Ryles found four sticks of dynamite in a paper bag, the fuses burned down to the blasting cap. Whatever his technical deficiencies, the bomb maker had an uncanny sense of timing. Maurice Ryles was about to become a behind-the-scenes player in the nonviolent revolution being plotted that day by the Southern Christian Leadership Conference in Georgia. Ryles was a black bail bondsman who would have a crucial role in managing the traffic in and out of Bull Connor's jail come spring.

Project X

BLACK PEOPLE had an old saying that it would take a hundred years to get freedom: from 1863, when the Emancipation Proclamation was issued, to 1963. With no intimations of liberation, Fred Shuttlesworth flew to Georgia on January 10 to join Martin Luther King, Ralph Abernathy, Wyatt Walker, and a handful of seasoned strategists, including Stanley Levison and Jack O'Dell, at a retreat in Dorchester, just south of Savannah. SCLC was about to embark on its first premeditated campaign, Project X. It was time to shoulder the cross and go into Birmingham.

King was balking. The leader of the civil rights movement had yet to initiate a civil rights action, having been shanghaied into every Movement port back to Montgomery. "We've got to move in Birmingham," Shuttlesworth said impatiently to his colleagues gathered at a former Congregational missionary school that the Highlander Folk School's Myles Horton had acquired for SCLC from the National Council of Churches. "We've been hammering away for seven years with no impact," Shuttlesworth continued. "If segregation is going to fall, we've got to at least crack the wall in Birmingham."

A cautionary example of gradualism at its best had issued three days earlier from the Supreme Court, which consented to hear the *New York Times*'s appeal of the *Sullivan* verdicts. The *Times* did not see much of a constitutional precedent at stake; libel law had always been strictly a state matter, and no libel judgments, even ones as fantastic as those under appeal, had been overturned on First Amendment grounds.

But neither had direct action "redeemed the soul of America"—the goal SCLC had proclaimed at the time of its founding. It had not even done much for a small town in Georgia. Before taking on Birmingham, SCLC would have to figure out what had gone wrong in Albany, which seemed to have everything going for it except success. The "lessons of Albany" that emerged from the Dorchester meeting would become a Movement mantra, and they generally boiled down to too many chiefs (SNCC, SCLC, and the Albany natives) and too many targets. Instead of Albany's scattershot attack on public facilities, the Movement clearly needed to pick smaller, winnable battles so that it could *declare* victory—sort of the reverse m.o. of the white southern politician, for whom "winning" lay in the act of defiance rather than the outcome. Defiance, of course, had been the refuge of Albany's city commission against the Movement's demands. Another lesson of Albany: In the absence of black voting strength, it made no sense to pressure politicians. Segregation's vulnerable belly, as had been clear as far back as the Montgomery bus boycott, was the economic establishment.

To Shuttlesworth, these lessons were beside the point. They had indeed been implemented in Birmingham, even as SCLC was learning them in Albany. The department store boycott of 1962, a model of intramural cooperation between Shuttlesworth and Lucius Pitts's Miles College gang, had ignored city hall and targeted the business leaders, and its aims had been the same limited ones that SCLC would now, a year later, propose for its Birmingham project—desegregation of store facilities, job opportunities for blacks, and the establishment of a biracial civic task force. The only thing wrong with the Birmingham campaign of 1962 was that it hadn't worked.

The real lesson of Albany was that nonviolence could not succeed without violence—segregationist violence. The Georgia town's ingratiating police chief, Laurie Pritchett, had, the saying went, killed the Movement with kindness. After reviewing the law enforcement lapse at Birmingham's Trailways station on Mother's Day 1961, Pritchett had concluded that the police had harmed their own segregationist cause, provoking the federal government as well as the public conscience in a way that the integrationists' actions alone were not able to do. So he had studied up on Gandhi and had prepared for the Mahatma's "fill the jails" mandate by busing his prisoners to cells in neighboring counties, thereby removing the bodily witness from Albany proper. Pritchett's hostile comments had remained private. Publicly, he was the perfect gentleman—removing his hat and bowing his head as if in prayer before arresting kneeling ministers.

Albany's "gentle" apartheid had not aroused the public. Robert Kennedy had wired Pritchett congratulations for his restraint. Unless the federal government intervened and ordered segregationists to behave—as it had during the mob scenes at Little Rock, Montgomery (after the Freedom Rider riot), and Oxford—blows for civil rights were nothing but sucker punches. In the absence of government intercession in Autherine Lucy's behalf, the University of Alabama had remained white. And the only progress Albany blacks could claim was that they were now occasionally called "Mr." and "Mrs."

The segregationists of Birmingham had "cooperated" with the Movement in the way that Laurie Pritchett hadn't. But ultimately, all Shuttlesworth's "publicity stunts"—the chain-beating in front of Phillips High School, the jailings that had gotten him nicknamed "the Stonewall Colonel"—had yielded no meaningful publicity. In a culture obsessed as much with celebrity as with violence, some magic formula of both was required to elevate victims to martyrs. And that was why Shuttlesworth needed Martin Luther King. "Go where the Mahatma goes" was the news editors' instructions to their correspondents covering King. "He might get killed." In acknowledgment of the perhaps fatal violence invited by direct action in Bull Connor's town, Project X would become Project C, for "Confrontation": huge, jail-filling, history-making demonstrations, during the symbolically freighted Easter season.

A junior strategist at Dorchester sat silent as the practical planning of the

Birmingham confrontation was deferred to Wyatt Walker. Twenty-four-year-old James Bevel, a veteran of the Nashville Movement, who had recently married Diane Nash (to the great sorrow of her many admirers), had left SNCC during the Albany campaign to become SCLC's field secretary in his native Mississippi, where whites had seized his father's land because he had sent a son and a daughter to college. (Bevel had spent half his childhood in his father's adopted city of Cleveland.) A teenage religious conversion had made him turn his back on a rock-and-roll recording contract and head for Nashville's tuition-free American Baptist Theological Seminary, where one of his comrades was the practitioner of nonviolence John Lewis, of Troy, Alabama. Bevel's first "Gandhian" protest, as the Movement's most eccentric charismatic, had been to liberate the rarely circulated books on the Mahatma from the library, explaining, "Gandhi was about changing the world, books on the shelf ain't never changed nothing."

By the time of the Dorchester meeting, Bevel wore a yarmulke on his shaved head—"I consider myself a rabbi"—in deference to what he called the "science" of Judaism. Although Bevel did not scorn King as did the "young SNCC guys who were not *basically* Christian," he did share their dislike of Wyatt Walker—and the *creased* blue jeans he wore. Watching him run the strategy meeting at Dorchester, Bevel was dumbfounded that none of the grown men there would state that the real trouble with Albany was the "psychological problem" of Walker himself.

Walker, Bevel believed, was "spiritually a boss" rather than a "brother." This bent had undeniably benefited SCLC, which he had transformed from a letterhead to a fully staffed organization. Walker's defect was that he thought of the Movement in terms of "getting hired hands to get something done." Bevel understood that the critical ingredients of a nonviolent campaign were "community and commitment"—to which he considered black males generally allergic. The fractious ministers of Birmingham were a case in point, and yet, when the Dorchester discussions addressed whether Project X could count on the black clergy's support, Shuttlesworth was dismissive: "Don't worry, Martin, I can handle the preachers."

Bevel knew that Shuttlesworth could be counted on because he was "very clear on personal righteousness, social responsibility, and the absolutely guaranteed outcome of that." But in view of the Walker problem, Bevel determined then and there that if the Birmingham campaign was going to work, he, rather than Walker, would have to be in charge.

This planning session for SCLC's first mass execution of nonviolence ended in the contemplation of violence. King looked around at his dozen friends and said that some of them might not make it back from Birmingham alive. Then, with his marvelous ability to turn sanctimony on its head, he preached irreverent mock eulogies for each one. Some believed that King was preparing for his own death in Birmingham by joking about it. It didn't strike anyone as ironic that, with the arrival of King, SCLC, and the national media, Fred Shuttlesworth would be the safest he had been in his career.

Chafing to catch his flight back to Birmingham, Shuttlesworth asked King and Abernathy to drive him to Savannah. Arriving at the airport just as the plane for Birmingham was taking off, King said with humorous sympathy, "Ralph, I be-*lieve* Fred has missed his plane." Inside the terminal, Shuttlesworth said, "Gentle-men, I'm powerful hungry," and led them into the all-white lunch room, instructing them, "Leave some stools between us. Some white folks may want to sit down." To the waitress who was sullenly ignoring the leaders of the civil rights movement, Shuttlesworth called, "Little lady, if you don't want your airport to make the history books, you better serve me." But the only record for posterity was the rolls of surveillance film that the FBI shot of the SCLC members' com-ings and goings at the airport, assuming the revolutionary plot being hatched at Dorchester to be Marxist-Leninist.

Hosea's Vindication

THE FBI BELIEVED it had gotten to the bottom of the Communist conspiracy inside the civil rights movement, and it was none other than Birmingham's old proletariat hero from the 1930s and 1940s, Hosea Hudson. If there was anyone who was a personal testament to the American Communist Party's devolution from the overtaxed engine of "Negro liberation" to a marginal sect of internecine intrigue, it was Hudson, now husbanding his meager Party paycheck in the New York area. In May 1962, a bureau Teletype to J. Edgar Hoover from Atlanta's spe-cial agent in charge had made the first documented connection between Hudson and Martin Luther King, warning that Hudson might join the imminent SCLC activity in Shreveport, Louisiana, through the machinations of Jack O'Dell. There immediately followed a summary of the FBI's dossier on Hudson, from his firing by Stockham Valves in the early 1930s, to his ousting by the Steelworkers union in 1947, to his support of the Southern Negro Youth Congress's 1948 protest against the anti-labor Taft-Hartley bill. In August, FBI agents went down to SCLC's Dorchester retreat and showed a picture of Hudson to someone con-nected with the center, to see if he had been part of the training going on there.

The photographs and film the FBI netted in January of the small, dapper Stanley Levison greeting King, Shuttlesworth, Abernathy, Joe Lowery, and Wyatt Walker at the Savannah airport (Levison, who did not like to fly, had arrived ear-lier by train) would have been reward enough for J. Edgar Hoover. But then there was the added bonanza of Jack O'Dell's attendance at the retreat, even though he had supposedly resigned from the SCLC staff. Robert Kennedy forwarded the FBI's memo on this surprise finding to his civil rights chief, Burke Marshall, an-notated: "Burke—this is not getting any better."

A week after the Dorchester conference, Hoover circulated a document col-lating various tidbits proving King's Communist associations. Among items on the order of a 1961 editorial in *The Worker* supporting SCLC's voter registration efforts was the statement of a man—an informant perhaps—who had said the previous fall that "most of the South's racial troubles could be solved by the elim-ination of Martin Luther King" and that his "underworld contact in New Orleans" said he would murder King for $2,000. There is no indication that the FBI alerted King or did anything to discourage the would-be assassin.

Segregation Forever!

ON JANUARY 14, George Wallace, natty in striped pants and cutaway, stepped up to the microphone in the portico of the state capitol. Preparing for this inaugural moment, the governor-elect had told a group of state senators, "I'm gonna make race the basis of politics in this state, and I'm gonna make it the basis of politics in this country." The vulgarity of Wallace's speech, the obsessiveness of its racism, astonished even his closest advisers. "Today I have stood where Jefferson Davis stood, and took an oath to my people," he said. "It is very appropriate then that from this Cradle of the Confederacy, this very heart of the great Anglo-Saxon Southland, that today we sound the drum for freedom. Let us rise to the call of the freedom-loving blood that is in us. In the name of the greatest people that have ever trod this earth, I draw the line in the dust and toss the gauntlet before the feet of tyranny. And I say, Segregation now! Segregation tomorrow! Segregation forever!"

The closing stemwinder of the inaugural address had a lush romanticism normally lacking in Wallace's mean and sinewy rhetoric, and it confirmed an unheralded political comeback by one of Alabama's most infamous segregationists. Ace Carter, the old Big Mule Citizens Council hand turned redneck redeemer, had come out of semi-retirement on his cattle farm (since the 1957 shoot-out that cut short his career as a Klan leader) to write speeches for Wallace during the previous spring's gubernatorial primary. Frightened by the almost physiological fury, fueled by cigarette after cigarette, that gripped Carter while he composed his harangues, Wallace's aides had paid him secretly, through middlemen. The more temperate members of the staff tried to keep his prose out of the hands of the governor-elect as the swearing-in approached. But Carter had gotten to him and, pointing to the "Segregation forever!" finale—an echo of the old Klan motto "Here Yesterday! Here Tomorrow! Here Forever!"—told Wallace, "Here's the lines that are gonna catch everybody."

The man assigned to make Carter's pledge legal was Jim Simpson. The governor credited his first job, as Simpson's fifteen-year-old gofer in 1935, as "probably the key to much of my later interest in politics." And now the Great Man was serving Wallace, as the chairman of his Committee on Constitutional Law and Sovereignty, a new blue-ribbon group of lawyers dedicated to preserving segregation. In his old page, Simpson had latched on to a proxy who would finally make a national success of his old anti–New Deal race agenda. And not a moment too soon, now that Simpson's municipal franchise was slipping away.

Anointing a Mayor

BULL CONNOR had announced that he was running for mayor under the new form of city government he had declared communistic. When Commissioner

Jabo Waggoner also threw his hat into the mayoral ring, Vincent Townsend sent over one of the *News*'s senior reporters to ask him to withdraw, dangling a high appointment under a Townsend-approved administration. As the city's rough-around-the-edges public works commissioner (though the owner of a diploma from North Carolina's Elon College, where he had played right halfback under the quasi-legendary Peahead Walker), James T. "Jabo" Waggoner was a career street-sanitation man, never so happy as when he was taking over routes for garbage collectors who called in sick. He had proved so indifferent to the higher functions of leadership that Townsend called him "Ironhead." True to his name, Waggoner refused to bow out.

As for Art Hanes, he had long since come to regret the long-distance call from Lew Jeffers on Kennedy's inauguration day directing him to seek office. On commission business, Bull and Jabo had ganged up on him unmercifully. And Clint Bishop, the scheming executive secretary he had inherited from the outgoing mayor, Jimmy Morgan, had been a constant vexation ever since Hanes, either forgetting or not understanding that the support he had gotten from the "House of Morgan" was contingent upon Bishop retaining his job, had tried to fire him. Though Hanes had quickly backed down, Bishop had made him pay, enlisting his old "black-hand" collaborator, the *News*'s Tom Lankford, to tape and photograph Hanes on his lengthy lunchtime assignations at the Tutwiler. It was only when Bishop played some tapes for the husband of one of the mayoral appointments that Hanes figured out who had been calling Lankford's shots on those particular assignments. "You've hurt me enough," he begged Bishop. When the election mooted his office, Hanes performed the one principled act of his mayoralty and fired his executive secretary. Marking time till he could pack up and leave, Hanes busied himself with such official duties as sending auto tags with the city slogan, "It's Nice to Have You in Birmingham," to the Lord Mayor of Birmingham, England. Sadly he insisted that he would have been better off as a football coach than a public official.

The intrigue settled on whom the reformers would tap to run for mayor and lead Birmingham into the post-segregation era. The moderates' old man on horseback, Tom King, was now working as an arbitrator for the National Labor Relations Board and struggling in private practice. Eager to be back in the saddle, he pleaded his candidacy before Vincent Townsend, who tersely explained that priorities had changed. The goal now was simply to get rid of Bull Connor. And to do so the forces of progress had decided to go with a proven bigot.

The Boutwell Dilemma

ON GROUNDS of charisma alone, fifty-eight-year-old Albert Boutwell ought to have been disqualified from running. He was short, bespectacled, and sickly looking, his presentation screaming "fishy handshake." He donned a chef's hat during backyard barbecues, and for a hobby he bowled, badly.

Boutwell had begun his political career as an outsider, the poor, country Goddamn Independent candidate for student government president at the Uni-

versity of Alabama in the mid-1920s. He defeated the Greek machine, but in contrast to his fellow South Alabamian Jim Folsom, who had engineered the election
upset, Boutwell had dedicated his political talent to upward mobility and opened
a law practice under the wing of the future Dixiecrat Frank Dixon. Elected in
1946 as the Big Mules' surrogate to succeed Jim Simpson in the state senate, he
became the slick commander of the bloc of lawmakers who crushed Folsom's
program during both terms. His legislative claim to fame was the Pupil Placement
(or Freedom of Choice) Act that had neutralized the *Brown* decision—and impelled Fred Shuttlesworth to take a beating in front of Phillips High School. As
the lieutenant governor–elect in December 1958, he had convened a regionwide
segregationist think tank, including Governor-elect John Patterson and a Georgia lawyer (and future moderate U.S. attorney general) Griffin Bell, to "carry this
fight to the people nationally."

Boutwell had been the intellectual adviser to the White Citizens Councils, delivering the council-sponsored radio address against the Civil Rights Act
of 1957 ("monstrous legislation"), and he had been a prominent figure in the
Methodist Layman's Union—in other words, a Dixiecrat through all their modern permutations. Yet he had a way of appearing to be all things to all people. His
fellow Citizens Council honcho Sid Smyer took the lead in drafting Boutwell to
run for mayor. But he was also promoted by the liberal lawyer Abe Berkowitz, his
roommate at the University of Alabama, who had remained a close friend despite
Boutwell's coziness with the union-busting anti-Semitic propagandists of the
1940s, who considered him "as one" with them on the Jewish question.*

Boutwell was touted as the most successful politician in Jefferson County
history (seven for seven races). But did he have the wiles to "seg"—the polite form
of the verb "nigger"—his way to victory at the same time he was accepting the inevitability of desegregation?

Competence

"WE HAVE HEARD from the Little House in Montgomery," the Reverend Ed
Gardner quipped at the Alabama Christian Movement mass meeting on the night
that George Wallace drew his line in the dust. The speaker of honor, Emory O.
Jackson, advised the Movement, in the words of Joe Louis's manager, to "move in,
hit high, and keep your punches high for 1963."

March 14 had been set as the kickoff date for SCLC's Birmingham Project X.
The strategists had wanted to begin the campaign earlier, to peak during the
Easter shopping season, but Shuttlesworth had reversed his position since Dor-
chester and insisted on delaying till after the March 5 mayoral race between Bull
Connor, Albert Boutwell, and Tom King, to deprive Connor of any winning

---

* Even Emory O. Jackson had seen fit, two weeks before the announcement of the *Brown* decision
Boutwell was sabotaging, to praise in the *World* his "sense of fairness and justice to all people," citing his fight against the poll tax and his support of Jackson's sister's lawsuit to equalize black and
white schoolteachers' salaries.

propaganda. The organizers took *noms de guerre* to baffle Connor's wiretaps. King was "JFK," Walker "RFK," Abernathy "Dean Rusk," the secretary of state. Shuttlesworth answered both to Defense Secretary "McNamara" ("Mac") and to "Bull." But Project X was still very much a work on paper.

Its most hopeful asset at this point seemed to be the sympathy between its field marshal, Wyatt Walker, and Shuttlesworth, its host and sponsor. Of all SCLC's key members, Walker would say later, "Shuttlesworth and I were most akin. The difference was that Fred was absolutely fearless. He would walk into the teeth of the Klan in the middle of the night without alerting AP and UPI. I was calculatedly fearless. I tried to wait until some TV cameras were there to make it worthwhile." As the self-avowed "king of ego, dahlin'," Walker approved of the "Wild Man from Birmingham" with less ambivalence than his colleagues and meant no offense in decreeing Project X's policy of "tiptoeing around Fred's ego." Walker understood that "the only reason we had Birmingham was Shuttlesworth."

Shuttlesworth was not bothering himself with the organizational details, on the theory that, with a little help from Walker, "God was directing it." Walker continued to treat Project X as a military maneuver, making reconnoitering trips to draw up the "battle plan" for a four-stage campaign of sit-ins, marches, and store boycotts. Leaving it to the ACMHR's workhorse secretaries, Julia Rainge and Georgia Price, to round up the first "baptismal candidates" (the demonstrators' designations), Walker studied the city code covering parades, identified the local bail bondsmen, and scouted various routes from Sixteenth Street Baptist Church to city hall, calibrating how long it would take a child, an adult, and an old person to make the march. At potential sit-in sites, he counted the stools and diagrammed the exits. Competence could substitute for vision, up to a point.

The only sure thing Walker thought he had for the Birmingham campaign was the solid infrastructure of the ACMHR. But Shuttlesworth's unstable Movement was now on the verge of mutiny. At a February board meeting at Ed Gardner's humble church in the eastern Birmingham neighborhood of Woodlawn, a cold front swept through the room as Nelson Smith, the Movement's Big Preacher secretary, and his parishioner Lola Hendricks, the corresponding secretary, asked if it was all right for the board to make decisions when the president was away. Suspicious, Shuttlesworth demanded some for instances. Smith muttered about a fundraising plan that he had left at home. Shuttlesworth surveyed his comrades and said, "Everyone come clean, and lay the cards on the table." Charles Billups, the tough-sweet Shuttlesworth loyalist with the steel plate in his head, threatened to say right there what his fellow board members (a "bunch of hypocrites") had "been saying on the outside." Smith and another board member talked loudly until Billups fell silent.

On the morning of February 7, Martin Luther King, Ralph Abernathy, and Wyatt Walker appeared at the Gaston Motel to discuss Project X. Had they been intimate with the personalities of the ACMHR, they might have been troubled when Shuttlesworth arrived only with Herb Oliver. There was a white man in the motel's Masters Lounge, suggesting why Oliver had been invited into this inner sanctum. The U.S. Civil Rights Commission had scheduled hearings in Birmingham for April 22 and 23, on the basis of the painstaking affidavits on police brutality Oliver's Inter-Citizens Committee had sown around the country. Arnold Treback, a commission member, had come down from Washington to determine how SCLC's plans might affect the hearings. He urged the ministers to cancel the Birmingham project.

Oliver was jealous for his own show, but he was also genuinely skeptical about the coming "boycott," as he understood SCLC's campaign, and predicted failure if one of two conditions was not met. The white powers would have to make a "mistake" like jailing Shuttlesworth, which had sparked the spring department store boycott, in order to mobilize a "spontaneous" protest. Otherwise, a situation would have to be created to stir up the community. When King said that Albany was an example of the Movement creating the unity, Oliver incredulously pointed out that Albany had been a failure. Wyatt Walker, the tactician, asked if Oliver was against direct action under any circumstances, or only if the community was not properly unified. (The latter.) Oliver expressed the same doubts Jim Bevel had about Walker: The "field marshal" was going to be leading an army of deserters.

Delay

THE STRATEGISTS behind Albert Boutwell's campaign had had a piece of good news. George Wallace was supporting Bull Connor. This played perfectly into their hopes of tying Connor to the "outsider" (Wallace had not carried Birmingham) whom one newspaper editor was too optimistically calling "the loneliest man in Alabama." The state's Responsible Citizens had mobilized against Wallace—including Big Mules, reactionary newspapers, and even the University of Alabama's Dixiecrat-dominated board of trustees—urging him to enforce "law and order," the old Bourbon warning cry against Populist insurrection now a euphemism for integration. Wallace replied that he had heard enough about "law and order."

A most unlikely moderate spokesman—a local U.S. Steel executive—charged that Wallace and Connor were giving Alabama a reputation for "reaction, rebellion and riots, of bigotry, bias and backwardness ... trouble with a capital 'T.' " In a city-limits version of Wallace's "Stand in the Schoolhouse Door," Connor was pledging to close the public schools rather than integrate them. In other Wallace echoes, he brayed at the Supreme Court and offered to personally fight the attorney general of the United States. Wallace's comments on Robert Kennedy during his own campaign had been so obscene as to be unprintable.

On a tornado-swept primary day, March 5, Albert Boutwell led the mayor's race with 39 percent of the vote. There would be a runoff between him and the second-place Bull Connor, who had beat Tom King by only 2,000 votes.

Wyatt Walker's *i*'s came undotted. Although launching Project X as scheduled on March 14 would give Connor a fabulous "niggering" opportunity leading up to the April 2 runoff, postponement might kill the campaign altogether. Jim

Bevel thought that the Movement should begin the campaign when the people were ready, and that was now. Some 250 "baptismal candidates" had signed commitment cards to keep the ten commandments of nonviolence ("Refrain from the violence of fist, tongue or heart"; "observe with both friend and foe the ordinary rules of courtesy"). Shuttlesworth agonized between his own impulse for rash action and the locals' importunings for delay. Lucius Pitts, who was frantic to avert the demonstrations now that they were no longer his fictional threats, pressed on Sid Smyer the names of five black people who might be amenable to negotiation. Apparently, Smyer never made the overtures.

As it turned out, SCLC's Atlantans had begun to lose their zest for a showdown with Connor and would just as soon conduct Project Confrontation in the relatively nonconfrontational environment of a Boutwell administration. King had his own worries about what he was calling "the Birmingham thing," given the *News*'s past interest in Jack O'Dell. "They are going to do everything they can to destroy the image of SCLC," he told Levison over the phone. The two agreed to keep paying O'Dell through the subterfuge of a middleman. The gleanings from the FBI's wiretap of the conversation were sent to the field office in Birmingham as well as to J. Edgar Hoover.

Perhaps the most compelling reason to delay the campaign had nothing to do with either Birmingham or SCLC. New York was in the midst of a months-long newspaper strike. Without the *New York Times*, Birmingham's sins might remain hidden not only from the outside world but from its own white citizens as well. SCLC decided to hold up till after the runoff.

Boutwell indulged in the doublespeak of the moderate politician, pledging to "defend and maintain" segregation as long as Birmingham didn't become "a city of unrestrained and unhampered mockery of the law." But he was no longer pretending to himself that the race was other than a referendum on segregation. In the office of his old college roommate Abe Berkowitz, in perhaps what would be the high point of a career that would sink into ambiguity, Boutwell met with attorney Arthur Shores's black political "machine." Accompanying him there, David Vann heard words he had doubted a southern politician would utter in his lifetime. Boutwell, once segregation's brightest custodian, promised the assembled black lawyers, undertakers, dentists, and preachers, including Fred Shuttlesworth, that when he took office Birmingham's Jim Crow ordinances would be repealed. Jaded by his recent experience with the power structure, Shuttlesworth gathered that what Boutwell was offering was the same old "progress, but we cain't make commitments, like desegregated toilets, on behalf of the merchants." As far as black people were concerned, Shuttlesworth said, Boutwell was "a crying bull" to Connor's "roaring bull."

The next day, Tuesday, March 19, during a layover in Atlanta, Shuttlesworth met with King. From a pay phone, he checked in with the ACMHR's secretary Georgia Price, who held the receiver up to her radio. Bull Connor was making a campaign speech, accusing Shuttlesworth of cooking up something with Martin Luther King to disrupt the coming election. Shuttlesworth dictated a press release to Price disguised as a directive to his constituents, warning that Connor planned to stage a racial incident and blame the ACMHR. Shuttlesworth urged King and Walker to "lay low, with no visible signs of forthcoming action" until election day. The "Move-Off" as Shuttlesworth called the launch of the Birmingham project, was now April 3, the day after the runoff.

Men on Horseback

THE BIRMINGHAM MUNICIPAL AUDITORIUM had been the scene of Bull Connor's two greatest triumphs, the Southern Conference for Human Welfare founding session in 1938 and the Dixiecrat convention ten years later. At the first he had managed to make democratic progress seem a subversive alien ideology, and at the second he had dressed up a recipe for fascism as a legitimate third-party platform for president. Now in the spring of 1963, thanks to Birmingham, the most radical part of the agenda of that 1938 liberal front—the racial equality advanced by the Communists—was about to become a national priority. And so it seemed fitting that the remains of the once awesome reactionary resistance—ranging from Birmingham City Hall to the committee rooms of Congress to the board rooms of Wall Street and even to the Reichstag—came back to the Municipal Auditorium to shore up the waning career of its old mascot, Bull Connor.

On March 8, the auditorium was the boisterous scene of a rally by the Reverend Billy James Hargis, the Tulsa-based evangelist who generated radio broadcasts and all manner of print propaganda based on his reading of Acts 17:26 proving that segregation was ordained by God. The board of his Christian Crusade had become a haven for the most infamous of the old Roosevelt-era anti-Semites. This evening was part of Hargis's twenty-seven-city "superpatriotic" tour, Operation Midnight, to audition former Major General Edwin "Ted" Walker, the headline speaker (and the celebrity of the Ole Miss riots), as the "man on horseback" for the movement. But, though tall and handsome, Walker was proving to be too ineffective a speaker—incoherent sometimes—to command a movement, and soon Hargis would become part of the national right-wing brain trust that would coalesce around George Wallace's presidential aspirations.

Tonight's rally had been turned into a campaign opportunity for Bull Connor, drawing the city's most committed segregationist battlers. Besides the predictable Eastview contingent, there were Dr. Edward Fields of the National States Rights Party and Ace Carter, making his first public appearance in some time. Robert Chambliss parked himself at the auditorium door, host and greeter, wearing his blue suit rather than khakis, smoking and handing out literature for Connor.

These vestiges of the heyday of reaction would always find a sentimental welcome in Birmingham—if not at the country club any longer, at least, for a time, at city hall. Bull Connor was looking ahead to his last stand, but it would also be his most memorable.

Beginning to Live

AT A LITTLE BEFORE nine o'clock on the evening of March 24, 1963, a bomb exploded at the residence of Elizabeth Williams on a back alley of a black downtown neighborhood. After Williams and a friend were taken to University Hospital to be treated for injuries, a police wagon carried off the Negroes who had gathered to sympathize with the families. On the basis of a Negro girl's assertion that a black man had threatened to blow up the place during a fight with a black woman, the police would classify the bombing as "non-racial." Gary Thomas Rowe's FBI handlers would suspect otherwise because of the immediacy with which their informant had notified them of the blast. No TV cameras showed up at the crime scene. The Mahatma had not yet come.

Martin Luther King arrived quietly on the Friday night before the election—two days after the birth of his fourth child, Bernice Albertine—to meet with the very few local men and women in on the Move-Off. King asked Herb Oliver (who was not among the informed) for his Inter-Citizens Committee affidavits on police brutality, which he needed for a meeting whose nature and location he did not divulge.

On Sunday, March 31, King and Oliver's affidavits were in the Manhattan apartment of Harry Belafonte, the Jamaican-born singer who acted as one of SCLC's most reliable fundraisers in between concerts. "Dr. King and Reverend Shuttlesworth are meeting with some of their friends at Harry's apartment," Belafonte's secretary had cryptically said in inviting some seventy-five New Yorkers, an advance guard of radical chic. Belafonte had suggested to King that donors might be more generous if they felt they were included in the planning of a campaign rather than called in at the point of crisis—if they were apprised, in other words, that the crisis was intentional.

Sworn to secrecy for this briefing, three days before Project X's Move-Off, were off-duty journalists (the *New York Post*'s James Wechsler, whose brother Herbert, a Columbia Law professor, had written the successful Supreme Court *cert* petition for *The New York Times* v. *Sullivan*), clergymen, actors (Anthony Quinn), an aide to New York governor Nelson Rockefeller, and William Kunstler, the radical New York lawyer involved in the appeals of Shuttlesworth's 1962 jailing. To many of them, King appeared to be more a cocktail party companion than an oppressed Negro as he discoursed dispassionately on the goals of the campaign—relief from the brutality of the Birmingham police described in Oliver's affidavits—and its timing ("If Boutwell is elected, we'll probably be criticized for not giving him a chance").

Fred Shuttlesworth stood by, run-down and sniffling from a brutal airplane itinerary. When it was his turn to speak, he said, "You have to be prepared to die before you can begin to live." He had merely articulated a daily fact of black southern life, but the roomful of New Yorkers greeted his speech with "a silence," King would recall, "almost like the shock of a fresh discovery." Belafonte closed the pitch by naming a committee to raise the huge bail fund needed to float a campaign predicated on filling the jails.

As if Shuttlesworth's hands-on fundamentalist God had given the campaign His go-ahead, the New York newspaper strike ended the next day. That night, Wyatt Walker appeared before the regular Monday meeting of the ACMHR; he had performed his role so discreetly that the Birmingham police identified him as "Wayne Walker, who is Martin Luther's secretary." Most of the 250 "baptismal candidates" he had rounded up earlier to be arrested were nowhere to be found. Walker hastily called up new troops—"prospective voters"—for private briefings in a back office of the church.

Election Day

BULL CONNOR seemed to have decided that his best campaign strategy was to run against the *Saturday Evening Post*. Within the space of three weeks in March, the magazine published two devastating assaults on Alabama's most precious institutions. Writing in sadness more than outrage, Joe David Brown, a former *Birmingham Post* reporter who had fictionalized Art Hanes's father, the flamboyant Methodist circuit rider, in his novel *Stars in My Crown,** went after Our Way of Life and its chief guardian, "Ole Bull," finding little to praise in his hometown except the new Bank for Savings skyscraper. In its March 23 issue, the *Post* struck again, against an even more sacred target, Bear Bryant. An article alleged that the Crimson Tide's fall win over the University of Georgia Bulldogs had been a "fix" between coaches Bryant and Wally Butts; the accuser was a Georgia man who, through some fluke of technology, had patched into the two coaches' telephone discussion of game plans. Bryant submitted to the indignity of a lie detector test and then, refusing to turn the other cheek, sued the *Post*.

Hoping to bask in Bryant's martyrdom, Connor added the *Post* to the list of "outside agitators" who were out to get him. These also included the "Mountain Brook–controlled Chamber of Commerce," whose tyrant for the past half century, U.S. Steel, was his most prominent remaining supporter. His pokes at Boutwell as the candidate of the "Negro bloc vote" seemed wondrously understated.

On April 2, an election day inspiring the largest turnout in the city's history, Martin Luther King and Ralph Abernathy flew to Birmingham. Spotting Shuttlesworth at the airport, they shot each other cynical looks: The greeting committee consisted only of three Shuttlesworth yes-men. "Where's Ware?" King asked, darting his eyes meaningfully around the terminal.

J. L. Ware had been busy that spring making a quixotic run for the new city council, and Shuttlesworth did not tell King that there was no way on God's earth that he would trust Ware with information about Project X. He merely explained

---

* His more famous novel would be *Addie Pray,* made into the movie *Paper Moon.*

that Ware was holding the regular Tuesday meeting of his ministers, accounting for the absence of "the others."

King, Abernathy, and Shuttlesworth went to the preachers' meeting straight from the airport. Their entrance stopped Ware in midsentence. The other ministers parted with no smiles. When King asked for the opportunity to say a few words about why he was in town, Ware was so afraid of appearing to endorse him that he sought the group's permission. King floundered, his excuses for the campaign's secrecy eliciting not a single amen.

King, Abernathy, and Shuttlesworth drove in silence to the Gaston Motel, where Wyatt Walker's crisp presentation of street maps and city ordinances could not overwhelm the truth that, as he himself would later admit, "We decided to launch a movement, *then* put the pieces together." It looked as if Birmingham might not be another Albany after all; it would be worse.

New Day

DAVID VANN'S UNCLE had also flown to Birmingham that day, from New York, to eyewitness a revolution, he hoped, and to give his nephew moral support in case the coup failed. Vann had suffered plenty since assuming the task of ending Our Way of Life. The partners at White, Bradley, Arant, such as Hobart McWhorter, had been grumbling that he wasn't pulling his weight, was neglecting the real business of a City of Lawyers. Vann had read the signals and agreed to separate from the firm. Douglas Arant, the closet liberal partner, had managed to secure a few months' salary for him while the firm officially loaned him out to the new administration, at long last moving into Birmingham City Hall.

By a margin of 8,000 votes, Albert Boutwell unseated Bull Connor. Virtually all 10,000 of the city's Negro votes went to the victor. The black people had turned Connor out of office, and still no one dared articulate that segregation had been repealed.

Vincent Townsend busted the *News* budget to put color on the front page the following day, April 3. A bright drawing of a golden sun rose over a city skyline dominated by Vulcan: "New Day Dawns for Birmingham." In a statement underneath, Mayor-elect Albert Boutwell promised to meet—even secretly, was the implication—"with our citizens in all sections of the city." With obvious relief, he proclaimed, "We are on our way to better things."

The post-segregation era seemed to be arriving in style. But the city's old motto persisted: Hard times come to Birmingham first and stay longest.

McWhorter 1963

MY FIRST INKLING of political anxiety had come a month earlier, when my Camp Fire troop took a field trip to the state capital. We were apprehensive about visiting the Governor's Mansion. The dads at the country club had been muttering that the new governor "wudn't anything but a damn populist." His gut-grinding "Segregation forever!" inaugural had given offense, though the most objectionable things about George Wallace as far as we urbane ten-year-olds could tell were his patent-leather hair and oil-slick suits.

I was convinced that Wallace was waiting at the mansion to terrorize us Camp Fire Girls. During the governor's race, we had swallowed our confusion over Wallace's political shortcomings and marked up our blue canvas school binders with various misspellings of the name of his unsuccessful opponent, Ryan deGraffenried. It was a character weakness to be caught without an opinion in Birmingham. Standing in the lobby, I composed the grim, tight-jawed look my uncle got when he wanted to convey Toughness or Principles. Several years earlier, Uncle Hobart had seen enough tenacity in my budding character to nickname me Bear Bryant. I cherished that virile legacy, even as I had begun plotting my wedding to Bama's quarterback, number 12, Joe Willie Namath.

Mrs. George Wallace appeared. It was rumored that all the Wallaces had brought with them to these new velvet-and-gilt surroundings was their suitcases. She wore a high-necked dress, the kind country women favored when they got dressed up. Her mouth had the hillbilly scrawniness that one might see in a Kresge checkout girl, which Lurleen Burns had been when she met her future husband. She talked so slow to ears attuned to the progressive drawl of Birmingham, but she seemed nice, asking us if this was our first trip to the mansion, and all.

On the train ride back to Birmingham, we maliciously stretched out the diphthongs of "Luhr-laaiin" and made fun of the first lady's Self-Styling Adorn hairdo. This was a rehearsal of the scorn we would display to our parents about the meeting with the enemy. Who among the children could have guessed that Sam Upchurch's grandfather had slipped Wallace some serious campaign money, or that my uncle Hobart's blue-blood father-in-law, Kirkman Jackson, was one of the lawyers Wallace had handpicked to serve on his blue-ribbon segregation committee? Or that the new governor was the latest redneck political ward of Birmingham's own Great Man, Jim Simpson?

I felt utterly alone with the shame that my father had voted for Wallace. My father, it made my eyes sting to realize, was a Wallace man—next to a Kennedy man the worst sort of person a fifth-grader at the Brooke Hill School for Girls could imagine. In a traumatic diary entry of unprecedented length that night, I tried to atone: "We met Mrs. Wallace. (I didn't want to.)" And soon after, my diary went blank.

There was some sort of blackout of consciousness that spring of 1963, encrypting meaning that would still be making its way to the surface a generation later. The last notation my mother made in her datebook was on March 16, the day she returned from her first trip to New York, with a group of locals. The highlight of the visit was an evening in the studio audience of *The Tonight Show with Johnny Carson*. I hope Johnny asked, "Is there anyone from Birmingham here tonight?" For those were the final weeks that our city could still be owned with any esteem.

ELECTION DAY was a turning point in my life, though it was related to the momentous results at the polls only insomuch as it, like almost everything in our city, concerned race. The entire Brooke Hill fifth grade had a dinner party that evening at the home of Studie and Walker Johnson, the twin girls of the local Coca-Cola franchisee (Pepsi's daughter was also in our class). The menu featured all the six-and-a-half-ounce Cokes we could drink and grown-up food: hollandaise sauce on broccoli and chicken breasts in a sauce involving sour cream and Campbell's cream of mushroom. The guest of honor was our classmate Mary Badham.

The previous summer, at an audition held in Birmingham, Mary had beat out her best friend, a pig-iron heiress named Elizabeth "Bimi" Woodward, for the role of Scout in *To Kill a Mockingbird*, starring Gregory Peck. In the trophy house behind the Woodwards' main mansion, where Bimi entertained her friends amid the stuffed mementoes of her parents' African safaris, she swore to us that *she* had been the filmmakers' first choice over Mary but her mother had nixed acting as "tacky." Perhaps Mrs. Woodward had merely read the novel on which the movie was based, by the South Alabama native Nell Harper Lee.

After dinner, Brooke Hill seniors, on whom we all had crushes, chauffeured us downtown to the Melba Theater for a sneak preview of the movie—the official premiere was taking place the following night. At the beginning of the show, we nodded appreciatively when Atticus Finch (Gregory Peck) told his daughter, "Don't say nigger, Scout," and we recognized Calpurnia, the family maid, as a dead ringer for the fussy black women of our own kitchens. But soon our minds balked at the racial world of Scout's South Alabama. For the first time, we came face-to-face with the central racial preoccupation of the southern white psyche, the dynamics that justified and ennobled Our Way of Life: the rape of a white woman by a black man. We had only a technical understanding of the crime, but neither did we know the meaning of southern justice, and so we did not see how the movie's black martyr, wrongly accused of raping the pellagra-skinned Mayella Ewell, could fail to be acquitted, especially since his lawyer was Gregory Peck. When Tom Robinson was convicted of rape and then shot dead while "trying to escape," I summoned all the toughness I had learned in ten years of being Martin McWhorter's daughter but still could not contain my tears.

In the halls of Brooke Hill the next day, the talk of fifth grade was how *cute* Scout was and what a shame our Mary had suddenly gotten so gawky and stringy-haired. We went around saying such Scout-isms as "What in the Sam Hill are you doing?" and "Cecil Jacobs is a big wet hen!" (as well as Mayella's "chiffa*robe*"). But in acknowledgment of our secret bond—the racial guilt we shared in rooting for a Negro man—almost everybody in the class could recite the speech Scout delivered on the steps of the jailhouse to avert the lynch mob. "Hey, Mr. Cunningham. I said, hey, Mr. Cunningham...."

For the next few Saturdays we would go to matinees of *To Kill a Mockingbird* and weep clandestinely. But suddenly our mothers stopped us from going downtown. It was the Year of Birmingham. The past made it possible, but the worst was still ahead.

12.

MAD DOGS AND
RESPONSIBLE NEGROES

Project C

VINCENT TOWNSEND's newsprint sunrise had not even hit the stands on the afternoon of April 3 when history embarrassed him again. As soon as he heard about SCLC's plans, he called Burke Marshall, the civil rights chief at the Justice Department, and asked him to stop Martin Luther King. At ten that morning, Marshall telephoned the Gaston Motel and, in King's absence, conveyed to Wyatt Walker Townsend's opinion (which was shared by the attorney general) that they ought to give the new city government a chance. When Walker agreed to "pass the message on to Dr. King," Marshall translated to himself, "Like hell."

Lola Hendricks, the ACMHR's corresponding secretary, had been selected to break the news of Project X to Bull Connor, who would retain his office as a lame duck until April 15. The thirty-one-year-old daughter of a TCI tin mill worker who preferred not to know about her involvement in "that mess," Hendricks had a reputation for fearlessness that did not fail her when she arrived on the third floor of city hall and encountered a familiar man standing at a desk. "We came to see Commissioner Connor," she said.

"You looking at him," he replied. She inquired about getting a permit to picket.

"You will not get a permit in Birmingham, Alabama, to picket," he said, twice. "I'll picket you over to the jail." Hendricks thanked him and left, the minister who had accompanied her still mute at her side.

Wyatt Walker had raised about sixty-five of the lost "baptismal candidates." After "workshopping" them that morning, he had them coordinate their watches and fan out with military rigor to his five target lunch counters. Project X had become Project C.

The ACMHR's security chief, James Armstrong, had been on Walker's early list of recruits, but now he was sitting at the Gaston Motel, voicing vague doubts about the campaign's "timeliness." Herb Oliver was not so bashful about his dismay. Still, the inveterate worrier was unable to resist circulating among Pizitz, Loveman's, Kress, and Woolworth's to check out the sit-ins, and he felt a surge of pride in seeing the protesters roosting in semi-darkness, the management having cut out the lights and shut down. Among the spectators at one site Oliver spied a white face that filled his heart with sorrow. Arnold Treback of the U.S. Civil Rights Commission had come down to deliver the crushing news that the hearings into Oliver's police-brutality charges had been sacrificed to the dubious enterprise before them.

Delegates from the Eastview 13 klavern who greeted the first sit-ins were shouldered away by another white man, a plainclothes cop perhaps, before they could do anything more brutal than baptize the Reverend Calvin Woods with a gob of spit to the face. Woods, the minister whom Bull Connor had had arrested five years earlier for advocating Birmingham's bus boycott from the pulpit, smiled and said, "Thank you."

Project C had opened on a decidedly dim stage. Bull Connor—it almost seemed as if he was taking lessons from Chief Laurie Pritchett of Albany—was saying he wouldn't arrest the scofflaws unless the store management complained. Newberry's was the only store to challenge the sit-ins, many of whom took one look at the hefty bouncers and heeded the old saying, "A coward don't tote no broke bones." This first "demonstration" of Birmingham netted a mere twenty jailbirds, although like Governor John Patterson during the Freedom Rides, Connor was aiding the Gandhian objective by assuring the press that he would "fill the jail."

Cruel and Vicious

DIRECT ACTION was a frontier of fragile alliances. The Movement's natural white allies had cold shoulders. With the exception of the maverick businessman Jim Head, who wrote Mayor-elect Boutwell practically demanding that he convene a biracial committee, the moderates were furious over "outside agitators" spoiling an orderly changing of the political guard.

David Vann took the "betrayal" personally. This most liberal Christian of the white men in Birmingham had taken on the segregationists in his beloved Methodist church, sacrificed his car tires and risked his personal safety to join the Alabama Council on Human Relations, and finally nailed Connor himself. He believed that the Negro community should be in the streets rejoicing rather than demonstrating, even if the new mayor had made his name as a segregationists' segregationist, standard-bearer of the anti-*Brown* resistance. From Vann's white perspective, King's arrival was "the most cruel and vicious thing that has ever happened to Birmingham."

To plead Vann's case with SCLC, a Catholic priest named Albert S. "Steve" Foley, a longtime officer of the Alabama Council, had come up from Mobile, where he taught sociology at Spring Hill College. Early Wednesday evening at the Gaston Motel, Foley jumped all over Shuttlesworth and King for recruiting "outsiders" to take advantage of Vann's service in booting Bull Connor. "Do you Negroes want progress or attention?" he asked. Shuttlesworth shot back, "Go over to the city jail and ask twenty-one Negroes in jail what they want."

To complete the day, police sirens screamed toward another "demonstration" taking place in front of the Melba Theater amid bunting and klieg lights. Ignoring the motorcycle escort, the crowd engulfed a car carrying two local youths, Mary Badham and Philip Alford, to the "Hollywood-type premiere" of the movie in which they were starring. *To Kill a Mockingbird* had been released in 1962, but it was only now, months later, after lobbying from the Junior Chamber of Commerce, that a local theater had agreed to show this spectacle of southern justice, just in time for the reckoning to come to our streets. After the outgoing commissioner Jabo Waggoner presented the children with keys to the city, Mayor-elect Boutwell took the stage to say, "There doesn't seem to be anything I can give at this time, but I hope to give them a greater Birmingham."

Shuttlesworth left the motel for the mass meeting, where he led off with that punch line of Negro derision, "As I came into Birmingham I walked underneath a sign that said, 'It's Nice to Have You in Birmingham.' . . ." But then he went on the defensive and, in tacit response to Foley's objections, dismissed Boutwell as merely a distinguished version of Connor. Following Shuttlesworth to the pulpit, King also had to deal with negatives, first the "outside agitator" rap. ("Shuttlesworth called on us and we were glad to come." . . . "If there is injustice in Birmingham, then the world is not right.") Then he went on to address the rebuke that had haunted him since Albany, the charge that would recur bitterly in Shuttlesworth's mouth as he came to regret his exuberant opening-night introduction of King: "In the end he will lead us to freedom." That criticism was that King never stayed till the end; his traveling circus departed early and left a community stranded with false hope and huge legal fees. But King assured the Birmingham crowd that he had told his wife, still in an Atlanta hospital with their four-day-old daughter, "It might take three days and it might take three months. But however long it took, that's how long I would be gone."

On the other side of black Birmingham's tracks, at a banquet of the conservative businessmen of Frontiers International (a sort of black Kiwanis), Father Foley, who two years earlier had expressed his "highest admiration" for the Freedom Riders, was accusing King of money-grubbing opportunism. "If he's really bent on leadership," he said, "he has a lot to learn."

Cement

THE FIRST DAY had barely ended, and Project C was already confronting Jim Bevel's unspoken reservations about Wyatt Walker's tactician's mentality. Walker had basically written off "the classes," who had made peace with (and money off) segregation, and expected little to come of the honeyed call King put in earlier that day to A. G. Gaston—"obstructionist," as Walker saw him, though Gaston had unwittingly provided SCLC with its temporary office in the heart of the black commercial section. (The local minister who was the go-between did not reveal who his client was.) But how was Walker even going to engage the masses, who had adjusted to segregation in their own, self-destructive way?

By day, the Fourth Avenue Negro business district that Gaston ruled was a somewhat poignant spectacle of black people emulating the white man's preoccupation with money. But come nightfall, Fourth Avenue was the beat that cops called Scratch Ankle, a roost of pimps, prostitutes, pool sharks, gamblers, and Saturday nighters. This subterrain was ruled by one of segregation's other black success stories, A. G. Gaston's equal when it came to official white approval. He was known as Rat Killer, or "Bull Connor's right-hand man"—and not with contempt. "Everybody loves Rat Killer," said Rat Killer himself, a small and indeed ferret-like man christened Charles Barnett, who had gotten his nickname working for Orkin Exterminators.

Rat's current place of business was the Seventeenth Street Shine Parlor, just off Fourth Avenue North. Though the Movement preachers got their shoes shined there, most of his clientele came for the liquor he sold in the back. Rat Killer was one of the select perpetrators of "victimless crimes"—bootlegging, pimping, prostitution—who made up Connor's network of informants and ensured the Birmingham police's famed efficiency. As a hangout for the Negro "criminal element" (as well as a popular after-hours spot for visiting black entertainers—the Staples Singers, Jackie Wilson, Sam Cooke, the Temptations, B.B. King—and ballplayers), his parlor was so vital to the system that the police were careful not to question him about frivolous crimes, lest he lose clientele and effectiveness. Rat's jet-setting leisure style—the World Series and the All Star Game almost every year, as well as the big fights (he had seen Cassius Clay)—was a testament to his status. "Bull is a humdinger," Rat affirmed. "I admire him, I like him. He is *my* right-hand man."

Though Rat Killer himself was protective toward the Movement's secretaries coming and going in the neighborhood—"Hey, you walking too close to that lady," he sometimes called out to patrons—the Negroes of his world were likely to wear the doctrine of nonviolence about as comfortably as Gandhi's diapers. As the ACMHR vice president Ed Gardner pointed out, if there was a bulldog in the middle of the road, a white man would walk around it, but a Negro would want to fight it. To some, the campaign simply meant "I got a chance to kill me a cracker." At mass meetings, King began passing around a box for people to deposit razors, knives, ice picks, and pistols, and salted his inspirational calls to dignity with reminders that being black did not in itself constitute a virtue. But Negro violence was a permutation of Negro fear. "A lot of Negroes in Birmingham don't know that the Civil War is over," Gardner said. "They don't seem to care what happens to them. They don't even know F. L. Shuttlesworth."

The Movement was going to have to give people courage and hope in order to give them nonviolence. That process would later get lost in the anecdotal lore of the Movement, the danger and the comedy of the showdowns. In fact, religion was what the activist Miles College professor Jonathan McPherson would call "the magnet that attracted people to the Movement and the cement that held it together." The path to Bevel's goal of commitment was a spiritual odyssey that defied the precision of Wyatt Walker's typed notes on the nightly mass meetings' format and often lofted, as the Albany Movement had proved, on a song. Walker too considered music the "primary ingredient which has binded us together as a surviving people." The Movement choir, which the ACMHR had established in 1960, would have to lead endless wails of gospels, incantations of "Free-e-e-dom," "Ain't gonna let nobody turn me around," and "We shall overcome" until Bevel's science transformed the angry Negroes of Birmingham into nonviolent soldiers.

In light of the pressing tasks of community-building, King scrapped his plans for an early arrest. It fell to Fred Shuttlesworth to man the front line. On Saturday, April 6, after three days of straggly sit-ins and mass meetings, he and Charles Billups, the minister who had helped him organize the 1960 sit-ins, led forty-five men and women, dressed as if for church, two by two out of the Gaston Motel, down Fifth Avenue North. Their march was silent and somewhat awkwardly paced, like an old film clip. The lack of any placards was perhaps a concession to Shuttlesworth's impatience finally to begin Birmingham's "demonstrations." And despite Wyatt Walker's "blueprint," he and Shuttlesworth had decided on *where* to march only right before the demonstrators left the motel: to city hall to pray.* After they had marched for two and a half blocks, past uniformed police to the Federal Building, Bull Connor ordered a subordinate to call the wagons. "I'm hungry," he added, as if Project C were just an intrusion on his lunch hour.

Chief Jamie Moore picked up a bullhorn and twice told the marchers that they were violating a city ordinance against parading without a permit. Shuttlesworth and Billups dropped to their knees, followed by the rest of the marchers, who remained still as bird dogs while Billups prayed out loud. Then Shuttlesworth took over: "Lord, give us grace to do what we have to do, and bless the men who are oppressing us in the guise of protecting us. Bless this city." The performance transcended its script, into a realm of tears that commemorate truth.

Denim

THE MASS MEETING at St. James Baptist—attendance a mere two hundred—had been going for forty-five minutes of warm-up when King, Abernathy, and two Birmingham ministers unfamiliar to the ACMHR crowd bounded down the aisle. (Shuttlesworth was in jail.) Ordinarily SCLC's wardrobe-conscious officials favored dark conservative suits, but on this Saturday night the civil rights court of Camelot, "JFK" and "Dean Rusk," had on overalls to promote the Easter boycott.

---

* "Bull Connor had something in his mind about not letting these niggers get to city hall," Walker would say later. "I prayed that he'd keep trying to stop us.... Birmingham would have been lost if Bull had let us go down to the city hall and pray."

Among ambitious blacks, the epithet "bib overall wearer" connoted not simply poverty but a subservient mentality, and even if privately the two friends put on little minstrel shows that mocked the "whooping" preachers of the masses, tonight they embraced those "churchpeople," symbolically promising to toil with the field hands until segregation was broken. "I will wear them as long as I am in Birmingham and until we are free," King told the crowd.

Was there a tinge of condescension in the denim? Abernathy confessed that his "old clothes" were actually new: The SCLC leaders had had to go out and buy their overalls, which couldn't possibly have come from downtown Birmingham with a brand name like Liberty, Abernathy joked, showing off the down-home irony that had earned him the nickname Mr. Rough to King's Mr. Smooth. (King had called the clothes a "serious, symbolic expression of our sacrifice.") "Abby's *mean*," the Birmingham folks had begun to say after he asked the cops at Friday's mass meeting if they knew what KKK stood for. "You may think that stands for Ku Klux Klan, but now it stands for Kennedy, Khrushchev, and King."

Tonight Abernathy's meanness seemed to contain gratuitous contempt for Birmingham, as if the Alabama Black Belt native couldn't resist preening over the superiority of his adoptive town of Atlanta, where, he boasted, he had shared the airport's restroom with a white man the other day. "He smelled," he said, "and why the hell can't I smell if he smells?"

Some Birmingham blacks, not only the predictable "responsible leaders," took umbrage at the Atlantans. "Do what Martin Luther King tells you," Abernathy had ordered an earlier mass meeting. The *World*'s race man, Emory O. Jackson, was despondent, again. "I am no longer involved in civil rights," he wrote his confidante Anne Rutledge, a former student from his days teaching high school, two days into the campaign, and he failed to mention Project C in his paper except as an aside in a UPI story about the black comedian Dick Gregory marching with SNCC in Greenwood, Mississippi. The *World*'s front page featured Boutwell's victory, a man scalded by his wife during a fight, and a picture of Angela Davis,* who had just made the dean's list at Brandeis University. On page 2, printed without comment, was the "Birmingham Manifesto," Project C's eloquent declaration of resistance ("We act today in full concert with our Hebraic-Christian tradition, the laws of morality and the Constitution of our nation"), which Wyatt Walker would claim to have written in forty-five minutes on the opening day and to have signed the names of Shuttlesworth and the ACMHR's secretary, Nelson Smith.

The other key local naysayer, Herb Oliver, recalled his admonition to SCLC in February—that if the segregationists didn't make a "mistake," the organizers would have to invent one. King had said to Walker during the planning stages, "Wyatt, you've got to find the means by which to create a crisis, to make Bull Connor tip his hand." But four days into Project C, the biggest crisis Walker faced was

---

* Her parents upheld the legacy of their Southern Negro Youth Congress activism by becoming silent benefactors of the Movement.

that his colleagues had started buying their clothes from a farm-supply store. The overalls, which were, after all, SNCC's uniform, "rubbed me the wrong way," said Walker, who continued to wear suits.

Walker had "calculated for Bull Connor's stupidity," not for his present demureness. It was no surprise that Vincent Townsend's paper was ignoring the campaign, which was preferable to his printing another exposé on O'Dell. But the action was so tame that the *New York Times* editors were also running the stories about the campaign deep inside the paper.

On Palm Sunday, at four o'clock, fewer than thirty marchers congregated at St. Paul Methodist Church. Their leaders were the local preachers who had joined King and Abernathy at the pulpit in overalls the night before. One of them was King's younger brother, Alfred Daniel Williams King, known as A.D., who had arrived in Birmingham a little over a year before to take over First Baptist Church of Ensley, after the previous pastor "took the night train," as Ed Gardner described his dropping dead in the middle of an announcement at a Movement meeting. If M.L. had made the more profound rebellion against Daddy King's old-school, paternalistic Southern Baptist ministry, it was A.D., the rebel without a cause, who bore the brunt of his harsh patriarchy. Daddy King chewed him out for smoking; M.L. kept his nicotine habit under wraps. By the time he got to Birmingham, A.D. was an alcoholic. The only area in which he kept up with his older brother harked back to his childhood envy of M.L.'s adroit "flitting from chick to chick," and most of what the Birmingham police wiretaps picked up on his phone were adulterous rather than integrationist plots. "I loved A.D. because I loved Martin," Shuttlesworth said, tactfully.

A.D.'s fellow novice at the head of the Palm Sunday march was a big, open-faced minister, John T. Porter, a Birmingham native with Atlanta polish. While attending Alabama State, he had been King's assistant pastor at Dexter Avenue Baptist the year before the 1956 Montgomery bus boycott, and then as a student at Morehouse, he was Daddy King's factotum at Ebenezer, where his co-janitor, A. D. King, was always in trouble with his father. When Porter was installed, in December 1962, as pastor of Birmingham's largest black church, Sixth Avenue Baptist, Martin had flown in for the ceremonies. But Porter, who had a Ph.D., remained aloof from Shuttlesworth. "You couldn't have more than an eighth-grade education to be a member," he said of the ACMHR. Standing on the sidewalk of St. Paul Methodist on Palm Sunday, Porter looked as uncomfortable in his clerical robe as he had in his Liberty overalls the night before. Having left Montgomery just before the boycott and Atlanta just before the sit-ins, he was thinking that "the Lord had been sparing me for a quick death in Birmingham."*

Porter, together with A. D. King and Nelson Smith, led the thirty marchers east along Sixth Avenue North toward city hall, singing, "Hold My Hand While I

---

* Like my father, John Thomas Porter was named after Thomas Martin, longtime president of the Alabama Power Company, for whom Porter's father also worked, as a gardener. Robert Porter, who had previously warned John not to "get involved in this mess," walked up to his son on Palm Sunday and simply shook his hand.

Run This Race." A thousand spectators bunched behind them like a storm cloud. At Kelly Ingram Park, the square block of grass and elms dividing black from white Birmingham, Bull Connor pointed at the only recognizable "radical" and said, "There's Smith. Get him." The police captain on duty was Glenn Evans, mentor to the force's anti-Connor Young Turks, who had undergone a conversion on a city bus one day in the fifties watching a young black mother scold her toddler for taking a seat up front. Evans ordered the marchers to "desist." That was the ministers' cue to kneel. Porter, feeling overwhelmed by the shame of his impending jail sentence, was startled by A.D.'s cackle behind him: "Pray, Porter!"

Wyatt Walker, pacing like a field marshal on the margins, recognized the coveted crisis. When a policeman placed his hand on one of the ministers leading the marchers toward the police wagon, the spectators went wild, jeering and jostling. "Fight 'em," somebody urged the nonviolent marchers. "Do something about this!" a female onlooker screamed. As she was being arrested, the people surged toward the police cars and the patrolmen rushed toward them, swinging their clubs.

If the Movement couldn't provide the masses, nonaligned black Birmingham would. Walker decided to schedule marches right after work, to reap a premium of spectators ("If we missed 'Huntley-Brinkley,' we could still get on the news at eleven"). The white newsmen could be counted on to inflate the Movement troop count. "Marchers, spectators?" Walker recalled. "To them we all looked alike." But Bull Connor still was not providing the necessary brutality to make righteousness graphic. The police remained courteous despite the clubs— "You go on home, Billy," one cop told a lame, drunk black bystander. Even Connor's K-9 Corps, making its Project C debut, merely sniffed at the crowd.

Eighteen-year-old Leroy Allen, a spectator, went at a police dog, swinging a large knife, as a white *New York Times* reporter saw it. Allen was choking the dog when four cops threw him to the ground. A dog lunged at another man, who swung back with a penknife ("I don't know whether I cut him or not," he reported, "but I hope I did"). "Look at that dog go," Connor said. "That's what we train them for—to enforce the law—just like we train our officers."

Wyatt Walker, perhaps remembering the hopeful subtext of King's warning at the opening-night mass meeting—"They may set the mad dogs on us"—immediately called King: "I've got it. I can't tell you on the phone, but I've got it." The white Leftie lawyer from New York, William Kunstler, who had just arrived to cook up diversionary legal tactics, caught Walker's drift and was telling the press that Leroy Allen had stepped protectively in front of a dog charging a woman and baby. Someone added that Chief Jamie Moore himself had repeatedly kicked the prostrate Allen.

The local stringer for *Life*, who had been covering the protests all week, was skeptical of Kunstler and Walker's performance. In a class of machismo apart from his colleagues on the beat, Albert "Buck" Persons, a cousin of the writer Truman Capote (né Persons, and fictionalized in *To Kill a Mockingbird*), had been a member of the American commando force invading Cuba's Bay of Pigs in 1961, and two years later, resentful that four of his fellow pilots from Alabama had made the ultimate sacrifice with no show of appreciation from their government, he became the first of the CIA mercenaries to reveal his role. His two articles in the *Chicago American* that March had prompted *Life* to recruit him to freelance. Persons knew that Chief Moore had been nowhere in the vicinity of Leroy Allen.

After the reporters left the motel, Walker jumped up yelling, "We've got a movement. We've got a movement. We had some police brutality. They brought out the dogs. They brought out the dogs. We've got a movement."

Another potential bonus for the Movement, featured in that day's *Birmingham News,* was nearly lost in the euphoria over the dogs. Bull Connor and his fellow commissioners had taken an ad to announce that they had no intention of leaving office on April 15. Their four-year terms ended in 1965, and they planned to serve them out.

The Advantaged

THE FIRST CRACKS in what Fred Shuttlesworth liked to call Fortress Segregation were starting to appear, on the side of the segregated. The city's prominent black businessmen had begun to debate the consequences of an alliance with King. Was it worth risking the retribution of their white creditors? A. G. Gaston worried that if he opposed King he might be caught on the losing side. On Monday, April 8, he summoned the black men he considered "local leaders" to his motel for an early-evening audience with King. They told him, in the same language that the white city fathers used when they were put on the spot by outsiders: "We can do it ourselves."

Observing his peers at the meeting, Shuttlesworth's physician, James T. Montgomery, felt entitled to express his disgust. He was from one of the high-society families of Rosedale, where his father was principal of the high school. (Jim had admired Shuttlesworth's football-playing at Rosedale, impressive for "such a little fellow.") He had been shipped off to the black "Ivies"—Morehouse, where he had known Martin Luther King as an apolitical younger student, then to Howard Medical School—and finally to Harvard for a fourth-year residency in cardiology. Montgomery was in the middle of a personal civil rights battle: seeking admission as the first black doctor in the all-white Jefferson County Medical Society—the only way he could become a member of the American Medical Association. Local white doctors had declined to give him the requisite endorsements for admission (five), but had been happy to recommend him for national board certification in cardiology. "I understood their problem," Montgomery would admit, aware that a "nigger lover" was worse than a "nigger." "I just never told them I understood."

Montgomery now confronted the black Big Boys, "Have all y'all lost your minds? We've been trying to get these things done all these years and someone comes in to help and y'all want to get rid of him? Y'all just want to go backward." King was now emboldened to scold rather than woo: "Man cannot ride your back if you can stand up." Still, the men couldn't bring themselves to gamble their "advantages" on civil rights unless a favorable outcome was more or less guaranteed. King would have to take his case directly to the various black constituencies.

King left Birmingham's black royalty for the masses waiting at Ensley's First Baptist, whose pastor, his younger brother, A. D. King, had gone to jail the day before. Wyatt Walker was at the microphone, raging that on Palm Sunday he was just a few feet from this Negro that the police dogs got hold of—a *nonviolent* Negro! he said, figuring no one had seen the *New York Times* headline, "B'ham Protest Ended as Negro Attacks Dog."* *Five* police dogs had to subdue this man, he said, selling the machismo of nonviolence. Then he added, "It may be tomorrow or Wednesday, but the dogs *will* be put on someone else."

Abernathy noted how strange it was that Birmingham police wouldn't let any Negroes on the police force even though the police dogs were integrated—"five black ones and a white one." But most of his gibes hit those he and King had recently addressed: "Get rid of the Uncle Toms, get them out of the church, and let someone in who is willing to go to jail for freedom." The crowd was excited by the time he invoked the names of Birmingham's newest political prisoners—Nelson Smith, John Porter, and A. D. King.

Jailhouse Martyrs

"BAPTISM" had not come easily to the three ministers. On the way to jail in the police wagon, A. D. King had countermanded an officer's orders for them to stop singing and launched into the chorus of "We Shall Overcome." Scrunched up in front by the police, Nelson Smith told A.D. to "come here and sit where I'm sitting and see whether you feel like singing." A.D.'s specialty, as his friend John Porter observed, was to stand in the background and get *your* head whipped. "He took life very lightly," Porter said.†

A.D. had been pacing around his cell, demanding a drink of water. "You're in jail, A.D.," Porter said. "You're not a guest in someone's home." Presently, King called his church to find him a bondsman. Porter protested, "If you lead the people into jail, you've got an obligation to stay with them." But Nelson Smith watched A.D. with an open mind. This was his first "baptism," too. "He always had to go see about a dead minister" when it came time to volunteer for jail, a Movement colleague explained. Smith had been hoping to continue the jail-less streak by lobbying Martin Luther King to tap him as the Birmingham Abernathy, the nightly warm-up act, so that he could show off the "Fireball" roar and timing that had been known to set a dozen women in the audience to screaming and fainting. But King had decided to let the hilarious Ed Gardner (he even looked a bit like

---

*Leroy Allen, who denied having any weapon, was taken to the hospital from jail, where twenty-five cops came to eye him, to get a good look at him, they said, so that they would recognize him on the street. Another K-9 victim being treated at the hospital, seventy-year-old Raymond Coleman, was told that the dog that bit him was not a police dog.

†In 1969, King would be found dead in his new swimming pool in Atlanta.

Groucho Marx) continue as Birmingham's Abernathy, perhaps because of the fundraising skills that had earned him the nickname Late Money for his mercilessness toward those who "holler Amen till the collection time and then get hot and have to go outside until collection is over."

At one o'clock on Monday morning, only several hours after his arrest, Smith had phoned Gardner. As the "day-to-day man," Gardner kept track of the commitment cards Walker collected from march volunteers, specifying how long they were willing to stay in jail. He asked Smith where he was calling from. Smith replied, nonchalantly, that he was at his church office. "You supposed to stay in jail, aren't you, brother?" Gardner said, the "brother" not quite as pointed an admonition as "doctor" would have been.

As Abernathy was chanting their names Monday night, as if they were Matthew and Mark, building the crowd to indignation over their lockup, Nelson Smith and A. D. King were halfway down the aisle of A.D.'s church.

Falling In

MARTIN LUTHER KING went on the offensive the next morning at the regular Tuesday meeting of J. L. Ware's Baptist Ministers Conference. He condemned the "dry as dust" gospel of individual salvation and shamed the two hundred or so preachers into taking a stand as influential men immune from white reprisals. Finally, Ware's men voted to back King. It was the crucial "black establishment" endorsement SCLC needed to get the rest of the community to fall in. That same day, King addressed the black businessmen of the Frontiers Club, appealing to their insecurity by announcing the imminent arrival of Jackie Robinson, Sammy Davis Jr., and Harry Belafonte.

Perhaps the team from Atlanta was beginning to lose its tact, alienating old friends as it shamed the new ones. Herb Oliver suddenly found himself being treated like a child. On Sunday night, he had been chatting with Foster Hailey of the *New York Times* about what was, from the press's point of view, a stalled campaign. Oliver's extemporaneous opinion appeared in the paper that Tuesday, April 9, as a semi-official "statement" that the Movement was "operating in a vacuum," given that there was "no one to go to to negotiate grievances" until the repudiated commissioners left office. King, Abernathy, and Walker summoned Oliver.

Over lunch at the Gaston Motel, King slammed his hand down on the table. Abernathy applied some soothing words, but Oliver was taken aback at a side of King he was unaware of. "I have always spoken my mind and will continue to do so," he told the men evenly. "I do not have to ask anyone's permission."

"What You Niggers Really Want"

THE FIRST BREAK in the white power structure's hostile indifference to Project C also came that day. Sid Smyer called the Alabama Council's Jim Jimerson and asked him to gather some representatives from the other side and come to the Church of the Advent. The meeting marked the initiation of a gentleman-preacher new to the SCLC inner circle. Andrew Young, a Congregational minister (the demurest, whitest of the black denominations) tempered in Connecticut and New York, had cheerfully accepted the assignment of dealing with the white folk; his father, a New Orleans dentist, had taught him "that putting white people at ease was a survival skill that signaled my superior intellect rather than inferior social status." His Movement colleagues called him, usually humorously, Uncle Tom.

Through a white woman he knew who worked for the diocese, Young had made early contact with the state's number two Episcopalian, Bishop Coadjutor George Murray. The son of a TCI ceramics engineer, Murray had begun his clerical career as chaplain of the University of Alabama, from which position he officiated the wedding of Chuck and Camille Morgan. His professional track—he was now the conservative Bishop C.C.J. Carpenter's designated successor and co-pastor at Birmingham's rarefied Church of the Advent—had been unimpeded by a functioning conscience. He was the only white clergyman to have publicly condemned the Autherine Lucy mob and it was he who had opened up his boss's study to a series of interracial negotiations, including the one that Tuesday afternoon.

Shuttlesworth arrived at the Advent with Nelson Smith. Jimerson had also invited A. D. King. The only Atlantan on hand was Andy Young, who had on his best suit. Besides Smyer and Jimerson, the whites included a refreshing surprise: Chuck Morgan. So far, Morgan had been content just to work the phones, keeping the Justice Department apprised of the happenings in "our scenic little community." Burke Marshall routed Morgan's occasional droll notes to his fellow Birminghamian Lou Oberdorfer in the tax division, "for information and entertainment." Otherwise preoccupied with another looming crisis—Governor George Wallace's vow to "Stand in the Schoolhouse Door"—Morgan had no great desire to rescue the businessmen from SCLC and had considered it a "major imposition" when Jimerson asked him to come along. But Smyer had insisted he be there as security, figuring that the Negroes wouldn't expose Morgan to further charges of "nigger lover" by blabbing about the secret meeting.

Morgan took a seat next to Shuttlesworth, opposite Smyer, in the pastor's study. The slight Shuttlesworth shivered in the chilly room. Morgan, who like most beefy white southern boys preferred his indoor climate down in polar bear range, took off his seersucker jacket and draped it over Shuttlesworth's shoulders. Smyer, who did not own a department store and probably had not given much thought to Negroes putting on clothes that a white person might subsequently wear, looked as if he was going to be sick. Then he opened the meeting by stating, "The one thing we've got to know is what you niggers really want."

Shuttlesworth, whom Smyer had dignified the previous fall as "Doctor," responded contemptuously. "You know what our demands are," he said, and refreshed Smyer's memory about those previous negotiations: desegregated toilets, water fountains, and lunch counters, plus job promotions at the department stores, and a biracial committee. He also asked for an immediate plan for school desegregation, something Abernathy had thrown in for the whites to reject out of hand. When Shuttlesworth invited the white men to join in the demonstrations, they concluded that they were dealing with "a group bent on exploiting the situation" and agreed only to another meeting, on Thursday. Smyer accused Shuttlesworth and his colleagues of creating nothing but chaos. "It's dark in Birmingham now and it's going to get darker," Nelson Smith replied, at least in the retelling, "but when it is the darkest that's when you can see the stars of freedom."

"I Had a Dream Tonight"

THE CATHOLIC PRIEST from the Alabama Council on Human Relations, Steve Foley, was brought to heel at the Tuesday-night mass meeting, signaling an erosion of white solidarity. "How did I get myself in this mess?" a policeman heard him whisper as he walked to the pulpit to receive King's teasing forgiveness. "We still love Father Foley, don't we?" he asked the crowd. With one arm draped around Foley and another around the South's most prominent Black Muslim, the Atlanta-based Jeremiah X, King said, "We don't love what Brother X advocates, black supremacy, we don't love white supremacy, but we love our white brother and we love integration."

And then he rhapsodized about little Negro boys and girls walking to school with little white boys and girls, playing in the parks together and going swimming together. Those who heard the speech—the old Miles College activist Charles Davis made a tape of it—would still be marveling twenty years later over its repeated phrase, a leitmotif that seemed to hang in the Sixteenth Street church's sanctuary. "I had a dream tonight," he said, "I had a dream."

The Atlanta momentum was building into a whirlwind, causing A. G. Gaston to suffer the passion of the Responsible Negro—as one black newspaper had uncharitably described the species, someone who "can shuffle his feet and keep his eyes on the ground when he's talking to white people, and at the same time stand up before colored people and demand immediate racial equality." Torn between loyalty to his race and love of his city, he issued a statement to the newspapers. "We want freedom and justice," he said, adding some Booker T. Washington language about "dignity in all endeavors where we are qualified." But he did not want "outsiders" like Martin Luther King and SCLC fighting for freedom and justice in Birmingham.

The Atlantans were furious. Shuttlesworth—the "local" authority for SCLC's presence—had flown home to Cincinnati after the mass meeting that night. An urgent message awaited him when he arrived at his church. He turned around and headed back to the Cincinnati airport.

For the first time, the tension between the Atlantans and the Birminghamians broke the surface. Some SCLC staffers threatened to picket Gaston right along with the "downtown merchants." Speaking for the Birmingham Movement in Shuttlesworth's absence, Ed Gardner was appalled. "I'm proud of the old man," he said of Gaston. "If he's broke, I can't get nothing from him." As one who owed his first job after college to the old man—as a deejay at a Gaston-owned Montgomery radio station—Abernathy should have been sensitive to the ambivalent loyalty the locals felt toward him.* In an atypical burst of independence, Gardner told the SCLC staff, "If you picket Gaston, we'll send every one of you back to Atlanta." And then he more subtly challenged the Atlantans' moral authority. Referring to the Movement's huge bar tab at the Gaston Motel, he said, "Get the ministers to send the bill to their churches."

Shuttlesworth rushed into an unhappy scene in Room 30—the "war room"—at the Gaston Motel. The conflict between Shuttlesworth and Gaston was complex and as difficult to characterize as Gaston's mispronunciation of his name as "Shullyworth." There had been a rumor that Lucius Pitts had actually had to separate the two men during a showdown at the Metropolitan A.M.E. Zion Church. But Shuttlesworth was far less hot about Gaston, whose position was clear, than about the selectively supportive lawyer Arthur Shores, and it was with more dismay than anger that he now reminded Gaston, who had been summoned to his motel, that the middle-class folk were under no Movement pressure to take any official stands, for or against the campaign: "Just let whoever chooses to go to jail go." When Gaston did not return the favor, Shuttlesworth lit into him for making money off a movement he failed to support. "These prices you putting on me are out of sight," he said, referring to the minimal break Gaston was giving the Movement in motel fees. (Gaston refused to do business with the controversial Atlanta outsiders and insisted on charging the bill to the ACMHR.†) Finally, Shuttlesworth got so worked up that he said, "You are a *super* Uncle Tom," though he begged Gaston's pardon on the spot.

Birmingham's black conservatives followed the chastened Gaston on board Project C. "Negroes Uniting in Birmingham," the *New York Times* announced on Thursday, April 10. To keep the classes hitched, King appointed a "central committee" of around twenty-five men and women who would meet at the Gaston Motel every morning to approve the day's strategy, worked out by the civil rights pros the night before over chicken or ribs. (Andy Young had noticed that the "elemental act of chewing on bones" seemed to suspend the usual jockeying for King's ear.) The deference the new committee would pay to Gaston, Shores, and Pitts made Shuttlesworth's heart sink, and not simply out of resentment that his former resisters had been handed, unearned, the power he had risked so much for. One of the earliest agreements he and King had struck was that only the two of them and

---

* Many years later, after Abernathy published some crude revelations about King's sexual appetite, Gaston would call Abernathy "an unusually stupid kind of fellow" and "usually broke," and complain about "always lending him money for one thing or another."
† Over time, Gaston would be given credit for putting up the Movement for free. Gardner, who handled the expenses ($1,500 a week for room, and the same for food), would say, "We paid him every cent. He gave us just enough of a break to save face."

Abernathy had veto power over day-to-day decisions. To turn Project C into a committee effort seemed to him disastrous.

There were other signs that Shuttlesworth was losing his grip on the Birmingham Movement. In the first days of Project C, the *New York Times* had showcased him as the active director of the campaign, with King his "principal adviser," who "flew in from Atlanta last week to help local leaders." By April 11, Shuttlesworth had become one of "the local leaders allied with" King. Worried that Shuttlesworth's star was in eclipse, Emory O. Jackson editorialized in the *World* against the Atlantans' intrusions—he considered SCLC the "upside-down civil rights crew." He endorsed Gaston's equivocation, perhaps as a sly way of tricking the Birminghamians into closing ranks around Shuttlesworth. His April 10 editorial terming the direct action thus far "both wasteful and worthless" was taken as a slap at Project C, but in his perverse way, Jackson seemed to be egging on "sincere and serious" direct actionists to prove him wrong. Perhaps Jackson recognized that sometimes it was better for the homegrown leaders to let outsiders do their dirty work. Then again, maybe he was having another bout of Jim Crow craziness. "This is a hard struggle," he wrote his friend Anne Rutledge, with uncharacteristic understatement.

13.

BAPTISM

Chapel

THE SEASONED MARCHERS were calling it "Connor's Chapel for Freedom." The city jail was one of Birmingham's generic public buildings, a grayish, dull concrete box sharing a stretch of urban refuse south of downtown with the city pound, the city warehouse, the city crematory, and the city garage. When the jail was built, in 1911, newspaper writers portrayed it as a germ-proof place with "the aspect of a Carnegie library," serving "crisp and sweet" cornbread irresistible to officials there on business. The jail could indeed be sort of a benign second home to revolving-door drunks, brawlers, prostitutes, and bootleggers such as the legendary balladeer Jimmy Tarlton, who begged his beloved Bessie to "Write me a letter/Save it for mail/Send it care of/The Birmingham Jail."* Tarlton vowed to "Walk out this jail house/To do wrong no more," but doing no wrong hardly indemnified black Birminghamians, not when the crime of "vagrancy" could be defined as behavior in any way disagreeable to white people.

The jailhouse was the proverbial boil on the diseased segregationist community, to borrow one of Martin Luther King's favorite metaphors. The way nonviolent direct action worked was to expose the system to the light of public conscience. Fred Shuttlesworth had pierced the boil many times, but in obscurity and in isolation, and was more deterrent than example to prospective jailbirds— he made surviving jail seem like a miracle. With his appeal to the mass media, King would be able to demystify the Birmingham jail enough to make it seem safe and to mystify it enough to make it sacred.

His own jail plans averted by the chores of coalition-making, King had hoped to send Al Hibbler, the blind jazz singer who was the first of the outside "celebrities" to arrive in Birmingham, into the brig as a sort of canary. King had heard that Hibbler, who had socialized with the King family while touring with Duke Ellington, was coming to Birmingham later that month for a concert at A. G. Gaston's Hall Auditorium, and had called him up in New Jersey and asked him to

---

* Hard-core criminals on their way to the state penitentiary were held in the county jail.

come early. At a recent mass meeting, Hibbler promised "to free the people from discrimination and sing a song"—his trademark guttural rendition of "Nobody Knows the Trouble I've Seen."

But on Tuesday, April 9, leading pickets in front of Loveman's on Integration Corner (the intersection of Nineteenth Street and Third Avenue North), Hibbler had been frustrated from his goal of jail. While the other marchers were carted off in police wagons, he was chauffeured back to the Gaston Motel, his police escort explaining, "We could not leave a blind man alone on a street corner."

The next day, Bull Connor, who was blind in only one eye, accosted Hibbler: "Nigger, I'm taking your sign from you, and I'm taking your eyes away from you," whereupon he pulled away the woman holding Hibbler's free hand. Hibbler tried to follow his twenty-five jail-bound colleagues into the wagon. Connor ordered him "back against that wall."

"Don't tell me to get back against the wall. I'm a free man."

"You can't work and anyone who goes to jail has to earn his food," Connor said, adding, "You can't do anything, even entertain."

Hibbler said, "I'll be back tomorrow."

"Nigger," Connor said, "you just don't know when to quit."

Pritchett's Errand

LAURIE PRITCHETT WONDERED how much longer Bull Connor could resist the cheap shot that would stir up the national news media. The now-celebrated police chief of Albany, Georgia, was an old friend of Jamie Moore, the lanky country boy who had become Birmingham's police chief under Robert Lindbergh on the same day the Alabama Christian Movement for Human Rights was founded, in June 1956. By the time Connor reclaimed his office in 1957, the civil service system safeguarded Moore's job against Connor's usual ploy of firing chiefs in their first probationary year. So the commissioner simply circumvented Moore through handpicked proxies and personally took charge of the big assignments, as when he had encouraged the chief to take off Mother's Day 1961.

Moore had discussed the Birmingham police's "mishandling" of the Freedom Riders' bloodbath with Pritchett, who was his guest at the Alabama–Georgia Tech game at Legion Field the following fall. When Pritchett's own reputation was soon after tested by "agitators," Moore—accompanied by Detective Tom Cook, the "subversives" specialist who reported directly to Connor—went over to Albany in late July 1962 to observe his friend's smooth moves and fraternize with the cops billeted in a local motel. As soon as King moved on to Birmingham, Moore invited Pritchett up to brief Bull Connor in person.

The first thing Connor did in the company of the second most famous lawman in the South was brag about cementing up the holes in the closed-down public golf courses. Pritchett, aware that black people were not stereotypically passionate about golf, thought Connor should save "this stage stuff" for the voters. Then Connor boasted that he was prepared to use the K-9 Corps and the fire department, with their riot-dispersing fire hoses. "Deactivate them immediately," Pritchett advised.

In subsequent meetings, Pritchett outlined the theory of nonviolence for Connor, Moore, and Captain J. H. Woolley: It was "designed to put them over the edge," it was "intimidating and coercive." Woolley, in turn, gave his men a daily lecture at roll call: "If a camera catches you beating anyone, you'll be in Atlanta in twenty-four hours." In this case, "Atlanta" was the federal penitentiary.

Nonviolence was every bit as revolutionary for the Birmingham police as it was for the black masses. Although some Movement regulars were convinced that the detectives spying on their mass meetings were converted to the cause, more typical were the police lieutenant who awarded patrolmen a couple of days off for shooting a black burglary suspect and another lieutenant who liked to say, "If you arrest a live burglar, you have to work on two of your off-days." * Jim Parsons, the Connor-bashing reformer who had at long last made detective, believed that the basically decent men of the department, entrusted with protecting an "honest," law-abiding society, lost self-respect when they became party to policies that caused them to act counter to their personal values. So they found a scapegoat to blame for their feelings as well as to absorb the punishment they themselves deserved. Blacks were forced to give policemen a fraudulent version of the respect they could not give themselves, cowering and calling them "boss man"; even the African-Americans' private nicknames for them—coy expressions of contempt like "Mr. Blinky," "Mr. Clean," "Mr. Kid Gloves"—endowed the lawmen with a certain grandiosity.

Laurie Pritchett's transfusion of professionalism—"If they violate the law, arrest 'em"—did seem to be boosting police morale. Cops had even begun to countermand Connor. A lieutenant had intervened when the commissioner jostled Al Hibbler: "Mr. Connor, you can call him all the names you want to, but don't lay your hands on him." Driving "Mr. Hibbler" back to the Gaston Motel, the lieutenant had explained, "I like to hear you sing" and boasted that his arm had been broken as he helped Nat King Cole during the 1956 attack by Ace Carter's men at the Municipal Auditorium. Like Pritchett, Connor's men seemed well on their way to becoming media darlings. The *New York Times* had noted their impartiality in clearing spectators: "They have been charged in the past with using force only against Negroes." (The somewhat disappointing headline in *Jet* read, "Southern Policemen Adopting King's Non-violent Method.") So encouraged were the city fathers that Hayes Aircraft chief Lew Jeffers and a fellow Democrat operator, federal judge Clarence Allgood, took Connor to dinner at La Paree and advised him to get out of the way and let the demonstrations peter out on their own.

Before heading home, Laurie Pritchett paid a call on his "friend" Martin

---

* In Birmingham, it was held a fact of criminal science that the surest way to stop a crime wave—burglaries, rapes, whatever—was to go out and shoot a few suspects. ("This thing's getting out of hand," a lieutenant might say. "You know what we've got to do.")

Luther King, ascertained that he would not be coming back to Albany anytime soon, and paused at the Tutwiler Hotel to toast old battles with his other friends, in the civil rights press corps.

The Fall of Eastview

BULL CONNOR'S DILIGENCE had exceeded Pritchett's wishes. He had ordered the Klan to stay away from his confrontation with Martin Luther King. This time, he didn't trust his main man, Tom Cook, to deliver the message. Instead, he sent his homicide ace, Maurice House, to give the orders directly to two top Klan leaders. "Can't we help?" the Klansmen protested. House replied, "We want to keep our friendship with the Klan, but if you try to help us you'll be arrested."

Connor's final rebuff signaled that Klansmen's ties to the institutions of their society had officially unraveled. As old alliances dissolved, so too did old enmities. Ivan's restaurant, the former scene of police-Klan confidences, now provided the caffeine fuel for an unprecedented alignment: Hubert Page, Billy Holt, and Eastview's Exalted Cyclops, Robert Thomas, had begun to hold meetings, recorded for posterity by FBI informant Gary Thomas Rowe, with the old pariahs from the National States Rights Party, "Dr." Edward Fields and his mentor, J. B. Stoner.

March

AT EIGHT-THIRTY WEDNESDAY NIGHT, April 10, Martin Luther King went before the mass meeting at St. James A.M.E. Church and announced, "We are not here to do something for you, but to do something with you. . . . Everyone in the movement must live a sacrificial life." He was ready to march, he told the gathering. The failure of Project C to find a newsworthy crisis virtually compelled it. His planned surrender to the Birmingham authorities, two days hence, would finally bring the Movement's messiah to his Golgotha. "I can't think of a better day than Good Friday for a move for freedom," he said.

The police microphones had scarcely transmitted this scoop to the squad car parked outside the church before Bull Connor dispatched his two top city attorneys to the home of Judge William A. Jenkins Jr. in Mountain Brook's modest neighborhood of Crestline. A former criminal lawyer who hadn't had the stomach for jailhouse conferences with clients, forty-three-year-old Jenkins was a civil rights virgin; he disagreed with *Brown* on the ground of stare decisis, and his understanding of the Montgomery bus boycott consisted of "some woman got out of the back of the bus and moved to the front." It was Jenkins's reputation for granting employers temporary injunctions against striking workers that had singled him out for the honor of this visit on Wednesday night from attorneys James "Mack" Breckenridge and Earl McBee, career public servants. His ready signature restrained Walker, King, Abernathy, Shuttlesworth, A. D. King, 133 other named persons, and "Richard Roe and John Doe" from any further "plans or projects commonly called 'sit-in' demonstrations, 'kneel-in' demonstrations, mass street parades," etc.

The law enforcement official delegated to serve the injunction was Deputy Ray Belcher, one of the Klan's friendlier contacts inside the Jefferson County sheriff's department. When he arrived at the motel, Shuttlesworth, King, and Abernathy were waiting in the ground-floor restaurant drinking coffee, casual in shirtsleeves, as if they were not sitting amid a crush of reporters and it were not 1:15 in the morning. Wyatt Walker had alerted the press and the TV stations. Cameras flashed as the three read from the piece of paper. Shuttlesworth called the order "a flagrant denial of our constitutional rights." *Newsweek*'s Karl Fleming understood that this impromptu news conference was a turning point, an "electric event. One knew that the talk was over, that people were going to get hurt, possibly killed." At the very least, the injunction would bankrupt the campaign: Demonstrators violating the order could be charged with contempt of court on top of parading without a permit and moved out of city court into state court, significantly increasing the penalties and draining the bail fund. And if SCLC chose not to violate it, the Movement would be over anyway.

At noon the next day, Thursday, Shuttlesworth, King, and Abernathy took their places at a microphone-bordered table in the courtyard of the motel. Amid the rustle of the working press, King, in his Liberty overalls, read from the press release Walker had written in the early hours: "We cannot in all good conscience obey such an injunction, which is an unjust, undemocratic and unconstitutional misuse of the legal process." The black supporters jamming the motel balconies cheered his conclusion that the Movement was aware "of the possible consequences involved." Shuttlesworth nodded challengingly at a policeman taking notes and stated that if the police couldn't handle it, the mob would. Abernathy took care of the religious imagery: "Almost two thousand years ago Christ died on the cross for us. Tomorrow we will take it up for our people and die if necessary." There was no doubt as to which one in the trio was the Christ analog. "I am prepared to go to jail and stay as long as necessary," King said, creating news that would at last land Birmingham on the front page of the *New York Times.*

The two local newspapers continued to run aloof, unsigned stories about Project C on page 2 or deeper inside. The *Birmingham News*'s day-to-day coverage was being directed by managing editor John Bloomer, the journalist at the Trailways station two years earlier who had not recognized the freedom bus because it was so sleek and new. ("Those Freedom Riders—they were asking for it," he believed. "They came with the idea of stimulating a confrontation and they got it.") A native of Wabash, Indiana, Bloomer was an arch-conservative whose certainties were often inflamed by alcohol. On the grounds that segregated conditions here were no different from those of any other southern city, he forbade any mention in his paper of *why* Negroes might be demonstrating and what conditions would have to be met in order to end their protest. He insisted that their sole aim was to raise money for Martin Luther King. When Shuttlesworth tried to take out an ad to publicize the Movement's demands, the paper refused it.

King's Passion

ON THURSDAY AFTERNOON, the black and white "negotiators" who had convened on Tuesday repaired to Bishop C.C.J. Carpenter's study at the Church of the Advent for their second meeting. Even as the talks began, a dozen pickets materialized on the sidewalk in front of Pizitz department store, the first violators of Judge Jenkins's injunction. A passing truck driver called out to a TV cameraman, "Why don't you put buckshot in those things and shoot those black bastards?"

Inside the Advent, Sid Smyer—who had enlisted the incoming Chamber of Commerce president, William Spencer, and another Young Turk lawyer, George Peach Taylor, to replace Chuck Morgan—seemed miffed that Shuttlesworth had brought the same radicals, as if he were expecting Martin Luther King to come despite the whites' insistence on dealing only with locals. King's brother, A.D., checked the time. "You keep looking at your watch," Smyer said. "I'm going to speak last, and I want you to be here listening to me when I do." Nothing came of the meeting except a growing rapport between A. D. King and the liberal Episcopal bishop George Murray—Shuttlesworth warned his colleague not to be snowed by the white folks—and an agreement that both groups would put together separate negotiating committees of ten to twelve representatives for a conference the following Tuesday.

At city hall that day, Bull Connor smiled for the first time ever at the foe he had, at least twice, tried to have assassinated. "Shuttlesworth," he said, "if you wear those overalls to jail, they're going to work you real hard over there." Shuttlesworth said he was hoping to "save the city a few pennies' worth of workclothes."

That night, it became clear why Connor had been smiling: The city notified the Movement's local bail bondsmen—one of them was Hugo Black's old Klan boss from the 1920s, Jim Esdale—that no further bonds could be posted for the demonstrators because of SCLC's inadequate assets to cover them. With the jails not even close to full, this was a catastrophic blow. It was already tough enough to recruit demonstrators; now anyone who pledged to go to jail would have to stay indefinitely.

King had been on the phone with Harry Belafonte, wondering why the commitments made in his apartment two weeks earlier had not turned into cash. Wyatt Walker had planned for many contingencies, but the one area in which King was irreplaceable was fund-raising. Belafonte made it clear that his philanthropic task would be difficult if King was unavailable for personal appearances. "This means you can't go to jail," an aide reputedly told King.

A. G. Gaston seemed to be enjoying the reversal of SCLC's fortunes. On an hour's notice, he had canceled the concert at his auditorium that Al Hibbler had long been scheduled to play that Thursday afternoon. He explained to the singer that he "didn't want to go against the good white folks in Birmingham." Hibbler appeased the throng of fans with an a cappella performance of "He" in Kelly Ingram Park, and after the mass meeting gave his concert at the Star Bowling Alley as a Movement fund-raiser.

On Good Friday morning, Gaston arrived for the meeting of the central committee wearing his usual three-piece suit and watch chain. The injunction had given him and the other Big Boys a legal handle for criticizing the campaign, and they freely condemned King's intention to march in violation of a court order. Lucius Pitts also joined in the apparently well-rehearsed appeals for a "cooling-off period," which Abernathy assumed meant till "sometime after the Easter sales," in deference to the Big Boys' "white friends."

SCLC's critics had hit upon a sensitive dilemma for the Movement. Apart from the bail crisis, disobeying the injunction would undermine the South's white moderates who invoked "law and order" to urge compliance with unpopular Supreme Court rulings such as *Brown*. Selectively discounting court orders as morally and constitutionally wrong was also what the "Christian" white segregationists were doing in defying *Brown*. During the planning sessions for Birmingham, King, who had not yet disobeyed a court order, had argued, "Not every judge will issue an injunction," and Shuttlesworth had responded: "Where are those converted judges? Where did niggers ever move and law was not used to beat our heads, with the judges helping?" Shuttlesworth had insisted on both an SCLC board decision and a personal agreement with King that, as he put it later, "under no circumstances would we let the Ku Klux Klan, the police, or the courts stop this Movement. Even if there had been a federal injunction, we were going to violate it."

A few hours before King was supposed to march, twenty-five men and women were crammed into the "war room" of the Gaston Motel. King pulled on a cigarette while the strategists debated the damned-if-you-do-or-don't fine points of their leader getting arrested. As far as Shuttlesworth was concerned, this was a dog-and-pony show. He knew they were obliged to "hear some of the middle class" on the coordinating committee, but incredibly, many of King's aides were also agonizing over the merits.

Walker seemed to be the only person besides Shuttlesworth operating on the assumption that the decision had been made long before Judge Jenkins signed his injunction. Walker thought King "should have gone to jail earlier." Up for three nights without sleep, he had recently snapped for the first time at "Mr. Leader," as he half-seriously called King, slamming down his clipboard and saying he couldn't be everywhere at once.

Now, against what seemed to be the mounting consensus among the Atlanta lieutenants, Calvin Woods, the young ACMHR minister who had been spat upon during the first sit-in, spoke up. Woods said he had had a dream the night before. His fellow Birminghamians cringed, knowing of Calvin's tendency toward "visions" and trancelike pulpit rantings, begging God to save Bull, Wallace, and Khrushchev. "Something told me to tell you," he said to King, " 'Fear not the deprivation.' " King left his colleagues in the sitting area of the suite and closed himself in the bedroom to pray. The sounds of cheering and hymn-singing breezed through the open window from the mass meeting at Zion Hill Baptist.

Shuttlesworth recognized the symbolic value of King's Hamlet routine. He understood that making the press wait, making the public wait, created suspense. But as the minutes passed, Shuttlesworth began to worry that King did not understand that he *had* to march or else risk his authority as the leader of the Movement.

When King reemerged half an hour later, he was wearing his denim marching clothes.* M. L. "Daddy" King Sr., who had flown in from Atlanta, tried to talk some sense into his son. Never one to shy from hypocrisy, he who the night before had criticized Birmingham ministers for having "nothing to give to the movement" now urged his son to obey the injunction. His son turned to his best friend. Abernathy demurred—he did not want to go to jail; he wanted to be in his pulpit on Easter Sunday. "I am asking you to go with me," King said. Before Abernathy went into the bedroom to put on his workclothes, the twenty-five men and women joined hands and sang "We Shall Overcome."

The Meaning of Utter Darkness

CHEERING NEGROES thronged the streets around Zion Hill Baptist as King and Abernathy made their way there from the motel at around one-thirty. They walked unnoticed past a police car whose passengers were engrossed with the sound coming from their radio—the chants and hymns being piped in from the church via the electronic bug Abernathy had begun to berate at mass meetings as "that doohickey." SCLC had been trying to round up an impressive showing of ministers to march with King, but the big preachers had seized—embraced, it seemed—the injunction as an argument to end Project C. Robert Fulton, a peripatetic middle-aged white Presbyterian clergyman doing a year's stint on the Miles College faculty, shamed the black ministers by volunteering.

At 2:40, King and Abernathy walked down the church aisle toward the exit, leading a double-file column of fifty marchers at a leisurely pace. "There he goes, just like Jesus," someone called out, as if cued. The group proceeded three blocks

---

* Among the statements King is credited with: "I have decided to take the leap of faith. I have decided to go to jail. I don't know what's going to happen. I don't know if the movement will continue to build up or whether it will collapse. However if we obey Judge Jenkins' injunction the civil rights movement will be dead. . . . It's better to go to jail in dignity than to accept segregation in humility." Nichols, " 'Cities Are,' " p. 287.

• "I don't know what will happen; I don't know where the money will come from. But I have to make a faith act." M. L. King, *Why*, p. 73.

• "The path is clear to me. I've got to march. I've got so many people depending on me. I've got to march. . . . If we obey [the injunction], then we are out of business." Garrow, *Bearing*, p. 242.

• "Look, I don't know what to do. I just know that something has got to change in Birmingham. I don't know whether I can raise money to get people out of jail. I do know that I can go into jail with them." Williams, *Eyes*, p. 186, quoting Andy Young.

• "There's no point in going on a speaking tour. We've already raised all the money we can right now. The only thing to do is for me to go to jail, and join those people already there. And stay there until people see what we're dealing with. Those who're going with me, get ready." Young, *Burden*, pp. 214–15.

• "Gentlemen, thank you for your words of advice, but we're going to have to march. Now." Abernathy, *Walls*, p. 249.

east on Sixth Avenue North. At Seventeenth Street, the corner of Kelly Ingram Park where the dogs had attacked on Palm Sunday, the police awaited with a blockade, having been briefed by Walker on the route. King and the marchers turned right at the wall of police and headed south toward downtown. Onlookers clapped, skipped, and sang. From the sidelines, Wyatt Walker snapped pictures. The column turned back east on Fifth Avenue, but by then the police had redeployed. *Newsweek*'s Karl Fleming had visions of "the Charge of the Light Brigade." After the marchers had traveled another four and a half blocks, Bull Connor shouted to his men, "Stop them there." Two patrolmen wheeled their motorcycles in front of the line as if on a big vice raid and threw up their hands: "Halt!" King and Abernathy paused before kneeling.

The policemen and two detectives collared King and Abernathy and shoved them into the patrol wagon, providing the first memorable photographs of the campaign, men in blue manhandling men in blue. The work shirts being snatched by the police (no overalls today, but crisp denim jeans, rolled schoolboyishly at the cuff) looked starched and creased as if just unwrapped from cellophane, and the white visible in the photographs under the work-shirt collars appeared to be not T-shirts but the kind of cotton dress shirt the Movement leaders wore with their suits.

The car holding Abernathy and King was stalled for several minutes in the tumult of screeching motorcycles, shouted commands, and eerie wails from a woman or child. The cops were having a hard time telling the demonstrators from the hundreds of spectators who were singing and yelling encouragement. The official marchers lined up and waited to be loaded into the police wagon. All except Fred Shuttlesworth, who had marched only the first few blocks for the appearance of solidarity as well as the practical purpose of nailing down the last-minute details with King and Abernathy. The plan was for him to stay out of jail as long as the two others were in. When policemen appeared at the Gaston Motel later that day and took him to jail anyway, there were no cameras to capture his arrest.

Andy Young would call King's decision to go to jail in Birmingham "the beginning of his true leadership." Shuttlesworth said later, "I am sure that had I not been in Birmingham, he would not have marched. My position was forthright, and almost came down to an ultimatum."

At the Southside jail, the cops saved their worst insults—"Bullshit, bullshit!"—for the traitor to his race, the white Miles teacher Bob Fulton. The fifty-odd little-name marchers, including Miles professor Jonathan McPherson, were herded into the drunk tank with the hundred or so demonstrators already there. King, Abernathy, and Shuttlesworth were segregated from the other Movement folk in the new wing of the jail, a taupe-brick box erected in 1962; a plaque acknowledged its public sponsors—Connor, Hanes, and Waggoner—in a fitting memorial to the last city commission of Birmingham.

Shuttlesworth had earlier called Constance Baker Motley at the New York headquarters of the NAACP Legal Defense Fund (known as the "Inc. Fund") and, telegraphing his mistrust of Arthur Shores, asked her to send down someone to choreograph the expanding legal footwork. When Motley's envoy, a young Columbia Law graduate named Norman Amaker, arrived at the jail, Connor refused to let him see his clients. Amaker gave up and left the jail at eleven, and went to Wyatt Walker's "command post," a suite of offices in Gaston's sleek new office building overlooking Kelly Ingram Park. Walker had fired off telegrams to the Kennedy brothers: "Use the influence of your high office to persuade the city officials of Birmingham to afford at least a modicum of humane treatment. Neither of these men have mattress or bed linen." (The "neither" suggested that Shuttlesworth was no longer in the lead cast.) Upon receiving Amaker's report, Walker placed a 1 a.m. phone call to the Justice Department's Burke Marshall, who repeated what he'd been telling reporters: The federal government had no legal standing to get involved in Birmingham.*

The only way King could tell that his first night of penitence had ended was when slants of daylight appeared through the window high on the wall. "You will never know the meaning of utter darkness until you have lain in such a dungeon," he would observe, "knowing that sunlight is streaming overhead and still seeing only darkness below."

Shuttlesworth, Jonathan McPherson, and many other marchers made bond on Saturday, heralded by one of Shuttlesworth's picturesque statements: "The strange Stars of Segregation have fallen on Alabama, and they seem to have blinded the eyes of its judiciary." King and Abernathy remained in jail, prisoners as much to Wyatt Walker's PR imperatives as to Bull Connor.

Federal "Intervention"

Attorney General Robert Kennedy's renowned "ruthless" side had begun to chafe against his carefully cultivated passivity toward SCLC's mission in Birmingham. He began pestering Burke Marshall about why they couldn't intervene. Marshall would answer, "Well, who do you want to lead the Army—me or you? One step leads to another, and if you don't understand where you're going you've got to resist starting." On Saturday morning, when the President telephoned Marshall from his Palm Beach getaway to find out what could be done about King's jailing, Marshall took the hint and put in a call to Arthur Shores to inquire if King was in physical danger.

This first affirmative "intervention" by the federal government wasn't much, but Shores, accompanied by the NAACP Inc. Fund's Norman Amaker, took it to Bull Connor, who relented. When Amaker appeared at the jail, an official told a guard, "Bring that nigger King down here." Only Walker was not thrilled with the breakthrough: Now he would have to drop the adjective "incommunicado" from his description of King's predicament. Still there were other publicity angles to pursue.

---

* Marshall's contention was that since King et al. were only having their First Amendment rights to free speech and assembly violated, the federal government had no enforcement authority as it did in a statutory violation of, say, voting rights.

Soon after the last biracial meeting on Thursday, Bishop Coadjutor George Murray decided to take his frustration public. The previous January, he and some other white clergymen had released an unprecedented statement criticizing George Wallace on moral (rather than "bad for business") grounds, and perhaps he felt he had the authority now to condemn the demonstrations as "unwise and untimely" in light of the post-Connor "days of hope." Signed by seven ministers and a rabbi, Murray's statement urging "our own Negro community to withdraw support" from the "outsiders" had been published in the *Birmingham News* on Good Friday. Walker had assured the *New York Times,* which quoted liberally from it on Sunday, that a response would be forthcoming.

The battle seemed to be finally transcending the minutiae of Walker's dubious blueprint. As the white clergymen would soon learn, the Movement's God worked in ironic ways.

McWhorter 1963

EASTER SUNDAY DAWNED as only an Alabama spring morning can, with the fragrance of lilies thick upon the land. At eleven o'clock, a corps of pious black militants, in Sunday best despite the denim vogue, appeared at white churches around the city and spoiled the Resurrection mood. Andy Young and two women in Easter bonnets were admitted to services at First Baptist, and after an usher refused Young's extended hand and offering, the Reverend Earl Stallings demonstrated that he had not been defending segregation itself when he signed the published statement asking Martin Luther King to leave town. He shook hands with all three.

Easter was the occasion for the Mountain Brook Club's biggest Sunday lunch of the year. It was the opening day of white-shoe season, and pastels bloomed in the dim downstairs grill. I had gotten my pale green Easter dress at Loveman's in the nick of time, though the main wardrobe concern of my peer group that spring was our leisure wear: denim overalls, cut off above the knee, with fathers' cast-off shirts underneath. We made trips downtown to a tiny plank-floored store on Second Avenue North called Creidman's to get Liberty overalls—the brand that Vulcan wore during his commercial stint at the Fairgrounds. To be really cool, one's back-bib label had to say "Give me LIBERTY" rather than just "LIBERTY."

The men at the club were working on a consensus. There was nothing to the "trouble downtown." It was quiet as a tomb there. Still, mothers were beginning to rethink Saturday-matinee privileges for their children, especially those of us making return visits to *To Kill a Mockingbird.* (Mary Badham went to Hollywood that month for the Oscars, losing out in the best supporting actress category to Patty Duke, who had played another Alabama girl, Helen Keller, in *The Miracle Worker.*) No one quite knew what to make of the demonstrations. The only black "mass movement" white people had ever seen was the molasses-like tide of maids rolling through the Mountain Brook streets to the bus stops every afternoon at four. What had now come over them, our colored people whom we took such pride in "knowing"?

We were living in a racial interregnum. Birmingham had never permitted the early-childhood camaraderie common among blacks and whites in old slave societies—and miscegenation was something most Birminghamians learned about when they read William Faulkner in high school. My generation barely had even the "know-your-place" relationships that had been conscience savers for my parents and grandparents. "Why, Edward raised the boys!" my grandmother often said of her housekeeper Ruby Thornton's son, and proudly recounted the guest cottages Edward shared with Martin and Hobart on vacations to the Gulf Coast. As for Mama Ruby, it wasn't until I saw a picture of my aunt and her bridesmaids, with a lace cap–framed black face in the background, that I realized what my grandmother meant when she said, "Ruby was practically *in* Gail's wedding." My friends and I had to make do with "loving our maid" (never say "the maid") from an awkwardly formal distance and with the furtive kick we got out of using the maid's bathroom.

My family wasn't rich enough for full-time help, and our series of part-time cleaning women, some barely out of their teens, had nothing in common with my friends' matronly maids, who were as passively accommodating as furniture. When the demonstrations began, our maid was Thelma, barely twenty, beautiful, and fun. White women often declared utter dependence on their cleaning women to properly iron their husbands' shirts, but Thelma's claim to fame was that she sounded like a white person. "Oh, you have company," callers would say to Mama if Thelma had answered the phone. Mama was tickled over having a maid about whom everyone said, "But she talks so nice," and passed the compliment on to her. Right before Thelma left us in 1963, to marry a steelworker, Mama had called her about working an extra day and heard her summoned to the telephone as Velma. She insisted that we stick with Thelma, though. Servants were always being called by names that weren't quite theirs, much as the slaves had inherited the names of their masters.

It was at the Mountain Brook Club that the illusion of interracial fellowship remained whole. Our beloved waiters were all there on Easter Sunday, acting as if Martin Luther King did not exist. I basked in the head waiter Lindsay Gaines's usual greeting—"Hello, Missy" (after a more unctuous "Miz McWhorter?" to my grandmother)—and our mutual regard hardly compared to the relationship my father had had with the club staff. As a teenager he had spent a few hours in jail—the jail that now housed King—for two Mountain Brook Club waiters. Martin and Hobart had witnessed the waiters' car collide with a carload of white boys downtown one night, and when the McWhorters informed the police that the whites had run a red light, a brawl ensued between the white factions over the fighting words "nigger lover." In a measure of how drastically my father had bucked the norm in taking the side of the waiters, he and Hobart rather than "nigger haters" were taken to jail.

I HAD BEGUN to die a thousand deaths when my mother's car—the current one a scruffy old black-and-white Dodge station wagon—pulled up among the Cadillacs and wood-paneled air-conditioned station wagons at Brooke Hill. Papa bought these secondhand wonders at auctions held in Attalla, a tough town east of Birmingham. (He insisted on Chrysler, saying that Ford—his father's preferred automobile maker—stood for "Fix or Repair Daily" or "Found on the Road Dead.") Perhaps the only reason my chagrin wasn't reciprocated by my classmates as contempt was that the school we all went to had been founded by my father's parents, along with two other couples, because they had been worried that daughter Gail might be unprepared for Wellesley.

At first I believed Papa would eventually make his way back to Mountain Brook, as he had come home in time for Gail's debut. I had thought Crestline Park was just another one of his "experiences," like cooking shoats by the Pearl River. I had begun to disdain the good-natured Crestline Park moms who let me call them by their first names; they wore pants that emphasized their bottoms, popped their gum, and used bad words like "crap." My older brother, Craig, reported back to me the word on the street: I was "stuck-up."

For a few months, my parents had been talking seriously about moving out of the little house on Hoadley Drive. My spirits rose, but Papa found fault with every prospect Mama looked at in Mountain Brook. His particular objection, which ruled out nearly every house there, was that he did not want to climb any steps to reach the front door, whether because of the liquid hobby that was making him come home later and later or because he refused to end up in a house on a hill.

What Mama had managed to keep from us was that Papa did not want to move into a house at all. He wanted to move into a trailer. One Saturday in early 1963, he took her to see the model unit at a trailer park just off a bleak commercial strip in Irondale, a lowly suburb Mama and I referred to as Arndale, mocking the pronunciation of its residents. Martin McWhorter wanted to settle his family there.

I was covered with shame. Could even the granddaughter of "Miz Mc-Whorter," as my friends' mothers referred to Marjorie with hushed respect, withstand the disgrace of having her address listed in the Brooke Hill handbook as "The Irondale Trailer Park"? This was my trauma in the spring of 1963, and it was not wholly unrelated to the social breakdown that was taking place on the streets.

14.

TWO MAYORS AND A KING

Fighting

Late on Easter afternoon, A. D. King, John Porter, and Calvin Woods led thirty official marchers out of Thirgood C.M.E. Church through a parting sea of singing, clapping, and laughing onlookers. Their destination was Southside jail, to pray for King and Abernathy. The crowd that the *New York Times* put at two thousand began to sing "We Shall Overcome," further blurring the line between spectators and protesters.

Police reserves checked the marchers in a vacant lot to await the patrol wagons. As they drove the prisoners away, the crowd bridled. The *Times* would headline its story "Fighting Erupts at B'ham." The reporter placed equal blame on the three black rock throwers arrested and the policemen who clubbed to the ground a young boy trying to flee. But nonviolent law enforcement was becoming an oxymoron. While escorting one out-of-town newsman away, a cop shoved aside another reporter. The police were giving Wyatt Walker one more reason to praise the Lord that holy day.

Trigger Fingers

Tommy Blanton's Catholic neighbor had awakened Easter morning to find her car covered with red paint; several weeks earlier, the decapitated head of a lawn jockey had been placed on her car seat. Bobby Cherry, the old Ace Carter Klansman now part of the hardest core of Eastview 13, spent Easter night with Klan brothers Wyman and Wallace Lee. After putting a new grip on Cherry's .38 Smith and Wesson, Wyman, a gas station attendant who had reportedly accompanied Cherry on the Krystal mission, told him to check the hammer to make sure it hadn't jammed. Cherry pulled the trigger, discharging a bullet into Wyman's gut. They drove him to Carraway Hospital, where a surgeon removed one kidney.

One frustrated Eastview Klansman proposed bombing one of the churches where the Movement was meeting. But a police officer warned that if they got within fifty feet of it they would be killed. To prove his point, the policeman drove

Tommy Rowe and a few Klansmen by the church and shined his flashlight on a second-floor window. A black man raised a window and showed his shotgun. "Just wanted to see if everything's all right," the cop called.

Two Mayors

THE MORNING AFTER EASTER, Mayor-elect Albert Boutwell and the new city council were sworn into office. Foster Hailey, the *Times* reporter, saw the ceremony through a mist of false hope. "A warm sun was shining" on Boutwell and the councilors on the steps of city hall, and a "picnic" atmosphere infected the two hundred spectators standing in Woodrow Wilson Park, about a fourth of whom were blacks Wyatt Walker had urged to welcome the man their vote had elected. The media were buying the white moderates'—and the Kennedy administration's—position that Boutwell, rather than King or Shuttlesworth, was the legitimate savior of Birmingham.

Inside city hall Bull Connor was stage-directing Ralph Abernathy and Martin Luther King's first excursion outside the jail in three days, for a court hearing. Earlier that morning, Clarence Jones, the smooth black New York entertainment lawyer who raised money for SCLC, had appeared at King's cell with good news: Harry Belafonte had raised $50,000 for bail bonds and promised to come up with "whatever else you need." The prospect of continued battle with SCLC seemed to have buoyed Connor. "I'm surprised you got tied to these Communists," he said to Ed Gardner, Shuttlesworth's right-hand man, in the hall. "I thought you were my best friend."* To Orzell Billingsley, the Movement lawyer far less inhibited than his cousin Arthur Shores, Connor remarked, "Orzell, if any more of my police get hurt, we're gonna have some trouble." Though proud of his versatility (he had "friends in the Klan," a soft spot for George Wallace dating from the "little judge"'s warmth toward black lawyers, and a friendship as well as an attorney-client relationship with Rat Killer, the informant-bootlegger), Billingsley had recently had to act fast to avoid being seen talking shop with Connor on the street by ducking into a fraternal order dining room.

With his truest antagonist, Connor was playful. Fred Shuttlesworth was at the water fountain about to sample some white water when Connor came out of his office and called, "Awww, I got you." As it turned out, the city hall fountains had been shut off and the restrooms locked, forcing Shuttlesworth to walk across the street to the Greyhound station, where he encountered four or five cops also using the facilities. "Bull has got us in the same position you Negroes are in," one said. Another agreed, "Yeah, Reverend, you got this damn town rocking."

The payoff for Wyatt Walker's efforts to liberate Project C from the parochial concerns of city hall came that afternoon. The previous day, a worried

---

* A city court judge, searching madly for the Communist plot behind the demonstrations, had sent Connor a copy of "Commands for the Volunteers," which had been taken from a juvenile girl arrested in the early sit-ins. The only sinister thing that he could find was commandment number 10, "Follow the directions of the movement and of the captain on a demonstration."

Coretta King had called him to report that her husband had not phoned her from jail. Walker had suggested that she appeal to the President of the United States. John Kennedy returned her call late on Monday to say her husband was safe and would be phoning shortly. Police Chief Jamie Moore denied to reporters that presidential intervention led to the ensuing phone call. In fact, he said King hadn't even *asked* to speak to his wife, which Moore implied was kind of strange, considering that Mrs. King had just had a baby. But perhaps it was action from another quarter that had gotten the phone privileges. Connor had bragged to his adviser Judge Clarence Allgood that his prisoner was asking to call his wife but that he wasn't going to let him. "You better let him," the federal judge ordered unofficially, "or I'm going to make you." Connor sent Judge Allgood a police tape of the call.

Among the first things King had asked his wife was if the President had called her directly.

"Yes, and he told me you were going to call in a few minutes. . . ."

"Is that known?" King asked anxiously and told her to inform Wyatt Walker right away. Then he asked about the new baby.

Walker jubilantly alerted the press to the President's overture and told the night's mass meeting that the campaign was going into its "second phase" of federal engagement. Shuttlesworth sang a song that went on for a good fifteen minutes. Around that time Chuck Morgan dropped by the Gaston Motel for a drink. While gassing with Clarence Jones, he sized up the mood of the Movement leaders. They knew they were going to win; they just didn't know how.

Morgan's view of the city's two-mayor dilemma was this: "Added together, they'd hardly make one." When Mayor Boutwell and the council arrived at city hall the next day, Bull Connor and Jabo Waggoner ignored them; as far as they were concerned, their terms expired on October 1, 1965. (The deposed commission president, Art Hanes, made room for Boutwell in a cubbyhole off his office.) At the last fall of the gavel at the commission's regular Tuesday meeting, the new officials tackled the agenda all over again. Until the courts ruled on the legitimate officeholders, in an estimated two weeks, all decrees and checks would have to be signed by both governments. The few whites whose sense of humor had not deserted them would jest that Birmingham had two mayors, a King, and a parade every day.

The Jailhouse Epistle

DESPITE THE MOMENTUM, Project C was still struggling to surmount the tactics, and the tactics weren't even working. Press coverage of the presidential call to Coretta ranged from unimpressed (the *New York Times*) to unbelieving ("Just a Bit Phony," a *Washington Star* editorial was headlined). *Time* titled its story "Poorly Timed Protest," and *Newsweek* implied that King was as much an extremist as Bull Connor. The Kennedy administration was still publicly deploring SCLC's timing, and the Reverend Billy Graham would soon tell his "good personal friend" King to "put the brakes on." Far from redeeming himself for Albany, King was still being portrayed by the press as a spoilsport for raining on Boutwell's parade.

The previous July, during the ill-fated Albany campaign, Harvey Shapiro, an editor of the *New York Times Magazine,* had called SCLC's Atlanta office to propose that King write a "letter from prison," after the example of earlier saints who were political prisoners. The assignment had been queered by the unexpected brevity of that jail stay. Now, King began a letter from prison, addressed to "My dear fellow clergymen," on the margins of a five-day-old *Birmingham News* that published the local clergymen's criticisms of SCLC's campaign.

King started off wearily, explaining that if he made a habit of answering his critics, he would have time for nothing else. But he believed these to be "men of genuinely good will," singling out First Baptist's Earl Stallings for his courtesy during the "kneel-ins" of Easter morning. The opening was a gambit for the tour de force that followed, a just-short-of-condescending lesson in the discipline of nonviolence combined with an awesome exhibition of spiritual scholarship. The quotations from St. Augustine, St. Thomas Aquinas, Socrates, John Bunyan, Martin Buber, Reinhold Niebuhr, T. S. Eliot, and on and on, suggested the frustration of someone too often obliged to justify himself to his intellectual inferiors, who was exhilarated at the chance to cut loose with his peers. Conspicuously neglecting the main source of his identity as preacher-protester—the black church—King was adroitly selling himself as a citizen of the world, like Apostle Paul, that circuit-riding troubleshooter and quintessential author of jailhouse epistles.

The letter's most topical passage concerned the defiance of the court injunction, a forceful defense concluding that "everything Adolf Hitler did in Germany was 'legal' and everything the Hungarian freedom fighters did in Hungary was 'illegal.' " His most trenchant yet almost offhanded insight was into what Virginia Durr liked to call the "Sweet People," the average decent citizen of Birmingham. King wasted little time detailing the city's "ugly record of brutality." It was not this, he pointed out, but the broken promises of the city fathers the previous fall that had led to direct action. "I have almost reached the regrettable conclusion that the Negro's great stumbling block in his stride toward freedom is not the White Citizens' Counciler or the Ku Klux Klanner, but the white moderate, who is more devoted to 'order' than to justice; who prefers a negative peace which is the absence of tension to a positive peace which is the presence of justice; who constantly says: 'I agree with you in the goal you seek, but I cannot agree with your methods of direct action.' . . . Shallow understanding from people of good will is more frustrating than absolute misunderstanding from people of ill will."

King's lawyers—Jones, Shores, Billingsley—sneaked the scraps of paper on which King had written over to Wyatt Walker's command post in Gaston's office building. Walker deciphered the manuscript for his secretary, Willie Pearl Mackey. ("Dr. King does not have a Spenserian hand," Walker said. "I was the only one who could translate that chicken scratch.") When Mackey fell asleep over her typewriter, Walker continued the typing. Drafts were sent back to King through the lawyers, with queries of "Is this what you meant?" A long section on how the civil rights movement would also liberate the white man was cut, as was a discussion of how it would enhance U.S. moral authority in the Cold War. When the last draft was completed on Thursday, April 18, King reputedly had no idea of its moment. But legend would have Walker declaring, "This is going to be one of the historic documents of this movement. Call it 'Letter from a Birmingham Jail.'"

Martin Luther King's "Letter" was a masterpiece, a triumph of tone as much as of exposition, *the* statement of purpose for the modern civil rights movement and probably the most eloquent treatment of the nexus between law and injustice since Henry David Thoreau's essay "Civil Disobedience." King had placed the black struggle into the archetypal American drama of religious persecution. But Wyatt Walker could find no accomplices for turning it into a PR opportunity for the Movement. Harvey Shapiro could not get the letter past his bosses at the *Times.* It would not be published in full for nearly two months, and it became a sacred civil rights document only in the afterglow of Birmingham.*

As he later settled into obscurity, Fred Shuttlesworth would say that his name ought to have been on the "Letter," in keeping with the policy of jointly signed statements. The clergymen whom King addressed claimed never to have received a personal copy and smarted as their reputation as bigots grew with the fame of the essay.

Marchless

BY PREARRANGEMENT WITH KING, on the afternoon of his jailing Jim Bevel had roared in from Mississippi in his 1959 Rambler and found a campaign in trouble. He immediately informed his SCLC brethren, "You guys are running a scam movement. In a movement you don't deal with the press. You act like there is no press. Otherwise you end up staging it. A movement is when people actually do out of conviction." His speech at the mass meeting that night was more lye in the face. "Some Negroes don't want to get well," he said. "If they do, they would have to compete with the white man. There are some Negroes who want segregation as much as Bull Connor." He called the detectives present in the church "white trash" and served notice on his fellow blacks: "If God can feed the cockroach, he can feed the Negro." His closing exhortation could barely be heard over the noise of the crowd: "The Negro has been sitting here dead for three hundred years. It is time he got up and walked."

So began Bevel's call to the masses. The fallacy of building a movement around the personality of King was clear in the fallout from his jailing. Once he was removed from the action (and the press's assassination watch suspended), fear had returned to the locals. On Tuesday night, April 16, four days into King's jail

---

* For years to come, scholars would dissect its classic rhetorical form, comparing it to Lincoln's Gettysburg Address and Zola's *J'accuse* in defense of Dreyfus. It would be printed in the *Atlantic Monthly, Christian Century,* the *New Leader,* and *Liberation.*

stay, only 9 seasoned "jailbirds" out of the 700 people at the mass meeting agreed to march. The next night, Andy Young called for volunteers for twenty minutes before netting 7 teenagers. Barely 300 people (fewer when the repeaters were taken into account) had gone to jail, compared with 738 imprisoned in the first phase of the Albany marches. "There are more Negroes going to jail for getting drunk," the Reverend J. S. Phifer (visiting from White Plains) had scolded an earlier mass meeting. Rumors of inmates being stuck with needles for "blood tests" had robbed jail of some of its glamour. Wyatt Walker desperately began playing up the store boycott, putting together a "Grapevine Squad" to squeal on illicit shoppers. Project C was hemorrhaging.

The white folks had also begun to smell the Movement's failure. That Tuesday, Sid Smyer was to have brought a dozen white representatives to the bargaining table with the Movement's spokesmen. Late the night before, the Alabama Council's Jim Jimerson and David Vann met at a Movement minister's home with an unnamed King aide—probably Andy Young—who was pleasantly surprised that Vann's concern was not simply to end the demonstrations but also to seek just solutions. One black observer had thought the meeting marked the start of meaningful negotiations. Then, on short notice the next morning, Smyer and his men canceled the scheduled gathering; the *News*'s Vincent Townsend had advised them to hold out because the demonstrations were fading away on their own.

Walker sent Shuttlesworth to Washington to appear before the National Press Club because the media had been ignoring Birmingham all week. SCLC's man in Washington, the Reverend Walter Fauntroy, who was on tap to fly to Birmingham if Walker was jailed, judged Shuttlesworth's performance "tremendous," especially in defusing the criticism of the campaign's timing. Shuttlesworth then went to see Burke Marshall at the Justice Department. Though Walker had launched an impromptu voter-registration drive to draw the administration into the Birmingham campaign, Marshall stuck so unflappably to his no-basis-for-federal-action refrain that Shuttlesworth threatened to go back to jail with King and Abernathy and stay indefinitely. The next day, Saturday, April 20, however, King and Abernathy posted $300 cash bonds and left jail. Abernathy somewhat apologetically assured the press that they were not "the Castro brigade," despite their jailhouse beards, and flew straight home to Atlanta. Shuttlesworth returned to Cincinnati.

Smelling defeat, A. G. Gaston evicted the Movement from an office in his building on Fifth Avenue and Sixteenth Street, accusing workers of carrying on with dope and whiskey. Walker could no longer afford to alienate him and attempted to defuse this newest incident by announcing, "Those here on the scene know that Dr. Gaston has supported the movement from its inception." Walker was touting himself, King, Abernathy, and Shuttlesworth as the "Four Horsemen of Civil Rights," failing to take into account that the original horsemen represented Conquest, Slaughter, Famine, and Death. Reporters were turning to Andy Young for official statements, some having come to the conclusion that Walker

was the epitome of SCLC's nickname, "Slick"—"a man who was not to be believed, a minister though he was," said the *Times's* Claude Sitton, who had a special affection for "the SNCC kids" and their SCLC cousin, Bevel.

Even with King and Abernathy returning to action on Monday, April 22,
there was an air of resignation at the mass meeting that night. John Porter, the reluctant activist, had volunteered his big church, although some ACMHR regulars
noted that the minister himself was not in attendance, and Abernathy needled
him about locking up his Bible before the masses arrived. Ed Gardner was losing
his sweet touch, telling the people that if they turned their money loose fast (and
he always preferred "quiet money," bills), they could leave. Donations came to
$700, a far cry from the $7,000 collected a week earlier. King gave a speech that
betrayed depression. "Don't worry about it and don't think we are going to lose in
Birmingham," he said. "Our destiny is tied up in the destiny of this nation." The
Reverend Calvin Woods countered with a more realistic view: "As soon as one of
us gets to the top of the mountain, someone is there to pull us back down into the
valley." Only ten people volunteered to demonstrate.

Lawyers

As Project C faltered, the bulwark of segregation that had gone by the name of
"Me and Jim" also seemed to be teetering toward an anticlimax. Ironically, Jim
Simpson was not present for his protégé's last stand—he was off touring the
Greek Isles with his wife, Florence. Once the Great Man, Simpson had now be-
come a prodigal son and spoiler, unwittingly identifying with the anti-
establishment father whom he had designed everything about his life to reject.
The elite men of his adopted social class had finally abandoned the consensus he
had so long ruled, had put their brains and money together to oust the dictator
Simpson had created and propped up for twenty-five years, and did even still.

The previous January, Simpson had filed suit challenging the November referendum that abolished Connor's office. Though he lost his case, the commission
remained alive on a technicality when a majority of four state supreme court justices declined to rule on when the new government should take over. Thus, the
mayor and the city council had had to file suit to eject the commissioners whom
the Movement humorously called the "sit ins" at city hall.

On Tuesday, April 23, Judge Edgar Bowron ruled that Connor, Hanes, and
Waggoner were not the legitimate city government. Simpson's firm was ready on
the draw to appeal the decision to the Alabama Supreme Court, which brought
"Me and Jim" a final reprieve.

Down the corridor from Judge Bowron in the county courthouse, King,
Abernathy, Walker, Shuttlesworth et al. went on trial for contempt of court, having willfully violated an injunction. The NAACP had stepped in conspicuously to
represent them, signaled by the presence of Roy Wilkins, the organization's president, and the Inc. Fund's Constance Baker Motley. Some years back, a local black
lawyer had squired Motley around the Saturday-night hangouts in search of

Tuxedo Junction, the Ensley dance hall commemorated in a tune of the same name by Erskine Hawkins, a black trumpeter from Birmingham who became the toast of New York's Savoy Ballroom. (His Big Band number had not become a household tune until it was recorded by Glenn Miller, who was white). The reserved product of New Haven, Connecticut, Motley had been staggered by the sheer number of black people in Birmingham; "anything could happen here," she felt. Now she and her colleagues saw a way to edge the masses off the Movement forefront: They proposed shifting the focus of the campaign to King's trial, a courtroom drama that would expose the legal side of segregation.

King declined. After all, the SCLC strategists joked, though they were happy to reveal their plans to the police and the press, their lawyers were kept in the dark for as long as possible. Yet the truth was, the trial was now the most sensational thing going, what with detectives telling Judge William Jenkins that Shuttlesworth was spitting in their faces out in the halls. But King's attempt to explain what an injunction was to the Tuesday, April 23, mass meeting only emphasized that it would take more than a show trial to salvage the campaign.

A Mind Unchained

PROVIDING AS USUAL the Movement's theatrics, Shuttlesworth impishly put his arms around the two white female Birmingham-Southern students who had come to the mass meeting. "Of course, when he did that every Negro in the church came out of his seat hollering, screaming, and applauding," a police detective commented tolerantly.

With the meeting still in progress, the national press broke camp in Birmingham and rushed forty miles east to Attalla. William Moore, a white postman in his thirties from Baltimore, was seventy miles into his one-man Freedom Walk from Chattanooga to his native Mississippi. Moore had apparently been driven crazy by the racial horrors he saw growing up there; after being confined to a New York State mental hospital for more than a year, he wrote a book, *The Mind in Chains,* explaining, "I believed the world was wrong and so did not adjust my behavior to reality."

Earlier that Tuesday, he had marched on swollen, blistered bare feet down U.S. Highway 11 wearing a signboard that read "Eat at Joe's Both Black and White." His effects were in a two-wheel postal cart. Toward evening, a Gadsden radio reporter asked him how he felt about all the threats against his life. "I don't believe the people in the South are that way," Moore said. "I think a lot of this stuff is just made up." Within the hour, the husky ex-Marine, still wearing his signboard, lay faceup by the side of the road, with two .22-caliber bullet holes in his head.*

Upstaged, the Klansmen of Eastview almost lost their nonviolence the next

---

* The bullets were traced to a rifle that belonged to a store owner named Floyd Simpson, who had earlier asked Moore to explain his views on integration. No one was ever indicted for the murder.

day, April 24, orders or no orders from city hall. Some klavern regulars were patrolling the department stores downtown when Martha Turnipseed, a white Methodist minister's daughter who was one of Birmingham-Southern's Christian radicals, participated in a lunch counter sit-in at Woolworth's. In light of the Klansmen's fury, Turnipseed was whisked out a side door to safety. In the crowd, the *News's* Tom Lankford spotted the familiar face of Howard Thurston Edwards, the Irondale man identified by police as the pipe-armed assailant at the center of Tommy Langston's photograph of the Mother's Day attack at the Trailways station two years earlier.

Disc Jockeys

JIM BEVEL FINALLY DECIDED that he had no choice but to force democracy on the Birmingham project. It was not incidental, Bevel believed, that he and Diane Nash "practiced democracy" in their marriage, as soul mates and equal partners, whereas the other SCLC ministers, with the exception of Shuttlesworth (domestic tyrant though he was), excluded their wives from joining their "real work." Bevel told his SCLC colleagues, "You guys are playing like you have a movement."

Since the week of King's jailing, Bevel had been conducting a countercampaign to the chief-laden event Birmingham had become. Essentially he was retracing the twenty-year-old footprints of the Southern Negro Youth Congress. The key to saving Birmingham, he believed, was kids, free of the material burdens that made their elders cautious. And Bevel made a perfect Pied Piper. With his bib overalls (the pockets made "an excellent office filing system"), shaved head, and yarmulke, he was a militant out of Dr. Seuss—an ordained minister who "could get teen-age girls to take him home and then would seduce their mothers," according to his former SNCC colleague Julian Bond.* Bevel sought out what he called the student "influence leaders," and the most efficient access to them was through a hitherto untapped Movement resource—the black disc jockey.

Around the corner from the Gaston Motel down Fourth Avenue, at the studios of WENN, the premier black radio station, Bevel found his deputies: Birmingham's best-known black show-biz personalities. Black entertainers had not generally used their favored status in white America to promote their race. Nat King Cole had refused even to participate in anti-Klan rallies, which perhaps explained why his beating in Birmingham did not draw much sympathy from Thurgood Marshall, who said that all Cole needed to complete his Uncle Tom act was a banjo. Though singers Lena Horne and Harry Belafonte were discreetly radical, their appeal was more to rich white liberals and their own "talented tenth" than to a mass audience. Disc jockeys such as Shelley Stewart were a breed apart.

Stewart had experienced the ache of intraracial inferiority in Rosedale, the bourgeois Negro preserve where Shuttlesworth had been bused to high school.

---

* Bond was the son of the prominent educator and author Horace Mann Bond, who had been red-baited into resigning from SNYC's advisory board in the 1940s.

His father, an alcoholic TCI laborer, had killed four-year-old Shelley's mother—a "nigger crime" that went unpunished. Middle-class neighbors would not let their children play with the four Stewart boys, but they did call in the health department to inspect some traps in the chicken yard, which caught the rats that their father's girlfriend fried for the boys' supper. Shelley ran away from home not long after his arm was broken by his drunk father and found grunt work and a bed of straw at a Tennessee walking horse stable outside Crestline Village—hence his facetious claim to have grown up in Mountain Brook.

A wealthy client, impressed with "the little colored boy who could read," placed him in a congenial black home, and Shelley graduated from Rosedale at the top of his class. He borrowed a suit to consult his principal, B. M. Montgomery (whose son Jim was now Shuttlesworth's doctor), about the best way for him to get to law school. Montgomery took one look at Shelley's dark complexion and counseled him to become a mechanic. Instead, he took the *Silver Comet* to New York City, worked as a house painter, and enrolled at the Cambridge School of Broadcasting. In 1949, he was hired by a black Manhattan station to do a weekend show, on which he rhapsodized about his Magic City.

Stewart returned to Birmingham, conked his hair with a straightening solution of lye and grease, aspiring to the Nat King Cole waves in vogue among black performers, and took the "handle" demanded of black deejays. But Shelley the Playboy (after his female fan club known as the Playgirls) was no conformist. He preferred a "crazy nigger" falsetto—"Ooh! Good goobly woobly!"—to the School of Broadcasting hyperenunciation that had black announcers speaking of "senatoars in Washingtahn." Cuing a hot record ("Tim-berrr, let it fall!"), he seemed on the verge of either euphoria or violence, and by and by the white kids who listened to black radio stations for the rowdiest of James Brown began to appropriate Stewart's slang. "Shelley, you're white," they told him at the platter parties he deejayed.

The Klan cut down his radio tower in 1958. Bull Connor called him "Shelley the Plowboy." Stewart referred to his fellow radio announcer as "Eugene" and snickered on the air about Connor's morals trials. His listeners reaped his sarcasm too. "Get some education," he said. "Someday we may want to drive the bus instead of ride in the back of the bus." When Jim Bevel showed up at his station, they found they spoke the same language.

The other hot jock, "Tall Paul" Dudley White (after the eminent white physician of the same name), had grown up in a rough Southside neighborhood and did not readily make friends. Though his lean six-foot-three frame was his most striking feature, closer inspection yielded insight into his aloof "outsiderness." He had kinky black hair and blue eyes. Tall Paul did, however, cultivate his young fans, holding court with them at the Gaston Motel, and at Bevel's request, he and Stewart were happy to go on the radio and announce "hot luncheon" at the motel for some of their friends—beauty queens and football stars they had gotten to know at school dances. Twenty or thirty high school big shots and church youth leaders showed up for a strategy meeting with Bevel. Their assignment was to start a "whisper campaign" on upcoming workshops and youth rallies. To "make them feel like they were doing something half-sneaky, half-devilish," Bevel passed out small palm cards to conceal from the adults. ("Fight for freedom," they said. "Then go to school.") Andy Young and Bernard Lee, the old Alabama State sit-in leader who was now King's aide-de-camp, helped Bevel break in a corps of young lieutenants, recent high school graduates like Andrew Marrisett and James Orange, who would go on to become minor legends as SCLC staff members.

Young folk began arriving in vast waves at Sixteenth Street Baptist to hear Bevel's afternoon harangues. First he had them admit their part in the existing social problem: Your grandmama went along with disfranchisement. When blacks vote, he explained, " 'niggers' become 'colored constituents.' " Bevel had been known to take his young trainees to a graveyard and say, "In forty years you are going to be here. Now, what are you going to do while you're alive?"

The schoolchildren went nuts. No one had ever talked to them like that, goading them to freedom rather than coaxing them into "gittin' an education." Despite the collection of weapons—knives, razors, nail files—that was taken up at those first youth rallies, Bevel had no doubt that the students could be converted to nonviolence. He screened for them a two-year-old NBC White Paper hosted by Chet Huntley (it had been spiked locally by Vincent Townsend) on the 1960 Nashville sit-ins, culminating in the famous march of four thousand and Diane Nash's triumphant showdown with Mayor Benjamin West. This was Bevel's vision for Birmingham, dwarfing the pitiful demonstrations that Walker was trying to charm from the dried-up pool of adults.

After the youth rally on Wednesday afternoon, April 24, many of the children went directly to the night's mass meeting at St. James Baptist, flooding the aisles to make this the first standing-room-only meeting since King's jailing. Fire marshal Aaron Rosenfeld ordered those without seats to leave. A discussion ensued between the fireman ("My good people, this is a law") and Shuttlesworth ("Is this a law, or are you just trying to harass us?"), until the preacher salvaged the situation by addressing the whites in the audience: "Mr. Detective, I don't know where you going to sit. But if you going to stand, then I'm going to call these other people back." The detectives stepped outside and put their ears to the door as Shuttlesworth riffed, the Movement choir sang, and the short life of the postman William Moore was held up as a rather forbidding inspiration to those who would take to the streets of Birmingham.

After more than half an hour of cajoling, Martin Luther King was unable to scare up more than twenty foot soldiers. Most of them were Bevel's kids and King was having no truck with the idea of children going to jail. He repeatedly urged the young people to sit down. Bevel bit his tongue.

The Courtesy Capital of the Country

ROBERT KENNEDY MOVED the dateline for the civil rights press south ninety miles on Thursday, April 25, when he flew to Montgomery to sound out George

Wallace on his pledge to Stand in the Schoolhouse Door. Ten days before, Arthur Shores had forced the governor's hand by filing papers in federal court to have two black plaintiffs admitted to the University of Alabama that summer. The Kennedy administration had already taken elaborate behind-the-scenes precautions to prevent Tuscaloosa from becoming the next Oxford, and was now playing its hand so cryptically that speeches had been arranged for Kennedy in South Carolina and Atlanta to camouflage the trip to Montgomery.

In the Washington delegation's honor, the Confederate battle flag had been hoisted atop the capitol dome.* On the capitol portico, a wreath of red and white carnations (Bama colors) had been laid over the Jefferson Davis memorial brass star to prevent its desecration by Kennedy soles. A group of Klansmen and National States Rights Party hangers-on greeted Kennedy with pickets: "No Kennedy Congo Here" and "Kosher Team: Kennedy, Kastro, Kruschev [*sic*]." Some roughly handwritten leaflets billed "The Giant, Jew-Communist Race Mixing TRAINED NIGGERS Road Show and Travelling Circus . . . Niggers Fresh From New York. . . . Now Exclusively Appearing in Birmingham." ("See Ape Martin Luther Koon actually use a telephone and call Atty. Gen. Robert Kennedy and see Robert Kennedy send FBI agents to Birmingham to help keep the trained niggers from falling off the lunch counter stools!") Ace Carter's signature ellipses suggested that one of the governor's own men was behind the pickets, and that the anti-Semitic nuts of the lunatic fringe now enjoyed the official privileges that had historically belonged to the Klan.

Climbing the steps, Robert Kennedy and Burke Marshall passed through a column of steel-helmeted state troopers; one pressed his stick into the attorney general's stomach and then belted him "not for laughs," Kennedy later said. Right before this encounter, when a journalist asked the attorney general how he felt about paying a courtesy call on a man who had recently described him as "a pugnacious sapling," Kennedy deadpanned, "I think he's entitled to his opinion."

Wallace greeted his visitors defensively. "If you want to pay a courtesy visit, this is the courtesy capital of the country," he said. He pointed out the various flags in his office, the state flag, the Confederate flag. "You all know what the American flag is, we all recognize that," he said. Kennedy accepted the most basic of southern courtesies—"I might have a Coke"—before the governor began pursuing his agenda: To reap full political advantage from the Second Reconstruction in progress, federal troops would have to occupy his "sovereignty." On Mississippi governor Ross Barnett's advice, a tape recorder had been placed on the governor's desk to record the attorney general's coveted threat to send troops into Alabama if Wallace defied the federal order to integrate the university.

"You seem to want me to say I am going to use troops," Kennedy said, not taking the bait. Wallace insisted that he had no desire to "make a show of resis-

---

* Twenty-nine years later, the state was embroiled in a major controversy over the official display of this racist and historically incorrect symbol (the Confederate national flag, not this battle flag, would have been flown from a public building).

tance and to be overcome." Perhaps that last word reminded him of the "phony" up in Birmingham. "Well, Martin Luther King said you have a right to disobey unjust laws," Wallace added.

Kennedy and Marshall went from the governor's office to the *Montgomery Advertiser* to talk to its colorfully iconoclastic editor, Grover C. Hall Jr., a Wallace confidant. Hall assured them matter-of-factly that the governor had enough pull with the Klan to prevent violence in Tuscaloosa.

Contempt

JIM BEVEL HAD INFORMED King right after he bonded out of jail that he had figured out a way to fill the jails: with children. King deferred to Shuttlesworth, who had begun a children's section of the ACMHR two years earlier. Shuttlesworth gave one of his realpolitik replies—"whatever"—and King took the matter to the central committee. These middle-class locals who theoretically got to approve all SCLC strategies were aghast. Bevel scared the wits out of A. G. Gaston, Arthur Shores, and J. L. Ware. Soothing words from the mild-mannered Andy Young, a co-conspirator on the recruitment of children, could not neutralize the Bevel effect. Gaston was horrified that King would "use" young people. Injured children (or worse) would reflect as badly on the adults who had put them in danger as it would on the assailants. Besides, another businessman argued, the kids wouldn't understand why they were marching, opening up the Movement to charges of opportunism. The Reverend John Porter, whose attitude toward Shuttlesworth was "Anything that Fred asked me to do, I wasn't about to do," was not much more impressed with Bevel—"a radical of the worst kind, with no sense of public relations." But Porter's friend A. D. King pointed out that the kids were dying to march. Shuttlesworth framed the argument succinctly: "We got to use what we got."

Martin Luther King was struggling to sustain his renowned touch for conciliation. ("I asked you, twice, kindly to do it," he had said icily to an aide, a reprimand far more devastating than a cussing from Shuttlesworth.) Reporters found King different from the composed figurehead of Albany, who had exuded the quality he described as "peace at the center." He was preoccupied with the imminent jailing of all the Project C leaders on contempt charges.

There was some suspense in the Movement over what form of contempt they would be charged with. Civil contempt was worse than criminal since it entailed an indefinite jail stay until the defendant basically apologized and promised never to be bad again. According to Movement legend, the strategists were rooting for the civil charge because it would allow King to languish melodramatically in jail. On Friday, April 26, Judge Jenkins surprised everyone and dismissed the civil contempt charge and gave Walker et al. five-day sentences for criminal contempt. SCLC's apparent disappointment over the lesser conviction seemed like another one of Walker's bluffs, given that King had harvested from his first stay only a presidential phone call and an as yet undiscovered jailhouse treatise. They appealed their convictions, unable to risk any more time in jail. Shuttlesworth, Abernathy, and King flew home for the weekend, leaving Birmingham to Bevel.

No executive approval had been issued for a children's march, but a youth rally was called for Saturday morning to prepare for just that. At the night's mass meeting, Bevel gave a speech, complete with blackboard illustration, comparing segregation to a water tank "built to withstand storms and tornadoes." Andy Young announced that on either Thursday or Friday there would be a march on city hall, the likes of which Birmingham hadn't seen. When he called for twenty-seven volunteers, sixty rushed forward. "You're too young to go to jail," Young said. "But you can go to the library. You won't get arrested there, but you might learn something."

On Monday, a blizzard of leaflets hit Parker, Ullman, and other black high schools around the county. They instructed students to leave their classes and re-port to Sixteenth Street Baptist at noon on Thursday, May 2, regardless of whether they had permission from teachers or parents. The FBI informed the Bir-mingham police, who alerted Bull Connor. In his capacity as the commissar of public education, Connor ordered his school superintendent to instruct the black principals that any student over sixteen involved in the walkout would be "sum-marily and permanently expelled from school."

While the finishing touches were being put on the stage of Birmingham, the marquee once again moved east toward Attalla. The murder of William Moore had galvanized SNCC, as the bludgeoning of the Freedom Riders had done two years earlier. SNCC regulars from Nashville joined the pregnant Diane Nash, in from Greenwood, Mississippi, to complete Moore's Freedom Walk. The group of nine was setting out that day from the spot where William Moore's body was dis-covered, a single-file trudge through the onion grass along Highway 11. After fif-teen minutes, state troopers charged up, threw the marchers' signs ("Love!" and "All Men Are Equal") in the trunk, and drove them off to the county jail. SNCC had once again put their clerical elders on the spot, pressuring them finally to bring to a climax what one reporter called the "month of minor sorties and skir-mishes" in Birmingham.

Taking in the panoramic historic spectacle from the shoulder of the highway was the Southern Conference Educational Fund's executive, Jim Dombrowski. It was exactly twenty-five years since he had witnessed the end of Alabama's first era as the epicenter of mass militant youth. On May 1, 1948, at the Southern Negro Youth Congress's last convention in Birmingham, Dombrowski had been one of the first political prisoners taken from Herb Oliver's tiny church—his jailing a minor flap compared with that of Senator Glen Taylor. His arresting officer that day had been a patrolman named Jamie Moore.

15.

D-DAY

Keeping Cool

CHIEF OF POLICE Jamie Moore had been going around saying—how iron-ically his men weren't sure—"What's them niggers doin' in the street?" The demonstrations were a month old, and the police department still had no system for handling them. Bull Connor planned the day's strategy every morning in the bar of the Molton Hotel, knocking back two shooters of 100 proof Old Grand Dad with the long-time assistant Jim Simpson had picked for him. He seemed confident that King would "run out of niggers." The detectives were proud of their network of black informers—one female had been assigned to get close to Wyatt Walker. The ACMHR regulars equally prided themselves on knowing who the snitches were: "Go tell 'em this." Besides, what was the point of informers when Walker himself was giving the cops daily briefings?

The policemen were exhausted and demoralized, bunking at headquarters, sometimes allowed to go home to their families between 4 and 6 p.m. When they weren't chasing demonstrators, they were keeping tabs on the members of George Lincoln Rockwell's American Nazi Party hanging out in Montgomery, who had threatened to come up for the previous week's trial of Martin Luther King.

One day after Captain J. H. Woolley gave his orders to "keep cool" or be sent to the Atlanta penitentiary, two out of the eighty patrolmen present took off their badges and flung them at him. The rank and file adjourned to a sandwich shop to take a vote on a walkout. Though the loyalists prevailed, some cops revolted out of camera range. On the night of May 1, a patrolman roughed up a black motorist who said "That's right" instead of "Yes sir." ("Any time an officer stops a black S.O.B., whether he is violating the law or not, he can put anything he wants to against him," the policeman reminded his victim.)

In a more perverse rebellion, a cop declined on the witness stand to identify Ed Gardner, explaining that they all looked alike to him. Another officer told Fred Shuttlesworth at his contempt trial, "I'm not going to testify against you today, because I know you are right." Bull Connor cursed one of his men who shared a sandwich with a Movement marshal on a street corner, but the officer did not so much as flinch. After all, only an appellate brief stood between Connor and unemployment.

May Day

THIRTY YEARS AGO TO THE DAY, on May 1, 1933, Birmingham's first civil rights heyday had peaked at Kelly Ingram Park. City officials then had also denied a permit for a rally—this one organized by the Communist Party for May Day. Nonetheless, Hosea Hudson and his block committee captains had shepherded some three thousand Depression-worn demonstrators into the park. As cops were trying to sweep the crowd out onto the sidewalk, a black male bystander had walked up to an armed officer and hit him on the head with a stick. When another policeman tried to retaliate with his own stick, Hudson grabbed it. Guns were drawn. "Shoot me, and you'll shoot a thousand more," a black woman taunted. A sergeant shouted orders to his men: "Put them guns up and use them sticks!" That night, fifteen cops reportedly turned in their badges when they were told they couldn't use guns on unarmed reds. At a Party meeting the next day, black women asked brightly when the next demonstration would be, so they could "whip them a cop."

Jim Bevel was calling May 2 "D-Day." Schoolchildren woke up that morning and tuned their radios to WENN. Shelley the Playboy was offering some jive encouragement: "Kids, there's gonna be a party at the park. Bring your toothbrushes because lunch will be served." The toothbrushes, of course, were for jail hygiene. When Joe Lackey, the white manager of the white-owned station (and Tall Paul White's only discernible close friend), arrived at work, he gave his revolutionary jocks an indulgent smile.

Nearly eight hundred kids missed roll call that Thursday. The third-grade teacher of the ACMHR secretary Lola Hendricks's daughter Audrey cried over her pupils' plans to march—out of admiration, Audrey guessed, though schoolteachers had never been supporters of the Movement. ("They had a blocked mind," said one of the few teachers in the ACMHR, though to be fair, they also had white bosses.) R. C. Johnson, the principal of Parker High School—once pictured on local postcards as the "Largest in the World for Colored Pupils," as if this were an honor rather than a symptom of the duress under which blacks were educated in Birmingham—locked the school's front gates. His students scampered over the fences to follow Bevel. What kept going through the mind of seventeen-year-old Robert McClain was the time he had heard his father "Yessir" a little white boy.

By 8 a.m., Sixteenth Street Baptist was filled with young black people, aged six to twenty. Each arriving regiment shouted the name of its school, as if for a citywide pep squad competition. To conquer one of the last obstacles to "commitment"—fear of the police—Bevel had taken a couple of students over to Bull Connor's office. "Mr. Connor, I explained to them that the policemen's job is to arrest them, and as long as they don't cuss them, there's nothing for them to be afraid of," Bevel said. "That's right," Connor agreed, not imagining that the number of kids waiting at Sixteenth Street exceeded a thousand.

Close to one o'clock, the WENN deejays were giving the signal to march. "It's really c-o-o-old," one said, shivering his voice on the eighty-plus spring day. In an atmosphere that the *New York Times* compared to that of "a school picnic," the first column of marchers came clapping out of Sixteenth Street church, with adults applauding from the sidelines. The sight of approaching policemen made some very small children turn hide and drop their hand-lettered signs proclaiming "Freedom" and "I'll Die to Make This Land My Home." But most knelt like pros and prayed. Andy Young wanted them on their knees, eyes closed, because he knew that "people get excited when they are standing." Bevel waited just long enough to make the police think that was all for the day before sending out the next column of a dozen or so kids. After several waves, a policeman asked Shuttlesworth, "Hey, Fred, how many more have you got?"

"At least a thousand more," replied Shuttlesworth.

"God A'mighty," said the cop.

"Sing, children, sing," called an elderly woman, as she followed one group down Sixth Avenue past the park toward city hall. With at least four simultaneous marches pursuing different routes, Birmingham resonated with baby-voiced choruses of "We Shall Overcome," "Ain't Gonna Let Nobody Turn Me Around," and some songs perhaps directed at their elders as much as the white folks—"Which Side Are You On?" and "Will You Join Us or Will You 'Tom' for the Big, Bad 'Bull'?" Almost before they could be informed of their arrests, the kids ran gleefully toward the patrol wagons. Jail at last!

School buses had to be brought in to carry the children. Struck by the absurdity of his law enforcement role, a policeman leaned down to address a demonstrator of no more than eight and said in the tenderly stern tone that southern daddies take with their daughters, "What do you want?" White people had high affection for colored children, even if the axiom that "pickaninnies are so cute" contained the unspoken corollary, "Too bad they have to grow up." There was a white conviction that black adults had somehow "earned" their oppression, but the little girl's reply—"F'eedom"—defined as if for the first time the idea of "innocent victim."

Watching the school buses being loaded, an officer turned to Captain Glenn Evans, the mentor to the force's Young Turks, and said, "Evans, ten or fifteen years from now, we will look back on this and we will say, 'How stupid can you be?' "

In a Movement first, three battalions of marchers made it out of the "colored section" and down to the main shopping district. A group of twenty even got to city hall, where their arrests were supervised by Bull Connor, his arms whirling. Then he deployed fire trucks to strategic corners. Their hoses swelled on the street, but remained idle.

A newsman witnessing this first big "demonstration" asked Jim Bevel, who seemed to be giving the orders, "Who did this?" Bevel hedged. "Well, I'm just a field organizer." The skeptical newsman pressed him: Had Dr. King passed on the plan? King spent most of D-Day out of sight at the Gaston Motel, still trying to make up his mind about whether or not to use the children.

Wyatt Walker had a fit over Bevel's insubordination, even though he had been an early advocate of child demonstrators. He demanded that Bevel be disciplined, but by evening King himself had jumped on Bevel's bandwagon. For the first time in American history, the prize of Gandhian strategy had been won: The jails were filled, with some six hundred kids. "I have been inspired and moved today," King said at the night's mass meeting. "I have never seen anything like it."

Two thousand people were jammed into John Porter's church, the most "militants" Birmingham had ever claimed. Ed Gardner's opening remark captured the blend of elation and apprehension. "This has been a great day in Birmingham. We are going to change the name of the Tragic City to the Magic City." He said not to worry about dying, "because you are going to die someday anyway." Then, perhaps referring to the fire department's debut, "We are going to go wade-in, sit-in, and after a while we are going to walk-in."

"The whole world is watching Birmingham tonight," Shuttlesworth cried.

Bevel was on a "you ain't seen nothing yet" tear. He asked for a show of hands of all who had gotten inspired by the Movement. "Now I want everybody that held up their hand to go to jail between now and Sunday because I want to be back in Mississippi chopping cotton Tuesday." As Bevel began to sing, two thousand got out of their seats, waving, stomping, and screaming. Three hundred, too impatient for the morrow, began marching up and down the aisle.

Firemen

BEVEL HAD NAMED Friday, May 3, "Double D-Day." Fifteen hundred kids were absent from school. Governor George Wallace threatened to have their teachers investigated for collaboration. At ten o'clock the truants converged on Sixteenth Street Baptist. A block away, in the Gaston Motel, SCLC had just concluded another difficult session with the central committee. "Let those kids stay in school," A. G. Gaston had told King. "They don't know nothing."

King replied, "Brother Gaston, let those people go into the streets where they'll learn something." He and Shuttlesworth left confidently for their press conference in the courtyard. King told the reporters that the demonstrations were going to get more intense until they got "promise and action" from the city.

Wafting out of the Sixteenth Street church was the sound of mass praying and singing and responsive chanting, led by Bevel and Andy Young. With them was a veteran-newcomer, Glenn Smiley, the old Fellowship of Reconciliation hand who had come to workshop the young troops, amazed at the handiwork of the "Wild Man from Birmingham," whose leadership he had so damagingly criticized four years earlier. The elders were warning the kids not to be caught carrying so much as a peach pit, whereupon half a trashcanful of knives was surrendered. "Negroes have been throwing bottles and cussing for the last hundred years and it hasn't ended segregation," one leader reasoned.

At around one o'clock, the children began filing out of the church. Two decoy marches tried to lure the policemen west while the main column headed east toward city hall. Mayor Art Hanes, in a straw hat, stood at an intersection with Bull Connor and a dozen cops. He turned to Connor and said, "Here they come."

The students this day were older, mostly teenagers, and did not seem as coltish as the D-Day kids. A couple of the decoy columns walked right around a policeman who was ordering them to halt. The main group of children, singing their way down Fifth Avenue North, made it to the threshold of "white Birmingham," Seventeenth Street. To their right were more than two hundred black adult spectators. To the left a crowd was gathering among the elms of Kelly Ingram Park. The marchers hesitated. The entire black district around Sixteenth Street Baptist was blockaded with police lines and squad cars and fire trucks. Firemen stood next to their rigs, sweating in their dun-colored slickers. "Do not cross," Connor intoned. "If you come any further, we will turn the fire hoses on you."

The fire department had little more in common with the police department than with the public safety commissioner's other chief responsibility, the board of education. Firemen were accustomed to sitting in their folding chairs outside one of the downtown stationhouses and laughing at the cops breaking up the nightly drunken brawls on the Buzzard's Roost beat. They were not used to busting heads. If "law and order" was structured around corruption and brutality, the fire department ran like a collection of snug households. The men took pride in polishing their engines, cleaning their hoses, and trying out recipes for chili at the firehouse. Most firemen kept their distance from Connor, following the example of Chief John L. Swindle, who had begun performing his job three years after the merit system had given him the top post, in 1958; that was how long it had taken the personnel board to dislodge Connor's handpicked, functionally illiterate fire chief.

Throughout April, Swindle had been hearing that Connor didn't want "them" to cross Seventeenth Street, come hell or high water. But the chief had not realized he was going to provide the high water until Thursday, May 2, when city hall requested some trucks down on Seventeenth Street. Swindle had stalled Connor: The national union officially disapproved of using fire equipment to "control" crowds. You can't herd anyone with fire hoses, he explained. They're tied to hydrants and the crowd can walk away from you.

This day, Swindle was still insisting that the demonstrations warranted "police action," which was a way of saying *his* department had not been conditioned to treat blacks as adversaries. "We didn't hate them," a battalion chief recalled. "All we was doing was waiting on them all the time." By now Connor had heard enough about fire department policy. "Turn 'em on, or go home," he told Swindle. Surrounding Kelly Ingram Park, named after another accidentally famous firefighter—the first sailor to die in World War I—the firemen stood by the hydrants, hoses loosely poised. Police captain Glenn Evans yelled through a bullhorn at the demonstrators and the adult spectators wagging them, "Disperse, or you're gonna get wet." The children resumed their march.

Leo

BOB ZELLNER, SNCC's white field secretary, was approaching the Alabama state line on day 3 of a "Freedom Walk" sponsored jointly by SNCC and CORE—a second protest, in addition to Diane Nash's memorial march—to complete William Moore's journey from Chattanooga to Jackson. Before Zellner left Chattanooga, a telegram had arrived from his mother in Mobile: "In the unlikely event that George allows you to walk through Alabama, please drop out in Birmingham as your grandfather and uncle will kill you." The grandfather and uncle were the diehard Klansmen on Zellner's father's side, and George was, of course, the governor. Though a family friend of the Zellners, Wallace had already had Bob arrested in January amid false rumors that he was in Montgomery to demonstrate at the inaugural festivities. The only hitch had been that Wallace had not yet taken office, and the unamused lame duck, John Patterson, reputedly threatened to testify on Zellner's behalf.

Zellner had been selected to be the spokesman for the five SNCC members on the ten-man "William L. Moore Memorial Trek." Even though Double D-Day was proceeding back in Birmingham, the first-string national press corps had followed the *New York Times*'s Claude Sitton to the state line. The ten trekkers trailed pedestrians, state police, and FBI men training movie cameras on the white harassers as the border loomed ominously ahead, Wallace's line in the dust.

Charles Moore, *Life*'s photographer, was following in a Hertz rental car, parking at intervals to walk alongside the marchers. Moore had left the *Montgomery Advertiser* the year before, with the most memorable shots of the Movement's Montgomery phase to his credit, and had made his debut as a freelancer in *Life* the previous fall photographing the desegregation of Ole Miss. Added to Bob Zellner and his SNCC recruit, former Birmingham-Southern student Sam Shirah, Moore brought to three the total of white Alabama preachers' sons on Highway 11. On his car radio, Moore listened to a report that discussed the children's demonstrations about to begin in Birmingham in a way suggesting the authorities were not viewing them as the romp of the day before. He decided to head west for Birmingham. He drove up to Kelly Ingram Park and jumped out of the car as Chief Swindle was finally relaying Bull Connor's order to his men.

The firemen kept their fogging nozzles on, misting their human targets as if they were prize flowers. Some marchers backed off. When a dozen plopped down on the sidewalk, the firemen switched to their monitor guns, fed by two hoses for maximum pressure. The sound of the hose spray shattered the singing like automatic machine-gun fire.

The children flung their hands to their faces and then embraced, holding their ground for a few seconds before sprawling across the sidewalk. Those trying to flee were pinned against doorways, and a group leader took the high-powered spray until his shirt was ripped from his body. The marchers who continued to pour out of the Sixteenth Street church were sent skittering down the gutters. One girl surfaced with a bloody nose, another with scratches around her eyes.

In his office atop his tallish building, A. G. Gaston was on the phone with David Vann, exchanging wishes that SCLC would leave town and give the new city administration a chance. Through his window he saw a little girl being turned end over end by hose spray. "Lawyer Vann," he said, "I can't talk to you now or ever. My people are out there fighting for their lives and my freedom. I have to go help them."

A woman holding the hand of her four-year-old son led the next wave of marchers. "This baby is mine and he's in it too!" she shouted at the police line. Charles Moore was jarred by the sight of adults exposing children to such dangers, and said so to Andy Young. The Fellowship of Reconciliation's Glenn Smiley sat on the church steps, holding two conflicting ideas at once. This was one of the most horrifying things he had seen, and it was also the culmination of his life work in nonviolent strategy.

The mass of 1,000 to 1,500 onlookers booed the police. The hoses rotated their way. They gasped in mock horror; some wagged their backsides at the spray. Those who had ringside seats on a corner rooftop rained bricks, stones, and Coke bottles on the men in uniform. Charles Moore, who had gotten his training as a Marine combat photographer, was hit in the ankle with a chunk of concrete. Even as his foot swelled, he continued to click his camera. In the background of his crowd shots was the Carver Theater's marquee advertising the war picture *Damn the Defiant!*

"Bring the dogs," Connor said to Captain Evans, the symbol of police progress. Evans and his Young Turk protégés thought that the K-9 Corps (mostly used to chase burglars) was overrated and the officer in charge of it a showboat. "Clear the park out," Evans ordered the K-9 Corps.

K-9's six German police dogs, including Rebel, Leo, and, of course, King, pulled their handlers to the front of the police line. A twenty-three-year-old black man, Milton Payne, was bitten in the heel, calf, and thigh. The spectators subsided from Seventeenth Street as the dogs pressed against them on taut leashes. Some folks poured into Kelly Ingram in retreat back to the Sixteenth Street church. As Henry Lee Shambry, thirty-four, cut diagonally across the park, a policeman kept bumping him with his motorcycle. Then two canines jumped Shambry, ripping his pant leg off, and bit his arm, leg, and hip. The elderly Rosie Lucius Bell, trying to get out of the path of the stampede, fell and broke her eyeglasses. A dog charged at seven-year-old Jennifer Fancher and knocked her down. Three Negroes were taken away from the scene in ambulances. The fleeing crowd stopped on the sidewalk in front of the church, where some boys took off their shirts and waved them at the dogs like matadors. Others barked in the dogs' faces.

The Associated Press's Bill Hudson, down from his base in Memphis, was apparently the only out-of-town photographer on the scene besides Charles Moore. He hadn't had time to react to what his 35mm Nikon—concealed under his coat while idle—was shooting, his only priorities being "making pictures and staying alive" and "not getting bit by a dog." He hardly noticed when Walter Gadsden, a six-foot-tall Parker High sophomore, stepped in front of him. The youth seemed barely fazed by the police dog lunging at his chest.

On the human end of the leash, the K-9 Corps was known for attracting straight arrows who wanted none of the scams and payoffs that often came with a regular beat. Nor were the dog handlers known for being race ideologues. Officer Dick Middleton, the southpaw son of a TCI crane operator, with a secret passion for cooking, was the quietest, most reserved man on the K-9 detail. He had a German wife as well as a German shepherd, Leo. Inscrutable behind sunglasses, he reached out to grab Walter Gadsden's cardigan sweater as Leo charged his torso. The youth was arrested and taken to jail for "parading without a permit."

Just as Hudson had not registered the presence of Gadsden, Middleton, and Leo in his viewfinder, neither did Bull Connor yet understand that his show had just entered the realm of myth. "Why did you bring old Tiger out?" he jested over his bullhorn to the K-9 cops. "Why didn't you bring a meaner dog—this one is not the vicious one."

By three o'clock, Jim Bevel had joined the policemen in trying to move the crowd off the streets and back into the church, where the police had barricaded a thousand more prospective marchers. Better yet, Bevel shouted to the spectators, just go home. He knew that, paradoxically, "creative tension"—the Gandhian dynamic King had spelled out in his jailhouse epistle—became truly creative at the moment it threatened to become destructive. Things were getting hairy on Sixteenth Street. A white man had tried to drive his car into some marchers. Police took him into custody. A Negro youth grabbed an officer's pistol from his holster; Negro "suspects" had been killed for less, but the cop merely chased him till he dropped it.

A fire inspector went into the packed church and said he would open the doors if the demonstrators promised to call it a day. The young people filed quietly out of the church. Double D-Day ended barely two hours after it began, but that was enough time to bring an epoch to a close.

As the authorities saw it, a few people got wet—there hardly existed the fireman who hadn't taken some hose spray, and department tradition called for dousing the chief if he arrived late for a big fire. As for the K-9 Corps's work, Double D-Day had yielded more torn clothes than broken skin, and very little of either.

Firemen quickly resumed their fix-it role, repairing the window their water had broken at a black insurance company on Sixteenth Street. Lola Hendricks had been inside the office working her regular secretarial job when the glass shattered. She who had been so cool earlier in the face of Bull Connor's curses came undone over the dogs and hoses. "Don't cry," her boss said. "That's what they want you to do. This may be the best thing that ever happened to the Movement."

Alabama Won't Ever Stand for It

As the SNCC and CORE marchers drew within sight of the state-line road-blocks, a Bama boy sitting on his car advised, "You won't make it. Georgia may take it, but Alabama won't ever stand for it." A crowd numbering at least 1,500 streamed over a fence and across the creek that separated Georgia from Alabama. The white preacher's son Sam Shirah was at the head of the march, wearing the sandwich board with Moore's messages: "Eat at Joe's Both Black and White" and "Equal Rights for All, Mississippi or Bust." One spectator observed, "Well they may bust, by God. The other'n did."

"Colonel" Al Lingo, the state's public safety chief, ordered the marchers arrested. "Get the goddamn communists," a white man agreed. Bob Zellner and two of his white colleagues dropped down on Highway 11 in dead nonviolent weight. Troopers jabbed electric cattle prods into their genitals. "Kill him! Kill him! Kill him!" screamed a woman in plastic curlers. Zellner was still limp when he was dragged upstairs to his cell at the De Kalb County Jail, from which his friend George Wallace would presently have him transferred to Kilby Prison, home to the hard core.

Television's Finest Hour

Charles Moore was sickened by what he had photographed at Kelly Ingram Park, which included a sensational series of two dogs ripping Henry Lee Shambry's clothes. He knew how ugly segregationists could be, having endured then governor John Patterson's comments (while Moore was still at the *Montgomery Advertiser*) that the reason he photographed so many racial episodes was so he could have carnal knowledge of "nigger gals." But growing up poor and rough in North Alabama, he also knew plenty of white southerners who had operated in an evil system with unself-conscious decency. His own father, known as Brother Mo' to the black townsmen of Tuscumbia (Helen Keller's birthplace), had welcomed an old Negro man into his sanctuary every Sunday, and was a frequent guest preacher at black churches. But the film now on the plane to New York, Moore sensed, was likely to obliterate in the national psyche any notion of a "good southerner."

The first shot he had gotten that day would grace the double-truck opening of *Life*'s spread—firemen thrusting their hose in a common purpose that recalled another era-defining picture, of the Marines planting the American flag at Iwo Jima. In the background their targets blurred behind the spray of a hundred pounds of water per square inch making impact. The headline would be, "They Fight a Fire That Won't Go Out."

The dogs and fire hoses dominated the evening news. The scene had been a cameraman's dream, nothing like the previous race melees—Mother's Day at the Trailways station, for example. Two years after that event, which had provided the payoff in "Who Speaks for Birmingham?" white people were still going up to

CBS's southern correspondent, a thirty-one-year-old Texan named Dan Rather, and saying, "Now, y'all better watch what you say, after what happened to Howard K. Smith." But in the end Connor and the police had done the journalists' job for them, providing uniformed brutality that seemed almost staged for the screen. If commercial time on Huntley-Brinkley—the NBC team outdrew CBS's new replacement for Douglas Edwards, Walter Cronkite—was worth $30,000 a minute, Andy Young calculated that the Movement stood to get millions of dollars worth of "educational TV."

Huntley-Brinkley's man in Birmingham was a twenty-eight-year-old Ohioan named R. W. "Johnny" Apple Jr., who had concluded while getting a master's in history at Columbia that the South was at the crux of much of American history. But watching the day's history being made, he had simply said to Charles Moore, "I've never seen anything like this in my life." Even after he became a legend in his trade as a *New York Times* correspondent, Apple would maintain that none of the many war zones he covered upset or frightened him as much as Birmingham. He was spat upon by civilians and rousted in the middle of the night by policemen acting on reports of women or narcotics in his motel room. Apple's old Princeton roommate, Senator Lister Hill's son, had needled him before he came to Alabama, "Don't worry, I'll get you out of jail." Until now, Apple had thought he was kidding.*

Apple and Dan Rather jockeyed over the fifteen- or twenty-minute window of opportunity for filing their pieces from Vincent Townsend's TV station, applying their pancake makeup (and in Apple's case, a sheen of black shoe polish on his crew cut) while putting the finishing touches on their scripts. Watching their reports on the evening news up in New York, Bayard Rustin reveled in "television's greatest hour."

Nevertheless, the melodrama of the news film had its built-in denouement. The dogs stopped lunging, the hoses went flaccid; the children gained their footing and walked away, and a sponsor came on selling Geritol. No one had seen anything quite like it in America, but SCLC had not changed the world yet.

The supervising photo editor in the AP's Atlanta bureau, a gentlemanly veteran named Jim Laxon, had taken Bill Hudson's film back to the *Birmingham News* darkroom. Some of Hudson's hose-spray shots captured the "fair atmosphere" he had discerned before the K-9 Corps was called out. But one of them—the saintly calm of young Walter Gadsden in the snarling jaws of the German shepherd— gave Laxon the same surge he had felt when he processed his first Pulitzer winner, a shot of a woman jumping from an upper-story window in Atlanta's Winecoff Hotel fire of December 1946.

---

* Apple's other roommate was Hodding Carter III, son of a prominent liberal Mississippi newspaper family and future journalist himself, whose college thesis on the White Citizens Councils had been published as a book, *The South Strikes Back,* in 1959.

Little Lies, Big Truth

IN THE DAWN HOURS of Saturday, the Birmingham police removed an effigy of Martin Luther King from a tree in the courtyard of St. Paul's Catholic Church, where a priest had been shot to death with impunity by a Klansman forty-two years before. The morning papers were about to hit the stands across the country. For a wire-service photographer, the play one received in the New York dailies, particularly in the picture-allergic *Times*, was the ultimate measure of success; often the New York office would send "attaboy" tearsheets to hinterland bureaus when they broke into that winner's circle. Bill Hudson's picture of Walter Gadsden and Leo spanned three columns above the fold on page one of the May 4 *Times:* "DOGS AND HOSES REPULSE NEGROES AT BIRMINGHAM." The K-9 Corps of Birmingham took its mystical place next to the bloodhounds chasing Eliza across the ice floes in *Uncle Tom's Cabin.*

Wyatt Walker could not have hoped for more. Connor had finally acted as the epic anti-hero, and the children had provided the biblical multitudes. In a sense, the Birmingham police had the most heroic assignment: pantomimes of graphic violence, which yielded no serious injury. "Sure, people got bit by the dogs!" Walker said later. "I'd say at least two or three. But a picture is worth a thousand words, dahlin'."

The picture of Walter Gadsden had captured the Big Truth about segregation, but in many of its particulars it was as much a fiction as Harriet Beecher Stowe's slavery-beating novel had been. Gadsden was not even a demonstrator; he was merely watching his classmates file out of Sixteenth Street Baptist. The one-time honor student had been playing hooky even before the demonstrations made truancy morally correct, "running with the wrong crowd," he would admit, and thinking about dropping out of school. His father, L. A. Scott, belonged to the family that owned the *Atlanta Daily World* and the *Birmingham World,* and had such an aversion to King that it refused to mention him on the front page of the flagship paper. Walter shared his class's resentment of King's intervention.

At first glance, the picture looked like a textbook study in nonviolent acquiescence, Walter's body stooped, the head slightly bowed and eyes lowered. Closer inspection, however, revealed that Gadsden, who had a big dog at home, had not only thrust his knee into the dog's chest but had grasped Officer Middleton's wrist with his left hand.* This stunning effrontery was the gist of a countermythology now spreading along the black grapevine. Herb Oliver, who had drawn up affidavits within the hour documenting the K-9 brutality, was proudly noting that Gadsden's own lunge had broken the dog's jaw. Another rumor had dogs fleeing their handlers and being cut to death by the Movement's shock troops.

---

* After years of trying to track Walter Gadsden down, I finally located him in a large southern city. When I tried to talk to him about his history-making photograph, he told me that he didn't want to "get involved" and hung up on me.

In truth, the K-9 Corps's dogs were too well trained to get away from their masters, as Wyatt Walker could attest. In one of his "I don't believe I told Dr. King about that" offensives, he would deploy Miles College students to stand on street corners and blow dog whistles. But the animals were not distracted, and it was only in the imagination of black Birmingham that the streets were littered with bloodied German shepherds.

"Let 'Em Have It"

ON SATURDAY MORNING, children filled up Sixteenth Street Baptist and a nearby church, as eager to march as if there had been school to skip and no dogs to brave. At the same time Walker was selling the K-9 Corps to the outside world as the dogs of war, he had to convince the Movement participants that they were nothing. At the previous night's mass meeting, Andy Young had addressed the possibility that people might be losing too much of their fear of the police. "We must not boo the police when they bring up the dogs or call them names—we must praise them," he said. Indeed, after getting a rabies shot for the dog bite she had suffered that day, the seven-year-old Jennifer Fancher had begged her mother to let her return to the action.

Today there was a new strategy: The kids weren't marching but "strolling," straggling out of the church in groups of two—no orderly, placard-labeled columns. After ambling aimlessly, they coalesced into a line, unfurling the banners ("Love God and Thy Neighbor") concealed under their raincoats—the raincoats thanks to deejays Shelley Stewart and Paul White, who had been forecasting showers and urging the kids to wear their rain gear, even though the skies were smoggy gray-blue. In a new strategic development, the Movement's activist black society matrons carpooled fifty youngsters into the "white" shopping district— six blocks from the usual action. A school bus was dispatched by the police department to carry them off to jail, its windows leaking escapees. Another group made it to city hall just as Bull Connor was coming out the door on his way to Kelly Ingram Park. As his men herded them down the ramp to police headquarters in the basement, the children turned to the television cameras and smiled their hearts out.

Two blocks west, at the corner of Kelly Ingram at Fifth Avenue and Seventeenth Street, the mounting fearlessness of Birmingham's famously well "contained" black community was producing a different photogenic sensation. Some three thousand students occupied the park, and the usual crowd of older spectators crammed the sidewalk across the street. One young marcher suspended his chants of "Freedom!" to flail his arms at the K-9 Corps and shout, "Get white dogs!" When two black men armed with rocks climbed onto a car top, the police dogs were given some slack on their leashes but never summoned for duty. A youth ran up to a policeman and hit him in the chest with a rock; the cop thwacked him across the back with his billy club but made no arrest. From the park, a mass of grinning students wagged their fingers at the policemen and chanted, "Send us to jail!" A pretty black teenager called out to the uniforms, "Y'all don't like us but you like our pussy." The two black prostitutes who hung out at the Gaston Motel's restaurant after their nocturnal calls on city hall told a similar story about the private tastes of the commission's public segregationists.

Connor arrived to see his firemen and policemen impassively absorbing the jeers. "Let 'em have it," he said to the firemen.

A lone girl came forward and taunted the line of blue shirts and brown slickers. Hose spray hit her knees, knocking her down in the street. A policeman hustled her—gently, it appeared—across the park. Waiting for the next target, firemen aimed their dual-hose monitor guns at some Kelly Ingram elms a hundred feet away and flicked off the bark, then eased the spray down the tree trunks onto a slim girl in white, who set her feet stubbornly for a split second before keeling over in slow motion. A number of boys were sprayed shirtless, and two girls, their dresses having been peeled off like the bark, scurried away in their slips.

Standing behind the police lines, a few hundred white spectators clapped and whistled. A competing gallery of black adults, some of whom were, as Shuttlesworth might say, "spirit-ed," answered, "Go home, white people." For once, Connor agreed with the blacks. "Goddammit, that's what causes trouble, them white people," he said. "Run 'em off!" He then explained loudly, "I don't want anybody here to get hurt."

The black spectators hurled the standard fare of rocks, bricks, and Coke bottles at the policemen, now wearing hard hats. The *New York Times*'s Foster Hailey interpreted the missiles as retaliation for the hoses. The local newsmen concluded that the hoses were used against the rock throwers. Police orders to disperse elicited a shower of more debris. To whites, the flying Coke bottles had come to symbolize the barbarism of the Negroes, who in truth preferred Pepsi and Royal Crown, in consideration of ancient rumors that storekeepers would not sell Coca-Cola to blacks for fear that the cocaine would make them savage.

Drunks swung their arms at no one in particular. Knives glinted. Jim Bevel, in yarmulke and overalls, counted at least twenty-five guns. He walked up and down the avenue surveying his handiwork, then turned to Captain George Wall and said, "If you let me borrow your bullhorn, I can quiet them down; they're my own people." He began exhorting the crowd in his "preacher voice." ("People preach in absolutes, not relatives, and your tone of voice changes; it's quite different from a 'maybe' type language.") As Wall stared placidly ahead, Bevel said, "Everybody get off this corner. If you're not going to demonstrate in a nonviolent way, then leave." Only 127 marchers had been arrested—the 250 jailed on Double D-Day had nudged the political prisoner census toward a thousand—but Bevel called off the demonstrations with an all-in-a-day's-work casualness. He did not want to be "manipulated into a riot" because it would take three or four days to get people psyched to hit the streets again.

Moments later, Mayor Art Hanes strode into A. G. Gaston's Smith Building, on the east side of the park, whose plate glass had afforded Wyatt Walker a perfect view of the action. A detective stopped Hanes as he climbed the stairs to Walker's post: "Mayor, it's dangerous." But Hanes for once knew better. He conferred with Walker and the ACMHR's Reverend Charles Billups, warning, "There's a fine line between a crowd and a mob. Violence begets violence. Let's keep this thing under control."

"We believe in nonviolence," Walker replied, betraying none of the exhilaration of the play-by-play account of "The Battle of Ingram Park" that he had just given a New York radio station. Off the air and out of earshot of the press, he would describe how the children had been frolicking in the hose spray and sucker-punching the K-9 Corps. "There was no battle," he would say with satisfaction. "It was a Roman holiday." One young participant later summed it up, saying, "We thought it was fun. We didn't know it was going to be history, or progress."

Gunnar Myrdal, the Swedish social scientist whose seminal 1944 work on race relations, *An American Dilemma,* had had twenty-six printings, was in Detroit that day for an Emancipation centennial on "The Negro in a Changing Society." Reacting to the news from Birmingham, he predicted that legal segregation would be abolished within ten years. The national news corps did not yet comprehend either that what they were conveying to the world would cut Myrdal's estimate by nine years.

16.

MIRACLE

S.O.S.

W HEN THE *Birmingham News*'s photographers brought back pictures of
Bull Connor's fire hoses and police dogs, the media czar Vincent
Townsend realized that he had wheeled and dealed himself into a box again. He
put the photos in a drawer, and under the story (inside the paper) headlined "Police Use Water, Dogs on Marchers," ran a head shot of Mayor Albert Boutwell.
The *News* devoted more ink to canine than to human casualties—a police car
door had slammed on a dog's tail—and Townsend's ultra-conservative managing
editor, John Bloomer, would insist that no one was bitten "despite visually strong
baiting postures." (He also said that "those putting themselves in front of the dogs
wore three or four pairs of pants and three or four coats"—as if they had known of
Connor's riot-control plans as they got dressed that morning.)

The local dailies answered the national page-one dogs and hoses with front-
page articles on Governor George Wallace's speech at a Civil War battle centennial in Mississippi, Happy Murphy and Nelson Rockefeller's scandal-wedding,
and Jayne Mansfield's divorce. The story of Birmingham unfolded on page 2 or 8
or 24, without bylines. "Had the demonstrations been taking place on Fifth Avenue in New York City, it is doubtful that the *New York Times* would have printed
it on page one," explained Bloomer, who was convinced that the *Times*'s Claude
Sitton was "one of King's chief consultants," meeting with him every evening to
outline the next day's activities.

Unlike his true-believer managing editor, Townsend was a pragmatist.
Though he had been counseling the city fathers to stall, the pictures made him realize that the "trouble" was not going to go away on its own. The whites, too, might
benefit from an "outside agitator," who, by forcing them to act, could take the rap
for reform. The obvious candidate for the role was Townsend's own favorite
whipping boy, the federal government. But given that he had been reassuring the
Justice Department, often a few times a day, that the city had things under control, it would have been embarrassing for him to put out the S.O.S. personally.

On Saturday, May 4, Townsend tapped his newest proxy, Sheriff Mel

Bailey, to call the Justice Department. Bailey's 1962 run against the longtime Klan-tolerant incumbent had marked Townsend's and the Young Turk lawyers' return to politics after Tom King's mayoral defeat. (Now wise to the lethal PR of a "Negro bloc vote," Chuck Morgan had gone to key black politicos before the primary and asked them to make sure *all* their boxes didn't go for Bailey.) Thirty-eight-year-old Bailey, a veteran cop who had been one of the best car-theft detectives in the South (and had made the first arrests in the Freedom Riders assault—of the non-Eastview brawlers), did as he was told.

Burke Marshall took his call. Starting his third year as the chief of the civil rights division, Marshall was acquainted with the situation in Birmingham, having spoken the day before to Townsend, David Vann, Vann's boss Douglas Arant, A. G. Gaston, Arthur Shores, and Martin Luther King. In a sense, Marshall had been preparing for this moment since he gave up his white-shoe antitrust practice at Washington's Covington and Burling to enter government service. After being ambushed (while in bed with the mumps) by the Freedom Rides a few months into the job, he had made an effort to anticipate the coming crises. First, he checked the Eisenhower file on Little Rock and, finding it empty, began making reconnoitering trips to the hot spots on his short list—Oxford, Memphis, New Orleans, and of course, Birmingham, where his favorite sources were Chuck Morgan and Abe Berkowitz. On one visit Douglas Arant, who managed to maintain a conservative local profile and a liberal national one, had taken him to dinner at the Mountain Brook Club, hoping like hell, Marshall was sure, that none of the clubmen would discover that Robert Kennedy's henchman was in the grill overhearing the joke du jour. ("Why does Alabama have so many Negroes and Massachusetts so many Kennedys? Because Alabama had first choice.") As for his caucuses with Townsend, who received him at home, Marshall was never clear on who was manipulating whom.

The smallish, bespectacled product of Exeter and Yale, Marshall was the last person the average white southerner would suspect of being a civil rights lawyer from the Justice Department, which was precisely why the administration had picked him for the job. He had become so indispensable to the Kennedys on civil rights that he had reputedly been passed over for the 1962 Supreme Court appointment that went instead to Deputy Attorney General Byron White. But the Justice Department had not yet patented a southern strategy. In both the Freedom Rides and the Ole Miss emergencies, Robert Kennedy had handled southern governors naively by what one critic would call the Code of the Ivy League Gentleman, assuming that underneath the racist ravings were men willing to cut off-the-record deals. Barely a week before Sheriff Mel Bailey called Marshall, the Kennedys had still been pursuing that discredited code, dispatching the attorney general and Marshall to call on George Wallace.

The shared memory of that recent charade lent a gallows irony to Marshall's conversation with Robert Kennedy about Sheriff Bailey's plea for help. The relationship between the two had come a long way since their first interview, arranged

by Marshall's former Covington and Burling colleague Harris Wofford, who as
the presidential campaign's civil rights expert (and Martin Luther King's sometime adviser) had been too closely identified with the cause to get the job himself.
At their first meeting, Kennedy had awkwardly reciprocated Marshall's taciturnity. But even though the *New York Times* noted that Marshall "wholly lacks the
extroverted football-player qualities said to be admired by the Kennedys," his So-
cratic method had become a valued complement to the headlong Kennedy style.
He was said to be one of the few people Robert Kennedy looked on as a mentor.

"Do you think you should go down?" Kennedy asked Marshall on Saturday,
May 4.

"I think I could," Marshall said.

"See you later," Kennedy said. "Want anyone to go with you?"

"Joe," Marshall said.

Joseph Dolan, a former Senate committee counsel for John Kennedy, was
now Deputy Attorney General Nicholas Katzenbach's* top aide. He had considered Robert Kennedy's appointment as attorney general the worst in history, and
he had gone to Justice because he "thought the country needed to be protected
from Bobby." That opinion had gradually changed, and Dolan gave credit for the
boss's enlightenment to Marshall, "best lawyer, brightest human being." Because
he shared the Kennedys' ability to laugh at serious things, Dolan (though his official responsibility was federal judiciary appointments) had become a fond member of the civil rights "riot squad," on the scene in Montgomery for the Freedom
Rides and in Oxford for Meredith.

Dolan and Marshall hopped an FAA plane. Landing in Birmingham, Dolan
turned his watch back two hours to the local time—central standard. It was fifteen
minutes before they had taken off in Washington, on eastern daylight savings
time. In retrospect, that would symbolize for him the down-the-bunnyhole absurdity of what was to come.

The first thing Marshall did when he arrived was call Martin Luther King at
the Gaston Motel to find out what concessions, besides desegregation of lunch
counters and restrooms, would stop the demonstrations. The Movement's demands had been spelled out, in Wyatt Walker's "Birmingham Manifesto," as of
day 2 of the campaign, and had been reported in the *New York Times* as of April 12.
On Friday, the eve of Marshall's arrival, King had enumerated them before the
mass meeting: the desegregation of lunch counters, drinking fountains, and restrooms; the upgrading of Negro employment; and the formation of a biracial committee to address school and parks desegregation. The fourth demand was that all
charges against the demonstrators be dropped. Somehow, Marshall got the impression that King, incredibly, had not come up with any negotiating points, and
in the history of the Kennedy Justice Department it would be written that Mar-

---

* Katzenbach was promoted to the job when Byron White went on the Supreme Court.

shall saved the day by advising the Movement that it couldn't make a deal unless it knew what the deal was about.

Guests in the Region

ON SATURDAY AFTERNOON in Abe Berkowitz's law office, where Bull Connor's ouster had been plotted less than a year earlier, Burke Marshall repeated the Movement's demands to the only men in a position to grant them, the downtown merchants. Retail sales were off 30 percent or more that spring, and more stores were for rent than had been in the Depression. On top of "the trouble downtown," there was a new, ultimately more threatening commotion outside town: The Eastwood Mall—Alabama's first such innovation in shopping, referred to in news headlines as "Fabled"—had opened in the very white eastern section and was accurately being touted as the "magnificent Merchandise City of the future," so dazzling a landmark that its customers were referred to as "sightseers."

Although Marshall understood that the downtown retailers had absorbed more than their share of the costs of segregation, he was unprepared for their response. They kept shaking their heads and talking about something called the power structure. They couldn't make any move without the Big Mules. Eventually, the meeting went quiet. Marshall would later marvel over how "really remarkable" it was "how much these people did not have a mind of their own."

With a couple of exceptions, the men in Berkowitz's office were Jewish. And as Jews, they were the most vulnerable members of the city's elite. The most prominent Jewish Big Mule, a coal operator named Morris Adler, had lost his stomach for heavy industry after his son was shot dead in a battle between labor and management during the coal strike of 1920. Adler's fellow coal barons sent a floral arrangement to the funeral. It was in the shape of a cross.

The impotence of Birmingham's 3,900 Jews reflected a decades-long journey from progressive activism to passive isolationism, through the crucible of Scottsboro. Birmingham's Jewish pioneers had been eminent in local government and were featured in the Blue Book of 1929, a sort of local Social Register. Otto Marx, an investment banker who built the city's second skyscraper, the Brown-Marx Building, had been an investor in Robert Jemison's Mountain Brook Club, and so exquisitely fit the bill of what Jemison called a "pet Jew" that, out of consideration for his gentile friends, he reputedly never set foot in the clubhouse he helped build.

The reborn Klan in Birmingham had done most of its violence against Catholics and, to a lesser extent, blacks, but the TWK signs (for "Trade With Klansmen") in the windows of gentile-owned emporia were directed at the Jewish store owners. Jewish lawyers could not get a verdict in the courts. When one of them, Yale-educated Irving Engel, proud of his boyhood in the "Jew Hollow" pocket of a tough mining settlement, decided to move to New York in 1924, the Klan sent an emissary—the deputy clerk of the circuit court—to assure his friend that he was "not the kind of Jew they were after."

In 1933, Alabamians identified the wrong kind of Jew. He was Samuel Lei-bowitz, the dapper Cornell-educated Rumanian-born New York lawyer—said to be the heir to Clarence Darrow—who had agreed to defend the Scottsboro Boys in their second, Supreme Court–ordered trial after the Communist Party bowed out. During the trial, he produced medical evidence that no rapes had occurred as well as a "victim" who recanted. The county prosecutor countered by tying Lei-bowitz to the Communist-Jewish-Negro juggernaut, saying in his summation that if one of the defense's chief witnesses, a white man named Lester Carter ("Maybe it is Carterinsky now!"), had hung out with the Communists any longer, "he would have been down here with a pack on his back a-trying to sell you goods." And then the challenge: "Show them that Alabama justice cannot be bought and sold with Jew money from New York."

That speech (followed by more death sentences for the Boys) alienated the local Jews not only from their fellow Alabamians but also from their co-religion-ists. Someone in the office of the great progressive governor Bibb Graves went through the Scottsboro protest mail and annotated certain signatures as "Russian Jews." Birmingham's German-Jewish aristocracy began to further distance itself from those Eastern European newcomers. In 1955, fifty of Reform Temple Emanu-El's more cautious members, chiefly proprietors of stores with Mountain Brook branches, seceded into the Congregation of Reform Judaism, which met without a rabbi, in Mountain Brook churches.

That year, Irving Engel had invited fellow southern Jews to a New Orleans hotel to discuss the rift in American Jewry caused by the 1954 *Brown* decision. Since leaving his native Birmingham for New York, Engel had become head of one of the national Jewish advocacy groups that had endorsed the ruling—the old-line (non-Zionist) American Jewish Committee, formed in New York in 1906 to combat discrimination. Engel was taken aback by his fellow Jews' vehement sense of betrayal over his committee's pro-integration stance. A Montgomery man wept as he described how his gentile business associates had at last begun taking him on hunting and fishing trips, though they had not yet invited him and his wife to evening functions. Engel's accusers were joined by his own brother, William, who had remained in Birmingham and become a successful real estate man and one of its most assimilated Jews, though he had been the only property owner in the city to rent to the CIO's Steel Workers Organizing Committee in the 1930s. Irving had forgotten the adage: The southern Jew is like a guest in the re-gion, bending over backward to conform to the racial rites. As Bernard Lewis, a Jewish plumbing contractor, liked to reassure Art Hanes and his Christian drink-ing buddies, "It wasn't the Birmingham Jews who killed Jesus. It was the Miami Jews."

The fear of being taken for Miami Jews—the sixties version of Scottsboro's "Russian Jews"—seemed to motivate the community's spiritual leader as well. "My biggest interest in Birmingham was in better Jewish-Christian relations," said Emanu-El's Rabbi Milton Grafman, his proudest achievement the annual In-stitute on Judaism for Christian Clergy. When the (Negro) Reverend John Porter sought permission to attend, Grafman wrote back saying he could not invite him because the institute was open only to members of the Birmingham Ministerial Alliance, which was all white (and, despite Grafman's entreaties, persisted in ending its meetings "In Jesus' name").

Grafman had been one of the eight signers of the pastoral statement that gave King the reason for his jailhouse masterpiece and had consequently been recruited by the Episcopal liberal George Murray to meet with King and Shuttlesworth on April 25. Bishop C.C.J. Carpenter, in the pseudo-British accent Shuttlesworth loved to mimic, had reiterated the arguments of the published statement, until finally Murray said, "I confess, all of us have been guilty; we have not done what we ought to have done." Shuttlesworth retorted, "You confess just like white folks confess and go right on doing the same thing."

Grafman, the only Jew in the group, had felt the most picked on. King's references to "merchants" made him wince. Louis Pizitz, Isadore's father, had been "wonderful to them"—a big Tuskegee supporter. King "implied that the problem was the Jews," Grafman complained, "and they were not the power structure!" When the Movement representatives pressed Grafman to make a commitment on behalf of the retailers, he said, "I don't speak for my people," adding, in what was taken as a slap at King, "I don't speak for God." Shuttlesworth shot back, "Well, who in the hell are you speaking for? In our church, we try to speak for God."[*] As King would say of the white clergymen, "We have to be patient with them. They are all pitiful. They think we outsiders are Communists."

Of the Jewish men who convened on Saturday afternoon to meet with Burke Marshall, only the host did not claim Grafman as his rabbi. Abe Berkowitz, a member of Conservative Beth El, was so comfortable with his Russian Jewishness that his friends were aghast when he joined the elite Jews' Hillcrest Country Club (because it had a golf course, unlike the more modest Fairmont club). He had been a gadfly on the Reform crowd ever since his youth, when he had sent arms to his fellow Jews in Palestine as the leader of Birmingham's Zionist movement—the divisive class issue of the day, with the Reform assimilationists opposed to any separatist militancy. Among the ardent anti-Zionists were the Loveman family and the brilliant lawyer Leo Oberdorfer, who had been a pillar of the snooty Congregation of Reform Judaism.

Oberdorfer's son, Louis, had been keeping tabs on the race crisis in his hometown for his Justice Department colleague Burke Marshall, regularly consulting Vincent Townsend, a Southside neighbor of his father, and Emil Hess, the

---

[*] The Jewish journalist Harry Golden observed, "In the Negro Movement, the Negro understands that the Jew is the weak point in the white power of the South. By instinct the Negro launched his strongest demonstrations in Birmingham, Atlanta, and Richmond against the Jewish-owned department stores. Tragicomically, Jews clutch my arm to tell me Negroes are anti-semitic." Shuttlesworth, however, apparently did believe that the merchants controlled the power structure. There was an old theory among blacks, as Hosea Hudson had once expressed it, that white people are so busy keeping Negroes down that they have allowed Jews and Italians to possess all the wealth.

1

Vulcan, Birmingham's fickle, crippled god of fire and industry, was domesticated into a patron saint of traffic safety.

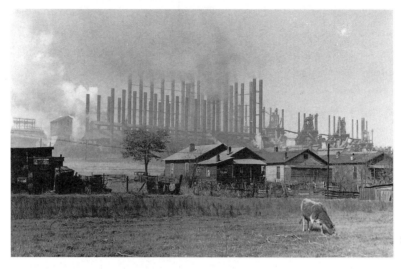

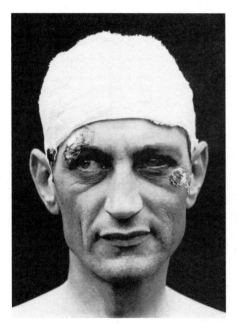

U.S. Steel's blast furnaces were photographed by Franklin Roosevelt's Farm Security Administration in 1937, not long after the corporation's "security" hands beat up a radical union advocate named Joe Gelders. State prisoners sentenced to toil in Birmingham's coal mines had assured the industrialists of a strike-proof labor force until the "convict lease" system was outlawed in 1927.

To sway the public against the "socialism" of the New Deal promoted by the likes of Alabama Senator Hugo Black (above left), coal magnate Charles De-Bardeleben (above right) used propaganda and machine guns, while Big Mule lawyer-politician Jim Simpson (below left) installed in city hall a popular cracker-barrel baseball announcer named Bull Connor.

The local anti–New Dealers, led by the plainspoken Sid Smyer (left) and the elegant former governor Frank Dixon (below left), coalesced into a national political movement in 1948: the Dixiecrats. Meanwhile, the state's equally inventive progressives rose up behind the magnetic new governor, a "redneck" integrationist named Big Jim Folsom.

12

As a civil rights movement gained footing through the efforts of Louis Burnham of the Southern Negro Youth Congress (seated to left of speaker at the SNYC's 1948 convention) and James Dombrowski of the Southern Conference Educational Fund (right of speaker), the Dixiecrats turned to intermediaries to keep the Negroes "in their place." Among them were "Dynamite Bob" Chambliss (with his wife, Flora, in 1947) and, later, the volatile rabble-rouser (and future best-selling author) Ace Carter.

13

14

15

16

Autherine Lucy's desegregation of the University of Alabama in February 1956 coincided with a Negro boycott of buses in Montgomery sparked by Rosa Parks (pictured in the 1980s with her white comrade in arms, Virginia Durr) to make Alabama the cradle of a modern civil rights movement, led by a young minister named Martin Luther King Jr.

In Birmingham, the Movement was ushered into its direct-action phase by Fred Shuttlesworth (opposite, top left), who was beat up in 1957 while escorting his children to an all-white high school. To the right of Shuttlesworth is Charles Billups, behind him is J. S. Phifer, to the left of Shuttlesworth (head averted) is Edward Gardner and Shuttleworth's daughter Pat. Communist Party member Jack O'Dell (opposite, top right) took part in the Birmingham movement before becoming Martin Luther King's embattled aide. Shuttlesworth's other co-conspirators included the jaded *World* editor, Emory O. Jackson (bottom left), and the NAACP's cautious lawyer, Arthur Shores, standing in front of his bombed house.

17

18

19

20

The bludgeoning of the Freedom Riders at Birmingham's Trailways station on Mother's Day, 1961 (above left), and the burning of their bus outside Anniston engaged the Kennedy administration in the civil rights struggle and inaugurated the scandalous career of the FBI's informant inside the Ku Klux Klan, Gary Thomas Rowe Jr. (above right, and in the foreground, above left).

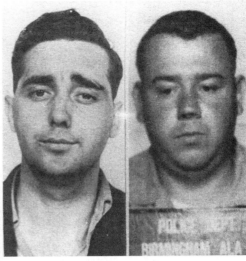

Rowe's brothers in the Klan's flagship Eastview klavern included the veteran bomber Robert Chambliss (above left) as well as newcomers John "Nigger" Hall and Charles Cagle (above right). With their segregationist franchise under siege, the rough-and-ready Klansmen desperately joined forces with wellborn neo-Nazis of the National States Rights Party, Edward Fields (left, wearing tie) and dynamite ace J. B. Stoner (below).

28

29

Early in the Southern Christian Leadership Conference's do-or-die Birmingham campaign to end segregation, the blind jazz singer Al Hibbler led pickets in April 1963. As the demonstrations faltered, Martin Luther King (with Ralph Abernathy to his immediate right, and Fred Shuttlesworth) shouldered the burden of true leadership on Good Friday and marched in violation of a court injunction. His subsequent confinement at Birmingham Jail yielded the "Letter" that consecrated his reputation.

The Movement's recruitment of schoolchildren as demonstrators (opposite, bottom) tested the nonviolence of the Birmingham police. Photographs by *Life*'s Charles Moore (top) and the AP's Bill Hudson (center) shifted international opinion to the side of the civil rights revolution and branded the man responsible for the imagery, Public Safety Commissioner Bull Connor (leading policemen), as the villain of the era.

34

3

The Justice Department's "riot squad"—civil
rights chief Burke Marshall (above, briefing
Attorney General Robert Kennedy on the
Birmingham crisis) and Joe Dolan (above
right, advising an Alabama state trooper)—
headed south to force negotiations between
blacks and whites. Liberals Chuck Morgan
(right) and David Vann (below left, pictured
as mayor in the 1970s) maneuvered behind
the scenes, while Big Mule Sid Smyer reluctantly spoke for white Birmingham.

36

37

It's nice to have you
...IN BIRMINGHAM

38

Martin Luther King, a disgruntled Fred Shuttlesworth, and Ralph Abernathy announced Birmingham's "accord with its conscience" on May 10, 1963. Hours after Imperial Wizard Bobby Shelton denounced the whites' settlement with King at a Ku Klux Klan rally (left), bombs exploded at two Movement targets and triggered the first postwar race riot. In the aftermath (below), Birmingham resembled a war zone.

42

The Kennedy administration's confrontation with Alabama's segregationists escalated in June, when Governor George Wallace halted Deputy U.S. Attorney General Nicholas Katzenbach as he attempted to register two black students at the University of Alabama. The governor's failed "Stand in the Schoolhouse Door" launched his national career. At summer's end, the freedom cause dramatized in the streets of Birmingham became a national priority at the March on Washington, where the protest's organizer, Bayard Rustin (below), extended his arms to the multitudes demonstrating for the passage of the Birmingham-inspired bill that would become the Civil Rights Act of 1964, abolishing legal segregation.

43

44

The death throes of segregation proved to be violent. Klansmen's dynamite blew a hole in the east wall of Birmingham's most venerable black church, Sixteenth Street Baptist, on Sunday morning, September 15, 1963. Under the rubble were the corpses of (below, left to right) Denise McNair, Carole Robertson, Addie Mae Collins, and Cynthia Wesley.

2 Charged in 1963 Church Blast That Killed 4 Birmingham Girls

Hint of New Testimony but No Details Are Given

By KEVIN SACK

BIRMINGHAM, Ala., May 17 — Nearly 37 years after a bombing that horrified the nation, the authorities here charged two longtime suspects with murder today in the deaths of four black girls in the explosion at Birmingham's 16th Street Baptist Church.

Thomas E. Blanton Jr. and Bobby Frank Cherry, both of whom were affiliated with the Ku Klux Klan and have been considered suspects for decades in the 1963 bombing, turned themselves in this morning after being indicted by a state grand jury on

Associated Press
Bobby Frank Cherry

Jefferson County Sheriff's Department
Thomas E. Blanton Jr.

Tuesday. They are being held in the Jefferson County jail here without bond.

Only one man, Robert Chambliss, has ever been tried in the case, and that was not until 1977, 14 years after the bombing. He was convicted of murder, sentenced to life and died in prison in 1985. Herman Cash, another man named as a suspect in early Federal Bureau of Investigation case files, died in 1994 without ever being charged.

Federal authorities reopened their investigation of the bombing in 1996, but they declined today to discuss the evidence they have gathered against Mr. Blanton, 61, of Birmingham, and Mr. Cherry, 69, of Mabank, Tex.

Several of Mr. Cherry's relatives, including an ex-wife and a granddaughter, have said they told grand jurors that Mr. Cherry had boasted of taking part in the bombing. But there is little information about what additional new evidence, if any, investigators may have found to implicate either Mr. Cherry or Mr. Blanton, whose indictment came as more of a surprise.

Asked about the evidence at a news conference today, Doug Jones, the United States attorney here, would only say, "We expect the evidence today to be a good bit different than it would have been 36 years ago."

Though some witnesses have died and there have been no reports of new physical evidence, prosecutors said today that they were optimistic about their chances to win convictions in the Birmingham case. "The witnesses that we have, we believe, are sufficient to sustain the charge," Mr. Jones said.

The prosecutions of Mr. Blanton and Mr. Cherry are the latest in a series of dusty civil rights cases that have been reopened in recent years as a new breed of Southern prosecutors have come to power, as new witnesses have come forward to relieve guilty consciences, and as changing times and demographics have made it easier to impanel jurors willing to convict whites for the

Continued on Page A28

47

owner of Parisian Department Store. That Marshall's intelligence had come from Hess, by far the most liberal of the retailers, may explain why he was so stunned by the reaction he was getting.

"Why doesn't the President order King to leave Birmingham?" one store owner asked him. Why us? the men demanded. Why Birmingham? Berkowitz stared at the men with the whites-only lunch counters; he always cringed at the country club when some of them wondered "where was that nigger with my bacon, lettuce, and tomato sandwich." Now he told them, "I don't know why anyone would want to eat your lousy soup."

The store owner Shuttlesworth had called "the most recalcitrant"—a characterization not disputed by Marshall—was Isadore "Bud" Pizitz, who had been standing in front of his store when the pickets arrived the first week of the campaign. He had asked them why they were picking on him and noted that he liked colored people "in their place." It was he who finally articulated his colleagues' position for Marshall: "I'm not going to put myself in the middle."

Peacekeeper

DESPITE ITS PROMISE of "federal intervention," Burke Marshall's arrival was greeted with suspicion at the Gaston Motel. Robert Kennedy was still questioning the timing of the campaign, lamenting that "an injured, maimed, or dead child is a price that none of us can pay." When President Kennedy said the dogs-and-hoses pictures made him "sick," it was conceivable that he meant this in the spirit of "this is going to make America look bad in Russia, Nigeria, etc."

As far as the Movement was concerned, Marshall's "peace-keeping" mission was pursuing the kind of "negative peace" that King described in the letter from jail. Wyatt Walker could barely maintain his cool on the subject of Marshall. After several hostile telephone encounters beginning with the Freedom Rides, Marshall had admonished Walker for using Robert Kennedy to get publicity for King. Walker was a bit quick on the offensive when he snarled back, "How dare you question the integrity of Dr. King!" As Walker later described his position on Marshall: "I didn't want to see him. He'd already torn his ass with me. I thought it was a bad sign that he was the broker. He was weak, naive, and uninformed."

Nor was Fred Shuttlesworth pleased with Marshall's visit. Though Shuttlesworth liked and admired him, his presence spoke for itself: How meaningful could "negotiations" be when the whites would not deal with blacks except through an intermediary? White folks listened to the truth only during demonstrations, as Chuck Morgan liked to say. And if a deal was to be struck behind closed doors in Abe Berkowitz's office, it was only because of what was going on in the streets.

"Blessed are the peacemakers," read a sign in Marshall's office, "for they catch hell from all sides."

Miracle Sunday

Jim Bevel's "science" of nonviolent direct action as community-building was about to clash with Wyatt Walker's strategic maneuvering. Walker was in another tiff over Bevel's unilateral and insubordinate cancellation of demonstrations for Sunday, May 5. "You don't argue with people" was Bevel's attitude toward authority, "you outwork them."

At 4 p.m. that Sunday, after a morning of integrating white churches, the crowd of faithful gathered for a prayer meeting at Nelson Smith's New Pilgrim Baptist. Bull Connor was threatening to arrest any white person who crossed Sixth Avenue South, and that included the celebrities drawn to the spotlight on Birmingham. The twenty-two-year-old folksinger Joan Baez had flown in to give an evening concert at Miles. ("Greenwich Village comes to Birmingham," the *World* noted.) Two of her albums were among Billboard's top-forty LPs, on a fully desegregated list that mixed James Brown, Ray Charles, Little Stevie Wonder ("The 12 Year Old Genius"), and Nat King Cole with such ultra-white acts as the Beach Boys and Allan Sherman, of "Hello, Mudduh" fame, at the top of the chart. The musical mongrel Elvis Presley was at number 9.

Policemen blocked Baez from entering the church. Highlander's Guy Carawan, Pete Seeger's protégé and heir as the school's folkie laureate (he had introduced "We Shall Overcome" at the 1960 organizational meeting of SNCC), had come to Birmingham as the Movement's music historian, to record the ACMHR choir—the most polished of the Movement's singers, with vocalists like Cleo Kennedy and Mamie Brown destined for national careers. Inside New Pilgrim, Andy Young announced that Carawan and his wife, Candie, had just been arrested on the church steps. The only white person who had made it inside, the *Nation* reporter Barbara Deming, was smuggled up to the balcony as a black man piped in a good-natured falsetto of fake panic, "Don't you worry, honey! We'll get you out! Won't let Bull Connor get you!"

Bevel entered, fussing that the detectives would have to comply with Connor's ban on whites. He exited to address the large crowd outside the church, then returned to the standing-room-only sanctuary with Bernard Lee. To the irritation of Wyatt Walker, Bevel declared himself "tired of this mess" and called off his moratorium on demonstrating. "Let's not march," he said. "Let's walk."

At around six o'clock, a group estimated at between one thousand and three thousand left the church and walked west into the setting sun on Sixth Avenue. The Southside jail was a few blocks away. This was the largest demonstration of the campaign so far, and proof that the children had finally gotten their parents behind the Movement. Its leader was Charles Billups, Nelson Smith's co-pastor and Shuttlesworth's co-conspirator. Billups had been with Shuttlesworth at the head of the very first march in Birmingham, that silent, placardless ritual a month before, when the C in Project C might have stood for Choke. Since that Saturday, when King and Abernathy tried to lecture Birmingham into obedience, SCLC's brass had been operating as if they were the Movement, needing only bodies to follow their commands. But "Miracle Sunday," as this would go down in the annals, was an overwhelmingly local production. The humble Billups, the pride of the masses, was about to preside over the campaign's spiritual climax.

As the road dipped under a viaduct, Bevel, standing next to Billups, could make out fire trucks straddling the side streets ahead. At first sight, he thought the hoses, mounted on tripods at six stations, were machine guns. Bevel sensed that Billups "knew my courage had happened" when he grabbed Bevel's shoulder and told him to go bring up the back of the line. The men and women proceeded, singing "I Want Jesus to Walk with Me." Spectators jamming the porches of neighboring houses were hushed in contrast to past onlookers. When the first marchers reached the police barricade two blocks from the jailhouse, they knelt and began to pray, as their wake of churchpeople billowed to the ground. Flanked by firemen, Captain Glenn Evans ordered them to disperse.

Billups stood and looked into the nozzles of the hoses. "We're not turning back," he said. "We haven't done anything wrong. All we want is our freedom. How do you feel doing these things?" Then he began to chant, "Turn on your water, turn loose your dogs, we will stand here till we die." Tears streamed down his face. The crowd chimed in, a chorus swelled.

As with most miracles, the particulars of that Sunday are difficult to document, especially since reporters were among the white people Connor had barred from the scene. What the press did observe from a distance was that the demonstrators retreated across the street to Julius Ellsberry Park—named after Jefferson County's first (Negro) World War II casualty, at Pearl Harbor—where they prayed and sang for half an hour, with water guns trained on them.

Movement participants would swear that Connor barked at his firemen, "Turn on the hoses," and the firemen had just stood there. "Dammit!" Connor said, "turn on the hoses." But the firemen fell back. Nelson Smith believed they had caught the marchers' "spiritual intoxication." Some firemen were crying, and one was heard to say, "We're here to put out fires, not people." Connor would insist that the firemen were simply being considerate of the marchers' Sunday clothes. But most of the Negroes felt what Smith called "the hand of God" as never before, as they arose from their prayers singing "I Got Freedom over My Head" and strode through a line of policemen and firemen parting like the Red Sea.

Fire Chief John Swindle would not advertise his hand in Miracle Sunday. He had arrived on the scene late, after the protesters were bunched in the park, and observed that they "weren't creating any problems." When Connor said to turn on the water, Swindle "didn't hear him." Neither did his nozzlemen: After the heavy hosing the day before, the chief had instructed the fire department to ignore orders that did not come directly from him. Had Connor personally ordered Swindle to give his men the command, the chief later admitted, he "probably would have, because I didn't have enough time [of service] to go on a pension."

Martin Luther King called the demonstration "one of the most fantastic events of the Birmingham story. . . . I saw there, I felt there, for the first time, the pride and the *power* of nonviolence." But King was not at Miracle Sunday. He was at home in Atlanta, being hailed at Ebenezer as "Moses on earth." Charles Billups was the Moses of this miracle. He had told Shuttlesworth when he joined the Movement, with the steel plate in his head from his war wounds, that he was "living on borrowed time," with "nothing to go for but life," and on this day he staked his corner of heaven.*

A Christian Problem

THE MERCHANTS RECONVENED in Abe Berkowitz's office that Sunday. A consensus was taking shape. As a secular Jewish leader would soon put it in writing, "the Jewish community leadership generally believes that Jews, as such, ought to stay out of the desegregation fight on the ground that it is a 'Christian problem' between whites and Negroes and not simply a racial problem." This would have come as a surprise to the Christian ministers busy positing that civil rights was a political rather than a moral issue. But at any rate, as the retailers continued to discuss their predicament before Burke Marshall and Joe Dolan, they turned increasingly to the Christian among them, Roper Dial.

As Sears, Roebuck's man in Alabama, Dial was the merchant closest to the power structure. He was a member of the Birmingham Country Club, handsome and courtly, his daughter a Brooke Hill graduate and debutante. When Sears had expanded from catalogues and begun opening stores in the 1920s, the company had bought up large lots on the outskirts of the retail district to allow for its innovation of "ample free parking." Disgruntled established merchants watched trade being pulled off their blocks, and southerners still thought of Sears as such a modernist alien that Sears and Roebuck were rumored to be Negroes—perhaps out of some vague awareness of Sears founder Julius Rosenwald's philanthropies that subsidized Negro education.

Despite his free parking and his Memphis roots, Roper Dial had become popular with the natives, particularly Bud Pizitz. He was also Vincent Townsend's point man in retail. He had a bit more incentive than his peers to settle the thing; his Sears store was situated on Sixteenth Street, near a dense black residential neighborhood and just a few blocks south of Kelly Ingram Park. Dial was the merchant who had broken the impasse in the previous fall's negotiations—his janitor having "accidentally" painted over the "White Only" restroom sign—and so that Sunday morning Pizitz again turned the Christian problem over to him.

Pizitz told Dial that the only man he figured could speak for the white power structure was Sid Smyer. Dial knew someone who might speak for the black power structure: David Vann. Since no one made a move without Vincent

---

* Within seven months of King's own assassination, Billups would be found in his car dead of head injuries from a blunt instrument. He had moved to Chicago and was at the time of his death on November 7, 1968, director of human relations for the National Food Stores. His murder was never solved. His body was brought back to Birmingham and led to the grave site in a mule-drawn cart. The sermon, "Mission Possible," was delivered by his pastor, Nelson Smith.

Townsend, he was called upon to arrange Vann's first audience with the retailers. When Vann arrived at Abe Berkowitz's law library on Sunday, Dial informed him that the plan was for Vann and Smyer to head a biracial "negotiating committee" on behalf of but not including the merchants. Vann telephoned Arthur Shores and asked him if he could get together some Negroes to meet. A few hours after Charles Billups had parted the waters of Miracle Sunday, Sid Smyer left his over-the-mountain home and drove to Birmingham Realty, to play host to the first negotiating session.

Smyer's and Vann's white companions were a couple of Young Turk lawyers—Erskine Smith, Vann's main co-conspirator on the Citizens for Progress petition, and George Peach Taylor, a lawyer on the landmark reapportionment case who was now Sheriff Mel Bailey's staff attorney (and had been at an earlier biracial meeting at the Church of the Advent). Billy Hamilton, the wheezy, alcoholic, extremely intelligent assistant to the maybe mayor Boutwell, was sitting in, unofficially. And there was the unassuming man in glasses, Burke Marshall.

Arthur Shores had gotten up a group of what the whites would once have called Responsible Negroes—Lucius Pitts, an insurance executive named John Drew, and A. G. Gaston. The only Atlanta ringer was Andy Young. Shuttlesworth was not there—his vice presidents, Ed Gardner and Abraham Woods, were representing the ACMHR—but this was no group of Big Boys "all-righting" the white men. Since watching the girl being hosed on Friday, Gaston had stood up to his "white friends" and found it liberating.

The black negotiators presented their minimal demands. One, immediate desegregation of all store facilities. Two, immediate promotion of black employees and a nondiscriminatory hiring program. Gardner turned to Marshall, "We need to be demonstrating against y'all, because y'all don't have any Negroes anywhere but the post office." Smyer said he would provide all the jobs they needed—Birmingham Realty had that quarry. "No," Gardner said, "what about these other folks," referring to the merchants. Demands number three and four were that the merchants pressure the city to drop charges against demonstrators and to establish a biracial committee to push for desegregation of the police department, schools, parks, movie theaters, and hotels.

Smyer bristled. There was absolutely no way private businessmen were going to speak for the city government. The black men accused the whites of bad faith. Smyer began to tell the group of that Rotary convention in Tokyo, of his embarrassment and shock at seeing the bus station business through international eyes. As he spoke of his love for his city, tears spilled onto his cheeks.

Realizing how unappreciated was his courage in hosting this meeting, Smyer ordered everyone out of his office. "There will be no more meetings here," he said.

One of the black negotiators, John Drew—perhaps the only man in Birmingham with the social standing to call Martin Luther King "Mike"—took particular offense at Smyer's high-handedness. John ("Pope John" in the Movement's telephone code) and his Pennsylvania-born wife, Addine (or Deenie)—so "high yaller" that she had attended the Dixiecrat convention as a spy—had become friendly with King when Drew was the only insurance man willing to insure the Montgomery Improvement Association's station wagons during the bus boycott. King usually stayed in the guest room of the Drews' luxurious ranch house atop Dynamite Hill when he was in town, enjoying steak dinners and "Mr. John Walker (he's become a very good friend) or Mr. Beefeater."

Drew said to Smyer, "Well, this ain't so hot," and pointed out sarcastically that this wasn't the only place in town to meet. He suggested that they adjourn to his house.*

In the quickening dispute over who was more beholden to whom, Smyer and Drew took off their jackets and squared off. "You're not going to tear up my office," Smyer said, and proposed that they step outside. The group trooped through the Birmingham Realty Company's dingy marble lobby and out onto the First Avenue sidewalk, where the dudgeon drained out of the two men.

George Peach Taylor called Deenie Drew to alert her that some of them were coming over to continue the meeting on Dynamite Hill; she had a friend bring over a ham and some booze. Smyer retreated back over the mountain.

Doable

ON MONDAY MORNING, Parker High's principal, R. C. Johnson, stood at the school's main entrance. At night Johnson had been sitting by his own front door with a shotgun to protect his new grandbaby and his daughter Alma, who had moved back home while her Bronx-bred husband, Colin Powell, was in Vietnam earning his first stripes in a distinguished Army career.

Jim Bevel's young lieutenants had blanketed the school building with handbills reading, "It's up to you to free our teachers, our parents, yourself, and our country." Students thronged the halls, singing "Freedom" to the tune of "A-a-a-men." Eleanor Roosevelt had visited Parker in 1937 when it was still called Industrial High, and after 2,500 students sang "Swing Low, Sweet Chariot" for her, she told them, "I hope that you will look upon your gift of music as one of the things you have which will smooth your way through life." Now a chant rolled over the melodies, as students streamed past their principal and out the door, "Gotta GO, Mister Johnson, gotta GO."

As the children headed for Sixteenth Street Baptist, David Vann, under the silent watch of Burke Marshall and Joe Dolan, was giving the retailers a report about the previous night's meeting. By standing their ground on the "non-negotiable" items involving city government, the store owners could rationalize

---

* In a curious dissent from conventional Movement history, Deenie Drew would claim that on his fifth or sixth day in jail, King had sent for her through attorney Orzell Billingsley, had her sit in his cell while he finished what he was writing on some scraps of paper, and then asked her to get them to a typist. She took them to Rose White, Lucius Pitts's assistant at Miles. After typing up "Letter from Birmingham Jail," White threw away the scraps, never thinking in years to come that archivists would be cursing her or scholars doubting her.

the other concessions, even the promotion of Negroes onto the floor—most of them had some fine colored employees who got along well with the white workers. The negotiating point that most worried Dolan was the fitting rooms. It was only a fairly recent development for white merchants to let black people try on clothes before buying them, though Negro purchases were still usually nonreturnable. Dolan feared a sudden vogue in store-provided plastic undergarments.

"Well, you never put two women in the same fitting room anyway," Parisian's Emil Hess said, pointing out that this amounted to "segregation." One of his colleagues said, "You're holding something back." Hess hesitated, weary of having his liberalism imputed to his store's lack of a lunchroom. Finally he said, "Well, I desegregated my fitting rooms two years ago."

A gasp. "What happened?" someone asked.

"No one noticed," Hess said.

There was silence. Another man spoke. "I already desegregated mine too."

That was when Dolan realized that a settlement in Birmingham was "doable," although he did not quite understand how Sid Smyer was going to be the man to do it.

Ain't Scared of Your Jail

THE FIRE DEPARTMENT'S red pumpers appeared at Kelly Ingram Park around noon. In his latest "I don't believe I mentioned that to Dr. King" intrigue, Wyatt Walker had dispatched Miles students around the city to decoy the fire department with false alarms, but Chief Swindle sent reserves out to the suspicious "fires," pulling none of his trucks off demonstration duty. Cops stood atop the low-rise buildings along Fifth Avenue. Short-wave radios crackled. Joan Baez had arrived at the church facedown on the back seat of a car and then, accompanied by her blond, waifish traveling companion, joined the singing, clapping, and around-the-pew parading. A speaker announced that since the city had run out of jail space, some rich white folks were donating their tennis courts to pen them in. The crowd cheered and hooted.

Outside, as a roar from the sanctuary roused the neighborhood, the policemen, wearing white World War I–type helmets, turned expectantly toward the church. The Muslim leader Jeremiah X stood on the sidewalk with Len Holt, Shuttlesworth's favorite lawyer, who had just flown in from his home in Virginia. "At any moment those cops expect three hundred years of hate to spew forth from that church," Jeremiah said.

Instead, Jim Bevel walked out. He went over to a police captain and asked, You're not going to turn those hoses on the children, are you? The move was calculated to disarm the opposition more than to spare the kids the hose spray, which by now fell under the category of recreation, unworthy of comment beyond Bevel's casual advice to wear raincoats. The officer declined to shake Bevel's extended hand but smiled and said, "I think you've had enough experience with us to know that we are not going to use any more force than necessary."

At the marching hour of one, Dick Gregory, sporting a gray Italian-cut suit, led the first column of nineteen boys and girls out of the church, carrying a sign reading "Everybody Wants Freedom." Gregory, barely past thirty, had broken into entertainment's color-blind big time as one of the great, brazen young nightclub comedians, pulling down $1,500 a week: He knew the South very well—"I spent twenty years there one night." By the time Martin Luther King had called him at home in Chicago for help, Gregory was a Movement folktale as the first celebrity to join SNCC's campaign in Greenwood, Mississippi, a month earlier. When a cop there spit in his face, he had let it run into his mouth. "I guess that makes me as white as you now, boy," he said. "I got your spit inside me." The cop threw him into his car but admitted en route to jail that Gregory was "a better man than I am," and returned him to the battlefront.

At three on Monday morning, hours before he was to leave for Birmingham, Gregory had come home drunk, only to be ordered by his wife to return the urgent calls of the President of the United States. "*Please*, don't go down to Birmingham," Kennedy said to Gregory. "We've got it all solved. Dr. King is wrong, what he's doing."

Gregory replied, "Man, I will be there in the morning." The thing that had upset him most about Birmingham was the fire hoses. He expected the worst from the police, but firemen had been his childhood idols.

Now, staring into the face of a police captain in a war helmet, Gregory noticed the same expression he was used to seeing on black faces: fear. Captain George Wall asked him if he understood that he was in violation of a city parade ordinance and a state court injunction.

"No."

"No what?" said Wall, accustomed to the ministers' polite "sirs."

"No, no, a thousand times no," Gregory said.

"Call the wagon," Wall announced into his bullhorn.

The children broke into what Len Holt saw as "a hybrid of the turkey-trot and the twist," as they belted out to the tune of "The Old Grey Mare": "I ain't scared of your jail/'Cause I want my freedom!/Want my freedom." More and more paraders of twenty and thirty lined up to be arrested. King, who had not been visible around Ingram Park during the preceding days of violence, stood at the church door and greeted each group of youngsters, "The world is watching you." Joan Baez, with the dark complexion of her Mexican-American father, marched out with a group of girls, a scarf concealing her straight hair, and walked back to the Gaston Motel, past houses whose porches were jammed with women singing, "Black and white together/We shall overcome someday."

The kids seemed to be having the time of their lives. They shadowboxed the police as they piled into the school buses, toothbrushes periscoping from their pockets. Some kids had worn bathing suits as if to play in the sprinkler. It was hot and muggy, up near ninety. To the disappointment of some, the fire hoses remained slack.

At the Birmingham jail, Guy and Candie Carawan were making good professional use of their stay, gathering material for a new chorus to Jimmy Tarlton's ballad—"Birmingham jailhouse, Birmingham jail;/ Waiting for Freedom in Bull Connor's jail." A sample verse went: "Pushed by the policemen, herded like hogs—/Some got the fire hose, some got the dogs."

Bull's Hour

KIDS HUNG OUT THE WINDOWS of the school buses cum police wagons and to the chants of "Freedom! Freedom!" shook their index fingers at Commissioner Bull Connor. "If you ask half of them what freedom means," he said, "they couldn't tell you."

Until the dogs, Connor's Birmingham had been the trivial side of the story, tacitly condoned by the reporters who stayed away from mass meetings at Connor's request. The news media were so focused on King and his Golgotha that their distress at his use of children had initially offset their shock at Connor's use of fire hoses and police dogs. But since Double D-Day, the well-rehearsed, coat-and-tied Mr. Connor of the knowing commentary had reverted to the ole Bull, grimy straw hat cocked jauntily over his bad eye, working the audience like a vaudevillian doing his last shtick.*

While chauffeuring the commissioner around King's theater, Captain George Wall had asked him whether he thought the Supreme Court—"They're conservative"—might rule in his favor. "Hell no, buddy," Connor replied, "they're gonna get rid of me. But they'll know Bull Connor for many years in this world."

Alabama Is All Right

THERE HAD BEEN no civilian violence to bring out the fire hoses and the dogs that Monday afternoon, but the police were on a roll. Five uniformed cops provided another memorable photograph by subduing a black woman in a flowered dress. As the photograph moved over the UPI telegraph to the *New York Times,* the paper's lawyers were rejecting Stanley Levison's attempts to place a fund-soliciting ad for SCLC unless he agreed to delete all references to brutality and discrimination, including direct quotations from the *Times*'s own news stories. The *Times*'s Supreme Court brief for *Sullivan*—the outcome of the last ad for King in the paper—was now being written, longhand on yellow legal pads, by the constitutional scholar and Columbia professor Herbert Wechsler, who as a young

---

* One of Connor's most memorable lines may have been given to him. During a press post-mortem on Saturday at the Tutwiler, *Time*'s Dudley Morris told colleagues that Connor had ordered a sergeant to let the whites come up to the corner. "I want 'em to see the dogs work," Morris claimed Connor said. "Look at those niggers run." Albert "Buck" Persons, the local *Life* stringer (and Bay of Pigs veteran) who had earlier become skeptical of Wyatt Walker's account of police brutality, had observed Connor trying to move white spectators from the scene and asked Morris if he had actually heard the statement. Morris admitted that he hadn't, and Persons was outraged when the quotation appeared unqualified in *Time,* and was picked up by *Life* in a caption for one of Charles Moore's pictures.

lawyer had worked on the winning brief in the black Communist Angelo Herndon's Supreme Court appeal of his sedition conviction; at the time, his brother James, the *New York Post* editor who had reputedly been one of Project C's benefactors at Harry Belafonte's gathering, was having an unhappy dalliance with the Communist Party. The line between that civil rights epoch and this one had long since been expunged by the Cold War.

A Coke bottle came sailing from the crowd of bystanders and crashed on the sidewalk near some policemen, triggering street-clearing maneuvers from cops and ministers. A Movement messenger ran out of Sixteenth Street church and declared it "all over for today."

Later that afternoon, Shuttlesworth, King, and Abernathy encountered Art Hanes as they were leaving the Gaston Motel. "There goes Shuttlesworth," Hanes said, as though he had spotted a celebrity.

"Yeah, there we go," Shuttlesworth called back. "We got the town, friend."

The three ministers got in a car and cruised around Eighteenth and Nineteenth Streets. They liked what they saw: pandemonium. Grinning kids were still swarming around; some carried lunch bags and suitcases, hoping to join the 2,500 in jail, by the police's probably low estimate. Despite the helmets and sunglasses, the cops looked helpless, more like school crossing guards beside the yellow buses. A policeman fell off his motorcycle as he cut sharply to avoid a demonstrator. "Don't kill yourself, brother," Shuttlesworth called out the car window. Turning to King, Shuttlesworth said, "All we have to do is hold this pressure for three days, and we got it."

Shuttlesworth went off to a "negotiating session"—a term he objected to, given that the white principals would not meet him face-to-face. David Vann presented his retail clients' opening gambit: Five or six Negro employees could be "justifiably promoted"—after the demonstrations ended. The store owners would desegregate the fitting rooms immediately. The lunch counters, restrooms, and water fountains would require a delay. The black men insisted on prompt desegregation of all facilities, with pressure from retailers on the city to "wink" at the segregation ordinances. The whites said absolutely not, and threatened to resign as negotiators.

As the committee met, Abernathy and King made the rounds of the mass meetings that had filled four churches. Grassroots specialists from SNCC had been arriving since the weekend—their guru, Ella Baker, had just flown in. SNCC's best administrator and fund-raiser, James Forman, a Chicagoan, blew into St. James Baptist and seized the microphone from the ACMHR minister Charles Billups: At the jail, students had been herded into a pen outside in the rain. Parents got up from their pews to undertake a mass delivery of blankets. King urged them to hold off. Forman accused him of insensitivity. King excused himself and accompanied Forman, Billups, and Bevel to the open jail compound, where the girls still had on the white dresses seniors wore every day in May leading up to graduation. There, Bull Connor received a piece of Bevel's mind, and then King, who proposed that they solve the crisis by calling Burke Marshall, received a piece of Forman's. "The constant calls to the Justice Department lessen the militancy of the people," he lectured King. Bevel and Billups sided with Forman.

As a motorcade of five hundred cars was rumored to be conveying blankets and food to the jailyard, King made his third mass-meeting appearance of the evening. "I have never in my life had an experience like I am now having in Birmingham, Alabama," he said. "This is the most inspiring Movement that has ever taken place in the United States of America." Perhaps in a nod to the prominent black journalist and Movement chronicler Louis Lomax, in the audience taking notes, King continued, "There are those who write history, there are those who make history, there are those who experience history. I don't know how many historians we have in Birmingham tonight, I don't know how many of you would be able to write a history book. But you are certainly making history and you are experiencing history, and you will make it possible for the historians of the future to write a marvelous chapter."

If there was a note of condescension here, the conclusion of King's talk—on *agape*—seemed out of touch. To distinguish his favored Greek platonic love from the selfish romance of *eros*, he said, "You love your lover because there is something about your lover that *moves* you."

Ralph Abernathy seemed to sense that his friend was losing his audience, that the much invoked "hand of God" had anointed mass Birmingham over classy Atlanta. Envy had inevitably gnawed at Abernathy's love of King, and now the sidekick took advantage of the chance to show him up. After stressing his close friendship with King, he said, "There's one thing we have that's different. He is a native of Georgia, and I am a native of Alabama. And I have been telling him all along that Alabama was all right, that the people of Alabama are all right. I've been telling him that we know the meaning of the word that he called e-ros," he said. "He said that eros is that type of love that mo-o-o-ves ya." Laughter intervened. "And he went on to say what it *might* be. It might be the way yo' luvah"—he paused lasciviously—"walks. And it might be the way your lover talks. I was glad that he didn't tell ya what it really is! But that's the way people talk from Georgia. In Alabama, we'll take the 'it might be' out and let you know just plainly what it is."

17.

MAYDAY

The Photographs

THE ALABAMA CHRISTIAN MOVEMENT for Human Rights's officers Ed Gardner and Bill Shortridge took a room at the Gaston Motel to count the collection from the Monday-night mass meeting—a $40,000 tribute to the dogs and hoses that were also keeping Jack O'Dell busy cashing donation checks at SCLC's New York office. The photographs from Birmingham had passed into the archive of universal metaphor. The theme emerging from the mail pouring into Birmingham City Hall was expressed by the ninth-grade teacher from Brooklyn who condemned the "policy of racial superiority (otherwise known as genocide) less than a score of years after so many Americans died to thwart the same plans of Hitler and his Nazis." On the Senate floor, Wayne Morse, of Oregon, compared Bull Connor's police to "the Nazi storm troopers against the Jews." Germany's leading magazine, *Der Spiegel*, was devoting half a coming issue to the American freedom movement.

The photographs came as an ironic boon to Birmingham's retailers. Until "Double D-Day," the polite white people of Birmingham had been seen around the country as reformers on the side of the angels and the Kennedy administration. The responsibility for ending the demonstrations had been the store owners' private agony. By Monday, however, their plaint, "We can't make a move without the power structure," had become a positive summons for the city fathers to take action. Under persuasion from Bud Pizitz, Sears's Roper Dial urged Sid Smyer to call a meeting of the seventy-seven white Brahmins of the Senior Citizens Committee—excluding its twelve black members in order to do away with segregation.

The Fulfillment of a Dream

SNCC's JIM FORMAN had been unimpressed with the format of the demonstrations—the police's "containment" of the marches within the Negro district made Project C look simply like "people walking from the church and into waiting police vans." And so on Monday night at the Gaston Motel, he and a variety of leaders—a couple of SNCC comrades, SCLC's ranking woman, Dorothy Cotton, lawyer Len Holt, CORE field secretary Isaac Reynolds (one of the original Freedom Riders), and, of course, Jim Bevel—sat up into the early hours plotting a surprise: Operation Confusion. By six o'clock Tuesday morning, May 7, as Gardner and Shortridge were counting the last of the "quiet money," Movement organizers were at Parker High School. The real D-Day had dawned.

On the way to his and Martin Luther King's ten o'clock press conference at the Gaston Motel, Fred Shuttlesworth saw Forman shepherding the young troops toward the Sixteenth Street Baptist Church and told the out-of-towner he didn't appreciate outsiders coming in and trying to organize a "SNCC chapter." His displeasure was probably displaced territorial anxiety over the fact that the only "joint leader" being quoted in the papers was King. The motel courtyard was jammed with journalists from around the world—more than a hundred—who had followed Bill Hudson's photograph of Walter Gadsden and the police dog Leo to Birmingham. ("You got a bonus, didn't you?" a British reporter asked him. "Not so much as a nickel," Hudson answered, or even a thank-you from New York.) The foreigners making their first visit to the American South joined the beat veterans who had recently formed their own acronymous band, the Southern Correspondents on Racial Equality Wars, or SCREW.

King stepped up to the microphone and claimed the moment. "Activities which have taken place in Birmingham over the last few days, to my mind, mark the nonviolent movement coming of age," he told the press. "... In a very real sense this is the fulfillment of a dream."

In the church around the corner, a SNCC worker asked a group of kids, "Who wants to go to jail?" All hands shot up. Soda money was dispensed to the sit-ins. Following the plans that SNCC and company had hammered out the night before, children headed nonchalantly out the door and got into cars manned by Miles students and "Movement moms," including Deenie Drew. Carloads headed via different routes to the post office, the bus stations, and eight department stores. At twelve o'clock, the cars disgorged six hundred young people into the "white" retail area. This was a turning point in the war. In all previous marches, with a few isolated exceptions, "they" had been kept to their "own" section, confined to within a couple of blocks of the staging area around Kelly Ingram Park.

A decoy march took the customary route out of Sixteenth Street Baptist around Kelly Ingram, but there were few policemen to fool: In the practiced minuet that the Battle of Ingram Park had become, the partners had never assumed their positions before twelve-thirty and the dance had never begun before one. The full law enforcement contingent was half an hour away from duty when a patrolman alerted headquarters of the new development, seeming to confirm the message Wyatt Walker had already phoned in, affecting a cracker drawl, that "niggers are on their way" to Sears and other nonexistent targets.

Connor's oaths crackled over the police radio. His squad swarmed the center of town, already teeming with demonstrations. Sit-ins had taken their positions at some stores, while at others "flying squads" created confusion by approaching the lunch counters, suddenly changing course, and vanishing.

The arriving police tore up the marchers' signs, but made no arrests. There was no vacancy at the jail. This marked the first time that Gandhi's "fill the jails" axiom of nonviolent strategy had been executed in America.

Singing "We Shall Overcome," the children headed back to Sixteenth Street Baptist for further instructions.

The Power Structure

THE SIRENS OF Connor's fleet could be heard inside the Chamber of Commerce building, where Sid Smyer had managed to assemble seventy-seven of his Senior Citizens, those rarefied men in suits who did not feel they could indulge in the short-sleeves-and-necktie cheat attire of lower-rung Deep South businessmen. It was probably the most impressive group ever assembled outside a country club—the presidents not just of the big manufacturers (including TCI's president Art Wiebel and Hayes Aircraft's Lew Jeffers) but also of the banks, utilities, textiles, insurance and lumber companies, auto dealerships, Coke and Pepsi, plus the name partners from the major law firms and ex-governor Frank Dixon. The businessmen considered this meeting an imposition. Most were convinced that the "trouble" was the invention of outsiders, staged by the television networks—with an anti-CBS contingent bucking the majority, who blamed NBC's Huntley-Brinkley. As for the K-9 Corps, there was a rumor that some of the Negroes had put T-bone steaks up their sleeves to get the dogs to bite.

Because of the local newspapers' policies against printing Project C's modest goals, no one at the Chamber of Commerce knew that all that was necessary to stop the protests was the desegregation of the lunch counters and restrooms at the downtown department stores and the promotion of a few Negro employees out of the janitorial ghetto. Still, it would have made little difference if the city fathers had known why the black people were demonstrating: They had been conditioned by a lifetime at the center of a segregated universe to see "Negro demands" as unacceptable by their very existence. But now, unknowingly, they were about to officiate the end of segregation.

As the outside agitator in the Chamber of Commerce meeting room, Burke Marshall was making an effort to blend into the furniture. His always wry funnybone had been struck by the designation the men around him went by, Big Mules—perfect, without his quite being able to say why. Marshall was tired. For three days, relieved only by lunch at the Hillcrest Country Club with Lou Oberdorfer's formidable father, he had been taxied—by David Vann or Chuck Morgan, who thought Marshall was "the coolest man in the whole town"—from Smyer's realty company, to Abe Berkowitz's office, to Vann's bungalow in Crestline Park, to John and Deenie Drew's house on Dynamite Hill, and back to his own stale Holiday Inn room, which potentially concealed bugs from the city, the state, the *Birmingham News*, and maybe even the FBI. Marshall had avoided telling anyone what to do, had just sat and taken notes. To the Negroes he had suggested that the whites' proposed delay in desegregating the facilities didn't really make a difference. To the whites he had explained how unrevolutionary King was by the lights of the U.S. Constitution. What he had wanted to say was, "It isn't like they are going to integrate the country club."

Like the ACMHR's negotiators, some of the store owners had noticed that the Internal Revenue offices a few blocks away were as white as their lunch counters and suggested to Marshall that the segregationists were only doing what the government was doing. One new verse to "Birmingham Jail" asked, "When will we live by/The law of the land?/President Kennedy/ Where do you stand?"

On hand to answer the Senior Citizens' questions were Mayor Albert Boutwell, members of the newly elected city council, and Sheriff Mel Bailey. David Vann took his seat between Marshall and Judge Edgar Bowron, whose ruling declaring Boutwell the legitimate city executive was under appeal. Marshall turned to Vann and whispered his amazement at seeing a city "come together in one room like this." Vann's Pollyannaish outlook made him process the comment as a full compliment, though this was certainly a dubious superlative. Most cities did not find themselves chronically on the brink, in need of such attention, but this was the most recent in a series of Big Mule councils that had been kicked off by Sid Smyer's uncle E.J. more than half a century before, on August 12, 1908. He and other prominent citizens had called a mass meeting at the Bijou Theatre to arouse public opinion against the 16,000 local coal miners then on strike. One normally dignified city father after another got up and professed his hatred of the United Mine Workers of America, and passed a resolution all but granting the industrialists the right to murder if their privileges were threatened.

Those had been the days when the Big Mules had felt emboldened to speak for Birmingham. And now, fifty-five years later, it had come down to this rearguard capitulation.

Room Service

FOUR BLOCKS AWAY from the Chamber of Commerce, two thousand blacks crammed the Sixteenth Street Baptist Church. Shuttlesworth announced another mass invasion of downtown. "Who's going to lead them?" SNCC's Jim Forman carped. Shuttlesworth said King wanted them to "just go" again. Forman, offended that his careful tactics had been mistaken for a spontaneous outburst, decided to go over to the Gaston Motel to appeal to King. Forman found him on the phone, wearing a robe and pajamas, and about to tuck into a steak dinner from room service. Forman stalked back to Sixteenth Street.

A policeman entered the church and asked a Movement leader to get the people to leave. The whole sanctuary emptied into Kelly Ingram Park. "We want to go to jail," some kids told a cop. "Jail's that way," he answered, pointing south. The kids broke across the park, screaming, "We're going to jail!" A singing and laughing stampede of two thousand spectators swept along with them toward the "white" retail district, under the banners proclaiming "It's Nice to Have You in Birmingham."

Whites on their lunch breaks froze on the sidewalk amid demonstrators kneeling to pray or high-stepping to the beat of freedom songs. *Newsweek*'s Atlanta bureau chief, Joe Cumming (who had organized SCREW over dinner that week), stopped at a pay phone to alert his editors to the developing free-for-all. He hailed a passing black youth and said, "Tell my bosses in New York what this is all about."

"It's about freedom," the teenager said into the conference call, giving the home office what Cumming was sure was its first encounter with an authentic southern Negro voice.

The Last of the Dixiecrats

AS THE MEETING at the Chamber of Commerce got under way, the first Big Mule rose to speak. It was Frank Dixon, the grandest of the Dixiecrats. Unlike his old co-conspirator Sid Smyer, Dixon had not kept up with the times; as the head of Associated Industries, he still lobbied aggressively for the interests of a heavy-manufacturing industry he refused to acknowledge was in decline. And he tried to turn back the clock before the assembly of Senior Citizens on May 7, 1963, some of whom had heard him deliver the keynote at the Dixiecrat convention fifteen years earlier. He proposed that Governor Wallace send in the National Guard to quell the demonstrations. That was the old way of handling things, back when the state militia served as the industrialists' private army for putting down threats to business, as when the Guard tore down the coal strikers' tent village in 1908.

Burke Marshall's heart sank. This was the worst scenario he had envisioned: The Guard would arrest thousands of black people, put them in camps, and then greet a flood of protesters, hundreds of thousands, from around the country. Marshall would go down himself if he were a civilian. The President would have to federalize the National Guard—then what? Marshall thought he had already disabused the merchants of that nightmare.

When Vincent Townsend stood up, Marshall allowed himself a twinge of optimism; if nothing else, the wheeler-dealer could be counted to have a program. As Townsend began to speak, Marshall felt himself go numb with disbelief. "The people out there in the streets are the creation of Bobby Kennedy," Townsend said. "It's all Bobby Kennedy's doing and J.F.K.'s doing. And the man sitting right over there, Burke Marshall, could call them off immediately if he wanted to."

Marshall knew Townsend to be an adept hypocrite, but he also was aware that Townsend knew his bidding had been done on the first day of Project C when Marshall asked Wyatt Walker to call off the demonstrations. Townsend had made a reference to it that almost suggested that he had overheard the conversation (it hadn't occurred to Marshall that the *News* itself might have wiretapped the Gaston Motel telephones).

Townsend turned to Marshall and said, "Mr. Marshall, the problem is that the President won't come down and take a little girl by the hand. If he did, then everything would be all right."

As Marshall composed himself, his colleague Joe Dolan, sitting nearby, mulled over this strangely evocative "little girl." Usually that kind of argument came from liberals, who thought the President should escort black schoolchildren into newly desegregated schools. He watched Marshall stand up. He was no orator, but now, with feeling Dolan had rarely witnessed, Marshall explained that the President of the United States had no authority to tell people when to get on and off the streets. The freedom of assembly was a right guaranteed by the First Amendment. Marshall said it seemed to him that what these people were demonstrating for was basic constitutional rights.

David Vann made a move to salvage Marshall's mission from Townsend's aberrant speech with some sophistry of his own. It was Townsend himself who had delegated Vann essentially to put one over on the Senior Citizens, many of them major clients of his law firm, men he still yessirred. Vann presented the most controversial of SCLC's demands—the desegregation of lunch counters and restrooms—as if they had already been met. After all, Vann reasoned, the city itself was taking the position that segregation was unenforceable. Why else would Connor be arresting sit-ins for trespassing rather than for violating segregation ordinances? Basically, Vann explained, that left only the promotion of a few black employees to the position of *clerks* to end the demonstrations.

The dilemma Vann now had to finesse had a classic Birmingham logic to it: The local citizens in the hot seat—the store owners—happened to be men who had been excluded from the elite fraternity of Senior Citizens (though few men in the room knew that it was at the insistence of Isadore Pizitz that no Jews had been put on Smyer's committee). The problem was, Vann said, these good men who had shouldered the burden of ending Birmingham's racial troubles had merchandise that was vulnerable to the bomb, the torch, and the razor. Vann's task was to persuade the men—the gentiles—before him, insulated in their tall buildings, to come to the rescue of people they had banned from their country club. At the same time, he had to make them feel they were risking nothing in return. All the Senior Citizens had to do, Vann said offhandedly, was just sort of endorse an end to the demonstrations. "The minute we announce our decision, the hounds will start chasing the foxes," he said. "We need to give them some good foxes to chase that are fairly invulnerable foxes"—the mortgage bankers, the real estate folks, the power company.

Albert Boutwell stood to give Vann's proposals the city's blessings, but none of the Big Mules seconded him. Nor did anyone even urge that there be a settlement.

Wedding Dresses

BUD PIZITZ LEFT in the middle of the Senior Citizens meeting that he was sitting in on as the proverbial guest in the Protestant household. He decided to go check on the store. Picking his way through a milling black chorus, he took the elevator to his remodeled fine women's apparel department. Lying on the brand-new wall-to-wall carpeting was a young boy in blue jeans, T-shirt, and dirty sneakers, his eyes shut tight while his mouth belted out "Freedom, Freedom, Everybody Wants Freedom." As the Movement legend would come down, Pizitz stepped back into the elevator before the doors closed and headed back to the Chamber of Commerce.

On a sidewalk in front of one of the department stores, white pedestrians got into a fistfight with some of the black protesters. It was the campaign's first combat involving civilians. The ordinary logic of this occurrence suddenly clarified the most extraordinary feature of the brutal show Bull Connor had put on for the world: Despite those pictures of tooth-baring dogs, there had been no real violence against Martin Luther King's troops. White mob conditions brewed as a rumor took hold that "the little niggers" had gone into Loveman's and spit on wedding dresses.*

Shuttlesworth's Moment

THE CARS in the retail district purred at a standstill. As CBS's Dan Rather said in summing up the effectiveness of the demonstrations, "This country will tolerate almost anything as long as you don't block traffic." A pink Thunderbird belonging to WBRC-TV idled, its driver a recent Miss Alabama finalist and young comic talent named Fannie Flagg, who would ultimately find fame writing fiction. For now she was the kooky sidekick to the host of Channel 6's *Morning Show*. Recently she had asked her bosses why the station wasn't covering the demonstrations. In reply, they gave her explicit orders *never* to mention the trouble on the air. When the Movement kids saw Flagg's pink car, they got boisterous and pounded the windshield and fenders, not in anger, she recognized, but in fun. All the same, she rolled down the window and called in her best clipped-Yankee, acting-class voice: "I'm with you, I'm with you all the way!"

Fred Shuttlesworth, too, was watching the pandemonium in the streets through a car windshield. He, King, and Ralph Abernathy were out on a reconnaissance cruise. Seeing his people finally in motion, Shuttlesworth was overcome with a sense of personal and historic fulfillment.

---

* Pizitz and Emil Hess would say that no merchandise at any department store was damaged during the sweep.

Law Enforcement

AT THE CHAMBER OF COMMERCE BUILDING, Mel Bailey took the floor. The new sheriff was emerging as Alabama's best public relations asset. Devoted to church and Little League, he was also a beautiful-looking man, with a lantern jaw, blond hair, a giant's physique, and a smile that begged for a cartoon sparkle. On Saturday, the day after Bull Connor called up the K-9 Corps, he had risen to the mandate of his recent election and, after interrupting a shouting match between Bull Connor and Albert Boutwell, informed the men that he had "no alternative but to take charge of law enforcement at this time." His "walking intelligence machine" on the demonstrations was Vincent Townsend's own reporter-operative, Tom Lankford, who had also reputedly written many of his campaign speeches the previous year.

The day before, Bailey had taken Burke Marshall and Joe Dolan on a tour of the county jail because some demonstrators complained of mistreatment. After interviewing the inmates and ascertaining only that the food was undersalted, the Justice lawyers were treated at Bailey's insistence to a jailhouse meal. The food supervisor came out to receive their compliments. "If you think that's good, you ought to come tomorrow," he said, beaming. "We're having chicken and dressing, lima beans, mashed potatoes, apple pie and ice cream. Except those demonstrators. They're gonna get wings and necks."

Today, Bailey was painting a different picture of the accommodations. Eight hundred girl prisoners were being held in 4-H Club dorms at the state fairgrounds. Any more arrests and barbed-wire fences would have to be erected at Legion Field, the shrine of Coach Bear Bryant and his star quarterback, Joe Namath. It's not going to look pretty on TV, Bailey said; it was going to look like a concentration camp. The "freelance photographers"—a species that had become more sinister than SCLC—would have a field day.

The city's lucky casualty record couldn't hold up forever, Bailey continued somberly. The local law enforcement capacity was already stretched too thin. And George Wallace, pronouncing himself "tired of the lawlessness in Birmingham," had just sent up 375 state troopers. The Birmingham police had offended the nation by using dogs and billy clubs; the troopers favored sawed-off shotguns, carbines, and submachine guns.

Outside the Chamber of Commerce building, sirens keened on cue. Someone came in to report that some debris thrown from a rooftop had broken a lawman's collarbone.

Shuttlesworth Down

THE YOUNG BLACK MARCHERS had completed their second foray into the retail shopping district and were skipping back to Sixteenth Street Baptist. Kelly Ingram Park was surrounded by some three hundred public safety officers, and an eight-block area had been sealed off. Patrolmen swung billy clubs. Fire department nozzlemen paced in every intersection. The K-9 Corps scurried from their cars. Bull Connor roared up and down Sixteenth Street in the Army-surplus armored car that everyone called "the tank," the loudspeaker blaring orders to disperse; Martin Luther King had earlier remarked ironically on its color, white. The young demonstrators seemed motivated less by the Holy Spirit than by the hormone that renders adolescents immortal. "Bring on the dogs," they yelled. "Bring on the water."

The Yale chaplain William Sloane Coffin, the Ivy League Freedom Rider, led a column of marchers out of the church. Impelled to return south by the police dog pictures and a copy of King's "Letter from Birmingham Jail" that Wyatt Walker had mailed him, Coffin felt his knees buckling as a motorcycle cop bore down on him on the sidewalk. But the marchers with him did not break rank, and at the last second the policeman veered into the street. Bull Connor's "tank" was also heading their way. When it sputtered to a stop, two mechanics in Coffin's line offered to fix it.

The *New York Times*'s Claude Sitton timed the beginning of the "rioting" at 2:45. Black spectators who were wadded up on the sidewalk opposite the north side of the park began heaving rocks and Coke bottles at the policemen and the firemen. The fire hoses, idle since Saturday, let loose on the crowd. More missiles rained back on the firemen's slickers. In return, they hydraulically teased one man like a cat with a bird before shooting him down the flooded gutter. The day seemed poised on the point of no return.

Shuttlesworth had just stopped in at the Gaston Motel to give a progress report to King and Abernathy. "Martin, this is it," he said. "If we get those kids back out there one more time, we got the battle won."

King said, "Well, maybe we ought to just let them rest up."

Shuttlesworth insisted on pressing on, "before the city can recoup from this." As he left the motel, Shuttlesworth hailed an agitated Jim Forman. "Jim, try to get the people back into the church!" he said.

"Get 'em back yourselves," Forman answered.

In the mounting chaos, the Movement leaders were beginning to identify with the cops. A. D. King was yelling at the mob through a police megaphone, "You're not helping our cause." One of the fire-hose guns had spun out of control on its tripod and downed a couple of officers. Shuttlesworth feared for the cops' composure after watching a kid sucker-punch an officer. He decided he would have to get the children back into the church and began walking east on Sixth Avenue to go around the park. "Although you are young, you're soldiers," he called out to the kids. "You mustn't taunt the police; don't act like you intend to strike them." At around three o'clock, with some three hundred kids in tow, he turned west on Fifth Avenue, waving a white handkerchief. Before heading north toward the church on Sixteenth Street, he talked a little shop with the assistant fire chief, O. N. Gallant. Shuttlesworth considered it a show of professional respect that the nozzlemen had avoided hitting him—opposing generals do not cross swords.

Shuttlesworth was heading down the stairwell into the basement of Sixteenth Street Baptist Church when a white voice near the fire trucks on the street
said, "Let's put some water on the Reverend." Shuttlesworth looked up to see
water arcing toward him: one hundred pounds per square inch. He put his hands
over his face and "spoke heart to heart with the Lord," saying, "If You're ready for
me, I'll come." Then, a jet of water swept him down the stairs and slammed him
against the wall. "Oh, my God, Reverend Shuttlesworth is struck," someone said.
He was still trying to catch his breath when he was piled on a stretcher and loaded
into an ambulance.

Bull Connor came over from his post a block away to see what the ruckus was
about. "I waited a week to see Shuttlesworth get hit with a hose," he said. "I'm
sorry I missed it." Informed by a newsman that he had left in an ambulance, Connor said, "I wish they'd carried him away in a hearse."

The Man from the Corporation

THREE BLOCKS AWAY, David Vann was pleased that Mel Bailey's speech had
"quieted the objections greatly." Vann sweetened his offer to the Big Mules. They
did not actually have to make any decision. All they had to do was work out a
timetable for *delaying* implementation of the terms already conceded by the merchants, none of which would go into effect until the court ruled on the legitimate
city government. Would they fall for it—give their O.K., without dictating any of
the conditions?

A familiar and dreaded figure stood. It was no surprise that Art Wiebel, the
man from U.S. Steel, would be the first to offer his opinion of Vann's proposal, like
an oracle. Wiebel, the hardest pill from Pittsburgh that Birmingham had yet had
to swallow, once actually called the president of General Motors in Detroit to
complain about the Cadillac he had bought from a local dealer. Stiff and slickly
Brylcremed, he marched around "*my* steel company" like a brigadier general. Behind his back the locals called him a "cold fish" or "the Prussian," but left the social extermination to their wives, who had denied Mrs. Wiebel membership in the
exclusive Little Garden Club. Since Martin Luther King had been in town,
Wiebel had been taking a tough-guy stance in interviews with out-of-town reporters, shimmying his shoulders and digging down into his chair, as if to say, "Hit
me again, big boy." *Newsweek*'s Joe Cumming was referring to him as the "Evil
Weasel."

On this Tuesday, May 7, Wiebel aired his objection to making any settlement with King. Burke Marshall was dismayed but not surprised. Winning over
the Corporation had hardly been any more plausible than seducing Bull Connor,
into whose mayoral campaign TCI had reportedly poured considerable funds.
On April 2, Robert Kennedy's office had announced the indictment of U.S. Steel
and four other steelmakers on charges of price-fixing conspiracies, culminating
the year of bad blood since U.S. Steel violated the administration's wage and price

freeze in the spring of 1962. "My father always told me that steel men were sons of bitches," the President had famously said, citing the conclusion that Joe Kennedy had drawn on the basis of the La Follette committee hearings.

Still, when the Birmingham situation got out of hand, the administration had worked the old-boy network to put pressure on U.S. Steel chairman Roger Blough.* Robert Kennedy had persuaded the dean of Yale law school, Eugene Debs Rostow, to call Blough, an alumnus, but the most Rostow had been able to persuade him to do was have Wiebel meet with Burke Marshall. Marshall had come away from their talk with the inevitable "cold fish" impression and the conviction that Wiebel would be "utterly useless."

Wiebel now said that U.S. Steel would do what was best for U.S. Steel. He saw no reason to involve *his* plant in resolving this political matter or any other. Or as he had told a delegation from the President's Committee on Equal Employment Opportunity that had come down the previous August to investigate complaints of discrimination at TCI and other federal contractors: "I'll not have any burr-headed niggers telling me how to run my plant."

The Aristocracy of Damn Fools

SID SMYER WATCHED his colleagues shift in their seats. To his surprise, some members of the power structure began to buck Wiebel. They were the ones who had gotten direct phone calls from Secretary of the Treasury Douglas Dillon, or Labor Secretary Willard Wirtz, or Defense Secretary Robert McNamara, or Commerce Secretary Luther Hodges: Do it for the nation, the Cabinet members had said, but do it for yourselves too; you have no way out. Edward Norton, a paper magnate turned chairman of Royal Crown Cola, who had been phoned by Dillon, was ready to settle. When the bankers, too, began to accede cautiously, Smyer allowed himself to believe for the first time that they might pull together a deal.

Bud Pizitz, recalcitrant as usual, became irritated by the bankers' presumption of solving the merchants' problems and proposed that the bankers hire black tellers. The outburst underscored the relative triviality of what was being demanded of these businessmen: They didn't have to *do* anything, just take a little of the heat. Judge Edgar Bowron summed up the absurdity of the deliberations over unpublicized "Negro demands" that no white newspaper reader in Birmingham could have known about. "You mean," he asked, "that's all they want?" Still, no one was willing to publicly endorse the settlement.

Smyer's thoughts kept turning to his black housekeeper of twenty-five years, Eliza Whitfield. A few days earlier, she had announced that she had to have a new

---

* As a boy, Blough, a Swiss-Lutheran from Pennsylvania, had lived for a time amid Birmingham's Ensley blast furnaces with his aunt, the wife of a steel mill superintendent, after his parents' marriage broke up. Blough's daughter Jane now lived in Birmingham and had been a favorite teacher of mine at Highlands Day School. Her father-in-law, a local hardware magnate, was a member of the Senior Citizens Committee.

dress but needed Frances Smyer to go downtown shopping with her. "I'm scared to go down there alone," she explained. The "civil rights" issue that finally brought the war home to Smyer was the violation of his maid's freedom to shop.

His voice shaking, Smyer offered to take full responsibility for the settle-ment. He would make sure the Senior Citizens' names were not published for at least a week, and by then Martin Luther King would be gone. All they had to do was agree in principle to let a subcommittee carry out the remaining negotiations. "I'm a segregationist," Smyer said, "but I'm not a damn fool."

History would record that the seventy-seven most powerful men in Bir-mingham committed their first progressive act that day by agreeing to come to terms with King. Some accounts would even say there was a vote. But Burke Mar-shall and Joe Dolan were not sure that an agreement had been reached. Certainly no vote had been taken, no paper signed, and no subcommittee officially ap-pointed.* Unwittingly, the Big Mules of Birmingham had joined the tiny sector of racially progressive southern whites that a prominent liberal once called "the aristocracy of damn fools."

Vincent Townsend found himself backed into an uncharted corner of PR hell. That morning, he had fired off a telegram to the President of the United States. The message was a dress rehearsal for the point he had made in the meet-ing: It was all the Kennedys' fault. Townsend had prominently printed his telegram in the Tuesday-afternoon paper—the first time Project C made the local front page. One of Townsend's problems was that he had as usual signed his boss's name to his handiwork. And Clarence Hanson, publisher of the *Birmingham News,* was a member of the Senior Citizens Committee that had just theoretically collaborated not only with the Washington enemy Townsend had denounced in his name, but also with the far more controversial interlopers from Atlanta.

Endgame

IN THE HEART of black Birmingham, there were signs that segregation was falling. After getting a call from Sixteenth Street's furious pastor, Fire Chief John Swindle had personally appeared at the church. "We put the water in," he said, surveying the flooded basement, "and we're going to get it out." The firemen were threatened by black bystanders as they waded in with their buckets and squeegees, but the basement was dry within twenty minutes. Watching his public safety colleagues, Captain Glenn Evans recalled the words his fellow captain George Wall had said at the beginning of the demonstrations: How stupid can you be?

As the fire department was working for the civil rights movement, the police department was dissolving a cherished interracial alliance. A couple of blocks away from the church, policemen burst into Charles "Rat Killer" Barnett's

* The positive-thinking David Vann thought it was "sort of like a Quaker meeting—they arrive at a consensus and someone announces it."

"shoeshine parlor" and pulled a shotgun on the bootlegger who was "Bull Connor's right-hand man." Barnett, who had always supplied his police friends with free nips, had been spotted earlier among the rowdy spectators. "Rat Killer, what was that you said to me?" one of the cops yelled. Shocked that his friends on the force would take his actions amiss, Rat explained that he was just out watching them "skeeting the fire hoses at everyone." He pleaded, "Sergeant, I didn't say anything to you."

In the past, as one of the local civil rights leaders observed, Rat Killer didn't have to be concerned with the Movement because he was already free. But the old etiquette of "niggertown" was obsolete. The policeman held his gun against Rat's head and said, "Hush, or I'll blow your brains out."

McWhorter 1963

THE FINAL BELL had rung at the Brooke Hill School for Girls. To say that we fifth-graders, in our modern brick schoolhouse on the perch of Red Mountain, were cut off from what was going on downtown did not really do justice to the intensity of our alienation from the city in the valley. My most frequent spend-the-night host, Nancy Spencer—her family had just taken me to see *The Miracle Worker*—was the most up-to-the-minute of my friends; it was she who introduced me to the best candy (Sugar Daddies, because they lasted so long) and the best Friday-night TV show (*Rawhide:* "Who do you like better, Rowdy or Gil?").

But as we went to our lockers to gather our things on Tuesday, Nancy had no privileged information about the meeting of Senior Citizens that her daddy, the incoming president of the Chamber of Commerce (and also the president of the Mountain Brook Club), was attending at the Chamber building that afternoon. Mr. Spencer was a ball-bearing manufacturer painfully familiar with the rough persuasion U.S. Steel put on clients like him to enforce civic conformity, and the only thing that mitigated his distaste for having to make a deal with Martin Luther King had been watching Art Wiebel throw his weight around and realizing that the Corporation might not get its way this time.

My friends and I knew that Birmingham was the "Pittsburgh of the South," but we did not understand that TeeCeeEye was one and the same as U.S. Steel. The industry that had made Birmingham was an abstraction, like the pink nimbus of air pollution around the city you saw when you arrived by plane. I had never met a steelworker, and had no idea what misty pedigree made everyone covet the approval of a Brooke Hill sixth-grader named Margaret DeBardeleben Tutwiler, other than the downtown hotel with her last name. Even Charles DeBardeleben, Margaret's great-grandfather, had left behind little residue outside the Eastview Klan.

Instead of workshops, we children were obsessed with suburban houses. One in particular had become a frequent destination on our exploring expeditions. It was an Italianate villa that seemed the very definition of the "estates" that had been dropped from Mountain Brook's name once the hard-luck developer Robert Jemison sold out with heavy losses in the mid-1940s to an erratic Shreveport man. (He developed Glencoe, the middle-class neighborhood of Mountain Brook abutting the villa, and soon after killed himself in a Memphis parking lot.) The once grand house was now a ruin we called "the Spanish castle," fooled by the yellowish stucco. Where elegant horse-riding parties had roamed, now boys exploded cherry bombs in Coke bottles. My friends and I would tiptoe over rotting floorboards trying to find a clue to explain the desecrated landmark. I did not know that the answer was in my family.

Margaret Crawford Jackson, Uncle Hobart's mother-in-law, was a flamboyant presence at all our holiday events. Peggy was tall, skinny, and witty, wore expensive flats and big jewelry, and used to warn me that scented beauty creams caused facial hair. We heard offhanded remarks about her childhood of extreme privilege—a *white* (Irish) nanny and tutors instead of school. Her mother, a famously snobbish New Orleans belle, had once been engaged to Prince Umberto Raspoli of Italy, who was shot in the heart by a peasant on his property. Her portrait, by Howard Chandler Christie, hung in the Birmingham Museum of Art.

Years later, all grown up, I sat in Peggy's sunroom looking through her scrapbooks. She had, it turned out, been raised in a huge house on the side of Red Mountain, where U.S. Steel chairman Elbert Gary, a dinner guest, once asked her how many stars she figured were in the sky and two weeks later sent a set of encyclopedias to provide an answer. Peggy's father, George Gordon Crawford, had been a thirty-eight-year-old wunderkind engineer running one of U.S. Steel's big three—National Tube, outside Pittsburgh—when Gary tapped him to take over TCI.*

One of the photographs in Peggy's scrapbook prickled the hair on the back of my neck; it was of the Crawfords' country estate, with formal gardens and riding stables to house her mother's favorite horse, Stellita. The place where Peggy had spent her childhood weekends and summers, it turned out, was the Spanish castle. I found it remarkable that the villa had long since been razed to make way for a housing development before I learned that we had such a local luminary in the family, but no one had considered it worth mentioning that Peggy's father, my first cousins' great-grandfather, was the golden boy of the Corporation, U.S. Steel's first man in Birmingham. Peggy did, however, occasionally boast that her father had bailed out his snakebit friend Robert Jemison's Mountain Brook Club when it fell into bankruptcy during the Depression.

When I was growing up, I observed my father at McWhorter gatherings having grave yet animated conversations with Peggy and her similarly blue-blooded husband, Kirkman Jackson, who I had no idea was George Wallace's fancy legal

---

* Peggy had no use for her father's graceless successor. "The Wiebels live in a little bitty house, and they have no help," she explained.

adviser. Clearly, Martin still felt entitled to be in such high-toned company and amid such graceful appointments, as he also seemed completely at ease around the black man who had "raised" him, Edward Thornton, now launching a prosperous catering career that kept him in close company with the McWhorters and their peers. I had been confused then by Papa's place in the world. But by the time I learned that Peggy's luxurious manor was our "Spanish" ruin, I was beginning to understand how a single family could encompass such clashing creatures of Birmingham. For I now knew that genteel adults *did* use the word "nigger," that country clubbers and Klansmen had had interests in common, that ideals and sin were sometimes indistinguishable, and that fathers earned their prodigal sons and daughters. My family was simply a metaphor for the city around it, submerged in the epic of the United States Steel Corporation: passive yet volatile, complacent and unrequited, promising and defeated. We were all, indeed, as Martin Luther King had recently written (in a different context) from Birmingham Jail, part of an "inescapable network of mutuality."

18.

THE THRESHOLD

Mysterious Ways

THE MOVEMENT LEADERS were scared. At Sixteenth Street Baptist, host to one of three simultaneous mass meetings that Tuesday evening, May 7, Ed Gardner was so preoccupied that he forgot to take up the collection. Mothers had been worrying him about their locked-up children—some 2,600 at last count. "They could go to jail for shooting or stealing," he told them. "They went to jail for freedom."

The hospitalization of Shuttlesworth seemed to have reverted the troops to what Gardner called "a lot of dissension and a lot of foolishness." He told them they were at war, what with the state policemen arriving "just like John Dillinger broke loose." Gardner praised Shuttlesworth and said, "I am not in this for fortune or fame, I am in for freedom"—a dig at Martin Luther King, whose absence from the daily battles of Ingram Park had caused the *New York Times*'s Claude Sitton to observe that he "appeared to have little control of the demonstrations."

King reached out awkwardly to the masses at the meeting. "I heard about your president," he said, referring to Shuttlesworth's "foot injury" with strange indifference (though maybe he had absorbed the children's insouciant attitude to the hose spray). Then, enigmatically, "God works in mysterious ways." He dropped names, singling out Bill Coffin as the son-in-law of the famous pianist Arthur Rubinstein, along with the "wonderful comedian of this day and age" Dick Gregory, and Jackie Robinson, who was raising money for the Movement in New York. He revisited his tour of the White House that he had described at a mass meeting more than a year before. "We need to call on the President to sign a paper saying that segregation is unconstitutional," he said—the "Second Emancipation Proclamation."

That evening, John Kennedy was dining with his brother at the White House, awaiting word from Birmingham. The extent to which the administration was manipulating the power structure was hinted at in Burke Marshall's call—the

President himself took the phone—at 8:02 Washington time: "The meeting worked," he said. "Now if it will only hold, we're over the worst."

"Negotiations"

AT THE INSURANCE OFFICES of John Drew on Tuesday night, the first meeting between black negotiators and the Senior Citizens "subcommittee" putatively authorized to carry out the will of the Big Mules convened. In a show of no hard feelings, Drew asked Sid Smyer to open the session with a prayer, and the old Methodist obliged.

The "new" subcommittee consisted largely of the same whites, Smyer and Vann, with Mayor Albert Boutwell's executive assistant, Billy Hamilton, as an observer. One new face was not a Senior Citizen at all, but the merchant closest to the power structure, Sears's Roper Dial. A new black participant joined Drew and Andy Young: Lucius Pitts had finally become Birmingham's ranking civil rights leader, by the grace of the fire hoses that put Shuttlesworth in the hospital.

Much of the negotiators' work had been achieved in the previous meetings. The delayed desegregation of the store facilities had been nailed down, and Hamilton had already let it be known that Boutwell's administration would repeal the segregation ordinances and appoint the biracial committee requested by the Movement. Now he implied that the city would even lead the way for the private sector in nondiscriminatory hiring if the store owners would pledge to promote black employees to positions that required them to "wear a tie." The remaining problem was the handling of the demonstrators' arrests. Hamilton was not open to doing anything about getting the charges dropped, and when the black negotiators proposed that the white men drum up some loans to cover the bail bonds, they again drew the line.

Young, Pitts, and Drew headed back with Marshall and Dolan to the Drews' house. There Jonathan McPherson, the Miles professor and activist, put the heavily armed contingent of ACMHR guards through military paces amid a gauntlet of reporters. The press corps was in knots over the secret meetings. As soon as one reporter's inside source hailed "progress," another's pronounced a stalemate. Lucius Pitts gave *Newsweek*'s Joe Cumming a look and said, "Someday I'll tell you what we *really* said in those meetings."

Martin Luther King was also at the Drew home. He had already put in his nightly call to Robert Kennedy—the FBI had trucked a mobile communications unit to the Drews' backyard, to allow for conversations unmonitored by Bull Connor (or Vincent Townsend). For the first time, Deenie Drew heard her friend reply to the usual question about how Washington could help: "I think you're going to need some federal marshals."

The strategists got down to the finer points of diplomacy: how to create an agreement specific enough to satisfy the Movement (and the press) but vague enough to give the whites a little face-saving maneuverability. And there was still the problem of the bail money. Deenie Drew's duties as Movement host and gatekeeper kept her in motion until the small hours of Wednesday morning, delivering sandwiches and coffee to McPherson's troops, pouring cocktails for the brass inside, "sweeping the porch clean of groupies," and otherwise guarding the inner sanctum. A black female who claimed to operate a beauty shop in Chicago had been hanging around the Gaston Motel insisting on a private meeting with King. When a pistol was spotted in her pocket, the Movement security detail feared she was a Black Muslim on an assassination mission.

A few miles west, Shuttlesworth fretted in bed at Holy Family Hospital. General chest injuries was the diagnosis. Dr. James Montgomery gave him two hypodermic sedatives and recommended three or four days of hospitalized rest. But Shuttlesworth, nearly delirious, kept trying to get out of bed to go to the Gaston Motel. Sister Marie, the white nun who was nursing him, instructed Shuttlesworth's young factotum, Carter Gaston, to "stay with him, and don't let anyone in." Later, Herb Oliver arrived, bearing a troubling rumor: Apparently some meeting was going on where they were talking about calling the demonstrations off.

Sister Marie went to Shuttlesworth and said, "There's something fishy going on. Do you feel strong enough to take care of some business?" Though Shuttlesworth was in no condition to move, his anxiety fought off a third powerful sedative. Why hadn't Martin or Ralph come to the hospital to see if he was dying? Why hadn't they even called?

Mr. Shit

As the central committee reported to the motel on Wednesday morning for its regular meeting in Room 30, the war room, Lucius Pitts slipped easily into the cockpit. He had, of course, never been a demonstration man; his specialty had been to "call them off," even when they had never been planned. Now he proposed a novel carrot-and-stick approach: Why not halt the demonstrations if the Movement extracted commitments from the merchants only on the two main points—to desegregate the facilities and to promote the employees. Pitts reasoned that a truce would put them "in a good position to effect continual change in the community." The argument went against all of black experience since long before Frederick Douglass observed, "Power concedes nothing without a demand." But King and Abernathy embraced it with relief.

As the committee met, Shuttlesworth resisted another sedative injection. Dr. Montgomery told Ruby Shuttlesworth, who had flown down from Cincinnati in the middle of the night, to take her husband back to the Gaston Motel, where his heart was. No sooner had Shuttlesworth gotten tucked in at the motel than Andy Young appeared to say that King was waiting to see him at the Drews' house. Shuttlesworth felt "a wave of revulsion to get out of my sickbed to go to John Drew's."

The Drew house was a tormenting reminder of a social gap he would never close. He referred to the Drews as "tea sippers." Deenie considered Shuttlesworth "the bravest man" she had ever known, but found him "always on, nervous and driven," not a candidate for cocktail chat or the merciless teasing that bonded the Drews with King. The Drews' hospitality toward Shuttlesworth generally had urgent motives, as when they had offered him shelter after his parsonage was bombed out from under him. Perhaps because Shuttlesworth sensed that John Drew considered him "an ordinary nobody," he had been interested less in housing than in whether "Doc" Drew had seen him on TV.

Flanked by Ruby and his loyal vice president Ed Gardner, Shuttlesworth descended into the sunken living room of the Drews' elegant Center Street house and settled beside Ralph Abernathy on a yellow velvet couch. John and Deenie Drew sat at opposite ends of the room. Burke Marshall kept quietly to a corner, his arms folded. King had his back to them, thumbs in his hip pockets, staring out the picture window at the valley.

Shuttlesworth let the silence roar for a few minutes. "Why do you need to send and get me out of my sickbed?" he eventually asked. No answer. Shuttlesworth repeated the question and looked around the room to see if anyone would let him in on the big secret.

Finally King spoke. "Well, Fred, here it is. We have decided to call off the demonstrations." Shuttlesworth thought his hazy mind might be tricking him. "Say that again, Martin. Did I hear you right?

"We who?" Shuttlesworth said. "It's hard for me to see with our understanding how anybody could decide that without me." He reminded King of their agreement to make all decisions jointly. "But you didn't do that, you didn't even come see me in the hospital. You were busy or something. If that's what you called me out here for, out of my sickbed, I'm going back. Hell, no, we're not calling anything off."

Unable to bring himself to say that it had been the Movement's idea to call off the demonstrations, King explained that the merchants said they couldn't negotiate with all the demonstrations going on. Shuttlesworth pointed out that the whole reason SCLC was in Birmingham was that the merchants to whom King was showing such good will had broken their promises the previous fall.

King did not mention the other, more legitimate motive for stopping the demonstrations: fear. The Movement's amazing casualty-free record was not likely to survive the state troopers. George Wallace had threatened to prosecute the Movement participants for murder if the demonstrations resulted in any fatalities. But SCLC was also frightened by the potentially wild and uncontrollable power of the young people, whom only Bevel seemed able to harness. "We wanted to get out of it, as bad as Birmingham was," Wyatt Walker later said simply. It was so bad that a stickler for protocol like Walker had allowed such a momentous decision to be made without Shuttlesworth.

Shuttlesworth knew that for the people of Birmingham there was no "getting out." As he later said, "Whether or not I had a beautiful democracy, I certainly had people following me." He said to King, "Here in Birmingham, the people trust me. I've never lied to them. And you and I promised that we would not stop demonstrating until we had the victory."

Deenie Drew spoke up. "I want to know *why* we can't call the demonstrations off."

"Well, you can't pull 'em out, because you don't have the troops," Shuttlesworth replied. He turned back to King. "Martin, you know what they said in Albany, although I know it was different: You get things stirred up and then you pull out and leave the community with sickness and death and lost jobs. Your own brother has said that you should have gone further and stuck with it longer. A snake half dead is as bad as a snake all alive—it'll still bite you. You've been Mr. Big, Martin, but you'll be Mr. Shit if you pull out now. You'll be a nobody. If you want to call it off, you call it off, but I'm marching."

Burke Marshall spoke for the first time. "What about the press conference?" The President wanted to be able to announce some "resolution" at his regular news conference that day—Tass, the Soviet news agency, was delighting in the Birmingham problem as "part and parcel of the American way of life." King was to make a simultaneous announcement that the demonstrations were ending, pending settlement.

"Oh, I see, y'all got it all worked out," Shuttlesworth said. "Well, I'm going to go get in bed and wait till I see you and the President on TV calling off the demonstrations. And then with the little strength I've got left, I'm going to lead three thousand students into the streets, if I die in the street.... The President doesn't live here; you don't live here."

From another room in the house could be heard a white man talking on the telephone. He was saying that the "frail one" was holding things up. Shuttlesworth called out, "Tell the Attorney General that I'm frail, but I'm not that frail."

Ralph Abernathy rested his hands supplicantly on Shuttlesworth's legs. "Fred, we're friends," he said. "You and I went to school together."

"Get off your knees," Shuttlesworth snapped. "It doesn't matter whether you are on your knees or your damn belly, I'm not going to call it off."

"I made promises," Marshall said.

Shuttlesworth turned: "Burke, who gave you the authority to make promises to anybody? If you've made any promises that I didn't agree to, they're not promises. While I would like to agree with you, and I'd like to be with Martin, I cannot at this time. You all have pressured him. I don't think it's his heart to do this, but I'm not going to let him make this mistake, because this would kill his reputation. And if it's to be killed by this action, I'm going to kill it, by being what I'm supposed to be in keeping faith with the people."

Shuttlesworth made his way to the door, steadied by Ruby and Gardner. King turned back to his window, "deeply pained," Shuttlesworth believed. "Burke," King said, "we've got to have unity. People have suffered. People will suffer."

As the confrontation threatened to end in the slam of a door, Marshall went over to Shuttlesworth. "Fred," he said solicitously, "the merchants are going to agree to it."

Truce

THE PAGE-ONE HEADLINE in Wednesday's *New York Times* defined Tuesday's action as a "riot." The now traditional fire hose shot was joined by a picture of Bull Connor's armored car, or "tank." Birmingham looked like a war zone. The state police, joined by Sheriff Jim Clark's horseback posse from Dallas County, had been standing guard at Seventeenth Street, the boundary between white and black Birmingham.

The militant Miles College graduate Charles Davis showed up at Sixteenth Street Baptist with his marching shoes on. More than a thousand young people were awaiting word from Shuttlesworth. Davis now worked for the U.S. Postal Service, the only federal agency besides the Veterans Administration hospitals that employed blacks in numbers. Like most black adults with jobs, he had not yet officially demonstrated, instead creeping into line like a spectator. But that day, Davis was ready to risk losing his job, possibly his life. He did not feel that the coming battle was one that children should be sent to fight. He believed that the firemen had tried to kill Shuttlesworth with the fire hose, and today's demonstration was going to be an "anti-what-you-did-to-Shuttlesworth" march, potentially a mass human sacrifice.

Some thirty police cars were double-parked on the north side of Kelly Ingram Park, their trunks holding carbines and submachine guns. Reporters availed themselves of the helmets the cops were handing out. As Bull Connor circled the block in a squad car, Negro spectators shouted, "Hey, Bull, hey, Bull," and laughed.

At the Gaston Motel, Andy Young was trying to sweet-talk Shuttlesworth, the first SCLC leader with his own power base to openly flout King's authority. "Now, Reverend," Young began.

"Don't give me any of that Reverend shit," Shuttlesworth interrupted. "And if you mean call off the demonstrations, hell, no." He hadn't yet said what it would take to make the agreement acceptable to him, only: "We can't end this movement until Birmingham is freed."

Ultimately, thanks to semantic vagueness and his genuine love for King (plus, according to one theory, a sedative slipped in his coffee by some SCLC colleague), Shuttlesworth improvised an ingenious compromise. Before the microphones in the courtyard of the Gaston Motel, with the temperature climbing toward ninety, Shuttlesworth was accorded center stage between King and Abernathy, to avoid any hint of a rift. The demonstrations would not be canceled, merely postponed for twenty-four hours. At Sixteenth Street Baptist, more than a thousand marchers were standing by, in case Shuttlesworth changed his mind.

Shuttlesworth tersely endorsed the truce. King said that a settlement was expected within twenty-four hours. President Kennedy echoed the twenty-four-hour deadline at his regular press conference, its agenda topped by Birmingham. "Same old shit," said a cop listening over a transistor radio to Kennedy's confidence in whites and Negroes working out their problems.

"They haven't talked to Bull Connor," Connor said to the *Times's* Claude Sitton. Within an hour of the presidential press conference, Connor's rubber stamp in the recorder's court, Judge Charles Brown, retroactively set appeal bonds at $2,500 (the new maximum recently legislated to bankrupt the demonstrators) on the old convictions of parading without a permit on Good Friday. King seemed almost relieved to take the high road to jail, a detour from his collision course with Shuttlesworth, who got the news of Brown's action in the war room suite at the Gaston Motel and charged out of bed, saying he was on his way to Sixteenth Street Baptist to lead a march.

Young had already confirmed to Claude Sitton that the marches were off— "It's too hot. We couldn't have controlled this crowd." In Room 30, Young, who thought Shuttlesworth was delirious from "freedom high" as much as from the sedatives, bodily clamped him to a halt, and was prepared to tackle him to the floor if that's what it took to stop him from "embarrassing Martin Luther King in front of the whole world." Justice's Joe Dolan returned to the war room just as Shuttlesworth was cussing at Young. Dolan picked up the phone and dialed the Justice Department. With Shuttlesworth still hollering, Dolan whispered to Robert Kennedy, "Fred's sort of gone off the deep end. Could you try to calm him down?" He grabbed Shuttlesworth and handed him the phone. Dolan had no idea what the attorney general said to Shuttlesworth (who himself would not recall) because Kennedy never, ever, talked about anything after it was over. But it worked.

Shuttlesworth not only decided not to move, he even calmed down his irate colleagues. Wyatt Walker was now calling for marches, and A. D. King was saying, "The negotiations are off and plans are being made for the biggest demonstrations this city has ever seen." But with King-like composure, Shuttlesworth told the Birmingham press that the jailing of King and Abernathy "does not destroy our faith in the people we are dealing with. . . . We hope the latest incident will spur the merchants to reach a settlement by tomorrow."

In New York, Bill Kunstler and Harry Belafonte scrounged up the $5,000 bond money for Abernathy and King from what was essentially their friends' loose change, the banks being closed. Kunstler, who had booked a seat on the next day's 2 a.m. from Newark to Birmingham, reached Belafonte's apartment just as Walker called to say that A. G. Gaston had put up the money. Gaston's infrequent spasms of magnanimity were never simple, and it is possible that he thought he was pulling a fast one on the Atlantans, after the example of the mythical "well-dressed Negro" who had paid their fine at Albany. Indeed Jim Bevel had been insisting that King would stay in jail until all the children were out.

The Rabbis

DAVID VANN MET with the merchants to relay Burke Marshall's opinion that they wouldn't *all* have to hire Negroes in noncustodial jobs. He managed to get commitments for five promotions.

The merchants moved on to a more urgent crisis: Nineteen conservative rabbis had flown into Birmingham to show their support for King, and on Wednesday evening were sweltering on the platform at John Porter's overflowing Sixth Avenue Baptist. "Our people are your people," said Rabbi Alex Shapiro, of Pennsylvania. They taught the congregation a short Hebrew song and, at around midnight, went to the offices of the largest "Jewish law firm" in town for their confrontation with the natives. Rabbi Milton Grafman, the spokesman for the locals, stifled the urge to point out that if the Yankees really wished to make a dent in local affairs, the rabbinate at Beth El was still vacant after many months of recruiting efforts. Eventually, the locals believed, they had convinced some of the rabbis that their "visit to Birmingham was a mistake." Meanwhile, the prominent real estate man Bill Engel warded off "another Scottsboro" by persuading his friend Vincent Townsend not to divulge the rabbis' presence at the mass meeting.

Bailing Out

DAVID VANN REPORTED to the Drews' house on Thursday morning to close the deal. Though he and his bride, Lillian Foscue, a liberal young *Post-Herald* reporter, used to visit the Drews while they were courting, this was Vann's first trip to Dynamite Hill since the demonstrations began. The housekeeper served him bacon and eggs at the table with the Drews' young son Jeff, who was being shipped off to a New York prep school in the fall, out of fear for his safety. Vann had one last consultation with Burke Marshall in the kitchen. Of the five employees the merchants had pledged to promote, Vann was prepared to offer King three, to allow for attrition. Marshall argued against any precise number. King was satisfied with keeping the pledge equivocal. Only Shuttlesworth was pressing for specifics; he even wanted it in writing that one of the five promotions would be to a cash register. But Shuttlesworth was well on his way to being neutralized.

Vann walked into the living room, filled with the usual SCLC gang and Burke Marshall, to meet Martin Luther King in person for the first time. After courtesies were exchanged, Vann offered King the three promotions, thinking that the settlement would then be acceptable. King said fine, but they still had the problem of all the demonstrators in jail. Vann was surprised; it had been made clear that this had nothing to do with the men he represented. He said anyone who had enough on the ball to pull off these demonstrations also ought to be able to solve the bail problem.

Deenie Drew, too, wondered aloud what the big deal was with raising the bail money, given the huge check—$32,692—that had just been sent by the National Maritime Union, the old Communist-led institution that had radicalized

Jack O'Dell. Everyone laughed. It was only a fraction of the roughly quarter of a million dollars they needed to spring the nearly eight hundred demonstrators still in custody. Getting them out was a must if SCLC was to shake its reputation for seducing and abandoning black communities. There were rumblings in the press of "another Albany." And from Washington that day, the Black Muslim leader Malcolm X said, "Birmingham is an example of what can happen when the Negroes rely on the whites to solve their problems for them." On King's tactics: "We believe that if a four-legged or two-legged dog attacks a Negro he should be killed."

The Atlantans began to take out their frustrations on David Vann, with Wyatt Walker playing a particularly enthusiastic and profane bad cop. When Vann sat down in the Drews' living room and cried, they turned to the other peacemaker, Burke Marshall. The razzing of Marshall started out with good-natured hints that if the Kennedys chose not to take care of the bail problem, the Movement might have to indebt itself to a Republican—Nelson Rockefeller, say. Someone pointed out that the President had had no trouble raising the ransom money for the political prisoners of the Bay of Pigs. Then Ralph Abernathy started to get mean with Marshall, reminding him bluntly that he and his administration were in this too.

The government's monitors of world opinion were concluding from the headlines in Seoul, Dar es Salaam, Djakarta, Amsterdam, Paris, Rio, Santiago, Montevideo, and, of course, Moscow, that public sympathy supported sending federal troops to aid the marchers. African nationals were preparing to picket the United Nations in New York, urging UN intervention in Alabama. Burke Marshall got a secure line to Washington from the FBI mobile unit in the Drews' backyard and enlisted his department in the bail hassle.

King stood at the Drews' great picture window and reassured David Vann, letting him know that he understood how unusual it was for businessmen to take *any* position on the mildest controversy. Then he made the prediction that Vann would be quoting for years to come, especially after he himself became mayor: They would live to see the day that Birmingham would be the symbol of the best race relations in America.

The 11 a.m. deadline for the settlement came and went as the bail crisis remained unresolved. SCLC postponed its scheduled press conference. Shuttlesworth was tactfully not on hand to enforce the threat of demonstrations, having withdrawn to the home of a Movement churchwoman. Waiting for Washington to pull the strings releasing the bail money, the SCLC hierarchy, accompanied by Joe Dolan, made a big production of calling on Shuttlesworth "like it was the last time we were going to see him," according to Dolan. ("Maybe King thought he was faking too," Dolan would say.)

The Justice Department's Birmingham expert, Lou Oberdorfer, had suggested to Robert Kennedy that the labor unions might be willing to put up the bail money. Kennedy called the United Auto Workers president, Walter Reuther, an early supporter of civil rights. Reuther called his Washington lawyer, Joseph L.

Rauh Jr. He was soon on the phone with attorney Erskine Smith, the twenty-nine-year-old former county chairman for Kennedy's presidential campaign, who was the only white in Birmingham radical enough to be attending the negotiating sessions with blacks simply because he wanted to. "Is this the Joe Rauh I think it is?" Smith, assigned to coordinate the bail money with Movement lawyers, asked his caller. "God, if they ever knew we were dealing with people like you!" The UAW was putting up $40,000, and the United Steelworkers were being pressed for another $40,000.

The merchants' other crisis had lifted at noon: The northern rabbis had decided to leave.

Steelworkers

JEROME "BUDDY" COOPER took the long-distance call from David Feller, the Steelworkers' national counsel who had succeeded Arthur Goldberg, now Kennedy's secretary of labor. Cooper was the longtime CIO lawyer in Birmingham, the only job he could get because none of the establishment firms would hire him, out of Harvard Law School, because he was Jewish and had been Hugo Black's first law clerk. Feller described to Cooper Kennedy's appeals to the UAW's Walter Reuther and to David McDonald, who was the head of the Steelworkers and a big Kennedy supporter.

"Davy, why don't the damn merchants put up the money?" Cooper asked Feller. He was the only Jewish lawyer in town with no Jewish clients, for they were all afraid of the CIO. (The DeBardeleben-subsidized Constitutional Educational League had baited him, assigning him the diminutive "Jerry" in an attempt to telegraph his ethnicity.) "I don't know if we can do this—it's union money," Cooper said.

"The President wants us to do it," Feller said.

Cooper considered it ironic that Robert Kennedy, who had made a career of denouncing union corruption and "getting Hoffa," was now asking union bosses to commit tens of thousands of dollars to something that could not remotely be termed union business. But that did not compare to the irony of the workers putting up their nest egg to come to the rescue of the Big Mules—now "Senior Citizens"—who had exploited them for decades.

Dutifully if resentfully, Cooper called the top two local Steelworker officials, who only that week had been removing the last racial lines of promotion from union policy. ("What are you going to do if 'they' start shoving you off the sidewalk?" was the classic question the white rank and file asked the more liberal of the officials. "Same thing I'd do if you shoved me off the sidewalk," he replied. "I'd knock hell out of you.") Predicting the white reaction to Feller's request, Cooper said, "All three of us will be looking for a job, but the President wants it."

One of the bail fund's administrators, Arthur Shores, had twenty-six years earlier called the CIO "one of the greatest social movements of our times." By bailing out Martin Luther King's movement, it was finally fulfilling that promise, if at the risk of also achieving what the Big Mules had spent so much money and bad faith trying to do: annihilate the union.

On the Threshold of Becoming Great

LATE ON THURSDAY AFTERNOON, after three postponements, King and Abernathy took their places behind microphones in the Gaston Motel courtyard. King made a point of explaining that Shuttlesworth's absence was due to his injuries, hoping to stanch the leaking rumors of his unhappiness with the peace terms. King's announcement that two out of four of the Movement's demands had been met seemed anticlimactic. Showing the barest hint of meanness, Abernathy promised that if the negotiations failed to progress, people would be at church tomorrow "with their marching shoes on."

By the time the evening's overflowing mass meeting began, the magical bail fund had become, Abraham Woods proclaimed, "one-half million dollars on the way from up North." Woods noted that Shuttlesworth was out sick, and Abernathy said King wasn't feeling well either. "King and Shuttlesworth told me to tell you to just hold on," Abernathy said. The negotiating committee working on the exact wording of the agreement had pinched down to a fateful few—Arthur Shores, David Vann, and Andy Young. By the time their late-night strategy meeting broke up, the only setback was that the whites were balking at announcing their end of the bargain. Sid Smyer was having second thoughts about publicly assuming the white man's burden. If he lost his nerve, there would be no deal. But one way or another, the social order was going to collapse.

On Friday morning, a committee representing the broadest spectrum of local blacks—including Gaston on the right, Pitts and Drew at the center, and Gardner and Abraham Woods, proxying for the still recuperating Shuttlesworth—headed for the final meeting with the white negotiators. It took place at the office of a white realty mortgage banker whom Treasury Secretary Douglas Dillon had called. Vann and Smyer led the usual white participants. The four-point agreement was read. The fitting rooms—the nonissue for the merchants—would be desegregated within three days after the end of the demonstrations. Within thirty days of the establishment of the new city government, the signs would be removed from restrooms and water fountains; within sixty days, the lunch counters would be desegregated. The employment program called for "one sales person or cashier," not specifying whether this was for each store. After the agreement was read, no one said anything.

The bail problem was not mentioned. Joe Rauh was wiring $160,000 worth of union funds, which Erskine Smith arranged to deposit at the Birmingham Trust National Bank, the only bank in town with a Jewish board member, and only because Bill Engel had threatened a proxy takeover as a major stockholder. The balance of the quarter-million-dollar bail fund had been raised on SCLC's end by Harry Belafonte and Nelson Rockefeller, who had ordered an after-hours visit to the vaults of the family bank, Chase Manhattan.

Wyatt Walker announced a noon press conference. Sixteenth Street Baptist was crowded with marching shoes, just in case. At one-thirty, reporters were still waiting on the Gaston Motel's sunbaked patio. Inside the motel, Chuck Morgan and the New York lawyer Clarence Jones were putting the finishing touches on Shuttlesworth's and King's official statements. Robert Kennedy had Shuttlesworth on the phone to make sure there would be no last-minute balk. Belafonte called King and said he had three thousand people ready to go to Washington to picket the White House in the event of a derailment.

Two o'clock came and went before Walker appeared in the motel courtyard, with Shuttlesworth, King, and Abernathy. They sat down, visibly tired, at a round metal table. Walker ceremoniously introduced Shuttlesworth, whose opening words had been written by Morgan and Jones. "Birmingham reached an accord with its conscience today," Shuttlesworth read. "The acceptance of responsibility by local white and Negro leadership offers an example of a free people uniting to meet and solve their problems. Birmingham may well offer for twentieth-century America an example of progressive race relations, and for all mankind a dawn of a new day, a promise for all men, a day of opportunity and a new sense of freedom for all America."

Shuttlesworth laid out the terms of the settlement. As a courtesy to the merchants, there was no mention of specific department stores that would desegregate their facilities "in planned stages within the next ninety days." Likewise, the hiring and promotion of Negroes was stipulated as "throughout the industrial community of Birmingham." As for the Senior Citizens Committee's part in all this, it would take the rap for the public reestablishment of biracial communication "within the next two weeks."

Shuttlesworth lurched a little as he yielded the microphone to King. After Shuttlesworth's skeptical definition of progress—the absence of "the necessity for further demonstrations"—King seemed effusive. Easily wearing the genius of his leadership, he heralded "the moment of a great victory" and counted the whites and the city itself among the victors. He credited the local masses and Shuttlesworth—who "stands clear as the magic name in this magic city," who "has walked a long and often lonesome road to reach this day." He reprised his private comments to Vann: "Birmingham now stands on the threshold of becoming a great, enlightened symbol, shedding the radiance of its example throughout the entire nation."

As reporters fired questions about the sincerity of the white negotiators, Shuttlesworth said he wasn't feeling well and walked away to applause from a crowd of Negroes. After taking a few steps, he fainted. King did not pause from his remarks as Shuttlesworth was carried away.

19.

EDGE OF HEAVEN

The Winning Team

AT THE BANKHEAD HOTEL, waiting to present the white version of the settlement, Sid Smyer and David Vann found it hard to enjoy the idea that they were entering history on the side of the angels. Crudely handwritten mail on the order of "Jew merchants control Birmingham" was arriving at city hall. As he often did in times of racial distress, Smyer turned red and said, "Hell, I'll do it." Vann and Andy Young had one last caucus. The two of them agreed to work out a supplemental statement if either party said something the other couldn't live with.

Most of the press was with the victors at the Gaston Motel when Smyer announced the whites' surrender in a shaky voice: "It is important that the public understand the steps we have taken were necessary to avoid a dangerous and imminent explosion." He deplored the demonstrations, discouraged recriminations, and thanked God "for a chance to re-establish racial peace." Concluding with his trademark brusqueness, he said, "It is up to all to help preserve it by doing nothing which would destroy it." Birmingham, Smyer said optimistically, had averted a "holocaust."

Smyer joined Vann back in the hotel room. The telephone rang. "Yes, Mr. President. Yes, Mr. President," Smyer said into the receiver, accepting Kennedy's appreciation. Vann hung around for several minutes, waiting for the call from Andy Young; it never came. As for the accursed peacemaker, Burke Marshall was on his way to Washington. He didn't want to be around as an invitation to reopen the negotiations.

The first radio reports of the accord plunged white Birmingham into panic. "Everyone knows, I believe that everyone knows, that Negroes carry a very high rate of venereal diseases," one man said to a reporter. "And myself, I don't wish to catch 'em. If this self-appointed committee is all hopped up over the idea and they want to use the restroom with them and catch all this, well that's fine, just as long as I don't have to do it." Mayor Art Hanes called the white negotiators "a bunch of quisling, gutless traitors." Bull Connor—though he insisted that the Negroes "didn't gain a thing"—said, "I would have beaten King, if those damn merchants and their over-the-mountain friends would not have given in."

King and SCLC had to figure out how to gracefully exit Birmingham, now that they had betrayed its legitimate civil rights leader to the Responsible Negroes who had been the bane of Shuttlesworth's career. When King took the pulpit at the Friday mass meeting as the crowd chanted "King" under orders from Abernathy, his talk was filled with mollifying appeals to "my fellow citizens of Birmin'ham." After reading the statement he had made at the press conference, he noted that the exact schedule of desegregation was not being announced, in order not to arouse the opposition—"you know, the Klan, they still live somewhere." But since the press wasn't there, he would let everyone in on a little secret: The fitting rooms would be integrated by Monday.

King used many words to frame the victory as more than just the right to spend money at the white man's store, but the biggest applause of the evening greeted his simple "I'm thankful to God for Fred Shuttlesworth." In the final speech, however, Nelson "Fireball" Smith, the ACMHR officer weary of Shuttlesworth, suggested that Birmingham now belonged to SCLC. One of his crowd-pleasing metaphors described freedom's winning team. Though Shuttlesworth was pitcher, King was general manager and Abernathy catcher. Wyatt Walker was manager, Andy Young first-base coach, and Jim Bevel third-base coach. Accompanying Smith (shortstop) in the infield were, surprisingly, rookies A. D. King at first and John Porter at third. The crowd hardly had time to wonder why the hero of Miracle Sunday, Charles Billups, was out in left field, or why the indefatigable Ed Gardner was not in the lineup at all, before the cascade of names ended in a worthy Fireball punch line: "Governor Wallace hasn't had a hit all season. Mayor Art Hanes has a charley horse. Commissioner Waggoner has been benched. And Bull Connor has a sore knee, an ailing back, a sick head, and a twisted heart."

Herb Oliver, another veteran left off the team, departed early from the mass meeting for Holy Family Hospital. Shuttlesworth awoke to his silent presence. "I tried to do a good job," Shuttlesworth said. Oliver told him he had done a great job. Shuttlesworth wanted to know what the press was saying about the settlement, in which he took so little pride. Oliver said not to worry about the press, just get some sleep. Shuttlesworth glided back into unconsciousness. Oliver sat with him till morning.

Stiff-Backed Men

BY DAYBREAK ON SATURDAY, May 11, Governor Wallace's army of state troopers had pulled out of Birmingham. State investigator Ben Allen had argued for staying through the weekend. A reliable Klan informant had told him that the Gaston Motel was going to be bombed. "Colonel" Al Lingo, Wallace's public safety director, brushed aside Allen's concerns, saying that he could "take care of" the Klan leader. It wasn't clear whether he meant that he would, or merely could, call off the bombing.

The day's editorial in the *Birmingham News* assured the citizens that none of the whites' pledges in the accord was binding: "Birmingham remains stable." The paper ran a page-one report on riots—in Syria. The *Post-Herald*'s front page also carried a story of rioting—by Yale and Brown students. Riots were hopefully seen as the prerogative of white people from very far away.

By noon, when Martin Luther King and Ralph Abernathy met with reporters at the Gaston Motel before catching a flight home to Atlanta, the staging ground of Project C looked bare and benign. At Kelly Ingram Park, the picnic benches Connor had set up for the state troopers—amenities alien to a "nigger park"—were occupied by snoozing elderly blacks. A newsman asked King if he expected any more "trouble."

"Well, I don't think so," King replied. "Of course, the Klan is meeting today. We'll have to see what they do."

The first Klan rally in North Alabama in some eight months was taking place in Bessemer that night. The princes of the Invisible Empire had all come: Georgia Grand Dragon Calvin Craig and his counterparts from Tennessee, South Carolina, and Mississippi. At nightfall, the family picnic and barbecue segued into the rally portion of the evening, as cries of "Fight the niggers" wafted across the park beside the Moose Lodge.

The atmosphere recalled a big homecoming game. The Eastview elite had paired up, as if with a favorite "date." Robert Chambliss arrived with Troy Ingram in Ingram's 1953 maroon Cadillac. Charles Cagle picked up the always-ready-for-action bookbinder Gene Reeves and his family. Arthur "Sister" White brought his wife and a beautician friend. Wyman Lee was hanging out with Bobby Cherry (who had accidentally shot him on Easter). Feisty Billy Holt was there with his equally feisty wife, Mary Lou. The Birmingham police had spotted Tommy Blanton's white-over-blue Chevy and J. B. Stoner's similar sedan. Hubert Page was walking around like the rising executive he was, now the Alabama Grand Dragon of Bobby Shelton's United Klans. Tommy Rowe strutted, too, in the uniform of the Klan's elite security detail—white shirt with red shoulder braids, white crash helmet with stars and bars, jump boots, and a holstered pistol.

Imperial Wizard Bobby Shelton formally opened the rally: "Good evening, ladies and gentlemen, and fellow Klanspeople." The faces of several thousand men, women, and children, glowing in the light of two flaming crosses, turned expectantly toward the flatbed truck laden with Klan royalty. As he lit into the Communist conspiracy of "Martin Luther King, Abernathy, Shuttlesworth, Walker, and the others," a feminine voice rang out from the audience—"That's about it"—in unwitting imitation of an audience dialoguing at a black church service. Shelton urged his fellow Christians to resist "bowing down to any concessions or demands from any of the atheist so-called ministers of the nigger race or any other group here in Birmingham." But the crowd was not rising to the rhetoric, and Shelton was nonplussed. "I thought we had some real rebels out there; that wudn't no rebel yell," he said. "Let's stand back and yell for the white people of Alabama."

Shelton's inability to rev up this family crowd was perhaps the truest reflection of the sea change that had been inspired by Birmingham that week. In the growing consensus that segregation had to go, the Klan was losing its mainstream appeal and shrinking into a purely terrorist cell. The real rebels that night were busy making other plans. At 8:08 p.m., the switchboard at the Gaston Motel lit up. A white male asked the operator if Martin Luther King was staying there and said they were going to shoot him. Five minutes later, a second male asked the operator if she had a casket to fit King. If they couldn't get him with a gun, he said, they had plenty of dynamite.

Back at the rally, a better-trained speaker, a Klan clergyman, took the microphone and used his "preacher voice" to call for "some good stiff-backed men who are able to shoulder the load and willing to go out to fight the battle for the Lord Jesus." But Shelton was unable to take advantage of that outburst of real inspiration, and he reinstated the tone of a Lions Club meeting, making gracious introductions of the dignitaries "with us tonight" from all around the South. Though Georgia's Calvin Craig assured the crowd that the Atlanta-bound Martin Luther King would "be met with force as he was met the last time he was in Albany, Georgia," he turned to lighter fare—a description of a "Cleopatra program" at black Atlanta University, which was to end in a kiss between a white boy and a Negro actress. A member of the audience called out, "I hope she's a blue-gum nigger." The other Grand Dragons offered similar titillations—references to Washington, D.C., as "Hersheytown, 90 percent black and 10 percent nuts." There was a brief digression about the "nigger curse" of sickle-cell anemia, including warnings of black baby-sitters cutting their fingers and dropping blood into the food of white babies.

Bobby Shelton steered the program back to the crisis at hand, wishing the blessings of God on "your governor and Bull Connor, and also the fire department." For the finale, he tried one last time to stir up the audience. "Now just let me remind you of this, and irregardless of what the news media says, irregardless of what television or Martin Luther King or the businesspeople say, Martin Luther King has not gained one thing in Birmingham because the white people are not going to tolerate the meddlesome, conniving, manipulating moves of these professional businessmen." And then after the obligatory call for converts— "If you're twenty-one years old and white, and want to be a white man, a real man . . ."—a preacher dismissed the crowd with a prayer for "traveling mercies back to their homes." A speaker, probably Shelton, added, "Take your time getting out. We certainly don't want to see any accidents whatsoever." A man from the audience yelled, "And run over every nigger you see." Shelton's responsive laugh— "Next year," he said—was sheepish, perhaps because he was thinking of the plans his stiffest-backed men had for later that night.

Bombs

AT HOLY FAMILY HOSPITAL in Ensley, a few miles from where the Klan rally had ended at around 10:15, the Alabama Christian Movement's Carter Gaston was keeping vigil over Shuttlesworth. Sometime between 10:30 and 11, Sister Marie, the nurse who had developed a proprietary attitude toward her patient's Movement, motioned Gaston to the window and said, "Watch this." Three carloads of police were in the parking lot. Some officers got out of their cruisers and piled into an unmarked car and headed in the direction of A. D. King's house a few blocks away.

Roosevelt Tatum, a laborer at a pipe company, was walking near Twelfth Street and Avenue H and spotted a regular squad car—Car 22—pull up in front of A. D. King's house. A uniformed policeman got out, according to Tatum, and walked up to King's front porch, where he stooped and placed a package next to the steps. He returned to his car and, as he drove away, Tatum claimed, tossed something out the window that landed a couple of feet from the sidewalk.

The thrown object exploded, knocking Tatum down. It seemed to have been mostly fuse caps detonating, more noise than impact, and the hole it made in the ground was the size of a bathroom sink. But it drew the usual crowd. After eight or nine minutes, when the streets were thronged, a bomb went off to the right of the porch. This one uprooted a shrub, blew the brick veneer off the house, collapsed the ceiling, and blasted the front door back into the kitchen. A. D. King was in bed, his wife was sitting in the living room. But, amazingly, no one was hurt.

Police lieutenant Maurice House eased his car through the mob and into King's yard, noticing that the *News*'s Tom Lankford had beat him there. House, who had been assigned to a newly created civil rights detail a week before the Easter march, was a law enforcement pro, friendly with Bull Connor without being branded as one of his stooges (though shortly after the Tutwiler Hotel scandal Connor had gotten House to check into a North Alabama motel under the name of Connor, with some magazines and a fifth of whiskey for company, to provide the trysting commissioner with an alibi). House had delivered Connor's stay-away message to the Klan at the beginning of Project C, but he was also a congenial figure among blacks and had teased Shuttlesworth about stepping out of the firing line during the Good Friday march to direct traffic from the sidelines. Tonight, however, bricks and stones and bottles pelted him from the darkness of this black neighborhood, typical for having no streetlights. House put on his helmet and ran into King's house.

Wyatt Walker, who had been called from his motel bed by Bernard Lee, went outside with A. D. King to try to quiet the crowd. People were grumbling that the policemen had known there was going to be a bombing. A small group was singing "We Shall Overcome." King shouted through a police bullhorn over the din, "Why must you rise up to hurt our cause? You are hurting us, you are not helping." A loud yell—and rocks—answered. "I'll go home on one condition," an angry woman shouted, but was drowned out before completing the threat.

Arriving fire trucks had their beacons extinguished by flying debris. A piece of wrapping paper was set on fire and thrown into the front seat of a patrol car. Walker physically restrained rock throwers. Police Chief Jamie Moore, who had also come to the scene, called Ed Gardner and told him he'd better get down there.

Inside the bombed house, among the indignant well-wishers, Roosevelt Tatum told A. D. King what he had seen before the explosions. King called the FBI. It seemed that, at long last, the bureau might get around to investigating a bombing in Birmingham.

Midnight

SPECIAL AGENT BYRON MCFALL must have been sweating over his prize informant. Gary Thomas Rowe was supposed to have checked in with the FBI from the Klan rally at 10 or 10:30, but McFall hadn't heard a word. Rowe had left the event with Hubert Page, Billy Holt, and Mary Lou Holt's nephew, an obese con artist named Don Luna, who was a member of the Klan Bureau of Investigation in Montgomery. They were part of the après scene at Jack Cash's Barbecue, a cafe on Third Avenue West that was a hangout for Klansmen and cops; the latter were charged only a quarter for meals and given unlimited free coffee. The proprietor, William Hurshel "Jack" Cash, who was barely literate enough to write his name, had been a Klansman for a good half of his fifty-plus years, a disciple of Ace Carter before becoming the Eastview and Bessemer Klans' favorite host; the abandoned theater that had served as Carter's headquarters was just down the street. Six years earlier, Cash had been charged with assault with intent to murder for attacking Fred Shuttlesworth at Phillips High School, and though Shuttlesworth identified him as the assailant with the brass knuckles, the arresting officers said they could not positively identify him.

On the night of May 11, Cash's Barbecue was an indiscreet cacophony of plans to break windows downtown. At the end of the Klan rally, three members of the Bessemer klavern, including Exalted Cyclops Robert Creel and his sidekick Eugene Thomas, had tapped five of their men and around fifteen Eastview regulars, including John "Nigger" Hall and Charles Cagle, to deploy themselves around the shopping district. At the stroke of midnight, they were to begin busting windows at the department stores of the Jewish merchants who had caved in to Martin Luther King. As the hour approached, Cash's Barbecue cleared out.

Nigger Hall and some Klan brothers were positioned on the street corners downtown, bats cocked to shatter glass. Minutes before midnight, they heard the night sky thunder with the sound of exploding dynamite. Realizing that they were decoys, the frustrated window-breakers took off, though not before Cagle (according to Rowe's report to the FBI) got in some licks at Parisian's plate glass.

At the juvenile detention center on the western side of town, the sound of the blast halted the freedom singing of the children still waiting for their $300 bond to be posted. A competing melody came over the P.A. speakers, sung over and over by white male voices: "Dixie."

Further west at A. D. King's house, Maurice House was roaming around the yard with the Movement men looking for evidence when they were interrupted by the noise. Bombs in Birmingham always sounded close if the air was heavy and humid.

"Oh, my God," King said. "That's my church."

"That's the motel," said Wyatt Walker, whose wife and two of his four children were there waiting for him.

An Assassination Attempt

THE BOMB HAD BEEN hurled from the back left window of a car traveling east down Fifth Avenue North between Fifteenth and Sixteenth Streets. It hit the west wall of the Gaston Motel—right under Room 30, the large corner suite on the second floor where SCLC strategists had been meeting for thirty-eight consecutive days. It sparkled to the ground and exploded, leaving a five-by-five-foot hole in the steel-reinforced concrete wall and destroying two adjacent house trailers. Members of Eastview's action squads had been knowingly mentioning Room 30, but the Klan's spies had been misinformed that King was attending an integrated dinner that night at the motel restaurant and would be back in the suite by midnight.

Orzell Billingsley Jr. had claimed Room 30 for Saturday night. Billingsley was the Movement's most free-spirited lawyer, who got some of his "brainiest ideas" while drinking whiskey. He handled the nuts and bolts of his cousin Arthur Shores's practice, but hardly shared Shores's cautious temperament. He had served as Jack O'Dell's counsel before HUAC in the summer of 1958, patiently spelling his first name for the incredulous committee, and he was a fan of Shuttlesworth's. Billingsley had been working around the clock processing the union bail money with the young white lawyer Erskine Smith, grousing all the while about the ambitious men of his own race, like his cousin Arthur and the NAACP lawyers who "fuck everything up." By Saturday, so sick of the nonviolent movement that he was calling himself Zellie X, Billingsley wanted nothing so much as a soft bed, a stiff drink, and quiet. He was displeased to discover that his wife, Giselle—once showcased in a *Pittsburgh Courier* feature on "More Beautiful Tan Girls"—was having a soiree at their house. He decided to take Room 30 to get some rest and would have been on top of the bomb if he had not fallen asleep while stopping home to get a change of clothes.

Still, the war room's fortuitous vacancy did not blunt the certainty that the bombing had been an assassination attempt.* A room below the suite, the perma-

---

*As with white southerners who claim to have been touched by Sherman's March, there seems to be an unlimited supply of people who were supposed to be at the Gaston Motel that night. King had offered Room 30 to Joe Lowery, the SCLC co-founder from Mobile who was now living in Nashville, but he had decided at the last minute to take the train back home. Al Hibbler said he vacated it the day before, or had the room next to it, but it seems more likely that he had been back in New Jersey for weeks. Working late that night, Emory O. Jackson considered stopping by the motel, as was his habit, but was too tired and went home.

nent residence of the motel manager's invalid mother, had been destroyed; its inhabitant was dug out from the crumbled plaster, miraculously alive.

At Holy Family Hospital, Fred Shuttlesworth's guardian nun, Sister Marie, became convinced that they would be coming after her patient next. She locked the doors on the floor and sent guards into the stairwells.

The Saturday-Night Crowd

THE FIRST COP to arrive at the bombing scene was Dick Middleton with his dog, Leo, the stars of Bill Hudson's photograph. By now, the "Saturday-night crowd" from Rat Killer's and the pool halls near the motel had been taking advantage of Saturday night for upwards of twelve hours. The social drinkers had been enjoying the state-store brands served at Rat's, but plenty of others were full of Joe Louis moonshine, consumed for knockout value only. They were out partying, conspicuously armed, when Wyatt Walker, Nelson Smith, and the other Movement leaders arrived from A. D. King's house, joining the police contingent pulling in. Walker grabbed a megaphone, climbed on top of a car, and pleaded with the crowd to go home. The tipplers weren't bothering to drink up the pints before pitching the bottles at the squad cars. An Italian grocery on Fifteenth Street and Fifth Avenue was set on fire. A "white" taxicab was flipped on its side and torched. The residential neighborhood abutting the commercial strip fed its occupants to the mob. "This is it," a black man yelled.

"Where's Bull Connor?"

"Let's go get Bull Connor's house."

"Let's kill him."

"If they bomb us, why can't we bomb them?" a black man said. "How come we have to go home every time they start violence?" And then he began to lead a chant: "Stop! An eye for an eye and a tooth for a tooth, an eye for an eye and a tooth for a tooth."

"Wait, wait, listen," a Movement man said, trying to quiet him. "Even in the Army, you got a leader. You got one now, you better listen."

The K-9 Corps was making no impression on the rioters. "It has gone too far," a woman said. "We gon' take over violence just like they turned the dogs loose, we gon' turn loose some bricks." Gravel hailed down on the dogs and their handlers. "You'd better get those dogs out of here," a man screamed.

Miles graduate Charles Davis had reported to the post-bombing scene feeling a certain vindication—white violence was good for the Movement, and a little black violence wouldn't do it any harm either, as long as it could not be pinned on SCLC. His feelings of gratification evaporated as three black men jumped Officer J. N. Spivey in the middle of the street and stabbed him in the ribs. Davis decided to leave. It didn't take a lot of imagination to guess how the police would react to the knifing of their own.

Davis was wrong, however. Instead, the police pleaded with the rioters, "We're your friends." A black man emerged from behind one of A. G. Gaston's office buildings and shook a long knife at a policeman. "I want that suit you got on," he said. The officer didn't move to defend himself. He just looked at his assailant as if transfixed. The black man's voice lowered to the soft menace of someone with the upper hand. "You come on back here," he said, as if he thought the cop might actually follow him. The policeman stood stock-still until the black man backed off into the crowd.

The white-black equation of police brutality and Negro fear that for so long passed for racial peace in Birmingham had come apart.

"Come and Go to That Land"

THE NEW YORK TIMES'S Claude Sitton, Newsweek's Karl Fleming, Time's Dudley "Do Right" Morris, and a couple of other national reporters were having their first celebratory meal in a month: They were leaving Birmingham the next day. Chuck Morgan had taken them to a popular steakhouse. Except for helping write the Movement's accord statement, Morgan had played a mostly social and philosophical role in Project C, and tonight he held forth on the significance of Birmingham. The use of children was "an excellent technique, but it is not nonviolence," he said, repeating the rampant rumor that the kids had damaged store merchandise. He ridiculed the City of Churches' cowardly clergy. The church, he explained, was "under the illusion that this is 'a world of sweetness and light,' " and it wasn't until Harrison Salisbury published his "Fear and Hatred" article in the New York Times that Birminghamians had "realized that somebody out there didn't like them."

Whiskey had lifted spirits high by the time Morgan was called to the phone to be informed of the Gaston Motel bombing. The reporters piled into a rental car. At the mob scene, sirening fire trucks appeared in their rearview mirror and the driver pulled over reflexively to let them pass. Karl Fleming looked out the window at the angry pandemonium and said, "Get the fuck out of here with this car."

But dutifully the newsmen got out of the car. Fleming found a pay phone and was talking to his editor in New York when the mob uprooted the booth. A brick hit a trash can in front of Claude Sitton. A rookie from AP started to leave. "You signed on for the cruise," Sitton called out. "This is part of it."

The police cars stalled in a quagmire of 2,500 bodies. Whenever the cars inched forward, they were bombarded with missiles, including the inevitable Coke bottles. Sitting with the officers inside one car was Albany's police chief Laurie Pritchett, who had returned to Birmingham when "everything tore loose" on Double D-Day. Earlier on Saturday, informing Bull Connor of the Klan meeting, he had warned, "They're going to blow King up. And if anything ever happens to him, wherever he's at, the city's going to burn. Cities all over the United States are going to burn."

"Let them blow him up," Connor had replied. "I ain't going to protect him."

The fire trucks were immobilized. A fireman hustled over the back of engine number one to elude a man wielding a four-by-four and a knife. The blazes were starting to show through the windows of the stores. Abraham Woods and other Movement ministers got into the police cars and stuck their black faces out the window to sell law and order to the mob.

Wyatt Walker had tied a white kerchief of peace—or truce—around his left arm and was patrolling the crowd with an electric bullhorn, trying to organize a human cordon to guard the firemen.

Ed Gardner stood on top of a parked Cadillac and shouted into a bullhorn, "Overcome evil with good. Everybody go home." Bricks shattered the windshield. A. D. King was hoisted up onto the car top beside Gardner. "We're not mad at anyone," he pleaded. "We're saying, 'Father, forgive them for they know not what they do.' " The roof caved in.

A guy next to a gas pump at the service station owned by Angela Davis's father, Ben, yelled, "Say, Rev, I want to sing."

"What do you want to sing at a time like this?" Gardner said.

"I want to sing 'Come and Go to That Land.' "

Gardner "thought we were all going to the land that night." Wyatt Walker decided that if he ever wrote a book about Birmingham, this would be the first chapter, titled "Edge of Heaven."

Near the motel, a group of black men waved brickbats, and across the street a band of fifty whites taunted them. Connor's nemesis on the police force, Detective Jim Parsons, drove up in his brand-new white Corvair, got out, and said, "Put those bricks down, and don't hit my new car." He had found his "preacher voice." They obeyed.

The city of Birmingham's "tank" rolled up and down, half on the street, half on the sidewalk, spreading tear gas. Rumors that Bull occupied the passenger's seat assured a barrage of the largest bricks and stones, but Connor had decided not to show up at the finale of his long career.

The fire at the Italian grocery store had spread to two houses. A telephone pole burned like a fiery cross. The mob seemed to be spending itself.

"We got hot," a black man said remorsefully. "We hate that."

"Why they burning up that man's store?" another said with disgust.

"Fire department won't come," a woman said.

An older man lamented: "We gone too far. We gone too far."

"Yeah, but they was led to do it," the woman countered.

The grocery store collapsed.

"That's a doggone shame, you know that?" one of the men said.

"It's just a shame before the righteous God."

"Give us our civil rights," the angry woman said. "They won't give us our civil rights. What's wrong with them? They must be crazy."

The group couldn't understand why the fire department wasn't doing its job. A man explained, "They don't come out until they get ready to shoot water on you."

The paralyzed fire trucks began to stir and eased toward the fires—an entire block was now ablaze. An Army tank, a real tank with treads, rolled down Fourth Avenue. Only later, when daylight returned, did people wonder where it came from, where it went, or if it had been an apparition.

The firemen hosed the houses and the stores—six now burning—and an apartment building and the flickering carcasses of cars, including the "white" taxicab whose driver had been stabbed and then fled on foot. People were still milling around, but the drunks and the hoodlums had been taken to jail. Observing from a police car, Laurie Pritchett learned from a Birmingham colleague that the state troopers were coming back in. That was his cue to leave.

At around 2:30 a.m., with their sleeves rolled up and their double-barreled shotguns and carbines leveled, the blue-helmeted troopers made their entrance. Detective Maurice House's partner got his camera out and began filming. It was like a John Wayne movie in which the posse shows up on a gauzy horizon. At first, only a few were visible, and then the line filled in as if by time-lapse photography. Around a hundred of them—those under the leadership of Dallas County sheriff Jim Clark—were on horseback.

Colonel Al Lingo, Wallace's director of public safety, drove up to the corner of Fifth Avenue and Seventeenth Street, where Police Chief Jamie Moore was standing with Mayor Art Hanes. Lingo got out of the car dragging a shotgun. His bodyguards carried Thompson submachine guns—a precaution that led some of his men to suspect that the pills Lingo popped "by the handful" were bringing on paranoid delusions. Moore assumed that he was simply "half drunk." At any rate, Lingo had no law enforcement experience—he was a cabinetmaker, specializing in doors, who had piloted Wallace's campaign plane. The main qualification for his current job was the vulgarity with which he expressed his views of Negroes.

Eyeing Lingo's weapons, Jamie Moore, said, "Put that back. You're liable to start a race war."

Lingo looked at Moore as if he were a poodle and said, "Get your cowardly ass back to your office or your house because I'm in charge now and my orders are to put those black bastards to bed." The "colonel" ordered Moore and Hanes into his car while he called the governor and asked him to supersede Sheriff Mel Bailey's authority and turn direct control over to him. Hanes, taking advantage of being in earshot of the *Times*'s Claude Sitton, blamed Robert Kennedy for the mayhem. "I hope that every drop of blood that's spilled he tastes in his throat," he said, "and I hope he chokes to death."

Back on the street, Lingo poked his shotgun at a black man trying to calm the mob—"Git!" Troopers prodded Negroes toward the nearest house, over protests of "But this isn't where I live." Sheriff Jim Clark's mounted deputies from Selma, wearing GI helmets and carrying hunting rifles, charged the Gaston courtyard. A state investigator turned to a colleague on a street corner where concrete blocks were pouring down from a roof and said: "Corporal, next time you see a head up there, shoot 'im." Sitton would dictate to New York, "The 'thonk' of clubs striking heads could be heard across the street." Lingo shoved his shotgun into the stomach of *Newsweek*'s Karl Fleming and threatened to blow him away.

The troopers were Birmingham's newest wave of "outside agitators." They acted out the segregationist brutality that white South could no longer get away with, in the way that Martin Luther King had forced the black community to act in its best interest. The Reverend Calvin Woods joined the local police he now considered "angels" in trying to calm the crowd and was hit in the shoulder by a trooper's gun butt. The butt of another trooper's carbine gave Wyatt Walker's wife a head wound that sent her to the hospital in an ambulance. As Walker—a tactical rather than philosophical practitioner of nonviolence, who in college had dreamed of "going around with a band of blacks exterminating Eastlands"—was about to take a lunge at the trooper, a UPI reporter from Mississippi tackled him and, Walker said later, "saved my life."

The journalists were marched at gunpoint into the Gaston Motel's glass-littered lobby. On orders that he did not fully understand, the deputy fire chief, O. N. Gallant, kept the press and the Movement leaders company. A reporter called the White House and left a message with the operator. A. D. King phoned the Justice Department as well as the White House without raising anyone of importance and finally settled on the FBI. "This whole town has gone berserk," he shouted into the receiver. After hanging up, King reported to the crowd in the lobby, "They say they'll look into it."

"You wasted your money," someone replied.

Finally King called his brother in Atlanta, while SCLC's songmaster Dorothy Cotton led a chorus of "We Shall Overcome."

The Informant

AT THREE IN the morning, the FBI finally found Gary Thomas Rowe—not far from the Gaston Motel at the VFW Hall. Rowe's principal handler, Byron McFall, who had gone down to "cover" the post-blast riot, finally let his misgivings about his informant show when Rowe told him he was with Billy Holt, Hubert Page, and Don Luna, and had been with them since the rally.

Any investigator who knew Rowe would have immediately deduced that the bombing of the Gaston Motel was the best-planned Klan action since the Freedom Riders were ambushed on Mother's Day, 1961. For as the FBI knew, much bad blood had come between Rowe and Holt since that day of fellowship, when they had beat up WAPI's Clancy Lake. Holt not only had doubts about Rowe's ideological fidelity, having accused him of being an FBI informant, but he also had suspicions that Rowe was sleeping with his flashy flirtatious wife. (Mary Lou Holt, who had once had dreams of going to Emory University to study medicine, had indeed grown disillusioned with Billy since falling for him when he was the star pitcher for Dr Pepper's softball team. She would say, insincerely, that she didn't suspect him of any violence because he wouldn't stand up to his own mother.) Mary Lou had told Billy that Rowe was calling her—and promising that if she was nice to him he would protect her husband from the FBI.

It is rumored that Rowe and Holt pulled their pistols on each other earlier on the night of the motel bombing—at a phone booth in the vicinity of Jack Cash's cafe, which would have been on the route between the Klan rally in Bessemer and downtown. Possibly the fight was related to the arrival of Don Luna from Montgomery. Flaunting his Klan Bureau of Investigation credentials, Luna may have been looking into his uncle Billy's misgivings about Rowe, and they had decided to test Rowe's allegiance to the Klan: Would he go through with a bombing?

The other clue to the advance planning of the bombing was Billy Holt's alibi. At two or three that afternoon, one of Eastview's eager-to-please rookies, George Lee Pickle, a chronically drunk trucker who idolized Robert Chambliss, had cruised through downtown in a car festooned with Confederate flags, seemingly looking for trouble. Near Fourteenth Street and Second Avenue South—due south of the Gaston Motel—some blacks had pulled up beside him and asked him where the parade was. Either serendipitously or by plan, policemen drove up, found a rifle inside Pickle's car, said it had been fired, and took him to jail. As dedicated a Klansman as Pickle ought to have made arrangements to bail out in time for the big rally, but he remained in jail, apparently for the good of the white brotherhood.

Police records would show that Billy Holt and his Exalted Cyclops, Robert Thomas, appeared at the Southside jail and signed Pickle's bond at midnight, right around the time the Gaston Motel was being bombed. That Eastview's top executive would have come down in the middle of the night to bail out a lowly rank and filer suggests an urgent need for documentation of his whereabouts. It is possible that the police did the Klan VIP the favor of also letting him sign for Holt. Of all the mischief makers, Holt would have been the most vulnerable, as a suspected collaborator of Robert Chambliss's in the 1956 dynamiting of Shuttlesworth's church.

Chambliss, too, had established an alibi. After the rally, he claimed, he and Troy Ingram had driven in Ingram's Cadillac to a nightclub and "watched them dance until 2 o'clock Sunday morning." The FBI would later suspect that Ingram had provided the license plates for the bombing car—off one of the junked autos he kept for parts in his yard. Ingram would have been a likely candidate to make the bomb, since he, with Chambliss, was considered the best in the business.

During the coming months, evidence trickling in to the FBI would point to the conclusion that the bombing of the Gaston Motel was indeed a fully coordinated Klan event, planned at the highest levels. An FBI "confidential source" later reported Chambliss saying that if anyone ever ratted on him, he would expose the roles of Exalted Cyclops Robert Thomas and Imperial Wizard Bobby Shelton in the motel bombing. Chambliss further threatened Billy Holt: If he, Chambliss, went to jail, Holt and Luna would go with him.

Chambliss would later insist on the craziest scenario, which despite all its fantastic turns would prove to be the one that made the most sense. He would say that Tommy Rowe, Hubert Page, Don Luna, and Billy Holt had bombed the motel. Chambliss would also say that the bombers' car had had an escort: his nephew Floyd Garrett, an officer for the Birmingham Police Department. According to Chambliss, after the dynamite was thrown, Garrett led the bombers' car back west toward the Birmingham-Southern neighborhood where Rowe had lived since separating from his wife the year before. At Arkadelphia Road, Chambliss said, the bombers peeled off, Garrett giving a little wave as they doubled back toward town. In later versions of his story, as age eroded his internal censors, Chambliss would allow that he had been riding with his nephew in the police car.

Chambliss's story received independent corroboration on the night of the bombing. Reporters from a radio station operated by New York's Riverside Church, the institution John D. Rockefeller had created for the influential liberal theologian Harry Emerson Fosdick, had brought their tape recorders to the riot (having scored an exclusive interview with Imperial Wizard Bobby Shelton after the Klan rally). They interviewed twenty-year-old Holman Turner Jr., a Dynamite Hill resident who was active in SCLC as a student at Alabama A&M in Huntsville. He had been in the motel at the time of the bombing, flirting with the young woman behind the desk. What he told the Riverside reporters diverged from Chambliss's account only in the position of the police car. "Now here's a 1953 Chevy that the bomb come out and throwed it in there." He saw three white men. "They went down, and the police right behind him, Car 25 was right behind him." Then he clarified the relationship between the squad car and the bombers' car: "No, they weren't chasing him. They acted like they were escorting it."

Car 25 belonged to Floyd Garrett. It had been his car, too, on Mother's Day, 1961, when he had received orders to check on a "32," or fight, and upon coming across Tommy Rowe and Billy Holt smashing Clancy Lake's car had radioed back, "Nothing to it." The Birmingham police never talked to Turner; his name turned up, enigmatically, in their files. Perhaps the FBI agents who interviewed Turner at his college dorm a bit later alerted the police to the potential trouble his testimony would create for them.

If Tommy Rowe had been put to a test, he had apparently passed it. As Robert Chambliss said, you could trust Rowe to "kill a nigger and never talk." Rowe's handlers had perhaps begun to sense this, too. At three o'clock on the morning of May 12 when Rowe finally called the bureau, McFall ordered him to get down to headquarters. There he was asked a seemingly frivolous question about Nigger Hall's wife. Rowe said that Nelda Hall and the kids had left the Klan rally in the car of another Klansman's wife. The FBI's "independent surveillance"—perhaps Nelda's own account, since she was said to inform occasionally for the FBI—had determined otherwise. The FBI had confirmed that Rowe's account of the evening was not to be trusted.

As if to flaunt his disingenuousness, Rowe told the FBI that the Black Muslims had done the bombing.* For a change, the FBI noted in its report the contradictions in Rowe's statements and even went out of the way to say that Rowe did

---

*Bobby Shelton accused Wyatt Walker of the crime.

not divulge his whereabouts between 10:30 p.m. and 3 a.m. The record does not indicate whether the FBI asked him whether he had bombed the motel.

The Moment of Truth

BY DAYLIGHT, the state troopers had reclaimed the picnic tables in Kelly Ingram Park and were drinking coffee and listening to the radio. A twenty-block area around the motel, strewn with broken plate glass and smashed squad cars, was sealed off and closed to white people, including the press. Blacks and reporters from the night before remained quarantined without food or water inside the motel, whose water main had been destroyed by the bomb.

Sunday, May 12, was Mother's Day again in Birmingham. As he had two years before, Vincent Townsend editorialized on the *News*'s front page: "This is a sabbath of sorrow." If the beating of the Freedom Riders in 1961 had proved how important white brutality was to the campaign for civil rights, this Mother's Day introduced black violence as an ingredient of the struggle. It was the first race riot of the modern civil rights era. In Boston, a white clergyman said, "Birmingham removes our fear of the future, for the crisis is here and now. This is the moment of truth. We have presumed too long on the long, long patience of the dispossessed." ACMHR vice president Abraham Woods had stood in the middle of the Saturday-night riot and realized that it wasn't "going to be long till this thing is going to take a new turn."*

For now, the country was not ready to accept the possibility of a black uprising. NBC's Johnny Apple did not come back with any film of rioting Negroes to offset the previous week's police dogs and fire hoses. The only widely circulated shot—of a fireman with blood streaming down his face—was once again the work of the AP's Bill Hudson. But otherwise no published photographs of black violence—no cabdriver being bludgeoned, no police lieutenant being stabbed—undermined his photograph of Walter Gadsden and Leo.

Nor could an organization grounded in nonviolence afford to recognize the new turn things had taken: The Movement's line on the riot—"freedom tensions," Emory O. Jackson was calling it—came swift and unswerving. Wyatt Walker acted as if the question of whether the violent "riffraff" was part of the Movement was beneath consideration. "The Saturday night crowd wasn't a member of nothing!" Ed Gardner insisted. "We don't need to keep a drunk head to keep us going. We won't be turned around."

But how could they be so sure about the rioters? There had been 2,500 people on the streets. Many were the "basic churchpeople" who lived in the surrounding shotgun houses. Most of the voices captured on the Riverside Church

---

*"What I saw at Sixteenth Street, what I saw at the motel, was the forerunner of what happened," Woods would say. "Later it was 'Burn, baby, burn.' . . . That came later and I saw it coming. I saw it coming." A 1966 study concluded, "The passivity and nonviolence of American Negroes could never again be taken for granted. The 'rules of the game' in race relations were permanently changed in Birmingham."

radio tape did not sound drunk or irrational. The Miles College veteran Frank Dukes believed there was "no difference between the people who were demonstrating and going to jail and the people who were throwing rocks." His former schoolmate Charles Davis agreed: "We kept 'em nonviolent while marching. But we knew in our hearts that they were violent. A lot of winos on Fourth Avenue marched."

"And really, those were the people who put the Movement over," Dukes said.

From his leftist perspective, Shuttlesworth's lawyer Len Holt considered the riot the "bread demonstration." He viewed the right that Project C had pursued for Negroes to sit at lunch counters as tantamount to the cake Marie Antoinette had offered the starving French peasantry.

Intervention

THE KENNEDY ADMINISTRATION was in national emergency mode. At six Sunday evening, Robert Kennedy, his deputy Nicholas Katzenbach, and Burke Marshall (who had been awakened at two in the morning at his West Virginia retreat and coptered to Washington) left Justice for the White House, where Secretary of Defense Robert McNamara was already caucusing with the President. Three thousand integrated pickets were in front of the Justice building, demanding that the attorney general rescue the schoolchildren of Birmingham. Earlier that day, Wyatt Walker had warned Robert Kennedy that, come nightfall, the blacks of Birmingham were going out "headhunting" for some cops.

Now that dynamite had jeopardized Marshall's deal—"that paper agreement" the administration was acknowledging privately while publicly aggrandizing it as the Birmingham Agreement—the next logical form of federal intervention was the Army troops that had been put on alert around the South. But, Robert Kennedy explained, unlike the "clear-cut situation" of a Montgomery or an Oxford, in Birmingham the "people who've gotten out of hand are not the white people, but the Negroes by and large"—apparently he considered the bombers a minor part of the equation. The government did not want to call out the Army against blacks who were rioting over real abuses, but, as President Kennedy bluntly put it, it would not do to "have the Negroes running around the city."

Governor Wallace, Marshall cautioned, would like nothing more than to be able to claim that "the President had invaded the state of Alabama. I think at the moment the governor and the outgoing city government are doing everything they can to make that agreement blow up," said Marshall, who believed that Wallace's troopers were trying to provoke the blacks to violence. The President wondered where the Senior Citizens would come down on federal occupation. "They want Birmingham to look like Atlanta," Marshall replied dryly, "and solve its own problems."

Smyer's Freedom High

SID SMYER and his phantom "subcommittee" were said to be meeting at the same time as the President's advisers. The Senior Citizens were standing by the accords, though judging from the threats Smyer was getting, the next bombing target might have an over-the-mountain address. "It seems to me if anybody needs to go to jail it would be 'Sidney Smyer,' " a citizen wrote Mayor Albert Boutwell. "He must be a *nut.*"

The old Dixiecrat was indeed experiencing a strange identification with the civil rights movement. He was referring to his Senior Citizens program as "nonviolent." He was praising the fairness of the national news media. And when he repeated the city fathers' motto in a Sunday-night statement to the press, "We're taking care of this thing ourselves," he included George Wallace's state troopers among the outside agitators who were exposing the city to the "heel of the military."

Mahatma

A. D. KING soothed the crowd at the Sunday-evening mass meeting at Nelson Smith's New Pilgrim Church: "When the Lord is with you, even bombs can't hurt you." The reporters filed out of the sanctuary, on standing orders to "Go where the Mahatma goes." A.D.'s brother had come back, little more than twenty-four hours after his departure. The Justice Department's Joe Dolan, also back, had picked him up at the airport.

Burke Marshall had already had a few telephone conversations with King, leaving the Cabinet Room at one point to feel him out on the likelihood of more rioting. King thought that if there were no other incidents, meaning bombings, he could control the people. He added reflexively that a lot of the rioters had been drunk, it being Saturday night.

In Nelson Smith's office, reporters found King sitting meditatively at the desk awaiting the next call from Washington. Marshall phoned with the administration's plan. He was coming back to Birmingham. Preliminary steps were being taken to federalize the Alabama National Guard. The President's men had decided to hedge the troop question: Soldiers trained in riot control (plus three hundred Airborne troops coptered in from Fort Benning, Georgia) would stand by at Fort McClellan outside Anniston. Katzenbach had argued against any air-to-ground maneuvers because when they landed at the Birmingham airport, they wouldn't know where to go. "They're going to mess it up," he said, stopping short of warning against "another Bay of Pigs."

Marshall had asked King what kind of statement he was looking for. Kennedy had been fretting about King's barbed suggestion from Atlanta that the President take "a forthright stand against the indignities which the Negro citizens still face." Marshall was a bit surprised that all King had in mind was your basic "men of decency must deplore this heinous act." The administration seemed to have been willing to commit to more, if only King had had an idea of what.

The popular leader of a finally popular civil rights movement—and his brother—had been the object of an assassination attempt. Instead of using the resulting outrage as political leverage, King seemed concerned more about the public's reaction to the black rock throwers than to the white bomb throwers. He went before the waiting masses at New Pilgrim and told them not to expect "the millennium" from the Birmingham Agreement, but to essentially behave themselves: "We must work passionately and unrelentingly for first-class citizenship, but we must not use second-class methods to gain it."

The President, who King contended had all but missed the boat on civil rights, meanwhile, was steering his administration toward choppier waters. He was toying with making national law an instrument of King's revolution. "If the agreement blows up," he had said in the Sunday-night meeting, before briefing the reporters on the Birmingham situation, "the other remedy we have under that condition is to send legislation to the Congress this week as our response to that action."

A Civil Rights Bill

IN THE MEMPHIS AIRPORT, Justice lawyer Ramsey Clark pondered the significance of Birmingham. A Texan raised mainly in Washington, Clark headed the department's lands division with such efficiency that he was able to direct his budget surplus toward the needy civil rights division. As an understudy member of Justice's "riot squad," he had just been in Oxford, Mississippi, reconnoitering for Robert Kennedy on whether troops should remain at Ole Miss (he thought not). On an "as long as you're south of the Mason-Dixon line" principle, he was ordered to Birmingham.

Clark was the son of Supreme Court Justice Tom Clark, Thurgood Marshall's best friend in official Washington. In a speech a year before, Tom Clark had acknowledged the capriciousness of the list of "subversive" organizations he had released as Truman's attorney general in 1947, and now Ramsey was about to vindicate one of the groups his father had condemned, the Southern Negro Youth Congress. Waiting in the Memphis airport overnight for the morning flight to Birmingham, he sat down in a plastic chair and began writing a memo to Robert Kennedy: It was time for federal civil rights legislation that would bring a definitive end to discrimination in public accommodations and employment. When he boarded the plane for Birmingham, he had in his briefcase an outline of the Movement's coveted "Second Emancipation Proclamation."

20.

NO MORE WATER

The King

FINALLY OUT OF the hospital on Monday, May 13, Fred Shuttlesworth told Herb Oliver that SCLC was trying to push him aside. He had a good mind to spike the shaky Birmingham Agreement by renewing demonstrations. Oliver nodded in sympathy and bemoaned the Friday-night victory mass meeting, where Ralph Abernathy had called Shuttlesworth "a great man" but had singled out Martin as the only divinely approved "King"—descended through Paul in the Philippian jail, Daniel in the lion's den, Moses in Midian. Oliver was so struck by the wounding irony of things that he recorded it in his diary: What the white people had tried to do for so long, neutralize Shuttlesworth, had just been achieved in the name of freedom.

While the two commiserated, the national news media tracked King on a peace tour (cooked up with Burke Marshall the previous day) of the dives that had supplied Saturday night's more spirited rioters. Or as Bull Connor pontificated to a reporter, "King's running around trying to get you people to get a picture and put it in the paper, running around down there on Fourth Avenue teaching nonviolence. But that son of a bitch, he's the only one that's caused any violence. You can quote me as saying that if you put 'son of a bitch' in front of it."

In the smoky underground of the New Home Billiard Parlor, Abernathy demanded, "Do you know who our leader is?"

"King!" came the pool players' reply.

"Are you willing to do whatever Martin Luther King tells you to do?"

"Yes!"

And then King (or "the King," as Abernathy introduced him) told them to lay down their weapons because violence was impractical as well as immoral. Their "amens" led to a halting linked-arm chorus of "We Shall Overcome." In the context of the Saturday-night riot, an unsettling question arose: Overcome what?

That afternoon brought Shuttlesworth a Pyrrhic vindication. The embattled Sid Smyer announced that the settlement called for promoting only one black employee, total, in all the downtown stores—not one in each store, as the Movement was interpreting it. This was the point of negotiation that had been left vague at Burke Marshall's recommendation, and over Shuttlesworth's objections. But Smyer was not simply dealing in the semantics of injured white pride: The merchants who had given David Vann commitments to promote five workers had reneged.

Shuttlesworth took to his bed and boycotted the Monday mass meeting, forgoing the Movement's biggest celebrity draws yet: Floyd Patterson, former heavyweight champion of the world, and Jackie Robinson, now retired from baseball, who said he had had no notion of coming down until he saw The Photographs. "I can't explain exactly how I feel," he said with emotion. The celebrity trail to Birmingham was becoming so crowded that the efficient Wyatt Walker lost B. B. King's offer to do a benefit blues concert.

Operation Oak Tree

IN WASHINGTON, the Justice Department phones were manned around the clock to receive calls from Birmingham. Barely forty-eight hours after leaving his hometown, the tax division's Lou Oberdorfer had been awakened in Washington on Sunday by the black man who worked for his father calling to say there had been a terrible riot. Oberdorfer had returned to Birmingham by military plane. Ed Guthman, Robert Kennedy's spokesman, had come down with Marshall to handle the delicate PR end of the administration's new interpretation of "federalism." That day, a reporter asked the attorney general how the situation in Birmingham had changed since last week, when the President said there was no authority for federal action. Kennedy offered tortured references to Little Rock and Oxford, hoping no one would ask which federal statutes or court orders had been violated by a motel bombing.

On Tuesday, Kennedy met with twenty Alabama newspaper editors to sell them on King's nonviolence, lest "worse leaders" take his place. The attorney general did not have to mention any names. Malcolm X was ridiculing King's strategic breakthrough ("Real men don't put their children on the firing line") and his goal of "integration," saying, "We don't want to have anything to do with any race of dogs. Two-legged white dogs siccing four-legged dogs on your and my mother!"

Oberdorfer was not thrilled to be sharing temporary headquarters with General Creighton Abrams, who had been put in charge of the Army's Birmingham detail—Operation Oak Tree. Abrams had also handled the military backup at Ole Miss eight months before. From the government command post in Memphis, he had groused over the phone to Army Secretary Cyrus Vance about the ragtag team of marshals Oberdorfer—given his similar experience during the Freedom Rides in Montgomery—had been charged with training, and then in the crunch, it had been the military that goofed, unable to find helicopters to get the soldiers to Oxford. After Ole Miss, Abrams thought better of coming into an area without reconnaissance and had brought a dozen or so people for Operation Oak Tree—its makeshift headquarters in the FBI's offices, high atop the 2121 Building, with vistas of the riot scene, Kelly Ingram Park, and Sixteenth Street Baptist.

By Monday, uniformed officers were riding, fully armed, up and down the elevators. A concerned call came from the White House, demanding a troop count. Abrams temporized, but the President's insistence on an exact number set off an exodus of soldiers to Anniston. Still, that a major general of the largest army in the Free World was on Eighth Avenue North, that 17,793 combat troops remained on two- or four-hour-alert status, was the ultimate statement on the crisis of Birmingham. It was the first time in modern memory that federal troops had been called out to calm civil insurrection rather than to enforce a court order, as at Little Rock and Oxford.

Ramsey Clark was circling the scene in a military prop plane, providing a civilian check on the Army's enthusiasm. The Texan was not completely grumpy about being in Birmingham. Across from his motel was an excellent barbecue joint, with real cornbread.

Shuttlesworth's Return

"OLD SOLDIERS don't fade away, they die away," Fred Shuttlesworth said. "This is one soldier that won't." On Tuesday night, May 14, flanked by bodyguards and two other men who seemed to be helping him walk, he made his first appearance at a mass meeting since before the Friday accord. King, Abernathy, and Walker were being feted in Cleveland. If King had seemed to be holding his breath and hoping the truce wouldn't fall apart, Shuttlesworth restored a sense of the upper hand. "Birmingham is not going back on the agreement we made or we will demonstrate again," he said. "Twenty-eight hundred of us went to jail this time and four thousand will be ready to go next time." And then he blasted Sid Smyer's version of the employment terms. "Burke Marshall was present when the agreement was worked out," he said. "... They had better have [black clerks] in all stores."

Smyer was telling anonymous callers threatening to "git" him that he'd be armed and waiting, and they'd have to guess what tree he was behind. President Kennedy had had his brother call Smyer and summon him up to Washington for a little pep talk, though it wasn't clear who was assuring whom. Smyer told the Kennedys, "We're working it out, don't you worry," having decided along with his local confidants that "it would be a black eye to us to have to call on the President of the United States to run the city of Birmingham."

The Mayor's Valedictory

ART HANES was about to move on to a legal career that would boldly advertise his sympathy with the Ku Klux Klan, but when he took the stage of the Municipal Auditorium on Wednesday afternoon, May 15, it was to address the Klan's respectable political front: the United Americans for Conservative Government.

Core members of the Klan had organized the group the year before, its biggest activists the men of Eastview 13: Robert Chambliss, Billy Holt, the Blantons, Hubert Page, Arthur "Sister" White, Gene Reeves, Nigger Hall, Bobby Cherry, Robert Thomas, and the contingent of old DeBardelebenites—Troy Ingram, Earl Thompson, and Bessemer Exalted Cyclops Robert Creel. More than a thousand segregationists turned out to hear the lame-duck mayor heap picturesque curses upon the "Congolese mob" (the demonstrators), "the witch doctor" (King), and the "weak-kneed quisling traitors" (the Senior Citizens Committee). Hanes said he would "never negotiate or meet with the Communists or the rabble rousers of the King type because they haven't got anything to negotiate with. They haven't got a thing that we want. We have what they want." To survey the perpetually hungover truckers in the audience, the hopeless dental cases and abused wives, was to wonder what they had that someone else might want.

The Next Threshold

ON THURSDAY, May 16, the city's best names, an Anglo-Saxon elite that preferred to confine press appearances to the social pages, were arrayed in the *Birmingham News*. Smyer's sympathetic few co-conspirators had lobbied for releasing the names of the Senior Citizens, to give a few more hounds to the foxes. True to form, the Big Mules had "taken responsibility" by denying it: Not every one of the seventy-seven men on the list attended the meeting, their statement noted, and not all of those who did attend agreed with "the method by which the subcommittee was to re-establish racial peace."

The Birmingham campaign seemed to be winding down to the ultimately unimportant fine points, with Martin Luther King and Sid Smyer bickering publicly over the number of clerks the department stores were to promote. Alabama's next racial spectacle was getting ready for prime time. Throughout the spring, Arthur Shores and Constance Motley, for the NAACP's Inc. Fund, had been discreetly performing the rites for resurrecting the old Autherine Lucy court order.* The two latest candidates for integration had sailed through the grueling application process, which involved detectives digging up dirt on the applicant in order for the university to persuade her to withdraw. Twenty-year-old Vivian Juanita Malone was a model student who had been in the civil rights orbit of SCLC's Joe Lowery as a youth in Mobile. James Hood was a boy preacher and son of a CIO man at Goodyear, who had helped organize an SCLC chapter in his hometown of Gadsden after consorting with SNCC and SCLC while attending Clark College

---

* The University of Alabama had hoped to force the NAACP to reargue the case's constitutional merits, on the ground that the dean of admissions named in the old, 1955 injunction, William Adams, had resigned. The circumstances of his resignation, in November 1960, presented a bit of a problem, however. A month earlier, he had made "obscene suggestions" to a male vice-squad lieutenant in a Memphis hotel room. The university was afraid that the details of his departure might expose them to charges of hypocrisy for rejecting Pollie Anne Myers on moral grounds.

in Atlanta. Hood would bring a bit of dry wit to the burlesque already titled the Schoolhouse Door. When a reporter asked him if he had pets at home, he amended his negative reply to say, "We have a police dog imported from Birmingham."

On Thursday, May 16, Judge Hobart Grooms reiterated his 1955 ruling desegregating the University of Alabama. George Wallace was delighted. He recognized that carpetbaggers were essential to the psychic innocence of southern segregationists. Just as occupying northerners had morally justified the anti-Negro terrorism of Bedford Forrest's Reconstruction Klan, so nearly a century later would the federal government stand in for the South's "beloved colored people" as the enemy. The Kennedy administration had played straight into Wallace's hands back in December, when, under orders from his superiors in Washington, Reid Doster, commander of the Alabama National Guard and the brains behind the Bay of Pigs air operation, sent a training jet to take reconnaissance photographs of the Tuscaloosa campus, as if the government was preparing for a military takeover.

One of Wallace's antagonists, however, understood the southern psyche as well as the governor whose job he aspired to. Chuck Morgan had developed a sort of blood-feud enmity toward his (former) fellow populist and was looking forward to the Schoolhouse Door because he wanted to see Wallace go to jail. He had been undermining the governor behind the scenes, politicking with the state's business leaders and opinion shapers. But in mid-March, Morgan had been forced once again into the main drama, the lone white on the "black side" of the Schoolhouse Door.

The university had an extension center in Huntsville that had been the beneficiary of the one-horse town's transformation into a space research mecca, where the National Aeronautics and Space Administration had created a laboratory for the German rocket scientists spirited away by the U.S. government after World War II. (The head of the Huntsville space center, Wernher von Braun, had not publicized his previous affiliation with Hitler's SS.) Morgan was being asked to represent a missile research technician named David McGlathery, a Huntsville sharecropper's son who had aced his way through the local black college, Alabama A&M, and now wanted to master applied mathematics at the University of Alabama extension, most of whose graduate students were government employees. Snubbed by the Inc. Fund, with its eye on the Tuscaloosa prize, McGlathery's case had been fobbed off on Chuck Morgan. He had the predictable reservations about becoming the first southern white lawyer to desegregate his state's university, and when Judge Grooms's May 16 ruling scheduled the Stand in the Schoolhouse Door for the opening of the summer session, June 11, Morgan consoled himself with the knowledge that with two campuses being desegregated, Wallace would be hard-pressed to be in both doorways at once.

A Prayer for Brother Brown

FRED SHUTTLESWORTH seemed to be recovering his appreciation of the ridiculous. At the mass meeting on Wednesday, May 15, he draped his arms around two white women ("I have really been integrated today") and commented on Bull Connor's favorite city court judge, "When Judge Brown dies and goes to hell, he is going to get a hundred dollars and a hundred and eighty days."

Within twenty-four hours, this standard Movement joke had joined the embarrassment of miracles that was this Year of Birmingham. On Thursday, nine of the Movement chiefs were to begin serving their five-day sentences for contempt of Judge William Jenkins's injunction but had received a stay from the state supreme court pending appeal. Most were sitting in Judge Charles Brown's court as he tore through the docket, processing the demonstrators arrested on charges of parading without a permit. King, Abernathy, and Shuttlesworth began to get worried. It was Brown who had slapped the $2,500 bail on King and Abernathy to imperil the truce.

"Where is Wyatt?" Abernathy said. "He needs to make some preparations to get us out of jail." Shuttlesworth asked his protégé Carter Gaston to go to the motel to get him. "It won't be necessary," Gaston said. "Nobody is going to jail. That judge is going to fall dead." He had dreamed it the night before.

"You're losing your mind," Shuttlesworth replied.

Gaston dutifully headed toward the motel and found Walker in the dining room. "I'm working on it," Walker said. Except for chewing his food, he was motionless. He was still eating his lunch when Gaston returned to Judge Brown's courtroom.

A police officer was testifying that he had arrested "one black male," and Orzell Billingsley objected to the insulting term "black." Brown sustained him and turned to the defendant, Eddie Upshaw: "Nigguh, I told you to answer my question right. I put all you nigguhs out yesterday and I'll do it again today." With that, the judge dropped dead of a heart attack.

Frank Dukes said to his neighbor, "A.D., lead a prayer for Brother Brown." Heads were bowed, lips were bitten.

"I wonder what he will tell the Big Judge up there," the Reverend Abraham Woods said at the mass meeting that night. Despite the now routine presence of a national celebrity—the actor and Jewish folksinger Theodore Bikel—the Birmingham Movement belonged on this night to the anonymous local Negroes who had suffered for a century under small white men like Judge Brown. The shape of Carter Gaston's future suddenly became clear to him after Martin Luther King spoke to him that day for the first time: "When are you going to stop running from the ministry?" In twelve years, he would be the pastor of Shuttlesworth's old church.

The Bill

JOE DOLAN, the "riot squadder," and Ed Guthman, Justice's press spokesman, left Birmingham that Thursday on a military Lockheed Jet Star. With them was Norbert Schlei, a thirty-four-year-old Californian and a former clerk to Justice John Marshall Harlan who had chosen law over a promising career in professional golf. As chief of the twenty-two legal whizzes who made up the Office of Legal Counsel, Schlei had drafted the executive orders calling out the troops at Oxford and at Birmingham.

Everyone on the plane agreed that something had to give. There were sure to be copycat Birminghams all over—even the scourge city of England had held a rally against its southern American namesake. Sit-ins had been resumed in Greensboro. In Raleigh and in Cambridge, Maryland, demonstrators had challenged the police to shoot. A Harlem rally on behalf of Birmingham had become disorderly, and a new Freedom Walk had begun from Chattanooga to Gadsden. At this rate the federal government would become a full-time race relations mediator.

But the logistical headaches weren't the main concern of the men on the plane. It was time for federal civil rights legislation—a real law rather than the weak bill the administration had futilely sent up to the Hill in February. It would not be easy to persuade the President to endanger the programs he could push through, including a pet tax-cut bill, by throwing himself at these windmill blades. But the consensus among the men from Justice was "No matter what." They went straight to the office after landing and told Robert Kennedy, "We've got to have the bill." The memo Ramsey Clark had written in the Memphis airport was already on the attorney general's desk. Kennedy had a speech to make in Asheville, North Carolina, the next day and said they could come along and discuss it en route.

It was Friday, May 17, the ninth anniversary of *Brown* v. *Board*. Kennedy, Guthman, Burke Marshall, Nick Katzenbach, and Lou Oberdorfer abandoned their regular assignments to go with the attorney general. Even the normally noncommittal Marshall was adamant: It had to be resolved now, by federal law. On the flight down aboard an Air Force plane, they discussed what should be covered in the bill, continued the debate as Kennedy left with Guthman to speak to the North Carolina Cold War Seminar, and refined a manageable list of basics on the trip back. The President had the outline on his desk that afternoon.

On Saturday, the Justice brain trust joined the Asheville barnstormers in Robert Kennedy's office. Their most urgent priority was to end discrimination in "public accommodations": the restrooms and the restaurants that the Birmingham campaign had zeroed in on. Norb Schlei assured Kennedy that a public accommodations bill would pass constitutional muster if they based it on the commerce clause rather than on the Fourteenth Amendment. But the lawyer's challenge was different from the politician's.

Chief Executives

THAT SATURDAY, for a ceremony marking the thirtieth anniversary of the Tennessee Valley Authority, President Kennedy was to rendezvous at Muscle Shoals, Alabama, with George Wallace, who had just called him a "military dictator" for authorizing troops in Birmingham. From talks with his hometown sources, Lou Oberdorfer had concluded that it wasn't safe for the President to go to Alabama. And worse, on the day of the trip, Birmingham attorney Kirkman Jackson, Hobart McWhorter Jr.'s father-in-law, filed suit in federal court on Wallace's behalf against the United States and Defense Secretary Robert McNamara, claiming that the movement of troops into Alabama was illegal. (The government would argue that troops hadn't actually been sent into Birmingham, causing Oberdorfer to observe wryly that they must not have found out about the 130 uniformed men in the FBI building.) Fearing that the governor might use the TVA ceremony to hit the President with the lawsuit, the Secret Service was prepared to intercede physically, although Norb Schlei recommended that the President rely on his best political weapon, humor.

Coptering with Wallace from Muscle Shoals to NASA's space center in Huntsville, Kennedy waited fifteen minutes before bringing up Birmingham, breaking the ice by thanking Wallace for seeing his brother Bob a few weeks before. Wallace replied that he had been happy to talk to the attorney general "for an hour and twenty-two minutes." The President asked Wallace how many men he had in Birmingham. Wallace's assurances that the thousand law enforcers on the scene had things under control invited Kennedy to say that things would never be under control until some progress was made on rights. Why couldn't Negroes be hired to work in some downtown stores when the very people who objected had Negroes serving their tables at home? Wallace insisted that the trouble with Birmingham was the outsiders—King was a "faker," he and Shuttlesworth rode "around town in big Cadillacs smoking expensive cigars" and vied with each other over "who could go to bed with the most nigger women, and white and red women too." That both heads of state were cigar aficionados and bedroom decathletes perhaps explained why Wallace changed the subject and offered the President a reminder that he, yet another "great pal in the South," had campaigned for the Democratic ticket in 1960.

Public Accommodations

SINCE THE TRUCE, the Movement leaders had been holding their breath about the fate of the schoolchildren who had demonstrated under threat of expulsion. The previous Sunday, Ralph Abernathy had told the kids to report to school the next day "just like nothing happened" and, if pressed, to say that they "learned in your school system that our nation was created under God and dedicated to the principle that all men are created equal . . . and we believed it because the white folk told us so." ("And look 'em dead in the eye as you tell them that.") Now, a week later, on Monday, May 20, the school board—appointed and overseen by Bull Connor and represented by Jim Simpson's firm—officially expelled the demonstrators.

Jim Bevel and his seconds mimeographed four thousand handbills urging a school boycott. U.S. Army troops in Anniston, Montgomery, and Fort Benning were ordered to be on fifteen-minute alert one hour before the school walkout. David Vann phoned Andy Young and called the boycott a violation of the settlement. Young called King, who had been in Chicago for the weekend. Facing the scenario that Shuttlesworth had warned him about—a generation of uneducated children—King returned to Birmingham to countermand Bevel. He called the kids to the courtyard of the Gaston Motel. Anyone who did not receive an expulsion notice, he told them, should go back to school. "Are you with me now?" The response was weak. The kids had been delighted to get out of school to march, and some were even more delighted to be out for good. "Are you with me?" he said and repeated, "I can't hear you," until the "yeahs" came back loud enough.

The Inc. Fund's Constance Motley joined Arthur Shores and Orzell Billingsley in representing the students' case before a judge. The Columbia-trained Motley was the only NAACP lawyer whom Billingsley considered "worth a damn," the stately daughter of a Yale University cook who had made her first trip to Alabama as an undergraduate at Nashville's Fisk University to attend the Southern Negro Youth Congress's 1942 convention, at Tuskegee. While in Birmingham she usually stayed with Shores, whom she had assisted over the years on the big cases, including Autherine Lucy. Lately she had found it hard to get any sleep, having noticed that the garage of his brick ranch on Dynamite Hill was packed with guards and their firearms.

That Monday of Motley's arrival, the Movement scored a great victory in a case she had argued before the Supreme Court. In an opinion written by Chief Justice Earl Warren, the Court overturned the conspiracy convictions of Shuttlesworth and Charles Billups in the 1960 sit-ins. "I only wish that Reverend Shuttlesworth were here tonight because the Supreme Court has turned him loose once again," Motley told the mass meeting. "You know, they say the cat has nine lives, but Shuttlesworth has nineteen, I think." Their appeals, combined with those of the ten local students arrested, had become one of the NAACP's test cases for the three thousand or so convicted sit-ins around the South, and Monday's outcome rendered segregation ordinances unenforceable.

This, the judiciary's first significant step to ending segregation of "public accommodations," vindicated the visionary campaign that Arthur Shores had begun exactly twenty-five years before, when Senator Glen Taylor tried to enter Herb Oliver's church through the "Colored" door. If there was a blemish on Birmingham's latest landmark, it was that the city's magnificent civil libertarian, Hugo Black, had deserted the democratic vanguard. In his dissent, he had gone atypically sentimental about "my Pappy's store" and his right to serve whomever he pleased. He would continue to be the Court's most strenuous critic of direct action.

As the Kennedy administration was aware, having the Supreme Court say it was so did not make it so in the South. Norb Schlei's draft of the civil rights bill that would convert such decisions into national law was on the attorney general's desk on May 20, the Monday the Court's decision came down. In a meeting that day between the attorney general and his men and the President and his men, the presidential aides seemed deaf to the significance of Birmingham, what Schlei called the "sea change" in the white public attitude. They balked especially at the meat of the bill: the public accommodations section. The President instructed his brother to keep has distance from Martin Luther King until the bill was in its final stages. "King is so hot these days," he said, "that it's like Marx coming to the White House."

As of May 10, Moscow had been devoting a quarter of its international radio output to Birmingham. Thirty-five years had passed since the Communist International contemplated the Magic City as the staging ground of a civil rights revolution in the American South, but it had been worth the wait.

Allgood

ON TUESDAY MORNING, Constance Motley, Arthur Shores, and Orzell Billingsley took their brief against the school superintendent into the courtroom of Clarence Allgood. As Motley spoke, the federal judge interrupted her: "You got this one by yourself?" His surprise at a woman doing the talking for perfectly able-tongued men was not the first instance that prejudice toward her gender had trumped racial bigotry. Then he told her that when he was a child, "a colored man"—he gave his last as well as first name—used to spank him whenever he did anything wrong. Motley sensed that this was his way of declaring that he was no racist.

Allgood had indeed been in the inner sanctum of Alabama's New Deal liberal establishment, Lister Hill's informant on the nefarious goings-on inside the "tall buildings" of Birmingham. But he also claimed Jim Simpson as a close friend, and when the anti–New Dealers fielded Simpson in the 1944 Senate race, Allgood had gone diplomatically behind the scenes for Hill, handling campaign contributions. Two years later, following the funeral of Alabama's senior senator, John Bankhead, Allgood had held a cocktail caucus of Democrats at the Mountain Brook Club to cut off a Simpson bid for the vacant seat by anointing John Sparkman, a New Deal–friendly congressman.

Though more recently Allgood took some credit for pressuring Connor to let Martin Luther King make the jailhouse phone call to his wife, his brand of "liberalism" was moldering. Lister Hill himself was publicly calling on the President to remove the "outside agitators" from Birmingham. And Allgood, a beneficiary of the glut of federal judgeships that the new administration had to fill in 1961,* was about to become one of the most discredited members of Kennedy's

---

* The Omnibus Judgeship Bill, signed in May 1961, created more than eighty new judgeships.

scandalous lineup of southern judiciary appointees, who reflected the wishful belief, as one observer put it, "that every redneck who came down the pike was another Hugo Black."*

"Would you have your children out in the streets demonstrating?" Allgood scolded Motley. His indignation seemed strange for a former juvenile delinquent who himself had been expelled from high school and had suffered hugely for his youthful mischief—still suffered, Motley could see from his limp. At eighteen, Clarence had hopped his last freight train: A swinging door from a boxcar struck him from behind and threw him under the train. He now walked on cork legs.

Motley asked Allgood to deny her motion officially so that she could appeal it. Allgood refused to do so without a hearing, and recessed the court for lunch. Motley called the Atlanta office of Elbert Tuttle, the chief judge of the Southeast's appellate forum, the Fifth Circuit Court of Appeals. Although he had been a Republican pillar of Atlanta since 1923, Tuttle was not a southerner, had attended interracial schools while growing up in Hawaii, and had been standing up to the country club set since serving as the local lawyer for the Communists' constitutional test plaintiff, Angelo Herndon.

Tuttle and Motley were old friends, but even so, what she was asking of him was highly unusual: an injunction against the school board *before* the appeal of the expulsions was heard. Tuttle said he would stay at the courthouse to hold a hearing at seven.

Before catching the five o'clock flight to Atlanta, Motley looked around the crowd of Movement folks at the courthouse and grabbed the Reverend Calvin Woods to go with her as the plaintiff on the affidavit verifying the complaint.

"Who, me?" the diminutive Woods said. "I've never been on a plane in my life." He stalled: "I've got to go home to tell my wife."

"You don't have time."

The named plaintiff would actually be Woods's eleven-year-old daughter, Linda Cal, a fifth-grader at Booker T. Washington, who had hidden in the back of her father's Cadillac to get to Sixteenth Street to join the marchers. Like most of the Movement ministers, Woods had been all for the children marching as long as his own were not among them.

Over the objections of Jim Simpson's law partner, representing the school board, Tuttle summarily struck down the board's action and ordered the children back to school, citing Motley's Supreme Court victory of Monday in the Shuttlesworth sit-in case. The following night, Wednesday, May 22, 1,500 children entered the mass meeting carrying small flags. "Tonight was their victory night," the detectives on Movement surveillance observed sportingly. Caught up in the delicious fine print, no one had noticed the epoch-making treaty that the President

---

* The administration had already used considerable muscle persuading the American Bar Association to upgrade its "not qualified" rating of Allgood after he was nominated. The NAACP had weighed in with an endorsement, and Burke Marshall's back-channel caucuses with Chuck Morgan yielded Allgood a thumbs-up, although he would later surmise that Morgan was "comparing him to Bull Connor."

had placed before the public in a news conference that day: a "legal remedy" for "those who feel themselves—or who are, as a matter of fact—denied equal rights . . . and therefore they take to the streets and we have the kind of incidents that we have in Birmingham."

The post-segregation era was beginning. On Thursday, May 23, Bull Connor was sitting at a picnic table in Kelly Ingram Park enjoying the sun with the state troopers when one of his men brought him the news: The Alabama Supreme Court had unanimously evicted him from city hall. "Well, I'm just going on up there and draw my pennies and get in line [for welfare] with the rest of the niggers," he said.*

One of Major Albert Boutwell's first official acts would be to present Burke Marshall a key to the city. The hasty ceremony was performed in what Marshall would later describe as "some closet," without witnesses.

Parallel History

ALREADY THERE WERE distinct versions of the Year of Birmingham, parallel truths each with its own authenticity. The history the city had made was being shoved into the closet of Birmingham proper, while simultaneously being shaped for posterity as a chapter—perhaps the climax—of Martin Luther King's epic story. The previous Sunday, King's until now obscure "Letter from Birmingham Jail" had been featured on the front page of the *New York Post*. Smaller magazines rushed versions of it into print, and the *Atlantic Monthly* prepared it for a summer issue, placing it in the same august New England sphere as Henry David Thoreau's "On Civil Disobedience." Meanwhile, a New York publisher urged King to include the letter in a larger book explaining Birmingham to the world, suggesting the title for what would be an instant classic, *Why We Can't Wait*. The fame of the Birmingham Jail would be no longer a lover's letter to it, but a martyr's letter from it.

On the last weekend in May, King went to Hollywood. Nearly 50,000 people, the largest number of civil rights enthusiasts in a single spot ever, jammed old Wrigley Field in Los Angeles, holding programs printed with Bill Hudson's picture of Walter Gadsden. King's warm-up act, Paul Newman, spoke for a glittering roster of movie stars, and then King kept the audience on its feet for an exultant speech ending in a recitation from the "Battle Hymn of the Republic"—"Mine eyes have *seen* the glory."

The Fire Next Time

LIKE THE WITCH at the fairy tale princess's christening, a black voice disrupted the euphoria of the post-Birmingham run of rallies that raised some $150,000 for

*Connor's last vote before leaving city hall was to approve trucking priority for Walter "Crack" Hanna, the vigilante turned steel fabricator who had preceded Connor as the industrialists' valet.

SCLC within a week. The writer James Baldwin, who had adopted Fred Shut-tlesworth as his "guide" on his first trip South, in 1957, had followed the Birmingham saga as a prophet follows the fulfillment of a prophecy. The previous November, *The New Yorker* had published his "Letter from a Region in My Mind," a savage description of the time bomb that was the black American male, racked with fear, sorrow, and a "hatred for white men so deep that it often turned against him and his own, and made all love, all trust, all joy impossible." The only thing that Baldwin believed would move white people ultimately was the expression of this black rage. His essay had ended with a cautionary line from a spiritual, "God gave Noah the rainbow sign. No more water, the fire next time!" The water hoses of Birmingham, followed by flaming grocery stores and the taxicab burning right in front of the Sixteenth Street Baptist Church, had lent Baldwin's metaphor an eerie literalness. The essay had been published in book form as *The Fire Next Time* the month the Birmingham campaign began.

Now, after Birmingham, Baldwin chided, "For a Negro there's no difference between the North and South, there's just a difference in the way they castrate you, but the fact of the castration is the American fact." Baldwin had essentially told Robert Kennedy the same bad news about the American nature of the South's problem at a breakfast discussion that spring. In the wake of Birmingham, Kennedy had asked him on short notice to gather a few influential Negroes to brainstorm with him about some government-sponsored remedies for the urban problem.

The summit took place on Friday, May 24, in New York. Burke Marshall and Lou Oberdorfer were in town with Kennedy for a secret, off-the-record meeting with representatives of national theater, restaurant, and hotel chains, to persuade them to voluntarily desegregate their southern branches. Two days earlier, Robert Kennedy had served lunch in his office to a group of owners of chain stores—Woolworth's, Kress, J. C. Penney, McCrory, Sears—in the first attempt to enlist the private sector behind the still-veiled civil rights bill. The gathering had been so promising that Oberdorfer was assigned to coordinate a series of such meetings. But on Friday, Kennedy noticed that the businessmen were reacting to him as the "devil incarnate," so worried about having their collaboration publicized (hence the meeting in New York rather than Washington) that they had hidden downstairs until they determined that the attorney general had not brought along any television cameras.

Kennedy and Marshall were looking forward to a restorative embrace afterward with their new black allies. Awaiting them at Kennedy's father's apartment on Central Park South were Baldwin, Harry Belafonte, Lena Horne, playwright Lorraine (*A Raisin in the Sun*) Hansberry. The Justice men had been expecting to meet with urban race experts, but the only people who vaguely qualified were King's (and Baldwin's) lawyer Clarence Jones, the Chicago Urban League's Edwin Berry, and Kenneth Clark, the sociologist who had supplied the NAACP the academic underpinning for the *Brown* case. There was also a young black CORE field secretary named Jerome Smith, a college dropout from Louisiana who had been on the first freedom bus into Mississippi, and was in New York getting medical treatment for the beatings since received in the southern trenches.

Smith resented the "movie stars" of the civil rights establishment who went to the White House for pictures rather than frank talk, and he pounced on Robert Kennedy's nervous opening about the rise of the Black Muslims. Smith countered that the whites had nothing to fear from that bunch, unwilling to risk anything but rhetoric. It was people like him, a Gandhian pacifist, whom they'd better start worrying about.

He had a specific turning point in mind. A few hours after the Gaston Motel bombing, he had called his CORE colleague Ike Reynolds, who had been blown out of bed by the dynamite, and told him that black folks had probably reached the end of this nonviolent thing. Unless the white man had something to fear— loss of his life or money—he was not going to give up anything. Smith now warned Kennedy that the nonviolent revolution was effectively over: "When I pull the trigger, kiss it goodbye."

Kennedy took Smith's challenge—and his profession of an urge to vomit— as a personal insult. For the other African-Americans, however, it spoke directly to what Lena Horne would call "the common dirt of our existence." The "movie stars," too, began to blast away at the Kennedys' civil rights tour de force: Birmingham. When Kennedy informed them of his close working relationship with King during the crisis (something Belafonte and Jones could have confirmed), they hooted, "That's not true." Why hadn't troops been sent in to protect those children? Burke Marshall pointed out that martial law would have resulted in the arrest of all demonstrators, and King, Abernathy, and Shuttlesworth would have ended up in jail. After three hours of what Kenneth Clark called "one of the most violent, emotional verbal assaults" he had witnessed, the blacks retreated into "hysterical laughter," Clark said: "the laughter of desperation."

Lou Oberdorfer debriefed his shaken colleagues back at the Waldorf. The classic white fear of the "black mob" had overcome Kennedy. "They seemed possessed," he said. "They reacted as a unit." Oberdorfer did not know what to make of the debacle either, but as he looked into his friends' ashen faces, he reached a conclusion: The race issue was not going to be solved by lawyers.

21.

THE SCHOOLHOUSE DOOR

The Expert

NERVOUS ABOUT HIS impending debut on the American political stage, George Wallace boarded a plane for New York on June 1 to appear on *Meet the Press.* He emerged swaggering from his first national TV forum: "All they wanted to know about was niggers, and I'm the expert."

In preparation for Wallace's Stand in the Schoolhouse Door on June 11, the Kennedys had reprised the old-boy-network strategy they had used in Birmingham. In late May, Cabinet members and other top administration officials had begun pressing their Alabama business contacts—128 in all—to urge moderation upon their governor. The Federal Aviation Administration even called David Rockefeller because he held stock in B. F. Goodrich, Tuscaloosa's Klan haven and Bobby Shelton's old employer. The state's own Rotarians had posted five different businessmen for several mornings running to await the governor's arrival at the office with a little law-and-order speech. But they threw up their hands and told the men in Washington that Wallace was a raving lunatic.

On June 5, acting on a request from the Justice Department, Judge Seybourn Lynne forcefully enjoined Wallace from obstructing the orders of the federal court. Because the ultra-segregationist Lynne was "no Frank Johnson," Burke Marshall permitted himself an inkling optimism that Tuscaloosa would not be "another Oxford." Wallace's lawyers, who included Jim Simpson and Kirkman Jackson, seemed to understand that it was all over but the client's shout, though that would resonate across decades.

Arsenal on Wheels

GOVERNOR WALLACE now found himself caught in a political version of suspended animation, between the violence of his rhetoric and the dignity of his office—and the higher one to which he aspired, the U.S. presidency. The national reporters covering him were wise to the self-consciousness of his political passion. After spewing some quotable venom in an interview with *Newsweek*'s Joe

Cumming—the Supreme Court "cruelly emasculated the orderly processes of government," or something—he put his feet up on his desk, lit a cigar, and said with a smile, "Isn't it good somebody has some spirit." But Wallace's rougher constituents were not as sophisticated as the news media, and now he faced the possibility that a white mob would rise up behind his words.

The governor began to plead over statewide TV for his fellow segregationists to stay home and let him be their stand-in at the Schoolhouse Door. Bobby Shelton obeyed. The Klan had "no intention of bringing any form of violence on the campus," the Imperial Wizard said, in a turnaround from his prediction in early May of "the bloodiest rioting ever seen in the U.S." Shelton would be rewarded with the time-honored currency of the gubernatorial favor bank: He became a contractor for the state highway department.

Ace Carter (another Wallace beneficiary of the taxpayers' money) passed along the governor's instructions to Dr. Edward Fields and the National States Rights Party before beginning to work on the Schoolhouse Door script. Wallace's newly idle pal, Bull Connor, delivered the stay-at-home message to the Tuscaloosa Citizens Council. Afterward, Connor, who was himself rumored to be going on the state payroll to organize a boycott of insufficiently segregationist businessmen, met with Klan contacts and asked them to spread the word.

It is not clear, then, who issued the orders that accounted for the party mood at Jack Cash's Barbecue on Saturday afternoon, June 8. The Klansmen of Eastview 13 were about to make their way to a big statewide Klan rally in Tuscaloosa, and if Gary Thomas Rowe is to be believed, his squad had instructions to "tear the place up and bomb the place up," referring to the University of Alabama. They were taking an arsenal with them to Tuscaloosa, including a bazooka, a submachine gun, some shotguns and pistols, and a cotton hook that Herman Cash—Jack's forty-five-year-old alcoholic little brother—used for loading freight at his trucking job. Besides Herman Cash and Rowe, the elite Eastview men tapped for this honor were the preacher's son Charles Cagle, the baby-faced Trailways (and Krystal) enforcer Gene Reeves, and Ellis Raymond "Pap" Dinsmore, a boyhood friend of Robert Chambliss's who had retired as foreman of butchers at the local Armour packing plant.

The most eager member of the delegation, Ross Keith, was the latest ward of Charles DeBardeleben to join Troy Ingram and Earl Thompson in Eastview 13. It had been a year almost to the day since the stockholders of the last remaining DeBardeleben coal-mining concern liquidated the company because of declining profits, and now the family's legacy was this concentration of DeBardelebenites, defying the laws of probability, in the most violent klavern in history. Like Ingram and Thompson, Keith was the son of one of DeBardeleben's evicted unionist traitors. (Robert Creel, the Exalted Cyclops of the Bessemer klavern, seemed the exceptional DeBardeleben Klansman who was the child of a company loyalist.) Unlike Ingram's father, William Keith did not take his firing with equanimity. He denounced Charles DeBardeleben to his growing sons and seemed especially sympathetic to the black "shirkers" whom DeBardeleben had chained to a railroad spur and let bake in the sun until they begged to go back into the cool mines. When William got a job with Sloss supervising convict miners, he had once intervened on behalf of a black convict who was being attacked with a pick handle by a white prisoner. His gallantry had not been transmitted to his son.

Ross had been recruited into the Klan in the summer of 1961 by his fellow alcoholic truckdriver John "Nigger" Hall. Because of his friendship with Hall and another Eastview trucker, Arthur "Sister" White, Keith had risen quickly through the ranks to squad leader. He was a severe diabetic who masked his sickliness through drinking, sexual conquest, and a big Harley-Davidson. His friends Nigger (for his dark skin) and Sister (for his effeminacy) may too have been overcompensating by becoming the most enthusiastic members of Eastview.

As the Klansmen prepared to leave Jack Cash's on Saturday a few hours before the rally, Keith walked up to Tommy Rowe, who was on the phone with one of his girlfriends, an insurance clerk named Helen Metcalf. She was to alert the bureau that the boys were about to leave. Keith asked who was on the phone, and when Rowe said it was Helen, he said, "Ah, bullshit." Billy Holt had been spreading his suspicions about Rowe's being an informer, and Keith had been trying to exorcise his doubts by joking about them. "Get off that goddamned phone, man," Keith said. "You're going to get us all killed."

"I can talk to my girl if I want to." Then he said, "Here, take the goddamn phone and say hello to her."

Keith accepted the receiver. Day broke over his worried face. "I'll be a son-ofabitch," he said, handing the phone back to Rowe.

Keith walked over to a table of Klansmen and said to Gene Reeves, "Yeah, yeah, it's Helen, all right."

Reeves said, "Goddamn, I thought I had him."

Rowe's latest test was not over. As the Klansmen left the cafe to caravan to Tuscaloosa, Reeves intercepted Rowe and said, "Why don't we go in Cagle's car." Rowe protested that Cagle's car was falling apart. (The bureau was going to be on the lookout for Rowe's green Chevrolet.) But then he acquiesced, acting "really pissed off." Rowe got into Herman Cash's 1958 Chevy, with Keith and Dinsmore. Reeves and Cagle ferried the rest of the weapons.

On Highway 11 just outside of Tuscaloosa, the roadblocks awaited them. A state trooper flagged the two cars over. A lieutenant walked up and said, "This is not the fucking car," meaning Rowe's Chevy. The trooper said he knew that, but since it had a whip antenna on it, he figured he'd better pull it over. (The Klan Bureau of Investigation, or KBI, had furnished key Klansmen two-way CB radios.) The men's attire—the spanking white regalia of the "security squad"—also spoke to the patrolman's instincts.

As the Klansmen stepped out of the car, the roadside ditches emptied what seemed to Rowe to be a battalion of officers. Rowe recognized the ace state investigator Ben Allen by his crippled arm. The troopers began confiscating the weapons and bandoliers of ammunition. Rowe would claim that a high-ranking officer started to take the bazooka out of the trunk, hesitated, then said, "Ah, crap, there are too many news reporters around here. We've got to give them some-thing, fellows." He took six loaded pistols, two sabres, two bayonets, two night-sticks, and Cash's cotton bale hook—only part of the inventory Rowe would claim was in the car. The officer left the bazooka.

The interrogation of the six suspects, which took place for some reason on the University of Alabama campus, was handled by Ben Allen, veteran of Big Jim Folsom's Klan crackdown of 1949, who had recently conducted the state's investi-gation of the university's soon-to-be black student Vivian Malone and pro-nounced her "good people." He knew Rowe and had occasionally tried to recruit him as a spy. Rowe believed that Allen suspected that he was an FBI informant and was looking to find out how much the bureau knew about state law enforcement. But the Klan chiefs, Bobby Shelton and Hubert Page, had assured Rowe that Allen, too, was "good people." He was the friendly emissary Wallace sent to visit Shelton at the Bell Café, to make sure that their deal of no-violence-at-the-schoolhouse-door was still on.

As Allen began questioning him, the alcohol-addled Herman Cash, with no front teeth to boot, looked as if he was about to faint. His Klan brethren had lately been calling him "Fearless" and "Ole Blood and Guts," his nerves were showing so. Allen took Rowe aside, Rowe would claim repeatedly under oath, and said, "You better get that guy to shut his goddamn mouth. Man, he's going to crap out everything he knows on you guys within five minutes." Perhaps Cash had the Klan's last major operation on his mind; investigators would conclude that his car transported the bombers to the Gaston Motel on the night of May 11. There was a good chance that Allen himself had a fair idea of what went down that night, since his Klan informant had alerted him to the motel bombing in advance.

Rowe would claim that at Allen's insistence he went up to Cash and said, "Hot sucker, if you don't straighten up, I'm gonna kill your goddamn ass when we leave here. You won't never see home. Knock that shit out."

"I can't help it, man, that they got us," Cash said, crying boozy tears. "They gonna hang us all."

"How in the fuck are they gonna hang you for riding in a goddamn car with a machine gun?" Rowe asked. "They ain't going to hang you for that."

Ben Allen, according to Rowe, separated Rowe and Cash from the rest of the group (and hence from the other officers). Then, according to Rowe, Allen said to Cash, "Hey, you're not worried about that bombing, are you?"

Cash said, "I don't know nothing, I don't know nothing. Please, please, look, I'll get on my knees. Just let me go. If you let me go you'll never see me again." The six men were taken to jail. The master of ceremonies for the Klan rally of 3,000 (mostly teenagers) posted bond for his brothers—and was himself arrested when two pistols were found in his car.

The next day, according to Rowe, he and Eastview Exalted Cyclops Robert Thomas drove back down to Tuscaloosa to pick up their weapons. Shelton intro-duced him to a judge who had twice let his courtroom be used for nighttime Klan meetings, with Shelton sitting on the judge's bench and the KBI security guards in the jury box. "I want to congratulate you for being an outstanding American," Rowe claimed that the judge said before sending them on their way back to Birmingham. "Take your weapons, and use them well."

"You can't have those weapons back," Rowe's handler at the FBI said after getting the day's report, and insisted they were locked in an evidence vault. Rowe invited him to look in the trunk of the car and pointed out the serial numbers, which matched those of the "confiscated" weapons. The cases never came to trial.

Rehearsal

Two documentary filmmakers, Robert Drew and Ricky Leacock, who had been given special access to candidate John Kennedy in 1960 to produce their breakthrough cinema vérité documentary, *Primary,* had gotten permission from all the principals to film the University of Alabama desegregation crisis. This added to the growing sense that the Stand in the Schoolhouse Door was a show.

Lou Oberdorfer, the administration's advance man in his home state, was rounding up extras for the government's side. He had called his friend the CIO lawyer Jerome "Buddy" Cooper to see if he could send some "reliable" union men, thug impersonators presumably, to Tuscaloosa to keep a lid on Shelton's rubber workers. That turned out not to be necessary. The state-provided security around the university was so tight that the school administration had to issue Deputy Attorney General Nicholas Katzenbach a faculty card so that he could get on campus when he arrived on Monday, Schoolhouse Door Day Minus One. In the hope of preventing "another Oxford," the federal men had brought a high-tech military communication system—red phones and all—so sophisticated that Katzenbach "could talk to Berlin."

U.S. troops quartered at an abandoned school in a nearby town had found a soldier roughly Wallace's pint size and practiced yanking him up by the armpits and walking him off Groucho Marx style. General Creighton Abrams was again in command of the military. At Foster Auditorium, the governor's press secretary, Bill Jones, had the grounds crew paint a white line several yards from where Wallace's lectern would be planted, beyond which reporters would not be allowed. The eager crew had also drawn a line that the federal authorities were not supposed to cross.

Meanwhile, the students, James Hood and Vivian Malone, were being prepped by Justice's John Doar. Perhaps thinking of Autherine Lucy's peach outfit, he told them to "dress as if you were going to church, for example—modestly, neatly."

At a White House meeting that Monday, John Kennedy asked his brother what he had planned if Wallace didn't step aside.

"We'll try to get by him," Robert said.

"Pushing?" the President asked.

Robert said, "By pushing a little bit."

Act One

ON TUESDAY, show time, George Wallace summoned two favored reporters to his Tuscaloosa hotel room, chewed on last night's stogie, and japed, "Boys, I feel a little sick this morning; I think I'll stay in bed today."

Downstairs in the Stafford Hotel's lobby, Bobby Shelton exchanged pleasantries with the town's "best people." Finally, Wallace made his way to an air-conditioned office at Foster Auditorium to await his opening scene. His entourage sensed he was in a sweat. He kept asking investigator Ben Allen if he thought they would put him in jail. Now and then, he walked over to the ground-level window and clowned for the press corps crushed together outside. Pretending that some burglar wiring was jail bars, he wailed, "This where the federal government gon' have me."

Katzenbach, who was driving Vivian Malone and James Hood down from Birmingham, was late for the ten-thirty curtain. The university's president, Frank Rose, and the trustees watched the auditorium from Coach Paul Bryant's office forty or fifty yards away. Since the respected Oliver Cromwell Carmichael had vacated the presidency on New Year's Eve, 1956—a casualty of the Autherine Lucy riots—Rose, the unimpressively credentialed young former president of Transylvania College in Kentucky, had presided over the educational equivalent of a tinpot dictatorship. Faculty worth the name had fled, and Shelton's spies had infiltrated the university enough to silence any remaining liberal professors. Alabama was the last state in the country with an all-white state university, but Rose had managed to create a magical universe apart from the social and academic strife by a single hire: Coach Bryant, owner of a National College Football Championship. But the Bear had refused Robert Kennedy's entreaties to stand up to Wallace.

Four hundred reporters toed the white line, among them the Associated Press's Bill Hudson, the still largely anonymous media hero of May 3. He wasn't broadcasting his proprietorship of the picture of Walter Gadsden and Leo, since even his sister, a married student at the university, had shot him a look on campus that said, "Get away. Y'all are causing us a lot of problems."

The federal motorcade finally pulled up to Foster Auditorium and Katzenbach lumbered out. He was six feet two, two hundred pounds, with a prominent bald pate and a lurking quality—perhaps a certain Princeton insouciance that belied his having survived a German POW camp. Wallace, all adrenaline and vinegar, stepped out from the shadows of the columned facade of the auditorium built with New Deal funds, in an era when Wallace and a progressive federal government were on the same side.

Malone and Hood remained in the car. Katzenbach approached, demonstrating his contempt for the theatrics by stepping over the white line in the dust.

Wallace signaled him to halt by holding up his hand like a traffic cop. The only instruction Katzenbach had received from the President—via the attorney general, over a pay phone at a shopping center en route from Birmingham—was to make Wallace "look silly." That much he had accomplished without saying a word.

Katzenbach's dome glistened under the ninety-five-degree sun, and his pants leg shook. Katzenbach would later say that the reason he was nervous was that he knew the President was watching. Amid the bank of hostile Alabamians, about ten feet to Wallace's left in the second row, was a friendly face: Joe Dolan, his own deputy, had been waiting inside the auditorium for the grand gubernatorial entrance and had simply walked in with the Alabama cast. Katzenbach handed the governor the presidential cease-and-desist proclamation and asked if he would abide by it. "No," Wallace said. Katzenbach folded his arms across his chest and countered brusquely. Wallace cut him off. "Now you make your statement because we don't need your speech," he said. Katzenbach retorted in kind.

In Bear Bryant's office, Frank Rose was on the phone with President Kennedy. "What's happening?" Kennedy asked. "When's he going to leave?" Rose didn't know. Kennedy said, "We're going to send in troops."

Wallace was making his prepared statement. Ace Carter was apparently its principal author. The governor said, "I stand before you today in place of thousands of other Alabamians whose presence would have confronted you had I been derelict and neglected to fulfill the responsibilities of my office." After denouncing the "central government" twice, Wallace ended his first scene with a little stutter-step backward into the fold of a couple of burly bodyguards.*

Katzenbach smiled. "I'm not interested in a *show*," he said to Wallace. "I do not know what the purpose of the *show* is. I am interested in the orders of this court being enforced. That is my only responsibility here. I ask you once more. The choice is yours. There is no choice that the United States government has in this but to see that the lawful orders of this court are enforced." Wallace extended his jaw in reply. Act One ended with Katzenbach leaning forward, as if the governor's hearing were acting up again, and enunciating carefully that the students "will register today to go to school tomorrow and go to school this summer." The line did not quite have the ring of segregation tomorrow and forever, but at least it had truth on its side.

Sad Duty

AT INTERMISSION, Vivian Malone and Jimmy Hood were taken to their dormitories; Katzenbach had procured their room keys in advance. Several girls joined Malone for lunch in the dining room, by prearrangement with the Justice Depart-

---

* They appeared to be state troopers, not Klansmen, despite Gary Thomas Rowe's claim that Eastview Exalted Cyclops Robert Thomas's wife, Mildred, had informed him that one of the bones Wallace had thrown to Shelton was to let Klansmen be his bodyguards for the Stand.

ment, which was hoping to avoid the kind of food fight that had broken out during James Meredith's first cafeteria appearance at Ole Miss. Wallace sat down to a lunch of iced tea and steak covered with ketchup. In Washington, Burke Marshall had finally had enough of humoring cryptic Alabamians. Rather than agonize any further over federalizing the National Guard, he said to Robert Kennedy, "Why don't we just go ahead and do it?"

Henry Graham, the National Guard general who had brought some courtliness to martial-law Montgomery during the Freedom Rides, was observing soldiers train at Fort McClellan outside Anniston, a couple of hours from Tuscaloosa by car, when he got word that his presence was wanted at the university. Perhaps Lou Oberdorfer, as the family friend of Joe Gelders, had warned his colleagues to bypass Graham's superior, General Walter "Crack" Hanna, on the grounds that they might have to worry about which side he would be on. Hanna had been sent to Atlanta on some make-work mission.

Though the Wallace camp was getting reports that the "central government" was approaching this little charade like "Eisenhower's invasion of Europe," Graham marched up the auditorium steps at three-thirty leading only four enlisted men. He stopped three feet from the governor. One of Wallace's more moderate aides thought federalizing the National Guard was a brilliant solution: much better for Wallace to step aside for General Graham than for Katzenbach or the Union Army. Graham would muster the day's only real eloquence when he saluted his former commander in chief and said, "Sir, it is my sad duty to ask you to step aside under orders from the President of the United States."

As the governor exited, one of the sharpshooter troopers posted atop Foster Auditorium waved a flag. It was, in William Faulkner's sardonic description of the Confederate battle flag, white.

For now, the administration's biggest fear about Wallace was that Judge Seybourn Lynne would insist on jailing him for disobeying his injunction. Katzenbach believed that Wallace technically *was* in contempt of court, but he also thought, "What difference did it make? We didn't want to arrest the governor." Katzenbach's enduring regret would be that instead of making Wallace look ridiculous, he had "launched him on his presidential campaign." By pitting Wallace against an ancient carpetbagging enemy rather than against two young black Alabamians, Katzenbach had resanctified the old racist agenda of "states rights," whose currency Wallace would draw out into the next decades, and into the rest of the country.

A Moral Issue

AT SIX O'CLOCK, President Kennedy personally called the television networks and asked them to give him fifteen minutes beginning at eight. In the jubilant mood after Joe Dolan and John Doar escorted Vivian Malone and Jimmy Hood into Foster Auditorium to sign up for their classes, the President had decided to make the civil rights address the attorney general had urged him to make the night before, even though it was unanimously opposed by his own staff. Robert Kennedy took time out to scribble notes to his children. "I hope when you are Attorney General, these kind of things will not go on," he wrote to his son Michael.

In fact, the speech had almost been made a month earlier, after the Gaston Motel was bombed and the President's men huddled in the Cabinet Room trying to figure out how to send troops to Birmingham without making it look like the Second Reconstruction. That Sunday night, Robert Kennedy, Nick Katzenbach, Burke Marshall, and the President's press secretary, Pierre Salinger, had sweated out the statement the President was going to make on national television about the Birmingham situation. The speech had been passed among them like a hot potato, with abrupt switches of handwriting and tone in the middle of a page. The most distinctive words were written in a bold script that none of the principals would be able to identify in later years. They had seemed too warm and moist for the dryly ironic President and had not made it into the final draft: "One of the great moral issues of our time is the achievement of equal opportunity for all citizens. Too long have negroes been denied fair treatment and equal opportunity in all parts of our land. . . . These are problems which must concern all of us and to which all of us have a moral obligation to put right."

Now, a month later, the mantle of resistance having passed from Bull Connor to the more resourceful George Wallace, the time for those discarded ideas had come. The President would finally have to speak from his heart rather than his head. There was a model for the speech, from an unlikely source. In October 1921, President Warren Harding had journeyed to Birmingham for the pageantry honoring the fiftieth birthday of what a booster called "the Magic City of the World, the marvel of the South, the miracle of the Continent, the dream of the Hemisphere, the vision of all Mankind." It was perhaps because Hugo Black had just won an acquittal for the Klan parson who assassinated Father James Coyle that Harding was inspired to abandon his boilerplate congratulations and discourse instead on "the problem of democracy everywhere," race. "Whether you like it or not," Harding told the white members of his segregated audience, "unless our democracy is a lie, you must stand for that equality." It became known locally as "Harding's Negro Speech," and Birmingham was still cross about it.

Forty-five minutes before President Kennedy was to go on air, his speech was not written. A draft that Robert had sent over from Justice was unsatisfactory. The President jotted down notes "on the back of an envelope or something." Generating pith in another room was his speechwriter Theodore Sorensen. Burke Marshall sat enclosed in his famous quiet, wondering how a speech could possibly be pulled together in time. President Kennedy relaxed by watching TV. The only anxiety he betrayed was when he walked down the hall to Sorensen's office—for the only time in his life—and asked, "How's it coming?" Sorensen returned to the Oval Office at five to eight, and the President spent three minutes reading the draft.

As the TV cameras rolled, Kennedy began rather curtly with the announcement that "the presence of the National Guard was required on the campus of the

University of Alabama." He then moved quickly beyond the facts: "I hope that
every American, regardless of where he lives, will stop and examine his conscience about this and related incidents." The speech's Golden Rule theme
mounted to the point: "Who among us would be content to have the color of his
skin changed and stand in [the Negro's] place?"

The address was in many respects a reply to Martin Luther King's "Letter
from Birmingham Jail," which had been privately sent to the administration.
Kennedy's rationale for federal invention relied on the same "interrelatedness of
all communities" argument that King had made to dismiss the "outside agitator"
charges against him. King's homiletic "Injustice anywhere is a threat to justice
everywhere" became Kennedy's terse "And this nation, for all its hopes and all its
boasts, will not be fully free until all its citizens are free." But while King had
made sure his letter avoided folk-preaching, keeping to a high theoretical plane,
Kennedy struck an evangelical tone unusual for him. "We are confronted primarily with a moral issue. It is as old as the Scriptures and is as clear as the American Constitution."

And for that reason he was sending up to Congress legislation that would
"make a commitment it has not fully made in this century to the proposition that
race has no place in American life or law."

It was a knock 'em dead performance, extemporized ending and all. And
John F. Kennedy had accepted the possibility that it might be his political swan
song, the death of his effectiveness as president.

Medgar Evers

AS THE PRESIDENTIAL address jockeyed with the Schoolhouse Door for the
next day's banner headlines, Dan Rather of CBS News was enjoying the post-
battle letdown with the rest of the nation's first-string field reporters in
Tuscaloosa. Late that Tuesday night, a source called him from Jackson: Medgar
Evers, the NAACP's civil rights lone ranger of Mississippi, was dead.

When President Kennedy had spoken earlier in the evening of "the events of
Birmingham and elsewhere" that had occasioned his bold action, the "elsewhere"
he had principally in mind was Jackson. Immediately after the Birmingham settlement, Evers had proclaimed in an unprecedented broadcast over local television, "In the racial picture things will never be as they once were. History has
reached a turning point, here and over the world." He asked Jackson's mayor to
appoint a biracial committee to hammer out the Birmingham blueprint for desegregation. The predictable double crosses by the city fathers had followed, and the
NAACP's chief Roy Wilkins had flown down to Jackson on June 1 and gotten
himself arrested with Evers in front of Woolworth's. Thanks to Birmingham, direct action had suddenly been switched from the "radical experiment" column to
"standard operating procedure."

By the time the front-page civil rights dateline moved to Tuscaloosa, Evers
was in a stalemate with the city of Jackson. The night of Kennedy's address, he re-

turned home late from a strategy session, buoyed by the prospects of a federal civil rights act. Across the street, Byron de la Beckwith, a white fertilizer salesman active in the Citizen Councils, was concealed in a tangle of honeysuckle. He leveled his deer rifle at Evers's white-shirted back and fired. Evers's last words, uttered to neighbors and policemen trying to pile him into a station wagon, were as allegorical as the spirituals: "Turn me loose!"

Dan Rather chartered a plane out of Tuscaloosa and was the first national reporter on the scene. At around dawn, he filed his first report, for radio, from a pay phone down the street from the Evers house. When Rather got back to his motel, his heart leaped when he saw a message from "Volunteer." While covering Birmingham, he had rather bumptiously told Martin Luther King that if he ever needed to reach him, instead of leaving his own name with a segregationist switchboard operator, he could just say he was "Mr. Volunteer." King's question to Rather when he returned the call might have struck more naive souls as paranoid: Did Rather have any evidence that police were involved—not merely the Jackson police, but other law enforcement agencies, like the FBI?* The object of an FBI conspiracy himself, King had let his mind race ahead to the ultimate demonic plot—a political assassination engineered by his own government.

In Saigon that day, a Buddhist monk set himself on fire in protest of the suppression of Buddhists by Vietnam's Catholic government. Malcolm Browne's photograph of that suicide would join Bill Hudson's shot of Walter Gadsden, Dick Middleton, and Leo in the finals for the Pulitzer Prize for photography, two images that would equally define their decade.

George Wallace declined a curtain call the following day, June 13. Chuck Morgan's "young scientist," as he had encouraged the press to call Dave McGlathery, drove his own Buick up to the university's Huntsville campus, trailed discreetly by Joe Dolan and Chief U.S. Marshal James McShane. In deference to his lonesome walk to the schoolhouse door, the Kennedy men lay on their bellies in the lawn to observe. Beside them Ricky Leacock's cameraman shot the scene through leaves of grass.

---

* Byron de la Beckwith (called DeeLay after his middle name) would be tried, twice, for the murder, both trials ending in hung juries, before a fresh generation of Mississippians convicted him of the assassination of Medgar Evers in 1994.

22.

THE END OF SEGREGATION

The Second Reconstruction

PRESIDENT KENNEDY had second thoughts about his June 11 speech. Suddenly, even Democrats the administration had taken for granted, not merely the expected southern legislators, were reneging on unrelated Kennedy programs like public works. Space, agriculture, and foreign aid legislation hung in the limbo of the civil rights bill. When the President needled his brother, Robert would say, with more admiration than blame, that "it was Burke Marshall who had gotten both of us in trouble." Marshall broke his reserve to say of the speech, "I thought it was great. He put the problem very well." For once, Martin Luther King found no fault with his President: "He was really great."

Marshall went to pick the brain of the administration's legislative maestro, Vice President Lyndon Johnson. So far Johnson had been only passingly consulted on the civil rights bill, perhaps because of Robert Kennedy's dislike of him. In a June 3 meeting with Norb Schlei, the Justice lawyer in charge of drafting the bill, Johnson had argued passionately that the President should speak out for civil rights in moral terms, tell the nation that we had to do the right thing. "Let's talk about God and morality and goodness and simple justice and patriotism and get that involved in this thing." Perhaps it was Johnson's advice that had made the President go so atypically spiritual in introducing the bill a week later. But the Vice President's fervor had subsided by the time Marshall appeared in his office after the speech. He now believed that the administration ought to frame the issue in economic terms, as the civil rights crusade at the core of his future presidency would be called a War on Poverty.

Johnson's ideal for government action was based on his formative experience during the New Deal working with Aubrey Williams's racially progressive National Youth Administration in Texas. Williams, Johnson's mentor and a white godfather of the current civil rights movement as the Montgomery-based president of the Southern Conference Educational Fund, had been the principal author of the twentieth century's last significant civil rights initiative, the Committee on Fair Employment Practice. The FEPC had been created by the executive order of Franklin Roosevelt in 1941 to end race discrimination in defense industries. President Kennedy was acutely mindful of the tumultuous career of the FEPC. It had been the federal insult that launched the previous Birmingham movement, the States Rights backlash that culminated in the Dixiecrat revolt of 1948. And in the case of the FEPC, the South had won: The committee had been put on ice after the segregationist outcry against its first southern hearings, in Birmingham in 1942. Kennedy knew how Truman's attempts to make the FEPC into a permanent agency had reaped him a whirlwind, and that was not the least of the symmetry between then and now.

The spark that had led to the creation of the FEPC was a great demonstration Philip Randolph had begun planning in 1940 with help from sleeping car porters around the country. It was to be a massive descent along the nonviolent principles of Gandhi of tens of thousands of Negroes on the capital to protest racial discrimination in war industries and the armed forces. He was calling it the March on Washington. As the day approached, July 14, 1941, Randolph's new assistant, Bayard Rustin, was arranging the bus transportation for young people while Randolph negotiated behind the scenes with Aubrey Williams, whom Roosevelt had sent over to forestall the demonstration. "Hell, Williams will join them," a presidential aide complained. And indeed Williams had been only too happy to give Randolph Executive Order 8802, establishing the Committee on Fair Employment Practice. In return, Randolph canceled the march.

Rustin had been critical of Randolph for abandoning the protest, and now he was about to be acquitted. Since late 1962, Randolph had been plotting, again with Rustin as his deputy, another March on Washington. Going through Fred Shuttlesworth, he had persuaded Martin Luther King to put SCLC behind it, and the breakthrough at Birmingham now gave Randolph a specific reason to march—the passage of the civil rights bill—that elegantly circled back to his original dream.

After a June 18 meeting with Randolph in New York, Shuttlesworth, King, and Ralph Abernathy flew to Birmingham, where the Alabama Christian Movement's officers were furious that their organization was operating in the red despite the fund-raising bonanza that Bull's dogs and hoses had brought SCLC. But the fortunes of one city's Negroes now seemed but a minor piece of the meaning of Birmingham. At the mass meeting on Thursday, June 20, the day after Kennedy sent his civil rights bill up to Capitol Hill, King was bursting with the bold new plans to help pass it. "As soon as they start to filibuster," he said of the congressional southerners, "I think we should march on Washington with a quarter of a million people." From New York the following morning came the official announcement that the March on Washington would take place in August.

Problems

PRESIDENT KENNEDY had been keeping King at arm's length since Birmingham. The Kennedys were terrified that the "Communist influences" on the Movement—J. Edgar Hoover's idée fixe—would taint their bill. On Saturday, June 22, the President subtly minimized King's stature by including him in a group appointment with the civil rights board of directors—Farmer, Wilkins, Randolph, SNCC's new chairman, John Lewis. Before the meeting, the President took King into the Rose Garden and told him to get rid of Stanley Levison and Jack O'Dell. King did not challenge Kennedy's characterization of O'Dell as the "number five Communist in the United States." But about Levison he insisted on proof—proof that the FBI would not and could not provide.

Shortly after, at ten-thirty, the President greeted the civil rights leaders. He was legitimately concerned that the March on Washington would give fence-sitters in Congress a "not at gunpoint" excuse to vote against his—their—civil rights bill. King agreed that the march might seem "ill-timed." But he had never engaged in a direct-action movement that did not seem ill-timed. "Some people thought Birmingham was ill-timed," he said.

"Including the attorney general," the President said, and added, "I don't think you should be totally harsh on Bull Connor. After all, he has done more for civil rights than almost anybody else." *

The following day, June 23, embracing the simpler obligations of the Cold War, Kennedy left for a European tour that would climax in a speech at the Berlin wall in which he proclaimed himself *"ein Berliner."*

The End of O'Dell

ON JUNE 29, the Justice Department leaked a story to James Free, the longtime Washington correspondent for the *Birmingham News* and the popular steward of the Gridiron Club's famous annual roast of politicians. Free had recently left Burke Marshall a message that he was "being very hard, harsh, and mean to Governor Wallace by not letting him stand in the Schoolhouse Door"—flaunting the camaraderie that characterized his relationship with Justice. Free had been a trusted friend of the department's press spokesman, Edwin Guthman, since the two were reporters together covering Robert Kennedy's work on the McClellan Rackets Committee. Free's front-page story in the June 30 *News* was more than a scoop; it was Justice's ransom note to Martin Luther King. Headlined "King's SCLC Pays O'Dell Despite Denial," it detailed the suspected Communist's continuing presence in SCLC's Manhattan office and his attendance at the Dorchester retreat where Birmingham had been planned.

Six days earlier, in response to the President's Rose Garden warning, O'Dell had been called to an emergency tribunal in New York consisting of King, Wyatt

---

* Standing to close the meeting, Kennedy had remarked, "We all have our problems. You have your problems, I have my problems." His were connected to the ruinous scandal that British War Minister John Profumo had brought on the government of Prime Minister Harold Macmillan by having an adulterous affair with a prostitute named Christine Keeler, who also happened to be sleeping with the Soviet naval attaché in London. The Profumo investigation had turned up the name of Mariella Novotny, a beautiful Anglo-Czech prostitute suspected of being part of a Soviet vice ring operating at the United Nations. Two years earlier, Kennedy's brother-in-law Peter Lawford had reputedly procured Novotny for a presidential tryst in New York.

Walker, Andy Young, and Clarence Jones, among others. Whether O'Dell had formally severed his affiliation with the Communist Party is uncertain; that he had no intention of repudiating it was clear. When Andy Young reported Burke Marshall's suggestion that Levison and O'Dell, if falsely accused, could sue the FBI for slander, O'Dell exploded that he did not consider the "Communist allegations" slander. "Hoover can kiss my ass!" he said. "I am not the issue!" O'Dell warned his colleagues that Hoover would not be content with this pound of flesh. And it would take less than a week for O'Dell's prediction to come true. But what was perhaps most alarming about the leak about O'Dell to the *Birmingham News* was that it had Robert Kennedy's fingerprints on it, rather than J. Edgar Hoover's.

Four days after the SCLC meeting, King sent Marshall a copy of his letter dismissing O'Dell; it read like the jailhouse manifesto of a political prisoner who accepted the punishment while refusing to concede the crime. On the problem of Stanley Levison, however, King balked. For one thing, Levison was not an employee but an unpaid confidant. And even if Levison was (as Hoover told his bosses) a paid agent of the international Soviet espionage "apparatus," what secrets could the civil rights movement possibly hold for the Russians?

Red Bait

FRED SHUTTLESWORTH'S REACTION to the *News*'s "exposé" of O'Dell typically flew in the face of Cold War protocols: "All I can say is that we are going to work with whoever wants to work with us." For the past month, he had been periodically luring the national media to Danville, Virginia, whose mayor was a disciple of Bull Connor's. ("We will hose down the demonstrators and fill every available stockade.") In early July, Shuttlesworth was greeted there by a U.S. marshal with an injunction banning further protests. Shuttlesworth defiantly delivered one of what he called his "riproaring speeches," quoted in *Newsweek*, promising to disturb the peace with a "joyful noise" of loud singing. "If singing 'We Shall Overcome' is upsetting, let's upset the hell out of the community." To his surprise, the authorities didn't bother him, and he headed for the airport to catch a plane to Chicago, to speak at the NAACP's annual convention. When a crowd at Grant Park booed Mayor Richard Daley and J. H. Jackson, the head of the National Baptist Convention, who had come out against the March on Washington, Shuttlesworth calmed the hecklers and soothed the targets as well.

On July 12, Fred and Ruby Shuttlesworth boarded a boat for a five-week tour of Europe and the Holy Land, courtesy of an elderly white New Yorker who contributed to the Southern Conference Educational Fund and had decided the Shuttlesworths needed some R & R. The day of his departure, Fred challenged King via telegram to add the red-baited SCEF to the sponsoring organizations for the March on Washington, preempting any buck-passing by reporting that Philip Randolph, Bayard Rustin, and Wyatt Walker favored it.

Robert Kennedy perhaps had not had the grasp of the Left's interlocking directorate to absorb the warning raised discreetly in a letter from Shuttlesworth on

June 6, seeking the attorney general's blessing for his new position: He had just been elected president of SCEF. The predicament posed by SCEF, as with its cousin the Highlander Folk School, was its nonsectarianism, its leadership's blind eye to the left-wing affiliations of its hardest workers. Given the number of Communist executive directors who had run SCEF's progenitor, the Southern Conference for Human Welfare, what seemed remarkable was that the current SCEF staff apparently contained no Communists. Jack O'Dell seemed to be the only major black Communist to have bridged the old fight for the masses with the new. But that was not how the red-hunters were likely to see things.

In his letter to Kennedy, Shuttlesworth, whose old SCLC mate Ella Baker had joined SCEF as a consultant, noted that though he himself had "never observed anything but complete support for the U.S. Constitution and the American Way of Life" at SCEF, he wanted the attorney general's "opinion of this organization, both as to its past and present status." There is no record of a response from Kennedy, but Martin Luther King had immediately understood the significance of his colleague's new office. When Shuttlesworth broke the news of his SCEF title to him and Abernathy as they drove to an SCLC board meeting in Louisville, they had nearly swerved off the road in their haste to plead with him to resign. Shuttlesworth offered to resign "from SCLC."*

Wallace's Revenge

IT WAS GEORGE WALLACE who brought home to the Kennedy administration the potential for mischief in Shuttlesworth's affiliation with old subversives. The governor had already begun to capitalize on his Schoolhouse Door debut, traveling to Gettysburg on July 1, the hundredth anniversary of the Civil War battle, and announcing that what the country needed was "a Southern President in the White House." On July 15, Wallace came to Washington to testify before Congress against the civil rights bill (or "program of civil wrongs"). He singled out Martin Luther King's "top lieutenant in Alabama, Fred L. Shuttlesworth, a self-styled 'Reverend,'" as the president of SCEF—chartered to "promote communism throughout the South"—and displayed a poster-sized version of the infamous photograph of King at the "Communist training school" (Highlander) taken in 1957 by a professional segregationist on the Georgia state payroll. Wallace was so authoritative that Senators Warren Magnuson of Washington and Mike Monroney of Oklahoma wrote to J. Edgar Hoover for comment.

Upon seeing Wallace's charges as a front-page story in the *New York Times,* Burke Marshall and Robert Kennedy gave their FBI liaison, Courtney Evans, an hour to identify the people in the Highlander photograph. The report that came back was not comforting: Abner Berry had at the time been basically who Wallace said he was, "a Negro member of the Central Committee of the Communist

---

* Anne Braden believed that Shuttlesworth's post-1963 loss of stature in SCLC came as a result not of his disputes with King in Birmingham but of his unapologetic prominence in SCEF.

Party." The good news was that King had been at Highlander only that once. In the allotted hour the bureau had not discovered that Highlander had "trained" some of King's key staff members.

With exquisite bad timing, on July 16, as the papers reported Wallace's conviction that King belonged to more Communist groups than anyone else in America, King's lawyer Clarence Jones, who was negotiating with a Los Angeles filmmaker about a documentary on Birmingham, came calling on Burke Marshall to propose a compromise with the administration in the matter of Stanley Levison, his own mentor as well as King's. Levison and King would suspend all direct contact, but would stay in touch through an intermediary. Jones hinted that Marshall might clue him in on which were the unwiretapped channels of communication. Marshall reported the conversation to the attorney general.

Robert Kennedy was stupefied. Moreover, he was still furious that Jones had remained silent during the horsewhipping at the James Baldwin meeting in May yet afterward privately offered his praise of Justice's work in Birmingham. "He is a nice fellow & you have swell friends," Kennedy had written of Jones to Marshall, his characteristic drollery cut with bitterness. As one who rarely reaped any of Kennedy's famous "impatience," Marshall was perhaps discharging some guilt over having arranged the Baldwin meeting when he entered a temporary truce with J. Edgar Hoover and, at the director's request, provided a list of those who had attended. FBI dossiers on each of them soon appeared on his and the attorney general's desks.

Robert Kennedy's response to Jones's latest impertinence was to order a wiretap on him. The attorney general astounded even the FBI's Courtney Evans by including Martin Luther King in the order. Evans mentioned "the repercussions if it should ever become known that such a surveillance had been put on King." Kennedy said this "did not concern him at all." The government was cutting less slack to disobedient integrationists than it had to obstructionist segregationists such as George Wallace, who had essentially gotten away with defying Federal Judge Seybourn Lynne's order not to stand in the schoolhouse door.

Integration

MAYOR ALBERT BOUTWELL was trying to be as cagey an integrationist as he had been a segregationist. The first institution he had desegregated, on June 29, was the mootest he could find: the city golf courses. The most avid black golfers were the country club caddies, who had their run of the city's greatest greens by sacred custom every Monday.

But finally the illusion in Birmingham that integration was still something that might happen sometime in the future ended on July 16. On the same day that Robert Kennedy decided to wiretap Martin Luther King, Boutwell made good on his off-the-record deal with him and appointed a biracial commission. The Community Affairs Committee would have 212 members so that the blame could be spread among many: representatives from the Lions Club, Rotary, the Chamber of Commerce, the Garden Club. Only twenty-seven were black; one of them, Fred Shuttlesworth's right-hand man, Ed Gardner, would complain that "some of the Negroes who were not connected with the demonstrations are trying to be big now." But in fact the white city fathers had come a long way in their perception of "Responsible Negro Leadership," and the *New York Times* editorial page would give Boutwell a pat on the back. "This is an historic event," he said in his address at the committee's inaugural meeting in the city council chamber as Klan pickets patrolled outside. "It could be the beginning of our finest hour."

Hoover's Degenerates

ROBERT KENNEDY thought better of spying on Martin Luther King once the FBI paperwork had been rushed back to him on July 25. The tap on Clarence Jones's home in Riverdale, New York City, went through, however, even though Stanley Levison had ended up breaking off communication with King to spare his relationship with the President. The Jones tap's early gleanings was the conversations of his houseguest, King, who was in town to work on his book about Birmingham—the last big project that had been on Levison's plate. The taps would prove to be Hoover's winning lottery ticket, all he needed to pursue King to the end. In between editorial sessions in a Riverdale motel with his ghost writer, Al Duckett (the pen behind Jackie Robinson's newspaper column), King found time to fit in his regular New York mistress. Hints of their assignations imprinted on the FBI's tape recorder. The SCLC inner circle was acquainted with the leader's secular alter ego. But this was news to Hoover, excellent news. If King was not a subversive, he was a degenerate hypocrite.

At least King kept his personae as libertine and "national security risk" separate, which was more than could be said for his President. Robert Kennedy had sent Hoover's latest report on King to his brother with a note saying, "I thought you would be interested in the attached memorandum." Earlier in July, FBI agents had paid a call on Ellen Rometsch, an East German who had come to Washington in 1961 as the wife of a West German soldier assigned to the embassy. She soon made a name for herself among the President's buddies as the girl who had given Kennedy "the best time he ever had in his life." Rometsch's lack of discretion tended to undermine the bureau's line on her as a possible East German spy, but on July 23, Courtney Evans filled in Robert Kennedy. The attorney general made plans to have Rometsch quietly deported.

Fields Anointed

JUST AS ROBERT KENNEDY and J. Edgar Hoover were making their accommodation over the civil liberties of Martin Luther King, so had the détente between the Ku Klux Klan and the National States Rights Party warmed into friendship. As Bobby Shelton admitted, "there is not too much difference in philosophy" between the two organizations. It was simply the degree of their fixation on Jews. A recent edition of the NSRP's *Thunderbolt* had reprinted the 1934 "Ritual Murder" issue of *Der Stürmer* (whose editor, Julius Streicher, was sentenced to death by the Nuremberg tribunal) with drawings of Jewish elders using straws to suck the blood of a dead gentile child.

The Klan had always been the regular guys with friends in high places, the descendants of the vigilantes who had fought organized labor. But now Edward Fields, J. B. Stoner, and their NSRP were moving to the center of a racist intrigue so tangled that its various strands were unaware of one another. That summer, the party had hired a spy-courier, Phillip Thomas Mabry (code-named Mockingbird). He was also, he claimed, acting as a messenger between Stoner and Ace Carter (code-named Ace Deuce), who was in contact with Shelton's United Klans. Apparently, Mabry was also supplying information about Carter to Public Safety Director Al Lingo. Mabry believed that Carter, too, was feeding information on Stoner and Shelton to Lingo. Bringing some institutional memory to the new coalitions, Detective Tom Cook, coordinator of the Stoner sting that had resulted in the 1958 bombing of Shuttlesworth's church, attended (undercover) an NSRP rally in early June at which Stoner explained how to make a bomb using a candle as a timing device. "A collection was taken up," Cook noted dryly in his report, "and you owe me $1.00."

In late July came the ultimate anointment of the NSRP. After a rally outside Anniston, a plainclothes state investigator escorted Edward Fields to a motel room to meet with Colonel Al Lingo. The governor needed a reason to close the public schools when they were integrated come fall, Lingo explained, and he wanted the National States Rights Party to provide it. They were to use any means necessary, from petitions to demonstrations, to disrupt the opening of the school year.

In Heaven with the Angels

ON JULY 23, the dismantling of Our Way of Life officially began in Birmingham. The new city council, amazingly, repealed segregation ordinances for restaurants and other places of "public accommodation," such as hotels and motels. The Johannesburg of America was voluntarily enacting the most controversial piece of Kennedy's civil rights bill.

Swastikaed members of the NSRP greeted the trickle of Negroes heading that day for the lunchrooms of Loveman's, Woolworth's, and Kress along Integration Row. Those black would-be diners reflected a technical glitch in the desegregation program being hammered out by the man who had negotiated it with Martin Luther King, David Vann. He had been spending his last six months on the White, Bradley, Arant payroll in an office away from the firm, orchestrating the integration of his city. Such was Vann's reward for having gotten rid of both King and Bull Connor.

Though the merchants now had no intention of promoting *any* Negroes to clerical positions, Vann had managed to convince them that their hands were tied on desegregating lunch counters: The city had repealed the relevant segregation ordinances. He had kept the actual target date of desegregation—July 30—such a secret that the Movement was largely unaware of it, and until then Negroes were turned away from the restaurants.

On Monday, July 29, Martin Luther King and Ralph Abernathy flew in to be at Integration Row the following day, when handpicked black adults braved the NSRP men in storm trooper uniforms and went out to lunch in white Birmingham. The first targets—Pizitz, Newberry's, Loveman's, Kress, Woolworth's—were covered by two detectives inside, with a police contingent on the streets. The black sit-ins were all couples—to preclude any imagery of "mongrelization." At Woolworth's, a white man explained to some white gawkers, "They are Kennedy's kinfolk."

Sympathetic white ringers from the Alabama Council on Human Relations already sat at the lunch counters. The black couples ordered their food, were served, and left after twenty minutes. The following day, lunchrooms were desegregated in outlying Roebuck, Five Points West, Five Points South, and at the fabled Eastwood Mall. The police arrested Edward Fields and two of his Confederate flag–waving followers for "parading without a permit."

The Reverend Calvin Woods, the lunch counter coordinator for the black community, reported, "There were no incidents. The waitresses were very cordial, while the clerks looked on with quiet amazement." And so it went for a few weeks. Every morning, Vann phoned Woods to get the day's lineup. To his surprise, Vann began getting calls from managers of untargeted lunchrooms, asking him to integrate them while he was at it. Woods recorded the reactions of the black lunchers: "They didn't think of me as a Negro, they served in order first come first serve."

"The waitress couldn't have been any nicer, unless she was in heaven with the angels."

McWhorter 1963

MY MOTHER'S DATEBOOK, which went ominously blank during the spring days of Project C, had been reactivated on Monday, May 20, noting the first day of swimming practice for us three children. We had recently become members of the Jewish Community Center, and Mama, conditioned by the Depression to maximize any paid-for opportunity, made my brothers and me join the JCC swim team. Her datebook did not reflect what a big day May 20 had been for Birmingham: The Supreme Court handed down its landmark ruling on Fred Shuttlesworth's sit-in case, which effectively outlawed segregation in public accommodations; and the board of education expelled more than a thousand black schoolchildren for marching with Martin Luther King. It was the simple challenge of a new sport that brought me closer to these historic events, still beyond my personal history.

The JCC's top administrator, Harold Katz, was the boogeyman of our summer vacation. We had no idea that he had more on his mind than shooing us brats out of the center's air-conditioned facility on our noisy retreats from poolside—hence the dreaded words, "Here comes Mistercats." But he was also the point man for Birmingham's besieged Jews. The unwelcome visit from the Yankee rabbis during the demonstrations had thrown the American Jewish leadership into turmoil, and as executive director of the Jewish Community Council (an umbrella over most of the national Jewish organizations represented in the city), Katz had been called upon to provide an accounting for the local Jews' hostility toward the civil rights struggle. It was he who had concluded, in his confidential memorandum to the National Community Relations Advisory Committee, that the desegregation fight was not the business of Jews, but " 'a Christian problem' between whites and Negroes."

Until we joined the center, the subject of Jews had never come up directly in my family, beyond the casual anti-Semitism that made "Jew down" a socially acceptable verb and "Jewish" an adjective for cheap or, you know, loud. I had noticed that my several Jewish classmates at Highlands Day School did not follow the rest of us girls to Brooke Hill, although I would never have dreamed that the school my grandparents founded had an unwritten policy of excluding Jews (because, as one board member explained, they would academically embarrass "our girls"). My grandfather, I would learn later, was an anti-Semite, and upset his wife by complaining about the "Jewish friends" with whom she worked on charity fund-raising drives.

My father, in his continuing rebellion against his father, considered himself something of a semitophile, boasting that the Jewish suppliers of surplus parts for his air compressors referred to him collegially as "McWhorterstein." He claimed Dickie Pizitz as "one of my best friends." Dickie had lived in a mansion down the street from the McWhorters' Hastings Road house and was now Richard, being groomed to take over the store. But of course I should have guessed that he, as one of my father's boyhood pugilistic targets—slight and Harvard bound—did not share Papa's view of their great friendship.

In the summer of 1963, as the National States Rights Party's brownshirts were acting out the fine distinction between attitudes that had been merely considered merely "conforming" for all those years and behavior that was possibly psychopathic, I was working out the third-generation response to my grandfather's anti-Semitism. In a version of my father's sympathy with Jews, I was obliquely refusing to participate in the history of the oppressor. I was "integrating," excited by my new Jewish friends, even if this was partly because of their fascination with me. Wizened grandmothers at the pool rubbed their hands down my chlorine-enhanced blond hair and crooned, "Just like spun gold."

Shame over "mixing" never surfaced in the privacy of my new world of

Jews—I simply worried about them going to hell. But when I ran into my friends from the Birmingham Country Club at a swim meet, I sometimes felt compelled to abandon my own team and sit with the gentiles. I hoped that the BCC kids assumed that I had joined the JCC team because my club, the Mountain Brook, didn't have a swim team, and when they sometimes asked me in lowered voices if I was Jewish, I would snort sarcastically and say, "Yeah, with a name like McWhorter"—and then, "It's really McWhorterstein." I felt caught in the act of some social taboo, discovering (as the South's liberals inevitably did) that it wasn't the minorities the Anglo-Saxon majority feared. It was being stigmatized by one's own tribe.

But then I was learning that the best antidote to social anxiety was winning. During my first weeks on the team, I mastered the hardest stroke of all, the butterfly, with Papa's unorthodox frog kick. As I became more confident, I began cultivating more quirks, like deliberately false-starting off the block and scissoring my legs right before I hit the water. I never took off the shark's-tooth necklace Papa brought me back from Florida, this charm of our shared toughness, even though his perverseness had now taken a troubling turn.

23.

THE BEGINNING OF INTEGRATION

Eastview Unbound

ROBERT CHAMBLISS'S STRUT had become the swagger of desperation. The sky had been falling since the Freedom Riders' beating in 1961—the Klansmen's last hurrah as establishment vigilantes. But if that international embarrassment had alienated the old industrial sponsors, now even the Klansmen's political patron, Bull Connor, was gone. As Eastview 13 became more marginal, dissension ruled the klavern. There was friction between Chambliss and his best friend, Troy Ingram, the source of it dynamite. Chambliss had long been considered the best bomb maker in Birmingham, but something had made Ingram pretend to the title—maybe it was the Gaston Motel dynamite package. Their shoptalk now had bursts of cryptic boasting, as if they were rival Cold War superpowers eyeing the nuclear brink.

The ultimate sign of Chambliss's frustration with Eastview 13 was that he had joined up with the National States Rights Party crowd. He was helping Edward Fields get signatures for the petition George Wallace had requested to protest school desegregation. That proud, red-blooded Klansmen like Chambliss were openly allying themselves with neo-Nazis they had always considered perverts demonstrated how little they had to lose. Something seemed to have snapped in place: the critical mass that occurs before fission.

In another destabilizing development, the dawn of Birmingham's new, desegregated civilization had ushered in a generation of Klan young bloods who flouted the conventions of the brotherhood. The rising hotspur of Eastview was Ronnie Tidwell, a redheaded, freckle-faced twenty-eight-year-old electrician (usually unemployed) with a record of grand larceny and firearms violations. Tidwell's wife had recently left him, and he bunked in a trailer on the property of his father, Ira, a lawyer who lived in DeBardeleben coal country outside Birmingham and had hauled timber supports into the mines before putting himself through night school. One of Ira's kin, Bit Tidwell, a miner at Acmar, had been part of a company posse that in May 1934 fired more than five hundred shots into a unionist's house. And it was perhaps the DeBardeleben legacy that accounted for Ronnie's knowledge of dynamite.

At the Thursday-night Eastview meeting of August 1, Tidwell gave a lesson on how to manufacture a bomb. Tommy Rowe was aghast—"real business" was never discussed at an open meeting. (Or perhaps Rowe was feeling competitive: Tidwell, too, was a judo amateur, who also claimed to be a CIA man, recently solicited by the agency to do "missionary work" in Africa.) The bomb makers were an elite brotherhood unto themselves, like the Army's Special Forces. Tidwell was breaking discipline by sharing the skill with regular grunts.

According to Rowe, his handlers at the FBI "went completely ape" over Tidwell's performance. At the next week's meeting, Tidwell demonstrated how to build a much more destructive bomb: a small box containing bolts and screws and metal shards. The idea, he said, was to draw a crowd with the smaller bomb demonstrated the week before, in order to maximize the victim count of the second's flying shrapnel.

This time, Rowe said, he spoke up. He pointed out the problems of not controlling the sources of bombs. Then, performing what the FBI called a little "counterintelligence," Rowe pointed out that there was "power structure going between" the National States Rights Party and the Klan and warned, "The States Righters will go out and pull a bunch of bullshit when we isn't prepared for it and it will fall back on us and we will catch all hell and go to prison for something they did." Rowe had hit a nerve. Loud arguments over the legitimacy of the NSRP suggested that the end of segregation had produced a consensus with which the Klan did not feel comfortable. And Rowe's prophecy of NSRP copycatting soon proved to be on the mark.

Publicity Stunts

AS THE KLAN spun out-of-bounds, the civil rights movement's "extremists" on the other side held the limelight. On August 5, an integrated planeload of entertainers landed at the Municipal Airport. A representative of the American Guild of Actors and Entertainers sat on the mobile runway staircase and introduced each celebrity, the headliner clearly Sammy Davis Jr. "It seemed to be a big publicity stunt," a detective on hand noted. Martin Luther King arrived on the 6:35 Eastern flight from Atlanta. And then Ray Charles's private plane taxied up, carrying thirty-five more artistes. Marian Anderson, the great contralto, arrived to carry on the fight she had begun twenty-four years earlier when she sang "America" at the Lincoln Memorial after the Daughters of the American Revolution barred her from performing in their Constitution Hall. Rounding out the icons were James Baldwin and Joe Louis.

They had come for a "Salute to Freedom, 1963," to raise money for the Birmingham movement's expenses to attend the March on Washington. "The $5 tickets will put you close up front," Ed Gardner had told a mass meeting, "and the

$4 tickets will put you next to the person that is close up." After the Municipal Auditorium and Legion Field rebuffed these international stars, the concert went on before an integrated audience at the Miles College stadium, whose makeshift stage collapsed after Johnny Mathis finished his number.

The next day at Integration Row, a white crowd vowed to answer the March on Washington with one of its own showcasing George Wallace and Governor Ross Barnett of Mississippi. Classic riot conditions were fanned by rumors that the manager of the Loveman's tearoom had held a chair out for a black female customer. Merchants discovered racks of ladies' dresses cut beyond repair.

Heat

DR. EDWARD FIELDS held an NSRP event at the Cascade Plunge on the evening of August 9, while the true-blue Klansmen rallied at a National Guard armory across town, in one last effort to assert mainstream status. Art Hanes and Bull Connor had come to grace the stage, but it soon became clear that they had lost hold of their constituents along with their offices. The air was warm with the fellowship of three or four hundred men and women. News reporters were beginning to catch some of the heat. A man lunged toward a newsman with a chair, and another got so close to the working press that Connor jumped out of his seat to restrain him. Bull tried to seize the mob's attention with boasts of how well he had handled the recent trouble. Hanes accused David Vann of being a Communist. Even if anyone had been listening, the staticky sound system would have prevented them from hearing, and at eleven o'clock the rally ended in the conviction that the Klan no longer spoke for anyone but itself.

Preview

FROM THE TOWN OF WARRIOR, northwest of Birmingham, came a flash of Klan violence, like a tracer bullet giving a glimmer of heavy artillery fire to follow. In a vacant lot next to a new community center, the annual carnival was in full swing. Word had gotten out that Negroes were being admitted for the first time. As the all-white Kiddielands had provided the racial epiphany for many a black parent, including Martin Luther King, so did such amusements constitute a last stand for the racists. Why did "they" need to encroach on these carefully planned zones of pleasure?

The hard-core Eastview Klansmen, who had regarded Warrior as their unregulated playground, decided to attend the carnival's closing night, August 10. Thirty-five men, among them the seasoned missionary Gene Reeves, Exalted Cyclops Robert Thomas, and allegedly Tommy Rowe, gathered at the Warrior bus station. There they were supposed to create a decoy ruckus so that Charles Cagle (who had lost his welding job as a result of his arrest for transporting arms to Tuscaloosa—the only punishment meted out for the incident) and Levie "Quickdraw" Yarbrough (a prison guard at a county work camp whose car had been spotted near the Gaston Motel just before it was bombed) could attend to some unfinished business.

At around nine, an informant would later tell the FBI, Cagle and Yarbrough drove a pale blue Ford that investigator's would conclude belonged to Gene Reeves over to St. James Methodist, a church they had thrown a jar of gasoline into the previous November only to have the jug break and the wick burn out. Stopping at the east side of the building, they got out of the car and heaved a five-gallon can of gasoline through the window. One of them lit a rag and tossed it inside. This time the fire did not go out.

The Reverend L. B. Bolling arrived at nine-thirty to watch the pumpers try in vain to save his church. The police couldn't figure out why anybody would go after St. James Methodist, which had suffered the same fiery fate back in the Klan heyday of 1926. Popular among blacks and whites, Bolling had never been involved in any integration mess.

Copycats

TWO DAYS AFTER the Warrior church torching, on Monday, August 12, Albert Francis DeShazo told his landlady not to shop at any of the integrated downtown stores on Thursday or Friday because she "might get hurt." DeShazo was typical of the neurotics who made up the youth end of the still sparse official ranks of the National States Rights Party. He had lost two of his childhood guardians—his father and an uncle—to Bryce, the state mental hospital, and, at age twenty-three, had a rap sheet that included desertion from the Army, burglary, and robbery. DeShazo had been captivated by the NSRP's paraphernalia—the uniforms and other Naziana—in the way that other post-teens were drawn to the trappings of college Greek life.

On Thursday, August 15, according to his landlady, DeShazo put on a dark blue suit and dark-framed glasses. At 11:25, a clerk in the men's department of Loveman's saw a man in a blue suit and glasses riding the down escalator. Nearing the first floor, he tossed a beer-can canister into the garbage. It thocked with a flash of fire and then spewed yellowish-green tear gas. A large black woman with several children hollered and bolted up the down escalator. The bomb thrower hurried through the men's department and left the store. As customers fled, coughing and gagging, the house detective, Martin Emanuel, fished the fizzling bomb out of the trash and took it to the door. The manager closed the store at noon.[*]

Compared to the Ku Klux Klan's dynamite attacks on churches, the States Righters' tear-gas canister seemed second-rate. But for the white mainstream, it was the reckoning. In the collapse of segregation, even the bombers had ceased to observe Jim Crow and were striking at the national pastime, shopping. Accord-

---

[*] Though the investigation would focus on the NSRP, police detectives initially showed witnesses photographs of the *News's* mischievous reporter, Tom Lankford.

ingly, Mayor Albert Boutwell seemed to draw a distinction between "innocent" and deserving targets in his statement of unprecedented outrage against the bomber—"a human being so totally indifferent to innocent human lives."

Accustomed to dynamite, the Movement was unfazed by tear gas. "If you are at the lunch counter eating and a tear-gas bomb explodes," Ed Gardner told a mass meeting, "just blow the gas out your nose and keep on eating."

The Arrival of *Brown*

THE INTEGRATION OF the Birmingham public schools moved into the "inevitable" column on August 19, when Judge Clarence Allgood approved the Birmingham Board of Education's desegregation plan, as demanded in July by the Fifth Circuit Court of Appeals. Allgood seemed not to have quite appreciated the momentousness of this token integration program, which would admit no more than five black children to the formerly white schools, until Robert Kennedy called with his congratulations and asked how many troops and marshals he would need to enforce his order.

The following morning, Tuesday, August 20, Jack Cash departed on a fishing trip on the Tennessee River. It seemed a strange time to be leaving his cafe shorthanded. The Klan was holding a meeting in Bessemer that evening, which meant there would be a big drinking crowd late into the night. By the end of the day it became clear that his was only one of the alibis multiplying like mushrooms.

The Harley aficionado Ross Keith, an Eastview squad leader and member of the security guard, joined several other klavern members at the Bessemer meeting, after which he went with Nigger Hall and Sister White to the Log Cabin Cafe and insulted his diabetic system with a fifth of whiskey. Since shortly after his arrest outside Tuscaloosa in June, Keith, who had a wife and children, had been dating a Log Cabin waitress named Wyvonne Lavelle Fike, a twenty-seven-year-old mother of three who was divorced from a burglar serving his time. Klan meeting night was "girlfriend night," since the wives weren't expecting their husbands home anytime in particular. Usually, Fike and Keith parked after "church" (as Klan sessions were called) in his Chevy; he always removed his .45 automatic from the glove compartment and put it on the dash. But on that night of August 20, Keith drove Fike straight home from the Log Cabin.

As they turned onto Third Avenue West, he said, "I might need your help after tonight." Savoring his importance, he added, "I might need you to prove where I was and that I was with you." Fike looked at her watch. It was nine o'clock. At her house in Bessemer, Keith walked her to the door and left.

At 9:26, a bomb blew up the front of Arthur Shores's fashionable three-year-old brick ranch house on Dynamite Hill, collapsing the garage onto his Cadillac and his Plymouth. The bombers must not have realized that the previous day's school desegregation victory had been one of Shuttlesworth's projects shunned by Shores, who had been inside his home alone watching television in bed and was not injured by the blast.

Apparently, as he would later tell Rowe, Ross Keith had gotten his motorcycle after dropping off Fike, and possibly Sister White had ridden his own motorcycle to Dynamite Hill. According to Rowe, Keith and White placed the bomb while Charles Cagle and Nigger Hall, sitting on Keith's Harley, served as lookouts. Before Keith and White could get away, the dynamite exploded with such force that it "ricocheted" Keith down the alley behind Shores's house. "That goddamned Sister stumbled and I liked to fell all over her," Keith would say. He had thought his "whole head was going to get blown off," and with his ears still ringing half an hour later, he went to a doctor to see if his hearing was damaged permanently.

For the first time in more than three months, the Movement's leaders rushed toward the scent of nitroglycerin and the angry noises of their people. When the Reverend Nelson "Fireball" Smith arrived, A. D. King and Charles Billups were already on the top of a police car making pleas for peace. "If you are going to kill someone, kill me," A. D. King shouted at the crowd. "The police are mad; now y'all go on." Detective Maurice House said, "A. D., don't say we're mad, you'll get us all killed." Some officers, expecting as much, had been issued submachine guns. "They stand here with pistols and other magic power," King persisted. "We can't beat them tonight. We are going to win this town regardless of what they do. Stand if you must—stand in love, not violence." A barrage of rocks answered him. A policeman positioned between two parked cars was felled by a flying rock, and Smith's leg was hit. He and King went into Shores's house to attend to a chip fracture on Smith's shinbone, leaving the mob to its momentum.

Troy Ingram came in from over the mountain. Tommy Rowe would later claim that Ronnie Tidwell had made the bomb in Ingram's garage, and perhaps Ingram wanted to see his protégé's handiwork. But as Sister White, who had almost gotten blown up by the effort, complained repeatedly thereafter, "Ronnie Tidwell was a piss-poor bomb maker."

The Shores bombing was obviously a pan-Eastview undertaking. Exalted Cyclops Robert Thomas virtually admitted to FBI agents that he had purposely established an alibi: Eastview had called a special "physical training" class that let out at 9:20, six minutes before the explosion. But the first team of seasoned "missionaries" had hung back, content to watch the novitiates, such as Sister and Nigger, and bide their time for their turn. Throughout the evening, Robert Chambliss and Tommy Blanton had engaged in a flurry of phone calls in front of witnesses, as if following a manual for "Creating an Alibi."* Bobby Cherry, Eastview's other explosives ace, who had recently fired his .22 at the feet of some Negroes throwing rocks on his lawn, claimed to have heard about the Shores bombing while watching TV at home in Ensley. "I hope it killed him," he said.

The headline in the next morning's *Post-Herald* was a classic display of

---

* Chambliss had supposedly been seen in the vicinity of the Shores house, but was at home after the bombing, to await the inevitable visit from the FBI. A later polygraph test would indicate that Blanton, who had taken the day off from work, as was his wont around dynamite dates, knew about the bombing though he didn't personally do it.

community priorities: "Rocks Hurled at Police After Negro Lawyer's Home Bombed." The afternoon's *Birmingham News* brought even more mind-boggling headlines. The U.S. attorney for North Alabama, Macon Weaver, had made what the paper boasted was "an unprecedented disclosure of Justice Department secrets" to assign blame in what he too apparently considered the major offense of the night before: the stoning of the police. According to Weaver, the riot had been provoked not by the bombing itself but by the "false charges" that Roosevelt Tatum, the black laborer, had made in May when he accused the Birmingham police of complicity in the dynamiting of A. D. King's house. Tatum had become the object of a puzzling government vendetta since informing the FBI that he had seen a policeman plant the bombs in front of King's house. Deciding to pursue the witness rather than the alleged bombers, the bureau had accused Tatum of making a false statement to an FBI agent under Title 18, Section 1001.

To consider charges, the government had convened a federal grand jury a month ahead of schedule, on June 28. But in July, the head of the Justice Department's criminal division denied U.S. Attorney Weaver permission to prosecute him. Weaver went after Tatum anyway, with an indifference to the chain of command suggesting that he was operating under an authority higher than his division chief. It seemed unlikely that the attorney general himself would have gotten involved in the prosecution of a lowly Birmingham Negro, even if Tatum's lawyer was Kennedy's nemesis Clarence Jones, but undoubtedly the case represented a new low in the dubious record of the FBI. The agency was selectively pursuing a cipher who was only alleging a police-Klan conspiracy that its own star informant had already uncovered, and for a crime that the FBI, if it had wanted to establish federal jurisdiction over the Klan, could have slapped on virtually every Klansman it had ever interviewed.*

Meanwhile, the FBI's reports to Justice about the Shores bombing peddled the segregationists' favorite inside-job theory, noting that an informant saw an "unknown Negro male by Shores's residence acting strangely." Carrying the Big Lie to its logical end, the bureau notified the local police.

The Cahaba River Group

THE BREWING SPLIT in Eastview 13 had centered on one of those badges of authenticity that acquire out-of-scale significance among revolutionaries when the

---

* On the day that Weaver's amazing statements prejudging Tatum's guilt ran in the *News,* the FBI wiretap on Clarence Jones's phone in New York picked up a conversation in which he instructed A. D. King to say that there was a widespread belief among Negroes in Birmingham that the police were not neutral and that he was conducting his own investigation of the May bombing. On August 24, A. D. King called the *News* reporter Tom Lankford in an attempt to get Tatum's story out. He told Lankford of the rigged lie detector test Tatum had been given by the FBI and the bureau's threats of a five-year jail sentence if he didn't repudiate his story about the police. Lankford was even directed to an eyewitness who corroborated the essentials of Tatum's story—a Negro named Shelby "Sheets" Webb. In response to Lankford's story, the FBI considered issuing a press release "denying allegation of intimidation," but decided against it.

cause seems lost. The personal had become the political, as Exalted Cyclops Robert Thomas, a relatively unassuming man not cut out for controversy, was painfully realizing. A faction of the klavern was pressuring him to fire his black cleaning woman. It once had been fashionable for Klansmen to brag that their maids ironed their robes, but the Eastview radicals now believed that Negroes did not even deserve what amounted to prisoner-of-war status. Nor did it help the Exalted Cyclops's position that he worked alongside Negroes repairing railcars for Southern Railway.

Tommy and Pop Blanton were Thomas's leading detractors. The old man shot his mouth off about internal Klan affairs, and Tommy seemed to be moving from Eastview into the camp of the NSRP, picketing with the neo-Nazis down on Integration Row. Blanton's neighbor, Mrs. Freeman Brown, grabbed her binoculars whenever the bark of Tommy's collie signaled the arrival or departure of his car. Over the past few weeks, she had watched the Blantons take things from the car and lock them in the house trailer and sheds in their backyard. One night she looked through the binoculars as Tommy stood in front of a mirror inside his apartment practicing quick draws with his revolver.

The Blantons had become an official Klan problem. Bobby Shelton branded them "undesirables" but offered them leniency if they would agree to cut their ties with Dr. Fields and the NSRP crowd. They refused and were expelled from the United Klans of America.

The Blantons' fellow loudmouth and chief co-conspirator, Robert Chambliss, created a dilemma for Shelton. Like Pop, Chambliss had begun to direct some of his wrath at other Klansmen rather than at the black enemy. His doubts had also centered on the man whose fidelity he had once admired, Tommy Rowe. Acting on his duty as "the oldest Klansman in the United Klans of America," Chambliss had stood up at a Thursday-night meeting and said, "We got a CIA son of a bitch in here we better get rid of before it's too late." Rowe jumped up and asked him what he meant. Chambliss quieted down, but he would claim that the outburst marked him.

But Chambliss, the Klan's continuity to the golden age of the 1920s as well as to the glory days of Dynamite Hill, could not be simply banished. Shelton would attempt to reeducate him before kicking him out. The Imperial Wizard said he was hoping to discourage Chambliss from forming a rival rump group. An FBI informant would later glean a somewhat different interpretation of Shelton's behavior, one that suggested that a rump group was just what the Imperial Wizard wanted, to perform extreme operations that the Klan was too vulnerable to execute.

The Blantons were out of Eastview, and Chambliss was going. So was George Pickle, the malcontent loser who had gone to jail in order to provide his buddies an alibi for the Gaston Motel bombing. Pickle had recently gotten into trouble with the Eastview brass for shooting tires off a Negro's car, and had been squawking about the secrecy of the Klan's financial records. These four men alone—an alcoholic drudge, two white-whiskered veterans of the next-oldest Klan wars, and a sociopath—were unlikely to start any bona fide organization. But there was a leader, a proven statesman, waiting over the mountain for the right brigade. Troy Ingram's moment as Exalted Cyclops had rearrived, now six years after his first crack at the job had been made all too brief by the castration of Judge Aaron.

Ingram's true life passion—coal mining—had finally been spent. He had abandoned his patrimony with little more to show for it than a spot of black lung. His home auto-mechanic business had been good enough to allow him to build a brick house on his property that year, and he still worked free on the jalopies of the Negroes who had remained nearby in the old Overton neighborhood, Uncle Charlie's other "children."

Ingram just might have enough personal stature to turn a motley band of outlaws into an organization. He also provided them their handle as the "Cahaba River group." For their first meeting, on Sunday, August 25, he lured them over the mountain, down Highway 280 through Mountain Brook, past the Birmingham Water Works to a spot right under the bridge where 280 crossed the Cahaba River. Perhaps fifty yards below the highway, about eighteen men sat on the riverbank. Along with Chambliss, the Blantons, Pickle, and possibly Bobby Cherry, there were representatives from the National States Rights Party. The coalition was now official. Ingram was the hands-down choice for Exalted Cyclops.

The confab had the meandering vehemence of most open Klan meetings. Some men went along with an "all niggers should be exterminated" approach, countered by those who agreed with Pickle that only the "top echelon" should be eliminated, Shuttlesworth and "Martin Lucifer Coon." There was little to suggest that the leaders already had an agenda, a surefire scheme for winning the coveted charter from Bobby Shelton's United Klans of America.

The next day, the federal government obtained its first indictment in a bombing case in sixteen years of racial dynamitings in Birmingham. It was against the A. D. King bombing witness, Roosevelt Tatum, and the charge was lying. In a matter of weeks, the FBI would realize how misplaced its diligence was.

The Last Days of Summer

ON TUESDAY, Boutwell's executive secretary, Billy Hamilton, gave the FBI the names of the three white schools that would be integrated in a week. News from the higher-education front hinted at how difficult the transition was going to be. James Meredith had gotten his diploma from Ole Miss on August 18; he wore the same suit he had on his first day of school (but with one of Ross Barnett's "NEVER, NEVER" buttons on upside down), and left Oxford with the entourage of U.S. marshals who had been his constant companions.

The University of Alabama's new black student Jimmy Hood had ended his studies prematurely. After publishing a guest editorial in the college's *Crimson-*

White caustically suggesting that the civil rights movement ought to move off the streets and into the classroom, Hood had tried to neutralize the ensuing black backlash by claiming, at a Movement rally in Gadsden, that the piece had been written by a cousin of the governor's. He added that Al Lingo's men were treating him "like a slave." Lingo's men were there recording Hood's words, and George Wallace used them to pressure the university trustees to expel Hood. Arthur Shores persuaded him to withdraw voluntarily on grounds of mental and physical stress. And then there was one, Vivian Malone. Wallace asked a university administrator in the presence of the man's nine-year-old son how much longer it would take "to get that nigger bitch out of the dormitory."

On the last Tuesday in August, six buses idled in front of Sixteenth Street Baptist Church, waiting to take a delegation to Washington. It was a rather small group, considering. But many of the pioneer demonstrators of Birmingham had not understood what purpose yet another march would serve.

24.

ALL THE GOVERNOR'S MEN

The March

F RED SHUTTLESWORTH had seen his first stabs at direct action finally turn into the quantum thrust behind a new legislative Reconstruction in the Kennedy civil rights bill. The March on Washington, which was to be an affirming echo of what Wyatt Walker was calling the watershed of Birmingham, was for Shuttlesworth more valediction than validation. At a summit meeting on the march in early July, the NAACP's Roy Wilkins had taken one look at the fifteen places set in New York's Roosevelt Hotel dining room and banished the nine guests who were not his titular peers. Shuttlesworth was among them, although he certainly couldn't match the outrage of the also rejected Bayard Rustin, whom Philip Randolph had put in charge of day-to-day planning. Leaks about Rustin's 1953 morals charge in Pasadena, including word that he had played the "active" part in the homosexual event, trickled through the press, and the FBI intercepted an August 11 conversation between King and a friend worrying that Rustin might "take a drink before the march" and "grab one little brother."

The march came together in defiance not only of its sundry critics but also of the pickup team of organizers working out of Rustin's makeshift Harlem office. On Tuesday, August 27, the participants began arriving in the capital by planes, trains, cars, bikes, skates, and the vehicular civil rights archtype, buses, ringing with the melodies of freedom: the Movement according to Cecil B. DeMille.

The next morning, the actor Sidney Poitier was standing in the lobby of Washington's Willard Hotel with the writers John Killens and James Baldwin. Someone came up to them and reported, "The Old Man died." No one had to ask who the Old Man was. W.E.B. Du Bois had passed away in his sleep the previous night at the age of ninety-five, in Ghana, where he had moved at the invitation of its socialist president, Kwame Nkrumah. The founder of the NAACP, the man who had wrested the post-slavery idea of black liberation from Booker T. Washington, had two years earlier joined up with the shrunken Communist sect whose own pioneering civil rights fronts had been consigned to the dustbin of history.

So many of the roads to this march led from Birmingham, not least Du Bois's prophecy at the Southern Negro Youth Congress's 1946 convention that the Southland would be the cradle of black freedom. Du Bois's SNYC protégés James and Esther Cooper Jackson—it was through them that he had joined the Party—were among the 250,000 hugging the Reflecting Pool along the Washington Mall, and they had gasped with the crowd at Roy Wilkins's announcement of Du Bois's death. Esther was now the editor of one of Du Bois's last American achievements, the quarterly *Freedomways,* of whose 1961 debut the FBI had made due note. The newest staff member Esther had recruited completed this reunion in Washington of stars from the SNYC: Jack O'Dell had his first article in the current *Freedomways* issue, on the economic structure of Birmingham. O'Dell was lonely in this crowd, having come down from New York by himself, and he steered clear of the old SCLC colleagues with whom he had so recently been planning this milestone.

For Birmingham's Aubrey Williams, the March on Washington was the fulfillment of a wish he had made twenty-five years earlier, after Bull Connor enforced the color line at the founding meeting of the Southern Conference for Human Welfare, and Williams had hoped out loud that he would "live to see the day when we will be allowed to sit down together with our black brothers in Birmingham." Williams had suffered many disappointments since parlaying Randolph's original March on Washington plan into the Committee on Fair Employment Practice, but the most devastating had been his exclusion from the modern civil rights movement because of the red-baiting of the Southern Conference Educational Fund. Fred Shuttlesworth, who now held Williams's old job as president of SCEF, had done his utmost to restore his white colleagues' honor, pressing the march's organizers to officially recognize their spurned forebears. After a long delay, on August 7, Rustin had written SCEF's executive director, Jim Dombrowski, an excuse-filled apology saying that the fund would be listed as a "participating organization."

Williams was now terminally ill with stomach cancer, but on this glorious end-of-summer day, he pushed the rented wheelchair of Dombrowski, too arthritic to walk down the Mall. The handsome devil still visible in his emaciated face, Williams held hands with "a beauteous gal from Ohio" named Donna and got caught in the rapture of the freedom songs that had been spilling out from the Washington Monument staging area all morning, courtesy of Odetta; Joan Baez; Bob Dylan; Peter, Paul and Mary; and the old comrade Pete Seeger. Williams's and Dombrowski's heroic service would remain concealed in the folds of the Movement, but Williams had assured his colleague, "My friend, you had more to do with bringing this about than any other white man. . . . I don't want to die of course, but I do thank whatever Powers there be that I have lived long enough to see this happen."

The aura of Birmingham hung over these festivities, down to the Justice Department's orders to the District police to leave their police dogs at home. The march harked back to the great demonstrations of the spring and looked forward to the landmark legislation they had inspired. It was no wonder that Fred Shuttlesworth had become visibly agitated to learn that he had been excluded from the roster of speakers. What of the letter Rustin had written him nine days earlier inviting him to "say a few words from the Lincoln Memorial between one and two pm"? What sort of show-biz mentality dictated that Shuttlesworth would be silenced when actor Marlon Brando would be allowed to show off the cattle prod he had ascertained "really worked" when he joined a demonstration in Gadsden, Alabama, the week before?

Shuttlesworth got in his licks at the civil rights establishment as the cast of thousands surged down the Mall toward the Lincoln Memorial for the beginning of the official speeches. In a guard's room at the memorial, Shuttlesworth was the only elder siding with the youths in an argument dividing the march leaders over the speech that SNCC chairman John Lewis was planning to deliver. Some of its ghostwritten sections were deemed excessive, and the SNCC hothead Jim Forman had insisted on a line about marching through the heart of Dixie "the way Sherman did." Burke Marshall arrived in the sidecar of a police motorcycle, bearing a new draft. On principle, Lewis and his SNCC colleagues resisted the pressure from the Kennedys. Shuttlesworth, too, "didn't think we went up there to be sweet little boys." Randolph countered them with appeals based on seniority. "I have waited twenty-two years for this," he told the SNCC kids. "Would you young men please accommodate an old man?" But it was King who finally made the truest observation: "John, I know who you are. I think I know you well. I don't think this sounds like you."

Those commonsensical, almost offhanded words masked the worries King had been harboring throughout the planning of the march. He knew, certainly after the riot around the Gaston Motel, that violence was a real possibility now that the Negro had begun to shed his fear. Inflammatory words from SNCC might set something off. "If that happens, Ralph," King had said to Abernathy, "everything we have done in Birmingham will be wiped out in a single day." Federal troops had been put on alert. Perhaps recalling mobs of a different color, Justice Hugo Black was convinced that the march would turn into a full-scale riot. "You better tell your friend Martin Luther King to stop marching," he wrote his sister-in-law Virginia Durr. Meanwhile, Malcolm X was in a D.C. hotel denouncing the "Farce on Washington" to any reporter who would listen.

The bickering over Lewis's speech had thrown Rustin's program off schedule. He hastily tapped Shuttlesworth. Justice, it seemed, had ultimately prevailed in the often undemocratic arena of intraracial privilege. The polish of his "impromptu" speech, "Echoes from the South," suggested that Shuttlesworth had known it would all along.

To students of Movement politics, Lewis's sanitized but still militant speech, and the elders' clash with the angry young men, would be the most significant event of the day, marking the beginning of the end of nonviolence. The last major speech would come to symbolize that receding era. Martin Luther King discarded the sober homilies he had brought to the podium and found a universal tune. Parts of his speech were indirect quotes from his "Letter from Birmingham Jail," and other passages had been in his repertory when he raised the rafters of the Sixteenth Street Baptist Church at a mass meeting in April. "I have a dream" was the motif, "I have a dream." The "Let freedom ring" finale was the ending he had used in his oratorical debut as a civil rights celebrity, at the end of the bus boycott in December 1956. But the refrain went back further than that, to Easter of 1939, when Marian Anderson had stood at the Lincoln Memorial and sung "Let freedom ring" in her performance of "America" before the multitudes on the Mall. And the dream reached back still further, to the first great black abolitionist, Frederick Douglass, whom the Southern Negro Youth Congress had quoted at its founding convention: "I had a dream of freedom."

The Governor's Ambassador

IN CONTRAST to the day's other orators, with their list of grievances and appeals for remedies, King had avoided earthbound particulars. But there had been one small man who compelled him to suspend his noble reverie: The governor of Alabama was the only living public figure whom he referred to specifically. George Wallace had returned the compliment and sent his personal emissary to the march. He was a high school dropout named Ralph Roton, who had recently been hired as the investigator for the Legislative Commission to Preserve the Peace (or Peace Committee), a sort of state version of HUAC that the Alabama legislature had created in response to the Birmingham uprising. Roton's qualification for the job was that, as a member of the United Klans of America's Montgomery klavern, he had done undercover work for Imperial Wizard Bobby Shelton—under orders to infiltrate SCLC, CORE, and the Southern Conference for Human Welfare (which the Klan apparently did not know was defunct). Wallace had personally recommended Roton to the committee, and this was his first big assignment, to photograph and tape-record "as many known Communists as I could" at the March on Washington. It was understood that all the information Roton gathered for the Peace Committee would be shared with Shelton, thus effectively making the Ku Kux Klan a subsidiary of the state of Alabama even after the rest of its respectable sponsors had deserted it.

Déjà Vu

NOT LONG AFTER the march, puzzled FBI agents from the New York City area appeared at the apartment of Hosea Hudson, the Communist Party's aging black working-class hero. Having assumed that Birmingham's oracle of the masses from the 1930s and 1940s had masterminded the new revolution, they wanted to know why he hadn't been in Washington. Hudson's arthritic knees were the literal answer, but he also explained that there were young people now to harvest the seeds he and his comrades had sown. "That's right, Mr. Hudson," an agent said with unassuming eloquence. "You have done enough."

Back to Birmingham

A HOT LINE had just been hooked up to connect the White House with the Kremlin in order to avert a nuclear catastrophe. Meanwhile, at home, America deployed the military for civil war. At Fort Campbell, Kentucky, 1,350 battle-ready troops were put on alert in preparation for the opening of school in Birmingham on Wednesday, September 4.

On Thursday, August 29, the Justice Department's friend from the spring, Sheriff Mel Bailey, "invited" two hundred Birmingham clergymen, including Herb Oliver and four other black ministers, to the Municipal Auditorium to discuss school integration and warned them, "You better start preaching reconciliation." Rumors raced through the resistance that Bailey was planning to deputize the ministers. The Klan's political front, the United Americans for Conservative Government, wired George Wallace that its "6300 members" (one of them was the governor's spy Ralph Roton) urged him to send the state troopers to Birmingham to "relieve the incompetent deputized preachers that they may revert to their pulpits and the Lord's work." Bailey understood that Wallace was setting him up, even without knowing what the FBI had just ascertained: The governor would indeed be sending his own police up to the Birmingham schools.

Wallace's constituents were working on a fallback plan in case his state troopers failed to stop integration. On Saturday, Ross Keith was riding around on his Harley with his girlfriend, Lavelle Fike, and asked her if she minded going by Robert Chambliss's house on some business. Chambliss was in a particularly bad mood, so Fike excused herself to go to the bathroom. She guessed the wrong door and ended up in the Chamblisses' bedroom. On the floor were four or five bundles of what looked like giant firecrackers the color of masking tape, tied together with string.

That afternoon, the National States Rights Party paraded to Montgomery, a convoy of seventy-five cars flying Confederate flags. They were delivering Wallace's requested petition—30,000 names—asking the governor to close "mixed schools." Though Wallace was not available to receive the neo-Nazis, he had written Fields a warm apology and arranged for his top lieutenants, including Colonel Al Lingo, to give them an extensive private audience.

Back in Birmingham that night, Fields addressed an NSRP rally in Cahaba Heights. It was something of a comedown from the capitol steps, where he had declaimed earlier against Kennedy and "Martin Lucifer Coon." Only 250 attended, but the quality of the participants, including J. B. Stoner and his sidekick Richard Bowling from Atlanta, had attracted the FBI. Possibly Stoner had come to seek out a Cahaba Heights citizen present at the rally: Troy Ingram, the brains behind the new Klan group that was creating ripples in the resistance.

Trial Run

CAHABA HEIGHTS was to be the scene on Sunday, September 1, of the second meeting of Ingram's Klan, which was still identified by the river on whose banks it met. Ingram had collected some blank application forms and was taking steps to seek a charter from Bobby Shelton. Somewhere, someone was putting the finishing touches on the task one informer would say Shelton had set for the new klavern to earn its right to exist.

That afternoon, the National States Rights Party took over the Vulcan and the Amber Rooms at the Redmont Hotel for its "national party convention." Undercover detective Marcus Jones—known as "Two Tones" Jones for the way his voice cracked spontaneously—and one of his informers, "T," perused the Nazi literature on display, and a bit later a female informer, "M," went to the hotel with a bug in her purse and got a complete tape of Edward Fields's explanation of how the Jew had taken over the Kennedy administration and the FBI.

Robert Chambliss was helping Willie Mae Walker, the crippled daughter of his sister, and her fourth husband, Harry Eugene Walker, a diabetic high school dropout, move into their new home in Trussville. A few weeks earlier, Uncle Robert had personally secured the $1,500 bank loan for their down payment. Later that Sunday, it would become apparent that Chambliss's good deed carried an ulterior motive.

At midnight, "Tall Paul" Dudley White, the deejay who had enticed the children to Kelly Ingram Park for those "picnics" in May, drove the short distance from the Gaston Motel to the rooming house where he lived, across the alley behind the Sixteenth Street Baptist Church. James Lay, a black Civil Defense captain, was standing on the east side of Sixteenth Street across from the church. Parked directly across the street was a dirty black 1956 or 1957 Ford Tudor sedan, facing the wrong direction, under a mimosa tree next to a stairwell leading to the church basement where Fred Shuttlesworth had been skeeted by the fire hose in May. A white man was sitting in the car. A second white man, in a suit with no tie, was on the sidewalk near the church steps. He held a black grip.

Spotting White nearby, Lay at first thought the men might have given the deejay a ride home—entertainers received special favors in the white world. But as soon as the man with the bag realized he had been spotted, he returned to the car. Its headlights extinguished, the car went north up Sixteenth Street. Lay looked for the license number, but there was no plate on the car. If there had been, it probably would have been traced back to Harry Eugene Walker, Chambliss's nephew-in-law.

Lay and White went to White's rooming house and at 12:40 phoned the police and Sixteenth Street's pastor, John Cross. Car 25 responded to the call, with its headlights off; it was Chambliss's nephew Floyd Garrett's car, but he was not on duty. Lay told his story to Officers R. F. Reese and L. R. Cockrum. Sometimes Lay was treated as an honorary policeman, but tonight, he would say, the cops said, "You didn't hear a [obscenity] thing. Get back up to Shores' house. We ought to kill you, nigger." They did not file a report. Their failure to do so would become relevant in two weeks, when the FBI showed Lay photographs of Robert Chambliss and Tommy Blanton. The driver of the car Lay had spotted bore a strong resemblance to Chambliss. The passenger who carried the bag to the steps looked like Blanton. A police investigator later judged that a third man, Bobby Cherry, had also been in the car.

The next day was Labor Day. A neighbor of Pop and Tommy Blanton noticed that the Confederate flags hanging from their house for the past year had been removed.

The End of a Marriage

IN BIRMINGHAM for a holiday appearance at a Civitan barbecue in Ensley, George Wallace, who had adopted the Confederate flag as an unofficial state insignia, greeted nearly ten thousand of his supporters, including most of the Klansmen in the metropolitan area. In a twenty-minute speech, he blasted the March on Washington as "planned and led by Communists and atheists" (notably "sex offender" Bayard Rustin), said the Kennedy administration was full of Communists and atheists, and boasted that he had closed the schools in Tuskegee. As of 6:25 that morning, more than a hundred helmeted state troopers personally commanded by Al Lingo ringed the high school there. The governor had "other secrets for Birmingham."

The second big-name speaker, Bull Connor, chose as his main topic Roosevelt Tatum. He loftily told the newsmen present to print Tatum's story about the cops bombing A. D. King's house and let the FBI worry about proving it false. It was almost as if he knew that the FBI couldn't afford to reveal what it had on his past collaboration with the Klan.*

Yet since Connor's departure, the Klansmen had begun to keenly feel the alienation of the police's affection. The department's latest directives to the Klan—to stay out of the school business—had not contained the customary "We'll handle the niggers ourselves" understanding. Klan egos further smarted when Connor and Wallace beckoned the upstart Edward Fields onto the Civitan speakers' platform.

At the United Klans of America rally that drew many Civitan picnickers to the Graymont Armory later that evening, Bobby Shelton, his arm in a cast, threw down the gauntlet at Police Chief Jamie Moore, and told the crowd of nine hundred that he had pictures of police training against white mobs—firing squads, trucks with machine guns mounted on them, snipers on buildings.

---

* Meanwhile, Bull's policemen had become poster boys for the John Birch Society's most enduring campaign, the "Support Your Local Police" bumper stickers; as an example of "what the police are up against," the organization had cited the Birmingham demonstrators "who kicked police dogs."

Crazy

IT HAD NOT BEEN a rewarding three months for the man who had once thought of himself as Alabama's best-liked politician. The public's attacks on Mayor Albert Boutwell had zeroed in on his sickly appearance ("yellow consumptive") and suggested, "Why in hell don't you blow your damn brains out?" The grassroots disgust for Boutwell was turning into an organized movement. Klansman Billy Holt's industrious wife, Mary Lou, in addition to being the main spark plug in the Klan's alter ego, United Americans for Conservative Government, had been gathering signatures for a referendum to bring back the commission form of government (and Bull Connor), essentially a Boutwell recall. Robert Chambliss had been threatening to slap Boutwell in the mouth. Boutwell tried to recover some dignity by denying press credentials to a photographer working for Black Star, one of the world's eminent photo agencies, because he deduced that it must be a Negro outfit.

George Wallace phoned the mayor at ten Tuesday morning and after meager formalities sought his blessings for sending the state troopers to Birmingham. Wallace wanted the city council to ask the federal court to delay the next day's opening of school "on the grounds that violence might erupt." Boutwell assured Wallace that he was "as strong for segregation as I have ever been," but refused to consider the troopers. "I don't think there is going to be the violence that you anticipate," he said. "I hope and pray there will not be."

"Albert, you can hope and pray," Wallace snapped. And then he said, chillingly, "What about dynamiting, blowing up? I would be derelict in my duty if I did not do all within my power to prevent or try to prevent such a situation." He told Boutwell that if *he* had been at Ensley Park the day before and seen the mood of the crowd, he would understand. "There is no way of knowing who the bombers or terrorists might be," Wallace said, but immediately backed away from his implicit indictment of his Klan friends, saying that they might be "Negroes or maybe Communists."

In Washington, Senator Wayne Morse of Oregon joined a chorus of Wallace detractors. Someone, either in the Pentagon or the Veterans Administration, had leaked to him the Army's psychiatric evaluation of Wallace—"severe anxiety state (chronic)" and anorexia—when he was hospitalized during World War II for a nervous breakdown after serving as a flight engineer on eleven B-29 missions over Japan. The V.A. still paid him a $20-a-month pension for a 10 percent service-related psychological disability. Wallace—with no shame about accepting money from the federal hand he was biting—retorted that he had been certified 90 percent *sane*, which was more than he could say for most of the people in Washington.

Schoolhouse Door Day II

BY 6:45 A.M. on Wednesday, September 4, police lines had been established around West End and Ramsay High Schools and Graymont Elementary, the three white schools destined to have a total of five new black students. Wallace's 450 state troopers were for now secreted away in motel rooms, waiting for Edward Fields and the NSRP to provide them the pretext to charge into battle.

The NSRP, which had attracted two thousand to a rally the night before at a go-cart racetrack, had mustered a sixteen-car motorcade, joined by Tommy Blanton. At the first stop, West End High, Movement strategists had pulled a fast one: The three black high school students—West End–bound Josephine Powell and Patricia Marcus and Ramsay's Richard Arnold Walker, all seniors, their identities still a secret—would not report to class until September 6, Friday. The demonstrators marched around with their placards ("Communist Jews Behind Race Mixing," "NAACP Is Jewish Financed") and taunted the police as "nigger lovers," but left after ten minutes.

At the front door of Graymont Elementary, Mary Lou Holt and a fellow Eastview wife, Wilda Rogers, were picketing ("Keep Alabama White," "Close Mixed Schools") and telling the students that if they attended school with Negroes now they would bear children with them later. Forty-five pupils had showed up, out of the total student body of 345. At 8:05, Dwight and Floyd Armstrong, the sons of the Alabama Christian Movement's chief of security, James Armstrong, and seasoned Movement jailbirds, were escorted through a side door of the Graymont school by their father, Fred Shuttlesworth, and attorney Oscar Adams. They left ten minutes later with enrollment blanks, the first Negroes legitimately inside a white Birmingham public school. A little white girl shouted over the jeering, "I haven't seen this much excitement since the Freedom Riders."

The arrival of the NSRP caravan brought the first violence of the school year. The demonstrators pulled the police ropes out into the street and began throwing rocks at the school. Captain George Wall called out the reserves standing by in Legion Field. As the police drove the protesters back, one rock thrower ran up to the line and heaved a half-brick into Detective Marcus Jones's chest. James Konrad Warner, the associate editor of *The Thunderbolt*, was arrested. The police drew their guns.*

Standing in the door of a nearby church, out of the hard rain that began to fall at around nine, were two stalwarts of Eastview—Ross Keith, who was on vacation from his job at Campbell's 66 Express, and his fellow trucker Sister White.

The NSRP men had gotten back in their cars and gone to Ramsay High School, unaware that it was still technically all white. A patrolman raised his billy club in greeting and was swamped by the mob. "Where's Bobby Kennedy?" someone shouted. The States Righters charged the officers. One got right in a captain's face and said, "We'll be here tomorrow morning and every morning until they get the niggers out! We're going to start a civil war!" The reserves were again summoned. Four members of the NSRP's "Security Guard," wearing wide leather belts with shoulder straps and thunderbolt armbands, were arrested.

---

* One officer on the newly reformed police force decided to concentrate on black scofflaws and made the day's only arrest of a black person. That policeman was Floyd Garrett, Robert Chambliss's nephew.

"Where's Wallace?" came the muffled voice of a suspect inside a police van. The governor would indeed come to the aid of his fall guys, for they had given him his prize: a picture in the paper of one of the two NSRP protesters whose faces had been bloodied by billy clubs. Wallace issued an executive order forbidding the integration of the public schools, "for the sole and express purpose of preserving the peace...."

Heading home from the demonstration, Tommy Blanton heard over his CB radio that the police were looking for his father's tan 1955 Ford—something about a bunch of guns being in it. When Tommy arrived at their building, Pop Blanton was driving off. Police stopped him and detained him for half an hour. Meanwhile, neighbors later told the FBI Tommy went to the locked shed behind his house, removed a grayish box around eighteen inches long, put it in the trunk of his car, and sped off. One neighbor jested to another, "Tonight there will probably be a bombing."

McWhorter 1963

OUR FIRST HALF-DAY was coming to an end at the Brooke Hill School for Girls. In the office, Mrs. Twining, the elderly administrator, had had the radio on listening to bulletins from the valley. "Blood is going to run in the streets," she kept muttering. Among some faculty members—wives of professors from Birmingham-Southern, primarily—there was the feeling that school integration was long overdue, although political commentary on the issue was on the order of Mrs. Gage's droll warnings. The formidable but beloved history teacher pronounced in a small, mirthful voice on George Wallace, "Beware of little men."

We lower-school students had a fond ritual with Mr. Cash, the grizzled and jovial custodian. He was white; his assistant, Roosevelt, was black. We would sneak up on him and, with gotcha sound effects, wave our hands with our fingers crossed, hoping to catch him with his fingers uncrossed. Mr. Cash had never been caught yet, but today he seemed preoccupied. He had wanted to wear his gun into the school, but the headmistress had persuaded him to keep it in his car. He was convinced that the first place "they" had in mind to integrate was Brooke Hill, which had the city's highest concentration of white girls.

To the extent that we girls would register the "trouble" it would be in the pressing question of sixth grade: "Are you prejudiced?" (Only it came out, "Are you prejudice?") I had no qualms about taking part in the prank calls my peer group liked to make to "colored-sounding" people listed in the phone book; it was a badge of pride to be able to convince them that we truly were "Will'Ida Jones from Pah-kuh High School" and keep them on the line chatting. But I had come up with what I thought was a humane and semantically brilliant answer to the "prejudice" question. "I'm a white supremacist," I would say, "but I'm not *prejudice* against them."

25.

A CASE OF DYNAMITE

Negron's Dynamite

AFTER NOON on Wednesday, Robert Chambliss drove northwest to the mining community of Blossburg to buy dynamite from one of his favorite sources, a store called Negron's. Leon Negron, known as the "Frenchman from Daisey City" though he was born in Alabama in 1911, supplied dynamite and blasting caps to the hundred or so small "wagon mines," including his own, within a ten-mile radius. His dynamite sales were not restricted to miners; as a member of the United Americans for Conservative Government, Negron did not object to other uses for the stuff.

Chambliss's ulcers were acting up that day, but a trip to Negron's was always tonic. This time, he would claim, he was buying an entire case of dynamite, around 140 sticks, on orders of Exalted Cyclops Robert Thomas. It was supposedly to be used to clear land the Klan had just bought off Highway 31 north of town as the site for a fancy new Klan hall. Negron drew his own conclusions about Chambliss's plans for the dynamite. "If you are going to blow up some niggers, I will throw in a few extra sticks," he said.

Chambliss put that case in his car trunk, plus the leftovers from another, a box of caps, and a roll of fuses, and drove home. That evening, as he left for an emergency meeting of the United Klans' Big Three klaverns—Eastview, Tuscaloosa, and Bessemer—he told his wife and her relatives, "Everyone watch TV."

The meeting was held at the Primitive Baptist church in Bessemer, near the Dixie Speedway in Midfield, the scene of a simultaneous rally of the West End Parents for Private Schools, which the resourceful Mary Lou Holt had helped spin off from the United Americans for Conservative Government. The most serious of the proposed schools was Hoover Academy, named after its bankroller, William Hoover, the insurance magnate who had been prominent in the Dixiecrats' American States Rights Association, had funded the Citizens Councils, and, officials suspected, had supervised the Dynamite Hill bombings. The other force behind the academy—the son of an old Hoover crony who had been a loud Robert E. Lee Klansman implicated in the Dynamite Hill explosions—was one of six parents Wallace had persuaded to petition the appellate court to stop school desegregation on the grounds of "grave risk of physical harm." Representing the petitioners at the taxpayers' expense were Wallace's sterling legal advisers, including Hobart McWhorter's father-in-law, Kirkman Jackson.

More than seventy-five men were at the Primitive Baptist church, including the Eastview all-stars. The attendance of the Imperial Wizard, Bobby Shelton, signaled that there was more to this meeting than the billed agenda of planning demonstrations against the integrated schools. The emergency was equally an intramural one. The Klan's ranks were bleeding into the other organizations taking the lead in the school integration fight, notably the National States Rights Party, which was holding a meeting (its second in two days) at the Redmont Hotel's Vulcan Room. Many of the Klansmen present had been planning to attend until Shelton disciplined them, and then they repaired to the Midfield rally and paraded their presence—alibi-making being the other purpose of the Klan event.

The National States Rights Party gala across town had drawn an audience of of only seventy, including Albert DeShazo, the suspected Loveman's tear-gas bomber, who had gotten married earlier that day to the daughter of the Trussville police radio operator. Despite the fact that the NSRP's official membership still consisted largely of borderline personalities and police informants, Edward Fields had never enjoyed such mainstream authority. He assured the crowd that he had just talked to Governor Wallace, who promised him that Al Lingo would see to it that the police—Boutwell's "storm troops"—did not manhandle their people the next day at the schoolhouse door.

And then, in the ultimate flattery, two Klan grandees, Robert Creel and Hubert Page, arrived fresh from the Bessemer meeting, while Fields looked on like a proud younger brother.

Lightning Strikes Twice

THE POLICE AND the sheriff's department had concentrated their manpower at the three hot schools, but at nine-thirty, two Birmingham detectives recognized a couple of FBI agents on surveillance at the base of Dynamite Hill near Center Street. The cops spoke to them and drove off. A few minutes later, a '56 or '57 Chevy cruised past Arthur Shores's house going north up Center, then turned around and went back; it was apparently the same car, a pale blue station wagon, that a witness had seen speed by the house over Labor Day weekend, with one of the three white male passengers peering at his watch. Perhaps, however, it was a decoy—its missing door made it kind of conspicuous. Another witness would see a light blue 1962 Ford in the alley behind Shores's house. Investigators believed that Gene Reeves had also lent that car to Charles Cagle and Levie Yarbrough the previous month for the burning of the St. James church in Warrior.

At 9:35, Shores was in his living room reading the *Wall Street Journal.* He began to feel apprehensive. "The old saying that lightning doesn't strike twice in the same place may be all right," he thought, "but I'm goin' sit out on the porch a little while with my double-barreled shotgun." He'd barely gotten up from his chair when his front door was blown into the living room. His wife, in the bedroom reading, was hurled onto the floor, as the familiar smell of dynamite filled the house.

Robert Chambliss's nephew Floyd Garrett was among the first policemen at the bombing scene. He was soon engulfed by the usual audience from the Smithfield apartments at the base of Dynamite Hill, the model federal housing project that Eleanor Roosevelt had personally given her blessing to in 1937. As Birmingham now hurtled into its third riot since the Gaston Motel bombing, the police arrived armed with revolvers, carbines, and twelve-gauge shotguns to cope with the brickbats.

Fred Shuttlesworth had been in Birmingham all week. That Wednesday night, he and some Movement ministers were meeting in the chapel of the Smith and Gaston Funeral Home to draft a statement backing up Mayor Boutwell, who was being barraged by hostile telegrams for going along with the desegregation of the schools. Miles president Lucius Pitts had come to help, bringing along his houseguest, John Monro, the white dean of Harvard College, who was in town giving Pitts professional advice. When the explosion interrupted their deliberations, Pitts and Monro followed Shuttlesworth to Dynamite Hill. But, quick as usual, Pitts taxied to safety after sensing that the mob might catch a blood scent for Monro. Despite this introduction to Birmingham, Monro would leave Harvard three and a half years later to become director of Miles's freshman studies.

Shuttlesworth muscled his way toward Shores's house through black folks throwing rocks, bricks, and bottles at the officers. The police were pushing them back, with bayonets if necessary, firing for now at the tops of houses. ("I reckon when it rains those roofs will leak," one cop said to another.) Shuttlesworth had raised his preacher's voice to try to calm the crowd, which was armed with conventional firearms, when Bull Connor's "tank" zigzagged up the street.

Hedrick Smith, a reporter for the *New York Times,* dodged the tank to find a pay phone and dictate his story to New York. His fellow *Times* men, Claude Sitton and Fred Powledge, were crawling on their bellies up the gutter, out of respect for gunfire so thick that Powledge would swear it came from machine guns.

Twenty-year-old John Coley, who had hopped a ride to the riot scene with his close friend Eddie Coleman, happened into a barrage of gunfire and collapsed facedown on the ground. Coleman called his friend's name. Coley raised his head and tried to say something but couldn't.

It was ten o'clock, only twenty-four minutes since the bomb had gone off. The Justice Department's Joe Dolan had arrived in the car of Jim Lay, the black Civil Defense captain who had seen the suspicious white men at Sixteenth Street Baptist a few nights before.* Dolan was walking along the police line when he saw

---

* Justice's press officer, Ed Guthman, an ex-GI, would later confront Dolan: "There was a rumor that you were lying on the floor of the car. That true?"

"You bet, but the ASAC was under me," Dolan replied, referring to the FBI's assistant special agent in charge.

Coley go down. He got back into Lay's car. The FBI assistant special agent in charge with Dolan said let's get out of here. Dolan was relieved to see his colleague Thelton Henderson standing among the black leaders in the melee. Henderson had become the newest member of Justice's riot squad in Birmingham, after Dolan explained to Robert Kennedy that the white government lawyers he was sending down were too conspicuous to hang out with the Movement leaders at the Gaston Motel. A Los Angeles native recruited by John Doar as the first black lawyer in the civil rights division, Henderson had listened to radio reports on the violent integration of Ole Miss while driving his Volkswagen beetle cross-country to Washington, wondering if this was the sort of thing he might expect to be involved in.

The crowd surged east closer to Shores's house. Shuttlesworth ran west and got behind a tree. A thirty-five-year-old laborer, Thomas Lymon, fell in the street and tried to get up, but a policeman beat his chest with a rifle butt. Lymon told him he was hurt. The policeman replied, "All you black bastards need to be dead; we ain't got no use for you anyway." Lymon grabbed the cop and threw him against one of the Smithfield project houses. A woman ran out of the house and began pounding the policeman with a broom. Shuttlesworth ordered another black man to intervene in the cop's behalf. Lymon had collapsed.

Lymon and John Coley were taken away in ambulances. Lymon had been shot in the head with buckshot, but would survive. Coley had also been hit in the head, though it was the #0 buckshot lodged in his liver that would account for his being dead on arrival at University Hospital. Several officers stationed in Coley's vicinity had been using that size pellet, and for the time being the police were so confident of their right to fire on the rioters that they told the *News*'s Tom Lankford that they shot Coley when he "burst from a house firing a gun," as if they had not been surrounded by hundreds of eyewitnesses who could contradict them. Floyd Garrett had been standing near Coley, but would claim to have been carrying a .44 revolver rather than his shotgun; he would lie about that shotgun in connection with a future bombing.

What the blacks who had gathered around Coley's corpse noticed was his dead-on resemblance, despite a twenty or so–year age difference, to Fred Shuttlesworth. They had no doubt that Coley was a victim of mistaken identity, that his murder had been another assassination attempt. The police would have to settle for merely kicking Shuttlesworth as he lost his footing and fell. After that, he ran to a porch to watch.

The riot had spread for blocks. NBC News correspondent Johnny Apple and his crew were still some distance away when a shotgun blasted out their rear window, almost hitting the driver. The police were not about to let *Post-Herald* photographer Tommy Langston get a second shot at a Pulitzer. A cop broke Langston's headlight as he approached Shores's house and insisted that he leave.

Gary Thomas Rowe "happened" to be driving his car down Eighth Avenue while the riot was in full roar. Just as he passed Parker High School, a brick smashed his side mirror. He looked to his left and saw a "great big ass black man" shouting, "Kill him!" As the man reared back with what appeared to be a brick, Rowe drew his .38 pistol, he claimed, and fired. The black man grabbed his chest; his legs buckled. The crowd exhaled a thunderous "Aaah!" Rowe floored the accelerator until he ran up against a roadblock manned by a motorcycle cop, the rare policeman who didn't recognize him.

Rowe claimed that he told the officer, "Whew! Better get some people back there. I think I just killed a man."

The cop surveyed him "nonchalant as shit" and then rested his arm on Rowe's window and said, also according to Rowe, "You all right?" Rowe said he was, and then the officer said, "What's going on?" Rowe says he said, "You better get some people in there. There's a lot of people getting killed down there." The officer asked him again if he was all right, and had anyone taken down his license plate number. Rowe says he exploded, "How the hell do I know if anybody got my tag number? There was a thousand goddamn niggers back there." The cop made sure one last time that Rowe was all right and said, according to Rowe, "Hey, get the hell on out of here, O.K.? Good shooting."

Colonel Al Lingo was pacing in his Birmingham headquarters, the St. Francis Motel over the mountain in Homewood. "My men are ready, already dressed," Lingo had been telling Police Chief Jamie Moore throughout the night, but Moore had insisted that he had the riot under control and everyone was beginning to disperse. Joe Dolan had a somewhat different prognosis. He called Burke Marshall in Washington and told him they had better start talking about troops. "The town is going to blow," he said. When Marshall told him to keep cool, Dolan felt as if they were "leaving me in Bataan."

Dynamite

It was now past eleven, an hour and a half after the Shores bombing, and the man known as Dynamite Bob was still in possession of what would become the most famous case of dynamite in history. At the Klan meeting in Bessemer earlier that evening, Exalted Cyclops Robert Thomas had instructed Nigger Hall and Charles Cagle to go by Chambliss's house late that night to pick up something. Hall and Chambliss arranged to find each other at Jack Cash's after the meeting, but Chambliss, after waiting awhile over barbecue and a cup of coffee, went home. Hall, it turned out, had stopped with Sister White and Ross Keith at the Blue Bird Restaurant on the Bessemer Super Highway and drunk a fifth of vodka. Upon arriving at Cash's, Hall had a few beers and left for Chambliss's house, with Cagle following in his car.

Flora Chambliss answered the door, told Hall her husband was asleep, and gave him the keys to the 1960 blue Falcon. In the trunk was the case of dynamite, weighing more than fifty pounds, but the rattling told Hall it might be missing a couple of sticks.

In two years, an FBI informant would hear Robert Chambliss say that he had used one and a half sticks on the Shores house. His involvement in the bombing was already old news to his family. He had bragged when he got home that it wouldn't do any good to repair the house and that he had never made a bad bomb.

Hall put the dynamite in his trunk. Cagle also took a canvas sack of loose dynamite from Chambliss's car. Hall asked Cagle if he had any ideas what to do with the explosives, and Cagle said, Lord no. (A polygraph would later suggest that Cagle, along with Gene Reeves—whose car had been spotted in the alley behind Shores's house—had been involved in the bombing.) They drove north toward Gardendale. By the time Hall stopped to urinate by the side of the road, Cagle had come up with a plan. About a mile from Hall's house, the men turned off Highway 31 onto Mockingbird Lane and set the dynamite thirty feet into the woods under some kudzu. Cagle told Hall he would get in touch with "Quickdraw" Yarbrough, the prison camp guard who Hall would inform the FBI had helped Cagle burn the Warrior church, to see if he knew of a better stashing place. This was only the beginning of the case of dynamite's tour of Birmingham.

An Excellent Shot

FBI SPECIAL AGENT BYRON McFALL called Gary Thomas Rowe at dawn to ask where he had been. Rowe would claim that he confessed to having possibly committed a murder. McFall phoned the Birmingham police, according to Rowe, and called back to say that the riot's only fatality, John Coley, had been hit in the head. Rowe insisted that he, "an excellent shot," had "hit the nigger right in the chest." McFall ascertained that the Birmingham policeman at the roadblock hadn't recognized him and told him, according to Rowe, to forget about the incident "to the day you die."

Dolan's Epiphany

ON THURSDAY MORNING, September 5, Superintendent of Schools Theo Wright, under pressure from Wallace that included a state trooper banging on his door in the middle of the night, closed the schools. Informed of the decision at 8:07, Police Chief Jamie Moore was not amused, and he was further annoyed to find that Al Lingo had deployed twenty-five unauthorized state troopers to each of the three schools. In front of Ramsay High, Lingo gave an interview to the press.

Over at West End High, Joe Dolan was prowling about in his rental car. A block and a half from the school, he saw an FBI agent sitting in his government sedan listening to the news on the car radio. The night before, after leaving the Shores scene, the assistant special agent in charge had taken him to police headquarters, where two agents were already there, again listening to the radio. "The way they covered the bombing was to get information from the Birmingham police," Dolan later said scornfully.

Dolan slipped into West End High to use a pay phone to call Justice. To the extent that he understood it, his assignment in Birmingham was this: "I could do what I wanted. I just had to be right." He felt a hand on his shoulder, and a man in uniform said he was going to arrest him for disturbing the peace. Dolan said to the officer, "Why don't I just go away?" As he walked back to his car, a policeman taunted him, "Did you call Boooobby yet?"

The NAACP Inc. Fund's Constance Baker Motley added George Wallace as a party defendant to the suit she had filed against the school authorities. "Don't refer to me as that Negro lawyer," she told reporters, as if to admonish them that this was no parochial fight. Her efforts to round up affidavits from those who had witnessed the barring of the students revealed to Joe Dolan the ulterior benefits of the FBI's surveillance by radio: The agents refused to provide any affidavits because they weren't eyewitnesses. Dolan gave her a statement.

Wallace's Dilemma

GEORGE WALLACE WAS living up to the mythic status Martin Luther King had conferred on him at the March on Washington, pushing his Faustian bargain to the limit. On Thursday, as the powder lingered over Dynamite Hill, Wallace told a *New York Times* reporter—unfriendly ears—that "what this country needs is a few first-class funerals, and some political funerals, too." He did not seem to comprehend that the difference between a crime against property and murder was as random as where Arthur Shores happened to have been reading his newspaper. He also publicly hailed the NSRP protesters (who turned out on Friday, September 6, even though the schools were closed) as martyrs to the Birmingham police: "It takes courage to stand up to tear gas and bayonets." Martin Luther King and Fred Shuttlesworth telegrammed President Kennedy, flashing their understanding that it was Negro violence rather than white terrorism that attracted the attention of the authorities: "Something must be done to apprehend the bombers and curtail the irresponsible action of Governor George Wallace, or realism impels us to admit that Birmingham and Alabama will see the worst race riot in our nation's history."

On Saturday, Wallace traveled to Birmingham to make the keynote address at a big fund-raising banquet for the United Americans for Conservative Government, the Klan's political arm that had served him so diligently. The ladies had outdone themselves on the artificial flower arrangements. And the turnout— 489—rewarded their efforts. Imperial Wizard Bobby Shelton was there, along with his lapsed stalwarts, Robert Chambliss and Troy Ingram. Rounding out the governor's entourage, Edward Fields—who had been boasting to the *New York Times's* Fred Powledge that his party hoped to draft Strom Thurmond for President in 1964—had been given a table of honor, at Wallace's invitation, directly in front of the podium.

As Wallace entered the Redmont Hotel's Emerald Room, one of the tuxedo-clad well-wishers greeting him was the black headwaiter, a fellow Barbour County man. As they hugged each other's necks, Wallace said, "Doc, I'm so glad to see you." The waiter said, "I'm so glad to see you, Judge," adding, "Skeeter's working out here too." Skeeter was summoned from the kitchen to integrate a bit with his old friend from Clio.

Eyebrows raised. In Birmingham, where the practice of segregation had always been sincere (and the continuing rift in Eastview was over Robert Thomas's maid), few shared Wallace's conviction that the political was not the personal, and he would soon get a Birmingham-postmarked letter denouncing his "nigger"-hugging transgression. And if that had been the worst of Wallace's hypocrisy, his followers might have eventually lost their spirit. But in his speech that evening, Wallace referred indignantly to the suspicious absence of fatalities in the Birmingham bombings. He could only conclude that the "nigras" were slinging dynamite to further their own cause. The audience of accomplished bomb makers applauded.

The Castle

TOO FIRED UP by the governor to let the evening end, a few dozen Klansmen repaired to Bessemer headquarters, the Primitive Baptist church. Bessemer Exalted Cyclops Robert Creel told Tommy Rowe, "Baby Brother, we got a goody. You'll like this. Right up your alley. There's gonna be some ass-kicking." Another Klansman presented the layout of A. G. Gaston's residential spread, a big colonial house out in the country north of town that the Klan was under the impression Gaston referred to as "The Castle." For a few weeks now, Officer Lavaughn Coleman, the Klan's biggest sympathizer on the force, had been telling Rowe that guns and ammunition were arriving at Gaston's motel in caskets, and that he was supplying the Black Muslims.

The Klansmen decided against dynamite in favor of firebombing the house. According to Rowe, Eugene Thomas, a Bessemer Klansman active in the Steelworkers union, disappeared for a while and came back from a nearby police station with some incendiary devices. At 3 a.m. thirty men piled into cars and headed toward Tarrant; they included, by Rowe's account, Thomas, Creel, Billy Holt, Herman Cash, Hubert Page, Earl Thompson, and W. O. Eaton. Gaston had returned home only a few hours earlier from Washington, D.C., where he had attended a White House dinner for the king and queen of Afghanistan. After watching the Miss America Pageant with his wife, he retired at around midnight.

The white boys crept through the woods toward the estate and hurled a glass jug of diesel fuel through the living room window, igniting curtains, a rug, and a lampshade. Amid flares and whooshing sounds, a second, smaller jug knocked against a windowsill and fell to the ground, scorching the wall before burning out.

Gaston and his wife were not hurt. The FBI did not investigate the bombing and has no record that Rowe discussed it with his superiors or that he was suspected of being involved, though Rowe would embellish this incident for a popular book he would write about his exploits as a G-man.

Enough

AT THE SIXTEENTH STREET BAPTIST CHURCH ON the following evening, Sunday, September 8, a new pipe organ was being dedicated. Two bomb threats had been phoned into the church that morning, and just before services, a member saw an unkempt white male in a blue shirt loitering across the street. She later picked out a picture of Tommy Blanton as someone who looked like him. A group of guards, pillars of the church, stationed themselves around the building.

George Wallace already seemed to be doing penance for his Saturday-night fling with the Klan. On Sunday, he went up to a TV station on Red Mountain and taped an hour-long appeal for "law and order," to air statewide that night. His elite legal advisers, including Kirkman Jackson and Jim Simpson, were arranged around him on the set. Wallace assured "all the citizens of this state—both white and Negro—that my fight is not against anyone. I am one who believes that there is a Supreme Being and that He made each and every one of us in this state regardless of our color and I have never made a single reference or statement in public in my life that reflected upon any man because of who he happened to be."

Simpson said on the program, in the foggy language normally favored by cornered moderates, "Let us go no further and no faster in the direction of error than we are forced to go by the overwhelming power of the federal government. As soon as the pressure is relaxed, let us recede as far and as rapidly as we can to a posture of common sense." At dawn the next day, the meaning of those words became clear. Wallace issued an executive order permitting the opening of the schools but denying entry to the black students. At Ramsay High, sixty troopers were waiting to repulse Shuttlesworth, two black attorneys, and their ward, Richard Walker; Al Lingo himself turned students away from West End and then Graymont.

Wallace had finally reaped the can-do, full-court Kennedy pressure. Faced with similar schoolhouse door scenarios in Mobile and Tuskegee, Burke Marshall asked Judge Frank Johnson if the government could file in his middle district to get relief over the entire state. Johnson was willing to chew his own tough meat, he replied, but he was damned if he was going to chew everybody else's. Oberdorfer and Dolan called four other federal judges, and on Monday afternoon the first five-judge restraining order, dictated by Johnson, enjoined the governor and "everyone acting in his behalf" from interfering with the court's desegregation order.

U.S. marshals headed to the capital to serve the governor. Wallace locked himself in his office. At nine at night, his finance director, Seymore Trammell, summoned to the capital twenty-five National Guardsmen, who began sticking bayonets in the bushes and, as the legend evolved, flushed out fifteen federal marshals like quail.

In Cahaba Heights that night, Troy Ingram was sitting in the dark by his garage with his nephew Carey "Cotton" Isbell, also contemplating the enemy. Ingram had been somewhat morose since the previous day's meeting of his Cahaba

River Klan. He had hoped it would be the big occasion that his splinter group officially formed a new klavern, and Bobby Shelton had been interested enough to have sent spies to the meeting. But despite the number of informants, the meeting had still failed to draw the necessary twenty-five brothers to form a new club. As morale fizzled, six hard-core men, including Chambliss and the Blantons, and possibly Herman Cash and the munitions ace Bobby Cherry, had repaired to Ingram's house to get down to business.

Ingram's conversation with his nephew now turned to explosives. Ingram said he had twelve to fifteen sticks of dynamite in his garage. He got a flashlight and went to make sure, reappearing in a few minutes. "O.K.," he said, "I've got enough."

Kennedized

AT THREE-THIRTY in the morning, the FBI learned that Wallace had decided to call out the National Guard—three hundred troops—to keep black children out of the schools in defiance of the federal court. At 7 a.m., 5 a.m. Alabama time, President Kennedy signed an order federalizing the Guard. Defense Secretary Robert McNamara ordered the Guardsmen back to the armory. Even though Kennedy's purpose was to remove the soldiers from the scene, Wallace acted as if they were the aggressors, telling the TV cameras that he couldn't "fight bayonets with my bare hands"—a hardship from which he had not spared the U.S. marshals the night before.

Burke Marshall phoned Chief Jamie Moore from Washington at 7:30 Birmingham time to make sure that the police didn't need the troops to help him enforce the peace. Robert Kennedy picked up an extension phone to give Moore a pep talk but did not mention that in addition to the three hundred Birmingham Guardsmen on standby, he had a hundred troops coming in from Tuscaloosa and heading for the Green Springs Armory. Seven hundred reinforcements were on standby to leave Fort Campbell, Kentucky, at noon, with 8,300 more troops on four-hour alert. Mayor Boutwell had met the crisis by scheduling an official trip to Tampa, where he was touring a Schlitz brewery.

Fred Shuttlesworth escorted Dwight and Floyd Armstrong into Graymont Elementary. Lillian Foscue, David Vann's wife, on assignment for the *Post-Herald*, observed white youngsters pepper the two brothers with "adult obscenities in the soft treble voices of little boys." But then, too, there was a well-dressed white man holding his daughter's hand. "We'll come to school tomorrow," he said. "Today I want her to see there is nothing to fear. I told her I played with Negroes when I was a boy. There are good ones and bad ones."

All was quiet at Ramsay when Richard Walker skipped up the steps and went into a classroom segregated by sex. A policeman who was also a member of the National Guard joked about going to get his other uniform—"I been Kennedized." The Popsicle Man rolled up his truck in front of the school, and, with the clear sense that the party was ending, Captain Jack Warren invited the reporters and neighbors to "have some ice cream, courtesy of the Birmingham Police Department."

At West End, the post-segregation ceremonies extended for a while longer. NSRP-trained teenagers led the student body onto the football field in response to the arrival of Josephine Powell and Patricia Marcus, for a "spontaneous demonstration" that went on nearly two hours. A student played "Dixie" on his bugle, like a requiem.

There was an explosion in the street that night in the 1500 block of Twentieth Street. The FBI determined that it "may have been nothing more than a large firecracker, and the police saw nothing to investigate."

Parade of Racists

AN HOUR INTO the school day on Wednesday, September 11, the Armstrong brothers were sent home for wearing short pants. Almost preferable to this petty harassment by professionals was the rock heaved by a white teenager through the window of the car taking Patricia Marcus and Josephine Powell home from West End that afternoon. (Only because Joe Dolan asked them to, FBI agents interviewed the girls and their driver before turning the case over to the police.)

All three schools opened quietly the next day, Thursday, September 12, despite two NSRP motorcades with a total of 150 cars snaking from school to school.

The heavy turnout at Eastview's regular meeting that night reflected the seriousness of the week's developments. In addition to the loyalists—Earl Thompson, Ross Keith, Robert Creel of Bessemer, Billy Holt, Harry Walker, Charles Cagle, Sister White, and Nigger Hall—Robert Chambliss and Troy Ingram made an enigmatic appearance. Tommy Rowe, who was also there, did not tell his handlers what a police informant told Birmingham detective Marcus Jones: that there was a demonstration of a bomb with a delayed fuse that night in the Klan hall. Were Ingram and Chambliss hoping to implicate the old klavern, or was Eastview complicit in the Cahaba River group's plan to "prove" itself to Bobby Shelton?

Signs

THE CAFE OWNER Jack Cash was in a bit of hot water. A cop had stopped him in Thursday's NSRP caravan, pulled him out of his 1954 Cadillac, and confiscated a derringer pistol, a straight razor, a baling hook (perhaps the same cotton hook supposedly taken from his brother on the trip to the Schoolhouse Door in June), and a fishing tackle box containing a sawed-off shotgun. Cash had always received a good deal of slack from the police—he had gotten off easy on the 1957 beating of Shuttlesworth at Phillips High School. But this time, perhaps because of his new affiliation with the NSRP, he was arrested.

Integration had turned Cash paranoid—he checked his car for booby traps every morning before heading to the farmers' market to buy the day's vegetable menu—and on Friday the thirteenth, his suspicions were rewarded. One of Cash's suppliers was having a bowl of chili at the cafe at around two o'clock when he noticed the proprietor walk over to the pay phone. For reasons he would never fully explain, the salesman copied down the number Cash dialed. He heard Cash ask for "Joe," whom he told to "leave the case at the Powderly church." Cash said he would pick it up.

The number Cash had called was that of a filling station on the outskirts of downtown, across from the terminal from Baggett Transportation, where the company parked the trucks that carried its explosives. Baggett had contracts with the U.S. government and Du Pont to haul dynamite and dynamite caps. In-city truckdrivers such as Cash's brother Herman and Bobby Cherry, who had driven for Baggett, used the station as a rest stop. So many of the truckers who hung out there were named Joe that the call had to have been prearranged so that "Joe" was waiting to take it. Or perhaps Cash had asked for Jones and bit off the final consonants in the lazy southern fashion. One of Cherry's best friends, Johnny Frank Jones, who was with him on Easter night when he accidentally shot Wyman Lee, hauled explosives for Baggett. At the time, it did not occur to the eavesdropping salesman that the case might have referred not to beer or whiskey but to dynamite, or that the "church" was a euphemism for klavern headquarters. Powderly was a community between Cash's barbecue and Bessemer, named after the leader of the Knights of Labor, the earliest of the labor unions, in tribute to the high aspirations of the workingmen of the Birmingham district.

That evening, Robert Chambliss came into Cash's Barbecue, had a sandwich, and made a call from the pay phone. Then he compared notes with Cash about the previous day's demonstrations and may have checked discreetly on the whereabouts of the "case" while griping loudly that the cops had stopped him, too, during the NSRP demonstration and taken his Confederate flags.

The place where those Confederate flags were made was becoming a nerve center of the resistance. The Modern Sign Shop, on the corner of Third Avenue North and Sixteenth Street, had outfitted the NSRP's school pickets and was still churning out signs to "Defeat Boutwell" and "Boycott Schools." Not that the owner, Merle K. Snow, was profiteering from segregation; he let the NSRP and the Klansmen operate his presses and silk-screening equipment at cost.

As it happened, the mainstays of the Cahaba River splinter group were at the shop that night, supposedly to help Snow make signs. Chambliss stopped by. Bobby Cherry arrived at around five-thirty. He had broken his back in May and still wore a brace, but he had been at the sign shop the night before as well, with his friend Johnny Frank Jones, the explosives trucker. Tommy Blanton broke a date with his girlfriend, a Jones Valley high school senior named Jean Casey, saying he had to "work." But apparently he decided to skip the trip to Snow's and go only to the later meeting that so urgently demanded this public synchronizing of alibis.

26.

THE EVE

Elizabeth

Elizabeth Hollifield Hood had felt a horrible self-loathing around her uncle Robert Chambliss ever since she was four years old, back in 1944, and he spoke directly to her for the first time. "Whose little boy are you?" he asked as she played on the sidewalk in front of her house. She reminded him that she belonged to John and Libby, his wife's sister, and was not old enough to understand that her shame at having her gender confused had been his intention. By 1949, when she attended her first Klan rally with Robert and Aunt Flora—the Labor Day affair at which he assaulted the *Post-Herald* reporter and ended up losing his city job—she had grown to fear her uncle, and not just because of his tendency to sexually fondle his nieces and nephews.

Now twenty-three, separated from her violent husband, and the mother of a young son, Elizabeth had come to accept Chambliss as a fact of life. She had learned to compose the noncommittal look that the rest of the in-laws assumed when he "shared"—bragged about some racial mayhem or displayed sticks of dynamite. In a strange way, it was his political authority—who were they to second-guess the gentlemen lawyers who had sued the NAACP on his behalf after the Autherine Lucy riot?—that made them doubt their own instincts for right and wrong. Then, too, there was the Klan code known as the "kiss of death," the curse of fatal retribution that kept Klan brothers from informing on one another. Elizabeth knew the kiss of death was on her aunt Tee (as she had christened Flora as a child trying to pronounce the family pet name, Sister).

Chambliss summoned Flora, whom he still called Mommy, though they had no children, with an ear-splitting whistle. And she was always there for him, with a cup of coffee laced with Eagle Brand sweetened condensed milk. Even on this morning of Saturday, September 14, when she was ill with the flu. Elizabeth Hood had come by at seven on her way to work to check on her aunt and joined Robert at the kitchen table.

Hood mentioned an item she had read in the morning paper. Chambliss's good friend Bob Gafford, a used-auto-parts dealer who was a big cheese in the

United Americans for Conservative Government, had put up a $100 reward for the arrest of a black male who had allegedly slashed the arm of a white girl on her way to a high school football game the previous night. Chambliss snapped, saying that he had been fighting a one-man battle since World War II and that if the boys had backed him up, they would have had the "goddamn niggers" in their place by now. George Wallace was a lily-livered coward—couldn't even keep the "niggers" out of the schools. "We got him elected, and he's not going to do what's right," he told his niece.

Chambliss ordered Flora to comb his hair so that he could go out to buy the paper to read the story for himself. He boasted between expletives that he had the address of "the nigger girl that was going to integrate the school." His niece told him to be careful now, he might get caught, and what would Tee do without him? He said that the FBI could come and do all the searching they wanted. He had enough "stuff put away," he said, "to flatten half of Birmingham."

"What good do you think any of that would do?" Hood asked. He looked his niece squarely in the face. "You just wait till after Sunday morning," he said. "They will beg us to let them segregate."

"What do you mean by that?" she said.

"Just wait," he said. "You will see."

Business

DOWNTOWN THAT SATURDAY, as black diners trickled into the lunch counters of Woolworth's, Loveman's, and Newberry's, Integration Row was for once devoid of the National States Rights Party storm troopers and their Klan reinforcements. Tommy Blanton flitted around on errands, apparently restless for his seven-thirty date with Jean Casey. Troy Ingram stopped by Chambliss's house with a Cahaba Heights neighbor, a brickmason named Henry Glass. Chambliss was still peeved over the credit Ingram was getting as the master bomb maker. He had been Dynamite Bob when Ingram was using the stuff just for blasting coal. But the two men had decided to pool their talents. The end of segregation demanded something more than the nocturnal throw-and-blow fare—something activated on a timer, perhaps, that could be planted in advance and exploded in daylight.

That day, one of Flora Chambliss's sisters, Mary Frances Cunningham, came by to visit. Sometime between six and seven, Chambliss got up to leave the house and told the women that if he got any calls, "Tell them I'm going to Troy Ingram's to a meeting." The family knew that "going over to Troy's house" was code for Klan work under way. Bob Gafford, whose auto parts store was just down the street, intercepted Chambliss on his way out and the two conferred before Chambliss drove off.

Chambliss and Troy Ingram had been working on a timing device involving acid and had probably been experimenting the night before, once alibis were established at the Modern Sign Shop. But by Saturday night, they weren't completely confident of their expertise. They went out to Highway 280, near the Cahaba River meeting place, and spoke with a lieutenant from the National Guard who knew something about acid detonators used with a short fuse. According to one theory, the men decided to put sulfuric acid in a small plastic pill bottle and submerge in it a gelatin capsule filled with sugar and chlorate or perchlorate. Once the sulfuric acid ate through the gelatin, the combination of the ingredients would produce an instantaneous reaction of heat and rapid burning hot enough to ignite a standard commercial safety fuse or to detonate a #6 blasting cap. The whole package fit inside a shoe box.

Mary Frances Cunningham

AN OMNISCIENT NARRATOR would have looked down on Birmingham this Saturday night and observed an unusual amount of suspicious activity among the South's notable racists. Right after Robert left the house—and despite his waning popularity around town—the Chamblisses' phone started ringing. Earl Thompson, his suspected accomplice in the 1956 Shuttlesworth bombing, called, as did Ross Keith, a suspected bomber of Arthur Shores's house. Then both Blantons and Gene Reeves, whose car witnesses placed at the scene of the Warrior church burning, called. Hubert Page, who returned at eight-thirty from the funeral of an in-law in Montgomery, checked in with Chambliss before embarking on a night jam-packed with alibis. Bobby Cherry, who had also been one of Chambliss's callers, was out late, although it was understood that a man with seven children under the age of eleven didn't need much of an excuse to get out of the house.

The anti-Semitic branch of the resistance was also represented. J. B. Stoner's car was parked, under continual police surveillance, in front of Edward Fields's house. Ace Carter was also in town, perhaps reconnoitering for the governor.

But there was no omniscient narrator, and consequently we may never know what really happened during the hours leading up to Sunday morning. There were only Flora Chambliss and her sister Mary Frances Cunningham at the Chambliss house fielding phone calls from Klansmen. Flora's attitude toward her husband had not yet progressed from ambivalence to abhorrence, for the couple had some strange, tender connection. Chambliss still talked about how he took her over to Loveman's shortly after their marriage, in 1937, and told her to get a fur coat. "Mr. Chambliss, I don't believe in furs," she had said. "I'm just a plain little old country girl." But the feisty Cunningham hated her brother-in-law, thought he was killing her sister, and she had begun sharing damaging information about him with a sheriff's deputy named James Hancock. (Although the informant-deputy relationship seemed to be based, in part, on intimacy of a different sort.) This was risky, considering the breadth of the Klan's law enforcement contacts (and it was not clear where Hancock's sympathies lay). Also, most of the material Cunningham was passing on came from Flora, whom Chambliss did not hesitate to "straighten out" with violence.

On Saturday night, Cunningham heard enough to make a leap of faith. She claims she called Hancock: "They are up to something. I believe they are going to bomb something." But, she says, he hung up on her.

Policemen

POLICE CHIEF JAMIE MOORE might have had a hunch of his own, for he had assigned two special cars to patrol the downtown staging ground of the spring's revolution—the Gaston Motel (protected also by Movement guards), Kelly Ingram Park, and Sixteenth Street Baptist. Or perhaps he did not have full confidence in the officer ordinarily assigned to the beat. The driver of Car 25 was Robert Chambliss's nephew Floyd Garrett. At 10:40, twenty minutes before Garrett's shift ended, a police cruiser radioed headquarters to send a plainclothesman to Merle Snow's Modern Sign Shop, on the flank of Garrett's beat. There was no record as to who answered the call, or why it was made. Later, some theories would hold that Snow's business, not Troy Ingram's garage, was the bomb factory; or perhaps the device made there the night before, when half the dynamite enthusiasts in town seemed to have moved through the shop, was being fine-tuned at Ingram's.

Waiting

AT AROUND ELEVEN, Ross Keith, one of Chambliss's many callers, showed up at his girlfriend Lavelle Fike's house with Sister White and Nigger Hall, all of whom Tommy Rowe later claimed had been drinking with him at a bar in North Birmingham. Fike left her six-year-old daughter, Reginia, and went with the men to the G and H Restaurant in Bessemer to look for girls to pair off with White and Hall. Keith told her to be quick because "we are in a stolen car."

Bobby Shelton was still in his Tuscaloosa office. Eastview's Gene Reeves and Bill Morgan, the colorless plumber who was the titular head of the United Americans for Conservative Government, had gone there from Birmingham to use the Klan press to run off some pamphlets for a big segregationists' meeting in Midfield the next day. At around eleven, Shelton received a tip, he would claim, that a carload of Negroes with rifles was heading toward Tuscaloosa—or maybe it was toward Birmingham. Shelton alerted the authorities as well as Eastview Exalted Cyclops Robert Thomas, who Shelton knew was at Billy and Mary Lou Holt's house, along with Wilda and Loel Roosevelt Rogers, an Eastview Klansman who was a diesel mechanic (and sometimes disguised his middle name as Rosvelt). Thomas, Rogers, and Holt, who had alibied one another on September 4, the night of the second Shores bombing, repaired with their weapons to the "Y" Cafe and Truck Stop in Bessemer, avowedly to lie in fruitless wait for the armed Negroes, an appropriate distance from the Sixteenth Street Baptist Church.

The Souls of White Folks

DAVID "WOODY" EVANS, who had provided some corroboration of Roosevelt
Tatum's story about the A. D. King bombing, was hanging out in front of the
Jockey Boy restaurant, where Walter Gadsden and the police dog Leo had been
historically photographed the previous spring. It was across the street from Sixteenth Street Baptist. Sometime between eleven and eleven-thirty, Evans
watched a white man in a black suit circle the block three times in his 1963 white-
on-red Pontiac Bonneville before stopping in front of the Jockey Boy. He turned
out to be "a homosexual with ten dollars to spend," Evans told the bartender.

So far, this Saturday night was holding out no more than the usual indignities
for Negroes in Birmingham. At around midnight, police officers drove up to the
Jockey Boy and told Evans and his friends that they would not have them "laying
around on the sidewalks like hogs and pigs." A few minutes later, a carload of
white teenage girls, just out of a movie downtown, decided to try the feminine
version of "nigger knocking" and drove into the neighborhood to yell at black
pedestrians.

"Tall Paul" White was just arriving at his rooming house behind the Sixteenth Street church, carrying a hundred 45 rpm records from a platter party in
Leeds, where 103 white fans had paid fifty cents apiece to hear him deejay.

Girlfriends

TOMMY BLANTON and Jean Casey were having a tryst at a popular lovers' lane
at Vulcan's base. They got out of Blanton's white-on-blue 1957 Chevy and walked
to the escarpment of Red Mountain overlooking Twentieth Street, where a fence
prevented pedestrians from jumping into the traffic below. At around midnight
they drove toward Casey's house in West Birmingham.

Other Klan girlfriends were also working overtime. Pat Clark checked in at
Bob's Tourist Court with her recently divorced paramour, George Pickle, and a
case of beer; for some reason they registered as New Yorkers, though Pickle was
so drunk he would barely be able to reconstruct his whereabouts.

Ross Keith asked Lavelle Fike what time it was and was told it was midnight.
The couple, still with Nigger Hall and Sister White, stopped briefly at the Blue
Bird Truck Stop on the Bessemer Super Highway, and left with three cans of
Schlitz and three Burger ales. Eventually, they headed down the Bessemer Short-
cut toward a viaduct a mile out of town. Parked there was an unoccupied white-
on-green 1956 Ford. Since this was apparently Hall's car, the men must have
orchestrated this destination earlier.

Hall got out of Keith's car and threw up. Sister White walked him down to a
small branch. After they had been by the water for fifteen minutes, Hall was on
edge enough to yell back to Keith and Fike, "Watch it, Ross, there is a car pulling
in—it might be the boys." Fike assumed he meant cops. But nobody arrived.

Perhaps there had been a plan for policemen to appear and confirm the men's alibi, for the choreography that often aligned vigilantes and law enforcers before a racial milestone seemed to be in play. Across town in the Eastern Section, Police Car 21 radioed into headquarters the license plate number of a 1959 Chevrolet spotted at the Roebuck Shopping Center. It turned out to be registered to Robert Creel, the Bessemer Klan chief, who was quite a way from his home turf. Police records do not reveal why the license check was made, but it did help establish Creel's presence well outside the vicinity of Sixteenth Street.

With his ties to Bobby Shelton (his immediate Klan boss), George Wallace (through the United Americans for Conservative Government), and the Birmingham police (through Detective Tom Cook now that Bull Connor was gone), Hubert Page was in a position to implicate a lot of powerful people if he should ever get caught in a bombing plot. He had arranged for himself a mature, solid alibi, as befit the elder statesman he played inside the Klan. At around ten or so, he and his friend (and fellow UACG honcho) Bob Gafford had taken their wives to the Eastwood Bowling Alley, one of the few places in Birmingham that stayed open all night. Soon after midnight, by coincidence, Robert Chambliss's employer, Herman Siegel (the rare Jew the Klansman had no profane words for), came by after a movie at the Alabama and kidded Gafford, one of his customers, about the reward money he had put up in the arm slashing.

If Page seemed on edge that night, there were two reasons. One, he was falling in love. His extra-Eastview role in the UACG had given him the opportunity to be with the group's fun-loving secretary, Mary Lou Holt, around whom important men, including George Wallace, seemed to light up. (She would later sweet-talk the governor into making Eastview's Loel Rogers a justice of the peace.) And second, his alibi lasted from 10 p.m. to 2 a.m., the window (as Mary Frances Cunningham would gather later) during which he had been expecting to hear about a big explosion downtown. But when he got home, it was as quiet as a tomb.

Bomb Threat

ON THE SIXTEENTH STREET BEAT, Officer Ernie Cantrell had taken over Car 25 from Floyd Garrett at eleven. Cantrell, who belonged to the same church as Mary Lou and Billy Holt (Minor Heights Baptist, which was pastored by the UACG's spiritual leader, Ferrell Griswold), saw two white men he didn't recognize sitting in their parked car. Upon spotting the police radio hanging off the dash, he greeted them, assuming that either the feds or the state had a stake. A block away from the church, a street sanitation worker who happened to be an old friend and tenant of Earl Thompson was filling his truck at a fireplug. A man in a black Chevrolet—a plainclothes officer probably—shined his hand spotlight on him. The sanitation worker repaired to the downtown branch of the Krystal hamburger chain and looked out the window onto a dreamscape: a twenty-car caravan traveling west, on Second Avenue North, fluttering Confederate flags.

It was around 1:15—a strange hour for a demonstration. Around ten cars turned north up Sixteenth Street, past the Modern Sign Shop toward the Baptist church. One of them, an older model, had a Confederate flag tied to a high whip antenna, just like Tommy Blanton's car. If Blanton had needed to stop by the sign shop to pick up a package—or a person—this would have been a deceptively brazen way to camouflage his presence in this black neighborhood. And as it happened, his friend Robert Chambliss also had business in the neighborhood at around that time.

Chambliss had gone home for a while after the meeting at Ingram's and then had left again, apparently to meet Floyd Garrett after his shift ended at eleven. Chambliss claimed to own two police uniforms and may have put one of them on in order to join his nephew inconspicuously. At around the time the white supremacist caravan was traveling through downtown, Chambliss would say, Garrett put a handkerchief over the mouthpiece of a pay phone and called headquarters to report anonymously that he heard two guys saying that a bomb was going to explode at the Downtowner Holiday Inn at 3:30 a.m.

At 1:29, Sergeant W. E. Wilson called off the stakeout at the Gaston Motel, six blocks away from the Downtowner. Wilson flagged down the two special patrols and assigned them to platoon each other at the all-white motel, which lodged NBC's Johnny Apple and the rest of the news reporters who hadn't gotten home for the weekend. That meant that there would be only one car alternating between the church and the motel.

The Holiday Inn bomb threat would not appear on the radio log that the Birmingham Police provided to the FBI six weeks later, and for some reason the call had not been put out over the police radio. This omission may have had something to do with the fact that the radio dispatcher on duty was Officer "Six Pack Jack" LeGrand, considered to be a Klan sympathizer, and a close friend of Tommy Rowe.

Two O'Clock

BACK AT THE BESSEMER VIADUCT, Ross Keith thought he heard a noise. He left Lavelle Fike in the car and joined Sister and Nigger at the branch. They stood there talking for forty-five minutes. Keith took out his pistol and shot it two times. After a minute he fired twice again. Fike wondered what he was shooting at. Perhaps, as a product of the old DeBardeleben "family," he was practicing an old miners' tradition of celebrating with firearms, as on a really big day like Christmas.

It was two in the morning. Ernie Cantrell, in Car 25, was just about to take his next break, as Floyd Garrett, off-duty owner of the beat, would know.

The Seamstress

FOR THE NEXT nearly four decades, investigators would try to recover from randomness these snippets of Klan activity. And the most sophisticated crime-

solving techniques in the world would probably have been defeated by this motley band of brothers if a woman named Kirthus Glenn had not decided to take a
vacation from her job in the laundry department at a Detroit hospital to visit her
hometown of Birmingham. She was a seamstress like another black woman of
Movement fame.

At 2:10 on the morning of September 15, Glenn pulled up in front of the
house where she was staying, on Seventh Avenue North between Fifteenth and
Sixteenth Streets. She and her host's son, Henry Smith, were returning after driving a friend over to West End. As Glenn slowed her red Chevy sedan, she spied a
smudge of light to the right, in front of Poole's Funeral Chapel. A parked car's interior dome light illuminated three white men, possibly four. The driver's back
was to her, but she got a good look at the man sitting in the back seat, passenger's
side. "They must have a phone in there with such a high wand on the left rear
fender," Glenn said to Smith.

Immediately after Glenn pulled into a parking space, the car with the white
men departed. It moved east on Seventh Avenue and stopped at the stop sign at
Sixteenth Street. The Baptist church was immediately to the right, but the car
swerved into the left lane and turned north. Before it disappeared, Kirthus Glenn
got a good look at it. She took it to be a 1955 or 1956 Chevrolet sedan, white over
turquoise. She was a year off on the model, and the darkness had made the blue
car look a bit greener than it was, for the car Glenn would later pick out as identical to the one she saw was Tommy Blanton's 1957 white-on-blue Chevy.

Investigators would later suspect that Glenn had arrived while a Klansman,
perhaps wearing one of the police uniforms in Chambliss's possession, was planting the bomb. That would explain why two of the three men Glenn saw were sitting in the back seat. They had probably let their confederate off on Fifteenth
Street, at the mouth of the alley that ran directly behind the church. Mary Frances
Cunningham would later tell the FBI that Bobby Cherry had carried the bomb, although having him do the deed would have been a bold move, given that the brace
for his broken back posed something of a handicap. Investigators would believe
that, after the arrival of Glenn and Smith, Blanton drove around the block, avoid-
ing passing by the church by going north up Sixteenth Street to Eighth Avenue
and back around the block to a vacant lot on Seventh behind the church, near
where Glenn had spotted the car. Then, investigators would guess, the man who
planted the bomb cut through the lot to reunite with his three co-conspirators:
Blanton, Chambliss, and Herman Cash. Troy Ingram perhaps still retained too
many compunctions as a citizen and family man to appear at the crime scene.

At 3:44 came the familiar Birmingham music: an explosion. Police converged
on the north-of-downtown scene prepared for a riot. Gary Thomas Rowe would
claim he awoke and braced for a call from the FBI. The blast, however, turned out
to be an accident at the Alabama Gas Company on Huntsville Road.

Perhaps the men who had recently been parked near the Sixteenth Street
Baptist Church thought their timing device had malfunctioned. For six minutes
later, beat cops spotted a 1957 Chevrolet, white top, blue bottom, with two men in

the front seat, speeding through Ensley. It turned up Avenue I, but then the driver hightailed it to Warrior Road and then to Avenue P, where the Chevy finally shook Car 41—the same police cruiser that had arrived at A. D. King's house immediately after it was bombed. Cherry lived on Avenue I.

Saturday night was nearly over, and only two black people in Birmingham had a glimmer of history in progress. Kirthus Glenn had worried enough about the three white men to write down the license plate number of their car and put the scrap of paper on a desk by the phone. But she did not call it in. Her companion, Henry Smith, had suggested that they "sit on the porch and watch them," and they went back out to look for a sign of the Chevrolet. When the FBI interviewed Smith later, he would say that he had been drinking and that the car he saw was red. His account was dismissed. And so the seamstress would become the only official witness to the crime of the era.

McWhorter 1963

BECAUSE MY FATHER had gotten in the habit of working weekends when he was struggling to get his new business going, we never expected to see him on Saturday night. At around five-thirty, he usually walked up the hill from "the plant" and started drinking at Weems Place, which we children would call the "Shoot 'em Up" after the occasional gunfights that broke out there. If Mama asked him where he went afterward that kept him out till midnight, he would say, "Civil rights."

I had vague but sinister visions of what my father might be doing, and when I tried to imagine where he was doing them, I pictured him driving in his car around Woodlawn. It was the only off-limits part of Birmingham I was familiar enough with to know that Papa's dusty Dodge would have blended right in. One had to go through Woodlawn to get to the airport, and that was the extent that anyone I knew spent time there. Over-the-mountain residents were so phobic about those neighborhoods that anyone who had an unavoidable errand on the wrong side of town—the best fabric store, for example, was in low-rent Avondale—preempted the disapproval of friends by rolling her eyes in reference to "the bunch of rednecks" over there.

But the Martin McWhorter family's doctor was in Woodlawn. Dr. Somerset was the father of a Dean Martin look-alike who had been a classmate of my father's at Battle Ground Academy. Sitting in his waiting room, in a converted wood-and-fieldstone "country-style" house, I always felt as if my identity were being sucked out of me. I looked hard at "What's Wrong with This Picture?" in the children's magazine *Highlights*, fearing the caste confusion that would result from eye contact with any of the other patients. Sometimes after doctor's visits we stopped for some ten-cent hamburgers at the Krystal, sitting amid the vortex of greasy air stirred up by fans over the grill. As bad as it was, I had no idea that I was eating in the dining hall of the most violent bunch of rednecks in the country, a stone's throw away from the headquarters of Eastview 13.

My father's shop was a few miles northeast of Woodlawn. On the days we had to be there with Mama while she did her secretarial duties, I loved answering the phone at the "McWhorter Engineering Company," not understanding that the fact of someone my age playing receptionist might cancel out the importance of the name. Papa's "plant" was really no more than a machine shop. And aside from being the son of Hobart Amory McWhorter Sr. and Marjorie Westgate McWhorter, Papa did not seem that much different from the machinists, electricians, power company linemen, and mechanics who belonged to Eastview 13. Among the *Skin Diver* magazines in his office we sometimes found some primitively produced literature from the Klan.

People who worked with machines seemed to see the world as a mechanical system, in which processes were a means to an end. The civil rights movement could not exist for its own integrity any more than a carburetor could vaporize gasoline for its own satisfaction. Did these men really believe that the Movement was a Communist conspiracy to mongrelize America? I think Papa did, and was not simply looking for a noble excuse to get away from his family at night.

MY FATHER HAD MADE his first bombs with miniature whiskey bottles he retrieved from the Dumpster at the Mountain Brook Club. He filled them with nitroglycerin and sold his minibombs to the neighborhood kids for fifty cents a pop. Back in the blind road off Hastings, they would light them under hastily assembled cairns to see how far the rocks would blow. Martin liked to point out that his mother, the chemistry major at Wellesley, had taught him how to make the bombs and that his father took nitroglycerin in tablet form for angina caused by job pressure "he didn't have the mental bridgework to handle."

Way in the future, I would often review this Saturday night in September 1963. I would wonder if, on a night when I had fallen asleep with nothing more on my mind than what I was wearing to church the next day, my father might have found some marvelous opportunity to identify with fate: to out-tough his father, yet also be true to the bigoted principles of his community, and once and for all prove that a boy from Mountain Brook could keep up with the real men of Birmingham.

27.

DENISE, CAROLE, CYNTHIA,
AND ADDIE

Sunday Morning

IT BEGAN AS AN OVERCAST, unusually cool September day. On the western side of town, Mrs. Freeman Brown, Tommy Blanton's tormented neighbor, left her house at seven to go to mass at Blessed Sacrament Catholic Church. She glanced toward the Blantons' apartment building and noticed that neither the father's nor the son's car was there.

Willie Green arrived at Sixteenth Street Baptist at around seven. He had been the church janitor for two weeks. Entering through the Sixteenth Street side door, he began his rounds of the building, making sure that all the clocks conformed to his watch.

Robert Chambliss was just waking up. He had a pious streak, insisting on grace before meals, delivered with unvarying inflection—"Kiiind heavenly father/We thaaank thee/For theeeese table blessings." But he hadn't gone to church in nearly five years—not since his pastor at Thirty-fifth Avenue Baptist had announced from the pulpit that he had recently visited the Sixteenth Street Baptist Church and had returned the invitation to its members. Chambliss and three other Klansmen had showed up at the minister's apartment the next evening and informed him that he was under Klan investigation as a suspected Communist. Chambliss never set foot in the church again. Sixteenth Street Baptist had cost him his faith.

Chambliss went next door for a cup of coffee with his dominoes buddy Clarence Dill, an auto mechanic in the advanced stages of alcoholism. Chambliss and Dill went to the newsstand, but soon after his return Chambliss left again, saying he had forgotten to buy cigarettes.

Mary Frances Cunningham, who had come back to the Chambliss house, officially to tend to her sister, began trying to get in touch with her friend Deputy James Hancock to repeat her warnings of the night before. The sheriff's office relayed her messages, and Hancock agreed to meet her at around eight-thirty north of Tarrant City. Cunningham spoke in ominous generalities. She said she had a feeling that there was a bomb out there, that something was supposed to have happened at midnight. That morning, she told Hancock, Chambliss had put on one of his favorite disguises, a floppy old hat and a walking cane, to complete the picture of an old man. Later she would say that he had gone down to Sixteenth Street. Now, she did not say why she suspected that the target was the Sixteenth Street Baptist Church, other than Chambliss's periodic comments that "they ought to blow that church up."

What happened then between Mary Frances Cunningham and James Hancock remains one of the mysteries of the case. She would claim that he drove her around town and into the countryside, questioning and teasing her, stopping for a cup of coffee as though this were a date. He effectively prevented Cunningham from taking her information to anyone who might have acted upon it.

The Children

AT AROUND TEN O'CLOCK, Herbert E. Oden Jr., a schoolteacher and the Sixteenth Street Baptist's assistant pastor to John Cross, left the church by its east door to guest-preach at J. L. Ware's Trinity Baptist. He headed down the stairs where Fred Shuttlesworth had been swept by fire hoses four months before. If Oden had noticed a package under the steps, concealed by a magnolia bush, this Sunday morning might have been like most other Sunday mornings in the City of Churches.

The Reverend John Cross was acutely aware of the ambiguous glory of the church he had taken over the previous year. Sixteenth Street Baptist was still the snootiest black congregation in the city, a bastion of schoolteachers and administrators who deferred to their "white friends." Its founding minister was known for working with the industrialists to discourage Negroes from joining the union. The events of the spring had underscored the church's mounting irrelevance. Seeing his sanctuary filled with the hope of Birmingham, the thousands of young black people putting their bodies into the struggle, Cross had been struck by how strange it was for stuffy old Sixteenth Street to be harboring a youth movement. Freedom songs had reverberated against walls that had never heard even gospel music, only the sedate hymns of white Christianity. The church had been the only one in the city to charge the Movement for using its facilities. Cross was still after SCLC for the electrical bill it had run up at its 1962 convention.

Cross had decided to expand his youth ministry and hold youth fellowship every month rather than once a year. September 15 was the inaugural Youth Day. The musical chores at the eleven o'clock service would be handled by the youth choir, and Cross's sermon was entitled "The Rock That Will not Roll."

Many of the young choristers were attending Sunday school classes in the church basement. One of them was eleven-year-old Denise McNair, a sheltered child of the middle class, the devoted owner of a dog named Whitey, and the recent author/illustrator of a story titled "The Boy Who Wanted a Pet," featuring black and white children and a chicken. Her only care in the world that morning was that her parents belonged to different congregations. It was a mark of Sixteenth Street pride that quite a few female members refused to switch churches in submission to their husbands. Chris McNair, a Tuskegee graduate and freelance photographer, was superintendent of the Sunday school at St. Paul's Lutheran and had to leave for church earlier than his only child. Denise already showed a take-charge bent for leadership, whether it was in helping the infirm cross the street or making the sort of decision of faith that had brought her recently to join the church of her mother, Maxine, a schoolteacher.

Another young singer, fourteen-year-old Cynthia Wesley, was an accidental member of the black bourgeoisie. Claude Wesley, a grade school principal, and his wife, Gertrude, a nursery school teacher, had grieved over their childlessness until a teacher friend told Gertrude she could get her a child. The Wesleys were taken to visit a hard-up family with eight children, and as Gertrude was getting into her car to leave, the six-year-old daughter had stood before her, rocking with hands on hips, and said, "When I go with you, you gonna buy me one of those stiff underskirts."

Soon, Cynthia had not only a hands-on acquaintance with the word "petticoat" but other trappings of middle-classness—dance lessons, music lessons. She played the saxophone in the Ullman High School band and was an honor student whom her pastor considered "brilliant." Nor had her new abundance gone to her head; she dispensed gifts and her old music books to those left behind. Her parents, however doting, had given her perspective on the petticoats. "Cynthia, your slip is hanging," the mother had told her daughter at home on Dynamite Hill that morning as she headed out with her father for Youth Day, and then repeated one of her favorite maternal maxims: "Always put your clothes on right, 'cause you don't know how you might be coming back."

Cynthia Wesley and three other members of the youth choir left Ella Demand's intermediate Sunday school class to freshen up for their roles as ushers at the main service. The lesson for the day had been on "The Love That Forgives." Denise McNair, also excused by her teacher, met Cynthia and her classmates in the women's lounge, in the northeast corner of the basement opposite the exterior stairwell.

Mabel Shorter, filling in for the vacationing church secretary, was upstairs in the main office trying to complete the Sunday school rosters, but she hadn't been able to get anything done all morning. The phone kept ringing, and when she answered, the caller wouldn't say anything. It was as if someone was just checking to see if anybody was there—a strange thing for a Sunday.

Normally after Sunday school, the girls who were in the women's lounge this morning would have gone to a drugstore to wait for church to begin, but because they were part of the service, primping was in order. Fourteen-year-old Carole Robertson, another product of a "mixed" Sixteenth Street marriage (her father was a Methodist), was the most mature of the girls, even more mentally advanced than her precocious close friend, Cynthia Wesley. She was wearing medium-high heels for the first time, shiny black ones bought the day before at a downtown department store. Mrs. Robertson had gotten Carole a necklace to go with the shoes and put a winter coat on layaway for her.

Also in the lounge were Addie Mae and Sarah Collins, perhaps the least "Sixteenth Street" of the congregation that liked to refer to itself as the elite. Their father, Oscar, worked at Joy Young's, the city's beloved Chinese restaurant, whose black staff had turned table waiting into ballet. One of eight children, fourteen-year-old Addie was a little on the shy side, but she looked radiant in her white usher's dress. Cynthia and Carole also wore white. The three ushers were standing with young Denise over by the window, whose sill began at about four feet above the lounge floor and gave onto Sixteenth Street at ground level; so elegant was this church that even that restroom window was made of stained glass.

Addie's younger sister Sarah stood at the washbowl. On orders from a Sunday school teacher, fifteen-year-old Bernadine Mathews came into the lounge to encourage the girls to return to their classrooms. Denise's hair was perfect, with a gold barrette anchoring a French roll, but Cynthia Wesley said she needed to push her hair up one more time. Bernadine chided her, "Cynthia, children who don't obey the Lord live only half as long."

Seventy-five-year-old Joel Boykin, the dentist whose home-office had gone up in dynamite in 1950, was sitting in his parked car several yards north of the church, where he had dropped his wife off; he was killing a little time before services at his own church, St. John's A.M.E. Leo "Jabo" Cleveland was putting a coin in the jukebox at his restaurant, the Silver Sands, across the street from the church. Deacons were gliding up the grand front steps that led to the sanctuary. Around 125 people were inside.

William Sturdivant's adult class, upstairs in the dining room of the old parsonage, was interrupted by what sounded like a loud ticking. Someone said, "Reckon that was—" At 10:22 there was a resonant thud, as if someone had hit the world's largest washtub, followed by a ripping blast that sent a streak of fire above the church. Closed doors flew open, and the walls shook. As a stale-smelling white fog filled the church, a blizzard of debris—brick, stone, wire, glass—pelted the neighborhood. Some of those inside belived that the Russians were coming.

A motorist was blown from his car. A black pedestrian calling his wife from a pay phone across the street was whooshed, the receiver still in hand, into the Social Cleaners, whose front door had been whipped open. Johnny Apple, the NBC correspondent, felt the blast as he was having breakfast at the White Castle hamburger joint not far from the church.

Thirty blocks away, Nigger Hall and Ross Keith were sitting in a car at Hall's brother's junkyard, recovering from the previous night's drunk. Keith observed, "I guess it's somebody discriminating against them niggers again."

Accounts differ on how Mary Frances Cunningham and Deputy James Hancock heard about the blast. Hancock would later imply that Cunningham's tip had not been acted on because the two had been enjoying the illicit privacy of his car, and Cunningham (who would allow that she had been pounding his aching back at the moment of the explosion) would insist that this was just a way of turning on her the blame that was his. Neither would be forthcoming about the events of the morning of September 15. Hancock gunned the car toward Sixteenth Street.

Maxine McNair, who had been attending her adult Sunday school class upstairs in the choir stand, was the only member of her group to scream hysterically. A few blocks away, Claude Wesley, who was getting a shoe shine, said to himself, "I know it's our church," and raced through Kelly Ingram Park toward the noxious gray cloud billowing from the building's northeast corner.

In the basement, Sarah Collins lay in darkness, surrounded by rubble. The last thing she had seen was Addie by the restroom window, tying the sash of Denise McNair's purple plaid winter-cotton dress.

Sarah called her big sister. "Addie, Addie, Addie."

"The Goddamn Church Just Went Down"

GARY THOMAS ROWE would claim that he was waiting at his apartment for Nigger Hall to show up so that they, Sister White, and Ross Keith could go monitor blacks who might be trying to integrate the white churches downtown. Mary Lois McCord, a dispatcher for the Birmingham police who was one of his many girlfriends and law enforcement contacts, called at ten-thirty. "Thank God, honey, you're home," she said. "At least you wasn't down there." Rowe wanted to know what the hell she was talking about, and she said, "The church just went down." McCord was always teasing him with her hopeful suspicions that he was working for the FBI rather than the Klan, and she said, "Get ahold of the bureau—if you haven't already." Then she laughed in relief that her two-timing boyfriend was not a church bomber.

Rowe reached the dispatcher at the FBI and said, "Goddamn, have you got ahold of my man? The goddamn church just went down." The dispatcher replied, "It's so quiet ain't nothing up here but me and the mouse." He told Rowe to hold on a sec. Six minutes later, he came back: "Jesus Fucking Christ, our switchboard is lit up like a Christmas tree." He said people were lying all over the place, some dead. "Get off the line, and get dressed."

When Special Agent Byron McFall called, Rowe offered a few suspects off the top of his head: Charles Cagle, Ross Keith, Nigger Hall, Sister White, and maybe Earl Thompson, because they were all riding together.* But Rowe said that he did not think Klansmen were involved because the church was in such a heavily black neighborhood.

* Rowe would not tell his FBI handler until seven months later that Hall, White, and Keith were supposed to have picked him up that morning; he had apparently forgotten that he had named these men as suspects on the morning of the bombing.

Return to the Scene

MOMENTS AFTER THE EXPLOSION, two black construction workers, Dallas and John Cunningham, were making their way home after having a few slugs of Golden Spur wine at a cafe. They saw two casually dressed white men run out from between two houses onto the Seventh Avenue sidewalk. It was precisely the spot, between Fifteenth and Sixteenth Streets, where Kirthus Glenn had noticed Tommy Blanton's car parked the night before. The men were holding hands and stumbling, sweaty and winded. One appeared to be pulling along the other, who was limping. "Those are the bombers," John Cunningham yelled, but by the time they could stop the car and jump out, the whites had disappeared.

The Cunninghams had not gotten a good look at the limping man because his head was down, but the FBI quickly suspected that he was Troy Ingram, who had recently broken a toe. The witnesses had a better description of the man helping him: He had black hair and a crew cut, like Tommy Blanton.

A couple of doors west, Kirthus Glenn got something of a jolt when she looked out the window and spied the car she had seen the night before in front of Poole's Funeral Chapel, cruising Seventh Avenue. In the hysteria that followed the blast, she apparently did not think to find the scrap of paper on which she had written the license plate number.

Final Embrace

FIVE MINUTES AFTER the explosion, the telephone at the church office—the lines somehow remained intact—rang again. A church member answered. "There's been a tragedy at the church," he explained to the silence on the other end.

A church elder, eighty-four-year-old John Henry Pullin, appeared at the church's side doorway with blood streaming down his face. Normally a staircase connected the door to the sidewalk, but it had been obliterated. From his experience in the mines, Pullin estimated fifteen sticks of dynamite.

Jim Lay, the black Civil Defense captain, arrived, mindful of the white man with a grip he had spotted two weeks earlier by the church's now leveled side stairs. Through a bullhorn he shouted orders to clear the streets to let the ambulances through. Soon he was joined by a black Civil Defense sergeant, Hosea Hudson Jr., whose father, the star of Birmingham's Communist Party, had once epitomized the sort of "bomb thrower" who brought about social breakdown.

Another early arrival at the scene was Ralph Roton, the Klansman who served as the investigator for the legislature's Peace Committee. He was to take pictures of the bystanders, perhaps to help George Wallace make the inevitable case that Communists or Negroes had bombed the church.

Inside, the Reverend John Cross followed parents of small children to the basement. Cross's thirteen-year-old daughter had suffered only minor injuries. She had declined to accompany her friend Cynthia Wesley to the restroom, but had promised to hold her purse till she returned. Cross stopped in every class to shepherd the children out and after a quick survey said to himself, "Good, I don't see a single person trapped."

Cross made his way back upstairs and stood on the front steps of the church, looking down upon the angry crowd of black sympathizers. Handed a megaphone by a Civil Defense worker, he said, "We should be forgiving as Christ was forgiving as He hung from the cross and said, 'Father, forgive them, because they know not what they do.' " He began to recite, " 'The Lord is our shepherd. We shall not want.' " Then he turned his megaphone over to the Reverend Charles Billups to try an even more extreme tactic. "Go home and pray for the men who did this evil deed," Billups said. "We must have love in our hearts for these men."

Cross moved toward the fog that clung to the northeast side of the church. There was a seven-by-seven-foot hole in the wall of what had been the women's lounge. The bomb had made a crater two and a quarter feet deep and five and a half feet wide, demolishing a foundation that had been a thirty-inch-thick mass of stone facing over a brick-and-masonry wall. The solid limestone windowsill and the heavy-gauge-wire protective screens had been destroyed. Debris that had once been the church's east wall was now piled against the opposite wall of the basement: brick, concrete, stone, wood, and mortar.

Cross walked through the gaping hole. Turning around and looking across Sixteenth, he could see the sign of a contracting company, named Liberty. Some deacons and Civil Defense workers with Cross began digging into the wreckage. Strewn about were blood-spattered leaflets printed with a child's prayer: "Dear God, we are sorry for the times we were so unkind." After a couple of layers of bricks had been removed, someone said, "I feel something soft."

A gingerly excavation uncovered four bodies. They were stacked horizontally like firewood. Cross had no idea who they were. They looked like old women, and he knew that the basement had been filled with Sunday school children.

"Lord, that's Denise," said Deacon F. L. Pippen, owner of the Social Cleaners, across the street. Denise McNair was Pippen's granddaughter. It was only then that Cross realized that the corpses were young girls. Pippen had recognized Denise's no-longer-shiny patent-leather shoes. The clothes had been blown off the girls' bodies.

Samuel Rutledge, looking for his three-and-a-half-year-old son, instead found a female buried alive, moaning and bleeding from the head. He told her that the church had been bombed and carried her through the hole toward the street. "Do you know who she is?" people asked one another. Again, Cross thought she had to be forty or forty-five years old. But Sarah Collins was only twelve. Her face was spurting blood, and to a witness across the street, it looked as if the skin had been peeled from her face. After being loaded into an ambulance (colored), she sang "Jesus Loves Me" and occasionally said, "What happened? I can't see." She was hoping that the reason her sister Addie hadn't answered when she called her name was that she and the other three girls at the restroom window had fled.

The ambulance driver delivered Sarah to a doctor at University Hospital and, when his assistant fainted, returned alone to the church to pick up his next cargo, the corpse of Addie Mae Collins.

Elizabeth

ELIZABETH HOOD WAS at home in North Birmingham with her young son, Robin, and her grandmother, Mama Katie. She had ruled out a bombing when she felt the ground rumble—it was daylight—and decided something was going on over at the ACIPCO cast-iron pipe foundry. The TV set was tuned to a church service, and suddenly the singsong drone of the preacher was interrupted by the crisp diction of a newsreader. The only words she caught were "apparently a bomb." When she heard the words "Sixteenth Street Baptist," she called her aunt Tee, but was confused to hear her uncle Robert talking in the background, assuming that he would not have had time to get home from Sixteenth Street. But Hood knew, in her mind as well as her gut, that Chambliss had to have been involved. Sunday morning had come.

The Shoe

APPROACHING HER FATHER in the crowd on the sidewalk, Maxine Pippen McNair cried, "I can't find Denise." F. L. Pippen told his daughter, "She's dead, baby. I've got one of her shoes." Later, Pippen would say that he was glad that he, and not some stranger, had been the one "who lifted those big, sharp chunks of concrete off of her" and carried her to the ambulance. But that morning, watching his daughter take in the significance of the shoe he held up, he screamed, "I'd like to blow the whole town up."

Where Did Freedom Go?

A RIOT WAS BREWING around the church. Helmeted cops fired over the heads of brick throwers, prompting a chorus of the "We Are Not Afraid" verse of "We Shall Overcome." A black spectator was spreading the rumor that police had been parked the night before in Sixth Alley between Sixteenth and Seventeen Streets, keeping all Negroes out.

Before long, rubbernecking white tourists began showing up. Newlyweds from Chicago, returning north from their Nassau honeymoon, cruised past sidewalks seven deep with black people, some with bottles cocked. Their next stop was University Hospital, where the bride had her head sewn up.

Joel Boykin Jr., the son of the bombed-out Dynamite Hill dentist, who himself now had the biggest black dental practice in Birmingham, had come to his church to check on his mother, the organist for the youth choir. Joel Jr. had played a role in the spring demonstrations, pressuring his fellow professionals to put up property bonds for the imperiled bail fund and to sign a statement of solidarity with King, his old Morehouse schoolmate, that had been published in the *Bir-mingham News* late in the campaign. Boykin's young son had asked him that spring, "Who is that Freedom everyone is looking for, and where did Freedom go?" Boykin had laughed and thought, "That's a tough one; where *did* freedom go?"

Outside the wreckage, Boykin ran into one of his patients, Alpha Robertson. She asked him to try to find out if Carole was O.K. Boykin relayed the message he had heard from another man: Her daughter was safe.

Shoes

CLAUDE WESLEY had searched and searched the church for his daughter, Cynthia. He joined his wife, Gertrude, at the hospital, where a makeshift morgue had been set up. Claude Wesley spied a hand dangling out from under a sheet. He recognized the imitation class ring. "That's her," he said. He also saw her black-patent-leather shoes and white socks. There wasn't much else to go on. It was Cynthia whose head James Lay had pulled out of the wreckage, unable to "tell whether it was a human head from a dog's head."

Chris McNair, who had thought the bomb blast that morning was thunder to match the gray day, had gone to the hospital to look for his daughter after a cousin told him that his wife was safe. In the waiting room, McNair was shown a list of more than a dozen parishioners admitted, including Bernadine Mathews, the girl who had chided Cynthia for primping. He was enjoying his relief at not seeing his surname when a staff member led him to a room where four dead children lay under sheets. "I saw a little foot sticking out from under one of the sheets. A scarred patent-leather shoe covered with dust," McNair said later. "I suppose every little girl's foot looks about the same, but I knew it was Denise. I didn't need to look under the sheet to know it was her."

It is not known whether the fourth casualty was still wearing her shoes, but they were in mint condition when the funeral home returned them to her family: strapless pumps, day-old, with medium heels, in honor of the young woman Carole Robertson was on the verge of becoming.

Suspects

GARY THOMAS ROWE was telephoning the usual suspects. He called Nigger Hall and got his wife, Nelda, who said Hall was out doing missionary work in the bread truck cum Klan security mobile. Then he phoned the Exalted Cyclops Robert Thomas's house, and Mildred Thomas said, "Honey, they're out working, but Robert's not with them. His dad is here today and he had to run off with him for a while." She said that "Earl Thompson and them" had been there. Rowe then called Thompson, Herman Cash, and Billy Holt, and found no one home. He dialed Jack Cash's Barbecue, where the police radio had been turned up to allow patrons to listen to the dispatching of the squad cars.

Suspects had already been informally identified. One of Pop Blanton's tenants was hanging laundry in the backyard when a neighbor told her about the explosion. The tenant automatically looked over to see if the Blantons' cars were there. A newly enlisted WAC named Waylene Vaughn also thought immediately of Tommy Blanton, the boyfriend who had tried to run down the black pedestrian on their New Year's date.

Chambliss called Ronnie Tidwell, the electrician who was emerging as the new Eastview generation's leader in explosives. Chambliss's gloating tone in informing him of the bombing hadn't been lost on Tidwell, who had called a neighbor of Chambliss's and asked him to check to see whether Chambliss's car was in front of his house. Tidwell apparently didn't believe that Chambliss could have pulled off a delayed-action bombing.

Unable to stay away from the scene of the crime, Bobby Cherry came down to Snow's sign shop with his oldest boy, Frank, and found Merle Snow standing on the corner looking three blocks north toward the swarm of fire trucks and cruisers. When Cherry returned home, he told a neighbor that this was not the end of the bombings in Birmingham.

Garrett

OFFICER FLOYD GARRETT had a professional contempt for alibis and saw no reason to take them seriously even when one was needed. His accounts of how he learned about the church bombing would revolve erratically around what was clearly a bigger lie—in some versions he was home alone when the call came from headquarters; under oath, he would say that the phone had awakened him and his wife. Never would he mention the outing a witness saw him make before ten that morning, out of uniform, to one of Flora Chambliss's sisters, Viola Hillhouse. He told her that there was a bomb out at the church. "Keep your damn mouth shut," Hillhouse's daughter heard him say. "If anybody asks, you don't know anything. Understand?" If something got out, he promised her, "we will put it on Jim."*

On his way to headquarters after the explosion, Garrett had taken a detour by his uncle Robert's and charged into the house. The bond between the two men was clearly based on something more compelling than their blood ties, for there was little love lost between them. They had reputedly come to blows over Garrett's suspicion that his uncle was sleeping with his wife.

"What's the matter?" Chambliss greeted Garrett. "More nigger trouble or bombing?"

"They will get your ass on this one," Garrett replied. "You have gone too far."

It was the latest in a series of signs—beginning with the hang-up calls to the church—that the bomb had not gone off on schedule, or that those peripherally involved in the conspiracy had not been under the impression that the exploding

---

*Viola's husband, Jim Hillhouse, was still feuding with his brother-in-law Robert Chambliss, now fourteen years after Chambliss had tried to frame him for one of the Klan's crimes of 1949, apparently because he had regretted his decision to join the brotherhood and tried to resign.

church was to have been occupied. If, as Chambliss would claim, Garrett had phoned in the fake bomb threat to the Downtowner Holiday Inn, then he had conspired in murder. Which still did not persuade him to come up with a convincing alibi for his whereabouts the night before.

Garrett—a loud, beefy man nicknamed Fat Daddy, who was known for his interest in "women of either race"—would tell the FBI that after going off duty at 11 p.m. September 14, he had picked up his girlfriend, who worked the seven-to-eleven shift at the Melrose Dairy, and they had gone grocery shopping at the Liberty Supermarket a few blocks from the church-motel area. It was the same alibi he'd had on a Saturday night four months earlier, when someone had spotted his car, number 25, escorting the bombers of the Gaston Motel.

The FBI had arrived at Chambliss's house by the time Garrett came over Sunday morning. They watched their fellow officer of the peace come and go.

Senior Citizens

IT WAS AN HOUR OR SO LATER, at noon, when David Vann left Highlands Methodist on the Southside and headed for Sixteenth Street to see the smoke his year of toil had become. At the mouth of Fifth Alley was Robert Chambliss. The floppy hat disguise and old-man posture did not fool Vann.

The Senior Citizens who had been Vann's reluctant clients that spring had gone from church to the country club. Some of the Mountain Brook Club waiters, having heard the explosion on their way in to work, wore that look of shame that inexplicably overcomes those who have experienced tragedy. It was perhaps the misery on the waiters' faces rather than the growing body count that brought home the cruelty of the moment to the Big Mules, who had always extended gentle courtesies to their black retainers.

Rally

BY TWO O'CLOCK, the Cahaba River insurgents—Chambliss, the Blantons, Ingram—mingled with two thousand other citizens at the Dixie Speedway in Midfield at a rally of the West End Parents for Private Schools. Some of them came from services at West End Methodist, where the Reverend Dr. O. S. Gamble had coaxed the congregation to the altar to pray and weep for the bombing victims. The rally's organizers decided to cancel the cavalcade through the city planned for later that day—it might be dangerous because the "niggers" were so upset.

It was difficult to interpret Bobby Shelton's presence in the crowd. Blanton and Ingram came up to him and, with what might have been a did-we-prove-ourselves-good-enough swagger, asked him whether he would now grant the Cahaba group a charter in the United Klans of America. Shelton claimed to have turned his back on them and walked away. James Hancock, the shifty deputy, would insist to investigators that a wiretapped conversation among several Klan conspirators revealed that Shelton had said the bomb had to go off at midnight.

The Blood of Our Little Children

WORD OF THE BOMBING had reached Martin Luther King in Atlanta as he was about to step up to the Ebenezer pulpit. "Dear God, why?" he had silently asked. Then he appealed to secular powers, wiring President Kennedy that unless "immediate federal steps are taken," the "worst racial holocaust this nation has ever seen" would come to pass in Alabama. His telegram to George Wallace charged, "The blood of our little children is on your hands."

King prepared to go back to Birmingham, to another riot scene. The now familiar assortment of law enforcement officials stood guard with their shotguns at the Sixteenth Street Baptist Church while two FBI lab men flown down on a military jet sifted through the debris.

One of the stained-glass windows had survived the explosion. Only the face of Jesus had been blown out, recalling the city fathers' decision decades earlier to discard the marble head of Christ that Giuseppe Moretti had sculpted as an essential companion piece to his god of industry.

28.

AFTERSHOCKS

Peanut and Johnnie

THE DEATH TOLL for September 15, 1963, was not yet complete. Two white sixteen-year-old Eagle Scouts, Michael Lee Farley and Larry Joe Sims, had left the truncated rally of the West End Parents for Private Schools disappointed that the afternoon's parade had been canceled. They headed over to the National States Rights Party's untidy headquarters near the fairgrounds and bought a forty-cent Confederate flag. Larry hopped on the back of Michael's red motor scooter, and they drove to the western outskirts of town, reaching the neighborhood of Sandusky.

Virgil Ware, the thirteen-year-old son of an unemployed black TCI coal miner—known to his five brothers and sisters as Peanut—had just gone with an older brother to pick up a bicycle for their paper route and was riding on the handlebars as they headed home. When the white Eagle Scouts passed the black paperboys, Larry Sims, a straight-A student at Phillips High School, pulled out a pearl-handled pistol and fired it. Virgil Ware fell off the handlebars.

"Get up, Virge," his brother said. "You trimmin' me." And Virgil said, "I'm shot." Two bullets had pierced his cheek and his lung and punctured his aorta.

The murder of Virgil Ware would be submerged in the tragedy of the white Eagle Scouts—"these two raw, grieved untutored boys, who have had this unfortunate thing come into their lives at their age," as their attorney, Roderick Beddow, the best criminal lawyer in the city, would describe them. Larry, the murderer, would be sentenced to six months in a juvenile detention center, and Michael got probation. But Virgil's was not the last unpunished death of September 15.

Johnnie Robinson, a black sixteen-year-old, was shot in the back by Officer Jack Parker as he ran up a downtown alley after throwing rocks at a car shoe-polished with such messages as "Negro, go back to Africa." He was dead on arrival at University Hospital. Neither the police department nor Robinson's family challenged Parker's shotgun retort to a rock-throwing transgression.*

---

* A sixty-four-year-old black curiosity seeker named Charlie Lane was shot in the head by one of the state troopers George Wallace sent to surround the church, but he survived.

Denise, Carole, Cynthia, and Addie, however, were surviving the furious background checks on them, the search for some flaw deserving of punishment. For all the advantages the McNairs had given Denise, they had not wanted her to be "vain," their delicate word for the superiority accorded the light-skinned bourgeoisie, and their refusal to indulge her wish (and she had begged) to march with Martin Luther King was coming in handy. As it would turn out, more than any other feature—their youth, their gender, their humanity—the victims' aloofness from the "mess" of the spring would compel commentators of all bents to certify their "innocence." One of the white families who came to Denise's grandfather's house to pay their respects even had a Confederate flag on its car.

Caucusing

As dusk descended, there was barely a car on the streets downtown. The brave men of Cahaba River, however, had no fear of being abroad. In various combinations, they caucused into the night. After visiting with Troy Ingram, Tommy Blanton stopped by Bobby Cherry's house. Before heading out on his rounds, Robert Chambliss rang the doorbell at the home of his mother-in-law, Mama Katie. Her live-in granddaughter, Elizabeth Hood, stepped into the hallway and froze. Before he saw her, Hood went into Mama Katie's room; the grandmother said not to let him in. They were afraid not of what he might do to them, but "afraid that we could not hide our certainty that he had placed the bomb."

Hood spoke to her uncle through the screen. He said his wife wanted to know how Mama Katie, who had taken to her bed, was doing. He tried the door handle. Elizabeth refused to unlock it, bracing for his anger. She knew he had come by to gauge their reaction to him. Hood, concentrating on looking normal, saw rage flicker across his face. Then he ducked his head, ran his hand through his hair, and composed a grin: "If y'all need us, call."

Working the beat that night, Chambliss's nephew Floyd Garrett looked in on Tank's bootleg joint on Eighth Alley, perhaps to collect his payoff in money or nips. Willie Henry Gary, a black dishwasher at a local cafeteria, got into an argument with a female customer named Barbara. She summoned Garrett and told him Gary had bombed the church. Garrett arrested Gary and took him down to headquarters.

Dynamite Hill

Martin Luther King had been rushed from the airport in a high-speed caravan to John and Deenie Drew's house on Dynamite Hill. Burke Marshall and Joe Dolan, who had arrived from Washington, asked an FBI agent to take them over to the Drews', but the special agent in charge said, "No, it's too dangerous." A black contractor drove them in his car, handing them hard hats to "put a shadow" on their faces.

The conference at the Drews' was coming to a decision: King and some black

Birmingham leaders would seek an audience with the President. The other consensus, which Dolan and Marshall had been unable to discourage, was the need for federal troops. King was still turning the other cheek—letting the Movement absorb the violence against its cause—but the growing unfeasibility of that position had begun to make him go a little Jim Crow crazy. "What murdered these four girls?" he said to reporters. "The apathy and the complacency of many Negroes who will sit down on their stools and do nothing and not engage in creative protest to get rid of this evil." Perhaps sensing that King was blaming her for her own daughter's death, Alpha Robertson, a schoolteacher, refused his bedside plea on Monday that she join the three other families in a mass funeral for the girls. "Carole lost her life because of the movement," she said.

Evidence

KIRTHUS GLENN got into her red Chevrolet Biscayne early Monday morning and headed home to Detroit. Surely it occurred to her that the suspicious-looking Chevy she had seen Saturday night and Sunday morning might have had some bearing on the carnage she was leaving behind. Had she thought to look for the scrap of paper on which she had jotted down the license plate number? And even if she hadn't been able to find it, why hadn't she given her account to the authorities? The answer may lie in her belief that the police had not been put on earth to protect black folk and to pretend otherwise only made things worse. In any case, a scrap of brown paper placed on a desk next to a telephone would take its place among the "if onlys" of Birmingham's history.

Another piece of evidence had already succumbed to intrigue. At the crime scene, a police officer had picked up a fragment of red plastic and wire that had been part of a fishing bobber. He turned it over to the FBI. But the bureau's forensic report to headquarters declared that nothing useful had been unearthed (and usually all that a bomb leaves of itself is evidence of a timing mechanism). As rumors about the bobber persisted and were denied by the FBI, the signs of friction among law enforcement agencies surfaced along with a theory about the bomb's timing device—a leaking bucket that activated the blasting caps when the water level reached a certain low.

Maurice House, the detective heading the local end of the investigation, had already gotten lost in the labyrinth created by the superimposed interests of the Birmingham police, the FBI, and the Klan. He had gotten Floyd Garrett to admit that he had gone by Chambliss's Sunday morning to see if he was at home, because he suspected him of being involved. But for House, the obvious trail that led to Dynamite Bob was covered over Monday morning, when an FBI man came by his office and told him a lie. He said that their surveillance had put Chambliss at home all Saturday night. The bureau, so miserly with information, would probably not have volunteered this telling falsehood unless it wanted to baffle a police department it knew to be unreliable in such affairs. House threw himself into the assignment that would prove to be his ultimate frustration, facing a virtually endless pool of suspects, thanks to the demolition skills acquired indiscriminately in the local coal mines. "Asking how these guys know about bombs," he would say, "is like asking how a farmer knows how to drive a tractor." As a kid on the farm, House himself had discharged dynamite, even making a primitive delayed bomb. It wasn't especially hard to do.

On the basis of the FBI's tip, House turned his magnifying glass away from Chambliss onto Howard Thurston Edwards, the pompadoured battler of the Freedom Riders, and the inevitable Stoner crowd. The local urge to blame "outsiders" soon produced a "get-away car" with a Tennessee license plate and three perpetrators, professional bombers from Georgia, Tennessee, and Virginia.

A suspect of perpetual promise was born on Monday when police took the Sixteenth Street custodian, Willie Green, who had walked down the church's side steps moments before they were blown up, to headquarters for questioning: The janitor did it.

A Dead City

AS GRIEF AND RAGE poured into Birmingham from around the world, the rapturous baptism of the civil rights movement at the Lincoln Memorial eighteen days earlier turned into a mass wake. On the Monday morning after the bombing, Chuck Morgan wrote down his thoughts. Forty-seven bombings since 1947, according to the newspapers' count, would make these first deaths seem long past due, inevitable. But in Birmingham, the casualty-free record had assigned the bombers some magic quality; like stuntmen, they were illusionists whose pyrotechnics did no real harm. Only Morgan seemed to remember that less than a year earlier they had almost killed those black kids at Bethel Baptist Church as they rehearsed for a Christmas pageant.

At noon Monday, church bells tolled around the city to signal a moment of silent prayer. That "Let us pray" reaction frosted Morgan, particularly when the first carillon he heard came not from a church but from the Protective Life Building, headed by the reactionary William Rushton, who had resigned from the Senior Citizens Committee to protest the accord with Martin Luther King. The song it was playing, dirgelike, was "Dixie."

The Young Men's Business Club was holding its regular luncheon meeting that day at the Redmont Hotel. Morgan was thinking about making a speech about the bombing and asked his friend, the liberal medical center scientist Roger Hanson, originally from Minnesota, if he thought he should. Hanson, who had gotten Morgan to take his first big civil rights case—the defense of the Alabama Council's Bob Hughes during the Harrison Salisbury flap—looked over the notes Morgan had taken, a scolding of all those who had ever attributed Birmingham's problems to its "image," to "outside agitators," to isolated lunatic extremists. Through tears at his press conference the day before, Mayor Albert Boutwell had said, "It's just sickening that a few individuals could commit such a horrible atrocity." And: "All of us are victims, and most of us are innocent victims."

Hanson told Morgan, Do it. Morgan's memoir of the ensuing turning point in his life would take pains to distinguish between the talk he delivered that day "from the heart" and the one that he would put into "final form" for publication. That written version of the speech would add the epithet "opportunist" to the standard charge against Morgan, "nigger lover." The debate over whether he had "really given the speech" obscured the matter of its merits. For in attempting to answer the question on everyone's lips—Who did it?—he had charged, "The 'who' is every little individual who talks about the 'niggers' and spreads the seeds of his hate to his neighbor and his son. The jokester, the crude oaf whose racial jokes rock the party with laughter. . . . It is all the Christians and all their ministers who spoke too late in anguished cries against violence. It is the coward in each of us who clucks admonitions. . . . We are a mass of intolerance and bigotry and stand indicted before our young." The speech concluded, "What's it like living in Birmingham? No one ever really has and no one will until this city becomes part of the United States. Birmingham is not a dying city. It is dead."

From the City Too Busy to Hate came an echo directed at the entire region. Speaking of Denise McNair's shoe, the *Atlanta Constitution* editor Eugene Patterson wrote, "We hold that shoe in our hand, Southerners. Let us see it straight and look at the blood on it."

BAPBOMB

ROBERT KENNEDY CANCELED a speech in Philadelphia to stay in the office on Monday and keep in constant contact with Dolan and Marshall in Birmingham. The many telegrams to the White House were urging the administration to do whatever was necessary to bring the perpetrators to justice; a third of the messages requested that troops be sent to Birmingham. The country seemed to be back in the mood for Reconstruction, which at least meant support for Kennedy's civil rights bill.

J. Edgar Hoover was representing the bombing investigation—code-named BAPBOMB—as the most intense operation since the Dillinger manhunt of the thirties. This was quite a departure for the bureau, whose kid-gloves attitude toward segregationists was reflected in its policy of having agents inform hostile whites being interviewed in a civil rights case that they were acting at the request of Robert Kennedy and Burke Marshall. Still, when the Justice Department released specific details about the FBI's special BAPBOMB team of eleven agents, Hoover furiously instructed his men not to "give a 'blow by blow' account" to Justice because it "will appear in the *Star* or the *Saturday Evening Post*." George Wallace, meanwhile, accused Justice of ordering the FBI to cover up any evidence implicating "the wrong people," like blacks or civil rights advocates.

Hoover's inside man in Birmingham, Gary Thomas Rowe, was busy. He paid a visit to Eastview Exalted Cyclops Robert Thomas on Monday. In front of his wife, Thomas denied any knowledge of the bombing and then maneuvered Rowe out into the front yard and told him to keep quiet around Mildred. Thomas had always been ambivalent toward his authority, contented to be "Mr. Shelton's" yes-man. And when Rowe said to him, "Robert, goddamnit, the shit has hit the fan," Thomas answered opaquely, according to Rowe, "Amen, just play it cool."

The Governor

ON TUESDAY MORNING, September 17, the country's opinion makers read Chuck Morgan's who-did-it indictment of his city in the *New York Times*. An emerging national consensus seemed to agree with the line in the "speech" that said, "The 'who' is every governor who ever shouted for lawlessness and became a law violator." George Wallace was reaping much blame for the bombing. President Kennedy remarked obliquely that "public disparagement of law and order has encouraged violence which has fallen on the innocent." *Time*'s cover would superimpose Wallace's scowling face over the faceless Christ from Sixteenth Street Baptist's damaged stained-glass window. But it must have been dawning on the Kennedy administration that it had permitted the governor's continuing Stands in Schoolhouse Doors. As Ralph Abernathy put it at the Monday-night mass meeting, "If the federal government had done its job [in Tuscaloosa], Governor Wallace would be in jail right now."

The unlikely potential agent of Abernathy's wishes was Clarence Allgood, the federal judge who had upheld the expulsion of the demonstrating school-children in May. He convened a special session of the federal grand jury and, in a passionate fifteen-minute condemnation of Sunday's "blackening sin against humanity," ordered the jurors to investigate and indict anyone who had interfered with or obstructed his August order to desegregate the schools. It took a full day for the *Birmingham News* to realize that, if taken seriously, Allgood's charge would result in the indictment of Colonel Al Lingo, as well as the man who gave him his orders, George Wallace. Not surprisingly, the grand jurors opted for Wallace's most expendable proxies: the nutcases of the National States Rights Party.

Unmerited Suffering

THE SOLO FUNERAL of Carole Robertson took place at three o'clock Tuesday at St. John's A.M.E. Church, amid rumors that either NBC or CBS had offered to foot the expenses if Alpha Robertson would agree to a mass funeral. Confounding the Movement Kremlinologists who thought the Robertsons were Tomming in snubbing King, the family had asked Fred Shuttlesworth to join Sixteenth Street's minister in eulogizing Carole, whose death, he called "another installment" paid on "this precious thing called freedom." Otherwise, the affair was sufficiently ag-itation free for the *News* to put it on its front page, along with the death of the oak that had inspired Joyce Kilmer to write his poem "Trees."

On Wednesday, September 18, several thousand people arrived at John Porter's Sixth Avenue Baptist for the funeral of Denise, Addie, and Cynthia. The large sanctuary was stifling with grieving flesh, and an overflow crowd collected on the sidewalk—many more whites than had attended Carole's funeral, though most of them seemed to be out-of-towners—such as the delegation from the World Council of Churches led by the Reverend Dr. Eugene Carson Blake, one of the five official sponsors of the March on Washington.* SCLC's left wing of advisers—Stanley Levison, Clarence Jones, and Bayard Rustin—had debated calling for a national work stoppage during the funeral, but Rustin had decided that there wasn't time to organize it properly and they would be better off just letting Martin Luther King do what he did well.

King took the pulpit to deliver unto history these "heroines of a modern crusade for freedom and human dignity." The children's miracle of the spring might have turned into this blasphemy, but, King insisted, " 'A little child shall lead them.' " He pounded the politicians, the federal government, the Negro on the sidelines, and the peculiar cruelties of Birmingham. "At times, life is hard, as hard as crucible steel." But King was bent on the life-affirming lesson of so many of his past speeches, up to and including the most recent one in Washington, that "unmerited suffering is redemptive." By invoking their "spilt blood," King was elevating the girls' supreme sacrifice into the realm of religious communion: "They did not die in vain."

Some women collapsed as white-clad classmates of the dead girls preceded the caskets out of the church. A male voice signaled a shift in the crowd's mood. "Where are we safe?" he said, "Not in our homes, not in school, now not even in church." On the sidewalk, the hordes closed in behind the departing hearses and sang "We Shall Overcome," loudly.

Standing out among the well-dressed mourners were SNCC workers in trademark bib overalls. "Let's go," one of them yelled, and the crowd began marching behind him, clapping and singing, "Ain't Gonna Let Nobody Turn Me Around," up tempo and defiant. SNCC's leaders—Diane Nash, John Lewis, and Julian Bond—had arrived in Birmingham the day before in a mood to escalate their challenge of the Movement elders at the Lincoln Memorial. They had debated blocking the streets around the funeral to tie up the city until Fred Shuttlesworth convinced them that the caskets would speak louder than their getting beat up by cops.

The march they now led toward the graveyard bore little resemblance to the recent protest in Washington that had fused whites, blacks, and a government in one great symphony of hope. This one recalled the mass funeral the Communist Party had held in Birmingham some thirty years earlier for two black men fatally shot during one of the "uprisings" of sharecroppers the Communists had led in Tallapoosa County.† Then, three thousand people, including a number of whites, marched six miles to the cemetery behind caskets draped with banners of crimson

---

* Rabbi Milton Grafman attended but was complaining that King's "Letter From Birmingham Jail" was "very unfair to us. He made us look ridiculous." He and a group of local clergy, prodded by the liberal Episcopalian George Murray, had met the afternoon before to set up a fund to pay for the victims' funerals.
† One of the sharecroppers wounded in the shoot-out, Ned Cobb, would be immortalized as Nate Shaw in Theodore Rosengarten's classic oral history *All God's Dangers*.

hammers and sickles. SNCC would be heading to the old haunts of the share-croppers' union in the Alabama Black Belt and in a few years would launch a militant movement behind the sign of the black panther.

Diane Nash had just drawn up an agenda for the new phase of the revolution. The news of the church bombing had filled her and her husband, Jim Bevel, with a visceral need either to find the bombers and kill them or to strike out against George Wallace. At Shuttlesworth's urging she channeled her vigilante rage into a detailed blueprint for mass nonviolent action—a military takeover of the Alabama capital. Overall-uniformed troops would surround the statehouse, blocking traffic, tying up the phone lines, and lying down on railroad tracks, airport runways, and bus driveways to cut off all transportation in and out of Montgomery.

Nash first ran the plan by Shuttlesworth—"she looked upon me as I guess a great leader," he explained. But he was busy calling on the federal government to "take over Birmingham" and referred her to King. At the Gaston Motel Wednesday night after the funeral, flanked by SNCC comrades, Nash presented a typewritten "Proposal for Action in Montgomery" to King. He found it so bizarre as to be on the level of a joke. He laughed. The contempt was mutual. "He was old," Julian Bond would say wryly of King. "He was supposed to be made fun of. That's what old people are for." King was thirty-four and once again found himself playing catch-up with the vanguard, as SNCC began to build on the events of Birmingham for the Movement's next milestone, a massive march to Montgomery.

The Coach and the General

HAVING EXHAUSTED the capacities of its own "riot squadders," the Justice Department had come up with the only man it considered up to the job of Birmingham: General Douglas MacArthur. The attorney general called Earl "Red" Blaik, the retired football coach at West Point, and asked him if he could approach MacArthur. Blaik said that would be asking too much of an eighty-year-old man. He suggested another former general, Kenneth Royall, who had been Truman's secretary of war. Though Royall now practiced corporate law on Park Avenue, he passed the Mason-Dixon test, as a North Carolina native who on his first day in Felix Frankfurter's class at Harvard Law had moved to the back of the room, explaining to his professor, "There was a nigger sitting by me."

Royall agreed to be the administration's emissary to Birmingham, and at three o'clock Robert Kennedy called Blaik back and asked him to go down with him. "Well, you're talking to the wrong person," Blaik said. "My image in this country is that of a football coach." But that was what made Blaik an inspired choice for the Football Capital of the South. Kennedy told Blaik the President wanted him to go and that he had to make up his mind quickly "because we're going to announce something within an hour."

The timing apparently had to do with the imminent arrival of Shuttlesworth, King, Abernathy, J. L. Ware, A. G. Gaston, and Lucius Pitts for a late-afternoon conference at the White House. The men had come to ask the President to send troops to Birmingham, not a retired general and a football coach. But Kennedy's reply to their request was querulous, nonresponsive: "What's the hope of Birmingham?" Both Kennedy and King seemed to have been rendered timid by the blast from Alabama. The country's Cassandra on the race front, James Baldwin, was furious over the Movement's dutiful pilgrimage to Washington. "I blame J. Edgar Hoover in part for the events in Alabama," he told the *New York Times,* but privately he was repeating the shocking observation that his sister had made to his mother: "Negroes are thinking seriously of assassinating Martin Luther King." Nonviolence, it seemed, had not only been vindicated in Birmingham; it had been made obsolete.

The very mainstream *Jet* ran a picture of Birmingham Negroes in business suits holding rifles and pistols, their faces blacked out so that they could not be identified.

More Suspects

EASTVIEW 13'S FIRST REGULAR meeting since September 15 took place on Thursday night. The only surviving description of that event, when the most violent men in Birmingham were not quite sure who among them had participated in the church bombing, comes from an unreliable source. Robert Chambliss would claim that Tommy Rowe complained that "we" hadn't put enough out there, that they should have "put out enough to level the damn thing."

At around eleven that night, dynamite exploded in a yard several blocks from Chambliss's house, across the street from a still segregated school in North Birmingham. The police went straight to the neighbor who had alerted them, drove him to an isolated spot, beat him, then took him to jail and charged him with drunkenness. The man whose front yard had been bombed, Mose Leonard Jr., had the good sense to call the FBI instead of the police. Agents who came to the scene collected a few debris samples and advised Leonard and his family to move out of their home for a while.

This was the first sign that the bombers had not been fazed by the death of four girls, and rather than heed it, the FBI and the police, with varying degrees of diplomacy, had decided to blame the victim.

Tribunal

THE SIXTEEN-YEAR-OLD NEGRO BOY shot in the back by the police was buried Sunday following a funeral at Nelson "Fireball" Smith's New Pilgrim Baptist Church. "Not only are we here for the funeral of Johnnie Robinson," the ACMHR's Abraham Woods said, "I think we can say we are here for the funeral of Birmingham." Martin Luther King and Ralph Abernathy attended, along with a mob of out-of-town journalists, capping a week of funeral observances for Birmingham's young all over the country, from Foley Square in New York to the World's Fair "Space Needle" in Seattle.

A simultaneous white pep rally was taking place at the Municipal Airport, where Mary Lou Holt was about to depart for Washington with some United Americans for Conservative Government petitions to present to Burke Marshall and Alabama senator John Sparkman. Klansmen had turned out in force for the exuberant Mary Lou—Billy Holt, of course, and the rival for his wife's affections, Hubert Page, along with Nigger Hall and Tommy Blanton. Probably Mary Lou did not realize that she was functioning as an alibi for those heading on to an important powwow at the Cahaba River bridge.

Tommy and Pop Blanton picked up a barber named Billy Levaughn Jackson, who had pleaded guilty to bigamy charges in the spring, a few months after one wife accused him of beating and choking her. He had been angling for membership in the Cahaba River Klan, but he had been turned away from a pre-bombing meeting at the river. To earn future admission, he had promised Chambliss, "I'll help in any way that I can." It was he whom investigators would suspect of securing the acid that ended up in the detonator of the Sixteenth Street bomb. Also at the bridge was the old Du Pont employee Pershing "Pud" Mayfield, who had earlier shared with Chambliss his knowledge of acid detonators.

Chambliss had made a point to be at the bridge, even though he had to leave town that night on a delivery trip to South Alabama. There was still tension between him and his best friend, Troy Ingram, a sense that the competition over who was the better bomb maker had soured into a substantive grievance. Elizabeth Hood had heard her uncle call Ingram "stupid"—perhaps he had fouled up the bomb's timing device. It is possible that Chambliss was dumping onto Ingram the blame he himself was getting from on high. As Mary Frances Cunningham would tell the FBI, Hubert Page was complaining that the bomb had gone off hours earlier than it was supposed to, that it wasn't meant to kill anyone. "*I* meant for it to kill someone," she claims Chambliss said.

Page made a grand appearance at the bridge that day—along with the UACG's Bob Gafford and Bill Morgan, according to the state informant present. This seemed to be a tribunal of sorts, an accounting to the racist establishment that had been aware of the church bombing plot but surprised by its timing. Himself an electrician, Page was said to have worked on the detonating device, perhaps during the Friday-night meeting that the FBI hadn't gotten his alibi for. Billy Holt had needled Page the previous Thursday about what he planned to do with the reward money that was being pledged for the capture of the bombers.

If Page, Morgan, and Gafford were at the Cahaba River for some answers, all they apparently got was the vague embittered speeches of open meetings. At one point Chambliss became agitated when Ronnie Tidwell, Eastview's rising Young Turk, showed up at the bridge with some non-Klansmen, one of them a Catholic. The gathering broke up and the hard core—Chambliss, the Blantons, and perhaps Page, with Billy Jackson tagging along—adjourned to Ingram's house, where they sat in the driveway, away from electronic bugs. This was probably the gathering that investigators would come to refer to as the "kiss-of-death meeting," the ceremonial invocation of the Klan code. "If any one of you ever talks, it will be the kiss of death for you," the leader—perhaps it was Chambliss, or Page—said. "We join hands here and now in swearing that each of us takes a vow to kill the man who gives anything away to the police."

"You People"

A DELEGATION of five prominent white men from Birmingham, who had been on the flight to Washington with Mary Lou Holt, arrived at the White House at around noon on Monday for an audience with President Kennedy. Besides Boutwell's top aide, Billy Hamilton, there were the head of the still all-white ministerial alliance, a city councillor, and a couple of Senior Citizens. They came armed with prepared statements about "our great department stores" encouraging customers over their loudspeakers to pause and pray for the bombing victims, who, they proposed, might have accidentally set off the cache of dynamite themselves.

Kennedy had by now held many meetings with community leaders to rally public opinion behind his civil rights bill. He usually opened with a description of a Negro child—his slim chances of growing up and earning a decent living, of reaching a normal life expectancy, and on and on, and then he would refer to Birmingham. But now that Birmingham was here before him without shame, and the example of truncated Negro lives so gruesomely concrete, his tone of high statesmanship slipped. Having absorbed his brother's outrage, he practically jumped on the men for resisting such basic concessions as hotel and restaurant desegregation. "Oh, public accommodations is nothing!" he said. He even addressed these civic paragons as "you people," normally the prerogative of whites toward Negroes. The Birmingham delegates were almost disrespectful in return, as if worried that word might get out that they were cutting a deal with the enemy. Kennedy tried to appeal to their conservatism, urging them to honor the accords with SCLC or live with SNCC—"real sons of bitches."

Ultimately it was the President who blinked, his renowned vigor reduced to pleas for even a "public relations action" that would reassure the Negroes, much as he was doing in his own response to the bombing. The "Blaik-Royall mission" had already hit some PR snags. Red Blaik's national championship teams at West Point had been all-white, and Kenneth Royall had fought against desegregating the military as Truman's Army secretary. And on Tuesday, September 24, when the coach and the general flew by private plane into Birmingham, they were greeted by an all-white delegation of VIPs. Mayor Boutwell welcomed these outsiders with a prepared statement denouncing "professional outsiders" (black) before whisking them off to a segregated luncheon.

Endgame

AT THE HOME of the UACG's plumber-president Bill Morgan, the debriefing reception following Mary Lou Holt's return from Washington was breaking up at around midnight. Flushed with importance, Holt had described her meetings with Congressman George Huddleston Jr. and Burke Marshall, whom she had told that the church bombing had been planned right there in Washington, D.C., by a department of the United States government. Marshall proposed the Birmingham Police Department as a more likely candidate—or so she said.

As the Klansmen at Morgan's house were lingering over conspicuous, alibi-worthy goodbyes, Robert Chambliss was steering his truck up Highway 31 into Birmingham, coming back from his delivery trip to South Alabama. At 12:15 a Catholic priest returning home from Huntsville was driving down Second Avenue North near Center Street when he saw, traveling east at a snail's pace, a car matching the description of Tommy Blanton's Chevrolet, with two young men in the front seat. At Second Street, the Chevy turned right, heading south. At 1:31, eighteen blocks south of where the Chevy had been sighted, there was an explosion in a black residential neighborhood that anchored Center Street on the south side of town as Dynamite Hill did on the north.

Gary Thomas Rowe just happened, he said, to be in the vicinity after taking his girlfriend home. He stopped his car at a phone booth and at 1:34 notified the FBI that he had heard an explosion. Heading toward the scene in Car 24. Officers, J. D. Allred and Jimmy Vines, spied Rowe, who occasionally "rode with" them. He called to them from the phone booth, "I don't know nothing," and they drove on. Still talking to Special Agent Byron McFall, Rowe said he thought he heard another thunderclap and stepped outside the phone booth to listen.

Thirteen minutes after the first blast, and fifteen feet west, a bomb such as Birmingham had not yet experienced detonated on the sidewalk at South Center Street. A wooden utility pole was sheared off at its base, toppling into a vacant lot. An eighteen-inch-deep, two-by-three-foot hole was blown into the pavement. In addition to flinging chunks of concrete from the sidewalk, the bomb itself spewed nails, bolts, scrap metal, and pipe sections. The shrapnel shattered windows and lodged in the siding of surrounding houses.

Two cops had passed by the bomb a minute or two earlier, and a crowd also had gathered, looking for the first explosion. It always seemed amazing when no one was hurt by the dynamite, but here "amazing" had achieved a new level.

It did not strike the FBI as suspicious that for the second time that year Rowe had reported a bombing practically from the scene—the earlier one the dynamiting of row houses on March 24. Instead, his handlers concluded that he was "doing a good job if he's there somewhere where he's knowing what's going on."* The Klan's investigator, Don Luna, would claim that Rowe, with the help of his good friend Officer Lavaughn Coleman, had pulled off the shrapnel bombing. Rowe's involvement had a certain logic if one calculated that no Klansman would attempt a fatal bombing so soon after J. Edgar Hoover initiated his manhunt un-

---

* Rowe would be renowned for "remembering" tidbits he had neglected to tell the bureau previously, and what he had most recently "forgotten" to mention was that during a coffee break at the heavily attended Klan meeting three days before the church bombing, Nigger Hall told Harry Walker that a syrup bucket or an old toolbox and half a stick of dynamite would make a good shrapnel bomb—the deadly kind that flung nails and scrap metal. Troy Ingram asked Hall if he could make a shrapnel bomb, and Hall said no problem. Chambliss proposed that there should be two bombs, as there had been at A. D. King's house in May—"one to draw the niggers out and one to kill them."

less he had indemnity from the FBI. But Rowe put together a plausible scenario that let him off the hook, even though it never made it into his FBI file.

Rowe said Sister White would later complain to him over drinks that Ronnie Tidwell had made "a piss-poor bomb *again*"—the "again" a reference to the earlier putative Tidwell concoction that Rowe said White had thrown at Arthur Shores's house on August 20. For the shrapnel bomb, Rowe would claim, Tidwell had sought the guidance of Troy Ingram and Robert Chambliss. But the first bomb had been so dainty, White told Rowe, "only about a dozen niggers just stuck their head around." Sister said he was riding on the back of Nigger Hall's motorcycle and "almost pissed on Johnny" when the second one went off. "That son of a bitch was a good one," Rowe reported White said.

Was the shrapnel bomb Eastview's way of anteing up to stay in the game with the Cahaba River gang? Or was it a pan-collaboration, as the church bombing may have been, suggesting that Ingram's group had become the terrorist arm of Eastview? Or was it the even stranger scenario proposed by Deputy James Hancock? He said that the bomb was his idea: that under his instructions, Mary Frances Cunningham proposed the dynamiting of some "nice nigger homes around Center Street" to Chambliss, the Blantons, and two other men. The goal was for Hancock to catch Chambliss redhanded and get him convicted on at least one bombing. But as with an uncanny number of other bombings, the deputy was on his way to the scene when the blast occurred. (Cunningham dismissed this tale altogether.)

While discussing the shrapnel bomb the following day, Chambliss boasted that he could make a better bomb than Troy Ingram. That could have meant either that his shrapnel bomb had been better than Ingram's misfiring church bomb or that Chambliss's deadly church bomb was better than Ingram's nonfatal shrapnel bomb. The debris gathered at the scene included a piece of fishing tackle identical to that FBI agents would discover in Ingram's tackle box, and the clutch assembly of a circa 1940 Hudson, such as had recently been parked among the junked cars in Ingram's yard.

Whoever its authors—and one polygraph-supported theory would have Tommy Blanton placing the bombs—the shrapnel operation defied reason. Even the church bombing might have been extenuated as a miscalculation. But the shrapnel bomb proved unequivocally that the civil rights movement had launched a counterinsurrection intent upon maiming or killing. And the lapse of time between the crowd-luring "firecracker" and the lethal metal thrower—more than ten minutes—suggested that the shrapnel bombers were hoping to strafe some cops and journalists. As Officers Allred and Vines told Rowe, they didn't mind the Klan killing "niggers," but this one liked to have hurt some policemen.

The terms of engagement had shifted. As if to acknowledge that war had been declared, Brigadier General Reid Doster, commanding officer of the Alabama National Guard (and air strategist for the Bay of Pigs invasion), led troops to the crime scene that night.

29.

BAPBOMB

Shuttlesworth's Bow

BIRMINGHAM REIGNED at the seventh annual SCLC convention in Richmond, where Fred Shuttlesworth was billed with Martin Luther King at the top of the program, and the Alabama Christian Movement choir gave freedom concerts every night. The tragedy at Sixteenth Street, followed by the twin insults of shrapnel and Blaik and Royall's white greeting committee, had somewhat cramped the spirits of the "I Have a Dream" team. And behind the scenes, Wyatt Walker was making waves demanding a threefold salary increase, in line with his enhancement of the SCLC budget. The more likely source of his job dissatisfaction, however, was the executive prestige he had lost when King refused to discipline the insubordinate Jim Bevel during Project C. Birmingham had, in effect, ended the controversial but brilliant SCLC career of Wyatt Walker, who would submit his resignation in a matter of weeks.

It became clear at the board meeting on Wednesday that SCLC's business in Birmingham was unfinished, tempting as it was to move on to a new civil rights theater—like Gadsden or Danville, Virginia—with new characters to enliven the monotonous plot line of desegregating. What with the department store owners refusing to promote any black workers, a subdued Shuttlesworth agreed that demonstrations might have to resume in Birmingham. Nelson Smith, whose church had just held Johnnie Robinson's funeral, said it was going to be tough to restrain their people when bombs were still being thrown at them. King seemed overcome with battle fatigue and proposed that they table Birmingham—"the acid test of whether the revolution would succeed"—for his special meeting with Shuttlesworth in Atlanta the following week. Of the SCLC founders, Shuttlesworth and King were the fateful two who remained, bound together in the awkward three-legged race that accounted for their organization's only momentum. Ralph Abernathy, the other original still in the leadership, had turned his energies to the care and feeding of his vanity. Wounded by his best friend's anointment at the Lincoln Memorial, he spent the SCLC convention in a snit over having been assigned a hotel room inferior to King's.

Thursday, September 26, the next-to-the-last night of SCLC's celebrity-studded four-day affair, belonged to Shuttlesworth. After his vice president Ed Gardner accepted the Affiliate of the Year Award on behalf of the Alabama Christian Movement, Shuttlesworth received the Rosa Parks Freedom Award. Parks had moved into the secure haven of "legend," her actual service as a Movement figure having been abridged by the Big Boys in the Montgomery Improvement Association. Shuttlesworth, whose personality did not invite the adjective "beloved," refused to be shelved as an icon. But this would be the closest to a pat on the back his colleagues would give him for bringing about an end to legal segregation. When Martin Luther King won the Nobel Peace Prize the following year for his work in Birmingham, Shuttlesworth was not included in the large entourage that accompanied him to Oslo.

Tips

ALBERT BOUTWELL was fielding "tips" about the church bombers from a variety of reward seekers, including a kook from Memphis who called to confess to the bombing—and also to having voted for Boutwell. ("Bless your soul," Boutwell said.) Though the city's Lieutenant Maurice House was still off on his wild-goose chase after Stoner and company, the solution to the crime had quickly become obvious to both the state and the FBI. The suspense would be over what would permit the perpetrators to get away with it: the state's malevolence or the FBI's negligence.

For the next three decades, the church-bombing case would be a marvel of frustration, as a band of barely functional outlaws toyed with the best crime-solving minds of the country. The exact meaning of the investigative events following the explosion may never be understood completely, but they reveal much truth about the long tradition of enmeshment between law enforcers and Klansmen that made those ensuing encounters more ordinary than extraordinary.

Eastview's kingpin, Hubert Page, was proving to be the co-conspirator whom many parties—the state of Alabama, the city of Birmingham, and maybe even the FBI—seemed to want to remain unindicted. State investigator William Ray Posey had apparently identified Page's supervisory role in the bombing through an informant he had developed inside the Cahaba River group, most likely the barber Billy Levaughn Jackson. The informer's credibility was enhanced by his knowledge of the aborted attempt to bomb the church on the Labor Day eve—reported to the hostile police department by Jim Lay and Tall Paul White. This fact had not been released to the public, and the informer had probably gleaned during the September 22 "kiss of death" meeting. He also made knowing comments about Chambliss's possessing two police uniforms and Officer Floyd Garrett being his relative. This seemed to be a veiled allusion to a rumor that Chambliss had been wearing a uniform during the hours before the bomb was planted, when he and Garrett were decoying the police with a bomb threat against the Downtowner Holiday Inn.

Posey relayed his informer's account of the meeting to his superiors on September 26, and the intelligence on Page got dramatic results. Two days later, in the late-night hours of Saturday, September 28, one of Posey's superiors, a captain named R. W. Godwin, who was known to be no enemy of the Klan, drove Page to Huntsville to see Lee C. Greene, a veteran polygraph expert. Greene proceeded with a three-part, thirty-five-question lie detector test. Page's negative answer to "Do you know who bombed the Sixteenth Street Baptist Church?" brought a "strong reaction" of deception. "Extreme reaction" characterized his denials of "assisting" in the church bombing (as well as the bombing of Arthur Shores's house). Page had tipped his cards, asking Greene to clarify "assist"—did it mean actual participation or merely prior discussion of the plans? Greene also asked, "Did Robert Chambliss bomb the Sixteenth Street Church?" Page gave a definite no, which—even if the answer had not shown "extreme" deception—might imply that he knew who did do it. And then there was the clue about what the state had on Page: "Did you work on the detonating device for the bomb at the Sixteenth Street Church?" His denial showed "definite" deception.

Lee Greene concluded that Page "definitely has knowledge of the bombings, Arthur Shores' residence, 16th St. Church, and the [shrapnel] bombing at Center St. South. He is lying about his participation in these bombings and definitely attended the Cahaba Meeting. The man is a fanatic."

It would soon become clear that the point of the Page polygraph was not to build a case against him. To the contrary, Page was about to enter a compact with the state. The FBI would not learn of the polygraph for two years, by which time its agents had assured Page that he was not a BAPBOMB suspect. The U.S. government might have had its own reasons for not delving into Page's criminal history: The evidence suggests that he and the FBI's Gary Thomas Rowe were accomplices in the Gaston Motel bombing the previous May.

State investigator Ben Allen, meanwhile, was working on a hunch about the identity of one of the men in the white-on-blue Chevy in the early hours of September 15. The same Saturday that Page was taking his test, Allen showed up at the home of Herman Cash. Perhaps Allen was wondering whether Denise, Carole, Cynthia, and Addie might be alive if he hadn't taken pity on Cash in June, when the alcohol-impaired Klansman was arrested on Rowe's tip for carrying firearms to the Schoolhouse Door. Allen had helped Cash fight off the urge to confess to his part in the Gaston Motel bombing.

The FBI at Work

FOR ALL THE DILLINGER HYPE, the FBI's BAPBOMB investigation seemed to be proceeding with very deliberate speed. On Saturday evening, September 28, while Hubert Page was undergoing his secret polygraph, the FBI made its first contact with Chambliss since opening its BAPBOMB investigation. When Chambliss pulled into a filling station in the neighborhood where the dynamite from Negron's store had supposedly been hidden, Special Agents Bernard Cashdollar and Timothy Casey drove in behind him and flashed their shields. They seemed surprised, almost flattered, that he agreed to accompany them to FBI headquarters. In a rambling interview, Chambliss discussed his long career with the Klan, his employment history, his ulcers, and his whereabouts on the evening of September 14 and the next morning: at home.

Earlier that day, two FBI agents in Detroit had been dispatched to Harper Hospital to interview an employee in the laundry department, Kirthus Glenn. The agents did not give the impression of urgency. Nor did Glenn betray any sense of moment when she told them that at approximately 2:10 to 2:15 on the morning of September 15, she had observed a 1955 or 1956 white-on-turquoise Chevrolet parked on the street behind the Sixteenth Street Baptist Church. Inside the car she had seen three hatless white men. She offered no additional description of them or the car. Nor did the agents ask.

The FBI's leisurely pursuit of witnesses was playing into the Klan's hands. The longer the agency took, the more time the Klansmen had to coordinate alibis, and the greater the chance there was of another law enforcement agency mucking up the case. But perhaps the bureau had its own reason for pursuing the evidence cautiously. Gary Thomas Rowe had been instructed by his handlers to stay away from the scene of the crime for at least a week, probably to keep him from turning up in the suspect files of their investigative rivals. In showing photographs of suspects to witnesses, the FBI never included a picture of Rowe or his car, a 1959 white-on-green Chevrolet Biscayne with a whip antenna on the left rear fender: not appreciably unlike the car Glenn spotted.

But Rowe did not return the favor to the bureau. Drinking at the VFW Hall on Saturday night, Rowe passed along to his old protector from the Trailways deal, Detective Red Self, a tip from his state sources that he had neglected to tell his FBI handler about: Al Lingo and his guys were coming to Birmingham to arrest Chambliss, Charles Cagle, and Nigger Hall. Self would say that Rowe added, "I'll tell you one thing: they will never solve the Sixteenth Street bombing because me and another guy handled it."

Lawmen and Klansmen

HOURS AFTER RETURNING from his polygraph in Huntsville, on Sunday, September 29, Hubert Page was part of the rogue aristocracy of Klansmen—including Bobby Shelton, Robert Thomas, Nigger Hall, and Bobby Cherry—summoned to a meeting with Lingo. It took place at the house of UACG president Bill Morgan, a big supporter of George Wallace's who was rumored to be a concealed Klansman. Apparently Lingo was impressing upon the Klansmen that a deal needed to be struck: The FBI was close to making arrests. Cherry, who had so far eluded all law enforcement radar and could not have been pleased about being summoned by the head of the state department of public safety, must have felt a combination of elation and guilt when he realized what was taking place: A scapegoat was being arranged to take the heat off the rest of the Klansmen who had either known about the bombing or participated in it. Cherry gathered that Shelton and Thomas were trying to put Chambliss in the electric chair. Hubert Page, thanks to the warning of the previous night's polygraph, had probably persuaded his fellow Klan muck-a-mucks that sacrificing Chambliss was the tidiest available solution to their common problem, though Cherry had overestimated the penalty they had in mind for him.

To build its case against Chambliss, the state had enlisted the help of Don Luna, the portly, furtive member of the Klan Bureau of Investigation. Luna (who had initially been helping the highway patrol develop a case against Birmingham's Black Muslims) guessed that the state was after the information he had gleaned from his Klan brothers about the dynamite that Charles Cagle and Nigger Hall had moved from Chambliss's car to the kudzu patch on September 4, the night of the Arthur Shores bombing. Cagle claimed that the next day he had asked his fellow suspect in the Warrior church burning, Levie "Quickdraw" Yarbrough, to move the "muscadines," as he called the explosives, to yet another, undisclosed hiding place.

Predictably, this most fingerprint-covered case of dynamite in Klan history had become the focus of attention by both the FBI and the state. On Thursday, September 26, Cagle had taken FBI agents to the field and showed them where the case had initially been hidden. Whether the dynamite was evidence of a church bombing or a decoy, Al Lingo seemed to feel that it gave the state enough ammunition to scoop the FBI.

By Sunday evening, the plans for Chambliss's downfall—or perhaps it was really his salvation—had acquired an official imprimatur. In his favorite room at the St. Francis Motel in suburban Homewood, Lingo convened the same Klansmen from the afternoon caucus at Bill Morgan's house to meet with his own people: his top officer, Major William R. Jones, a lawyer named Wade Wallace (a distant cousin of the governor's and a member of the UACG), and former mayor and onetime Eastview applicant Art Hanes, a friend of both Hubert Page and Billy Holt. Also there were the two men the Klan had assigned to investigate the bombing, Don Luna and Gene Reeves—a suspect in the second Shores bombing.

Major Jones was skeptical about the plan being discussed at the motel: the immediate arrests of suspects in the church bombing. It wasn't that he found anything unseemly about collaborating with the Klan: "Preachers don't tell you who criminals are." It was just that he did not believe that it made sense to charge someone with a crime without any evidence. Nevertheless, the meeting at the St. Francis Motel adjourned, and all the governor's men—state troopers as well as Kluxers—fanned out in a dragnet of the lowliest neighborhoods of the city in a valley.

Joint Operation

WHEN THE EVENING NEWS broke the story that Governor Wallace was flying back from Miami to announce arrests in the church-bombing case, Birmingham

Police Chief Jamie Moore called Lieutenant Maurice House, perplexed. House confirmed that he had developed nothing solid. But Chambliss, also watching the news, turned to his wife and said, "That Bill Holt has talked." Chambliss summoned his doctor, complaining of severe stomach pain, and begged to be hospitalized for X rays. The doctor opted for injecting him with a sedative, perhaps remembering another time Chambliss had checked into the hospital amid a tussle with the law. He was asleep when state investigator W. R. Posey knocked on the door and hustled to the bedroom past Flora Chambliss and her sister Mary Frances Cunningham. Accompanying the state were Klansmen Gene Reeves and Don Luna. They slapped Chambliss's face to wake him up and told him to get dressed. On the way to the car, Luna reassured him that they would "get him out of it."

Most of the group from the St. Francis Motel meeting had moved over to state police headquarters in Bessemer to await the arrival of the suspects: Chambliss, Charles Cagle (in the car with Chambliss), Levie Yarbrough (picked up by Lingo himself), and Nigger Hall (brought in by Bobby Shelton and Reeves). All of them were connected with the dynamite in the kudzu field. Yarbrough was released, but Cagle and Chambliss—Nigger Hall would join them in a couple of days—were held for lockup. "Hold for investigation" was the "charge." The roundup of suspects was characterized in an unsigned memo by one of the participants as a "joint operation" between the Klan and the state police.

Another Scapegoat

"WE CERTAINLY BEAT the Kennedy crowd to the punch," Governor Wallace announced. The FBI icily refused comment on the arrests. There had been bad blood between the state and the feds since FBI agents had blocked Wallace's investigators from the crime scene on the Sunday of the bombing. J. Edgar Hoover privately informed Robert Kennedy, "They have certainly 'flushed' the case and I doubt that they will be able to hold these two men." But Hoover found it painful to concede that his men were not close to cracking the case either. And in response to that failing, he reached for a scapegoat. It was not the Justice Department's favorite, Al Lingo, but his personal obsession: Martin Luther King.

In an interview with the *New York Times* the previous November, King had commented broadly on SCLC's fumbled campaign in Albany, and even though his toughest criticism was directed at the Kennedy administration's passivity, an editor had extrapolated from the most provocative of his remarks—that FBI agents in the South tended to be southerners with close ties to local authorities—to write the headline "Dr. King Says F.B.I. in Albany, Ga., Favors Segregationists." An incensed Hoover had embarked on a campaign to prove that King was not only a Communist but a "vicious liar," even if the civil rights leader's claims paled beside what the career of the FBI's own informant, Gary Thomas Rowe, had already positively established.

In his memo to Kennedy following the church bombing, Hoover blamed

King's ten-month-old remarks to the *New York Times* for queering the FBI's "close contacts or connections with the local authorities" in the South. And this estrangement, he insisted, explained why the BAPBOMB case had not been solved.

Hoover's tantrum was only part of a bureau-wide escalation of animus toward King. On September 16, with the agency riveted on perhaps the worst race crime of its history, one of Hoover's men proposed a counterintelligence program, COINTELPRO, not against the presumed church bombers but against King, to "expose, disrupt, discredit, or otherwise neutralize" the civil rights movement.

Liars

THE FBI HAD IDENTIFIED a major suspect left out of Lingo's sting. As the news of the arrests of Chambliss and Cagle gratified the country, Troy Ingram received a summons for a polygraph exam. On Monday, September 30, he was hooked up to the lie detector and interrogated for two hours. The last question— "Did Robert Chambliss help you bomb the church?"—set off all the graphs measuring blood pressure, breathing, pulse, and skin response. Privately, the polygraph administrator said he would stake his career on the fact that Ingram knew something about the crime and would further venture that he had made the bomb in his machine shop. Confronted with the results, Ingram insisted that he was telling the truth, his confidence boosted by the moral support of an old friend who had accompanied him to the test, a fellow miner's son from the DeBardeleben camp who had become an assistant U.S. attorney.

The luck of the DeBardelebens seemed to be shining on Ingram's best friend, Robert Chambliss, as well. Within hours of their lockup, a Klan lawyer named Matt Murphy had come to the jail and calmed their fears. Murphy was Charles DeBardeleben's nephew—a great-grandson of Birmingham's founding "King Henry" DeBardeleben, grandson of Walker Percy, the lawyer who had created the city's commission form of government. A handsome graduate of the University of the South at Sewanee, Murphy had at first seemed destined for the discreet practice of the Dixiecrat politician-lawyer, but had instead become the first-string attorney not only for the Klan but also for the National States Rights Party. He was a true believer and severe alcoholic, the only nod to his upbringing the wellborn mistress he kept in an apartment on the Southside.*

It was perhaps Murphy as much as anyone else who saved Chambliss from

---

* Murphy's first cousin Walker Percy—also Henry DeBardeleben's great-grandson, Charles De-Bardeleben's nephew, and the namesake grandson of Walker Percy—had rebelled against the family as well. He was writing a novel, *The Last Gentleman,* set partly in the hometown he had come to despise, in the mansion by the Birmingham Country Club where his lawyer-father, LeRoy, had succumbed to the depression he called "The Crouching Beast" and in 1920, committed suicide, like his father before him. Young Walker had articulated an existential version of that family depression in his National Book Award–winning first novel, *The Moviegoer,* published in 1961. Percy had by now achieved a relatively elevated civil rights consciousness, expressed in his passionate essays on the southern race crisis, and was unabashedly a Kennedy fan.

serious legal difficulties. He had sized up the state's case against his client and had ordered him not to talk. Chambliss was so cocky the next day that he consented anyway to a lie detector test, stopping by Chief Jamie Moore's office to chat on the way to his appointment as if he still owned city hall. While the polygraph was being administered, Chambliss fell asleep in his chair.

Square One

FOR ITS ARCHITECTS, the end of segregation was seeming like a momentary trick of the mind. Sid Smyer, who would earn a place in history as the lone Big Mule to negotiate with Martin Luther King, was entering his long, ambiguous denouement following the spring climax, when he had said grace with black men and spoken the language of nonviolent revolution. He never quite seemed to make peace with his membership in that "aristocracy of damn fools," protesting that his strange heroism had been just "a dollars-and-cents thing." And in a way he was telling the truth. His odyssey, however dramatic, had really been the transformation that power makes in order to preserve itself.

Now, falling back on the "extremists on both sides" equation between civil rights activists and rabid racists, Smyer made front-page news by saying, "If Martin Luther King, Fred Shuttlesworth, Edward R. Fields, and the other outsiders really want our local problems solved, the best service they can render to the local Negroes is for them to keep hands off." Furthermore, Smyer said, "the four Negro children that were killed in the church bombing and the others would be living today" if King hadn't demonstrated.

King had come back to Birmingham on Monday to put down the latest insurrection by A. G. Gaston and Arthur Shores—an anti-"outsider" statement that finally got some "black leaders" on the front page of the local paper. King's speech on the last night of the SCLC convention had basically been an apology to Shuttlesworth, conceding their bitter argument in May at John and Deenie Drew's house. "I have acted contrary to the wishes and the frustrations of those who have marched with me in the dangerous campaigns for freedom," he said, admitting that he was "naive enough to believe that the proof of good faith would emerge." Unknowingly concurring in the Kennedy administration's own impulse to send MacArthur to the battlefront, he had said, "But I serve notice tonight, that *I will return* to Birmingham."

King now vowed that if the presidential team of Blaik and Royall did not come up with some results by the end of the week, he would recommend demonstrations. SCLC had added an item to its Birmingham agenda—the hiring of Negro police—as a face-saving way to revive the old items that had not been disposed of. Thousands of Movement handbills called for a boycott of the downtown department stores unless the promise to hire Negro clerks was honored the next day. It was back to square one.

From Washington, the Kennedy administration gloomily followed the fate of the Birmingham Agreement, which was, after all, the test run for its civil rights bill. The Community Affairs Committee that Mayor Boutwell had appointed to oversee the new era of race relations had become simply another instrument of the *News* executive Vincent Townsend's machinations. One CAC member, Rabbi Milton Grafman, suspected him of bugging the meetings. "Typical Birmingham psychosis," Burke Marshall said of Grafman's suspicion, "although it may be true."

The administration's own contributions to a Birmingham solution, Coach Blaik and General Royall, seemed to have become part of the problem. Justice's Lou Oberdorfer was worried that the men were being brainwashed in Birmingham, particularly since their visit was being stage-managed by Townsend. Aware of how easy it was to lose touch with the rest of the world in his hometown, Oberdorfer had arranged to have the *New York Times* flown down every day and delivered to their hotel rooms. "They were very vulnerable," he explained later, and noted morosely that they "almost did get brainwashed." Blaik and Royall seemed to be identifying with their country club peer group, behaving as if race were too indelicate a subject to broach.

The Kudzu Patch

LINGO WAS SUCKING WIND. Police Chief Jamie Moore and Sheriff Mel Bailey refused to rescue him from humiliation. "We have been aware of some of the suspects questioned by state investigators and had knowledge of their activities," Moore said. "However, at the time of their arrests we felt that we did not have enough evidence on any of them for a conviction."

In his haste to beat the FBI (and perhaps to minimize the exposure of Hubert Page and Bobby Shelton to prosecution), Lingo seemed to have forgotten that he needed a crime with which to charge the suspects. He didn't even have the famous case of dynamite as physical evidence. But Charles Cagle was about to help him fix that. On Tuesday, October 1, as Matt Murphy was preparing to represent Chambliss in a habeas corpus hearing, Lingo, along with Major Bill Jones and state investigator Ben Allen, took Cagle out of jail to the kudzu patch in Gardendale where he and Quickdraw Yarbrough had supposedly returned the dynamite on Sunday. There, they came upon a new prop in the shell game of the moving dynamite: On the spot where Cagle said he and Yarbrough had placed the case was now a sack that held only two and a half sticks of dynamite. Neither he nor Nigger Hall had mentioned to the authorities that in addition to the case of explosives Hall had gotten from Chambliss's trunk on the night of September 4, Cagle had taken a canvas bag of dynamite. Was this what remained from Cagle's bag, and if so, who had put it in the field? And where was the original case?

Major Jones walked a hundred yards into the woods and found a box of dynamite—Monobel B-1¼ × 8, certified as "Permissible Dynamite" by the Bureau of Mines because the flash of the explosive would not ignite any gases present in a coal mine. It had been manufactured by the Du Pont Powder Company's nearby Watson plant on August 28. Du Pont had sold four cases of that lot to Leon Negron on September 3, the day before Chambliss said he had bought it, and turned it over to Cagle and Hall. There were only 130 sticks in the stash, meaning that at least nine sticks were missing. Bomb experts had estimated that the church blast had been caused by around ten sticks. But that seemed too straightforward an explanation for the missing dynamite. Nigger Hall would inform the FBI that Cagle had told him that the case-from-the-trunk had supplied the dynamite for the shrapnel bomb, a crime for which Cagle's friend and co-arsonist Levie Yarbrough was a main suspect.

However the dynamite came to be in the kudzu patch—and the KBI's Don Luna suspected that his fellow investigators from the state police had put it there—Lingo could now at least file some charges against Chambliss and Cagle. At his habeas corpus hearing Tuesday, Chambliss was charged with possession of dynamite—a misdemeanor—and, after posting $300 bond, strutted out of jail.

Chambliss's luck seemed almost uncanny: When FBI agents tried to administer a polygraph to his nephew-in-law Harry Walker, whose car he and Blanton were suspected of using in the aborted September 2 attempt to bomb the church, the subject's diabetes and insulin use rendered the test inconclusive.

Out of Circulation

ALABAMA JUSTICE had prompted the Kennedy administration to call on an old friend for a favor. That Tuesday, Floyd Mann, Lingo's predecessor as Alabama's public safety director and the native hero of the Freedom Riders disaster, appeared in Burke Marshall's office to discuss a matter too sensitive for the telephone. What, Marshall wanted to know, could Mann find out about Lingo's bizarre law enforcement move?

Mann sought out one of his old lieutenants, still with the state. The lieutenant told Mann that the arrests had been made to muddy the FBI's investigation by taking the suspects out of circulation. The source believed that Chambliss and Cagle had conspired with the state troopers to create the possession-of-dynamite charge, in order to preempt a murder charge or a federal charge. The conclusion from Mann's report was that the state of Alabama was obstructing a criminal investigation and protecting church bombers.

Given George Wallace's obvious interest in a case with such implications for his political ambitions, there is a temptation to see something more than Kluxer big talk in the report that Gary Thomas Rowe would submit to the FBI a few months later about the governor and the Klan's well-connected Hubert Page: "The Klan met and discussed Page getting $15,000 from Gov. Wallace and there was a large shortage with some believing that Page embezzled some of it."

Blowing the Blanton Case

UP IN DETROIT, the FBI returned to Harper Hospital to talk to Kirthus Glenn that Tuesday, October 1. This time, she recalled that the white-on-turquoise

Chevy she observed between 2:10 and 2:15 a.m. had an eight- or nine-foot antenna on the rear left fender. She did not mention writing down the license plate
number, perhaps for fear that the Man would get her for losing it, but it was clear
when the FBI closed in on Tommy Blanton later that day that they had already
formed an opinion about who owned the car.

Blanton had not been very fastidious about covering his tracks. The previous
week, he had dropped by to see his West End neighbor (and mother figure) Mary
Lou Holt and found her on the phone talking about the church bombing. He had
burst out laughing, saying, "I could tell you something about that bombing." Now,
under the questioning of two FBI agents, he test-drove his alibi, which apparently
had not been thought through beyond the fact of his date with Jean Casey. He
kept changing his mind about what they had done before going to Jean's house at
midnight, and he said that he had stayed there until around 1:45 on the morning of
September 15—which would have allowed him to get to Poole's Funeral Chapel
in time to encounter Kirthus Glenn at 2:10.

Blanton submitted to a polygraph test that same day. The general questions
about various bombings climaxed in the final series, which switched from the
rather insipid ("Did you ever buy dynamite to use in bombs?") to the bone-
chilling: "On 9/15/63 were you parked in your car near 7th Avenue North and
16th Street about 2:00 a.m.?" Blanton's reaction went from strong to extreme and
stayed there on the following question: "Was Robert Chambliss with you?" His
strong reaction subsided on the next question, "Was Troy Ingram with you?" and
went to normal on "Was Ross Keith with you?" The FBI had now identified a cast
of characters for Sunday morning. The problem was that Tommy Blanton knew
what his role in it was.

The FBI waited an entire day to question Jean Casey. By then Blanton had
gotten to his girlfriend to "refresh his memory." The two coordinated their stories
to the extent of saying that they had stopped at Ed Salem's drive-in. But Blanton
had neglected to tell her that he had run into Mary Lou Holt when he went there,
and not only would Casey say Blanton had talked to no one, but Holt would confirm that Blanton had been alone when she saw him. It is possible that much of the
date with Casey was fabricated, but both now insisted that he had left her house
around 2:30 rather than 1:45.

Six FBI agents swarmed the Blanton residence on Friday, October 4. Agents
found three pistols and a shotgun but no explosives. Tommy took a swing at Special Agent Bernard Cashdollar and then thrust his hand in his pocket. While an
agent trapped Blanton's hand, Cashdollar removed a black pocketknife. Blanton
was placed under arrest for attempted assault of a federal agent. The bureau now
had a trophy to match the highway patrol's.

The FBI continued its interrogation of Blanton at headquarters. Tommy had
not thought up an excuse for his absence from work on the days of both Arthur
Shores bombings, nor had he come up with an alibi for the critical meeting of Cahaba boys on Friday the thirteenth—the night he had broken his date with Casey.
After more than six hours into the interrogation, Blanton suddenly remembered

that he had been at the Modern Sign Shop that Friday night, painting signs with his friend Bobby Cherry. Three minutes later, Blanton asked for permission to call a lawyer. He phoned Matt Murphy at both his home and his country house, but could not reach him.

After a night in the county jail—where Blanton told a sheriff's deputy posing as a prisoner, "I have got people looking after me; at least they better be"—Blanton appeared to hear the charges against him before a U.S. commissioner. Her name was Louise Charlton, and twenty-five years earlier she had helped launch a crusade that was to have been the salvation of poor white southerners like Blanton along with the race that was his ferocious obsession. Charlton had been the founding chairwoman of the Southern Conference for Human Welfare.

Ingram

STRESS FRACTURES were beginning to show in the Cahaba River group's inscrutable facade. While in custody, Blanton mentioned three or four times that Chambliss had told him he was going to make a bomb that would throw metal, the technical name for which was a "shrapnel bomb." Chambliss arrived at the Cahaba River bridge meeting on Sunday, October 6, cussing Bobby Shelton for being in cahoots with George Wallace to sell him down the river. Shelton, he believed, wanted to collect the bombing reward money—some $92,000 had been pledged, to be matched by the city government—to finance the Klan village that Don Luna was hoping to build out in DeBardeleben country near Lake Purdy. Chambliss claimed that Luna, the Klan's go-between with the state, had set him up: "And, buddy, I'm going to kill him too." Exalted Cyclops Robert Thomas was acting as Shelton's proxy, Chambliss believed, in "trying to put me in the chair." Troy Ingram was fretting about the black Ford Falcon with no license plate and a whip antenna that had been circling his house—state or county lawmen, Ingram was convinced, trying to plant some bombing evidence. Jitters, however, were not the same as remorse. To his intimates Ingram would say that the only thing wrong with the church bombing was that it didn't kill all the black bastards. And Bobby Cherry's way of denying involvement in the dynamiting would be to say that somebody had beat him to it.

Hoping to improve his standing with the FBI, Ingram underwent a second polygraph at his own request. The addition of new questions revealed the progress of the BAPBOMB investigation. "Did you use fishing bobbers in the bomb?" divulged the latest theory about the timing device. "Do you know if Tommy Blanton bombed the church?" elicited a sharp deceptive response, and even stronger was the reaction to "Did you have a meeting to plan or make the bomb on Friday night?" As for the shrapnel bomb, Ingram set the machine off when he was asked if he had ever put a clutch plate in a bomb.*

* Both of Ingram's tests also indicated that he had had some involvement in one or both of the Shores bombings.

Perpetual Paradox

MARTIN LUTHER KING was engulfed by the media when he arrived at the Birmingham airport late Monday afternoon, October 7. He wanted badly to be finished with Birmingham, knowing that a renewed campaign would be sabotaged by the law of Guinness: The demonstrations would not be perceived as a success unless they topped those of the spring. It seemed, however, that the Kennedy administration might have finally come to the Movement's rescue. Through a little Rotary-style cajolery, Blaik and Royall had on October 3 gotten a commitment from the power structure to support the hiring of Negro police. It was a replay of the open-parks movement, with change being decreed from a segregated Olympus, but this time city hall was cooperating. The council had quietly agreed to pass a resolution in favor of hiring Negro police on Tuesday. An endorsement of Negro police in Monday's *Birmingham News* was seconded by forty-four "nonresident" Big Mules, including Art Wiebel, Prince DeBardeleben Jr., Charles's heir, at least one bankroller of the Citizens Councils, and a founder of the Methodist Layman's Union.

As Blaik and Royall confidently packed their bags, Fred Shuttlesworth put the millennium spirit into perspective at the Monday-night mass meeting: White bombers, he said, were under $300 bond for possession of dynamite; he was under $2,500 bond for walking the streets. Chambliss, Cagle, and Nigger Hall went on trial in city court for their misdemeanor on Tuesday night and Wednesday. They were convicted, but when they decided to appeal the fine of $100 and sentence of 180 days, the judge suspended their sentences. Chambliss left the courthouse with a smile for the cameras.

In the perpetual paradox of Birmingham, the conspicuous presence of Shuttlesworth and King scotched the turning point that their conspicuous presence had inspired. Suddenly the city council refused to buckle down to what even Blaik and Royall had called "the threats and ultimatums of non-residents": No Negro police.* For once public opinion seemed to be on Birmingham's side. Letters from all over the country urged Boutwell to stand up to King and Shuttlesworth. The problem of Birmingham, as President Kennedy had taken pains to say, was not confined to Birmingham, especially as it was becoming clear that King and Shuttlesworth did not intend to confine themselves to Birmingham.

The Kennedy administration seemed to have grown battle-weary too. Although Burke Marshall had gotten Herbert Harris, the economist and sociologist

---

* The Negro police campaign had accomplished one thing: It got U.S. Steel chairman Roger Blough off the hook at his quarterly news conference in New York in late October, when reporters badgered him to explain why the corporation did not use its economic influence to ease the racial tensions in Birmingham. Blough's reply might have brought tears to a few of his Birmingham customers. He said that "economic compulsion to achieve a particular end" was "quite beyond what a corporation should do, and I will say also, quite beyond what a corporation can do." Noting that Art Wiebel had recently supported the employment of Negro policeman, he closed his end of the age of segregation: "We have fulfilled our responsibility in the Birmingham area." The next year, Wiebel would be gone, reclaimed by Pittsburgh in a corporate reorganization.

who had helped orchestrate the Marshall Plan, to work with Blaik and Royall in preparing a meaningful report to the President, it would never get beyond a draft deploring "the extremists on either side." The only thing lasting to come out of the Blaik-Royall mission was a photograph taken when the two men appeared at the Oval Office on Thursday. The President's young children had scampered in, and the White House photographer got a winsome shot of John John peering out from under the desk that had once belonged to General Grant.

Cherry Bomb

BOBBY CHERRY was considered by even his fellow Klansman Nigger Hall as being practically insane. But over the years he had shown an undeniable gift of the gab, whether in an ability to talk his way into jobs or, now, fabricate Tommy Blanton's alibi for Friday night, September 13. He vouched that Tommy had been at the Modern Sign shop with him. Cherry's FBI polygraph on October 9 elicited a strong reaction of deception on the question. "On Friday night, was Tommy Blanton with you making a bomb?" But his autonomic functions showed a low level of sensitivity otherwise, and his reaction to "Did you bomb the Sixteenth Street Baptist Church?" would not lead agents to conclude (as they would later from Flora Chambliss's reports via Mary Frances Cunningham) that Cherry had planted the bomb. He boasted to Edward Fields and J. B. Stoner that he beat the lie detector.

That friendship between the Klansmen and the neo-Nazis remained solid in desperation—Fields issued Robert Chambliss a free subscription to *The Thunderbolt*—but Fields's own constituency was said to be deserting him. The rumors that Fields, a husband and father, had a second "wife"—a nurse who had followed him from Louisville to Birmingham with their young daughter—would within two years help split the organization apart. The National States Rights Party's brief moment as a pet of the governor of Alabama had passed, its remaining trace of institutional support a comment on the vicissitudes of power. The man police believed had put up the money to bond Fields and his followers out of jail on the federal obstruction charges was a Dothan banker and anti-Semite named Wallace Malone Sr., who had once ruled over state politics as an architect of the Dixiecrat revolt.

Informers

LIKE ITS QUARRIES, the FBI was being forced further into risky alliances. Gary Thomas Rowe was proving a disappointment as an informer. He claimed to have stepped up his contacts with Robert Thomas's wife, Mildred, in order to find out what the Exalted Cyclops knew about the bombing. She either did not know or did not say what the FBI would later hear—that Thomas had tried to cancel the Sixteenth Street mission. Mildred's guess was that Earl Thompson and Ross Keith, the DeBardelebenites, were involved, along with Billy Holt. Thompson had indeed been taking the church bombing badly. Perhaps he was wondering whether the chemical detonator he was said to have recently tested with Ingram, Cherry, and Holt might be relevant to the crime. As one of the suspected bombers of Bethel Baptist on Christmas 1956, perhaps he too had come to believe that God was guarding men like Fred Shuttlesworth against death. And Thompson turned to God for forgiveness.

As for Ross Keith, his girlfriend and alibi, Lavelle Fike, gave a marathon interview to the FBI to get back at him for slapping her face and grabbing her jaw to pop her dentures—all because she had gotten jealous that he was dancing with another woman at Club 280, near the Cahaba River bridge. To her threat of tattling, Keith had replied—perhaps referring to the Schoolhouse Door firearms contretemps—that he had gotten out of trouble before and would get out of any she might cause. And indeed Keith would prove to have inherited the immunity of the DeBardelebens and was never punished for his crimes.

A Birmingham policeman ran into Rowe drinking at the Brown Derby and asked him about the church bombing, "Aren't you a little shaky about this deal?" It wasn't a Klan deal, Rowe told him, and said that the man who had put up the money to have the church bombed was Harry Belafonte.

The worthlessness of its prize informant prompted the FBI to turn to another Klansman. The new Eastview man the agency was grooming for government service was Nigger Hall, drunkard, burglar, wife beater, and suspected bomber, whose dark skin had prompted fellow Klansmen to kid him about being a "spy from King's bunch."

30.

GENERAL LEE'S NAMESAKES

Kiss of Death

O
N THE EVENING OF FRIDAY, October 11, Elizabeth Hood slipped into the back seat of a government sedan in the parking lot of the insurance company she worked for. In a sense, this was the moment she had been living for since her uncle Robert had humiliated her when she was four. Her beloved Aunt Tee had not only not protected her kinfolk from Robert; she had allowed them to become secondary beneficiaries of the kiss of death. That summer, Flora Chambliss had taken Elizabeth to an empty house in Fountain Heights—seemingly an innocent adventure to see what the owners had left behind. In the basement, they found a workbench covered with electrical wire, glass jugs of a liquid that looked like gasoline, and boxes of what Tee announced were dynamite and blasting caps. As they left "the bomb factory," Tee told Elizabeth, "If anybody knew we'd been here, it could get us killed. You can't tell anybody, not even Robert." Yet Elizabeth now had the feeling that Tee had taken her there precisely in order to create a legacy of information sources.

Hood's aunt Mary Frances Cunningham had already talked to the FBI. She had urged Elizabeth to do so as well, assuring her that everything she said would be kept a secret. Still, Hood was sweating when she climbed into the car. One of the two FBI agents in the front seat, Robert Womack, told her that they knew who had done the bombing but needed physical evidence and testimony to build a court case. They showed her a piece of fabric they believed had been used to tie sticks of dynamite together in a recent bombing, and asked if she recognized it as anything she had ever seen her aunt Flora wear. They showed her a picture of a fishing bobber and explained how it could be used as a timing device, floating atop a slow-leaking liquid until it was low enough to exert the pressure that would break a chemical capsule or trip a fine wire.

Hood poured out the story of her life of fear: of her heart's certainty that her uncle had done evil, including this evil; of her frustration over not being able to offer anything more concrete than his outburst on the Saturday before the church bombing, ending with "Let them wait till after Sunday morning. They will beg us to segregate." This bloodletting felt so tonic that for a moment Hood lost her own fear and said that she worried only about the "kiss of death" Chambliss might put on his mother-in-law, Mama Katie, and her own son, Robin.

The agents told Hood that they planned to interview her family, and perhaps it would be best, for her safety, if she joined them as though she had not had previous contact with the FBI. It was then that Hood realized that she had embarked on a dangerous, clandestine relationship. The bureau created code names for her and Mary Frances Cunningham—Abingdon Spaulding and Dale Tarrant—to accommodate the double life that they would lead for another thirty years, culminating for Hood in a drastic personal decision that seemed to make her uncle Robert's first comment to her prophetic.

There was plenty of celebrating that Friday at J. Edgar Hoover's "seat of government" in Washington, but not over the new witness in the BAPBOMB case. The day before, Hoover had won the prize he had been angling for since July—Robert Kennedy's signature authorizing a wiretap on Martin Luther King. Kennedy's acquiescence may have been related to the ordering that day of a Senate investigation into Bobby Baker, Vice President Lyndon Johnson's old fixer on his Senate staff, whose back-channel services included pimping the President's deported East German–born mistress, Ellen Rometsch.

Commuting seamlessly from sexual to political intimidation, Hoover received on Monday the revisionist monograph his domestic intelligence division had done at his insistence on "Communism and the Negro Movement." The FBI's deputy director, Alan Belmont, was startled by the virulence behind the predictions that "as the Communist party goes, so goes Martin Luther King, and so also goes the Negro movement of the United States." He warned of the attorney general's displeasure. But Hoover had the report sent not only to both Kennedys but also to the Central Intelligence Agency, the secretaries of state and defense, and all branches of the military. When Robert Kennedy indeed became furious, especially that it had gone out to the Army, Hoover blandly recalled all copies. They had served their purpose.

On to Selma

AS MARTIN LUTHER KING colonized more and more of the national imagination, his career seemed to be going around in circles within the Movement itself. "There comes a time when people get tired of being kicked around," he said at the Monday, October 14, mass meeting in Birmingham, reprising his memorable speech pairing fatigue with inspiration that had kicked off the Montgomery boycott eight long years before. But the "tired" this time—of bombings and second-rate jobs and schools—sounded different from the regenerative weariness of the earlier call to arms, more like exhausted resignation. He said he would like to stay home with his wife rather than demonstrate, but concluded, "If they force it on us, we will regroup our souls and march again." Observing him now from afar,

Stanley Levison said that King's desire to get out before the battle was won was "like a child who can't finish something and moves on to some other game."

The next day, King was to go to Selma, where SNCC had migrated its campaign to avenge Denise, Carole, Cynthia, and Addie. To focus their rage against Wallace, SNCC's aging youths were embarking on a voter registration drive to vote him out of office. A week earlier, John Lewis had been bowled over to see hundreds of Selma Negroes confront Sheriff Jim Clark at the Dallas County courthouse in an attempt to register, many of them elderly and presumed brainwashed, but perhaps old enough to remember the young Communists who had organized sharecroppers there in the 1930s. Lewis would consider that date "the turning point in the right to vote," the campaign that would reach a climax two years later in the Movement's nonviolent valedictory: the Selma-to-Montgomery March.

From Birmingham, King was going to Selma to buck up the troops, and as usual he was behind schedule. Nelson "Fireball" Smith had agreed to drive him. Outside the Gaston Motel, Smith spied Thelton Henderson, the black Justice Department lawyer, who was in town on some voting cases. Smith rolled down his window and said there was something wrong with his tire. Henderson offered his Hertz rental. The Movement ministers had long since overcome their wariness of Henderson, once he disarmed them during the spring demonstrations by saying that they shouldn't tell him anything they didn't want Robert Kennedy to know. Henderson, in turn, was showing signs of going native.

Someone warned Smith that folks had been by taking pictures of Henderson's blue Chevy Impala, but Smith decided to borrow it anyway. And he felt a little safer being in a Justice Department car when some "rosin chewers" began following him and King down the two-lane highway to Selma.

Bad Faith

GEORGE WALLACE's reaction to Al Lingo's bungled dynamite case—which surely he had not undertaken without the governor's approval—had been to propose that the reason Chambliss and company hadn't been charged with the bombing was that they were innocent. Maybe the real bombers were "communists or other Negroes who had a lot to gain by the ensuing publicity." Wallace ordered Major Bill Jones to increase his coverage of "subversives," a designation not for the Klan but for the civil rights establishment. That explained why Captain R. W. Godwin had slacked off on his pursuit of church bombers since escorting Hubert Page to his polygraph test. The men in Godwin's unit had been spying on King since he had arrived at the Birmingham airport and were the "rosin chewers" following him and Smith in Thelton Henderson's car to Selma.

On Wednesday, October 16, Wallace had the "not surprising" information leaked, without further elaboration, that King was being chauffeured at the taxpayers' expense. Justice categorically denied the charge. Henderson assured his superior John Doar that the story was untrue—he hadn't actually been in the car—and began the longest week of his life.* From Detroit the next day, King confirmed that he had gone to Selma in Smith's Chevrolet. Burke Marshall called Wallace's claim "either a gross mistake or a deliberate attempt to mislead the people." Henderson decided he needed a vacation and went home to his mama in Los Angeles.

Sport

AT THE NATIONAL STATES RIGHTS PARTY'S "White Rally" Saturday night, October 19, effigies of King, Shuttlesworth, and Kennedy hung in the Mount Olive Ball Park in Gardendale, the resting ground of the famous case of dynamite. Robert Chambliss seemed to regard the heavy surveillance on him as a kind of joke. He drove into the field behind one of the unmarked police cars, pretending to be tailing it. He boasted to Detective Marcus Jones that he had been having sport with the FBI agents following him—dirty people. J. B. Stoner lectured the crowd of 100 or 150, mostly Klansmen, on the history of Jewish control of the FBI, which, he claimed, had bombed the church. Stoner was still the Birmingham police's favorite suspect.

Those Who Shake the Apple Tree

AT 2:45 ON TUESDAY, October 22, the reporters crowding the patio of the Gaston Motel stirred as Fred Shuttlesworth and Martin Luther King descended the stairs to take their places in front of the microphones. "I guess you know who we are," they opened with a rueful familiarity. Shuttlesworth said that they would honor the city's request to leave the date of police hiring up in the air "if they will do something on the ground." The demands seemed flat. Even when King said that Marlon Brando and other actors, as well as 110 rabbis, were awaiting their call, the detectives present were not much impressed, noting that Shuttlesworth jumped in and answered questions directed at King. There would be no black policemen in Birmingham until 1966.

In contrast to the spring, only a dozen or so black people were on hand, mostly motel employees. The word on the street had always been that the May settlement was about as good as "the promises the white man made to the Indians." The Movement lawyer Len Holt, who had termed those concessions "cake" for Negroes who don't have the "bread" to buy it, had come to share Malcolm X's view that it was the fear of " 'bread' demonstrations," such as the Gaston Motel riot, that had made officials around the country rush "to integrate places that most Negroes don't even know exist."

A related irony emerging from the Year of Birmingham was that those who

---

* That same day, West End Parents for Private Schools, received $1,200 from Wallace as seed money for the private school they were organizing—suggesting that the governor's sensitivity about taxpayers' money was selective.

would reap the rewards of the social revolution were not the revolutionaries themselves. As Abraham Woods, the Alabama Christian Movement for Human Rights vice president, liked to say, "Those who shake the apple tree are not those who generally get to eat the apples." The Sixteenth Street Baptist pastor John Cross, a lukewarm supporter of the Movement, had been taken to task by some parishioners after initially depositing in his personal account a $13,000 check that the city of Seattle sent to cover the bombing victims' hospital and burial expenses (which had already been paid out of other funds). Meanwhile, a young chemistry professor at Miles College, Richard Arrington, kept his nose out of the Movement "mess"; in fifteen years he would unseat David Vann to become Birmingham's first black mayor.

An immediate casualty of the curse of being right was Chuck Morgan. The Speech, which had been broadcast over Voice of America, had earned him a pat on the back from the United States attorney general and death threats from his fellow Birminghamians. He called five lawyers to his office in that skyscraper of hope, the Bank for Savings Building, parceled out his furniture and law books, and packed up his family to move to Atlanta. The razzle-dazzle legal career ahead of him would never quite make up for his disappointment at not becoming governor of Alabama.

The Pantheon

ON TUESDAY, October 22, at Harper Hospital in Detroit, FBI agents showed the seamstress Kirthus Glenn photographs of Tommy Blanton's Chevrolet, which she pronounced identical to the car parked in front of Poole's Funeral Chapel in the early morning of September 15. Later that day, reading a recent issue of *Jet*, she saw a story about Robert Chambliss's release from jail and called the FBI. The accompanying picture of Chambliss resembled one of the men who had been sitting in the back seat of the Chevy.

On October 24, the FBI finally showed Glenn, its only eyewitness, photographs of the BAPBOMB suspects: the pantheon (Keith, the Cashes, Thomas, Holt, Thompson, Reeves, Ingram, Cagle, Blanton, White, Tidwell, Yarbrough, Hall); the B-team, who probably knew about the bomb but didn't help plan it (George Pickle, Billy Levaughn Jackson, Loel Rogers); the kooks (Stoner, Fields, Bowling). Glenn recognized only Chambliss; the two other men she had seen in the car had had their faces averted from her. As usual, the FBI lineup included no picture of Gary Thomas Rowe.

This was the FBI's case against the Sixteenth Street Baptist Church bombers, and the further evidence against the suspects gleaned largely by Mary Frances Cunningham through her sister Tee Chambliss would not stand up in a court of law.

Malice

ON WEDNESDAY, October 23, George Wallace announced that he was conven-
ing a state grand jury to determine the facts of the Thelton Henderson car case,
given that the Justice Department's denials had "impugned the honesty and integrity of state and county law officials." There was an echo here of former Montgomery commissioner L. B. Sullivan's now three-year-old defamation suit against
the *New York Times*, whose lawyers had filed their ninety-five-page brief with the
Supreme Court in September. The *Sullivan* case had now been stripped of racial
connotations. Freedom of the press, not Negroes' civil rights, was the cause being
pressed by the *Times* lawyers, who had split their case off from the appeal
mounted by Shuttlesworth and the three Alabama ministers in *Abernathy* v. *Sullivan*. Both parties were due to present their oral arguments before the Supreme
Court in January.

Thelton Henderson knew that his hide was not going to be saved by high-
minded constitutional apologies. He was having an "out-of-body experience, like
watching this happen to another person." John Doar called him at his mother's in
Los Angeles and said, "We've got to sort this out." When Burke Marshall received
Henderson's confession, he must have had the same feeling the *Times* editors had
had when they discovered the inaccuracies, however benign, in Bayard Rustin's
fateful "Heed Their Rising Voices" ad, a gift to a foe who happened to be the malicious party. Marshall accepted Henderson's resignation, his raw feelings on the
matter clear in how close he came to also firing Henderson's champion, Doar, who
had a four-month-old son named Burke.

Among the many people who applauded George Wallace for thus embarrassing the Kennedys was a budding politician from Kennedy's Boston named
Louise Day Hicks. She wrote the attorney general, sarcastically asking him to
have "one of your big black Justice Department limousines" at the Montgomery
airport to meet her when she went there to make a series of speeches on "Why I
am not going to vote for Kennedy the next time." Hicks would become the
George Wallace of the following decade's civil rights watershed, as the most vehement of the politicians leading the resistance to court-ordered school busing in
Boston.

Playboys

THE *DES MOINES REGISTER* of Saturday, October 12, reported the August de-
portation of Ellen Rometsch, the East German "party girl," in its front-page story
on the Senate hearing scheduled for the following Tuesday on the Bobby Baker
scandal. The author of the article was Clark Mollenhoff, a frequent beneficiary of
J. Edgar Hoover's leaks. Robert Kennedy, whom a bureau memo that day also tied
to "playgirls," spent the weekend stanching the flow from his brother's personal
life, going so far as to send one of the family valets to Germany with a budget to
keep Rometsch out of sight.

On Monday morning, October 28, while supplicating Hoover to help him bury the Rometsch affair,* Robert Kennedy seemed to acknowledge the reckless way in which he and his brother had put the important things in jeopardy, for he changed the subject from the President's sex life to the Birmingham church bombing. Hoover's priorities, too, were momentarily jolted. Instead of blaming Martin Luther King for the bureau's failure to crack the BAPBOMB case, he faulted the state of Alabama.

Hoover's agents in Birmingham, meanwhile, had been reduced to taunting Robert Chambliss as he cursed them from the loading dock at his place of work; they told him that he was not acting like an innocent man. And so it must have come as a relief when on Tuesday, October 29, after a few weeks of courtship, Chambliss's Eastview Klan brother Nigger Hall pledged his full cooperation with the FBI in solving the church bombing. The following night he went to FBI headquarters in the 2121 Building and offered a theory: There were two sets of bombers working independently. One was the Chambliss-Ingram axis. The second, he believed, consisted of Quickdraw Yarbrough and Charles Cagle.

Soon Hall would join Gary Thomas Rowe on the government payroll, as Huey Lipscomb. Hall was approved by Washington despite the field office's acknowledgment that he "undoubtedly participated in some of Birmingham's minor bombings" and, as noted by his September polygraph, had "some knowledge of the bombing of 16th Street Baptist and may have participated in some way in the bombing or the planning thereof." The bureau also knew that he had volunteered to kill Fred Shuttlesworth in 1962 and had probably played a major role in the hardly "minor" shrapnel bombing. Rowe had complimented him on being "the granddaddy of the shrapnel bombs." On December 2, even before he became an official informant, Hall would name the three prime suspects in the bombing—Chambliss, Ingram, and Blanton—a full year before Rowe would produce the same list.

The Great Man's Legacy

THE GROWING REWARD FUND for the church-bombing case was being administered by the law firm of Jim Simpson. That is, the incentive for the capture of the bombers had been entrusted to the mentor of Dynamite Bob's own handler. Bull Connor was, with Simpson's help, about to be elected to the state's Public Service Commission, which set the rates for Simpson's utility clients, but the Great Man's attentions were now diverted onto his new ward, George Wallace. On Monday, November 4, Simpson accompanied the governor to Harvard University, where he was making a heavily attended and lavishly picketed appearance under the auspices of the campus Young Democrats. In deference to the hoity-toity crowd,

---

* Fortunately for the Kennedys, the Bobby Baker investigation had unearthed enough dirt to fill a bipartisan cemetery of randy lawmakers, and Hoover agreed to use his authority with the senators to tamp down the Rometsch scandal. Perhaps acknowledging his debt to Hoover, Robert Kennedy authorized a wiretap on Bayard Rustin three days later.

Simpson had assumed some of the speechwriting chores from the talented Ace Carter.* It was one of Simpson's passages—"*Brown* did not, I assure you, as some seem to think, spring instantly into existence full grown and ready for action equipped with injunctive process, preferred appeal, set bayonets and all its accoutrements like Botticelli would have us believe Venus came to the shores of Greece full grown and full blown on the breath of Boreas"—that got the only, if unintentional, laugh of the evening.

Simpson would later say with rare levity about himself that this first "national" speech was the last he would write for Wallace. It was Wallace's ad-libs that inspired the electric moment of the Harvard performance. When the grandson of the late W. E. B. Du Bois stood up and informed the governor that he intended to run for president someday, Wallace smiled. "Between you and me both, we might kick out that crowd down in Washington," he said, and paused. "Maybe we should run on the same ticket."

On his third college lecture tour, the next February at the University of Wisconsin, George Wallace laid the groundwork for his 1964 presidential candidacy, in the kitchen of a former operative of Senator Joe McCarthy. He met the filing deadline to launch his campaign from McCarthy's hometown of Appleton. He would get a shocking 34 percent of the state's vote. The banner of ultrapatriotism had passed from the hands of Big Business to the little man's bantam friend.

New Dimensions

FRED SHUTTLESWORTH was moving beyond Martin Luther King, toward obscurity. With all the demands on his attention—New American Library was impatient for his manuscript on Birmingham—King did not have the focus to do what was necessary, Shuttlesworth thought. He prodded King by letter: "I hope, however, that you will consider that you as the Symbol of the Movement, must lead in planning and stirring up people in the South; and that writing and some speaking in the North may be less crucial at the moment."

Shuttlesworth was proposing "new dimensions" for the Movement. He was endorsing Diane Nash's radical plan, now being refined by the old master strategist Bayard Rustin. What they had in mind were mass demonstrations in Birmingham for the spring, followed by a procession of 35,000 or 40,000 to Montgomery. The aim would be to "effectively immobiliz[e] Birmingham and Montgomery." The ambiguous "victory" in Birmingham made it clear that moral witness was not

---

* Carter's writing career would peak on the *New York Times* best-seller list. Taking the name of his Civil War hero, "Forrest" Carter wrote first a novel called *Gone to Texas*, which became the Clint Eastwood movie *The Outlaw—Josey Wales*, and then a "memoir" of his boyhood under the care of made-up Cherokee grandparents. Called *The Education of Little Tree*, it featured a loving portrait of a Jewish peddler. Carter did not live to see his hoax become a New Age cult phenomenon in the early 1990s. His mysterious death, in 1979, is usually attributed to a heart attack, but the ambulance driver who took him to the hospital would say that he had aspirated his vomit after a drunken fist-fight with his son.

sufficient to meet the challenge of institutional racism. Shuttlesworth had seen the future of black power. "I have come to understand," he admonished King, "that we must either keep leadership or give it over to more active elements."

It was with a sense of excitement as much as apprehension that Shuttlesworth looked ahead to a split between the Movement's nonviolent integrationists and its militant separatists. And he continued to honor its controversial past. On November 9, he presided over the board meeting of the Southern Conference Educational Fund in the city of its birth, impervious to the recent front-page *Birmingham News* story about a police raid on SCEF's New Orleans headquarters: "Shuttlesworth Fund Offices Raided Under Anti-Communist Law."

A Bombing Verdict

ON NOVEMBER 18, 1963, the FBI got its first conviction in a bombing: Roosevelt Tatum, the poor black laborer who claimed to have seen a police officer plant the bombs at A. D. King's house the previous May, pleaded guilty in Judge Clarence Allgood's court to lying to an FBI agent. The mystery of why Orzell Billingsley, after so zealously fighting the indictment, would let his client plead might be explained by the futility of the case, the lawyer's workload, or his whiskey intake. Allgood sentenced Tatum to a year and a day.

The FBI's defense of the Birmingham police must have confounded Detective Maurice House: He believed that some of his fellow officers might have been "deeply involved" in the bombings, including the one he was currently investigating, of the Sixteenth Street Baptist Church.

The courtesy that FBI agents accorded Bobby Shelton on November 20 was a blunt contrast to their treatment of Roosevelt Tatum. In the first interview with the Imperial Wizard since the church bombing, the agents hewed to the bureau policy of apologizing to whites being questioned in connection with a race crime and "assured SHELTON," as they wrote in their report, "that as long as Mr. HOOVER was head of the FBI the organization would be in fact an investigative organization without malice or opinion and dedicated to serving the public without preference or discrimination. SHELTON stated he has always been an admirer of the Bureau and Mr. HOOVER and hoped that his leadership in the FBI would continue."

To Dallas

AS SHELTON PAID HOMAGE to Hoover on November 20, Robert Kennedy celebrated his thirty-eighth birthday at the office in typically casual style. Lou Oberdorfer went from the birthday party to a White House reception for the Supreme Court. He chatted with his first boss, Hugo Black, and he and the President reminisced about the ransom package Oberdorfer had put together for Fidel Castro to bring the Bay of Pigs prisoners home. The problem of Cuba was beginning to look refreshingly straightforward next to the quagmire in a distant hemisphere. On November 2, South Vietnam's corrupt president, Ngo Dinh Diem, had been assassinated in a coup of army generals. Kennedy's optimism about extricating himself from an Indo-Chinese guerrilla war—he had hoped to get all American military advisers out of Vietnam by 1965—now seemed unrealistic.

For the time being, there was the civil insurrection within his own country to deal with. A few weeks earlier, anti-Kennedy pickets in Dallas holding "Remember the Bay of Pigs" signs had spat upon the visiting UN ambassador, Adlai Stevenson. The President himself was about to leave for Dallas, to try to charm the hostile Texas Democrats.

River City

IWOULD HAVE NO MEMORY of where I was when I heard the news of the bombing of the Sixteenth Street Baptist Church. My mother's date book showed that my rehearsal for *The Music Man,* a community theater production in which I was a member of the chorus, was canceled, out of fear for the safety of white people abroad at night.

Papa told us the janitor had bombed the church and invoked "that Communist training school at Monteagle, Tennessee." I didn't believe him and wasn't sure whether he was serious, but it was an increasingly popular theory, as civic denial spread out from the Chamber of Commerce over the mountain. My good friend Nancy Spencer's father, the Chamber president and prominent Senior Citizen, had submitted a sort of position paper to Mayor Boutwell, proposing that the church bomb had been the work of "sleek, fat agitators" intent on fomenting "mobs of negroes."

The run of *The Music Man* had just ended, and so had a bit of my naiveté. I had encountered homosexual flamboyance (in the taskmaster who directed all Town & Gown theatrical productions); learned that the proper pronunciation of Pompeii was not "Pompy-eye," as the mayor of River City thought; and understood my first sophisticated joke, although not until the laughter of the live audience cued me that the line "The coward dies a thousand deaths but the brave man only five hundred" took liberties with the original. The fact that I had participated in the drama of a small-minded community ultimately saved by an "outside agitator" was not entirely lost on me, but I was oblivious of the history on my own doorstep. It would be twenty years before I learned that one of my fellow child cast members was the daughter of the state representative who had helped incorporate the ultra-segregationist West End Parents for Private Schools into a legal entity and had addressed its rally two days after the church bombing.

My eleventh birthday, on November 1, had fallen amid the busy run of the play, so we had postponed my party. It would now take place on the third Friday in November.

November 22, 1963

THE THELTON HENDERSON scandal had been too delicious for George Wallace to drop, better even than Robert Kennedy's 1961 call to "Mr. Greyhound." Two grand juries were now looking into Martin Luther King's ride in a government car. J. Edgar Hoover was peppering Burke Marshall with thirdhand reports of Henderson's romantic involvement with a white woman. The civil rights division won an appellate ruling that a state grand jury had no constitutional power to investigate a federal agency, but as a courtesy Marshall had agreed to let one representative of the Alabama grand jury question his staff about the Henderson affair. Wallace's aides figured that it would play better with the folks if all the jurors went up, so they had gotten travel agents to book the entire grand jury on a taxpayer-supported flight to Washington. They left for the capital on Friday, November 22.

For the second time that fall, the world came to an end. General Robert Edward Lee's other namesake, Lee Harvey Oswald, had outdone Robert Edward Chambliss.

My family decided to go ahead with my birthday party. My mother had bought cartons of sherbet for pastel ginger-ale floats and, for breakfast, frozen waffles, Log Cabin syrup, and link sausages. In gym class a few hours before arriving at my party, some of my guests, the daughters and granddaughters of Birmingham's Big Mules, had cheered at the news that the President had been shot—a reaction, it turned out, that had been repeated by schoolchildren across the city. The main reason I hadn't joined in was that I was standing next to my best friend, Caroline McCarley, a Kennedy admirer and political nonconformist who, a few years later, would name her dog after Hugo Black.

Our childhood was already being brought to an end by hormones. In October, a band of four long-haired British lads from Liverpool had gotten its first airplay in America. And two books published earlier in 1963—Betty Friedan's *The Feminine Mystique* and Sylvia Plath's *The Bell Jar*—hinted at the liberation movement that would shape our own future. But I would date the independence of mind and emotion that signals the onset of maturity from the all-night séances my friends and I conducted in my grandmother's living room on November 22, to reach our dead president, begging him to come back and identify his killer. It was the closest we came to mourning before we composed our game faces for the weekend of televised national grief.

"Why do we hate Kennedy?" I asked Papa as a riderless horse shied across the screen. "The Bay of Pigs," he explained and delivered a long, technical lecture on something called "air cover."

For once, the President's enemies did not invoke "civil rights" directly. Even George Wallace seemed to feel that the curtain had come down on his show. He was shaken, perhaps, by the same presentiment felt by Martin Luther King after the news of the assassination: "That is what is going to happen to me also."

After issuing a statement deploring Kennedy's murder and lowering the state's flags to half staff, Wallace joined King and his other foes in Washington for the funeral. During that weekend it seemed improbable that Wallace would launch a national counterrevolution against the last cause on which Kennedy had staked his administration. Or that his vigilantes would have so much murderous fight left in them. Ronnie Tidwell, the dynamite-savvy Young Turk, would soon replace the mild-mannered Robert Thomas as Exalted Cyclops of Eastview 13, declaring, "If we're going to be Ku Kluxers, let's Klux." By spring there would be talk of an all-Klan offensive similar to the Freedom Riders assault and a bombing of a new black-owned bank. Finally J. Edgar Hoover would be moved to act, targeting Bobby Shelton and his comrades that summer for the FBI counterintelligence program's dirty tricks.

The governor who shared Wallace's car at Kennedy's funeral, California's Pat Brown, told a reporter afterward that the governor of Alabama had confessed to him what the United Americans for Conservative Government had guessed a couple of months earlier, when he had embraced Doc and Skeeter: In his heart he was opposed to segregation.

And the tragedy of it is that Wallace was probably telling the truth. Segregation had created a society of untrue believers. Not just populist "bomb throwers" like Wallace who ended up harboring child killers and Klansmen who were loyal to their maids, but "honest men" who practiced bad faith and Christians who worshipped a crippled pagan god of industry.

Birmingham had begun as a vision of a post-bellum South, full of smoke and prosperity, but it became the site of a new civil war, in which the very tools of prosperity were used to murder the young. The Magic City was barely ninety years old. That was a short time to produce a history so terrible.

From it had come a gift, perhaps America's most stirring example of democracy.

EPILOGUE

O N JULY 2, 1964, President Lyndon Johnson signed into law the Civil Rights Act of 1964, abolishing legalized racism in America. Birmingham's foremost barbecue joint, Ollie's, whose owner, Ollie McClung, was a devout member of my mother's church, filed the unsuccessful constitutional test case against the public accommodations section of the law.

Guaranteed his place in history by Birmingham, Martin Luther King was *Time*'s 1963 Man of the Year and the following year's winner of the Nobel Peace Prize. Compelled to expose King as a " 'tom cat' with obsessive degenerate sexual urges," J. Edgar Hoover (who had long lobbied for the peace prize) sent audiotapes of King's "sex orgies" to the news media (which ignored them) and to Coretta Scott King, with a note urging King himself to commit suicide.

The most salacious of the recordings had been made in January 1964 at Washington's Willard Hotel, where King was staying while attending arguments at the Supreme Court for former Montgomery commissioner L. B. Sullivan's libel suit against the *Times* and Shuttlesworth et al. In one of its most landscape-altering decisions, the Court reversed Sullivan's lower-court victory in order to extend First Amendment protection to the public debate, thus preventing the state from effectively censoring controversial ideas. Henceforth, public figures would have to prove that any alleged libel against them was made with "actual malice," or "reckless disregard of whether it was false or not." Hugo Black, in a separate opinion concurring with William Brennan's landmark decision, made cautionary note of how the standards of malice might be skewed by the special racial climate of his native state; he had racially inflamed juries there himself once.

Fred Shuttlesworth (who says he was not in Washington for the arguments) grew more isolated from the Southern Christian Leadership Conference's inner circle of Atlantans, though he remained SCLC's secretary. As the nonviolent phase of the civil rights struggle approached its finale—the Selma-to-Montgomery March—Shuttlesworth became more conciliator than "wild man," dispatched by King to Selma to soothe the inevitable power struggles among the indigenous leadership, SCLC, and SNCC. But the Selma campaign caught

Shuttlesworth for the first time on the viewing side of the TV set. He was home in Cincinnati for the march's "Bloody Sunday" opener on March 7, 1965, when five hundred people were repulsed on the Edmund Pettus Bridge by Colonel Al Lingo's tear gas and billy clubs and the charging horseback posse of Sheriff Jim Clark—the law enforcement heavies of the Gaston Motel riot two years earlier. As the civil rights story converted into scholarship, Shuttlesworth became an incidental freak show—the freedom-fighting equivalent of a fire-eater—rather than the only member of the Movement who actually sustained a mass movement. His most lasting civil rights alliance, continuing to the present day, would be with the Southern Conference Educational Fund, which evolved into the Southern Organizing Committee for Economic and Social Justice in the 1980s under the leadership of Shuttlesworth's comrade Anne Braden.

BESIDES MARKING THE final collaboration between SCLC and SNCC around the doctrine of nonviolence, the Selma-to-Montgomery March led to the Voting Rights Act of 1965. As the Sixteenth Street Baptist Church bombing had hastened the passage of the Civil Rights Act of 1964, a racial assassination would also secure the quick legislative results of 1965—and finish Gary Thomas Rowe's undercover career with the FBI. At the conclusion of the four-day Selma march, Rowe and three longtime co-conspirators from the Bessemer klavern chased down the Oldsmobile of a white activist from Detroit named Viola Liuzzo, overtook her by the Big Bear Swamp on Highway 80 in Lowndes County, and shot her through the spinal cord. Back in Birmingham, Rowe explained to his police buddy, Lavaughn Coleman, "We had to burn a whore." Rowe's identity as an FBI informant was revealed soon after he and his friends were arraigned.

As the government's key witness against his Klan brothers, Rowe became a law enforcement hero. (They were ultimately sentenced to ten years for federal civil rights violations, having beat state murder raps.) Years would pass before it dawned on the public that Rowe had done nothing to prevent the cold-blooded murder of a woman whose cause was mainstream enough that one of her fellow marchers was the daughter of Secretary of Defense Robert McNamara. And as Rowe told and retold his outrageous story to congressional committees and Justice Department task forces, it began to seem that the violence of the Ku Klux Klan had been abetted by the bureaucratic negligence of the U.S. government. If the FBI had acted on Rowe's first scoop and stopped or punished the attackers of the Freedom Riders, Rowe might not have subsequently used his informant status as a shield for criminal activity, and Viola Liuzzo might be enjoying her grandchildren today.

Walter Bergman and James Peck, two of the original white Freedom Riders, successfully sued the Justice Department over the FBI's failure to protect them from the Birmingham Klan. The Liuzzo children lost a similar lawsuit against the department, in a trial notable for the hugs exchanged and lunch shared at the witness table by Fred Shuttlesworth and one of the alleged killers, Eugene Thomas, who had found God.*

Once exposed, Rowe became such a hated man among hate groups that the government put him in its witness protection program and on the payroll again, as a deputy U.S. marshal. He worked primarily as a security guard in his native Savannah, under the name Thomas Moore, until he died of a heart attack in 1998, his passing unnoticed by the media for months.

IN 1970, a twenty-eight-year-old with hair grazing his collar defeated Attorney General MacDonald Gallion, who had served the anti–Freedom Riding injunction on John Lewis as he bled in the streets of Montgomery in 1961. The new attorney general, William J. Baxley, was one of those Alabamians who had decided at an early age to become governor when he grew up, and he had all the earmarks of being the second coming of Folsom—for better and for worse, it turned out, as he was blessed not only with Big Jim's liberalism but also with his appetite.

In office for the next eight years, Baxley hired black assistant attorneys general, including future federal judge Myron Thompson. He secured a "full and unconditional pardon" for the last living Scottsboro "Boy," Clarence Norris. He sent the professional anti-Semite Edward Fields the following reply to a hostile letter: "Dear 'Dr.' Fields: My response to your letter of February 19, 1976 is—kiss my ass." And he wrote the names of Denise, Carole, Cynthia, and Addie on his state phone-calling card, one in each corner, to remind himself daily of the pledge he had made on Sunday, September 15, 1963, in the Kappa Sig house at the University of Alabama: to get the men who had murdered them.

Baxley reopened the investigation and rounded up the usual suspects, including Gary Thomas Rowe. Rowe submitted to a new round of interviews and "passed" his polygraphs. Herman Frank Cash, the least certain, fifth suspect, also passed a lie detector test. Amazingly (some thought suspiciously), within days of agreeing to talk to investigators, both Ross Keith and John "Nigger" Hall died, apparently of cirrhosis, soul mates till the end. Earl Thompson, the suspect in the 1956 Shuttlesworth bombing who found religion after Sixteenth Street, pleaded Christianity. The barber Billy Lavon Jackson agreed to undergo hypnosis to revive his memory of the Cahaba River Klan meeting of September 22, where he heard something he came to regret; but when he got to the incriminating discussion of the bombing that took place at Troy Ingram's house, he became agitated, repeating that he wanted to "go home." Ingram had died in 1973, suffering a heart attack at the wheel of his fire truck. He was the volunteer fire chief at the time.

---

* In 1978, Eugene Thomas and Collie Wilkins, the alleged triggerman, told the ABC News show *20/20* that it was Rowe who had fired at Liuzzo. Their charges were probably not true, but they were credible enough that the FBI had had similar doubts about its employee. It did not take any fingerprints from the murder weapon, Gene Thomas's .32-caliber pistol, in a lapse so egregious that J. Edgar Hoover personally demanded an explanation and continued to raise a fuss, ordering that murder weapons henceforth be routinely dusted.

The attorney general's investigation continued through protracted cat and mouse with the FBI over the release of the relevant records. In 1965, Hoover had forbidden his Birmingham field office to turn its evidence over to federal prosecutors, apparently not believing that it was strong enough to convict. In August 1977, when Chambliss learned that the grand jury was investigating his crime, he discounted the possibility that his niece, Elizabeth Hood, now thirty-seven and a Methodist minister, remarried as Cobbs, would testify against him. "One phone call to a certain number will take care of that," he said.

Chambliss was indicted for murder in September and went on trial on November 14. His attorney was Art Hanes, whose post-mayoral legal career had maintained its high profile since he got acquittals on the murder charges against the Klansmen accused of shooting Viola Liuzzo. In 1968, he briefly defended James Earl Ray, who had bought the rifle he used to assassinate Martin Luther King at a large sporting-goods store in Birmingham.

On the second day of the Chambliss trial, the courtroom was sealed in anticipation of Elizabeth Cobbs's dramatic surprise entrance, through a gantlet of armed sheriff's deputies. Chambliss looked at her and turned his head from side to side, "the way he would at a child who was both naughty and simpleminded." Her testimony about her uncle's "Wait till after Sunday" comments on the eve of the bombing, along with Kirthus Glenn's eyewitness description of the men in the car, were all the state had besides the notoriety of Dynamite Bob himself. On November 17, Baxley urged the jury—nine whites and three blacks—to "give Denise McNair a birthday present." She would have been twenty-six that day.

Chambliss was found guilty of murder. Flora Chambliss was lying on the couch in her darkened living room when she received the news. She, the indirect source of much of what we know about the bombing, threw the compress from her eyes, shouted "Hallelujah," and opened the shades to let the daylight in.

At four-thirty on the afternoon after the verdict was returned, Baxley's men served a subpoena on Tommy Blanton at the home he shared with Nellie, the half sister he still tormented. The prosecutors were hoping that the Chambliss conviction would throw a scare into him and loosen his lips, but Blanton (who now had a night-school law degree) got a lawyer and refused to talk.

Nor could Baxley break Bobby Frank Cherry, who he initially believed was the best candidate for turning state's evidence—and who had worried Chambliss most over the years, according to his sister-in-law Mary Frances Cunningham. Cherry was located in Grand Prairie, Texas, outside Dallas, the truck driver now the owner of some false front teeth. Baxley summoned him to the Grand Prairie police station and slammed an arrest warrant on the table. Prosecutors dogcussed him, repeating a remark that Cunningham said Chambliss made: that Cherry had walked down the alley carrying the bomb. At first he hemmed and hawed in a manner that reminded one investigator of the TV actor George Lindsey, Gomer Pyle's cousin Goober, but he seemed to regain his confidence after placing a collect call to Birmingham following Baxley's visit. The phone number in question belonged to Bob Gafford, the arch-segregationist auto parts dealer who had been Chambliss's confidant. That association had not prevented Gafford from moving into politics, as a member of the state house of representatives. The Jefferson County legislator who sat next to him was the first black elected from the district since Reconstruction: Chris McNair, the father of Denise.

Prosecutors made pilgrimages to Chambliss's cell at Kilby Prison to see if he would talk, but he would say only that he had given the dynamite for the church bombing to "Rowe and them." Chambliss, who knelt in prayer every night to ask God not to forgive Bill Baxley, became something of a media curiosity, particularly when he was assigned a new cellmate in 1985: J. B. Stoner had been convicted five years earlier of the 1958 dynamiting of Shuttlesworth's church, on the basis of Birmingham police memos that state investigators on the Sixteenth Street case had come across, describing the sting Bull Connor and his detective Tom Cook had tried to pull off.

On October 19, 1985, Robert Chambliss was rushed from prison to the hospital by ambulance and died later that day. By now, the woman who had put him behind bars, his niece Elizabeth Cobbs, had lived several lives. After leaving her marriage and her church, she served as the first pastor of the predominantly gay Metropolitan Community Church and in early 1979 moved to Texas under an assumed name to escape threats (including from family members) and the fear that her new lifestyle might be used by Chambliss's lawyers to appeal his conviction. That year, she entered a gender dysphoria clinic at the University of Texas medical school for gender reassignment and in 1985 returned to Birmingham as a man named Petric Smith, to work in a variety of civil rights causes. The new identity got him on *Oprah*. He died of cancer in 1998.

As for the man who put Chambliss behind bars, Bill Baxley lost the governor's race in 1978. And then, after serving a term as lieutenant governor, he went down in flames during the 1986 gubernatorial election, undergoing a career-ending extramarital sex scandal that anticipated the downfall of a 1988 Democratic presidential candidate, Gary Hart. My uncle Hobart grew fond of "Bullet Bill," as he called Baxley, once the young crusader matured into a lawyer representing the highest bidder. Still, Hobart continued to refer to him with heavy irony as his niece's "political hero," and Baxley would indeed join Big Jim Folsom in the broken hearts of Alabama's liberal romantics.

EARLIER IN THE YEAR of his death, Chambliss had refused my request for an interview through the state prison warden, saying, "I ain't going to help no woman make money by writing a book about my life." My attempts to talk to him had been more obligatory than heartfelt. I knew what to expect from him as a source, having read his erratically capitalized, occasionally pornographic stream-of-consciousness letters protesting his innocence to various public officials. Instead, I telephoned his relatives, hoping to gain some insight into what kind of family had produced him. Other than his mother's depression, I found little out of the ordinary about the Chamblisses. Robert's sister Margie Burke, the mother of Officer Floyd Garrett, portrayed the family as "normal; we had what we wanted," including a black nurse to help Mrs. Chambliss take care of the kids. We had been chatting for some time before Burke seemed to realize why I had called. "You know," she informed me, "they said Robert bombed that church up there."

In the end, Chambliss resisted nuance. It seemed to me that the only thing interesting and mysterious about his brand of evil had been buried with Bull Connor, who served out his political days on the state Public Service Commission and died in 1972, reputedly requesting a deathbed visit from Fred Shuttlesworth. And even Connor was only as interesting as Jim Simpson. The Great Man had died of a stroke in 1973, and within five years, whatever politely legal sins he had committed would be eclipsed by a more conventional family disgrace. In 1978, Simpson's drug-addicted namesake grandson—my old friend Popsie—was indicted for shooting his mother to death in the thirty-two-room mansion she lived in, a few doors down from my uncle Hobart. The charges against him were later dismissed for lack of physical evidence.

Robert Chambliss's best friend and co-conspirator, Troy Ingram, seemed to be closer to Birmingham's perverted destiny. Reading back issues of the Communist Party's *Southern Worker,* I came across a 1936 story on Troy Ingram, sixteen-year-old proletarian hero, who had sued Charles DeBardeleben for evicting his father because he had joined the United Mine Workers. Something I had only believed could now be documented: The dynamite that had blasted the coal of Birmingham's fortunes was the same as the church bomb.

In the spring of 1993, I drove out to Cahaba Heights, next to the old DeBardeleben Overton camp, to the brick house the Ingrams had proudly built in 1963. Troy's widow, Mary Ingram, was in the yard with a young granddaughter. A gray, depleted-looking woman, Ingram eyed me as if I were the Grim Reaper coming across her lawn, but she radiated decency as she answered my questions about her husband, who had been introduced to her by a fellow DeBardeleben alumnus. She told me that he had agreed to stop hanging around with Chambliss after she told him "there's something about that man I just don't trust." She had discussed the bombing with her husband, and he had assured her he hadn't done it.

The Ingrams' granddaughter, running around with a jelly jar of iced tea, looked at me suspiciously. Ingram turned to me and said she didn't want her husband to be in any book, because she didn't want her grandchildren and great-grandchildren to find out.

I had been dreading the inevitability of making actual contact with the remaining veterans of Eastview 13. While interviewing a policeman early on, I had asked whether I should be "concerned" about calling on the bombing suspects. The cop squinted. "I don't know if you should be 'concerned,' " he said, "but you should be *scared.*" By 1993, I had read tens of thousands of pages of investigative documents on the Eastview Klansmen, had pored over old city directories to find out what kinds of jobs they had, what their fathers did. I knew their cover stories better than my own father's. And finally it was time to begin my cold calls on them.

I drove out to Earl "Shorty" Thompson's house outside Birmingham in Leeds. He was in the driveway washing his car with the spray attachment of the hose. He still had red hair and a fireplug body. He turned off the spray when I approached. The date was September 16, 1993, and the local papers had recently done recaps on the church bombing, but I decided to cut to the chase and asked, "Will you talk to me about the Eastview Klan?"

"If I can?" he said. The question mark made me unsure as to whether he was answering me or repeating what he thought I had said.

I asked again, and when he looked more bewildered, I realized he was hard of hearing. I glanced around the wide-open spaces around us, and the Leeds locale, near the old DeBardeleben mines, made me impulsively ask him if his father had worked for the family. This time he heard me. His father had dug coal for DeBardeleben, and he told me that as a boy he had even attended United Mine Workers meetings at Bumstead Hall in Irondale with his dad before the family was ejected.

Thompson said that since getting out of the Klan and giving up alcohol he had "signed on with the Lord's team and have been living it ever since." As we chatted about Bull Connor—he said he had known him as a neighbor in Crestwood—I asked if Connor had had anything to do with the 1956 bombing of Fred Shuttlesworth's church, for which the FBI suspected Thompson of driving the getaway car. His face clouded, the eyes turned mean, and said, "You hear a lot of stories and don't go striving on them."

The statistically fantastic predominance of DeBardeleben connections in Eastview 13 struck me as something you might read in Aeschylus, and so I called on the old man who had once done the ideological violence in the light of day. Prince DeBardeleben, the son who had assumed the anti-union mantle after his father, Charles, was buried on Labor Day of 1941, was in his late eighties when he received me in his dim living room on the crest of Red Mountain. I felt the familiar scruples that gnawed at me when characters in my story invited me into their homes as a family friend rather than a journalist. Prince's daughter and my aunt had been in each other's weddings, and his granddaughter had been my old TKD "sorority sister." Margaret DeBardeleben Tutwiler had become the most visible DeBardeleben descendant, a high-ranking woman in the Reagan and then the Bush administrations, on whom Libyan president Muammar Qaddafi became romantically fixated when she served as State Department spokesperson.

DeBardeleben did not flinch when I began asking him about the union, and in fact a little fire lit up the frail, closed face when we got to the United Mine Workers' famous march on Acmar and Margaret in 1935, which had been met, fatally in the case of one unionist, by machine-gun fire. DeBardeleben succinctly described the sequence of the violence: "Our men started shooting, they started running, and we started shooting some more." I fumbled for the $64,000 question: "Were you aware . . . did you, like, see the confrontation?" He interrupted me impishly: "I was in it!"

AFTER I TALKED TO Earl Thompson, I drove out to Center Point, the suburb of working-class white flight north of the city, to the modest redbrick neighborhood that was home to Robert Thomas, the Exalted Cyclops of Eastview's heyday. "Come in!" answered my knock, and as I pushed the door open, I said, "But y'all don't know me." After some awkward introductions to Thomas, his wife, Mildred, and his grown daughter, I settled on the couch for an hour-and-a-half-long visit. What struck me about the Thomas living room, with its chintz-draped, glass-topped side tables covered with framed photographs, was how much it looked like the homes of my friends in Mountain Brook.

The former Exalted Cyclops was a wiry, bowlegged, formerly handsome man, his jeans drifting off his recessed butt. And his wife, whom Gary Thomas Rowe claimed as a close friend and an information source for the FBI, looked like just another heavyset, bespectacled grandmother. Thomas, rumored to have been an FBI informant himself, knew now to frame his Klan past in terms of states' rights "politics" rather than race. When I asked him if it would be a violation of his Klan oath to talk about the church bombing even if he knew about it, he said that he could hardly see how you could have something like that on your conscience for all these years and not talk about it. His sincerity was so convincing that I did not recall until after I had left that one of the investigative reports I had read said that Thomas had tried to call off the bombing.

Stuffed animals were piled on the back of the sofa, and my startled reaction when one fell on me was the most genuine moment of the visit. Thomas fell into knee-slapping laughter as he said, "I can hear you telling it now—here you are in this ex-Klansman's house and something hits you on the shoulder. . . ." By the time I stood to go, the self-consciousness we all felt was so out in the open that Thomas's daughter asked me how I was going to remember everything her father told me. I answered truthfully that as soon as I left I would write down everything in my notebook, explaining that if I started taking notes while he talked, her dad would clam up.

The daughter's son came in from outside with a friend. "I'm Pat," he said to me. His mother moved us tactfully off Klan talk. "He's getting ready to go to college"—the University of South Alabama, in Mobile. I congratulated him and asked him if he knew what he was going to study. Not quite hearing the reply, I begged his pardon. "Nursing," he repeated, and all my uneasy feelings crystallized in my regret that he might think I considered his choice unorthodox (or unmanly), this first-generation college man setting off into a healing profession, oblivious of the wounds his grandfather had inflicted.

It seemed that all of us were actors fulfilling roles in reaction to our fathers and our fathers' fathers, as I now discharged my own historic obligation by driving to the nearest parking lot and making my notes on the visit. I checked my map and found the address of my next stop, Thomas's Center Point neighbor Billy Holt,* one of the gamest of the Eastview hard core. In front of the Holt house was a car with a "Perot for President" bumper sticker, but I was somewhat relieved to find no one home.

By the time I returned nearly two years later, in June 1995, Billy Holt had died (only seventeen months earlier) under an oxygen tent in a nursing home, of asbestos silicosis caused by his work as a brickmason. His widow, Doris Holt, a squat woman with a contorted face, opened the door, and I realized how mistaken I had been to assume that Billy might have lost his ideological starch after Mary Lou Holt left him for Hubert Page.

The first thing out of Mrs. Holt's mouth was something about Oklahoma City and the bombing of the Alfred P. Murrah Federal Building there in April that had killed 169 people, many of them children. Her face furrowed, her eyes intense and intelligent, she told me that the federal government was behind the Oklahoma bombing ("You're probably one of those that loves the government") and that the United Nations was preparing for a "one-world government" by training Russian troops in this country.

The parallels between that recent explosion and the bombing I would have interviewed her husband about were uncanny, down to the resemblance between Billy Holt's Klan and the right-wing paramilitary movement that provided the political ambiance of the Oklahoma bombing—with Speaker of the House Newt Gingrich standing in for George Wallace. Doris Holt was a veteran of the sixties counterrevolution; she told me mysteriously that she had worked for Wallace in a position that required security clearance. She still seemed exuberant with the class rage that had fueled the Wallace phenomenon. In response to the social gulf she sensed between us, she declared, "I'm not a hick." (She had stayed in the best hotels growing up as the daughter of a businesswoman; had played the accordion in her youth for Franklin Roosevelt at Warm Springs, Georgia.)

She urged me to stop looking into Birmingham's history. Then she paused. Was I investigating any of my relatives? I laughed and said, "Yeah, my father." She wanted to know if he was in the Klan. I said I didn't know. "Is that why you're writing this book?" she said, and again I had to laugh at what a strange hometown we shared, so many different kinds of prodigal children in search of a fatherland.

THE YEAR I BEGAN my research, only five years after Chambliss was convicted, Papa told me, "I know Chambliss didn't bomb the church because I was with him that day."

---

*There had been only one Klansman I visited who refused to talk to me. Nelda Hall, Nigger Hall's widow, had assured me that Gene Reeves, the activist (busted for transporting weapons to the Schoolhouse Door) who had become Eastview's Exalted Cyclops, was "a fine Christian man, over in Fultondale"—the drab suburb where the Klan had bought property to build its compound on. Reeves, a well-preserved, compact man, with a pebble-smooth tan offsetting his white hair, walked out to meet me in the yard of his unornamented red-shingled bungalow, with two American flag decals on the door. Firmly, but with a cautious smile playing on his lips, he told me he would not talk to me and would not be moved as I stalled in his driveway checking out the cloud formations.

"You knew Chambliss?" I said.

"I knew 'em all," he said.

"You knew Gary Thomas Rowe?"

"I knew 'em all."

"So who bombed the church?"

He gave me a half-lidded look and trotted out the old chestnut: "It was the janitor."

My father's break with Mountain Brook was now fairly gothic. He had even made it, at last, to the trailer park. For a few years in the 1970s, he lived in the London Village mobile home community with his second wife and her young daughter, who called their (black) dog "Nigger" and, after her mother and my father divorced, became pregnant at fifteen or sixteen. I had found my sporadic forays from my home up north into Papa's new life both funny and dismaying. But once I started my book—he had now moved back into a proper house, with furniture that looked as if it had been designed by R. Crumb—the class alienation I felt around him converted into professional purpose.

I accompanied him to his latest hangout, Velma's Place, where he played dominoes after work with men whose first names were appliquéd on their uniforms. The man from Mountain Brook had such a reputation for cheapness that someone had put a dated sign behind the bar: "Mack bought Rock a beer." (Papa confirmed for me that the correct spelling of his nickname was "Mac," explaining that Mack "is the Jewish spelling.") But he retained traces of his breeding. When a man everyone called Cosell wagged his finger and said "hey" to get my attention, Papa rebuked him, "Her name is Diane."

"You're really writing a book about Birmingham?" one man said.

"Well, tell them what it's about," Papa said to me.

"It's mostly about 1963," I said.

"It's about the nigger movement," Papa translated.

For the next hour I was treated to comments like "You know, as far as I'm concerned, you can take all the niggers and put 'em on a boat and ship them all back to Africa. And you know what, you could send all the Jews right after them."

"Aw, now, I think niggers are all right. I think everybody should own two or three of them."

A Coca-Cola truck driver described how stupid one of his fellow (black) drivers was, and my father said, "I'll tell you one thing, I'll bet you that nigger who drove the truck never read Shakespeare."

That exchange alone probably contained the class history of Birmingham, with my father's atavistic love of Shakespeare being summoned out to assert a barely literate white truck driver's superiority over a black colleague. But my research was moving beyond my father's rebellion against his suburban background, and I was now determined to find out what he had *really* been doing at night during my childhood when he was working against civil rights. Reading Gary Thomas Rowe's informant reports, I had gone clammy when I came across the name of the Eastview member and beer hall regular who had recruited Rowe into the Klan: Loyal McWhorter. "Loyal" seemed like the perfect nom de guerre for my mythomaniac father, who was fastidious enough to try to buffer his family from his nocturnal identity.

When I tried to pin Papa down, he was so slippery that I finally resorted to tape-recording him. ("I'm not ready to play with you yet," he scolded his Boston terrier, one of a series of Charlies. "I'm being interviewed.") He told me that the group he belonged to was a combination of the FBI, the CIA, and the John Birch Society. Sometimes he implied that he had served as a liaison between his drinking buddies and the industrial princes he had grown up with. "People I knew very closely from earlier in my life," he explained. "I found out what their thoughts were and what their ideas were and everything else. But I was in a situation where most of the people I was finding out information from, they believed just like I do. They didn't believe in Russian domination of this United States, and they didn't believe in the hierarchy of the union. They believed that everybody was responsible for what they did, for their own actions. I always thought that everybody's responsible for their own actions. If their actions ain't too good, they may need to do a little bit more praying."

"What was the name of the group you were in?"

"Well, we really didn't have a name. It was just a group of us from Mississippi and Alabama and Louisiana who got together to fight Communism."

"So why did you meet in West Blocton?" (This was the town next to Bessemer where he always told Mama he had to go at night.)

"Ohhh! Well, one of the people in the group had a farm there, and we met at his house."

He told me that he was active in the cause from 1961 or 1962 to 1969 or 1970. "Our primary objective was information supply, to the CIA and the FBI," he said, presumably information about the "subversives" they had identified. "The Klan already knew about it. We didn't have to supply it to the Klan."

"Did you use your own car?" I asked, still upset that he would expose the family to embarrassment.

"We usually doubled up."

"That's how they find out who people are, you know. They look at your license plate."

"Oh, I know. We usually doubled up. I'd park my car at my friend's place, and we'd get into another car and go places. The people we were watching weren't that smart. Niggers ain't ever that smart."

"It seems that you would be kind of conspicuous spying on black people," I said.

"Oh, we did both, whites and blacks. 'Cause you had a white faction in there favorable to the black movement. And we used to get out there and talk them out of it."

"Who were these white people?"

"Lot of 'em I didn't know their names, but a lot of 'em had an awful lot of flat tires. Lot of 'em had no carburetors in their cars. Lot of bad things happened to those types of people. You'd be surprised at how effective it was, 'cause they got the message. If they didn't, we told the KKK about it and they did the rest. If a flat tire didn't do it, the next thing they knew their automobile was burned up."

Papa told me that the FBI approached him.

"Who were your contacts at the FBI," I asked him, "the Birmingham office?"

"Right straight to Washington."

"Were you an official informant?"

"Yeah, in a way I was, but I was kind of one-sided. I supplied the information the FBI wanted to hear."

"Which wasn't necessarily true?"

"Oh, it was always true. It was just kind of slanted."

"Did you call the FBI?"

"Didn't have to. I supplied it to another informant."

"Did they know your name?"

"No-o-o-o. Nobody knew my name."

"Why?"

"I was subject to get shot by both factions."

"Because you were supplying stuff to the FBI and the Klan?"

"Right."

"Well, Papa, are you afraid of getting shot if I write that in my book?"

"No, it won't make any difference. The only thing, just don't name me."

"Don't name you? Papa! We have the same name!"

"Well, whatever, all right, too much water has gone under the bridge."

In an attempt to see if my father had any remorse over his past actions, I set up a reunion between him and the old childhood friend whose "ass" he had supposedly "run out of town." Chuck Morgan had moved on from celebrity civil libertarian (the lawyer for Cassius Clay in his famous draft case), having left the helm of the American Civil Liberties Union after becoming the first public figure to call for the impeachment of Richard Nixon, in violation of ACLU policy against political stands. Still in Washington, he was now an equally flamboyant lawyer for the Interests, including the smoking lobby. When I tweaked him for representing Sears in a much-watched class-action sex-discrimination case, he earnestly began reciting a history of the store founder Julius Rosenwald's foundation that had given artistic and scholarly grants to promising young blacks. I was amused by his appeal to both our better impulses, when I knew that what motivated him was the nagging example of Mountain Brook, the need to beat the old peers at their own game: making money.

I arranged for my father to come to the pied-à-terre Morgan had bought outside Mountain Brook Village. ("Well, you know, you *can't* have a telephone exchange other than 871 or 879," Morgan said only half ironically, referring to the essential signifier of a Mountain Brook address.) When Papa greeted Chuck's wife, Camille, whom he had dated as a teenager, he as usual showed no sense of disjunction from the days of Chi Sigma Chi, when Chuck had been "one of my best friends, doll baby." And the chitchat between these two big men was the aimless remem-

brances of frat brothers who have gone separate ways, no mention of the racial conflict that had informed both their adult lives.

Sometimes, Papa flogged me with some of the scorn for do-gooders that had
gotten Chuck into trouble with the old crowd. "Don't ever—*ever!*—make yourself
a member of the Amalgamated Association of World Savers!" he warned me. And
though he would come to bug me, as did most people close to me, about how long
it was taking me to "save" my hometown—longer, in fact, than the career of Martin Luther King—he had once lowered his voice and said, "You're going about it
right. You've got to have the glue. The glue is sticking with it."

Thus I labored to nail down Papa's relationship with the Klan. "Well, you had
Klan plus and you had Klan minus," he obfuscated. "We were Klan minus. There
were very few of us who thought that way, only six. We were in favor of what the
Klan was doing, but we couldn't be associated directly with the Klan." His claim
that he wore a straw hat while on his missions threw a brief panic into me when I
examined Tommy Langston's photo of the Trailways bus station on Mother's Day,
1961, and saw the profile of a man wearing a straw hat, a beefy, grave-faced match
for my father. But the FBI had identified him as a Klansman from Bessemer.

I had now read enough FBI files also to know that Loyal McWhorter was not
Martin McWhorter's Klan alter ego. Loyal may have been a distant cousin. He
was the oldest of four sons who grew up on a cotton farm in Arab, only a couple of
counties away from Cherokee. Besides moonlighting as a bartender at the VFW
Hall, Loyal held down two jobs, as a Sears salesman and in the sheet metal department at Hayes Aircraft (and had been listed as a reference on Tommy
Blanton's successful Hayes job application). But he had not been a well-adjusted
man since earning four battle stars under Patton in World War II. "They go in
scared boys and come out like they died anyway," his brother Dewitt explained to
me. Loyal battered his German wife when he was "not in his normal mind but his
drinking mind," Dewitt said. In 1968, Loyal was shot dead by his girlfriend while
lying in bed.

And so my quest for my father went, teetering like the city around me between pathos and farce. Often Luciano Pavarotti was on the stereo while we
talked. "Looseeahno's bigger than the best quarterback in the NFL," Papa said.
"He could be singing 'Ave Maria' and make a touchdown—that's the picture I get
of him." He digressed into disquisitions on the dangers of anti-gun legislation or
the recent discovery of mammoths encased in ice in the Arctic or his incompre-
hension of why his younger brother rather than he had been named after his father. I felt in the thrall of some roughneck Scheherazade, continually postponing
the moment of truth.

On my next research trip home, I went out to the plant to talk to Papa while
he was stone sober. The enclosed office area that had once been a scrubbed
linoleum, air-conditioned oasis against the noise and grime and danger of the
workshop outside was a shambles. Short-sleeve polyester shirts hung on the hat
rack, and the brown vinyl sofa was stacked with catalogues such as "Specialty
Gases and Equipment." Other artifacts of my father's life included his skin-diving

trophies ("King Spearfisherman 1971 Championship Class"), the photograph of him with Jacques Cousteau, a Styrofoam Wallace hat, a full set of *Encyclopaedia Britannica*, his books on the occult (Ruth Montgomery, Jess Stearn), and, I discovered with a pang of affection, his subscription copies of *Writer's Digest.* Everything was covered with filmy dust. I doubt the place had been cleaned since one of his skin-diving pals came there one night to kill himself, but the rifle had been too long, and after taking off part of his neck and ear, he called my father, apologized for the mess and for not dying, and asked him to call an ambulance. Papa came in the next day and cleaned up the blood.

I hoped finally to reconcile my father's competence and intelligence, and his sense of his destiny, with the desperate, disordered milieu he had chosen. "Papa, this is it," I said to him in his office. "I have to know what you were doing." I got out my Eastview 13 roster and began with the most "genteel" member, who worked at the L&N switching yards that Papa passed every day on the way to work.

"Did you know Robert Thomas?" He considered a second and shook his head.

"Herbert Eugene Reeves?"

"Naw, I don't believe so."

I ran through the names that to me had become like disreputable members of the family. Occasionally he brightened and said, "Sounds familiar." It was a typical Klansman mind game. They either lied about how little they knew or they lied about how much they knew, and my father was clearly in the first camp.

I returned the list to its manila folder. "You don't know anybody in the Klan," I said. He thought for a moment and said that he did know one Klansman, and that was a man named Harry Kepplinger who occasionally rented space from him and tried to recruit my brothers into the Klan Junior. I felt that I had gotten to whatever bottom there was. It was Kepplinger who had been responsible for the Klan pamphlets in Papa's office that had made me feel so ill as a child.

"I'm afraid I'm not going to turn out to be the kind of hero you think I am," he said.

I couldn't quite grasp the grandiosity that would make someone falsely claim intimate knowledge of the most horrible crime of his time. My father's warped all-knowingness predated my book project, but I believe that the prospect of being immortalized in print gave these stories meaning, and then a certain pressure to top them.

"I didn't get involved in any rough stuff," he almost apologized. "If I got involved any deeper, I would have had to kill people, but primarily because of my religious background, I don't believe in taking another man's life, unless it's absolutely necessary. Going around bombing people wadn't my cup of tea. I might stick a needle in 'em, but I wouldn't bomb 'em."

At least one of my childhood fears had been laid to rest: My father had not killed anyone. What he had been doing on those nights he said he devoted to "civil rights," I may never know. But a mystery that is insoluble often has a way of revealing a much larger truth. I did not understand my father, but because of that I learned to see the world in a new way. For in order to define him, I had to invoke the history of a race, of two races, and of a place.

I was twenty-seven years old—and had not lived in Birmingham for ten years—before I first laid eyes on the Sixteenth Street Baptist Church. As I drove through the once bustling, now forlorn "Negro business district" along Fourth Avenue, I felt the "black neighborhood alert" reflex to roll up the car window and then covered up my motive by saying to myself, "Jeez, it's hot. I should turn on the air conditioner." On Sixteenth Street, I spied the red neon sign, the kind you see on windowless cafés, identifying the large amber-brick building with the traditional Baptist dome and tower: "16th St. Baptist Church." I parked catty-corner from the church, in front of Kelly Ingram Park, and tried to compose some appropriate thoughts. But I did not then know enough, with my windows still rolled up, to understand that this was the neighborhood, host to death and redemption, that would finally carry me home.

Instead I watched some black children playing in Kelly Ingram Park and marveled at how that hallowed landmark could be so utilitarian, living on ordinarily beyond its extraordinary moment. This was only the beginning of my civil rights tour of the city I grew up in. Had I known that the children in the park would be grown by the time it ended, I wonder if I ever would have begun.

And now it is over. This is my monument to the Movement, but it is a monument to my father, too: another enemy disarmed by nonviolence, another lost soul, now consecrated to history.

In 1982, I joined the federal judges, civil rights leaders, and assorted other "sissybritches" on George Wallace's enemies list. Condemned to a wheelchair by a would-be assassin's bullet, Wallace had just repented of his segregationist sins and was elected, with the black vote, to an unprecedented fourth term as governor. ("Black people are very forgiving," said the Reverend Abraham Woods, the old ACMHR lieutenant who had become the tenured head of Birmingham's SCLC chapter. "Sometimes they are more forgiving than they ought to be.") I wrote a couple of articles recalling the blood on Wallace's hands dating back to the fall of 1963, and he telephoned my uncle, whose late father-in-law had been part of his segregationist brain trust in 1963. "Hobart," the governor said, "are you any kin to that Diane McWhorter?"

And my favorite uncle, whose law firm handled most of the state's bond business, said he replied, "Never heard of her in my life, George."

But even the conservative Hobart, who calls me the "Com symp," has had to play by the new rules. In 1990, he turned into the unlikeliest of civil rights collaborators when Birmingham, true to destiny, became the nation's acid test for country club desegregation. After SCLC threatened demonstrations, the local Shoal Creek Country Club underwent emergency desegregation to prevent the Professional Golf Association from pulling its annual tournament out of the club. Amid the ensuing national publicity, the most exclusive clubhouses in the country located "qualified" blacks in order to comply with the PGA's new egalitarian guidelines. The dismantling of institutionalized segregation that began with the Birmingham-inspired Civil Rights Act of 1964 was, in theory, complete.

My uncle Hobart, because he was invulnerable to charges of "nigger lover," was assigned the job of hosting the first Negro guest at the Mountain Brook Club—where the wait staff, too, has now been "desegregated," by Latinos and perhaps even a non-Hispanic white or two. Few of the old-timers remain. Otis Pitts, the long-suffering waiter who for years parried Hobart's summonses of "Preacher," retired after a serious illness. Hobart had gone to see him in the hospital, only to be informed that visitors were restricted to family members. "I'm his uncle," Hobart told the hospital gatekeeper and was motioned right in.

Vulcan, too, has progressed, from unintentionally camp to knowingly so. A local deejay proposed putting him on a lazy Susan to spare the suburb to his south the continual indignity described in the local hit he recorded: "Moon over Homewood, it's so unrefined,/ We have to get mooned with Vulcan's behind." In the mid-eighties, when the red/green torch blew its neon lights, the community began reexamining its obsession with traffic safety. "Bad for Image," reads the classic headline of a letter arguing that "an Iron Man" should not be holding "something that looks like a cone of pistachio ice cream." Vulcan's torch was changed to a color that somehow did not surprise me: white.

By the 1980s, Vulcan's industry had been eclipsed by the now world-class University Medical Center, the city's longtime symbol of progress finally overwhelming the smokestack pall. U.S. Steel had greatly curtailed its local operations, blaming the hardships imposed by the Environmental Protection Agency, though the more likely cause was the landmark 1972 Birmingham consent decree that the corporation signed in a federal class-action suit by black employees. It effectively ended systematic discrimination in the factory, the great CIO vindicated at last.

For many years, the Chamber of Commerce quaked every time a civil rights anniversary brought the national press back to Birmingham, but finally the white leaders decided to stop denying what had taken place and, if not quite embrace it, put it under glass in a museum. The Birmingham Civil Rights Institute opened across the street from the Sixteenth Street Baptist Church and Kelly Ingram Park in 1992, with dubious bronze likenesses of Martin Luther King and Fred Shuttlesworth welcoming sightseers to the battleground where African-Americans waged a nonviolent civil war and threw off the chains of segregation.

And finally, in the last year of the old millennium, it seemed that Birmingham's white people might finally rid themselves of their burden of collective guilt. Bobby Frank Cherry and Tommy Blanton, the last two living suspects in the BAPBOMB file, were charged with murder in the bombing of the Sixteenth Street Baptist Church. It seemed that personal sins—Cherry as an alleged molester of a stepdaughter and abuser of at least one of his five wives—had moved new witnesses to speak up.

I will never forget where I was on May 17, 2000, when I heard the news that Cherry, age sixty-nine, and Blanton, age sixty-one, had been arrested. It was a moment I never expected to experience. Like the tragedy in Dallas that same fall, the Sixteenth Street Baptist Church bombing had ceased to feel like a murder case and had become a piece of the culture, abstract yet powerful and permanent, as haunting as the work John Coltrane recorded two months after the crime. "Alabama" is "a frightening emotional portrait of some place, in these musicians' feelings," wrote the playwright LeRoi Jones (Amiri Baraka). "If that 'real' Alabama was the catalyst, more power to it, and may it be this beautiful, even in its destruction."

Birmingham was America's city in a valley, but out of the depths rose a city upon a hill. Beauty from destruction. There is magic in that.

AFTERWORD

THE TRIAL OF TOMMY BLANTON for the murder of Denise McNair, Carole Robertson, Addie Mae Collins, and Cynthia Wesley opened on April 24, 2001. Suddenly I had joined the human race's "inescapable network of mutuality," described by Martin Luther King in the "Letter from Birmingham Jail." By uncanny coincidence, *Carry Me Home* had been published a month earlier—after nineteen years in the works. Over those two decades of solitary toil, my driving aim had been to "solve" the church bombing, to bring the murderers if not to justice then at least to truth. That the case might end up before an actual judge had never seemed possible outside the contingency of a miracle.

The trial—the culmination of a six-year-long investigation reignited by a local FBI official as a conciliatory gesture to the black community—was to have been the joint day in court for Blanton *and* Bobby Frank Cherry. But true to Birmingham's name, "The City of Perpetual Promise," little more than a week before the trial date, a judge ruled on the basis of two independent psychiatric evaluations that seventy-year-old Cherry was incompetent to stand trial. And so instead of the last two living suspects facing justice, Blanton reported alone to a handsome, wood-paneled Jefferson County courtroom that the judge predicted would "give a doggone nice image of Birmingham." Robert Chambliss had been convicted in this same room twenty-four years earlier.

Globally, the Blanton trial was seen as an American expiation drama, the most stirring in a series of last-chance prosecutions of old civil rights crimes around the South. The country's obsession with below-the-Mason-Dixon-Line racists has sometimes seemed to be an attempt to geographically isolate a systemic national problem and, by focusing on hooded villains and decapitated victims, reduce it to a caricature that more subtle practitioners of prejudice cannot recognize. Just before the trial, there had been disproportionate media coverage of a referendum in Mississippi to replace the state flag, the last in the nation to showcase the Confederacy's Stars and Bars. The subtext of the stories was, Will those racists down there ever repent? As long as the South remained unreconstructed (the referendum failed), the rest of the country was assured of its innocence—what Robert Penn Warren called "the murderous innocence of the American people."

Birmingham itself was having a hard time figuring out its role in the unfolding redemption saga. The *Birmingham News* ran a brief mea culpa for its less than constructive contribution to the city's racial past, but most citizens had no sense of any institutional sin to atone for. Apathy toward the trial ran so high that civic groups had to call out their members to fill the embarrassingly empty courtroom pews. For the many journalists on hand, trying to tap the meaning of Tommy Blanton's judgment day was like stepping on their own shadows. Even I, who had not only been part of this story as a child but had relived it for twenty years as an adult writing my book, could barely make sense of it when it was recurring in the moment.

Perhaps the most jarring lesson of this new chapter of the Sixteenth Street story was how difficult it is for the individuals who live history to experience its harsh, abstract truths. Though this trial was about the most horrible crime of the civil rights era, it often felt like a surreal family reunion, hinging more on intimacy than on hate, like the final moments of the four girls, flung together by the bomb blast into their fateful embrace. The judge, James Garrett—an outgoing, slightly rakish Rip Torn look-alike, proud of his tough upbringing in coal-mining country north of Birmingham—chatted about camera equipment with Denise's father, Chris McNair, a professional photographer, who had abruptly retired from his long career in politics right before the trial. Blanton's attorney paused on his way out to a press conference to inform me that my mom was looking for me. During conferences at the bench, he and the prosecutor laid tender hands on each other's shoulders. They too were part of the inescapable network of mutuality: good friends and former law partners.

Doug Jones, the forty-seven-year-old U.S. attorney who argued the government's case in state court under a special arrangement with the district attorney, had had that mark of destiny ever since his name was flashed on the electronic marquee atop a local skyscraper as the Kiwanis Club's 1972 Youth of the Year. He grew up in a household of George Wallace supporters in the U.S. Steel milltown of Fairfield, his father promoted off the tin mill floor into management. His subsequent political education was recorded in framed photographs on his office wall—Jones as a long-haired University of Alabama undergraduate with Supreme Court Justice William O. Douglas, as state manager for Delaware senator Joseph Biden's 1988 presidential campaign. After being appointed by Bill Clinton in 1997, Jones was sidetracked from the Sixteenth Street case by another fatal Birmingham bombing, an explosion at an abortion clinic that killed a policeman and maimed a nurse. (The suspect, Eric Rudolph, a white-supremacist survivalist also accused of the Atlanta Olympics bombing in 1996, is still at large.)

The defense lawyer, Jones's old partner John Robbins, was, at the time of the church bombing, a four-year-old budding juvenile delinquent known as Butch who was being raised by a grandmother he thought was his mother in Trenton, New Jersey. If Jones exuded the peppy charm of a boy politician, Robbins could have been a character drawn by Charles Schulz, with a quizzical frown, scruffy facial hair, and a permissive attitude toward his inner smart aleck. Yet even though

Jones was the obvious protagonist of the Sixteenth Street case's latest drama, it was Robbins—appointed by the court eight weeks earlier, after Blanton's original lawyer withdrew—who became the trial's narrator, providing the outsider's fresh (in every sense of the word) reaction to the tricky moral calculations that have kept Birmingham from settling its accounts with history.

"IT HAS BEEN A long time, ladies and gentlemen," Doug Jones addressed the jury in the inaugural words of the *State of Alabama* v. *Thomas E. Blanton Jr.* Since pretrial research found no great community awareness or outrage about the Ku Klux Klan, the prosecution decided to keep the focus on the "four little girls," as Carole, Denise, Addie, and Cynthia have come to be memorialized (that was the title of Spike Lee's 1997 feature documentary), even though three of them were teenagers. Jones told the jury, "Nineteen sixty-three in Birmingham was about children": the young black demonstrators recruited by Martin Luther King's organization as well as the non-marchers killed at Sixteenth Street. Jones had fought back tears when he noted that this day, April 24, 2001, would have been the fifty-first birthday of Carole Robertson. She had been wearing her first pair of heels on the day she died.

John Robbins dispassionately countered in his opening statement: "This is not a popularity contest between Mr. Blanton and four girls." His guy, he admitted, was "annoying as hell." Then he broached the true challenge that he—and the jury—faced: the pressure to bring this case to a historically gratifying resolution. Invoking the cliché that was the media's only purchase on the story, Robbins said, "This is not about 'closure.'"

THE KIWANIS CLUB HAD invited me to share my thoughts about the trial at the lunch recess; and all morning, I had been racking my brain about how to avoid the "Chuck Morgan speech"—the one the brash young lawyer had made the day after the bombing, charging the whole city with collective guilt. But instead of guilt, the civic neurosis I decided we Birminghamians shared was shame. We all bore the stain of the city's reputation—and felt compelled to rub it out, to call it unjustly inflicted. Hence, the prevailing "lone gunman" theory of the bombing: A handful of "rednecks" had given an entire law-abiding people a bad name.

The shame had prevented Birmingham from engaging with its history—with the antecedents of the explosion. The dynamite, I told five hundred Kiwanians and their guests, was the medium of our urban destiny. It not only blasted the coal that forged the iron, but also enforced the doctrine of the industrial status quo: white supremacy. When I had finished, the Kiwanis Club gave me a standing ovation, seemingly laying to rest the ghost of Chuck Morgan. It took three days for a rumor to get back to me that half the audience had stood up in the middle of my speech and walked out.

THE TRIAL PROCEEDED IN an atmosphere of light camaraderie—the defense lawyer referred to the U.S. attorney as "Doug"; Judge Garrett urged out-of-town reporters to visit the art fair going on in the park next to the courthouse—that jarred with the life-and-death grimness of the testimony. One witness, the FBI agent who had conducted Blanton's "alibi interview," was accompanied by his cardiologist, while the Birmingham Rescue Squad stood by with a defibrillator. Because a stroke had incapacitated James Lay, the Civil Defense worker who had arrived at the church with the first ambulance (and would die within days of the trial's end), his testimony* was read in court by Shelley Stewart, the deejay who had broadcast signals to the child demonstrators in 1963 and was now an advertising mogul. Hearts stopped at Lay's description of how he dug through the church wreckage and pulled out a head that was barely recognizable as belonging to a human.

Sitting at the defense table, the man accused of such mayhem looked unassuming and a bit abashed, the stocky, swaggering body of youth having turned to post-middle-aged pulp, and his distinctive shock of black hair now reduced to a comb over. He wore a muted jacket over an open-collared shirt. His lawyer had waived the obligatory defendant's tie, which seemed awkward on a man who at the time of his arrest had been a clerk at Wal-Mart, living in a five-by-ten-foot trailer. When I had first set eyes on Blanton in court, my throat constricted. After he scowled at me a couple of times, I wondered whether he knew who I was. Later I learned that he had read the relevant parts of this book and considered me a "bitch."

But I was the least of his female troubles. Jean Casey Blanton Barnes, who had been his seventeen-year-old girlfriend in 1963 and the alibi for his whereabouts on the eve of September 15, loomed over these proceedings as the much-anticipated star witness, inspiring hope and dread on both sides of the aisle. The government had an FBI surveillance tape of her and Blanton discussing "the bomb" ten months after the explosion, by which time the two had married.† Yet the defense had subpoenaed Jean, too. For despite the incriminating tape, her position on whether Blanton was involved has always been hear no evil.

The challenge for the government was to impose a plausible narrative on that July 1964 conversation fragment between Tommy and Jean Blanton, captured by a rubber-encased mike that an FBI agent had placed under the newly-weds' kitchen sink. But witnesses leading up to the playing of the tape, instead of offering a glimpse into the South's heart of darkness, insisted rather raucously on the great American themes of sex and violence. A third motif would further ease the courtroom mood from tragedy into farce: The message emerging from the government's witnesses was that the Ku Klux Klan was an organization fully committed to racial tolerance.

Waylene Vaughn, a girlfriend of Blanton's in 1963, now wearing school-marmish glasses and a navy blazer, took the stand to describe some of their

---

*This was the testimony he had given earlier to the grand jury.
†They were divorced after several years and then remarried in the early 1970s, when the state attorney general Bill Baxley reopened the church bombing investigation. After divorcing Blanton a second time, Jean married her current husband, a minister.

courtship activities: Tommy pouring skin-searing acid on the seats of black-owned cars; tossing a jar of noxious liquid into a crowd at a black nightclub; and, on their New Year's date in 1963, trying to run down a black pedestrian because he "wanted to kill one of those black bastards." Under cross-examination Vaughn asserted her lifelong disgust for racists, prompting an outburst of incredulity from defense attorney John Robbins. He counterproposed that she found the Klan "se-e-e-xy." Indeed, he pointed out, she used to "shack up in motels around town" with Blanton to "perform oral sex on him." An October 1963 FBI interview with Vaughn (marked "obscene"), from which Robbins drew that information, contained details that could have gratuitously embarrassed his client as well: Vaughn had told the FBI that Tommy admitted to having had sex with men.

Another government witness, Billy Jackson, the barber who had attended what investigators believed was the bombing conspirators' "kiss of death" meeting a week after the crime, introduced the concept of the racially benevolent Klan—Robbins took to calling it the "all-inclusive Klan." Jackson, now a white-haired friendly giant sort, had a month earlier come to a book signing I was doing at a local mall and stood guard outside the store in case "some people showed up"—meaning, I assumed, old Klan colleagues who might not have liked what I had written. Jackson apparently had no problem with my description of him as a bigamist who had been accused of choking one of his wives. But he did complain that I had misspelled his middle name. He thrust his fist toward my face to reveal the proper spelling, tattooed on his wrist: Levaughn. He assured me that I didn't have any reason to be afraid of Blanton (as I had told a local newspaper I was). "He threatened to kill me twice, but he wouldn't hurt you," Jackson said, suggesting that chivalry was not dead.

Blanton had become angry with Jackson after he testified for the prosecution at Robert Chambliss's trial in 1997, and the state's purpose in calling him this time was again to cast doubt on the defendant's alibi for the eve of the explosion. (Jackson insisted that Blanton was at the Modern Sign Shop that Saturday night.) But Jackson had told such a variety of tales over the years, and had apparently lost some memory after electroshock treatments, that on cross-examination Robbins got him to affirm that he was "a big fat liar." Like Waylene Vaughn, however, Jackson felt the need to disavow ever having had any racist thoughts. This claim summed up as well as anything the change that had taken place in Birmingham since the bombing: Where once the good people felt compelled to keep silent, now the bigots repudiated their true selves. Which somehow helped me understand why, after leaving the witness stand, Jackson walked up to me and gave me a bear hug.

On Friday, April 27, the courtroom was filled for the first time, in anticipation of the "kitchen tape." Prosecutor Doug Jones believes that when he is on his death bed he will still be hearing the voice of eighteen-year-old Jean Casey Blanton piercing the static of the vintage tape, a mixture of teenybopper inanity and shrewish purpose.

"Weeeelllll"—her voice rises sassily—"you never bothered to tell me what you went down to the river for, Tawmee."

The river was the Cahaba, where Blanton's rump Klan group had met by the bridge in the weeks leading up to the bombing. And "what Tommy went down to the river for" was the prosecution's only real link between the defendant and the Sixteenth Street explosion. (Kirthus Glenn, the seamstress who had spotted a car identical to Blanton's near the church in the early hours of September 15, had died since testifying at the Chambliss trial.) And even that connection depended on the jury's accepting that "the bomb" could, in the Birmingham of 1964, refer to only one crime. The meeting at the river was "the big one," Blanton explains to Jean: "the meeting where we planned the bomb." And, one more time, he says distractedly, since he's trying to decide which shirt to wear: "We had that meeting to make the bomb."

"I know that," Jean says. "It's what you were doing that Friday night when you stood me up." And—with the remark that will surely earn her a place in the "banality of evil" hall of fame—she says that her bigger fear on that evening, when she had called the Modern Sign Shop and been told Tommy wasn't there, was that "you stood me up to go out with Waylene." She seems relieved that all he was doing was making "the bomb."*

The following day, the prosecution played recordings made by an FBI informant from the old Warrior Klan named Mitch Burns, a meatpacker (bacon department) who for nine months in 1965 drank and chased women with Blanton on the government payroll. Among Blanton's taped comments:

"They ain't going to catch me when I bomb my next church."

"Boomingham, Boomingham, that's my kind of town."

"I'm going to stick to bombing churches."

From the witness stand, Burns—who, to the government's relief, had forgone his all-black Johnny Cash look in favor of a bright peach shirt and bolo tie—parried John Robbins's cross-examination about a girlfriend of his, insisting, lasciviously, that she was "my waitress" and that he "did not have sexual relations" with her. After Robbins acknowledged the allusion to Bill Clinton, Burns returned to the other theme of the trial. "I've never been a racist," the ex-Klansman said, "never said anything bad about black people, never been mean to them."

Looking like a man trying to find his way out a bunny hole, Robbins said, "Somebody should have told Martin Luther King that... Tommy Blanton was the only racist in Birmingham."

---

*Interestingly, Waylene Vaughn told the FBI, in her October 1963 interview that was omitted from the master BAPBOMB file, that she was indeed with Blanton that Friday night—that they had trysted at the Blue Bird Motel. (Vaughn's trial testimony about the large black woman who had come to the car and given them a room key thrilled the Fleet Street reporter in the press gallery—grist for what his editors were calling "lifestyles of the Klan" stories.) That Blanton never produced this alibi for that critical night, when I concluded he *was* attending a meeting to plan the bomb, is puzzling enough to make me wonder whether Vaughn was confused about the timing of their date.

DOUG JONES HAD PROMISED the jurors in his opening statements that they would hear from Jean Blanton Barnes, and the decision about whether to call her became his most agonizing. He had played the tape for her a few months earlier and sensed that she might cooperate, especially after he informed her of Blanton's favorite name for her: "my alibi." But since then she had gone so dumb that her current husband had been accusing her of caring more about Blanton than their marriage. ("You're not the one going to jail," she reputedly said.) Ultimately ruling out any chance of Jean coming through on the stand in "a Perry Mason moment," Jones passed.

The final witnesses for the prosecution were the victims' families, those silent, stoic figures in the front pew, their isolation underscored by the laughter that had greeted the ex-Klansmen's testimony. ("The horrible can be not only ludicrous but outright funny," Hannah Arendt observed in *Eichmann in Jerusalem*.) Of the parents, only Chris and Maxine McNair and a wheelchair-bound Alpha Robertson are still alive, and there were usually some sisters in attendance. Sarah Collins Rudolph, the only girl in Sixteenth Street's ladies' lounge to survive the blast, took the stand last. Now a fifty-year-old housekeeper with a glass eye, Rudolph told the court of the moments after the explosion, as she lay in the rubble, and she spoke the words that I had always found the most tragic in my manuscript. "I called out to my sister. I said, 'Addie. Addie. Addie.'"

Did she answer? Jones asked.

"No."

On Saturday afternoon, April 28, after twenty-two witnesses and five days of testimony, the state rested.

JOHN ROBBINS REPORTED to his no-frills Southside office to work on Tommy Blanton's defense after the 8:30 mass on Sunday morning—a Catholic plotting the salvation of man who had once despised Catholics more than blacks, though the subject of religion has never come up between attorney and client. "We're praying for you," the deacon had told Robbins, who thought, "Yeah, praying that your client will burn in hell."

"Praying that the riots stay on *their* side of the mountain," said the thirty-year-old junior defense counsel, Dave Simpson, whose shaved head and minibeard made him look like the baddest member of the college swim team—and may have been sending a subliminal "skinhead" message to the jury.

If this had been an ordinary, nonpolitical case, Robbins would have put on what he calls an is-that-it? defense and just said the government had proved nothing. But this historic jury would want to hear something from the accused. On Monday Robbins called two witnesses. One was intended to cast doubt on the Civil Defense worker James Lay's account of seeing Blanton—with Chambliss—toting a valise to the side door of the church late at night two weeks before the bomb exploded there. (The man Lay identified as Blanton, Robbins contended, also fit the description of the neo-Nazi Edward Fields.) The other witness, a black teenager in 1963, who now carried an oxygen tank to the stand, introduced an alternative bomb scenario—two white men in a Rambler who sped off at the time of the explosion.

The lawyer's dilemma once again came down to the ex-wife, the alibi. Jones had been trying to bait his old partner into calling Jean, but in the end Robbins bowed to the certainty that the prosecution would destroy her on cross-examination. Her subpoena gone cold, Jean Casey Blanton Barnes, now a plus-size middle-aged woman, retained enough of the minx to park herself, conspicuous in purple, on the front bench next to the victims' families.

Robbins rested on a prayer, not for a grand-slam acquittal but for a base hit of reasonable doubt to hang the jury.

AT DUSK ON Monday, April 30, the effervescent Doug Jones was taking a break from preparing his closing arguments, having changed out of his jury suit into a short-pants Atlanta Braves "uniform" bearing the name and number of the third baseman Chipper Jones. He sat cross-legged, barefoot, outside the U.S. attorney's office, which is in the federal courthouse named after Robert Vance, a liberal judge murdered in December, 1989, by a bomb delivered by letter. In 1963, Vance had been a star lawyer in Chuck Morgan's cadre of activist Young Turks. Jones is very much their legacy, a bright progressive Democrat who, after the trial, launched a campaign for the U.S. Senate.

In the strange lovefest that this church bombing reprise has become, Jones did not get the first crank call or letter. The only creepy touch had been the dynamite charges going off across the street from the courthouse while Jones's team got ready for trial inside; the blasts came from a construction site, for the new Taj Mahal being built by my uncle Hobart's law firm, the still-resplendent Bradley, Arant, Rose & White.

The atmosphere in Jones's office on the eve of the trial's last day was marginally upbeat, as in the dugout of the team with a slight edge. Andy Sheldon, the government's consultant from Atlanta, opened what he called his "Wells Fargo bag" and took out the shoes in which eleven-year-old Denise McNair walked into her last Sunday school class—surprisingly large patent leather flats that Judge Garrett had not let the jury see, though he did overrule Robbins and allow the mortar that was pulled from Denise's head. Sheldon has become the keeper of the sacraments, having assisted on the belated prosecutions of three civil rights crimes in Mississippi, including the successful 1994 trial of Byron de la Beckwith for the murder of Medgar Evers. Sheldon calls these "reconciliation cases," and, despite the underwhelming evidence against Blanton, he said hopefully, "If you believe in the reconciliation script, they have one destiny."

ON THE LAST DAY, the courtroom finally had a buzz equal to the event. Along with representatives of the civic groups, those ever-fretful guardians of Birmingham's image, were baby boomers who—like me and Doug Jones—had no recollection of hearing about the bomb that exploded only two months before the JFK assassination was branded in our memory. Students cutting class leaned against the balcony railing, giving the courtroom a *To Kill a Mockingbird* feel. Virtually none of the children on hand were black; the Reverend Abraham Woods, veteran of the 1963 demonstrations and still Birmingham's designated rabble-rouser, explained that the young people at his church were otherwise preoccupied—Tiger Woods had been in town for a golf tournament.

Jones's deputy—a career federal prosecutor named Robert Posey, with whom I had grown up over the mountain—delivered the government's first closing. The consultant Andy Sheldon had advised him, "Go as far as you feel comfortable, and then take it a step further." When the normally buttoned-up Posey's voice cracked during his invocation of the four girls, many spectators broke down too.

John Robbins lumbered over to the jury box. Since this was his last shot—the prosecution's two closing arguments sandwiched his—he took nearly an hour, grave and deliberate. As he settled into his summation, he was at last rewarded with eye contact from the denim-jacketed juror the press had nicknamed the Mad Liberal. He told a children's story, about an emperor walking around naked. The kingdom had been convinced that the "good" people could make out clothes where none existed. The jurors, Robbins said, must not similarly feel that seeing through the prosecution's fancy wardrobe made them "bad." He had gestured to the gallery, the media pressing the burden of history down on them. "Don't get caught up in it," he said quietly. "There is no shame in this case in saying to the government, 'Try as I might, I can't see your new clothing. I don't see your magic suit ... The emperor has no clothes.' And that is justice."

The rough consensus of the press was that the prosecution had not surmounted the handicap of reasonable doubt. Aired in open court, the kitchen tape was only intermittently intelligible, and its incriminating impact had not registered with the reporters or in their stories. (The jury had been provided a transcript.) To finesse his reasonable doubt problem, Doug Jones, in the prosecution's second closing, took the jurors back one last time to childhood. The government's essential metaphor was a jigsaw puzzle. Even when some pieces were missing, Jones said, you could still tell what the picture was. The basic figure was clear: Tommy Blanton, church bomber.

True to the reconciliation script, the jurors—eight white women, three black women, one black man—opened their deliberations with a prayer. They listened to the kitchen tape again, and just before 5:30, after less than two and a half hours, filed back into the jury box. Robbins told his client that a quick return was a not a good sign—especially from this white-male-free jury. The prosecution had struck ten of the eleven white men in the jury pool of forty-four people, and Robbins got rid of the eleventh after he said he would hold it against the defense if the trial made him miss his scheduled trip to Disney World.

The foreman, a black woman whom the press had christened "the Sleeper," was so overcome that she could barely choke out the verdict: guilty on all counts of murder in the first degree. As a court employee ordered that the SWAT team be alerted, Blanton was handcuffed and, with nine dollars in his pocket, led away to an eternity of penitence. One of the prosecutors noted that his "face was tense, but there was fire in his eyes."

Doug Jones hugged Chris and Maxine McNair; Alpha Robertson was already at home in her pajamas. Then he embraced Robbins.

AT THE END OF the day, sitting with a quietly elated government team in the bar of the Tutwiler Hotel, I felt sad. Maybe my mood was a sign that the system worked, that the protocols of jurisprudence, along with a cleaned-up defendant, really do cast a spell of innocent-until-proven guilty on the courtroom. I asked the connoisseur of reconciliation, Andy Sheldon, if that had been his experience in the previous cases he consulted on. "Always," he said. He thought it was the swift and utter demarcation between freedom and imprisonment. Judge Garrett himself had seemed a bit taken aback by the sudden resolution of this thirty-eight-year-old case and had at first asked the lawyers gathered at the bench whether he should wait until morning to sentence Blanton. But then he had answered his own question, with four consecutive life sentences.

The general disorientation was part of the conundrum of Birmingham and probably of any place that has been singled out by history: the near impossibility of taking in the magnitude of its own story. Even I, the Sixteenth Street specialist, was unable get my emotional bearings about the latest headlines out of my hometown. As I recorded everything going on around me in my reporter's notebook, Kevin Sack, a southern correspondent for the *New York Times,* came down to the hotel bar from his room, carrying the laptop on which he had just written his verdict story; it had made page one of the following day's paper. After displaying the screen to Doug Jones, Sack brought the computer over to me. It was only upon reading this first draft of history that the moment hit me, and I burst into tears.

I think my sadness was the recognition, too, that justice cannot force truth, and without truth there is no real, redemptive "closure." The next-to-the-last living suspect now protests his innocence from a cell "segregated" from the rest of the prison population (the verdict is under appeal), and it seems unlikely that we will ever have an honest, firsthand story of a political crime that changed America—and stranded four girls in a cold, perpetual youth.

Throughout the trial, the national news had been swirling with the ghosts of dead babies searching for "closure": from the Vietnamese children former Senator Bob Kerrey confessed to have killed as a young soldier at war in 1969, to the "collateral damage"—Timothy McVeigh's term for his youngest victims—of the 1995 Oklahoma City bombing. Within days of the Blanton verdict came the latest echo linking Oklahoma City to Birmingham. Soon after former Alabama attorney general Bill Baxley publicly condemned the FBI for withholding the crucial kitchen tape from him in the 1970s, preventing him from seeking a conviction against Blanton along with Robert Chambliss, McVeigh's execution was postponed because the bureau had failed to hand over required documents to the defense.

And then Birmingham's perpetual promise rallied yet again. The Bobby Frank Cherry case was resuscitated when the government got a psychiatric evaluation that contradicted both the defendant's and the court's doctors, saying that his "vascular dementia" was not severe enough to exempt him from justice. In July 2001, a skeleton crew of the church-bombing media squad materialized in Judge Garrett's court for a hearing on the conflicting opinions. Cherry, who wore his best blank stare, had by now exceeded his early sociopathic potential, abandoning his eight children after his battered wife died of cancer, allegedly molesting a young stepdaughter and a granddaughter, and abusing a few more wives, his grand total: five.

The outcome of the hearing seemed a foregone conclusion. With no state law spelling out the standard of proof, the burden on the prosecution established by case law was to prove the defendant competent by "clear, convincing, and unequivocal" evidence. With the bar set so unrealistically high, no one was surprised when on July 16 Judge Garrett pronounced Cherry incompetent. In a strange, perpetually promising coda to the ruling, however, Garrett set a further hearing date to order a state-administered evaluation of the defendant, its purpose unstated.

The church bombing case seemed to have limped to an anticlimactic finish.* The prosecution, though contending that Cherry was faking, did not appear sorry to see it go away. Doug Jones had stepped down as U.S. attorney after the Blanton conviction to make way for the appointee of George W. Bush. And the case against Cherry was not strong—basically two witnesses.†

Just as the community seemed to be acquiescing in the outcome, Fred Shuttlesworth returned. Still a resident of Cincinnati, he had been in town on the opening day of the trial to speak to one of the many educational groups that have made Birmingham a prime history-hunting destination. He took a seat in the press balcony after lunch, causing a little a stir at the prosecution table. Shuttlesworth had just faxed a message to Martin Luther King III, who now had his father's old job as head of the Southern Christian Leadership Conference. The letter's exasperated contents carried me back to my days in the archives, where I had found Shuttlesworth's pushy dispatches to Martin Luther King Jr., chiding him for dragging his feet. Lately Shuttlesworth had been urging SCLC to hold

*As a member of the committee of judges charged with writing the state's rules on criminal procedure, Garrett vowed to address the flaws in Alabama's competency-setting standards, bringing them in line with other states' burden of a "preponderance of evidence."
†One of them, a boyhood friend of Cherry's eldest son, recalled overhearing Cherry and some men discussing a bomb and a church days before the explosion. The other was a Texas acquaintance who said Cherry had boasted of killing the girls. The granddaughter he molested told the grand jury that she too had heard him brag about the bombing at a family gathering, but no other relatives present would corroborate her claim.

mass demonstrations to protest the disfranchisement of blacks in Florida during the recent disputed presidential election, but his old comrade's also reluctant son was not in favor of them.

Instead of Florida, it was back to Birmingham for SCLC. Within days of the Cherry ruling, Shuttlesworth, with his former vice president from the Alabama Christian Movement for Human Rights, Abraham Woods, staged demonstrations outside the courthouse, drawing from that venerable, telegenic pool: children. At first the indignation had focused on Alabama's many indigent black borderline-retarded defendants who had managed to clear the competency bar all the way to death row. But rising black frustration turned the rhetoric personal. Judge Garrett was hit with the label that had replaced "nigger lover" as most dreaded bait: racist. The full circle from 1963 to now closed when moderate whites (as well as some blacks) deserted the civil rights militants over their "extremism." But the dialectic prevailed—the demonstrations, once again, "worked."

On August 10, the day after Martin Luther King III led a nostalgic march through downtown Birmingham to the Sixteenth Street Baptist Church, Bobby Frank Cherry reappeared before Judge Garrett, who committed him to the state mental hospital for a controlled, in-patient evaluation of up to ninety days. Whatever the outcome—and the defense bar predicted "competency" on the basis of the facility's track record—there will be yet another hearing to sort through the opinions, and on this second go-round, for some incomprehensible reason, the prosecution's burden of proof to establish his fitness will convert from "clear, convincing, and unequivocal" to "preponderance of evidence." As of this writing, the Bobby Frank Cherry case could be headed for an indefinite future on life support, but without the political pressure of demonstrations, it would have most likely met a premature death.

Yet this victory, too, carries a depressing sense of déjà vu. Its impact on real black lives is slight. Indeed, if the ultimate result is a lowering of the competency standard, it will, if anything, make it easier for the "average" (read black) suspect to be railroaded through the system. Black "gains"—at least for Shuttlesworth's beloved masses—so often amount to two steps backward for every step forward. It sometimes seems that the struggle for black equality in America is Sisyphean. The promise of Birmingham's shining moment remains perpetual.

THE EXTENDED WRAP-UP of the Sixteenth Street church bombing case has been an unusual opportunity for a city to revisit its defining historical event. But the outcome has been confusion as much as resolution. How *does* a community atone for collective evil in which the average individual was only passively complicit? What are the means by which "coming to terms with the past" is achieved?

There is a word in German for this process—*Vergangenheitsbewaltigung.* The efforts of Germany to recover from the disgrace of Nazism were greatly enhanced, if not specifically induced, by defeat and occupation. The official history of that era has been sternly overseen by the victors. But in the case of Birmingham (as well as postwar France and Austria, on which moral rehabilitation was not forced), "closure" has been an impulse to forget the past rather than to examine and preserve it. And "reconciliation" has too often been a goal sought in a vacuum, with no corresponding pursuit of understanding.

Perhaps the reason the South has not had to face its guilt is that it really did not lose its war. Certainly, it conceded the battle over legal segregation, and stopped condoning dynamite-happy vigilantes. But the southern outlook was simply exported in code to the rest of the country. George Wallace, who seemed to be a lonely barker at a departing carnival in 1963, turned out to be John the Baptist, the inspiration for Richard Nixon's presidency-winning "southern strategy." The Solid South has moved from the Democratic ledger to the Republican, its largely poor citizens casting their lot with a party that offers them little besides the fellowship of white men.

As I WRITE THIS, the thirty-eighth anniversary of the Sixteenth Street Baptist Church bombing approaches: September 15, 2001. President Bush designated the days leading up to it National Birmingham Pledge Week. The Birmingham Pledge—essentially a chain letter whose signers promise to eradicate racism from their hearts—was conceived by a Bradley, Arant lawyer in 1998. It was evolving from an image-healing placebo to a pretext for making Birmingham a laboratory for racial justice based on redemption rather than retribution. A series of events had been planned that week, to turn ceremony into action. But they were abruptly suspended.

On September 11, the unthinkable happened once again, in my adopted hometown, New York City. America's innocence was lost beneath the rubble of another landmark building.

Birmingham has behaved over history as if it, too, was the victim of some alien agent of evil, even though the mad terrorists who struck the Sixteenth Street Baptist Church were homegrown. Local resistance to confronting the past has sometimes bordered on defiance. The white folks' classic reaction to the Blanton trial was "Why open old racial wounds?"—as if they bore any of the scars. And within Birmingham, Doug Jones was hailed not as a local hero but as an "opportunist," especially when he announced for the Senate. That had also been the charge leveled more than a generation ago at Chuck Morgan.

On a beautiful Sunday afternoon the summer after the Blanton conviction, I took Jones to meet Morgan at the apartment outside Mountain Brook Village where I had arranged the reunion between Morgan and my father almost twenty years earlier. When I told Jones that Papa might join us there, he quipped, "Should I bring a subpoena?" (During the trial Jones had jokingly refused to let me interview his father—"After what you did to yours? I don't want you saying *my* father was in the Klan.") Papa, who showed up before the Morgans got home and left, had been handling the celebrity my book had inflicted on him with singular grace, expressing his pride in me to reporters and patiently fielding questions from acquaintances about whether he had had anything to do with that church bombing.*

I think that his equanimity reflected the recognition that this vast prose tribute to our relationship grew out of total acceptance. I hope the quality of *Carry Me Home* that some readers found pitiless is also a form of acceptance, a refusal to substitute "image" for the complex molecular structure of a city that contained both the best and the worst of America. The civic DNA has been passed from the parents to the children, and now it is our turn, the grown daughters and sons of the epoch, to take its imprint, invisible at the time, and, through example and action, make of it a living language of historical memory.

Chuck Morgan, brilliant and controversial, who was one of the few members of his Birmingham generation insightful enough to shape the narrative as it was being lived, now has Alzheimer's disease. As Jones and I sat in his beautifully appointed living room, Morgan sometimes did not know where he was or whether it was summer or winter. But he did have a fine understanding that this book was his vindication and that Jones's recent triumph was the continuation of his own story. But not the resolution of the story, never a resolution. In the dying of the afternoon light, Morgan's face took on the squinty intensity of the old king-making days, and he asked what "we" were going to do to force progress on the city he had pronounced dead nearly four decades earlier.

And that is the moral of the story: The corpses of that past gave meaning to the lives of people like Jones, and me, and with any justice to the city itself. Robert Penn Warren described the merger of the personal with the public—the individual with history—as "identifying with fate." The network of mutuality, happily, remains inescapable.

Diane McWhorter
New York City
September 2001

---

*My uncle Hobart, meanwhile, though he has supported me privately, has distanced himself from the book among his country club cohort. (He has gotten facetious hate mail about his appraisal of the Birmingham Country Club, to which his standard reply is, "I didn't say it was a roadhouse. I said it was *like* a roadhouse.") The *Birmingham News* published, without giving me a chance to respond: "Diane has written an effective, largely fictional book." Though he later told me he had read only the first chapter, his dear friend Jimmy Simpson quoted this in a letter to the *News* editor condemning my portrait of his father, James A. Simpson.

Abbreviations Used in Source Notes

AA	*Baltimore Afro-American*
AB	Albert Boutwell Papers, BPL
ACHR	Alabama Council on Human Relations Papers, SRC
ADAH	Alabama Department of Archives and History, Montgomery
AH	Birmingham *Age-Herald*
AJC	American Jewish Committee Papers, Yivo Institute for Jewish Research, New York City
ASRA	American States Rights Association Papers, BPL
Bapbomb	FBI investigative file on the Sixteenth Street Baptist Church bombing (FBI file no. 157-352), BPL
BC	Eugene "Bull" Connor Papers, BPL
BM	Burke Marshall Papers, JFK
BN	*Birmingham News*
BP	*Birmingham Post*
BPH	*Birmingham Post-Herald*
BPL	Birmingham Public Library Archives, Birmingham
BPSF	Birmingham Police Surveillance Files, BPL
BUK	Martin Luther King Jr. Papers, Special Collections Department, Mugar Library, Boston University
BW	*Birmingham World*
BWC	*Birmingham World* Collection, BPL
CCJC	C.C.J. Carpenter Papers, BPL
CD	*Chicago Defender*
Chambliss trial transcript	*Alabama, State of,* v. *Robert E. Chambliss,* C.C. 1977-01954
COH	Oral History Collection, Columbia University Library, New York City
DV	David Vann Papers, BPL
DW	*Daily Worker*
EOJ	Emory O. Jackson Papers, BPL
EOJAR	Correspondence between Emory O. Jackson and Anne Rutledge, BPL
FOR	Glenn Smiley Papers, Fellowship of Reconciliation Peace Collection, Swarthmore College, Swarthmore, Pa.
Freebus	FBI investigative file on Freedom Rides (file no. 149-16), BPL
FS	Fred Shuttlesworth Papers, KC
IC	Inter-Citizens Committee affidavits, in various locations, chiefly CCJC and courtesy of C. Herbert Oliver
ILD	International Labor Defense Papers, SC
JFK	John F. Kennedy Library, Boston
JM	Jimmy Morgan Papers, BPL
JY	John Yung Papers, courtesy of John Yung

KC	Martin Luther King, Jr., Library and Archives, Martin Luther King, Jr., Center for Nonviolent Social Change, Inc., Atlanta
Klan HUAC hearings	House Un-American Activities Committee. *Hearings on Ku Klux Klan Organizations.* 89th Congress, 1st session. Washington, D.C., 1965
Klan HUAC report	House Un-American Activities Committee. *Report: The Present-Day Ku Klux Klan Movement.* 90th Congress, 1st session. Washington, D.C., 1966
La Follette hearings	U.S. Senate Committee on Education and Labor (La Follette subcommittee). *Violations of Free Speech and Rights of Labor: Hearings Before Subcommittee.* 74th Congress, 2nd session. Washington, D.C., 1938
LeGrand int. with Rowe	Captain Jack LeGrand and Officer Ernie Cantrell int. with Gary Thomas Rowe, Sept. 12, 1977, BPSF 9.1
Levison FBI	FBI wiretap of Stanley Levison (file no. 100-111180), SC
MA	*Montgomery Advertiser*
MLK	Martin Luther King, Jr., Papers, KC
MSOH	Oral History Collection, Civil Rights Documentation Project, Moorland-Spingarn Research Center, Howard University, Washington, D.C.
NLRB report	Oscar Smith to G. L. Patterson, National Labor Relations Board Report on Alabama Fuel and Iron Company, Case No. X-C-1102, May 23, 1942, in Philip Taft Papers, BPL
NYT	*New York Times*
PC	*Pittsburgh Courier*
POF	President's Office Files, JFK
RB	Ralph Bunche Papers, SC
RFK	Robert F. Kennedy Papers, JFK
Riverside tape	WRVR-FM radio documentary, "Testament of Nonviolence," 1963, Michigan State University Library, East Lansing
Rowe Baxley deposition	deposition of Gary Thomas Rowe by Bill Baxley, Dec. 1, 1975, BPSF 9.1
Rowe California deposition	deposition of Gary Thomas Rowe, Oct. 17, 1975, BPSF 9.1
Rowe Church committee testimony	testimony of Gary Thomas Rowe before U.S. Senate Select Committee to Study Governmental Operations with Respect to Intelligence Activities, chaired by Frank Church, 94th Congress, 1st session, Dec. 2, 1975
Rowe Dees deposition	deposition of Gary Thomas Rowe for *Beulah Mae Donald* v. *United Klans of America, Inc.,* April 27, 1985, courtesy of Morris Dees
Rowe Peck deposition	deposition of Gary Thomas Rowe for *Peck* v. *U.S.A.,* Nov. 29, 1979, courtesy of Edward Copeland
SC	Schomburg Center for Research in Black Culture, New York Public Library, New York City
SCLC	Southern Christian Leadership Conference Records, KC
SK	Stetson Kennedy Papers, SC
SK/SLA	Stetson Kennedy Papers, SLA
SLA	Southern Labor Archives, Georgia State University Library, Atlanta

SRC	Southern Regional Council Papers, BPL
State Freedom Rider Investigation	State of Alabama Department of Public Safety Investigation on Freedom Rider Movement, Aug. 15, 1961, Box 4, BPSF
Stoner trial transcript	*Alabama* v. *Jesse Benjamin Stoner,* 10th Judicial Circuit Alabama, Jefferson County, Division 6, 1980
SW	*Southern Worker*
Task Force Report	U.S. Department of Justice. *The FBI, the Department of Justice and Gary Thomas Rowe, Jr.: Task Force Report on Gary Thomas Rowe, Jr.,* Washington, D.C., 1979
TCSH	Tutwiler Collection of Southern History, BPL
Vann, LeGrand speech	David Vann speech at Duard LeGrand Conference, Birmingham, Nov. 15, 1978
VN	Victor Navasky Papers, JFK
WH	William Hamilton Papers, BPL
WP	*Washington Post*
WSJ	*Wall Street Journal*

NOTES

A Note on Sources

MUCH OF THE NARRATIVE of the Ku Klux Klan has been drawn from the FBI's interviews with Klansmen. Though their accounts must be used with caution, I have established patterns of consistency through painstaking cross-referencing and have supplemented the FBI records with the Birmingham police's surveillance files and the investigative files of former attorney general William J. Baxley's office, as well as interviews of my own. Since I went through the police surveillance files (BPSF) before they had been inventoried, I should alert fellow scholars that some of the box numbers I have cited may be out of date.

Preface

16 *only one man would agree:* V. Hamilton, *Alabama,* p. 142.
16 *Lucy Haynie Harris:* Marjorie McWhorter, *Hobart Amory McWhorter* (privately published, Birmingham, 1972), pp. 9–10.
16 *My great-great-grandmother:* ibid., p. 14. Like French people who all claim to have been in the Resistance, every southerner seems to have a personal encounter with General Sherman in the family. So I was somewhat surprised to learn in Sherman's memoirs that he was indeed in Gaylesville in October 1864, after chasing General John Bell Hood through Alabama and Georgia, and he had just formulated his scorched-earth strategy for winning the war. See William Tecumseh Sherman, *Memoirs of General W.T. Sherman* (New York: Library of America, 1990), pp. 631, 633.
16 *"smashing things,"* and *"make Georgia howl":* Sherman, *Memoirs,* pp. 629, 627.

Introduction: September 15, 1963

20 *hired out half its prisoners: Survey,* Jan. 6, 1912, p. 1541.
20 *tuberculosis-breeding coal mines:* Thomas D. Parke, *Report on Coalburg Prison,* p. 11, Thomas Parke Papers, BPL.
20 *majority of them black:* E. B. Clark, "Convicts," p. 19. Between 1904 and 1912 more than 80 percent were black.
20 *"all the evils":* A. B. Moore, *Alabama,* pp. 814–15.
20 *Slackers were hung:* E. B. Clark, "Convict," p. 21; D. Harris, "Racists and Reformers," pp. 71–72; R. Lewis, *Black Coal Miners,* p. 31.
20 *teach ignorant Negroes:* ibid., p. 33. This argument was reminiscent of the prewar slaveholders' claim that they were saving the African heathens from savagery by introducing them to Christianity. Bond, *Negro Education,* p. 11.
21 *"son of a bitch":* int. Marie Jemison, Nov. 11, 1982, who heard him say this. This was the comment President Franklin Roosevelt had made in the 1930s about Nicaragua's new dictator, Anastasio Somoza.
21 *"a heart as hard": Jet,* Dec. 25, 1958.
22 *"A snarling police dog":* quoted in Wade, *Fiery,* p. 320.
24 *"most prestigious club"* and *Lindsay Gaines:* int. Lindsay Gaines, Oct. 6, 1983.
25 Uncle Tom's Cabin and *police dog: Jet* magazine (April 25, 1963) made this connection after a dog attack on a young man earlier in the campaign.
25 *"The world outlook was bad":* Percy, *Last Gentleman,* p. 193.

1. The City of Perpetual Promise: 1938

31 *"The City of Perpetual Promise":* Leighton, "Perpetual Promise."
31 *original squatters:* Armes, *Coal and Iron,* p. 41; White, *District,* p. 15. The earliest settlers came in 1815.
31 *Millner was struck:* Armes, *Coal and Iron,* pp. 113, 218–19.
31 *built a railroad:* ibid., pp. 108–109, 116.
31 *who tried to born in:* ibid., pp. 216, 218–21, 243–44; Bond, *Negro Education,* pp. 37–38.
31 *"best workshop town":* Armes, *Coal and Iron,* p. 223. "Brummagen," the nickname for Birmingham, England, was a synonym for "showy, inferior, phony."
31 *The iron man: BPH,* Feb. 27, 1986; *BN,* Aug. 15, 1936; "Spotlight on Vulcan," Birmingham Historical Society lectures, March 3, 1986; "Vulcan" vertical file, TCSH.
32 *"hard flat incurable sore":* James Agee, *Let Us Now Praise Famous Men* (Boston: Houghton Mifflin, 1941), p. 197. They went through Birmingham in 1936.
32 *Murder Capital of the World: BP,* Dec. 20, 1934.

32 *haven for loan sharks:* Leighton, "Perpetual Promise."

32 *"Before God":* Survey, Jan. 6, 1912, p. 1461.

32 *"improved estate section":* Jemison prospectus on Mountain Brook Estates, Inc., Robert Jemison Papers, BPL.

32 *hardest-hit city in America:* "worst hit town in the country," according to Leighton, "Perpetual Promise."

32 *hundreds of millions:* ibid.; the government had lent or spent $361 million over four years.

33 *marble head of Christ:* John Lusko speech, "Spotlight on Vulcan," Birmingham Historical Society lectures, March 3, 1986.

33 *forbidding the workers to grow corn:* SW, June 1935.

34 *dwindling Ruskin:* Mary Louise Bennett, "Ruskin: Ware County's Vanished City," *Georgia Review,* Summer 1951; Francelia Butler, "The Ruskin Commonwealth: A Unique Experiment in Marxian Socialism," *Tennessee Historical Quarterly,* undated; Charles Kegel, "Earl Miller's Recollections of the Ruskin Cooperative Association," *Tennessee Historical Quarterly,* March 1958, all courtesy of Henry Simpson.

34 *"corn as a substitute for coffee":* Simpson's memoir of Ruskin, courtesy of Henry Simpson.

34 *"capitalist system":* BN, Sept. 28, 1932.

34 *"Old Ego"* and *"Look at that son of a bitch":* Black Jr., *My Father,* p. 46.

34 *including convicts leased:* E. B. Clark, "Convict," pp. 89–94; Black and Black, *Mr. Justice,* p. 35. Newman, *Black,* pp. 66–67.

34 *outrageous jury awards:* e.g., $3,000 for a hernia sufferer. V. Hamilton, *Black,* p. 76.

35 *excuses Hugo Black:* Newman, *Black,* pp. 94–96.

35 *Populism:* O. Stone, "Agrarian," pp. 394–98; Grady McWhiney, "The Revolution in 19th Century Alabama Agriculture," *Alabama Review,* January 1978, in Wiggins, *Civil War,* pp. 109–32; William Warren Rogers, "The Alabama State Grange," *Alabama Review,* April 1955, in Wiggins, p. 137.

35 *Hugo's father was an enemy:* Fayette "Fate" was a business partner of the brother of the founder of the People's Party of Alabama, Joe Manning—the brother also rejected Populism. Black and Black, *Mr. Justice,* p. 7.

35 *"colonel and carpetbagger":* O. Stone, "Agrarian," p. 118, coined by John Temple Graves II.

35 *the poll tax:* Gaither, *Blacks,* p. 110; Hamilton, *Black,* pp. 16–17; Hackney, *Populism,* p. 208.

35 *"nigger lovers":* Gaither, *Blacks,* p. 28. See also A. B. Moore, *Alabama,* p. 636, for dissension in communities.

35 *"communistic ring"* and *"outside agitators":* O. Stone, "Agrarian," p. 508, quoting *Moulton Advertiser* and *Montgomery Advertiser* from March and July 1887.

35 *the Klan, fallow:* Wade, *Fiery,* pp. 138, 147–48, 150; BN, Oct. 13, 1921; Chalmers, *Hooded,* p. 78.

35 *"American hotbed":* Charles P. Sweeney, "Bigotry Turns to Murder," *The Nation,* Aug. 31, 1921.

35 *Black won an easy acquittal:* BN, Oct. 7–22, 1921; Newman, *Black,* pp. 85–86.

36 *humoring the Klan:* This is my conclusion from William R. Snell, "Masked Men in the Magic City: Activities of the Revised Klan in Birmingham, 1916–1940, *Alabama Historical Quarterly,* Fall and Winter 1972.

36 *Know-Nothing Party:* William H. Skaggs, *The Southern Oligarchy* (New York: Devin-Adair, 1924), p. 336. At the height of Know-Nothing strength, in 1854, the compromise was repealed.

36 *"Super Government":* Charles N. Feidelson, "Alabama's Super Government," *The Nation,* Sept. 28, 1927. He called it "the most completely Klan-controlled state in the Union."

36 *equally unanticipated:* BN, Aug. 8, 1926, dismissed his candidacy.

36 *Bibb Graves:* William E. Gilbert, "Bibb Graves as Progressive, 1927–1930," *Alabama Review,* January 1957, in Wiggins, *Civil War.*

36 *"We don't have to kiss":* Alabama, Sept. 20, 1937. The plaques signified "life memberships."

36 *sole anti-Klansman:* Newman, *Black,* p. 115.

36 *"every man and woman":* Leah Rawls Atkins, "Senator James A. Simpson and Birmingham Politics of the 1930s," *Alabama Review,* January 1988, p. 9.

36 *Simpson had become:* int. Florence Evans Simpson, March 22, 1989.

36 *list "Country Club":* BN, Aug. 8, 1926.

36 *abolition of the convict lease:* E. B. Clark, "Convict," p. 63; *The Nation,* July 18, 1928; R. Lewis, *Black Coal Miners,* pp. 20, 25.

36 *governor's reforms:* Gilbert, "Graves as Progressive," in Wiggins, *Civil War,* pp. 336–38; BN, Aug. 8, 1926.

36 *Black waved:* V. Hamilton, *Black,* p. 214.

37 *Roosevelt acolytes had also captured:* BN, Dec. 2, 1935; *Alabama,* Dec. 14, 1936. They were Lewey Robinson and W. O. Downs.

37 *Simpson's work:* Details, though not interpretation, are drawn from Atkins, "Civil Service." This is, of necessity, an oversimplified portrait of Simpson, who stood out among the hack pols as a gifted legislator and a hard worker, even shying away from the conflict of interest that was in the job description of most Big Mule legislators. And he was not so rigid that when "progressive" served the aims of Birmingham, as in Graves's futile fight for reapportionment, he could be an enthusiastic "administrationist" himself. See *BP,* Aug. 17–19, 22, and Sept. 4 and 13, 1935.

37 *"Simpsonize":* Atkins, "Civil Service," pp. 27, 29, 30.

37 *rather hear a game:* int. Beara Connor, Dec. 28, 1984.

37 *Bull was his nickname:* ibid.; BN, Oct. 18, 1931, and Oct. 31, 1937; unpublished article on Connor, January 1935, courtesy of *The Sporting News; The Sporting News,* Feb. 25, 1932.

38 *"Ouuuuuuuuuut!":* and other quotes in BN, Oct. 18, 1931.

38 *opiate of the mine and mill masses:* The biggest baseball day of the season, was Labor Day, with company-provided barbecue for the fans. Fullerton, "Striking Out Jim Crow," p. 154.

38 *Black Barons:* ibid., pp. 63–66. Paige was with the Barons from 1926 to 1930.

38 *Rickwood Field:* A. H. "Rick" Woodward, "The Memoirs of the Man Who Built Rickwood," reprinted in Birmingham Barons' 1985 souvenir program.

38 *Lindbergh's Birmingham touchdown:* Zipp Newman, "September Memory," a 1968 *BN* article reprinted in Birmingham Barons' 1985 souvenir program. Lindbergh stopped in Birmingham in 1927.

38 *the Barons' batboy:* Boston Herald, Sept. 9, 1987.

38   *casualty of an air rifle:* int. Beara Connor, Dec. 28, 1984.
38   *"going to tell the truth":* BN, Oct. 31, 1937.
38   *spent only $64:* Alabama, Feb. 1, 1937.
38   *"Sunny Jim":* BP, Sept. 10, 1935; Alabama, May 17, 1937.
39   *signed into law:* Atkins, "Civil Service," p. 95.
39   *blocking funding for a passenger elevator:* BP, Sept. 3, 1935. Intriguingly, Connor sponsored the Graves administration's failed constitutional amendment that would cancel all back poll taxes except for the last three years.
39   *They wanted him to run:* Atkins, "Civil Service," p. 39 (her citations do not have any reference to this, however).
39   *charge of "outside agitator":* BN, May 9, 1937; Alabama, May 10, 1937. Connor's actual words were that Graves's henchmen had come up from Montgomery and were "moving heaven and earth" to beat him.
39   *not to improve his grammar:* BN, Oct. 31, 1937.
39   *Simpson . . . now would use:* On virtually every important bit of city business, Connor consulted Simpson, usually by telephone. His fellow commissioners knew that "Let's hold off on this till next week" meant "I've got to ask Jim." Int. James "Jabo" Waggoner, May 27, 1984.
39   *the police Connor controlled:* police interviews; Nichols, "Cities Are," p. 61.
39   *Sidney Smyer:* int. Sidney W. "Billy" Smyer, Dec. 2, 1987; Smyer vertical file, TCSH.
39   *Alabama fever:* V. Hamilton, Alabama, p. 3.
40   *"Persons who are fortunate":* Daniels, A Southerner, p. 278.
40   *Negro peasants:* See Draper, American Communism, pp. 315–36; Kelley, Hammer, p. 14; John Beecher, "The Share Croppers' Union in Alabama," Social Forces, October 1934.
40   *"right of self-determination":* Draper, American Communism, pp. 345–56; Spero and Harris, Black Worker, pp. 427–29.
40   *launched from the South's industrial hub:* Kelley, Hammer, p. 14.
41   *few southerners had been moved:* Special House Committee on Communist Activities in the U.S., "Investigations of Communist Propaganda, 71st Congress, and Session, Washington, D.C., 1930.
41   *seized by sheriff's deputies:* Carter, Scottsboro, pp. 3–5.
41   *occasional prostitutes:* ibid., pp. 78–79.
41   *sentenced to death* and *"bursts empires":* Wilson, "Freight-Car Case."
41   *"nigger rape case":* Carter, Scottsboro, p. 12.
41   *Communist Party embarrassed:* ibid., pp. 53, 57, 61, 67; SW, June 13, 1931.
41   *fund-raising rallies:* Kempton, Part, p. 253.
41   *"Negro liberation":* "Thesis and Resolution for the Seventh National Convention of the Communist Party of the United States," quoted in Wilson, "Freight-Car Case."
41   *martyr Angelo Herndon:* Herndon, "You Cannot Kill the Working Class, in Grant, Protest, pp. 227–28; other sources date arrest in June.
41   *"This is no life":* Herndon, Let Me Live, pp. 57–58. A fellow miner had replied: "There are no men—there are no Christians, nowhere. Only pigs."
41   *claimed a membership:* Kelley, Hammer, pp. 76, 90.
41   *Joe Gelders:* Esther Gelders Zane, "Professor, How Could You?" The New Republic, March 2, 1938; int. Dora Sterne, Dec. 9, 1987; telephone int. Marge Gelders Frantz, Nov. 18, 1993; Ingalls, "Antiradical Violence."
42   *strikers and strike breakers had been murdered:* SW, 1934; Taft, Dixie, p. 111.
42   *"Reds Linked"* and *"Outbreak Believed":* BN, May 9 and 10, 1934, quoted in Kelley, Hammer, p. 71.
42   *sought out the Communist Party:* telephone int. Marge Gelders Frantz, Nov. 18, 1993. Gelders was cleared when the Popular Front era opened up the Party to the liberal bourgeoisie.
42   *become an American colony:* Mullins, "Corporation's Purchase," p. 30.
42   *John "Bet a Million" Gates:* Tarbell, Gary, pp. 75, 122; Fuller, "History," pp. 143–44; Woodward, Origins, p. 303; Josephson, Robber Barons, p. 426.
42   *Gates had vowed:* Fuller, "History," pp. 145–50; Armes, Coal and Iron, p. 511. This was in late 1905.
42   *"formidable industrial enemy":* Woodward, Origins, p. 127.
42   *last hurrah:* Chernow, House of Morgan, p. 122.
43   *The scheme Morgan proposed:* e.g., Mullins, "Corporation's Purchase," pp. 17–20; Fuller, "History," p. 162; Tarbell, Gary, p. 200. Morgan's latest biographer, Jean Strouse, offers a revisionist view of this episode.
43   *approve Morgan's instant monopoly:* Armes, Coal and Iron, pp. 517–18.
43   *stock market rallied:* Chernow, House of Morgan, p. 128.
43   *"fool or a knave":* M. Sullivan, Our Times, p. 304.
43   *"most important occurrence":* The U.S. Geological Survey's Edwin Eckel quoted in Fuller, "History," p. 163.
43   *worth a* billion *dollars:* Woodward, Origins, p. 301.
43   *Congress's aggressive antitrust investigations:* AH, May 28–Aug. 2, 1911. During a lengthy 1911 House investigation into the takeover, congressmen became facetious about the Corporation's claims of having grossly overpaid. (See Texas congressman quoted in House of Representatives' U.S. Steel hearings, AH, July 29, 1911.) The committee wondered why Morgan would overpay by many millions to bail out a concern, Moore & Schley, vulnerable for only $6 million. In its separate investigation, the Senate concluded that the Corporation had acted to seize control of the national iron-ore supply, the production of open-hearth steel rails, and the southern iron and steel trade in general. *Absorption of the Tennessee Coal & Iron Co.,* in Senate Documents, 62nd Congress, 1st session, no. 44, p. 66, quoted in Woodward, Origins, p. 301. In October 1911, President William Taft's attorney general filed an antitrust suit to dissolve the United States Steel Corporation. The suit was resolved in 1920 in the Corporation's favor in a much-debated split Supreme Court decision. Mullins, "Corporation's Purchase," pp. 63, 66–75. The government's suit had been pending at the same time U.S. Steel was producing many of the guns of World War I. Theodore Roosevelt died before seeing himself and his "good trust" so vindicated, as did J. P. Morgan.
43   *offended the Corporation's new southern subjects:* AH, July 2, 1913.
43   *imposed immediate layoffs:* Hackney, Populism, p. 317.

43 *clear to a trade analyst:* Armes, *Coal and Iron,* p. 523.

43 *potential would remained untapped:* Woodward, *Origins,* p. 315.

43 *supplied the propaganda:* The Interchurch World Committee's Report on the Steel Strike of 1919, quoted in Levin, *Political Hysteria,* p. 42. Ninety percent of all radicals taken into custody were reported by one of the large corporations, either of the coal or steel industry.

43 *three worst cities:* Ingalls, "Antiradical Violence."

43 *Gelders's first project:* ibid.; Gelders's statement to state police, Sept. 24, 1936, folder h18, ILD.

44 *Logan had been sentenced:* SW, October 1936.

44 *"committee" from TCI:* La Follette hearings, Part 3, p. 779; Belle Barton affidavit.

44 *four men clubbed:* Ingalls, "Antiradical Violence"; Gelders's statement to state police and National Committee for the Defense of Political Prisoners press release, undated (November 1936), folder h18, ILD.

44 *"fishing trips":* La Follette hearings, Part 3, p. 752.

44 *became a cause célèbre:* Ingalls, "Antiradical Violence"; *Alabama,* Jan. 25, 1937.

44 *Walter J. Hanna:* Ingalls, "Antiradical Violence"; La Follette hearings, Part 15, p. 6319.

44 *pitching rocks at cans:* int. James Head, June 6, 1984.

45 *"royal family on progress":* Leighton, "Perpetual Promise."

45 *protected right of workers:* This was Section 7(a) of the National Industrial Recovery Act. See, e.g., Taft, *Organized Labor,* pp. 416–23.

45 *La Follette's staff understood:* ILD press release, Sept. 26, 1936, folder h18, ILD.

45 *second investigation:* Auerbach, *Labor and Liberty,* pp. 93–94.

45 *leaped to the defense:* Ingalls, "Antiradical Violence."

45 *"Whippings, I believe"* and *taken off ACLU's list:* La Follette hearings, Part 3, p. 798; Ingalls, "Antiradical Violence."

45 *audience with Eleanor Roosevelt:* Durr, *Magic Circle,* p. 119; Rob Hall, "Those Southern Liberals," *Dissent,* Fall 1979; Krueger, *Promises,* pp. 16–19.

46 *Popular Front:* Klehr, *Heyday,* pp. 186–206; Isserman, *Hammer,* p. 12; Schlesinger, *Upheaval,* pp. 565–66; Kelley, *Hammer,* p. 122.

46 *"the Fascist system":* Michie and Ryhlick, *Dixie Demagogues,* p. 190.

46 *"Unquestionably a large factor":* *Amalgamated Journal,* Sept. 2, 1937, quoted in Auerbach, *Labor and Liberty,* p. 108.

47 *Gelders divulged:* telephone int. Marge Gelders Frantz, Nov. 18, 1993. Lewis's southern deputy was a former radical Socialist from Indiana named William Mitch.

47 Report on the Economic Conditions: Egerton, *Speak Now,* p. 180; Reed, "SCHW," p. 8.

47 *first elected mayor, James Powell:* Armes, *Coal and Iron,* pp. 223–25, 231–32.

47 *darkest underground labor* and *"Dumb Beasts":* Kulik, "Black Workers," pp. 25–27.

47 *few lumps of coal:* V. Hamilton, *Black,* p. 39.

48 *Fred Shuttlesworth:* ints. Fred Shuttlesworth; Shuttlesworth oral histories, KC and MSOH; conversation with Alberta Webb (Shuttlesworth's mother), Oct. 9, 1983; Manis, *Fire,* p. 31. I conducted numerous interviews with Shuttlesworth between 1985 and 2000, and since they often went over the same ground, I have in some cases cited them in the aggregate.

48 *community called Rosedale:* prospectus on Mountain Brook Estates, Inc., Robert Jemison Papers, BPL; *BN,* June 2, 1929.

48 *Ruby Kenon Thornton:* conversations with Marjorie McWhorter, Ruby Thornton, and Edward Thornton.

49 War of the Worlds: Manchester, *Glory,* pp. 232–37.

49 *more than 1,500 delegates:* Southern Conference for Human Welfare convention, *BN,* Nov. 21–23, 1938; Ashby, *Graham,* p. 156; Reed, "SCHW," pp. 33–34, 48, 57; Durr, *Magic Circle,* pp. 120–21; Egerton, *Speak Now,* pp. 179–97; int. James Jackson, Nov. 13, 1990; Robert Hall, "Those Southern Liberals," *Dissent,* Fall 1979; Painter, *Hudson,* pp. 290–91; Kelley, *Hammer,* p. 186; *Alabama,* Dec. 5, 1938. Accounts vary. So discreet was Gelders that Jim Simpson attended early planning meetings on the conference.

49 *"shares in promise":* Daniels, *A Southerner,* p. 273.

49 *decision of his career:* Carter, *Scottsboro,* pp. 380–81.

49 *Hosea Hudson:* See Painter, *Hudson;* Kelley, *Hammer,* pp. 24–25.

50 *"new and unique adventure":* Reed, "SCHW," p. 48. He was referring to the courage of the middle-class white liberals.

50 *"not to segregate":* Harrison E. Salisbury, "Fear and Hatred Grip Birmingham," *NYT,* April 12, 1960.

51 *wife of the President . . . browbeaten:* When asked to comment on the enforcement of segregation, she backed down, "I would not presume to tell the people of Alabama what to do." *BN,* Nov. 23, 1938.

51 *swirling his "medicine":* Carter, *Scottsboro,* p. 394.

52 *largest commercial producer:* *Alabama,* Aug. 30, 1937.

52 *Henry Fairchild DeBardeleben:* Cruikshank, *Birmingham,* p. 368; M. McMillan, *Yesterday's Sketches,* p. 23; Armes, *Coal and Iron,* pp. 162–63, 239–41, 267, 275; 1987 Alabama Business Hall of Fame program (unpaginated), in author's possession.

52 *"King of the Southern Iron World":* Armes, *Coal and Iron,* p. 423.

52 *toppled by stock market rascals:* Fuller, "History," pp. 122–23.

52 *"clawed the rocks":* Armes, *Coal and Iron,* p. 427.

52 *To stop John L. Lewis:* DeBardeleben's anti-union measures in La Follette report, Part 3, p. 793; NLRB report on Alabama Fuel & Iron Company, Philip Taft Papers, BPL, p. 14; Taft, *Dixie,* p. 86.

52 *"mystery man":* "Mystery Man" affidavit signed by Luther Burnham et al., in NLRB report.

52 *drove out to "organize":* AH, Oct. 29, 1935.

52 *personally headed:* showdown between DeBardeleben and UMW in NLRB report, pp. 9–10; *BN,* Oct. 28,

1935; *AH,* Oct. 29 and 31, 1935; *BN,* Dec. 4, 1935; telephone conversation with Gertrude Thomas, victim's sister-in-law, Dec. 6, 1995.

52   *Nine DeBardeleben employees were: BN,* Dec. 8, 1935; *BP,* Dec. 3 and 4, 1935.

52   *beat the rap:* Their attorney, Borden Burr, contended in the face of absolutely contradictory evidence that the unionists had been trespassing on private property. The company's lawyers also squashed the half-million-dollar civil suit the widow had filed. *BP,* May 11, 12, and 14, 1937.

52   *hero to his class:* Huie, *Mud,* p. 215.

52   *"greatest believers of White Supremacy":* Kelley, *Hammer,* p. 188.

53   *weekly* Alabama: Stoney to Bunche, Jan. 24, 1940, RB, 29.11.

53   *"dyed-in-the-wool Communists": Alabama,* December 5, 1938.

53   *HUAC during the Cold War:* Abt, *Advocate,* p. 69.

53   *antidote to the left-leaning La Follette:* ibid., p. 69; Auerbach, *Labor and Liberty,* p. 167.

53   *Texas congressman Martin Dies:* Michie and Ryhlick, *Dixie Demagogues,* pp. 56, 58, 63, 65–66.

53   *"America for Americans": Alabama,* Dec. 5, 1938; Dec. 19, 1938; Norrell, "Labor at the Ballot Box," p. 218.

53   *asked committee to investigate:* Kelley, *Hammer,* p. 188.

53   *sent a spy:* Egerton, *Speak Now,* p. 190.

53   *if the playwright:* Michie and Ryhlick, *Dixie Demagogues,* p. 59.

53   *Lewis did not discriminate:* Taft, *Organized Labor,* p. 620. Though Lewis had been a red-baiter in the twenties, he eventually put more than sixty Communists on the CIO payroll.

53   *DeBardeleben had been high on the list:* NLRB report, p. 11.

53   *Constitutional Educational League:* Friends of Democracy, "Joe Kamp,"; testimony of Joseph Kamp before House Committee to Investigate Campaign Expenditures, Sept. 20, 1944, 78th Congress, 2nd Session in SK 3.1, p. 248, quoting from charter; Levin, *Political Hysteria,* p. 201.

54   *head of the league was Joseph Kamp:* Friends of Democracy, "Joe Kamp,"; Kamp testimony, before House committee, pp. 253–54; Forster and Epstein, *Radical Right,* p. 39.

54   *Fred Marvin: Rosika Schwimmer* v. *Fred Marvin and Commercial Publishing Company,* appellate records, 1928; American Civil Liberties Union, *The Case of Rosika Schwimmer: Alien Pacifists Not Wanted* (New York: ACLU, 1929); *NYT,* July 15, 1939; *Who's Who,* 1938–39; Carlson, *Under Cover,* p. 196; Marvin, *Are These Your Friends?* (Denver: Americanization Press Service, 1922).

54   *jotting down impressions:* Marvin quotations in Marvin, *Alabama Fuel and Iron,* pp. 57, 21, 22.

54   *"the Munich of Southern capitulation": Alabama,* Nov. 28 or Dec. 5, 1938.

54   *held a banquet:* "More on America's Moseley," typescript in SK 4.3; Carlson, *Under Cover,* pp. 137–39. The program is reproduced in Friends of Democracy, "Joe Kamp," p. 14.

54   *George Van Horn Moseley:* ibid., pp. 20–25.

54   *name joined in a litany:* Carlson, *Plotters,* p. 20.

54   *John Eoghan Kelly was a propagandist:* Friends of Democracy, "Joe Kamp," p. 3, 23; Carlson, *Under Cover,* p. 468.

54   *Lawrence Dennis, a disillusioned:* Schlesinger, *Upheaval,* pp. 74–78; Friends of Democracy, "Joe Kamp," p. 10; Stetson Kennedy memo, "More on America's Moseley," p. 4, SK 4.3.

54   *Philip Johnson:* Schlesinger, *Upheaval,* p. 72.

54   *"Democracy, hell!":* Carlson, *Plotters,* p. 20. This statement was made in 1940.

55   *union-fighting organization:* Wade, *Fiery,* p. 494 *n.* 262, *SW,* December 1934.

55   *"about three-quarters Negro":* NLRB report, p. 13.

2. Ring Out the Old: 1948

56   *"artless monstrosity": BPH,* Feb. 27, 1986. The remarks were made on April 4, 1947, by an artist and critic, Ralph Pearson.

56   *series of radio talks: BN,* Dec. 2, 1937.

56   *second-largest and fastest-growing city:* Barnard, *Dixiecrats,* p. 112.

56   *industrialist had to be arrested:* Beiman, "Steel Giant," p. 100. The ordinance was passed in 1946.

57   *"The Lottery":* Shirley Jackson, "The Lottery," in Stanley Edgar Hyman, ed., *The Magic of Shirley Jackson* (New York: Farrar, Straus, and Giroux, 1966), p. 142.

57   *Victorian where Lionel Hampton:* L. Hampton, *Hamp,* p. 4.

57   *Black Barons caravaned:* Fullerton, "Striking Out Jim Crow," p. 79.

57   *Ruth Jackson:* Ruth Jackson oral history, Jan. 9, 1981, Birmingfind Papers, BPL.

58   *"All segregation laws":* Richards, "Youth Congress," p. 186.

58   *executive secretary, Louis Burnham:* ints. James Jackson and Esther Cooper Jackson, Nov. 13, 1990; int. Dorothy Burnham, Nov. 13, 1990; int. Sylvia Hall Thompson, Nov. 29, 1990.

58   *audience with Bull Connor:* Richards, "Youth Congress," pp. 187–89.

58   *Connor rounded up the minister,* and *"strike the church down":* ibid., pp. 188–90.

59   *"dream of freedom":* Proclamation of Southern Negro Youth Congress, quoted in Strong, "Southern Youth's," p. 35.

59   *moved their headquarters . . . to Birmingham:* ibid., pp. 42–43; Richards, "Youth Congress," pp. 43, 118.

59   *attending the 1938 founding:* int. James Jackson, Nov. 13, 1990.

59   *most historic development:* Richards, "Youth Congress," p. 140.

59   *Notable . . . for being black owned:* See Anne Braden, "The White Southerner in the Integration Struggle," *Freedomways,* Winter 1963.

59   *"Cast down your bucket":* speech reprinted in Grant, *Protest,* p. 197.

59   *"them asses":* Virginins Dabney, *Below the Potomac* (New York and London: D. Appleton-Century, 1942) p. 58. He was apparently quoting a white snob.

59 *"flower of the Negro race":* Richards, "Youth Congress," p. 41; Strong, "Southern Youth's," p. 44. This was F. D. Patterson, who presided from 1940 to 1947.

59 *SNYC advisory board:* Richards, "Youth Congress," p. 158. Its major institutional benefactors were the Marshall Fund, American People's Fund, and the Rosenwald Fund.

59 *"If the Party coughed":* int. Junius Scales, March 7, 1994.

60 *conference that Paul Robeson:* int. Esther Cooper Jackson, Nov. 13, 1990.

60 *Roosevelt telegrammed:* Richards, "Youth Congress," p. 56.

60 *voter registration drives, anti–poll tax campaigns . . . puppet theater:* ibid., pp. 91, 98, 100–101, 119, 121; ints. Esther Cooper Jackson and James Jackson, Nov. 13, 1990.

60 *When Bechtel . . . SNYC cranked out handbills:* ints. James Jackson and Esther Cooper Jackson, Nov. 13, 1990; int. James Jackson, Dec. 20, 1990; Strong, "Southern Youth's," p. 45. The firm was then known as Bechtel, McCone and Parsons.

60 *Arthur "Duke" Wolff:* Wolff, *Duke of Deception,* pp. 72–76.

60 *Fred Shuttlesworth had plummeted:* ints. with Fred Shuttlesworth; Shuttlesworth oral histories, KC and MSOH.

61 *"freest man":* Lee Bains int. with Fred Shuttlesworth, courtesy of Bains.

61 *member of the Southern Negro Youth Congress Advisory Committee:* Richards, "Youth Congress," p. 74. His name was William Dinkins.

61 *record thousand delegates:* 1946 SNYC convention, program of Columbia conference, Oct. 18–20, 1946, courtesy of James and Esther Jackson; int. Esther Cooper Jackson, April 8, 1992; ints. James Jackson and Esther Cooper Jackson, Nov. 13, 1990; Richards, "Youth Congress," p. 159; Scales, *Cause,* pp. 164–65.

62 *Du Bois, gave his speech:* reprinted in *Freedomways,* First Quarter 1964, pp. 8–15.

62 *name was Hunter Pitts O'Dell:* int. Jack O'Dell, March 16, 1993.

62 *Dies's Committee:* Richards, "Youth Congress," p. 137.

62 *"the most active communist:* ibid., pp. 137, 140–42.

62 *Central Intelligence Agency:* ibid., p. 137.

62 *moderate base was scattering:* ibid., p. 151.

62 *gamely conceded bore a marked resemblance:* Manchester, *Glory,* p. 561. However, the Communist Party at the time was in its post-Browder phase, hardline to the point of irrelevance.

62 *"Jim Crow in America":* P. Sullivan, "Gideon," pp. 241–43.

63 *senator Glen Taylor:* Abt, *Advocate,* pp. 147–48; Manchester, *Glory,* p. 527.

63 *"fast dying clique":* BN, May 1, 1948.

63 *pledged to arrest:* BW, April 30, 1948.

63 *the use of his church:* Beard to Burnham, April 27, 1948, BWC 1.11; BW, April 30, 1948.

63 *Hotels canceled:* BW, May 4, 1948.

63 *ascended to the U.S. Party's:* Painter, *Hudson,* pp. 308, 384n.6.

63 *"gonna arrest":* Richards, "Youth Congress," pp. 143–44.

63 *Taylor decided:* BN, May 2 and 4, 1948; *Time,* May 10 and 17, 1948, p. 24; BW, May 4, 1948; Richards, "Youth Congress," p. 193.

63 *major burglary:* Rowan, *Freedom,* p. 165.

64 *hospitality tour:* Richards, "Youth Congress," pp. 193–94.

64 *at the house:* int. Sallye Bell Davis, May 20, 1991.

64 *180-day suspended sentence:* Richards, "Youth Congress," p. 196.

64 *NAACP had assumed charge:* Lomax, *Negro Revolt,* p. 119.

64 *"Maybe the Hitler":* North, *No Men,* p. 195.

64 *first constitutional challenge:* press release from Senator Taylor's office, June 6, 1950 (petition for certiorari was filed on June 5), in "Birmingham Communal Issues, 1944–1962," AJC; Cochran, "Shores," p. 67; BN, March 10, 1950; Abt, *Advocate,* pp. 156, 159.

64 *sung "Birmingham Jail":* BN, May 4, 1948.

64 *wig manufacturing:* Abt, *Advocate,* p. 147.

65 *"not enough room":* Time, May 10, 1948.

65 *pundits would pronounce:* See Harry Ashmore's postmortem, reprinted in BN, Dec. 6, 1948.

65 *"program of the Communist Party":* Cohodas, *Thurmond,* p. 130.

65 *southerners to believe:* Time, May 17, 1948; Alabama, July 23, 1948.

65 *tiny poll tax–reduced fraction of those they governed:* S. Kennedy, *Southern Exposure,* pp. 98–99.

65 *League to Maintain White Supremacy:* Alabama Sun, March 24, 1944; "League to Maintain White Supremacy" memo, undated, SK; Alabama, July 24, 1942, p. 9; ADL report, "The Visible Empire" (1942–46), pp. 2–3 SRC (this was written by Stetson Kennedy); memo on "Artcrafters, Southern Citizens League, etc.," Oct. 16, 1945, and "Southern Citizens League," undated notes, SK 3.9; telephone int. Carl H. Perkinson (a league member), April 21, 1994.

65 *league retaliated:* Alabama Sun, April 14, 1944; Richards, "Youth Congress," pp. 80, 104 (calling it League of White Supremacy).

65 *named Vance Muse:* Michie and Ryhlick, *Dixie Demagogues,* pp. 185–87; Schlesinger, *Upheaval,* pp. 520–23; S. Kennedy, *Southern Exposure,* pp. 128, 249–50, 252–53; George Wolfskill, *Revolt, The Revolt of the Conservatives: A History of the American Liberty League, 1934–1940* (Boston: Houghton Mifflin, 1974), pp. 166–67, 241; Carlson, *Plotters,* pp. 270–71; undated memos ("He first gained renown" and "Excerpt from Secretary Muse's Report"), "Purposes and Activities of Christian Americans," (1945) memo, "Excerpt from Secretary Muse's Report . . . ," undated memo, and Muse to Christian American, June 23, 1943, all in SK 5.

66 *"You ties in the niggers":* Carlson, *Under Cover,* p. 322.

66 *"preaching only what Jesus taught":* Marvin, *Alabama Fuel and Iron,* p. 90.

66 *the group's seasoned propagandists:* "The Artcraft Network," undated memo; "Facts, Inc," memo, Feb. 11, 1946, undated, untitled memo "The charter shows . . ."; "Artcrafters, Southern Citizens League, etc.," all in SK 3.9.

66 Alabama Sun *carried:* Alabama Sun, March 24, 1944 (first issue).

66   *issued knowing threats:* memo on "Artcrafters, Southern Citizens League," Oct. 16, 1945, p. 2, SK 3.9.
66   *"big industrialists of Germany":* V. Hamilton, *Hill,* p. 128.
66   *reputedly funneled some liberal outside funds:* ibid., p. 122.
66   *"sharp repudiation":* BN, May 3, 1944.
66   *"vindictive and vicious":* Crow to Marie Bankhead Owen, May 22, 1944, Charles B. Crow Papers, ADAH.
66   *"better people of the state voted":* int. Florence Simpson, March 22, 1989.
67   *his sponsored legislation:* Beiman, "Steel Giant," pp. 119–20.
67   *precedent-setting obstruction:* S. Kennedy, *Southern Exposure,* p. 269.
67   *coming race Armageddon:* See *Alabama,* April 14, 1944.
67   *"candidate acknowledges defeat":* ibid., May 5, 1944.
67   *"plump associate":* Malone to Dixon, April 2, 1949, quoted in Feldman, "Wilkinson," p. 385n.42.
67   *"Brooklyn overseer":* V. Hamilton, *Hill,* p. 79.
67   *"Huns have wrecked":* Barnard, *Dixiecrats,* p. 98. He said this after the November general election.
67   *his uncle Thomas Dixon:* See Raymond Allen Cook, *Fire from the Flint: The Amazing Careers of Thomas Dixon* (Winston-Salem, N.C.: Blair, 1968).
67   *named* The Birth of a Nation: Schickel, *Griffith,* p. 268
67   *Dixon later denounced:* ibid., p. 76.
68   *Connor whooped:* Lesher, *Wallace,* p. 80.
68   *"devil's own loudspeaker":* Grafton and Permaloff, *Big Mules,* p. 119.
68   *The "walkers" stalked:* Only half of Alabama's twenty-six-person delegation bolted. Senator Lister Hill was a delegate at the convention, and thirteen "loyalists" remained there. Too scared of Truman, Hill and the loyalists had ended up supporting Georgia's aging wunderkind senator, Richard Russell, who had led the Senate fight against the Fair Employment Practices Committee in 1944.
68   *christened by a derisive editor:* Cohodas, *Thurmond,* p. 142.
68   *"knife in the heart":* BN, July 15, 1948.
68   *"They crucified us":* BN, July 16, 1948.
68   *empty war plants:* Beiman, "Steel Giant," p. 107.
69   *one of the last diehard activists: Alabama,* July 23, 1948; telephone int. Marge Gelders Frantz, Nov. 18, 1993. She was Polly Dobbs.
69   *Anglo-Saxon heritage:* Dixon speech and reaction in BN, July 18, 1948. See also BW, July 20, 1948.
69   *"Virile Governor":* Cohodas, *Thurmond,* p. 122 and photograph no. 16.
70   *"sons of bitches' nuts out":* Grafton and Permaloff, *Big Mules,* p. 28.
70   *he called Buttermilk Road:* G. Sims, *Little Man's,* p. 21.
70   *cedar suds bucket* and *"green breeze":* Grafton and Permaloff, *Big Mules,* p. 60.
70   *Strawberry Pickers: Alabama,* April 5, 1946.
70   *Folsom's landslide victory: Alabama,* June 14, 1946, and Jan. 24, 1947.
70   *"revolt of the 'outs' ":* Grafton and Permaloff, *Big Mules,* p. 74.
70   Life *published pictures:* G. Sims, *Little Man's,* p. 46.
70   *Folsom's truly radical politics:* ibid., p. 26; *AH,* March 24, 1939.
70   *"integratin' goin' on at night":* Grafton and Permaloff, *Big Mules,* p. 68.
70   *"most liberal state":* Barnard, *Dixiecrats,* p. 4.
70   *red-baited him:* ibid., p. 105.
70   *his illegitimate son:* Huie, "Draughts of Old Bourbon," pp. 757–58; Barnard, *Dixiecrats,* p. 107; telephone int. Gould Beech, April 1, 1994.
70   *greeted with boos: BN,* July 18, 1948. What was perhaps more meaningful was the number of cheers the speaker still commanded in this crowd.
71   *last Deep South chief:* int. Sylvia Hall Thompson, Nov. 29, 1990. He was Sam Hall, of Anniston.
71   *fathered a daughter:* Jack Bass and Marilyn W. Thompson, *Ol' Strom: An Unauthorized Biography of Strom Thurmond* (Atlanta: Longstreet, 1998) pp. 273–87.
71   *"ugly carnival scene": MA,* July 20, 1948, quoted in Starr, " 'Dixiecrat' Convention," p. 46.
71   *"Ku Klux Klan convocation": Anniston Star,* July 18, 1948, quoted in ibid., p. 38.
71   *mob had set upon a booster: BN,* July 18, 1948; Feldman, "Wilkinson," p. 266.
71   *American Broadcasting Company bailed out:* Starr, " 'Dixiecrat' Convention," p. 39.
71   *"howling, screaming savages": BN,* July 17, 1948.
71   *Thurmond winced:* He told reporters, "We do not invite and we do not need the support of Gerald L.K. Smith." *Christian Science Monitor,* July 20, 1948; Cohodas, *Thurmond,* p. 178.
71   *Gerald L. K. Smith:* Walter Davenport, "The Mysterious Gerald Smith," *Collier's,* March 1944; "In Fact" newsletter, Sept. 27, 1948, courtesy of Stetson Kennedy.
71   *Constitutional Educational League had sponsored:* Joseph Kamp testimony, Sept. 20 and Oct. 6, 1944, before House Committee to Investigate Campaign Expenditures, 78th Congress, 2nd session, p. 287.
71   *J. B. Stoner, who believed:* Stoner trial transcript, pp. 394, 349, 353; Stetson Kennedy typescript (1948), SK/SLA 1518.62; FBI int. with Stoner, Sept. 1, 1950; S. Kennedy, *Southern Exposure,* p. 207; P. Sims, *Klan,* pp. 152, 156, 158; Stetson Kennedy int. with Stoner, July 26 and Aug. 3, 1944, and June 15, 1946, SK; Kennedy int. with Stoner's aunt, Sept. 7, 1946, SK; Stoner to Kennedy, Aug. 26, 1946, SK; *Atlanta Constitution,* July 5, 1946; "J. B. Stoner," "Bethel Baptist Church 6/29/58," in Box 1, BPSF.
71   *"conspicuous failures":* Ashmore reprinted in BN, Dec. 6, 1948.
72   *Pratt City:* White, *District,* pp. 245–50; BN, March 12, 1989.
72   *huge prison stockade:* R. Lewis, *Black Coal Miners,* p. 29.
72   *Jack Daniel's temporarily relocated its distillery:* White, *District,* p. 249.
72   *Epidemic disease was the leading cause of death:* Mitchell, "Birmingham," p. 160.
72   *Chambliss had reached adulthood:* FBI ints. with Chambliss, Oct. 1, 1963, and with John Ollie Chambliss, Nov.

5, 1963, Bapbomb; telephone conversation with Margie Chambliss Burke, Feb. 8, 1993; telephone conversation with Ollie Chambliss, Feb. 8, 1993; City Directory, 1934; FBI int. with Chambliss, Oct. 1, 1963, Bapbomb; Chambliss to Graddick, Aug. 17, 1979, Alabama Attorney General's Office.

72 *unhappily married:* Chambliss to Bailey, Feb. 5, 1981, George Beck Papers, courtesy of Beck.

72 *joining the Robert E. Lee klavern:* FBI int. with Chambliss, Oct. 1, 1963, Bapbomb.

72 *treadmill of subsistence:* Birmingham City Directory, 1904.

72 *disrupt the CIO:* S. Kennedy, *Southern Exposure,* p. 167; Wade, *Fiery,* p. 262.

72 *an arm of management:* Norrell, "Caste," p. 15.

73 *Klan disbanded:* Wade, *Fiery,* p. 275; Carlson, *Plotters,* p. 42.

73 *led fifty black veterans: BN,* Jan. 23 and 24, 1946; ADL report, "The Visible Empire," SRC.

73 *Klan announced:* "The Artcraft Network," p. 6, and "Ned" to "AF," Feb. 12, 1946, SK 3.9; ADL report, "The Visible Empire," SRC; ADL report, "Ku Klux Klan," 1949, SRC; Stetson Kennedy int. with Imperial Wizard E. D. Pruitt, Aug. 14, 1946, SK.

73 *Chambliss was now working in the city garage:* Personnel Board of Jefferson County, Employment Record and Examination Record, Box 3, BPSF; FBI int. with Herman Siegel, Oct. 20, 1963, Bapbomb.

73 *cussing out a group of Negroes:* Robert Edward Chambliss FBI Identification Record, Oct. 7, 1963, Bapbomb.

73 *"You-all might need me":* FBI ints. with W. E. Coleman, Nov. 25, 1963, and June 29, 1964, Bapbomb.

73 *bootlegging sideline:* int. Maurice House, Spring 1985; FBI int. with Frank Hollifield, Feb. 3, 1966, Bapbomb.

73 *his second wife:* Chambliss to Bailey, Feb. 5, 1981, George Beck Papers; Chambliss trial transcript, p. 602.

73 *brick tiles* and *Sport:* Cobbs/Smith, *Long Time,* pp. 34–35.

73 *zoning law unconstitutional: BW,* undated (August 1947), BPSF 7.24. FBI has date as August 4.

73 *dynamite exploded:* Lewis et al. to Eddins, Aug. 20, 1947, State Bureau of Investigation and Identification report, Sept. 25, 1947; Willie Patterson statement, James Monteith statement, and Sam Matthews statement, all in Box 4, BPSF; *BN,* April 4, 1965.

74 *Girl Scout training session:* This was on June 10, 1948. Amerman to Stickney, June 11, 1948, "Statement of Visit by Unauthorized Personnel," undated (June 1948), David Smith's Statement on Trip to Birmingham, undated (July 1948), *BN,* June 25, 1948, and miscellaneous clippings, in Katrine Nickel Scrapbook, BPL.

74 *"Red Henry":* Feldman, "Wilkinson," p. 284.

74 *patrolled the courthouse:* P. Sullivan, "Gideon," pp. 331–32; *BN,* Sept. 1 and 2, 1948.

74 *"fresh eggs": BN,* Sept. 2, 1948.

74 *"take him to Harlem":* P. Sullivan, "Gideon," p. 333.

74 *was recognized:* FBI ints. with W. E. Coleman, Nov. 25, 1963, and June 29, 1964, Bapbomb. Connor had assigned Coleman to sit in Wallace's car.

74 *Wallace delivered: BN,* Sept. 2, 1948; P. Sullivan, "Gideon," pp. 334–37.

74 *Klansmen paced around: BN,* Sept. 2, 1948.

74 *"eyes of fascism":* Wallace had said this at his previous stop, at the Republic Steel stronghold of Gadsden, where steelworkers banged on his car with bats and chanted, "Kill Wallace." P. Sullivan, "Gideon," pp. 330–31; *BN,* Sept. 1, 1948.

75 *bombing houses with abandon:* Between the spring of 1949 and the end of 1950, eight houses were bombed. Chambliss was apparently involved in all but one of them. For description of bombings, see FBI Summary of Bombings, Bapbomb; *BPH,* Oct. 1, 1963; FBI ints. with Paul McMahan, July 16, 1964, and Aug. 12, 1965, Bapbomb; FBI int. with Hugh Morris, Aug. 5, 1965, Bapbomb; McMahan interrogation of Chambliss, May 23, 1949, statement of Milton Curry, June 8, 1949, police statement of DeYampert, Aug. 16, 1949, and statement of J. H. Coleman, Aug. 23, 1949, all in Bishop Green bombing file, Box 4, BPSF; *BN,* Aug. 13 and 14, 1949; "Confidential-Source Material," Sept. 23, 1977, attorney general's notes on FBI files, JY. In *BN* interview, July 26, 1979, Chambliss admits that one night he "stationed himself in a building to watch the bombing of three vacant houses."

75 *moved to "break up the Klan":* ADL report, "Ku Klux Klan," 1949, p. 13, and ADL report, "Alabama," p. 9, SRC; *BN,* July 20, 1949, and March 28 and Oct. 4, 1950; int. Coleman "Brownie" Lallar, June 12, 1995.

75 *notables in the Dixiecrat movement:* See especially state investigators Lamar Allen and Ben Allen int. with Robert E. Lee klavern's Exalted Cyclops E. E. Campbell, April 28, 1950, BPSF 6.13. For police collusion with Klan, see FBI int. with Paul McMahan, Aug. 12, 1965, Bapbomb; "Confidential-Source Material" memo, Sept. 23, 1977, JY. Roderick Beddow, the most famous criminal lawyer in the state, and two other top lawyers, George Rogers and Jim Gibson, represented some of the defendants for a dollar apiece. Int. Coleman "Brownie" Lallor, June 12, 1995.

75 *active in anti–New Deal politics: BN,* Nov. 25, 1938.

75 *Olin Horton:* Birmingham City Directory, 1947–1951; Atkins, "Civil Service" p. 46.

75 *wrote to his friend Senator Lister Hill:* Carmichael to Hill, July 21, 1949, Lister Hill Papers, Special Collections, University of Alabama Libraries.

75 *Exalted Cyclops:* telephone conversation with E. E. Campbell Jr., Nov. 16, 1995; Birmingham City Directory, 1937–1949.

76 *Jack O'Dell:* int. Jack O'Dell, March 16, 1993.

76 *Louis Burnham had sensed:* Abt, *Advocate,* p. 156.

76 *poachers from both Right and Left:* Manchester, *Glory,* p. 561. Thurmond got 1,169,021.

76 *Burnham dissolved:* int. Junius Scales, March 7, 1994; Scales, *Cause,* pp. 152, 193.

76 *anti-Communist investigations:* and Reed, "SCHW," p. 116; P. Sullivan, "Gideon," p. 151; Joseph Kamp, *The South vs. the Smear* (New York: Constitutional Educational League, 1946), SK 3.3.

76 *to answer charges of Nazi collaboration:* Carlson, *Plotters,* p. 278. The league had twice been named as a "factor" in the sedition indictments the U.S. government had brought in 1944 against thirty collaborators. Phillips, *The 1940s,* pp. 118–21.

77 *longtime SCHW board member:* P. Sullivan, "Gideon," pp. 184–85.

77 *post-election inter-racial conference:* Salmond, *Rebel,* p. 224; Krueger, *Promises,* pp. 189–91.

77 *"next great liberal movement": NYT,* March 2, 1947.

78   *"cradle of a reviving faith":* Kelley, *Hammer,* p. 202.
78   *"Mr. Connor's bluff":* BN, May 2, 1948.
78   *"Non-Violence":* Kelley, *Hammer,* p. 222.
78   *"grateful to Mr. Connor":* BN, May 2, 1948.
79   *"education, enlightenment, culture":* Powergrams, Oct. 26, 1936, in Martin vertical file, TCSH.
79   *counsel with the House of Morgan:* Leighton, "Perpetual Promise," p. 238.
79   *experiment in electricity-making:* The TVA was to be a "yardstick" to prevent the private power monopolists from gouging the consumer. At 4.6 cents per kilowatt hour, Alabama Power had the cheapest rates of all C&S southern subsidiaries and was below the national average of 5.5 cents. McCraw, *TVA,* p. 61.
80   *"barefoot Wall Street lawyer":* Chernow, *House of Morgan,* p. 448, quoting Harold Ickes.
80   *corporate lawyering a fulfilling challenge:* Hobart would be outlived by the dazzling mortgage bond deal he put together to comply with the restrictions Senator Hugo Black slapped on holding companies. Commonwealth & Southern survived the Public Utility Holding Company Act of 1935 and remained a going concern until legislation in 1947, calling for the geographical integrity of holding companies, split the bottom half of C&S into the Southern Company.
80   *halted construction on the wire mill:* For story of Fairfield (formerly Corey), see "Fairfield—1909," Robert Jemison Papers, BPL. Construction was stopped in 1911.
80   *"arrogant gesture":* Carmer, *Stars Fell,* p. 79.
81   *"Nothing has been done":* prospectus on Mountain Brook Estates, Inc., Robert Jemison Papers, BPL.
81   *library and a grander mansion:* Tolson, *Pilgrim,* p. 38.
83   *eloquent but measured letter:* McWhorter to Graham, Oct. 14, 1939, and Graham to McWhorter, Dec. 1, 1939, Frank Porter Graham Papers, Wilson Library, University of North Carolina.

3. Mass Movements: 1954–1956

84   *signature ordinance:* The infamous Section 597 of the city code forbade whites and blacks to "play together or in the company with each other any game of cards, dice, dominoes, checkers, softball or basketball, baseball, football, golf, track and swimming pools or beaches, lakes or ponds." Quoted in Breckenridge to Ingalls, Nov. 15, 1955, JM 24.25.
84   *police corruption scandal:* Citizens Committee report, February 1952, JM 22.2; *Alabama,* Dec. 28, 1951; BN, Jan. 9, 1952, JM 22.1.
84   *"small-time gestapo":* Eskew, *But for Birmingham,* p. 95, quoting a radio station executive.
84   *controlling the force:* int. James Parsons, Spring 1984; int. James D. Smith, Spring 1984; confidential police interview, March 1985; Citizens Committee report, February 1952, JM 22.2.
84   *"my niggubs":* Nunnelly, *Connor,* p. 26.
84   *disenchanted detective, Henry Darnell:* int. Maurice House, Spring 1985; int. James D. Smith, Spring 1984; BPH, Oct. 3, 1952, JM 22.5.
84   *hollering for Commissioner Connor:* BN, Dec. 22, 23, and 24, 1951; BPH, Dec. 22 and 27, 1951.
85   *quite the public moralist:* Southern News Almanac, Jan. 23, 1941; Eskew, *But for Birmingham,* pp. 91–92.
85   *office Christmas party:* conversation with Barbara Percer and Sarah Naugher, May 1984.
85   *popularity could not offset:* BN, Jan. 16, 1952.
85   *five sticks of dynamite:* BN, Jan. 6 and 7, 1952.
85   *amended the notorious "checkers" ordinance:* Gilliam, "Second Folsom," p. 19. It allowed for interracial competition in "baseball, football, or similar games."
85   *Mel Allen: Look,* Sept. 28, 1960; BPH, April 26, 1957; telephone int. Mel Allen, June 12, 1990.
85   *"Doing away with segregation":* Gilliam, "Second Folsom," p. 20.
86   *Birmingham's Dixie Walker:* I am indebted to Ira Glasser ("The Baseball Guide to Character and Politics," *NYT* op-ed, May 3, 1983) for the baseball-politics analogy. Walker was actually from the suburb of Leeds.
86   *had even lost control:* V. Hamilton, *Hill,* p. 169.
86   *the county sewer system:* BN, Feb. 7, 1949, in Smyer vertical file, TCSH.
86   *practically every newspaper:* BN, March 25, 1954. Ads ran in every daily and forty weeklies.
86   *canvassers went door-to-door:* BN, March 16, 1954. "Do you want your child to go to school with a Negro?" was how the issue was put to prospective signers.
86   *get "red hot":* BN, March 16, 1954.
86   *death of his wife:* See Newman, *Black,* pp. 406–08.
86   *flagship case:* This was the first school case that the NAACP had brought, *Briggs* v. *Clarendon County.*
87   *"Hitler's creed":* Newman, *Black,* p. 429.
87   *"We conclude, unanimously":* e.g., Williams, *Eyes,* p. 34.
87   *voted separate and unequal baseball back in:* BN, June 2, 1954.
87   *shook hands with the janitor:* Frady, *Wallace,* p. 106.
87   *only scripted line:* "George C. Wallace, A Change in the Heart of Dixie," *MA* special section, Jan. 11, 1987, p. 12.
87   *"underscoring the changing patterns":* NYT, May 4, 1954, quoted in Gilliam, "Second Folsom," p. 51.
88   *one of whose deacons:* ints. with Fred Shuttlesworth; Shuttlesworth oral history, KC, and MSOH, p. 7; Manis, *Fire,* pp. 51–67.
88   *activists who brought him down:* Sears vs. Communists in *SW,* July 12, 1933; Painter, *Hudson,* pp. 169–79; Robert N. Washington oral history, Birmingfind Papers, BPL; int. H. D. Coke, Nov. 5, 1990.
89   *initial euphoria:* BW, May 21, 1954; Suggs, *Black Press,* p. 45; Stewart, "Reaction," pp. 63–64.
89   *"ought to be run":* Rowan, *Freedom,* p. 170.
89   *escorted to his workshop:* int. H. D. Coke, Nov. 5, 1990.
89   *escorted out of the Dixiecrat convention:* Emory O. Jackson oral history, MSOH, p. 6.
89   *"Jim Crow crazy":* ints. James and Esther Cooper Jackson, Nov. 13, 1990.
89   *objections to* Brown: Clarke, *These Rights,* Appendix, p. 134; Lomax, *Negro Revolt,* p. 126; BW, May 25, 1954.

89 *Southern Negro Improvement Association:* Moore to Morgan, July 11, 1954, JM 18.39; *BPH,* July 23, 1954; *BN,* Aug. 1, 1954; *Alabama,* Jan. 28, 1955.

89 *alienated its own constituency:* Louis Lomax, "The Negro Revolt," *Harper's,* June 1960, p. 42.

89 *"the fat boys":* Rowan, *Freedom,* pp. 169–71.

89 *"solid thinking":* int. Fred Shuttlesworth, March 6, 1989.

90 *Civic Leagues:* George Stoney, "Field Notes for Southern Trip," November 1939, and int. Dr. Taggart, Nov. 18, 1940, p. 37, RB 34.3; Edward Strong int. with Emory O. Jackson, May 1940, RB 34.1.

90 *a black woman:* [Rosa Parks], Thornton, "Bus Boycott"; Williams, *Eyes,* pp. 63–66; Abernathy, *Walls,* p. 134. Legally, black passengers in the sixteen middle seats were not obliged to defer to later-boarding whites–a concession resulting from a Negro boycott of the newly segregated Montgomery buses in 1900.

90 *"push us around":* Abernathy, *Walls,* p. 134.

90 *The* Zeitgeist: M. L. King, *Stride,* p. 44.

91 *had boarded a Birmingham streetcar:* ints. James Jackson and Esther Cooper Jackson, Nov. 13, 1990; telephone int. Joe Edelman (McAdory's widower), Dec. 18, 1990; Robin D.G. Kelley, "Congested Terrain: Race, Space, and Resistance on Birmingham Public Transportation During World War II," unpublished ms., p. 29. Kelley's article dates this in 1942.

91 *founder of the local chapter:* The *Montgomery Advertiser* called him the "NAACP Mau Mau chief." *MA,* Oct. 2, 1955, quoted in Gilliam, "Second Folsom."

91 *"For Common Courtesy":* ints. James Jackson and Esther Cooper Jackson, Nov. 13, 1990.

91 *radicalized by Senator Robert La Follette:* Durr, *Magic Circle,* pp. 108–11.

92 *"available pink Alabamians":* Alabama, Dec. 5, 1938.

92 *not flinched from the Communists:* During the campaign she had unabashedly attended a big Communist rally in Paris, even ascending to the podium to join Moscow's French mouthpiece, Jacques Duclos. Durr, *Magic Circle,* pp. 196–97.

92 *Myles Horton:* Adams, *Unearthing,* pp. 7, 12, 10, 14.

92 *handful of functional radicals:* Painter, *Hudson,* pp. 23, 204; Adams, *Unearthing,* pp. 25–27; Horton, *Haul,* p. 63.

92 *"paid the price":* Horton, *Haul,* p. 27.

92 *"best radical work":* Kelley, *Hammer,* p. 120. This quote is from 1935.

92 *Highlander exhibit A:* Joseph P. Kamp, *The Fifth Column in the South,* Constitutional Educational League, 1940, SK.

92 *put up $5,000:* Carlson, *Under Cover,* p. 135. Carlson says that a wealthy southerner put up the money. See also *BP,* Feb. 25, 1941, in SK/SLA 1514/39.

92 *progressive frontier was race:* Horton, *Haul,* p. 86. Horton was committed to this new agenda by 1953.

93 *nominated her seamstress, Rosa Parks:* Durr, *Magic Circle,* p. 279; Cynthia Stokes Brown, "Rosa Parks," *Southern Exposure,* Spring 1981.

93 *Montgomery was hopeless:* Anne Braden oral history, COH, p. 64; see also Adams, *Unearthing,* p. 150.

93 *The Durrs and E. D. Nixon:* Durr, *Magic Circle,* p. 280; E. D. Nixon oral history in Raines, *My Soul,* pp. 43–45; int. with E. D. Nixon in *Down Home,* Fall 1982, pp. 30–31; Peck, *Freedom Ride,* p. 52; E. D. Nixon, "How It All Started," *Liberation,* December 1956. Accounts vary slightly. E. D. Nixon would sometimes overstate his role ignoring the crucial role of an Alabama State professor and activist, Jo Ann Robinson.

93 *"dog 'em":* Rowan, *Sorrow,* p. 117.

93 *except as a defendant:* int. with E. D. Nixon in *Down Home,* Fall 1982, p. 31.

93 *"gonna be mens":* Branch, *Parting,* p. 136.

93 *"a big deal":* int. Fred Shuttlesworth, March 6, 1989.

93 *"big nigger's church"* and *"Plato or Socrates":* Branch, *Parting,* pp. 104, 107.

94 *"we got Moses":* The *New Republic,* July 6, 1963, p. 16.

94 *his first speech:* Williams, *Eyes,* p. 76; Branch, *Parting,* pp. 139–41.

94 *Columbia conference of 1946:* int. Esther Cooper Jackson, April 8, 1992.

94 *"refuse-to-ride movement":* BW, Jan. 10, 1956.

94 *tumblers of bourbon:* Rowan, *Breaking,* p. 136.

94 *"a great questioning":* BW, Dec. 16, 1955.

95 *raising money for the Scottsboro Boys:* Cynthia Stokes Brown, "Rosa Parks," *Southern Expos..re,* Spring 1981.

95 *blacks still filled the buses from the rear:* PC, Jan. 14, 1956. This was called the Mobile plan, after that city's policy.

95 *King had quoted:* Gilliam, "Second Folsom," p. 238. "Let no man pull you so low as to make you hate him."

95 *"despicable features":* BW, Jan. 10, 1956.

95 *indigenous leadership:* BW, Dec. 16, 1955.

95 *"emaciated emancipator":* BW, Dec. 23, 1955.

95 *"know very little about"* Gandhi: Garrow, *Bearing,* p. 68.

95 *black tide:* Durr, *Magic Circle,* p. 283.

95 *Shuttlesworth began traveling . . . Alabama State:* ints. Fred Shuttlesworth; Shuttlesworth oral history, MSOH, p. 3.

95 *God had chosen King:* Fred Shuttlesworth oral history, KC, tape 2.

95 *"speech before an NAACP-sponsored mass meeting":* BW, Jan. 10 and 27, 1956; Shuttlesworth's statement to the Civil Rights Commission, Spring 1961, Box 4, FS.

95 *Emancipation Day* and *"real centers":* BW, Jan. 3 and 6, 1956.

96 *named Juanita Lucy:* ints. Autherine Lucy Foster, March 2 and 16, 1992; BW, Feb. 10, 1956, reprinted from *New York Journal-American;* E. C. Clark, *Schoolhouse,* p. 17.

96 *Hobart Grooms:* NYT, March 1, 1956; int. Hobart Grooms, March 1987.

96 *To the amazement:* int. Constance Baker Motley, March 27, 1991.

96 *Black unilaterally upheld:* Black's biographer Roger Newman says Black anonymously ruled on the motion; E. Culpepper Clark (*Schoolhouse,* p. 47), however, maintains that he declined to act on October 3, saying he wanted the full court to make the decision.

96 *"Thank God":* BW, March 2, 1956.

96   *Myers's acceptance:* NYT, March 1, 1956; Grafton and Permaloff, *Big Mules,* pp. 196–97; E. C. Clark, *School-house,* p. 54.

96   *"Autherine would go":* int. Autherine Lucy Foster, March 2, 1992.

97   *Lucy had asked a special friend:* int. Autherine Lucy Foster, March 2, 1992; int. Fred Shuttlesworth, March 28, 1991.

97   *stopped to joke with Shuttlesworth:* E. C. Clark, *Schoolhouse,* p. 57.

97   *"Congratulations":* BW, Feb. 7, 1956.

97   *geography:* int. Autherine Lucy Foster, March 16, 1992.

97   *asked her name:* BW, Feb. 10, 1956, reprinted from *New York Journal-American* article by Lucy.

97   *"Everything fine":* BW, Feb. 7, 1956.

97   *Lucy's entrance:* NYT Magazine, Feb. 26, 1956; Grafton and Permaloff, *Big Mules,* pp. 196–97; G. Sims, *Little Man's,* p. 179.

97   *"a peach dress":* int. Autherine Lucy Foster, March 2, 1992.

97   *Leonard Wilson:* Anthony, "Resistance Groups," p. 19.

97   *"Keep Bama white!"* and *riot on Saturday:* Friday- and Saturday-night mob scenes in E. C. Clark, *Schoolhouse,* pp. 62–68.

98   *"Bolshevik Klans":* Wade, *Fiery,* p. 289.

98   *Klansmen had left:* BN, Aug. 2, 1949.

98   *fired from the city garage:* BP, Sept. 24 and 27, 1949.

98   *continued to protect:* FBI ints. with Paul McMahan Aug. 12, 1965, and Lamar Allen, Nov. 19, 1965. Bapbomb; telephone int. Lamar Allen, March 1985; Ben Allen interview, in Raines, *My Soul,* p. 168. A year after Chambliss's firing, a Klansman interrogated about who was behind the two most recent bombings told state investigators, "Find out who Dynamite Bob's friends are." They managed to have him jailed on August 29, 1950, as "a material witness" to the bombings. The police chief refused the state detectives access to Chambliss on orders from "higher up." The chief said rather enigmatically that Chambliss was "hired out," and under persistent questioning confessed to the state investigators, "By order of the commissioner." Chambliss had, in fact, already been released from jail.

98   *demolition of the new home office:* Dr. Joel Boykin's house was demolished by three bombs apparently made at Robert Chambliss's house. "Confidential-Source Material," Sept. 23, 1977, JY; Boykin investigative file, Box 2, BPSF; telephone int. Joel Boykin Jr., Dec. 8, 1995; Smyer to Green et al., Nov. 16, 1948, Cooper Green Papers, BPL.

98   *"going soft":* Cobbs/Smith, *Long Time,* p. 56.

98   *White Citizens Council:* J. B. Martin, "Deep South," June 15, 1957.

98   *"intend to make it impossible":* Bartley, *Resistance,* p. 193; J. B. Martin, "Deep South," p. 72.

98   *$25 fee:* Anthony, "Resistance Groups," Appendix, p. 2.

98   *Smyer transposed:* See *Alabama,* Feb. 11, 1955.

98   *"first one in Jefferson County":* E. C. Clark, *Schoolhouse,* p. 106, quoting threatening message Chambliss left for university president O. C. Carmichael.

98   *eggs came at her:* BW, Feb. 10, 1956; NYT Magazine, Feb. 26, 1956.

98   *praying for the courage:* int. Autherine Lucy Foster, March 2, 1992.

99   *fourth was Robert Chambliss:* BW, Feb. 10, 1956; E. C. Clark, *Schoolhouse,* p. 77; Murray Kempton in *New York Post,* March 5, 1956. The other men were Ed and Earl Watts (brothers) and Kenneth L. Thompson.

99   *thousand Negroes:* Woodward, *Strange Career,* p. 155; the estimate in an Immigration and Naturalization Service report in BW, Feb. 24, 1956, is five hundred, mostly graduate students, but undergraduates too in states without a large black population.

99   *"for her protection":* NYT, Feb. 17, 1956.

99   *"symbol of Southern resistance":* NYT, March 13, 1956.

99   *recent "nullification" resolution:* Woodward, *Strange Career,* p. 156; NYT, March 13, 1956; Gilliam, "Second Folsom," pp. 322–26; Cohodas, *Thurmond,* p. 281. Folsom neither vetoed nor signed the resolution.

99   *Southern Manifesto:* V. Hamilton, *Hill,* p. 213; Cohodas, *Thurmond,* pp. 283–86. The manifesto was issued on March 12.

99   *biggest rally:* J. B. Martin, "Deep South," June 15, 1957, p. 75; Rowan, *Sorrow,* pp. 155–57; NYT, Feb. 11, 1956; Bayard Rustin, "Montgomery Diary," *Liberation,* April 1956.

100   *Asa Earl Carter:* unless otherwise cited, in Anthony, "Resistance Groups" ("Biographies of Statewide and Significant Local Citizens Council Leaders"), int. Doug Carter, Spring 1984; telephone int. Louey Curry, April 15, 1994. Carter was rumored to have worked on *The Salt of the Earth,* the 1953 movie by the blacklisted Hollywood Ten director Herbert Biberman.

100   *"history we are making":* e.g., transcript of February 1955 broadcast on NCCJ, ASRA.

100   *Anti-Defamation League:* int. Roger Hanson, Dec. 8, 1987.

100   *denouncing the National Conference:* transcript, Feb. 21, 1955, ASRA.

100   *to devastate organized labor:* Mitchell, "White Citizens Councils"; Anthony, "Resistance Groups"; Corley, "Quest," p. 106; Hughes to Via, May 8, 1957, ACHR; *U.S. News & World Report,* April 6, 1956. For union leadership's concerns about the WCC, see union questionnaires (ca. 1956) in Emory Via Papers, SLA 1277.4.

101   *condemned the White Citizens Councils:* Gilliam, "Second Folsom," pp. 394–95.

101   *Big Mules recommissioned:* The Klansman on the industrialists' payroll (at a rumored $50 a day) was Elmer Bailey Brock, who had been instrumental in the Klan's 1946 revival as the Federated.

101   *Hanna announced:* Anthony, "Resistance Groups," pp. 2–3. "We've got to oppose integration in a lawful manner and we don't want a bunch of Ku Kluxers."

101   *Moseley banquet:* Mitchell, "White Citizens Councils," p. 22.

101   *read Carter out of the movement:* Anthony, "Resistance Groups," pp. 4, 9 and Appendix, p. 3; Gilliam, "Second Folsom," p. 372.

101   *"Number-One Do-Gooder"* and *"radical":* Frady, *Wallace,* pp. 96–98.

101   *"probably will be hostile":* ibid., p. 98.

102 *"How drunk?":* Benjamin Muse report, July 13, 1961, SRC.

102 *Folsom had deliberately abandoned Lucy:* G. Sims, *Little Man's,* pp. 181–82; Rowan, *Sorrow,* p. 170; Gilliam "Second Folsom," p. 309.

102 *"How far can I go":* Powell and Folsom in Grafton and Permaloff, *Big Mules,* p. 194; Gilliam, "Second Folsom," p. 287; *South* (formerly *Alabama*), Nov. 11, 1955; Gray, *Bus Ride,* pp. 42, 45.

102 *"recognize the Negro":* Grafton and Permaloff, *Big Mules,* pp. 57–58.

102 *"hard a lick":* "George C. Wallace, A Change in the Heart of Dixie," *MA* special section, Jan. 11, 1987, p. 10. He was the champion in 1937. This was the quote of a younger brother.

102 *began cussing Folsom:* Frady, *Wallace,* p. 109; G. Sims, *Little Man's,* pp. 207–208; Grafton and Permaloff, *Big Mules,* p. 194; Carter, *Wallace,* p. 85.

102 *begging Folsom to appoint him:* Frady, *Wallace,* p. 106.

102 *wartime service with Negroes:* Durr, *Magic Circle,* p. 315.

103 *Wallace was the featured speaker:* Norrell, "Labor Trouble," p. 252.

103 *organizational meeting:* *NYT Magazine,* Feb. 26, 1956; E. C. Clark, *Schoolhouse,* pp. 92–93; Norrell, "Labor Trouble," p. 252.

103 *members of the Lucy mob:* Helpfully, the union men wore red hats. Telephone int. Louey Curry, April 15, 1994; H. L. Mitchell, "The White Citizens Councils vs. Southern Trade Unions," March 12, 1956, SRC.

103 *White Citizens Council filled:* Carter, *Wallace,* p. 85.

103 *At the top of the list was Robert Chambliss:* statement of John A. Caddell, March 1, 1956, quoting NAACP complaint, CCJC; E. C. Clark, *Schoolhouse,* p. 79.

103 *motley defense table:* E. C. Clark, *Schoolhouse,* p. 105.

103 *conspiracy charge:* *NYT,* Feb. 14 and March 10, 1956; statement of John A. Caddell, March 1, 1956, CCJC; int. Hobart Grooms, March 1987; G. Sims, *Little Man's,* pp. 180–81; Rowan, *Sorrow,* p. 174; int. Constance Baker Motley, March 27, 1991.

103 *Grooms ordered the trustees:* *NYT,* March 1, 1956. She was to return to school by March 6.

103 *"baseless accusations":* *NYT,* March 10, 1956.

103 *filed suit against the NAACP:* E. C. Clark, *Schoolhouse,* p. 105.

103 *"filled with fear":* *BW,* Feb. 10, 1956.

103 *"never finish astonishing":* Paris office to Lukas, March 5, 1956, "Communal Issues Alabama," AJC.

104 *Eisenhower's refusal:* It was Judge Grooms who had divulged to the NAACP lawyers the staggering news: The Justice Department had informed him that President Eisenhower would not be sending in troops. Int. Constance Baker Motley, March 27, 1991.

104 *Eisenhower invited Hoover:* C. Hamilton, *Powell,* pp. 259–60; Powers, *Secrecy and Power,* pp. 329–31; O'Reilly, *"Racial Matters,"* pp. 41–42; Branch, *Parting,* p. 182.

104 *"massively overcome":* int. Fred Shuttlesworth, May 25, 1987.

105 *Bayard Rustin:* Anderson, *Rustin,* pp. 47, 51, 52, 54; Viorst, *Fire,* pp. 200–202; Branch, *Parting,* pp. 168–70; Isserman, *Hammer,* p. 131. Rustin's history with the Party remains somewhat murky.

105 *with A. Philip Randolph:* Viorst, *Fire,* pp. 22–23.

105 *Nixon . . . credited Randolph* and *"different type":* ibid., p. 22; Peck, *Freedom Ride,* p. 52.

105 *"George":* Kempton, *Part,* p. 242.

105 *Muste's Fellowship of Reconciliation:* Isserman, *Hammer,* pp. 128–32; Farmer, *Freedom—When?,* pp. 54–55.

105 *arrested for "copulating":* police report of incident reproduced in Albert C. "Buck" Persons, *The True Selma Story* (Birmingham: Esco, 1965), a pamphlet written on special assignment for Congressman Bill Dickinson of Montgomery in BPSF 7.1a.

105 *embrace the opposition:* Bayard Rustin, "Montgomery Diary," *Liberation,* April 1956.

105 *"Communistic rattlesnakes":* Eugene "Bull" Connor, "Birmingham Wars on Communism," *Alabama Local Government Journal,* August 1950. Rustin flippantly told the police that he was on assignment for *Le Figaro* of Paris or Britain's *Manchester Guardian.*

105 *press conference in New York:* *NYT,* March 2, 1956; int. Autherine Lucy Foster, March 16, 1992.

105 *driven to Detroit:* E. C. Clark, *Schoolhouse,* pp. 86–87.

105 *"damage and setback":* *BW,* March 2, 1956.

106 *"What do you mean?":* Senate Internal Security Subcommittee, "Scope of Soviet Activity in the United States," April 12, 1956, p. 765.

106 *faithful to leave:* see Scales, *Cause,* pp. 301–302.

106 *"the Baptist preacher":* int. Junius Scales, March 7, 1994; Scales, *Cause,* p. 304.

106 *"I didn't get in":* int. Jack O'Dell, Sept. 7, 1999.

106 *big lay supporters:* int. H. D. Coke, Nov. 5, 1990. Coke "didn't have enough sense," he would say sardonically, to fear and loathe Communists.

107 *Smith Act indictments:* O'Reilly, *"Racial Matters,"* p. 153; Abt, *Advocate,* p. 150.

107 *Jackson would be saved:* int. Esther Cooper Jackson, Dec. 18, 1990; int. James Jackson, Dec. 20, 1990.

107 *asked him to come work for him:* int. Jack O'Dell, March 16, 1993.

107 *Phenix City Alabama,* Dec. 17, 1954; *MA,* April 12, 1987; Gilliam, "Second Folsom," p. 87.

107 *tolerated the Communists:* Thurgood Marshall oral history, COH, pp. 53–54.

107 *Mason ring:* ibid., pp. 184–85, 146–47.

108 *legal hook:* This was borrowed from a similar suit filed in Louisiana a bit earlier. Gilliam, "Second Folsom," pp. 425–26.

108 *presided over the indictments: Alabama,* Dec. 17, 1954.

108 *ordered the NAACP:* Cochran, "Shores," pp. 87–89; *BPH,* July 26, 1956; Carter, *Wallace,* p. 92; Gilliam, "Second Folsom," pp. 427–28.

108 *the entire South followed:* Gilliam, "Second Folsom," p. 433; Murphy, "The South Counterattacks: The Anti-NAACP Laws," *Western Political Quarterly,* June 12, 1959.

108 *met to discuss their options:* origins of new organization in Clarke, *These Rights,* Appendix; ints. Fred Shuttlesworth; Shuttlesworth oral history, KC. A number of ministers discouraged him, and Shores again laid out the legal penalties.

109 *Jackson's church:* Its pastor, R. L. Alford, had driven Autherine Lucy to the University of Alabama for her first day of classes but had urged Shuttlesworth to back off this particular folly. *BW,* Jan. 6 and Feb. 10, 1956; Emory O. Jackson oral history, MSOH, p. 14.

109 *model established in Montgomery* and *Negroes of Tallahassee:* Clarke, *These Rights,* Appendix, p. 139.

110 *One of the old-guard ministers:* int. Fred Shuttlesworth, May 4, 1989.

110 *"believe in integration":* BN, June 6, 1956.

110 *"NAACP's work":* Eskew, "ACM," p. 8.

4. Rehearsal: 1956–1959

111 *Time's 1956 Man of the Year:* Manchester, *Glory,* p. 947. This was Harlow Curtice.

111 *Kant and Hegel: NYT,* March 21 and Dec. 22, 1956.

111 *"Hell, Nay":* ints. Fred Shuttlesworth.

111 *Two-thirds of the members:* Clarke, *These Rights,* Appendix, pp. 163–73.

112 *"almost taboo":* ibid., p. 146.

112 *one-half of one percent:* ibid., p. 173.

112 *"don't say nothing good":* int. Fred Shuttlesworth, March 26, 1989.

112 *meeting of the "Ware group":* ibid.

113 *set back race relations:* See Ambrose, *Eisenhower,* p. 327.

113 *"God Almighty":* C. S. King, *My Life,* p. 142; M. L. King, *Stride,* p. 160.

113 *"All that walking":* Wofford, *Kennedys,* p. 119.

113 *Through a prepared statement:* int. Fred Shuttlesworth, May 4, 1989. See Shuttlesworth to city commissioners, Dec. 20, 1956, *BWC* 1.1.

113 *"whatever action is necessary": NYT,* Dec. 21, 1956.

113 *"you are Dr. King":* C. S. King, *My Life,* p. 147.

114 *gas station:* Birmingham City Directory, 1954; City Directory, 1956 and 1957. He switched to selling ads for WBRC.

114 *FBI started to keep track:* Nunnelly, *Connor,* p. 51.

114 *Jim Simpson had never:* int. Florence Evans Simpson, March 22, 1989.

114 *single-name invocation:* See Newman to the commission, July 18, 1956, JM 24.32.

114 *Fred Jr. strutted:* Fred Shuttlesworth Jr. oral history in Levine, *Freedom's Children,* p. 8.

114 *six sticks of dynamite:* Eddy to Beck memo on "Bapbomb Confidential Informers Information," Aug. 15, 1977, and "Confidential-Source Material," Sept. 23, 1977, JY; Shanahan to SAC, July 16, 1964, p. 5, Bapbomb. Holt, Thompson, Chambliss are handwritten on FBI Summary of Bombing Incidents, p. 8, Bapbomb.

114 *They exploded:* ints. Fred Shuttlesworth; Shuttlesworth statement to Civil Rights Commission, Spring 1961, FS 4; police "Report of Injury—Bombing," Dec. 26, 1956, BPSF 9.1; *BW,* Dec. 29, 1956; *BN,* Dec. 26, 1956; Fred Shuttlesworth oral history, MSOH, p. 17; James Roberson and Fred Shuttlesworth Jr. oral histories in Levine, *Freedom's Children,* pp. 6–8. Manis, *Fire,* p. 110, has conversation with the policeman taking place inside the house.

115 *"Is he dead?":* int. Edward Gardner, Oct. 7, 1983.

115 *"blown into history":* Fred Shuttlesworth oral history, MSOH, p. 17.

115 *borrowed suit* and *"going to put you in jail":* int. Edward Gardner, Oct. 7, 1983.

115 *two hundred potential bus riders: BW,* Dec. 29, 1956.

116 *ride would take place:* Shuttlesworth had said so in his original announcement. *NYT,* Dec. 24, 1956.

116 *"Boys step back":* int. James Armstrong, Oct. 3, 1983.

116 *boarded the bus:* Clarke, *These Rights,* Appendix, p. 150; ints. Fred Shuttlesworth; int. James Armstrong, Oct. 3, 1983; *BW,* Dec. 29, 1956.

116 *city craftily changed the charges: BW,* Jan. 5, 1957.

116 *twenty-one southern cities: BPH,* Jan. 7, 1957.

116 *"fight is on": Jet,* Jan. 10, 1957.

116 *He had pushed the Movement:* The only mass direct-action precedent for Shuttlesworth's action that I can find was an ambiguous integrated bus ride in New Orleans by seventy-two black college students in January 1956. Because they were coming home from a basketball game when one of them removed the "For Colored Only" wooden partition, it isn't clear whether the mass arrests fell under the category of college prank or meditated direct action. In 1946 there had been, also in New Orleans, a mass arrest of twenty-five black front-of-the-bus riders en route home from a baseball game. *PC,* Jan. 14, 1956.

117 *completely indigenous:* Garrow, *Bearing,* p. 72.

117 *monthly brainstorming sessions:* telephone int. Joseph Lowery, September 1990; Lowery oral history, MSOH, p. 2; ints. Fred Shuttlesworth. Lowery had been agitating against the "Mobile plan" that the MIA was asking for.

117 *distaste for Baptist ministers:* ibid., p. 8.

117 *Stanley Levison:* Garrow, *FBI,* pp. 26–43. By 1957, Levison had been deleted from the FBI's list of "key figures."

117 *Depression contacts with Communists:* Ella Baker oral history, MSOH, p. 47.

117 *their confab:* Rustin, Levinson, and Baker meeting in Morris, *Origins,* p. 83; Fairclough, *Redeem,* pp. 30–32. Nearly a year earlier, the three had been moved by the lynching of Emmett Till (the previous summer) to form a group called In Friendship to raise money for "victims of racial terror."

117 *passive enough to be guided:* Rustin to King, April 15, 1960, Rustin and Levison to King, undated four-page briefing, BUK I.29; Wofford, *Kennedys,* p. 115.

117 *To prod King into action:* When King came to Birmingham on New Year's Day to make the Emancipation Day speech at the Sixteenth Street Baptist Church (*BW,* Jan. 5, 1957), Rustin had Shuttlesworth force his hand into issuing

the call for Rustin's first meeting of southern activists. Rustin had first asked C. K. Steele—the Tallahassee minister whose seven-month Montgomery-inspired bus boycott had ended inconclusively after the Supreme Court ruling—to call the meeting, but Steele said the initiative should come from King (Fairclough, *Redeem,* p. 32; Morris, *Origins,* p. 83). The first meeting of Rustin's southern preachers—some sixty, including a few laymen—was at Martin Luther King Sr.'s Ebenezer Baptist Church in Atlanta on January 10 and 11 (Garrow, *Bearing,* p. 85; Morris, *Origins,* p. 84; Fairclough, *Redeem,* p. 32).

117 *developed a stutter:* Fred Shuttlesworth Jr. oral history in Levine, *Freedom's Children,* p. 8.

117 *"get myself killed":* ints. Fred Shuttlesworth.

117 *"Let the people see":* [Braden], *People,* unpaginated.

117 *desegregate the white waiting room: BN,* March 7, 1956; *BPH,* March 7, 1956; ints. Fred Shuttlesworth. They were taking up the cause of Carl and Alexina (spelled variously in news accounts as Alexinia and Alezinia) Baldwin, arrested in December for sitting—with what end in mind was unclear—in the white waiting room. *BW,* Dec. 29, 1956; *NYT,* Jan. 26, 1957.

118 *Lamar Weaver:* Nichols, " 'Cities Are,' " p. 99; Nunnelly, *Connor,* p. 52; ints. Fred Shuttlesworth.

118 *the three men: BN,* April 7, 1989 (picture reprinted); int. Fred Shuttlesworth, March 28, 1991.

118 *"man of high morals":* Eskew, "ACM," p. 29. The commissioner's policemen made no attempt to apprehend Weaver's assailants, despite the *Post-Herald*'s page-one shot of them rocking his convertible.

118 *bomb exploded on New Year's Eve:* FBI int. with Connie V. Russo, Jan. 31, 1966, Bapbomb; list of bombings in "South Center St., Misc.", Box 2, BPSF; FBI Summary of Bombing Incidents, Bapbomb; *BN,* Jan. 1, 1957.

118 *in April, two more houses:* Oscar Hyde list of bombings, Box 2, BPS; FBI int. with George Dickerson, Dec. 16, 1965, Shanahan to SAC, July 16, 1964, p. 6, and Summary of Bombing Incidents, all in Bapbomb. The two houses, sold that spring to a black pastor and a rising entrepreneur, were bombed at ten-thirty on the night of April 10. The newspapers did not report these bombings.

118 *Chambliss was boasting:* Chambliss trial transcript, p. 603.

118 *the Georgia Klan he headed:* Klan HUAC report, pp. 11–12; Wade, *Fiery,* pp. 304–305.

118 *klavern voted to withdraw:* FBI int. with Morris Dixon, June 7, 1965, Bapbomb.

118 *Troy Ingram:* int. Edith Ingram Isbell Smith, March 23, 1993, and telephone conversation, July 11, 1993; conversation with Mary Ingram, March 23, 1993.

119 *summer of 1934:* NLRB report; int. Edith Ingram Isbell Smith, March 23, 1993. Sam Ingram was ordered to patrol the camp with a high-powered rifle and a shotgun, and to "shoot the hell out of" any union representatives.

119 *voted to join:* NLRB report; Taft, *Dixie,* p. 146.

119 *Sam was not bitter:* telephone conversation with Edith Ingram Isbell Smith, July 11, 1993. The federal Coal Labor Board would rule that the mine had been closed illegally. NLRB report; *BP,* Dec. 19, 1934.

119 *sued DeBardeleben, returned to Overton: SW,* February 1936.

119 *Angelo Herndon's first:* Herndon, "You Cannot Kill the Working Class," in Grant, *Protest,* pp. 229–30.

119 *Ingram's transformation:* Ingram worked amicably with Negroes in his wagon mine, and paid them the same wages as the white miners. Telephone conversation with Edith Ingram Isbell Smith, July 11, 1993.

120 *"Shorty" Thompson:* conversation with Earl Thompson, Sept. 16, 1993; FBI ints. with Earl Thompson, May 24, 1961, and with Walter Purvis, Nov. 14, 1963, Bapbomb.

120 *Thompson as the driver:* Eddy to Beck memo on "Bapbomb Confidential Informers Information," Aug. 15, 1977, and "Confidential-Source Material," Sept. 23, 1977, JY; Shanahan to SAC, July 16, 1964, p. 5, Bapbomb. This information was apparently relayed to the FBI from Flora Chambliss through her sister.

120 *"I wasn't guilty":* telephone int. Earl Thompson, Oct. 25, 2000.

120 *"higher-type individual":* FBI int. with Morris Dixon, June 7, 1965, Bapbomb.

120 *"put the persuasion":* int. Fred Shuttlesworth, April 9, 1991. Rustin had brought King to the Gaston Motel to meet with him. Shuttlesworth remembers that A. Philip Randolph was at the meeting. Shuttlesworth had named a May date, saying, "Martin, the only time I can participate is May, so I guess that's when it'll have to be."

121 *Prayer Pilgrimage:* Garrow, *Bearing,* pp. 90–94; Branch, *Parting,* pp. 217–18; Fairclough, *Redeem,* p. 40.

121 *"glad to be alive":* Pilgrimage program and Shuttlesworth speech, FS 4.

121 *"Fortress Segregation":* Shuttlesworth to King, July 27, 1957, BUK 71A.9A.2.

121 *"tagged as 'Red' ":* Ella Baker oral history, MSOH, p. 23.

121 *when she covered:* Anne Braden oral history, COH, pp. 2–17. The article appeared on page one, without a byline. *BN,* Jan. 23, 1946.

122 *Aubrey Williams:* Salmond, *Rebel,* pp. 4–5, 8–10, 83, 170–71.

122 *"most important thing":* ibid., p. 253.

122 *use Fred Shuttlesworth:* Reed, "SCHW," pp. 327–28; Anne Braden interview, COH; ints. Fred Shuttlesworth.

122 *favorite red-bait:* Salmond, *Rebel,* pp. 253, 261; O'Reilly, *"Racial Matters,"* p. 104.

122 *Communist, Abner Berry:* Naison, *Communists,* p. 135; Isserman, *Hammer,* p. 223.

123 *just "passing through":* Myles Horton oral history in Raines, *My Soul,* p. 397. This is a somewhat disingenuous account on Horton's part.

123 *exposé pamphlet,* Highlander Folk School, *billboards:* A copy of this is in BPSF 6.16; Adams, *Unearthing,* pp. 124–26. Adams says 250,000 were printed.

123 *Braden gave King a ride:* Garrow, *Bearing,* p. 98. Myles Horton's wife, Zilphia, had first heard the song in 1946 on a picket line of striking South Carolina tobacco workers. Horton, *Haul,* p. 158; Adams, *Unearthing,* p. 89.

123 *"the old class split":* quoted in Garrow, *Bearing,* p. 101.

123 *Nixon, had written* and *Parks had taken a job:* Branch, *Parting,* p. 200; Garrow, *Bearing,* pp. 95, 99. Although King refused to accept the resignation, Nixon had all but washed his hands of King's movement.

123 *"worst things I've done":* Newman, *Black,* p. 440.

124 *Ku Klux Klan of the Confederacy:* J. B. Martin, "Deep South," June 29, 1957; *BN,* Jan. 28, 1957; telephone int. Louey Curry, April 15, 1994; *Jet,* Nov. 15, 1956.

124 *not merely mean but "weird":* int. R. B. Jones, July 14, 1996.

124　*Carter's lieutenant: The Southerner,* September–October 1957.

124　*assault on Nat King Cole: BPH,* April 11 and 12, 1956.

124　*special order of business:* Klan castration, *BPH,* Oct. 8 and 30, and Nov. 6, 1957, and *BN,* Oct. 31 and Nov. 6, 1957, and Feb. 19, 1958, in Klan vertical file, TCSH; Corley, "Quest," p. 30; *Jet,* May 16, 1963; William Bradford Huie, "A Ritual 'Cutting' by the Ku Klux Klan," *True,* 1964, in DV.

126　*"hoodlumism in racial difficulties": BN,* May 2, 1957.

126　*steel, was in crisis:* Frank C. Porter, "Steel's Long, Deep Sleep," *The New Republic,* Jan. 5, 1963, pp. 13–16.

126　*U.S. Steel's local president (Art Wiebel) at Rotary: BN,* May 1, 1957.

127　*Lawyers from the NAACP immediately understood:* int. Constance Baker Motley, March 27, 1991.

127　*at Little Rock:* Harry S. Ashmore, *Hearts and Minds* (New York: McGraw-Hill, 1982), pp. 92–95; Billy Bowles and Remer Tyson, *They Love a Man* (Atlanta: Peachtree, 1989), pp. 191, 195–96.

127　*"foolish to decide":* Corley, "Quest," p. 137. Predictably, four of the original petitioners had dropped out.

127　*filibuster of twenty-four hours:* Cohodas, *Thurmond,* pp. 294–95.

127　*101st Airborne:* Ambrose, *Eisenhower,* pp. 417–20.

127　*lunged at Shuttlesworth: BN,* Sept. 9, 1957; *BPH,* Sept. 10, 1957; ints. Fred Shuttlesworth; Ricky Shuttlesworth oral history in Levine, *Freedom's Children,* pp. 43–44; *CD,* Sept. 28, 1957; film clip of attack in, e.g., Spike Lee's documentary, *4 Little Girls.*

128　*"moved as if by prearranged plan": BN,* Sept. 9, 1957.

128　*they never spoke* and *"Don't run the stop sign":* Ricky Shuttlesworth oral history in Levine, *Freedom's Children,* pp. 46, 44.

128　*At University hospital:* ints. Fred Shuttlesworth. This account differs from that in MSOH, pp. 24–25.

128　*heard the Lord:* Fred Shuttlesworth oral history, KC.

128　*"lead God's army": BPH,* Sept. 10, 1957.

128　*pulse and blood pressure normal:* int. James Montgomery, Dec. 4, 1987.

128　*forgave his attackers:* Shuttlesworth oral history, KC.

128　*"I shall be dead":* Nichols, " 'Cities Are,' " p. 100.

129　*a steelworker named Ivey Ford Gauldin: BPH,* Sept. 10, 1957; FBI ints. with Ivey Ford Gauldin, Oct. 29, 1963, and with Ellie T. Rouse, Oct. 18, 1963, Bapbomb.

129　*Ingram resigned:* FBI ints. with Troy Ingram, Nov. 15, 17, and 24, 1963, Bapbomb; FBI int. with Ingram, May 23, 1961, Freebus; FBI ints. with Jack Junior Howard, Nov. 21, 1963, with Elmer Bailey Brock, Dec. 30, 1965, and with Alexander Jackson Nelson, Nov. 22, 1963, Bapbomb. Several other charter members of the Alabama Knights resigned.

129　*two separate bombs:* FBI Summary of Bombing Incidents, pp. 10–11, and FBI int. with Elmer Bailey Brock, Dec. 30, 1965, Bapbomb.

129　*ordered them to fix:* Sasser to city commission, Dec. 30, 1957, JM 24.29.

130　*"suspicious quiet":* Emory Via's report on trip to Birmingham, April 2–4, 1958, SRC.

130　*upheld the state's masterly Pupil Placement Law: BN,* June 3, 1958.

130　*"I'm not gonna promise": BN,* June 3 and 4, 1958; ints. Fred Shuttlesworth.

131　*runoff between George Wallace:* Frady, *Wallace,* pp. 119, 125; Carter, *Wallace,* p. 91; Taylor, *Me 'n' George,* p. 13; "George C. Wallace, A Change in the Heart of Dixie," *MA,* special section, Jan. 11, 1987; *NYT,* June 4, 1958; Hughes to Fleming, Aug. 28, 1959, ACHR.

131　*vote for "the lesser evil":* int. Fred Shuttlesworth, June 21, 1991.

131　*"bald spot creeping": New York Post,* ca. May 23–24, 1961, reprinted in *Negro Digest,* September 1961.

131　*courted the support:* Lesher, *Wallace,* p. 124.

131　*banning black school marching bands: NYT,* Jan. 20, 1959.

131　*"if he had won":* Frady, *Wallace,* p. 126.

131　*working-class voters of Birmingham:* Norrell, "Labor Trouble," p. 262. AFL-CIO didn't officially endorse, but recommended four candidates, including Wallace and excluding Patterson.

131　*"like a hermit"* and *"out-niggubed again":* Frady, *Wallace,* p. 127. Wallace denied having made this statement, his most infamous quotation. See Lesher, *Wallace,* p. 129. But Carter, *Wallace,* p. 96, provides documentation.

132　*fifty-four sticks of dynamite:* FBI Summary of Bombing Incidents, Bapbomb; police memo on bombing attempt, July 17, 1958, pp. 1, 16; "Jewish Temple Bombing," Aug. 28, 1958; Moore to Hoover, May 15, 1958, all in BPSF.

132　*"We have just blown up": BN,* May 1, 1958.

132　*orchestrated regional bombing campaign, Southern Conference:* e.g., Birmingham police memo, "Investigation of Attempt [*sic*] Bombing on Temple Bethel," July 17, 1958, and T. E. Lindsey memo, May 6, 1958, on Charlotte attempt, in Box 1, BPSF.

132　*on a list* and *"clerical error":* Epstein to Connor, May 1957, Box 1, BPSF.

132　*On May 8:* Connor-Morris-Stoner transaction, Birmingham police investigative files on the case, Box 1, BPSF, and the state investigative file on the case, courtesy of John Yung, the state's attorney who successfully prosecuted Stoner in 1980.

132　*spent sixty-seven days in jail:* See *BN,* Sept. 21, 24, 25, and 26, 1949.

132　*Morris told Connor:* various memos in the files, including (from Box 1, BPSF) Eddy to Beck, Aug. 30, 1977, reporting on FBI file on Bethel Baptist bombing; Police memo, July 17, 1958; "Statement of Mr. X" (Hugh Morris), July 14, 1958, "Statement of Eugene 'Bull' Connor," July 15, 1958, and (in JY) "William Hugh Morris." Morris was sure that J. B. Stoner had lit the fuse himself in Florida.

133　*scrupulous about not abusing:* Eddy to Yung, Jan. 21, 1980, re ints. with Duggan D. Weaver and with Mable Thompson, JY.

133　*law degree:* He had passed the Georgia bar the year *before* finishing law school in 1952, but practiced for only a year.

133　*"pray for me":* Stoner trial transcript, p. 165.

133　*original price* and *discount bulk rate:* police memo, July 17, 1958, p. 17, Box 1, BPSF. When Morris came back to Connor with the price, the commissioner took the evidence to District Attorney Walter Emmett Perry. The seasoned prosecutor was unimpressed. "There was no crime," he pointed out, "and even if there was it would border on entrapment." Nonetheless, Connor proceeded with his scheme. Eddy to Beck, Aug. 30, 1977, Box 1, BPSF.

133   *June 21, Stoner met . . . parking lot:* Stoner trial transcript, pp. 222–28. Rather than let Stoner bring up the money, one of the detectives, Captain G. L. Pattie, quoted the $2,000 figure Morris had told him was Stoner's price—a big gaffe, it seemed, for law enforcement professionals who had already been warned about entrapment.

133   *Bull Connor and his buddy Clarence Kelley:* int. Maurice House, Spring 1985; int. Tom Cook, March 1985.

133   *Two more FBI agents:* Stoner trial transcript, pp. 235–36; int. Jamie Moore, Dec. 9, 1987.

133   *proposed to Stoner that he assassinate:* statement by G. L. Pattie ("Interview on Saturday, June 21, 1958, with Mr. 'S' "), Box 1, BPSF. It is clear from this contemporary memo that the two detectives, Pattie and Sergeant Tom Cook, broached the subject of assassinating Shuttlesworth; Cook's testimony in the trial differs from it in several self-serving ways. Pattie told Stoner point-blank that if blowing up Shuttlesworth's church didn't run him out of town, "our group would be willing to go further with another job that would eliminate Reverend Shuttlesworth completely." Stoner replied that he had some people who set bombs and some who "would do other type of work, but I could arrange either or both type of jobs." Stoner would say that, in that second meeting, after the Shuttlesworth church had been bombed, the detectives offered him $5,000 to $10,000 to have Shuttlesworth murdered.

Both Pattie and Cook's undercover conversations with Stoner—before and after the bombing—had been conducted under heavy surveillance monitored by experts. The chances of two out of two failures on a relatively unsophisticated assignment seem remote. It seems far more likely that the tapes were destroyed because of the incriminating material they contained about Connor and his police force.

134   *"nonviolent Winchesters":* Shuttlesworth to Connor, Aug. 9, 1958, JM 24.29.

134   *O'Dell volunteered:* int. Jack O'Dell, March 16, 1993. O'Dell's company had moved him to Montgomery in the spring of 1957, and he had recently left Alabama altogether.

134   *Richard Bowling:* "Thomas H. Cook (1958), p. 7, and Bowling rap sheet, JY; FBI Summary of Bombing Incidents, p. 12, Bapbomb.

134   *church's east wall:* E. H. Cantrell int. with Stone Johnson, Sept. 30, 1977, Box 1, BPSF; Stoner trial transcript, pp. 159–212; "Thomas H. Cook" (1958)," JY.

134   *guards, Will Hall:* George Stoney int. with Arthur Shores, "Field Notes for Southern Trip," November 1939, pp. 41, 50, RB 34.3; petition to Personnel Board of Jefferson County, June 24, 1939, RB 34.1; Cochran, "Shores," pp. 38–41; int. Arthur Shores, May 20, 1991.

134   *"Bull's record had preceded him":* int. E. C. "Bud" Watson, Dec. 7, 1987; Bull Connor statement, July 16, 1958, JY; int. Tom Cook, March 1985.

135   *miming dynamiters:* Shuttlesworth statement to Civil Rights Commission, Spring 1961, FS 4.

135   *Shuttlesworth wrote to the FBI:* Shuttlesworth to Connor, Aug. 9, 1958, JM 24.29. This letter detailing complaints against police was delivered to the FBI.

135   *close relations:* int. Maurice House, Spring 1985; int. Tom Cook, March 1985.

135   *"hold contacts with Connor":* Nunnelly, *Connor,* p. 79.

135   *to become SCLC's acting director* and quotes: Ella Baker oral history, MSOH, pp. 19, 37.

135   Stride Toward Freedom: A scholar would discover in the 1970s that sizable chunks of it had been lifted without credit from two books King had been assigned at seminary. Garrow, *Bearing,* p. 112.

135   *bus desegregation suit:* int. Arthur Shores, May 20, 1991; *AA,* Nov. 8, 1958.

135   *minted an ordinance:* Simpson to Willis, Oct. 15, 1958, and Willis to Simpson, Oct. 17, 1958, JM 17.38. It was passed on October 14.

136   *refused to let his children off:* Fred Shuttlesworth oral history, MSOH, p. 37.

136   *On Monday, October 20:* bus protest, *AA,* Nov. 1 and 8, 1955; *BN,* Oct. 21, p. 158.

136   *"to show 'Bull' ":* Clarke, *These Rights,* Appendix, p. 151.

136   *"commit suicide":* *BN,* Oct. 21, 1958.

136   *in silent prayer:* Hughes to Routh, Oct. 29, 1958, ACHR; *AA,* Nov. 1, 1958; [Braden] *They Challenge.*

136   *Tipped off by a wiretap:* Fred Shuttlesworth oral history, KC, side 3. Shuttlesworth's phone would ring even when it was off the hook.

136   *took the Montgomery men to headquarters:* Hughes to Routh, Oct. 29, 1958, and Hughes to Leadership Personnel, Nov. 6, 1958, ACHR.

136   *J. L. Ware:* *AA,* Nov. 22, 1958.

136   *little planning:* Glenn Smiley memo, "Birmingham and Its Recent Protest," Nov. 18, 1958, FOR.

136   *first national outcry:* James B. Carey, head of Electrical Radio and Machine Workers International, to Morgan, Oct. 30,1958; Patrick Murphy Malin, executive director of ACLU, to Morgan, Oct. 30, 1958; and Walter Reuther, President of UAW, to Morgan, Nov. 11, 1958, all in JM 25.1.

136   *to send telegrams:* King telegram to Carey, Oct. 30, 1958, SRC.

136   *"Your wise restraint":* King to Shuttlesworth, undated, BUK 71.2-3-4.

137   *King asked Glenn Smiley:* int. Glenn Smiley, April 26, 1989; *Fellowship,* November/December 1993.

137   *"shiny, new,":* *AA,* Nov. 22, 1958.

137   *Smiley was less enamored* and *"afraid of neither man nor devil":* ints. Glenn Smiley, April 26 and September 1989; Morris, *Origins,* p. 72.

137   *some doubt:* Smiley to Gussner, Nov. 10, 1958, FOR.

137   *imposing a blackout* and *"assisting in the bus boycott":* Hughes to Routh, Dec. 1, 1958, ACHR.

137   *detectives had started to attend:* *AA,* Nov. 22, 1958; Shuttlesworth and Smith to Commissioners, Dec. 1, 1958, FS 1.

137   *"fire we got here":* Shuttlesworth oral history, KC, side 3.

137   *walk in dignity:* int. Calvin Woods, July 15, 1987; Clarke, *These Rights,* Appendix, p. 142.

137   *Billups, was arrested:* *BPH,* Dec. 2, 1958.

137   *Ware went back to carping:* Hughes to Via, Dec. 1, 1958, ACHR.

137   *"Only God can tell me":* *PC,* Dec. 12, 1958.

138   *When William Rogers ordered:* *NYT,* Nov. 14, 1958; *Time,* Dec. 15, 1958.

138   *"Damn the law": AA,* Nov. 22, 1958. He also vowed to collect the $150 fine if Glen Taylor ever came back.
138   *Court upheld:* statement of Connor, Nov. 24, 1958, JM 24.29; Bartley, *Resistance,* pp. 290–92; Corley, "Quest," pp. 140–41.
138   *"generations, not years":* quoted in Corley, "Quest," pp. 140–41.
138   *"courageous leader, but devoid":* Smiley to Gussner, Nov. 10, 1958, FOR.
138   *"different drummer"* and *"craved publicity,":* ints. Glenn Smiley, April 26 and 27, and September 1989.
139   *"We are all neurotic":* int. Glenn Smiley, April 27, 1989.
139   *"runoff" fee:* police memo, Oct. 23, 1961, mass meeting, BC.
139   *Shuttlesworth accused Shores:* Clarke, *These Rights,* Appendix, pp. 153, 146.
139   *"good close friend":* int. Arthur Shores, May 20, 1991; Shores's daughter informed me that he was suffering from Alzheimer's disease, although nothing he said contradicted my research. In an interview conducted in the 1970s, Shores told Lee Bains, "We [Connor and Shores] had a pretty good relationship." Lee Bains int. with Shores, courtesy of Bains. "Arthur and Bull were friends," Orzell Billingsley told me (July 18, 1987). Connor had left standing instructions at the city jail to release any of Shores's clients on his signature, without bond (Cochran, "Shores," p. 112) "Arthur Shores is the nigra that I fear most," Connor said. "He's a smart nigra and he is honest." Lee Bains int. with E. C. Overton, courtesy of Bains.
139   *"glorified after-dinner speaker":* Branch, *Parting,* p. 250.
139   *Baker, who had now grown close to Shuttlesworth:* int. Fred Shuttlesworth, March 28, 1991.
139   *"cult of personality":* Fairclough, *Redeem,* p. 50. See Ella Baker oral history, MSOH, pp. 16, 17, 37–38, and Robert Terrell, "Discarding the Dream," *Evergreen,* May 1970, p. 72.
139   *Randolph had singled out Stanley Levison:* Branch, *Parting,* pp. 256–57; Garrow, *Bearing,* p. 117.
140   *SNYC membership of Dr. Charles Gomillion:* Thompson, "History of the Alabama Council," pp. 90, 92.
140   *But O'Dell had begun to sense:* int. Jack O'Dell, March 16, 1993.
140   *raised only around $25,000:* Garrow, *Bearing,* p. 121; King disputed this figure.
140   *"flowery speeches":* Shuttlesworth to King, April 24, 1959, BUK 71.2-3-4.
140   *Shuttlesworth began to promote:* "Dear Friend" letter from Shuttlesworth, with pamphlet, Nov. 30, 1959, BUK 71A.9B.
140   *Communist press covered: People's World,* Aug. 15, 1959, in police dossier on Shuttlesworth, Oct. 1961, BPSF 9.17.
141   *segregationist lay Methodist group: Alabama,* Dec. 24, 1954; *BN,* Dec. 14, 1954, May 12, 1955, and March 15, 1959; Corley, "Quest," p. 180.
141   *MLU would prompt: BPH* and *BN,* March 20, 1959; Corley, "Quest," p. 181.
141   *epicenter of "Christian" racism: NYT,* July 7, 1959.
141   *"big voice": Time,* Dec. 15, 1958.
141   *A strange scene occurred: BPH,* March 21, 1959; Carter, *Wallace,* p. 168. Connor explained to a friend at the meeting that Chambliss had been picked up for investigation after one of the bombings.
141   *Klan posted "Welcome" signs:* Hughes to Fleming, Aug. 28, 1959, ACHR.

5. Breaking Out

149   *B. Elton Cox:* State Freedom Rider investigation, p. 173.
149   *sat down at the lunch counter:* Cagin and Dray, *Afraid,* pp. 57–60; Morris, *Origins,* p. 99; Williams, *Eyes,* p. 127.
149   *Shuttlesworth was knocked out:* int. Fred Shuttlesworth, March 28, 1991.
150   *called the person, "You must tell Martin,"* and *"the new dimension":* ibid.; Shuttlesworth oral history, KC, side 5; Shuttlesworth oral history, MSOH, p. 33; Morris, *Origins,* p. 201.
150   *not some spontaneous plague:* See Viorst, *Fire,* p. 107; Williams, *Eyes,* p. 127; Cagin and Dray, *Afraid,* p. 57. Between 1957 and 1960 students in various partnerships with the NAACP, the Fellowship of Reconciliation, and its off-shoot CORE, and in one instance an SCLC affiliate had staged token sit-ins at segregated department-store lunch counters in sixteen mostly border-state cities.
150   *was the daughter* and *activist, Francis Grandison:* int. James Jackson, March 27, 1991.
150   *to report ecstatically:* State Freedom Rider investigation, p. 19.
150   *"Pardon me":* James E. Jackson oral history for Hatch-Billops Collection, April 5, 1992.
150   *On February 25:* George McMillan, "Racial Violence & Law Enforcement," Southern Regional Council, undated, in "Racial File," BC 9.16; *BN,* Feb. 26, 1960.
150   *and was charmed* and *will "John L" Hall:* ints. Fred Shuttlesworth.
151   *felony tax evasion:* Gray, *Bus Ride,* pp. 150–52; Branch, *Parting,* p. 269; Garrow, *Bearing,* p. 129.
151   *Moore got a clear shot:* int. Charles Moore, April 28, 1992; C. Moore, *Powerful,* p. 25.
151   *"not permit organized":* press release, Feb. 26, 1960, BC.
151   *four-year black college:* E. J. Kahn, "A Whale of a Difference," *The New Yorker,* April 10, 1971.
151   *college president, W. A. Bell:* Richards, "Youth Congress," pp. 61, 74, 187.
151   *"Negro betterment":* int. Jesse Walker, April 2, 1991.
151   *leader was Tommy Reeves:* int. David Vann, May 28, 1984; int. Henry King Stanford, Jan. 18, 1988; *BPH,* March 20, 1959; *BN,* March 22, 1959; Corley, "Quest," p. 181.
152   *with more spiritual verve:* int. Jesse Walker, April 2, 1991; Hughes to Fleming, March 2, 1960, ACHR.
152   *Hill, was fueling up: BN,* Feb. 29, 1960.
152   *"The Law of God": BN,* March 1, 1960; Hughes to Fleming, March 2, 1960, ACHR; leaflet also in BC 6.14.
152   *Shuttlesworth was there to greet them:* ints. Fred Shuttlesworth; int. Jesse Walker, April 2, 1991.
152   *"Signal 31-Green":* Jamie Moore to "all members of the police department," Feb. 26, 1960, BC 5.26.
152   *took them to headquarters:* Wall to Moore, Feb. 29, 1960, BC 6.14; *BN,* March 1, 1960; "Mob violence at a Bessemer, Alabama home," IC.
152   *433 firemen for riot training:* Alabama Council quarterly report, March–May 1960, ACHR.
152   *first dog cop:* Palmore to Connor, Feb. 26, 1960, BC 5.29.
152   *led half the Alabama State student body: BN,* March 1, 1960; Branch, *Parting,* p. 283.

153 *"a million dollars' worth"*: int. Fred Shuttlesworth, March 28, 1991.
153 *"not a dictator"*: Fred Shuttlesworth oral history, KC, side 7.
153 *Jug Jones had been beaten:* "Mob violence at a Bessemer, Alabama home," IC; *NYT,* April 12, 1960 (Harrison Salisbury's account, which is considerably more lurid); *BW,* April 2, 1960.
153 *did not object:* Branch, *Parting,* p. 286.
153 *In a private meeting:* int. Jesse Walker, April 2, 1991.
153 *"necessary tonic"* and *"firemen and fire hoses, and even dogs"*: press release, March 30, 1960, FS 1.
153 *Charles Billups:* "Who Speaks for Birmingham?" p. 18; program for Billups's funeral, FS 1; ints. Fred Shuttlesworth.
154 *Billups had been in the news:* BPH, Dec. 2, 1958.
154 *beat him numb:* ints. Fred Shuttlesworth; police memo, "Re: Beating of Charles Billups, BM," April 10, 1959, BC 2.22; James M. Lawson Jr., "The Man Who Escaped the Cross," *Fellowship,* November 1959; int. Glenn Smiley, April 26, 1989.
154 *the next morning: James Gober et al.* v. *City of Birmingham,* p. 374; *Shuttlesworth* v. *City of Birmingham;* Document no. 4, April 8, 1960, IC; Shuttlesworth's statement to Civil Rights Commission, FS 4; *BW,* April 2, 1960.
154 *"transformed the jail"*: King to Shuttlesworth, April 4, 1960, BUK 71A.9B.
155 *drove up to Kidd's house:* ints. C. Herbert Oliver, Jan. 13, 1984, April 11, 1988, and Aug. 11, 1991; int. Jesse Walker, April 2, 1991; int. Robert King, April 4, 1991; minutes executive committee meeting of Birmingham-Southern board of trustees meeting, Apr. 18, 1960, courtesy of Henry King Stanford.
155 *sending Governor Patterson:* minutes of executive committee meeting of Birmingham-Southern board of trustees, April 8, 1960, courtesy of Henry King Stanford.
155 *forwarded photocopies:* typescript of names in BC 5.24. He also sent a copy to Birmingham-Southern's president, Henry King Stanford, who publicly stood up for Reeves against the trustees demanding his expulsion.
155 *C. Herbert Oliver:* ints. C. Herbert Oliver, Jan. 13, 1984, April 11, 1988, Aug. 11 and 12, 1991, and June 25, 1992; Vincent Harding oral history, MSOH, p. 29.
155 *"Fess" Whatley:* int. J. L. Lowe, Summer 1982; Birmingfind, *The Other Side;* Jazz Hall of Fame exhibit at BPL, May 1991.
155 *"Musical Extravaganza" fund-raisers:* Richards, "Youth Congress," p. 118.
156 *Burnham had tried to persuade:* int. C. Herbert Oliver, Aug. 11, 1991; *BW,* May 4, 1948.
156 *Walker played the bad cop:* int. Jesse Walker, April 2, 1991.
156 *Gregg called the Birmingham police:* Document no. 4, April 8, 1960, IC.
156 *slipped off the campus:* int. Robert King, April 4, 1991, and int. C. Herbert Oliver, Jan. 13, 1984. Accounts differ on how the men got off campus.
156 *NAACP and the Communist Party were paying Reeves's new church:* Hughes to Fleming, April 13, 1960, ACHR.
157 *Only upon checking:* Connor to Cook, March 28, 1960, BC 5.24.
157 *specialist, Detective Tom Cook:* int. Tom Cook, March 1985.
157 *"I guess I was guilty"*: int. Jesse Walker, April 2, 1991.
157 *battery of defense lawyers* and *Ella Baker on hand: BW,* April 9 and 14, 1960.
157 *Connor answered the challenge:* BN, April 5, 1960; *BW,* April 9, 1960; "Loitering Code Gets More Teeth" release, April 5, 1960, BWC 1.15.
157 *was found not guilty:* BN, April 5, 1960.
157 *Gregg was a witness for the prosecution:* BW, April 9, 1960.
157 *"a thorough situationer"*: Harold Faber's memo in *Times* v. *Sullivan,* p. 163.
158 *rabbi whom Salisbury disguised:* BPH, Sept. 22, 1964.
158 *"get a kick"*: int. Harrison Salisbury, Jan. 19, 1988.
158 *hysterical counteroffensive:* See Salisbury, *Fear or Favor,* p. 381; Salisbury, *Time of Change,* p. 44.
158 *"Radio Moscow"*: MA, April 15, 1960.
158 *compared the piece to* Uncle Tom's Cabin: Salisbury, *Time of Change,* p. 47.
158 *"cold water in the face"*: WP, Oct. 23, 1960, quoted in Corley, "Quest," p. 210.
159 *"honest self-appreciation"*: S. Lewis, *Babbitt,* p. 27.
159 *"good points,"*: Smyer et al. to Jemison, Jan. 12, 1959, Robert Jemison Papers, BPL.
159 *sue the* Times: Simpson to Morgan, Waggoner, and Connor, April 14 and 19, 1960, JM 24.31.
159 *demand for a retraction:* Morgan to Sulzberger, April 20, 1960, JM 24.31.
159 *Ella Baker formalize* and *handing the reins:* Wyatt Walker oral history, MSOH, p. 34; Ella Baker oral history, MSOH, p. 36.
159 *Wyatt Tee Walker:* Wyatt Walker oral history, MSOH, pp. 1–2, 9, 45; Walker to King, Dec. 3, 1959, BUK 74.16; R. Warren, *Who Speaks?,* p. 223.
159 *joined the Young Communist League:* int. Wyatt Walker, March 26, 1999.
159 *kept up his subscription:* State Freedom Rider investigation.
160 *"social relationship with white girls"*: int. Wyatt Walker, March 26, 1999.
160 *conference of young sit-in veterans:* Williams, *Eyes,* p. 136; Morris, *Origins,* p. 215.
160 *"feet of clay"*: Morris, *Origins,* p. 104.
160 *"Negro leadership"*: See Louis Lomax, "The Negro Revolt," *Harper's,* June 1960; Garrow, *Bearing,* p. 131.
160 *without a hitch:* Morris, *Origins,* pp. 216–17; Ella Baker oral history, MSOH, p. 46.
160 *Walker, who had driven up:* int. Jesse Walker, April 2, 1991.
160 *named to the coordinating committee:* State Freedom Rider investigation, p. 377.
160 *He encouraged the crowd:* int. Robert King, April 4, 1991; Adams, *Unearthing,* pp. 132, 153; telephone int. Guy Carawan, May 17, 1996. Student quoted is Jane Stembridge.
161 *"rednecks all stirred up"*: int. R. B. Jones, July 14, 1996.
161 *Gary Thomas Rowe Jr.:* Task Force Report, pp. 32–33; Rowe California deposition, pp. 3, 6; Rowe Peck deposition, p. 29.

162   *ever since becoming a player:* Hughes to Fleming, Aug. 28, 1959, and ACHR quarterly report, June–August 1959, ACHR.

162   *$1.6 million government contract:* Wade, *Fiery,* p. 313.

162   *Shelton incorporated the Alabama Knights:* Klan HUAC hearings, pp. 1676–77, 1682–83, 3942.

162   *Patterson was behind Shelton's power grab:* FBI int. with Elmer Bailey Brock, Dec. 30, 1965, Bapbomb.

162   *Rowe had added: Task Force Report,* pp. 31–33; int. Malcolm Kendrick, March 24, 1977, with rap sheet, BPSF 9.1.

162   *Washington had sent: Task Force Report,* p. 34.

163   *"Yankees" were fobbing:* Delany to Gray, April 22, 1960, BUK I.24; Gray, *Bus Ride,* p. 166.

163   *letterhead ornamented by:* e.g., Rustin to King, June 7, 1960, BUK 71A.9b; King to Jackie Robinson, undated (May 1960), BUK IX.1 "R."

163   *$10,000 toward its $200,000 goal:* press release, March 3, 1960, in Gray to Kilgore, Aug. 17, 1960, BUK I.16.

163   *"spiritual leader": NYT,* March 29, 1960.

163   *commissioner, L. B. Sullivan: New South,* November 1960, pp. 22–23; telephone int. Mike Sullivan, Nov. 14, 2000.

163   *praised the spirit of "cooperation":* ibid., p. 23; Dan Wakefield, *Revolt in the South* (New York: Grove, 1960), p. 27; *NYT,* March 7 and April 10, 1960.

164   *named as co-defendants:* testimony of John Murray, *Times v. Sullivan,* October 1963, pp. 804–13.

164   *using the* Times *as a pretext: MA,* Feb. 2, 1961.

164   *"Absolutely no truth":* telegram from Don McKee, April 14, 1960, in *Times v. Sullivan,* pp. 207–10.

164   Chicago Daily News *fretted: MA,* May 22, 1960. The retraction was on May 17.

164   *Chamber of Commerce's "rebuttal": MA,* May 4, 1960.

165   *"contempt, ridicule, shame":* Simpson to Morgan, May 6, 1960; copy of complaint, JM 24.31.

165   *so many celebrities:* Shuttlesworth testimony in *Times v. Sullivan,* pp. 796–800.

165   *Shuttlesworth's co-defendants . . . were pained: Times v. Sullivan,* p. 795.

165   *Shuttlesworth felt that Rustin's:* ints. Fred Shuttlesworth, March 28 and April 9, 1991.

165   *Jack O'Dell had begun:* ints. Jack O'Dell, March 16, 1993, and Sept. 7, 1999.

165   *as Cornelius James:* Garrow, *FBI,* p. 50.

165   *"slavery of the Negro people":* O'Dell testimony, July 30, 1958, House Un-American Activities Committee hearings in Atlanta on "Communist Activities in the South," pp. 2714–15.

166   *Arens was a paid consultant:* O'Reilly, *Un-Americans,* p. 8. The millionaire was Wycliff Draper.

166   *O'Dell took the First and Fifth:* O'Dell testimony, February 1960, before House Un-American Activities Committee hearings in Washington on "Communist Training Operations," pp. 1390–91.

166   *went straight to Rustin:* int. Jack O'Dell, March 16, 1993.

166   *O'Dell's first official signature:* Garrow, *Bearing,* p. 653n.4.

166   *immaculate financial records* and *"Something happened":* Branch, *Parting,* pp. 294, 311.

166   *mixed up in any Klan violence: Task Force Report,* p. 4.

166   *between the reigning Eastview 13:* FBI int. with Charles Edward Tyler, Nov. 30, 1963, Bapbomb.

167   *"ignorant idiots":* FBI int. with Elmer Bailey Brock, Dec. 30, 1965, Bapbomb.

167   *"Kennedy is a member": Task Force Report,* p. 36.

167   *Hubert Page:* FBI ints. with Hubert Page and with Dorothy Page, Oct. 2, 1963, Bapbomb; conversation with Dorothy Page, Nov. 26, 2000.

167   *Morgan's Department Store: BN,* Feb. 21, 1988.

167   *write a report* and *get his cash payment:* Rowe California deposition, p. 13; *Task Force Report,* p. 38.

167   *elected Night Hawk: Task Force Report,* p. 36; Klan HUAC report, p. 23.

167   *brief reprise of sit-ins:* "Who Speaks for Birmingham?," p. 20.

167   *"Wholesale Day"* and *"modified" baseball bats: Task Force Report,* p. 45; Rowe report, Sept. 1, 1960, Freebus.

168   *"Klan could go along with the Communists":* Rowe report.

168   *rent a room overlooking Phillips:* FBI memo referring to September 1 report: "Re Racial Situation, Birmingham Division," Oct. 7, 1960, Freebus.

168   *director of Detective Tom Cook:* "Thomas H. Cook," [1977] Attorney General's files.

168   *"criminal libel" charges: SW,* September 1934.

168   *playwright John Howard Lawson:* Kempton, *Part,* p. 195; Victor Navasky, *Naming Names* (New York: Penguin, 1981), p. 174.

168   *was thrown in jail: SW,* September 1934; Kelley, *Hammer,* pp. 71–72.

168   Times *ordered its reporters:* Salisbury, *Fear or Favor,* p. 384. Salisbury was indicted on September 6, but the charges were never served on him.

168   *"most important challenges":* quoted ibid., p. 384.

169   *prosecutor was a member:* "Background on Recent Events Concerning the Reverend Robert E. Hughes," Alabama Communal Issues, 1950–1951, AJC; Hughes to Fleming, April 13, 1960, ACHR.

169   *Unitarian Church. Dr. Joseph F. Volker:* ints. Roger and Bette Hanson, Dec. 8, 1987.

169   *only local white clergyman:* Stewart, "Reaction," pp. 88–89.

169   *That was . . . Bob Hughes:* ints. Robert Hughes, Aug. 10, 1991, and Oct. 10, 1994; Hughes résumé in SRC.

170   *meet with city commissioners:* int. Robert Hughes, Aug. 10, 1991; M. L. King, *Stride,* p. 112; *BW,* Dec. 13, 1955. See also Thompson, "History of the Alabama Council," p. 37.

170   *Hughes had been standing* and *at Phillips High School:* int. Robert Hughes, Oct. 10, 1994; int. Bette Hanson, June 19, 1992. Hughes had hoped that Ware would take the civil rights helm. Hughes to Routh, Oct. 29, 1958, ACHR.

170   *"slightly in love":* int. Frederick Kraus, March 28, 1988.

170   *stormed a council meeting, attendance fell to five,* and *disciple William Miller:* Corley, "Quest," pp. 184–85; int. Roger Hanson, Dec. 8, 1987; ints. Robert Hughes, Aug. 10, 1991, and October 10, 1994.

170   *"preaching full racial integration": BN,* May 26, 1959.

170   *"anticipation of which":* Hughes to Fleming, May 26, 1959, ACHR.

170   *the burning cross: BPH,* July 27, 1959.
171   *"Jesus Christ was here":* int. Robert Hughes, Oct. 10, 1994.
171   *noticed that Hughes:* int. Harrison Salisbury, Jan. 19, 1988; int. Robert Hughes, Aug. 10, 1991; Hughes to Fleischman, May 17, 1960, Alabama/Birmingham 1960–63 file, AJC.
171   *had come out for dinner:* Hughes to Fleming, April 13, 1960, ACHR.
171   *ordering him to surrender:* int. Robert Hughes, Aug. 10, 1991; "Background on Recent Events Concerning the Reverend Robert E. Hughes," Alabama Communal Issues file, 1950–1951, AJC; Hughes to Fleming, April 13, 1960, ACHR. For fuller treatment of this episode, see Morgan, *A Time,* pp. 71–85.
171   *office of Frederick Kraus:* int. Frederick Kraus, March 28, 1988.
171   *Chuck Morgan was shaping:* Unless otherwise noted, Morgan material from ints. July 14, 1982, Aug. 12, 1983, December 1985, and many other conversations.
172   *"Try your case":* Campbell, *Dragonfly,* p. 210.
172   *"veiled double-talk"* and *"fearful of the KGB":* Salisbury, *Fear or Favor,* p. 381; Salisbury, *Time of Change,* p. 53.
172   *holed up in their office:* Morgan, *A Time,* p. 76.
172   *"Lord is your jurisdiction":* ibid., p. 77. Also waiting out in the hallway to testify were Salisbury's other supposedly anonymous sources—a rabbi, lawyers, a reporter, whose names had been obtained from the Tutwiler Hotel phone records.
172   *he spoke to the Klansmen:* ibid., pp. 78–79.
172   *He was sent to jail:* BN, Sept. 3, 1960; "Background," AJC; Morgan, *A Time,* pp. 80–81.
173   *Will Campbell, the poor-white* and *"Those bastards":* Campbell, *Dragonfly,* pp. 209–10. And off they went to The Club, stopping by the Tutwiler Hotel to retrieve Campbell's sensitive documents in the likely event of a police search.
173   *boy kicking a can* and *"called on to be faithful":* Morgan, *A Time,* p. 85, quoting a letter from Hughes.
173   *"out of kilter":* Southern Institute of Management, "The Birmingham Metropolitan Audit, Preliminary Report, 1960." (Louisville, Ky.: 1960), Report 2, p. 7, TCHS.
173   *"excellent qualities":* "Audit," Report 3, p. 22.
173   *"fearfully watch":* ibid., p. 13.
174   *"doubt of self":* ibid., p. 12.
174   *four most important goals:* ibid., p. 19.
174   *"consequent lack of taste":* "Audit," Report 2, p. 21.
174   *"defensive measures":* "Audit," Report 3, p. 25.
174   *"general social progress":* ibid., p. 21.
174   *"foreboding bald head":* int. Fred Shuttlesworth, April 9, 1991.
174   *"I Speak for the White Race": MA,* March 4, 1957, quoted in Gray, *Bus Ride,* p. 26.
174   *overrule the textbook:* A. Lewis, *No Law,* p. 26. This lent weight to the rumors that Jones had actually helped the plaintiffs cook up the lawsuits.
174   *"Negro, you trying":* int. Fred Shuttlesworth, April 9, 1991.
175   *young boys:* Salisbury, *Fear or Favor,* p. 385.
175   *under a fictitious name:* A. Lewis, *No Law,* p. 24.
175   *the plaintiff lawyers:* trial in *MA,* Nov. 2 and 4, 1960. At least the plaintiffs' lawyers had not figured out that Bayard Rustin was a former Communist and homosexual ("What does Rustin do? What is his profession?"): *Times* v. *Sullivan,* p. 813.
175   *"retract something": MA,* Nov. 4, 1960.
175   *Gray had threatened to withdraw:* Gray to Kilgore, Aug. 17, 1960, BUK I.16.
176   *largest sum: MA,* Nov. 4, 1960.
176   *state-sponsored censorship:* See A. Lewis, *No Law,* pp. 34–35.
176   *courtesy of singer-activist Harry Belafonte:* telephone conversation with Fred Shuttlesworth Jr.
176   *Greyhound suit* and *boycott: PC,* Nov. 26, 1960.
176   *was arrested after joining:* Branch, *Parting,* pp. 351–54.
176   *"I've got all my votes":* Theodore White, *The Making of the President, 1960* (New York: Atheneum, 1961), p. 323.
176   *as "Mr. K.": New York Courier* (edition of the *PC*), Oct. 22, 1960, FS 4.
176   *SCLC tussled with SCEF:* Braden to Dombrowski, Sept. 21, 1960, reprinted in State of Louisiana, Joint Legislative Committee on Un-American Activities, *Activities of the Southern Conference Educational Fund, Inc., in Louisiana,* April 13, 1964.
177   *named Len Holt:* telephone int. Len Holt, July 10, 2000; Ella Baker oral history, MSOH, p. 46; Forman, *Making,* p. 309.
177   *sued to desegregate: CD,* Oct. 8, 1960.
177   *guilty of delinquency: CD,* Oct. 1, 1960. The kids were put on indefinite probation.
177   *"file in pauperis":* int. Fred Shuttlesworth, April 9, 1991, and ibid.
177   *questioning Connor: BN,* Nov. 22, 1960. Connor's notable quote: "Police have attended meetings of the NAACP, this thing you [Shuttlesworth] head, the Ku Klux Klan and the White Citizens Council—we treat 'em all alike."
177   *histrionics of Kingfish:* int. Fred Shuttlesworth, March 28, 1991. "I'm the Kingfish who always gets Andy in trouble."
177   *Shuttlesworth's boilerplate: Shuttlesworth and Billups* v. *Connor and Moore,* Civil Action #9751, Nov. 22, 1960, FS 3. Simpson was assisting the city attorney, with his son Henry.
177   *"harass the harasser":* int. Fred Shuttlesworth, April 9, 1991.
177   *"prolix and redundant": BN,* Feb 1, 1955. This was a housing suit, filed with Shores.
177   *wrote Washington:* SAC Kelley to Director, Nov. 5, 1960, Freebus. There was no mention of the shady circumstances of Rowe's introduction to the FBI.
178   *judo demonstration:* Rowe report, Sept. 29, 1960, Freebus.
178   *"better wake up":* Rowe report, Dec. 15, 1960, Freebus.

178   *"crush" the black pickets:* Task Force Report, p. 46.
178   *wondered if Rowe:* ibid., p. 47.
178   *admitted that they did:* ibid., Appendix, pp. 39–40.

6. Action

179   *Rickwood Field was about to go dark:* The Barons did not play in 1962 and 1963.
179   *Jimmy Morgan: BN,* Oct. 31, 1937.
179   *"I used to enjoy":* Time, Dec. 15, 1958.
180   *"Come on up":* Connor-Jeffers transaction in Washington hotel, int. James Head (who was present), May 30, 1984.
180   *Lister Hill's large circle:* int. Clarence Allgood, May 16, 1991.
180   *Hayes Aircraft: BN,* March 10, 1986. The founder was Harry T. Rowland.
180   *Art Hanes:* int. Art Hanes, May 24, 1984; *BPH* (obit), May 10, 1997. Hanes had emceed a statewide Citizens Council rally in 1955 that drew a record (probably inflated) 5,000 to the Municipal Auditorium.
181   *"has become one of us":* Ed Gardner quoted in police memo, Oct. 23, 1961, mass meeting, BC.
181   *At the January 23 meeting:* police memo, Jan. 23, 1961, mass meeting, BC 9.24.
181   *the second plaintiff:* James trial, *MA,* Feb. 2, 1961; A. Lewis, *No Law,* p. 35.
181   *father carried the Confederate truce flag:* A. Lewis, *No Law,* p. 25.
182   *$6,150,000:* Salisbury, *Fear or Favor,* p. 382.
182   *Abernathy's five-year-old sedan: MA,* Feb. 5, 1961; Gray, *Bus Ride,* pp. 168–69.
182   *replaced the good tires:* ints. Fred Shuttlesworth.
182   *featured speaker:* police dossier on Shuttlesworth, October 1961, BPSF.
182   *prosecutor had raided:* Adams, *Unearthing,* pp. 131–32; Horton, *Haul,* p. 158.
182   *martinis in Vienna sausage cans:* Young, *Burden,* p. 130.
182   *Sewage problems:* int. Fred Shuttlesworth, Summer 1985; Shuttlesworth oral history, KC, side 5.
182   *turned down a job:* police memo, Feb. 6, 1961, mass meeting, BC 9.24.
182   *"in the name of Jesus":* police memo, Feb. 13, 1961, mass meeting, BC 9.24. The ACMHR even offered to supplement his weekly $75 salary from Bethel, but Shuttlesworth did not believe in taking money from the Movement.
182   *King privately pleaded:* Branch, *Parting,* p. 393.
182   *largely an Alabama phenomenon:* Alabama had the most representation of any state on the board—8 of the 33 members (Fairclough, *Redeem,* p. 34). Its officers were mostly from Alabama by the summer of 1958. The Louisianians among the original leadership had dropped out, casualties of the widening chasm between King and J. H. "Big Jack" Jackson, the Machiavellian Chicago minister who reigned over the almighty National Baptist Convention. ("Revised list of Board members," June 22, 1959, BUK 58.44.) Jackson was blocking overtures to bring his organization of more than 5 million, including 10,000 black Baptist ministers, into the struggle for civil rights.
183   *1954 lashing:* Sperber, *Murrow,* p. 441.
183   *"Johannesburg or Capetown":* ibid., p. 604.
183   *switched from one room to another:* int. Harrison Salisbury, Jan. 19, 1988.
183   *"atmosphere of Moscow":* Salisbury, *Fear or Favor,* p. 381.
183   *fear in Birmingham was worse:* int. Harrison Salisbury, Jan. 19, 1988; Salisbury, *Fear or Favor,* p. 386.
183   *Vincent Townsend, the editorial boss:* int. James Head, May 30 and June 6, 1984; telephone int. Peggy Roberson, Dec. 12, 1984; int. David McMullin, Nov. 23, 1982; *BN,* Feb. 12, 1965, Dec. 13, 1978, and Nov. 5, 1979, in Townsend vertical file, TCSH.
184   *"kick 'em in the butt":* int. Irving Beiman, April 30, 1986.
184   *Townsend invited the reporter:* int. David McMullin, Nov. 23, 1982. The year was 1957.
184   *confer with the outdoors columnist:* int. Irving Beiman, April 30, 1986.
184   *mandate directly from:* telephone int. Peggy Roberson, Dec. 12, 1984.
184   *"big lie": MA,* April 15, 1960.
184   *dynamite attempts:* Also, Salisbury had said both attempts had taken place within the last eighteen months, when the other had taken place nearly two years before.
184   *instructed his reporters:* int. Irving Beiman, April 30, 1986.
185   *businessmen who filed into Stanton's:* ints. James Head, June 6, 1984, and May 29, 1988; telephone int. Frank Stanton, Spring 1987.
185   *blacked out all Negro speakers:* Branch, *Parting,* p. 323.
185   *Stanton with a Ph.D.:* S. B. Smith, *Glory,* pp. 130–32, 368–69; telephone int. Frank Stanton, Spring 1987. See also Kendrick, *Prime Time,* and Sperber, *Murrow.*
185   *Kennedy, wanting to know if Murrow:* int. C. Herbert Oliver, April 11, 1988; ints. Roger and Bette Lee Hanson, Dec. 8, 1987. Oliver recalled that it was at another motel, however.
185   *bureau chief, Howard K. Smith:* telephone int. Howard K. Smith, May 11, 1988; Sperber, *Murrow,* p. 618.
185   *great concession from the network:* int. James Head, May 30, 1984. Smith, however, said that it was Murrow who called him from Washington and asked him to take over.
185   *fingered by McCarthyites:* Sperber, *Murrow,* p. 242; H. K. Smith, *Events Leading,* p. 224. *Red Channels: The Report on Communist Influence in Radio and Television* listed Smith as one of the 151 people in the media having ties to Communist organizations.
186   *best southern accent:* telephone int. Howard K. Smith, July 11, 1988.
186   *Women's Committee:* int. Margaret Sizemore Douglass, Spring 1983.
186   *Eleanor Bridges:* ibid.; int. Bettye Shepherd, Spring 1983; int. Cecil Roberts, Spring 1983.
186   *"soft and sweet":* This was part of Bridges's standard speech called "The Eternal Feminine," covered in *BN,* Jan. 30, 1946.
186   *"a saturate solution," I think that's one,"* and *"heard Negroes":* "Who Speaks for Birmingham?", pp. 5–7.

187 *Bridges had been one of the funders:* Richards, "Youth Congress," p. 118.

187 *he showed up:* police memo, March 14, 1961, mass meeting, BC; "Who Speaks for Birmingham?," pp. 19, 18, 21.

188 *TCI's president was a supporter:* int. Clint Bishop, May 28, 1984.

188 *named J. Thomas King:* int. Tom King, March 16, 1987.

188 *of the Machine:* Philip Weiss, "The Most Powerful Fraternity in America," *Esquire,* April 1992; Pepper, *Pepper,* p. 24.

188 *brought to the Alabama campus:* V. Hamilton, *Hill,* p. 26; *MA,* Feb. 7, 1993.

188 *freshman, Chuck Morgan:* int. Chuck Morgan, July 14, 1982; Morgan, *A Time* and *One Man;* int. Tom King, March 16, 1987; conversations with Martin and Hobart McWhorter, Morris Hackney, David McMullin, and other contemporaries.

188 *"spontaneous demonstrations":* Morgan, *A Time,* p. 26.

188 *to the consternation:* ibid., p. 32.

188 *"them goddamned Dixiecrats":* Morgan, *One Man,* p. 78.

189 *Young Men's Business Club:* Atkins, *Valley,* p. 156.

189 *Young Hugo:* Newman, *Black,* p. 393; details courtesy of Newman.

189 *"old Justice Harlan's dissent":* Black Jr., *My Father,* p. 208.

189 *When the justice appeared:* detail courtesy of Roger Newman; int. Norman Jimerson, on Riverside tape, Part 5, side 8. He was also booed by a table of lawyers; the year was 1955.

189 *His father had:* See Nancy Huddleston Packer, *In My Father's House* (Santa Barbara, Calif.: John Daniel, 1988). He had started off as a "bolshevik," "anarchist," and "rabble rouser," in the words of the Bourbon *Age-Herald,* fighting steel imperialism (as well as U.S. imperialism in the Philippines and later Nicaragua).

189 *heavy breathers phoning in death threats:* Morgan, *A Time,* p. 84.

190 *their correspondence went on:* int. Tom King, March 16, 1987.

190 *"giant psychiatrist":* int. Chuck Morgan, April 25, 1991.

190 *telegram from Congressman George Huddleston:* SAC to Director, Feb. 17, 1961, Freebus.

190 *"Tweedledee or Tweedledum":* Morgan, *A Time,* p. 89.

190 *At a meeting:* ints. Clint Bishop, May 28, 1984, and March 1985.

191 *Coca-Cola crate:* int. Tom King, March 16, 1987.

191 *Bay of Pigs:* Wyden, *Bay of Pigs,* and AP report, Feb. 16, 1998, on the CIA's report on the invasion, finally released that month.

191 *assassination of Castro was foiled:* Hersh, *Camelot,* pp. 203, 211.

191 *"just to be quiet":* int. Art Hanes, Jan. 2, 1990.

191 *King had been shocked:* int. Tom King, March 16, 1987.

191 *"here comes Jesus":* int. Irving Beiman, April 30, 1986.

192 *sent headquarters a summary:* SAC to Director, Feb. 18, 1961, in *Task Force Report,* pp. 37–38.

192 *earned $155:* Task Force Report, p. 38.

192 *One of the applicants:* LeGrand int. with Rowe, p. 24; Rowe Peck deposition, p. 39. See also Rowe California deposition, p. 10. Rowe called Hanes a "card-carrying Klansman." He said he personally gave the bureau his application, and the local office had Washington verify the signature.

192 *Rowe told his FBI handlers:* "Garry Thomas Rowe, Jr.," Nov. 25, 1975, p. 1, BPSF 9.1; Rowe Peck deposition, pp. 49–50; Rowe Church Committee testimony, p. 1865; *Task Force Report,* p. 45.

192 *"move some heavy equipment," Klan Kodes:* Rowe reports, March 23 and April 6, 1961, Freebus.

192 *out to Odenville:* Rowe Peck deposition, pp. 52–58; Rowe report, April 10, 1961, Freebus; *Task Force Report,* pp. 42–43.

192 *what looked like CIA credentials:* LeGrand and Cantrell int. with Robert Chambliss (notes), ca. 1976, BPSF 9.1.

193 *instructed Rowe to get in touch:* Task Force Report, pp. 48–49.

193 *Cook had helped make:* Cook and McMahan interrogation of David Cunningham, April 30, 1951, BPSF 10.7.

193 *"mixed up in this Shuttlesworth crowd":* Connor to Cook, Feb. 2, 1959, BC 2.16.

193 *Cook met Rowe:* Task Force Report, pp. 48–49; "Garry Thomas Rowe, Jr.," Nov. 11, 1975, BPSF 9.1; LeGrand int. with Rowe, p. 54.

193 *Cook handed Rowe his file:* Kemp to SAC, May 15, 1961, Freebus.

193 *produced a memo:* Cook to Connor, "Re: Martin Luther King, Jr., and Communism," May 17, 1960, BC 5.24.

193 *someone was leaking information:* Rowe report, April 25, 1961, Freebus. *Task Force Report,* p. 49, has slightly different timing.

194 *canceled his address:* BPH, March 7, 1961.

194 *taken oaths to God:* Rowe report, March 16, 1961, Freebus.

194 *"sent to the penitentiary":* Task Force Report, p. 49. This, Cook said, was assuming that the culprit was not associated with the Civil Rights Commission or other federal agency.

194 *sent photocopies to Washington:* Kemp to SAC, May 15, 1961, Freebus.

194 *summoned Rowe to a meeting:* Rowe Peck deposition, pp. 75–76, 78–79; "Garry Thomas Rowe, Jr." Nov. 25, 1975, p. 25, BPSF 9.1; Rowe Dees deposition, p. 18. There are discrepancies in his accounts, some of which have Billy Holt, Hubert Page, and Bobby Shelton at the meeting. Sometimes Rowe says that Self introduced Rowe to Cook.

194 *Page, announced grimly:* FBI memo re "Congress of Racial Equality, Racial Matters," May 5, 1961, Freebus.

195 *charismatic Negro:* Morris, *Origins,* p. 230.

195 *James Farmer, another key pivot:* Farmer, *Lay Bare,* pp. 70, 102–104, 129, 132, 142, 160, Appendix A, pp. 355–60.

195 *"Journey of Reconciliation":* Viorst, *Fire,* p. 138. Rustin was arrested on the journey and served twenty-two days on a chain gang in North Carolina.

195 *Black's* Boynton *decision:* ibid., p. 140; Peck, *Freedom Ride,* p. 114.

195 *"create a crisis":* Williams, *Eyes,* p. 147. The sit-ins, violating state laws, technically afforded the federal government no entree.

195 *named John Lewis:* J. Lewis, *Walking,* pp. 36–40.

196   *"last supper"*: James Farmer oral history in Raines, *My Soul*, p. 111; Farmer, *Lay Bare*, p. 198.
196   *"Keep Birmingham White"* and *"cesspool of integration"*: Benjamin Muse report, July 13, 1961, SRC; Nichols, " 'Cities Are,' " p. 140.
196   *"make Birmingham into another Atlanta"*: Morgan, *A Time*, p. 91.
196   *arranged a summit meeting* and *"You got"*: int. Tom King, March 16, 1987.
197   *assumed Bull Connor was its mastermind:* There were rumors that he had plucked the Negro stooge from jail, trading the handshake for freedom.
197   *Bishop and a photographer:* ints. Clint Bishop, May 28, 1984, and March 1985.
197   *"our bus riders will be here"*: police memo, May 8, 1963, mass meeting, BC.
197   *"By God, if you are going"* and *"like a bulldog"*: SAC to Director, May 12, 1961, Freebus.
198   *sixty would be called:* ibid.
198   *possibility that Rowe was a double agent:* Task Force Report, p. 50.
198   *Jenkins teletyped Rowe's report:* SAC to Director, May 12, 1961, Freebus.
198   *making them scheme and manipulate:* ints. Clint Bishop, May 28, 1984, and March 1985; *BN,* May 17, 1961; Benjamin Muse report, July 13, 1961, SRC.
198   *meeting with Vincent Townsend:* int. Tom King, March 16, 1987.
199   *"baked us a cake"*: Farmer, *Lay Bare*, p. 199.
199   *"are you Gandhi?"* and *Mrs. Farmer was convinced:* ibid., p. 80; James Farmer oral history in Raines, *My Soul*, p. 113.
199   *Moore informed:* SAC to Director, May 14, 1961, Freebus; int. Jamie Moore, Dec. 9, 1987. Moore said he was not ordered to go away; Connor "gave me permission to go."
199   *as an unpaid staff person:* telephone int. Howard K. Smith, July 11, 1988.
199   *conversation at The Club:* ibid.; ints. James Head, June 6, 1984, and May 29, 1988; ints. Bernard Monaghan, May 26 and 28, 1984; ints. Cecil Roberts, many over Spring 1983.
199   *"going to see action"*: telephone int. Howard K. Smith, July 11, 1988.

7. Freedom Ride

200   *Stoner had gone into hibernation:* Fulton County solicitor Carl Copeland int. with Hugh Morris, Nov. 24, 1958, in JY.
200   *caller was Edward Fields:* SAC to Director, July 17, 1961, Freebus; FBI int. with James Atkins, May 23, 1961, Freebus.
200   *Fields was handsome:* "Confidential Edward R. Fields" Memorandum from Navy apparently, in Box 2, BPSF; Davenport Police Report re: Edward Reed Fields, March 20, 1954, and "Edward Field File" in Box 3, BPSF. While earlier attending a Catholic prep school, he had become smitten with the Columbians, a brown-shirted Nazi-esque youth group founded in Atlanta after World War II. The Columbians had tried to cajole Major General George Van Horn Moseley to lead their putsch. Stetson Kennedy ("Snow James") article in *PC*, ca. September 1963, SK/SLA 1518.64.
201   *Connor wrote Fields:* int. Henry Simpson, Nov. 17, 1982.
201   *an ingratiating letter:* Fields to Connor, Jan. 17, 1961, BC 8.10.
201   *his producer, David Lowe:* C. Herbert Oliver's diary, May 13, 1961, courtesy of Oliver; int. Oliver, Aug. 13, 1991. The police had ruled it an accidental drowning.
201   *Shuttlesworth and Oliver telegrammed Bull Connor:* SAC to Director, May 24, 1961, Freebus; *BN,* Nov. 8, 1961.
201   *Cook asked Rowe how he was dressed:* Rowe Peck deposition, p. 113.
201   *saw dozens of officers:* Rowe Church Committee testimony, p. 1867.
202   *Jim Crow Bibles:* Peck, *Freedom Ride,* p. 25. But the most surprising impression he took away was how many drivers and passengers seemed tolerant of integration (p. 27).
202   *now around sixteen:* *NYT,* May 16, 1961.
202   *follow the CORE leaders back to their hotel:* SAC to Director, May 12, 1961, Freebus.
202   *treated as "poison":* FBI int. with Billy Holt, May 23, 1961, Freebus.
203   *planned to deal with the States Righters:* SAC to Director, May 15, 1961, Freebus.
203   *had cooperated by rustling:* *MA,* May 31, 1961. Rumors would persist that Eastview men had been in on the Anniston detail.
203   *thrashing at the bus:* SAC to Director, May 18, May 22, and May 16, 1961, Freebus; statement of Albert Bigelow to Marvin Rich (of CORE), May 25, 1965 CORE Papers, BPL; Raines, *My Soul*, p. 113; John Patterson oral history, p. 32, JFK; Hank Thomas interview in *MA,* undated (ca. 1994), courtesy of John Yung; *BN,* May 15, 1961; *NYT,* May 15, 1961.
203   *Eli Cowling:* e.g., *Jet,* June 1, 1961.
203   *Troy Ingram had driven:* FBI int. with Troy Ingram, May 23, 1961, Freebus.
204   *no local radio station reported:* FBI ints. with radio station personnel, Oct. 16, 1961, Freebus.
204   *bus made it to Anniston:* SAC to Director, May 17 and 18, 1961, memo, Freebus; FBI ints. with John Olan Patterson (bus driver), May 17, 1961, and int. with George Edward Webb (victim), May 25, 1961, Freebus; AP story on Bergman, March 4, 1983; *NYT,* May 15, 1961; *Jet,* June 1, 1961.
204   *an old Socialist:* State Freedom Rider investigation, p. 150, citing *Detroit News,* May 15, 1961.
204   *"like pancakes"* and *"no lawsuits":* *Jet,* June 1, 1961.
204   *detoured through Oxford:* SAC to Director, May 15, 1961, Freebus.
205   *hoping just to arrest Dr. Fields's crowd:* ibid.
205   *motorcycle policeman received orders:* confidential police int., March 1985.
205   *Tom Lankford:* telephone int. Peggy Roberson, Dec. 12, 1984; int. Lew Wilkinson, Dec. 18, 1984; ints. James Parsons, Spring 1984; and April 13, 1993, int. Mel Bailey, May 1984, int. Earl Morgan, Spring 1986; int. Maurice House, Spring 1985; int. James Parsons, April 13, 1993. When the police got around to updating their equipment, they reputedly sent Lankford to Miami to buy it.
205   *"just another bus":* FBI int. with William Mobley, May 27, 1961, Freebus.
205   *chilly, per Townsend's orders* and *"those niggers":* telephone int. Howard K. Smith, July 11, 1988.

205 *half expected to see:* "Garry Thomas Rowe, Jr.," Nov. 25, 1975, BPSF 9.1.

206 *Conrad Creel, father of:* SAC to Director, May 17, 1961, Freebus; memo on Robert Milton Creel, Bapbomb; FBI int. with Conraid Creel, Nov. 20, 1963, Bapbomb. It is not known whether the Creel family, like the other De-Bardeleben legacies in the Klan, was forced to leave for sympathizing with the union.

206 *were drinking Cokes:* FBI ints. with John Bloomer, Bud Gordon, and E. L. Holland, May 19, 1961, Freebus. Tom Lankford was nearby.

206 *didn't figure it was:* FBI int. with John Bloomer, May 19, 1961, Freebus.

206 *"you Communists":* FBI int. with Herman Harris (Freedom Rider), May 18, 1961, Freebus.

206 *holding Coke bottles:* FBI int. with George Webb, May 25, 1961, Freebus. Peck was brained with a Coke bottle.

206 *Peck gave his black partner, Charles Person, a look:* Peck, *Freedom Ride,* p. 128.

206 *"escort" from:* This was Rowe's word.

206 *"Before you get my brother":* SAC to Director, May 17, 1961, Freebus.

206 *set upon Person:* Peck, *Freedom Ride,* p. 128.

206 *"Let's get them"* and *smashed Webb's ear:* FBI int. with George Webb, May 25, 1961, and with Mary A. (Spicer) Webb, May 25, 1961, Freebus; FBI statement of Ivor Moore (Freedom Rider), May 16, 1961, Freebus.

206 *Spicer recognized:* FBI int. with Mary A. (Spicer) Webb, May 25, 1961, Freebus.

206 *Langston entered:* int. Tommy Langston, March 29, 1988; FBI int. with Langston, May 21, 1961, Freebus.

206 *"Get that camera":* FBI ints. with George Webb, May 25, 1961, and with Tommy Langston, May 21, 1961, Freebus.

207 *reporter heard a man of Page's description:* FBI int. with Jerry McCloy, May 20, 1961, Freebus.

207 *"Run, nigger":* FBI int. with Ivor Moore, May 18, 1961, Freebus.

207 *"knock hell out of" Gordon:* FBI int. with Bud Gordon, May 19, 1961, Freebus.

207 *volunteered his film:* FBI int. with Thomas Dygard, May 19, 1961, Freebus. In the account he gave the FBI, Lankford said two of the men forced him into the alley and demanded his camera. However, according to Dygard, a local reporter for the AP, Lankford "ran up" to the thugs. "There was no struggle for the film," he said. Earl Thompson denies his involvement.

207 *third camera to sanitize:* FBI ints. with Bud Gordon, May 19, 1961, with Tommy Langston, May 21, 1961, with Tom Lankford, May 20, 1961, and with Earl Holland, May 19, 1961, Freebus; *Task Force Report,* pp. 58–59.

207 *"Hey, get the fuck":* Rowe Peck deposition, p. 139; Rowe California deposition (for slightly different language), p. 29; "Garry Thomas Rowe, Jr.," Nov. 25, 1975, BPSF 9.1.

207 *Smith snagged three bloodied Negroes:* telephone int. Howard K. Smith, July 11, 1988.

207 *Smith's roughest assignment:* H. K. Smith, *Events Leading,* p. 271.

208 *had been riding lookout:* Eddy to Beck memo on "Bapbomb Confidential Informers Information," Aug. 15, 1977, and "Confidential-Source Material," Sept. 23, 1977, JY; Shanahan to SAC, July 16, 1964, p. 5, Bapbomb (Holt, Thompson, Chambliss are handwritten on it); FBI Summary of Bombing Incidents, p. 8, Bapbomb.

208 *attack on Lake:* John Hall statement to Attorney General's Office, Dec. 18, 1975, BPSF 6.9; SAC to Director, May 14 and 17, 1961, and FBI int. with Clancy Lake, May 18, 1961, Freebus; *BN,* May 15, 1961; *Task Force Report,* p. 59. Descriptions of Rowe's activities also in Rowe California and Peck depositions.

208 *Garrett, radioed:* Radio log, p. 3, BPSF 7.3.

208 *beating up some Negro men:* FBI ints. with Johnnie Ayers, May 17, 1961, and Walter Elder, May 24, 1961, Freebus.

208 *marred by the wrath of Dot Rowe:* Rowe Peck deposition, p. 141.

208 *wiring him $500:* SAC to Director, May 24, 1961, Freebus. Western Union informed the local authorities of "outside money."

209 *"as bloody":* ints. Fred Shuttlesworth; Shuttlesworth oral history, KC; Peck, *Freedom Ride,* p. 129; Isaac Reynolds statement in *BPH,* March 1, 1983; *BN,* May 15, 1961.

209 *beat up their own kind:* James Roberson oral history in Levine, *Freedom's Children,* p. 87.

209 *Morgan, had fallen asleep:* Morgan to Edwards, May 15, 1961, JM 24.26.

209 *move his first big story: NYT,* May 25, 1961.

209 *"aren't getting any signals":* telephone int. Howard K. Smith, July 11, 1988.

209 *photo desk tracked down Tommy Langston:* int. Tommy Langston, March 29, 1988; FBI int. with Langston, May 21, 1961, Freebus.

210 *Lamar Weaver, the white:* Nichols, " 'Cities Are,' " p. 99; [Braden], *They Challenge.*

210 *"I'm a nonviolent man":* ints. Fred Shuttlesworth; Hank Thomas oral history in Raines, *My Soul,* p. 115.

210 *James Armstrong, the Movement's:* int. James Armstrong, Oct. 5, 1983.

210 *33,715 black schoolchildren: BN,* Dec. 18, 1988.

210 *outfitted his men with rifles:* Though it is always romantically told in accounts of the Movement, Shuttlesworth calls the tale of the armed convoy "a dirty lie."

210 *Negro from the old DeBardeleben mining "family": NYT,* May 15, 1961. He was from the Margaret camp.

210 *gave an interview: BN,* May 15, 1961.

211 *picked a fight:* int. Mary Lou Holt Page, Nov. 17, 1995; int. Tom Cook, March 1985; *Task Force Report,* pp. 59–60.

211 *Klansmen intercepted a second wave:* Rowe Peck deposition, p. 142; "Garry Thomas Rowe, Jr.," Nov. 25, 1975, BPSF 9.1.

211 *"It's a goddamn shame":* Rowe Peck deposition, pp. 167–68.

211 *"If we're not back":* ints. Fred Shuttlesworth; Shuttlesworth oral history, KC, side 6.

211 *threatened to arrest him for vagrancy:* Peck, *Freedom Ride,* p. 130.

211 *"What's you' name":* ints. Fred Shuttlesworth; Shuttlesworth oral history, KC, side 6.

212 *Cook called Rowe, "a goddamn good job," "I thought you boys,"* and *"Some asshole":* SAC to Director, May 17, 1961, Freebus; *Task Force Report,* p. 60.

212 *"The Old Man's going":* Rowe Peck deposition, p. 89; Rowe California deposition, p. 30; *Task Force Report,* pp. 248–50. When Rowe's various handlers were later asked by Justice Department investigators about whether they coached Rowe as he claimed, they all denied it. One said, inconceivably, he had never seen the photograph. One agent

did allow that Rowe had told him at the time that the FBI had instructed him not to own up to being in the picture, and he even said that he should say it was another Klansman. When the Justice investigator asked the agent what his reaction was to Rowe's assertion, he replied, "I didn't react at all."

213 *"was not personally involved":* SAC to Director, May 16, 1961, Freebus.

213 *"Jesus Christ, I can't believe this":* Rowe Peck deposition, p. 89; Rowe Dees deposition, pp. 21–22.

213 *taking movies:* "Garry Thomas Rowe, Jr.," Nov. 25, 1975, BPSF 9.1; Rowe Dees deposition, p. 21; Rowe Peck deposition, p. 115; Rowe Church Committee testimony, p. 1867; *Task Force Report,* p. 63. Sometimes Rowe says they were taking pictures. In the reams of paper that would be devoted to this turning point in Rowe's undercover career, one thing would remain firm in his shifting but essentially consistent accounts: his wounded professional pride over the bureau's failure to intervene in the Freedom Rides' ambush.

213 *rival paper's coverage: BPH,* May 15, 1963.

214 *"newspaper has full confidence": BN,* April 19, 1961.

214 *Smith had made a radio report: NYT,* May 15, 1961.

214 *with whom the* News *men had been discussing the Freedom Rides and breezed into the station:* FBI ints. with John Bloomer, May 19, 1961, and with Bud Gordon, May 19, 1961, and SAC to Director, May 15, 1961, Freebus.

214 *chided a public:* Sperber, *Murrow,* p. 39.

215 *"have meant death": BN,* May 15, 1961.

215 *cosseting his police sources:* FBI int. with Tom Lankford, May 20, 1961, Freebus. He refused to furnish FBI agents with the names of any policemen on the scene.

215 *photograph of Lankford's and Gordon had paid $20:* int. Clint Bishop, May 28, 1984.

215 *rejected Rustin:* Carson, *Struggle,* p. 29. SNCC had disinvited him from attending its recent convention after one of its labor union benefactors threatened to withdraw.

215 *he knew of the Freedom Ride:* R. Kennedy, *Own Words,* p. 83; *Jet,* May 25 and June 8, 1961. *Jet* reporter Simeon Booker says that Kennedy had "Justice Dept. sleuths following the 'bus testers' " throughout the ride.

215 *"Stop them":* Wofford, *Kennedys,* p. 153.

215 *led Freedom Riders to the Greyhound station: MA,* May 16, 1961; Peck, *Freedom Ride,* pp. 129–31; police memo, May 15, 1961, mass meeting, BC; Robert Kennedy telegram to John Patterson, May 20, 1961, RFK; ints. Fred Shuttlesworth.

216 *Patterson had fallen in love with the Kennedys:* R. Kennedy, *Own Words,* pp. 90–91; John Patterson oral history in Raines, *My Soul,* pp. 307–308; Patterson oral history, JFK; Benjamin Muse report, Nov. 30, 1960, SRC; telephone int. John Patterson, Dec. 19, 2000.

216 *death of the Kennedy candidacy:* police memo, June 22, 1959, mass meeting, JM 24.30.

216 *training the Alabama Air National Guard:* Hersh, *Camelot,* pp. 175–78; telephone int. John Patterson, Dec. 19, 2000. Kennedy used the information to advocate an overthrow of Castro, forcing Nixon—worried that the Eisenhower administration's cover was about to be blown—to take a dovish position.

216 *Patterson blamed:* G. Sims, *Little Man's,* p. 217.

216 *"looking for trouble":* Williams, *Eyes,* p. 148; *BN,* May 15, 1961 (for Connor's).

216 *phone with Robert Kennedy:* ints. Fred Shuttlesworth; Shuttlesworth oral history, KC, side 5.

216 *"Surely somebody":* transcript "From the Office of the Atty. General of Ala. MacDonald Gallion," May 15, 1961, BM.

217 *FBI office was the intermediary:* Burke Marshall/Louis Oberdorfer oral history, JFK.

217 *Page phoned a bomb threat:* SAC to Director, May 15 and May 17, 1961, Freebus.

217 *showed up at the airport:* Peck, *Freedom Ride,* p. 132; *MA,* May 16, 1961; *NYT,* May 16, 1961.

217 *John Seigenthaler, a former reporter:* John Seigenthaler oral history, COH, pp. 40–49.

217 *"hold their hand":* Branch, *Parting,* p. 428.

217 *"Our commissioner sends":* police memo, May 15, 1961, mass meeting, BC.

218 *"you was from Birmingham":* Lee Bains int. with Sidney Smyer, courtesy of Bains.

218 *improved stock coverage: BN,* May 20, 1961.

218 *Khrushchev munched:* undated cartoon from *Minneapolis Tribune,* in JM 24.26.

218 *"Your city is sick!": BN,* May 25, 1961.

218 *The suspects that the FBI began interviewing:* See suspects interviews in Freebus.

219 *did not take down the customary physical description:* FBI int. with Hubert Page, May 24, 1961, Freebus.

219 *arrested three men:* FBI int. with Mel Bailey, May 28, 1961, Freebus; *MA,* May 17, 1961; *NYT,* May 17, 1961.

219 *Edwards's U.S. Klans:* FBI ints. with Richard Bearden, May 26, 1961, and with John Thompson, May 26, 1961, Freebus; police memo, Dec. 5, 1975, BPSF 7.3.

219 *was charged with assault:* police memo, May 17, 1975, BPSF; FBI int. with Jessie Faggard, May 23, 1961, Freebus.

219 *Melvin Dove:* FBI ints. with Melvin Dove, May 17, 1961, and with two unnamed fellow employees, May 20 and 21, 1961, Freebus.

219 *The pipe holder, Howard Thurston Edwards:* FBI int. with Hubert Kilgore, Oct. 11, 1963, Bapbomb; FBI int. with Mary A. (Spicer) Webb, May 25, 1961, Freebus.

219 *board the bus in Anniston: Jet,* June 1, 1961, mentions a white man who "opened a paper bag and pulled out a piece of pipe."

220 *Nash told Fred Shuttlesworth:* ints. Fred Shuttlesworth; FBI int. with Mary A. (Spicer) Webb, May 25, 1961, Freebus. Shuttlesworth oral history, KC; Birmingham police interrogation of James Zwerg, May 17, 1961, Box 5, BPSF.

220 *"comely coed,"* Miss America trials: *Jet,* June 15, 1961.

220 *had his daughter:* Nichols, " 'Cities Are,' " p. 126.

220 *"Truth Ride":* Zwerg interrogation; Lucretia Collins int. in *Southern Exposure,* Spring 1981.

220 *"Are you a Christian?":* Forman, *Making,* p. 151.

221 *called Robert Kennedy's secretary:* "Mr. Kennedy" memo to "Jayne," May 17, 1961, RFK.

221 *"I will not drive": MA,* May 18, 1961; *NYT,* May 18, 1961.

221 *"guarantee the safety of fools": BN,* May 17, 1961; *MA,* May 18, 1961.

221   *At 4:05:* ibid.; *NYT,* May 18, 1961; Viorst, *Fire,* p. 149; J. Lewis, *Walking,* pp. 151–52; SAC to Director, May 17, 1961, Freebus.

221   *"I am the Kingfish":* police memo, May 22, 1961, mass meeting, BC.

221   *"love is color-blind":* Alabama *Journal,* May 18, 1961.

221   *dinner party.* Louis Falk *Oberdorfer:* int. Louis Oberdorfer, Oct. 21, 1992; Oberdorfer oral history, JFK.

222   *whose bylaws:* conversation with Hobart McWhorter Jr., June 13, 1995.

222   *John Kennedy put in a call to:* BN, May 19, 1961; Manchester, *Glory,* p. 1150; Burke Marshall/Louis Oberdorfer oral history, JFK.

222   *Oberdorfer's marshal plan:* Louis Oberdorfer oral history, JFK, pp. 27–28.

222   *mind kept turning to:* Louis Oberdorfer oral history, JFK, pp. 24–25.

222   *gone out on a date:* telephone conversation with Marge Gelders Frantz, Sept. 20, 2000.

222   *"enlarge its membership":* Chamber of Commerce resolution, May 18, 1961, JM 24.27; *BN,* May 19, 1961; Corley, "Quest," p. 219.

223   *$40 million plant investment:* WSJ, May 26, 1961.

223   *"Eat with niggers?":* Clark Foreman, quoted in Durr, *Magic Circle,* p. 122.

223   *Townsend, the power broker:* ints. James Head, May 30 and June 6, 1984.

223   *"define the city's policies":* BN, May 18, 1961.

223   *"I'm amazed":* "Who Speaks for Birmingham?," p. 3.

224   *"the rope, the knot":* ibid., p. 1.

224   *CBS executive had complained:* Fred Friendly profile by Thomas Whiteside in *The New Yorker,* Feb. 17, 1962; telephone int. Thomas Whiteside, June 13, 1988; telephone int. Howard K. Smith, July 11, 1988; *NYT,* May 29, 1961.

224   *Smith's friend Newton Minow:* H. K. Smith, *Events Leading,* p. 265.

224   *"a vast wasteland":* on May 9, 1961. S. B. Smith, *Glory,* p. 419.

224   *ramrod personality:* Gary Paul Gates, *Air Time: The Inside Story of CBS News* (New York: Harper & Row, 1978), pp. 108–28.

224   *"men in sports shirts":* "Who Speaks for Birmingham?," p. 30.

224   *"Fear and hatred":* BN, May 15, 1961. Smith had impishly quoted that concession right after Townsend's all-knowing on-air defense of Connor's efficiency.

225   *bureau's contrasting treatment:* McGowan to Rosen, May 14, 1961; SAC to FBI lab, May 18, 1961; Rosen to Parsons, May 22, 1961, all in Freebus.

225   *wife of a state investigator:* Rosen to Parsons, May 18, 1961, Freebus.

225   *"got what they deserved":* FBI int. with Billy Holt, May 23, 1961, Freebus.

225   *hunger strike* and *met at Shuttlesworth's:* police memo, May 22, 1961, mass meeting, BC; *MA,* May 19, 1961. Also there were Len Holt and Nashville's top SCLC minister, J. Metz Rollins.

225   *"The challenge has to be made":* MA, May 19, 1961; *BN,* May 18, 1961.

225   *"That's Reverend Shuttlesworth":* police memo, May 22, 1961, mass meeting, BC.

225   *"he has to talk loud":* "Who Speaks for Birmingham?," p. 23.

226   *"You people came in here from Tennessee":* BN, May 19, 1961.

226   *singing was driving him crazy:* Burke Marshall/Louis Oberdorfer oral history, JFK.

226   *"Two cars awaited them":* BN, May 19, 1961; *NYT,* May 20, 1961; Forman, *Making,* p. 152; John Lewis oral history in Raines, *My Soul,* p. 118; J. Lewis, *Walking,* p. 153; police memo, May 22, 1961, mass meeting, BC. The story of Connor's interaction with the riders during the trip to Tennessee has been widely told, yet according to the immediate eyewitness account of *News* reporters Lankford and Gordon, Connor was in his personal car, accompanied only by two detectives, and the students were all in the rental limousine, with a detective and a reporter.

226   *"white women of immature age":* quoted in Benjamin Muse report, July 13, 1961, p. 5, SRC.

226   *a car that Diane Nash sent:* Lucretia Collins int. in *Southern Exposure,* Spring 1981.

226   *A mob of thousands:* MA, May 20, 1961.

226   *"Birmingham has good dogs":* police memo, May 22, 1961, mass meeting, BC.

226   *"eternal law":* MA, May 20, 1961.

226   *"Old Temp died":* police memo, May 22, 1961, mass meeting, BC.

226   *CBS's unfair editing:* BN, July 3, 1961.

226   *Patterson had finally agreed:* R. Kennedy, *Own Words,* p. 85; *NYT,* May 24, 1961; R. Kennedy telegram to Patterson, May 10, 1961, RFK; *MA,* May 21, 1961; Guthman, *Band of Brothers,* p. 170; Hampton and Fayer, *Voices of Freedom,* pp. 85–86.

226   *"dripping sorghum and molasses":* Seigenthaler int. in *Eyes on the Prize,* PBS.

227   *"got the spine to stand up":* Williams, *Eyes,* p. 152. He said that he was more popular than John Kennedy.

227   *public safety director, Floyd Mann:* MA, May 28, 1961.

227   *Shuttlesworth was arrested:* MA, May 20, 1061; *PC,* June 17, 1961; *NYT,* May 20, 1961.

227   *crying "Fire!":* BN, May 18, 1961.

227   *"washed their faces"* and *"nice benches":* police memo, May 22, 1961, mass meeting, BC.

227   *K-9 Corps kept the mob:* MA, May 20, 1961; *BN,* May 20, 1961.

227   *"I don't have but one life":* BN, May 20, 1961.

227   *"An armed escort to take a bunch of niggers":* Wofford, *Kennedys,* p. 154.

228   *"Friend, why don't you":* police memo, June 27, 1961, mass meeting, BC.

228   *"refusing to move":* press release from Southern Conference Educational Fund, June 20, 1961, Shuttlesworth file, VN 32.

228   *"Why don't you hit me?":* police memos, May 22 and June 27, 1961, mass meetings, BC.

228   *SceniCruiser pulled:* trip to Montgomery, *BN,* May 20 and 21, 1961; *MA,* May 30, 1961; John Lewis int. in *Eyes on the Prize,* PBS; Forman, *Making,* p. 154; Stuart H. Loory, "Reporter Tails 'Freedom' Bus caught in Riot," *New York Herald Tribune,* May 21, 1961, in Grant, *Protest,* pp. 318–23.

228   *in the original CORE crew:* Lewis had missed the Atlanta-to-Birmingham leg, having taken a leave of absence to be interviewed for a foundation grant, but had been on Bull Connor's midnight ride to the Tennessee line.

228   *Jim Zwerg:* Birmingham police interrogation of James Zwerg, May 17, 1961, Box 5, BPSF.

228   *"Filthy Communists":* bus station mêlée, BN, May 20, 1961 (Tom Lankford's story); MA, May 21 and May 30, 1961; Forman, *Making,* p. 154; NYT, May 21, 1961; Frederick Leonard int. in *Eyes on the Prize,* PBS; Loory, "Reporter," in Grant, *Protest,* pp. 321–22; Lucretia Collins int. in *Southern Exposure,* Spring 1981; Durr, *Magic Circle,* pp. 296–98.

228   *writing his description of the flying bodies on a bureau notepad:* int. Joe Dolan, November 1986.

229   *"We want these outside meddlers":* Dan Wakefield, *Revolt in the South* (New York: Grove, 1960), pp. 24–25.

229   *pedestrian was doused:* NYT, May 21, 1961.

229   *Frederick and Anna Gach:* Southern Patriot, June 1961; Durr, *Magic Circle,* p. 289. Anna was fired from her job in the composing room of the *Montgomery Advertiser.*

229   *dragged out and smashed:* BN, May 20, 1961; MA, May 21, 1961; Seigenthaler int. in *Eyes on the Prize,* PBS; Williams, *Eyes,* p. 154; John Patterson oral history, JFK; Seigenthaler oral history, COH.

229   *"I'll shoot":* BN, May 21, 1961.

230   *Bob Zellner fled:* telephone int. Bob Zellner, July 16, 1991; *Southern Patriot,* June 1961; Durr, *Magic Circle,* pp. 297–98.

230   *Mitford was a comrade of:* Mitford, *Fine Old Conflict,* pp. 137–38.

230   *no one was arrested:* As L. B. Sullivan laconically explained, nobody had sworn out any warrants against members of the mob (MA, May 30, 1961). The NYT/AP, May 21, 1961, says four white people were arrested.

230   *Floyd Mann wept:* Branch, *Parting,* p. 452.

230   *"if my mother would let me":* telephone int. Bob Zellner, July 16, 1991.

230   *He became convinced:* ints. Fred Shuttlesworth.

231   *Oberdorfer returned:* int. Louis Oberdorfer, Oct. 10, 1986.

231   *summoned from a baseball game:* NYT, May 23, 1961.

231   *"We will both go":* int. Louis Oberdorfer, Oct. 10, 1986.

231   *scoured the law books:* NYT, May 23, 1961.

231   *Oberdorfer stayed up:* Louis Oberdorfer oral history, JFK, pp. 25, 28–30. Navasky int. with James McShane, chief of marshals (VN), said the marshal force numbered 750.

231   *Claude Sitton:* int. Claude Sitton, May 5, 1992.

232   *Patterson was meeting with Byron White:* MA, May 22, 1961; Raines, *My Soul,* p. 310; Guthman, *Band of Brothers,* pp. 172–73.

232   *"We asked for Federal intervention":* BN, May 21, 1961.

232   *"like he was the president":* Schlesinger, *Robert Kennedy,* pp. 309–10; NYT, May 24, 1961.

232   *Awaiting him at Abernathy's First Baptist:* MA, May 22, 1961; NYT, May 22, 1961.

232   *"a living mass of formless hate":* Southern Patriot, June 1961.

232   *"Can you get me":* ints. Fred Shuttlesworth; Shuttlesworth oral history, KC, side 6; telephone int. with James Farmer, Dec. 1, 1989; MA, May 22, 1961; Farmer, *Lay Bare,* pp. 204–205; Viorst, *Fire,* pp. 154–55; Farmer oral history in Raines, *My Soul,* p. 122.

233   *"I'm only a little fellow":* police memo, June 27, 1961, mass meeting, BC.

233   *"perfect Southern lady":* Durr, *Magic Circle,* p. 300.

233   *"We'll get you":* MA, May 22, 1961.

233   *"go to church with the niggers":* ints. Joe Cumming, June 21 and 22, 1992.

233   *get some bats:* Joseph Lacey oral history in Levine, *Freedom's Children,* p. 90.

233   New York Times *profile by David Halberstam:* NYT, May 23, 1961.

233   *"We have been cooling off":* Farmer, *Lay Bare,* p. 205; Schlesinger, *Robert Kennedy,* p. 311.

233   *monitored by a switchboard operator:* John Patterson oral history in Raines, *My Soul,* p. 310. She was the wife of a state trooper.

233   *how to transport:* Louis Oberdorfer oral history, JFK, p. 30; R. Kennedy, *Own Words,* p. 88; Burke Marshall oral history, p. 30.

234   *"another Bay of Pigs":* int. Joe Dolan, November 1986. RFK aide Dolan said that this was Oberdorfer's line, but Oberdorfer has always given it to White. "Another Cuba" in Oberdorfer oral history, JFK, p. 31.

234   *1,500 Negroes:* NYT, May 23, 1961.

234   *advancing mail trucks:* Joseph Lacey oral history in Levine, *Freedom's Children,* p. 90.

234   *many of the Revenooers* and *"Whose side?":* R. Kennedy, *Own Words,* p. 95; Burke Marshall oral history, JFK, p. 85.

234   *"and mean every word of it":* NYT, May 22, 1961.

234   *hit L. B. Sullivan's car:* ibid.

234   *"sunk to a level of barbarity"* and *"It's a sin and a shame":* MA, May 22, 1961; police memo, May 22, 1961, mass meeting, BC; *Eyes on the Prize,* PBS; Williams, *Eyes,* p. 158.

234   *Guardsmen took sentry posts:* NYT, May 23, 1961; BN, June 3, 1961; R. Kennedy telegram to Patterson, May 21, 1961, RFK; MA, May 22, 1961.

234   *"say that on television":* Guthman, *Band of Brothers,* p. 178.

234   *"for your own safety":* NYT, May 22, 1961.

234   *"dead as Kelsey's nuts":* R. Kennedy, *Own Words,* p. 89.

234   *"Oh, you made it":* int. Fred Shuttlesworth, June 21, 1991. "I thought you weren't going to Montgomery," Kennedy said. Shuttlesworth said, "I'm going to be wherever problems are."

235   *"You look after your end":* BN, June 3, 1961.

235   *"Mickey Rooney":* quoted in Williams, *Eyes,* p. 158. The Reconstruction picture is mentioned in George Stoney int. with local chairman of Democratic executive committee, March 1940, RB 37.6.

235   *"All right, nigger":* Navasky int. with James McShane, VN.

8. Pivot

236 *grafted his prejudices:* Levin, *Political Hysteria,* p. 52. "The Reds have done a vast amount of evil damage by carrying doctrines of race revolt and the poison of Bolshevism to the Negroes," Hoover early articulated his idée fixe.

236 *Hoover's first black target:* O'Reilly, *"Racial Matters,"* pp. 11–13, 16. He used several previous strategies, including the Mann (or White Slave Traffic) Act.

237 *Robeson, even Mary McLeod Bethune:* ibid., p. 39.

237 *investigation of CORE:* ibid., p. 82.

237 *"We have enough":* Navasky, *Justice,* p. 14.

237 *"an attack on me personally":* Navasky, *Justice,* p. 6.

237 *mobsters had evidence:* Summers, *Official and Confidential,* pp. 256–58. This has been challenged by Athan Theoharis in *J. Edgar Hoover, Sex and Crime: An Historical Antidote* (Ivan R. Dee, 1995).

237 *"presents a greater menace," Kennedy practically laughed:* ibid., p. 282.

237 *spotty intelligence:* Garrow, *FBI,* pp. 23–25; Branch, *Parting,* p. 468. Branch also makes the connection with Tom Cook's report (p. 469).

237 *"latest form of the eternal rebellion":* Powers, *Secrecy and Power,* p. 343.

238 *showdown between:* Farmer, *Lay Bare,* pp. 206–207; Forman, *Making,* pp. 147–48.

238 *black leader of choice was Shuttlesworth:* Forman, *Making,* p. 148. The students had some reservations.

238 *"make Shuttlesworth very big":* police memo, May 22, 1961, mass meeting, BC.

238 *"to keep all the symbols all together":* Fred Shuttlesworth oral history, KC, side 6.

238 *Twelve hundred National Guardsmen:* NYT, May 24, 1961; MA, May 23, 1961.

238 *insisting that they report:* Fred Shuttlesworth oral history, KC, side 6.

238 *they took a bus:* MA, May 25, 1961; NYT, May 25, 1961.

239 *"represented by competent counsel":* MA, May 23, 1961.

239 *a foot-dragging Jim Farmer:* James Farmer oral history in Raines, *My Soul,* pp. 123–24. Farmer had been hoping to shake their hands through the window as King had done earlier that morning and send them on their way.

239 *Kennedy dismissed these trips as unauthorized:* MA, May 25, 1961. He pledged not to give the riders any more marshal protection.

239 *William Sloane Coffin:* Coffin, *Every Man,* p. 151; NYT, May 25, 1961. The Montgomery native was John Maguire, who was teaching at Wesleyan.

239 *took a testy call from Robert Kennedy:* notes from telephone conversation in Navasky int. with Ed Guthman, VN. See also Guthman, *Band of Brothers,* pp. 154–55.

239 *didn't have a clue:* Wofford, *Kennedys,* pp. 155–56.

239 *escorted them through the barricade:* scene at Trailways station, MA, May 26, 1961; NYT, May 26, 1961; int. Fred Shuttlesworth, June 21, 1991; Shuttlesworth oral history, KC, side 6.

239 *voice had broken:* Jet, June 8, 1961.

240 *"You need not think":* SAC to Director, May 24, 1961, Freebus. This phone conversation allegedly took place on Tuesday, May 23. "I don't think you should try to bust us up after we backed you up," the Klansman retorted.

240 *a novel injunction:* NYT, May 21, 1961.

240 *"errand boys":* BN, Dec. 5, 1958.

240 *house was being guarded:* NYT, May 22, 1961.

240 *hosted the Ku Klux Klan:* NYT, May 27, 1961; BN, May 27, 1961.

240 *National States Rights Party:* William Engel to Irving Engel, June 1, 1961, "Communal Issues, Birmingham, 1944–1962," AJC. An Eichmann Trial Facts Committee sprung up as a fundraising front for the NSRP. Joseph Wilson and Edward Harris, "Hucksters of Hate—Nazi Style," *The Progressive,* June 1964, p. 15.

240 *Cook had just counseled Shelton:* summary of Rowe report, May 24, 1961, BPSF 9.1.

241 *Claude V. Henley:* Morris Dees, *A Season for Justice* (New York: Touchstone, 1992), pp. 77, 84–85.

241 *boarded a plane:* MA, 27, 1961.

241 *Still in the Montgomery jail:* Fred Shuttlesworth oral history, KC, side 6; undated news clip, "It's glorious! Negroes and Whites Are Being Beaten Up Together," FS 4; MA, May 28, 1961.

241 *by posting his $1,000 bond:* MA, May 28, 1961; undated news clip, "It's glorious!," FS 4; police memo, May 29, 1961, mass meeting, BC. The June 1 issue of *Jet* announced that he had decided to accept the pulpit in Cincinnati, so the decision had obviously been made by the time he was in jail in Montgomery.

241 *Robert Kennedy petitioned:* Justice Department press release, May 29, 1961, Box 29, VN; MA, May 30, 1961.

242 *arrangement with Mississippi senator:* R. Kennedy, *Own Words,* p. 96.

242 *neglected to divulge:* O'Reilly, *"Racial Matters,"* pp. 89–90. See SAC to Director, Aug. 18, 1961, Freebus.

242 *his restraining order:* MA, May 25, 1961; Department of Justice press release, May 24, 1961, Box 10, RFK.

242 *Connor mugged for the gallery:* BN, May 31, 1961.

242 *made a special trip:* police memo, June 12, 1961, mass meeting, BC.

242 *restraining order, against Shuttlesworth:* MA, May 31, 1961; restraining order, June 2, 1961, BUK I.42.

243 *"intense embarrassment":* BN, June 1, 1961.

243 *fleeting aberrations:* William Engel to Irving Engel, June 1, 1961, "Communal Issues, Birmingham, 1944–1962," AJC.

243 *critic Jack Gould, "Smith at his best":* NYT, May 28, 1961.

243 *policy of "fairness":* S. B. Smith, *Glory,* p. 370.

243 *to suspend Smith:* telephone int. Howard K. Smith, July 11, 1988. Smith said that his bosses cited articles in the *Birmingham News* alleging that he hadn't been present at the scene of the bus station riot. I can find no such story in the *News,* though it may have been implied in other southern reports.

243 *foolproof "racial incident":* e.g., BPH, May 31, 1961.

243 News *tried to refute:* e.g., BN editorial, May 21, 1961.

243 *stooges of the paper's owner:* Morgan, *A Time,* p. 95.

244 *"I'm catching hell for being somebody":* police memo, June 12, 1961, mass meeting, BC.

244 *doing all SCLC's work and getting none of the money:* Shuttlesworth to King, June 8, 1961, BUK 58.44 (1); see Walker to Shuttlesworth, July 11, 1961, BUK 58.44b.

244 *"My native state would like to disown me":* Fred Shuttlesworth's annual address, June 5, 1961, FS 1.

244 *"tremendous job in Birmingham":* Walker to Shuttlesworth, July 11, 1961, BUK 58.44b.

244 *"Fred, we've had our differences":* int. Fred Shuttlesworth, Summer 1985.

244 *"very little money":* police memo, July 31, 1961, mass meeting, BC.

244 *Connor hatched a state law:* BN, Aug. 25, 1961.

244 *officer most dry-eyed:* Smith was absent even from the roster of speakers at the going-away "Program in His Honor." "Program in His Honor," in FS 1.

244 *esteem for J. L. Ware, pantomiming at the steering wheel:* int. Fred Shuttlesworth, March 6, 1989.

245 *Frank Dukes, one of the instigators:* Osborne, "Boycott"; Ben Bagdikian, "Negro Youth's New March on Dixie," *Saturday Evening Post,* Sept. 8, 1962; int. Frank Dukes, Oct. 4, 1983.

245 *spiritual father, Charles Davis* and *classifications of Uncle Toms:* int. Charles Davis, Oct. 6, 1983.

245 *he had been part of a flying wedge:* telephone conversation with Nelson Smith, Aug. 2, 1991.

245 *NBC's annual convention, in Kansas City:* Branch, *Parting,* pp. 501–507.

245 *Lucius Pitts:* E. J. Kahn, Jr., "A Whale of a Difference," *The New Yorker,* April 10, 1971; *BN,* April 8, 1962.

245 *Ella Baker had wooed him:* Ella Baker oral history, MSOH, p. 20. Bell had already resigned, but he died before his resignation took effect.

246 *"not an intellectual Uncle Tom":* police memo, Oct. 2, 1961, mass meeting, BC.

246 *"a reading Negro":* "Who Speaks for Birmingham?," p. 25.

246 *"most courageous man":* Reddick to King, May 9, 1961, BUK 56A.39; typescript of newsletter, undated, BUK 58.44b.

246 *what remained of Eldon Edwards's Atlanta-based United Klans:* Klan HUAC report, pp. 20–22, 83.

246 *"jet-age Klan":* ibid., p. 81.

246 *Rowe's grandiosity grew:* See *Task Force Report,* pp. 39–40.

246 *Justice Department saw:* SAC to Director, Sept. 19, Oct. 11, Oct. 31, and Nov. 1, 1961; Nov. (mislabeled Oct.) 6, 1961, memo "Re: Cecil Lamar Lewallyn"; Belmont to Rosen, Oct. 31 and Nov. 13, 1961, all in Freebus.

246 *cases against Cecil Lamar Lewallyn and Ken Adams:* "Re: Cecil Lamar Lewallyn," Nov. 29, 1961, Freebus; *BPH,* Nov. 28, 1961; int. R. B. Jones (the attorney), July 14, 1996. Acker would subsequently be killed in an accident in Georgia.

247 *memo depicting John Doar:* Navasky int. with Burke Marshall, VN; O'Reilly, *"Racial Matters,"* p. 85.

247 *Rowe received a $125 bonus: Task Force Report, NYT,* Feb. 17, 1980.

247 *harassed members of the jury:* Rosen to Belmont, Oct. 31, 1961 (two memos), and SAC to Director, Nov. 1, 1961, Freebus.

247 *"semi-segregated":* BN, Oct. 24, 1961.

247 *"a good conservative":* int. Hobart Grooms, March 1987.

247 *closing of the public parks:* for general background, Benjamin Muse report, Jan. 11, 1962, SRC; Jimerson to Muse, Nov. 14, 1961, ACHR; int. James Head, May 30, 1984; int. Bernard Monaghan, May 26, 1984; int. Henry King Stanford, Jan. 18, 1988.

248 *James Head:* ints. James Head, May 30 and June 6, 1984.

248 *inviting Ralph McGill:* William Engel to Irving Engel, May 15, 1961, "Communal Issues, Birmingham, 1944–1962," AJC.

248 *happy to do something about the race problem:* William Engel to Irving Engel, June 5, 1961, "Communal Issues, Birmingham, 1944–1962," AJC.

248 *Nat Turner:* Bond, *Negro Education,* p. 15.

249 *continued to do his Sunday radio "analyses":* telephone int. Howard K. Smith, July 11, 1988; telephone int. Blair Clark, March 24, 1992; telephone int. Richard Salant, March 24, 1992; telephone int. Frank Stanton, Spring 1987; Gates, *Air Time,* p. 38; S. B. Smith, *Glory,* p. 418. An article in *Variety,* quoted appreciatively in the *Birmingham News* of November 9, 1961, cited the Birmingham documentary as the crux of the dispute, but other contemporary news accounts of Smith's departure did not mention it. See *Newsweek,* Nov. 1, 1961; *Saturday Review,* Nov. 18, 1961. Frank Stanton later said flatly that the Birmingham report was not the cause, but would not comment further. Smith would say unequivocally that it was Birmingham that led to his parting.

249 *"a small amount of revenge":* Wilson to Connor, Dec. 14, 1961, BC.

249 *libel suits against CBS: NYT,* Dec. 9, 1961.

249 *"take a picture of":* Ivan Allen Jr. and Paul Hemphill, *Mayor: Notes on the Sixties* (New York: Simon & Schuster, 1971), p. 64.

250 *Bernard Monaghan:* ints. Bernard Monaghan, May 24 and 28, 1984.

250 *Vulcan Materials:* White, *District,* pp. 61–62; ints. Bernard Monaghan, May 24 and 28, 1984; *BPH,* Oct. 13, 1987.

250 *through his purchasing department:* int. William Spencer, Spring, 1983.

250 *absurdly nominal assessments:* C. Harris, *Power,* pp. 115–16.

251 *Monaghan, could not bring himself:* Rilling to Dunbar, March 5, 1962, SRC.

251 *called a biracial meeting:* ACHR quarterly report, December 1961–February 1962, ACHR; C. Herbert Oliver diary, Dec. 21, 1961, courtesy of Oliver; Rilling to Dunbar, March 5, 1962, SRC. This memo has apparently conflated the parks biracial meetings and similar ones that took place somewhat later.

252 *crossed their fingers:* conversation with Jo Hicks, Fall 1982, who was at the swearing-in.

252 *"I'm not a summertime soldier":* Nichols, " 'Cities Are,' " pp. 142–43.

252 *"nigger mayor or a nigger police chief": Time,* Dec. 22, 1961; Morgan, *A Time,* pp. 109–11.

252 *"a minor problem": WSJ,* March 12, 1962.

252 *"not miss what we have never had":* police memo, Oct. 31, 1961, mass meeting, BC.

252 *"let's pretend":* police memo, Jan. 15, 1962, mass meeting, BC.

253 *Head had gone:* int. James Head, May 30, 1984; int. Henry King Stanford, Jan. 18, 1988, who was at the meeting with Grooms.

253 *December 21 meeting:* C. Herbert Oliver diary, Dec. 21, 1961, courtesy of Oliver.

253 *"selling them down the river":* BW, Dec. 23 and 27, 1961. The highly prized "communication" meant that "the white folks do all the talking and the Negro does all the listening."

253 *froze white onlookers:* C. T. Vivian int. in *Eyes on the Prize,* PBS.

253 *"sell 'em merchandise and refuse 'em service":* Ben West int. in ibid.

253 *"tenth fastest booming city":* Howard Zinn, "Albany, A Study in National Responsibility" (Atlanta: Southern Regional Council, 1962), p. 1.

253 *Sherrod had staged the first Albany sit-in:* Carson, *Struggle,* pp. 57–58; *Eyes on the Prize,* PBS.

254 *Interstate Commerce Commission ruling:* ICC press release, Sept. 22, 1961, Marshall file, Box 29, VN.

254 *for the first time, the entire system:* See Wyatt Tee Walker's address, "The American Dilemma in Miniature, Albany, Georgia," at Conference on Civil Disobedience and the American Police Executive, March 26, 1963, SCLC 37.8.

254 *had gone demonstration crazy:* telephone int. Bob Zellner, July 16, 1991; Carson, *Struggle,* p. 59, Branch, *Parting,* pp. 534, 536, 553, 557; Garrow, *Bearing,* p, 188. On November 25, bystanders at the courthouse where the first bus station sit-in convictions were being handed down marched en masse.

254 *Abernathy bailed out, Men's Day speaker:* Abernathy, *Walls,* pp. 213, 208.

254 *King changed his mind:* Carson, *Struggle,* p. 60; Garrow, *Bearing,* p. 187; Branch, *Parting,* p. 556. He gave as his reason the city government's agreement to abide by the new ICC regulations.

254 *"one of the most stunning defeats":* quoted in Branch, *Parting,* p. 557.

254 *jailing the Greyhound station manager:* Jimerson to Dunbar, Nov. 7, 1961; int. Jabo Waggoner, May 27, 1984. Connor also threatened to throw a visiting Justice Department official in Southside jail, warning, "Instead of probing Bull Connor, they'd better be probing the Communists in this country who seem to have more rights than we in the South."

254 *both Fred Shuttlesworth and Emory O. Jackson:* BW, April 9, 1960; police memo, June 26 and July 31, 1961, mass meetings, BC.

254 *tried back in 1934:* Emory O. Jackson oral history, MSOH, p. 11.

255 *Bob Zellner* and *recruited him was Anne Braden:* telephone int. Bob Zellner, July 16, 1991; Anne Braden oral history, COH, p. 139; Carson, *Struggle,* p. 53.

255 *courthouse in McComb:* telephone int. Bob Zellner, July 16, 1991; Tom Hayden, "Revolution in Mississippi," 1962, in Grant, *Protest,* p. 308.

255 *received him politely:* Benjamin Muse report, Jan. 11, 1962, SRC.

255 *"This We Believe"* and *"wait complacently for those rights":* "This We Believe," reprinted in Nichols, " 'Cities Are,' " Appendix, p. 111; Osborne, "Boycott"; Benjamin Muse report, Jan. 11, 1962, SRC; int. Frank Dukes, Oct. 4, 1983. The statement was adopted at a December meeting attended by some 700 of the college's 800 students, and was printed inconspicuously in *Birmingham News* on January 3.

255 *investigation of local department stores:* int. Frank Dukes, Oct. 4, 1983; Benjamin Muse report, Jan. 11, 1962, SRC.

255 *Shuttlesworth had never proposed demonstrations:* ints. Fred Shuttlesworth.

256 *"tipping off" his new white acquaintances:* Benjamin Muse report, Jan. 11, 1962, SRC. Pitts's self-consciously inflammatory tactics are extrapolated from the fact that he's the only black source named for this memo.

256 *Ingram had recently returned:* summary of Rowe report, Nov. 8, 1961, BPSF 9.1.

256 *didn't want to hear about it:* FBI statement of Ronald "Cotton" Lowe, Nov. 2, 1963, Bapbomb.

256 *"niggers at the Krystal":* summary of Rowe report, Nov. 2 and 3, 1961, BPSF 9.1; FBI int. with Earl Thompson, Oct. 29, 1963, BPSF 10.3; Rowe Peck deposition, pp. 64–66; int. Ann Robertson, March 1985; *Task Force Report,* p. 68; FBI ints. with Gary Webb Gregory, Oct. 26, 1963, and with Arthur White, Nov. 12, 1963, Bapbomb; Lowe statement, Nov. 2, 1963, Bapbomb; Rodney B. Cooper statement to FBI, Oct. 23, 1963, BPSF 7.48.

256 *"mentally deficient":* FBI int. with Evelyn Peeler, Oct. 9, 1963, Bapbomb.

257 *1,500 acres:* WSJ, March 12, 1962.

257 *making an appointment:* int. James Head, May 30, 1984.

257 *"Plea for Courage":* attached to Benjamin Muse report, Jan. 11, 1961, SRC.

257 *including Marjorie McWhorter's:* petition in BC 8.12.

257 *breakfast to caucus . . . meeting with Bull Connor:* int. Henry King Stanford, Jan. 18, 1988; int. Bernard Monaghan, May 26, 1984; int. James Head, May 30, 1984; BN, Jan. 1, 1962.

9. The Full Cast

259 *Three churches were dynamited:* NYT, Jan. 17, 1962; FBI Summary of Bombing Incidents, p. 14, Bapbomb; summary of Rowe report, Jan. 17, 1962, BPSF 9.1.

259 *journeyman members of the action squad:* LeGrand int. with Rowe, p. 19, and summary of Rowe report, Feb. 23, 1962, BPSF 9.1. They were Harry William Walker, a twenty-six-year-old open-hearth helper at U.S. Pipe's by-products plant, and Earnest Falkner, who soon after was elected Province Titan of the United Klans.

259 *Bobby Frank Cherry:* FBI ints. with Cherry, Oct. 16, 1963, and Nov. 6, 1964, and with Virginia Cherry, Oct. 15, 1963, Bapbomb; Birmingham police int. with Cherry, March 31, 1965, Bapbomb; Cherry rap sheets, Bapbomb; George Beck int. with Virgil Cherry, Aug. 12, 1977, Box 3, BPSF; LeGrand int. with Rowe, p. 67; telephone int. Tom Cherry, Dec. 2, 2000.

259 *checklist of suspects:* handwritten "Check List" in Box 1, BPSF.

259 *If the bureau had found a reason to investigate:* Kirkpatrick to Vann, Feb. 25, 1976, Bapbomb.

260 *written by Stanley Levison:* Garrow, *FBI,* p. 26; see also New York SAC NY to Director, April 12, 1962, Levison FBI.

260 *"Just wait":* Powers, *Secrecy and Power,* p. 357.

260   *Hoover recovered* and *warn King about Levison's:* Garrow, *FBI,* pp. 26, 44–45; Summers, *Official and Confidential,* p. 287. Kennedy's aide John Seigenthaler and Burke Marshall, head of the Justice civil rights division, did warn King, through Harris Wofford.

260   *prevented from making:* Benjamin Muse report, Jan. 11, 1962, SRC; police memo, Oct. 2, 1961, mass meeting, BC.

260   *bus protest* and *"Calhoun":* Fred Shuttlesworth's statement to the Civil Rights Commission, Spring 1961, FS 4; Kunstler, *Deep,* pp. 80–84; police memo, Jan. 8, 1962, mass meeting, BC.

261   *threw Shuttlesworth and Phifer in jail:* The timing was related to a stern letter Connor had gotten that morning from the local U.S. attorney revealing the results of an FBI investigation into the vagrancy arrests of Shuttlesworth, Charles Billups, and Herb Oliver during the 1960 sit-ins. Connor forwarded the letter to Jim Simpson, confessing that he received it "before we arrested Shuttlesworth and Phifer." U.S. Attorney Macon Weaver to Hanes, Jan. 24, 1962, with note from Connor to Simpson attached, BC 12.15.

261   *staying in the new addition to the Southside jail:* police memo, Oct. 9, 1961, mass meeting, BC.

261   *King wired* and *fired off a letter:* Walker to "Friend of Freedom," Jan. 27, 1962 (copy of King's telegram to Kennedy attached), MLK 1.6; SCLC press release, Jan. 31, 1962, MLK 22.30.

261   *the appeals:* King to "Dear Doctor," Feb. 6, 1962, MLK 22.15; King to Smith, March 6, 1962, MLK 22.18.

261   *into the wastebasket:* BPH, Feb. 7, 1962.

261   *Oliver, who saw his jailing:* C. Herbert Oliver diary, March 1962, courtesy of Oliver.

261   *Pitts had been inviting Oliver:* ints. C. Herbert Oliver, April 11, 1988, and Aug. 11, 1991.

261   *disunity of the black leaders:* Rilling to Dunbar, Feb. 28, 1962, SRC.

262   *manipulate his white "friends":* ACHR quarterly report, December 1961–February 1962, ACHR. Although Pitts later discreetly declined to name him, Head's subsequent role suggests strongly that he was the man Pitts phoned to get the "demonstrations" called off.

262   *rounded up a couple of store owners:* ints. James Head, May 30, 1984, and May 29, 1988; int. Frank Dukes, Oct. 4, 1983; int. Emil Hess, May 1984.

262   *C. C. J. Carpenter:* See Joel Williams to Carpenter, May 15, 1961, CCJC.

262   *"best nigger":* int. A. G. Gaston, March 28, 1988.

262   *"Let's have lunch":* int. A. G. Gaston, March 28, 1988; Benjamin Muse report, Dec. 12, 1960, SRC.

262   *laborer for Tennessee Coal:* int. A. G. Gaston, March 28, 1988; Gaston, *Green Power,* pp. 47–50, 53; *BN,* Sept. 9, 1985, and May 27, 1990.

263   *"to encourage thrift":* Gaston to Jimmy Morgan, April 13, 1956, JM 18.40.

263   *killers must have had good cause:* Gaston, *Green Power,* p. 7–8.

263   *first "Negro pool":* Strong, "Southern Youth's," p. 46.

263   *"never accept the status quo":* int. Art Hanes, May 24, 1984.

263   *on February 12:* ACHR quarterly report, December 1961–February 1962, ACHR.

263   *"Let's go see,":* ints. James Head, May 30 and June 6, 1984.

263   *Head was running against Smyer's son:* Paul Rilling report, March 5, 1962, SRC.

263   *"our beloved city"* and *"We're not talking":* int. A. G. Gaston, March 28, 1988; ints. James Head, May 30 and June 6, 1984.

264   *number of illegitimate children:* Since late 1959, when the state legislature stipulated that voters be "of good character," the county board of registration had been trying to disfranchise unwed mothers. Eskew, "ACM," pp. 59–60.

264   *desegregated the elevators:* Smyer's reforms in Rilling to Dunbar, March 5, 1962, SRC.

264   *"niggers" to "boys":* int. Frank Dukes, Oct. 4, 1983.

264   *banned by his peers* and *did not have a lunch counter:* ibid.; int. Isadore Pizitz, March 1983; int. Edward Gardner, Oct. 7, 1983.

264   *meeting on Lincoln's birthday:* police memo, Feb. 12, 1962, mass meeting, BC.

264   *criticizing Shuttlesworth:* Rilling to Dunbar, March 5, 1962, SRC.

264   *"naive"* and *"under the influence":* Anthony to Dunbar, interoffice memo, Jan. 21, 1963, SRC.

265   *King had spied:* police memo, Feb. 12, 1962, mass meeting, BC; SCLC press release, Oct. 18, 1961, BUK 58.44.

265   *Oliver urged:* int. C. Herbert Oliver, Aug. 12, 1991.

265   *"vise":* e.g., police memo, Oct. 23, 1961, mass meeting, BC.

265   *"better 'ham":* police memo, Feb. 26, 1962, mass meeting, BC. Although the Court also ruled unanimously that same day that no state could enforce segregated transportation facilities, Shuttlesworth's appeal of his arrest for challenging such statutes would not be resolved until December 1963, five years after the original arrest. Kunstler to King, Dec. 16, 1963, King to Kunstler, Dec. 30, MLK 14.21.

265   *Pitts had scheduled a putsch:* Rilling to Dunbar, March 5, 1962, SRC.

265   *Oliver's warnings:* C. Herbert Oliver diary, Dec. 14, 1962 (mentioning incident earlier in the year).

265   *"improving the human relations":* Dukes letter, March 6, 1962, in Nichols, " 'Cities Are,' " Appendix, p. 386.

265   *Hess replaced the dual drinking fountains:* Charles Wittenstein field report to Murray, March 23, 1962, "Communal Issues Birmingham," 1944–1962, AJC.

266   *"sandwich themselves between the white people," "Fred, I told":* int. Fred Shuttlesworth, Aug. 2, 1991.

266   *store boycott:* ACHR confidential report, "Birmingham," April 5, 1962, ACHR; int. Frank Dukes, Oct. 4, 1983; int. Charles Davis, Oct. 6, 1983.

266   *"sic the dogs":* undated clips on broadsheet titled "Selective Buying: Right of Protest" in FS 1.

266   *despite his disappointment:* C. Herbert Oliver diary, Dec. 14, 1962, courtesy of Oliver; int. Oliver, Aug. 11, 1991. Dukes claimed a success rate of 80 to 95 percent, slashing the stores' 12 to 15 percent profit margin.

266   *"it's hurting":* BN, April 4, 1962.

266   *"bunch of cannibals":* police memo, March 19, 1962, mass meeting, BC.

267   *"a hut in the cotton patch":* and details of testimonial in police memo, March 26, 1962, mass meeting, BC.

267   *surveillance photographs:* ibid.

267   *shots were fired:* Shortridge statement to FBI, Shortridge Papers, courtesy of Pinkie Lee Shortridge.

267   *"I am reliably informed":* Osborne, "Boycott."

267   *cut off its $45,000 contribution:* BN, April 3 and 4, 1962.
267   *"obstructing the sidewalk":* confidential report, "Birmingham, April 5, 1962," ACHR.
267   *lifted its traditional new blackout* and *"face facts":* BN, April 5, 1962.
267   *"freedom for which I fought":* Nichols, " 'Cities Are,' " p. 170.
268   News *published a collage:* BN, April 7, 1962.
268   *"would have a drastic":* ACHR quarterly report, March–May, 1962, ACHR; Fineberg to Emil Hess, April 4, 1962, "Communal Issues, Birmingham, 1944–1962," AJC.
268   *of the few moneymaking scams:* int. David Vann, May 28, 1984.
268   *"100 German police dogs":* BN, April 9, 1962. "All I got to do is say 'sic 'em' and the agitators will break their necks getting out of the way."
268   *as the frontrunner:* e.g., Benjamin Muse reports, Sept. 30, 1960, and Oct. 11, 1961, SRC.
268   *"pool-mixin' ":* Frady, *Wallace,* p. 133.
268   *"chicken thief":* Saturday Evening Post, March 17, 1962.
268   *men in denim:* Frady, *Wallace,* p. 133.
268   *"Stand in the Schoolhouse Door":* Saturday Evening Post, March 17, 1962. "I shall refuse to abide by any illegal Federal Court order even to the point of standing in the schoolhouse door."
269   *boys couldn't be topped:* John Patterson oral history in Raines, *My Soul,* p. 305.
269   *to put up Wallace signs:* FBI ints. with Robert Chambliss, Oct. 21, 1964, and with John Wesley Hall, Dec. 2 and 3, 1963, Bapbomb; LeGrand int. with Chambliss, undated (ca. 1976), Box 1, BPSF.
269   *letter to the ACMHR:* police memos, Jan. 29 and Feb. 26, 1962, mass meetings, BC.
269   *"Y'all come":* G. Sims, *Little Man's,* p. 220. This was MacDonald Gallion.
269   *to praise him:* phone message from Folsom, May 22, 1961, Box 10, RFK. He had reconsidered by the next day and decided it was time for the marshals to go. MA, May 23, 1961.
269   *"country bucks," "Metrecal":* G. Sims, *Little Man's,* pp. 219, 232.
269   *"George don't drink":* Billy Bowles and Remer Tyson, *They Love a Man in the Country* (Atlanta: Peachtree, 1989), p. 152.
269   *Folsom decided to go on the air:* G. Sims, *Little Man's,* p. 221. There are numerous accounts of this political legend. Folsom's faithful would always insist that dirty campaign tricks had done their candidate in. Some aides would further swear that Folsom had not been drinking heavily, for him, that he had been slipped a Mickey.
270   *Folsom wept* and *set out for Arkansas:* Grafton and Permaloff, *Big Mules,* p. 236.
270   *rode around the suburb:* Taylor, *Me 'n' George,* p. 18.
270   *relics of a moribund political / economic order:* The Dixiecrats' embrace of Wallace in 1958 was rumored to have been part of a deal whereby Wallace would help unseat Hill (and John Sparkman) from the Senate. V. Hamilton, *Hill,* p. 232.
270   *was horrified by the rumor:* int. James Head, June 1, 1988.
271   *"He* listens!": BN, April 8, 1962.
271   *"got to take the offensive":* Grafton and Permaloff, *Big Mules,* p. 232.
271   *to hear deGraffenried's pitch:* ints. Bernard Monaghan, May 26 and May 28, 1984. It was Alabama Power president Thomas Martin whom Monaghan persuaded to host the meeting.
271   *gazed triumphantly at the tall buildings:* Taylor, *Me 'n' George,* p. 18.
271   *most votes ever cast:* Frady, *Wallace,* p. 135. DeGraffenried had gotten the unfortunate endorsement of Folsom, and was labeled "Big Jim deGraffenried" by a hostile editorialist.
271   *propose raising the corporate tax rate:* BN, March 1, 1963. This apparently died in the legislative session.
271   *accused the Alabama Council:* ACHR quarterly report, December 1961–February 1962; Jimerson to Welch, Dec. 27, 1961; Jimerson to Rilling, Feb. 5, 1962, all in ACHR.
272   *Robert Coles:* Coles to Johnston, May 1962, Paul Johnston Papers, BPL.
272   *"exposé":* ACHR confidential report, "Birmingham," April 5, 1962, ACHR.
272   *called the Dallas Plan:* Jimerson to Rilling, Sept. 18, 1961, SRC.
272   *Hodges, to speak:* int. James Head, June 6, 1984; BN, April 9, 1962.
272   *"like an anchor of a ship":* int. James Head, June 1, 1988.
272   *Newberry's fired his black employees:* ACHR confidential report, "Birmingham, April 5, 1962," ACHR.
272   *Shuttlesworth warned the backsliders:* police memo, June 4, 1962, mass meeting, BC.
273   *"thirty-five-dollar segregated shoes":* police memo, June 11, 1962, mass meeting, BC.
273   *Oliver went home and cried:* police memo, May 14, 1962, mass meeting, BC.
273   *"most difficult big city":* Garrow, *Bearing,* p. 200. Statement was made in early June.
273   *May executive board meeting:* board meeting minutes, May 16, 1962, MLK 29.1.
273   *Come into Birmingham:* Martin Luther King interview, *Playboy,* January 1965; ints. Fred Shuttlesworth. Shuttlesworth persuaded SCLC to hold its annual fall convention in Birmingham, on September 25, 26, and 27.
273   *During a four-hour lunch:* Evans to Belmont, March 20, 1962, in Theoharis, *Secret Files,* p. 40; Summers, *Official and Confidential,* p. 290; Powers, *Secrecy and Power,* p. 360.
273   *The man who printed it, Fred Short:* "The Artcraft Network," pp. 2–4, SK 3.9; FBI int. with Fred Short, Oct. 15, 1963. In August 1944, he had organized an Alabama "convention" of the fanatically anti-Roosevelt Liberty League's latest stalking horse for the Republicans, a three-year-old "party" named the American Democratic National Committee, which also included fascist sympathizers. Carlson, *Plotters,* p. 290; "In Fact," Sept. 27, 1948, courtesy of Stetson Kennedy.
273   *Kennedy had had a brief marriage:* SAC New York to Hoover, Nov. 13, 1961, and Hoover to Personal Files, Nov. 22, 1961, in Theoharis, *Secret Files,* pp. 42, 43.
274   *Seymour Hersh concluded:* Hersh, *Camelot,* pp. 326–27.
274   *tapped his pet scribe:* Benjamin C. Bradlee, *A Good Life* (New York: Simon & Schuster, 1995), p. 239.
274   *Hoover's fingerprints:* See Summers, *Official and Confidential,* pp. 292–94; Hersh, *Camelot,* p. 336. The rumor surfaced in "Walter Scott's Personality Parade" column in the popular Sunday newspaper supplement *Parade.*

274   *secretary, Pamela Turnure:* DeLoach to Tolson, June 10, 1959, and Florence Kater to Hoover, April 5, 1963, in Theoharis, *Secret Files,* pp. 37–38; Summers, *Official and Confidential,* pp. 266–67, 293–94.

274   *appeared at the home of Marilyn Monroe:* Summers, *Official and Confidential,* p. 299; James Spada, "The Man Who Kept Marilyn's Secrets," *Vanity Fair,* May 1991; Richard Ben Kramer, *Joe Di Maggio: The Hero's Life* (New York: Simon & Schuster, 2000), pp. 403–405. Though the Monroe–Robert Kennedy relationship has been disputed, these claims are well sourced.

274   *"Dr. King's publicists," "let them be," "let King do it,"* and *"the entangled background":* BW, July 11, 1962.

274   *conversation between Levison and O'Dell:* int. Jack O'Dell, March 16, 1993; Garrow, *FBI,* pp. 46, 49–50. Levison hired O'Dell in early 1961 to help organize SCLC's fundraiser at Carnegie Hall.

275   *"Integration is what":* House Un-American Activities Committee hearings on "Communist Activities in the South," July 30, 1958, p. 2671. Braden, a radical socialist, had never been knowledgeably accused of being a Communist.

275   *Shuttlesworth had forced:* dossier on Shuttlesworth, October 1961, in BPSF 9.17. On King and SCEF, see Branch, *Parting,* p. 328. The Birmingham police identified Shuttlesworth as the petition's "initiator."

275   *had held a civil rights conference:* C. Herbert Oliver diary, April 13, 1962, courtesy of Oliver. The National Lawyers Guild, the much red-baited group dedicated to radical pro bono work—with which Len Holt was affiliated—also sent a representative.

275   *on the FBI's second-echelon:* Garrow, *FBI,* p. 49. This was just below the "Security Index" occupied by Levison.

276   *pledged their cooperation:* Task Force Report, pp. 68–71; NYT, Feb. 17 and 18, 1980. According to Rowe, Page also claimed that he had made arrangements with Governor Patterson to have the Klansmen pardoned if they were convicted. Patterson calls this an "absolute 100 percent untruth," and says that he would have had no authority over pardons in any case. Telephone int. John Patterson, Dec. 19, 2000.

276   *John Wesley Hall:* FBI "Re: John Wesley Hall," Bapbomb; FBI int. with Hall, Dec. 3, 1963, Bapbomb; Rowe Baxley deposition, p. 6, BPSF, 9.1.

278   *"The Founder":* Manchester, *Glory,* p. 1163.

279   *former FBI agent Art Hanes:* int. Art Hanes, May 24, 1984.

281   *in a book Chuck Morgan wrote:* Morgan, *One Man,* p. 21.

10. Progress

282   *tuned to Dave Campbell's call-in show:* Vann, LeGrand speech, p. 15.

282   *"weight of a chief deputy":* Morgan, *One Man,* p. 206.

282   *to throw eggs:* conversation with Jim Wall, December 1985.

283   *Arant—had forbidden him:* int. Roger Hanson, Dec. 8, 1987. Vann had unofficially helped Morgan draft the appeal to the Supreme Court that led to Hughes's summary release from Bessemer jail.

283   *confronted the Methodist bishop* and *Young Men's Business Club's resolution:* int. David Vann, May 28, 1984.

283   *peers was Walker Percy:* Thomas Cottingham, "Walker Percy," a typescript in Percy file, TCSH; Tolson, *Pilgrim,* pp. 32–33; C. Harris, *Power,* pp. 82–84.

284   *in the tidal wave:* Woodward, *Origins,* pp. 388–89.

284   *three "honest men":* BN, April 10, 1911. The Big Mule governor appointed three gentlemen, including Percy's law partner, to the commission.

284   *"Nothing is so sad":* William Alexander Percy, *Lanterns on the Levee: Recollections of a Planter's Son* (1941; reprint, Baton Rouge: Louisiana State University Press, 1981), p. 145.

284   *against a socialist druggist:* C. Harris, *Power,* p. 87.

284   *Smyer had asked, Jettison the commission:* Corley, "Quest," pp. 213–14; BN, Aug. 16 and 19, 1962.

284   *"watch the niggers":* int. David Vann, May 28, 1984.

285   *never vote to reapportion:* Morgan, *A Time,* pp. 102–104, 107; Cortner, *Apportionment,* pp. 162, 165; Vann, LeGrand speech, pp. 13–15. Half the legislators were currently elected by less than a quarter of the voters. Jefferson County claimed one-fifth of the state's entire population, but only 7 of the 106 members of the house of representatives.

285   *they had sued:* BN, April 9, 1962. The case was brought under the auspices of the Young Men's Business Club.

285   *Morgan made the plaintiff's closing arguments:* Morgan, *A Time,* p. 108; Cortner, *Apportionment,* p. 169.

285   *telephoned Mayor Art Hanes: Christianity and Crisis,* June 10, 1963; Morgan, *A Time,* p. 111.

285   *A special election:* Vann, LeGrand speech, pp. 15–27, unless otherwise noted. In two previous efforts to get up a vote on the form of government, petitions had all disappeared from the neighborhood gathering spots, confiscated presumably by Connor's policemen.

286   *Berkowitz had christened:* Berkowitz to Vann, Aug. 20, 1962, DV.

286   *to confront Bull Connor:* Frank Dukes's summary and petition "To the Birmingham City Commissioners, August 13, 1962," in Nichols, " 'Cities Are,' " Appendix, pp. 397–400; BN, Aug. 28, 1962; int. Frank Dukes, Oct. 4, 1983.

287   *guarded them overnight* and *seven names had been razored:* Vann, LeGrand speech, pp. 24, 25. The lawyer was Erskine Smith.

287   *Bank for Savings Building:* Morgan, *A Time,* pp. 3–4.

288   *"finest looking toilet":* Abernathy, *Walls,* p. 215.

288   *Their fine had been paid:* Garrow, *Bearing,* p. 203; Branch, *Parting,* pp. 603–607; Abernathy, *Walls,* p. 217.

288   *hung up their marching shoes:* Garrow, *Bearing,* pp. 214, 216; Branch, *Parting,* p. 628. The Albany Movement had won nothing. "Not a single racial barrier fell," reported one newsweekly, typical of a press that had framed Albany's struggle for human rights as though it were a pennant race between morally neutral segregationists and integrationists.

288   *to call SCLC "Slick":* int. Claude Sitton, May 5, 1992.

288   *Smyer formalized* and *On August 24:* ACHR quarterly report, June–August 1962, ACHR.

288   *Townsend did the white handpicking:* int. James Head, June 6, 1984.

288   *Navy veteran had "passed":* BN, Sept. 25, 1962.

288 *"humble ploughboy":* Lord, *Past,* pp. 140–41, 143; Manchester, *Glory,* p. 1157.
289 *traditional honorific: BN,* Sept. 26, 1962.
289 *As he met:* meeting with Kennedy, Fred Shuttlesworth oral history, KC, side 11; int. Shuttlesworth, Feb. 4, 1987; Paul Rilling memo, September 1962, SRC; police memo, Oct. 2, 1962, mass meeting, BC.
289 *had expanded his white contacts* and *conferences with Sid Smyer:* Paul Rilling memo, Feb. 28, 1962, SRC; int. Norman Jimerson, May 1988; Jimerson to Rilling, July 3, 1962, ACHR.
289 *"to take the bull":* Thompson, "History of the Alabama Council," p. 127.
289 *brought Jimerson into the current controversy:* int. Norman Jimerson, May 1988.
290 *showed up at SCLC's Atlanta office:* ibid.
290 *appealed to the American Jewish Committee:* "Martin Luther King's Visit to Birmingham, September 1962," John Slawson files, AJC; Hirsh to Fleischman, Nov. 27, 1962, "Birmingham," and Foley to Lukas, Sept. 17, 1962, "Alabama/Birmingham, 1960–1963," AJC.
290 *Pitts passed the buck:* Anthony to Dunbar, SRC interoffice memo, Jan. 21, 1963, SRC.
291 *Shuttlesworth, who had never:* negotiations with power structure, ints. Fred Shuttlesworth; Shuttlesworth oral history, KC; Shuttlesworth oral history in Raines, *My Soul,* pp. 155–57; int. Calvin Woods, July 15, 1987; int. Edward Gardner, Oct. 7, 1983; int. A. G. Gaston, March 28, 1988.
292 *first to have escalators:* Birmingfind calendar, 1981; on November 8, 1947.
292 *the German-Jewish family:* Elovitz, *Jewish Life,* p. 27; Robert G. Corley, *Paying "Civic Rent": The Jews of Emanu-El and the Birmingham Community* (Birmingham: Temple Emanu-El, 1982), unpaginated.
292 *he built replicas:* int. A. G. Gaston, March 28, 1988.
292 *Pizitz had delivered food:* Edmonds, *Parson's Notebook,* p. 216. During the Depression, he bought up mines and sold coal at cost, just to provide jobs for the destitute.
293 *Jewish agencies stay out of Birmingham:* Wittenstein to Murray, Nov. 2, 1962, "Visits, Birmingham, Ala. 1944–1962," AJC.
293 *worst of the rumors:* "Martin Luther King's Visit to Birmingham, September 1962," John Slawson files, AJC; Foley to Lukas, Sept. 17 and 21, 1962, and Alabama Advisory Committee of U.S. Civil Rights Commission, Special Memorandum, September 1962, in "Ala./Birmingham, 1960–1963," AJC. The advisory committee immediately phoned the Justice Department to request an injunction against the Klan and the presence of U.S. marshals and FBI agents to prevent another Mother's Day in Birmingham.
294 *really aimed at the whites:* R. A. Puryear Jr., president, to member, Sept. 19, 1962, Box 3, BPSF; see Art Hanes's comments in Riverside tape, Part 5.
294 *"connection man":* int. Pinkie Lee Shortridge, Aug. 10, 1990.
294 *"living in Birmingham":* Shortridge to King, Sept. 21, 1962, MLK 1.15.
294 *40 percent of the proceeds:* Walker to Shortridge, Oct. 10, 1962, MLK 1.15.
294 *he was joined:* int. Art Hanes, May 24, 1984.
294 *The convention seemed to be: BN,* Sept. 26, 1962; *NYT,* Sept. 26, 1962.
294 *Barnett had personally barred James Meredith:* Lord, *Past,* p. 155; Manchester, *Glory,* p. 1158; Schlesinger, *Robert Kennedy,* p. 332.
294 *Stanford telegrammed Barnett:* int. Henry King Stanford, Jan. 18, 1988.
295 *punching King in the mouth:* int. A. G. Gaston, March 28, 1988; int. Abraham Woods, June 19, 1992; telephone int. Joseph Lowery, September 1990; int. Lola Hendricks, March 26, 1989. Movement veterans would later claim that the man had come to Birmingham on a kamikaze mission, hoping to provoke King's people to kill him and thereby discredit the nonviolent movement. Edward Gardner int. in *BN,* Jan. 19, 1986.
295 *an immediate trial: BN,* Sept. 28, 1962. The judge gave him a 30-day jail sentence and a $25 fine.
295 *Ingram had been organizing:* FBI statement of Willis Crain, Nov. 18, 1963, Bapbomb.
295 *had been charged in the bombing:* Melissa Fay Greene, *The Temple Bombing* (Reading, Mass.: Addison-Wesley, 1996), pp. 276 and 287. The charges were eventually dropped.
295 *Stonerites at Ole Miss:* FBI memo, "Desegregation of University of Mississippi," Sept. 30, 1962, RFK; typescript of UPI dispatch in Box 24, VN.
295 *Barnett whipped up,* and *"big Nazi rally":* Lord, *Past,* p. 191.
295 *"Barnett, yes":* Manchester, *Glory,* p. 1160.
295 *Edwin A. "Ted" Walker:* Navasky int. with Joe Dolan, VN; Harry S. Ashmore, *Hearts and Minds* (New York: McGraw-Hill, 1982), pp. 285–86; Lord, *Past,* pp. 180–84; Guthman, *Band of Brothers,* p. 196. After Ole Miss, the general would be arrested for insurrection and spirited off for psychiatric observation. In 1976, he was arrested in a public rest room on a morals charge.
296 *160 Federal marshals had been injured:* Williams, *Eyes,* p. 217. Two hundred members of mob were arrested, only 24 of them students. Manchester, *Glory,* p. 1165.
296 *Colonial American history:* Lord, *Past,* p. 232.
296 *"Was it worth two lives":* Manchester, *Glory,* p. 1166.
296 *23,000 federal troops:* This was three times the town population. They would remain until Meredith left in the summer of 1963 with his bachelor's degree in political science.
296 *donated office equipment:* int. David Vann, May 24, 1984.
296 *Grooms gave $10 cash:* int. David Vann, May 28, 1984.
296 *an industrial Who's Who:* list in DV.
296 *contribution from the Stockham Valves family:* Rushton to Vann, Sept. 28, 1962, DV.
297 *Vann asked him to lunch:* int. James Parsons, Spring, 1984.
297 *Townsend was marshaling:* WAPI's Thomas M. Percer to Vann, Sept. 25, 1962, DV.
297 *"at a Jewish Club":* Charles Wittenstein memo, Oct. 23, 1962, quoting *BN,* Oct. 18, 1962, "Birmingham 1950–1962," AJC.
297 *elevator equipment* and *fireproofing:* Corley, "Quest," p. 239; Nichols, " 'Cities Are,' " pp. 175–76. In *The Reporter,*

June 6, 1963, p. 14, Vincent Harding writes that building inspectors threatened to close several stores and forced one proprietor to make $9,000 worth of repairs on his elevator system.

297   *evidence to back the stories:* None of the department store owners I interviewed, including Isadore Pizitz, could cite any specific threats from Connor. The deputy fire chief at the time, O. N. Gallant, said categorically of the rumor that the fire department leaned on the retailers, "That's not true. We didn't fine anyone. We don't have the authority to fine people. If it had happened, I would have known about it." However, Gallant's boss, Chief John Swindle, said Connor could have sent over a fire inspector unofficially because he had a lot of friends in the fire department. Int. O. N. Gallant, March 13, 1987; int. John Swindle, July 16, 1987.

298   *"We aren't doing anything":* int. Emil Hess, May 1984.

298   *"they'll put 'em up again":* Branch, *Parting,* p. 650, quoting Wyatt Walker.

298   *Birmingham had been resegregated:* Jimerson to Rilling, Oct. 25, 1962, ACHR.

298   *"getting with it":* Jimerson to Rilling, Oct. 3, 1962, ACHR.

298   *raise legal fees for the Movement:* Jimerson to Rilling, Oct. 25, 1962, ACHR. Shuttlesworth maintained that he proposed to the whites, "Let's all go and get an injunction against Bull. Y'all should be fighting with us."

298   *revive the "Selective Buying Campaign":* ACHR quarterly report, September–November 1962, ACHR.

298   *"Keep your black feet":* police memo, Dec. 3, 1962, mass meeting, BC.

298   *The Senior Citizens countered:* Jimerson to Rilling, Oct. 25, 1962, ACHR.

298   *SCLC's confrontation with segregation would begin:* Garrow, *Bearing,* p. 221.

298   *frenetic membership drive* and *wearing skullcaps:* police memos, Oct. 29 and Nov. 12, 1962, mass meetings, BC.

298   *dead of an overdose:* Summers, *Official and Confidential,* pp. 299–301; James Spada, "The Man Who Kept Marilyn's Secrets," *Vanity Fair,* May 1991, pp. 193–95.

299   *"I hope he will serve the country":* Branch, *Parting,* p. 627.

299   *"Communist in High Post":* BN, Oct. 26, 1962.

299   *U.S. naval quarantine:* Schlesinger, *Robert Kennedy,* p. 527; Manchester, *Glory,* p. 529.

299   *"If I was a Communist":* int. Jack O'Dell, March 16, 1993.

299   *"Like Ray Charles":* Wyatt Walker oral history, MSOH, p. 35.

299   *most effective staffer ever:* Garrow, *FBI,* p. 244n.64.

299   *O'Dell had resigned:* int. Jack O'Dell, March 16, 1993; BN, Nov. 2, 1962; *Long Island-Journal,* Nov. 2, 1962, quoted in Levison FBI.

299   *summoned the city's firefighters:* Vann, LeGrand speech, pp. 26–27; BN, Oct. 18, 1962.

299   *burst in on a meeting:* ACHR quarterly report, Sept.–Nov. 1962, ACHR. The report does not mention Lankford by name but says that there were two newsmen from the *News.* Tom Cook (int. March 1985) confirms that Lankford accompanied him on surveillance of "subversives."

300   *bugged the commissioners:* int. James Parsons, Spring 1984.

300   *"We took every nut":* Vann, LeGrand speech, p. 26.

300   *phoned Vann* and *prepared two statements:* int. David Vann, May 28, 1984.

300   *"historic day for Birmingham":* "Victory Statement" typescript in DV.

300   *barely a 700-vote majority:* ACHR quarterly report, September–November 1962, ACHR; Corley, "Quest," p. 229.

11. New Day Dawns

303   *shattered the windows of Bethel Baptist:* statement of Herbert Gillespie to Detective C. R. Jones, Dec. 18, 1962; "Re: Bombing of Bethel Church," Dec. 14, 1962; report by Detective E. K. Alley, Dec. 18, 1962; "Summary of Facts Regarding the Bombing," Dec. 17, 1962; memorandum of Bethel Church bombing re Ray McKiney; memorandum, Dec. 27, 1962; M. H. House memorandum re Bethel Bombing, Jan. 2, 1963: all in Box 1, BPSF; BN, Dec. 15, 1962. A nine-month-old girl from one of the many neighboring houses showered with shrapnel was also hospitalized.

303   *"We know that Negroes did it":* NYT, Feb. 1, 1962. Detective Maurice House's investigation of the bombing led to the mining town of New Castle, up near Klan-happy Warrior, where a gang of youths had bombed a black nightclub called Maxie Forge's Place a couple of weeks earlier, apparently using the same car and similar shrapnel.

303   *missed work at Hayes:* FBI ints. with D. R. Pike, Oct. 15, 1963, and with Loyal McWhorter, Nov. 18, 1963, Bapbomb.

303   *alerted a friend:* FBI int. with Mrs. Homer Jackson, Nov. 22, 1963, Bapbomb. The friend was Klan brother Wallace Lee.

303   *string of brief employers:* See Special Agents Richard Vivian and William Patton's ints. with former employers, Oct. 4, 1963, and FBI int. with B. L. Bobo, Oct. 5, 1963, Bapbomb.

304   *surveilling Catholic churches:* FBI memo, "Thomas Edwin Blanton Jr.," Bapbomb.

304   *constant "anonymous calls":* FBI ints. with Mrs. B. Freeman Brown, Oct. 4, 1963, and with Mabel Moore, Oct. 8, 1963, Bapbomb.

304   *raised Catholic:* FBI int. with Nellie Blanton, Oct. 9, 1963, Bapbomb.

304   *Klan friends seemed amused:* FBI int. with Wyman Stacey Lee, Oct. 11, 1963, Bapbomb.

304   *confided to a girlfriend:* telephone int. Waylene Vaughn, June 10, 2001. Vaughn also told this to the FBI in an interview on Oct. 17–18, 1963, which the Bureau marked "obscene."

304   *Both Blanton men accused Nellie:* FBI ints. with Thomas E. Blanton Sr., Oct. 5, 1963, with Nellie Blanton, Oct. 9, 1963, and with Mrs. B. Freeman Brown, Oct. 4, 1963, Bapbomb.

304   *talking about the ultimate Klan act:* FBI memo, "Thomas E. Blanton, Jr.," Bapbomb; FBI int. with Wyman Stacey Lee, Oct. 11, 1963, Bapbomb.

304   *not intelligent enough to make a bomb:* FBI statement of John Wesley Hall, Oct. 8, 1963, Bapbomb.

304   *Klan-connected private eye from Atlanta:* police memo re Earl L. Wright, Dec. 19, 1962, Box 1, BPSF.

304   *confinement in the psychiatric ward:* Jet, May 16, 1963.

305   *ignored Oliver's entreaties, Keating intervened, "when I was hurt":* William Bradford Huie, "A Ritual Cutting by the Ku Klux Klan," *True,* 1964, in DV.

305 *Pitts called a meeting for December 17:* C. Herbert Oliver diary, Dec. 14 and 17, 1962, courtesy of Oliver; ACHR quarterly report, December 1962–February 1963, ACHR.

305 *As Oliver was reciting a poem:* C. Herbert Oliver diary, Dec. 17, 1962, courtesy of Oliver; poem courtesy of Oliver; police memo, Dec. 17, 1962, mass meeting, BC.

305 *"by far the worst big city"* and *met with Kennedy:* Garrow, *Bearing,* p. 225; Branch, *Parting,* p. 684.

306 *"Governor Bryant":* Holland to Marshall, Dec. 20, 1962, BM. Holland had been one of the *News* men sipping Coke at the Trailways station when the freedom bus rolled in.

306 *Oberdorfer, had been in charge:* See Oberdorfer oral history on the subject, May 14, 1964, JFK.

306 *"a free Havana":* Schlesinger, *Robert Kennedy,* p. 562.

306 *"Guerra! Guerra!":* Wyden, *Bay of Pigs,* next to last picture page before p. 161.

306 *"Roll, Tide!":* Norman, *Showdown,* p. 92.

306 *Blanton liked to impress dates* and *toward the pedestrian:* FBI ints. with Wanda Grace Lee, undated, and with Waylene Vaughn, Oct. 21, 1963, Bapbomb.

306 *Ryles found four sticks of dynamite:* FBI Summary of Bombing Incidents, Bapbomb.

307 *take a hundred years:* e.g., Claudette Colvin oral history in Levine, *Freedom's Children,* p. 29.

307 *retreat in Dorchester:* int. Jack O'Dell, March 16, 1963; int. James Bevel, Sept. 18, 1988; int. Wyatt Walker, Jan. 13, 1984; telephone int. Joseph Lowery, September 1990; ints. Fred Shuttlesworth.

307 *"We've got to move in Birmingham":* Young, "And Birmingham," p. 22.

307 *Supreme Court, which consented to hear:* A. Lewis, *No Law,* pp. 103, 107, 112–13, 138. The Supreme Court ruled on January 7. Shuttlesworth and the three Alabama ministers had filed their own petition for certiorari. The two appeals—the *Times's* and the ministers'—would be heard separately, but simultaneously, a year later.

308 *Pritchett had concluded that the police had harmed:* telephone int. Laurie Pritchett, Aug. 17, 1991.

308 *hostile comments had remained private:* as when he said to SNCC's Charles Sherrod that their conflict was a matter of mind over matter—"I don't mind and you don't matter." *Eyes on the Prize,* PBS.

308 *he was the perfect gentleman:* Campbell, *Dragonfly,* p. 166; Young, *Burden,* p. 178.

308 *become Project C:* It's not clear exactly when X became C; notes apparently typed up after the Dorchester session still say Project X. While most accounts of this session—see Young, *Burden,* p. 188, and especially Branch, *Parting,* pp. 689–90—make it appear that Walker presented a detailed blueprint of the campaign, the archives and other participants' accounts suggest that the group was still very much feeling its way at this point, and much of Walker's nuts-and-bolts organizing came after the session.

309 *James Bevel:* int. James Bevel, Sept. 18, 1988; Lewis, *Walking,* pp. 70–71.

309 *to the great sorrow of her many admirers:* int. Julian Bond, ca. Spring 1984.

309 *"books on the shelf ain't never":* Young, *Burden,* p. 127.

309 *"I consider myself a rabbi":* Bevel quotes, unless otherwise noted, int. James Bevel, Sept. 18, 1988. "Engineering is for people who want to build bridges. Judaism is for whoever is going to live life profitably and serviceably."

309 *their dislike of Wyatt Walker:* int. Julian Bond, ca. Spring 1984; int. Wyatt Walker, Jan. 13, 1984.

309 *"Don't worry, Martin":* Branch, *Parting,* p. 691.

309 *mock eulogies* and *preparing for his own death:* Young, "And Birmingham"; Young, *Burden,* pp. 194–95. From his obsolete Old Left perspective, Stanley Levison invented a mythological past for Bull Connor as a steel company employee who had fought to keep the unions out of Birmingham in the thirties. Jean Stein with George Plimpton, *American Journey: The Times of Robert Kennedy* (New York: Harcourt Brace Jovanovich, 1970), pp. 112–13.

310 *"Ralph, I believe":* int. Fred Shuttlesworth. It was common for southern airports not to observe federal mandates to desegregate their terminals until sued.

310 *surveillance film that the FBI shot:* Savannah SAC to Director, Jan. 16, 1963, Levison FBI. The FBI has Shuttlesworth boarding the 8:25 a.m. flight to Atlanta on January 12 with King, Joe Lowery, O'Dell, and Walker, so his memory may be conflating two airport episodes.

310 *Hudson might join the imminent SCLC activity in Shreveport:* Atlanta SAC to Director, May 23, 1962, Levison FBI; "Supplemental Correlation Summary" on Martin Luther King, Jan. 18, 1963, Levison FBI.

310 *summary of the FBI's dossier on Hudson:* Atlanta SAC to Director, June 7, 1962, Levison FBI. In July, the bureau had the great notion that Hudson might be masquerading as Hosea Williams, the freewheeling chemist who was SCLC's man in Savannah. Atlanta SAC to Director, July 26, 1962, Levison FBI.

310 *FBI agents went down to SCLC's Dorchester retreat* and *showed a picture of Hudson:* Savannah SAC to Director, Aug. 29, 1962, Levison FBI.

310 *"this is not getting any better":* Garrow, *FBI,* p. 58.

310 *"most of the South's racial troubles":* "Supplemental Correlation Summary" on Martin Luther King, Jan. 18, 1963, Levison FBI.

311 *"make race the basis":* Frady, *Wallace,* p. 140. See also Tony Heffernan oral history in Raines, *My Soul,* p. 375.

311 *"Today I have stood":* e.g., Frady, *Wallace,* p. 142.

311 *to write speeches for Wallace:* int. Doug Carter, Spring 1984. For evidence of Carter's touch, see March speeches quoted in Lesher, *Wallace,* p. 157.

311 *paid him secretly, through middlemen:* Dana Rubin, "The Real Education of Little Tree," *Texas Monthly,* February 1982.

311 *But Carter had gotten to him:* int. Earl Morgan, Spring 1986; int. Doug Carter, Spring 1984. Taylor, *Me 'n' George,* p. 29. Another crony had gotten a college student who worked for him to deliver Carter's speech to Wallace's office.

311 *"probably the key":* "George C. Wallace, A Change in the Heart of Dixie," *MA* special section, Jan. 11, 1987, p. 11.

311 *chairman of his Committee on Constitutional Law and Sovereignty: BPH,* Jan. 21, 1963.

311 *Townsend sent over* and *Townsend called him "Ironhead":* int. Jabo Waggoner, May 27, 1984.

312 *had been a constant vexation:* ints. Clint Bishop, May 28, 1984, and March 1985.

312 *enlisting his old "black hand" collaborator:* ibid. On Hanes's womanizing, see also Duard LeGrand quoted in Nichols, " 'Cities Are,' " p. 14.

312 *sending auto tags: Congressional Record,* March 25, 1963.

312   *Tom King, was now working:* int. Tom King, March 16, 1987.
312   *Albert Boutwell:* Grafton and Permaloff, *Big Mules,* p. 8; *Alabama,* Feb. 22 and March 1, 1937.
312   *donned a chef's hat* and *he bowled: NYT,* April 17, 1963.
313   *segregationist think tank: BN,* Dec. 1, 1958. Governor-elect Ernest "Fritz" Hollings of South Carolina sent his blessings; telephone int. John Patterson, Dec. 19, 2000.
313   *adviser to the White Citizens Councils:* See *Alabama,* July 1, 1955.
313   *"monstrous legislation": BN,* March 23, 1957.
313   *Boutwell's coziness:* Stetson Kennedy, undated, untitled notes ("FDR greates [*sic*] imbecile"; "Blackmon has editorial defining anti-Semitism"; "He said he often had to take time out"); "Artcraft Publishers of Birmingham," Sept. 21, 1945, all in SK 3.9.
313   *Even Emory O. Jackson had seen fit: BW,* April 30, 1954. Boutwell had co-authored the bill that wiped out the cumulative feature and had helped get the appropriations for the state's two largest black colleges doubled.
313   *"We have heard":* police memo, Jan. 14, 1963, mass meeting, BC.
313   *insisted on delaying:* Initially he had wanted the campaign to begin before the city elections, because the moderate administration slated to take over afterward would not allow them to dramatize their cause. Int. Jack O'Dell, March 16, 1993.
314   noms de guerre: Wyatt Walker oral history, MSOH, p. 64.
314   *"Shuttlesworth and I were most akin":* and other details, int. Wyatt Walker, Jan. 13, 1984.
314   *"God was directing it":* int. Fred Shuttlesworth, Summer 1985. One extrapolates from Shuttlesworth's letter of March 15 that he was either not in on the details or that Walker's advance fastidiousness has been exaggerated in the telling of the campaign. So apparently oblivious was Shuttlesworth of the "lessons of Albany" that he suggested that they expand the targets from lunch counters to "the waterfront—including Parks Implementation (golf, Kiddie-Land), Roving squads to ride Taxis, Buses, etc.; picketing if necessary, Marches, and even a Prayer meeting at City Hall." Shuttlesworth to Walker and King, March 15, 1963, MLK 22.11.
314   *making reconnoitering trips:* int. Carter Gaston, July 15, 1987; int. Lola Hendricks, March 26, 1989; int. Wyatt Walker, Jan. 13, 1984; "Tentative Schedule for Project X," Box 1, MLK.
314   *February board meeting:* C. Herbert Oliver diary, Feb. 5, 1963, courtesy of Oliver.
314   *appeared at the Gaston Motel:* C. Herbert Oliver diary, Feb. 7, 1963, courtesy of Oliver.
315   *Wallace was supporting Bull Connor: BN,* March 9, 1963; int. Earl Morgan, Spring 1986.
315   *"loneliest man": Saturday Evening Post,* March 17, 1963.
315   *mobilized against Wallace:* ACHR quarterly report, September–November 1962, ACHR; *BPH,* Nov. 10, 1962.
315   *"law and order":* ACHR quarterly report, September–November 1962.
315   *"trouble with a capital 'T' ":* Corley, "Quest," p. 244.
315   *comments on Robert Kennedy:* Benjamin Muse report, Jan. 11, 1962, SRC.
315   *Boutwell led the mayor's race: BN,* April 1, 1963. He got 17,434 votes to Connor's 13,780.
316   *250 "baptismal candidates had signed commitment cards:* Harding, "A Beginning," p. 16; M. L. King, *Why,* pp. 63–64. The number of recruits varies in different accounts.
316   *pressed on Sid Smyer:* ACHR quarterly report, March–May 1963, ACHR. This happened in mid-March.
316   *lose their zest for a showdown with Connor:* ACHR quarterly report, March–May 1963, ACHR; Abernathy, *Walls,* p. 235.
316   *"the Birmingham thing"* and *"to destroy the image of SCLC":* New York SAC to Director and Birmingham SAC, March 13, 1963, Levison FBI. As of the tapped conversation between King and Levison on March 10, SCLC had decided to postpone the launch of the campaign till the day after the election.
316   *months-long newspaper strike:* MacNeil, *Way We Were,* p. 64. It began in December.
316   *black political "machine":* int. David Vann, March 2, 1989. Shuttlesworth recalled that his meeting was with Boutwell's main operative, Billy Hamilton.
316   *From a pay phone:* ints. Fred Shuttlesworth; Shuttlesworth oral history, KC; SCLC press release, "Shuttlesworth Blasts Vicious Political Tactics," March 19, 1963, with "special memo" attached, MLK 22.11.
317   *"lay low":* Shuttlesworth to Walker and King, March 15, 1963, MLK 22.11.
317   *scene of a rally: BN* and *BPH,* March 9, 1963; E. C. Clark, *Schoolhouse,* p. 189.
317   *Billy James Hargis:* Forster and Epstein, *Danger on the Right,* pp. 68–86. One of the anti-New Deal anti-Semites, the notorious Allen Zoll, had been on Hargis's staff as late as 1961, and it had been under the tutelage of Gerald Winrod, the "Jayhawk Nazi," that Hargis began "saving America" in 1952.
317   *Operation Midnight: BN* and *BPH,* March 9, 1963; E. C. Clark, *Schoolhouse,* p. 189.
317   *Hargis would become part:* Carter, *Wallace,* p. 299.
318   *a bomb* and *informant had notified:* March 24, 1963, Rowe: chronology of bombings, Box 2, BPSF; *Task Force Report,* p. 93.
318   *King asked Herb Oliver:* C. Herbert Oliver diary, April 3, 1963, courtesy of Oliver.
318   *"Dr. King and Reverend Shuttlesworth are meeting":* Kunstler, *Deep,* pp. 173–74; M. L. King, *Why,* p. 57. Though many accounts place the actor Ossie Davis at the meeting, he maintained that he wasn't there. Nor did James Wechsler's widow, Nancy Frankl Wechsler, recall anything about the meeting.
318   *run-down and sniffling:* police memo, March 18, 1963, mass meeting, BC. *
319   *"Wayne Walker, who is":* police memo, April 1, 1963, mass meeting, BC.
319   *went after Our Way of Life: Saturday Evening Post,* March 2, 1963.
319   *had been a "fix":* Kirby, *Fumble.* Kirby (p. 63) says that the *Post* did have a "special animosity toward Bear Bryant." He also concludes that something fishy did occur, though if there had been a fix it seemed technically inept.
319   *"outside agitators":* "From the Atlanta Constitution comes the Quisling, Ralph McGill who integrated Atlanta," read one ad, "to tell you how to vote." *BN,* April 1, 1963.
319   *U.S. Steel, was his most prominent remaining supporter:* Wittenstein to Murray, Dec. 5, 1963, Alabama, Birmingham, 1960–1963, AJC.
319   *"Negro bloc vote": BN,* April 1, 1963.

319 *"Where's Ware?"*: Abernathy, *Walls*, p. 238.
319 *making a quixotic run: BN*, April 3, 1963.
320 *regular Tuesday meeting:* Abernathy, *Walls*, pp. 238–39.
320 *Vann's uncle had also flown to Birmingham:* int. David Vann, March 2, 1989.
320 *loaned him out:* int. David Vann, May 24, 1984.
320 *"New Day Dawns": BN*, April 3, 1963.

12. Mad Dogs and Responsible Negroes

323 *he called Burke Marshall* and *Marshall telephoned:* int. Burke Marshall, October 1985.
323 *Lola Hendricks* and *"We came to see":* int. Lola Hendricks, March 26, 1989; *Walker v. Birmingham.*
323 *voicing vague doubts* and *Oliver was not so bashful:* C. Herbert Oliver diary, April 3, 1963, courtesy of Oliver.
324 *check out the sit-ins:* ibid.; B. Richardson, "That's All Right," *Freedomways,* First Quarter 1964, p. 67; int. Calvin Woods, July 15, 1987; police memo, April 8, 1963, mass meeting, BC.
324 *delegates from the Eastview 13 klavern: who greeted:* FBI ints. with Wyman Stacey Lee, Oct. 8 and 11, 1963, Bapbomb; "Thomas Edwin Blanton, Jr." statement, Bapbomb; undated (1964), unsigned memo (Tom Lankford?), in Box 2, BPSF; Rowe Dees deposition, p. 50.
324 *wouldn't arrest the scofflaws: BN*, April 4, 1963. Then he accused the "merchants" of cowardice in closing their stores.
324 *"A coward don't tote":* Abernathy, *Walls*, p. 242.
324 *"fill the jail": BN*, April 4, 1963.
324 *wrote Mayor-elect Boutwell:* Head to Boutwell, April 6, 1963, AB.
324 *"the most cruel and vicious":* ACHR quarterly report, March–May 1963, ACHR. The speaker is not named, but is described as "one liberal white leader who worked actively to change the form of city government." In Brewbaker report to SRC, May 4, 1963, SRC, Vann (named) expresses a similar sentiment.
324 *Early Wednesday evening:* Shuttlesworth and King meeting with Foley, C. Herbert Oliver diary, April 3, 1963, courtesy of Oliver; police memo, April 3, 1963, mass meeting, BC.
325 To Kill a Mockingbird: *BN*, April 4, 1963.
325 *"As I came into Birmingham:* police memo, April 3, 1963, mass meeting, BC.
325 *at a banquet:* police memo, April 5, 1963, mass meeting, BC, for King's characterization of Foley's statement; *BW*, April 3, 1963; C. Herbert Oliver diary, April 3, 1963, courtesy of Oliver; *BN*, April 5, 1963.
325 *"highest admiration": Interracial Review: A Journal for Christian Democracy,* September 1961, p. 235.
325 *honeyed call:* Abernathy, *Walls*, p. 240.
326 *known as Rat Killer:* ints. Charles "Rat Killer" Barnett, Oct. 10, 1983; Frank Dukes, Oct. 4, 1983; John Nixon, Oct. 7, 1983; Orzell Billingsley, July 18, 1987.
326 *"Hey, you walking too close":* int. Julia Rainge, July 15, 1987.
326 *bulldog in the middle of the road:* police memo, Jan. 23, 1961, mass meeting, BC. Yet Gardner sometimes boasted of his race's handiness with a blade. Police memo, April 5, 1963, mass meeting, BC.
326 *"I got a chance to kill me a cracker":* Andrew Marrisett oral history in Raines, *My Soul*, p. 148.
326 *passing around a box:* Abraham Woods int. in *BN*, Feb. 18, 1988.
326 *reminders that being black:* police memo, April 5, 1963, mass meeting, BC. E.g., "Some Negroes I don't like as well as some white people."
326 *"don't know that the Civil War is over":* police memo, Sept. 11, 1961, mass meeting, BC.
327 *"magnet that attracted":* int. Jonathan McPherson, Oct. 5, 1983.
327 *"primary ingredient":* Walker interviewed in "The Story of Gospel Music," a BBC production for PBS's *Great Performances* series, Feb. 5, 1997. Walker would write his doctoral dissertation on Negro sacred music.
327 *led forty-five men and women: NYT,* April 7, 1963; *BW*, April 10, 1963; M. L. King, *Why*, pp. 68–69; ints. Fred Shuttlesworth. Contradicting Wyatt Walker's memory, Shuttlesworth did mention the city hall destination in the previous night's mass meeting.
327 *"Connor had something in his mind":* Nichols, " 'Cities Are,' " p. 286.
327 *"I'm hungry":* Dorman, *We Shall*, p. 171.
327 *mass meeting at St. James Baptist:* police memo, April 6, 1963, mass meeting, BC.
328 *Mr. Rough to King's Mr. Smooth:* Branch, *Parting*, p. 125.
328 *"You may think that stands for Ku Klux Klan":* police memo, April 5, 1963, mass meeting, BC.
328 *"and why the hell can't I smell?":* police memo, April 4, 1963, mass meeting, BC. "If we can't get our hands on some soap and can't find a bath tub, we will go on stinking, but we are going!"
328 *"I am no longer involved":* Jackson to Rutledge, April 4, 1963, EOJAR.
328 *The World's front page: BW*, April 6, 1963. The *World* made no mention of SCLC or Martin Luther King except in a news story about the resignation from SCLC of a black Atlanta dentist who accused King's group of having "sold out to Gov. Rockefeller" for personal gain. SCLC assumed that Jackson's hostility was simply part of the Scott newspaper chain's antipathy to King, but Jackson himself had been on mutinous terms with what he called "the parent newspaper"—always threatening to start his own paper. Shivery to Jackson, July 2, 1946, *BWC* 1.10.
328 *by becoming silent benefactors:* int. Edward Gardner, Oct. 7, 1963.
328 *written in forty-five minutes:* int. Wyatt Walker, Jan. 13, 1984. Andrew Young, "And Birmingham," p. 22, claims that the manifesto was hammered out soon after the Dorchester strategy meeting.
328 *"create a crisis":* int. Wyatt Walker, Jan. 13, 1984; Walker oral history, MSOH, p. 59.
329 *"calculated for Bull Connor's stupidity":* Nichols, " 'Cities Are,' " p. 286.
329 *"took the night train":* police memo, Feb. 22, 1962, mass meeting, BC.
329 *"flitting from chick to chick":* Oates, *Trumpet*, p. 16.
329 *minister, John T. Porter:* int. John Porter, Oct. 6, 1983. "M.L. ignored his father. Daddy King would get down—down, *down*—on A.D.," Porter observed.

329   *led the thirty marchers:* ibid.; Westin and Mahoney, *Trial,* p. 69; int. N. H. Smith, Oct. 3, 1983; *NYT,* April 8, 1963.

330   *to reap a premium of spectators:* R. Warren, *Who Speaks?,* p. 226; int. Wyatt Walker, Jan. 13, 1984; Walker oral history, MSOH, p. 60. The role of the spectators would assume increasing, sometimes apocryphal value in Movement memory.

330   *went at a police dog:* NYT, April 8, 1963; Leroy Allen's Inter-Citizens Committee affidavit, document no. 34, in MLK 1.15, denies that he had a knife or any other weapon; Forman, *Making,* p. 311, for a somewhat hyperbolic account; police memo, April 8, 1963, mass meeting, BC.

330   *"Look at that dog go":* BW, April 13, 1963, quoting wire service dispatch. Black witnesses would maintain that the teenager pulled his knife only after the dog attacked.

330   *"They may set the mad dogs":* police memo, April 3, 1963, mass meeting, BC.

330   *"I've got it":* Wyatt Walker oral history, MSOH, p. 60.

330   *Kunstler, who had just arrived:* Kunstler, *Deep,* pp. 179–80. Kunstler would represent Shuttlesworth and thirty-eight other jailed demonstrators in Judge Charles Brown's court at city hall, invoking an old Reconstruction criminal statute to get the cases transferred to federal court.

330   *kicked the prostrate Allen:* int. Albert Persons, May 1991; unpublished manuscript, by Albert C. "Buck" Persons, courtesy of Persons. A version of this was published in *The True Selma Story* (Birmingham: Esco, 1965), in BPSF 7.1a.

331   *"We've got a movement":* Forman, *Making,* p. 312. Forman puts this episode at a week later, but the documentation points to this incident. George Wallace mobilized a hundred state troopers—a third of his force—to Birmingham that night.

331   *taken an ad to announce:* BN, April 7, 1963.

331   *summoned the black men:* BW, April 13, 1963, for timing.

331   *his peers at the meeting:* int. Frank Dukes, Oct. 4, 1983; int. James Montgomery, Dec. 4, 1987; John Cross oral history, KC, p. 12. Along with the business leaders and prominent ministers were Frank Dukes and Emory Jackson.

331   *Montgomery, felt entitled:* int. James Montgomery, Dec. 4, 1987.

331   *known Martin Luther King as a younger apolitical student:* Montgomery int. in BN, Jan. 19, 1986.

331   *"Have all y'all lost your minds?"* and *"Man cannot ride your back":* ibid.; int. James Montgomery, Dec. 4, 1987.

332   *Allen . . . taken to the hospital* and *Coleman:* Inter-Citizens Committee documents no. 34 and 33, in MLK 1.15.

332   Five *police dogs:* police memo, April 8, 1963, mass meeting, BC.

332   *"Get rid of the Uncle Toms":* police memo, April 8, 1963, mass meeting, BC.

332   *on the way to jail* and *"You're in jail":* int. John Porter, Oct. 6, 1983; int. N. H. Smith, Oct. 3, 1983.

332   *King would be found dead:* NYT, July 22, 1969.

332   *"see about a dead minister":* conversation with Lincoln Hendricks, March 1986.

332   *Smith had been hoping:* int. Edward Gardner, Oct. 7, 1983.

332   *set a dozen women:* See police memo, Feb. 26, 1962, mass meeting, BC.

333   *"holler Amen":* police memo, March 27, 1961, mass meeting, BC.

333   *"day-to-day man," Gardner kept track of the commitment cards:* int. Edward Gardner, Oct. 7, 1983.

333   *Smith and A. D. King were halfway down the aisle:* ibid.; int. John Porter, Oct. 6, 1983.

333   *King went on the offensive:* M. L. King, *Why,* p. 67; int. C. Herbert Oliver, April 11, 1988; John Cross oral history, KC, p. 13.

333   *King addressed the black businessmen:* Kunstler, *Deep,* pp. 183–84; NYT, April 9, 1963. Kunstler was at the meeting, as was Shuttlesworth, who had bonded out of jail.

333   *"operating in a vacuum":* NYT, April 9, 1963.

333   *"I have always spoken my mind":* int. C. Herbert Oliver, April 11, 1988. Andy Young was also there.

333   *Smyer called the Alabama Council's Jim Jimerson:* ACHR quarterly report, March–May 1963, ACHR.

334   *"that putting white people at ease":* Young, *Burden,* p. 190.

334   *only white clergyman to have publicly condemned:* undated clipping from *Mobile Press,* in CCJC.

334   *"our scenic little community":* Morgan to Marshall, Jan. 23, 1963, BM. "At least," he would say later, looking back on the Camelot era, "the Kennedy Administration gave me someplace to telephone." Navasky int. with Morgan, Box 29, VN.

334   *Morgan took a seat:* int. Chuck Morgan, July 14, 1982; Morgan oral history in Raines, *My Soul,* p. 180; Navasky int. with Morgan, Box 29, VN.

335   *Shuttlesworth invited the white men:* int. George Murray, June 2, 1990.

335   *"a group bent on exploiting":* "Outline of Negotiations," unsigned memo in DV. Vann said he didn't write this memo. My guess is that Vincent Townsend wrote it.

335   *"It's dark in Birmingham":* police memo, April 10, 1963, mass meeting, BC.

335   *"I had a dream tonight":* police memo, April 9, 1963, mass meeting, BC; int. Charles Davis, Oct. 6, 1983; int. C. Herbert Oliver, Jan. 13, 1984. King had delivered a version of the speech in Savannah on Emancipation Day, shortly before the Kennedy inauguration (Branch, *Parting,* p. 689). Oliver considered Abernathy's speech right afterward much better.

335   *"can shuffle his feet":* quoted in Nathan Hare, *The Black Anglo-Saxons* (Chicago: Third World Press, 1991), p. 39.

335   *"We want freedom and justice":* text in BW, April 13, 1963, and reported in NYT, April 10, 1963.

336   *"I'm proud"* and *"If you picket Gaston":* int. Edward Gardner, Oct. 7, 1983. And the Atlantans' scorn for Birmingham's Uncle Toms was a little hypocritical, given that King had promised Atlanta's jealous black burghers that SCLC wouldn't undertake any local campaigns.

336   *owed his first job:* Abernathy, *Walls,* pp. 87–88; in the summer of 1950.

336   *"an unusually stupid kind of fellow":* A. G. Gaston int. in BN, Oct. 22, 1989, over Abernathy's published descriptions of King's sexual exploits in Memphis on the eve of his assassination.

336   *"Get the ministers":* int. Edward Gardner, Oct. 7, 1983.

336 *showdown at the Metropolitan A.M.E. Zion:* int. Jonathan McPherson, Oct. 5, 1983. Shuttlesworth (int. Summer 1985) denied that this took place.

336 *"These prices you putting":* int. Julia Rainge, July 15, 1987; timing of this remark is not clear.

336 *insisted on charging the bill to the ACMHR:* int. Edward Gardner, Oct. 7, 1983.

336 *"You are a* super *Uncle Tom":* This remark has been repeated by numerous witnesses, including Edward Gardner, Frank Dukes, Calvin Woods, and Abraham Woods, but Shuttlesworth said (int. Summer 1985), "I think that's been given to me. I may have said, 'If you persist then you will be a super Uncle Tom.' I let Mr. Gaston be Mr. Gaston. I never had a serious contradiction with him, let alone in public." Gaston himself denied that Shuttlesworth made the remark, attributing it instead to SCLC staffer Hosea Williams, who was not in town at the time the remark was alleged to have been made. Int. A. G. Gaston, March 28, 1988.

336 *"Negroes Uniting in Birmingham":* NYT, April 11, 1963.

336 *"central committee":* "Central Committee Members," SCLC 137.7. The SCLC/ACMHR members on the committee included Lola Hendricks, Bill Shortridge, Nelson Smith, Andy Young, and Dorothy Cotton.

336 *"elemental act of chewing on bones":* Young, *Burden,* p. 233.

337 *"principal adviser," who "flew in from Atlanta":* NYT, April 10 and 9, 1963.

337 *"upside-down civil rights crew":* Jackson to Rutledge, April 9, 1963, EOJAR.

337 *"both wasteful and worthless":* BW, April 10, 1963. See also editorial of April 13. In retrospect, Jackson would say simply that he did not "sign" with King "not out of any lack of enthusiasm or support or anything for Dr. King, I just have not felt like I had any reason to assign that anybody was my leader." Emory O. Jackson oral history, MSOH, pp. 22–23.

337 *"This is a hard struggle":* Jackson to Rutledge, April 12, 1963, EOJAR.

13. Baptism

338 *The city jail was:* "Hoosegow Home-Coming," undated clip and undated *BN* article in "Birmingham Jail" file, TCSH; C. Harris, *Power,* pp. 161–62.

339 *had been frustrated:* Hibbler: int. Al Hibbler, July 3, 1987; NYT, April 10 and 11, 1963; police memo, April 10, 1963, mass meeting, BC; *Jet,* April 25, 1963. Hibbler had gone solo in 1951 after touring with Ellington for eight years.

339 *safeguarded Moore's job:* int. Jamie Moore, Dec. 9, 1987. Instead, Connor filed forty-eight charges against Moore for allegedly condoning illegal liquor sales and for campaigning for Connor's opponent, Lindbergh. "We don't want that loud mouth talking up and down the hall," Moore had reputedly said of candidate Connor (*BN,* Jan. 16, 1958). Upheld by the personnel board, he became the first police chief to beat Connor.

339 *at Legion Field:* int. Jamie Moore, Dec. 9, 1987. For timing of trip to Albany, see Director to Attorney General, Aug. 11, 1962, Levison FBI.

339 *first thing Connor did:* telephone int. Laurie Pritchett, Aug. 17, 1991; Pritchett oral history in Raines, *My Soul,* p. 365.

340 *"If a camera catches you," lieutenant who awarded,* and *"If you arrest a live burglar":* confidential police int., March 1985.

340 *"Mr. Blinky":* ibid.

340 *boosting police morale:* Watters, *Down,* p. 206.

340 *"don't lay your hands on him":* int. Al Hibbler, July 3, 1987.

340 *"using force only against Negroes":* NYT, April 9, 1963.

340 *"Southern Policemen Adopting":* Jet, May 2, 1963.

340 *took Connor to dinner:* int. Clarence Allgood, May 16, 1991.

340 *Pritchett paid a call:* int. Laurie Pritchett, Aug. 17, 1991.

341 *"We want to keep our friendship with the Klan":* int. Maurice House, Spring 1985.

341 *unprecedented alignment:* LeGrand int. with Rowe, p. 5, BPSF 9.1; Finger to Jones, Sept. 9, 1963, Box 3, BPSF. In April, Page began communicating with Fields, whose ass he had sworn to whip two years earlier.

341 *"must live a sacrificial life":* police memo, April 10, 1963, mass meeting, BC.

341 *William A. Jenkins* and *"some woman":* int. William A. Jenkins Jr., Dec. 7, 1987.

341 *signature restrained:* ibid.; Westin and Mahoney, *Trial,* p. 69; telephone int. James "Mack" Breckenridge, March 11, 1987. Surprisingly, Breckenridge said that James Simpson had nothing to do with the decision to seek an injunction.

342 *Ray Belcher, one of the Klan's friendlier contacts:* Rowe Baxley deposition, p. 38, BPSF 9.1..

342 *"a flagrant denial":* Westin and Mahoney, *Trial,* p. 77.

342 *"electric event":* int. Karl Fleming, June 16, 1992.

342 *increasing the penalties:* Westin and Mahoney, *Trial,* p. 68. The state legislature had already passed a bill allowing city judges to set appeal bonds for misdemeanors at $2,500 instead of the previous limit of $300.

342 *"obey such an injunction":* Justice Potter's opinion in *T. Walker v. Birmingham,* Appendix B and p. 3; Westin and Mahoney, *Trial,* pp. 101, 79; NYT, April 12, 1963.

342 *managing editor John Bloomer:* int. John Bloomer, June 1984; Bloomer to author, June 8 and 14, 1984; Navasky int. with Chuck Morgan, ca. 1968, Box 29, VN; Lee Bains int. with Duard LeGrand, courtesy of Bains; telephone int. Peggy Roberson, Dec. 12, 1984.

343 *"Why don't you put buckshot in those things":* NYT, April 12, 1963.

343 *"I'm going to speak last:* int. Norman Jimerson, May 1988; int. William Spencer, Spring 1983; int. George Murray, June 2, 1990; ACHR quarterly report, March–May 1963, ACHR.

343 *Bull Connor smiled:* police memo, April 11, 1963, mass meeting, BC.

343 *King had been on the phone with Harry Belafonte:* Abernathy, *Walls,* p. 245.

343 *he had canceled the concert:* Revisionism would have it that a mix-up had caused Hibbler to be barred from Gaston's auditorium. Gaston would even claim in his autobiography, *Green Power* (pp. 124–25), that Hibbler had apologized for laying blame on him, although Hibbler maintains, "I did not apologize and will not apologize."

343 *Hibbler appeased the throng* and *concert at the Star Bowling Alley:* police memo, April 11, 1963, mass meeting, BC; int. Charles Davis, Oct. 6, 1983; int. Al Hibbler, July 3, 1987.

344 *three-piece suit and watch chain:* Young, *Burden,* p. 206.

344 *"sometime after the Easter sales":* Abernathy, *Walls,* p. 248.

344 *"converted judges"* and *"if there had been a federal injunction":* int. Fred Shuttlesworth, May 25, 1987.

344 *slamming down his clipboard:* Wyatt Walker oral history, MSOH, p. 49.

344 *had a dream* and *Calvin's tendency toward "vision":* int. Calvin Woods, July 15, 1987; int. John Porter, Oct. 6, 1983.

344 *save Bull, Wallace, and Khrushchev:* police memo, Feb. 11, 1963, mass meeting, BC.

344 *sounds of cheering:* Abernathy, *Walls,* p. 249.

344 *Shuttlesworth recognized the symbolic value:* int. Fred Shuttlesworth, May 25, 1987. "I appreciated his dramatizing it," he said, "when he used the significance of the Good Friday/Easter situation. I had no problem with that." Shuttlesworth stood ready to lead the Good Friday march himself if King backed out.

345 *wearing his denim:* M. L. King, *Why,* p. 73.

345 *did not want to go to jail:* Williams, *Eyes,* p. 186. For other versions see M. L. King, *Why,* p. 73, and Abernathy, *Walls,* p. 249.

345 *walked unnoticed past a police car:* Abernathy, *Walls,* p. 250.

345 *"just like Jesus":* C. S. King, *My Life,* p. 223.

346 *briefed by Walker:* Justice William Brennan's dissent, *Walker v. Birmingham.*

346 *"the Charge of the Light Brigade":* int. Karl Fleming, June 16, 1992.

346 *collared King and Abernathy:* NYT, April 13, 1963; *Jet,* April 25, 1963 (says shirts were gray); Abernathy, *Walls,* p. 252. One of the marchers arrested with them was seventeen-year-old Virginia Clark, who would grow up to be the borough president of Manhattan, Virginia Fields. Telephone int. Virginia Fields, Nov. 16, 2000.

346 *"the beginning of his true leadership":* Williams, *Eyes,* p. 186.

346 *"came down to an ultimatum":* int. Fred Shuttlesworth, May 25, 1987.

346 *At the Southside jail:* int. Jonathan McPherson, Oct. 5, 1983; McPherson oral history, Miles-Tuskegee Oral History Project; figures extrapolated from *NYT,* April 13, 1963; police memo, April 23, 1963, mass meeting, BC.

346 *Shuttlesworth earlier called Constance Baker Motley:* Westin and Mahoney, *Trial,* p. 77.

347 *Connor refused to let him see his clients:* Andrew Young, in *Burden,* p. 215, contends that the Inc. Fund had sent Amaker and Leroy Clark down to Birmingham from the beginning to be on the scene full-time. For example, Young says that once the decision was made to march, the lawyers began creating a paper trail to support their contention that this was not a parade, since they would be marching two by two and obeying all traffic lights.

347 *"Use the influence of your high office":* Walker to J. and R. Kennedy, April 12, 1963, MLK 1.8; *NYT,* April 15, 1963.

347 *1 a.m. phone call* and *no legal standing:* NYT, April 14, 1963.

347 *"the meaning of utter darkness":* M. L. King, *Why,* p. 74.

347 *"strange Stars of Segregation":* "Statement by Rev. F. L. Shuttlesworth," FS 1.

347 *"who do you want to lead?":* int. Burke Marshall, October 1985.

347 *took it to Bull Connor* and *"Bring that nigger King":* Westin and Mahoney, *Trial,* p. 86.

348 *"unwise and untimely":* "We the undersigned clergymen," (April 1963), in CCJC; also in *BN,* April 12, 1963; *NYT,* April 14, 1963.

348 *were admitted to services:* Andy Young at First Baptist and other church details, *NYT,* April 15 and 18, 1963 (corrects misidentification of First Presbyterian from previous report); Harding, "A Beginning," p. 15. The only other successful infiltrators were two black women admitted at First Presbyterian. "I'm so glad you came," they were told.

348 *for the Oscars:* Britannica Book of the Year, 1964, p. 688. Gregory Peck won best actor for his portrayal of Scout's father, Atticus, though the movie itself lost out to *Lawrence of Arabia.*

349 *waiters' car collide:* conversation with Hobart A. McWhorter Jr., Oct. 22, 1982.

14. Two Mayors and a King

351 *thirty official marchers:* NYT, April 15, 1963; *Walker v. Birmingham.*

351 *covered with red paint* and *decapitated head:* FBI ints. with Evelyn Shaffer, Oct. 12, 1963, with Mrs. B. Freeman Brown, Oct. 4, 1963, with Mabel Moore, Oct. 8, 1963, and with Terrance Moore, Oct. 4, 1963, Bapbomb.

351 *discharging a bullet into Wyman's gut:* FBI ints. with Johnny Frank Jones, May 29, 1965, and with Bobby Frank Cherry, Oct. 16, 1963, Bapbomb.

351 *policeman drove Tommy Rowe:* "Garry Thomas Rowe, Jr.," Nov. 25, 1975, p. 5, and Rowe California disposition, pp. 25–26, BPSF 9.1.

352 *"A warm sun":* NYT, April 16, 1963.

352 *Walker had urged:* police memo, April 14, 1963, mass meeting, BC.

352 *"whatever else you need":* M. L. King, *Why,* p. 75.

352 *"tied to these Communists":* int. Edward Gardner, Oct. 7, 1983.

352 *sent Connor a copy of "Commands for the Volunteers":* Ellis to Connor, April 9, 1963, BC.

352 *Connor remarked, "Orzell":* int. Orzell Billingsley, July 18, 1987.

352 *a soft spot for George Wallace:* Billingsley to Branch, Jan. 17, 1983, courtesy of Billingsley.

352 *"Awww I got you.":* police memo, April 15, 1963, mass meeting, BC.

353 *Kennedy returned her call:* C. S. King, *My Life,* pp. 225–26; Garrow, *Bearing,* p. 243; Jim Bishop, *The Days of Martin Luther King Jr.* (New York: Putnam's, 1971), p. 296.

353 *Jamie Moore denied to reporters:* NYT, April 17, 1963.

353 *"You better let him":* int. Clarence Allgood, May 16, 1991. Allgood implied that there was something controversial on the tape. In 1991, he came across the tape while cleaning out his files and burned it.

353 *"Yes, and he told me"* and *"Is that known?":* police transcript of call, April 15, 1963, included in police memo dated April 17, BC.

353 *"second phase"*: police memo, April 15, 1963, mass meeting, BC.
353 *knew they were going to win* and *"Added together"*: int. Chuck Morgan, December 1985; Navasky int. with Morgan, VN; int. Clarence Jones, Oct. 24, 2000.
353 *Hanes, made room for Boutwell*: int. Art Hanes, May 24, 1984.
353 *tackled the agenda all over again:* Lee Bains ints. with M. Edwin Wiggins and E. C. "Doc" Overton (city councilors), courtesy of Bains.
353 *"a Bit Phony"*: quoted in Branch, *Parting*, p. 736.
353 *"good personal friend"*: *NYT*, April 18, 1963.
354 *raining on Boutwell's parade:* e.g., "Racial Peace in Birmingham?," *NYT*, April 17, 1963.
354 *"letter from prison"*: telephone conversation with Harvey Shapiro, March 18, 1992.
354 *"men of genuinely good will"*: M. L. King, *Why*, p. 89. Subsequent quotations from "Letter from Birmingham Jail" are taken from the reprint of the letter in *Why*, pp. 76–95.
354 *selling himself as a citizen of the world:* This idea is pursued in Miller, *Voice*, pp. 65–66.
354 *"Spenserian hand"* and *"chicken scratch"*: Wyatt Walker oral history, MSOH, p. 73; int. Wyatt Walker, Jan. 13, 1984. William Kunstler read the letter sheet by sheet as it came out of the typewriter. Kunstler, *Deep*, p. 187.
355 *King reputedly had no idea of its moment:* See Garrow, *Bearing*, p. 671*n*.
355 *"one of the historic documents"*: Wyatt Walker oral history, MSOH, p. 73; int. Wyatt Walker, Jan. 13, 1984.
355 *Shapiro could not get the letter past:* telephone conversation with Harvey Shapiro, March 18, 1992. The *New York Post* published the first excerpts of the letter on May 19, 1963. The Quaker journal, *Friends*, published it in its June issue. The first mention of the letter I could find was in *The New Republic* of May 18, which quoted a piece of it.
355 *published in full:* in the *New Leader*, June 24, 1963.
355 *name ought to have been on the "Letter"*: ints. Fred Shuttlesworth.
355 *smarted as their reputation:* telephone int. Milton Grafman, March 18, 1992; int. George Murray, June 2, 1990. One copy of the "Letter" found its way into the hands of the Birmingham police. Box 4, BPSF.
355 *By prearrangement with King:* int. James Bevel, Sept. 18, 1988.
355 *"scam movement"*: and other Bevel quotes unless otherwise cited, ibid.
355 *His speech at the mass meeting:* police memo, April 12, 1963, mass meeting, BC.
356 *only 9 seasoned "jailbirds"*: police memo, April 16, 1963, mass meeting, BC.
356 *Young called for volunteers:* police memo, April 17, 1963, mass meeting, BC.
356 *compared with 738:* *NYT*, April 10, 1963; Oates, *Trumpet*, p. 218.
356 *"going to jail for getting drunk"*: police memo, April 10, 1963, mass meeting, BC.
356 *"blood tests"*: police memo, April 19, 1963, mass meeting, BC.
356 *met at a Movement minister's home:* Harding, "A Beginning," p. 15; int. Norman Jimerson, May 1988. Vann decided that Jimerson's public identification with the cause made it unwise to include him in any further negotiations.
356 *Townsend had advised them to hold out:* int. Norman Jimerson, May 1988; "Outline of Negotiations," DV. Their excuse to the blacks was that they had decided to sit tight until the courts named the legitimate city government.
356 *judged Shuttlesworth's performance "tremendous"*: Walker to King and Abernathy, "Progress report," undated (ca. Friday, April 19, 1963), MLK 1.8.
356 *Shuttlesworth threatened to go back to jail:* Marshall's "Monday Report," April 23, 1963, BM.
356 *Gaston evicted the Movement:* int. Julia Rainge, July 15, 1987. A tenant complained that one of the pickets had come in for lunch drunk. Gaston later apologized.
356 *"Dr. Gaston has supported"*: undated press release, "King Aide Terms Gaston Blast Unfair," MLK.
357 *"not to be believed"*: int. Claude Sitton, May 5, 1992. Karl Fleming (int. June 16, 1992) seconded Sitton's estimation of Walker.
357 *mass meeting:* police memo, April 22, 1963, mass meeting, BC.
357 *ACMHR regulars noted:* int. Julia Rainge, July 15, 1987. Porter (int. Oct. 6, 1983): "I was not an all-day everyday civil righter."
357 *Simpson was not present:* int. Florence Evans Simpson, March 22, 1989.
357 *Simpson had filed suit:* Simpson had found a 1959 state law holding that in the event of a change in the form of city government the incumbent administration should serve out its term. Three of the state supreme court justices had upheld a 1955 statute making the changeover immediate. *BN*, April 4, 1963; int. David Vann, June 16, 1992.
357 *"sit-ins"*: police memo, April 15, 1963, mass meeting, BC.
358 *Tuxedo Junction:* *NYT*, April 6, 1988.
358 *"anything could happen"*: int. Constance Motley, March 27, 1991.
358 *courtroom drama that would expose:* See Westin and Mahoney, *Trial*, pp. 101–102.
358 *lawyers were kept in the dark:* Young, "And Birmingham," p. 27.
358 *April 23, mass meeting:* police memo, April 23, 1963, mass meeting, BC.
358 *William Moore:* *NYT*, April 24 and 26, 1963; *Jet*, May 9, 1963; *BN*, April 24, 1963. Branch, *Parting*, pp. 748–49. In Jackson, Moore planned to deliver a letter to Ross Barnett asking him in essence to rise to the occasion of history.
358 *Floyd Simpson:* *MA*, ca. November 1989, courtesy of John Yung.
359 *sit-in at Woolworth's:* Ellard and Vance to Jamie Moore, April 24, 1963, BC; Young, "The Day," p. 8.
359 *Lankford spotted:* Lankford statement to FBI, Sept. 17, 1963, Bapbomb. It's not clear that this was on the same day as these particular sit-ins.
359 *"practiced democracy"* and other Bevel quotes, int. James Bevel, Sept. 18, 1988. "They married their sex partner; they didn't marry their brain partner."
359 *"seduce their mothers"*: int. Julian Bond, Spring 1984.
359 *Horace Mann Bond:* Richards, "Youth Congress," p. 183.
359 *Shelley Stewart:* int. Shelley Stewart, May 1984.
360 *Klan cut down his radio tower:* Emory Via's report on trip to Birmingham, April 2–4, 1958, SRC; int. Shelley Stewart, May 1984. They scrawled KKK in red on the station.

360   *"Tall Paul" Dudley White:* FBI ints. with Ulysses Jackson, Oct. 12, 1963, and with Robert Jones, Oct. 20, 1963, Bapbomb.

360   *happy to go on the radio:* int. James Bevel, Sept. 18, 1988.

361   *"In forty years":* Coffin, *Every Man,* p. 173; Deming, "Notes After Birmingham," p. 157.

361   *collection of weapons:* college student interviewed on Riverside tape, Part 4, side 7.

361   *White Paper:* int. James Bevel, Sept. 18, 1988; police memo, April 27, 1963, mass meeting, BC.

361   *spiked locally by Vincent Townsend:* Charles Wittenstein field report, April 26, 1961, "Visits to Alabama Cities," AJC.

361   *mass meeting:* police memo, April 24, 1963, mass meeting, BC.

362   *camouflage the trip to Montgomery:* Navasky int. with Edwin Guthman, VN.

362   *Confederate battle flag:* MA, Nov. 1, 1992.

362   *governor's own men was behind the pickets:* Carter, *Wallace,* p. 120, says that Carter had engineered it.

362   *"not for laughs":* R. Kennedy, Own Words, p. 185.

362   *"a pugnacious sapling":* Lesher, *Wallace,* p. 182.

362   *"If you want to pay a courtesy visit":* Navasky int. with Ed Guthman (who was present), VN; Carter, *Wallace,* pp. 121–23.

362   *Barnett's advice:* Taylor, *Me 'n' George,* p. 31.

363   *enough pull with the Klan:* Guthman, *Band of Brothers,* p. 211.

363   *children's section of the ACMHR:* Eskew, "ACM," p. 76. Largely, it seemed, *in loco parentis;* discipline of children was a theme of Shuttlesworth's—see also March 20, 1961, police memo, BC.

363   *Bevel scared the wits:* Lee Bains int. with John Porter, courtesy of Bains. They called him the "Young Turk." Int. Abraham Woods, June 19, 1992.

363   *on the recruitment of children:* int. Julia Rainge, July 15, 1987; Lee Bains ints. with John Drew and John Porter, courtesy of Bains; int. John Porter, Oct. 6, 1983; int. James Montgomery, Dec. 9, 1989; int. A. G. Gaston, March 28, 1988; int. Deenie Drew, May 1988.

363   *"no sense of public relations":* int. John Porter, Oct. 6, 1983.

363   *"I asked you, twice"* and *"peace at the center":* Rather, *Camera,* pp. 97–98, 90.

363   *sentences for criminal contempt:* Westin and Mahoney, *Trial,* pp. 141–42; int. William Jenkins, Dec. 7, 1987. Jenkins maintained that civil contempt was never a consideration because it has to occur during court proceedings.

364   *youth rally was called:* Whitehouse to Jamie Moore, "Mass Meeting on April 26, 1963," BC.

364   *mass meeting:* police memo, April 27, 1963, mass meeting, BC.

364   *"too young to go to jail":* The New Republic, May 18, 1963, pp. 3–4.

364   *blizzard of leaflets, FBI informed:* House to Moore, April 30, 1963, BC.

364   *Connor ordered his school superintendent:* Wright to Bell, April 30, 1963, BC.

364   *state troopers charged up:* "Action Memo" from Jim Dombrowski to "Friends of SCEF Everywhere," Southern Conference Educational Fund, Inc., May 6, 1963, BC. Paul Brooks of Nashville, one of the original SNCC Freedom Riders, was leading the march with Nash.

15. D. Day

365   *knocking back two shooters:* Wayne Greenhaw int. in MA, March 24, 1988.

365   *"run out of niggers":* Newsweek, May 18, 1963, p. 27.

365   *network of black informers:* int. Maurice House, Spring 1985. The informants were arrested right along with the other marchers, to protect their cover until their cases could be dropped.

365   *"Go tell 'em this":* int. Lola Hendricks, March 26, 1989.

365   *Nazi Party hanging out in Montgomery:* Moore to all members of police department, April 22 and 24, 1963, BC.

365   *took off their badges* and *some cops revolted:* confidential police int., March 1985.

365   *"Any time an officer stops a black S.O.B.":* Inter-Citizens Committee document no. 38, IC.

365   *they all looked alike:* int. Edward Gardner, Oct. 7, 1983.

365   *"I know you are right":* police memo, April 23, 1963, mass meeting, BC.

365   *shared a sandwich:* Harding, "A Beginning," p. 15; also Young, "The Day," p. 10.

366   *"Shoot me":* May Day riot, SW, May 9, 1933; Painter, *Hudson,* pp. 144–45; Kelley, *Hammer,* p. 33; Jane Speed affidavit in La Follette hearings, Part 3, pp. 961–62.

366   *White's only discernible close friend:* FBI int. with Ulysses Jackson, Oct. 12, 1963, Bapbomb.

366   *an indulgent smile:* int. Shelley Stewart, May 1984.

366   *eight hundred kids missed roll call:* BPH, May 4, 1963.

366   *The third-grade teacher:* Audrey Hendricks oral history in Levine, *Freedom's Children,* p. 95.

366   *"Largest in the World":* Davis, *Angela Davis,* p. 99.

366   *locked the school's front gates:* police memo, May 2, 1963, mass meeting, BC.

366   *"Yessir" a little white boy:* BN, Jan. 20, 1986.

367   *"nothing for them to be afraid of":* int. James Bevel, Sept. 18, 1988.

367   *"I'll Die to Make":* Jet, May 23, 1963.

367   *"people get excited":* Young, "And Birmingham," p. 27.

367   *"Hey, Fred, how many?":* police memo, May 2, 1963, mass meeting, BC.

367   *"Sing, children":* children's march, M. L. King, *Why,* p. 9; NYT, May 3, 1963; BN, May 3, 1963.

367   *"Which Side Are You On?"* and *"Will You Join Us?":* Jet, May 23, 1963.

367   *"Freedom":* Riverside tape, Part 1, side 2; M. L. King, *Why,* p. 98. Abernathy, *Walls,* p. 262, makes the point about innocence. King wrote that the "amused policeman" spoke with "mock gruffness." Little over a year later, when he gave his interview to *Playboy* (January 1965 issue), the policeman had "accosted" the little girl and "asked her gruffly."

367   *"How stupid":* Glenn Evans oral history in Raines, *My Soul,* p. 171.

368   *trying to make up his mind:* int. James Bevel, Sept. 18, 1988; int. Abraham Woods, June 19, 1992. Bevel said King, Walker, and Shuttlesworth had not come around to using children, although Shuttlesworth was on the scene approvingly.

368   *that Bevel be disciplined:* int. James Bevel, Sept. 18, 1988.

368   *jails were filled:* per King, police memo, May 2, 1963, BC 13.5. *NYT* (May 2, 1963) puts the count at over five hundred.

368   *"I have been inspired":* police memo, May 2, 1963, BC.

368   *Wallace threatened:* BPH, May 4, 1963.

368   *"Let those kids stay":* int. A. G. Gaston, March 28, 1988.

368   *press conference in the courtyard:* police memo on press conference, May 3, 1963, BC; *NYT,* May 4, 1963.

368   *had come to workshop:* ints. Glenn Smiley, April 26, 1989 and September 1989.

368   *peach pit* and *trashcanful of knives:* Fred Shuttlesworth oral history, KC, side 8; John Cross oral history, KC, p. 42.

369   *"throwing bottles and cussing":* Deming, "Notes After Birmingham," p. 16.

369   *"Here they come":* Newsweek, May 13, 1963.

369   *"Do not cross":* NYT, May 4, 1963; Bill Hudson's telegram to Pulitzer Committee, January 1964, courtesy of Hudson.

369   *laughing at the cops:* int. James D. Smith, Spring 1984. Since fire was the preferred assignment over police, candidates had to score higher on the civil service exam, resulting in the fire department having the better-caliber force.

369   *fire department ran:* ints. John Swindle, July 16, 1987, and July 13, 1993 (telephone); int. O. N. Gallant, March 16, 1987; and int. Robert Reeves, February 1986.

370   *First sailor to die:* BN, Dec. 2, 1974.

370   *Bob Zellner:* telephone int. Bob Zellner, Nov. 15, 1994; Morgan, *A Time,* pp. 140–41. He was merely recruiting for SNCC at his alma mater, Huntingdon College.

370   *press corps had followed:* int. Joe Cumming, June 20–21, 1992.

370   *Charles Moore:* telephone int. Charles Moore, April 28, 1992.

370   *automatic machine-gun fire:* Deming, "Notes After Birmingham."

371   *Gaston was on the phone with David Vann:* int. David Vann, May 24, 1984; Vann, LeGrand speech; int. A. G. Gaston, March 28, 1988.

371   *Smiley sat on the church steps:* ints. Glenn Smiley, April 26, 1989, and September 1989.

371   *gasped in mock horror, some wagged their backsides:* Newsweek, May 13, 1963.

371   *In the background of his crowd shots:* telephone int. Charles Moore, April 28, 1992. The photograph was not published at the time.

371   *"Bring the dogs":* Bill Hudson's telegram to Pulitzer Committee, January 1964, courtesy of Hudson.

371   *"Clear the park":* telephone conversation with Bobby Joe Danner, July 1987.

371   *bitten in the heel:* violent K-9 incidents, Inter-Citizens Committee's "Report on Police Brutality During the May 3, 1963 Demonstrations in Birmingham, Alabama," IC.

371   *took off their shirts* and *barked in the dogs' faces:* Newsweek, May 13, 1963.

372   *Press's Bill Hudson:* telephone int. Bill Hudson, July 29, 1992.

372   *Walter Gadsden: Jet,* Oct. 10, 1963; Gadsden's affidavit in "Documents on Human Rights in Alabama," special brochure on the demonstrations by the Inter-Citizens Committee, IC.

372   *known for attracting straight arrows* and *race ideologues:* int. James Parsons, April 13, 1993; confidential police int., March 1985. The notable exception of the K-9 officers was the racist Klan sympathizer Lavaughn Coleman, who did not stay with the corps long.

372   *Officer Dick Middleton:* phone conversations with R. E. Middleton, April 14, 1993, and C. R. Boyd, April 13, 1993. "You in New York?" Boyd (known as "Bunny Rabbit"), Major's handler, asked me. "You be good to us rednecks down here, OK?" The K-9 Corps had been in action for less than a half hour and would never be called out again against the demonstrators. But they had done their job. "We all got promoted because we were due for one," explained Bobby Joe Danner (telephone conversation, July 1987).

372   *"Why did you bring old Tiger out?":* int. Major Bill Jones, March 1985.

372   *came undone over the dogs and hoses:* int. Lola Hendricks, March 26, 1989.

373   *SNCC and CORE marchers:* NYT, May 4, 1963; BPH, May 4, 1963; Forman, *Making,* pp. 308–309; Watters, *Down,* pp. 243–47; int. Claude Sitton, May 5, 1992; Newsweek, May 13, 1963.

373   *Moore was sickened:* telephone int. Charles Moore, April 28, 1992.

373   *"nigger gals":* telephone int. Charles Moore, April 28, 1992. This occurred when Moore was on assignment on the governor's plane.

373   *a hundred pounds of water:* C. Moore, *Powerful,* p. 99.

373   *"They Fight a Fire":* Life, May 17, 1963.

374   *"y'all better watch what you say":* conversation with Dan Rather, Oct. 20, 1990.

374   *"educational TV":* Young, "And Birmingham," p. 25.

374   *R. W. "Johnny" Apple:* telephone int. R. W. Apple, March 7, 1993.

374   *"television's greatest hour":* Rustin int. on the short-lived ABC program *Our World* on the year 1963.

374   *Jim Laxon:* telephone int. Jim Laxon, July 30, 1992.

375   *"Sure, people got hit":* int. Wyatt Walker, Jan. 13, 1984.

375   *"get involved":* telephone int. Walter Gadsden, April 19, 1993.

375   *Gadsden's own lunge had broken the dog's jaw:* int. C. Herbert Oliver, Jan. 13, 1984. Oliver recalled that it was Henry Lee Shambry who did this, but the evidence suggests that he meant Gadsden.

375   *being cut to death:* int. Frank Dukes, Oct. 4, 1983.

376   *blow dog whistles:* int. Wyatt Walker, Jan. 13, 1984. Walker said one of his New York advisers brought down the whistles.

376   *"We must not boo":* police memo, May 3, 1963, mass meeting, BC.

376   *Jennifer Fancher: Jet,* May 23, 1963.
377   *Today there was:* May 4 march, *NYT,* May 5, 1963; *Newsweek,* May 13, 1963; Deming, "Notes After Birmingham," p. 14.
377   *"Y'all don't like us":* int. Robert Reeves, February 1986.
377   *two black prostitutes:* telephone ints. Paul Jones, Oct. 24 and 25, 1995.
377   *preferred Pepsi* and *ancient rumors:* conversation with Josephine Truss, July 1987. In 1955, the NAACP removed the Coke vending machine from its New York headquarters after a South Carolina Coke bottler made a "nigger" speech. Wilkins to Kendrix, Dec. 9, 1955, *BWC* 1.6.
377   *turned to Captain George Wall:* telephone conversation with George Wall, March 29, 1988; int. James Bevel, Sept. 18, 1988; *NYT,* May 5, 1963; *Newsweek,* May 13, 1963.
377   *Hanes strode into A. G. Gaston Smith Building:* int. Art Hanes, May 24, 1984; *NYT,* May 5, 1963, for timing.
378   *"Roman holiday":* int. Wyatt Walker, Jan. 13, 1984.
378   *"We thought it was fun":* conversation with Josephine Truss, July 1987.
378   *was in Detroit: NYT,* May 5, 1963.

16. Miracle

379   *"visually strong baiting postures":* and other Bloomer quotes, Bloomer to author, June 8, 1984.
379   *counseling the city fathers to stall:* ACHR quarterly report, March–May 1963, ACHR. After receiving his intelligence about the children's march, Townsend had tried to revive the biracial negotiations during the week leading up to D-Day. But one leading department store owner—the smart money would say Isadore Pizitz—was vowing that neither he nor his colleagues would negotiate with Negroes.
380   *Bailey, to call Justice:* Burke Marshall oral history, JFK, p. 97.
380   *having spoken the day before:* Marshall phone logs, May 3, 1963, BM.
380   *reconnoitering trips:* int. Burke Marshall, October 1985; Birmingham SAC to Director, Feb. 9, 1962, Levison FBI, mentions Marshall's trip to Birmingham on February 9, 1962.
380   *joke du jour:* Mississippi version of this joke in Lemann to Marshall, Feb. 11, 1963, BM.
380   *he had reputedly been passed over:* Navasky int. with Nicholas Katzenbach, Nov. 20, 1968, VN.
380   *Code of the Ivy League Gentleman:* See Navasky, *Justice,* pp. 159–242.
381   *colleague Harris Wofford:* Wofford, *Kennedys,* p. 93; int. Joseph Dolan, June 22, 1992. Wofford, who became an adviser to the President on civil rights, left the administration in November 1961 because Kennedy decided to delay until after the spring primaries signing his promised "stroke of the pen" executive order desegregating federal housing.
381   *reciprocated Marshall's taciturnity:* Navasky int. with Burke Marshall, VN. "I don't remember it as being a paragon of communication between us."
381   *"wholly lacks the extroverted": NYT,* May 10, 1963.
381   *looked on as mentor:* Navasky int. with Harold Reis, April 21, 1969, VN.
381   *"Do you think?":* and other Marshall material, int. Burke Marshall, October 1985.
381   *Dolan gave credit* and other Dolan material, ints. Joseph Dolan, November 1986, June 22, 1992, and Nov. 8, 1994.
381   *"best lawyer":* Navasky int. with Joseph Dolan, VN.
381   *King had enumerated them:* police memo, May 3, 1963, mass meeting, BC.
382   *in Abe Berkowitz's law office:* "Outline of Negotiations," DV; int. Joseph Dolan, November 1986; int. Burke Marshall, October 1985; int. Isadore Pizitz, March 1983.
382   *sales were off 30 percent* and *more stores were for rent: NYT,* May 10, 1963.
382   *Eastwood Mall: BN,* Aug. 31 and 22, 1960.
382   *Morris Adler* and *shape of a cross:* int. Julian Adler, March 31, 1988; Taft, *Dixie,* pp. 52–55; int. Dora Sterne, Dec. 9, 1987.
382   *impotence of Birmingham's 3,900 Jews:* In Birmingham as elsewhere, financial prosperity–the median household income of the local Jews was a hefty $30,000—did not translate into political power. Nichols, " 'Cities Are,' " p. 209.
382   *eminent in local government:* Robert G. Corley, *Paying "Civic Rent": The Jews of Emanu-El and the Birmingham Community* (Birmingham: privately published, 1982) unpaginated. Isaac Hochstadter, a member of one of Birmingham's three pioneer Jewish families, was elected to the first of four terms as alderman in 1875, when the "Jewish vote" was all of about twenty. There was also a Jewish police chief. Otto Marx had maintained his membership at the Birmingham Country Club fourteen years after he moved to New York in 1916.
382   *Irving Engel* and *"not the kind of Jew":* Irving Engel oral history, tape 1, pp. 7–8, 30–33, tape 2, p. 3, AJC.
383   *"Jew money":* Carter, *Scottsboro,* p. 235. A white moderate said that the prosecution's rantings of "Jew money" had "damaged the standing of Southern Jews" even more than the Klan rhetoric of the twenties.
383   *Congregation of Reform Judaism:* a copy of its statement of principles attached to Marvin Engel to Samet, Dec. 9, 1955, "Communal Issues, Birmingham, 1944–1962," AJC; Elovitz, *Jewish Life,* pp. 157–58.
383   *Engel had invited:* New Orleans meeting of Jews, Louis S. Breier's field report, March 21, 1950, "Visits, Birmingham, 1944–1962," AJC; Irving Engel oral history, tape 4, pp. 6–8, and William Engel oral history, tape 2, p. 102, AJC.
383   *old-line (non-Zionist):* Kesselman, *FEPC,* p. 104.
383   *guest in the region:* William Engel (paraphrasing Morris Abram) oral history, tape 3, p. 182, AJC.
383   *bending over backward to conform:* When in 1957, the AJC joined a friend-of-the-court brief in behalf of Alabama's outlawed NAACP, Birmingham's Jews became so embittered that they discussed boycotting the committee and filing a counterbrief. Harold Murray's field report, March 20, 1958, "Alabama Visits," AJC.
383   *"It was the Miami Jews":* int. Art Hanes, May 24, 1984.
383   *"My biggest interest":* Nichols, " 'Cities Are,' " p. 210.
383   *Porter sought permission:* int. John Porter, Oct. 6, 1983.
384   *"In Jesus' name":* int. Milton Grafman, July 1982.

384   *meet with King and Shuttlesworth:* ACHR quarterly report, March–May 1963, ACHR; Shuttlesworth oral history, KC, side 11; ints. Fred Shuttlesworth; int. George Murray, June 2, 1990; int. Milton Grafman, July 1982.

384   *"wonderful to them":* int. Milton Grafman, July 1982.

384   *"In the Negro Movement":* quoted in Nichols, " 'Cities Are,' " p. 164.

384   *believe that the merchants controlled:* Lee Bains int. with Fred Shuttlesworth, courtesy of Bains.

384   *old theory among blacks:* Ed Strong int. with Hosea Hudson, May 1940, RB 34.1, p. 5.

384   *"We have to be patient":* police memo, April 26, 1963, mass meeting, BC.

384   *friends were aghast:* Elovitz, *Jewish Life,* p. 225.

384   *leader of Birmingham's Zionist movement:* ibid., pp. 135 and 142–45.

384   *the divisive class issue:* Isaiah Terman's field reports, July 20, 1945, and April 1, 1946, and Lawrence L. Koch's field reports, July 9 and Aug. 10, 1948, "Visits to Birmingham, 1944–1962," AJC. Leo Oberdorfer and the other anti-Zionists issued a statement opposing "all propaganda and agitation which assert that Jews constitute a nation."

384   *consulting Vincent Townsend:* int. Louis Oberdorfer, September 1986; int. Emil Hess, May 1984.

385   *he always cringed:* int. Abe Berkowitz, ca. Spring 1983.

385   *"lousy soup":* int. Joseph Dolan, November 1986.

385   *Pizitz, who had been standing:* int. Julia Rainge, July 15, 1987.

385   *"put myself in the middle":* int. Isadore Pizitz, March 1983.

385   *"maimed, or dead child":* *NYT,* May 4, 1963. He did finally endorse the aims of the Negroes, but the gist of his comments echoed Mayor Albert Boutwell's first official statement, also printed in the May 4 *Times,* blasting the "irresponsible and unthinking agitators" for using children.

385   *pictures made him "sick":* Only the previous February, Kennedy had forbidden photographers to take pictures of Sammy Davis Jr. and his Swedish wife, Mai Britt, at a White House reception on Lincoln's Birthday. Simeon Booker oral history, JFK, p. 24.

385   *on the subject of Marshall:* int. Wyatt Walker, Jan. 13, 1984.

385   *"Blessed are the peacemakers":* Navasky, *Justice,* p. 177.

386   *"You don't argue":* int. James Bevel, Sept. 18, 1988.

386   *concert at Miles:* BW, May 15, 1963.

386   *top-forty LPs:* April list of Billboard's top LPs in MacNeil, *Way We Were,* p. 72. The Sherman album currently on the list was *My Son, the Nut.*

386   *had come to Birmingham:* telephone conversation with Guy Carawan, May 17, 1996.

386   *Andy Young announced:* and other details from meeting, in police memo, May 5, 1963, mass meeting, BC.

386   *"Don't you worry":* Deming, "Notes After Birmingham," p. 16.

387   *were machine guns* and *"knew my courage":* int. James Bevel, Sept. 18, 1988.

387   *What the press did observe:* ibid.; conversation with Laura Oden, March 1986; Dave Dellinger, "The Negroes of Birmingham," *Liberation,* Summer 1963; *NYT,* May 6, 1963; *BN,* May 6, 1963; int. Nelson Smith, Oct. 3, 1983; Myrna Carter oral history in Levine, *Freedom's Children,* pp. 106–107.

387   *his hand in Miracle Sunday:* int. John Swindle, July 16, 1987.

387   *"one of the most fantastic events":* *Playboy* int. with Martin Luther King, January 1965. In M. L. King, *Why,* p. 101, he uses similar language but does not claim to have been there.

388   *"Moses on earth":* *Negro Digest,* May 6, 1963.

388   *"living on borrowed time":* ints. Fred Shuttlesworth.

388   *a 'Christian problem' ":* Harold Katz's "Confidential Memorandum on Racial Problems Affecting the Birmingham Jewish Community," July 3, 1963, Mark Elovitz Papers, BPL.

388   *political and moral issue:* ACHR newsletter, May 1963, ACHR.

389   *Dial informed him:* "Outline of Negotiations," DV (it appears that Vann was at this meeting and the one the day before); ints. David Vann, May 24 and 28, 1984, and March 2, 1989; int. Burke Marshall, October 1985; int. Joseph Dolan, November 1986; int. Isadore Pizitz, March 1983.

389   *white companions were:* telephone int. George Peach Taylor, undated; ACHR quarterly report, March–May 1963; Lee Bains int. with David Vann, courtesy of Bains, says that Smith, Hamilton, Marshall, Smyer, and maybe Abe Berkowitz, plus Gaston, Shores, Shuttlesworth, Harold Long. Report says there were only three whites, which would leave out Erskine Smith. Joe Dolan (int. June 22, 1992) did not recall any blacks being there.

389   *stood up to his "white friends":* int. A. G. Gaston, March 28, 1988. When a local casket manufacturer who had overstocked Gaston's funeral home pressed him to get King out of town, Gaston refused. The creditor demanded payment in full. Gaston wrote a check, and asked First National's John Hand to cover it.

389   *black negotiators presented:* "Outline of Negotiations," DV; int. Edward Gardner, June 26, 1982; int. Abraham Woods, June 19, 1992; Woods oral history in Raines, *My Soul,* p. 151; int. Deenie Drew, May 1984.

389   *John Drew* and *Addine (or Deenie):* ints. Deenie Drew, May 1984 and June 18, 1992; John and Deenie Drew, int. in *BN,* Jan. 19, 1986; Wyatt Walker oral history, MSOH, p. 64.

390   *quickening dispute:* ints. Deenie Drew, May 1984 and June 18, 1992. George Peach Taylor did not remember this incident, but did recall meeting at the Drews' house once, with King, Young, Shuttlesworth, and Abernathy. Deenie Drew said that years later, Smyer wrote Drew "a love note" in which he apologized for this incident.

390   *Deenie Drew would claim:* Interestingly, details in Abernathy, *Walls,* p. 252, support Drew's story. He claims that upon their arrest, Connor ordered him and King put in Jefferson County Jail rather than Southside (city) jail, where history has placed him. But there are other mistakes in Abernathy's account (for instance, that the fairgrounds were being used to house prisoners at this point), and he mentions a barbed-wire prison yard (which the county jail did not have, only enclosed exercise rooms). Sheriff Mel Bailey said that King was not in his jail at that time (int. Mel Bailey, April 1, 1992). Also, the ACMHR's Lola Hendricks saw Walker's secretary type it up, and she even gave her a copy (int. Lola Hendricks, March 26, 1989). The copy of the original that found its way into Birmingham police files closed with MLK:wm, indicating that Willie Mackey was the typist (Box 4, BPSF). In the face of the contradictory evidence, Deenie Drew would simply insist, "All I can tell you is that I brought it out of the jail in my hands."

390   *"free our teachers":* Dorman, *We Shall,* p. 177.

390   *"look upon your gift of music": BN*, March 24, 1937, in Eleanor Roosevelt scrapbook, BPL.
390   *"Gotta GO": Negro Digest*, May 15, 1988.
390   *store owners could rationalize:* "Outline of Negotiations," DV. Smyer's Senior Citizens Committee had committed in principle to black promotions eight months earlier. As for desegregating the restrooms, some stores didn't even have signs up on theirs. To desegregate the lunch counters, they would opt for the "Atlanta plan," under which Mayor Ivan Allen had timed the integration of Rich's tearoom to coincide with school desegregation.
391   *"never put two women":* and discussion of fitting rooms, int. Joseph Dolan, November 1986.
391   *false alarms:* int. Wyatt Walker, Jan. 13, 1984; int. John Swindle, July 16, 1987. Swindle cheerfully acknowledged "a lot of trouble with fire alarms."
391   *rich white folks were donating their tennis courts:* Baez, *And a Voice*, p. 195.
391   *wearing white World War I–type helmets:* Dorman, *We Shall*, p. 177.
391   *"three hundred years of hate":* Len Holt, "Eyewitness: The Police Terror at Birmingham," *National Guardian*, May 16, 1963, reprinted in Grant, *Protest*, p. 345.
391   *advice to wear raincoats:* police memo, May 5, 1963, mass meeting, BC.
391   *"more force than necessary": Negro Digest*, May 7, 1963.
392   *pulling down $1,500 a week: The New Republic*, May 18, 1963, p. 4.
392   *"twenty years there one night":* Gregory, *Nigger*, p. 144.
392   *first celebrity to join:* ibid., pp. 169–75; Dick Gregory oral history in Raines, *My Soul*, p. 238.
392   *"Please, don't go":* Lane and Gregory, *"Zorro,"* p. 24; Raines, *My Soul*, pp. 291–92.
392   *firemen had been his childhood idols:* Lane and Gregory, *"Zorro,"* pp. 22–23. "There was something so beautiful, peaceful, and competent about the firemen's attitudes."
392   *Gregory noticed:* ibid., p. 26.
392   *Wall asked him:* Gregory-Wall confrontation and description of march, Holt, "Eyewitness," in Grant, *Protest*, p. 345; *Jet*, May 23, 1963; *NYT*, May 7, 1963.
392   *"The world is watching":* Dorman, *We Shall*, p. 178.
393   *"Birmingham jailhouse":* typescript for "Bull Connor's Jail," MLK 1.7. The actual lyrics were by Ernie Marrs. Candie Carowen to author, Nov. 9, 2000.
393   *stayed away from mass meetings:* Deming, "Notes After Birmingham," p. 14.
393   *Persons was outraged:* unpublished manuscript, courtesy of Albert Persons. A version, "How 'Images' Are Created," in *The True Selma Story* (Birmingham: Esco Publishers, 1965), in BPSF 7.1a. According to Karl Fleming's account of the same scene in *Newsweek*, "Bull's men prodded a crowd of whites back 100 yards for safekeeping." And later he "held off white bystanders with one hand ("Goddammit," he snorted, "that's what causes trouble, them white folks. Run 'em off!").
393   *"Hell, no, buddy":* telephone conversation with George Wall, March 29, 1988; Lee Bains int. with Wall, courtesy of Bains.
393   *subduing a black woman: Negro Digest*, May 7, 1963.
393   *lawyers were rejecting:* Branch, *Parting*, pp. 771–72.
393   *brief for* Sullivan: A. Lewis, *No Law*, pp. 104, 114–15.
394   *"all over for today":* Dorman, *We Shall*, p. 178.
394   *"There goes Shuttlesworth":* ints. Fred Shuttlesworth. Some handler, probably Vincent Townsend, had canceled the mayor's scheduled appearance on the *Today* show that morning. Int. Art Hanes, May 24, 1984.
394   *"negotiating session":* "Outline of Negotiations," DV; int. David Vann, June 16, 1992. On "Birmingham, Alabama, 1963: Mass Meeting," Folkways Record 5487, Abernathy mentions that Shuttlesworth couldn't be with us because he was working on problems. Shuttlesworth now claims he went to no session (though he remembers that he, King, and Abernathy met at least twice with Mayor Boutwell's deputy, Billy Hamilton, who couldn't make any promises. Vann, Gardner, and Woods all place him at at least one of the "negotiations."
394   *SNCC's best administrator:* Ella Baker oral history, MSOH, p. 58. Forman had been jailed at Fort Payne while acting as an "observer" on the William Moore Memorial Freedom Walk.
394   *herded into a pen, King urged them,* and *Forman accused him:* Forman, *Making*, p. 313; Holt, "Eyewitness," in Grant, *Protest*, pp. 346–47; police memo, May 7, 1963, mass meeting, BC; Navasky int. with Burke Marshall, VN.
394   *white dresses:* Judy Tarver oral history in Levine, *Freedom's Children*, p. 97.
395   *motorcade of five hundred cars:* Holt, "Eyewitness," in Grant, *Protest*, pp. 346–47, reports this as fact, but Forman, *Making*, doesn't mention it, and police memo of May 7, 1963, mass meeting, BC, says, "as far as we know there wasn't any mass formation in automobiles that went to the City Jail."
395   *"I have never":* King and Abernathy quotations from mass meeting, "Birmingham, Alabama, 1963: Mass Meeting," Folkways Record 5487, recording of May 6, 1963, mass meeting.

17. Mayday

396   *took a room at the Gaston Motel* and *$40,000:* int. Edward Gardner, Oct. 7, 1983.
396   *cashing donation checks:* Branch, *Parting*, p. 771.
396   *"policy of racial superiority":* Gordon to Boutwell, May 9, 1963, AB.
396   *"the Nazi storm troopers against the Jews":* quoted in Fairclough, *Redeem*, p. 137.
396   *Der Spiegel was devoting:* J. H. O'Dell, "How Powerful Is the Southern Power Structure?" *Freedomways*, First Quarter 1964.
396   *Dial urged Sid Smyer:* "Outline of Negotiations," DV; int. Isadore Pizitz, March 1983.
396   *"people walking":* Forman, *Making*, pp. 312, 314; Len Holt, "Eyewitness," in Grant, *Protest*, p. 347.
397   *Operation Confusion:* ibid.
397   *Shuttlesworth saw Forman:* Forman, *Making*, p. 314. Wyatt Walker had chewed out Forman for using the Birmingham crisis for some "narrow organizational work" (Wyatt Walker oral history, MSOH, p. 75).
397   *journalists from around the world:* O'Dell, "How Powerful?", p. 77.

397 *"You got a bonus"*: telephone int. Bill Hudson, July 29, 1992. Because the AP was a nonprofit organization, run as a collective among member newspapers, Al Resh, AP's executive news photo editor of that era, said there would have been no accounting of how many papers ran the picture or how much it made (telephone int. Al Resh, July 31, 1992).

397 *SCREW:* Dorman, *We Shall,* pp. 162–63.

397 *"the nonviolent movement coming of age"*: *NYT,* May 8, 1963.

397 *"Who wants to go to jail?"*: B. Richardson, "That's All Right," *Freedomways,* First Quarter 1964, pp. 67–69.

397 *"niggers are on their way"*: Wyatt Walker oral history, MSOH, p. 58.

398 *tore up the marchers' signs:* Richardson, "That's All Right," p. 71; Holt, "Eyewitness," in Grant, *Protest,* p. 348; Forman, *Making,* p. 314.

398 *Smyer had managed to assemble:* May 7 meeting at Chamber of Commerce, ints. Burke Marshall, October 1985 and June 25, 1992; ints. Joseph Dolan, November 1986, June 22, 1992, and Nov. 8, 1994; int. Isadore Pizitz, March 1983; int. William Spencer, Spring 1983; ints. David Vann, May 24 and 28, 1984, March 2, 1989, and June 16, 1992; Vann, LeGrand speech, pp. 32–34; int. Jimmy Lee, May 1984; int. Mel Bailey, May 1984; "Outline of Negotiations," DV; Corley, "Quest," p. 268; Burke Marshall oral history, JFK, pp. 99–101; *NYT,* May 8, 1963; Nichols, " 'Cities Are,' " pp. 322–23. Presiding was the former mayor Cooper Green.

398 *staged by the television networks:* This attitude is evident throughout Lee Bains int. with William Spencer, president of the Chamber of Commerce, courtesy of Bains.

398 *he had been taxied:* ints. Joseph Dolan, November 1986 and June 22, 1992; int. Burke Marshall, October 1985.

398 *"the coolest man"*: Navasky int. with Chuck Morgan, Box 29, VN.

398 *concealed bugs:* ints. Joseph Dolan, November 1986 and June 22, 1992; int. Burke Marshall, October 1985.

399 *sat and taken notes:* int. Abraham Woods, Summer 1985.

399 *"integrate the country club"*: int. Burke Marshall, October 1985.

399 *segregationists were only doing:* int. Joseph Dolan, June 22, 1992.

399 *"When will we live by?"*: transcript, "Bull Connor's Jail," MLK 1.7.

399 *mass meeting at the Bijou:* *AH,* Aug. 11 and 13, 1908; *BN,* Aug. 13, 1908; *Survey,* Jan. 6, 1912, p. 1536.

399 *coal miners then on strike:* Taft, *Dixie,* pp. 26–28, 30, 42; Elmore, "Strike of 1908," pp. 45, 47–48, 55, 59, 61–62, 64; *BN,* Aug. 10, 1908; R. Lewis, *Black Coal Miners,* p. 55.

399 *a steak dinner:* Forman, *Making,* pp. 314–15.

400 *demonstrators kneeling to pray or high-stepping:* Dorman, *We Shall,* p. 179.

400 *to alert his editors:* int. Joe Cumming, June 20 and 21, 1992.

400 *proposed that Governor Wallace:* Smyer brought Dixon in to one of the earlier meetings with the merchants to give their settlement his blessing. "Outline of Negotiations," DV; int. David Vann, June 16, 1992, and Vann, LeGrand speech, p. 33; ints. Burke Marshall, October 1985 and June 25, 1992; ints. Joseph Dolan, November 1986 and June 22, 1992.

400 *worst scenario* and *disabused the merchants:* Navasky int. with Burke Marshall, Box 28, VN; transcript of press briefing by Robert Kennedy and Marshall, May 10, 1963, Box 24, VN.

401 *insistence of Isadore Pizitz that no Jews:* Charles Wittenstein's field report, Nov. 2, 1962, "Visits, Birmingham, 1944–1962," and Wittenstein's field report, Oct. 23, 1962, "Birmingham 1950–1962," AJC. Cooper Green, the Senior Citizens head, assured Wittenstein that Jews would be added to the committee as it evolved, but they were not.

402 *check on the store.* Picking his way: See Harding, "A Beginning," p. 1; Coffin, *Every Man,* p. 176.

402 *spit on wedding dresses:* int. Art Hanes, May 24, 1984; int. Jabo Waggoner, May 27, 1984.

402 *"don't block traffic"*: Rather, *Camera,* p. 89.

402 *"I'm with you!"*: conversation with Fannie Flagg, Spring 1983.

402 *Shuttlesworth was overcome:* Fred Shuttlesworth oral history, KC, side 8.

403 *"no alternative," "walking intelligence machine,"* and *tour of the county jail:* int. Mel Bailey, May 1984; int. Joseph Dolan, November 1986.

403 *erected at Legion Field:* In fact, the stadium officials had denied the county permission to use the field to hold demonstrators, citing an upcoming Southeastern Conference track meet. Wagner to Boutwell telegram, May 3, 1963, AB.

403 *"tired of the lawlessness"*: BPH, May 8, 1963; *NYT,* May 8, 1963, says 250.

403 *Kelly Ingram Park was surrounded:* *NYT,* May 8, 1963; BPH, May 8, 1963; *Jet,* May 23, 1963; ints. Fred Shuttlesworth.

404 *remarked ironically on its color:* police memo, May 3, 1963, mass meeting, BC.

404 *led a column of marchers:* Coffin, *Every Man,* pp. 171–72, 175.

404 *"Jim, try to get the people back"*: Forman, *Making,* p. 315.

405 *"Let's put some water"*: ints. Fred Shuttlesworth; Shuttlesworth oral history, KC, side 8; int. Jonathan McPherson, Oct. 5, 1983.

405 *"carried him away in a hearse"*: *NYT,* May 8, 1963.

405 *"quieted the objections"*: int. David Vann, June 16, 1992.

405 *complain about the Cadillac:* int. Margaret Gordon Crawford Rives, July 3, 1982.

405 *denied Mrs. Wiebel membership:* int. Bettye Shepherd, Spring 1983.

405 *"Evil Weasel"*: int. Joe Cumming, June 20 and 21, 1992.

405 *poured considerable funds:* Wittenstein to Murray, Dec. 5, 1963, "Alabama, Birmingham, 1960–1963," AJC. Wiebel also donated cash.

405 *indictment of U.S. Steel:* Department of Justice press release, April 2, 1963, Box 32, VN.

405 *violated the administration's:* Schlesinger, *Robert Kennedy,* pp. 419–23; Schlesinger, *Thousand,* pp. 635–36.

406 *"sons of bitches"*: Schlesinger, *Thousand,* pp. 635–36. Joe Kennedy was referring specifically to the La Follette committee testimony of Republic Steel's hard-shelled Tom Girdler, whose guards had in May 1937 fired into a strikers' parade at his South Chicago plant, killing 10 and wounding more than 90.

406 *pressure on U.S. Steel:* Secretary of Defense Robert McNamara, one of Steel's major clients, was sicced on him as well. Int. Burke Marshall, June 25, 1992; Schlesinger, *Thousand,* p. 636.

406 *As a boy, Blough:* Roger Blough oral history, COH, pp. 1, 3, 15, 17, 42–43, 55, 58–59; int. Jane Blough French, Spring 1983.

406 *Rostow had been able to persuade him:* David Alan Horowitz, "White Southerners' Alienation and Civil Rights: The Response to Corporate Liberalism, 1956–1965," *Journal of Southern History,* May 1988, p. 190. Eugene Rostow (telephone conversation, June 25, 1992) did not remember making the call.

406 *"cold fish":* int. Burke Marshall, October 1985.

406 *"burr-headed niggers telling me":* int. Howard Strevel, December 1987. The remark was made in front of Strevel, a local union official, and the committee's representative (former House Speaker Sam Rayburn's nephew).

406 *became irritated:* int. Isadore Pizitz, March 1983; telephone int. George Peach Taylor, undated.

406 *"that's all they want?":* ints. David Vann, May 24 and 28, 1984; int. Burke Marshall, October 1985.

406 *his black housekeeper:* "Birmingham Now a Long Way from 'Bombingham,' " undated UPI story on Smyer (ca. 1967), in Smyer vertical file, TCSH.

407 *"not a damn fool":* int. Burke Marshall, October 1985. AP report of May 17, 1963, has quote, "I'm still a segregationist but I hope I'm not a damn fool." Slightly different version is in Harold Katz, "Memorandum on Racial Problems Affecting the Birmingham Jewish Community," July 3, 1963, Mark Elovitz Papers, BPL.

407 *"sort of like a Quaker meeting":* int. David Vann, June 16, 1992. Smyer would claim that "the committee voted unanimously to appoint a subcommittee." *BN,* May 10, 1963.

407 *"the aristocracy of damn fools":* Osborne, "Boycott." "If you recite the tribal rites, you are accepted by the people in town," an anonymous resident who sounds like Chuck Morgan told a reporter for *The Nation* one year before, "but if you express any concern with the state of race relations, you immediately become a member of what James McBride Dabbs has called the 'aristocracy of damn fools.' "

407 *fired off a telegram:* BN, May 7, 1963; original telegram in Box 96, POF.

407 *"We put the water in":* int. John Swindle, July 16, 1987.

407 *Evans recalled the words:* Glenn Evans oral history in Raines, *My Soul,* p. 174.

407 *policemen burst into Charles "Rat Killer" Barnett's:* int. Charles "Rat Killer" Barnett, Oct. 10, 1983.

408 *already free:* int. Frank Dukes, Oct. 4, 1983.

409 *erratic Shreveport man:* "Mountain Brook Land Company," Robert Jemison Papers, BPL.

409 *how many stars:* int. Margaret Gordon Crawford Rives, July 13, 1982.

18. The Threshold

411 *meetings that Tuesday:* May 7 mass meeting and quotes, police memo, May 7, 1963, mass meeting, BC.

411 *"little control of the demonstrations":* NYT, May 8, 1963.

411 *Robinson, who was raising money:* ibid.

412 *"The meeting worked":* unsigned mostly handwritten notes, May 7, 1963, in Box 24, "Birmingham," VN. Edwin Guthman's notes on conversation, cited in Branch, *Parting,* p. 780, have a slightly different version. Marshall had no recollection of whether the idea for the Senior Citizens meeting came from him or someone in Birmingham (int. Burke Marshall, June 25, 1992).

412 *first meeting between black:* "Outline of Negotiations," DV; "My personal opinion," unsigned memo, probably written morning of May 8, 1963, SCLC 139.7; Harding, "A Beginning," p. 17; Dorman, *We Shall,* pp. 183–84. Dorman places this meeting at Drew's house, but Smyer was never there by all accounts. Harding places the meeting at the office of a leading insurance broker, who would be Drew.

412 *The "new" subcommittee consisted:* If an actual Senior Citizen was in attendance—and that would remain one of the many murky particulars of the "negotiations"—it was probably Royal Crown Cola's Ed Norton. Curiously, David Vann said in one interview that he was not part of the negotiating committee formed after the meeting, and mentioned yet another member, *Post-Herald* editor Jimmy Mills (Lee Bains int. with Vann, courtesy of Bains).

412 *appoint the biracial committee:* John Brewbaker report to SRC, May 4, 1963, SRC.

412 *lead the way for the private sector:* Fred Shuttlesworth's news bulletin, "Why We Must Demonstrate," March 19, 1964, AB. This contains a recap of the agreements of May 1963.

412 *"wear a tie":* telephone int. Edwin Guthman, June 23, 1992.

412 *"Someday I'll tell you":* int. Joe Cumming, June 20–21, 1992.

412 *"need some federal marshals":* int. Deenie Drew, May 1984.

413 *"clean of groupies":* int. Deenie Drew, June 18, 1992.

413 *insisting on a private meeting with King:* statement of the Reverend Sammy C. Perryman to Birmingham police, Oct. 1, 1963, BPSF 7.1a.

413 *two hypodermic:* ints. Fred Shuttlesworth; int. Julia Rainge, July 15, 1987.

413 *Why hadn't Martin or Ralph come?:* ints. Fred Shuttlesworth.

413 *regular meeting:* "My personal opinion," unsigned memo, May 8, 1963, SCLC 139.7; Abernathy, *Walls,* pp. 267–68.

413 *Montgomery told Ruby:* int. Fred Shuttlesworth, Summer 1985.

413 *"tea sippers":* int. Lola Hendricks, March 26, 1989.

414 *"an ordinary nobody":* Lee Bains int. with John Drew, courtesy of Bains.

414 *whether "Doc" Drew had seen him:* int. Deenie Drew, May 1984.

414 *"Why do you need":* King-Shuttlesworth confrontation, ints. Fred Shuttlesworth; int. Ed Gardner, June 1982 (although Gardner said that he was not there, he did recall parts of the conversation in question); Shuttlesworth oral history in Raines, *My Soul,* pp. 158–61; Shuttlesworth oral history, KC, side 10; int. Burke Marshall, October 1985; int. Deenie Drew, May 1984; Abernathy, *Walls,* p. 268.

414 *Movement's idea:* Garrow, *Bearing,* pp. 255–56, argues that it was King's own idea to call off the demonstrations and that Pitts was his local front. Birmingham had so skewed the political axes that King was not only to the right of Shuttlesworth, he was also to the right of Roy Wilkins, who had just called on one hundred key NAACP branches to launch demonstrations in sympathy with the Birmingham martyrs, whom the NAACP was urging to "continue their

protests in increasing strength until victory is won" (*NYT,* May 8, 1963). Yet the same day Wilkins issued his call, he turned down King's request for bail funds, on the specious grounds that the NAACP had been outlawed from doing business in Alabama (Corley, "Quest," p. 271).

414 *Wallace had threatened to prosecute:* BPH, May 8, 1963.
414 *uncontrollable power of the young people:* Vincent Harding oral history, MSOH, pp. 18–20.
414 *"beautiful democracy":* int. Fred Shuttlesworth, July 28, 1992.
415 *"part and parcel":* BPH, May 9, 1963.
415 *"frail one":* Fred Shuttlesworth (oral history in Raines, *My Soul,* p. 160) says this was John Doar, who was not there at the time. However, Joe Dolan told me he did not make this call, and it's unlikely that he would have referred to Shuttlesworth by anything other than his name. I don't know who made the call.
416 *that employed blacks in numbers:* U.S. Civil Service Commission to Vice President, May 20, 1963, BM; Geoghegan to Attorney General, May 8, 1963, Box 96, POF.
416 *Davis was ready:* int. Charles Davis, Oct. 6, 1983.
416 *carbines and submachine guns, "Hey, Bull":* Gutwillig, "Six Days."
416 *"any of that Reverend shit":* int. Joseph Dolan, November 1986.
416 *"until Birmingham is freed":* Young, *Burden,* p. 246.
416 *ingenious compromise:* Shuttlesworth's memory is faulty about how this all came about; he claimed that the demonstrations were never called off. The compromise is Fairclough's interpretation (*Redeem,* p. 129), and the one that makes most sense.
417 *"Same old shit":* Gutwillig, "Six Days."
417 *set appeal bonds at $2,500:* BPH, May 9, 1963; *NYT,* May 9, 1963; Dorman, *We Shall,* p. 185.
417 *King seemed almost relieved:* This is Taylor Branch's interpretation (*Parting,* pp. 785–86).
417 *"embarrassing Martin Luther King":* Young, *Burden,* p. 247.
417 *Shuttlesworth was cussing* and *"Fred's sort of":* int. Joseph Dolan, November 1986; int. Calvin Woods (who was there), July 15, 1987; *NYT,* May 9, 1963; Young, *Burden,* p. 247.
417 *"negotiations are off"* and *"does not destroy our faith":* BPH, May 9, 1963.
417 *Kunstler and Harry Belafonte scrounged:* See Kunstler, *Deep,* p. 192; Branch, *Parting,* p. 784, for fuller treatment.
417 *pulling a fast one on the Atlantans:* int. Deenie Drew, June 18, 1992; int. A. G. Gaston, March 28, 1988. Gaston would later boast (*Green Power*) that he put up the money against the wishes of the civil rights leaders, who he thought wanted to keep King in jail for symbolism.
417 *Bevel had been insisting:* police memo, May 8, 1963, mass meeting, BC.
418 *Vann met:* "Outline of Negotiations," DV; ints. David Vann, March 2, 1989, and June 16, 1992. Vann said he had nothing to do with getting Gaston to put up the bond money.
418 *rabbis had flown into Birmingham:* NYT, May 8, 1963, William Engel to Sonnabend, May 21, 1963, "JSX-Ala., A–Z, 1962–1967," AJC. Four hundred Conservative rabbis had been attending the sixty-third annual Rabbinical Assembly in New York.
418 *"Our people":* police memo, May 8, 1963, mass meeting, BC; Dorman, *We Shall,* p. 186; notes of *News* reporter (Tom Lankford, perhaps) in Irving Engel to Slawson, May 14, 1963, "JSX-Ala., A–Z, 1962–1967," AJC. They sang the song several times and for the last round invited the congregants to put an arm around the person next to them. The Movement people surrounding the two cops laid it on thick—"of course," the detectives observed.
418 *confrontation with the natives:* int. Milton Grafman, July 1982; Elovitz, *Jewish Life,* p. 171; Rittenbaum to Friedman, June 13, 1963, Mark Elovitz Papers, BPL. A committee of prominent local Jews, including Abe Berkowitz and Rabbi Grafman, had "welcomed" them at the airport at 2:15 the previous morning but had been unable to persuade them to turn back.
418 *by persuading his friend Vincent Townsend:* Irving Engel to Slawson, May 14, 1963, "JSX-Ala., A–Z, 1962–1967," AJC.
418 *Vann reported to the Drews', and young son, Jeff:* int. David Vann, May 28, 1984; int. Deenie Drew, June 18, 1992. Deenie had grown tired of bundling him up at the drop of a bomb threat and making him sleep in the car deep into their property, out of flying debris range.
418 *last consultation with Burke Marshall:* ints. David Vann, May 28, 1984, and June 16, 1992.
418 *to meet Martin Luther King:* int. James Montgomery, Dec. 4, 1987; ints. David Vann, May 28, 1984, and June 16, 1992; ints. Deenie Drew, May 1984 and June 18, 1992. Andy Young also refers to Vann crying in *Eyes on the Prize,* PBS, and in *Burden,* p. 244, which has an incorrect account (he has Chuck Morgan as one of the negotiators).
418 *wondered aloud what the big deal was:* int. Deenie Drew, June 18, 1992. She recalled that the check came from the Fellowship of Reconciliation, but *NYT,* May 10, 1963, and *BPH,* May 10, 1963, mention NMU check.
419 *"another Albany":* See Claude Sitton's skepticism in *NYT,* May 10, 1963.
419 *"when the Negroes rely on the whites":* NYT, May 10, 1963.
419 *razzing of Marshall:* Harding, "A Beginning"; telephone int. Harold Long, June 19, 1992.
419 *monitors of world opinion:* USIA's Donald Wilson to R. Kennedy, May 9 and May 13, 1963, Box 10, RFK; "Summary of Foreign Reaction to Racial Tension in Birmingham, Alabama," May 17, 1963, "Civil Rights Alabama May 17–Oct. 10, 1963," Box 96, POF.
419 *African nationals were preparing:* NYT, May 10, 1963.
419 *made the prediction:* int. David Vann, May 28, 1984; Vann, LeGrand speech, p. 35.
419 *calling on Shuttlesworth:* int. Joseph Dolan, November 1986.
419 *Oberdorfer had suggested:* Louis Oberdorfer oral history, JFK, p. 36.
419 *lawyer, Joseph L. Rauh Jr.:* telephone int. Joseph Rauh, July 23, 1992.
420 *Erskine Smith:* obit, BN, July 26, 1973.
420 *coordinate the bail money:* Dorman, *We Shall,* p. 189; Navasky, *Justice,* p. 208.
420 *Cooper took the long-distance call:* ints. Jerome Cooper, Dec. 17 and 18, 1984, December 3, 1987.
420 *Constitutional Educational League had baited him:* Joe Kamp, *The South vs. the Smear* (New York: Constitutional Education League, 1946), SK.

420   *ironic that Robert Kennedy:* ints. Jerome Cooper, Dec. 17, 1984, and December 3, 1987.
420   *"What are you going to do?":* int. Howard Strevel, December 1987.
420   *"greatest social movements":* Arthur Shores, H. D. Coke et al. to Philip Murray, Sept. 28, 1937, Box 7, United Steelworkers of America District 36, Penn. State University Library.
421   *on Thursday afternoon* and *leaking rumors: NYT* and *BPH,* May 10, 1963.
421   *"one-half million dollars":* May 9 mass meeting, police memo, May 9, 1963, mass meeting, BC.
421   *committee working on the exact wording:* Harding, "A Beginning." Vincent Harding was apparently also present.
421   *whites were balking: NYT,* May 10, 1963.
421   *final meeting with the white negotiators:* int. David Vann, June 16, 1992; "Outline of Negotiations," DV. Though Vann recalled that the pastor of Birmingham's only black Congregational church, Harold Long (who had a doctorate from Yale Divinity School), read the agreement, Long did not remember being at any specific negotiating session.
421   *Rauh was wiring:* Louis Oberdorfer oral history, JFK, p. 36. Lawyer Jerome Cooper was also involved in handling the money on the Birmingham end.
421   *bail fund had been raised:* For an amusing account, see Branch, *Parting,* p. 789.
422   *Kennedy had Shuttlesworth on the phone:* int. Frank Dukes, Oct. 4, 1983.
422   *Belafonte called King:* Riverside tape, Part 1, side 2.
422   *"Birmingham reached an accord":* press conference statements, Dorman, *We Shall,* pp. 189–90. The statement does say ninety days even though a sixty-day timetable had been agreed upon.
422   *King seemed effusive:* Or "oleaginous" (Gutwillig, "Six Days").
422   *"the moment of a great victory":* King's statement, Dorman, *We Shall,* pp. 190–92; int. Charles Davis, Oct. 6, 1983.
422   *he fainted:* Gutwillig, "Six Days."

19. Edge of Heaven

423   *Crudely handwritten mail:* See AB 5.17.
423   *"Hell, I'll do it"* and *work out a supplemental statement:* int. David Vann, June 16, 1992.
423   *"important that the public understand":* and Smyer quotes, Dorman, *We Shall,* p. 192; *BN,* May 11, 1963.
423   *"Yes, Mr. President"* and *Vann hung around:* int. David Vann, June 16, 1992. In Navasky int., Box 32, VN, Vann says it was Robert Kennedy who called.
423   *Marshall was on his way:* int. Burke Marshall, June 25, 1992. He left, with Oberdorfer, at around noon on Friday.
423   *"high rate of venereal diseases":* Riverside tape, Part 1, side 1.
423   *"quisling, gutless traitors": NYT,* May 10, 1963.
424   *"didn't gain a thing":* Dorman, *We Shall,* p. 193.
424   *"I would have beaten King":* Nichols, " 'Cities Are,' " p. 314.
424   *the Friday mass meeting:* Riverside tape, Part 1, sides 1 and 2.
424   *Shuttlesworth awoke:* C. Herbert Oliver diary, May 10, 1963, courtesy of Oliver.
424   *A reliable Klan informant had told:* Ben Allen oral history in Raines, *My Soul,* p. 177.
425   *snoozing elderly blacks:* Dorman, *We Shall,* p. 194.
425   *expected any more "trouble":* Christianity and Crisis, June 10, 1963.
425   *Eastview elite:* summary of Rowe report, May 11, 1963, Box 2, BPSF; Chambliss statement, Sept. 29, 1963, Bapbomb; FBI ints. with Gene Reeves, Nov. 12, 1963, with Lucien Wayne Rawlins, Nov. 11, 1963, and with Hubert Page, Dec. 4, 1964, all in Bapbomb; "Gaston Motel Bombing," Box 4, BPSF.
425   *and fellow Klanspeople":* Klan rally, Riverside tape, Part 2, sides 2 and 3, and Part 6, side 10.
426   *at 8:08 p.m.:* threats at Gaston Motel, police memo on "Bomb Threats," May 23, 1963, BPSF 6.46. The motel manager, Earnest Gibson, called the police and sheriff's office, and, at Wyatt Walker's urging, the FBI.
427   *"Watch this"* and *officers got out:* int. Carter Gaston, July 15, 1987.
427   *Roosevelt Tatum:* Lane and Gregory, *"Zorro,"* pp. 33–34.
427   *A. D. King was in bed:* W. E. Berry report on bombing, May 14, 1963, BPSF 6.46.
427   *Maurice House:* House report on A. D. King bombing, May 16, 1963, BPSF 6.46; int. Maurice House, Spring 1985.
427   *small group was singing:* Golden report and Berry report on King bombing, May 14, 1963, BPSF 6.46; int. Maurice House, Spring 1985; Wyatt Walker oral history, MSOH, pp. 70–71; *Christianity and Crisis,* June 10, 1963; Riverside tape, Part 2, side 3.
428   *Tatum told A. D. King* and *King called the FBI:* Lane and Gregory, *"Zorro,"* pp. 34, 38. Two agents took Tatum down to headquarters to get his statement.
428   *Rowe had left the event:* FBI int. with Don Luna, March 23, 1964, Bapbomb.
428   *"Jack" Cash:* FBI ints. with William Hurshel Cash, Oct. 3 and 14, 1963, with Eugene T. Coleman, Nov. 22, 1963, with Dora Ireland, Oct. 7, 1963, with Bill Whitley, Oct. 15, 1963, and with Louie C. Richie, Nov. 26, 1963, all in Bapbomb; Rowe Baxley deposition, p. 5, BPSF 9.1.
428   *for attacking Fred Shuttlesworth: AA,* Oct. 5, 1957; Fred Shuttlesworth, "Statement to the Civil Rights Commission in Birmingham," FS 4.
428   *plans to break windows:* FBI int. with Lonzo Foster, Jan. 29, 1965, Bapbomb.
428   *Nigger Hall and some Klan brothers* and *got in some licks:* FBI statement of John Hall, Nov. 19, 1963, Bapbomb; summary of Rowe report, May 11, 1963, Box 2, BPSF; "Charles Arnie Cagle" memo in BPSF 9.12(d). Cagle now refuses to comment on how Klan activities (telephone conversation, Oct. 28, 2000).
428   *"Dixie":* Myrna Carter oral history in Levine, *Freedom's Children,* p. 106.
429   *"That's my church":* int. Maurice House, Spring 1985.
429   *"That's the motel":* Wyatt Walker oral history, MSOH, pp. 70–71.
429   *knowingly mentioning Room 30* and *Klan's spies:* LeGrand int. with Rowe, pp. 53–54, BPSF 9.1. The Klansman

Rowe believes infiltrated King's organization was Glenn Wheeler, who also spied on the Alabama Council on Human Relations.

429 *Orzell Billingsley:* int. Orzell Billingsley, July 18, 1987; ACMHR incorporation papers in W. E. Shortridge Papers, courtesy of Pinkie Lee Shortridge; Clarke, *These Rights,* Appendix, p. 141; 1958 HUAC hearings, p. 2713.

429 *"More Beautiful Tan Girls":* PC, Sept. 6, 1958, courtesy of Orzell Billingsley.

429 *people who were supposed to be at the Gaston Motel:* telephone int. Joseph Lowery, September 1990; Abernathy, *Walls,* p. 270; Jackson to Rutledge, May 14, 1963, EOJAR; int. Al Hibbler, July 3, 1987.

430 *dug out from the crumbled plaster:* Isaac Reynolds oral history, MSOH, p. 25.

430 *locked the doors:* int. Carter Gaston, July 15, 1987.

430 *first cop to arrive:* police memo, May 17, 1963, "Re Blast A. G. Gaston," BPSF 6.46.

430 *Walker grabbed a megaphone:* AP photo in Alabama Civil Rights, May 1, 1961–May 12, 1963, Box 96, POF.

430 *was set on fire:* riot, BPH, May 13, 1963; NYT, May 13, 1963; *Christianity and Crisis,* June 10, 1963, Riverside tape, Part 2, sides 3 and 4; Dorman, *We Shall,* pp. 196–99; BW, May 15, 1963 (UPI report); int. Edward Gardner, Oct. 7, 1983; int. Nelson Smith, Oct. 3, 1983; int. Wyatt Walker, Jan. 13, 1984; int. James Parsons, Spring 1984; int. James D. Smith, Spring 1984; int. Claude Sitton, May 5, 1992; int. Karl Fleming, June 16, 1992; int. Jamie Moore, Dec. 9, 1987; int. Maurice House, Spring 1985; int. Charles Davis, Oct. 6, 1983; telephone int. R. W. Apple, March 7, 1993; int. Calvin Woods, July 15, 1987; Abraham Woods oral history in Raines, *My Soul,* p. 152.

431 *Morgan had taken them:* int. Karl Fleming, July 21, 1992; int. Claude Sitton, May 5, 1992.

431 *"an excellent technique":* Morgan quotes, *Christianity and Crisis,* June 3, 1963.

431 *inside one car:* telephone int. Laurie Pritchett, Aug. 17, 1991.

431 *"going to blow King up":* Powledge, *Free,* p. 512.

431 *fireman hustled:* Birmingham Fire Department memo, "Investigation of Explosion," May 15, 1963, BPSF 6.46.

432 *titled "Edge of Heaven":* Wyatt Walker oral history, MSOH, p. 72.

432 *Connor had decided not to show up:* int. Jamie Moore, Dec. 9, 1987.

433 *Moore was standing* and *Lingo got out of the car:* Moore-Lingo confrontation, int. Art Hanes, May 24, 1984; Ben Allen oral history in Raines, *My Soul,* pp. 176–77; int. Jamie Moore, Dec. 9, 1987; Dorman, *We Shall,* p. 197; BPH, May 13, 1963. Accounts of this encounter vary.

433 *"Corporal, next time":* telephone int. W. L. Allen, March 1985. Allen had been one of the six state officers to remain on duty in Birmingham.

434 *"exterminating Eastlands":* int. Wyatt Walker, Jan. 13, 1984.

434 *"saved my life":* Wyatt Walker int. in Hampton and Fayer, *Voices,* p. 138.

434 *the Gaston Motel:* int. O. N. Gallant, March 16, 1987; *Christianity and Crisis,* June 3, 1963; BW, May 15, 1963.

434 *Rowe was sleeping:* int. Mary Lou Holt Page, Nov. 17, 1995.

435 *took him to jail:* FBI ints. with George Pickle, Oct. 10, 1963, and Oct. 23, 1964, Bapbomb.

435 *appeared at the Southside jail:* LeGrand int. with Rowe, p. 28, BPSF 9.1; state investigators' memo, "Robert Sidney Thomas," BPSF 9.12(d); Cantrell int. with Billy Holt, May 2, 1977, Box 4, BPSF. The Pickle transaction is very fishy. Thomas would claim that he left the Klan rally early to bail Pickle out, which would put him at the jail far earlier than midnight. Maybe neither Klansman went to the jail. Only a few months after the incident, Pickle would claim that he had stayed in jail overnight, and left the next afternoon after paying a $15 fine and $5 costs. And he would complain bitterly that the Klan did not pick up the bill, suggesting that his arrest had been part of a grand Klan plan (FBI ints. with George Pickle and with Patricia Pickle, Oct. 10, 1963, Bapbomb). Also mysteriously, when the FBI drew up an "Identification Record" of Pickle's arrests the following October, the lengthy list of felony assault and driving while intoxicated charges did not include the May incident (Identification Record of Pickle, Oct. 18, 1963, Bapbomb).

435 *"watched them dance":* Robert Chambliss statement, Sept. 29, 1963, Bapbomb.

435 *Holt and Luna would go with him:* Eddy to Beck, Aug. 15, 1977, "Bapbomb Confidential Informers Information," Aug. 17, 1977, JY. Although Chambliss could apparently have nailed Holt for helping him bomb Shuttlesworth's parsonage on Christmas 1956, the reference to Don Luna could only have meant he was talking about the Gaston explosion.

435 *insist on the craziest scenario:* David Barber int. with Robert Chambliss, Oct. 12, 1978, and Bob Eddy notes on int. with Chambliss, Dec. 11, 1978, Box 3, BPSF; also in numerous rambling letters, e.g., Chambliss to Bailey, Feb. 5, 1981, courtesy of George Beck. There is some evidence that William Otto Perkins, a Tuscaloosa National Guardsman who was a close friend of Bobby Shelton's, was suspected of being involved in the bombing—or perhaps the police were trying to pin it on him as a favor to Eastview. See police int. with Sylvester Norris, May 20, 1963, Box 4, BPSF.

436 *Holman Turner Jr.:* telephone int. Holman Turner Jr., Nov. 19, 2000.

436 *"Car 25 was right behind him":* Riverside tape, Part 2, side 3. Turner's account is more logical than Robert Chambliss's placement of the police car in the lead, since it would make it difficult to see the license plate. Turner's name is listed, without elaboration, in the police files of witnesses to the bombing. Handwritten list, "Automobiles Seen," Box 4, BPSF.

436 *"kill a nigger":* Eddy int. with Mary Frances Cunningham, Aug. 19, 1977, JY.

436 *question about Nigger Hall's wife* and *Black Muslims:* LeGrand int. with Rowe, pp. 31, 29, BPSF 9.1.

436 *Shelton accused Wyatt Walker:* FBI int. with Bobby Shelton, Aug. 21, 1964, Bapbomb.

437 *first race riot:* Watters, *Down,* p. 269.

437 *"fear of the future":* BW, May 25, 1963, quoting dean-designate of Boston University's Marsh Chapel, Robert Hamm.

437 *"take a new turn":* Abraham Woods oral history in Raines, *My Soul,* p. 153.

437 *"The passivity and nonviolence":* Donald Matthews and James Prothro, *Negroes and the New Southern Politics* (New York: Harcourt Brace and World, 1966), quoted in Lesher, *Wallace,* p. 196.

437 *NBC's Johnny Apple:* police memo, May 14, 1963, BPSF 6.46; int. Maurice House, Spring 1985, telephone int. R. W. Apple, March 7, 1993. Apple does not share House's recollection that a cameraman was there.

437 *photographs of black violence:* AP's photographs are in Civil Rights Alabama, May 1, 1961–May 12, 1963, Box 96, POF. There is a picture of a burning taxicab.

437   *"freedom tensions":* e.g., *BW,* May 25, 1963.
437   *"wasn't a member of nothing!"* and *"drunk head":* int. Edward Gardner, Oct. 7, 1983; police memo, May 13, 1963, mass meeting, BC.
438   *"no difference," Davis agreed:* int. Frank Dukes, Oct. 4, 1983; int. Charles Davis, Oct. 6, 1983. Indeed, during one march, Shuttlesworth himself had gone up to a group of blacks stockpiling brickbats and said, "Now folks, if y'all want to join the demonstrations, come out and join us. But no rocks will be thrown." The men joined the Movement.
438   *"bread demonstration":* Leonard W. Holt, "Birmingham's Harlem," *Freedomways,* Summer 1963. The riot was the desperate act of the vast black majority who didn't have the "bread" to buy any cake at the lunch counters.
438   *for the White House:* meeting, audiotape 86.2, JFK; AP dispatch, May 12, 1963, in "Alabama Civil Rights, May 12–14, 1963," Box 96, POF.
438   *Three thousand integrated pickets:* Navasky, *Justice,* p. 133.
439   *"must be a* nut*":* Howe to Boutwell, undated, AB.
439   *"heel of the military":* Riverside tape, Part 5, side 9; *BN,* May 13, 1963.
439   *reporters filed out: Christianity and Crisis,* June 10, 1963.
439   *Joe Dolan* and *Burke Marshall:* UPI and AP dispatches, May 12, 1963, in "Alabama Civil Rights, May 12–14, 1963," Box 96, POF; Durman, *We Shall,* p. 200.
439   *"forthright stand":* UPI dispatch in "Alabama Civil Rights, May 12–14, 1963," Box 96, POF.
440   *"We must work passionately":* Riverside tape, Part 3, side 6.
440   *direct his budget surplus:* Navasky int. with Ramsey Clark, VN.
440   *Marshall's best friend:* Thurgood Marshall oral history, COH, p. 84.
440   *acknowledged the capriciousness:* Richards, "Youth Congress," p. 184.
440   *writing a memo:* int. Ramsey Clark, Sept. 28, 1992. Navasky has notes on such a memo, though its emphasis is on education. June Payne of the Kennedy Library kindly "looked high and low" to try to locate such a memo in Burke Marshall's and RFK's papers and was unable to do so.

20. No More Water

441   *Shuttlesworth told Herb Oliver:* C. Herbert Oliver diary, May 13, 1963, courtesy of Oliver.
441   *"a great man":* Riverside tape, Part 1, side 1.
441   *descended through Paul:* from Sunday, May 12, 1963, mass meeting, in Riverside tape, Part 3, side 5.
441   *on a peace tour:* Dorman, *We Shall,* pp. 204–205; int. Charles "Rat Killer" Barnett, Oct. 10, 1983.
441   *"son of a bitch":* Riverside tape, Part 2, side 2.
442   *had reneged:* Navasky int. with David Vann, Box 32, VN. Vann had initially gotten commitments for five promoted employees, but it's not clear how many merchants had pledged these.
442   *Floyd Patterson* and *Jackie Robinson:* details from mass meeting, Riverside tape, Part 6, side 10, and Part 2, side 4; police memo, May 13, 1963, mass meeting, BC; Dorman, *We Shall,* p. 205; Confidential Situation Report, May 15, 1963, "Civil Rights Alabama, May 17–Oct. 10, 1963," Box 96, POF.
442   *B. B. King's offer:* Wyatt Walker oral history, MSOH, p. 24.
442   *Justice Department phones:* Geoghegan to Lee et al., undated (May 13, 1963), in "Civil Rights—U. of Ala., April 9–May 31, 1963," Box 10, RFK.
442   *Oberdorfer had been awakened:* Louis Oberdorfer oral history, JFK, pp. 42–44.
442   *tortured references:* transcript of televised statement made by attorney general on May 13, Box 24, "Birmingham, Ala., 1963 Riots and Bombings," VN.
442   *Kennedy met:* Navasky, *Justice,* p. 218; Rosenthal to Salinger, May 13, 1963, re "Background material for luncheon with Alabama editors," in Burke Marshall file, Box 29, VN.
442   *"Two-legged white dogs":* Marshall Frady, "The Children of Malcolm," *The New Yorker,* Oct. 12, 1992, p. 64.
442   *Operation Oak Tree:* Confidential Situation Report for Birmingham, May 16, 1963, "Civil Rights Alabama, May 17–Oct. 10, 1963," Box 96, POF.
443   *set off an exodus:* ibid. Only Abrams, his two assistants, and a twenty-man Air Force detachment remained.
443   *Clark was circling* and *barbecue joint:* int. Ramsey Clark, Sept. 28, 1992.
443   *"Old soldiers":* and quotes from May 14 mass meeting, police memo, May 14, 1963, mass meeting, BC.
443   *he'd be armed and waiting:* int. Sidney W. "Billy" Smyer Jr., Dec. 2, 1987.
443   *call Smyer and summon:* The only source for this meeting is Sidney Smyer's interview in Raines, *My Soul,* pp. 163–64. Raines places this before the crucial May 7 meeting and cites it as its impetus, but given the urgency of the tone and the talk of federal troops, it seems more likely that the meeting took place around this time.
444   *its biggest activists:* FBI int. with Mary Lou Holt, March 28, 1966, Bapbomb.
444   *heap picturesque curses:* Riverside tape, Part 5, sides 8 and 9; Dorman, *We Shall,* p. 207.
444   *the city's best names: BN,* May 16, 1963.
444   *Smyer's sympathetic few co-conspirators:* int. David Vann, March 2, 1989. Vann believes this was Dick Puryear, president of the Alabama Gas Company.
444   *King and Sid Smyer bickering:* In a press conference, King asserted seven clerks for seven stores and misrepresented a few other fine points of the agreement.
444   *Adams, had resigned:* E. C. Clark, *Schoolhouse,* p. 179.
444   *digging up dirt:* ibid., pp. 125–26. The university had scuttled three strong black candidates since Pollie Anne Myers.
444   *Malone was a model student, Hood was a boy preacher:* ibid., pp. 175–77.
445   *take reconaissance photographs:* ibid., p. 167. On his first ex officio visit to Washington, in February, Governor Wallace japed that he "took some aerial views" of the capital as he flew in.
445   *wanted to see Wallace go to jail:* Anthony to Dunbar, Jan. 21, 1963, SRC.
445   *Wernher von Braun:* Tom Bower, *The Paperclip Conspiracy: The Hunt for Nazi Scientists* (Boston: Little, Brown, 1987), p. 119.

445   *McGlathery's case:* E. C. Clark, *Schoolhouse,* pp. 171–72, 187; Morgan, *A Time,* pp. 151, 157.
446   *mass meeting on Wednesday, May 15:* police memo, May 15, 1963, mass meeting, BC.
446   *Judge Charles Brown's court:* int. Carter Gaston, July 15, 1987; int. Orzell Billingsley, July 18, 1987; int. Frank Dukes, Oct. 4, 1983; police memo, May 16, 1963, mass meeting, BC.
446   *"tell the Big Judge":* police memo, May 16, 1963, mass meeting, BC.
446   *"When are you going to stop running?":* int. Carter Gaston, July 15, 1987.
447   *Lockheed Jet Star:* trip, telephone ints. Edwin Guthman, Sept. 28 and June 23, 1992; telephone int. Norbert Schlei, Sept. 29, 1992; int. Burke Marshall, June 25, 1992; pp. vii–viii.
447   *Norbert Schlei:* telephone int. Norbert Schlei, Sept. 29, 1992; N. Schlei oral history, JFK, pp. 1–2, 15, 21; Navasky int. with Nicholas Katzenbach, VN.
447   *Sit-ins had been resumed in Greensboro:* Confidential Situation Report for Birmingham, May 16, 1963, "Civil Rights Alabama, May 17–Oct. 10, 1963," Box 96, POF.
447   *pet tax-cut bill:* Richard Rovere, "Letter from Washington," *The New Yorker,* June 1, 1963. JFK's recent fight to enlarge the Rules Committee had revealed that the administration's margin in the House of Representatives, even on such a sterile matter of housekeeping, was precisely one vote.
447   *come along and discuss it:* telephone ints. Edwin Guthman, Sept. 28 and June 23, 1992; Louis Oberdorfer oral history, JFK, p. 33.
448   *wasn't safe for the President:* Louis Oberdorfer oral history, JFK, p. 37.
448   *filed suit in federal court:* NYT, May 19, 1963; Louis Oberdorfer oral history, JFK, p. 44.
448   *Secret Service* and *Schlei recommended:* Schlei to Lee White, May 17, 1963, "Civil Rights Alabama, May 17–Oct. 10, 1963," Box 96, POF.
448   *by thanking Wallace:* Kennedy-Wallace conversation, Pierre Salinger memo on trip, in ibid.
448   *"just like nothing happened":* and other Abernathy quotes, Riverside tape, Part 1, side 2.
449   *expelled the demonstrators:* The order, which could not be appealed until June, meant that 1,081 kids either would not be promoted to the next grade or, in the case of seniors, would be deprived of the most important secular rite of many a black person's life, high school graduation. Int. Constance Motley, March 27, 1991.
449   *four thousand handbills:* Newsweek, June 3, 1963.
449   *on fifteen-minute alert:* Cyrus Vance to Attorney General, May 20, 1963, Box 24, VN.
449   *Vann phoned Andy Young:* int. David Vann, May 28, 1984.
449   *"Are you with me now?":* ibid.; Vann, LeGrand speech, p. 36.
449   *"worth a damn":* int. Orzell Billingsley, July 18, 1987.
449   *daughter of a:* Constance Motley oral history, COH, pp. 21, 107–10; int. Constance Motley, March 27, 1991. While living at the Harlem Y in the summer of 1941 and taking French and biology at New York University, she had moved into the orbit of the charismatic Louis Burnham, just before he departed to head the SNYC offices in Birmingham.
449   *"cat has nine lives":* and Motley quotes, Riverside tape, Part 4, side 8.
449   *NCAAP's test cases:* Gober v. Birmingham (argued as part of a similar case, Peterson v. Greenville). int. Constance Motley, March 27, 1991. The decision did not address what might happen in a city without such laws where store owners refused service to blacks. Newsweek, June 3, 1963; Richard Rovere, "Letter from Washington," The New Yorker, June 1, 1963; Newman, Black, pp. 544–47.
449   *In his dissent:* Newman, Black, pp. 541–42. Though Black, who was joined by Kennedy's former deputy attorney general, Byron White, was not averse to laws prohibiting merchants from discriminating, he did not believe that in their absence shopkeepers could be forced to accept customers against their will. It was time, he would say in conference, "to clamp down on the Negroes."
450   *In a meeting that day:* audiotape 88.4, JFK. The President's aides preferred remedies like Title 3—the one omitted from the 1957 act, which would have allowed the Justice Department to initiate civil rights suits.
450   *Moscow had been devoting:* "Summary of Foreign Reaction," May 17, 1963, "Civil Rights Alabama, May 17–Oct. 10, 1963," Box 96, POF.
450   *into the courtroom of Clarence Allgood:* int. Constance Motley, March 27, 1991; int. Orzell Billingsley, July 18, 1987.
450   *Allgood had indeed:* int. Clarence Allgood, May 16, 1991; Coleman and Coleman, Allgood, pp. 9, 11, 14, 15, 17, 18.
450   *"outside agitators":* Lister Hill press release, May 9, 1963, AB. He also commended local law enforcement for "great and admirable restraint" in the face of "continual and calculated provocation and outside agitation."
451   *"that every redneck":* Navasky, Justice, p. 251.
451   *"comparing him to Bull Connor":* Navasky int. with Burke Marshall, Box 28, VN.
451   *Elbert Tuttle:* Bass, Unlikely Heroes, pp. 36–37.
451   *highly unusual:* int. Constance Motley, March 27, 1991.
451   *grabbed the Reverend Calvin Woods:* ibid.; int. Calvin Woods, July 15, 1987.
451   *daughter, Linda Cal:* int. Linda Woods Smith, July 20, 1987.
451   *Tuttle summarily struck down:* int. Constance Motley, March 27, 1991; Bass, Unlikely Heroes, pp. 207–208.
451   *"victory night":* police memo, May 22, 1963, mass meeting, BC.
452   *"legal remedy":* Bass, Unlikely Heroes, p. 210.
452   *"draw my pennies":* Newsweek, June 3, 1963.
452   *Connor's last vote:* int. Jimmy and Henry Simpson, Nov. 17, 1983.
452   *key to the city:* int. Burke Marshall, June 25, 1992.
452   *New York publisher urged:* Branch, Parting, p. 804. The letter had also been lightly quoted in the current New Republic.
452   *jammed old Wrigley Field in Los Angeles:* Branch, Parting, pp. 804–805. Demonstration logs, in RFK, put the number at 30,000. At a reception at the Beverly Hills mansion of Burt and Norma Lancaster, Newman wrote a $1,000 check, which was topped by Marlon Brando's $5,000. Sammy Davis Jr. matched the $20,000 raised at the party, which did not include the rally's gross of $35,000.
453   *adopted Fred Shuttlesworth as his "guide":* conversation with James Baldwin, ca. Spring 1983.

453   *taxicab burning right in front of the Sixteenth Street Baptist:* BPH, May 13, 1963.
453   *essay had been published:* MacNeil, *Way We Were,* p. 67.
453   *"no difference between the North and South":* Riverside tape, Part 6, side 10.
453   *Kennedy had asked him:* Navasky int. with Burke Marshall, Box 28, VN.
453   *meeting with representatives* and *Oberdorfer was assigned to coordinate:* Louis Oberdorfer oral history, JFK, pp. 33–34; R. Kennedy, *Own Words,* p. 181.
453   *Baldwin, Harry Belafonte:* meeting with Baldwin et al., int. Louis Oberdorfer, Oct. 21, 1992; R. Kennedy, *Own Words,* pp. 223–26; Navasky int. with Burke Marshall, Box 28, VN; *Jet,* June 13, 1963; Schlesinger, *Robert Kennedy,* pp. 344–48; Guthman, *Band of Brothers,* pp. 220–21; *Newsweek,* June 3, 1963; Clarence Jones letter to *NYT,* June 7, 1963.
454   *Smith resented:* int. with Jerome Smith ("Louisiana Story"), *Freedomways,* Second Quarter 1964, pp. 251, 248.
454   *called his CORE colleague Ike Reynolds:* Isaac Reynolds oral history, MSOH, pp. 25–26.

21. The Schoolhouse Door

455   *appear on* Meet the Press: Lesher, *Wallace,* p. 211; E. C. Clark, *Schoolhouse,* pp. 199–200.
455   *reprised the old-boy-network:* R. Kennedy, *Own Words,* pp. 189–90; Orrick to Attorney General, May 29, 1963, Box 24, VN (also in BM).
455   *Lynne forcefully enjoined Wallace:* E. C. Clark, *Schoolhouse,* p. 203. Lynne stopped short of prohibiting Wallace from being in Tuscaloosa on June 11.
455   *Marshall permitted himself:* Navasky int. with Burke Marshall, Box 29, VN.
456   *"has some spirit":* quoted in David Lawrence, "Wallace and Defiance of the Law," *New York Herald Tribune,* ca. June 4–11 1963, in BM.
456   *"the bloodiest rioting":* Klan HUAC report, p. 83.
456   *contractor for the state highway department:* Lesher, *Wallace,* p. 204.
456   *Carter . . . passed along the governor's instructions:* Carter, *Wallace,* p. 139.
456   *Connor delivered . . . message to the Tuscaloosa Citizens Council:* ACHR quarterly report, June–August 1963, ACHR; *BN,* June 8, 1963. The man who had led the riots against Autherine Lucy, Leonard Wilson, was the master of ceremonies at the Citizens Council meeting.
456   *rumored to be going on the state payroll:* Wittenstein to Lukas, June 14, 1963, "JSX—Alabama A–Z," AJC.
456   *met with Klan:* ACHR quarterly report, June–August 1963, ACHR; *BN,* June 8, 1963.
456   *Jack Cash's Barbecue* and *taking an arsenal:* Rowe Baxley deposition, pp. 17–20, 33–35; LeGrand int. with Rowe, p. 69; Rowe Peck deposition, pp. 172–75; Rowe Church Committee testimony, pp. 1897–98, all in BPSF 9.1; FBI int. with Herman Cash, Oct. 15, 1963, Bapbomb; *Task Force Report,* p. 72; *BN,* June 9 and 10, 1963.
456   *Herman Cash:* FBI ints. with R. L. Hasty, Oct. 7, 1963; with Kenneth Jones, Oct. 16, 1963; with Herman Frank Cash, Oct. 8 and 15, 1963; and with Laura Woods, Oct. 14, 1963, all in Bapbomb.
456   *DeBardeleben coal-mining concern liquidated:* Birmingfind calendar for 1982. This was DeBardeleben Coal, on June 11, 1962.
456   *Keith was the son:* telephone int. Harlan Keith (Ross's brother), Sept. 15, 1993; FBI ints. with Ross Keith, Oct. 7 and Nov. 11, 1963, Bapbomb.
458   *sent to visit Shelton:* Ben Allen oral history in Raines, *My Soul,* p. 331.
458   *"Fearless"* and *"Blood and Guts":* Wyman Lee ints. in *BN,* Sept. 7 and 21, 1997.
458   *his car transported:* See Sylvester Norris statement "Re Gaston Motel," police memo, May 20, 1963, Box 4, BPSF; Attorney General's Memo "Thomas E. Blanton Jr.," July 21, 1977, summarizing FBI files on motel investigation, Box 2, BPSF; FBI int. with William Otto Perkins, Jan. 14, 1964, Bapbomb; state memo "Herman F. Cash," BPSF 9.1(d); int. George Beck, March 1985.
458   *"worried about that bombing":* Rowe Church Committee testimony, p. 1898; "Garry Thomas Rowe, Jr.," Nov. 25, 1975, p. 4; Rowe Baxley deposition, pp. 20–22; Rowe Peck deposition, pp. 173–74, all in BPSF 9.1. In all his accounts of this scene, Rowe says that Cash was about to spill the beans about the Sixteenth Street Baptist Church bombing. However, this event took place three months before the church bombing. Since I can find no other incidence of Ben Allen being in the room with Rowe, Cash, and other Klansmen (though he did interrogate Cash at his residence on September 28), I assume the bombing in question was at the Gaston Motel, in which Cash's car was suspected of being used.
459   *documentary filmmakers* and *breakthrough cinéma vérité:* E. C. Clark, *Schoolhouse,* p. 201; B. Ruby Rich, "Is There a Narrator in the House?" *Village Voice,* Film Special, May 23, 1995. Film historians would later assert that the trend away from conventional narrator-driven filmmaking (which had achieved the state of the art in Edward R. Murrow's "Harvest of Shame," made the same year as *Primary*), in favor of cinéma vérité's "objective" camera's eye, was attributable to the fear of expressing political opinions that had come out of the McCarthy era.
459   *He had called his friend:* int. Jerome Cooper, Dec. 17, 1984.
459   *"could talk to Berlin":* BN, June 5, 1983.
459   *walking him off:* Ben Allen oral history in Raines, *My Soul,* p. 331.
460   *On Tuesday:* Stand in the Schoolhouse Door, *NYT,* June 12, 1963; E. C. Clark, *Schoolhouse,* pp. 223–31; Nicholas Katzenbach oral history in Raines, *My Soul,* pp. 340–42; Carter, *Wallace,* pp. 146–51; Lesher, *Wallace,* pp. 216–33; Guthman, *Band of Brothers,* p. 215ff.; *BN,* June 5, 1983; Wittenstein to Lukas, June 14, 1963, "JSX—Alabama A–Z," AJC; int. Earl Morgan, Spring 1986; int. Claude Sitton, May 5, 1992; int. Bill Hudson, July 29, 1992; int. Joseph Dolan, Nov. 8, 1994; int. Burke Marshall, October 1985.
460   *Faculty worth the name had fled* and *Shelton's spies:* E. C. Clark, *Schoolhouse,* pp. 151–52.
461   *knew the President was watching:* Katzenbach had already come a cropper by asking the Pentagon to get him those aerial views of the campus. Navasky int. with Edwin Guthman, VN; Navasky, *Justice,* pp. 111–12.
461   *Carter was apparently its principal author:* int. Doug Carter, Spring 1984. Usually the speech is attributed to another bug-eyed Wallace adviser, attorney John Peter Kohn, and its numerous legalisms would bear out his involvement.
461   *Klansmen be his bodyguards:* Rowe California deposition, pp. 19–20, BPSF 9.1.

463   *"I hope when you are Attorney General":* Schlesinger, *Robert Kennedy,* p. 256. Michael would die in a skiing accident in 1997, not long after creating a public scandal by having an affair with his children's baby-sitter.

463   *speech had almost been made:* May 12 drafts in Civil Rights, Alabama, May 12–14, 1963, Box 96, POF. I showed the handwriting in question to Ed Guthman, Nicholas Katzenbach, Ted Sorensen, Pierre Salinger, and Burke Marshall and none recognized it. Louis Martin, the President's "Negro adviser," has been given credit for the moral language, but he was not at the White House meeting of May 12.

463   *"the Magic City of the World":* Blaine A. Brownell, "Birmingham, Alabama: New South City in the 1920s," *Journal of Southern History,* February 1972, p. 48.

463   *and discourse:* Harding speech, *BN,* Oct. 26, 1921. Harding's appeals to "an end of prejudice and of demagogy" did seem a bit much, coming from the man who had recently welcomed the Klan's "Imperial induction team" into the White House to administer the Klan oath. Wade, *Fiery,* p. 165.

463   *Kennedy relaxed by watching TV* and *"How's it coming?":* telephone int. Theodore Sorensen, May 27, 1999.

463   *"the presence":* Kennedy speech, transcript in *NYT,* June 12, 1963.

464   *got himself arrested: BW,* June 5, 1963.

465   *"Turn me loose":* Adam Nossiter, *Of Long Memory* (Reading, Mass.: Addison-Wesley, 1994), p. 62.

465   *Dan Rather:* conversation with Dan Rather, Oct. 20, 1990; Rather, *Camera,* pp. 106–107.

465   *Buddhist monk:* Britannica Book of the Year 1964 has this on June 11. The winner of the Pulitzer was Hector Rondón of *La República* (Caracas), for a picture of a wounded Venezuelan soldier.

22. The End of Segregation

466   *"both of us in trouble," "put the problem very well":* R. Kennedy, *Own Words,* p. 201.

466   *"He was really great.":* FBI memo "Re Martin Luther King," June 12, 1963, Levison FBI.

466   *Marshall went to pick the brain:* Burke Marshall oral history in R. Kennedy, *Own Words,* pp. 177–78.

466   *Johnson had been only passively consulted:* Graham, *Civil Rights Era,* pp. 71–73, 77; telephone int. Norbert Schlei, Sept. 29, 1992; Schlei oral history, JFK, pp. 46–49.

467   *President Kennedy was acutely mindful:* telephone int. Norbert Schlei, Sept. 29, 1992. Kennedy was hung up on the employment discrimination section of the bill because of the FEPC controversy.

467   *the March on Washington:* Kesselman, *FEPC,* pp. 94–95.

467   *Randolph negotiated:* Williams to King, Summer 1963, reprinted in State of Lousiana, Joint Legislative Committee on Un-American Activities, *Activities of the Southern Conference Educational Fund, Inc., in Louisiana,* April 13, 1964, p. 89; Salmond, *Rebel,* pp. 172–76. NAACP Chief Walter White and New York mayor Fiorello La Guardia were in on the negotiations.

467   *Randolph canceled:* Kesselman, *FEPC,* p. 97. The March on Washington Movement continued, upstaging the established black organizations, for another year before flagging. Rustin and others were critical of Randolph for calling it off.

467   *Going through Fred Shuttlesworth:* Anderson, *Rustin,* p. 240.

467   *officers were furious:* Shuttlesworth to Shortridge, June 1, 1963, FS.

467   *fund-raising bonanza:* FBI memo "Re Martin Luther King," June 10, 1963, Levison FBI. King had sent out a fundraising appeal while still embroiled in Project C. King to friend, May 1963, Levison FBI.

467   *"I think we should march":* police memo, June 20, 1963, mass meeting, BC.

467   *On Saturday, June 22:* meeting at the White House, e.g., Schlesinger, *Robert Kennedy,* pp. 371–73; R. Kennedy, *Own Words,* p. 141; Garrow, *FBI,* pp. 60–61; Branch, *Bearing,* pp. 836–38. The FBI's informant on Stanley Levison, Jack Childs, had in March reported that Levison was "disenchanted" with the Party.

468   *Lawford had reputedly procured Novotny:* Summers, *Official and Confidential,* pp. 305–306; Hersh, *Camelot,* p. 391.

468   *James Free:* telephone int. Edwin Guthman, July 2000; *Alabama,* May 10, 1937. Free, who had tried to unionize the *News* staff in the 1930s, took care not to show many liberal impulses in his dispatches.

468   *"mean to Governor Wallace":* Burke Marshall phone logs, May 24, 1963, BM.

468   *O'Dell had been called:* int. Jack O'Dell, Sept. 7, 1999; Young, *Burden,* p. 268; Branch, *Parting,* pp. 844–45.

469   *"going to work with whoever":* police memo, July 8, 1963, mass meeting, BC.

469   *he had been periodically luring* and *When a crowd at Grant Park:* ints. Fred Shuttlesworth; *Newsweek,* July 15, 1963; police memo, July 8, 1963, mass meeting, BC.

469   *tour of Europe and the Holy Land:* Fred Shuttlesworth oral history, KC, Part 2; police memo, July 8, 1963, mass meeting, BC; *Jet,* Sept. 19, 1963.

469   *Fred challenged King:* Shuttlesworth to King, July 12, 1963, FS 22.111.

469   *letter from Shuttlesworth:* Shuttlesworth to R. Kennedy, June 6, 1963, FS.

470   *Baker had joined SCEF:* Ella Baker oral history, MSOH, p. 69.

470   *When Shuttlesworth broke the news:* ints. Fred Shuttlesworth; Anne Braden, "A View from the Fringes," *Southern Exposure,* Spring 1981.

470   *"a Southern President":* ACHR quarterly report, June–August 1963, ACHR.

470   *Wallace came to Washington:* NYT, July 16 and 17, 1963; Carter, *Wallace,* pp. 157–59. Lesher, *Wallace,* pp. 242–43. Three days earlier, Mississippi's governor Ross Barnett had earned front-page headlines by attacking Highlander: "Barnett Charges Kennedys Assist Red Racial Plot."

470   *wrote to J. Edgar Hoover:* Garrow, *FBI,* p. 63.

470   *gave their FBI liaison:* Evans to Belmont, July 16, 1963, Levison FBI. Robert Kennedy would draft a carefully worded letter to the inquiring senators stating that neither King nor any civil rights leaders were "Communists or Communist-controlled," leaving open the possibility of Communist influence. He sent Nicholas Katzenbach, Burke Marshall, and Courtney Evans to personally brief Monroney, Magnuson, and Georgia's Richard Russell. R. Kennedy, *Own Words,* pp. 144–45; Garrow, *FBI,* p. 66.

471   *documentary on Birmingham:* Strick to Jones, July 9, 1963, MLK 13.13.

471   *propose a compromise:* int. Clarence Jones, Oct. 24, 2000; Garrow, *FBI,* p. 63; Branch, *Parting,* p. 853.

471   *he was still furious:* See R. Kennedy, *Own Words,* p. 224; FBI memo on Stanley David Levison, June 3, 1963, Levison FBI. Kennedy had received Jones and Levison's wiretapped comments that Kennedy "really needed" the grief he had gotten and was "the worst illustration of white arrogant liberalism."
471   *"a nice fellow":* Jones to Editor of the *Times,* June 7, 1963, BM. It was on a copy of this letter that Kennedy wrote the note to Marshall.
471   *provided a list:* Mills to Marshall, June 7, 1963, BM. Marshall requested the list of Robert Mills of the General Artists Corporation and forwarded it "in accordance with your request" to the FBI's Al Rosen.
471   *FBI dossiers:* O'Reilly, *"Racial Matters,"* p. 102.
471   *"repercussions if it should ever":* Evans to Belmont, July 16, 1963, in Theoharis, *Secret Files,* p. 95.
471   *Community Affairs Committee:* Justice Department Monday Report, July 8, 1963, BM; Vann, LeGrand speech, p. 37.
472   Times *editorial page: would give Boutwell:* NYT, July 20, 1963.
472   *Jones tap's early gleanings:* Evans to Belmont, July 25, 1963, in Theoharis, *Secret Files,* p. 96; Garrow, *FBI,* p. 65; Schlesinger, *Robert Kennedy,* p. 619; Branch, *Parting,* pp. 859–60.
472   *"I thought you would be interested":* Garrow, *FBI,* p. 67.
472   *Ellen Rometsch:* Evans to Belmont, July 24, 1963, in Theoharis, *Secret Files,* p. 41; Summers, *Secret and Confidential,* pp. 309–11.
472   *"not too much difference":* Lee Bains int. with Bobby Shelton, courtesy of Bains.
473   *Phillip Thomas Mabry:* FBI ints. with Phillip Thomas Mabry, Oct. 27 and 30, 1967, Bapbomb.
473   *how to make a bom* and *"you owe me":* Tom Cook memo on NSRP rally, July 1, 1963, City of Birmingham Law Department Papers, BPL.
473   *escorted Edward Fields:* Carter, *Wallace,* pp. 166–67.
473   *desegregation program:* Vann, LeGrand speech, p. 37; int. Frederick and Anny Kraus, March 28, 1988; Marcus Jones memo, Aug. 7, 1963, AB; int. David Vann, May 24, 1984.
473   *Arant payroll:* int. David Vann, May 24, 1984.
473   *merchants now had no intention:* Navasky int. with David Vann, Box 32, VN.
474   *braved the NSRP men:* Marcus Jones memo, September 1964, BPSF 7.20.
474   *police arrested Edward Fields:* Fields's arrest record in NSRP file, Bapbomb; Marcus Jones memo, Aug. 7, 1963, AB.
474   *Woods recorded the reactions:* Woods to SCLC, July 31, 1963, Aug. 1, 5, and 8, 1963, MLK 1.9.
475   " *'Christian problem' ":* Harold Katz, "Confidential Memorandum on Racial Problems Affecting the Birmingham Jewish Community," July 3, 1963, Mark Elovitz Papers, BPL.
475   *did not share Papa's view:* int. Richard Pizitz, March 1983.

23. The Beginning of Integration

477   *Chambliss's frustration:* FBI int. with Robert Gafford, Oct. 7, 1963, Bapbomb.
477   *Ronnie Tidwell:* "Tidwell Ronald Jefferson" employment history, BPSF 9.1; Klan HUAC hearings, p. 3071; FBI int. with Ronald Tidwell, Dec. 7, 1964, Bapbomb; telephone conversations with Ernest Tidwell, Dec. 15, 2000, and with Thad Tidwell, Dec. 17, 2000.
477   *fired more than five hundred shots:* NLRB report.
478   *Tidwell gave a lesson:* Rowe Baxley deposition, pp. 8–10; Yung investigative notes, BPSF 7.2; state interview with Robert Thomas, March 25, 1976, p. 7, BPSF 10.2. Special Agent Neil Shanahan, who became Rowe's primary handler in March 1964, says that the Tidwell demonstration took place in 1964 (Eddy summary of int. with Shanahan, May 3, 1977, JY).
478   *an integrated planeload of entertainers* and *"Salute to Freedom":* Marcus Jones memo, Aug. 7, 1963, AB; Burke Marshall phone log, July 15, 1963, BM; *AA,* Aug. 17, 1963; police memos on July 19 and 29, 1963, mass meetings, BC.
479   *riot conditions were fanned:* ACHR quarterly report, June–August 1963, ACHR.
479   *Fields held an NSRP event* and *Klansmen rallied:* police memo, "Friday, August 9, 1963," AB.
479   *From the town of Warrior:* church burning, LeGrand int. with Rowe, pp. 37–38, BPSF 9.1; FBI ints. with Howard Guthrie, Nov. 26, 1963, with L. B. Bolling, Nov. 12 and 26, 1963, and with John Wesley Hall, Nov. 19, 1963, all in Bapbomb; Billy Neil Tipton statement, Nov. 20, 1963, Bapbomb; state memo on Charles Cagle, BPSF 9.12(d). Investigators also suspected that Hall was involved. Gene Reeves (conversations Sept. 15, 1993) and Charles Cagle (telephone conversation Oct. 28, 2000) refused to comment on their Klan activities.
480   *DeShazo told his landlady* and *DeShazo put on:* Loveman's teargas bomb, Sims to Jones, Oct. 16, 1963, BPSF 1.23; FBI ints. with Charles Thompson and with James D. Robertson, Oct. 2, 1963, Bapbomb; Jones police report, Aug. 19, 1963, AB 5.7; Jones police report, September 1964, BPSF 7.20; Finger to Jones, Oct. 11, 1963, Box 3, BPSF.
480   *police detectives initially showed:* Jones police report, Aug. 19, 1963, AB 5.7.
481   *Boutwell seemed to draw:* statement in AB. In response to the mayor's moral indignation over this "sick, rabid animal," an anonymous caller informed Boutwell's son that the mayor's house was going to be bombed.
481   *"just blow the gas out":* police memo, Aug. 19, 1963, mass meeting, BC.
481   *Allgood approved:* BPH, Aug. 21, 1963; Coleman and Coleman, *Allgood,* pp. 34–35; Reid Barnes statement, Sept. 3, 1963, AB; int. Clarence Allgood, May 16, 1991.
481   *Cash departed on a fishing trip:* FBI int. with Dora Ireland, Oct. 7, 1963, Bapbomb.
481   *Since shortly after his arrest:* FBI ints. with Virginia Gantney, Nov. 8, 1963, with Ross Keith, Nov. 11, 1963, and with Wyvonne Lavelle Fike, Oct. 15, 1963, Bapbomb.
481   *a bomb blew up:* Rowe Baxley deposition pp. 12–13; LeGrand int. with Rowe, pp. 10–11, 33–34; summary of Rowe report for Aug. 20, 1963, all in BPSF 9.1. In one account, Rowe names these four as the suspects in the second Shores bombing, but his contemporaneous report to the FBI specifies this one. Not long before the blast, Rowe had given eleven blasting caps to Billy Holt, a member of the Shores bombing squad who evidently was not at the crime scene.

482 *For the first time:* riot, *BPH,* Aug. 21, 1963; Fire Chief Swindle, "Bombing Damage," AB; int. Maurice House, Spring 1985; police memo, Aug. 21, 1963, Re "Injury sustained by Reverend Nelson Smith," Box 2, BPSF.

482 *Ingram came in* and *made the bomb in Ingram's garage:* LeGrand int. with Rowe, pp. 10–11, BPSF 9.1; FBI ints. with Bobby Lowe, Nov. 29, 1963, with Clyde Hill, Jan. 21, 1964, and with Willis Crain, Nov. 18, 1963, all in Bapbomb.

482 *"piss-poor bomb maker":* LeGrand int. with Rowe, p. 10, BPSF 9.1.

482 *Thomas virtually admitted* and *"physical training":* FBI int. with Robert Thomas, Nov. 3, 1963, BPSF 6.18. He said he "considered it good judgment to procure witnesses to his activities" at the time of a bombing.

482 *Chambliss and Tommy Blanton had engaged:* Eddy memo, "Thomas E. Blanton," July 21, 1977, Box 2, BPSF; FBI ints. with George Pickle and with Patricia Pickle, Oct. 10, 1963, Bapbomb.

482 *polygraph test would indicate:* handwritten memo, "Polygraph says," Box 2, BPSF.

482 *fired his .22* and *"I hope it killed him":* FBI int. with Bobby Frank Cherry, Oct. 16, 1963, Bapbomb.

483 *"Rocks Hurled":* BPH, Aug. 21, 1963.

483 *Roosevelt Tatum:* Marlin to Marshall, Aug. 21, 1963, BM; Lane and Gregory, *"Zorro,"* pp. 38–39. Tatum's lawyer Clarence Jones had accompanied him to the polygraph test that had led to his continuing investigation by the grand jury.

483 *rigged lie detector* and *corroborated the essentials:* After the bombing, Tatum had been flown to Washington for interviews with Justice Department lawyers and, he thought, a member of Congress from New York. Back home, FBI agents asked him to take a lie detector test. Before the exam, according to Tatum, the agents told him to answer no to all questions about his family, regardless of their accuracy, so that the polygraph operator could establish a base line for deception. But after completing the polygraph, Tatum would say, he was pressured by the agents to sign an admission that he had made false statements. These were the charges for which the government convened a federal grand jury a month ahead of schedule. As the disenchanted chief deputy U.S. marshal explained the special treatment: "It was to get Tatum. To indict him. He was a problem. They had to get him out of the way" (Lane and Gregory, *"Zorro,"* p. 37). Still, the prosecution's own witnesses ended up corroborating key elements of Tatum's story: A policeman admitted that he was immediately at A. D. King's house even though the area was not his beat; a neighbor revealed that he too had seen a police car parked in front of the King house; the polygraphist from Memphis agreed that he had questioned Tatum about his family and unrelated subjects for about an hour before the test was given.

483 *"unknown Negro male":* Marlin to Marshall, Aug. 26, 1963, BM.

484 *Thomas's leading detractors:* FBI int. with Hubert Page, Dec. 4, 1964, Bapbomb.

484 *grabbed her binoculars:* FBI int. with Mrs. B. Freeman Brown, Oct. 4, 1963, Bapbomb.

484 *The Blanton's had become* and *Chambliss, created a dilemma:* FBI memo "Thomas Edwin Blanton, Jr.," Bapbomb, places the timing of this as August. FBI int. with Troy Ingram, May 19, 1965, Bapbomb, suggests that Chambliss was also expelled, but Shelton (FBI int. Aug. 21, 1964, Bapbomb) says that he kept Chambliss in longer and attempted to reeducate him. He did remain in Eastview.

484 *"CIA son of a bitch":* David Barber int. with Robert Chambliss, Oct. 12, 1978, Box 3, BPSF; LeGrand int. with Chambliss, ca. 1976, Box 1, BPSF. This confrontation may have taken place in 1964.

484 *rump group was just what the Imperial Wizard wanted:* An informant would tell the FBI that Shelton ordered Robert Thomas to evict two people from the Klan—probably either both Blantons, or Blanton and Chambliss—and then bomb the church. "Confidential-Source Material," Sept. 23, 1977, JY.

484 *Pickle had recently gotten:* Ben Allen and Willie Painter int. with Patricia Pickle, Oct. 7, 1963, BPSF 1.23.

485 *worked free on the jalopies:* conversation with Mary Ingram, March 23, 1993.

485 *For their first meeting:* deposition of William L. Jackson, March 2, 1976, Box 4, BPSF; FBI ints. with George Pickle, Oct. 10, 1963, and Jan. 25, 1965, and with John Thomas Coker, Sept. 18, 1964, all in Bapbomb.

485 *Hamilton, gave the FBI:* Wasserstrom to Marshall, Aug. 28, 1963, BM.

485 *"NEVER, NEVER":* MacNeil, *Way We Were,* p. 134.

486 *Hood had ended his studies* and *"get that nigger bitch":* E. C. Clark, *Schoolhouse,* pp. 243–46.

486 *not understood what purpose:* int. Deenie Drew, May 1984.

24. All the Governor's Men

487 *Walker was calling the watershed:* Walker to Potoker, June 7, 1963, SCLC 33.18.

487 *banished the nine guests* and *outrage of . . . Bayard Rustin:* Branch, *Parting,* p. 847.

487 *"grab one little brother":* ibid., p. 861. Hoover sent Robert Kennedy a four-page narrative of Rustin atrocities, some of which, including his membership in the Young Communist League, were enumerated three days later on the Senate floor by Strom Thurmond.

487 *"The Old Man died":* D. Lewis, *Du Bois,* p. 3.

488 *Du Bois's SNYC protégés:* ints. Esther Cooper Jackson, June 20, 1995, and James Jackson, July 25, 1995.

488 *O'Dell was lonely in this crowd:* int. Jack O'Dell, Sept. 7, 1999.

488 *Rustin had written:* Rustin to Dombrowski, Aug. 7, 1963, reprinted in State of Louisiana, Joint Legislative Committee on Un-American Activities, *Activities of the Southern Conference Educational Fund, Inc., in Louisiana,* April 13, 1964, p. 62.

488 *"you had more to do":* Salmond, *Rebel,* p. 280.

488 *leave their police dogs:* Schlesinger, *Robert Kennedy,* p. 65.

489 *"say a few words":* Rustin to Shuttlesworth, Aug. 19, 1963, FS.

489 *"the way Sherman did":* Hampton and Fayer, *Voices,* p. 166. The manifesto-esque parts were probably drafted by Bayard Rustin's assistant, a white socialist named Tom Kahn.

489 *"John, I know who you are":* Garrow, *Bearing,* p. 283.

489 *"everything we have done":* Abernathy, *Walls,* p. 275.

489 *Federal troops had been put on alert:* O'Reilly, *"Racial Matters,"* p. 126.

489 *"You better tell":* Newman, *Black,* pp. 542–44; Durr, *Magic Circle,* p. 293.

489 *Malcolm X was in a D.C. hotel denouncing:* Ossie Davis int. in Hampton and Fayer, *Voices,* p. 162.

489 *"Echoes from the South":* Fred Shuttlesworth oral history, KC, Part 2.

489 *sober homilies:* Wyatt Walker oral history, MSOH, p. 74. Walker, Andy Young, and others had buffed them into the early hours.

489 *quotes from his "Letter":* G. Jack Gravlee, "A Black Rhetoric of Social Revolution," in Calvin M. Logue and Howard Dorgan, *A New Diversity in Contemporary Southern Rhetoric* (Baton Rouge: Louisiana State University Press, 1987) pp. 75–76.

490 *ending he had used in his oratorical debut:* "Annual Address at Institute on Nonviolence and Social Change," Dec. 3, 1956, BUK I.15.

490 *only living public figure:* See Miller, *Voice,* pp. 149–50.

490 *Ralph Roton:* Roton testimony, Klan HUAC hearings, pp. 3189–210; int. Ralph Roton, Nov. 26, 2000.

490 *Peace Committee:* Carter, *Wallace,* p. 231.

490 *FBI agents from the New York City area* and *"You have done enough":* Hosea Hudson, *Black Worker in the Deep South* (New York: International Publishers, 1972), pp. 109–10. Then the agents invited him to become an informant. Hudson appears to have been living in either Newark or Brooklyn.

491 *hot line had just been hooked up:* MacNeil, *Way We Were,* p. 128; Schlesinger, *Thousand,* p. 920.

491 *Bailey "invited"* and *Klan's political front:* Jones memo, ca. Sept. 1, 1963, BPSF 7.29; Morgan to Wallace, Sept. 3, 1963, AB 30.28; Wasserstrom to Marshall, Aug. 29, 1963, BM; *BPH,* Sept. 4, 1963. "For your information," Bailey coldly informed the governor in a telegram, "this information is completely false."

491 *giant firecrackers:* Lavelle Fike Young testimony, Chambliss trial transcript, pp. 470–76.

491 *paraded to Montgomery:* Joseph Wilson and Edward Harris, "Hucksters of Hate—Nazi Style," *The Progressive,* June 1964, p. 12; police memo, Sept. 5, 1963, Box 23, AB; Carter, *Wallace,* p. 167.

491 *NSRP rally* and *attracted the FBI:* Wasserstrom to Marshall, Aug. 31, 1963 (two memos), BM.

491 *present at the rally:* Troy Ingram: FBI int. with Troy Ingram, Sept. 25, 1963, Bapbomb.

492 *September 1, of the second meeting:* FBI int. with Bobby Shelton, Aug. 21, 1964, Bapbomb; Eddy to Beck, Sept. 23, 1977, George Beck Papers, courtesy of Beck. Bobby Shelton would be told that the meeting was canceled, but a Klan police informer said the meeting took place.

492 *"national party convention":* FBI int. with Ruby Palmer, Oct. 10, 1963, Bapbomb; police memo, Sept. 5, 1963, Box 23, AB.

492 *Chambliss was helping Willie Mae Walker:* FBI ints. with Harry Eugene Walker, Oct. 6, 1963, with Willie Mae Walker, Oct. 25, 1963, and with Robert Chambliss, Oct. 1, 1963, Bapbomb.

492 *At midnight:* White, Lay, and white men in Ford, int. Maurice House, Spring 1985; police int. with James Lay, Nov. 6, 1963, BPSF 9.12; ints. with Paul White and John Cross in Oct. 25, 1963, state investigative report by R. W. Godwin, BPSF 9.12; FBI memo beginning "Officer E.H. Cantrell was contacted," Bapbomb; FBI int. with Paul White, Sept. 19, 1963, Bapbomb; FBI "Interview of People in Vicinity at Time of Bombing," BPSF 9.1; Eddy memo, "Thomas E. Blanton, Jr.," July 21, 1977, and memo to state file, "Suspect Thomas Blanton, Jr.," Box 2, BPSF; police memos, Nov. 5, Sept. 15, and Dec. 4, 1963, in Lay file, Box 4, BPSF. The Birmingham police would develop an alternative scenario: Two weeks before, Edward Fields, J. B. Stoner, and Jerry Dutton of the NSRP met with Bessemer Klansman Eugene Thomas and a couple of his men and made plans to bomb the church over the Labor Day weekend. Police memo, Jan. 23, 1967, "Re: the Bombing of the Sixteenth Street Baptist Church," BPSF 7.10. In the April 2001 trial of Tommy Blanton, Lay's testimony (contradicting his contemporaneous accounts) suggested that White had not been on the scene but had been sought out by Lay after the car drove off.

492 *"You didn't hear a":* James Lay int. in *BN,* July 7, 1997.

493 *flags . . . had been removed:* FBI int. with Terrance Moore, Oct. 4, 1963, Bapbomb.

493 *at a Civitan barbecue:* police memo, Sept. 5, 1963, Box 23, AB; Wasserstrom to Marshall, Sept. 3, 1963, BM.

493 *As of 6:25:* Lesher, *Wallace,* p. 245.

493 *"who kicked police dogs":* Bulletin of the John Birch Society, July 1963, in Box 1, BPSF.

493 *At the United Klans of America rally:* FBI teletype, "9/2 KKK sponsored rally, " AB.

494 *slap Boutwell in the mouth:* FBI int. with Hubert Page, Oct. 3, 1963, Bapbomb.

494 *Wallace phoned the mayor:* quotes in "Gist of Telephone Conversation 9/3/63," AB 20.40.

494 *Morse of Oregon joined* and *Wallace . . . retorted:* NYT, Sept. 6, 1963; Lesher, *Wallace,* pp. 59–62.

494 *on Wednesday, September 4:* NSRP demonstrations, police memo, Sept. 5, 1963, WH 3.39; NSRP flyer, "Boycott Mixed Schools," in AB 34.1; Finger to Jones, Sept. 9, 1963, Box 3, BPSF; *BPH,* Sept. 5, 1963; *NYT,* Sept. 5, 1963; Evans to Moore, Sept. 4, 1963, Warren to Moore, Sept. 4, 1963, AB; FBI int. with Barnie Carmack, Sept. 24, 1963, Bapbomb.

495 *At the front door of Graymont Elementary:* Wall to Moore, Sept. 4, 1963, AB; FBI int. with Arthur Shores, June 29, 1964, Bapbomb; *BPH,* Sept. 5, 1963; police memo, Sept. 5, 1963, AB.

495 *were two stalwarts of Eastview:* FBI int. with Ross Keith, Nov. 11, 1963, Bapbomb.

496 *Wallace issued an executive order:* Executive Order No. 10, George Wallace Papers, ADAH.

496 *Blanton heard over his CB radio:* FBI int. with Tommy Blanton, Oct. 15, 1963, Bapbomb.

496 *"probably be a bombing":* FBI int. with Terrance Moore, Oct. 4, 1963, Bapbomb.

496 *at the Brooke Hill School:* int. Margaret Gage, Spring 1983.

25. A Case of Dynamite

497 *Leon Negron:* FBI ints. with Leon Negron, Oct. 3, 1963, and June 3, 1965, with James Hancock, Oct. 4, 1963, with Mary Lou Holt, March 28, 1966, and with Elmer Bailey Brock, Dec. 30, 1965, all in Bapbomb; int. James Parsons, Spring 1984.

497 *"throw in a few extra sticks":* Ernie Cantrell testimony in Chambliss trial transcript, p. 247.

497 *Chambliss put that case:* FBI int. with Robert Chambliss, Jan. 22, 1965, Bapbomb.

497 *"Everyone watch TV.":* "Confidential-Source Material," probably from informant Mary Frances Cunningham, Sept. 23, 1977, JY. Memo on confidential material, Aug. 17, 1977, JY, has this statement on August 20, but it is more consistent with the evidence to have it on September 4.

497 *rally of the West End Parents:* FBI int. with Hubert Page, Oct. 3, 1963, Bapbomb.

497 *was Hoover Academy:* FBI int. with Walter Monteith, Jan. 28, 1964, Bapbomb. The father was James Monteith; both father and son were longtime residents of Dynamite Hill.

498 *Wallace had persuaded to petition: BPH,* Sept. 5, 1963.

498 *More than seventy-five men:* Klan meeting, FBI ints. with Robert Creel, Nov. 26, 1963, with Don Luna, March 23, 1964, and with Robert Thomas, Nov. 9, 1963, Bapbomb; FBI int. with Robert Thomas, Nov. 3, 1963, BPSF 6.18; Charles Cagle statement to Bill Jones, Oct. 1, 1963, Bapbomb.

498 *gala across town:* FBI ints. with Ruby Palmer, Oct. 10, 1963, with Lawrence McCrae, Oct. 10, 1963, with Charlotte DeShazo, Sept. 28, 1963, with Hubert Page, Dec. 4, 1964, all in Bapbomb; police memo, Sept. 9, 1963, AB 20.38.

498 *detectives recognized a couple of FBI agents:* int. Maurice House, Spring 1985; int. Ernie Cantrell, March 21, 1985.

498 *"lightning doesn't strike twice":* Arthur Shores oral history in Raines, *My Soul,* pp. 348–49.

498 *at the bombing scene* and *its third riot:* police memo, Sept. 9, 1963, AB 20.38; Pierce to Moore, Box 2, BPSF; ints. Joseph Dolan, November 1986, and June 22, 1992; int. Claude Sitton, May 5, 1992; int. James D. Smith, Spring 1984; int. Maurice House, Spring 1985; ints. Fred Shuttlesworth; int. Arthur Shores, May 20, 1991; affidavit of Eddie Coleman, Inter-Citizens Committee document no. 44, Sept. 15, 1963, and affidavit of Thomas Lymon (also spelled Lyman), Inter-Citizens Committee document no. 45, Sept. 15, 1963, IC.

499 *Pitts had come to help, bringing along his houseguest:* E. J. Kahn, "A Whale of a Difference," *The New Yorker,* April 10, 1971, pp. 47–48.

500 *Thelton Henderson:* telephone int. Thelton Henderson, March 4, 1997.

500 *noticed his dead-on resemblance:* int. Frank Dukes, Oct. 4, 1983. Former detective Maurice House (Spring 1985) agreed, but told me, "You said it, not me." Former officer James D. Smith, however, readily acknowledged the resemblance.

500–1 *Rowe "happened"* and *drew his .38 pistol:* Eddy to Beck, Oct. 11, 1977, BPSF 9.1; *Task Force Report,* pp. 97–99; *NYT,* July 8, 9, 11, 1978. There are several contemporary eyewitnesses who corroborate much of Rowe's story up to the shooting.

501 *Lingo was pacing* and *Moore had insisted:* statements of Jamie Moore, re call with Lingo and re school board meeting, both Sept. 5, 1963, AB; September 5 statement re Cecil Jackson call, AB; int. Major Bill Jones, March 1985.

501 *"leaving me in Bataan":* int. Joseph Dolan, Nov. 8, 1994.

501 *Hall and Charles Cagle to go by Chambliss's* and *case of dynamite:* FBI ints. with John Hall, Dec. 3, 1963, and Oct. 8, 1965, Bapbomb; Cagle statement to Bill Jones, Oct. 1, 1963, Bapbomb; Chambliss statement to Bill Jones, Bapbomb; Sims to Jones, ca. September–October 1963, BPSF 9.1; statement of Hall to state investigators, Sept. 29, 1963, BPSF 1.23; police memo re "dynamite found by state investigator," Oct. 16, 1963, BPSF 7.48.

501 *used one and a half sticks:* state memo on FBI confidential material, Aug. 17, 1977, JY. This was gleaned in August 1965.

502 *never made a bad bomb:* "Confidential-Source Material," Nov. 23, 1977, JY.

502 *canvas sack of loose dynamite:* Eddy to Beck, "Bapbomb Confidential Informers Information," Aug. 15, 1977, JY; FBI int. with John Hall, Oct. 8, 1965, Bapbomb.

502 *Cagle, along with Gene Reeves:* state memo, "Charles Arnie Cagle," BPSF 9.12(d).

502 *McFall called Gary Thomas Rowe:* In one version, Rowe said he called McFall as soon as he got home and told him all the details. McFall, he said, arranged to meet Rowe at a lumberyard not far from where Rowe said the shooting occurred. *Task Force Report,* p. 99–100. the name of Rowe's handler is blacked out in my copy of the report, but McFall is named in Eddy to Beck, Oct. 11, 1977, BPSF 9.1. In the Justice Department report. Rowe's handler called the story "an absolutely untruthful statement."

502 *"hit the nigger right in the chest":* **Task Force Report,** pp. 99–100; Eddy to Beck, Oct. 11, 1977, BPSF 9.1. Like most of Rowe's stories, this one has flaws, the key one being that the coroner found no corpse other than Coley's, and his wound was definitely from a shotgun, not a .38 pistol (*Task Force Report,* pp. 101–104). Perhaps Rowe's victim was merely wounded, although one is hard-pressed to conceive of an ego that would admit to a murder that hadn't happened. Federal investigators would later discount Rowe's claim because his FBI file contained no evidence that the bureau had investigated this confession to a murder. Yet the only thing perhaps as fantastic as Rowe's story was the absence of any record in his FBI file that the bureau had even spoken to him at all the day after the bombing. Interestingly, former sergeant Ernie Cantrell (int. March 21, 1985) said that three people were killed at the Shores riot. There has been some speculation that Rowe was confessing to this murder at the time he did, 1977, so that it would be covered under any immunity deal he struck with the state attorney general then prosecuting Robert Chambliss. Investigating Rowe's claim in 1978, Birmingham police would suspect that Thomas Lymon was the man he had shot, nonfatally (*BPH,* Sept. 23, 1978), but Lymon was hit with shotgun not pistol fire.

502 *closed the schools* and *Moore not amused:* Wasserstrom to Marshall, Sept. 5, 1963, BM; Moore statements re conversation with board of education president Robert Arthur and re meeting with board, both dated Sept. 5, 1963, AB.

502 *"get information from the Birmingham police":* int. Joseph Dolan, Nov. 8, 1994.

502 *Dolan slipped into West End High* and *"Did you call Boooobby yet?":* ints. Joseph Dolan, November 1986 and June 22, 1992.

503 *Motley, added George Wallace:* Barrett to Marshall, Sept. 6, 1963, BM.

503 *"Don't' refer to me":* BW, Sept. 14, 1963.

503 *"first-class funerals"* and *"tear gas and bayonets": NYT,* Sept. 6, 1963.

503 *"Something must be done":* King and Shuttlesworth to Kennedy, Sept. 5, 1963, MLK 1.9.

503 *And the turnout:* FBI ints. with Ruby Palmer, Oct. 10, 1963, with Hubert Page, Oct. 3, 1963, and with Troy Ingram, Nov. 7, 1963, all in Bapbomb.

503 *boasting to the* New York Times's: *NYT,* Sept. 16, 1963.

503 *given a table of honor:* Carter, *Wallace,* p. 173.

503–4 *Wallace said, "Doc," "Skeeter's working"* and *Birmingham-postmarked letter:* int. Earl Morgan, Spring 1986.

504 *"nigras" were slinging dynamite:* FBI int. with Mary Lou Holt, June 6, 1964, Bapbomb.

504 *firebombing the house: BPH,* Sept. 9, 1963; Rowe, *Undercover Years,* pp. 94–95; LeGrand int. with Rowe, pp.

39–40, 59, BPSF 9.1; *Task Force Report,* pp. 75–76. Rowe embellishes this incident considerably in the telling. The smoke caused an estimated $5,000 to $10,000 worth of damage, about the same as Shores's first bombing.

504 *attended a White House dinner: BW,* Aug. 31, 1963.

504 *a popular book he would write:* Rowe, *Undercover Years.*

505 *bomb threats* and *unkempt white male:* FBI ints. with Vivian Lesley Williams, Oct. 5 and 16, 1963, Bapbomb.

505 *taped an hour-long appeal:* FBI transcript of speech, Sept. 8, 1963, BM. Wallace told the fable that would become the disingenuous refrain of his career: "I have never provoked any violence in this state," and again, "There has been no violence in this state between Negro and white, thank goodness; we have had some demonstrations but I am glad that we have had no race riots."

505 *sixty troopers were waiting* and *Lingo himself turned students away: BPH,* Sept. 11, 1963; Jamie Moore summary of phone conversation with Thelton Henderson, Sept. 9, 1963, AB; Wasserstrom to Marshall, Sept. 9, 1963, BM.

505 *Marshall asked Judge Frank Johnson* and *first five-judge restraining order: Washington Evening Star,* Sept. 11, 1963; Lesher, *Wallace,* p. 250; Bass, *Taming,* p. 209.

505 *twenty-five National Guardsmen who began, sticking bayonets:* int. Earl Morgan, Spring 1986. This account is corroborated, remorselessly, by Wallace himself, in Lesher, *Wallace,* p. 251.

505 *meeting of his Cahaba River Klan:* FBI ints. with Wyman Lee, Oct. 8, 1963, and Jan. 26, 1965, with Carey Isbell Jr., Nov. 18, 1963, and with Bobby Shelton, Aug. 21, 1964, Bapbomb. Herman Cash was there, along with the Blantons, George Pickle, and the NSRP's Jerry Dutton. Wyman Lee, the gas station attendant who was one of Eastview's more easily led members, was spying for Bobby Shelton. Lee suspected that Billy Holt was attending as Robert Thomas's eyes and ears.

506 *"I've got enough.":* FBI int. with Willis Alfred Crain, Nov. 18, 1963, Bapbomb.

506 *call out the National Guard* and *Kennedy signed an order:* Wasserstrom to Marshall, Sept. 10, 1963, BM; *Washington Evening Star,* Sept. 11, 1963; *BPH,* Sept. 11, 1963. Wallace suggested that Kennedy was planning to jail him because "I might participate in some of the presidential primaries. When we get around to jailing political opponents, we will have taken another long step toward a military dictatorship."

506 *Marshall phoned Chief Jamie Moore* and *Robert Kennedy picked up an extension:* police memo on conversation, Sept. 10, 1963, AB, "Summary of Plan for Tuesday, September 10," BM.

506 *touring a Schlitz brewery: BPH,* Sept. 11, 1963.

506 *"adult obscenities,": BPH,* Sept. 11, 1963.

507 *"have some ice cream":* ibid.

507 *"spontaneous demonstration,":* Wasserstrom to Marshall, Sept. 10, 1963, BM; *The Examiner,* Sept. 12, 1963.

507 *explosion in the street* and *"nothing to investigate":* Wasserstrom to Marshall, Sept. 11, 1963, BM.

507 *wearing short pants:* second memo, Wasserstrom to Marshall, Sept. 11, 1963, BM.

507 *rock heaved by a white teenager:* SAC Roy Faisst to Moore, Sept. 19, 1963, BPSF 6.23a; Marlin to Marshall, Sept. 13, 1963, BM.

507 *schools opened quietly* and *NSRP motorcades:* Wasserstrom to Marshall, Sept. 12, 1963 (two memos), BM.

507 *Eastview's regular meeting:* summary of Rowe report, Sept. 25, 1963, BPSF 9.1; Eddy to Beck, Oct. 11, 1963, JY; LeGrand int. with Rowe, p. 49, BPSF 9.1.

507 *Jack Cash . . . was arrested:* int. Maurice House, Spring 1985; FBI ints. with Jack Cash, Oct. 3, 1963, with A. J. Needham, Oct. 18, 1963, with T. M. Cuniff, Oct. 7, 1963, with LaNelle Driver, Oct. 7, 1963, and with Eugene Coleman, Nov. 22, 1963, all in Bapbomb; int. Clarence Allgood, May 16, 1991. In addition to state charges of carrying a pistol without a permit and a concealed weapon, the sawed-off shotgun qualified Cash for federal charges, landing him in the court of Judge Clarence Allgood.

508 *ask for "Joe"* and *"leave the case at the Powderly church":* Rabbi Milton Grafman statement, Sept. 25, 1963, and Marcus Jones memo, Sept. 25, 1963, Box 2, BPSF.

508 *best friends, Johnny Frank Jones:* FBI ints. with Wyman Lee, June 22, 1965, and with Johnny Frank Jones, Oct. 17, 1963, and May 29, 1965, Bapbomb.

508 *named after the leader of the Knights of Labor:* White, *District,* p. 209.

508 *Chambliss came into Cash's:* FBI int. with Jack Cash, Oct. 3, 1963, Bapbomb.

508 *Merle K. Snow:* FBI int. with Captain W. E. Berry, May 20, 1965, Bapbomb.

508 *were at the shop that night:* September 13 meeting, David Barber int. with Robert Chambliss Oct. 12, 1978, Box 3, BPSF; FBI ints. with Tommy Blanton, Oct. 5 and 11, 1963, with Bobby Cherry, Oct. 13 and 16, 1963, with Johnny Salter, Oct. 18, 1963, and with Jean Casey, Oct. 10, 1963, all in Bapbomb; FBI memo "Thomas Edwin Blanton, Jr.," Bapbomb; "Bobby Frank Cherry's Alibi," Box 3, BPSF.

26. The Eve

509 *Elizabeth Hollifield Hood:* Cobbs/Smith, *Long Time,* pp. 27, 29, 43–44, 53, 67–68, 74.

509 *"kiss of death":* ibid., p. 59.

510 *slashed the arm: BPH,* Sept. 14, 1963. She was hanging it out the window of a van bus. Elizabeth knew the victim, a detective's daughter.

510 *"flatten half of Birmingham":* Hood testimony, Chambliss trial transcript, pp. 257–76; Cobbs/Smith, *Long Time,* pp. 87–89, FBI int. with Elizabeth Hood, Oct. 12, 1963, Bapbomb; "Confidential-Source Material," Sept. 23, 1977, JY.

510 *Blanton flitted around:* FBI ints. with Tommy Blanton, Oct. 4 and 11, 1963, Bapbomb.

510 *Ingram stopped by Chambliss's house:* Eddy to Beck, Oct. 11, 1977, JY.

510 *code for Klan work:* Cobbs/Smith, *Long Time,* p. 60.

511 *spoke with a lieutenant:* Eddy to Beck, "Bapbomb Confidential Informers Information," Aug. 15, 1977, JY. The FBI speculated that this was James T. Perkins, a friend of Bobby Shelton's from Tuscaloosa, who had been assigned to the Schoolhouse Door detail in June (having worked the concession stand at the big Klan Tuscaloosa rally that Rowe and company had missed because of their arrests). Perkins had been sent to Birmingham to be on standby during the school

opening and was also there on May 11, at the Klan rally before the Gaston Motel bombing. He had mentioned to a fellow Guardsman that by putting acid in a balloon and letting it slowly leak out, a delayed dynamite charge could be set off at a specific time. FBI ints. with James T. Perkins, Jan. 10, 1964, and with William Emory Roughton, Dec. 23, 1963, Bapbomb.

511   *capsule filled with sugar and chlorate:* FBI int. with Fred Hendon (plant manager for Du Pont), Nov. 2, 1964, Bapbomb.

511   *Chamblisses' phone started ringing:* "Confidential-Source Material," Sept. 23, 1977, Eddy to Beck, Oct. 11, 1977, Eddy int. with Mary Frances Cunningham, Aug. 19, 1977, "Statements made to Mrs. R. E. Chambliss by Bob Chambliss," Oct. 6, 1977, and "Mrs. R. E. Chambliss," all in JY.

511   *Page, who returned at eight-thirty:* FBI int. with Hubert Page, Oct. 2, 1963, Bapbomb.

511   *Cherry, who had also been one of Chambliss's callers, was out late:* FBI int. with John Edward Kaiser, April 13, 1965, Bapbomb.

511   *Stoner's car was parked:* Marcus Jones memo, Sept. 18, 1963, AB. Stoner had been in town for much of the week and met on Friday with a Negro contact at Liberty Supermarket, in the heart of the black downtown district. "File No. 41-61," "States Rights Party," BPSF 1.23; FBI int. with Phillip Thomas Mabry, Oct. 30, 1967, Bapbomb.

511   *Carter was also in town:* Finger to Jones, Sept. 24, 1963, Box 3, BPSF.

511   *'little old country girl':* Chambliss to Bailey, George Beck Papers, courtesy of Beck.

512   *'bomb something':* Eddy to Beck, Sept. 28, 1977, JY. For alternative version see Eddy to Beck re int. with James Hancock, Aug. 17, 1977, and Eddy to Beck, Aug. 30, 1977. Attorney General's files.

512   *plainclothesman to Merle Snow's:* Roy Osborne memo, Oct. 27, 1963, George Beck Papers, courtesy of Beck; int. George Beck, March 1985.

512   *showed up at at his girlfriend Lavelle Fike's house:* FBI int. with Wyvonne Lavelle Fike, Oct. 15, 1963, Bapbomb.

512   *wait for the armed Negroes:* FBI int. with Robert Thomas, Nov. 3, 1963, BPSF 6.18; FBI int. with Bobby Shelton, Nov. 29, 1963, and with Gene Reeves, Oct. 14, 1963, Bapbomb; FBI memo, Oct. 9, 1963, Bapbomb. Shelton puts this at approximately eleven, but Thomas says the women were back at the Holts' house at ten-thirty or eleven, which would put the escapade considerably before. The men returned to the Holts' house to discover that their wives were gone. That some mischief was being covered up was clear from Wilda Rogers's statement to the FBI that no one other than she and Loel had visited the Holts that night, and that all they had done was eat cake and drink coffee.

513   *David "Woody" Evans, who provided some corroboration:* FBI int. with David Evans, Oct. 21, 1963, Bapbomb; state memo on confidential informants, Aug. 17, 1977, JY. Evans, who was living two blocks from A. D. King's house, saw a beige Chrysler leave the scene. (Sister Marie at Holy Family Hospital had seen policemen get into an unmarked car.)

513   *white teenage girls:* FBI int. with Bill Webb, Nov. 5, 1963, Bapbomb.

513   *tryst at a popular lover's lane:* FBI ints. with Tommy Blanton, Oct. 5, 11, 4, and 15, 1963, and with Jean Casey, Oct. 10, 1963, Bapbomb; House int. with Jean Casey, Oct. 23, 1963, BPSF 7.48. How much of this date took place is debatable.

513   *Pat Clark checked in at Bob's Tourist Court:* FBI int. with George Pickle, Oct. 16, 1963, and with Pat Clark, Oct. 15, 1963, Bapbomb.

513   *The couple, still with Nigger Hall and Sister White:* FBI int. with Wyvonne Lavelle Fike, Oct. 15, 1963, Bapbomb.

514   *license plate number of a 1959 Chevrolet:* Roy Osborne memo on police radio activity, Nov. 27, 1963, George Beck Papers, courtesy of Beck.

514   *taken their wives to the Eastwood Bowling Alley:* FBI ints. with Herman Siegel, Oct. 20, 1963, with Hubert Page and with Dorothy Page, Oct. 2, 1963, and with Frances Gafford, Oct. 7, 1963, all in Bapbomb. Page's account—that the Gaffords came to his house and a couple of other details—is flatly contradicted by his wife and Mrs. Gafford, but the FBI did not follow this up. Nor did Siegel say he saw anyone of Page's description. Don Luna claimed his aunt Mary Lou had borrowed his car for an assignation with Page. Eddy int. with Don Luna, April 26, 1977, George Beck Papers, courtesy of Beck. However, Dorothy Page (conversation Nov. 26, 2000) said that she herself was with Page all night. Mary Lou Holt (int. Nov. 17, 1995) claims that she was not having an affair with Page (whom she later married) before the church bombing.

514   *Ernie Cantrell:* Roy Osborne memo, Oct. 27, 1963, George Beck Papers, courtesy of Beck; Cantrell testimony, Chambliss trial transcript, pp. 516–17; "Bombing Sixteenth Street Baptist Church," ints. with officers, BPSF 8.22; FBI ints. with police officers, Bapbomb; int. Ernie Cantrell, March 21, 1985; int. Mary Lou Holt Page, Nov. 11, 1975.

514   *twenty-car caravan:* FBI ints. with William Knighten, Nov. 20, 1963, and with Mike Praytor, Oct. 7, 1963, Bapbomb. It was reputedly the brainchild not of the NSRP or the Klan but of a twenty-five-year-old white female.

515   *put a handkerchief over the mouthpiece of a pay phone:* Chambliss to Bailey, Feb. 5, 1981, George Beck Papers, courtesy of Beck. Chambliss calls it the Ramada Inn, but the address he gives for it is that of the Holiday Inn. He also puts the bomb threat call at ten-thirty and has it on the night of the Gaston Motel bombing, but in a letter to U.S. District Court, Dec. 1, 1981 (Sikora, *Until Justice,* p. 158), he puts this on September 14, then grafts on details from the Gaston bombing.

515   *bomb threat would not appear on the radio log:* Roy Osborne memo, Oct. 27, 1963, George Beck Papers, courtesy of Beck; Cantrell testimony, Chambliss trial transcript, pp. 517–18; FBI int. with Daniel W. Smith, Nov. 25, 1963, Bapbomb. Sergeant Wilson would be vague about how he learned about the threat; perhaps, he said, he had picked it up while stopping by headquarters.

515   *Keith took out his pistol:* FBI int. with Wyvonne Lavelle Fike, Oct. 15, 1963, Bapbomb.

515   *about to take his next break:* int. Ernie Cantrell, March 21, 1985.

516   *"They must have a phone in there":* FBI ints. with Kirthus Glenn, Sept. 30, Oct. 2, 22, and 25, 1963, Bapbomb; Glenn testimony in Chambliss trial transcript, pp. 312–23; Yung ints. with Glenn, Aug. 17, 1977, JY.

516   *let their confederate off on Fifteenth Street:* int. Ernie Cantrell, March 21, 1985; memo on confidential informers, Aug. 17, 1977, and "Confidential-Source Material," Sept. 23, 1977, JY. In January 1965, Mary Frances Cunningham—probably from information she got from Tee Chambliss—told the FBI that Chambliss had said, "Cherry walked down the alley with the bomb."

516–17   *accident at the Alabama Gas Company* and *speeding through Ensley:* FBI int. with Officer Bobby York, Nov. 2, 1962, Bapbomb; Roy Osborne memo, Oct. 27, 1963, George Beck Papers, courtesy of Beck.

517   *scrap of paper on a desk* and *"sit on the porch":* Yung int. with Kirthus Glenn, Aug. 17, 1977, JY.

517   *car he saw was red:* FBI int. with Henry L. Smith, Oct. 6, 1963, Bapbomb, courtesy of private source. This interview is not in the Bapbomb file that has been released publicly.

27. Denise, Carole, Cynthia, and Addie

519   *glanced toward the Blantons' apartment:* FBI int. with Mrs. B. Freeman Brown, Oct. 4, 1963, Bapbomb.

519   *began his rounds:* FBI ints. with Willie Green, Sept. 20 and 21, 1963, Bapbomb.

519   *"Kiiind heavenly father":* Cobbs/Smith, *Long Time,* p. 36.

519   *hadn't gone to church:* FBI int. with Robert Chambliss, Oct. 1, 1963, Bapbomb; Chambliss trial transcript, pp. 588–89, 599–602.

519   *Chambliss and Dill:* FBI ints. with Robert Chambliss, Oct. 1, 1963, and with Clarence Dill, Oct. 3, 1963, Bapbomb. Their stories do not conform.

519   *Hancock agreed to meet her:* Eddy to Beck, Oct. 6, 1977, JY; Cobbs/Smith, *Long Time,* pp. 90–91. Eddy to Beck re int. with James Hancock, Aug. 17, 1977, and Eddy to Beck, Aug. 30, 1977, Attorney General's files. There are discrepancies in the accounts. Hood says that Hancock had hung up on Cunningham the night before but then agreed to meet her at 6 a.m. the next day.

520   *floppy old hat* and *"blow that church up":* Eddy memo on int. with Mary Frances Cunningham, Aug. 19, 1977, JY; *NYT,* July 16, 1978.

520   *remains one of the mysteries:* Cobbs/Smith, *Long Time,* pp. 90–91; int. Ernie Cantrell, March 21, 1985.

520   *left the church:* FBI int. with Herbert Oden, Sept. 21, 1963, Bapbomb.

520   *package under the steps:* memo on Eddy int. with Mary Frances Cunningham, Aug. 19, 1977, JY.

520   *concealed by a magnolia bush:* int. Maurice House, Spring 1985.

520   *working with the industrialists:* Fuller, "History," p. 283.

520   *stuffy old Sixteenth Street:* ints. with the Reverends John Crutcher, John Cross (telephone), and Abraham Woods, July 1982.

520   *Youth Day* and *"Rock That Will":* church program for September 15, BPSF 9.12; telephone int. John Cross, June 1982.

520   *Denise McNair:* Sikora, *Until Justice,* p. 4; Wil Haygood, "The Four Girls," *Boston Globe Magazine,* Feb. 3, 1991, p. 35; Chambliss trial transcript, p. 184.

521   *Cynthia Wesley: Jet,* Sept. 26, 1963; Haygood, "Four Girls," p. 1; Sikora, *Until Justice,* p. 59; funeral program, Box 4, BPSF; *BN,* Sept. 16, 1963.

521   *left Ella Demand's:* FBI ints. with Ella Demand, Oct. 2, 1963, and with Mrs. Clevon Phillips, Oct. 3, 1963, Bapbomb.

521   *phone kept ringing:* FBI ints. with Carolyn Maull, Oct. 7, 1963, and with Mabel Shorter, Oct. 4, 1963, Bapbomb. Shorter had been receiving strange calls all week, and puts some of the hang-ups at the previous week.

521   *would have gone to a drugstore:* FBI int. with Marsha Stollenwerck, Oct. 7, 1963, Bapbomb.

522   *wearing medium-high heels:* Sikora, *Until Justice,* pp. 16–17.

522   *worked at Joy Young's:* Pierce to Moore, Sept. 15, 1963, Box 2, BPSF.

522   *three ushers were standing with young Denise:* Sarah Collins testimony, Chambliss trial transcript, pp. 94–95; FBI ints. with Marsha Stollenwerck, Oct. 7, 1963, with Sarah Collins, Sept. 17, 1963, and with Bernadine Mathews, Sept. 20 and Oct. 18, 1963, all in Bapbomb; William Bradford Huie, "Death of an Innocent," in *Look,* March 24, 1964.

522   *sitting in his parked car:* FBI int. with Joel Boykin in "Interview of People in Vicinity at Time of Bombing," BPSF 9.1; FBI int. with Juliette Boykin, Oct. 4, 1963, Bapbomb.

522   *there was a resonant thud:* explosion, FBI ints. with the Reverend Howard Scott, Oct. 20, 1963, with John Henry Robert Kelly, Sept. 20, 1963, with John Cross, Sept. 18, 1963, with Marius Munden, Sept. 20, 1963, with William Sturdivant, Oct. 2, 1963, with Eugene Webb, Oct. 11, 1963, with Mamie Grier, Sept. 25, 1963, with Earline Tankersley, Sept. 30, 1963, with Claude Wesley, Sept. 18, 1963, with Ella Harris, Oct. 1, 1963, and with John T. Smith, Oct. 2, 1963, all in Bapbomb; telephone int. R. W. Apple, March 7, 1993.

522   *"somebody discriminating":* FBI ints. with Ross Keith, Oct. 7 and Nov. 11, 1963, Bapbomb; John Hall "Statement," BPSF 6.9.

523   *pounding his aching back:* Eddy to Beck, Aug. 30, 1977, JY. This is from Cunningham's statement to Eddy. Cobbs/Smith, *Long Time,* pp. 90–91, says that Hancock had dropped her back at her car by ten, saying he would "check it out."

523   *"Addie, Addie, Addie":* Sarah Collins testimony, Chambliss trial transcript, p. 95.

523   *waiting at his apartment:* summary of Rowe report, Sept. 15, 1963, and LeGrand int. with Rowe, p. 42, BPSF 9.1. Rowe made this statement in April 1964, so it should be regarded with skepticism.

523   *"church just went down":* LeGrand int. with Rowe, p. 16; "Garry Thomas Rowe, Jr.," Nov. 25, 1975, pp. 3–4; Rowe Baxley deposition, pp. 2–3, all in BPSF 9.1. If the dispatcher was at FBI headquarters, only six city blocks from the church, it is not very plausible that he wouldn't have heard the explosion. McCord was not working at the station that day, as Rowe insisted she was, though it is possible that she called him from home.

523   *offered a few suspects:* LeGrand int. with Rowe, p. 42, BPSF 9.1; *Task Force Report,* p. 79.

524   *"Those are the bombers":* FBI ints. with Dallas Cunningham, with John D. Cunningham, with Willie Lee Germany, and with Walter Williams, Oct. 3 and 19, 1963, all in Bapbomb. The FBI would have the witnesses observe Troy Ingram in person, and though none could positively identify him, all said he looked similar to one of the men. For some reason, the agents apparently did not show them pictures of Tommy Blanton.

524   *spied the car she had seen the night before:* Yung int. with Kirthus Glenn, Aug. 17, 1977, JY; Glenn testimony, Chambliss trial transcript, p. 319.

524   *telephone at the church office:* police int. with John Henry Robert Kelley, Nov. 5, 1963, BPSF 9.12.

524   *Pullin appeared:* FBI ints. with Thelma Finch, Oct. 1, 1963, and with John Henry Pullin, Oct. 8, 1963, Bapbomb.

524 *Jim Lay* and *Hosea Hudson:* FBI ints. with Reuben Ellis, Sept. 24, 1963, and with Hosea Hudson Jr., Sept. 15 and 20, 1963, Bapbomb.
524 *Cross followed:* FBI ints. with Thelma Finch, Oct. 1, 1963, and with John Pullen, Oct. 8, 1963, Bapbomb.
524 *Ralph Roton:* Klan HUAC hearings, p. 3210; int. Ralph Roton, Nov. 26, 2000.
525 *"We should be forgiving":* post-bombing scene, FBI ints. with John Cross, Sept. 18, 1963, with Thomas Hill, Sept. 30, 1963, and with H. D. Coke, Oct. 11, 1963, Bapbomb; Haygood, "Four Girls," pp. 29–30; *BPH,* Sept. 15, 1993; FBI memo on damage, Sept. 17, 1963, Bapbomb; *BPH,* Sept. 16, 1963; Cross testimony, in Chambliss trial transcript, pp. 66–69; "Admitting Reports" of victims on Death Certificate, Bapbomb; Morgan, *A Time,* p. 162.
525 *seven-by-seven-foot hole:* report of Special Agent James R. Logan Jr., Oct. 4, 1963, and memo on damage, Sept. 17, 1963, Bapbomb; Aaron Rosenfeld testimony, Chambliss trial transcript, p. 496.
525 *Sarah Collins:* statement of Sylvester Norris, ambulance driver, Sept. 19, 1963, BPSF 1.23; statement of Samuel Warren Love, Sept. 18, 1963, Box 4, BPSF.
526 *Elizabeth Hood:* Cobbs/Smith, *Long Time,* pp. 94, 96.
526 *spectator was spreading the rumor:* FBI int. with Robert Green, Sept. 15, 1963, Bapbomb.
526 *Newlyweds from Chicago:* FBI int. with Michael A. Allen, Sept. 24, 1963, Bapbomb; *BN,* Sept. 16, 1963.
527 *"where did Freedom go?":* int. Joel Boykin Jr., Dec. 8, 1995.
527 *recognized the imitation class ring:* FBI ints. with Claude Wesley, Sept. 18, 1963, and with Gloria Oliver, Oct. 7, 1963, Bapbomb; Death Certificate, Bapbomb; *Presbyterian Life,* Oct. 15, 1963; *Jet,* Oct. 3, 1963.
527 *Chris McNair:* Huie, "Death of an Innocent."
527 *Rowe was telephoning:* Rowe Baxley deposition, pp. 3–5, and "Garry Thomas Rowe Jr.," Nov. 25, 1975, p. 4, BPSF 9.1; Yung notes, undated, BPSF 7.2.
527 *police radio had been turned up:* FBI int. with Billy Strickland, Oct. 18, 1963, Bapbomb.
527 *tenant automatically looked over:* FBI int. with Joyce Hyde, Oct. 20, 1963, Bapbomb. Apparently the cars were there.
528 *Vaughn also thought:* FBI int. with Waylene Vaughn, Oct. 20, 1963. Vaughn would tell the FBI (and testify at Tommy Blanton's April 2001 trial) that she had spent time with Blanton at the Blue Bird Motel on the previous Friday night, when he broke the date with Jean Casey. Blanton, however, never claimed this as an alibi.
528 *Chambliss called Ronnie Tidwell:* FBI int. with Ronnie Tidwell, Dec. 7, 1964, Bapbomb.
528 *Cherry came down to Snow's:* FBI int. with Bobby Cherry, Oct. 22, 1963, and with Merle Snow, Aug. 12, 1977, Bapbomb; Beck int. with Virgil Cherry, Aug. 12, 1977, Box 3, BPSF.
528 *"We will put it on Jim.":* Cobbs/Smith, *Long Time,* p. 95. Cobbs (Hood) says that the daughter heard her mother relaying the conversation to Mary Frances Cunningham, right after the visit, which would cast doubt on the story that Cunningham was with Hancock at the time of the explosion.
528 *"gone too far":* FBI int. with Floyd Garrett, Oct. 9, 1963, Bapbomb; Garrett testimony, Chambliss trial transcript, p. 572; int. Ernie Cantrell, March 21, 1985; Eddy to Beck, Oct. 11, 1977, JY. In the trial, Garrett says the Dills were at Chambliss's house. According to the FBI, he said an unknown woman with curlers was there.
529 *Fat Daddy* and *"women of either race":* telephone conversation with Jamie Moore, July 29, 2000; telephone conversation with James Parson, July 29, 2000.
529 *Vann left Highlands:* int. Ernie Cantrell, March 21, 1985; Vann int. in Hampton and Fayer, *Voices,* p. 174.
529 *rally of the West End Parents:* FBI ints. with Tommy Blanton, Oct. 11 and 13, 1963, with Troy Ingram, Oct. 11, 1963, and with Thomas Blanton Sr., October 5, 1963, all in Bapbomb.
529 *interpret Bobby Shelton's presence:* Many years later, Elizabeth Hood would claim that one of her cousins, another of Tee and Robert Chambliss's nieces or nephews, had driven with Robert to the airport on the evening of Saturday, September 14, to pick up Shelton. In the car on the way back to Chambliss's house, the youngster would say, the two men had discussed the bombing of the church. Then they had dropped the child off and gone to Troy Ingram's house. Cobbs/Smith, *Long Time,* p. 90.
529 *Hancock, the shifty deputy would insist:* Eddy to Beck re int. with James Hancock, Aug. 30, 1977, Attorney General's Files.
530 *"Dear God, why?":* police memo, Sept. 16, 1963, mass meeting, AB.
530 *"worst racial holocaust":* *Detroit News,* Sept. 16, 1963; *BN,* Sept. 16, 1963.

28. Aftershocks

531 *Virgil Ware:* conversation with Lorraine Ware, Oct. 2, 1983; Mary McGrory, "Question in Killing Is Why," Sept. 21, 1963, and "Truce Team Is Arriving Late," *Washington Evening Star,* Sept. 23, 1963; *BN,* Sept. 16, 1963; *BW,* Sept. 21, 1963.
531 *Johnnie Robinson:* police memo, "Shooting of Johnny Robinson," Sept. 15, 1963, statements of Ann Shirley, Sidney Howell, Jack Parker, and Officer J. E. Chadwick, Sept. 15, 1963, AB; conversation with Josephine Truss, Robinson's cousin, July 1987; *Washington Evening Star,* Sept. 23, 1963; *BN,* Sept. 16, 1963. The police department declared the shooting both "accidental" and "in the line of duty."
531 *shot in the head:* Inter-Citizens Committee affidavit of Charlie Will Lane, Sept. 21, 1963, IC.
532 *Confederate flag:* *Jet,* Oct. 3, 1963.
532 *Chambliss rang the doorbell:* Cobbs/Smith, *Long Time,* pp. 97–98.
532 *Garrett arrested Gary:* FBI int. with Willie Henry Gary, Oct. 11, 1963, Bapbomb.
532 *conference at the Drews':* int. Joseph Dolan, Nov. 8, 1994; int. Burke Marshall, October 1985; Marshall int. in Hampton and Fayer, *Voices,* pp. 175–76.
533 *"lost her life because of the movement":* *Jet,* Oct. 3, 1963. The entire quote was: "We realize Carole lost her life because of the movement, but we feel her loss was personal to us."
533 *headed home to Detroit:* Yung int. with Kirthus Glenn, Aug. 17, 1977, JY.
533 *fishing bobber:* int. Maurice House, Spring 1985; James R. Logan Jr. report, Oct. 4, 1963, and Zimmers and Killion memo on investigation of site, Bapbomb. The least sinister explanation for what became of the bobber was that the agent pocketed it, forgot about it, and, once he discovered it, did not introduce it for fear of incurring the top bureaucrat's displeasure. Eventually its existence would be conceded in an FBI report.

533   *Garrett to admit that he had gone by Chambliss's:* int. Maurice House, Spring 1985; House testimony, Chambliss trial transcript, p. 648. Elizabeth Hood, who later questioned why Garrett had come to Chambliss's house in mufti rather than in official blue, would suspect that he had stopped by Chambliss's house to pick up the police uniform he had left there the previous night after arranging the bomb threat. Cobbs/Smith, *Long Time,* p. 96.

533   *surveillance had put Chambliss at home:* int. Maurice House, Spring 1985.

534   *a "get-away" car:* Wittenstein to Murray, Sept. 17, 1963, "JSX—Ala. 1962-1967," AJC.

534   *police took the Sixteenth Street custodian:* FBI int. with Willie Green, Oct. 4, 1963, Bapbomb; G. McMillan, "Church Bomber," p. 16.

534   *grief and rage poured into:* e.g., Flenniken to Boutwell, Sept. 16, 1963, AB. New York City mayor Robert Wagner pronounced Birmingham a "synonym for barbarism and brutality."

534   *Young Men's Business Club:* int. Chuck Morgan, Aug. 12, 1983; int. Roger Hanson, Dec. 8, 1987; Morgan, *A Time,* pp. 9-14.

534   *"All of us are victims":* BN, Sept. 16, 1963.

535   *"We hold that shoe":* editorial reprinted in *Jet,* Oct. 10, 1963.

535   *many telegrams to the White House:* memo on telegrams in Box 24, VN.

535   *"give a 'blow by blow' account":* Task Force Report, pp. 77-78.

535   *"wrong people":* BN, Sept. 17, 1963.

536   *yes-man:* Klan HUAC report, p. 3062; statement of Ronald "Cotton" Lowe, Nov. 2, 1963, Bapbomb.

536   *"the shit has hit the fan,":* Yung notes, undated, BPSF 7.2; int. Robert Thomas, March 25, 1976, BPSF 10.2; conversation with Robert Thomas, Sept. 16, 1993.

536   *emerging national consensus:* Wallace put up a $5,000 reward, an amount that struck nearly everyone as outrageous—whether inflated or, as the *Oklahoma City Times* editorialized (Sept. 17, 1963), "insultingly small when four lives were lost." The chairman of Americans for Democratic Action said, "In fact, Wallace is as guilty as if he himself planted the bomb" (*BN,* Sept. 16, 1963).

536   *"public disparagement of law":* NYT, Sept. 17, 1963.

536   *Time's cover:* Time, Sept. 27, 1963.

536   *special session of the federal grand jury:* Coleman and Coleman, *Allgood,* pp. 36-38; *BN,* Sept. 16 and 17, 1963. Copy of charge is in AB.

536   *funeral of Carole Robertson: Washington Evening Star,* Sept. 19, 1963; *BN,* Sept. 18, 1963; *BW,* Sept. 21, 1963.

536   *rumors that either NBC or CBS:* Godwin report on bombing, Oct. 25, 1963, BPSF 9.12.

536   *funeral of Denise, Addie, and Cynthia: Washington Evening Star,* Sept. 19, 1963; *Presbyterian Life,* Oct. 15, 1963; *BW,* Sept. 21, 1963; Wittenstein to Murray, Sept. 17, 1963, "JSX—Ala. 1962-1967," AJC; *BN,* Sept. 18, 1963.

537   *"made us look ridiculous":* Jet, Oct. 3, 1963.

537   *national work stoppage* and *Rustin had decided:* FBI memo "Re: Martin Luther King, security matter," Sept. 16, 1963, Levison FBI.

537   *"heroines of a modern crusade":* Washington, ed., *Testament,* pp. 221-23; Miller, *Voice,* pp. 152-53.

537   *Shuttlesworth convinced them:* Fred Shuttlesworth oral history, KC, Part 2.

537   *"uprisings":* John Beecher, "The Share Croppers' Union in Alabama," *Social Forces,* October 1934, p. 131; Kelley, *Hammer,* p. 51. Some fifteen unionists and the sheriff's posse had a shoot-out, in which three black sharecroppers were killed.

538   *"take over Birmingham":* NYT, Sept. 18, 1963.

538   *"Proposal for Action":* Diane Nash and James Bevel ints. in Hampton and Fayer, *Voices,* pp. 172-73; "Proposal," Box 4, SCLC; *Jet,* Oct. 10, 1963.

538   *"He was old":* int. Julian Bond, Spring 1984.

538   *approach MacArthur:* Louis Oberdorfer oral history, JFK; Earl Blaik oral history, JFK. A few months earlier, the Kennedy brothers had used Blaik to enlist MacArthur to help arbitrate a dispute between the Amateur Athletic Union and the National Collegiate Athletic Association over Olympic eligibility. *Britannica Book of the Year 1964,* pp. 75, 771. (MacArthur was actually eighty-three.)

538   *Kenneth Royall:* Kenneth Royall oral history, COH, pp. 18-19, 109-10, 180-89; *BW,* July 30, 1948.

538   *"talking to the wrong person":* Earl Blaik oral history, JFK.

539   *"What's the hope?":* audiotape 112.1, JFK.

539   *Baldwin was furious* and *"Negroes are thinking":* FBI memo "Re Communist Party USA, Negro Question," Sept. 20, 1963, and FBI memo "Re James Baldwin," Sept. 24, 1963, Levison FBI.

539   *Negroes in business suits: Jet,* Oct. 10, 1963.

539   *Rowe complained that "we":* David Barber int. with Robert Chambliss, Oct. 12, 1978, Box 3, BPSF. This is after Rowe had been exposed as an informant when the Klan tried to pin everything on him.

539   *dynamite exploded:* Inter-Citizens Committee document no. 49, affidavit of James O. Richardson, and document no. 50, affidavit of Mose Leonard, Sept. 24, 1963, IC.

539   *funeral of Johnnie Robinson: BW,* Sept. 25, 1963.

539   *a week of funeral observances:* ibid.

540   *Klansmen had turned out in force:* FBI ints. with Hubert Page, Oct. 3, 1963, with Robert Venus, Oct. 10, 1963, and with Tommy Blanton, Oct. 4, 1963, Bapbomb; FBI int. with Billy Holt, Sept. 26, 1963, BPSF 6.18.

540   *Billy Lavon Jackson:* FBI ints. with John Lee, Dec. 18, 1963, and Nov. 12 and 24, 1964, with Billy Jackson, Aug. 11, 1964, with Wyman Lee, Oct. 8, 1963, with Pop Blanton, Oct. 5, 1963, and with John Hall, Dec. 13, 1963, all in Bapbomb; records of the chancery court and the circuit court, cited in Bapbomb. Hall says that Jackson had been a member of Eastview, but had gotten out a couple of years earlier.

540   *"Pud" Mayfield:* "Confidential-Source Material," Sept. 23, 1977, JY; state memo on confidential informer, Oct. 7, 1963, BPSF 1.23. Mayfield was a suspected source of the church bomb's dynamite. See also FBI ints. with James Phillips, Sept. 24, 1963, and with Minnie Thomason, Sept. 28, 1963, Bapbomb.

540   *wasn't meant to kill anyone. "I mean for it to:* FBI int. with Mary Frances Cunningham, Dec. 15, 1964. This claim was made in a controversial statement Cunningham gave, and later recanted, that she and Elizabeth Hood had

driven down to the church at 2 a.m. September 15 and seen Chambliss, Blanton, and men she "felt sure" were Bobby Cherry and Herman Cash plant the bomb. Hood made a statement (also later recanted) at the same time that was identical except that she said she heard Chambliss say it wasn't meant to kill anyone. She would testify in the trial that she heard him say, "It wasn't meant to hurt anybody. It didn't go off when it was supposed to." (Chambliss trial transcript, pp. 276-78).

540   *at the bridge:* state memo on confidential informer, Oct. 7, 1963, BPSF 1.23; Allen and Posey to Jones, Sept. 26, 1963, Box 4, BPSF; FBI int. with Lee C. Greene (Page lie detector test results), July 13, 1965, Bapbomb. Other rumored participants were George Pickle and Levie "Quickdraw" Yarbrough. Henry Glass, the brickmason and neighbor with whom Ingram met on the Saturday before the bombing, was there.

540   *surprised by its timing:* Eddy to Beck, "Bapbomb Confidential Informers Information," Aug. 15, 1977, JY. Page would later be heard saying that the bomb was supposed to go off at 10:30 (not clear whether a.m. or p.m.) on Saturday rather than 1:21 on Sunday.

540   *worked on the detonating device:* state memo on Page, BPSF 9.12(d). See also lie detector results.

540   *Ronnie Tidwell:* FBI ints. with Joe Pinson, Jan. 14, 1965, with Eugene Adams, Oct. 3, 1963, and June 15, 1964, with Ronnie Tidwell, Dec. 7, 1964, and with Lewis Massey, Jan. 4, 1965, all in Bapbomb.

540   *adjourned to Ingram's house:* state interview with Billy Jackson, March 29, 1976, Box 4, BPSF.

540   *"If any one of you ever talks":* G. McMillan, "Church Bomber." This article has Stoner as the mastermind of the bombing.

541   *armed with prepared statements:* Statements are included with Boutwell to J. Kennedy, Sept. 21, 1963, Box 24, VN.

541   *usually opened with a description:* Louis Oberdorfer oral history, JFK, p. 46.

541   *"Oh, public accommodations is nothing!":* audiotapes 112.6 and 113.1, JFK.

541   *"Blaik-Royall mission":* Louis Oberdorfer oral history, JFK, p. 45; "General Royall and Colonel Blaik stated," Sept. 24, 1963, AB; Blaik and Royall's "Report to the President of the United States," Oct. 10, 1963, POF; *NYT,* Sept. 25, 1963; *Jet,* Oct. 3, 1963.

541   *reception following Mary Lou Holt's return:* FBI ints. with Billy Holt. Sept. 26, 1963, with Bob Gafford, Sept. 30, 1963, with Hubert Page, Oct. 2, 1963, with Dorothy Page, Oct. 2, 1963, and with Loel Rogers, Oct. 12, 1963, all in Bapbomb.

541   *church bombing had been planned:* int. Mary Lou Holt Page, Nov. 17, 1995.

542   *Chambliss was steering his truck:* Chambliss statement to Bill Jones, Sept. 29, 1963, Bapbomb.

542   *Catholic priest returning home:* FBI ints. with Kevin Dunigan, Nov. 13, 1963, and with Vernon Hart, Oct. 14, 1963, Bapbomb.

542   *Rowe just happened:* LeGrand int. with Rowe, pp. 47-49, 55-56, and Allred statement, March 17, 1976, BPSF 9.1; *Task Force Report,* pp. 90-95.

542   *shrapnel bomb:* FBI ints. with J. H. Woolley, Oct. 14, 1963, and with Norman Daniel, Jan. 19, 1964, Bapbomb; Hart memo, Sept. 27, 1963, Bapbomb; House and Hart memo, Sept. 25, 1963, Box 2, BPSF; *Task Force Report,* pp. 90-91.

542   *Don Luna, would claim:* Beck int. with Don Luna, April 18, 1977, George Beck Papers, courtesy of Beck. He would say that he and his uncle Billy Holt had seen Rowe in the phone booth three minutes after the bomb exploded.

543   *Sister White would later complain:* LeGrand int. with Rowe, pp. 26-27, BPSF 9.1.

543   *stranger scenario:* Eddy to Beck, Aug. 17, 1977, re int. with James Hancock, and Eddy to Beck, Aug. 30, 1977, Attorney General's files. The state gave Mary Frances Cunningham a polygraph to evaluate her denials of this story, and she showed not deception. Polygraph report, Sept. 1, 1977, Attorney General's files.

543   *he could make a better bomb:* "Confidential-Source Material," Sept. 23, 1977, JY.

543   *tackle identical:* unsigned, undated memo, perhaps by Tom Lankford, in Box 2, BPSF. The old Klansman Hugh Morris would tell the FBI that he believed Chambliss, Ingram, Jack Cash, and Pershing Mayfield were in on the shrapnel bombing. The FBI eliminated Cash and Mayfield as suspects, and could not believe that Ingram and Chambliss would commit another serious bombing after Sixteenth Street. Hubert Page's polygraph suggested that he participated in this bombing.

543   *polygraph-supported theory would have Tommy Blanton:* police memo, undated, "Polygraph says," Box 2, BPSF.

543   *didn't mind the Klan killing "niggers":* Summary of Rowe report, Sept. 25, 1963, BPSF 9.1.

29. BAPBOMB

544   *resignation in a matter of weeks:* Walker to King, Oct. 3, 1963, MLK 36.1. The resignation was supposed to be effective December 31, though King persuaded him to stay on for another six months. His job would go to Andy Young.

544   *board meeting on Wednesday:* minutes of meeting, MLK 29.2.

544   *"the acid test":* Garrow, *Bearing,* p. 298.

544   *hotel room inferior to King's:* Branch, *Parting,* p. 899.

545   *September 26:* program of SCLC convention, MLK 29.2.

545   *"Bless your soul":* transcript of call from Don Bryan to Boutwell, Oct. 1, 1963, AB.

545   *Posey had apparently identified:* Allen and Posey to Jones, Sept. 26, 1963, Box 4, BPSF.

546   *lie detector test:* FBI int. with Lee C. Greene, including test and results, July 3, 1965, Bapbomb. When I called Godwin (April 1, 1985) and asked him about the trip to Huntsville with Page, he said, "What are you getting at? ... I don't have any comment about it, lady. ... You're trying to dig up some dirt."

546   *showed up at the home of Herman Cash:* FBI int. with Herman Frank Cash, Oct. 8, 1963, Bapbomb.

546   *made its first contact with Chambliss:* FBI int. with Robert Chambliss, Oct. 1, 1963, Bapbomb.

547   *Kirthus Glenn:* FBI int. with Kirthus Glenn, Sept. 30, 1963.

547   *instructed by his handlers:* to stay away: LeGrand int. with Rowe, p. 17, BPSF 9.1.

547   *a tip from his state sources:* Morgan and LeGrand int. with Self, April 26, 1976, BPSF 9.1. Given the ubiquitous hatred for Rowe, I'm not sure how reliable this is, though Self would say there were witnesses.

547 *house of UACG president:* FBI ints. with Hubert Page, Dec. 4, 1964, and with Bill Morgan, Oct. 28, 1964, Bapbomb; Eddy to Beck, Aug. 15, 1977, JY. A confidential informant—Nigger Hall, perhaps—told the FBI about this meeting.

548 *move the "muscadines":* FBI memo by Zimmerman and McCormack, Oct. 6, 1963, Bapbomb; Cagle statements, Sept. 25 and Oct. 1, 1963, Bapbomb; FBI int. with John Hall, Oct. 20, 1963, Bapbomb. Cagle would claim that Levie Yarbrough found him at his father's house on Sunday morning, September 29, and said he had left the dynamite close to Cagle's house. Panicked, Cagle told him to get it out of his neighborhood and led him to the original kudzu patch. If, however, as Cagle claims, Yarbrough moved the dynamite from the kudzu patch, why would he have to tell him where to return it? Hall said Yarbrough had something on Cagle that prevented Cagle from coming through with information on Yarbrough.

548 *By Sunday evening:* meeting between Lingo and the Klan, "Persons in attendance at meeting in Colonel Al Lingo's room . . . September 29, 1963," AB; Chambliss trial transcript, p. 215; FBI int. with Don Luna, March 23, 1964, Bapbomb; int. Major Bill Jones, March 1985.

549 *Moore called Lieutenant Maurice House:* int. Maurice House, Spring 1985.

549 *slapped Chambliss's face:* "Statements made to Mrs. R. E. Chambliss by Bob Chambliss," Oct. 6, 1977, and undated notes, "Mrs. R.E. Chambliss," JY; FBI int. with Ronnie Tidwell, April 30, 1965, Bapbomb; Jones memo, Oct. 2, 1963, Box 3, BPSF.

549 *"get him out of it":* Cobbs/Smith, *Long Time,* p. 101.

549 *arrival of the suspects:* FBI ints. with Robert Chambliss, Oct. 21, 1964, with Don Luna, March 13, 1964, with Levie Yarbrough, Oct. 3, 1963, and with Ross Keith, Oct. 7, 1963, all in Bapbomb; LeGrand int. with Chambliss, Box 3, BPSF; *BN,* Oct. 1, 1963. Ross Keith was also brought in, but was released after offering to take a polygraph. Yarbrough stuck so hard to his denials that he was released at 5 a.m., in time for him to report to work.

549 *"beat the Kennedy crowd":* BN, Oct. 1, 1963.

549 *campaign to prove:* Garrow, *FBI,* pp. 55–56; DeLoach to Mohr, Jan. 15, 1963, Levison FBI.

550 *bureau-wide escalation:* Garrow, *FBI,* pp. 68, 88–91; O'Reilly, *"Racial Matters,"* p. 137; Powers, *Secrecy and Power,* pp. 374, 376, 379.

550 *set off all the graphs:* Ingram polygraph, Sept. 30, 1963, Bapbomb; unsigned, undated memo, probably Tom Lankford, re briefing by U.S. Attorney Macon Weaver, Box 2, BPSF.

550 *Dixiecrat politician-lawyer:* Murphy was elected vice chairman of the Dixiecrats' Jefferson County States Rights Committee in 1951. *BN,* April 24, 1951.

550 *Walker Percy:* Tolson, *Pilgrim,* p. 45, 274–75, 309.

551 *stopping by Chief Jamie Moore's office:* int. Jamie Moore, Dec. 9, 1987; *BN,* Oct. 1, 1963.

551 *"dollars-and-cents thing":* Sidney Smyer oral history in Raines, *My Soul,* p. 165.

551 *"best service they can render":* BN, Oct. 1, 1963.

551 *anti-"outsiders" statement:* BN, September 29, 1963; *BW,* Oct. 2, 1963.

551 "I will return": Branch, *Parting,* p. 901.

552 *suspected him of bugging* and *"Typical Birmingham psychosis":* Marshall to Oberdorfer, Oct. 28, 1963, BM.

552 *Coach Blaik and General Royall:* int. James Head, June 6, 1984; Louis Oberdorfer oral history, JFK, p. 46; Marshall phone logs, Sept. 25, 1963, BM; Wittenstein to Murray, Oct. 2, 1963, Fleischman to Wittenstein, Oct. 4, 1963, "CRS-R, Ala., 1960–1963," AJC; int. Jerome Cooper, Dec. 17, 1984; int. Howard Strevel, December 1987; Blaik to Marshall, Nov. 1, 1963, BM.

552 *"aware of some of the suspects":* BPH, Oct. 1, 1963.

552 *Kudzu patch in Gardendale:* FBI int. with J. M. McDowell, Oct. 6, 1963, Bapbomb; Cagle statement to Godwin and Painter, Oct. 1, 1963, Bapbomb; Eddy to Beck, "Bapbomb Confidential Informers Information," Aug. 15, 1977, JY.

553 *Luna suspected that his fellow investigators:* FBI int. with Don Luna, March 23, 1964, Bapbomb. Cagle was released the following day.

553 *rendered the test inconclusive:* House to Cashdollar, Dec. 3, 1963, Bapbomb.

553 *Floyd Mann:* Marshall to Attorney General, "Re: Birmingham Bombings," Oct. 4, 1963, Box 3, VN. The source said that on Sunday, September 29, a Klansman told Harry Sims, a state investigator in Anniston, that the federal government was about to arrest Chambliss and Cagle. Sims called Lingo, and the "colonel" moved that night. Of course, the FBI could have saved the state the trouble if they had had Chambliss, Hall, and Cagle arrested on the night of September 4–5. As was customary after a bombing, they had sent agents to watch Chambliss's house following the explosion at Arthur Shores's and had apparently seen the dynamite being transferred.

553 *"The Klan met":* summary of Rowe report, Jan. 16, 1964, BPSF 9.1.

553 *FBI returned to Harper Hospital:* FBI ints. with Kirthus Glenn, Oct. 2 and 22, 1963, Bapbomb.

554 *Blanton submitted to a polygraph:* FBI int. with Tommy Blanton, Oct. 4, 1963, and polygraph, Oct. 1, 1963, Bapbomb.

554 *question Jean Casey:* FBI ints. with Jean Casey, Oct. 10, 1963, and with Tommy Blanton, Oct. 4 and 11, 1963, Bapbomb; Eddy memo on Blanton alibis, July 21, 1977, Box 2, BPSF.

555 *"people looking after me":* FBI int. with J. C. Williams, Oct. 8, 1963, Bapbomb.

555 *Louise Charlton:* FBI memo re Blanton, undated (Oct. 6, 1963), Bapbomb.

555 *Blanton mentioned:* FBI int. with Tommy Blanton, Oct. 11, 1963, Bapbomb. Then he would reconsider and say Chambliss hadn't mentioned bombs.

555 *at the Cahaba River bridge:* LeGrand int. with Robert Chambliss, Box 1, BPSF; FBI ints. with Chambliss, Jan. 25, 1965, and with Tom Coker, (date minus), Bapbomb.

555 *Ingram was fretting* and *kill all the black bastards:* FBI ints. with Troy Ingram, Oct. 3, 1963, and with Willis Crain, Nov. 18, 1963, Bapbomb.

555 *Ingram underwent a second polygraph:* polygraph report and test, Oct. 5, 1963, Bapbomb.

556 *commitment from the power structure:* "Meeting with Gen. Royall and Col. Blaik," Oct. 3, 1963, AB. See Blaik and Royall Report to President, Oct. 10, 1963, pp. 4 and 6, POF.

556 *Chambliss, Cagle, and Nigger Hall:* BN, Oct. 9, 1963.

556 *Wiebel would be gone:* NYT, Oct. 30, 1963; Boutwell to Blough, July 28, 1964, AB.

556 *Letters from all over the country:* From San Francisco came several copies of a newspaper report on the suspension of a black police officer, the married father of six, who had allegedly had sex with a drunk cocktail waitress in her car. See, for example, Pittman to Boutwell, Oct. 16, 1963, AB 34.33 and 34.35.

557 *"extremists on either side":* Blaik and Royall Report to the President, Oct. 10, 1963, POF.

557 *practically insane:* FBI int. with John Hall, Dec. 13, 1963, Bapbomb.

557 *gift of the gab:* telephone int. Tom Cherry, Dec. 3, 2000.

557 *fabricate Tommy Blanton's alibi:* Cherry and the Klansmen apparently had tried to establish a retroactive alibi for Tommy Blanton by reconvening the suspects at Merle Snow's Modern Sign Shop—the place where they had gotten together early on Friday the thirteenth—on the Tuesday after the bombing. FBI ints. with Bobby Cherry, Oct. 13, 1963, with Merle Snow, Oct. 17, 1963, with James T. Stephens, Oct. 25, 1963, and with Billy Levaughn Jackson, Oct. 16, 1963, all in Bapbomb.

557 *boasted to Edward Fields and J. B. Stoner:* Eddy to Beck, "Bapbomb Confidential Informers Information," Aug. 15, 1977, JY.

557 *had a second "wife":* The White American, March 1965, p. 4, in WH 3.36.

557 *contacts with Robert Thomas's wife:* Rowe Baxley deposition, pp. 16–17, and LeGrand int. with Rowe, p. 18, BPSF 9.1.

557 *Thomas had tried to cancel:* "Confidential-Source Material," Sept. 23, 1977, JY.

557 *taking the church bombing badly:* conversation with Earl Thompson, Sept. 16, 1993; Sikora, *Until Justice,* p. 85.

558 *Lavelle Fike:* FBI ints. with Wyvonne Lavelle Fike, Oct. 15, 1963, and with Cletine Neal, Nov. 8, 1963, Bapbomb. For some reason she would neglect to tell them about the roomful of dynamite she had supposedly come upon in Chambliss's house not long before the church bombing.

558 *"a little shaky":* int. with confidential police source, March 1985.

558 *"spy from King's bunch":* Rowe, *Undercover Years,* p. 95.

30. General Lee's Namesakes

559 *"bomb factory":* Cobbs/Smith, *Long Time,* pp. 68–69.

559 *Hood poured out the story:* ibid., pp. 135–37; FBI int. with Elizabeth Hood, Oct. 12, 1963, Bapbomb.

560 *authorizing a wiretap:* Evans to Belmont, Oct. 10 and 21, 1963, in Theoharis, *Secret Files,* pp. 97, 98–99; Garrow, *FBI,* p. 74.

560 *Senate investigation into Bobby Baker:* Summers, *Official and Confidential,* p. 310; Branch, *Parting,* p. 906.

560 *"Communism and the Negro Movement"* and *blandly recalled:* Evans to Belmont, Oct. 25, 1963, and Hoover to Tolson et al., Nov. 7, 1963, Levison FBI; Garrow, *FBI,* pp. 73–75.

560 *"people get tired":* police memo, Oct. 14, 1963, mass meeting, WH.

561 *"child who can't finish":* FBI memo on "Communist Party," Nov. 8, 1963, Levison FBI.

561 *"turning point in the right to vote":* John Lewis int. in Hampton and Fayer, *Voices,* p. 213.

561 *Movement ministers:* telephone int. Thelton Henderson, March 4, 1997.

561 *"rosin chewers":* int. Nelson Smith, Oct. 3, 1983.

561 *"communists or other Negroes":* Lesher, *Wallace,* pp. 256–57, citing Godwin to Jones, Oct. 16, 1963, ADAH. "Subversives" were defined as anyone "suspected of teaching or advocating policies which were detrimental to the interests of the state of Alabama."

561 *chauffeured at the taxpayer's expense:* handwritten notes on conversations with Henderson, Bob Ingram, et al. on the days following the trip, in Box 28, VN; Lesher, *Wallace,* p. 258; telephone int. Thelton Henderson, March 4, 1997; ints. Burke Marshall, October 1985 and June 25, 1992.

562 *received $1,200 from Wallace:* FBI int. with Ferrell Griswold, Oct. 21, 1963, Bapbomb.

562 *"White Rally":* flyer in BPSF 7.48; Jones memo, Oct. 22, 1963, AB.

562 *"I guess you know":* King and Shuttlesworth's October 22 press conference, Hart memo, Oct. 22, 1963, BPSF 7.1.

562 *"bread' demonstrations":* Len Holt, "Birmingham's Harlem," *Freedomways,* Fall 1963.

563 *depositing in his personal account:* police memo, Nov. 21, 1963, BPSF 9.19 (and in WH 3.41). Cross had admitted doing so at a November 19 church board meeting but said he would try to get the people of Seattle to agree to putting it toward an education fund. Angry women in attendance cautioned him about using the bombing as a church fund-raising opportunity.

563 *move to Atlanta:* Morgan, *A Time,* pp. 171–73; int. Roger Hanson, Dec. 8, 1987; int. Chuck Morgan, Aug. 12, 1983.

563 *Kirthus Glenn:* FBI int. with Kirthus Glenn, Oct. 25, 1963, Bapbomb.

564 *Sullivan case:* A. Lewis, *No Law,* pp. 115–18, 143, 147, 150–51. Black (and Justices William Douglas and Arthur Goldberg) believed that absolute immunity should be given to critics of public officials, regardless of malice. It was Black who wanted to frame the case as First Amendment protection of attacks on public officials.

564 *"out-of-body experience":* telephone int. Thelton Henderson, March 4, 1997.

564 *Louise Day Hicks:* Hicks to R. Kennedy, Nov. 12, 1963, George Wallace Papers, ADAH. She sent a copy of the letter to Wallace.

564 *tied to "playgirls":* Summers, *Official and Confidential,* p. 310.

565 *Robert Kennedy seemed to acknowledge:* Hoover to Tolson et al., Nov. 7, 1963, Levison FBI; Branch, *Parting,* p. 913.

565 *not acting like an innocent man:* FBI int. with Robert Chambliss, Oct. 30, 1963, Bapbomb. Spying Agents Timothy Casey and Bernard Cashdollar, Chambliss had called his boss, Herman Siegel, and Siegel's wife to witness him yelling at the agents: "I'm going to tell the FBI where they can go. Seventy-two percent of the bastards are Roman Catholics under the control of that yellow traitor Bobby Kennedy." (The bureau, recruiting heavily at Notre Dame, was indeed thick with Catholics.)

565   *"undoubtedly participated":* and other quotes on Hall, *Task Force Report,* pp. 135–36, 141.
565   *"granddaddy of the shrapnel bombs":* Eddy to Beck, March 22, 1977, Box 4, BPSF.
565   *name the three prime suspects:* FBI int. with John Wesley Hall, Dec. 3, 1963, Bapbomb. Hall would also name George Pickle, assumed to have knowledge of it.
565   *Simpson accompanied the governor to Harvard:* int. Florence Evans Simpson, March 22, 1989; Carter, *Wallace,* p. 197.
566   *Carter's writing career:* Diane McWhorter, "Little Tree, Big Lies," *People,* Oct. 28, 1991; Dana Rubin, "The Real Education of Little Tree," *Texas Monthly,* February 1992.
566   *"as the Symbol of the Movement":* Shuttlesworth to King, Nov. 7, 1963, MLK 22.11. He wrote the letter on Wednesday, November 6, after waiting in Cincinnati for an 11 a.m. call from King to discuss an upcoming meeting of religious and civic leaders in Birmingham. The phone never rang.
567   *board meeting of the Southern Conference Educational Fund:* See police memo, Oct. 21, 1963, AB. Scheduled to join them was Shuttlesworth's close comrade Ella Baker.
567   *raid on SCEF's New Orleans headquarters:* Anne Braden, "Smoke Screen—The Red Scare," *Freedomways,* First Quarter 1964; State of Louisiana, Joint Legislative Committee on Un-American Activities, *Activities of the Southern Conference Educational Fund, Inc., in Louisiana,* April 13, 1964, p. 65; *BN,* Oct. 5, 1963. Under orders from the Louisiana Joint Committee, a HUAC clone, police had stormed the SCEF offices and arrested its executive director, Jim Dombrowski. A judge threw out all charges three weeks later, calling the raid and arrests illegal. The records seized ended up in the possession of Senator James Eastland.
567   *Roosevelt Tatum . . . :* Lane and Gregory, *"Zorro,"* p. 40.
567   *fellow officers might have been "deeply involved":* "Note File," March 1, 1977, based on interview by attorney general's staff with House, Attorney General's Files. Though House does not refer to Tom Cook by name, he describes the suspects as "officers in the department [who] have recently retired." Cook retired in 1976.
567   *pleaded guilty: Bobby Shelton:* FBI int. with Bobby Shelton, Nov. 29, 1963, Bapbomb.
568   *spat upon the visiting UN ambassador:* MacNeil, *Way We Were,* p. 164.
568   *"sleek, fat agitators":* Carter, *Wallace,* p. 183.
568   *West End Parents:* The state superintendent of schools, Dr. Austin Meadows, had pledged to help the private schools devise a curriculum within accepted educational standards. The group had established a bank account at Exchange-Security, the bank Jim Simpson founded.
569   *question his staff about the Henderson affair:* summary of memos, Oct. 21, 1963, Box 29, VN; McLeod to Marshall, Nov. 15, 1963, Marshall to McLeod, Nov. 20, 1963, BM. When the appellate ruling came down, the Dallas County district attorney had quickly changed course, telegramming Marshall that he would pursue whether government attorneys had "harbored known criminals and dope addicts," "associated with admitted sex perverts," contributed to the delinquency of minors, or fomented "riots, insurrection, and civil disobedience."
569   *"happen to me also":* C. S. King, *My Life,* p. 244.
570   *Ronnie Tidwell:* Klan HUAC hearings, p. 3072.
570   *counterintelligence program's dirty tricks:* O'Reilly, *"Racial Matters,"* pp. 199–200. COINTELPRO against the Klan began at the end of August 1964.
570   *Pat Brown, told a reporter:* Lesher, *Wallace,* p. 265. Wallace's parole board would parole one of Judge Aaron's castrators early in 1964, after he had served less than a fourth of his twenty-year sentence.

Epilogue

571   *expose King as a "tom cat"* and *sent audiotapes:* Garrow, *Bearing,* p. 310; Sullivan to Belmont, Jan. 27, 1964, in Theoharis, *Secret Files,* p. 100.
571   *urging King himself to commit suicide:* Anonymous (Sullivan) to King, undated (Nov. 21, 1964), in Theoharis, *Secret Files,* pp. 102–103.
571   *dispatched by King to Selma:* Garrow, *Bearing,* pp. 381, 387–88; Fred Shuttlesworth oral history, KC, Part 2. Shuttlesworth flew down to Selma the day after Bloody Sunday and was back on the front lines for the protest when it resumed, completing the historic four-day march to Montgomery.
572   *Viola Liuzzo: Task Force Report,* pp. 148, 172–73. Two of the Klansmen, Eugene Thomas and William O. Eaton, had participated with Rowe in the firebombing of A. G. Gaston's house. The third, the alleged triggerman, was the young, slow-witted Collie Leroy Wilkins. Rowe had by now earned $22,000 from the FBI.
572   *daughter of Secretary Defense Robert McNamara:* telephone int. Robert McNamara, Oct. 1, 1992.
572   *hugs exchanged and lunch shared:* int. Anne Robertson, March 1985.
573   *Rowe who had fired at Liuzzo: Task Force Report,* pp. 159, 213, 232.
573   *reply to a hostile letter:* The letter would turn up on the cover of the next issue of *The Thunderbolt.*
573   *wanted to "go home":* Sikora, *Until Justice,* p. 120.
573   *heart attack at the wheel:* conversation with Mary Ingram, March 23, 1993.
574   *"One phone call":* Eddy to Beck, "Phone Conversation with Mary Cunningham," Aug. 30, 1977, JY.
574   *"naughty and simpleminded":* Cobbs/Smith, *Long Time,* p. 26.
574   *served a subpoena on Tommy Blanton:* LeGrand memo, Feb. 14, 1978, JY.
574   *break Bobby Frank Cherry:* int. John Yung, March 1985; int. George Beck, March 1985; Sikora, *Until Justice,* pp. 109, 116–17. Baxley visited Cherry after Chambliss was indicted. It was following a state investigator's earlier visit to Cherry that he called Gafford.
575   *Chris McNair: BN,* Sept. 11, 1963; conversation with Chris McNair, Fall 1981.
575   *new cellmate in 1985: J. B. Stoner:* int. John Yung, March 1985. In another made-for-media detail, his prison neighbor and fast friend in the next cell was Tommy Lee Hines, a retarded black man from Decatur whose conviction in 1978 for raping three white women had become a cause célèbre of the Southern Christian Leadership Conference, now led by Joe Lowery (the conviction was subsequently overturned). The Ku Klux Klan's violent reply to a civil rights

march in Decatur in 1979 led a judge to order the offending Klansmen to undergo consciousness-raising workshops conducted by SCLC's Lowery.

575 *Petric Smith:* Cobbs, *Long Time,* p. 189; *BPH,* Nov. 5, 1994.

576 *Margie Burke:* telephone conversation with Margie Burke, Feb. 8, 1993.

576 *Simpson's drug-addicted namesake: BN,* Sept. 1 and 2, 1977; BPH, March 29 and 30, 1978. The murder was committed in late August 1977 and Popsie was charged in March 1978.

576 *Mary Ingram:* conversation with Mary Ingram, March 23, 1993.

577 *Earl "Shorty" Thompson:* conversation with Earl Thompson, Sept. 16, 1993.

577 *Prince DeBardeleben:* int. Prince DeBardeleben, Dec. 7, 1987.

577 *Qaddafi became romantically fixated: Esquire,* Jan. 1997.

578 *Robert Thomas:* conversation with Robert Thomas, Sept. 16, 1993.

578 *information source for the FBI:* Eddy to Beck, Oct. 11, 1977, JY; LeGrand int. with Rowe, pp 57–58. Though Rowe characterizes Mildred Thomas as "an informant to me," Detective Jack LeGrand's questions indicate that he has information that she was "an informant for the FBI."

579 *Doris Holt:* conversation with Doris Holt, June 13, 1995.

583 *Loyal McWhorter:* telephone conversation with Dewitt McWhorter, Nov. 20, 1995.

585 *"Black people":* Diane McWhorter, "Wallace's Rebirth," *The New Republic,* Nov. 29, 1982.

585 *Shoal Creek:* Diane McWhorter, "The White Man's Last Stand," *The Nation,* Oct. 8, 1990.

586 *"Moon over Homewood"* and *"Bad for Image": BPH,* Jan. 11 and Feb. 14, 1986.

587 *"beautiful, even in its destruction":* This was in the liner notes that Jones (Amiri Baraka) wrote for the album, *Coltrane Live at Birdland.* "Alabama" was recorded on November 18, 1963, and, Coltrane said, "represents, musically, something that I saw down there translated into music from inside me.""

Afterword

593 *Billy Jackson:* Jackson preceded Waylene Vaughn as a witness.

600 *Vergangenheitsbewaltigung:* The historian Nell Irvin Painter explores this idea in a review of this book in *The Journal of Higher Education,* Summer 2001.

SELECTED BIBLIOGRAPHY

Abernathy, Ralph David. *And the Walls Came Tumbling Down.* New York: Harper & Row, 1989.

Abt, John, with Michael Myerson. *Advocate and Activist: Memoirs of an American Communist Lawyer.* Urbana: University of Illinois Press, 1993.

Adams, Frank, with Myles Horton. *Unearthing Seeds of Fire: The Idea of Highlander.* Winston-Salem, N.C.: Blair, 1975.

Ambrose, Stephen E. *Eisenhower: The President.* New York: Simon & Schuster, 1984.

Anderson, Jervis. *Bayard Rustin: Troubles I've Seen, A Biography.* New York: HarperCollins, 1997.

Anthony, Paul. "A Survey of Resistance Groups of Alabama," July 1956, in SRC.

Armes, Ethel T. *The Story of Coal and Iron in Alabama.* Leeds, Ala.: Beechwood, 1987. Originally published by the Birmingham Chamber of Commerce in 1910.

Ashby, Warren. *Frank Porter Graham: A Southern Liberal.* Winston-Salem, N.C.: Blair, 1980.

Atkins, Leah Rawls. "A History of the Campaign for Civil Service Reform in Birmingham and Jefferson County," unpublished paper, courtesy of James E. Simpson.

———. *The Valley and the Hills: An Illustrated History of Birmingham and Jefferson County.* Woodland Hills, Calif.: Windsor, 1981.

Auerbach, Jerold S. *Labor and Liberty: The La Follette Committee and the New Deal.* Indianapolis and New York: Bobbs-Merrill, 1966.

Autrey, Dorothy. "The National Association for the Advancement of Colored People in Alabama, 1913–1952." Ph.D. dissertation, University of Notre Dame, 1985.

Baez, Joan. *And a Voice to Sing With.* New York: Summit, 1987.

Barnard, William D. *Dixiecrats and Democrats: Alabama Politics, 1942–1950.* Tuscaloosa: University of Alabama Press, 1974.

Bartley, Numan V. *The Rise of Massive Resistance: Race and Politics in the South during the 1950's.* Baton Rouge: Louisiana State University Press, 1969.

Bass, Jack. *Taming the Storm: The Life and Times of Judge Frank M. Johnson, Jr., and the South's Fight Over Civil Rights.* New York: Doubleday, 1993.

———. *Unlikely Heroes: The Dramatic Story of the Southern Judges of the Fifth Circuit Who Translated the Supreme Court's Brown Decision into a Revolution for Equality.* New York: Simon & Schuster, 1981.

Beiman, Irving. "Birmingham: Steel Giant with a Glass Jaw," in Robert S. Allen, ed., *Our Fair City.* New York: Vanguard, 1947.

Black, Hugo L., and Elizabeth Black. *Mr. Justice and Mrs. Black: The Memoirs of Hugo L. and Elizabeth Black.* New York: Random House, 1986.

Black, Hugo L. Jr. *My Father.* New York: Random House, 1975.

Bond, Horace Mann. *Negro Education in Alabama: A Study in Cotton and Steel.* 1939; New York: Atheneum, 1969.

[Braden, Anne.] *Birmingham: People in Motion.* Birmingham: Alabama Christian Movement for Human Rights and Southern Conference Educational Fund, 1966.

———. *They Challenge Segregation at It's Core!* Birmingham: Southern Conference Educational Fund, 1959.

Bradlee, Benjamin C. *Conversations with Kennedy.* New York: Norton, 1975.

Branch, Taylor. *Parting the Waters: America in the King Years, 1954–63.* New York: Simon & Schuster, 1988.

Brandes, Stuart. *American Welfare Capitalism: 1880–1940.* Chicago: University of Chicago Press, 1976.

Cagin, Seth, and Philip Dray. *We Are Not Afraid: The Story of Schwerner, Goodman, and Chaney and the Civil Rights Campaign for Mississippi.* New York: Macmillan, 1988.

Campbell, Will D. *Brother to a Dragonfly.* New York: Seabury, 1977.

Carlson, John Roy (pseudonym of Arthur Derounian). *The Plotters.* New York: Dutton, 1946.

———. *Under Cover: My Four Years in the Nazi Underworld of America.* New York: Dutton, 1943.

Carmer, Carl. *Stars Fell on Alabama.* New York: Farrar & Rinehart, 1934.

Carson, Clayborne. *In Struggle: SNCC and the Black Awakening of the 1960s.* Cambridge, Mass.: Harvard University Press, 1981.

Carter, Dan T. *The Politics of Rage: George Wallace, the Origins of the New Conservatism, and the Transformation of American Politics.* New York: Simon & Schuster, 1995.

———. *Scottsboro: A Tragedy of the American South.* Rev. ed., Baton Rouge: Louisiana State University Press, 1979.

Chalmers, David M. *Hooded Americanism: The First Century of the Ku Klux Klan, 1865–1965.* Garden City, N.Y.: Doubleday, 1965.

Chernow, Ron. *The House of Morgan: An American Banking Dynasty and the Rise of Modern Finance.* New York: Touchstone, 1990.

Clark, E. Culpepper. *The Schoolhouse Door: Segregation's Last Stand at the University of Alabama.* New York: Oxford University Press, 1993.

Clark, Elizabeth Boner. "The Abolition of the Convict Lease System in Alabama, 1913–1928." Master's thesis, University of Alabama, 1949.

Clarke, Jacquelyne Johnson. "Goals and Techniques in Three Civil Rights Organizations in Alabama." Ph.D. dissertation, Ohio State University, 1960.

———. *These Rights They Seek.* Washington, D.C.: Public Affairs Press, 1962.

Cobbs, Elizabeth H. (Petric J. Smith). *Long Time Coming: An Insider's Story of the Church Bombing That Rocked the World.* Birmingham: Crane Hill, 1994.

Cochran, Lynda Dempsey. "Arthur Davis Shores: Advocate for Freedom." Master's thesis, Georgia Southern College, 1977.

Coffin, William Sloane, Jr. *Once to Every Man.* New York: Atheneum, 1977.

Cohodas, Nadine. *Strom Thurmond and the Politics of Southern Change.* New York: Simon & Schuster, 1993.

Coleman, Stephen, and Stephen Coleman Jr. *Judge Clarence Allgood.* Birmingham: Birmingham Historical Society, 1991.

Corley, Robert G. "The Quest for Racial Harmony: Race Relations in Birmingham, Alabama, 1947–1963." Ph.D. dissertation, University of Virginia, 1979.

Cortner, Richard C. *The Apportionment Cases.* Knoxville: University of Tennessee Press, 1970.

Cruikshank, George M. *A History of Birmingham and Its Environs,* 2 vols. Chicago: Lewis, 1920.

Daniels, Jonathan. *A Southerner Discovers the South.* New York: Macmillan, 1938.

Davis, Angela. *Angela Davis.* New York: Bantam, 1975.

Deming, Barbara. "Notes After Birmingham." *Liberation,* Summer 1963.

Destler, Chester McArthur. *Henry Demarest Lloyd and the Empire of Reform.* Philadelphia: University of Pennsylvania Press, 1963.

Dorman, Michael. *We Shall Overcome.* New York: Delacorte, 1964.

Draper, Theodore. *American Communism and Soviet Russia.* 1960; New York: Vintage, 1986.

Dubofsky, Melvyn, and Warren Van Tine. *John L. Lewis: A Biography.* New York: Quadrangle, 1977.

Durr, Virginia Foster. *Outside the Magic Circle.* Tuscaloosa: University of Alabama Press, 1985.

Edmonds, Henry M. *A Parson's Notebook.* Birmingham: Elizabeth Agee's Bookshelf, 1961.

Egerton, John. *Speak Now Against the Day: The Generation Before the Civil Rights Movement in the South.* New York: Knopf, 1994.

Elmore, Nancy Ruth. "The Birmingham Coal Strike of 1908." Master's thesis, University of Alabama, 1966.

Elovitz, Mark. *A Century of Jewish Life in Dixie: The Birmingham Experience.* Tuscaloosa: University of Alabama Press, 1974.

Ely, Melvin Patrick. *The Adventures of Amos 'n' Andy: A Social History of an American Phenomenon.* New York: Free Press, 1991.

Emspak, Frank. "The Break-up of the Congress of Industrial Organizations (CIO), 1945–1950." Ph.D. dissertation, University of Wisconsin, 1972.

Eskew, Glenn. "The Alabama Christian Movement and the Birmingham Struggle for Civil Rights, 1956–1963." Master's thesis, University of Georgia, 1987.

———. *But for Birmingham: The Local and National Movements in the Civil Rights Struggle.* Chapel Hill: University of North Carolina Press, 1997.

Fairclough, Adam. *To Redeem the Soul of America: The Southern Christian Leadership Conference and Martin Luther King, Jr.* Athens: University of Georgia Press, 1987.

Farmer, James. *Freedom—When?* New York: Random House, 1965.

———. *Lay Bare the Heart: An Autobiography of the Civil Rights Movement.* New York: Arbor House, 1985.

Feldman, Glenn. "Horace Wilkinson and Alabama Politics, 1877–1957." Master's thesis, Auburn University, 1992.

———. *Politics, Society, and the Klan in Alabama, 1915–1949.* Tuscaloosa: University of Alabama Press, 1999.

Forman, James. *The Making of Black Revolutionaries.* New York: Macmillan, 1972.

Forster, Arnold, and Benjamin R. Epstein. *Danger on the Right: The Attitudes, Personnel and Influence of the Radical Right and Extreme Conservatives.* New York: Random House, 1964.

———. *The Radical Right: Report on the John Birch Society and Its Allies.* New York: Random House, 1966.

Frady, Marshall. *Wallace.* New York and Cleveland: World, 1968.

Friends of Democracy Inc. "Joe Kamp, Peddler of Propaganda and Hero of the Pro-Fascists," ca. 1944, SK.

Fuller, Justin, "History of the Tennessee Coal, Iron, and Railroad Company, 1852–1907." Ph.D. dissertation, University of North Carolina, 1966.

Fullerton, Christopher Dean. "Striking Out Jim Crow: The Birmingham Black Barons." M.A. thesis, University of Mississippi, 1994.

Gaither, Gerald. *Blacks and the Populist Revolt: Ballots and Bigotry in the "New South."* Tuscaloosa: University of Alabama Press, 1977.

Garrow, David J. *Bearing the Cross: Martin Luther King, Jr., and the Southern Christian Leadership Conference.* New York: Morrow, 1986.

———. *The FBI and Martin Luther King, Jr.: From "Solo" to Memphis.* New York: Norton, 1981.

Gaston, A. G. *Green Power.* Birmingham: Birmingham Publishing Co., 1968.

Gelders, Esther F. "Professsor, How Could You?" *The New Republic,* March 2, 1938, pp. 96–97.

Gilliam, Thomas J. "The Second Folsom Administration: The Destruction of Alabama Liberalism, 1954–1958." Ph.D. dissertation, Auburn University, 1975.

Goldstein, Harold Joseph. "Labor Unrest in the Birmingham District, 1871–1894." Master's thesis, University of Alabama, 1951.

Grafton, Carl, and Anne Permaloff. *Big Mules and Branchheads: James E. Folsom and Political Power in Alabama.* Athens: University of Georgia Press, 1985.

Graham, Hugh Davis. *The Civil Rights Era: Origins and Development of National Policy, 1960–1972.* New York: Oxford University Press, 1990.

Grant, Joanne, ed. *Black Protest: History, Documents, and Analyses, 1619 to the Present.* Greenwich, Conn.: Fawcett, 1968.

Grantham, Dewey. *Southern Progressivism.* Knoxville: University of Tennessee Press, 1983.

Gray, Fred. *Bus Ride to Justice: Changing the System by the System.* Montgomery: Black Belt Press, 1995.

Gregg, Richard Bartlett. *The Power of Nonviolence.* London: J. Clarke, 1960.

Gregory, Dick, with Robert Lipsyte. *Nigger.* New York: Pocket, 1965.

Guthman, Edwin. *We Band of Brothers.* New York: Harper & Row, 1971.

Gutwillig, Robert. "Six Days in Alabama." *Mademoiselle,* September 1963.

Hackney, Sheldon. *Populism to Progressivism in Alabama.* Princeton, N.J.: Princeton University Press, 1969.

Hamilton, Charles. *Adam Clayton Powell, Jr.: The Political Biography of an American Dilemma.* New York: Atheneum, 1991.

Hamilton, Virginia Van der Veer. *Alabama.* New York: Norton, 1977.

———. *Lister Hill: Statesman from the South.* Chapel Hill: University of North Carolina Press, 1987.

———. *Hugo Black: The Alabama Years.* Tuscaloosa: University of Alabama Press, 1972.

Hampton, Henry, and Steve Fayer. *Voices of Freedom: An Oral History of the Civil Rights Movement from the 1950s Through the 1980s.* New York: Bantam, 1990.

Hampton, Lionel, with James Haskins. *Hamp: An Autobiography.* New York: Warner, 1989.

Harding, Vincent. "A Beginning in Birmingham." *The Reporter,* June 6, 1963, pp. 13–19.

Hare, Frances Hutcheson. *My Learned Friends: Memories of a Trial Lawyer.* Cincinnati: Anderson, 1976.

Harris, Carl V. *Political Power in Birmingham, 1871–1921.* Knoxville: University of Tennessee Press, 1977.

Harris, David Alan. "Racists and Reformers": A Study of Progressivism in Alabama, 1896–1911." Ph.D. dissertation, University of North Carolina, 1967.

Herndon, Angelo. *Let Me Live.* 1937. Reprint, New York: Arno, 1969.

Hersh, Seymour. *The Dark Side of Camelot.* Boston: Little, Brown, 1997.

Hogan, William T. *An Economic History of the Iron and Steel Industry in the U.S.,* 5 vols. Lexington, Mass.: Lexington Books, 1971.

Hollis, Daniel Webster, III. *An Alabama Newspaper Tradition: Grover C. Hall and the Hall Family.* Tuscaloosa: University of Alabama Press, 1983.

Horton, Myles, with Judith Kohl and Herbert Kohl. *The Long Haul.* Garden City, N.Y.: Doubleday, 1990.

Huie, William Bradford. "Drafts of Old Bourbon: Pregnancy and Politics in Alabama." *American Mercury,* June 1951.

———. *Mud on the Stars.* New York: L. B. Fischer, 1942.

Huntley, Horace. "Iron Ore Miners and Mine Mill in Alabama, 1933–1952." Ph.D. dissertation, University of Pittsburgh, 1977.

Ingalls, Robert P. "Antiradical Violence in Birmingham During the 1930s." *Journal of Southern History,* November 1981.

Isserman, Maurice. *If I Had a Hammer . . . : The Death of the Old Left and the Birth of the New Left.* New York: Basic Books, 1987.

Josephson, Matthew. *The Robber Barons.* 1934; New York: Harcourt Brace and World, 1962.

Katz, Michael B., ed. *The "Underclass" Debate: Views from History.* Princeton, N.J., Princeton University Press, 1993.

Kelley, Robin D.G. *Hammer and Hoe: Alabama Communists During the Great Depression.* Chapel Hill: University of North Carolina Press, 1990.

Kempton, Murray. *Part of Our Time: Some Ruins and Monuments of the Thirties.* New York: Simon & Schuster, 1955.

Kendrick, Alexander. *Prime Time: The Life of Edward R. Murrow.* Boston: Little, Brown, 1969.

Kennedy, Robert. *Robert Kennedy: In His Own Words,* ed. Edwin Guthman and Jeffrey Shulman. New York: Bantam, 1988.

Kennedy, Stetson. *Southern Exposure.* Garden City, N.Y.: Doubleday, 1946.

Kesselman, Louis. *The Social Politics of FEPC: A Study in Reform Pressure Movements.* Chapel Hill: University of North Carolina Press, 1948.

King, Coretta Scott. *My Life with Martin Luther King, Jr.* New York: Holt, Rinehart and Winston, 1969.

King, Martin Luther, Jr. *Stride Toward Freedom.* New York: Harper & Brothers, 1958.

———. *Why We Can't Wait.* New York: New American Library, 1964.

Kirby, James. *Fumble: Bear Bryant, Wally Butts, and the Great College Football Scandal.* San Diego: Harcourt Brace Jovanovich, 1986.

Klehr, Harvey. *The Heyday of American Communism: The Depression Decade.* New York: Basic Books, 1984.

Kluger, Richard. *Simple Justice: The History of "Brown v. Board of Education" and Black America's Struggle for Equality.* New York: Vintage, 1977.

Kovel, Joel. *White Racism: A Psychohistory.* New York: Pantheon, 1970.

Krueger, Thomas A. *And Promises to Keep: The Southern Conference for Human Welfare, 1938–1948.* Nashville: Vanderbilt University Press, 1967.

Kulik, Gary. "Black Workers and Technological Change in the Birmingham Iron Industry, 1881–1931," in Merl E. Reed, Leslie Hough, and Gary Fink, eds., *Southern Workers and Their Unions, 1880–1975.* Westport, Conn.: Greenwood, 1981.

Kundahl, George G., Jr. "Organized Labor in Alabama State Politics." Ph.D. dissertation, University of Alabama, 1967.

Kunstler, William. *Deep in My Heart.* New York: Morrow, 1966.

LaMonte, Edward S. *Politics and Welfare in Birmingham, 1900–1975.* Tuscaloosa: University of Alabama Press, 1995.

Lane, Mark, and Dick Gregory. *Code Name "Zorro."* Englewood Cliffs, N.J.: Prentice-Hall, 1977.

Lawson, Steven F. *Black Ballots: Voting Rights in the South, 1944–1969.* New York: Columbia University Press, 1976.

Leighton, George R. "Birmingham, Alabama: The City of Perpetual Promise." *Harper's,* August 1937, pp. 225–42.

Lesher, Stephan. *George Wallace: American Populist.* Reading, Mass.: Addison Wesley, 1993.

Letwin, Daniel Lazar. "Race, Class, and Industrialization in the New South: Black and White Coal Miners in the Birmingham District of Alabama, 1878–1897." Ph.D. dissertation, Yale University, 1991.

Levin, Murray B. *Political Hysteria in America.* New York: Basic Books, 1971.

Levine, Ellen. *Freedom's Children.* New York: Avon, 1993.

Lewis, Anthony. *Make No Law.* New York: Random House, 1991.

Lewis, David Levering. *King: A Critical Biography.* New York: Praeger, 1970.

———. *W.E.B. Du Bois.* New York: Holt, 1993.

Lewis, John, with Michael D'Orso. *Walking with the Wind: A Memoir of the Movement.* New York: Simon & Schuster, 1998.

Lewis, Ronald L. *Black Coal Miners in America: Race, Class, and Community Conflict, 1780–1980.* Lexington: University Press of Kentucky, 1987.

Lewis, Sinclair. *Babbitt.* 1922; New York: Signet, 1961.

Lomax, Louis. *The Negro Revolt.* New York: Signet, 1963.

Lord, Walter. *The Past That Would Not Die.* New York: Harper & Row, 1965.

McCraw, Thomas K. *TVA and the Power Fight, 1933–1939.* Philadelphia: Lippincott, 1971.

McMillan, George. "The Birmingham Church Bomber." *Saturday Evening Post,* June 6, 1964.

McMillan, Malcolm C. *Yesterday's Birmingham.* Miami: Seemann, 1975.

McMillen, Neil R. *The Citizens' Council: A History of Organized Resistance to the Second Reconstruction, 1954–1964.* Urbana: University of Illinois Press, 1971.

MacNeil, Robert. *The Way We Were: 1963, The Year Kennedy Was Shot.* New York: Carroll & Graf, 1988.

Manchester, William. *The Glory and the Dream*. Boston: Little, Brown, 1974.

Manis, Andrew M. *A Fire You Can't Put Out: The Civil Rights Life of Birmingham's Reverend Fred Shuttlesworth*. Tuscaloosa: University of Alabama Press, 1999.

Marshall, F. Ray. *Labor in the South*. Cambridge, Mass.: Harvard University Press, 1967.

Martin, John Bartlow. "The Deep South Says 'Never.' " *Saturday Evening Post*, June 15 and 29, 1957.

Martin, Thomas W. *The Story of Electricity in Alabama Since the Turn of the Century, 1900–1952*. Birmingham, 1952.

Marvin, Fred. *Alabama Fuel and Iron Company and Its People: A Story of a Visit to Happy Communities*. Birmingham, 1939.

Mecklin, John Moffatt. *The Ku Klux Klan: A Study of the American Mind*. New York: Harcourt Brace, 1924.

Michie, Allan A., and Frank Ryhlick. *Dixie Demagogues*. New York: Vanguard, 1939.

Miller, Keith. *Voice of Deliverance: The Language of Martin Luther King, Jr., and Its Sources*. New York: Free Press, 1992.

Mitchell, H. L. "The White Citizens Councils vs. Southern Trade Unions," March 12, 1956, in SRC.

Mitchell, Martha. "Birmingham: Biography of a City of the New South." Ph.D. dissertation, University of Chicago, 1946.

Mitford, Jessica. *A Fine Old Conflict*. New York: Vintage, 1978.

Moore, A. B. *History of Alabama*. University: Alabama Book Store, 1934.

Moore, Charles. *Powerful Days: The Civil Rights Photography of Charles Moore*. Text by Michael S. Durham. New York: Stewart, Tabori & Chang, 1991.

Morgan, Charles Jr. *One Man, One Voice*. New York: Holt, Rinehart and Winston, 1971.

———. *A Time to Speak*. New York: Harper & Row, 1964.

Morris, Aldon. *The Origins of the Civil Rights Movement*. New York: Free Press, 1984.

Mullins, Betty Hamaker. "The Steel Corporation's Purchase of the Tennessee Coal, Iron & Railroad Company in 1907." Master's thesis, Samford University, 1970.

Murray, William M., Jr. *Thomas W. Martin: A Biography*. Birmingham: Southern Research Institute, 1978.

Naison, Mark. *Communists in Harlem During the Depression*. New York: Grove, 1983.

Navasky, Victor. *Kennedy Justice*. New York: Atheneum, 1977.

Newman, Roger K. *Hugo Black*. New York: Pantheon, 1994.

Nicholas, William. *The Bobby Kennedy Nobody Knows*. Greenwich, Conn.: Fawcett, 1967.

Nichols, Michael Cooper. " 'Cities Are What Men Make Them': Birmingham, Alabama, Faces the Civil Rights Movement, 1963." Senior honors thesis, Brown University, 1974.

Norman, Geoffrey. *Alabama Showdown: The Football Rivalry Between Auburn and Alabama*. New York: Holt, 1986.

Norrell, Robert J. "Caste in Steel: Jim Crow Careers in Birmingham, Alabama." *Journal of American History* 73, no. 3 (December 1986), pp. 669–94.

———. "Labor at the Ballot Box: Alabama Politics from the New Deal to the Dixiecrat Movement." *Journal of Southern History*, May 1991.

———. "Labor Trouble: George Wallace and Union Politics in Alabama," in Robert H. Zieger, ed., *Organized Labor in the Twentieth-Century South*. Knoxville: University of Tennessee Press, 1991.

———. *The Other Side: The Story of Birmingham's Black Community*. Birmingham: Birmingfind, undated.

North, Joseph. *No Men Are Strangers*. New York: International Publishers, 1958.

Nunnelly, William. *Bull Connor*. Tuscaloosa: University of Alabama Press, 1991.

Oates, Stephen B. *Let the Trumpet Sound: The Life of Martin Luther King, Jr*. New York: Harper & Row, 1982.

O'Reilly, Kenneth. *Hoover and the Un-Americans*. Philadelphia: Temple University Press, 1983.

————. *"Racial Matters": The FBI's Secret File on Black America, 1960–1972.* New York: Free Press, 1989.

Osborne, George R. "Boycott in Birmingham." *The Nation,* May 5, 1962.

Painter, Nell Irvin. *The Narrative of Hosea Hudson: His Life as a Negro Communist in the South.* Cambridge, Mass.: Harvard University Press, 1979.

Peck, James. *Freedom Ride.* New York: Simon & Schuster, 1962.

Peirce, Neal R. *The Deep South States of America.* New York: Norton, 1974.

Pepper, Claude D., with Hays Gorey. *Pepper: Eyewitness to a Century.* San Diego: Harcourt Brace Jovanovich, 1987.

Percy, Walker. *The Last Gentleman.* 1966. Reprint, New York: Avon/Bard, 1982.

Phillips, Cabell. *The 1940s: Decade of Triumph and Trouble.* New York: Macmillan, 1975.

Powers, Richard Gid. *Secrecy and Power: The Life of J. Edgar Hoover.* New York: Free Press, 1987.

Powledge, Fred. *Free at Last? The Civil Rights Movement and the People Who Made It.* Boston: Little, Brown, 1991.

Raines, Howell. *My Soul Is Rested: Movement Days in the Deep South Remembered.* New York: Penguin, 1983.

Rather, Dan, with Mickey Herskowitz. *The Camera Never Blinks.* New York: Ballantine, 1978.

Reed, Linda. "The Southern Conference for Human Welfare and the Southern Conference Educational Fund, 1938–1963." Ph.D. dissertation, Indiana University, 1986.

Richards, Johnetta. "The Southern Negro Youth Congress." Ph.D. dissertation, University of Cincinnati, 1987.

Rikard, Marlene Hunt. "An Experiment in Welfare Capitalism: The Health Care Services of the Tennessee Coal, Iron and Railroad Company." Ph.D. dissertation, University of Alabama, 1983.

————. "Take Everything You Are . . . and Give It Away: Pioneer Industrial Social Workers at TCI." *Birmingham Historical Society Journal,* November 1981.

Rogers, William Warren. *The One-Gallused Rebellion: Agrarianism in Alabama, 1865–1896.* Baton Rouge: Louisiana State University Press, 1970.

Rowan, Carl T. *Breaking Barriers.* Boston: Little, Brown, 1991.

————. *Go South to Sorrow.* New York: Random House, 1957.

————. *South of Freedom.* New York: Knopf, 1952.

Rowe, Gary Thomas. *My Undercover Years with the Ku Klux Klan.* New York: Bantam, 1976.

Salinger, Pierre. *With Kennedy.* Garden City, N.Y.: Doubleday, 1966.

Salisbury, Harrison. *A Time of Change.* New York: Harper & Row, 1988.

————. *Without Fear or Favor.* New York: Times Books, 1980.

Salmond, John A. *The Conscience of a Lawyer: Clifford J. Durr and American Civil Liberties, 1899–1975.* Tuscaloosa: University of Alabama Press, 1990.

————. *A Southern Rebel: The Life and Times of Aubrey Willis Williams, 1890–1965.* Chapel Hill: University of North Carolina Press, 1983.

Scales, Junius Irving, and Richard Nickson. *Cause at Heart: A Former Communist Remembers.* Athens: University of Georgia Press, 1987.

Schickel, Richard. *D.W. Griffith: An American Life.* New York: Simon & Schuster, 1984.

Schlesinger, Arthur M., Jr. *The Politics of Upheaval.* Boston: Houghton Mifflin, 1960.

————. *Robert Kennedy and His Times.* Boston: Houghton Mifflin, 1978.

————. *A Thousand Days.* Boston: Houghton Mifflin, 1965.

Sikora, Frank. *Until Justice Rolls Down: The Birmingham Church Bombing Case.* Tuscaloosa: University of Alabama Press, 1991.

Sims, George E. *The Little Man's Big Friend: James E. Folsom in Alabama Politics, 1946–1958.* Tuscaloosa: University of Alabama Press, 1985.

Sims, Patsy. *The Klan.* New York: Stein & Day, 1978.

Smith, Douglas L. *The New Deal in the Urban South.* Baton Rouge: Louisiana State University Press, 1988.

Smith, Howard K. *Events Leading Up to My Death: The Life of a Twentieth-Century Reporter.* New York: St. Martin's, 1996.

Smith, Sally Bedell. *In All His Glory: The Life and Times of William S. Paley and the Birth of Modern Broadcasting.* New York: Touchstone, 1990.

Sosna, Morton. *In Search of the Silent South: Southern Liberals and the Race Issue.* New York: Columbia University Press, 1977.

Sperber, A. M. *Murrow: His Life and Times.* New York: Bantam, 1987.

Spero, Sterling, and Abram L. Harris. *The Black Worker: The Negro and the Labor Movement.* 1931; New York: Atheneum, 1968.

Starr, J. Barton. "Birmingham and the 'Dixiecrat' Convention of 1948." *Alabama Historical Quarterly,* Spring and Summer 1970.

Stein, Judith. "Southern Workers in National Unions: Birmingham Steelworkers, 1936–1951," in Robert H. Zieger, ed., *Organized Labor in the Twentieth-Century South.* Knoxville: University of Tennessee Press, 1991.

Stewart, George. "Birmingham's Reaction to the 1954 Desegregation Decision." M.A. thesis, Samford University, 1967.

Stone, Katherine. "The Origins of Job Structures in the Steel Industry," in Richard C. Edwards, Michael Reich, and David M. Gordon, eds., *Labor Market Segmentation,* Lexington, Mass: Lexington Books, 1975.

Stone, Olive Matthews. "Agrarian Conflict in Alabama: Sections, Races, and Classes in a Rural State from 1800 to 1938." Ph.D. dissertation, University of North Carolina, 1939.

Straw, Richard A. "The United Mine Workers of America and the 1920 Coal Strike in Alabama." *Alabama Review* 48 (April 1975), pp. 104–28.

Strong, Augusta. "Southern Youth's Proud Heritage." *Freedomways,* First Quarter 1964, pp. 35–50.

Suggs, Henry Lewis, ed. *The Black Press in the South, 1865–1979.* Westport, Conn.: Greenwood, 1983.

Sullivan, Mark. *Our Times: America at the Birth of the Twentieth Century,* edited with new material by Dan Rather. New York: Scribner, 1996. Originally published in 1926.

Sullivan, Patricia. "Gideon's Southern Soldiers: New Deal Politics and Civil Rights Reform, 1933–1948." Ph.D. dissertation, Emory University, 1983.

Summers, Anthony. *Official and Confidential: The Secret Life of J. Edgar Hoover.* New York: Putnam's, 1993.

Taft, Philip. *Organized Labor in American History.* New York: Harper & Row, 1964.

———. *Organizing Dixie: Alabama Workers in the Industrial Era,* revised and edited by Gary M. Fink. Westport, Conn: Greenwood, 1981.

Tarbell, Ida. *The Life of Elbert H. Gary.* New York: Appleton, 1925.

Taylor, Sandra Baxley. *Me 'n' George: A Story of George Corley Wallace and His Number One Crony, Oscar Harper.* Mobile, Ala.: Greenberry, 1988.

Theoharis, Athan. *From the Secret Files of J. Edgar Hoover.* Chicago: Ivan R. Dee, 1991.

Thompson, Jan Gregory. "A History of the Alabama Council on Human Relations, from Roots to Redirection, 1920–1968." Ph.D. dissertation, Auburn University, 1983.

Thornton, J. Mills, III. "Challenge and Response in the Montgomery Bus Boycott of 1955–56." *Alabama Review,* July 1980.

Tolson, Jay. *Pilgrim in the Ruins: A Life of Walker Percy.* New York: Simon & Schuster, 1992.

Trilling, Diana. *The Beginning of the Journey: The Marriage of Diana and Lionel Trilling.* New York: Harcourt Brace, 1993.

Viorst, Milton. *Fire in the Streets.* New York: Simon & Schuster, 1979.

Wade, Wyn Craig. *The Fiery Cross: The Ku Klux Klan in America.* New York: Simon & Schuster, 1987.

Warren, Kenneth. *The American Steel Industry, 1850–1970: A Geographical Interpretation.* Oxford, Eng.: Clarendon, 1973.

Warren, Robert Penn. *Who Speaks for the Negro?* New York: Random House, 1965.

Washington, James M., ed. *A Testament of Hope: The Essential Writing of Martin Luther King, Jr.* San Francisco: Harper & Row, 1986.

Watters, Pat. *Down to Now: Reflections on the Southern Civil Rights Movement.* New York: Random House, 1971.

Watters, Pat, and Reese Cleghorn. *Climbing Jacob's Ladder.* New York: Harcourt Brace & World, 1967.

Westin, Alan F., and Barry Mahoney. *The Trial of Martin Luther King.* New York: Crowell, 1974.

White, Marjorie Longenecker. *The Birmingham District: An Industrial History and Guide.* Birmingham: Birmingham Historical Society, 1981.

"Who Speaks for Birmingham?" Transcript of May 1961 *CBS Reports* in Southern History Department, Birmingham Public Library.

Wiggins, Sarah Woolfolk, ed. *From Civil War to Civil Rights, Alabama 1860–1960: An Anthology from the Alabama Review.* Tuscaloosa: University of Alabama Press, 1987.

Williams, Juan. *Eyes on the Prize: America's Civil Rights Years, 1954–1965.* New York: Viking, 1987.

Wilson, Edmund. "The Freight-Car Case." *The New Republic,* Aug. 26, 1931, pp. 38–43.

Wofford, Harris. *Of Kennedys and Kings.* New York: Farrar, Straus & Giroux, 1980.

Wolff, Geoffrey. *The Duke of Deception.* New York: Berkley, 1980.

Wolfskill, George, and John A. Hudson. *All but the People: Franklin D. Roosevelt and His Critics, 1933–1939.* New York: Macmillan, 1969.

Woodward, C. Vann. *American Counterpoint: Slavery and Racism in the North-South Dialogue.* Boston: Little, Brown, 1971.

———. *Origins of the New South.* Baton Rouge: Louisiana State University Press, 1967.

———. *The Strange Career of Jim Crow.* 1955; New York: Oxford, 1966.

Worthman, Paul B. "Black Workers and Labor Unions in Birmingham, Alabama, 1897–1904." *Labor History,* Summer 1969.

Wyden, Peter. *Bay of Pigs: The Untold Story.* New York: Simon & Schuster, 1979.

Young, Andrew. "And Birmingham." *Drum Major,* Winter 1971, pp. 21–27.

———. "The Day We Went to Jail in Birmingham." *Friends,* Feb. 9, 1964, pp. 3–11.

———. *An Easy Burden: The Civil Rights Movement and the Transformation of America.* New York: HarperCollins, 1996.

Court Cases

Alabama, State of, v. *Robert E. Chambliss,* C.C. 1977–01954.

Alabama, State of, v. *Jesse Benjamin Stoner,* C.C. 1980–24 and 25.

Gober v. *City of Birmingham,* 373 U.S. 374, No. 66 (1963).

NAACP v. *State of Alabama,* 377 U.S. 288, No. 169 (1964).

New York Times v. *Sullivan,* 376 U.S. 254, No. 39 (1964).

Shuttlesworth v. *City of Birmingham,* 373 U.S. 262, No. 67 (1963).

Shuttlesworth v. *City of Birmingham,* 382 U.S. 87, No. 5 (1965).

Shuttlesworth v. *City of Birmingham,* 394 U.S. 147, No. 42 (1969).

Walker v. *City of Birmingham,* 388 U.S. 307, No. 249 (1967).

ACKNOWLEDGMENTS

THE LATE J. ANTHONY LUKAS'S belief in the Talmudic truths contained in cities and in my ability to unravel those of my hometown sustained me through many years of quiet panic. Tony was patron saint to a generation of nonfiction writers, and I hope that this is a worthy tribute to his memory.

The process of writing this book was something like the Hundred Years War, with periodic changes in the high command, and I have been lucky to serve under a brilliant and congenial succession of editors. The project was launched by Jim Silberman, one of the finest editors and publishers of his time. Ileene Smith, with her exquisite mix of seriousness and a sense of the absurd, saw me through the gestation not only of the book but of the children we each produced over our time working together. During the middle siege, Becky Saletan maintained her warmth as well as her phenomenal critical faculties when confronted with the mammoth first rendering of the story. And finally there is Alice Mayhew, so legendary that she has been compared to the Old Testament God. She commanded me to shrink the manuscript to a size that could be manipulated without the aid of a forklift— and then shined her life-enhancing approval on the result.

I wish I could adequately convey the debt I owe Paul Solman, who is a journalist the way Goya was a cartoonist. He stepped in during the final months, merged his mind with mine, and through intellectual force and tough love turned a period of duress into an exhilarating jailbreak.

In my transition from journalism to history, I had many wonderful guides. Foremost among them, Robert G. Corley provided me the essential map—and demonstrated in his life of community service how scholarship can be converted into citizenship. Robin D.G. Kelley generously shared his sources on the Communist Party in Alabama, and despite his growing status as a celebrity historian took the time to comment thoughtfully on a portion of the manuscript. Roger Newman, biographer of Hugo Black and a fellow Magic City aficionado, was always ready to hear the latest bulletin from my research—and once said, only half jokingly, that there were really only a few of us who understood that Birmingham held the key to the universe. Jeff Norrell has done groundbreaking work on labor in Birmingham and pointed me in rewarding directions. Other writers who provided scholarly ballast and moral support were Dan T. Carter, Culpepper Clark, David Garrow, Wayne Greenhaw, and Victor Navasky. And as the consummate mediums of the civil rights era, Taylor Branch and Howell Raines have been formidable and inspiring exemplars.

A number of my sources opened their private papers to me. John Yung, one of the key state prosecutors who put away both Robert Chambliss and J. B. Stoner, gave me access to his case files, without which I would not have been able to reconstruct the bombings. Besides being my personal clipping service, Yung was my intrepid companion on field trips into darkest industrial Birmingham. George Beck, another of the prosecutors, also shared his files with me. Lawyers Edward Copeland and Morris Dees provided depositions on Gary Thomas Rowe. Michael Nichols lent me material from the undergraduate work he did on Birmingham, as did Lee Bains. Pinkie Lee Shortridge allowed me to go through the records of her late husband, Bill Shortridge, the treasurer of the Alabama Christian Movement for Human Rights. Orzell Billingsley gave me the run of his office—and appointed me as his representative at Bayard Rustin's memorial service. C. Herbert Oliver permitted me access to his personal diary of the time.

Because my original manuscript was three times the present length of the book, the inevitable falling away of certain characters and story lines made me at times feel that I was standing in an avalanche. I will never forget the moment that the FEPC (Committee on Fair Employment Practice), which had been one of my story's big milestones, slid into oblivion along with the secret history of the National Guard and metallurgical developments in the steel industry. My more experienced colleague Dan Carter told me to grow up, pointing out that no matter how long the book was, anyone who knew a lot about my subject would look at my index and say, "My God, how can so-and-so not be in there?" I feel compelled to ask the forgiveness of some of those so-and-sos. Among the heroes I had to neglect, the late Charles Zukoski should be singled out for being the ultimate paradox: a Mountain Brook Club member who was a liberal so outspoken that he was forced out of his bank job. James and Esther Cooper Jackson, for their work in the Southern Negro Youth Congress (as well as the time and insights they lavished on me), deserve far more than their brief appearances here. Other lamented casualties are Larry Adler, Henry Edmonds, Clyde Johnson, William Mitch, Howard Strevel, Wirt Taylor, and rogues such as Admiral John Crommelin and Horace Wilkinson.

Two of my favorite sources are in classes by themselves. Stetson Kennedy, an amazing activist-writer, infiltrated right-wing groups in the 1940s and exposed their connections to the industrial elite. His archives at the Schomburg Center for Research in Black Culture were crucial, and his "attagirls" were uplifting. I also, like many "out-of-town" journalists before me, had the privilege of being taken under the wing of the late Cecil Roberts, whose sardonic view of her adopted city was bracing. Among the many sources who responded to repeated queries with enthusiasm, I salute Buddy Cooper, Joe Dolan, the late Virginia Durr, Roger and Bette Hanson, James Head, the late Maurice House, Chuck Morgan, Fred Shuttlesworth, and David Vann, who, sadly, did not live to read this account of his remarkable career.

Thanks to Patty O'Toole and the Hertog Research Assistants Program in the graduate writing division at Columbia University for providing me a semester's worth of fact-checking and research help from the talented, industrious, and charming writer Kendra Hurley. And my gratitude to John Egerton, Ed Crawford, and all the Popham Seminar's crusty veterans of the civil rights beat who allowed me to join in their favorite pastime of "drinking whiskey and telling lies."

With one or two exceptions, archivists were unfailingly helpful. The people at the Birmingham Public Library Archives—Jim Baggett, Theresa Ceravolo, Tom Haslett, Jim Murray, Don Veasey, and Marvin Whiting—extended me perfect hospitality during the years I took up residency there. Debbie Greene and June Payne went out of their way for me at the John F. Kennedy Library. Thanks also to Mimi Jones and Ken Tilley at the Alabama Department of Archives and History, Helen Ritter at the American Jewish Committee, and Francine Cooper, Yvonne Crumpler, Jim Pate, and George Stewart at the Birmingham Public Library. Expert help with photographs was provided by Marci Brennan and Ron Brenne at Corbis/Bettmann, Yvette Reyes at AP/Wide World, and Bob Farley at the *Birmingham Post-Herald*.

Magazine and newspaper editors helped keep my name and subject before the reading public over the years that I disappeared into the Heart of Dixie. David R. Jones, supreme mentor at the *New York Times*, retained me on his coveted lunch circuit long after I aged out of the "promising protégée" niche. As the *Times*'s Atlanta bureau chief, Bill Schmidt enlivened my research trips with cocktails and the Alabama–Notre Dame game. My indulgent editors at the *Times* have included Michael Anderson, Paul Delaney, Walter Goodman, Dona Guimaraes, Julie Just, Mike Levitas, Nancy Newhouse, Katy Roberts, and Alex Ward. My editor at *USA Today*, Glen Nishimura, has been a writer's dream and his op-ed page a welcoming forum.

The book of perpetual promise had many indispensable collaborators. Jane Hicks, world's greatest friend, served me as host, source, banker, wedding planner, and (during my months on the Klan's case) bodyguard. Freddi Aronov was an ever sensitive analyst of Alabama's racial rites. Michael Globetti, connoisseur of Birmingham's lighter side, kept me laughing. Lee Aitken solved all the world problems of the present while I was stuck in the past. Sally Cook took me on the team bus to the Alabama-Auburn game and introduced me to Coach Gene Stallings. James Isaacs was my human encyclopedia on music and sports. Pat Crow was a taskmaster and cheerleader during one of the rounds of cutting the book. Evan Cornog, brightest human being, signed off on portions of the manuscript. Stephen Molton kept me mindful of the metaphysics.

My friends, relatives, and colleagues provided hope, strength, scholarly aid, shelter, office space, technical computer support, photographic services, medical attention, typing, baby-sitting, and the book's title: Sue Adams, Jon Alter, James Atlas, Steve Atlas, Don Bacon, Jenny Baldwin, Ann Banks, John Banks, Allen Barra, Larry Bergreen, David Berridge, David Blankenhorn, David Bloom, Sid and Jackie Blumenthal, Ghislaine Boulanger, Cynthia Bowers, Ruth Bronz, Linda

Burgess, Bob Burns, Stephen Byers, Frances Caldwell, Ronn Campisi, Lincoln Caplan, Susan Carney, Marcelle Clements, Joe Conason, Bob Crosby, Charles Dawe, Angela DiCamillo, Janis Donnaud, Debbie Dorsey, Kelly Dowe, Bill Dunlap, Jan Egleson, David Fanning, Don Fehr, Glenn Feldman, Anna Fels, Jan Freeman, Joanna Freeman-Solman, Tom Friedman, Pam Galvin, Simon Gavron, Jody and Bill Geist, Peter Gethers, George Gibson, Kathy Griffin, Bill Harris, Grady Hartzog, Bobby Heilpern, Madge Huber Henning, the late Jo Hicks, Mark Higbee, Carol Hill, Alison Humes, Sandy Jaffe, Marie Jemison, Heather Kilpatrick, Kristin Kimball, Larry Kirshbaum, Emily Lazar, Dan Letwin, Tamar Lewin, Nim and Nancy Long, Caroline McCarley, Celia McGee, Cathleen McGuigan, Vicki McKinnon, David McMullin, Ellen McWhorter, Linda Malamy, Kate Manning, Ken Matthews, Paul Mattick, Tannen Maury, Cheryl Merser, Betsy Meyer, Carolyn Miller, Gabe Miller, Lois Morris, Christy Newman, Adam Nossiter, Nina Nowak, Rory O'Connor, Dan and Becky Okrent, Andrew Olstein, Ellen Pall, Peter Petre, Martha Pichey, Pauline Badham Pinto, Katha Pollitt, Jeanine Powell, Robert Reeves, Rachel Ritchie, Carol Ruderman, Robert Rummell, Andrea Schaffer, Stephen and Rebecca Schiff, Rebecca Scholl, Laura Shapiro, Michael Shnayerson, Jimmy Simpson, Donna Smith, Patty Soto, Judith Stein, Bonnie Stockwell, Elizabeth Stone, Jean Strouse, Annalyn Swann, Lola Taylor, the late Edward and Mae Julia Thornton, the late Ruby Thornton, Liz Welch Tirrell, Don Valeska, Dan Wakefield, Robin Wilkerson, and Studie Johnson Young.

Simon & Schuster has shown heroic patience over the years that this book has been under contract, and I thank Carolyn Reidy for her tolerance. In addition to my principal editors, I must applaud Roger Labrie not only for his talent with an editing pencil but also for his calm and good humor during the storm surrounding the last months of this process. The book's copy editor, Charlotte Gross, was sharp of eye and mind, and saved me from numerous embarrassments. Of the people I've worked with at Simon & Schuster, I would like to thank Victoria Meyer, Marie Florio, Lisa Rivlin, and Denise Roy.

Charlotte Sheedy, through her own commitment to the civil rights movement, enabled me to maintain my faith in this material; her nurturing and guidance have transcended her role as literary agent. Two other friends in the publishing business, Linda Healey and Gail Hochman, freshened my perspective with their advice and encouragement.

My family, Richard Rosen and Lucy and Isabel McWhorter-Rosen, were my boon companions on this journey, and made my life complete. My in-laws and big supporters, Sol and Carey Rosen, held out the grail that one day I might be the featured author in Sol's book group. Veronica Mair gave me peace of mind as I struggled to mix book writing with parenthood, and I thank Terrell Morgan for sharing her.

I'm sure that my Birmingham family never thought this day of publication would finally come. When my uncle Hobart—who is still my hero even though I know those Cokes really were contaminated—had a heart attack a few years ago, I called him in the hospital to encourage him not to die before my book came out.

"I'll never live long enough for your book to come out," he said. He has; I am sorry that my grandmother, to whom *Carry Me Home* is dedicated, is not alive to claim the great credit she is due for propelling me into the world of inquiry. Elizabeth Biggs, my mother and biggest fan, gave me the confidence to keep at it. My brothers, Craig and Stephen, and my sisters-in-law, Carol and Lorraine, have been loyal partisans and comrades despite their concerns that what I was writing might make them regret sharing a last name with me. My aunt Gail McWhorter Rummell modeled my life for me and accompanied me on much of my quest for the McWhorters. And even though I never quite got to the bottom of his infinite mystery, I thank my father, Martin Westgate McWhorter, for delivering me, as Robert Penn Warren wrote, "out of history into history and the awful responsibility of Time."

INDEX

PHOTO CREDITS